# The Management of
# Human Resources

A Pearson Custom Publication

# The Management of Human Resources

Compiled from:

*Human Resource Management 5<sup>th</sup> Edition*
by Derek Torrington, Laura Hall and Stephen Taylor

*Contemporary Human Resource Management:*
*Text and Cases*
by Tom Redman and Adrian Wilkinson

*Human Resources in Organisations*
by John Leopold

*Human Resource Management:*
*A Contemporary Approach 3<sup>rd</sup> Edition*
by Ian Beardwell and Len Holden

*Employee Relations 2<sup>nd</sup> Edition*
by Graham Hollinshead, Peter Nicholls and Stephanie Tailby

*Employment Relations*
by Ed Rose

*Employee Relations:*
*Understanding the Employment Relationship*
by Philip Lewis, Adrian Thornhill and Mark Saunders

PEARSON
Custom
Publishing

Pearson Education Limited
Edinburgh Gate
Harlow
Essex CM20 2JE

And associated companies throughout the world

*Visit us on the World Wide Web* at:
www.pearsoned.co.uk

First published 2004

This Custom Book Edition © 2004 Published by Pearson Education Limited

Taken from:

*Human Resource Management 5$^{th}$ Edition*
by Derek Torrington, Laura Hall and Stephen Taylor
ISBN 0 273 64639 7
Copyright © Prentice Hall Europe 1987, 1991, 1995, 1998
Copyright © Pearson Education Limited 2002

*Contemporary Human Resource Management: Text and Cases*
by Tom Redman and Adrian Wilkinson
ISBN 0 201 59613 X
Copyright © Tom Redman, Adrian Wilkinson and
Pearson Education Limited 2001

*Human Resources in Organisations*
by John Leopold
ISBN 0273 64399 1
Copyright © Pearson Education Limited 2002

*Human Resource Management: A Contemporary Approach 3$^{rd}$ Edition*
by Ian Beardwell and Len Holden
ISBN 0 273 64316 9
Copyright © Longman Group Limited 1994
Copyright © Financial Times Professional Limited 1997
Copyright © Pearson Education Limited 2001

*Employee Relations 2$^{nd}$ Edition*
by Graham Hollinshead, Peter Nicholls and Stephanie Tailby
ISBN 0 273 65586 8
Copyright © Financial Times Professional Limited 1999
Copyright © Pearson Education Limited 2003

*Employment Relations*
by Ed Rose
ISBN 0 201 34299 5
Copyright © Pearson Education Limited 2001

*Employee Relations: Understanding the Employment Relationship*
by Philip Lewis, Adrian Thornhill and Mark Saunders
ISBN 0 273 64625 7
Copyright © Pearson Education Limited 2003

ISBN 1 84479 026 6

Printed and bound by Antony Rowe

# Contents

# Introduction

The management of human resources has become an increasingly important subject in the past couple of decades, not least because of the importance attached to employees in providing one of the main sources of competitive advantage within organisations.

This module has been developed to provide an understanding of the role of people management in the achievement of organisational goals and in the environment in which the organisation functions. This means gaining an understanding of the impact of the wider social, political and economic factors on the management of human resources. It also means understanding that managing human resources can take place within an international context; may differ in relation to both size and sector; and may involve a variety of performance outcomes.

Each week will consist of a lecture, to introduce the topic, followed by a seminar, which will enable greater discussion and understanding of the topic. **Attendance at all seminars is a compulsory part of the module**. On at least two occasions, as part of your learning objectives, you will be required to give a five to ten minute presentation to the rest of the seminar group in order to introduce the topic and prompt further discussion. This you will do with a number of your peers. **Failure to present at your given date and time will result in the deduction of marks from your coursework.**

This textbook has been created to fill a need for a core text, which covers all of the lecture topics taught as part of this module. Each chapter has been chosen, not to cover directly the lecture presented each week, but to complement it. The text should provide you with the minimum of information needed to understand the subject covered by the lectures. In order to understand the topics fully **you must not solely rely on this text alone**. You will also receive a module guide, which includes other recommended texts and supplementary reading for each topic. **To get good marks on the course you must read as widely as possible**. Reading more widely is essential for seminar presentations, essays and subjects for exam revision. For full details of the module and all it entails please consult your module guideline.

Remember, this module has been designed, not as a prescriptive means of teaching you to manage human resources, but rather to enable you to critically evaluate and understand the role of human resource management in any organisation. Because dealing with human beings is a complex issue there are never 'right' answers – only a variety of opinions and facts. It is up to you, with the assistance of us, to be able to understand all of the opinions and facts involved and to make your own decisions based on this information. I hope you find the text interesting and a useful tool in assisting you with this process. I welcome any comments on the contents within.

# Chapter 2  Current issues in human resource management

The world in which human resource managers exist and with which they interact is continually changing, generating new issues and conundrums to consider. While in most cases managers have a fair degree of choice about how to deal with new ideas and new sets of circumstances, the choices themselves are often difficult. Our aim in this chapter is to introduce readers to a number of these issues in general terms. All raise themes to which we will return at various stages later in the book.

## Responding to intensified competition

The most significant general issue facing HR managers in the current environment concerns the appropriate response to intensified competition in product markets. For many, the gut reaction is to react by simply maintaining a continual downward pressure on costs. This may mean fewer people, in which case the HR function is faced with the need to cut jobs and develop new means of intensifying work. It may also mean keeping pay levels down at or below market rates. Where this second line is taken, it becomes harder to recruit and retain staff, and a good deal more difficult to maintain motivation and commitment. In the long run, however, depending on the nature of the competition faced, it may be the best way of ensuring the security of the jobs that are left. Provided the process of cutting out 'fat' does not go too far, so that the organisation becomes overly lean (i.e. weak and anorexic) for its own good, such an approach is feasible.

Cost cutting is not, however, the only approach available. The alternative involves seeking to compete on grounds other than cost, accepting that prices charged to customers will be higher than those of some competitors, but providing greater overall value. The result is the production of 'high value-added' goods and services, which appeal because of their high quality or because they are innovative in some shape or form. In such situations there remains a need to operate efficiently, but there is less continual downward pressure on staffing costs. Instead there is a need to find and subsequently motivate high-quality performers. A more sophisticated set of HR practices is thus needed. Recruitment happens less often than it does in an organisation competing primarily on cost, but it matters more when it does because of the need to secure the services of highly capable people. A sophisticated approach to employee development is also necessary, as is a commitment to employee involvement.

Whatever approach is taken, there is a clear need to develop a greater capacity for flexibility and agility than has previously been the case. Whether the 'low-cost' or 'high value-added' strategy is adopted there has to be a fundamental change in the expectations of employees about the role they play and what the organisation is able to give to them in return. A widespread development has thus been a change in what is known as 'the psychological contract' between employers and the people they employ. Whereas a legal contract of employment sets out terms and conditions of employment, remuneration arrangements and the basic rules that are to govern the employment relationship, the psychological contract concerns broad expectations about what each side will gain from the other. Unquestionably shifts in this area have been some of the most important in employment in recent years as organisations have had to face increased competitive pressure. Central to the shift is the ending of any expectation of long-term or life-time employment. The old psychological contracts can be summed up as follows from the employee perspective:

I will work hard for and act with loyalty towards my employer. In return I expect to be retained as an employee provided I do not act against the interests of the organisation. I also expect to be given opportunities for promotion should the circumstances make this possible.

By contrast, the new psychological contract takes the following form:

I will bring to my work effort and creativity. In return I expect a salary that is appropriate to my contribution and market worth. While our relationship may be short term, I will remain for as long as I receive the developmental opportunities I need to build my career.

Another significant effect of increased competition on the operation of the HR function has been greater pressure for it to justify its own existence. The presence of an HR department or HR managers in an organisation can no longer be accepted as a given necessity. They survive and gain influence only where they can show that they add value by making a real contribution to the achievement of business objectives. There has thus been an upsurge in interest recently in ways of measuring the HR contribution, or where this is not possible, in finding other means of carrying out effective evaluation. A range of alternative approaches is used, including benchmarking outcomes such as absence rates, employee turnover rates and productivity per head against those of other organisations. Attitude surveys among staff and line managers are also more frequently carried out to establish what their perception of the function is and how it can be improved, while HR managers are considerably more inclined to set targets for themselves against which their performance can subsequently be evaluated.

## Managing international operations

As was stated above, one of the chief causes of intensified competition in recent decades has been the growth of the global economy. Most organisations now have to compete, at least to some extent, with rivals based in other countries. If a firm itself is not a large exporter, it is usually faced with competition from overseas organisations importing products or services into the home market. Particular challenges are posed for organisations based in the older industrialised countries by competitors with far lower cost bases in newly industrialising areas of the world. An important consequence of globalisation is the growth in the number and size of multinational organisations. As a result, a growing proportion of HR specialists work in organisations which are owned and controlled from overseas or are home based with substantial international operations.

The key decision to take here is how far it is necessary or desirable to have in place HR practices which are cross-national and which operate in the same way in all divisions across the world. In principle it is often considered desirable to standardise policy, practices and philosophy in all countries so as to develop a clear, single international identity and corporate culture. Global standardisation also facilitates the movement of individuals from one country to another, as well as permitting the sharing of 'best practice' on an international basis. However, a number of problems arise when such a path is taken. First, it is not always possible to operate in the same way across the world because of important institutional variations between countries. Tax regimes are different, as are training and qualification systems. Above all there are diverse systems of employment law in place, requiring organisations to operate differently in different locations. In some countries, for example, collective agreements are legally binding, while in others (including the UK) they are 'binding in honour only'. There are also major differences in the areas of dismissal and discrimination law. In the USA the doctrine of 'employment at will' means that there is little by way of statutory protection for people who consider themselves to have been unfairly dismissed. In the UK there is a measure of protection for some but not for all, while in Holland employers can only dismiss lawfully once they have gained the permission of a state official so to do (Hepple 1998, p. 291).

In addition to institutional restrictions there is a need to take account of cultural differences. As has been shown by Hofstede (1980 and 1991) and others, the way that different peoples approach work and workplace relations can vary substantially from country to country. Approaches which seem entirely natural in one place thus often travel badly when they are transplanted abroad. A good example is the standard Anglo-Saxon approach to performance appraisal, with annual reviews at which managers and subordinates talk frankly about what individuals have achieved and ways in which performance can be improved. As a method of managing individual performance, appraisal works well in most UK-based organisations – but this is not always the case elsewhere. Across much of the world it simply does not fit with prevailing cultural norms, managers and staff being reluctant to speak frankly and directly to one another about such matters (see Ling Sing Chee 1994, p. 154; Sparrow and Hiltrop 1994, pp. 558–60; Fletcher 1997, p. 97). A balance therefore has to be struck between global and local HR practices. It is usually possible to put in place an international HR strategy and, with certain limitations, to develop a global HR philosophy. By contrast, their application at the local level has to vary considerably depending on what is appropriate in the country concerned.

**Activity 2.1**  In the literature on international HRM there is a divide between those who see institutional differences as being the most significant determinants of varying HR practices across the globe, and those who stress the importance of cultural differences. The former believe that working cultures can be altered by making institutional changes, while the latter argue that culture is deeply entrenched and that it is responsible for the shape that institutions take. What is your view on this debate?

**The Management of Human Resources**

## Riding waves of technological innovation

Developments in the fields of information technology, telecommunications, biotechnology and laser-based applications, often used in collaboration, continue to provide opportunities for organisations as well as posing problems. From an HR perspective it is possible to identify three distinct types of challenge that arise from these developments. First there are direct effects in the way in which the HR function goes about its business:

- the use of email and intranet as tools of information provision and communication;
- the rise of the internet as a major new method for recruitment;
- the development of web-based approaches to training and learning;
- the use of computer databases to hold staff information and to generate reports;
- the application of computer technologies to established tasks such as human resource planning and pay-roll administration.

Second, technology brings change more generally to an organisation in terms of its structure, job duties, work allocation and even its culture. Technological change thus drives organisation change, requiring action of different kinds from the HR function. Recruitment and selection processes have to reflect the need to bring in people with different skills and attributes, the purpose and type of training activities will often have to evolve in new directions, while it may also be necessary to make redundancies. In some situations technology can drive radical change in a short space of time, changing forever long-established ways of carrying out an organisation's core functions. A good example is the revolution that took place in newspaper and magazine publishing during the mid-1980s. Whatever the pace of technological development, there is a role for HR professionals to play in planning it and subsequently in its implementation.

The third way in which technological developments affect HRM activity relates to the need to find new ways of managing staff who are employed in research and development (R&D) functions, and whose job is to drive technological development to the advantage of the organisation. It has been convincingly argued that the nature of this work is fundamentally different in key respects from that performed by others in an organisation, and that established management practices are often inappropriate. The following quotation illustrates this point:

> The principles of high task specialization, unity of command and direction, high division of labour, and equality of responsibility and authority all address the problems of structuring work systems and information flows in clear, repetitive ways. They are geared toward the resolution of familiar problems and the facilitation of productivity and control through formal lines of positional and hierarchical authority or through job standardisation. And organizations that are designed and managed for doing the same things well repetitively, as in manufacturing, are not particularly appropriate for doing something well once, as in R&D.
>
> (Katz 1998, p. viii)

A theme of research carried out into the management of staff in research and development environments is the need to move away from approaches which serve to enhance management control and which tend to work against the development of teams. In their place there is a need for structures which promote collaboration between individuals, exchange of ideas and sharing of knowledge.

What are the main ways in which technological developments are currently affecting the management of human resources in your organisation or one with which you are familiar? What do you think will be the most significant new developments over the next ten years?

## Meeting the expectations of the law

Another major trend with which the HR profession has had to contend in recent years is the growth in the amount of legislation covering employment matters. Prior to 1970, with one or two exceptions, there was no statutory regulation of the employment relationship in the UK. An individual's terms and conditions of employment were those that were stated in the contract of employment and in any collective agreements. The law did not intervene beyond providing some basic health and safety protection, the right to modest redundancy payments and a general requirement on employers and employees to honour the contractual terms agreed when the employment began. Since 1970 this situation has wholly changed. The individual contract of employment remains significant and can be enforced in court if necessary, but there has been added to this a whole range of statutory rights which employers are obliged to honour. The most significant are in the fields of health and safety, equal pay, sex and race discrimination and unfair dismissal. The following have recently been added to these longer-established rights:

■ disability discrimination law (in operation since 1997);
■ working time regulations (since 1998);
■ the national minimum wage (since 1999);
■ new maternity regulations (since 1999);
■ parental leave and the right to time off for family emergencies (since 1999);
■ the right to trade union representation at serious disciplinary and grievance hearings (since 2000);
■ new trade union recognition procedures (since 2000).

Unfair dismissal law itself has also been strengthened with the reduction in the qualifying period to one year's service and in the raising of the maximum compensation level to £50,000 from 1999. Further new law on discrimination and consultation is due to be placed on the statute books before 2003.

The extent to which HR practitioners, and managers generally, should welcome the growth in regulation remains a matter of debate. One view, expressed most frequently by those working in smaller firms, deplores much of the legislation. While accepting the laudable motives behind it, they see the long-term effect as being to increase the costs associated with employing people, while decreasing the flexibility managers enjoy in the running of their businesses. This results in a reluctance to create jobs in the first place and a tendency for international organisations to site operations in other, less highly regulated countries. According to proponents of this school of thought, regulation provides more social justice, but does so at a price – namely higher unemployment than would otherwise be the case.

An alternative view starts with the proposition that the burden of regulation in the UK remains a good deal less onerous on employers than is common in many industrialised countries, and that it is not extensive enough to have a detrimental effect. Indeed it can be persuasively argued that UK employment legislation does no more than require employers to treat their employees equitably and reasonably, and that good employers thus have no reason to complain. A third point of view is that UK labour law does not in fact go far enough and that further, rather tougher legislation would be beneficial. The argument here rests on the belief that the UK can no longer compete globally by producing 'low cost – low value-added' products and services because of competition from the newly industrialising countries and the former eastern bloc. Instead there is a need to develop a more highly skilled labour force and to focus activity on producing quality goods and services, on new technologies and on the development of a knowledge economy. Legislation, in requiring employers to pay relatively high wages and in making it difficult to dismiss without good reason, helps force them down such a path. The result, so it is argued, is a situation in which a high level of statutory employment protection is entirely compatible with the operation of a successful economy.

**Activity 2.3**   What is your position in the debate about employment protection legislation? Would you like to see more or less regulation in this field? What additional measures would you welcome? Which would you like to see removed from the statute book?

## Managing with or without trade unions

The Employment Relations Act 1999 requires employers to recognise trade unions and to bargain with them in good faith where a majority of the workforce in an identifiable bargaining group indicate that this is what they want. To an extent the law thus now restricts how far managements can choose whether or not they deal with a trade union. However, for many there remains a choice because of the reluctance of employees in many sectors of the economy to become trade union members in sufficient numbers to force recognition. According to the most recent UK Workplace Employee Relations Survey (Cully *et al.* 1999, p. 87) as many as 47 per cent of workplaces employ no one at all who is a union member, while membership covers fewer than half the workforce in the case of a further 25 per cent of organisations. There is also scope within the legislation for employers to resist recognition, even where there are plenty of union members, by seeking to persuade them that a system of collective bargaining is not in the organisation's interests.

For many organisations a good management case can be made against the recognition of trade unions. For smaller firms particularly there is often a well-founded desire to manage employee relations informally and on an individual rather than a collective basis. In other situations the case is based on fears that unions will restrict the freedom of action enjoyed by managers, that they will resist necessary change, preventing it from occurring, or that a damaging adversarial relationship between employees and management will become established. There are also, however, good reasons for managers to welcome or even to encourage a trade union presence:

> Trade unions also fulfil a number of important managerial functions which help explain why a number of foreign-owned companies coming into the UK have been willing to recognise them. One is the agency function which is especially important where there are large numbers of employees engaged in relatively homogeneous activities: management escapes the time-consuming and costly process of dealing with employees individually and also avoids inconsistencies which can be a major problem. A second is that trade unions voice the grievances and complaints of employees (Freeman and Medoff, 1984). In the words of Henry Mond, who had a significant influence on ICI's early policy towards trade unions, 'the trade unions are extremely useful to us in bringing to our notice matters that we would not otherwise be aware of' (quoted in Reader, 1973: 66). A third, and in many respects the most important, function that trade unions perform is in helping to manage discontent by legitimating procedures and management prerogative. (Sisson and Storey 2000, p. 193)

What is important from a management point of view is that a healthy and productive relationship should be established with one or more unions which enhances rather than detracts from the long-term success of the organisation. Such thinking underpins the growth in interest over recent years in forms of **partnership** arrangement – an approach favoured and encouraged by government. The key factor which distinguishes partnership from more traditional types of union relationship is an acceptance that both sides are working towards the same ultimate goals. The role of the union is not one of perpetual opposition but is instead supportive and constructive of legitimate management initiatives. In return for such support, managers treat union representatives as partners in decision-making processes and employees as key stakeholders in the organisation's future. Consultation occurs before new programmes are announced, while in other areas there will be an element of joint decision making. Partnership agreements do not restrict a union's freedom to criticise management

**WINDOW ON PRACTICE**

An interesting effect of the recent legislation on union recognition has been the way it has encouraged employers to review their employee relations practices ahead of time in order to avoid being forced to make changes by the regulators. Much activity in this area occurred between February 1999 (when the government issued its White Paper entitled 'Fairness at Work') and July 2000 (when the new legislation became active). Two rather different examples were reported in *People Management* in June 2000. The first concerned Eurotunnel, which tried to pre-empt a claim for compulsory recognition by signing a single-union agreement of the 'partnership' kind with the Transport and General Workers Union. The aim was to avoid a situation in which the company dealt with several different unions representing different groups of staff. The other example concerned Richard Branson's empire, in which unions were recognised in the Virgin Trains company but not in the Virgin Atlantic Airline. Here, before possibly being forced to do so under the terms of the Employment Relations Act, Virgin themselves organised a ballot of staff in order to establish whether or not there is any great desire for union recognition among employees of the airline. The article reported that were the staff survey to indicate support for recognition, some form of single-union deal would be sought and signed.

or to seek better terms and conditions for employees, but they do imply the fostering of an understanding mindset on the part of representatives which respects management's right to manage and accepts that the ultimate goal of an enterprise is commercial success.

## Ethical questions

Personnel/human resource management has always had an ethical dimension. The odd thing is that practitioners have for so long been trying to bury this aspect, while academic commentators have grumbled that HR practitioners fail to deliver on it. Thirty years ago it was possible to write a chapter in a book on personnel management with the title 'The Social Role of Personnel' (Torrington 1968, pp. 147–60) and generate a series of reviews that all vehemently disagreed with the implicit proposition that there actually *was* a social role for the personnel manager in the business. Since then there has been a resurgence of interest in ethics, but now it is not a vain attempt of the 'nice' personnel people to act as the conscience of the company. Instead it is a much more general management interest.

On a practical day-to-day basis, as well as when determining issues of policy and strategy, human resource managers are faced with ethical dilemmas. Situations often arise in which there is a conflict of some kind between what is strictly in the interests of the organisation and what individuals consider to be 'right' according to their own consciences or ethical principles. Interestingly the lack of ethicality arises as often from a failure to act as from a positive decision to take a particular course of action. Some examples are as follows:

- dismissing someone for a reason other than gross misconduct, such as ill health;
- failing to dismiss a senior manager or a particularly able employee who has committed an act of gross misconduct (such as sexual harassment);
- maintaining payment arrangements in which groups which are predominantly female are less well remunerated than those dominated by men;
- offering training opportunities to some while denying them to others;
- putting pressure on someone to change working hours or to move location when this will be disruptive for them or their families;
- failing to compensate disabled workers or those from ethnic minorities for possible disadvantages suffered in appraisal or recruitment processes;
- discriminating on grounds of age;
- minimising pay awards despite the organisation having the ability to pay more;
- failing to tell the 'whole truth' when giving evidence at an Employment Tribunal;
- failing to give wholly honest answers about a workplace or job to potential recruits in order to secure their services;
- turning a blind eye to the need to make costly alterations for health and safety reasons.

More generally, an organisation's overall stance on HR issues can often be criticised on ethical grounds. Some of the recent developments outlined earlier in the chapter can be seen as being responsible for a reduced interest on the part of employers in managing ethically. Significant examples include the pressure placed on people to work longer hours than is good for them, the decline in job security resulting from increased competitive pressures, and investment in new technologies which directly result in job losses. Some forms of cultural change may also be considered unethical, an example being a shift away from a culture based on excellence in customer service to one which is oriented towards hard-selling.

How far then should HR practitioners allow ethical questions to colour their judgement when making decisions? For some commentators the answer is 'not at all', since they believe that the long-term interests of society in terms of wealth creation are best served by unfettered competition between firms. Milton Friedman went as far as to contend that managers who devoted corporate resources to pursue personal interpretations of social need might be misguided in their selection and would unfairly 'tax' their shareholders, employees and customers in the process:

> There is one and only one social responsibility of business: to use its resources and energy in activities designed to increase its profits as long as it stays within the rules of the game, engaging in open and free competition, without deception and fraud.
> (Friedman 1963, p. 163)

The problem with such a position is that it pushes to one side consequences, such as inequity, inequality, insecurity and abuse of power, that arise in organisations when the pursuit of profit is placed ahead of all other considerations. Whatever its merits in purely economic terms, in putting expediency before ethicality, Friedman's position ignores altogether the role employers can play in promoting social justice. It is also a position with which many managers are understandably uncomfortable.

Such is reflected in the stance of the influential Chartered Institute of Personnel and Development (CIPD). One of its key objectives is the establishment, monitoring and promotion of standards and ethics for HR practitioners in the UK. In pursuing this objective it is seeking to prescribe standards of professional conduct such as those that exist in the medical, legal and accountancy professions. The problem is that HR people do not have a separate professional existence from the management of which they are a part. Human resource management must be a management activity or it is nothing. Doctors, lawyers and accountants, even when employed by a large organisation, can maintain a non-managerial professional detachment, giving advice that is highly regarded, even when it is unpopular. Furthermore they advise; they do not decide. HR specialists are employed in no other capacity than to participate closely in the management process of a business. They can not, therefore, be expected to take up a full-fledged, independent, professional stance. Were they to retreat to an ivory tower and maintain a purist position on ethical matters theirs would be a voice in the management wilderness that no one wanted to hear, let alone provide a salary or provide a company car in order to hear.

The need therefore is for HR people to argue vigorously in favour of a combination of efficiency and justice, remembering that they can only argue vigorously if they are present when decisions are made. They must ensure that they are valued by their managerial colleagues for the wholeness of their contribution and be prepared to accept the fact that they will often lose the argument. They cannot do it by masquerading as an unrepresentative shop steward. In practice what has to be done is to make a strong business case for taking an ethical line wherever it is credible to do so. Invariably this will be based on the long-established ideas of the Human Relations School outlined above; namely the belief that a business can only maintain its competitive edge if the people who work there are committed to its success and that commitment is volitional. In order to maintain the good will and enthusiastic co-operation of employees while also attracting good quality applicants from outside the organisation, there is a need for fair dealing, openness and consistency in the way people are treated.

| Activity 2.4 | What ethical dilemmas have you faced in the workplace? How far were you able to influence the direction that events took? To what extent can you justify to yourself the course of action that you took? |
| --- | --- |

## Best practice v. best fit

The final general issue of significance we discuss at this stage is another that has consequences across the field of human resource management. As well as being a managerial issue it concerns one of the most significant academic debates in the HR field at the present time. At root it is about whether or not there is an identifiable 'best way' of carrying out HR activities which is universally applicable. It is best understood as a debate between two schools of thought, although in practice it is quite possible to take a central position which sees validity in both the basic positions.

Adherents of a best practice perspective argue that there are certain HR practices and approaches to their operation which will invariably help an organisation in achieving competitive advantage. There is therefore a clear link between HR activity and business performance, but the effect will only be maximised if the 'right' HR policies are pursued. A great deal of evidence has been published in recent years, using various methodologies, which appears to back up the best practice case (e.g. Pfeffer 1994; Huselid 1995; Wood and Albanese 1995; Delery and Doty 1996; Fernie and Metcalf 1996; Patterson *et al.* 1998; Guest *et al.* 2000). While there are differences of opinion on questions of detail, all strongly suggest that the same basic bundle of human resource practices or general human resource management orientation tends to enhance business performance in all organisations irrespective of the particular product market strategy being pursued. According to David Guest this occurs through a variety of mechanisms:

> human resource practices exercise their positive impact by (i) ensuring and enhancing the competence of employees, (ii) by tapping their motivation and commitment, and (iii) by designing work to encourage the fullest contribution from employees. Borrowing from elements of expectancy theory (Vroom 1964, Lawler 1971), the model implies that all three elements should be present to ensure the best outcome. Positive employee behaviour should in turn impact upon establishment level outcomes such as low absence, quit rates and wastage, as well as high quality and productivity. (Guest 2000, p. 2)

The main elements of the 'best practice bundle' that these and other writers identify are those which have long been considered as examples of good practice in the HRM field. They include the use of the more advanced selection methods, a serious commitment to employee involvement, substantial investment in training and development, the use of individualised reward systems and harmonised terms and conditions of employment as between different groups of employees.

The alternative 'best fit' school also identifies a link between human resource management practice and the achievement of competitive advantage. Here, however, there is no belief in the existence of universal solutions. Instead all is contingent on the particular circumstances of each organisation. What is needed is HR policies and practices which 'fit' and are thus appropriate to the situation of individual employers. What is appropriate (or 'best') for one will not necessarily be right for another. Key variables include the size of the establishment, the dominant product market strategy being pursued and the nature of the labour markets in which the organisation competes. It is thus argued that a small organisation which principally achieves competitive advantage through innovation and which competes in very tight labour markets should have in place rather different HR policies than a large firm which produces low-cost goods and faces no difficulty in attracting staff. In order to maximise competitive advantage, the first requires informality combined with sophisticated human resource practices, while the latter needs more bureaucratic systems combined with a 'low cost – no frills' set of HR practices.

The best fit or contingency perspective originated in the work of Joan Woodward and her colleagues at Imperial College in the 1950s. In recent years it has been developed and applied to contemporary conditions by academics such as Randall Schuler and Susan Jackson, John Purcell and Ed Lawler. In addition, a number of influential models have been produced which seek to categorise organisational contingencies and suggest what mix of HR practices are appropriate in each case. Examples are those of Miles and Snow (1978), Fombrun *et al.* (1984) and Sisson and Storey (2000) – a number of which we look at in more detail in Chapter 3.

To a great extent the jury is still out on these questions. Proponents of both the 'best practice' and 'best fit' perspectives can draw on bodies of empirical evidence to back up their respective positions and so the debate continues.

## Summary propositions

2.1 Organisations respond in different ways to intensified competitive pressures. Whatever the response there is a need to become more flexible and to place the employment relationship on a different psychological footing.

2.2 In international organisations it is necessary to strike a balance between human resource strategies which operate globally and human resource policies which vary from country to country to reflect local institutional and cultural expectations.

2.3 New technologies give HR specialists opportunities to develop fresh approaches to their work. They also require new thinking about change processes and the management of people in technologically specialised roles.

2.4 Developments in employment law over recent years have substantially restricted the freedom of employers to manage their workplaces. While the law does little more than require compliance with basic good practice, there are also administrative and procedural requirements which reduce flexibility and increase costs.

**2.5** While trade union recognition remains much less common than was the case in the 1980s, there remains a good business case for working with trade unions in certain circumstances. This is particularly true of relationships based on the principles of partnership.

**2.6** Human resource managers are regularly faced with ethical dilemmas. HR professionals must argue for justice and equity, but will not be listened to unless they put forward a convincing business case.

**2.7** Opinion is divided about whether or not it is possible to identify 'best practice' in the various activities that make up HRM. Adherents of the 'best fit' perspective argue that what is 'best' for some organisations is often inappropriate elsewhere.

## References

Cully, M., Woodland, S., O'Reilly, A. and Dix, G. (1999) *Britain at Work as depicted by the 1998 Workplace Employee Relations Survey*. London: Routledge.

Delery, J. and Doty, D.H. (1996) 'Modes of Theorising in Strategic Human Resource Management: Tests of Universalistic, Contingency and Configurational Performance Predictions', *Academy of Management Journal*, Vol. 39, No. 4.

Fernie, S. and Metcalf, D. (1996) 'Participation, Contingent Pay, Representation and Workplace Performance: Evidence from Great Britain', *Discussion Paper 232*, Centre for Economic Performance, London School of Economics.

Fletcher, C. (1997) *Appraisal: routes to improved performance*, 2nd edn. London: IPD.

Fombrun, C., Tichy, N.M. and Devanna, M.A. (1984) *Strategic Human Resource Management*. New York: Wiley.

Freeman, R.B. and Medoff, J.L. (1984) *What do Unions Do?* New York: Basic Books.

Friedman, M. (1963) *Capitalism and Freedom*. Chicago: University of Chicago Press.

Guest, D.E. (2000) 'Human resource management, employee well-being and organisational performance', Paper given at the CIPD Professional Standards Conference, University of Warwick.

Guest, D.E., Michie J., Sheehan, M. and Conway, N. (2000) *Employment Relations, HRM and Business Performance: An analysis of the 1998 Workplace Employee Relations Survey*. London: CIPD.

Hepple, B. (1998) 'Flexibility and Security of Employment', in R. Blanpain and C. Engels (eds), *Comparative Labour Law and Industrial Relations in Industrialized Market Economies*, 2nd edn. The Hague, Netherlands: Kluwer.

Hofstede, G. (1980) *Culture's Consequences: International differences in work-related values*. Beverly Hills: Sage.

Hofstede, G. (1991) *Cultures and Organizations: Software of the mind*. London: McGraw Hill.

Huselid, M. (1995) 'The impact of Human Resource Management practices on Turnover, Productivity and Corporate Financial Performance', *Academy of Management Journal*, Vol. 38, No. 3.

Katz, R. (ed.) (1998) *The Human side of managing technological innovation: A collection of readings*. Oxford: Oxford University Press.

Lawler, E.E. (1971) *Pay and Organizational Effectiveness. A Psychological View*. New York: McGraw-Hill.

Ling Sing Chee (1994) 'Singapore Airlines: strategic human resource initiatives', in D.P. Torrington (ed.), *International Human Resource Management: Think Globally, Act Locally*. London: Prentice Hall.

Miles, R.E. and Snow, C.C. (1978): *Organizational Strategy, Strategy and Process*. New York: McGraw Hill.

Patterson, M.G., West, M.A., Lawthom, R. and Nickell, S. (1998) *Impact of People Management Practices on Business Performance*. Issues in People Management No 22. London: IPD.

Pfeffer, J. (1994) *Competitive Advantage Through People*. Boston: Harvard Business School Press.

Reader, W.J. (1973) *The First Quarter Century 1926-1952. Imperial Chemical Industries: A History. Vol. 2.* Oxford: Oxford University Press.

Sisson, K. and Storey, J. (2000) *The Realities of Human Resource Management: Managing the Employment Relationship*. Buckingham: Open University Press.

Sparrow, P. and Hiltrop, J.M. (1994) *European Human Resource Management in Transition*. London: Prentice Hall.

Torrington, D.P. (1968) *Successful Personnel Management*. London: Staples.

Vroom, V.H. (1964) *Work and Motivation*. New York: Wiley.

Wood, S. and Albanese, M. (1995) 'Can We Speak of High Commitment Management on the Shop Floor?', *Journal of Management Studies*, Vol. 32, No. 2.

## General discussion topics

1 What other issues, aside from those discussed in this chapter, do you think are significant for human resource managers? Which do you consider will become more important in years to come?

2 How far do you think it is possible to agree with *both* the 'best fit' and 'best practice' perspectives on HRM? In what ways are they compatible with each other?

3 It could be argued that the most effective means of forcing employers to treat their employees ethically is to pass more restrictive employment law and to police it more rigorously. How far do you agree with this point of view?

# Chapter 1

# In search of human resource management

Tom Redman and Adrian Wilkinson

## Introduction

This book is about human resource management (HRM) and is concerned with the way in which organisations manage their people. In this introductory chapter we discuss our own approach to the study of HRM and the rationale underpinning the ordering and presentation of material in the book. Our aim is to chart some of the broad terrain of a rapidly developing field of study in order to prepare the reader for the more finely grained treatment of specific HRM topics to be found in the individual chapters. In particular we examine the recent rise of HRM, the effects of the changing context of work on HRM, what it involves, the strategic nature of HRM practice, its impact on organisational performance and the changing role of the HRM function. The chapter concludes with a consideration of our views on the audience at which the book is targeted and some thoughts on how it may best be used.

## The development of HRM

The last 20 years or so have seen the rise of what has been called the Human Resource Management new orthodoxy (Guest, 1991). In the mid-1980s in the UK, and earlier in the USA, the term 'HRM' became fashionable and gradually started to replace others such as 'personnel management' (PM) and 'industrial relations' (IR). The practitioners of people management are no longer personnel officers and trainers but are HR mangers and human resource developers (and, importantly, line managers – see below). The 1990s saw the launch of new journals and the flourishing of university courses in HRM. The then Institute of Personnel

Management, the main professional body for personnel practitioners, relaunched its journal *People Management*, but subtitled it 'The magazine for Human Resource professionals'. The millennium has now witnessed the professional body receiving a Royal Charter to become the Chartered Institute of Personnel and Development. The HRM bandwagon is well and truly rolling.

Early contributions on the implications of the rise of HRM were concerned to define it and to compare it with the more traditional British approach to personnel management (e.g. Fowler, 1987; Guest, 1987; Miller, 1987). HRM was in turn both heralded as 'a new era of humane people-oriented employment management' (Keenoy, 1990: 375) and derided as a 'blunt instrument to bully workers' (Monks, 1998). There has been considerable ambiguity in the use of the term, with various commentators using 'HRM' as simply a more modern label for traditional personnel management, as a 're-conceptualising and re-organising of personnel roles', or as a new and distinctive approach, attempting to develop and utilise the potential of human resources to the full in pursuit of the organisation's strategic objectives. It is the promise that is held by this latter view that has most excited practitioners and attracted the attention of management academics.

There has been a long debate over whether HRM is no more than a relabelling of personnel management, the 'old wine in new bottles' critique, or something more fundamental (Legge, 1989; Gennard and Kelly, 1997). Traditionally, personnel management is often characterised as having little focus on broader business links and being overly concentrated on the activities of personnel professionals and a range of operational techniques. Thus, personnel management was seen as a low-level record keeping and 'people maintenance' function. The HRM stereotype, in contrast, is characterised as being much more concerned with business strategy, and linkages with HR strategy, taking the view that HR is a, if not *the* most important organisational resource. Thus there has been much talk of an HRM 'revolution'. However, although evolution is less exciting than revolution, Torrington and Hall's (1998) view that HRM is merely the next stage in the development of personnel management is persuasive. Torrington (1993), a staunch defender of 'good' personnel management, has also suggested that much of what is now labelled 'HRM' may be seen much more simply as long-standing good people management practice, whilst what was less effective has been relegated to remain, rather unfairly it seems, with the 'personnel management' brand.

To a large extent the rise of HRM reflects the changing concerns of management more generally. In the 1970s, following the Donovan (1968) report, senior management tended to concentrate on formalisation of relations with unions, and national issues such as incomes policies put personnel into a position of entrenchment. In the 1980s, with a changing balance of power in the workplace following from reforming Conservative governments with an ideological distaste for trade unions, management concerns turned to efficiency and productivity, which many felt were best dealt with at line management level.

Even the more 'upbeat' HRM work such as that of Storey (1992) indicates that changes in the arena of HRM did not come from initiatives designed directly to do this. Change was driven by broader organisational initiatives and personnel specialists have not been seen as the key drivers of change. Similarly, Wood's (1999) work on high commitment practices suggests that innovations in HRM tend to accompany changes in production concepts and that innovations on humanistic grounds are unrealistic. Thus in part HRM can be seen as a consequence of managing in 'uncharted territory', with new rules governing the employment relationship (Beardwell, 1998). Furthermore, the changing nature of the context of work clearly has had a significant effect on the development of HRM. The next section briefly sketches some of the main developments in this area.

## The changing context of work

> Things are happening in employment that are neither a cause nor an effect of HRM but which could have some impact on it. These include the intensification of work, the choices of work location provided by technology and the divisive nature of a society in which many are idle and impoverished while many others are seriously over-worked.
>
> (Guest, 1998b: 51)

In the main, developments in HRM, as we argue above, have been driven by large-scale organisational changes as employers adjust to a much more competitive global economic environment. To meet some of the challenges posed by intense competition organisations have been downsized, delayered and decentralised. Organisations are now less hierarchical in nature, have adopted more flexible forms, and have been subjected to continuing waves of organisational change programmes such as total quality management, business process re-engineering, performance management, lean production, learning organisation and a seemingly relentless series of culture change initiatives. The type of staff employed and the way they are organised has also undergone considerable change in the new organisational form. Employees are often now more likely to be female, work part-time, away from the workplace (e.g. teleworking and the so-called 'hot desking'), and be subcontractors, consultants, temps and interims, etc. The boundaries between work and home are now much more blurred (Cully *et al.*, 1999).

Such pressures have not been restricted to the private sector and we have seen the rise of the so-called 'new public management', with its emphasis on economy and efficiency (Rocha, 1994). The public sector has undergone many similar changes, with new organisational forms emerging in the wake of 'marketisation', compulsory competitive tendering and most recently 'Best Value'. For example, the civil service has experienced downsizing, delayering, market testing, and citizen's charters as well as the creation of next step agencies. The NHS has seen the advent of trusts, the creation of an internal market via the separation of purchasers from providers of healthcare, and the introduction of performance league tables and patient's charters. Healthcare provision has changed from being a citizen's right to a customer service. The traditional NHS culture has moved from one based on professionalism to one imbued with the rhetoric of the market, with hospitals and clinics 'franchised' by the Department of Health to sell health-care services (see Dent, 1995).

Some of these changes are seen as facilitating more discretion for staff while at the same time retaining control of performance. Here the relevance of HRM comes to the fore; new forms of work and organisation demand new HRM strategies and practices. The new work context also brings new HRM challenges; not the least of these derives from the impact of such changes on the stresses and strains involved in working under such conditions. Here the growing literature on stress at work paints a rather disconcerting picture of organisational life in the new workplace. Typical of this work is the report by the ESRC Centre of Business Research at Cambridge University for the Rowntree Foundation, which found a rise in stress and anxiety, with a significant increase in job insecurity, especially for professional workers. Over 60 per cent of employees felt the pace of work has increased in the last five years. Job insecurity was linked to poor health. Workplaces were seen as lacking in trust, with only 26 per cent of workers saying they believed management and employees were on the same side, and, when asked if management could be expected to look after their best interests, 40 per cent said only a little or not at all.

Whilst HRM practices (e.g. employee assistance programmes, workplace counselling schemes, etc) are used in some organisations to provide a more supportive environment and there is evidence that these appear to have some potential to ease but not cure the impact of workplace stress, the general picture is rather bleak. Indeed, HRM practices may have added considerably to the stresses of modern work-life, with the increased use of such practices as performance management systems, contingent pay, and flexibilisation. For example, in relation to flexibility, one of the key dimensions of Guest's (1987) conceptualisation of HRM, a recent Citizens' Advice Bureau report finds numerous accounts of worker exploitation, with unilateral changes in contracts and forced reductions in hours and pay. The 1990s also witnessed the growth of 'zero hours contracts', particularly in retailing, whereby employers do not guarantee that any work will be offered but, should they require labour, the employee is expected to be available. Thus the number of employment complaints more than doubled between 1983–4 and 1992–3 (NACAB, 1997). The impact of organisational change on employees has been so considerable that commentators now argue there is a need to radically reconstruct the nature of the 'psychological contract' between employer and employee. The search is now on for new deals for new times (Herriot and Pemberton, 1995).

Thus HRM is clearly not a simple panacea, and may even contribute directly to some of the above problems, but it is relatively safe to speculate that it looks likely to play an increasingly important role in the workplaces of the future. However, in this discussion we must also be careful not to overstate the case for HRM. There is a danger that accounts of change in organisations are always portrayed as major paradigm-shifting events when the reality is rather different. The rhetoric of organisational change often relies too heavily on hype from unrepresentative examples (Thompson and O'Connel Davidson, 1995). Managers, it seems, often perceive themselves to be in the midst of massive organisational change. Eccles and Nohira's (1992) historical account of post-Second World War management traces how it has been the norm rather than the exception for practitioners and writers to view their organisational environment as turbulent and characterised by transformative change. Thus issues of continuity are in many respects overlooked in the brave new world of HRM (Noon and Blyton, 1998). As we note above, poor people management practice is not just a product of old management systems, such as that attributed to personnel management by HRM advocates. It may be that many commentators have been rather blinded by the glossy nature of the new HRM vision, but we would suggest that talk of the end of traditional career jobs and the demise of trade unions and the like is rather too premature. History generally has a fairly cruel way of treating such rash predictions.

In particular, the rose-tinted managerial accounts of HRM in practice have recently been tempered somewhat by a literature examining HRM 'from below'. Surprisingly, the voice of the worker in evaluating HRM's achievements has been rather silent. Where workers' views are mentioned, for example in Storey's work, the impression is one of scepticism that they would gain benefits. Workers' response to HRM initiatives have generally been limited in early studies to anecdotal evidence and some limited case study work (Mabey *et al.*, 1998; Collinson *et al.*, 1997; Scott, 1994; Wickens, 1987), with broader survey-based work taking some time to emerge (Guest and Conway, 1999).

Thus there is a danger, apparent in much of the prescriptive literature in HRM (Armstrong, 1987; Hendry *et al.*, 1988; Williams *et al.*, 1989), of focusing almost exclusively on the initiatives of management and thereby seeing employees as essentially passive beings, whose attitudes and behaviour are there to be moulded by HR strategy in the pursuit of competitive advantage. The feasibility of a 'top-down' approach to the management of organisational culture has already been challenged by a number of authors. Employees too may respond to changes in the competitive environment, and this suggests that the effective implementation of HRM may be more than simply a matter of management will. However, there is some evidence that the employee experience of HRM is not always negative and exploitative. According to Guest (1999: 23):

> it appears that workers like their experience of HRM. The more HR practices they are currently experiencing in their employment, the more satisfied they seem to be and the better their psychological contract.

Indeed, recent work by Guest and Conway (1999) found that management practices are more important than union membership in determining whether staff feel fairly treated. Interestingly, they argue that union leaders should overcome their natural scepticism and pressure management to adopt progressive HRM practices. Clearly more research is needed in this area.

## What then is HRM?

In order to address this question we examine some of the key works on HRM theory. Storey's (1992) study of HRM identifies 27 points of difference between HRM and PM (see Table 1.1) and divides this into four broad categories: beliefs and assumptions, strategic qualities, the critical role of managers and key levers. Sisson (1990) sees HRM in terms of four aspects of employment practice: an integration of HR policies with business planning; a shift in responsibility for HR issues from personnel specialists to line managers; a shift from the collectivism of management – trade union relations to the individualism of management–employee relations and, finally, an emphasis on commitment.

Guest (1987) theorises HRM as having four key dimensions: commitment, flexibility, quality and integration. Commitment is sought in the sense that employees are expected to identify closely with the interests of the organisation, and to go beyond mere compliance to management by internalising the goals of the organisation and behaving accordingly. Flexibility involves the ability and willingness of staff to adapt to change, within the context of flexible organisation structures. The quality of staff and management is also seen to be important in achieving high levels of performance. Finally, integration refers to the matching of human resource strategies to the needs of the business strategy, and requires that the various elements of human resource management are themselves consistent and mutually supportive. Integration also implies that line managers should be fully involved in the management of their staff. Such a transformation would involve the pursuit of each of the four goals, with the adoption of a more long-term, strategic perspective, and the treatment of staff as a resource to be utilised to the full, rather than simply as a cost to be minimised (Guest, 1987).

Legge (1989) finds more common ground between the ideal types of personnel management and HRM than other commentators but also identifies three significant differences in the HRM literature. HRM concentrates on managers rather than on what managers do with shopfloor staff; it emphasises the key role of line managers rather than personnel managers and the responsibility of top management for managing culture. All these approaches in adopting stereotypical conceptualisations, however, thus tend to exaggerate the difference between HRM and PM in practice. Indeed, it could be said that HRM is depicted as aspirational whereas PM is what actually happens in practice in many organisations, so like is not being really compared with like.

A strong central theme of HRM in these accounts is that of linking the people management practice to business strategy and we now examine this in the next section of this chapter.

**Table 1. The 27-item checklist**

| Dimension | Personnel and IR | HRM |
|---|---|---|
| **Belief and assumptions** | | |
| 1. Contract | Careful delineation of written contracts | Aim to go 'beyond contract' |
| 2. Rules | Importance of devising clear rules/mutuality | 'Can do' outlook: impatience with 'rule' |
| 3. Guide to management action | Procedures/consistency control | 'Business need'/flexibility/ commitment |
| 4. Behaviour referent | Norms/custom and practice | Values/mission |
| 5. Managerial task vis-à-vis labour | Monitoring | Nurturing |
| 6. Nature of relations | Pluralist | Unitarist |
| 7. Conflict | Institutionalised | De-emphasised |
| **Strategic aspects** | | |
| 8. Key relations | Labour–management | Business–customer |
| 9. Initiatives | Piecemeal | Integrated |
| 10. Corporate plan | Marginal to | Central to |
| 11. Speed of decisions | Slow | Fast |
| **Line management** | | |
| 12. Management role | Transactional | Transformational leadership |
| 13. Key managers | Personnel/IR specialists | General/business/line managers |
| 14. Communication | Indirect | Direct |
| 15. Standardisation | High (e.g. 'parity' an issue) | Low (e.g. 'parity' not seen as relevant) |
| 16. Prized management skills | Negotiation | Facilitation |
| **Key levers** | | |
| 17. Selection | Separate, marginal task | Integrated, key task |
| 18. Pay | Job evaluation: multiple, fixed grades | Performance-related: few if any grades |
| 19. Conditions | Separately negotiated | Harmonisation |
| 20. Labour-management | Collective bargaining contracts | Towards individual contracts |
| 21. Thrust of relations with stewards | Regularised through facilities and training | Marginalised (with the exception of some bargaining for change models) |
| 22. Job categories and grades | Many | Few |
| 23. Communication | Restricted flow/indirect | Increased flow/direct |
| 24. Job design | Division of labour | Teamwork |
| 25. Conflict handling | Reach temporary truces | Manage climate and culture |
| 26. Training and development | Controlled access to courses | Learning companies |
| 27. Foci of attention for interventions | Personnel procedures | Wide-ranging cultural, structural and personnel strategies |

*Source*: Storey 1992

**The Management of Human Resources**

## Strategy and HRM

More recently the study of HRM has adopted a cross-functional approach and expanded its breadth of analysis beyond the staple concerns of selection, training, reward, etc. In particular, one stream of research, strategic human resource management (SHRM) has emerged as being highly influential in this respect. In essence, SHRM theory posits that an organisation's human resource assets are potentially the sole source of sustainable competitive advantage. Much of the work in this area draws from the resource-based theory (RBT) of the firm (Barney, 1991, 1995). Here RBT suggests that competitive advantage depends ultimately on an organisation having superior, valuable, rare, non-substitutable resources at its disposal and that such resources are not easily imitated by others. The nonimitable nature of resources is a key aspect, otherwise competitors would be able to replicate them and the advantage would rapidly disappear. The subtleties of the human resource value creation process, however, are extremely difficult for competitors to imitate. The ambiguities and complexities associated with even the 'strongest' of organisational cultures, and how HRM practices are related to culture, are considerable and cannot be easily teased out by would-be imitators. Equally, any competitive advantage located in a codified and explicit set of HRM practices is also much less likely to be nonimitable than one based on the complex interaction of HRM policies and an organisation's 'social architecture' (Mueller, 1996). By social architecture Mueller is referring to skill formation activities, co-operative behaviour and the tacit knowledge organisations possess. Thus the value creation process arising from HRM competencies does appear to meet the criteria set out by RBT and consequently a growing body of empirical and theoretical work has emerged on SHRM (see Boxall, 1996; Boxall and Purcell, 2000 for reviews of this literature). However, our knowledge base of SHRM is still rather limited, not least by its somewhat fragmented nature and there is, as yet, little consensus in the empirical findings. In the discussion below we review some of the more influential debates and findings of SHRM research.

A classic early work by Kochan *et al.* examined the nature of 'strategic choice' in HRM and provides an example whereby changes in the competitive environment lead to business decisions which *'reverberate through the organisation and its industrial system'* (1983: 13). Whilst such a response is clearly connected with business changes, Miller (1987) is undoubtedly right to question whether, in such circumstances, 'strategy' is an appropriate term. The strategic management of human resources must be more than a mere knock-on effect: most business decisions will have some effects on the management of people, but such effects are not necessarily strategic decisions. For Miller operational linkages between the business strategy and the policy towards employees are the key, or in his words, the 'fit of HRM with the strategic thrust of the organisation'. This is clearly an important point but Miller's definition of SHRM:

> those decisions and actions which concern the management of employees at all levels in the business and which are directed towards creating and sustaining competitive advantage
>
> (Miller, 1987: 352)

while important in demanding that human resources be a corporate level concern, has a significant weakness because of its concentration on linkages to the neglect of content.

If we return to the work of Porter (1985), from which Miller borrows, we find that competitive advantage can be achieved *either* through cost leadership or differentiation. Thus Miller's definition of SHRM would cover firms adopting either of these two approaches, as long as there was a 'fit' of HRM with the business policy followed. Yet these two approaches are likely to embody very different strategies for the management of human resources: one being based on seeing employees as a commodity, with the emphasis on cost control, while the other may emphasise differentiation in terms of quality, with employees as a resource to be developed.

A more useful approach might be to characterise SHRM as entailing strategic integration and a 'positive' approach to the management of employees, with an emphasis on staff as a resource rather than a cost. Thus strategic integration is a necessary but not sufficient component of HRM. The emphasis on staff as a resource would be likely to embody policies designed to achieve the goals Guest (see above) has identified as being important, namely flexibility, quality and commitment, although Guest himself appears to regard integration as an outcome rather than a process. However, we would argue that an emphasis on staff as a resource without strategic integration is not SHRM either. For instance, the many customer care programmes owe much to the fact that other companies are doing them, rather than relating to the business strategy of the organisation concerned. Thus in circumstances whereby HRM programmes become ends in themselves it is hard to credit them with being strategic. Equally, it clearly fails one of the tests of resource-based theory, namely that of being nonimitable. In contrast, an 'accounting' view of labour management may well be strategic in that it may be related to competitive advantage through cost leadership and, as such, strategically integrated, but this is not what SHRM is supposed to be about (see Storey, 1992; Guest, 1987). Hence the latter approach sees the importance of staff in a 'negative' sense of not hindering existing business strategy as opposed to actively contributing towards it. Of course, many companies would fit neither category in that the management of staff may not be considered a strategic issue at all, and neither integrated into the strategic planning process nor considered as a resource (see Table 1.2). Thus there is generally much academic criticism of failure of SHRM in practice but we must ask whether our expectations are rather too high of what SHRM can deliver.

**Table 1.2**

|  | Strategic | Non-strategic |
|---|---|---|
| People as resource | HRM | PM |
| People as cost | Not HRM? | Traditional management |

One recurrent theme in the SHRM literature is that organisations need to 'match' their human resource strategies to their business strategies, so that the former contribute towards the successful implementation of the latter (Miller, 1987; Lengnick-Hall and Lengnick-Hall, 1988; Schuler and Jackson, 1989; Boxall, 1992). A growing number of sectoral and company-level studies have shown how organisations facing change in their competitive environment have responded with new business strategies, which in turn have required a transformation in the organisation's approach to the management of staff (see, for example, Hendry and Pettigrew, 1992; Hendry *et al.*, 1988; McKinlay and Starkey, 1992; Snape *et al.*, 1993; Boxhall and Steenveld, 1999).

This approach, the so-called '*matching model*' by Boxall (1992), argues for a fit, or match, between business strategy and a human resource strategy, which fosters the required employee attitudes and behaviour. In this sense, human resource strategy flows from the initial choice of business strategy (Purcell, 1989). Furthermore, to the extent that changes in the corporate environment evoke a particular business strategy response, human resource strategies can also be seen as being strongly influenced by environmental change (Hendry *et al.*, 1988). As Sparrow and Hilltrop (1994: 628) argue, 'HRM strategies are all about making business strategies work.' A closely related body of work has recently called for a *configurational* approach to SHRM. Here it is argued that it is the pattern of HRM practices that supports the achievement of organisational goals and that, in line with the contingency approach, fit with strategy is vital to explaining the HR-performance nexus. The configurational approach takes the best fit view a step further in that it argues there are a number of specific ideal types that provide both horizontal fit, between HR practices, and vertical fit, between HR practices and business strategy (Ferris *et al.*, 1999). The configuration of practices which provides the tightest fits is then seen as being ideal for the particular strategy. Although this work is still in its infancy there has been some recent theorising on the nature of the 'ideal types' of configurations for customer-, operations-, product-, etc. led organisations (Sheppeck and Militello, 2000).

However, there is an issue as to how far human resource strategies can simply be 'matched' with the requirements of a changing business strategy. As Boxall (1992: 68) notes, much of the 'matching' literature has implicitly assumed that employee attitudes and behaviour can be moulded by management strategy in the pursuit of strategic fit. Human resource outcomes cannot be taken for granted, though, and whatever the merits of the view that personnel managers must increasingly see themselves as 'business managers' (Tyson, 1987; 1995), it is important to recognise that personnel management and industrial relations are about more than simply selecting the appropriate fit with a given business strategy. Thus the best-fit approach can be criticised for failing to acknowledge the importance of social norms and legal rules in the search for alignment. Indeed, the notion of fit is rather static and an inappropriate metaphor in a fast-changing and chaotic corporate world.

A commonly expressed view is that since the purpose of businesses is to produce profit, not good HRM, and to the extent that such practices are essentially facilitative and not a stand-alone activity but must flow from corporate strategy, it is inevitable that they are indeed second- or third-order (see the work of Purcell here). However, the discussion on much of this debate has been rather unhelpful because of the assumption that it is only first-order strategies that are really 'strategic', and other concerns relate essentially to operational considerations and are hence non-strategic. This is potentially misleading as it assumes strategies are of one kind (partly stemming from the view that strategy relates to product market issues) and other matters are either strategic or non-strategic, whereas in fact it may be better to think of degrees of strategy. It is clear, for instance, that HR is downstream from the overall corporate mission, be it a return on assets or profits through business decisions. The common argument posed above is undoubtedly correct: businesses are not formed to create good HR practice. Nevertheless, this is rather unhelpful in examining the significance of the relationship with business issues. What is being called for is that such matters should be considered within the overall business strategy of the organisation rather than separate from it. In other words, HR should not merely be affected in a knock-on manner, but be located much further up in the business strategy process.

What appears to be demanded is integration at two levels: firstly at the level of implementation, where it is argued that much of the success of policy implementation depends on the effective management of human resources. Secondly, it is argued that this is not in itself adequate, that human resources should actually be considered further up the planning process, so that rather than just flowing from the business strategy, it should be part of it, in that the human resource dimension may constrain the type of business strategy adopted or provide opportunities. It is no good making a business decision (strategic) to relocate if the organisation finds it cannot recruit the workforce in the area. The existing skills of the workforce may well constrain business growth, etc. Either or both of these approaches would be consistent with SHRM. In other words, the first approach suggests that the human resource strategy should be consistent with business strategy and implementation should take account of human resource factors. The second approach demands rather more: that human resource factors be considered not just in the implementation of policy but actually influence which business strategy is adopted.

## Performance and HRM: it's the people, stupid!

For years, HR professionals have yearned for evidence to show that people were really the most important asset a company had, and that good HR practice delivered in terms of organisational performance. By the mid-1990s their prayers appeared to have been answered in that a growing number of studies appeared to demonstrate just that. For example, in research undertaken on behalf of the

Institute of Personnel and Development in the UK the Sheffield effectiveness programme (based on 100 SMEs in manufacturing) concluded that people management is not only critical to business performance but is also much more important than an emphasis on quality, technology, competitive strategy or R&D in terms of influence on the bottom line. Effective people management was found to account for 19 per cent of the variation in profitability and 18 per cent of the variation in productivity, whilst in comparison R & D accounts for 8 per cent and the others barely 1 per cent (quality, technology and competitive strategy). Thus according to Patterson *et al.* (1998) this finding in one sense validates the oft-quoted claims of CEOs that people are the most important asset but is also paradoxical in that HRM is the most neglected aspect of business:

> Overall, the results of this study clearly indicate the importance of people management practices in influencing company performance. The results are unique, since no similar study has been conducted, comparing the influence of different types of managerial practices upon performance. If managers wish to influence the performance of their companies, the results show that the most important area to emphasise is the management of people. This is ironic, given that our research has also demonstrated that emphasis on HRM practices is one of the most neglected areas of managerial practice within organisations.
>
> (Patterson *et al.*, 1998: 21)

There are various terms used in these studies, for example, 'high performance management', 'high commitment management', 'best practice HRM', 'high involvement management', but a common message: the adoption of HRM practices pays in terms of where it matters most, the bottom line. It is worth noting that it is primarily in the USA that the case for the new approach has been demonstrated. The main studies have been American and, according to Huselid (1995), demonstrate that progressive HRM practices produce a significant magnitude of return. A 1 per cent standard deviation increase in such practices is associated with a 7.05 per cent decrease in labour turnover and, on a per employee basis, $27,044 more in sales and $18,641 and $3,814 more in market value and profits respectively. Other American studies (Arthur, 1994; MacDuffie, 1995) appear to generally support this and an exhaustive review by Ichniowski *et al.* (1996) concluded that a 'collage of evidence suggests that innovative workplace practices can increase performance, primarily through the use of systems of related practices that enhance worker participation, make work design less rigid and decentralise managerial tasks'. They also note that individual work practices have no effect on economic performance but 'the adoption of a *coherent and integrated system* of innovative practices, including extensive recruiting and careful selection, flexible job definitions and problem solving teams, gainsharing-type compensation plans, employment security and extensive labour–management communication, substantially improve productivity and quality outcomes'. Similarly Pfeffer (1994: 27) emphasises that 'these are interrelated practices that seem to characterise companies that are effective in achieving competitive success through how they manage people'. Wood (1995: 52) argues that his list of 'high commitment practices' should be used together since 'it is through the combined effects of such practices that management can most hope to elicit high levels of commitment'. The general argument is that piecemeal take-up of HR practices means that many managements miss out on the benefits to be gained from a more integrated approach (Marchington and Wilkinson, 2000: 94–7). Thus such collections of reinforcing HR practices have begun to be referred to as a 'bundle', and the task of HR managers is to identify and implement such HR systems.

However, this appears to be rather more easily prescribed than achieved. Many authors produce lists of HR practices which should be included in these bundles, but there is little consistency yet and we still await a definitive prescription of the best 'bundle'. As Wood and de Menezes (1998) point out, reviewing these studies indicates that there is a somewhat 'pick and mix' approach to the HRM bundle. Storey (1992: 35) identified aspects such as integrated selection systems, performance-related pay, harmonisation, individual contracts, teamworking and learning companies. Pfeffer (1994: 30–59) provides a list of 16, which includes employment security, selectivity in recruitment, incentive pay, employee ownership, participation and empowerment, teamworking, training and skill development, wage compression and promotion from within. These are held together under an overarching philosophy with a long-term commitment and a willingness to engage in consistent measurement of whether or not high standards are being achieved. Delaney *et al.* (1989) identified ten practices, Hueslid (1995) 13, Wood (1999) 17 whilst Delery and Doty (1996) appear quite miserly in comparison in only identifying seven strategic practices. All this must seem at the very least confusing to the practitioner but, more than this, there appear to be some quite contradictory notions in the various lists. For example, on the one hand formal grievance systems appear in some bundles as an indicator of best practice, but are associated in others with trade unionism and thus seen as part of the bureaucratic 'personnel management' approach.

Aside from the inconsistencies in the HRM bundle, the best practice and universalistic approach has received considerable criticism. Purcell, for example, is critical of the claim for a universal application:

> The claim that the bundle of best practice HRM is universally applicable leads us into a utopian cul-de-sac and ignores the powerful and highly significant changes in work, employment and society visible inside organisations and in the wider community. The search for bundles of high commitment work practices is important, but so too is the search for understanding of the circumstances of where and when it is applied, why some organisations do and others do not adopt HRM, and how some firms seem to have more appropriate HR systems for their current and future needs than others. It is only one of many ways in which employees are managed, all of which must come within the bounds of HRM.
>
> (Purcell, 1999: 36)

Whitfield and Poole (1997: 757) point out there are unresolved issues of causality, problems with the narrow base of the work undertaken (largely manufacturing), concerns that much of the data is self-reported by management, as well as doubts about measures of performance which are used. Even if the data does indicate a causal link, we lack understanding of the processes involved and the mechanisms by which practices translate into desired outcomes. Equally problematic is the implicit assumption that a particular bundle of practices is feasible for all organisations. Some organisational structures and cultures will present major difficulties in implementing certain HRM practices, for example, high involvement practices in highly bureaucratic and formal organisations will be particularly problematic. The notion of a reinforcing bundle of practices cannot be fully convincing either, given the variation in the bundles noted above. It cannot yet be dismissed that the different HR practices have a differential impact on firm performance. The best practice approach thus appears somewhat of a black box and many questions remain as yet unanswered. Why is there a linkage? What is it about having these practices which delivers performance? What is the process by which these outcomes have occurred? It is unlikely that, say, the very act of introducing practices X, Y and Z will deliver benefits directly. Much will depend on the context of their introduction, the way they are implemented, the support provided, etc. – but what are the critical factors?

## The changing role of HRM

Despite the growing recognition of the importance of effective people management for organisational success, there are still a number of concerns about the future for HRM. Superficially, the HRM function seems to be in good health. The CIPD now claims over 100,000 members (CIPD National Conference, Harrogate, 2000) and WERS data found that the proportion of workplaces with personnel specialists, defined as managers whose job titles contain 'personnel', 'HR' or 'industrial', 'employee' or 'staff relations' and who spent at least a quarter of their time on such matters, rose by a third during the 1990s. In 1998 20 per cent of workplaces employed a personnel specialist, up from 14 per cent in 1984 (Cully *et al.*, 1999). However, deeper worries about the effectiveness of the HR function linger on.

According to Peter Drucker, there has been a tendency in the past for the HR department to be seen as something of a 'trash can' function, a repository for all those tasks which do not fit neatly anywhere else:

> Personnel administration . . . is largely a collection of incidental techniques without much internal cohesion. As personnel administration conceives the job of managing worker and work, it is partly a file-clerk's job, partly a housekeeping job, partly a social worker's job and partly fire-fighting to head off union trouble or to settle it . . . the things the personnel administrator is typically responsible for . . . are necessary chores. I doubt though that they should be put together in one department for they are a hodge-podge . . . They are neither one function by kinship of skills required to carry out the

activities, nor are they one function by being linked together in the work process, by forming a distinct stage in the work of the managers or in the process of the business.

(Drucker, 1961: 269–70; quoted in Legge, 1995: 6)

Table 1.3 lists some of the key functions that HR departments now provide. In part Drucker's critique that the HR function lacks coherence has been moderated by some recent organisational changes. In particular, the practice of outsourcing during the 1980s and 1990s saw many of the more peripheral HR responsibilities, such as catering arrangements and security, subcontracted to specialist firms. Equally, the practice of decentralising HR responsibility from corporate central departments to business unit level departments and further still to line management has seen much 'streamlining' of HR responsibilities. However, perhaps more worrying for the HR function is that these trends have also seen some traditional core personnel areas, such as recruitment, training, and employee welfare management, also outsourced to HR consultants. In some accounts these trends have been seen as part of a 'crisis' as HR struggled for legitimacy and status in cost-conscious times and the function has been described as being 'under siege from external consultants' (Clark and Clark, 1991). In Torrington's view this 'crisis' is nothing new and its recent intensity may owe rather more to critical academics than actual reality in the profession:

> There is a crisis of confidence among personnel specialists, as there always has been. Their results are almost impossible to measure and their successes and failures are largely the successes and failures of other people. Furthermore, they operate in a field – how people behave – in which everyone else is an expert with a personal point of view from which they will not depart. The difficulty for personnel people is that they know how intractable some of the people problems really are. They are not helped by the persistent disparagement of HRM academics, who go to considerable lengths to explain how badly their job is done.

(Torrington, 1998: 36)

Others have interpreted the increasing use of consultants as reflecting a sign that HR is now seen as being much more important and thus merits additional investment. Management consultants are argued to be an important conduit along which new and more sophisticated HR practices flow between organisations. Nevertheless, some recent trends suggest that a 'crisis' interpretation may be more in tune with the facts. In particular, the reduction of the HR domains appears to have been taken one step further and there is now a considerable debate on the benefits of outsourcing the entire HR function. In part such changes have been driven by further cost pressures in a period of corporate downsizing, but more worrying for the HR function is that outsourcing may also have been fuelled by senior management concerns about the quality and responsiveness of in-house HR functions (Greer *et al.*, 1999). For example, drawing from survey evidence from UK private sector organisations, Guest reports that chief executives and personnel managers both give low ratings to the performance of the HR department and the effectiveness of HR practices in the company (Guest and Baron, 2000).

**Table 1.3  Functions performed by the HR department**

- Job analysis
- Human resource planning
- Recruitment and selection
- Training and development
- Pay and conditions of employment
- Grievance and disciplinary procedures
- Employee relations and communications
- Administration of contracts of employment
- Employee welfare and counselling
- Equal opportunities policy and monitoring
- Health and safety
- Outplacement

Thus the rising recognition that HR issues are vitally important in organisations has, paradoxically, not been all good news for the HR department, given their 'Cinderella' image. It seems many senior managers may be of the view that people management is far too important to be left to the HR department. In a *Fortune* article one commentator urged CEOs to 'Blow the sucker (HR) up' (Stewart, 1996). Whilst others have not been as forthright as this, the HR function appears to be at a dangerous crossroads, with some suggesting ascendancy to a full business partner whilst others predict a painful demise. On the one hand, the ascendancy school sees the rise of HR following hard on the success of SHRM and the creation of competitive advantage for organisations. In contrast, the formula for demise often involves the failure of HR to understand the broader business agenda. The literature typically sees a need for the 'reinvention' of HR along such lines, and that HR must simply evolve or die. However, Ulrich (1997) has also warned that the literature is replete with premature death notices of the HR function.

What then is the 'formula' for HR success? Firstly, in addressing this question there is a real danger of slipping into unrealistic, wishful thinking – of which there is already an ample supply in the prescriptive HR literature. Secondly, there is rather more consistency in the literature on what the future for HR should *not* be based on than that on what it should be. Thus Rucci (1997) has suggested that the worst-case scenario for HR survival is a department that does not promote change, does not identify leaders, does not understand the business, does not know customers, does not drive costs and does not emphasise values. According to Pfeffer (1998: 195) 'if human resources is to have a future inside organisations, it is not by playing police person and enforcer of rules and policies, nor is it likely to be ensured by playing handmaiden to finance'.

In contrast, there are a wide variety of suggestions for what the HR department should do in the future. According to Brockbank (1997) the future agenda is that a successful HR department needs to be involved in framing not only HR strategy

**The Management of Human Resources**

**32**

but also business strategy, promoting growth rather than downsizing and building more credible relationships with key shareholders and board members. Beer and Eisenstat (1996) emphasise the need for a comprehensive HR vision, stressing that in the future HR managers will require co-ordination skills across functions, business units and borders following the increased globalisation of business, and general management, communication leadership, creativity and entrepreneurship competencies. Research by Eichinger and Ulrich (1995) on the top priorities that HR professionals believe need to addressed in the future emphasises organisational redesign, attracting new leaders, customer focus, cost containment, rejecting fads, addressing diversity and becoming a more effective business partner with their line management customers. Ulrich (1998) also reports the results of survey research on the key competencies managers believe will be necessary for future success in HR roles – see Table 1.4. The ability to manage culture and change coupled with personal credibility is seen as critical.

**Table 1.4  Key competencies of HR professionals**

| Relative importance to effectiveness | % |
| --- | --- |
| Understanding of business | 14 |
| Knowledge of HR practices | 17 |
| Ability to manage culture | 19 |
| Ability to manage change | 22 |
| Personal credibility | 27 |

*Source*: Ulrich (1998: 20–1)

Thus a key theme in much of the work is that HR needs to earn its place at the top, i.e. senior management, table. One danger in these accounts is that the emphasis is very much on the strategic and business aspects of the HR role. In particular the 'bread and butter' issues of effectively managing the recruitment, selection, appraisal, development, reward and involvement of staff have been rather pushed to the periphery. What is interesting about Table 1.4 is the relatively low rating of knowledge of HR practices. There is thus a real concern that HR managers could be neglecting 'the basics' in their search for legitimacy and status with senior managers. In short, HR could be accused of ignoring employees. Indeed, HR 'futurologists', it seems, need to be reminded of Giles and Williams' (1991) rejoinder to accept that the HR role is to serve their customers and not their egos. We feel that there is a danger that the senior management and shareholder customers will be getting rather better service than the 'employee customer' in the HR department of the future.

One of our aims in the presentation of material in this book has been to balance the discussion in terms of both employee expectations and management expectations of the HR function. So, for example, in accounts of topics such as downsizing, empowerment, performance management, reward, flexibility, etc. the approach has been not only to critically examine HR's strategic role in the process but to also review the impact of these practices on employees. The last section of this chapter now discusses in more detail the layout of the book and some suggestions on its use.

## The book

This book has been written primarily as a text for students of business and management who are studying HRM. It aims to be critical but pragmatic: we are wary of quick fixes, slogans, prescriptive checklists, and bullet points of 'best practice'. The authors are all prominent researchers and draw from a considerable depth of research in their field. Each chapter provides a critical review of the topic, bringing together theoretical and empirical material. The emphasis is on analysis and insight and areas of growing significance are also included in each chapter. At the same time we wish to look at the implications of HRM research and theory development for practice and to do so in a readable, accessible manner. The book does not assume prior knowledge on the part of the reader but seeks to locate issues in a wider theoretical framework. It is suitable for MBA students, and undergraduates who these days may be doing business studies alongside degrees in engineering, humanities, social science, etc. As such, this is appropriate for modular degree courses.

The book is divided into two parts; the first one: *Fundamentals of HRM* examines the core elements of HR practice (see Table 1.3 above). In this section there are chapters on selection and assessment, performance appraisal, employee development, reward, grievance and discipline, employment relations. The second half of the book: *Contemporary Themes and Issues* addresses some key areas of rising importance in HRM practice. Here there are chapters on flexibility, careers, downsizing, empowerment, ethics, diversity management and HRM practice in the increasingly important small and medium-sized business sector.

Each chapter is accompanied by a combination of case studies, role-plays and exercises for students. The intention is that students should be actively involved in the study of HRM. We believe that in this respect the book is unique in the UK, where the trend has been for the publication of separate text and case books. Our aim in combining these elements in a single volume is to permit a smoother integration of the topic material and supporting cases and exercises. In all chapters the authors have provided both text and cases, although in some we also include additional material from other authors. The cases and exercises are of different lengths, levels and type in order to serve different teaching and learning purposes, e.g. a long case study for students to read and prepare prior to seminars/tutorials as well as shorter cases and exercises which can be prepared in the session itself. The aim is to provide a good range of up-to-date, relevant material based upon actual practice in HRM.

# References to Chapter 1

Armstrong, M. (1987) 'Human resource management: a case of the emperor's new clothes?', *Personnel Management*, August.

Arthur, J. (1994) 'Effects of human resource system on manufacturing performance and turnover', *Academy of Management Journal*, 37: 670–87.

Barney, J. (1991) 'Firm resources and sustained competitive advantage', *Journal of Management*, 17 (1): 99–120.

Barney, J.B. (1995) 'Looking inside for competitive advantage', *Academy of Management Executive*, 9 (4): 49–61.

Beardwell, I. (1998) (ed) *Contemporary Industrial Relations*, Oxford: Open University Press.

Beer, M. and Eisenstat, R. (1996) 'Developing an organisation capable of implementing strategy and learning', *Human Relations*, 49 (5).

Boxall, P. (1992) 'Strategic human resource management: beginnings of a new theoretical sophistication?', *Human Resource Management Journal*, 2 (3), Spring: 60–79.

Boxall, P. (1996) 'The strategic HRM debate and the resource-based view of the firm', *Human Resource Management Journal*, 6 (3): 59–75.

Boxall, P. and Purcell, J. (2000) 'Strategic human resource management: where have we come from and where should we be going?', *International Journal of Management Review*, 2 (2): 183–20.

Boxall, P. and Steenveld, M. (1999) 'Human resource strategy and competitive advantage: a longitudinal study of engineering consultancies', *Journal of Management Studies*, 36 (4): 443–63.

Brockbank, W. (1997) 'HR's future on the way to a presence', *Human Resource Management*, 36 (1): 65–69.

Clark, I. and Clark, T. (1990) 'Personnel management and the use of executive recruitment consultancies', *Human Resource Management Journal*, 1 (1): 46–62.

Collinson, M., Edwards, P., Rees, C., and Innes, L. (1997) *Involving Employees in Quality Management*, DTI report.

Cully, M., Woodland, S., O'Reilly, A. and Dix, G. (1999) *Britain at Work*, London: Routledge.

Delaney, J.T., Lewis, D. and Ichniowski, C. (1989) *Human Resource Policies and Practices in American Firms*, Washington DC: US Government Printing Office.

Delery, J. and Doty, D. (1996) 'Modes of theorizing in strategic human resource management: tests of universalistic, contingency and configurational performance predictions', *Academy of Management Journal*, 39 (4): 802–35.

Dent, M. (1995) 'The new National Health Service: a case of postmodernism?', *Organization Studies*, 16 (5): 875–99.

Donovan (1968) *The Royal Commission on Trade Unions and Employers' Associations, 1965–1968: Report*, Cmnd. 3623.

Drucker, P. (1961) *The Practice of Management*, London: Mercury.

Eccles, R. and Nohira, N. (1992) *Beyond the Hype: Rediscovering the Essence of Management*, Boston, Mass: Harvard Business School Press.

Eichinger, B. and Ulrich, D. (1995) 'Are you future agile?', *Human Resource Planning*: 30–41.

Ferris, G., Hochwarter, W.A., Buckley, M.K., Harnell-Cook, G. and Frink, D.D. (1999) 'Human resource management: some new directions', *Journal of Management*, 25 (3): 385–416.

Fowler, A. (1987) 'When the Chief Executive discovers HRM', *Personnel Management*, January: 3.

Gennard, J. and Kelly, J. (1997) 'The unimportance of labels: the diffusion of the personnel/HRM function', *Industrial Relations Journal*, 28 (I): 27–42.

Giles, E. and Williams, R. (1991) 'Can the personnel department survive quality management?', *Personnel Management*, April: 28–33.

Greer, C.R., Youngblood, S.A. and Gray, D.A. (1999) 'Human Resource Management outsourcing: the make or buy decision', *Academy of Management Executive*, 13 (3): 85–96.

Guest, D. (1987) 'Human resource management and industrial relations', *Journal of Management Studies*, 24 (5), September: 503–21.

Guest, D. (1991) 'Personnel management: the end of orthodoxy?', *British Journal of Industrial Relations*, 29 (2).

Guest, D. (1998) 'Beyond HRM: commitment and the contract culture' in M. Marchington and P. Sparrow (eds) (1998) *Human Resource Management: the New Agenda*, London: FT/ Pitman.

Guest, D. (1999) 'Human resource management: the workers' verdict', *Human Resource Management Journal*, 9 (3): 5–25.

Guest, D. and Baron, A. (2000) 'Piece by piece', *People Management*, 6 (15): 26–31.

Guest, D. and Conway, N. (1999) 'Peering into the black hole: the downside of the new employment relations in the UK', *British Journal of Industrial Relations*, 37 (3): 367–90.

Hendry, C. and Pettigrew, A. (1992) 'Patterns of strategic change in the development of human resource management', *British Journal of Management*, 3: 137–56.

Hendry, C., Pettigrew, A. and Sparrow, P. (1988) 'Changing patterns of human resource management', *Personnel Management*, November: 37–41.

Heriot, P. and Pemberton, C. (1995) *New Deals: the Revolution in Management Careers*, London: Wiley.

Huselid, M. (1995) 'The impact of human resource management practices on turnover, productivity and corporate financial performance', *Academy of Management Journal*, 38 (3).

Ichniowski, C., Kochan, T., Levine, D., Olsen, C. and Strauss, G. (1996) 'What works at work: overview and assessment', *Industrial Relations*, 35 (3): 299–333.

Keenoy, T. (1990) 'HRM: rhetoric, reality and contradiction', *International Journal of Human Resource Management*, 1 (3): 363–84.

Kochan, T., McKersie, R. and Cappelli, P. (1983) 'Strategic choice and industrial relations theory', *Industrial Relations*, 23 (I): 16–39.

Legge, K. (1989) 'Human resource management: a critical analysis' in J. Storey (ed) *New Perspective on Human Resource Management*, London: Routledge.

Legge, K. (1995) *Human Resource Management: Rhetorics and Realities*, Basingstoke: Macmillan.

Lengnick-Hall, C.A. and Lengnick-Hall, M.L. (1988) 'Strategic human resources management: a review of the literature and a proposed typology', *Academy of Management Review*, 13 (3): 454–70.

Mabey, C., Clark, T. and Skinner, D. (eds) (1998) *The Experience of Human Resource Management*, Milton Keynes: Open University Press.

MacDuffie, J. (1995) 'Human resource bundles and manufacturing performance: organisational logic and flexible production systems in the world auto industry', *Industrial and Labour Relations Review*, 48 (2): 197–221.

Marchington, M. and Wilkinson, A. (2000) *Core Personnel and Development*, London: CIPD.

McKinlay, A. and Starkey, K. (1992) 'Competitive strategies and organizational change', *Human Resource Strategies*, G. Salaman (ed) London: Sage.

Miller, P. (1987) 'Strategic industrial relations and human resource management – distinction, definition and recognition', *Journal of Management Studies*, 24 (4) July: 347–61.

Mueller, F. (1996) 'Human resources as strategic assets: an evolutionary resource based theory', *Journal of Management Studies*, 33 (6): 757–85.

National Association of Citizens' Advice Bureaux (1997) *Flexibility Abused: A CAB Report on Empowerment Conditions in the Labour Market*, London: NACAB.

Noon, M. and Blyton, P. (1998) *The Realities of Work*, London: Macmillan.

Patterson, M., West, M., Hawthorn, R. and Nickell, S. (1998) 'Impact of people management practices on business performance issues', *People Management*, 22, London: IPD.

Pfeffer, J. (1994) *Competitive Advantage through People*, Boston, Mass: Harvard Business School Press.

**The Management of Human Resources**

Pfeffer, P. (1997) 'Does human resource have a future?' in Ulrich, D., *Tomorrow's Human Resource Management*, New York: Wiley.

Pfeffer, P. (1998) *The Human Equation*, Boston, Mass: Harvard Business School Press.

Porter, M. (1985) *Corporate Advantage*, New York: Free Press.

Purcell, J. (1989) 'The impact of corporate strategy on human resource management', *New Perspectives on Human Resource Management*, ed. J. Storey, London: Routledge.

Purcell, J. (1999) 'Best practice and best fit: chimera or cul-de-sac?', *Human Resource Management Journal*, 9 (3): 26–41.

Rocha, J.A.O. (1998) 'The new public management and its consequences in the public personnel system', *The Review of Public Personnel Administration*, Spring, 18 (2): 82–87.

Rucci, A.J. (1997) 'Should HR survive? A profession at the crossroads', *Human Resource Management*, 36 (1): 169–75.

Schuler, R.S. and Jackson, S.E. (1989) 'Determinants of human resource management priorities and implications for industrial relations', *Journal of Management*, 15 (1): 89–99.

Scott, A. (1994) *Willing Slaves?*, Cambridge: CUP.

Sheppeck, M.A. and Militello, J. (2000) 'Strategic human resource configurations and organizational performance', *Human Resource Management*, 39 (1): 5–16.

Sisson, K. (1990) 'Introducing the *Human Resource Management Journal*', *Human Resource Management Journal*, 1 (1): 1–11.

Snape, E., Wilkinson, A. and Redman, T. (1993) 'Human resource management in building societies: making the transformation?', *Human Resource Management Journal*, 3 (3).

Sparrow, P. and Hilltrop, J. (1994) *European Human Resource Management in Transition*, London: Prentice-Hall.

Stewart, T. (1996) 'Taking on the last bureaucracy', *Fortune Magazine*: 105–108.

Storey, J. (1992) *Developments in the Management of Human Resources*, Oxford: Blackwell.

Thompson, P. and O'Conner Davidson, J. (1995) 'The continuity of discountinuity: managerial rhetoric in turbulent times', *Personnel Review*, 24 (4): 17–33.

Torrington, D. (1993) 'How dangerous is human resource management?', *Employee Relations*, 15 (5): 40–53.

Torrington, D. (1998) 'Crisis and opportunity in HRM: the challenge for the personnel function', in Sparrow, P. and Marchington, M. (eds) *Human Resource Management: The New Agenda*, London: Prentice Hall.

Torrington, D. and Hall, L. (1998) *Personnel Management* (3rd edn), London: Prentice-Hall.

Tyson, S. (1987) 'The management of the personnel function', *Journal of Management Studies*, 24 (5), September: 523–32.

Tyson, S. (1995) *Human Resource Strategy Towards a General Theory of Human Resource Management*, London: Pitman.

Ulrich, D. (1997) *Tomorrow's Human Resource Management*, New York: Wiley.

Ulrich, D. (1998) *Human Resource Champions*, Boston, Mass: Harvard Business School Press.

Whitfield, K. and Poole, M. (1997) 'Organizing employment for high performance', *Organization Studies*, 18 (5): 745–64.

Wickens, P. (1987) *The Road to Nissan*, London: Macmillan.

Williams, A., Dobson, P. and Walters, A. (1989) *Changing Cultures*, London: IPD.

Wood, S. (1995) 'The four pillars of human resource management: are they connected?', *Human Resource Management Journal*, 5 (5): 49–59.

Wood, S. (1999) 'Getting the measure of the transformed high performance organisation', *British Journal of Industrial Relations*, 37 (3): 391–417.

Wood, S. and de Menezes, L. (1998) 'High commitment management in the UK', *Human Relations*, 51: 485–515.

# Chapter 3 Strategic human resource management

There is a strong lobby propounding the view that human resources are *the* source of competitive advantage for the business, rather than, say, access to capital or use of technology. It is therefore logical to suggest that attention needs to be paid to the nature of this resource and its management as this will impact on human resource behaviour and performance and consequently the performance of the organisation. Indeed Boxall and Steneveld (1999) argue that there is no need to prove the relationship between firm performance and labour management as it is self-evident that the quality of human resource management is a critical influence on the performance of the firm. It is not, therefore, surprising that the rhetoric of strategic human resource management has been readily adopted, especially as a strategic approach is considered to be one of the characteristics of HRM as opposed to personnel management, which is seen as operational. HR needs to be a strategic player and the role of business strategist will be a key role for HR specialists in the future (Cleland *et al.* 2000).

In this chapter we first discuss some basic issues in relation to the nature of human resource strategy and strategic human resource management, we then explore three different theoretical perspectives on strategic human resource management and conclude by considering the role of HR specialists in strategic HRM.

## Strategic human resource management and human resource strategy

Our understanding of HR strategy has changed considerably since strategy first became the subject of great attention. We have moved from viewing strategy as a physical document to strategy as an incremental process, affected by political influences and generating learning. Tyson's (1995) definition of human resource strategy is a useful starting point, although somewhat limited, as will be seen from our later discussion:

> **the intentions of the corporation both explicit and covert, toward the management of its employees, expressed through philosophies, policies and practices.**
> (Tyson 1995)

This definition is helpful because research on human resource strategy in the early 1980s tended to focus on seeking an HR strategy document in order to determine whether there was a strategic approach to HR and what that approach was. This was rather like searching for the Holy Grail. Not surprisingly few complete HR strategies were found and HR specialists berated themselves for having failed in this critical area. Gradually the thinking changed to encompass a view that HR strategy need not be written on a piece of paper or need not indeed, be explicit, as the Tyson quotation illustrates. Further developments in thinking began to take on board the idea that strategies are neither finished, nor complete, but rather incremental and piecemeal. There is compelling evidence to suggest that strategic HR tends to be issue based rather than the formulation of a complete and integrated strategy (for example Grundy 1998; Hall and Torrington 1998). Strategic thinking, strategic decision making and a strategic orientation (for example, Hunt and Boxall 1998) were gradually understood as much more realistic expectations.

In parallel with this thinking there were developments in the general strategy literature which viewed strategy as a process which was not necessarily rational and top down, but a political and evolutionary process (see, for example, Mintzberg 1994). Mintzberg argues that strategy is 'formed' rather than 'formulated' and that any intended strategy is changed by events, opportunities, the actions of employees and so on – so that the realised strategy is different from the initial vision. Strategy, Mintzberg argues, can only be identified in retrospect. Wrapped up in this view is also the idea that strategy is not necessarily determined by top management, alone, but can be influenced, 'bottom up' as ideas are tried and tested in one part of the organisation, and gradually adopted in a wholesale manner if they are seen to be applicable and successful.

This leads on to the concept of strategy as learning both in content and process (see, for example, Senge 1990; Pedler *et al.* 1991) which is supported by the notion of strategy as a process of change (see, for example, Hendry and Pettigrew 1992). Literature draws out the need to sense changes in the environment, develop a resultant strategy and turn this strategy into action. While the HR function has often found itself excluded from the strategy formation process, HR strategy has more often been seen in terms of the implementation of organisational strategies. However implementation of HR strategy has been weak, at best. Among the qualities of the most successful organisations is the ability to turn strategy into action quickly (Ulrich 1998), in other words to implement the chosen strategy (Grensing-Pophel 1999), and Guest (1987) maintained that the capability to implement strategic plans is an important feature of successful HRM. However a lack of attention to the implementation of HR strategy has been identified (Beaumont 1992; Lundy and Cowling 1996; Skinner and Mabey 1997), and the information that does exist suggests that this is a problematic area. Legge (1995) maintained that the evidence of implementation of HR strategies was patchy and sometimes contradictory, and Skinner and Mabey (1997) found that responsibility for implementation was unclear with only 54 per cent of respondents, in organisations with an HR Director, perceiving that the HR function played a major part in implementation. In their research Kane and Palmer (1995) found that the existence of an HR strategy was only a minor influence on the HR policies and procedures that were used.

This brings us to the final issue in this introduction – that of the link between organisational strategy and HR strategy. Figure 3.1 is a simple model that is useful in visualising these relationships and has relevance for the newer conceptions of strategy based on the resource-based view of the firm, as well as earlier conceptions.

In the *separation model* (A) there is no relationship at all, if indeed organisational and human resource strategy *does* exist in an explicit form in the organisation. This is a typical picture of twenty years ago, but it still exists today, particularly in smaller organisations.

The *fit model* (B) represents a growing recognition of the importance of people in the achievement of organisational strategy. Employees are seen as key in the implementation of the declared organisational strategy, and human resource strategy is designed to fit with this. Some of the early formal models of human resource strategy, particularly that proposed by Fombrun *et al.* (1984), concentrate on how the human resource strategy can be designed to ensure a close fit, and the same approach is used in the Schuler and Jackson example in Table 3.1.

This whole approach depends on a view of strategy formulation as a logical rational process, which remains a widely held view. The relationship in the fit model is exemplified by organisations which cascade their business objectives down from the senior management team through functions, through depart-

**Figure 3.1 Potential relationships between organisational strategy and HR strategy**

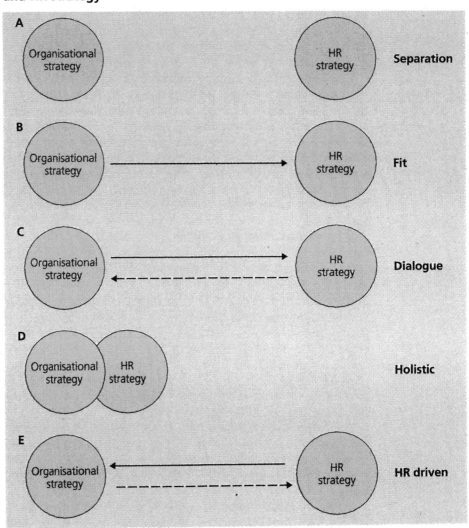

ments, through teams and so on. Functions, for example, have to propose a functional strategy which enables the organisational strategy to be achieved. Departments have to propose a strategy which enables the functional strategy to be achieved, and so on. In this way the HR function (as with any other) is required to respond to organisational strategy by defining a strategy which meets organisational demands.

The *dialogue model* (C) takes the relationship one step further, as it recognises the need for two-way communication and some debate. What is demanded in the organisation's strategy may not be viewed as feasible and alternative possibilities need to be reviewed. The debate, however, is often limited, as shown in the example in the Window on Practice which follows.

---

**WINDOW ON PRACTICE**

In one large, multinational organisation an objectives-setting cascade was put in place. This cascade allowed for a dialogue between the planned organisation strategy and the response of each function. In the organisation strategy there was some emphasis on people growth and development and job fulfilment. The HR Department's response included among other things an emphasis on line management involvement in these areas, which would be supported by consultancy help from the HR Department.

The top management team replied to this by asking the HR Department to add a strategic objective about employee welfare and support. The HR Department strongly argued that this was a line management responsibility, along with coaching, development and so on. The HR Function saw its customers as the managers of the organisation, not the employees. The result of the debate was that the HR Function added the strategic objective about employee welfare.

Although the approach in this case appeared two-way, the stronger of the parties was the management team, and they were determined that their vision was the one that would be implemented!

---

The holistic model and the HR-driven model (D and E) show a much closer involvement between organisational and human resource strategy.

The *holistic model* (D) represents the people of the organisation being recognised as the key to competitive advantage rather than just the way of implementing organisational strategy. In other words HR strategy is not just the means for achieving business strategy (the ends), but an end in itself. Human resource strategy therefore becomes critical and, as Baird *et al.* (1983) argued, there can be no strategy without human resource strategy. Boxall (1996) develops this idea in relation to the resource-based firm, and argues convincingly that business strategy can usefully be interpreted as more broad than a competitive strategy (or positioning in the marketplace). In this case business strategy can encompass a variety of other strategies including HRM, and he describes these strategies as the pieces of a jigsaw. This suggests mutual development and some form of integration, rather than a slavish response to a predetermined business strategy.

The *HR-driven model* (E) offers a more extreme form, which places human resource strategy in prime position. The argument here is that if people are the key to competitive advantage, then we need to build on our people strengths. Logically, then, as the potential of our employees will undoubtedly affect the achievement of any planned strategy, it would be sensible to take account of this in developing our strategic direction. Again this model is a reflection of a resource-based strategic HRM perspective. Butler (1988/89) identifies this model as a shift from human resources as the implementors of strategy to human resources as a driving force in the formulation of the strategy.

**The Management of Human Resources**

■ Which of these approaches to human resource strategy most closely fits your organisation? (If you are a full-time student read one or two relevant cases in *People Management* and interpret these as 'your organisation'.)
■ Why did you come to this decision?
■ What are the advantages and disadvantages of the approach used?

## Theoretical perspectives of strategic human resource management

Three theoretical approaches to strategic HRM can be identified. The first is founded on the concept that there is 'one best way' of managing human resources in order to improve business performance. The second focuses on the need to align employment policies and practice with the requirements of business strategy in order that the latter will be achieved and the business will be successful. This second approach is based on the assumption that different types of HR strategies will be suitable for different types of business strategies. Third, a more recent approach to strategic HRM is derived from the resource-based view of the firm. This view focuses on the quality of the human resources available to the organisation and their ability to learn and adapt more quickly than their competitors. Supporters of this perspective challenge the need to secure a mechanistic fit with business strategy and focus instead on long-term sustainability and survival of the organisation via the pool of human capital.

### Universalist approach

The perspective of the universalist approach is derived from the conception of human resource management as 'best practice', as we discussed in Chapter 1. In other words it is based on the premise that one model of labour management – a high-commitment model – is related to high organisational performance in all contexts, irrespective of the particular competitive strategy of the organisation. An expression of this approach can be seen in Guest's theory of HRM, which is a prescriptive model based on four HR policy goals: strategic integration, commitment, flexibility and quality. These policy goals are related to HRM policies which are expected to produce desirable organisational outcomes as shown in Figure 3.2.

Guest (1989a) describes the four policy goals as follows:

■ **Strategic integration** – ensuring that HRM is fully integrated into strategic planning, that HRM policies are coherent, that line managers use HRM practices as part of their everyday work.
■ **Commitment** – ensuring that employees feel bound to the organisation and are committed to high performance via their behaviour.
■ **Flexibility** – ensuring an adaptable organisation structure, and functional flexibility based on multiskilling.
■ **Quality** – ensuring a high quality of goods and services through high-quality, flexible employees.

Guest sees these goals as a package – all need to be achieved to create the desired organisational outcomes.

## Figure 3.2 A theory of HRM

| HRM policies ←——→ | Human resource outcomes ←——→ | Organisational outcomes |
|---|---|---|
| Organisational/ job design | | *High* Job performance |
| Management of change | Strategic integration | *High* Problem-solving Change Innovation |
| Recruitment Selection Socialisation | Commitment | |
| Appraisal training development | Flexibility/adaptability | *High* Cost effectiveness |
| Reward systems | | |
| Communication | Quality | *Low* Turnover Absence Grievances |

**Leadership/culture/strategy**

Source: D. Guest (1989a) 'Personnel and HRM: can you tell the difference?' in *Personnel Management*, January, p. 49. Reproduced with the permission of the author.

Clarity of goals gives a certain attractiveness to this model – but this is where the problems also lie. Whipp (1992) questions the extent to which such a shift is possible, and Purcell (1991) sees the goals as unattainable. The goals are also an expression of human resource management, as opposed to personnel management, and as such bring us back to the debate about what human resource management really is and the inherent contradictions in the approach (Legge 1991, 1995). Ogbonna and Whipp (1999) argue that internal consistency within such a model is extremely difficult to achieve because of such contradictions (for example the tension between flexibility and commitment). Because the prescriptive approach brings with it a set of values, it suggests that there is only one best way and this is it. Although Guest (1987) has argued that there is no best practice, he also encourages the use of the above approach as the route to survival of UK businesses.

Pfeffer (1994) and Becker and Gerhart (1996) are well-known exponents of this view. While there is some support for this perspective, which we consider in more depth in Chapter 16 on Strategic Aspects of Performance, there remains some debate as to which particular human resource practices will stimulate high commitment. The following Window on Practice gives an example of one interpretation of a high-commitment, high-performance approach to human resource management strategy.

Falling somewhere between the universalist approach and the fit approach is the Harvard model of HRM. This model, produced by Beer, Spector, Lawrence, Quinn Mills and Walton (1984), is analytical rather than prescriptive. The model, shown in Figure 3.3, recognises the different stakeholder interests that impact on employee behaviour and performance, and also gives greater emphasis to factors

| WINDOW ON PRACTICE | High performance teams at Digital, Ayr |

In an extremely competitive market the Ayr plant had to demonstrate that they could manufacture specified computer systems at a 'landed cost' competitive with other Digital plants, especially those in the Far East. To do this management had to rapidly introduce a package of changes. They had a strategic focus and a clear vision of the changes (both technical and organisational) required to promote success and they 'sold' this to the employees and corporate management. The high-performance team concept they sold had two great advantages – inbuilt quality and flexibility.

Supportive policies were put in place – such as a new skills-based pay system.

Employment policies in terms of career planning, training and development and other reward policies were also designed to be consistent with and reinforce the initiative. Management introduced unsupervised autonomous groups called 'high performance teams' with around a dozen members with full 'back to front' responsibility for product assembly, testing, fault finding, and problem solving, as well as some equipment maintenance. They used flexitime without time clocks and organised their own team discipline. Individuals were encouraged to develop a range of skills and help others in developing their capability. The ten key characteristics of the teams were as follows:

- self-managing, self-organising, self-regulating;
- front-to-back responsibility for core process;
- negotiated production targets;
- multiskilling – no job titles;
- share skills, knowledge, experience and problems;
- skills-based payment system;
- peer selection, peer review;
- open layout, open communications;
- support staff on the spot;
- commitment to high standards and performance.

Management had to learn to stand back and let the groups reach their own decisions – an approach that eventually released considerable management time. A great deal of attention was given to how the transition was managed and this was seen as critical to the success of the approach. Time was taken to ensure maximum formal and informal communication and consultation, and there was a critical mass of key individuals prepared to devote themselves to ensure success. Employees were involved to the fullest extent so they eventually felt they owned the concepts and techniques which they used. Training covered job skills, problem-solving techniques and 'attitude training' in the concepts of high-performance organisational design.

Source: Adapted from D.A. Buchanan (1992) 'High performance: new boundaries of acceptability in worker control', in G. Salaman et al. (eds), *Human Resource Strategies*. California: Sage.

in the environment that will help to shape human resource strategic choices – identified in the **Situational factors** box. Poole (1990) also notes that the model has potential for international or other comparative analysis, as it takes into account different sets of philosophies and assumptions which may be operating.

Although Beer *et al.*'s model is primarily analytical, there are prescriptive elements leading to some potential confusion. The prescription in Beer *et al.*'s model is found in the **HR outcomes** box, where specific outcomes are identified as universally desirable.

## Fit or contingency approach

The fit or contingency approach is based on two critical forms of fit. The first is

## Figure 3.3 The Harvard framework for human resource management

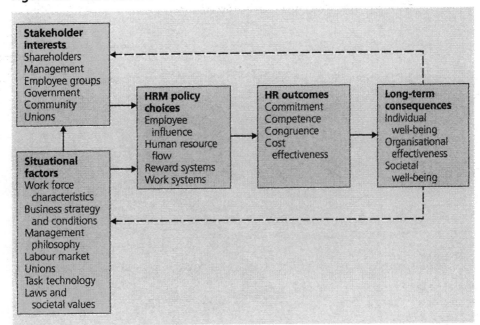

Source: Adapted with permission of The Free Press, a Division of Simon & Schuster, Inc., from *Managing Human Assets* by Michael Beer, Bert Spector, Paul R. Lawrence, D. Quinn Mills, Richard E. Walton. New York: The Free Press. Copyright © 1984 by The Free Press.

external fit – that HR strategy fits with the demands of business strategy; the second is internal fit – that all HR policies and activities fit together so that they make a coherent whole, are mutually reinforcing and one applied consistently. One of the foundations of this approach is found in Fombrun *et al.* (1984), who proposed a basic framework for strategic human resource management, shown in Figures 3.4 and 3.5. Figure 3.4 represents the location of human resource management in relation to organisational strategy, and you should be able to note how the Fit Model (B) is used. Figure 3.5 shows how activities within human resource management can be unified and designed in order to support the organisation's strategy.

The strength of this model is that it provides a simple framework to show how selection, appraisal, development and reward can be mutually geared to produce the required type of employee performance. For example, if an organisation required co-operative team behaviour with mutual sharing of information and support, the broad implications would be:

■ **Selection**: successful experience of team work and sociable, co-operative personality; rather than an independent thinker who likes working alone.
■ **Appraisal**: based on contribution to the team, and support of others; rather than individual outstanding performance.
■ **Reward**: based on team performance and contribution; rather than individual performance and individual effort.

There is little doubt that this type of internal fit is valuable. However, questions have been raised over the model's simplistic response to organisation strategy.

**Figure 3.4 Strategic management and environmental pressures**

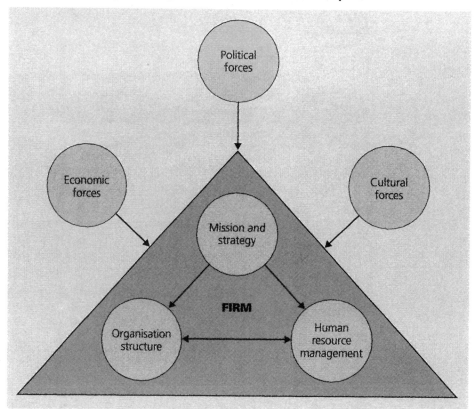

Source: C. Fombrun, N.M. Tichy and M.A. Devanna (1984) *Strategic Human Resource Management*, p. 35. New York: John Wiley and Sons, Inc. © John Wiley and Sons Inc., 1984. Reprinted by permission of John Wiley and Sons, Inc.

The question 'what if it is not possible to produce a human resource response that enables the required employee behaviour and performance?' is never addressed. So, for example, the distance between now and future performance requirements, the strengths, weaknesses and potential of the workforce, the motivation of the workforce and employee relations issues are not considered.

This model has been criticised because of its dependence on a rational strategy formulation rather than on an emergent strategy formation approach; and because of the nature of the one-way relationship with organisational strategy. It has also been criticised owing to its unitarist assumptions, as no recognition is made for employee interests and their choice of whether or not to change their behaviour.

Taking this model and the notion of fit one step further, human resource strategy has been conceived in terms of generating specific employee behaviours. In the ideal form of this there would be analysis of the types of employee behaviour required to fulfil a predetermined business strategy, and then an identification of human resource policies and practices which would bring about and reinforce this behaviour. A very good example of this is found in Schuler and Jackson (1987). They used the three generic business strategies defined by Porter (1980) and for each identified employee role behaviour and HRM policies required. Their conclusions are shown in Table 3.1.

**The Management of Human Resources**

**Figure 3.5 The human resource cycle**

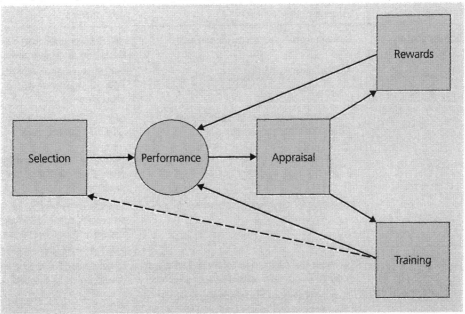

Source: C. Fombrun, N.M. Tichy and M.A. Devanna (1984) *Strategic Human Resource Management*, p. 41. New York: John Wiley and Sons, Inc. © John Wiley and Sons Inc., 1984. Reprinted by permission of John Wiley and Sons, Inc.

Similar analyses can be found for other approaches to business strategy, for example in relation to the Boston matrix (Purcell 1992) and the developmental stage of the organisation (Kochan and Barocci 1985). Some human resource strategies describe the behaviour of all employees, but others have concentrated on the behaviour of Chief Executives and senior managers; Miles and Snow (1984), for example, align appropriate managerial characteristics to three generic strategies of prospector, defender and analyser. The rationale behind this matching process is that if managerial attributes and skills are aligned to the organisational strategy, then a higher level of organisational performance will result. There is little empirical evidence to validate this link, but work by Thomas and Ramaswamy (1996) does provide some support. They used statistical analysis to investigate if there was a match between manager attributes and skills in organisations with either a defender or a prospector strategy in 269 of the *Fortune 500* companies in the United States. They found an overall statistical relationship between manager attributes and strategy. Taking the analysis a step further they then compared 30 organisations which were misaligned with 30 which were aligned and found that performance in the aligned companies (whether prospector or defender) was statistically superior. While this work can be criticised, it does provide an indication of further research which can be developed to aid our understanding of the issues. Sanz-Valle *et al.* (1999) found some partial support for the Schuler and Jackson model in terms of the link between business strategy and HR practices, but they did not investigate the implications of this link for organizational performance. The types of strategies described above are generic, and there is more concentration in some organisations on tailoring the approach to the particular needs of the specific organisation.

## Table 3.1 Business strategies, and associated employee role behaviour and HRM policies

| Strategy | Employee role behaviour | HRM policies |
|---|---|---|
| **1 Innovation** | A high degree of creative behaviour | Jobs that require close interaction and co-ordination among groups of individuals |
| | Longer-term focus | Performance appraisals that are more likely to reflect longer-term and group-based achievements |
| | A relatively high level of co-operative, interdependent behaviour | Jobs that allow employees to develop skills that can be used in other positions in the firm |
| | | Compensation systems that emphasise internal equity rather than external or market-based equity |
| | A moderate degree of concern for quality | Pay rates that tend to be low, but that allow employees to be stockholders and have more freedom to choose the mix of components that make up their pay package |
| | A moderate concern for quantity; an equal degree of concern for process and results | Broad career paths to reinforce the development of a broad range of skills |
| | A greater degree of risk-taking; a higher tolerance of ambiguity and unpredictability | |
| **2 Quality enhancement** | Relatively repetitive and predictable behaviours | Relatively fixed and explicit job descriptions |
| | A more long-term or intermediate focus | High levels of employee participation in decisions relevant to immediate work conditions and the job itself |
| | A moderate amount of co-operative, interdependent behaviour | A mix of individual and group criteria for performance appraisal that is mostly short term and results orientated |
| | A high concern for quality | A relatively egalitarian treatment of employees and some guarantees of employment security |
| | A modest concern for quantity of output | Extensive and continuous training and development of employees |
| | High concern for process: low risk-taking activity; commitment to the goals of the organisation | |
| **3 Cost reduction** | Relatively repetitive and predictable behaviour | Relatively fixed and explicit job descriptions that allow little room for ambiguity |
| | A rather short-term focus | Narrowly designed jobs and narrowly defined career paths that encourage specialisation, expertise and efficiency |
| | Primarily autonomous or individual activity | Short-term results-orientated performance appraisals |
| | Moderate concern for quality | Close monitoring of market pay levels for use in making compensation decisions |
| | High concern for quantity of output | Minimal levels of employee training and development |
| | Primary concern for results; low risk-taking activity; relatively high degree of comfort with stability | |

Source: R.S. Schuler and S.E. Jackson (1987) 'Linking competitive strategies with human resource management practices', *Academy of Management Executive*, No. 3, August. Reproduced with permission of the Academy of Management.

Many human resource strategies aim to target not just behaviour, but through behaviour change to effect a movement in the culture of the organisation. The target is, therefore, to change the common view of 'the way we do things around here' and to attempt to manipulate the beliefs and values of employees. There is much debate as to whether this is achievable.

We have previously recounted some of the concerns expressed about Fombrun *et al's* specific model; however there is further criticism of the fit or matching perspective as a whole. Grundy (1998) claims that the idea of fit seems naïve and simplistic. Ogbonna and Whipp (1999) argue that much literature assumes that fit can be targeted, observed and measured and there is an underlying assumption of stability. Given that most companies may have to change radically in response to the environment, any degree of fit previously achieved will be disturbed. Thus, they contend that fit is a theoretical ideal which can rarely be achieved in practice. Boxall (1996) criticises: the typologies of competitive advantage that are used, arguing that there is evidence that high-performing firms are good 'all rounders'; the fact that strategy is a given and no account is made of how it is formed or by whom; the assumption that employees will behave as requested; and the aim for consistency, as it has been shown that firms use different strategies for different sections of their workforce.

However, in spite of the criticisms of this perspective, it is still alive and kicking in both the academic and practitioner literature – see, for example, Holbeche's (1999) book entitled *Aligning Human Resources and Business Strategy*.

## Resource-based approach

The resource-based view of the firm (Barney 1991) has stimulated attempts to create a resource-based model of strategic HRM (Boxall 1996). The resource-based view of the firm is concerned with the relationships between internal resources (of which human resources are one), strategy and firm performance. It focuses on the promotion of sustained competitive advantage through the development of human capital rather than merely aligning human resources to current strategic goals. Human resources can provide competitive advantage for the business, as long as they are unique and can not be copied or substituted for by competing organisations. The focus is not just on the behaviour of the human resources (as with the fit approach), but on the skills, knowledge, attitudes and competencies which underpin this, and which have a more sustained impact on long-term survival than current behaviour (although this is still regarded as important). Briggs and Keogh (1999) maintain that business excellence is not just about 'best practice' or 'leapfrogging the competition', but about the intellectual capital and business intelligence to anticipate the future, today.

Barney states that in order for a resource to result in sustained competitive advantage it must meet four criteria, and Wright *et al.* (1994) demonstrate how human resources meet these. First, the resource must be *valuable*. Wright and his colleagues argue that this is the case where demand for labour is heterogeneous, and where the supply of labour is also heterogeneous – in other words where different firms require different competencies from each other and for different roles in the organization, and where the supply of potential labour comprises individuals with different competencies. On this basis value is created by matching an individual's competencies with the requirements of the firm and/or the job, as individuals will make a variable contribution, and one can not be substituted easily for another.

The second criterion, *rarity*, is related to the first. An assumption is made that the most important competence for employees is cognitive ability due to future needs for adaptability and flexibility. On the basis that cognitive ability is normally distributed in the population, those with high levels of this ability will be rare. The talent pool is not unlimited and many employers are currently experiencing difficulties in finding the talent that they require.

---

**WINDOW ON PRACTICE**

**Competing for best talent**

On the 'Today' programme (Radio 4), on 22 August 2000, there was a report about Arthur Andersen Consulting. In order to attract the best new graduates this company has begun to offer a £10,000 golden hello. This is not a new idea, as many competing firms are already offering around £3,000 to such graduates.

---

Third, resources need to be *inimitable*. Wright *et al.* argue that this applies to the human resource as competitors will find it difficult to identify the exact source of competitive advantage from within the firm's human resource pool. Also competitors will not be able to duplicate exactly the resource in question, as they will be unable to copy the unique historical conditions of the first firm. This history is important as it will affect the behaviour of the human resource pool via the development of unique norms and cultures. Thus even if a competing firm recruited a group of individuals from a competitor they would still not be able to produce the same outcomes in the new firm as the context is different. Two factors make this unique history difficult to copy. The first is causal ambiguity – in other words it is impossible to separate out the exact causes of performance, as the sum is always more than the parts; and second, social complexity – that the complex of relationships and networks developed over time which have an impact on performance is difficult to dissect.

Finally resources need to be *non-substitutable*. Wright and his co-authors argue that although in the short term it may be possible to substitute human resources with others, for example technological ones, in the long term the human resource is different as it does not become obsolete (like technology) and can be transferred across other products, markets and technologies.

Wright *et al.* noted that attention has often been devoted to leaders and top management in the context of a resource-based approach, and indeed Boxall (1996) contends that this approach provides the theoretical base on which to concentrate in the renewal and development of the critical resource of leaders in the organisation. However Wright and his co-authors view all human resources in the organisation as the pool of capital. This sits well with the view of strategy as evolutionary and strategy being influenced from the bottom up as well as from the top down. Also it is likely that top managers are more easily identified for their contribution to the organisation and hence are more likely to be mobile, therefore, than other employees who may not be so easily identified. However, different segments of the human resource are viewed differently by organisations in terms of their contribution to competitive advantage, so for some organisations the relevant pool of human capital may not be the total pool of employees.

**The Management of Human Resources**

**Figure 3.6 A model of human resources as a source of sustained competitive advantage**

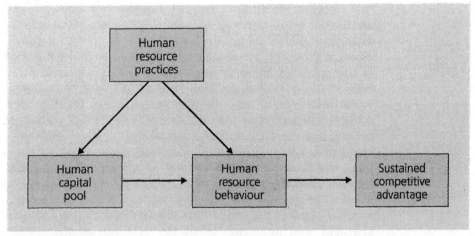

Source: P. Wright, G. McMahon and A. McWilliams (1994) 'Human resources and sustained competitive advantage: a resource-based perspective', *International Journal of Human Resource Management*, Vol. 5, No. 2, p. 318. Reproduced with the permission of Taylor and Francis Ltd.. See http://www.tandf.co.uk/journals.

Whereas fit models focus on the means of competitive advantage (HR practices) the resource-based view focuses on the source (the human capital). Wright *et al.* argue that while the practices are important they are not the source of competitive advantage as they can be replicated elsewhere, and they will produce different results in different places because of the differential human capital in different places. The relationship between human capital, human resource practices and competitive advantage is shown in Figure 3.6.

Boxall (1996) argues that this theoretical perspective provides a conceptual base for arguing that human resources are a source of competitive advantage, and as such valued as generating strategic capability. Thus there is a case for viewing HR strategy as something more than a reactive matching process. Indeed Wright *et al.* argue that it provides the case for HR to be involved in the formulation of strategy rather than just its implementation. They suggest that it provides a grounding for asserting that not every strategy is universally implementable, and that alternatives may have to be sought or the human capital pool developed further, via human resource practices, where this is possible. Hamel and Prahalad (1993), for example, talk about building distinctive competencies which enable the firm to learn faster and more effectively than competitors, and Grant (1991) identified the generation of firms becoming more intelligent and more flexible than their rivals. Human resource practices need to focus on the recruitment, utilisation, development and retention of the relevant human resource pool, and on embedding competitive practices into the organisation. However this approach also draws attention to the employee perspective and Boxall (1996) argues that there needs to be a congruence between employee interests and firm interests. It can be seen that this is a much more dynamic concept of strategy than the other perspectives we have discussed.

## The role of the HR function in strategy

The extent to which the personnel function is involved in both organisational and human resource strategy development is dependent on a range of factors, the most often quoted being whether the most senior HR person is a member of the Board of Directors. It is argued that there is a greater likelihood of involvement in strategy when the most senior HR person is at this level in the organisation. John Purcell (1994) found that only 30 per cent of companies in the private sector with 1,000 or more employees had such a Director. He found that many more had an executive with the title of Director, but without Main Board membership and the influencing potential that is allied with this. The IPM (1992) found two-thirds of personnel functions represented on the top management team, and Brewster and Smith (1990) found the same proportions in large organisations. They also found, however, that a smaller percentage (around half) were involved in strategic planning. Our research found a threefold increase in Board membership over the period 1984–94, and Board membership had risen to 63 per cent (Hall and Torrington 1998). However, not all of these HR managers had a decision-making role – 53 per cent did, compared with 10 per cent who did not. Our interviews also revealed that Board representation is not 'simply' increasing. Two businesses had previously had an HR Director on the Board but had one no longer, and in one organisation the title of HR Director was held by someone outside the function. Indeed, we found, as did Kelly and Gennard (1996), that Board membership, while generally identified as desirable, does not guarantee the involvement of specialists in strategy, and it was not necessarily seen as essential to strategic involvement:

> Thus whilst board membership is often treated as a proxy for strategic involvement, the reality of the situation is far more complex. Even looking at the most favourable evidence from the research, a picture emerges of limited involvement in strategic matters. The good news is that the IPM's survey found that representation on the top management team was predicted to increase, although there is contradictory evidence.
> (Tyson 1995)

Other factors influencing the role of the HR function in strategic concerns include the overall philosophy of the organisation towards the value of its people, the mindset of the Chief Executive, and the working relationship between the Chief Executive and the most senior HR person. Buller (1988) also found that in organisations placed in a more turbulent environment, the HR function were more likely to be involved in strategy, and our research supports this view.

These influences are not particularly easy to manipulate, but what the HR function *can* do is look for windows of opportunity in these areas, and *use* them. In order to do this the function needs to use business and financial language; describe the rationale for HR activities in terms of business benefits; act as a business manager first and an HR manager second; appoint line managers into the HR function; concentrate on priorities as defined by the business; and offer well-developed change-management skills that can be used immediately. In addition, the function needs to prepare itself by thinking strategically; identifying a functional mission and strategy and involving line management in the development of human resource strategy.

## Summary propositions

**3.1** The HR strategy can be viewed as the overall approach of the organisation towards its management of employees.

**3.2** It is more helpful to focus on the concept of strategic HRM than HRM strategy as this directs us to consider strategic thinking and a strategic orientation, rather than a 'strategy' which is written down and exists as a physical entity.

**3.3** Three theoretical perspectives on strategic HR management can be identified: universalist/best practice; contingency/fit; and the resource-based view.

**3.4** The extent to which HR specialists are involved in HR strategy is influenced by the environment of the business, its culture, the perspective of the Chief Executive, HR Board membership and the qualities, characteristics and working relationships of the most senior HR specialist.

## References

Baird, L., Meshoulam, I. and DeGive, G. (1983) 'Meshing human resources planning with strategic business planning: a model approach', *Personnel*, Vol. 60, Part 5 (Sept./Oct.), pp. 14–25.

Barney, J. (1991) 'Firm resources and sustained competitive advantage', *Journal of Management*, Vol. 17, No. 1, pp. 99–120.

Beaumont, P. (1992) 'The US human resource management literature: a review', in G. Salaman (ed.), *Human Resource Strategies*. London: Sage in association with OUP.

Becker, B. and Gerhart, B. (1996) 'The impact of Human Resource Management on Organisational Performance: Progress and Prospects', *Academy of Management Journal*, Vol. 39, pp. 779–801.

Beer, M., Spector, B., Lawrence, P.R., Quinn Mills, D. and Walton, R.E. (1984) *Managing Human Assets*. New York: Free Press.

Blyton, P. and Morris, J. (1992) 'HRM and the limits of flexibility', in P. Blyton and P. Turnbull (eds), *Reassessing Human Resource Management*. California: Sage Publications.

Boxall, P.F. (1992) 'Strategic human resource management: beginnings of a new theoretical sophistication?', *Human Resource Management Journal*, Vol. 2, No. 3.

Boxall, P.F. (1996) 'The strategic HRM debate and the resource-based view of the firm', *Human Resource Management Journal*, Vol. 6, No. 3, pp. 59–75.

Boxall, P. and Steeneveld, M. (1999) 'Human Resource Strategy and competitive advantage: A longitudinal study of engineering consultancies', *Journal of Management Studies*, Vol. 36, No. 4, pp. 443–63.

Brewster, C. and Smith, C. (1990) 'Corporate Strategy: a no-go area for personnel', *Personnel Management*, Vol. 22, No. 7.

Briggs, S. and Keogh, W. (1999) 'Integrating human resource strategy and strategic planning to achieve business excellence', *Total Quality Management*, July, p. 447.

Buchanan, D.A. (1992) 'High performance: new boundaries of acceptability in worker control', in G. Salaman *et al.* (eds), *Human Resource Strategies*. California: Sage Publications.

Buller, P.F. (1988) 'Successful partnerships: HR and strategic planning at eight top firms', *Organizational Dynamics*, Vol. 36, No. 1.

Butler, J. (1988/89) 'Human resource management as a driving force in business strategy', *Journal of General Management*, Vol. 13, No. 4.

Cleland, J, Pajo, K. and Toulson, P. (2000) 'Move it or lose it: an examination of the evolving role of the human resources professional in New Zealand', *International Journal of Human Resource Management*, Vol, 11, No, 1. pp. 143–60.

Fombrun, C., Tichy, N.M. and Devanna, M.A. (1984) *Strategic Human Resource Management*. New York: John Wiley and Sons.

Grant, R. (1991) 'The resource–based theory of competitive advantage: implications for strategy formulation', *California Management Review*, Vol. 33, No. 2, pp. 114–35.

Grensing-Pophel, L. (1999) 'Taking your "seat at the table" (the role of Human Resource Managers in companies)', *HRMagazine*, March, Vol. 44, No. 3, pp. 90–4.

Grundy, T. (1998) 'How are corporate strategy and human resources strategy linked?', *Journal of General Management*, Vol. 23, No. 3, Spring, pp. 49–72.

Guest, D. (1987) 'Human resource management and industrial relations', *Journal of Management Studies*, Vol. 24, No. 5.

Guest, D. (1989a) 'Human resource management: its implications for industrial relations and Trade Unions', in J. Storey (ed.), *New Perspectives on Human Resource Management*. London: Routledge.

Guest, D. (1989b) 'Personnel and HRM: Can you tell the difference?', *Personnel Management* (January).

Gunningle, P. and Moore, S. (1994) 'Liking business strategy and human resource management: issues and implications', *Personnel Review*, Vol. 23, No. 1, pp. 63–84.

Hall, L. and Torrington, D. (1998) *The Human Resource Function: The Dynamics of change and development*. London: Financial Times Pitman Publishing.

Hamel, C. and Prahalad, G. (1993) 'Strategy as stretch and leverage', *Harvard Business Review*, Vol. 71, No. 2, pp. 75–84.

Hendry, C. and Pettigrew, A. (1986) 'The practice of strategic human resource management', *Personnel Review*, Vol. 13, No. 3.

Hendry, C. and Pettigrew, A. (1992) 'Patterns of strategic change in the development of Human Resource Management', *British Journal of Management*, Vol. 3, No. 3, pp. 137–56.

Holbeche, L. (1999) *Aligning Human Resources and Business Strategy*. Oxford: Butterworth-Heinemann. © Roffey Park Management Institute.

Hunt, J. and Boxall, P. (1998) 'Are top Human Resource Specialists strategic partners? Self-perceptions of a corporate elite', *International Journal of Human Resource Management*, Vol. 9, pp. 767–81.

IPM (1992) *Issues in People Management, No. 4, The Emerging Role of the Personnel/HR Manager: A United Kingdom and Irish Perspective*. London: IPM.

Kane, B. and Palmer, I. (1995) 'Strategic HRM or managing the employment relationship?', *International Journal of Manpower*, Vol. 15, No. 5, pp. 6–16.

Kelly, J. and Gennard, J. (1996) 'The role of personnel directors in the Board of Directors', *Personnel Review*, Vol. 25, No. 1, pp. 7–24.

Kochan, T.A. and Barocci, T.A. (1985) *Human Resource Management and Industrial Relations: Text, Readings and Cases*. Boston: Little Brown.

Legge, K. (1991) 'Human resource management: a critical analysis', in J. Storey (ed.), *New Perspectives on Human Resource Management*. London: Routledge.

Legge, K. (1995) *Human Resource Management: Rhetorics and realities*. Basingstoke: Macmillan.

Lundy, O. and Cowling, A. (1996) *Strategic Human Resource Management*. London: Routledge.

Mabey, C. and Salaman, G. (1995) *Strategic Human Resource Management*. Oxford: Blackwell.

Mackay, L.E. and Torrington, D.P. (1986) *The Changing Nature of Personnel Management*. London: IPD.

Miles, R.E. and Snow, C.C. (1984) 'Organisation strategy, structure and process', *Academy of Management Review*, Vol. 2, pp. 546–62.

Mintzberg, H. (1994) 'The fall and rise of strategic planning', *Harvard Business Review* (February).

Ogbonna, E. and Whipp, R. (1999) 'Strategy, culture and HRM: evidence from the UK food retailing sector', *Human Resource Management Journal*, Vol. 9, No. 4, pp. 75–90.

Pedler, M., Burgoyne, J. and Boydell, T. (1991) *The Learning Company*. Maidenhead: McGraw Hill.

Pfeffer, J. (1994) *Competitive Advantage through People*. Boston: Harvard Business School Press.

Poole, M. (1990) 'Editorial: HRM in an international perspective', *International Journal of Human Resource Management*, Vol. 1, No. 1.

Porter, M. (1980) *Competitive Strategy*. New York: Free Press.

Purcell, J. (1991) 'The impact of corporate strategy on human resource management', in J. Storey (ed.), *New Perspectives on Personnel Management*. London: Routledge.

Purcell, J. (1992) 'The impact of corporate strategy on human resource management', in G. Salaman *et al.* (eds), *Human Resource Strategies*. London: Sage Publications.

Purcell, J. (1994) 'Personnel earns a place on the Board', *Personnel Management* (February).

Sanz-Valle, R., Sabater-Sánchez, R. and Aragón-Sánchez, A. (1999) 'Human Resource management and business strategy links: an empirical study', *International Journal of Human Resource Management*, Vol. 10, No. 4, pp. 655–71.

Schuler, R.S. and Jackson, S.E. (1987) 'Linking competitive strategies with human resource management practices', *Academy of Management Executive*, No. 3 (August).

Senge, P. (1990) *The Fifth Discipline: The Art and Practice of the learning organization*. London: Century Business, Random House.

Skinner, D. and Mabey, C. (1997) 'Managers' perceptions of strategic HR change', *Personnel Review*, Vol. 26, No. 6, pp. 467–84.

Storey, J. (ed.) (1989) *New Perspectives on Human Resource Management*. London: Routledge.

Storey, J. (1992) *Developments in the Management of Human Resources*. Oxford: Blackwell.

Thomas, A. and Ramaswamy, K. (1996) 'Matching managers to strategy: further tests of the Miles and Snow typology', *British Journal of Management*, Vol. 7, pp. 247–61.

Torrington, D. and Hall, L. (1996) 'Chasing the rainbow: Why seeking status through strategy misses the point for the personnel function', *Employee Relations*, Vol. 18, No. 6, pp. 70–6.

Tyson, S. (1995) *Human Resource Strategy*. London: Pitman.

Ulrich, D. (1998) 'A new mandate for human resources', *Harvard Business Review*, Jan.–Feb., pp. 125–34.

Whipp, R. (1992) 'Human resource management, competition and strategy: some productive tensions', in P. Blyton and P. Turnbull (eds), *Reassessing Human Resource Management*. California: Sage Publications.

Wright, P., McMahon, G. and McWilliams, A. (1994) 'Human Resources and sustained competitive advantage: a resource-based perspective', *International Journal of Human Resource Management*, Vol. 5, No. 2, May, pp. 301–26.

## General discussion topics

1 Is it feasible to link business strategy with the management of people in organisations?

2 Does it really matter whether the most senior HR person is on the Board of Directors, or are personal work relationships, political alliances and personal track records more important?

3 Human resource strategies can be stimulating to produce and satisfying to display, but how can we make sure that they are implemented?

## Chapter 16    Strategic aspects of performance

In our opening chapters we described the shift in emphasis away from the contract of employment towards the contract for performance. Even before the development of Taylor's Scientific Management methods a century ago, getting the most out of the workforce has always been a predominant management preoccupation, and the management literature is full of studies on the topic. Psychologists have studied motivation and leadership, ergonomists have dismantled and reconstructed every aspect of the physical environment in which people work, industrial relations specialists have pondered power relationships and reward, while sociologists discussed the design of organisations and their social structure, and operations experts have looked for ways to engineer process improvements.

In this chapter we review some major influences on our current thinking about performance. From this we explore in more detail some views on which human resource policies and practices result in high performance and then focus on understanding how this comes about. We shall conclude by briefly reviewing a range of popular strategic performance initiatives. The following three chapters look in more detail at organisational, individual and team performance.

## A change in perspective: from employment to performance

The traditional human resource management approach to enhancing individual performance has centred on the assessment of past performance and the allocation of reward (Walker 1992). The secret was seen to lie in the interplay between individual skill or capacity and motivation. There has also been a pattern of thinking which set reward as separate from performance: rewards were provided in exchange for performance. This has been powerfully influenced by the industrial relations history, as trade unions have developed the process of collective bargaining and negotiation.

The prime purpose of trade unions has always been to improve the terms and working conditions of their members, although there may be other objectives in addition to this. With that objective, the union has only one thing to offer in exchange for improvements in terms and conditions, that is, some opportunity for improvement in productivity or performance. With the steadily increasing influence of unions in most industrial countries through most of the twentieth century, it was inevitable that performance improvement was something of direct interest only to management. Performance therefore became stereotyped as something of no intrinsic interest to the person doing the work.

The influence of trade unions has altered and collective bargaining does not dominate the management agenda as much as it used to. This is the most significant feature in the general change in attitudes about what we go to work for. Managements are gradually waking up to this fact and realising that there is now scope for integration in a way that was previously unrealistic. Not only is it possible to say, 'Performance is rewarded', one can now begin to say, 'Performance *is* a reward.' The long-standing motivational ideas of job enlargement, job enrichment, and so forth, become more cogent when those at work are able to look for the satisfaction of their needs not only in the job, but in their performance in it.

**WINDOW ON PRACTICE**

Mavis has worked in a retail store for eighteen years and has recently attended a training course in customer care.

*'I always regarded the customer as some sort of enemy; we all did. In our coffee breaks we chatted away about the customer from hell, who was never satisfied, or who always put you down. Also I used to feel that I had to grin and bear it in trying to be nice to these enemies in order to earn commission.*

*Since the course I feel much more in control and have more self-respect. I really feel that most customers will respond positively if I approach them in the right way. It is my performance that largely affects how they behave. I actually enjoy what I am doing most of the time (and I never thought I'd say that!), because I can see myself doing a bit of good as well as selling more than I used to.'*

Although it may seem like playing with words, this subtle shift of emphasis is fundamental to understanding the strategic approach to performance.

## Influences on our understanding of performance

### The Japanese influence

The success of Japanese companies and the decline of Western organisations has encouraged an exploration and adoption of Japanese management ideas and practices in order to improve performance. Thurley (1982) described the objectives of personnel policies in Japan as performance, motivation, flexibility and mobility. Delbridge and Turnbull (1992) described type 'J' organisations (based on Japanese thinking) as characterised by commitment, effort and company loyalty. A key theme in Japanese thinking appears to be people development and continuous improvement, or 'kaizen'.

Much of this thinking and the specific management techniques used in Japan, such as JIT (just in time), have been adopted into UK organisations, often in an uncritical way and without due regard for the cultural differences between the two nations. It is only where the initiatives are developed *and modified* for their location that they appear to succeed.

### The American literature

Key writers from the American 'excellence' school, Peters and Waterman (1982), identified eight characteristics that they found to be associated with excellent companies – all American. These companies were chosen as excellent on the basis of their innovativeness and on a set of financial indicators, compared on an industry-wide basis. The characteristics they identified were:

- a bias for action – rather than an emphasis on bureaucracy or analysis;
- close to the customer – concern for customer wishes;
- autonomy and entrepreneurship – the company is split into small operational units where innovation and initiative are encouraged;
- productivity through people – employees are seen as the key resource, and the value of the employees' contribution is reinforced;
- hands-on, value-driven – strong corporate culture promoted from the top;
- stick to the knitting – pursuing the core business rather than becoming conglomerates;
- simple form, lean staff – simple organisation structure and small HQ staffing;
- simultaneous loose and tight properties – company values strongly emphasised, but within these considerable freedom and errors tolerated.

Peters and Waterman identified a shift from the importance of strategy and structural factors to style, systems, staff and skills (from the hard 's's to the soft 's's). In a follow-on book Peters and Austin (1985) identify four key factors related to excellence as concern for customers, innovation, attention to people and leadership.

Guest (1992) analyses why this excellence literature has had such an impact and identifies a range of methodological and analytical problems associated with the research, which question its validity. For example, he points out that no comparison was made with companies not considered to be excellent. We do not, therefore, know whether these principles were applied to a greater extent in excellent organisations. Hitt and Ireland (1987) go so far as to say that 'the data call into question whether these excellent principles are related to performance'. In addition, a number of the companies quoted have experienced severe problems since the research was carried out, and there remains the problem of the extent to which we can apply the results to UK organisations.

Whatever the reservations, the influence of the text on strategic thinking about performance remains profound. Even the use of the term 'excellence' means that there is a change of emphasis away from deadpan, objective terms like profitability, effectiveness, value-added and competitive advantage towards an idea that may trigger a feeling of enthusiasm and achievement. 'Try your best' becomes 'Go for it'.

More recently there has been considerable work in the USA that aims to identify HR practices which lead to high organisational performance, for example Huselid (1995) and Pfeffer (1998). The predominant method used to identify such relationships is quantitative analysis of large sets of statistical data. This type of approach is typical in research in the USA, but in the UK we tend to use a much greater mix of methods. However, the last few years have seen an increase in the use of quantitative methods in the UK, to attempt to establish the HR practices which are related to high performance, in other words to identify what are termed 'high performance work practices' in US terminology and 'high commitment work practices' in UK terminology.

## HRM and the strategy literature

The HRM strategy literature provides different ways to understand the contribution of HR policies and practices to organisational performance. We noted in Chapter 3 that three distinct approaches to HR strategy can be identified. The universalist or best practice approach presupposes that certain HR policies and practices will always result in high performance, and the question is to identify exactly what these are. The contingency or fit approach suggests that different HR policies and practices will be needed to produce high performance in different firms depending on their business strategy and environment. However, it is usually considered possible to categorise different business strategies and environmental influences, and, on the basis of these, to identify the HR policies and practices that will result in high performance. Finally the resource-based view of the firm suggests that neither of these approaches is sufficient, but that every organisation and its employees should be considered as unique and that the set of HR policies and practices that will result in high performance will also be unique to that firm. From this perspective no formula can be applied, and the way that people processes contribute to organisational performance can only be understood within the context of the particular firm. These three perspectives have resulted in different investigational approaches to understanding the impact of people management on organisational performance, as will become clear in the following section.

## Do people-management processes contribute to high performance?

The investigations to date have had a dual purpose, the first being to seek to establish a link between people-management practices and organisational performance. In other words, does the way that people are managed affect the bottom line? The second one follows logically from this, and is: 'If the answer to the first question is yes, then which particular policies and practices result in high performance?' Both these questions are usually investigated in parallel. A variety of different definitions of performance have been used in these studies. These range from bottom line financial performance (profitability), through productivity measures, to measurement of outcomes such as wastage, quality and labour turnover (which are sometimes referred to as internal performance outcomes). Sometimes the respondent's view of performance is used, on the basis that bottom line figures can be influenced by management accounting procedures. The studies have generally used large datasets and complex statistical analysis to determine relationships.

Much of the research has been carried out from the assumption of the universalist, or best practice approach to HR strategy. Reviewing the academic literature Richardson and Thompson (1999) come to the conclusion that the evidence indicates a positive relationship between innovative and sophisticated people-management practices and better business performance. Some researchers argue that the performance effects of HR policies and practices are multiplicative rather than additive, and this is often termed the 'bundles' approach (see, for example, MacDuffie 1995). In other words, a particular set of mutually reinforcing practices is likely to have more impact on performance than applying one or just some of these in isolation. Pfeffer (1998), for example, identifies seven critical people-management policies: emphasising employment security; recruiting the 'right' people; extensive use of self-managed teams and decentralisation; high wages solidly linked to organisational performance; high spending on training; reducing status differentials; and sharing information; and he suggests that these policies will benefit *every* organisation. In the UK the Sheffield Enterprise Programme (Patterson *et al.* 1997) has studied 100 manufacturing organisations over 10 years (1991–2001) and has used statistical techniques to identify which factors affect profitability and productivity. It has been reported that aspects of culture, supervisory support, concern for employee welfare, employee responsibility, training, job satisfaction and organisational commitment were all important variables in relation to organisational performance. It is worth noting that here variables associated with employee attitudes are included, that is, job satisfaction and commitment, in addition to the variables which comprise policies or practices. We will consider this mix in the following section. Also in the UK, Wood and de Menezes (1998) identify a bundle of HR practices which they term high-commitment management, and these comprise recruitment and selection processes geared to selecting flexible and highly committed individuals; processes which reward commitment and training by promotion and job security; and the use of direct communication and teamwork.

This avenue of work has a very optimistic flavour, suggesting that not only are people-management practices related to high organisational performance, but that we can identify the innovative and sophisticated practices that will work best in combination. On a practical level there are problems because different researchers identify different practices or 'bundles' associated with high performance (see, for example, Becker and Gerhard 1996). There have been many criticisms of this approach, partly based on the methods used – which involve, for example, the view of a single respondent as to which practices are in place, with no account taken of how the practices are implemented. A further problem is causality. It could be that profitable firms use best practice people-management methods, because they can afford to since they are profitable, rather than that such methods lead to profitability. A further issue concerns the conflict between different aspects of the bundle, along the lines of Legge's (1989) criticism of Guest's model of strategic HRM. Such contradictions are, for example, between individualism and teamwork and between a strong culture and adaptability. These contradictions can also be seen in some of the performance variables and strategic performance initiatives discussed below. Lastly, this approach ignores the business strategy of the organisation. Guest (2000) and particularly Purcell (1999) provide detailed expositions of the problems with this approach. While they recognise the value of the work they also see it as limited.

MacDuffie (1995) suggests that the best bundle is dependent on the logic of the organisation, and other researchers such as Wright and Snell (1998), have pursued the link between HR and organisational performance from the contingency, or fit, perspective. While this approach does bring the integration with business strategy to the fore, it fails to provide a more useful way forward. Attempting to model all the different factors that influence the appropriate set of HR policies and practices that lead to high performance is an extremely complex, if not impossible task. In addition to this Purcell *et al.* (2000) argue that the speed of change poses a real problem for the fit approach, and Purcell (1999) suggests that a more useful approach is to focus on the resource-based view of the firm, which is the third perspective on HR strategy that we considered in Chapter 3.

Becker and Gerhart suggest that it is more likely to be the architecture of the system, not just a group of HR practices, that results in high performance, and Purcell suggests that it is how practices are implemented and change is managed that makes the difference. The resource-based view would indicate that competencies in the implementation and management of change could form part of the basis of sustained competitive advantage. Hutchinson *et al.* (2000) term this 'idiosyncratic fit'. Part of the CIPD's major research project on investigating the link of HR to performance will involve longitudinal case studies that may shed some light on this issue.

## How do HR policies and practices affect performance?

On the basis that we have sufficient evidence to claim that HR policies and practices do affect company performance (although it should be noted that some studies do not support this, for example Lahteenmaki and Storey 1998), we need to understand better the processes which link these HR practices to business performance. As Purcell *et al.* (2000) point out, 'what remains unclear is what is actually happening in successful organisations to make this connection' (p. 30). The results from one part of the CIPD study, referred to above, should help us understand how, why and where certain HR policies and practices result in high performance. Currently our interpretation focuses on the central importance of commitment in mediating the impact of HR policies and practices on business performance, and we shall consider this in more detail.

### Commitment

Historically, some writers have identified commitment as resulting in higher performance. Commitment has been described as:

- **Attitudinal commitment** – that is, loyalty and support for the organisation, strength of identification with the organisation (Porter 1985), a belief in its values and goals and a readiness to put in effort for the organisation.
- **Behavioural commitment** – actually remaining with the company and continuing to pursue its objectives.

Walton (1985) notes that commitment is **thought** to result in better quality, lower turnover, a greater capacity for innovation and more flexible employees. In turn these are seen to enhance the ability of the organisation to achieve competitive advantage. Iles, Mabey and Robertson (1990) add that some of the outcomes of commitment have been identified as the industrial relations climate, absence levels, turnover levels and individual performance. Pfeffer (1998) and Wood and Albanese (1995) argue that commitment is a core variable, and Guest (1998, p. 42) suggests that:

> The concept of organizational commitment lies at the heart of any analysis of HRM. Indeed the whole rationale for introducing HRM policies is to increase levels of commitment so that other positive outcomes can ensue.

Hence we see the adoption of the terms 'high commitment work practices' and 'high commitment management' and their linkage with high performance. Meyer and Allen (1997) argue that there is not a great deal of **evidence** to link high commitment and high levels of organisational performance. Guest (2000) reports analyses of the Workplace Employment Relations Survey (WERS) data and the Future of Work Survey data to show some support for the model that HR practices have an impact on employee attitudes and satisfaction, which in turn

## Figure 16.1 A simple model of HRM and performance

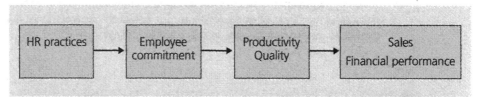

Source: D. Guest (2000) 'Human resource management, employee well-being and organizational performance'. Paper presented to the CIPD Professional Standards Conference, 11 July. Reproduced with the permission of the author.

has an impact on internal performance outcomes. He is, however, cautious about identifying causal links.

In this context Guest uses commitment as shorthand for employee attitudes and values, as shown in his model in Figure 16.1.

Some authors, however, have argued that high commitment could indeed reduce organisational performance. Cooper and Hartley (1991) suggest that commitment might decrease flexibility and inhibit creative problem solving. If commitment reduces staff turnover, this may result in fewer new ideas coming into the organisation. Staff who would like to leave the organisation but who are committed to it in other ways, for example through high pay and benefits, may stay, but may not produce high levels of performance.

As well as the debate on the value of commitment to organisational performance, there is also the debate on the extent to which commitment can be managed, and how it can be managed. Guest (1992) suggests that commitment is affected by:

■ personal characteristics;

---

**WINDOW ON PRACTICE**

Rebecca Johnson (1999) reports on performance initiatives at the Holiday Inn, Mayfair. Through a 'back to the floor' experience senior managers realised that front line staff did not have sufficient authority and autonomy to solve routine customer problems and that this was having an adverse impact on customer perceptions. A range of initiatives were thus implemented:

■ training to equip front line staff to take greater responsibility in solving customer problems;
■ new recruitment and selection strategies to help identify potential employees who are 'focused on going the extra mile', rather than those who have technical skills, which can be learned on appointment. Processes include 'auditions' to identify favourable attitudes;
■ demonstrating a genuine commitment to employees. Initiatives included attitude surveys, continued IIP recognition, a training resource centre and a network of mentors and 'buddies';
■ encouraging a sense of fun and openness;
■ a performance appraisal system which is also geared towards career development, and internal promotions where possible;
■ measuring customer feedback through a 'guest tracking system'.

Johnson reports that all these policies are paying off as profits have been increasing steadily for the last five years. She also reports the views of a recently appointed corporate sales executive who claims to have joined the organisation, partly because of the training programme, and who noted that 'the commitment is very strong'.

Source: Adapted from a case study by R. Johnson (1999) 'Case 2: Holiday Inn Mayfair', in A. Baron and R. Collard 'Realising our assets', *People Management*, 14 October.

---

The Management of Human Resources

- experiences in job role;
- work experiences;
- structural factors; and
- personnel policies.

Morris, Lydka and O'Creevy (1992/3) also identify that personnel policies have an effect on commitment. In particular they found career prospects as the most important factor in their research on graduates. This brings us to the link between commitment and the psychological contract and the role that trust and job security have on the experience of commitment.

One of the difficulties with the concept of commitment, as Singh and Vinnicombe (1998) suggest, is whether it is defined in the same way by employees and the organisation, and whether or not our general understanding of the term needs to be reviewed in the light of a different organisational environment which rarely allows for organisations to invest in the long-term careers of employees. They use a definition of commitment in their article which encompasses commitment, not only to the organisation, but to one's career.

Lastly, it is important to consider whether using commitment as a shorthand for attitudes and satisfaction is sufficient, and whether there are other important dimensions which may be lost, by focusing on commitment alone.

## Major performance initiatives

We have previously considered some HR policies and practices that have been identified as related to high performance, and have noted the idea of using practices in bundles. Many of the popular performance initiatives that companies have adopted represent similar (but not the same) bundles of HR policies and practices, and we now turn to these. There are many small initiatives every day that help to improve performance, but we are concentrating here on major strategic initiatives, 'big ideas', as described by Connock (1992). A big idea with the same label may, of course, mean different things in practice in different organisatons. Mueller and Purcell (1992, p. 28) reach the heart of the issue when they say:

> It is the integration of change initiatives with other aspects of organisational life which is the key to success. It is very rare for a single initiative, however well designed to generate significant or lasting benefit.

Moving to a performance culture is an all-or-nothing change in the way the business is run. This brings us to the concern that too many initiatives in the same organisation will give conflicting messages to employees, particularly when they are introduced by different parts of the business. There may, for example, be contradictions between the messages of Total Quality Management (TQM) and those of the learning organisation type of approach. We will explore these further in Chapter 17.

Table 16.1 lists some of the major performance initiatives. They are divided according to their primary focus: organisational, individual or team. Some of them partly cover the same ground, and it would be surprising to find them in the same business at the same time.

## Table 16.1 Some major performance initiatives

| Organisational focus | Learning organisation<br>Investors in people<br>Total quality management (TQM)<br>Performance culture<br>Lean production<br>Business Process Reengineering<br>Just in Time (JIT)<br>Standards:  BS5750<br>              ISO9000<br>Customer care/orientation |
|---|---|
| Individual focus | Performance management<br>Performance-related pay<br>Self-development/continuous development |
| Team focus | High-performance teams<br>Cross-functional teams<br>Self-regulating teams |

**Activity 16.1**

1 Identify the main performance initiatives in your organisation.

2 What/who is the source of each initiative?

3 In what ways do they mutually support each other, and in what ways do they conflict?

## Things that go wrong

The level of satisfaction with performance initiatives is typically low (Jacobs 1993; Antonioni 1994), so we close this chapter with a summary of the problems most often reported.

### The process/people balance

Schemes rarely strike the right balance between a people emphasis and a process emphasis. Concentrating on being brilliant at talking to the people, getting them going and talking them down gently if they don't quite make it will not suffice if there is not a clear, disciplined process that brings in the essential features of consistency and defining sensible goals. Getting the goals and measures right is a waste of time if there is not the necessary input to changing attitudes, developing skills and winning consent.

### Getting the measures right

On the basis of what gets measured gets done, it is critical that the organisation selects the most useful measure of performance for the organisaton as a whole and for the individuals within it. Single measures are unlikely to be sufficiently robust. Kaplan and Norton (1992) argue convincingly that the mix of measures which an organisation should use to assess its performance should be based around four different perspectives:

- **Financial measures** – such as sales growth, profits, cash flow and increased market share.
- **Customer measures** – that is, the customer perspective, which looks at, for example, delivery time, service quality, product quality.
- **Internal business measures** – cycle time, productivity, employee skills, labour turnover.
- **Innovation and learning perspective** – including such elements as ability to innovate and improve.

The focus must be on what is achieved: results are what count. At an individual level a focus on behaviour rather than results achieved can be unhelpful, leading to personality clashes, and misleading. Doing things in the right way is no substitute for doing the right things.

## Management losing interest

A constant axiom with any initiative is the need for endorsement from senior management. With a performance initiative there is the need to go a great deal further. First, senior managers have to accept that the initiative is something in which they have to participate continuously and thoroughly. They cannot introduce it, say how important it is and then go off to find other games to play:

> studies have shown that in organisations that utilise performance management, 90 per cent of senior managers have not received performance reviews in the last two years. Clearly the problem here is that PM is not used, modelled and visibly supported at the top of the organisation. Sooner or later people at lower levels catch on and no longer feel compelled to take the time to make PM work.
>
> (Sparrow and Hiltrop 1994, p. 565)

The second aspect is indicated in that quotation. Performance initiatives will not work unless people at all levels either believe in them or are prepared to give them a try with the hope that they will be convinced by the practice.

## The team/individual balance

Individuals can rarely perform entirely on their own merits; they are part of a department or team of people whose activities interact in innumerable ways. Trevor Macdonald may read the television news with a clarity and sureness that is outstanding, but it would be of little value if the lights did not work or the script contained errors. Most working people, no matter how eminent, are not solo performers to that extent. Somehow the performance initiative has to stimulate both individual and team performance, working together within the envelope of organisational objectives.

> Historically the individual has been the basis of performance management strategies. However, this may be problematic in that performance variation tends to be falsely attributed to individuals, and the enhancement of individual performance does not necessarily coincide with the enhancement of the greater unit or work system. (Waldman 1994, p. 41)

**Activity 16.2**

Think of situations in your own experience outside working life, where there has been a potential clash between individual performance and team performance. Examples might be:

(a) the opening batsman more concerned with his batting average than with the team winning the match;

(b) the person playing the lead in the amateur operatic society's production of *The Merry Widow* who ignores the chorus; or

(c) the local councillor more concerned with doing what is needed to earn an MBE than with supporting the collective view of the council.

How was the potential clash avoided, or not? How could it have been managed more effectively to harmonise individual and team performance?

## Leaving out the development part

A key feature of managing performance is developing people so that they *can* perform. This is the feature that is most often not delivered. It is often the lack of follow-up on development needs that is the least satisfactory aspect of performance management systems.

## Implementing and managing the change

If, as Purcell (1999) identifies, 'our concern should be less about the precise policy mix in the 'bundle' and more about how and when organisations manage the HR side of change', then the way that large and small performance initiatives are implemented and managed is critical. While this is well-trodden ground, there is considerable evidence of attempted changes which have failed for a wide range of reasons including: trust is low; change is seen as a management fad which will go away; change has been poorly communicated and understood; change is just a way to get us to work harder for the same money.

## Getting it right

Here are four suggestions for running a successful performance initiative:

1 Develop and promulgate a clear vision for the business as a framework for individual/team goals and targets.

2 In consultation, develop and agree individual goals and targets with three characteristics: (a) what to do to achieve the target; (b) how to satisfy the customer rather than pleasing the boss; (c) targets that are precise, difficult and challenging, but attainable, *with feedback*.

3 Do not begin until you are sure of: (a) unwavering commitment from the top; (b) an approach that is driven by the line and bought into and owned by middle and first-line managers; (c) a system that is run, monitored and updated by HR specialists; (d) an agreement that every development commitment or pay commitment is honoured, or a swift, full explanation is given of why not.

4 Train all participants.

## Summary propositions

**16.1** Central to understanding management interest in performance is understanding the subtle change in attitudes: not only is performance rewarded, performance is also a reward.

**16.2** In the UK our views of performance improvement have been influenced by the US literature, the Japanese experience and the HRM strategy literature.

**16.3** There has been considerable research effort devoted to investigating the link between a bundle of people management practices and organisational performance, and some would argue that the link has been successfully demonstrated.

**16.4** Much less clear are the processes by which the link is made, for example how, why and in what context? So far we see commitment as the moderating variable between HR practices and organisational performance.

**16.5** Things that typically go wrong with performance initiatives are getting the people/process balance wrong, not selecting the right performance measures, management losing interest and getting the team/individual balance wrong.

**16.6** Factors likely to produce success relate to a clear, understood vision, effective target setting, full management commitment, training and honouring commitments.

## References

Antonioni, D. (1994) 'Improve the performance management process before discontinuing performance appraisals', *Compensation and Benefits Review*, Vol. 26, No. 2, pp. 29–37.

Becker, B. and Gerhard, B. (1996) 'The impact of human resource management on organizational progress and prospects', *Academy of Management Journal*, Vol. 39, No. 4, pp. 779–801.

Connock, S. (1992) 'The importance of big ideas to HR managers', *Personnel Managers*, June.

Cooper, J. and Hartley, J. (1991) 'Reconsidering the case for organisational commitment', *Human Resource Management Journal*, Vol. 3, Spring, pp. 18–32.

Delbridge, R. and Turnbull, P. (1992) 'Human resource maximisation: The management of labour under just-in-time manufacturing systems', in P. Blyton and P. Turnbull (eds), *Reassessing Human Resource Management*. Beverly Hills: Sage.

Guest, D. (1992) 'Right enough to be dangerously wrong; an analysis of the "In search of excellence" phenomenon', in G. Salaman *et al.* (eds), *Human Resource Strategies*. London: Sage.

Guest, D. (1998) 'Beyond HRM: Commitment and the contract culture', in P. Sparrow and M. Marchington (eds), *Human Resource Management: The New Agenda*. London: Financial Times Pitman Publishing.

Guest, D. (2000) 'Human Resource Management, employee well-being and organizational performance'. Paper presented at the CIPD Professional Standards Conference, 11 July.

Hitt, M. and Ireland, D. (1987) 'Peters and Waterman revisited; the unending quest for excellence', *Academy of Management Executive*, Vol. 1, No. 2, pp. 91–8.

Huselid, M. (1995) 'The impact of human resource management practices on turnover, productivity and corporate financial performance', *Academy of Management Journal*, Vol. 38, No. 3, pp. 635–73.

Hutchinson, S., Purcell, J. and Kinnie, N. (2000) 'Evolving high commitment management and the experience of the RAC call center', *Human Resource Management Journal*, Vol. 10, No. 1, pp. 63–78.

Iles, P., Mabey, C. and Robertson, I. (1990) 'Human resource management practices and employee commitment. Possibilities, pitfalls and paradoxes', *British Journal of Management*, Vol. 1, pp. 147–57.

Jacobs, H. (1993) 'The ratings game', *Small Business Reports*, Vol. 18, No. 10, pp. 21–2.

Johnson, R. (1999) 'Case 2: Holiday Inn Mayfair', in A. Baron and R. Collard, 'Realising our assets', *People Management*, 14 October.

Kaplan, R. and Norton, D. (1992) 'The balanced scorecard – measures that drive performance', *Harvard Business Review*, Jan.–Feb., pp. 71–9.

Lahteenmaki, S. and Storey, J. (1998) 'HRM and company performance: the use of measurement and the influence of economic cycles', *Human Resource Management Journal*, Vol. 8, No. 2, pp. 51–65.

Legge, K. (1989) 'Human resource management – a critical analysis', in J. Storey (ed.), *New Perspectives in Human Resource Management*. London: Routledge.

MacDuffie, J. (1995) 'Human resource bundles and manufacturing performance: organizational logic and flexible production systems in the world auto industry', *Industrial and Labor Relations Review*, Vol. 48, No. 2, pp. 197–221.

Meyer, J. and Allen, N. (1997) *Commitment in the workplace: theory, research and application*. London: Sage.

Morris, T., Lydka, H. and O'Creevy, M.F. (1992/3) 'A longitudinal analysis of employee commitment and human resource policies', *Human Resource Management Journal*, Vol. 3, pp. 21–38.

Mueller, F. and Purcell, J. (1992) 'The drive for higher productivity', *Personnel Management*, Vol. 24, No. 5, pp. 28–33.

Patterson, J., West, M., Lawthom, R. and Nickell, S. (1997) *The Impact of People Management Practices on Business Performance*. London: IPD.

Peters, T. and Austin, N. (1985) *A Passion for Excellence*. New York: Harper and Row.

Peters, T. and Waterman, R. (1982) *In Search of Excellence*. New York: Harper and Row.

Pfeffer, J. (1998) *The Human Equation*. Boston: Harvard Business School Press.

Plachy, R. and Plachy, S. (1993) 'Focus on results, not behaviour', *Personnel Journal*, Vol. 72, No. 3, pp. 28–33.

Porter, M. (1985) *Competitive Advantage*. New York: Free Press.

Purcell, J. (1999) 'Best practice and best fit: chimera or cul-de-sac?', *Human Resource Management Journal*, Vol. 9, No. 3, pp. 26–41.

Purcell, J., Kinnie, N., Hutchinson, S. and Rayton, B. (2000) 'Inside the box', *People Management*, 26 October.

Richardson, R. and Thompson, M. (1999) *The Impact of People Management Practices – A Review of the Literature*. London: IPD.

Singh, V. and Vinnicombe, S. (1998) 'What does commitment really mean? Views of UK and Swedish Engineering Managers', *Personnel Review*, Vol. 29, No. 2, pp. 228–54.

Sparrow, P. and Hiltrop, J.-M. (1994) *European Human Resource Management in Transition*. London: Prentice Hall.

Thurley, K. (1982) 'The Japanese model: practical reservations and surprising opportunities', *Personnel Management*, February.

Waldman, D. (1994) 'Designing performance management systems for total quality implementation', *Journal of Organisational Change Management*, Vol. 7, No. 2, pp. 31–44.

Walker, K.W. (1992) *Human Resource Strategy*. New York: McGraw-Hill.

Walton, R.E. (1985) 'From control to commitment in the workplace', *Harvard Business Review*, March/April, pp. 77–84.

Wood, S. and Albanese, M. (1995) 'Can we speak of high commitment management on the shop floor?', *Journal of Management Studies*, Vol. 32, No. 2, pp. 215–47.

Wood, S. and de Menezes, L. (1998) 'High commitment management in the UK: evidence from the Workplace Industrial Relations Survey and employers' manpower and skills practices survey', *Human Relations*, Vol. 51, No. 4, pp. 485–515.

Wright, P. and Snell, S. (1998) 'Towards a unifying framework for exploring fit and flexibility in strategic human resource management', *Academy of Management Review*, Vol. 23, No. 4, pp. 756–72.

## General discussion topics

1 To what extent can the American excellence literature be applied in a UK setting?

2 Can commitment, empowerment and job flexibility be pursued together? If yes, how can this be achieved? If no, why not – what are the alternatives?

# Chapter 5 Motivation to work

Yvonne Leverment

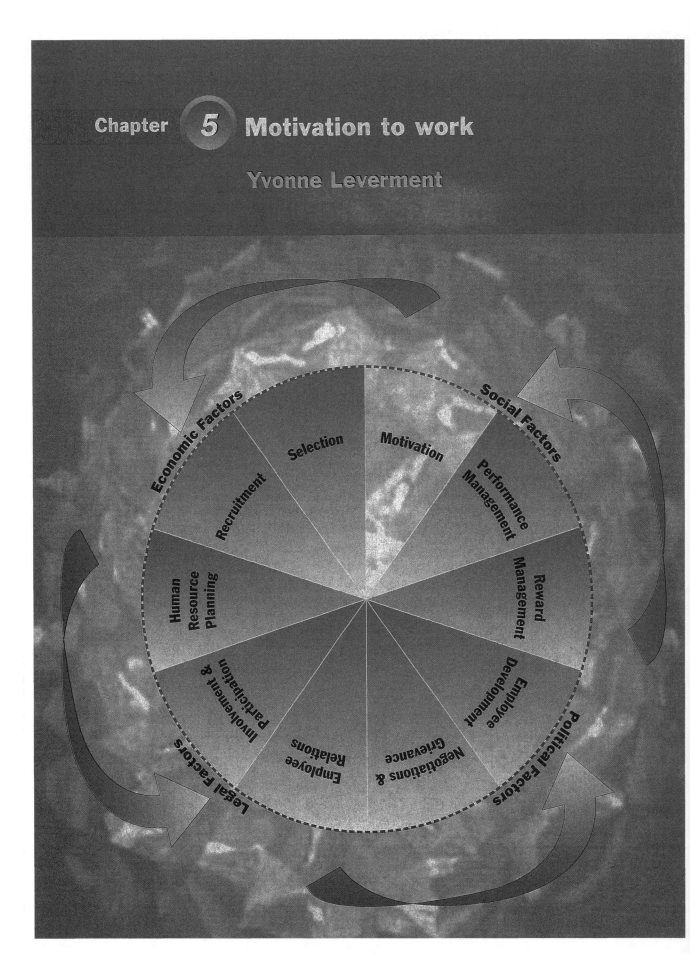

**The Management of Human Resources**

Having completed this chapter and its associated activities, readers should be able to:

- explain the main theories and concepts that underpin motivation to work
- identify the factors that contribute to the needs and expectations of people at work
- discuss and be able to evaluate their relevance in the work situation
- outline the key factors that contribute to a person's sense of job enrichment

## INTRODUCTION

This chapter considers the concepts of motivation and job satisfaction and examines the issues that are important in the creation of a stable and well-motivated workforce. What motivates people to work is a key issue for any organisation to address. This is because the relationship between the organisation and its workforce is governed by what motivates people to be fulfilled in the work that they do. The implication of this for the manager is the need to recognise how to elicit effective performance from their team of workers, in order to achieve the goals and objectives of the organisation. Although there is no single, universally accepted definition of motivation, what is clear is that people are usually motivated to do something. What should be remembered here is that this may not always be positive! A person may be motivated *not* to do something – a piece of work, communicate with colleagues – which may prove to be detrimental to the outcome. Also, factors that motivate one individual to perform well may not be the same factors that motivate another. Finally, it is important to accept that motivation is not the only important determinant of work performance and that factors such as ability, resources and interaction with others all play a part.

**Activity 5.1**

Think of your university work or current part-time job:

1 What motivates you as an individual?

2 What motivates you to carry out your work well?

3 How do you influence people in the work/university situation?

Early ideas on work motivation began with the scientific management approach taken by F.W. Taylor. In the late nineteenth century Taylor developed a science of work which involved the detailed assessment of work processes in order to improve efficiency and productivity (Taylor, 1947). In recommending the detailed division of skills into small fragmented tasks Taylor degraded the labour force by reducing its skilled component. The purpose of this was to simplify tasks in order to increase the flexibility of the labour force. This, in turn, allowed for greater efficiency and increases in productivity. At this time it was considered that workers were motivated by pay and working conditions above all else. Thus, research of the day concentrated on ways in which workers' productivity could be increased.

In the 1920s a group of experiments known as the Hawthorne studies challenged the notion that first, individuals acted only in isolation, and, second, that individuals were only responsive to rational economic and physical stimulation. The Hawthorne studies marked the beginning of the human relations approach to work which stresses the importance of social factors in the world of work. The role of management was to harness worker co-operation through team-building, improved communication and worker participation in the decision-making process.

From this time the development of many competing theories on the nature of work motivation began to emerge. Two contrasting approaches were adopted. The following part of this chapter outlines these two approaches.

## Theories of motivation

Motivational theories can be divided into two categories – *content* and *process*. Content theories or *need* theories are based on the assumption that all individuals possess the same set of needs and, as individuals, we behave in ways which satisfy these needs. In other words, this set of theories places importance on *what motivates* people to perform well at work. These theories consider human behaviour to be 'reflexive' and instinctive in nature, driven by unconscious drives. Process theories, on the other hand, acknowledge the differences in people's needs, focusing on the *processes* that create these differences. They assume that people are aware of their goals and behaviour and assume that people are purposive and rational. Also known as cognitive, the process theories identify how behaviour is initiated, directed and sustained. Each set of theories will be considered separately.

### The content theories

The major content theories of motivation are:

- Maslow's hierarchy of needs
- Alderfer's modified need hierarchy model
- Herzberg's two-factor theory

#### Maslow's hierarchy of need theory

Published in 1943, Maslow's theory was based on the basic assumption that people are always wanting, that is, they want more and what they want is dependent on what they already have. This basic assumption gives rise to what is known as Maslow's hierarchy of needs – a series of levels based on a hierarchy of importance.

The hierarchy comprises five levels beginning with physiological needs, which then ascend through safety needs, love needs, esteem needs and, at the highest level, the need for self-actualisation. Maslow argues that self-actualisation is the ultimate human goal, acknowledging the challenge for society is to enable individuals to develop their capabilities to the optimum. He believed that few people ever reached this level, thereby postulating that self-actualisation is a need that we, as individuals, strive for all our lives.

- *Physiological needs* – these include needs for food, warmth, clothing and shelter. Also, sleep, maternal behaviour and sensory pleasure.
- *Safety needs* – these include the need for safety and security, freedom from pain, protection from danger and deprivation and the need for predictability and order.
- *Social needs* – these include affection, a sense of belonging, social activity, friendships and relationships.
- *Esteem needs* – these include the need for recognition and belief in oneself. This may include self-respect and the esteem of others, together with the desire for confidence, strength, independence and achievement.
- *Self-actualisation needs* – this involves the need to develop one's full potential.

Maslow argues that once a lower need on the pyramid is reached or satisfied, it no longer acts as a motivator. Instead, the needs in the next level in the hierarchy demand satisfaction and become the motivating influence. Therefore, only unsatisfied needs motivate an individual. However, he also makes it clear that the hierarchy should not necessarily be a fixed order. Indeed, there may well be a reversal of the hierarchy. Some examples of this include:

- For some, the drive for self-actualisation may surface despite lack of satisfaction of more basic needs.
- For the unemployed, particularly those who can be classed as long-term unemployed, higher levels may be lost as the individual strives only to be satisfied at lower levels.
- Self-esteem may seem to be more important than social needs to some individuals.

Turning to the work situation, there are a number of problems relating to Maslow's theory:

1 Individuals do not necessarily satisfy their needs through the work situation alone. Therefore the manager needs to have some understanding of a person's private and social life as it may affect their behaviour in the work situation.
2 Individual differences and preferences means that people place different values on the same need.
3 Rewards or outcomes at work, such as higher salary or promotion, may satisfy more than one need.
4 Motivating factors between individuals may not be the same, as individuals seek satisfaction in different ways.
5 In Maslow's theory satisfaction is seen as the key motivational outcome. However, job satisfaction does not necessarily lead to improved performance.

Although Maslow's work was not originally intended as an explanation of motivation in the workplace, it has nevertheless been popular as a theory of motivation. It draws attention to a number of different motivators and provides a framework for viewing the different needs and expectations that individuals have. However, the theory holds little empirical support (Hall and Nougaim, 1968; Lawler and Suttle, 1972) and Maslow himself recognises the limitations of his theory as it provides no operational definitions of the needs he describes.

### Alderfer's modified need hierarchy

Alderfer's model (1972) suggests that individual needs can be divided into three groups, based on the core needs of existence, relatedness and growth (ERG):

- *Existence needs* – these include nutritional and material needs concerned with sustaining human existence and survival. In the work situation, working conditions and pay would fall into this group
- *Relatedness needs* – these include relationships which can be met through family and friends socially and through peers, colleagues and supervisors at work
- *Growth needs* – these include needs which are concerned with the desire for personal development

Whereas Maslow proposed a progression up a hierarchy, Alderfer suggests that these needs should be viewed as a continuum. More than one need can be activated at the same time and the individual can progress *down* as well as *up* the hierarchy. In what Alderfer refers to as the *frustration-regression* process he suggests that if an individual is frustrated at attempting to satisfy one set of needs, he can reassume a lower set of needs as important. In this way, unsatisfied needs become less rather than more important. Additionally, research carried out by Wanous and Zwany (1977) found that relatedness and growth needs become more important once satisfied. This suggests that employers can more easily satisfy the needs of their employees.

Work carried out by Mumford in 1976 used the broad categories of Maslow and Alderfer to identify more specific categories for workers' needs. The assumption underpinning these categories was that employees had needs which directly related to their work:

- *Knowledge needs* – work that utilises their knowledge and skills
- *Control needs* – these are satisfied by the provision of information, good working conditions and high-quality supervision
- *Psychological needs* – these include the need for recognition, responsibility, status and advancement
- *Task needs* – the need for meaningful work and some degree of autonomy
- *Moral needs* – the need to be treated in the way that employers would themselves be treated

### Herzberg's two-factor theory

Research carried out by Herzberg *et al.* (1959) involving interviews with 200 accountants and engineers, identified two sets of factors that affected motivation

**Figure 5.1** Hertzberg's two-factor theory of motivation
*Source*: Adapted from Mullins (1999: 495)

and work. One group of factors, which if found to be absent, caused dissatisfaction. This included working conditions, salary, job security, company policy, interpersonal working relationships. This grouping of factors was termed *hygiene* factors as they served to prevent dissatisfaction. The second group of factors, termed *motivators*, represented sources of satisfaction. This group included responsibility, recognition, promotion, achievement (see Figure 5.1).

Using this theory, it would appear that job satisfaction and dissatisfaction are caused by two different sets of factors. Motivational factors affect feelings of satisfaction or no satisfaction. Their absence did not cause dissatisfaction. Hygiene factors afford the workers an acceptable working environment. They do not lead to increased satisfaction or job involvement yet their absence leads to dissatisfaction, for example, low pay.

Herzberg's two-factor theory is more directly applicable to the work situation and this application can be used to incorporate more motivators when areas of work are redesigned (see Figure 5.1). The theory indicates that it is more likely that good performance leads to job satisfaction rather than the reverse. Although through his interviews Herzberg attempted to take an empirical approach to the study of work motivation, support for the theory is mixed. Two common criticisms centre on the validity of the methodology adopted in the research. First, the independent effects of hygienes and motivators is open to question. In addition, the interview approach may not have been the most appropriate way to determine people's reflection on their performance. Secondly, a study on accountants and engineers with interesting and lucrative jobs may not be applicable to people with largely unskilled work, which is uninteresting, repetitive and of limited scope. Later in this chapter we shall return to Herzberg's work when the motivational effects of job redesign are discussed in the section on job enrichment.

The content theories dominated work motivation for a number of years. Yet, evaluations of them reveal a number of significant flaws which Arnold *et al.* (1998: 248) summarise as follows:

- Needs did not group together in the ways predicted
- The theories were unable to predict when a particular need would become important
- There was no clear relationship between needs and behaviour
- Needs were generally described without sufficient precision
- The notion of need as a biological phenomenon is problematic as it ignores the capacity of people to construct their own perceptions of needs and how they can be met

### Activity 5.2

**1** Consider your own needs: do you recognise them in your own behaviour?

**2** Do your needs always drive your behaviour at work/and or at university?

## The process theories of motivation

In attempting to identify the relationships among the variables that make up motivation, the process theories provide a further contribution to understanding the nature of work motivation. The key process theories include:

- Expectancy-based models, such as Vroom, Porter and Lawler
- Equity theory
- Goal-setting theory

**The Management of Human Resources**

**76**

## The expectancy-based models

The basis of expectancy theory is that people are influenced by the expected results of their actions. Therefore, motivation is a result of the relationship between:

- the effort used and perceived level of performance, and
- the expectation that the desired outcome or reward will be related to the performance

For this to happen there must also be the expectation that a reward or desired outcome is available.

The most popular expectancy-based theory is that of Vroom. The publication of Vroom's study *Work and Motivation* in 1964 aimed to explain the links between people's perceptions of their role at work, with the amount of effort needed and the degree to which they felt rewarded for this effort. Also referred to as the *valence, instrumentality and expectancy (VIE) theory*, Vroom argues that people prefer certain outcomes from their behaviour over others. Satisfaction is felt when the preferred outcome is achieved. Definitions of these three variables are as follows:

1 *Expectancy* – If I try, am I able to carry out the action I am considering?
2 *Instrumentality* – If I carry out the action, will it lead to an identifiable outcome or reward?
3 *Valence* – How much do I value those outcomes and rewards?

According to Vroom, a person's motivation for a certain form of behaviour is determined by the combination of valence and expectancy. This is termed the *motivational force*. The strength of the force of the individual's motivation to behave in a particular way is evaluated in an equation as:

$$F = E \times V$$

Where $F$ = motivation to behave
$E$ = the expectation that a behaviour will result in a particular outcome
$V$ = the valence of the outcome

The motivational force of an action is unaffected by outcomes which either have no valence or are thought of as being unlikely to result from a certain course of action.

*An example of this:*
Imagine you are a professional tennis player, about to take part in a match. The first question you might ask is, 'How **capable** am I of winning?' (*expectancy*). The considerations you might make would be the amount of training you have done, your level of fitness, your level of experience in competition and the level and skill of your opponent. The next question you might ask would be, 'How **likely** is it that I will win?' (*instrumentality*). The considerations here might include your opponent's ability, the playing conditions, your present standard. Finally, you might ask, 'How much do I **value** winning?' (*valence*). The considerations you might make would be the amount of recognition you would receive, the progression and advancement of your career and the monetary rewards gained.

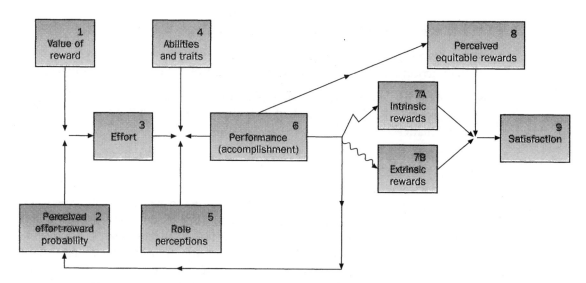

**Figure 5.2** Model from Porter and Lawler (1968)

Vroom's theory has been further developed by Porter and Lawler (1968) who go beyond motivational force and consider performance as a whole. From the work perspective the motivational force of a job is compromised by factors such as the individual's abilities, traits, perceptions of role and opportunities. They suggest *rewards* to be an intervening variable. In addition they suggest that motivation, satisfaction and performance are separate variables with a somewhat complex relationship (see Figure 5.2).

- *Value of reward* – similar to the valence in Vroom's model in that people wish for outcomes/rewards which they hope to achieve from their work. The value placed on this is dependent upon the depth and strength of people's feelings towards it.
- *Perceived effort-reward probability* – similar to expectancy in that it refers to a person's expectation that outcomes/rewards are dependent on the amount of effort given.
- *Effort* – is how hard the person tries. The amount of effort is dependent on the interaction of the variables such as the value of the reward and the perception of the effort-reward relationship.
- *Abilities and traits* – in suggesting that effort does not lead directly to performance, Porter and Lawler suggest that factors such as intelligence, skills, knowledge and personality contribute to a person's ability to perform an activity.
- *Role perceptions* – is the way in which a person views their work and the type of role that they should adopt. This not only influences the effort used but also the direction and level of action deemed necessary for effective performance.
- *Performance* – is dependent not only on the amount of effort used but also on the person's own abilities and traits and their perception of role. Therefore, if the person lacks either the ability or personality or does not have an accurate

**The Management of Human Resources**

78

perception of what is required, a large amount of effort may still result in poor performance.

- *Rewards* – these are the desired outcome of the task. They are both intrinsic, for example, sense of achievement, feelings of recognition and responsibility, and extrinsic, such as salary and working conditions. Porter and Lawler suggest that although both are important, intrinsic rewards are more likely to produce job satisfaction related to performance (rewards are discussed further in Chapter 7).
- *Perceived equitable rewards* – is the level of reward people feel they should fairly receive for a performance.
- *Satisfaction* – is seen as an attitude that is determined by the actual reward and the perceived level of award for a given task or performance.

What does all this mean to the manager in terms of how to motivate people in the work setting? While expectancy theory is helpful in identifying key factors that motivate workers, it pays little attention to the explanation of *why* an individual values or does not value particular outcomes/rewards. However, it does help to explain the nature of behaviour and motivation at work and thus can help to identify problems in performance. In order to achieve this, managers need to consider four key aspects of work:

1 The need to focus on the use of appropriate rewards for which to provide incentive for improved performance. It could be that in some instances workers may value recognition and praise rather than monetary reward.
2 The need to establish clear relationship between effort–performance and reward as perceived by the individual worker. This may mean improved training, guidance and support.
3 The need to take into account variables such as abilities and traits, perceptions of role, and organisational procedures, which may affect performance.
4 The need to minimise undesirable outcomes which may be perceived to be a result of high performance, such as short-term contract working, redundancy, and industrial accidents.

### Equity theory or organisational justice theory

The central theme in this theory is the notion that people's feelings of how fairly they are treated are assessed through comparison to others. This can be likened to a form of exchange process where a person expects certain outcomes in exchange for certain contributions or inputs. Equity theory is most associated with the work of Adams (1965). The assumption that underpins this theory is that social comparison in our relationships is governed by our concern as individuals for fairness or equity. In doing so, an individual perceives effort and reward in relative, rather than absolute terms. If the perception is one of inequity, the more distressed the individual feels, and the more tension this distress causes, and the more motivated they become to restore equity through changes in either perceptions, behaviour or both. A simple diagram to explain Adams's equity theory is shown in Figure 5.3.

**The Management of Human Resources**

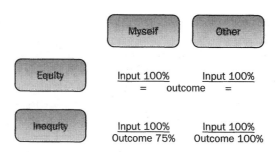

**Figure 5.3** Description of equity and inequity
*Source*: Adams (1965)

More recently, organisational issues such as downsizing, delayering and change in management programmes have impacted on how people view the organisations in which they work, and how committed and motivated they are within their work situation. In these incidences people may well express a sense of injustice in the work process and be less motivated and committed to the organisation. If a strong sense of injustice exists, people are likely to reduce their contribution to the organisation as a whole. A distinction can be made between *distributive justice* (whether people believe they have received or will receive fair rewards) and *procedural justice* (whether people believe that the organisational procedures that deal with rewards are fair). A good example of this is any form of assessment that you undertake as part of your undergraduate studies. Consider the work and effort that you would put in to preparing for an assessed seminar. You know that you have to prepare well in order to gain a good mark. You expect that the organisational procedures and systems are in place that will secure you a mark that is fair. Indeed, you are unlikely to prepare well for the assessment if you do not believe that you will receive a fair mark for your attempts. However, the resulting mark may not be what you had hoped for when you consider first, the amount of effort that you have made in your preparation, and secondly, if you begin to compare your mark with that of others. You may well begin to question the organisational procedures that are in place. These may include the provision of adequate and reliable assessment criteria prior to the assessment, the skill and depth of knowledge of the subject matter of the assessor, together with their level of experience of carrying out the assessment and subjective bias of the assessor.

### Goal-setting theory

Viewed as much as a motivational technique as a theory, work carried out by Locke (1976) is based on the notion that a person's goals or intentions determine their behaviour. The combination of goal difficulty, and the extent to which a person is committed to achieving a desired goal, determines the level of effort used in realising the goal. Thus, goals guide people's responses and actions, ultimately directing work behaviour and performance. To be effective goals need to be:

**The Management of Human Resources**
**80**

1 *Specific* – specific goals tend to lead to higher performance as they create a basis for a precise intention or form of behaviour. Here, the implication for the manager/employer is that specific goals should be identified by the manager in order to direct behaviour and maintain and enhance motivation.

2 *Realistic* – while difficult goals lead to higher performance than easy goals as they produce more effective behaviour, goals should be set at a challenging but realistic level.

3 *Achievable* – goals at the limits of a person's ability will not result in higher levels of performance. If goals are unachievable it will produce demotivational behaviour and reduce level of performance.

There is strong evidence to support goal-setting theory (Mento *et al.*, 1987; Locke and Latham, 1990) and Arnold *et al.* (1998: 258) points out that it is 'probably the most consistently supported theory in work and organisational psychology'. Feedback on behaviour and performance (also referred to as knowledge of results) is an important feature in goal-setting theory. Although it is well recognised that feedback on performance *is* motivational, it still remains that many organisations give little or no information regarding performance. More often, feedback and knowledge of results is only given when performance falls short of what is required. This gives rise to the fourth practical implication for the manager:

4 *Feedback* – feedback and knowledge of how an individual is performing is associated with high performance. Accurate and timely feedback acts as a progress check and can form the basis for revision of goals. In addition, feedback should be positive and any negative feedback should be dealt with in a sensitive manner.

A further issue in goal-setting theory concerns level of participation and its effect on performance. It is thought that goals set by others are more likely to be accepted if there is participation in determining the goals. It is assumed to be effective because it increases an individual's understanding of what is fair in the process. It also gives the individual a degree of control over the situation, thus enhancing their commitment to achieving the goal.

**Activity 5.3**

1 How far can you say that human beings are as rational as expectancy theory suggests?

2 What are your own goals at work or university? How do they motivate you to improve your performance?

## Job enrichment

The concept of job enrichment involves changing the design and experience of work in order to enhance satisfaction for the employee in the workplace. It anticipated that by doing this job satisfaction will lead to improved motivation

**The Management of Human Resources**

**81**

and a good performance output. Various aspects of a job may influence an individual's level of satisfaction with it. Extrinsically this may include factors such as pay, working conditions, peers and superiors. These factors are valued outcomes that are controlled by others. Intrinsic factors may include recognition, responsibility, advancement and achievement. The relationship between intrinsic rewards and performance are more immediate and more in control of the individual. It is argued by Lawler (1973) that it is these intrinsic rewards that are the most important influences on motivation to work.

An individual's role and job design can have a marked effect on how they experience work and achieve satisfaction in what they do. In their model Hackman and Oldham (1975) suggest that it is the *characteristics of the job* that lead to job satisfaction. Huczynski and Buchanan (1991) state that this model is the basis of Herzberg's expectancy theory of job enrichment strategy. In this model five core dimensions are used in which to analyse the job and role of an individual. These core dimensions are as follows:

- *Skill Variety* (SV): the extent to which a job makes use of different skills and abilities
- *Task Identity* (TI): the extent to which a job involves a whole and meaningful piece of work
- *Task Significance* (TS): the extent to which a job affects the work of other organisation members or others in society
- *Autonomy*: the extent to which a job gives the individual freedom, independence and discretion in carrying it out
- *Feedback*: the extent to which information is given about level of performance and which is related back to the individual

If the content of the job is assessed on these five dimensions a *motivational potential score* (MPS) can be calculated using the following equation:

$$\text{MPS} = \frac{\text{SV} + \text{TI} + \text{TS}}{3} \times (\text{autonomy}) \times (\text{feedback})$$

The motivating potential is low if one of the three main components is low. In addition, autonomy and feedback are considered to be more important in their influence over motivation. Thus a zero or near zero rating on either of these would result in a significantly greater lower score.

If jobs are redesigned in such a way that the presence of these five dimensions is increased, three critical psychological states can occur in workers:

- *Experienced meaningfulness of work*: determined by the level of skill variety, task identity and task significance and the extent to which work is meaningful, valuable and worthwhile
- *Experienced responsibility for work outcome*: determined by the amount of autonomy afforded and the extent to which an individual is accountable for the output of that work
- *Knowledge of results of work activity*: determined by the amount of feedback given and the extent to which an individual knows and understands how well they are performing

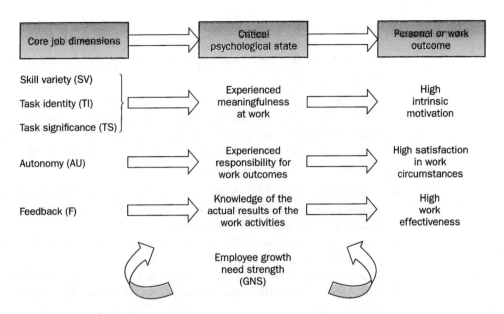

**Figure 5.4** Job enrichment

*Source*: Adapted from Hackman, Oldham, Jansen and Purdy (1975)

Work motivation and job satisfaction will be high when these three critical psychological states are experienced. In addition, behavioural outcomes such as work attendance and the quality of work produced may be improved. One further dimension to the model was a personal attribute termed the *growth need strength* (GNS). Hackman and Oldham (1975) believed that this moderated the extent to which the three critical psychological states could be experienced. If an individual has drive and potential their GNS will be high and they will experience the three critical psychological states strongly (see Figure 5.4).

It can be seen how Hackman and Oldham's model encompasses job characteristics, job satisfaction, principles of work design, psychological state and motivation. Although the model has been universally accepted over the years Roberts and Glick (1981) point to two major criticisms in its usage. First, that the model says little about how to change a job in order to increase the amount of core characteristics it offers and, secondly, the model says little about how to redesign jobs for people low in growth need strength. Huczynski and Buchanan (1991) illustrate how the model shows that the motivating potential of jobs *can* be improved by applying five implementing concepts. These, then, do have implications for managers in the workplace:

- *Combining tasks* – increasing the variety of the work carried out by an individual will increase the contribution that the individual makes
- *Forming natural work units* – increasing the contribution that the individual makes to the work will increase the significance of the job
- *Establishing relationships* – giving employees responsibility for establishing contacts both within and outside of the organisation increases variety and affords the individual more freedom. Furthermore, it increases the potential and opportunity for direct feedback

- *Vertical loading* – giving responsibility normally allocated to superiors increases individual autonomy
- *Opening feedback and communication* – allows improvement for the feedback of performance

These five concepts have a considerable impact on the nature of the relationship between employee and employer and reflect on what Schein referred to in 1988 as the **psychological contract**. This implicit contract is based upon a series of assumptions on this important employee–employer relationship. These assumptions are outlined as follows:

- That employees will be treated fairly and honestly. That they will be afforded information about changes in working conditions and practice and that they will be treated justly and with equity.
- That employees should be able to expect a degree of security in return for loyalty to the organisation.
- That employees should expect employers to recognise their work, value the contribution that they make and satisfy their needs of fulfilment and job satisfaction.

From these basic assumptions it can be seen that the contract is largely a tacit agreement between employee and employer – nothing is formally written down and agreed upon between the two. Even though the contract is at the core of the employee–employer relationship, it is neither fixed nor ever stable. In addition, it is an agreement between unequal parties. The input of the employee will be dependent on their skills and knowledge and what motivates and interests them as individuals. These will be influenced by factors such as class, education, family circumstances, gender and race. The priorities of the employee are to receive what *they* perceive to be appropriate rewards and recognition for their work effort. For the employer, economic forces and capital resources will be crucial factors in how they allocate reward and recognition.

The trend towards increased efficiency – the 'notion of more for less' – and the increased expectancy of 'what is reasonable' by the employee, threatens the stability of the psychological contract between employee and employer. Watson (1995) suggests that different types of contract are made between an individual and their employer, depending on their position within the organisation and the type of work carried out. Two broad categories are used by Watson to explain this:

- Managerial/professional positions. Individuals in these positions tend to use discretion in their work and so have a high trust relationship with their superiors. In return for a high level of reward (salary, opportunity, status, satisfaction) these individuals use their own initiative and comply with the requirements of the organisation.
- Less skilled manual work, routine clerical and service work. The generally lower level of monetary reward (often on an hourly or weekly basis) for these groups is characterised by a low trust relationship with superiors. Work tasks are monitored under a basic contractual commitment and there is less in the way of potential for career advancement.

Clearly, if either party fails to meet the basic assumptions and expectations of the psychological contract, serious consequences may develop. For the employee, these may include lack of morale, demotivation and lack of advancement. For the employer, it may include absenteeism, lack of employee effort and high employee turnover. In addition, it is reasonable to suggest that the psychological contract does not hold as true in the new millennium as it did in years gone by. In Chapter 2 we have seen how the concept of the 'flexible firm' has challenged the notion that the relationship between employee and employer, as described above, remains strong. Individuals now work longer hours, are more accountable, more flexible and more disposable than ever before and the psychological contract can no longer be taken for granted.

Due to the uncertain economic climate where competition is strong and change inevitable, the response from within organisations has been to focus on adaptability and responsiveness to change rather than continuity and stability. This has been reflected not only in the psychological contract as described above but also in the nature of the more formal employment contract. Today there are a variety of employment contracts other than full-time and part-time permanent positions (see Chapter 2). The use of part-time and short-term contracts limits the commitment of the employer to the employee and can be justifiably (by the employer) seen as a form of control. This control often precipitates the need for the employer to work harder and for longer hours, often working beyond contract in an attempt to gain a degree of security.

### Activity 5.4

In considering Hackman and Oldham's model, look for areas where your own work could be redesigned in order to increase your own motivation and work performance.

## Motivation, performance and commitment

If we refer back to the Guest model of HRM (1989) in Chapter 1, in discussing policy goals related to human resource management, he argues that the policy goal for commitment is to ensure that employees feel bound to their organisation and are committed to high performance via their behaviour. One of the more popular ways of dividing organisational commitment into various components is described by Allen and Meyer (1990):

- *Affective commitment* – concerns the individual's emotional attachment to the organisation
- *Continuance commitment* – the individual's perception of what it would cost and the personal risk involved in leaving the organisation
- *Normative commitment* – the individual's own feelings of obligation to the organisation as their employer

It is true to say that people can feel multiple commitments in the workplace. These may not only be to their particular organisation, but also to their department, locality, trade union or professional association (Aranya and Ferris, 1984; Barling *et al.*, 1990). It is believed that an individual's commitment to their work can be enhanced through affording them the opportunity to encounter positive experiences in the workplace. Aspects intrinsic to the job are more important than extrinsic factors such as pay and working conditions. For example, Matthieu and Zajac (1990) found autonomy to be positively associated with organisational commitment, which Iverson (1996) suggests has a positive impact on attitudes in the workplace. This would seem particularly pertinent for the affective component of commitment where commitment is based on emotional attachment.

The link between commitment and performance is a lot less clear. Iverson, Deery and Erwin (1994) suggest that role ambiguity, or lack of role clarity, role conflict or inconsistent demands of the role and role overload will have a negative impact on organisational commitment. While Meyer *et al.* (1993) found that workers with high affective commitment tended to be better performers, a person is unlikely to perform well if they are unable to achieve, either through lack of ability or any of the above. If this is so, it can be expected that there will be a stronger link between commitment and performance for aspects of performance that depend more on motivation than ability. Finally, intention to leave the organisation is the most cited reason for low organisational commitment. Additionally, as Matthieu and Zajak (1990) point out, a person who does not feel committed to his organisation is more likely to want to leave it, than a person who does feel committed.

---

**Case Study 5.1**

### Working for patients but demotivating the professionals?

Roymary NHS Trust is a large district general hospital undergoing a radical whole hospital change programme. The hospital's musculoskeletal process deals with any type of orthopaedic condition. The range of patient age and type of condition on these wards is enormous – from elderly fractures of the hip to young football players breaking legs, from traffic accidents to the less severe, but equally debilitating slipping and falling over, breaking arms, legs and backs. In the organisational change process four previously mixed acute/rehabilitation trauma wards have been restructured in order to accommodate two wholly acute and two wholly rehabilitation wards.

Previously on admission, patients had been admitted to one ward for the duration of their stay. Following the restructuring this no longer happened. The acute wards now accepted the patients on admission. It was from these wards the patients went to theatre and subsequently spent the initial few days of their post-operative recovery. The rehabilitation wards, as their name suggests, serve to accept the patients in preparation for discharge back into the community. Nursing staff worked in teams – two teams per ward – but all other health professionals, for example members of the therapy professions, treated patients on any of the four wards.

One of the jobs to be *formally* redesigned was that of the traditional ward sister. As a direct result of the organisational change programme this role no longer existed, having been replaced by Team Leaders. These newly created roles incorporated new job descriptions, which

Case Study continued

saw an extension in the roles and responsibilities beyond nursing itself and into the realms of middle management. In addition, a new role of Support Worker was added to the team, which nursing and therapy assistants had been encouraged to apply for. Underpinning this new Support Worker role was the introduction of a hospital-led training programme. This programme had a number of objectives. It was anticipated that by improving the support worker knowledge base the continuity of care, and handling and rehabilitation of the patient would be enhanced. In addition, the blurring of professional boundaries through the newly trained support workers role enhanced skill mix on the unit through providing some therapy intervention at weekends and promoting rehabilitation outside of formal treatment sessions. To further the concept of a skill-enhanced support worker, an in-house competency-based training package was developed, based on the National Vocational Qualification system. This centred on basic nursing, physiotherapy and occupational therapy skills which included dressing practice, wound care and simple exercise regimes. This specifically designed package allowed the support worker to concentrate on skills related to rehabilitation and allowed them to obtain a recognised in-house award – the one incentive they had received for taking on the new role.

Other than this the traditional team-based nursing existed. That is, nurses, including the support workers, were organised into teams comprising a mix of seniority and skill. Each team had responsibility for the welfare of a fixed number of patients. As far as possible the workload was organised such that patient allocation was based in bays. Each team took on the workload of two bays and a set number of side rooms.

Although attached to the ward through secondment, the physiotherapists and occupational therapists were actually based in their own departments in another part of the hospital. Located within their own small teams, both professions worked on the wards and in the gymnasium adjacent to the wards on a daily basis and for much of the day. The nature of the musculoskeletal work was such that the therapy professions were heavily involved in the treatment and recovery of the patients. To this end, a new initiative introduced by management had been the introduction of newly designated therapy treatment rooms within the confines of the musculoskeletal unit. This provided them with their own base close to the ward setting from where they could treat patients without taking them to their main department elsewhere in the hospital.

A further new initiative had involved the use of multiskilling. Professionals had been encouraged to identify tasks that could be 'shared' in order to enhance the treatment of the patient and speed up recovery. An example of this was the introduction of nurses being allowed to supervise exercise regimes on the wards – a role which had previously been performed by the physiotherapists. Another example was the ability of the nurses to assess patients attempting the stairs post-operatively – a pre-requisite for being discharged. Again, this had previously been under the umbrella of the physiotherapists.

The organisational change programme had brought about significant improvement in patient care in terms of level of care, patient recovery, theatre waiting times and increases in bed occupancy. The health professionals themselves, however, portrayed a mixed response to what was happening around them. For the most senior nurses, acceptance of change was more evident in those who experienced a sense of enrichment in their roles which tended to be confined to those whose jobs had been formally redesigned. For the nurse, the higher up the hierarchical ladder, the more upbeat and positive the attitude to change. For the more junior nurses, there was evidence of increases in workload among those whose jobs had not changed following the restructuring, but who were experiencing changes in role as a result of changes in the nursing hierarchy. In addition, increases in tasks and task variety were seen as intensification

Case Study continued

**The Management of Human Resources**
**87**

of work rather than increases in job satisfaction. Lack of recognition of this work intensification was often cited as a major concern. The new support worker role had provided variation and increases in scope of practice for nursing and physiotherapy assistants, but other than an in-house qualification had failed to provide little incentive for the role to succeed.

In spite of concerns over the intensification of work the nurses viewed the issue of multi-skilling more positively than the therapy professions. Much was made of the benefits to patients through providing a more comprehensive level of care and enhancing their own skill base. The therapy professions, although pleased with the management initiative of providing on-site treatment facilities, demonstrated a real of fear of losing their skills to other professions and viewed the whole process of multiskilling as 'deskilling'.

### Activity 5.5

1 Discuss how expectancy theory and equity theory contribute to the understanding of the situation described above for the:

    a) team leader
    b) nurses
    c) support worker
    d) therapy professions

2 What are the implications for management in dealing with the situation?

3 How can management enhance the commitment of the professionals to the change process?

### SUMMARY

In this chapter the following key points have been made:

- There are two contrasting approaches to the theory of work motivation
- Content or need theories are based on the assumption that psychological needs lie behind human behaviour
- Process theories concentrate on the cognitive process of determining levels of motivation
- Fairness and justice are becoming more prominent in organisational life
- The setting of goals that are specific, achievable yet sufficiently difficult can often improve a person's work performance
- An individual's role and job can affect how they experience work and achieve satisfaction
- The psychological contract is based on a series of assumptions and is an important element in the employer–employee relationship
- Individuals can have multiple commitments in the workplace
- Organisational commitment is encouraged by positive experiences at work

## DISCUSSION QUESTIONS

1 What are the differences between content and process theories of motivation? Outline and discuss the main motivational theories.

2 How far can management 'assume' a well-motivated, fully committed workforce?

3 Discuss the various considerations that a human resources manager would have to make when redesigning work and introducing new roles into the organisation.

## FURTHER READING

Students seeking further detail on the issues raised in this chapter should consult Arnold *et al.* (1998), Fincham and Rhodes (1999) or McClelland (1999).

# 4

# Human resource planning: control to seduction?

*Damian O'Doherty*

**OBJECTIVES**

- To critically assess the transition from the quantitative regime of manpower planning to the more qualitative practice of contemporary human resource planning, a transition that we have characterised in terms of a move from *control* to *seduction*. Do not be seduced by this text.

- To impart a comprehensive understanding of the technical and prescriptive components of traditional 'scientific' manpower planning, from the measurement of labour turnover to the use of Markov models.

- To impart an understanding of the assumptions and metaphorical figures that underpin and support the traditional vision and practice of manpower planning. This will allow us to open up those domains of organisation that are typically excluded and neglected in the discourse of manpower planning.

- To stimulate a critical awareness of the tensions between order and disorder in organisation, tensions that fracture the integrity of the employment relation and which manpower planning, and latterly human resource planning, attempt to address. As we shall see, manpower planning often compounds and amplifies these tensions, tripping off further rounds of struggle and discord.

- To locate and identify areas of dissension within organisations that contest the objectives and practice of manpower planning, and to evaluate the extent to which the more radically 'unitarist' human resource planning succeeds in transcending divergent 'stakeholder' interests. The chapter seeks to advance an explanation of this dissension.

- To provoke critical self-awareness in the reading and writing of human resource planning. In effect we question the legitimacy of 'objectives' and the capacity of instrumental and linear-rational calculation to manage organisation. We do aim to be interesting and relevant even if it appears at times irreverent and irresponsible. At times perplexing, if not amusing, this might contribute to the adumbration of that space where organisation is given chance, where we are given chance, and where anything might happen next.

# INTRODUCTION

Traditionally, manpower planning has been studied and taught from within a unitarist frame of reference. As a consequence, its practice is understood as a technical exercise performed exclusively by management. Consistent with this approach, management gets defined as a rational and politically neutral agent of organisation responsible for the execution of a series of business 'functions' in a perspective that abstracts management from issues of political struggle and negotiation (Cole, 1991; Torrington and Hall, 1995). Given this frame of reference, trade unions and shopfloor collective employee organisations were considered, at best, to provide a medium for securing managerial legitimacy. Outside personnel management departments, the activities of trade unions, for example, were generally looked upon as the antithesis of efficient manpower planning (Fox, 1985), deviant institutions that worked to prevent the most rational deployment and use of labour. By maintaining such things as customary norms, 'restrictive practices', and inefficient working routines, together with the publicity that certain manpower practices attracted in the public sector, in areas of manufacturing, and especially in the docks (Donovan, 1968; see also Turnbull, 1992; Turnbull and Sapsford, 1992), unions were seen as inimical to the 'acquisition, utilization, improvement and retention of an enterprise's human resources' (HMSO, cited in Bramham, 1990).

Where management was formally trained, this tended, in the main, to be a syllabus of neo-classical economics and 'organisation science' whose assumptions legitimised this sovereign and singular authority claimed by management (see Chapter 3). More commonly, however, the hegemony of neo-classical economics was established through the more informal processes of distillation and socialisation within work organisations, hegemony that finds only latent expression in the mundane assumptions and prejudices rehearsed in management discourse. The emergence of human resource management can be understood, to some extent, as a project to recover and extend the assumptions of unitarist management, especially in the domain of manpower planning. Following the collective challenge of labour and its prosecution of a pluralist agenda, pursued – in part successfully – through state institutions and the processes of social democracy, management seems to have been in need of a new discourse of legitimisation.

HRM is perhaps best seen as a complex hybrid product of its times (cf. Chapter 1) – the discourse of crisis (Eldridge *et al.*, 1991), Reagan economics, Thatcherism (see Hall and Jacques, 1983), and even the punk nihilism of the 1970s. In this chapter we shall explore the nature of this transition from manpower planning to 'human resource planning' in a way that seeks to restore the politics of the workplace as it is 'distilled' and 'socialised' through contemporary social relations and organisation.

Locating the technical procedures of manpower planning within the ambit of organisation struggle, we try, in a preliminary way, to open up an arena that mediates a whole force-field of order and disorder, a field of tension that embraces both the rational and the irrational, conscious organisation, unconscious organisation, and a complex series of heterogeneous struggles within power relations – including the economic struggle between capital and labour. We shall then be able to develop an understanding that attends to the co-implication of representational and practical dimension in manpower planning: that is, the *complicated* inter-articulation of theory and practice. Our chapter advances towards that boundary space **between representation and practice** where 'manpower planning' gets manifest as struggle, in perpetual self-crisis, internally and externally distracted. Manpower planning attempts to integrate this fractious tension in/of organisation, to bind the elements of manifold material and ideal phenomena and so render the world objective and utile.

125

Like the world of banking, manpower planning wants to secure confidence and credit. Manpower planning can be usefully thought of in terms of the analogy with banking: it 'banks' on prediction and control, anticipation and foresight; it banks on employees as currency and resource; stabilise-able as economic units of calculation; as an investment, employees are trained and developed, disciplined and shaped, bought and sold on the labour market, terminated or 'cashed in' at the most financially lucrative moment for an organisation. Manpower planning also banks on *making* organisation, on *making the whole*. It aims to secure a coherent *whole* out of the mobile heterogeneous *parts* of organisation/disorganisation (Cooper and Law, 1995), parts that move in agitated patterns, co-mingling and combining, assembling and disassembling in complex and unpredictable forms. From the recalcitrance of the subjects' will – 'I refuse to work hard today' and 'Sod it, I've had enough of this' – to dream of fantasy and escape, to gossip and rumour that spreads like wildfire to delay and suspend the seriousness of the working day. Economic calculation and efficiency in the use of manpower only ever achieves a precarious and partial outcome in organisation.

In order to approach these difficult issues, this chapter embodies a reflexive and ironic tone that, for many, might seem to mirror – or better *mimic* – contemporary practices in human resource management (cf. Taussig, 1993; O'Doherty and Roberts, 2000). Exploring what might appear inappropriate domains of study, the seemingly irrelevant, the out-of-bounds or off-limits, and mixing together texts from a dispersed range of disciplinary fields – industrial relations, personnel management, aboriginal folklore, the archive of functionalist prescriptive texts in manpower planning, labour history, and organisation studies – we invite you to read this text as a palimpsest. We want to catch you off your guard; juxtapose the unseemly and the unseen in-organisation; introduce strands of discourse that come from elsewhere and lead somewhere else, pathways and portals to other worlds and ways of being (see Burrell, 1997). Here, manpower planning can suddenly appear to take on the features of bank, a form of accountancy, or a military campaign, in a space where a unit of 'human resource' might become a 'wolf-man' (Freud, 1918/1991), and the employment relation a site of exploitation and the appropriation of surplus value.

Splicing the incongruous and the unexpected, the fragments of marginal phenomena, we illustrate, however, that manpower planning as 'banking' on the *whole* is not what it seems. As an introduction to human resource planning, this chapter represents an effort to think and write on manpower planning in novel and unconventional ways in order to stimulate *readerly* creativity (Barthes, 1977). For the successful human resource planner of the future, this ability to cope with the shock of the unexpected might well be mandatory. Moreover, the capacity to 'channel hop' – to negotiate and move across multiple domains of reality; to step through the classical marble banking hall and into the space of high finance, a world of *forked lightning* and the *Mae West* (Valdez, 1997: 242); to improvise and innovate – will prove invaluable. After all, isn't this how the discourse of what becomes 'traditional' manpower planning comes into being? It is *invented*. We are far from a calculation of the 'labour stability index' or a 'frequency distribution of leavers by length of service', a discourse we will need to leave behind and eventually abandon all together. Not that it offered anything real or enduring in the first place, or secured the (w)hole of organisation. As we shall see, *manpower planning as a banking hall is a knot-what of seams.*

This chapter can be watched, read alone in silence, or read aloud collectively in groups. It is not designed, however, for radio broadcast nor, unfortunately, is there any obvious musical accompaniment. In the first half of this chapter we shall mime an

126

orthodox and incremental form of thinking in manpower planning that takes us through its basic 'functions'. Before the construction of a plan it is necessary to know where the need for manpower planning originates. Once we know this we can then address how one might go about creating a simple manpower plan. From the calculation of labour demand to an analysis of labour supply, manpower planning proceeds to reconcile demand and supply so as to secure equilibrium, harmony, and organisation. Following this we can work out some complications to the basic model that allows for dynamics and change. Then we shall explore the 'evolution' of manpower planning as it 'matures' towards *human resource* planning and the 'management of change'. In the second half of the chapter we unpack this linearity by opening up some of the definitions and assumptions that underpin resource planning. Here, we enter that field of tension that subverts the practice of manpower planning as rationality and organisation, a space of knots and seams where order becomes disorder and organisation – disorganisation. Before we think about 'who' it is that is said to conduct manpower planning within organisation, let's think about why there is a need for manpower planning.

## THE NEED FOR MANPOWER PLANNING

For many years, the importance of manpower planning was seen to lie with the contribution it could make to reducing 'shocks' and 'disturbances' within the social relations of large organisations and, in the process, maintaining some kind of organisational stability and equilibrium. These shocks and disturbances might emanate from within the organisation, in response to changes in the outside world – in technology, the product, labour, and capital markets – or as the result of a complex interaction between the inside and outside.

Within the organisation wider corporate initiatives are seen to trigger off a number of manpower repercussions, and manpower planners are expected to respond in an appropriate manner in order to manage and contain its disturbance. While the kind of extensive productivity planning conducted at Fawley in the late 1950s and 1960s might have offered a model case study that illustrates the importance of involving specialist manpower planners (Flanders, 1964), in the main, manpower planning was conducted ad hoc within a system of industrial relations and personnel management that was 'largely informal' and 'largely fragmented'. Moreover, once we open up organisation and the employment relation more broadly, we shall see this informality and fragmentation writ large. So, for manpower planning it was more a case of 'muddling through' (Edwards *et al.*, 1992), rather than strategic direction and control.

Typically, one finds that issues concerned with personnel and specialist manpower planning are subordinate to the power of accountancy and finance within senior corporate management, a pattern of power relations and inequality that in recent years has become more hegemonic and disadvantageous for the pursuit of a distinctive set of values and ideals through personnel management (see Armstrong, 1995). In the past this has meant that when individual companies made plans for future product development, or drew up investment schedules for new technology, more often than not manpower planning was relegated to a relatively low status and downstream function. Left to pick up the pieces, manpower planning was preoccupied with 'firefighting', tackling the outbreak of consequences and repercussions arising from decisions taken within corporate management and other more powerful management specialisms.

127

This means that the need for manpower planning might be better thought of as a 'derivative need', something that followed and sought to correct for the mistakes and oversights of wider 'strategic' managerial decision-making. Subject to this wider pattern of organisational power relations, manpower planning then, has struggled to construct and promote an autonomous and distinctive set of practices and techniques. It has always found itself situated within the power politics of organisation and in competition with the claims of other management specialisms such that it is forced to adapt and modify, shape and develop its practices in an ongoing process of organisational negotiation and political lobbying. Subject to the winds of change, the 'need' for manpower planning remains an historically contingent phenomenon, and one partly constructed and promoted by manpower planners themselves.

When we unpack the functions and techniques of manpower planning we also find a whole series of tensions and problems that render its practice far less coherent and rational than commonly assumed, but which nonetheless contribute to this 'need' for manpower planning. In large organisations the understanding and measurement of even the most basic and simple numerical flows of individuals are tasks that quite clearly require detailed and careful monitoring. Over a number of years, it might well be expected that 'patterns' will emerge, reducing the anxiety and burden of persistent organisational monitoring. In many ways we can think of the role of manpower planning as one that involves a struggle to represent organisation and its 'movements' as a two-dimensional picture of resource flows. Manpower planning thought it was taking photographs (!?) – pull the trigger – flash – illuminate – bring the distant closer – capture movement as impression on a chemical surface – like those preparations, perhaps, for aerial bombing. Yet, as we shall see, the problems of 'time' and 'movement' – the processual dimensions of organisation – are complex, creating difficulties that are only partially amenable to the timeless abstractions, representation, and control of photography. Building up reliable long-term patterns of resource flows in organisation always remains a precarious and contingent accomplishment, an organisational exercise that can never relax, and one that is always subject to perturbation and mistake. Even with the so-called advanced sophistication of military hardware in the Gulf War, we know that bombs still missed their targets, and manpower planning mistakes were made in the calculation of civilian and NATO military casualties.

In the perpetual strife between movement/change in organisation and the representation/stasis of manpower planning, these mistakes and unintended consequences call out for further rounds of intervention, correction, and readjustment by manpower planning. This adds a further layer of 'need' for manpower planning, a vicious incestuous cycle that resembles the case of a dog chasing its own tail. Later in the chapter we delve into the organisation 'shadow' cast by the photographic illumination of manpower planning that opens up an irrecoverable space between the dimensions of movement and stasis, the body and head of organisation, and where the rationality of planning meets its limits. What we are concerned with here is how the 'need' for manpower planning emerges in part from the tension between the three-dimensional world of organisation and its two-dimensional representation in manpower plans.

In a stable environment, where the characteristics of product and labour markets might be expected to continue and persist in a predictable and orderly fashion, the conditions for modelling long-term patterns of employment within organisation are no doubt a little more propitious. This would allow the planner to calculate and predict such things as the number of retirements, the expected turnover of staff within departments, and the average number of staff leaving for 'involuntary reasons'. Yet models

128

such as these provide a broad and rather crude picture of numerical turnover, providing only rudimentary information on things such as replacement times and rates. In other words, in order to maintain numerically stable employment over time, management requires more sophisticated and focused data on when, where, and how many employees need to be recruited.

The precise statistical and qualitative complexities and details that contribute to a manpower plan will be considered in more detail later in the chapter. At this stage it is important to appreciate that manpower planning is a critical managerial function because it provides management with information on resource flows that is used to calculate, amongst other things, recruitment needs and succession and development plans. This has been described above as an attempt to reduce shocks and disturbances. With detailed study of past and projected trends in 'employment loss', management can seek to minimise the shock of unexpected shortages of labour, inefficient and costly surpluses, and needless redundancies.

For example, if historically you have always recruited two junior members in the marketing department, a retrospection that leads you, once again, to seek the recruitment of two employees, management would be 'shocked' if they found the marketing department understaffed and unable to complete work on time. Upon further enquiry it might transpire that in that particular year there were more retirements, an 'unusual' number of sabbaticals, a large amount of maternity leave, an unexpectedly high degree of sickness leave, or indeed a higher than expected number of deaths! On closer analysis of relevant variables one might find that the marketing department was increasingly becoming a top-heavy and mature department. Furthermore, consider what might happen if British Airways were offering free around-the-world tickets for that year, child allowances had trebled owing to a rather generous restructuring of the Treasury under a Labour administration, and an epidemic of typhoid flu had been sweeping across Western Europe! Although this is a rather humorous example, it highlights the importance of manpower planning and the endless possibility of variables that one could possibly consider. This is partly why the task of manpower planning is such a difficult and time-consuming process involving a considerable amount of research and knowledge of current events that may shape and affect the availability of internal resources and indeed the current stocks of human resources available for recruitment in the local and national labour market.

How many variables is it sensible therefore to consider in a detailed manpower plan? If all variables are not considered then it may well be the case that at some stage management will be 'shocked' by 'disturbances' in organisational employment patterns in response to both internal and external environmental changes. It was well known, for example, that in certain British car factories in the 1960s and 1970s there would be a heavier than normal rate of sickness and absence on Fridays! Being aware of the variables that affect manpower supply is a crucial area of concern for professional manpower planners, and as the examples above show, it can prove critical for the success of the organisation. If management remains ignorant of the ebb and flow of organisation, the movement of employment patterns and the variables that lead to change, then severe operational difficulties will emerge as management finds itself with some departments overstaffed, other departments suffering from a chronic shortage of employees, and possibly some departments that cannot function on Fridays because of the absence of staff. The need for manpower planning arises therefore from the operational needs of an organisation, and its importance lies in maintaining a sufficient supply of employees, in the right place and time, and at the right cost. Only through detailed observation and planning of many variables, both internal to the organisation

129

and external in the wider political socio-economic environment, can management ensure a reconciliation of labour supply and demand such that shocks and disturbances are avoided.

We can summarise the need for manpower planning as one that involves both a quantifiable and quantitative dimension leading to:

- *recruitment plans*: to avoid unexpected shortages;
- *the identification of training needs*: to avoid skill shortages;
- *management development*: in order to avoid bottlenecks of trained but disgruntled management who see no future position in the hierarchy, but also to avoid managerial shortages – this often requires careful planning;
- *industrial relations plans*: often, seeking to change the quantity and quality of employees will require careful IR planning if an organisation is to avoid industrial unrest.

In practice, 'manpower planning is concerned with the demand and supply of labour and problems arising from the process of reconciling these factors' (Tyson and York, 1989: 76). In sum, the need for manpower planning lies with the long-term and short-term practical operational needs of the organisation but also, critically, with the social, psychological, and financial needs and aspirations of individual employees within organisation. As we have seen, it also arises out of a complex process of political negotiation within organisation and is in part the self-serving product of what we might call a will-to-power by manpower planners. A basic strife between movement and representation in organisation compounds this paradox and contributes to the always unfinished ongoing need for manpower planning. Yet, who is it that does manpower planning? It seems an arduous and unenviable task, one that over time always ends in partial failure and incompletion.

## WHO DOES MANPOWER PLANNING?

Traditionally in large organisations the function of manpower planning was normally carried out by the personnel department or by a specialist manpower planner employed within the personnel department. In many smaller organisations, often in the absence of any well-defined separate personnel department, the process of manpower planning would have been conducted by the general manager of the organisation. In small family-owned firms, for example, it may well be that the manpower planner would also have been the wages clerk, the financial manager, the marketing and distribution manager. It is really only in large-scale and often bureaucratic businesses that specialised personnel departments and manpower planners maintained a distinctive identity. Therefore, it is large-scale organisations such as the Civil Service, the National Health Service, the Royal Air Force, and the large high street retail banks that have provided the conventional empirical sites for the study and practice of manpower planning.

In the UK economy of the 1950s and 1960s, with full employment and an expanding dynamic international economy, the emphasis within manpower planning was one of employment growth and organisational expansion. Anticipating employee turnover, and identifying those areas of organisation that required additional 'manpower', constituted the principal responsibility of manpower planners. Recruiting and selecting cost-efficient employees in the context of difficult 'tight' labour markets, where inflationary pressures and wage rises were beginning to cause some concern over company profitability, combined to promote the virtues of 'good' manpower planning. Quick

130

and efficient methods of replacing turnover through recruitment and selection were seen to be critical in securing and maintaining continued profitability.

In times of labour scarcity, the credibility and influence of manpower planning as a specialist domain of management expertise prospered. If a business suffered from a high turnover of staff in the 1960s, a series of organisation-wide consequences and repercussions would have created considerable operational difficulties for management. As a delicate eco-like system of relational phenomena, we know that organisations are vulnerable to a knock-on 'domino'-like effect of reverberation and complication in response to only small degrees of disturbance. So, what might seem a relatively minor change in one area of an organisation can rapidly spill over into other areas, aggravating and amplifying the initial agitation. Overworked departments and underresourced divisions within organisations might very quickly spark discontent and low morale amongst employees, pushing up rates of absence and sickness. Given the conditions of full employment in the 1960s and early 1970s, staff were difficult and costly to replace. As a consequence, large organisations sought to invest considerable resources in the management of manpower planning at a time when 'organisation structures were highly centralised and relatively stable, with the emphasis on promotion and upward mobility; and the main concerns were recruitment and retention' (Timperley and Sisson, 1989: 103). The scale at which such organisations were operating, both geographically and hierarchically, clearly necessitated some planning and coordination of human resources.

First of all, as manpower planners we would have needed to know where employees were in the organisation – which in the context of large complex organisations is not as simple as it first might appear. Once we have established the number of employees, and where they are currently being used, then we might be in a better position to think how they could be moved to where they are needed or where they could be more gainfully deployed. Yet the identification of 'shortages' and 'surpluses' is also not the simple technical exercise it might at first seem. Consider the difficulties involved, pre-computerisation, of establishing how many people are working within a large organisation.

An obvious answer might be employment records. Well, yes, this might give you a figure representing formal numbers employed. Yet how accurate are these records, and who maintains them? Within dockwork, the repercussions of 'welting' (Clegg, 1979:142) meant that while formal employment records might tell you how many people were employed, they didn't really tell you how many were actually *working*. In his highly influential study of manpower reorganisation and collective bargaining at the Esso Fawley plant, Allan Flanders notes that craftsmen's 'mates' worked at only about 40% of the productivity rate of the craftsmen they assisted (Flanders, 1964:170). So formal employment records might show that 216 employees worked as 'pipefitters' in 1960. Of these, however, 82 were 'mates' who worked, on average, only $3\frac{1}{2}$ hours a day. Therefore the formal record of numbers employed offers only a very limited reading of manpower utilisation. It doesn't really guarantee how many people are working, nor 'where' organisational resources are being deployed or used, let alone where they might be most efficiently employed.

When we think about who maintains these records we complicate the picture even further. For legal and tax reasons there are often incentives to overplay or underplay the number of employees. In transport for example, where the law restricts the numbers of hours a lorry driver can work, organisations might be tempted to fabricate employment records. 'Excessive' hours driven by one truck driver might reap wage benefits for the individual employee and avoid employment costs for the employer. In an

131

effort to avoid legal proceedings the employer might create the 'illusion' that two drivers were working together in the cab. The 'strategic' use of multiple tachographs will allow one driver to work a 14-hour shift, while 'recording' only seven hours. The other seven hours are worked by another named driver, who exists only as a formal paper record. In order to 'distribute' the total number of driver hours among a larger population of drivers in an effort to avoid infringing legal requirements, formal records may show a far greater number of employees than is actually the case. In other companies, the creation of employment records might be a way of avoiding tax. This means that we always need to be cautious when approaching official company documents and published statistics, and ask who maintains the records and whose interests they serve.

Record keeping is an expensive administrative and managerial activity. We might even say that organisation needs to manpower plan for manpower planners! Before we know where we are, the risk is that manpower planning departments have sprung up, employing huge armies of statistical planners and record keepers. Paradoxically, keeping a tight control on the cost of maintaining such a large and diversifying workforce required considerable time and effort in the planning and control of manpower. Centralised within the apex of specialised head office departments, incumbent with its hierarchical vantage point, it was assumed that manpower planners could literally provide an 'overview' of manpower flows throughout the entire organisation. This is the manpower planner as the brains of the organisation, its heroic masculine 'author'. From its vantage point in the 'head' office, the stocks and flows of manpower could be monitored and recorded in a form that allowed its intellectual reprocessing by the 'head' so as to work the body of organisation more rationally and efficiently. This was an era of specialisation and the growth of management science, management as the 'science' of universal principles, techniques, rules and procedures. This was also the age of mechanised regularity and control, of organisation as machine (Morgan, 1986), where the formal-rational principles of modem organisation, or 'Weberian' bureaucracy (Weber, 1948), shaped the development of manpower planning. In the 1950s and 1960s, from national economic labour market planning to internal manpower planning audits and reviews – whether in the Civil Service, local government, or the banks – the rationalisation of manpower planning consolidated hierarchies of authority in organisation while contributing to the delineation of clear lines of command and control, the specialisation of function, and the cultivation of elite expertise.

The era of the specialist manpower planner, then, was one of growth, large complex organisation, record keeping, expanding bureaucracy, administration and control. In the main, manpower planning was a quantitative science officiated by white-collar technicians who traced their ancestry back to Taylor's time and motion study. The influence of Henri Fayol (1949), as mediated and popularised in the UK by Lyndall Urwick (1947), led to the increasing technical abstraction of manpower planning from the domain of the 'Taylorite' managerial struggle focused upon the point of production – that 'point' of day-to-day 'negotiation' and contestation in the employment relation between manager and worker over the substantive content of the wage–effort bargain (Armstrong, 1996). This was the 'white heat' of scientific and technological revolution – the onward march of science and man's ever greater mastery of the social and natural world.

In the context of the 1980s, traditional quantitative manpower planning fell somewhat out of favour as management, in response to product market crisis and international economic competition, sought to redevelop its employee resource and reduce staffing levels. With its associated bureaucracy and red tape, manpower planning was forced to reorientate its contribution to organisation in an era that saw

132

large-scale rationalisations, redundancies and restructuring. It is said by some that manpower planning is becoming 'human resource' planning (Bramham, 1989), providing a more sensitive and qualitative approach to the acquisition, utilisation and development of employees, one that is not so fixated upon numbers and statistical calculation. In the 1987 report of the Manpower Services Commission, 'competence, commitment and the capacity to change' were deemed to challenge the quantitative traditions of manpower planning. As John Storey (1992) writes on the basis of his research of UK industry in the late 1980s, the 'mechanistic manpower-planning models have been superseded and there is very clear evidence of a type of planning which attends not only to regulating numbers but is proactive in respect of part-time work and annual hours contracts, and proactive in the realm of radically different forms of labour utilization' (p. 89).

We might think of this as the growth of a more 'open' authorship in manpower planning, in which manpower planners returned to the floor to make use of a more improvised and intuitive range of skills, tinkering with the 'culture' of organisation and the more qualitative aspects of the employment relation (Deal and Kennedy, 1982; Peters, 1993, 1994). If it was the growth of a more open authorship, it was also a period in which the identity and authorship of a specifically delimited elite practice of manpower planning was challenged. Manpower planning began to be devolved into the immediacy of the day-to-day employment relation, where it merged with other 'tacit' features of people management within expanded roles for first-line managers (Storey, 1992: 216–241). Now, while we say 'devolved' we should not forget that this was within a framework of tight budgetary control, more sophisticated performance monitoring, and the application of strict accountancy procedures in audit and control imposed by the centre – whether through the use of 'cash limits' in the public sector or through the diffusion of a logic of accountancy into the practice of shopfloor management (Armstrong, 1995; Brown et al., 1995).

There are further grounds for questioning whether manpower planning is simply becoming less 'quantitative' as it incorporates elements of a 'softer' and more qualitative form of management. The number of redundancies, early retirements, plant closures and reorganisations multiplied in the 1980s and 1990s, often accompanied by an organisational strategy that sought the replacement of full-time workers with novel forms of labour and labour contracts that maximised quantitative prediction and control. This might reflect, of course, the contradictions and tensions associated with 'hard' and 'soft' human resource management (Storey, 1987). Furthermore, during the late 1980s personnel managers were increasingly expressing concern over UK demographic changes, together with attendant fears over supply shortages and recruitment difficulties. For many there was the very real fear that there would be an insufficient number of young and qualified individuals, prompting management to seek new, and often controversial, forms of employment. This suggests a persistent obsession with numerical calculation and the abiding presence of a logic of quantification.

A more realistic interpretation of the state of contemporary manpower planning is one that is able to grasp the significance of **contradiction** and **paradox** in organisation and organisational change. To appreciate this, one needs to examine the role of organisational politics, the competition between the different management specialisms, and the networks of power-knowledge that build up across the domains of academia, business consultancy, the financial markets, the government, and the professional bodies that represent the various management disciplines (Cooper, 1998; Thrift, 1999). One needs to examine the growth of human resource management in the UK then, against the backdrop of the Conservative government (1979–97), the commercialisation of

133

**The Management of Human Resources**

higher education, the rise of management consultancy, and the increasing power of the accountancy profession. This takes us beyond the scope of this chapter, but in tracing out the main lines of this analytical space we capture some sense of the importance of tactics, manoeuvring, and networking – between institutions, and across the social relations of organisation – by means of which the 'authorship' of manpower planning is achieved. Authorship becomes a derivative phenomenon, a contingent product of particular historical and social relations. We therefore de-centre the priority granted to the individual 'scientific' manpower planner by those studies that focus myopically upon the instruments and techniques of manpower planning (e.g. Bramham, 1990).

We might say then, that 'manpower planning' has been forced to reorientate its own values and reassess the contribution it makes – and the way in which it 'promotes' its contribution – to the regulation of employment relations. Qualitative and quantitative dimensions in manpower planning cannot be simply severed and organisational history assessed in terms of its predilection for one or the other. Any planning of manpower inevitably involves a complex of qualitative and quantitative features. Manoeuvring between the two represents a 'tactical' play of forces wherein the relations between manpower planners and the rising tide of human resource management, and those wider relations between HRM, other management professions, organisation more broadly, and the financial markets, are renegotiated and resettled. A history of capitalist enterprise would reveal that the tension between measurement-quantification and the demand to provide space for the less easily measured qualitative features of organisation and work is both indelible and potentially catastrophic for management.

In our assessment of who does manpower planning it is also worth noting the findings of a recent study, where it is reported that organisations 'prefer neither to use the term "manpower" nor to return to the large and elaborate planning documents produced by head offices a decade ago' (Cowling and Walters, 1990: 3). This means that when we try to assess *who* does manpower planning, we need to be aware that it is being increasingly performed in diffuse and complex ways by a heterogeneous range of agents, as formalised large-scale bureaucracies give way to the more disaggregated and experimental organisational configurations of organisation (Clegg, 1990; Hatch, 1997). This is taken up in greater detail later in the chapter. Here, it is necessary to stress that while many organisations are seeking to redirect the responsibility for manpower planning away from centralised specialised departments and towards 'empowered' production line managers, they do so by maintaining strategic hold and direction at corporate level (Marginson *et al.*, 1988, Storey, 1991, 1992; Salaman, 1992).

With the current emphasis on flexible manpower use, novel forms and new contractual modes of employment, together with innovative approaches to career and succession planning, one might be tempted to suggest that the decline of 'manpower planning' and the rise of 'human resource planning' (Bramham, 1989) captures the essence of contemporary human resource management. As Bennison and Casson (1984) suggest, in a somewhat cavalier fashion, manpower planning 'belongs to the world of calculation, computers and big bureaucracies' (p. ix). In its place, many theorists are recommending strategies and policies that address 'labour skill shortages and cultural change rather than hierarchical structures, succession plans, and mathematical modelling' (Cowling and Waiters, 1990: 3). This section has taught us to exercise some caution and critical scrutiny in the face of this kind of managerial self-representation. In the light of this we might say that this quotation from Cowling and Walters reflects an aspiration and a claim for relevance – a tactical manoeuvre within the changing composition of power relations and organisation politics – as much as it represents a factual state of affairs in the empirical world of organisation.

134

# THE CREATION OF A MANPOWER PLAN

In this section we shall look more closely at those traditional techniques that contribute to the planning of manpower resources in terms of both internal considerations and external factors that influence the final outcome of the manpower plan.

## Internal considerations

### Wastage analysis

Initially the manpower planner will be concerned with the average number of employees that leave and therefore need replacing just in order to maintain a stable number of employees in the organisation. In large organisations, with many departments and complex demarcated lines of responsibility, this can become quite a difficult statistical task, one that requires considerable time and effort in the collection, synthesis and analysis of data. In smaller organisations it can often be calculated very simply. On a very simple level, everybody knows everyone else, and when someone leaves it is quite an important and visible event. In large organisations it is far more likely that an employee is simply seen as a payroll number, or a job code. The constant ebb and flow of 'numbers' within larger organisations requires a far more rigorous calculation of 'wastage' than the rule of thumb applied by management.

The simplest way of calculating wastage is through a turnover analysis. This can be calculated using the following simple formula:

$$\frac{\text{Number leaving in one year}}{\text{Average number of employees}} \times 100\% = x\%$$

However, this gives a somewhat crude and unrealistic picture of wastage. At its most basic it fails to locate *where* these people are leaving from. In general, though, it gives a broad picture of organisational turnover, where it is usual to consider a 25% turnover rate as perfectly respectable in modem large-scale businesses. Anything approaching 30–35% may well start alarm bells ringing. The cost of advertising, recruiting, and training of employees, for example, will be far in excess of the cost for those companies that are able to maintain a 25% turnover of employees, making the organisation uncompetitive and inefficient. However, as we suggested above, when the manpower planner comes to formulate plans and policies to address turnover, this figure does not provide much useful and practical information. For example, where are these people leaving from? What is the average age of the person who is leaving? It could be that your turnover figure has become distorted over the recent past because of the age profile of the organisation, and in any one year it may be that there are far more employees than on average reaching retirement age. As a consequence, it would be far more useful if we could disaggregate this figure in order to account for that proportion of turnover made up of retirements. In this way we might begin to identify that turnover which is 'voluntary' in nature and where 'better' management might be able to have an impact. Legally, there is very little management can do to prevent turnover on the basis of employees reaching the retirement age. What it can do is to isolate those areas of employee turnover in organisation where management *can* make a difference.

Furthermore, turnover might be limited to one particular category of employment, one department, a certain grade, or one geographical area. The variety of influences

135

**The Management of Human Resources**
**101**

that affect employee turnover are far too numerous to be captured by one calculation such as the labour turnover ratio. Thus, for practical reasons, we need a more subtle index of turnover, which is more closely identifiable with factoral influences.

An alternative to the labour turnover ratio is the Labour Stability Index (Bowey, 1974), which is calculated from the following formula:

$$\frac{\text{Number of employees exceeding one year's service}}{\text{Number of employees employed one year ago}} \times 100 = x\%$$

This calculation, by contrast, calculates and emphasises those who stay, and hence is known as a *stability index*. Its importance can be demonstrated through a calculation and comparison with the turnover ratio. Consider two companies:

- In January 2000 *Company* X employs 2000 assistants, but by January 2001 800 have 'voluntarily' left. This gives a turnover of $800/2000 \times 100 = 40\%$.
- *Company Y* by contrast employs 2000 assistants in January 2000. By January 2001 only 100 have actually 'voluntarily' left the company, although they have been replaced eight times during the year. This would, once again, give a turnover of 40%.

The Labour Stability Index by contrast would show that Company X has a stability rate of only 60%, whereas company Y has a far more impressive stability rate of 95%.

Far more sophisticated techniques than this have evolved in an attempt to more accurately plot and account for employee wastage. In recent years many companies have become interested in the 'length of service' of employees, and Figure 4.1 shows how it might be possible to develop a 'frequency distribution' of leavers by length of service.

From Figure 4.1 it is possible to identify three distinct phases in the analysis of turnover. Coming out of the work of the Tavistock Institute, Hill and Trist (1953, 1955), in two important papers reporting on the Park Gate Iron and Steel Company study, established the existence of a relationship between an initial 'induction crisis', a period of 'differential transit', and a concluding 'settled connection'. During the induction crisis it can be seen that the relationship between the individual and the organisation is unsettled and a little insecure. The frequency of leavers in this period was far greater in the first 18 months of service than during subsequent periods of employment. This is perhaps best seen as a 'trial period', where employees are not sure if they are going to stay. Moreover, the 'shock' of employment and its concomitant attention to discipline, hard work, and regular timekeeping takes some adjustment time. In the crisis period, therefore, there is likely to be a far greater incidence of inductees leaving than in subsequent periods.

Hill and Trist also found that other problems associated with manpower planning could be identified during this period. The rates of 'unsanctioned' absence and industrial accidents, for example, were found to be far greater during the induction crisis than during the period of settled connection. In attempting to explain and analyse this relationship the authors found considerable evidence to suggest 'that accidents are in part used, however unconsciously, as a means of withdrawal from the work situation' (Hill and Trist, 1955: 121). Over time the incidence of accidents would fall, and relatively 'sanctioned absences' would rise. This was explained as a result of the quality of the relationship established between the individual and the organisation. After the induction crisis a more stable and secure relationship was established such that a more positive relationship between the individual and the organisation helped to reduce accidents and transfer unauthorised absences to registered sickness leave:

136

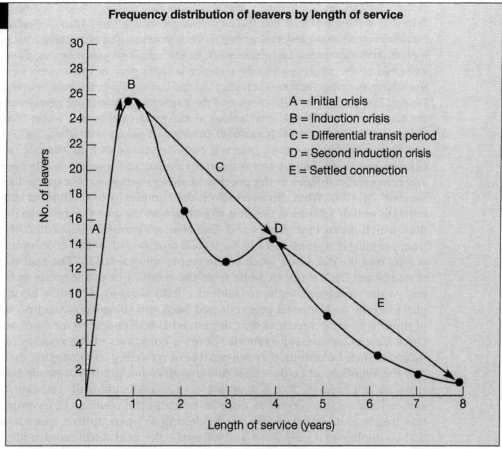

Figure 4.1    **Frequency distribution of leavers by length of service**

A = Initial crisis
B = Induction crisis
C = Differential transit period
D = Second induction crisis
E = Settled connection

Only sickness, therefore, remains; and the suggestion is that recourse is had to some kind of sickness when the individual, no longer able, in virtue of his [sic] improved relationship, to project his . . . bad feelings on to the firm as freely as he once did.                    (p.136)

Thus the authors conclude that employees internalise stress and dissatisfaction, and do not 'blame' the organisation after the induction crisis. The word 'blame' is used by the authors to denote a psychological reaction to the organisation such that the individuals are looking to punish or hit back at the organisation for the stress of employment by absenting themselves from work without authorisation. Accidents are also more likely to occur because of the same lack of commitment and dedication to the organisation. This also allows individuals to maintain the perception that it is the organisation which is at fault for their difficulties of adjusting to work rather than a problem for the individual employee. Therefore an overall fall in the level of absence after the induction crisis suggests 'a dynamic connectedness between sanctioned absence (in the form of sickness) and the phase of settled connection' (Hill and Trist, 1955: 136). Consequently the employee moves from being a victim at the psychological level to one who increasingly looks to him or herself for the cause of sickness or the need for absence.

The work of Hill and Trist is interesting because it suggests that manpower planning improves as individuals build up a positive working relationship with the organisation. Their work anticipates the interest among contemporary management in the 'psychological contract', and the increased concentration focused upon induction and settlement through forms of teamworking and cultural management. As a contribution to manpower planning, it demonstrates the importance of social, psychological, and existential factors at work in the employment relation. One needs to be attentive to the restless and often unpredictable play of these forces in pulling and stretching the wage–effort 'exchange' at the point of production between capital and labour. The retention, utilisation, and the capacity to labour are profoundly affected by the undercurrent of social, psychological and existential forces, forces that remain subterranean to the excessively rational practice of manpower planning. For Timperley and Sisson (1989), however, internal considerations such as absence, accidents and sickness can be measured and rendered rational and manageable because 'there are inherent predictabilities in the process, allowing wastage to be expected and therefore, forecast' (p. 109). What this overlooks is the complexity of the human subject, and the intricate web of relational ties that stretch across the putative boundaries of organisation, which mean that shocks and disturbances transmit unpredictably and rapidly from seemingly distant and disconnected domains of social, economic and cultural activity into the delimited space of the employment relation. The statistical modelling of manpower itself is not immune from the volatility of this intricate web of relational ties. As the sociologist Anthony Giddens (1976) suggests, a 'double hermeneutic' is in play whereby such models gets reflected back and reincorporated into the behaviour of those very same variables that the model is attempting to measure and formalise. Once human agents, for example, become conscious of the routine or predictable nature of their behaviour, they are capable of reflecting and changing their habits such that the simplicity of cause–effect thinking does not grant that much managerial perspicacity and control. The human subject remains stubbornly resistant to prediction and rationality, which renders organisation and the routines of its employment relation fragile and uncertain. We are beginning to open up that space in organisation that co-implicates – *complicates* and *subverts* – the neat distinctions traditionally made between 'theory' and 'practice', between re-presentation and the assumed a priori presence of organisation. Logic starts to break down in this space, and the procedural guidelines of rational manpower planning begin to sway and bend.

On one level, it is important to remember that rationality is 'bounded' (Simon, 1957), in part because there are far too many potential factors to incorporate and model. Manpower planners need not only accurate information on absence and turnover rates, but also statistical records and forecasts of retirements by department, sabbaticals, the average number of employees engaged at any one time in training and retraining, and even the fluctuating moods, sentiments and emotions of employees that affect performance and efficiency. This gives just a flavour of some of the factors that need to be taken into consideration in planning manpower, and we have already considered the difficulties involved in maintaining records. The work of Hill and Trist opens up the question of the human subject, and has stimulated us to think of the applicability and limitations of rationality and reason in explaining and accounting for its behaviour. Yet, if manpower planning is to be predictable and entirely accurate, rationality must observe no bounds!

## Business objectives

It may be of course that stability in employee numbers is not what is required, as the business may well be expanding or contracting in response to product market pressures. If an organisation is experiencing rapid product market growth, as it launches a

138

new innovative product for example, labour demand may well increase in order to respond and cover the extra workload. In the short term, organisations can adjust to unpredicted 'shocks' in the product market through making short-term adjustments to the supply of employees within the organisation.

The most obvious ways in which an organisation adjusts its manpower in response to growing demand include the increased use of overtime, the temporary extension in the hours of work of those employed, the use of subcontract labour, and the recruitment of short-term labour from temporary employment agencies. Of course, if manpower planning was integrated with business strategy and planning in a more 'human resource planning' mould, the launch of a new product and the projections for sales would have allowed manpower planners more time to make resourcing adjustments. One can never entirely predict the market response to new product launches. Who could have predicted the scale of success of the Rubik's cube? The film *Star Wars* was also widely expected to be a massive box office flop, and in order to secure the distribution of his film George Lucas was forced to sign an agreement that made him responsible for any losses incurred on merchandise. As we now know, not only was *Star Wars* one of the most successful films ever, it was precisely the merchandise that delivered the most profitability. The successful launch of a new product then often belies detailed planning and preparation. Even in more strategically integrated organisations professing to practise human resource management, the level of detailed resource planning that is needed to guarantee the elimination of 'shock' is almost impossible to calculate precisely. Indeed, it is this very unpredictability that provides the conditions for product market competition and the opportunity to make vast sums of money.

By contrast, organisations that are contracting or restructuring into new business areas may need to temporarily reduce the numbers of staff in old business areas. It may be that retraining and relocation packages are insufficient to resource the new plant or project, and consequently there will be a need to 'downsize' in one area of the business while expanding in other areas. This was the case for many UK organisations during the 1980s as they sought to respond to market and political pressures by restructuring their businesses. In the UK banking industry, for example, many of the old routine clerical and bookkeeping functions were being removed through the introduction of new technology while at the same time employment opportunities were increasing in the sales and insurance functions (Cressey and Scott, 1992; O'Doherty, 1993). Yet the limited scope of rationality and predictability is once again in evidence. A series of strikes in the financial services industry and rampant discontent and low morale spread deleterious effects in the capacity to utilise and develop manpower, while the reputation of the banks suffered further from a number of high-profile media stories. Alongside stories about overcharging customers and the withdrawal of local branch services, banks were also, perhaps unfairly, tainted by association with pensions and mortgage mis-selling within financial services more broadly. No amount of statistical modelling within the function of manpower planning could have forecast the compound and aggravated consequence attendant upon such rapid radiation and diffusion of effects across the complex interconnected web of social and political relations.

We have been arguing that it is undoubtedly necessary to take into account organisation-wide activity and wider business objectives during the process of manpower planning and in the creation of any competent manpower plan, but we have also illustrated the limitations of measurement and predictability. In the following section we take a look at so-called 'Markov' models, which offer an exceptional example of the role of calculation and prediction in the creation of a manpower plan.

139

### Markov models

These models are often used by manpower planners in addressing the internal factors that need to be considered in the development of a manpower plan. The Markov model, and variants of it, attempts to model the expected life flow of individuals within an organisation. It states that organisations have predictable wastage patterns according to length of service, for example, and that this pattern can be discerned early on in an individual's career. Once 'survival' rates have been calculated, and barring no future shocks, a fairly stable pattern of career progression and replacement needs over time can be calculated. Furthermore, adaptations of the basic Markov model can be used to project recruitment on the basis of stable patterns of both wastage and promotion. From this a manpower planner can predict the probability and the likely time span of an individual progressing from one grade to another in the hierarchy.

From a consideration of these factors, important planning information can be acquired and used in the recruitment and selection process, but also more significantly in preparing the training of individuals so that the organisation does not suffer from quantitative or qualitative supply shortages in the future. If a planner knows with some certainty that an individual tends to spend only two years in a particular managerial grade before being promoted to some other department, contingent training and recruitment plans can be made so that shortages in that area can be eliminated. Thus if 'recruitment, promotion and wastage patterns of staff are stable over reasonable periods of time, . . . the probability that someone in a particular grade at any time will be in some other grade at a later time can be established from the detailed recent career histories of staff' (Timperley and Sisson, 1994: 156).

Markov models attempt to map the 'throughput' of human resources in an organisation by predicting the patterns of entry and exit: entry and exit from the organisation as a whole, and entry and exit from particular grades. Elaborations on the basic model allow for the behavioural effects consequent upon changes in the distribution and flow of employees through an organisation. This model presents a view of organisation as one of predictability and regularity, organisation as 'institutions' that 'pass through staffing cycles', as Timperley and Sisson (1994) note in their review. Markov models work best under conditions of organisational stability, but begin to lack predictive accuracy under conditions of uncertainty and change. One of the most volatile sources of disturbance and change is found to emanate from external sources – changes in labour markets, in global product markets, and in government legislation. We now turn to examine the importance of some of these external considerations in the development of a credible manpower plan.

## External considerations

### State legislation

One extremely important area that needs to be considered while formulating a manpower plan is the restrictions that are imposed on organisations by the government in areas of individual and collective labour law (see Torrington and Hall, 1989, and Chapter 10). The evolution of the industrial system in the UK has been characterised by successive governmental interventions to redress power inequalities between capital and labour, and shape the way in which labour is recruited, deployed, trained, promoted, and made redundant. It is a long time since managers and employers could simply 'hire and fire' according to their own whim. The responsibility for the welfare of employees has been increasingly assumed by national and European government and secured by means of state legislation, to such an extent that today many organisations and manpower planners have found it prudent to establish specialist legal advisory departments to assist them in the development and management of manpower planning.

Increasingly this legislation is of a European-wide nature, enacted and passed by the European Parliament in Brussels and Strasbourg. This has been the cause of some considerable friction between the directives and legislation of the European Parliament and the traditions of economic and industrial regulation in particular member states. In the UK, many of the legislative initiatives, including those within the Social Chapter of the Maastricht Treaty, are seen by a considerable proportion of UK management (as articulated most vociferously by the Institute of Directors and certain sections of the CBI) to be overly onerous and restrictive. The role of European legislation has become far more important in the day-to-day activities of UK organisations and in particular in the management of manpower planning. We have seen most recently legislation, with some industry-specific exceptions, prescribing a maximum working week of 48 hours. Co-determination, consultation, and information rights on matters relating to manpower planning and use, particularly as regards management procedure in redundancy, have been granted to European Works Councils. Although John Major's Conservative government negotiated and secured a UK opt-out from the Social Chapter at Maastricht in 1991, UK companies, in part by virtue of employing workers in other European economies, have been steadily adopting the regulations of the social protocol (Hall, 1992, 1994). The Blair Labour government, elected in 1997, has adopted a far more progressive approach to the developing European Community, and the signs are that greater integration and legislative harmony across nation states will have a significant impact on domestic UK manpower planning.

In the recent past it was in the areas of sex discrimination and race relations legislation where European policy has had most impact. In response to European policy and EC directives UK legislation imposes a responsibility on manpower planners to recruit, train and promote employees on an indiscriminate basis, such that religion, race and gender cannot by law be considered a basis for employing, promoting, training or redundancy. Of course manpower planners can discriminate on the basis of being able-bodied! This rather bizarre practice is rare, but in recent press advertisements some councils have advertised for the recruitment of handicapped people only. At first sight this might appear somewhat discriminatory, but in fact there is no legislation proscribing discrimination on the basis of being able-bodied. Thus for manpower planners seeking to maintain the recommended 3% of handicapped employees within the organisation, they are quite within their rights to insist that only those deemed handicapped may apply for the advertised post. Moreover, manpower planning in local councils is affected by the responsibility to secure a 'representative' workforce that can be expected to be sensitive and attentive to particular community and sectional group needs.

Legislation on the hours that people can be expected to work, the time that can be spent working in front of a VDU, rest periods, the provision of basic medical facilities, and recently the necessity to provide facilities for pregnant employees, all imposes some restriction on the managerial prerogative in manpower planning. Organisations cannot simply consider their own operational and internal organisational needs. They are channelled within certain guidelines on what they can and cannot do in the management and employment of individuals. As we have seen, this has important consequences for those who are responsible for manpower planning. Yet it is not just through the use

141

of legislation that governments can make an impact on the conduct of manpower planning. A whole series of institutional mechanisms, and what are called 'supply-side' policies, can shape the development of company manpower planning, whether through changes to social security, unemployment benefits and taxation, or by means of company incentives, training schemes and regional development programmes. Manpower planners need to be aware of the interactions between the projects and institutions of national economic manpower planning conducted by the state and government and their company-specific manpower planning initiatives. We shall look at the use of regional development schemes in order to illustrate these connections between the wider political domain of manpower planning and company-specific management.

### Regional development schemes

Successive UK governments have attempted to influence the direction and level of investment through offering tax and other financial incentives for companies to establish new plants and outlets in particular regions of the economy. This is an economic and often a politically motivated policy initiative to boost employment in recession-hit areas. The North-West and the North-East, for example, have suffered disproportionately in the post-1945 UK economy as a result of protracted industrial restructuring and the decline of the heavy coal, steel and shipbuilding industries. In an attempt to boost new employment in these areas companies have been offered a package of financial incentives to move and locate new factories, departments and retail outlets in these areas. The growth of part-time, casual, and temporary employment in the former industrial heartlands of the UK economy is a direct consequence of legislative and manpower planning initiatives developed by successive governments in collaboration with foreign capital and domestic UK businesses.

The importance for manpower planners is that in the development of manpower plans the organisation needs to know where it is likely to trade more profitably. So, for example, if the development of a new product is going to necessitate the construction of a new site and the creation of 2000 new jobs, it will be the responsibility of the manpower planner to provide information on the most profitable location for this plant. It may well be that as a result of regional development schemes the company would be far better locating its new plant in the North-East, where cheap local reserves of labour are available, together with tax privileges that reduce the costs of production relative to constructing the new plant more locally. In the creation of a manpower plan it is important that such 'external considerations' are fully evaluated so that the organisation's manpower plan can provide information on the most profitable alternatives (Lee Clark, 1993).

### Micro-level factors

Finally, in the development of a credible manpower plan attention needs to be focused on the nature of the local labour markets. Successful manpower planning not only provides information on the immediate local labour market, but also needs to compare and contrast the age, skill and cost profiles of each local labour market. In this way the organisation plans the resource implications of organisational expansion, contraction and structural change in terms of quantity, quality and price. It may be the case, for example, that different local labour markets offer different average age profiles, which could be important for organisations seeking to recruit young employees. Alternatively, organisations might seek to locate new plants in areas where unemployment is high in

142

order to guarantee the availability of sufficient employees and also to benefit from the likely wage cost advantages. If supply exceeds demand, as characterises depressed regional economies, economic theory would predict a tendency for wages to fall. Thus in comparing the South-East with the North-West in terms of wage costs it has been a well-observed phenomenon for a number of years that cheaper labour is to be found in the North-West.

We have now established that there are a range of important internal and external factors that contribute to the development of a successful manpower plan. The construction of the Japanese Nissan plant at Washington in the North-East of England, for example, was a decision informed by the logic of manpower planning, one that illustrates the play of a whole series of internal and external considerations. In part the region provides vast reserves of low-wage employees, who were not steeped in the traditions and experience of shopfloor car manufacture. These offered critical manpower planning incentives for the Nissan Corporation, who wanted to avoid both high-cost labour and the risk of shopfloor trade union militancy that had typified significant sections of the UK car industry (Beynon, 1973). However, as a number of recent studies of Nissan and Japanese car production suggest (Garrahan and Stewart, 1992; Delbridge, 1995), total manpower planning predictability and calculation cannot be achieved even in the context of sophisticated Japanese manpower planning and technology management. Low morale, poor commitment, unrecorded employee unrest and resistance, and health and safety abuses stand as testimony to the limitations of manpower calculation and prediction, and once again provide evidence that employment relations remain an unstable and partially unpredictable component of organisation.

## ANALYSING DEMAND AND SUPPLY

Once the external and internal considerations have been brought together at the development stage of the manpower plan, our textbook manpower planner is held to be in a position to analyse the 'net demand' and 'net supply' of human resources. The manpower planner can then proceed to seek a reconciliation of demand and supply. This has been captured in Figure 4.2, which synthesises the major components of the human resource planning process.

From this diagram it can be seen that there are two distinct stages in the planning process: an analysis of the current state of play in the organisation's human resources, and an analysis of the future plans and requirements of the business.

It should be clear from the preceding section that manpower planning adopts a number of techniques that seek to predict and project the availability of current staff. Predictability arises because of the claim that manpower flows typically tend to follow a fairly orderly pattern when analysed and measured quantitatively. Thus a good manpower plan is able to locate those employees who are likely to leave, where they are likely to leave from, the rate at which they leave, and the training implications arising from the need to keep a constant flow of suitably qualified employees to fill vacant positions. Any change in this pattern should also be able to be predicted by the manpower planner, because at this stage they should have a fairly comprehensive understanding of the variables that impact on these patterns of employment. By carefully monitoring these variables, shocks should be avoided and adjustments made relatively slowly and smoothly in order to avoid difficulties in the conduct of the business. The science of manpower planning pursues the ideal of a self-regulating

143

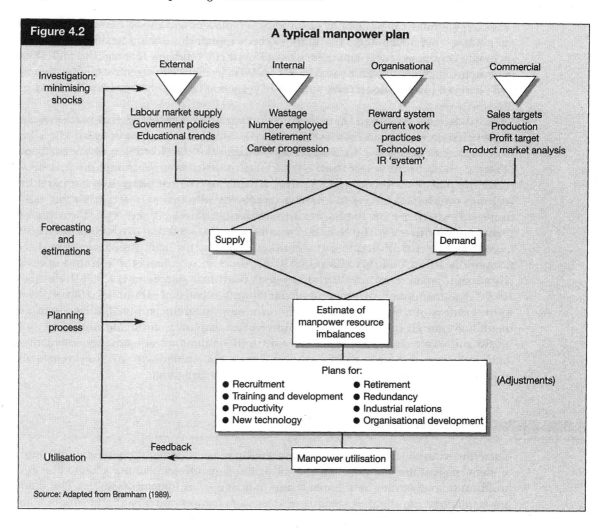

**Figure 4.2**      **A typical manpower plan**

Investigation: minimising shocks

External — Labour market supply / Government policies / Educational trends

Internal — Wastage / Number employed / Retirement / Career progression

Organisational — Reward system / Current work practices / Technology / IR 'system'

Commercial — Sales targets / Production / Profit target / Product market analysis

Forecasting and estimations

Supply      Demand

Planning process

Estimate of manpower resource imbalances

Plans for:
- Recruitment
- Training and development
- Productivity
- New technology
- Retirement
- Redundancy
- Industrial relations
- Organisational development

(Adjustments)

Utilisation      Feedback      Manpower utilisation

*Source*: Adapted from Bramham (1989).

organisation whole that automatically triggers a series of adjustments in response to signals and change in any one component of the organisation.

From the objectives of the business, the developmental, and relocation plans, the manpower planner has some basis within which to project the number of future staff that will be required by the organisation. At this stage the manpower planner is also in a position to advise on the strategic direction of the business in terms of what is possible strategically, given the constraints and opportunities in the internal and external labour market. For example, it is pointless to plan for organisational growth within a region that will be unable to supply the required number and skills of employees. In the absence of alternatives, organisational growth may be impossible given the future projection of labour supply availability. Good manpower planning can show how an organisation is best advised to develop and grow – where supply is available, the recruitment and training needs arising from growth, and the most profitable location for new plant and capital.

The third stage in Figure 4.2 shows the process of reconciliation. This arises because there is undoubtedly a mismatch between the quantitative and, importantly, qualitative demand for employees, based on future plans and projections, and what the current

144

projections of employee availability are likely to be able to deliver. Initially, organisations would be interested in the numerical surpluses or shortfalls in staff that are likely to emerge in the future. A shortfall of staff will result if business growth and increasing product market success has not triggered compensatory plans to resource the organisation. This would result in the all-too-familiar scenario of departments being run at overcapacity, such that the increasing use of overtime, subcontract and temporary agency staff eventually leads to longer-term and more chronic operational difficulties. Orders may start to be processed late, and consequently deliveries to customers become erratic. If this persists, customers will begin to search for alternative sources of supply, and the organisation may well find itself losing market share. This highlights the critical role that manpower planning plays. If it is able to project future shortfalls and surpluses, adjustments and contingency plans can be developed to reconcile the mismatch between net demand and net supply.

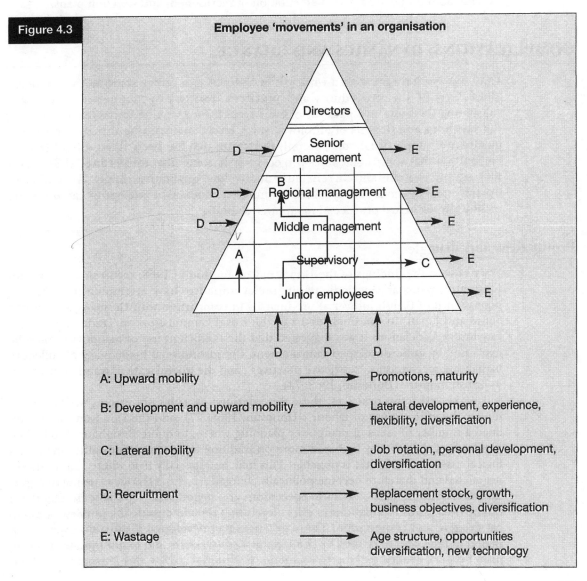

Figure 4.3 — Employee 'movements' in an organisation

145

**The Management of Human Resources**
**111**

The fourth stage in Figure 4.2 illustrates that function of manpower planning that is concerned with presentation and the evaluation of alternative policy routes in the management and reconciliation of shortfalls and surpluses. The final stage of the manpower planning process culminates in those changes that are made in the areas of recruitment and selection, training and development, redundancies and early retirements – in order to plug the gap between projected availability of staff and projected need. Figure 4.3 attempts to synthesise all the movements and flow of staff that typically exist in organisations. It reflects how difficult a task it is to track and monitor the complex movements of staff through an organisation, and at this stage we have not even really begun to consider the added complexity of the more qualitative dimensions of organisation.

In the next section of the chapter we address those factors that further complicate the process of manpower planning, factors that some would argue need to be taken into full account before the implementation of recruitment and selection plans.

## COMPLICATIONS: DYNAMICS AND CHANGE

Until now we have presented what will be defined as a rather static and decontextualised view of the procedures and practices involved in manpower planning – calculating the flows and patterns of employees through an organisation, reconciling the surpluses and deficits of employee stock levels, maintaining the qualitative and quantitative supply of labour. The only dynamism that has been allowed has been the recognition that some companies project growth, some plan for decline, while others seek simply to maintain current quantitative and qualitative supply. A number of dynamic qualifications can be added to this basic model that attempt to capture more realistically the actual practice of manpower planning.

### Productivity and struggle

Since at least the findings of the Donovan Commission in 1968, recurrent government pronouncements and periodic public policy initiatives have attempted to tackle the poor record of British industrial productivity in comparison with Germany, the United States and Japan. In the final report of the Royal Commission on Trade Unions and Employers Associations it was suggested that the inefficient use of manpower could be explained by underdeveloped management, the institutional inadequacy of collective bargaining mechanisms, 'restrictive practices', and the woeful state of training provision in British industry (Donovan, 1968: 74).

To take restrictive practices: these were defined as 'rules or customs which unduly hinder the efficient use of labour' (Donovan, 1968: 77), and the Donovan report outlined a number of areas of manpower planning where, to quote Bramham (1989), 'the standards of the job may be based more on tradition and expectation rather than on a logical assessment of what is possible. This may be especially true where standards are negotiated and therefore become politically charged' (p. 49). Of course, we might argue that all standards, workloads and expectations are 'negotiated' – in the sense that there can be no a priori foundations to effort levels that remain outside the purview of political struggle and contestation. These practices had developed historically over a long period of time, and were seen by Donovan as a conservative and inappropriate anachronism by work groups seeking to maintain 'traditional' rights and prerogatives in the

146

context of changing economic circumstances and technological advance. The kinds of restrictive practices to which Donovan was drawing attention can be seen in a review of the work practices, work group norms, values and attitudes that persisted in the British docks and shipping industry. In a series of articles Peter Turnbull and his colleagues have studied the history of changing work practices in the British docks (Turnbull and Sapsford, 1991, 1992; Turnbull, 1992; Turnbull *et al.*, 1992), where the practice of 'welting' was common, for example, allowing workers on the docks to secure time and leisure when they should have nominally been working:

> dock workers were able to indulge in the practice of 'welting', where only half the gang works the cargo at any one time. The other half might be playing cards, drinking tea or coffee, or in extreme (well organised) cases working at the local market or driving a taxi.
>
> (Turnbull and Sapsford, 1992: 306)

It is precisely these kinds of practices that were deemed to be widespread throughout British industry during the 1950s and 1960s, and acted as a serious brake on the pursuit of productivity and competitive advantage.

The reform of the industrial relations system can be seen as an integral and important component in the evolution of 'formally rational' (Weber, 1964) methods of manpower planning. By 'formally rational' we mean those principles and techniques of organisation and order that seek to increase the efficiency of business operations. Now, this definition of rationality ignores the *ends* to which these techniques and procedures are being used. Thus it might be suggested that the 'politically charged' (Bramham, 1989) negotiations of manpower planning reflect some disagreement and political struggle over the precise scope and meaning of the term 'rational'. For manpower planning, the importance of formal rationality can be seen in the importance attributed to what is called 'efficient techniques' and procedures of calculation, forecasting, and the reconciliation of the supply and demand of labour. Its rationality is assumed by the ends that it serves – namely the maximisation of output, efficiency and productivity. The pursuit of these ends, however, might be secured at the expense of group norms, informal practices, and tacit agreements reached on the shopfloor between work groups and their representatives and immediate supervisors and managers. In the context of industrial relations more broadly, this is what Donovan referred to as the conflict between the *formal* and *informal systems* of industrial relations. For example, it was not uncommon for shopfloor line managers to allocate overtime more generously than was strictly justified by the formally rational techniques of manpower planning to strong, powerful, and perhaps militant work groups. Yet we can understand the 'rationality' of these allocations and concessions only if we look elsewhere within the capital–labour relations. For Edwards (1986), these informal and tacit unwritten agreements are an example of 'informal accommodation', a means by which managers can ensure that jobs get done without causing too much friction and disorder in their relationship with workers. Once we recognise the 'structured antagonism' that characterises the employment relation – that labour and capital both require each other in order to secure their ends, but at the same time pull in opposite directions – the meaning of what might be 'rational' changes.

For our purposes, what is important here is to recognise the implications of competing in product markets, implications that impel management to seek ways of improving the quantity and quality of output while at the same time reducing costs. As labour costs represent such a significant proportion of total costs, especially in traditional manufacturing and service industries, productivity provides management with ways of thinking

147

how to increase labour output without incurring a concomitant increase in wage costs. The Donovan Commission was important because it identified the failings of British industrial competitiveness with the structure and conduct of management– labour relations. The pursuit of conflicting goals and values by labour and capital was the product of inadequate institutional means for bargaining and reconciliation. Productivity could be secured only within the framework of formal company-level collective bargaining. What Donovan recognised was that the need for change, which exists as an insatiable 'systemic' need in the context of free-market competition, interferes with the legacy of tradition and customary norms that congeal to form orderly and static arrangements in manpower use, deployment, and movement.

Those features of manpower planning that were considered in the sections on 'internal considerations' and 'external considerations' now need to be amended for the dynamic of productivity and its co-implication with the political struggle that wages over values and ends in the employment relation. If the basis for capital–labour antagonism runs deeper than the assumption made by the Donovan Commission – where the claim was that conflict and antagonism reflect institutional failures – productivity bargaining needs to be rethought in the terms of struggle. This assumption reflects the classic liberal-pluralist values of the authors of the Donovan report (Clegg, 1979). It may be that more recent moves to HRM reflect the failure of the institutional route to 'deliver' coherent 'political' integration and consensus in the employment relation. In other words, forms of productivity and efficiency in the conduct of manpower planning can be more effectively achieved in the absence of costly bureaucratic means of bargaining and negotiation.

This endemic and insatiable quest for productivity introduces a complex dynamic into manpower planning, one that raises a host of issues connected with politics, values, and struggle. In the study of manpower planning we open up one strand of its subject, only to find it weaves its way into a multiple set of relevancies. The productivity drive means that the performance of work accomplished through the day-to-day negotiations in the employment relation results in a situation where things are never stable for very long. We must expect change, upset and disturbance. Circumstances always change. A constant revolutionising of production, where 'all that is solid melts into air', as Marx once wrote (quoted in Berman, 1982: 15), characterises the dynamics of capitalist competition. It may be, for example, that a manpower assessment of the distribution of employees made five years previously, which had been used as a benchmark to guide future recruitment, training and succession needs, is no longer relevant or practical.

The rationalisations, redundancies, and restructuring of companies that have been witnessed throughout the public and private sectors over the past 15 years can be interpreted, in part, as a response to the persistence of outdated techniques, procedures and norms in the practice of manpower planning, norms that could no longer be sustained in the intensely competitive international economy of the 1980s and 1990s. Perhaps, in addition, this partly reflects the violence of what Foucault (1980) calls 'normalisation', or what we might call in the context of this chapter an increasing homogenisation of political values. In other words, where productivity might once have been seen as a contested political subject, it now appears to be an inviolable norm by which we all abide. Of course, it may well be that on the surface we submit to unitarist norms, but in the subterranean workings of organisation a whole series of tensions and repercussions are being played out, tensions that destabilise the functional stewardship of manpower planning.

148

Senior managerial initiatives seeking to drive productivity changes through are likely to seriously challenge, if not undermine, current manpower plans. It may be that an organisation's manpower plan dictates that in order to maintain demand and supply, three new employees are required each year in the accounts department to compensate for the anticipated turnover, promotions, and retirements. *Ceteris paribus*, if the department 'lost' three employees each year owing to turnover, promotions, or retirements, it would seem logical to seek to replace these employees. However, in the reality of manpower planning *ceteris paribus* can never really be assumed, and increasingly in the competitive environment of the 1990s and the new millennium, manpower plans are being constantly adjusted to satisfy productivity requirements and competitive needs. In the example above, although it would seem that the replacement of the three employees was required, management may seek to take advantage of the turnover to reduce costs, increase productivity, and hence increase market share and shareholder profitability. We might also expect the amplification of struggle and what some call 'dysfunctional' repercussion in response to these managerial initiatives.

Once again, we have begun to approach the limits of manpower planning as it is defined and understood by unitarism, to encroach upon the territory of politics, values and norms. In the section on the management of change below we seek to show that human resource planning, in contrast to manpower planning, is far more unitarist and unilateral in its planning and management of employee resource flows in an organisation, consistent with the 'unitarism' apparently characteristic of human resource management (Guest, 1989, 1990; Storey, 1995).

## THE MANAGEMENT OF CHANGE: HRP AND FUTURE DIRECTIONS

For some the practice of human resource planning is entirely different to manpower planning:

> In HRP the manager is concerned with motivating people – a process in which costs, numbers, control and systems interact and play a part. In manpower planning the manager is concerned with the numerical elements of forecasting, supply – demand matching and control, in which people are a part.
> (Bramham, 1989: 147, emphasis added)

A 1988 IPM survey attempted to establish and survey the use of 'systematic human resource planning', defined as a long-term, strategic planning of human resources concerned more with the development of skill, quality and cultural change than with statistical numerical forecasting, succession planning and hierarchical structures. This survey was an attempt to assess the extent to which resource planning was being practised in response to the cutbacks and cost-cutting of the 1980s, which for many had reduced the input of traditional manpower planning:

> Manpower planning by then had come to be associated in many people's minds with growth, five year plans, and bureaucracy, at a time when firms were having to contract and become more flexible.
> (Cowling and Walters, 1990: 3)

The results suggested that of the 245 respondents, in excess of 60% claimed that they were now practising forms of human resource planning that were more attentive to qualitative factors concerned with the identification of future training, retraining and development needs. The least popular practices were those associated with the 'analysis of the labour costs and productivity of competitors', the 'communication of future HRP plans and intentions to employees', and the 'monitoring of HRP practices to ensure

149

achievement of cost objectives' (Cowling and Walters, 1990: 7). Of course, they may have been unpopular but this doesn't mean that they were not being done, nor that they formed a significant part of the manpower planner's day-to-day responsibility. Of note is the finding that it was in the private sector that most of the practices associated with human resource planning were in evidence. It may be that the large and bureaucratic nature of most public sector organisations did not permit the exercise of radical and innovative techniques designed to develop the individual as a quality resource as counselled by human resource planning. Or that manpower planning in the public sector was pre-occupied with redundancies and simple cost control pursued through the channels of institutionalised collective bargaining. As Cowling and Walters go on to write:

> Modern style human resource planning, as outlined in the IPM guide, places considerable emphasis on a proactive strategy which anticipates and responds to changes in the environment, linked to a corporate strategy designed to enhance competitive advantage or quality of service.    (p.7)

Far more emphasis was placed by personnel departments on the importance of personnel and line management working together in a coherent manner, where both cooperate to jointly determine the role, function and implications for HRP emerging out of new corporate strategy. Now, what management might say it does, and what actually happens in practice, may be two very different things. Yet this emphasis on the importance of the line manager seems consistent with our earlier definition of human resource planning. Human resource planning is supposedly distinctive on the basis of the devolution of operational responsibility down to line managers, where line managers are encouraged to assume 'ownership' of resource planning. In contrast to the rules and procedural bias of old-style personnel management and manpower planning, line managers are persuade to 'go it alone', to innovate and experiment, to learn to live without a dependence on traditions and rule books (Peters, 1994).

HRP is also distinctive in its attempts to generate commitment and the integration of organisational departments and resources. These ambitions are pursued through attempts to develop cultural awareness and homogeneity, rather than the imposition and control of rules and procedures. The assumed advantages of this form of management are deemed to lie in the stimulus of employee creativity, commitment and flexibility, all those characteristics of the human resource that are deemed to be of crucial importance to productivity and competitive success (Peters, 1993). In this way human resource planning has a far more *developmental role* to play, in terms both of planning for flexibility (Atkinson, 1985), and of developing the attributes of quality, skill and 'excellence' within employees. It has become somewhat of a consensus among management gurus, consultants, and many academics (Peters and Waterman, 1982; Kanter, 1984) 'that markets, machinery and the money are available to everyone: success goes to those organisations which are able to recruit and develop the right people and not just at the top' (Timperley and Sisson, 1989: 120). Within the context of market competition, where success depends on failure, and for every winner the market needs a loser, these kinds of assumptions, to say the least, seem problematic.

The two main issues that have concerned human resource planners over the past decade have been the implications of demographic changes and the need for flexibility.

## Demographic changes

Towards the end of the 1980s many personnel departments began to express concern that demographic changes in the British economy meant that the number of young people coming onto the labour market was going to decline significantly. It is clear that

150

in a mature industrialised economy such as the UK the average age of the working population is likely to increase as the numbers of births and deaths decrease. Eurostat figures forecast a decline of 1.7% per annum in the supply of labour in the age group 20–30 throughout Western Europe (Eurostat 1990). The median age of the UK population was 34.6 in 1980 compared with 35.9 in 1990 and a projected 37.7 for the year 2000. In the old Federal Republic of Germany the figures were even more striking, rising from an average of 36.7 in 1980 to 41.1 in the year 2000 (IRDAC, 1990). These projections are largely explained by the increasing proportion of retirements, which is not compensated for by an equivalent number of young people coming onto the labour market, so that:

> Even if the forecasts mentioned should be used with caution, they indicate that the starting base for the next decade is far from excellent. If no corrective action is taken, there is a major risk that Europe will lose some of its competitive strength because of a lack of sufficiently qualified manpower.
>
> (IRDAC, 1990: 8)

This so-called 'demographic time bomb' has forced employers to look to their manpower planners to seek new and innovative forms of labour so that the projected difference between labour demand and traditional labour supply may be breached. In part, these observations help to explain the increasing proportion of part-time labour-use strategies, labour that in the main is composed of married female returners to the labour market. A cursory read through the pages of recent editions of *Personnel Review*, *Personnel Management, People Management*, and the *International Journal of Manpower Planning* would illustrate the interest among personnel managers in developing innovative forms of labour contract, part-time labour, job-sharing, school term time only working, annualised hours contracts, temporary employment contracts, and forms of employment tailored for mature returners to the labour market. These developments are supplemented by prescriptions and advice for manpower planners and human resource managers on the best ways to plan, manage, motivate, remunerate and regulate these novel forms of employment use.

In addition, it is generally argued that industry and business are increasingly demanding more skilled labour, and that relatively unskilled manual blue-collar jobs are in terminal decline, to be replaced by more highly skilled computer programmers, professional technically qualified managers, and other service sector functions. A 1993 Institute for Employment Research review of UK employment and the economy predicted on the basis of trends established over the previous two decades that occupational change will continue to favour the growth of corporate management and professional services in health, education, science, and engineering. Craft and skilled manual occupations, and plant and machine operatives, by contrast, declined on average by 1.3% and 1.9% respectively each year between 1971 and 1991. High-level professional and managerial occupations constituted 35% of total employment in 1991, and this was expected to rise to 41% by the year 2000 (IER, 1993).

The Institute for Employment Research at the University of Warwick projected similar labour market changes in the demand for highly qualified people with social science degrees and graduates of science and vocational subjects. An increase of some 1.5 million jobs is expected for the highly qualified by the year 2001 in comparison with 1991 (IER, 1995/6). Employment in primary industries would continue to decline throughout the 1990s. Projections anticipated a decline of some 14% between 1991 and 2000: a loss of 520 000 jobs. Figure 4.4 attempts to represent those jobs affected by changes in numbers and skill levels.

151

Based upon the research of Rajan (1993) and the Centre for Research in Employment and Technology in Europe (CREATE), Figure 4.4 suggests the emergence of the so-called new 'knowledge worker'. In addition to an increasing demand for highly skilled occupational employees, organisations are seeking to develop and require more flexibility and adaptability from their employees. Technological, organisational and broader macroeconomic changes are creating a situation in which employees need to have a heightened awareness of their own skills profile and status. Increased 'reflexivity', and the importance increasingly being attached to 'self-development', remain controversial but arguably predictable outcomes of recent management initiatives as organisations expect employees to exercise and demonstrate their own 'entrepreneurial' worth (Garsten and Grey, 1997; O'Doherty and Roberts, 2000).

It is also interesting to note that Rajan projects an increased demand for *deskilled* jobs in secretarial, junior clerical and recreational occupations. Such jobs will increasingly be filled by part-time employees, or, indeed, even more insecure and casualised forms of employment. This may suggest a contradictory series of outcomes in the labour

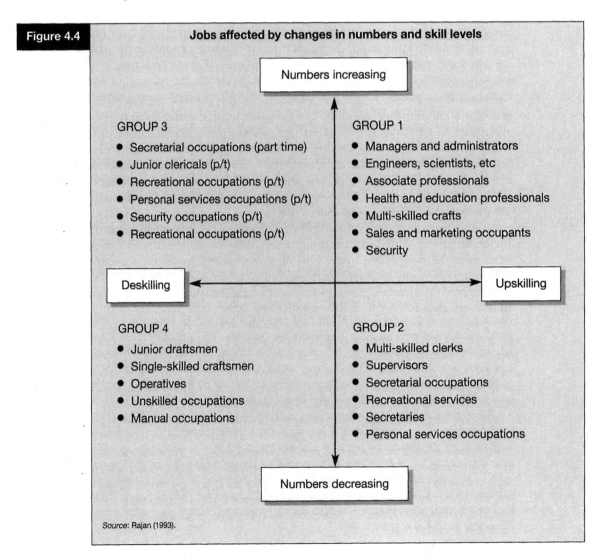

**Figure 4.4** — **Jobs affected by changes in numbers and skill levels**

Numbers increasing

GROUP 3
- Secretarial occupations (part time)
- Junior clericals (p/t)
- Recreational occupations (p/t)
- Personal services occupations (p/t)
- Security occupations (p/t)
- Recreational occupations (p/t)

GROUP 1
- Managers and administrators
- Engineers, scientists, etc
- Associate professionals
- Health and education professionals
- Multi-skilled crafts
- Sales and marketing occupants
- Security

Deskilling — Upskilling

GROUP 4
- Junior draftsmen
- Single-skilled craftsmen
- Operatives
- Unskilled occupations
- Manual occupations

GROUP 2
- Multi-skilled clerks
- Supervisors
- Secretarial occupations
- Recreational services
- Secretaries
- Personal services occupations

Numbers decreasing

*Source:* Rajan (1993).

152

**The Management of Human Resources**
**118**

market – highly trained and skilled professional employees, together with pockets of low-paid, 'ghettoised', deskilled employment, which offers few prospects for career progression or personal development. The complex relationship and causality between these contradictory labour market outcomes, and the emergence of 'hard' and 'soft' variants of human resource management, need to be carefully considered and researched. What contribution, therefore, does human resource planning make to the creation of low-paid and insecure temporary or part-time employment, which, we may note, tends to be filled by women workers? This remains an ethical and political question, but a question that nonetheless tends to be ignored by the majority of enthusiastic practitioner-based articles and writing, that celebrates the newsworthy and novel at the expense of careful scholarly research.

Nevertheless, even accepting an increased demand for professional and skilled employees, there remains the problem of supply (Keep, 1994; Keep and Rainbird, 1995). As economists have known for a long time, free markets have a tendency to fail in the provision of what are known as 'public goods'. A major problem facing UK organisations is that the free-market dynamic has a tendency to discourage investment in training by businesses operating in isolation. As one company unilaterally decides to invest in training another company will seek to reduce the costs of its training by buying in pre-trained employees. This cost-competitive dynamic operates to dampen down training investment as companies seek to pay slightly more for individuals who have been trained elsewhere and thus avoid the cost of training employees themselves. The market therefore fails. In recognition of this dynamic, governments often step in to support and counteract the deficiencies of pure market-based solutions to training and investment. This makes training and labour supply a macroeconomic and political problem, a domain of struggle and negotiation above and beyond those struggles that we have noted in the employment relation, but with implications and ramifications, nonetheless, for its conduct and management.

Unless educational opportunities are expanded in the UK, and the needs of training are seriously addressed at national level, it is argued that Britain will not only face a shortage of traditional sources of labour supply, but also a skills shortage will develop, creating a serious obstacle to future organisational growth and economic development (see Chapter 8). In response to these supply developments, and to cater for the increased demands placed on organisations to develop less bureaucratic and more responsible creative employees, manpower planners have sought to develop flexible manpower plans.

## Flexibility

There is some debate within academic journals over the precise nature of flexibility within the UK labour market and over organisations' use of flexible labour. A significant feature of this debate focuses on the novelty and progressiveness of using part-time labour, female returners, casual labour and temporary employees (Pollert, 1988, 1992; Hakim, 1990).

Of less contention is the observation that during the 1980s most of the employment growth was in the area of part-time employment, and specifically female part-time employment. John Atkinson and his colleagues at the IMS have suggested, in a series of papers (Atkinson, 1984, 1985), that one of the responses to the demographic and competitive changes in the British economy has been a notable increase in the use of more flexible forms of labour. Atkinson suggests that this is becoming

153

not only an increasingly popular form of manpower planning and practice but also one that needs to be seriously considered by other companies seeking to retain competitiveness in the market.

Essentially, flexible manpower plans have sought to introduce three forms of flexibility: numerical, financial and functional.

## Numerical

Here, organisations in response to fluctuations in the business cycle have begun seeking a more numerically flexible labour force. For example, in organisations such as banks and retail stores there are predictable and stable patterns in the fluctuation of business activity. In banks, for example, the lunch-time period is particularly busy, and therefore a more flexible and cost-efficient manpower plan would seek to accommodate the peaks and troughs of business activity more accurately with available labour supply. By having pools of labour resources that can be called in at short notice, often called 'key-time labour' by the banks, manpower planning can cut waste and inefficiency by only having labour in the organisation, or at least only paying it, when it is needed and actually being used. Thus manpower planning uses its employees like a tap that can be turned on and off at will in response to demand cycles, customer arrival patterns, and the peaks and troughs of business activity.

Numerical flexibility is also achieved through the use of annualised hours contracts, which allows management to alter the number of employees at very short notice in response to operational and business needs.

## Financial

Rather than paying individuals the 'going rate', or a collectively negotiated wage, companies are now seeking to pay employees and their labour a more flexible wage that, it is claimed, more accurately relates to their performance and productivity. In this way, manpower planning keeps cost under far greater control by using and deploying labour according to business needs and its measured contribution to output. This avoids the excessive rigidity in manpower plans that can arise when a fixed wage is paid for a set number of hours. This means that regardless of whether the employee resource is being used to full capacity or not, it is being paid. Financial flexibility therefore allows manpower planners to focus and contain the cost of employee utilisation. Performance-related pay and profit-related pay offer further examples of the way in which contemporary management is seeking to tie wage levels more accurately to the actual contribution that the employee makes to profit. The paradox here is that flexibility also decreases, in some sense, as reward is made ratio dependent on some measurement of addition to profit.

## Functional

This form of flexibility is heralded as one of the most important developments in manpower planning, and provides a lot of the justification for the claims made by *human resource* planners for their distinctive approach to labour utilisation. Functional flexibility attempts to remove what are understood to be organisational rigidities and demarcations, which prevent employees from being moved from one section of the organisation to another, performing a range of tasks and exercising a polyvalence of skills. It is here that we encounter the developmental potential of human resource planning where employees are required, because of operational needs, to be moved

154

through the shopfloor, or into other departments. This is often seen as part of the multi-skilling initiatives of many organisations, whereby employees are encouraged to develop a multiple range of skills and aptitudes so that they 'can be redeployed quickly and smoothly between activities and tasks. Functional flexibility may require multi-skilling – craft workers who possess and can apply a number of skills covering, for example, both mechanical and electrical engineering, or manufacturing and mainte-nance activities (Armstrong, 1992: 106). Whether these manpower, or rather, human resource plans amount simply to an extension of managerial prerogative, intensification and increased employee stress levels is a moot point (Wood, 1989; Elger, 1990). It is quite clear, however, that human resource planners have a vested interest in emphasis-ing the developmental potential and flexibility that these initiatives encourage.

One consequence of flexibility and flexible manpower planning is that with the attendant delayering of managerial hierarchies and the attempted breakdown in the typical pyramid structure of organisations, promotions and traditional hierarchical development may no longer be possible. Increasingly, human resource planners are having to develop alternatives to hierarchical succession planning in response to a rapidly changing business context that requires fluidity, rapid change and adaptability at the operational level. Hierarchies, therefore, and the functionally rigid structures of responsibility, seniority and status, can no longer be sustained because of the rapid change and flux in consumer demand, market fashion, and global product markets.

In order to resource this external volatility human resource planners are being forced to seek corresponding flexibilities and 'turnover' so that 'Workers, instead of acquiring a skill for life, can now look forward to at least one if not multiple bouts of deskilling and reskilling in a lifetime' (Harvey, 1989: 230). In the banking industry, for example, many of the traditional-style accountancy-biased branch managers are increas-ingly finding their skills redundant as banks seek to promote sales as the central focus of their business activities. The old-style paternalism in manpower planning, where employees were guaranteed, especially in the old large bureaucracies such as banks, 'cradle to grave' employment security, is being replaced by far more uncertainty and turnover. In terms of development, banks are now emphasising lateral development, or 'progression' *across* an organisation, rather than hierarchical promotion (Cressey and Scott, 1992; O'Doherty, 1993).

So far we have been following a fairly standard exposition of manpower planning. This programme has taken us through a number of stages, beginning with an explana-tion of the need for manpower planning, through to attempted identification of 'who' it is that actually does manpower planning, and then on to a discussion of the creation of a manpower plan that eventually took us on to a consideration of complication and complexity. Our discussion has challenged, at times, the scientific pretensions of man-power planning, illustrating the contested nature of the employment relation and the insecure nature of unitarist-style integration. What I want to do now is focus more explicitly on the assumptions, and what I call the 'field of vision', that inform the tradi-tional practice of manpower planning. Here we shall see that the pursuit of rationality, order, and control *borders* a domain or space of disorder, where the play of the irrational and the meaningless comes to wreak its damage on organisation. Paradoxically, the desire for order among manpower planners requires this very threat in order to consoli-date the need for its own existence. So this 'space' in organisation provides conditions of both possibility and impossibility for manpower planning. In recent years the fixation on control and regularity has subsided somewhat as manpower planning has evolved to assume the role of *human resource* planning. What we find here is that human resource

155

planning yields to the space of the irrational and disorderly as it seeks to pursue management less by means of control than by 'seduction' (Bauman, 1992: 48ff.). Corporate culture, new forms of teamworking, the discipline of enterprise and entrepreneurialism, and the discourse of learning and development, all open up the psychology of the individual human subject where the passions, anxieties, and fears of the unconscious act in often unpredictable and disorderly ways. By seeking to work on these areas of the human subject, human resource planning is playing with fire. Seduction remains a fragile and unstable means of securing organisation, and as a management strategy aggravates the play of chance, unpredictability, and the risk that anything might happen next in the employment relation.

## ASSUMPTIONS AND THE FIELD OF VISION IN MANPOWER PLANNING

The discourse of manpower planning has traditionally appropriated metaphors of 'stocks', 'flows', 'systems', 'state' and 'equilibrium' (Smith, 1976; McBeath, 1978), often directly from meta-sociological and economic theory. Such meta-theoretical work, and the values embodied in its discourse, remains at best contested and partial in contemporary social theory if not entirely discredited by developments and revisions in the understanding of the limitations not just of its theory but of all grand narrative 'catch-all' theoretical explanations (Lyotard, 1984).

Second-order business administration techniques and methodologies typically borrow indiscriminately from versions of Talcott Parsons' sociological model of structural functionalism (see Cole, 1991). This was contested within its own field in the 1950s and was subsequently subject to such revision and critique that contemporary students of social theory and the philosophy of social science may come across Parsons only in footnotes to textbooks (Game and Metcalfe, 1996). However, the husk of its discourse remains extant in the field of business administration, personnel management and the 'sciences' of marketing and accounting. This appropriation from social theory is forgotten, its contested nature suppressed, and its metaphors and methodology reified to an extent that it comes to take on the status of science and truth. The political and economic pressures that encourage this remain too complex to engage with here, but students should remain vigilant about the language, metaphors and world-views that are perpetuated in personnel management.

In George Cole's orthodox account of personnel management, this bias remains an integral, and even celebrated feature of his text in his claim that 'the approaches described throughout this book are firmly part of the functionalist approach, complete with managerial bias!' (Cole, 1991: 32). In terms of manpower planning, the assumptions of human behaviour and the human subject, the 'purposes' and values presumed to hold in something called organisation, and the nature of the employment relation, remain hidden if not actively suppressed.

If we consult the *Oxford English Dictionary* we appreciate the sense of divorce and *detachment* (Cooper, 1993) involved in many of the assumptions and practices of manpower planning. By divorce and detachment we mean that work of abstraction that is incarnate in the assumptions that enable orthodox manpower planning to proceed. To plan implies to *derive* or *contrive* by means and media to *control* and attempt to *tame* the active forces, energy, and agency of social relations at work, forces that remain only partially under the classificatory and designative capacity of 'planners'. To plan is also to construct an *imaginary* flat surface or plane, as in a perspective drawing, where 'several imaginary planes perpendicular to the line of vision form a grid within which the

156

objects represented appear to diminish in size according to the distance between the viewer and the planes' (*Oxford English Dictionary*). Here one can clearly see the abstraction and detachment involved in the planning process, which deploys, as the organisational theorist Keith Hoskin (1995) writes, 'a fixed point of view' so as to 'retheorize the world as disembodied or mathematical space' (p. 147). The social and natural world is rendered mathematical. It doesn't pre-exist in the form of mathematics but gets translated and understood through a mathematical frame of mind.

Planning derives from the root *plano*, derived in turn from the Greek *planos*, which captures a richer and more ambiguous sense – of wandering, of 'free living' and 'mobility', as in planetary movement – than has survived in the everyday usage of the contemporary word 'plan'. Over time this conceptual ambiguity of planning has been lost as it becomes increasingly equated with the rational, interventionist construction of active self-centred human subjects who incessantly seek to order, classify and organise the world around them. Robert Cooper (1993) explores a similar conceptual emaciation that has taken place today in conventional accounts of 'technology' and 'representation'. The sense of 'technology' derives from the Greek *techne*, a concept that implied the art of bringing something forward or present to the senses of the human body – as in making something available for use and understanding. However, the root of *techne*, namely *tech*, derives from the Greek *tuche*, which named that which was *not* under the control of the human being – in particular, the accidental, chance, and fate. This *tuche* takes place in that area of organisation we have previously called the organisation 'shadow', that shadow cast by the photographic activity of manpower planning. Therefore *techne* was that which controlled and ordered the vagaries of chance and accident, and hence that which *conquers* chance for the advantage of the human subject. Furthermore, *techne* was considered to be more detached from the interference of chance and accident:

> Human action expresses itself in relation to *tuche* in terms of attachment (at-tach-ment) and detachment (de-tach-ment). The more attached action is *tuche*, the more it is influenced by chance and vagary; the more detached it is, the more able it is to exert mastery and control.
>
> (Cooper, 1993: 279–280)

In modern uses of the word – technology – we tend to lose sight of this ontological relation as conceptually technology is confidently reduced by the human subject and equated solely with that which masters and controls.

This narrow rationalist frame of reference governs much of the manpower planning tradition, and remains explicit in the work of those concerned with the planning of manpower resources in the Civil Service (see Smith, 1976). The tone of the contributors to this text is that of an unquestioned faith in the rational and abstract principles of statistical forecasting. It is assumed that if these techniques are rigorously adopted and exercised across sufficient domains that impinge on the planning of resources, regularity and control can be achieved in the movement and distribution of labour. In reducing what is a complex and contradictory play of political, economic, and social-psychological relations, to one of quantified abstraction, where individuals appear simply as 'data' to be manipulated in a multivariable regression equation (Rowntree and Stewart, 1976), commits an analytical injustice upon the difficulty and practice of management.

That such statistical techniques are assumed to remain neutral and without value bias appears naive in the extreme. Following the logic of Rowntree and Stewart (1976), we are informed that staff numbers can be correctly calculated and projected only if the

157

manpower planner is able to 'de-correlate' the factors that are causally related to work-load levels. If, in calculating differing workload levels, for example $L_1$, $L_2$, $L_3$ and $L_4$, we fail to account for 'interrelated' forces that affect staffing requirements (p. 41), we fail to capture the underlying and essential factors that affect the workload level – and hence staff numbers. Manpower planning has a tendency to incorrectly isolate the contribution of forces $x_1$, $x_2$, . . . etc. by coefficients $b_1$, $b_2$, . . . etc., which results in a situation where the coefficient $b_1$ for example is not simply a measure of $x_1$ but picks up the influence of cross-correlated forces.

Here the adoption of multivariate regression in orthodox manpower planning takes account of a complex number of factors, which are positively or negatively related to staff requirements and which require both identification and measurement. So, for example, in a tax office processing tax claims, staffing levels will depend not only on the number of tax claims made ($x_1$) but on the complexity of the claims, which can be assessed, forecast and quantified by a variable ($x_2$) and the size of the claim ($x_3$). One member of staff may be required therefore for each 100 tax claims made of type $i$, and in a simplified regression analysis the $b_1$ coefficient would equate to 0.01. Staff numbers ($y$) would equal $b_i$, $X_i$, where $b_i$ represents the coefficient of $x$ that translates $X_i$ into staff numbers. In the example here, where $t$ = time period 1:

$$y^t = b_i X_i$$

Therefore:

$$y^t = 0.01(100)$$

and hence the calculation reveals we need one member of staff for each 100 tax claims made of type $i$. Cross-correlation would disturb our result if we calculated a figure for the numbers of individuals falling into a particular tax bracket, and then calculated this as a variable having an independent effect on staffing levels. There is likely to be a cross-correlation because an increasing number of individuals falling within a relevant tax bracket will affect the number of tax claims of $X_i$, and therefore the coefficient $b_i$ will not be measuring an independent variable. By measuring one variable, one $X$, and assuming its independence, we may wrongly calculate the number of staff required to service this demand. Our calculation would be wrong because there is a strong cross-correlation between the variables. Hence, according to this analysis, we may overestimate or perhaps underestimate our calculation of staff levels. What is required, therefore, is this decorrelation of the factors in order to arrive at the underlying fundamentals that can be measured directly in terms of their impact on staff levels:

> In theory staff numbers can be expressed in terms of these underlying factors, which may be projected into the future and used to derive forecasts of staff. (Rowntree and Stewart, 1976: 43)

On the basis of such apparently rigorous statistical techniques for developing forecasts and trend analysis, we are led to believe that staffing levels appear as some fait accompli consequent upon the neutral tools of science. But it is the very abstraction and detachment of these techniques from power relations and contestation within social relations that belie its neutrality. Moreover, no matter what effort we make to decorrelate and measure underlying factors, if these underlying factors are not predictable, but irrational and subject to the caprice of accident, chance or contingency, our statistics necessarily border on that *tuche* as identified by Cooper (1993).

Although most orthodox approaches to manpower planning pay tacit recognition to the contribution of trade unions, in the negotiation over issues such as productivity, expectations, norms, standards, work organisation and acceptable staffing levels, the acknowledgement tends to be couched in terms of order and predictability. Trade unions are seen to simply add legitimacy, to offer a medium through which the neutral techniques of statistical forecasting must proceed. This extends the managerial prerogative by drawing unions into the logic of the neutrality of these techniques and the procedures that support a normative commitment to the values of agreement, resolution, and regulation (Clegg, 1975, 1979; Hyman, 1978). Unions may contest the relative weight ascribed to particular variables but not the principles or logic of rationality and measurement. Today, more unions accept the principles of efficiency and competitiveness. If redundancies need to be made, unions today are more likely to contest the numbers or the level of staff compensation, rather than the logic of a system that periodically requires unemployment, redundancy and economic crisis.

Staffing levels may reflect the solidification over time cf contested, variable, and negotiable relations in the organisation, allocation and distribution of work. Thus the assumption of neutrality in the measurement of variables and forecasts of staffing levels is simply a projection from an assumed 'state of nature', a 'state' that may reflect simply a temporary consolidation or alliance in the struggles and caprices of human subjects and social relations. At any moment one could interpret this arrangement of relations and norms as only a temporary and partial condensation of what remains in tension, fractious, perhaps even chaotic. In the violent abstraction of planning, which detaches from these social relations and power inequalities, organisation is constructed and a 'balance of forces' regulated in the employment relation. Complexity gets diminished and disorder made orderly. The tradition of manpower planning is one that tends to construct analysis as if looking through an inverted telescope. Social relations and individual human subjects appear as 'entities' if we look this way through a telescope. Like a photograph we capture them as if like objects, timeless and abstract, with clear-cut lines of definition and boundary. As Foucault (1971) observes in his critique of the faith in the purity and singularity of origins in linguistic, conceptual and categorical thought, this represents almost a timelessness, a faith in the stable continuity of history. For Foucault, this commitment:

> is an attempt to capture the exact essence of things, their purest possibilities, and their carefully protected identities because this search assumes the existence of immobile forms that precede the external world of accident and succession. (p. 78)

The persistence of manpower planning techniques that maintain a commitment to the virtues of utilitarianism through the exercise of a singular, unitarist mode of rationality works to dim down those factors that cannot be subsumed within its logic. That which cannot be controlled gets relegated to a dustbin of error, deviance, and irrationality. Consider the work of McBeath (1978), who in discussing the necessity of control over recalcitrant subordinate managers urges the importance of vigilance in audit control (pp. 188ff). The rationality of the techniques of manpower planning are not called into question, and thus any deviance from the manning norms established by these methods must be the result of irrationality, a lack of understanding, or the irrational grandiose ambitions of managerial empire builders. The possibility that capitalist organisations are precisely about aggrandisement, growth, power, and empire building does not enter into his consideration. Deviance from prescribed standards must be punished and the managers 'red circled' (p. 189) for the convenience of the corporate gaze so as to enable it to quickly identify any likely future sources of transgression:

159

> Unfortunately, a few managers and supervisors are exceptionally able at maintaining their over strength establishments, somehow managing to get replacements even when someone does transfer or leave. It is these areas that the audit seeks to identify. (p. 189)

Such a perspective remains consistent with the command-and-control discipline of authority, hierarchy, and tradition, which perhaps until only recently governed the perspective and management of organisation. The manner in which discipline and authority are understood and the way in which it gets constructed in contemporary organisations may of course differ. Nonetheless, it is arguable whether the one-dimensional rationality (Marcuse, 1964) of technical utilitarianism is able to persist in the context of traditional and emergent corrosive forces and lines of division in contemporary organisation, forces that may have been unleashed by manpower planning and amplified through a more 'human resource'-style approach to planning.

The language of manpower planning also betrays this predilection for control and mastery. If we look at the texts of manpower planning we find a frame of reference that is predominantly masculine, with its discourse of 'power', 'efficiency', 'control' and 'man-power'. Organisation is synonymous with sobriety, control and exactitude. It is a kind of geometry, although one that can be disturbed and polluted, led astray, by the as yet unconquered, and perhaps unconquerable, forces of irrationality, conflict, deviance, and sheer bloody-minded stupidity. Thank a deity for stupidity?

Yet it is assumed that the exhaustive procedures and information-gathering techniques of manpower planning will eventually tend to order. A steady-state equilibrium is the natural state of affairs, which can be maintained in vitality and health, unified and coherent in order to allow further conquest and expansion. The language of 'conquest' pervades the texts on manpower planning – the conquest and control of nature we find in our assumption that precautionary contraceptive safeguards will guarantee 2.2 offspring together with the optimal allocation and distribution of domestic resources. This desire for completion and wholeness involves the repression and suppression of 'otherness' – whether competing frameworks, alternative rationalities, or novel modes of epistemology and ontology (see Inayatullah, 1990). That there may be different ways of being in the world is simply not entertained.

Let us consider the possibility that there *are* multiple ways of being in the world – a feminist mode of being, or an ecological mode, an aesthetic sensibility, or a queer way of being etc. To the native indigenous Australian population – what we have come to call 'aborigines' – there are *dream modes* of being in the world (Linstead and Banerjee, 1999) that offer access to understanding and truths closed off to the conscious daytime world. A greater sense of connectivity with the environment and with past and future family generations stimulates reflection on the limitations and potential dangers attendant upon the preoccupations of the ego-bound human subject. The human subject loses its sense of self-importance and is reminded of its temporary evanescent condition of transit through this world. Experience is enriched by the encounter with these shadowy domains, which exposes the constrictive bind imposed by our all-too-*modern* human rationality. Space and time lose their mundane, taken-for-granted presence; its defined and bounded state of coordination, which we routinely reify in the here and now, begins to unravel and dissolve. Consider the possibilities for alternative manpower planning – where the human subject might be 'distributed' across a range of space and time coordinates, some of which we might be conscious of, and others that remain unconscious. Do we slip across delimited boundaries in organisation while at work into reverie and dream

160

time? A number of contemporary writers on organisation would seem to think so, including Gabriel (1995, 1997), Linstead (1993), Linstead and Benerjee (1999) and Sievers(1994).

How might manpower planning think about managing the transgression associated with these movements? Opening up these subterranean features of work organisation, where the fears and anxieties of employees are played out, and where the unpredictability and chance of human behaviour exact their toll, confronts management with a complex set of problems.

The unconscious organisation does not easily lend itself to the appropriating reach of meaning and reason. Our world begins to appear less solid, and all the numbers of manpower planning begin to flicker and dance. We literally become *numb*-er to numbers, as the world presents itself anew – more unstable, less meaningful, a little vulnerable, and strange. What might be the significance of 'banana time' and 'coke time' (Roy, 1958) in manpower planning, or where managers begin to take on the guise of magicians (Cleverley, 1973), medieval court barons (Jackall, 1988), or even God (Gabriel, 1997)? We are not just making reference to the recently well-publicised appointments of corporate court jesters, or Bill Gates's employment of actors to add life to corporate entertainment exercises. What is more interesting is when the distinctions between these different domains begin to break down.

It is has been well documented that secretaries often come to act as substitute office wives for male managers (Game and Pringle, 1983; Pringle, 1990), and male bosses can assume the role of a father figure among subordinate women workers; but what happens to the rationality of manpower planning when the boundaries around the world of dream and fantasy break down, and agents act upon impulses drawn from these domains? Employees might then drift through the multiple space and time of organisation, struggling to make coherent that which is fractious and chaotic, to 'still' the strife of ontological instability, where they might suddenly find themselves confronted with a sexually attractive young male one day instead of what they had always appeared to be – an agent of oppressive work discipline. What might happen next? What might happen to motivation and productivity? Now then, this word 'productivity' . . . ? (cf: Bataille, 1957/1987). What might happen if we are no longer sure whether or not we are dreaming? What might become of the difference between dream and reality (Castenada, 1971), especially given the prospect of virtual organisations, the 'virtual' worker, artificial intelligence, cloning, and the cyborg worker (see *Organisation*, 1999)? Will we be able to tell when we are – and when we are not – working? Might our dreams become utilisable as a form of labour?

No doubt the world of the Disney Corporation, the Las Vegas economy, and vast swathes of labour in the entertainment and leisure industries, constructed around the seductive exploitation of fantasy and the selling of alternative realities, already stand as testimony to this speculation. Manpower planning might then come to assume the role of 'reality engineer', regulating access to the multiple domains of reality in order to secure a more efficient use of organisational time. Isn't this what is already happening through the development of corporate culture programmes (Willmott, 1993: Casey, 1995), where management seeks to tap into the existential insecurities of human subjects, to translate and re-bind – or 'cathect' as Freud would write – its energy into appropriate forms of corporate ritual and routine, myths and images, signs and symbols that stimulate excitation and passion in a careful regulation and deregulation of emotion?

In its traditions, manpower planning recognises none of this nonsense. When you're waging a war there is no time to entertain the extravagance of delusion and dream,

161

even if with all its mustard gas, chemical and biological weapons, our world might literally be disappearing. The metaphors of conquest and control that support the conventional perspective of manpower planning reflect and repeat the military and imperial history from which they derive. In fact, in many places in the manpower planning library, unashamed explicit reference is made to the linguistic roots of planning, recruitment, selection, training and regimen. It is not just linguistic roots, either. As Rose (1990) and Townley (1994) show, much of what has come to be the practice of personnel management finds its history in the military world of exercise and drill. According to Bartholomew and Forbes (1979), the 'statistical techniques of manpower systems must be as old as the planning of the military and building exploits of the ancient world' (p. 8). Acceptable statistical risks in trench warfare have been translated into the language of redundancy and wastage. Muscle, power, force, and productivity, a preoccupation with the physical body – 'put your back into it', 'how many hands have we got?' – provide the common currency of terms in manpower planning, mapping and constituting those human variables that come to form indispensable characteristics of employees and their social relations given the competitive nature of capitalist economies. The central planner at the apex of the organisation carefully calculates and calibrates, classifying and arranging, mapping movements and change, resolving the complexity of human relations by the application of the slide rule and mathematical calculation. As McBeath (1978) argues, manning systems require the constant attention and supervision of an elite of 'management':

> The regular attention of a systems man is essential, as much to ensure that some activities are discontinued or reduced in frequency, as to enable fresh demands to be made. (pp. 189–190)

This image of the white-coated male technician, omnipotent in his virility, rendering the world calculable for order (Kallinikos, 1995), seems today not only dangerous but in some ways rather sad. In the final section of our chapter we attempt to sketch some features of the contemporary workplace that are challenging some of these primordial assumptions and metaphors in manpower planning. One implication of the extension of interest in the management of the irrational and unconscious aspects of organisation and human interaction is the aggravation of the fragmentary tendencies inherent in the ongoing oscillation of organisation/disorganisation. This acts to limit the coherence and utility of the abstractions and techniques typically associated with manpower planning. We have seen how manpower planning remains an idealised abstraction from the struggle and contestation that characterise the day-to-day interaction of social and non-material relations. Now we shall find that the exercise of control by manpower planning is being made far more vulnerable by developments in post-bureaucratic, de-structured and networked organisation that amplify anxiety, insecurity and fear among employees.

## NEW ORGANISATION, TEAMWORKING AND SELF-DEVELOPMENT: THE EMERGENCE OF HUMAN RESOURCE PLANNING

The fracturing and disintegration of formerly unified bureaucracies and hierarchies represents an attempt to reconstitute organisation, in part through the reworking and devolution of responsibility for the discipline and planning of resources. Still subject to the financial control of senior corporate management (Marginson *et al.*, 1988; Sisson

162

and Marginson, 1995), these devolved 'business units' exercise far less autonomy, however, than some of the more enthusiastic management consultants and celebrants are likely to recognise. Yet there has been a discernible move in many sectors of the economy to shift the burden of day-to-day planning and management to 'empowered' team leaders and 'coaches' of small, team-based workgroups (Storey, 1992; IRS, 1995a, b, 1996).

According to Storey (1992, 1995), there has been a welter of HRM initiatives and restructuring programmes in an effort to reconstruct the balance of individual and collective forms of employment regulation, not simply in the new dynamic service sectors that emerged in the 1980s, but in the heartland of British industry. In an effort to encourage commitment and performance, much organisational restructuring has focused on the attitudes and expectations of the first-line supervisor–employee relation. From this point in the production process, organisational change seeks to remove the detailed layers of bureaucracy and management that service, monitor, discipline and plan from above. Those layers of middle management that hold in place the traditional command-and-control model of organisation have been eroded to refocus those activities in small workgroups or teams. The importance of the coach or first-line supervisor has been enhanced with added responsibilities, which now allow for a greater degree of middle-management delayering. In the place of these massed ranks of middle management, a more streamlined and flatter structure made up of supervisors, 'coaches', first-line managers, or 'heads' of shift, assumes responsibility for budgeting, planning and resourcing. This is the domain of that expanded supervisory role that Storey (1992) uncovers in his research, a role that 'embraced aspects of planning, scheduling, agreeing budgets, being responsible for a cost centre, ensuring quality and being the main managerial representatives in human resource management'(p. 239).

Research in human resource management has also discovered the importance attached to loyalty and commitment in generating motivation, but also coherence and meaning – given the fact that employees often work these days in smaller, more dispersed units of organisational activity. Teamworking provides an opportunity to foster communitarian values and commitment, which in conjunction with the adoption of performance appraisals, acts as a focus of a new disciplinary gaze. More extreme forms of devolution and empowerment have attempted to constitute the individual employee as a manager of themselves (Townley, 1994), in what Tom Peters has defined as the 'entrepreneurializing of every job' (Peters, 1994: 67). Ideally, those responsible for their own businesses will go anywhere, do everything, find anyone and break every barrier, procedure, and 'tradition' to get the job done and done well. Given the dispersal of work activity, binding more diffuse and heterogeneous elements might increasingly come to depend upon self-discipline and self-organisation. This is sold within the prescriptive literature as a means of generating new freedoms for individuals. By encouraging employees to continuously monitor and reflect upon their 'performance', in a context of team support and assistance, work becomes a preoccupation, a project of self-formation and mastery. The military overtones of manpower planning have not disappeared in human resource planning; they have simply refocused and reconstituted within organisation.

Some have noted that the type of organisational 'structure' that this kind of construction and management encourages (indeed Peters himself makes this observation) is one that comes to resemble the Jackson Pollock composition 'Autumn Rhythm'. Here, flexible lines of responsibility and authority continually shift and redefine, resting only temporarily to take form and shape before moving on. It remains difficult to identify a 'source' of manpower planning in these admittedly extreme, avant-garde and probably

163

idealistic, if not terroristic, postmodern organisations (Clegg, 1991; Hassard and Parker, 1994; Hatch, 1997).

In the film and television industry, Starkey and Barratt (1994; see also Lash and Urry, 1994) have identified the emergence of similar 'vertically disaggregated' forms of organisation and planning. Planning takes place within a diffuse heterogeneous network, assembled by reputation and personal contact. To produce a new drama series, for example, involving the employment and cooperation of thousands of employees, or rather a temporary network of labour brought together under multiple and myriad forms of contract association, involves the mobilisation of new forms of manpower planning that we might associate with moves towards human resource planning. Manpower planning now takes place at multiple points of 'intersection' – boundaries if you like – between specialist agencies representing actors, technicians, studios, and distribution outlets. Budgets and 'financial constraints' are subject to a complicated series of 'spot contracts' involving negotiation and movement – albeit at the margins and within some 'tolerance' level acceptable to the investors and financiers of the project. Yet we know that the production of films is associated with spectacular examples of over-budget projects. The 'negotiations' never stop as funds are sought through complex circuits of 'wheeling and dealing'.

Lash and Urry (1994) discuss the growth in these forms of 'structure' in the broadcast media – film, television and music – and in publishing and tourism. The key feature of this form of organisation is the temporary coalescence of organisational form – its 'just-in-time' character – and the temporary and shifting draft of labour that come to assemble organisation. Figure 4.5 attempts to represent the nature and form of 'manpower planning' within this kind of organisation. In this example we represent the design, production and broadcast of a new television drama series.

The 'producer choice' strategy embarked on by the BBC over the past few years has further encouraged this form of planning and organisation. Instead of using in-house production and editing, and BBC-employed actors and actresses, all paid under terms and conditions negotiated by the structures of union–management collective bargaining, producers can now recruit from outside the walls of the BBC. They may presage the future possibilities for the 'empowered' first-line managers identified in the study by Storey (1992), increasingly responsible for planning, management and the allocation of financial and human resources. With the freedom to manage their own budgets they do not remain constrained in the same way as traditional BBC producers, who were obliged to draw on resources and facilities pre-funded and provided by their own organisation.

## Foucault and power

Within these disaggregated and delayered, some would say *disordered*, organisations, teams of flexible and multifunctional alliances of labour, infrequently employees in the traditional sense, come to take on an increased responsibility and importance. Superficially, this might appear to resemble some utopian-empowered challenge to traditional hierarchical inequalities, with the planning and management of resources now performed closer to actual labour and the point of production. More extensive research, however, reveals the persistence of traditional forms of conflict, somewhat transformed, and the surfacing of many hitherto suppressed forms of antagonism and discontent.

Kondo (1990), and the work of Sewell and Wilkinson (1992), document the tremendous symbolic, discursive and material pressure that operate, often subliminally,

164

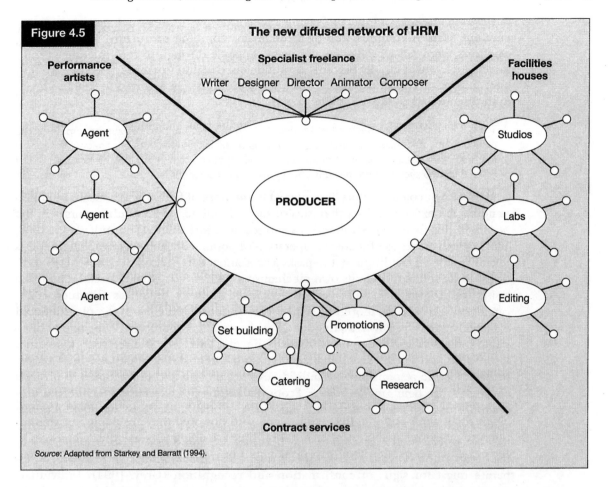

**Figure 4.5**      **The new diffused network of HRM**

Source: Adapted from Starkey and Barratt (1994).

through the discipline of manpower planning today, but the capacity for disruption and discontent is never far from the surface, and may actually have been aggravated by recent management initiatives. Given the decline of institutional regulation and the collective stability offered by trade union organisation, employment relations might well be expected to fracture and dissipate into a heterogeneous series of struggles throughout organisation. The imposition of new forms of discipline on workers 'can be expected – particularly if market conditions improve, or become accepted as the new normalcy', Hyman (1987) writes, to 'provoke unpredictable and disruptive forms of revolt' (p. 52).

The construction and constitution of team-based working brings with it new forms of vulnerability and volatility. While the intention of new forms of power-knowledge is to conscript individual employees as *objects* of discipline and control, the *seductive* aspects of these new forms of discipline work on cultivating *subjects* through the provision of 'opportunities' whereby individuals practise self-discipline and self-management. Empowered training regimes, through to performance appraisals, performance-related pay, and devolved schemes of career management, increasingly seek to turn work into a *reflexive project of self*. Employees are encouraged to reflect on their own performance, conduct, action and habits, to consider the ways in which they may benefit or hinder the performance of work. Increasingly, responsibility to one's self and one's team is

165

reflected in attitudes of guilt and shame and, conversely, attitudes of a pious and sancti-monious kind. A complex web of mechanisms combine to nurture these kinds of emotions, from self-surveillance and team vigilance through to zero tolerance group surveillance, which rapidly become institutionalised within workgroups as the responsi-bility for the successful completion of work is progressively devolved to self and team. According to Barker and Tompkins (1994):

> Team members expect each other to identify with the team and to behave according to the team's norms and rules. By violating team norms or exhibiting elements of 'dis-identification', a team member risks punishment by the team. The offending teammate may be accused of not being a team player or of not being faithful to the 'team's personality'. (pp. 225–226)

Many recent commentators have turned to the work of Foucault as a means of under-standing the process and mechanisms of such discipline. As Foucault has argued, the beauty of this form of discipline is its subtlety and invisibility (Foucault, 1977, 1980, 1984), which serves to obscure the operation of power. Foucault suggests that 'power is tolerable only on condition that it masks a substantial part of itself. Its success is propor-tional to its ability to hide its own mechanisms' (1980: 86). Quality circles, employee assistance programmes, and so-called 'employee wellness' initiatives (Townley, 1994) can all be seen as new, more powerful forms of self-surveillance in the planning and management of one's own 'manpower'. They represent a significant deepening of disci-plinary mechanics in comparison with the old paternal, welfare-style personnel institutions and schemes. Self-management and career development are increasingly being made the responsibility of individuals who, tied up and preoccupied in projects of the self, are being made *subjects*. From marketing and advertising to internal pro-grammes of corporate culture and enterprise, individuals are being made anxious about their status and identity – concerned with how well they are doing, or whether they are perceived as successful or not, how they are doing vis-à-vis other employees in the organisation or what their prospects might be – that animates, in response, a des-perate quest for signs of confirmation and recognition (Grey, 1994). Individuals exercise only an illusory sense of freedom in their preoccupation with making them-selves subjects, a complete whole they can project and present to the world of organisation. Foucault's work tells us that individuals can no longer simply be thought of as *objects*, repressed by power, shunted about through the guidelines provided by the overarching governance of organisational structure, rules, or procedures. Power is pro-ductive and seductive; it turns self upon self, stimulating anxiety and reflexivity so that individuals feel compelled to shape and secure themselves through corporate-provided images, ideals, and role models. Power is diffuse through a complex 'micro-physics' of capillary networks that 'wires up' social relations through regimes of truth that is found extant in our language and norms, our bodies and gestures. Organisation, and the indi-viduals and collectives who compose it, can be usefully thought of as occupying a field of tension that is spread out across a series of negotiations and agreements, settlements and struggles, an unsteady balance of forces that never ceases looking for ways to sta-bilise itself, confronted, as it is, by the play of multiple lines of fracture. Power is not simply a form of repression, but offers ways of doing and being within these lines of fracture. We exercise power, albeit in asymmetrical relations of opportunity and restric-tion, in the everyday mundane activity of our employment relation, through the sanctions and norms we aspire to and pass on to others in the ever circling relays of quotidian social relations.

166

One of the distinctive features of human resource planning is precisely the exercise of this mode of discipline. Yet, with the attention it confers upon subjects and their psyche, it opens up new areas of fragility and vulnerability. Lasch (1978) talks about the emergence of pathological narcissism among individuals in late capitalist societies, a selfishness that is paradoxically amplified by the lack of a sense of self, of completion and wholeness, which stimulates individuals to seek forms of gratification and confirmation in efforts to compensate for their diminishing sense of self. Yet individuals never find satisfaction. They crave ever greater degrees of confirmation and recognition as they become volatile and anxious, easily bored and agitated. We become less tolerant of others, and seek their company only if they can make us feel good about ourselves. Teams at work suddenly become fractious and fragile, a space of infantile regression through which complex emotions and anxieties get played out, often to the detriment of disciplined production. Management is made difficult. It is literally playing with fire.

## Interruptions, breakdowns, and conflicts

The 'directors' programme' at Royal Mail (IRS, 1995b) and the 'Development Partnership' scheme at the Trustee Savings Bank emphasise the importance of a shift in the conception of manpower and career planning. As one regional personnel manager at a large high street retail bank reported, 'We are moving away from a culture of "Do it to me" or "Do it for me" to one which emphasises self-development, empowerment, initiative and responsibility' (O'Doherty, 1994, 1996). In addition, the conception of a career as some progressive linear development through the ranks of middle management is now seen as anachronistic and redundant. In the fluid, delayered networks and alliances characteristic of contemporary organisational arrangements the old hierarchies are often no longer in place to the same extent or degree. Employees are being encouraged to broaden their understanding of career, to see a career as one that emphasises 'lateral development', which may be harnessed with the adoption of multiple and flexible forms of contract, exchange and relationship with the organisation. Temporary project work, part-time employment, job-sharing and service contracts across a range of business units, and even across different organisations, are seen by some to offer avenues for the future of career planning, development and management (Handy, 1989, 1994).

The entrepreneurial and Thatcherite rhetoric is barely disguised in the discourse of these new-style career-management strategies. In many ways this mirrors the withdrawal of institutional support and paternal welfare structures, the withdrawal of the 'nanny state', and the liberation of what is assumed to be a state of nature – competitiveness, entrepreneurialism, self-help, and the ideals of neo-classical economic liberalism. The Royal Mail 'directors' programme' is explicit in its efforts to encourage employees to view themselves as a project to be worked on and a self to be managed:

> The first aim of the directors' programme is to increase your awareness of who you are. What are your skills, strengths and abilities? What are your interests, weaknesses and values? One way of discovering where you want to go in the future is to look back at where you have been.
>
> (quoted in IRS, 1995b)

Most of the career planning initiatives of contemporary organisations remind employees, or contracted self-employed staff, that there are no guarantees: 'the only person that can make this work is you', and the only chance of success is a constant awareness and attentiveness to self and performance. This provides a clear example of the kind of disciplinary power that Foucault was talking about. Manpower planning

167

becomes individualised and empowered, but individuals find themselves exposed far more immediately and directly to the vagaries and dynamics of market forces. Rather than eliminating the conflict and tensions associated with the traditional power structures – the hierarchy and inequalities of the capital–labour relation – these new forms of manpower planning and organisation simply shift the 'space' within which discontent is constituted and expressed. From stress, to anxiety and disorientation (O'Doherty, 1994), these forms of organisation and employment relations are subject to a range of interruptions, breakdowns and conflicts. This is perhaps different in form from the traditional organisation and expression of conflict and tension, but arguably no less debilitating in terms of the efficient functioning and reproduction of organisation, profit and capital.

Research finds considerable evidence to support the claim that power remains marked by tension, disruption, and breakdown within contemporary forms of work relations. Barker (1993) details how in small, self-managing teams, new rules, regulations and normative expectations emerge around things like attendance, performance and commitment. These far more insidious forms of discipline replace the traditional and formal managerial directives of the 'command-and-control' variety. Prominent team members soon arise from within these so-called self-governing democracies, democracies that soon reproduce familiar patterns of power, authority and hierarchy.

Team leaders are able to maintain their position only with the support of a majority of the team, support that remains, however, tenuous and fragile. These 'elected' team leaders seek to manage, guide and steer the rest of the group into conformity with extant rules and norms, but their status remains insecure, partial and contingent on the day-to-day alliances of political traffic. What Tomkins and Cheney (1985) define as *concertive control* operates to regulate and manage work teams far more perniciously through informal hierarchies and seniority. Paradoxically this form of control can be seen to be both tighter and more powerful, but also more fragile in terms of the work and effort that employees must routinely invest to maintain discipline and order. Barker's (1993) ethnography of ISE reveals how this discipline operates with the example of 'Stephi', a short-term worker seeking to gain full-time employment status with the team. She was considered by the team to have a bad attitude and failed to identify sufficiently with the team. In Stephi's words:

> When I first started I really didn't start off on the right foot, so I've been working to re-prove myself as far as a team player. My attitude gets in the way. I let it get in the way too many times and now I've been watching it and hoping they [her team] will see the change in me and I can prove to them that I will make a good ISE employee. (p. 425)

Of course, this may simply represent self-interested guile and instrumentalism on Stephi's behalf in an effort to secure a full-time position. Indeed, Barker details the expression of tension and conflict in the arguments that regularly attend team meetings. Rivalries, personalities, disputes – and what we may speculate to be nascent political cliques and alliances – emerge as the social relations within the team attempt to tackle the exigencies of performance and market competition. In their efforts to plan, organise and discipline human resources, teams begin to resemble the Lord of the Flies (Golding, 1954). The work of Catherine Casey (1995) is also illustrative of these divisions and contradictions, where loyalty to one's team, one's identity as a worthy and productive employee, and the pressures of effort and performance requirements, combine to generate unstable work 'organisation'. In an exemplary rich ethnographic study, Casey begins to expose the weaknesses and lines of division that

168

accompany such corporate restructuring initiatives, which change the form and locus of manpower planning but not, it would seem, the inevitability of conflict and tension.

## CONCLUSIONS

We have found that traditional manpower planning attempts to present its practice as a pure scientific exercise. It is about statistical equations and differential calculus, and the belief that organisations can be made to resemble well-ordered machines. Derived from a history of warfare and murder, the discourse of manpower planning is a masculine prejudice, an illusion of quantitative mastery and representation that tries to translate the complexity and ambiguity of a three-dimensional world – and probably more than three, as we later discovered – into the flat cartography of two dimensions. As our chapter has evolved we have explored the ways in which this process of translation fails. The paper world of the scientific manpower planner is subject to continual dissolution by the encroachment of the material world, the world of work organisation and the employment relation. A constant relay between organisational presence and re-presentation gets continually interrupted and subverted and, almost like the dog chasing its own tail, the paper world of manpower planners and of those who write upon manpower planning spirals round and round in pursuit of ever greater representation and predictive accuracy. Yet the material world of organisation is nothing if not elusive, always just out of reach beyond the next horizon, and one step ahead. Perhaps manpower planners depend upon this elusiveness, this complexity, in order to provide a rationale for their own existence.

We have explored the categories of manpower planning and found them wanting. The idea that we can identify some heroic manpower planner occupied in an office at the apex of an organisation is another myth, an analytical convenience that fails to cultivate an awareness that it takes place everywhere – and therefore paradoxically nowhere – in organisation. This ontological problem has become more acute in the context of contemporary organisational form. We have tried to think of human resource planning as a method of restoring the discipline of manpower planning through new media and novel methods of organisational control. What we discovered was that the practice of human resource planning actually serves to aggravate tensions and conflict in organisation, adding to the antagonism that dislocates and disrupts the smooth economic exchange between capital and labour. Given the instability of many forms of organisation today, the fact that it mediates and generates a hypertrophy of realities – some that we remain conscious of and others that discharge their energy through subliminal and unconscious channels of existence – the hinges of order and disorder upon which organisation rests are made to oscillate more wildly and unpredictably. We see this in the dispersal of conflict and struggle among so-called empowered employees, who now increasingly work in teams, teams that resemble a viper's nest of accusation and counter-accusation, political back-biting, subterfuge, rivalry, and anxiety. Our chapter

169

suggests that the warp and weft of human resource management (see Chapter 2 by Collin) is being pulled and stretched, its seams frayed and unravelling. Not *what* any more – organisation is becoming dematerialised, less tangible and solid, more temporary and evanescent. This creates a fractious space wherein employees play out a whole series of fears and anxieties in ways that challenge the integrative capacities of human resource planning and its efforts to render the world economic and utile. The parts of organisation might literally be spinning out of control such that we can no longer see its whole. Who knows these days where they are going, what they will be doing next week, where they might be headed, or whether there will even be a job for them next month (see Chapter 12)?

Yet organisation persists, outrageous fortunes are made, inequality spreads, and the blight of economic poverty scars ever greater tracts of inner city space (Lash and Urry, 1994: 145–170). Is there anybody left still asking what all this has got to do with our humble manpower planner and human resource management? In the face of unpredictability and uncertainty one might be able to hear the tension and suspense in organisation today. Something or someone is about to fly off the handle. Banking on the whole is a knot-what of seams.

## SUMMARY

- This chapter has attempted to introduce students to the discursive, linguistic and theoretical suppositions that structure and inform traditional understandings in manpower planning. It was argued that a degree of suppression is evident in the myopic focus and reification of order. It was suggested that a process of undoing was simultaneously in play with the process of ordering through the practice of organisation and control.

- In seeking to reduce shocks and disturbances in the distribution and movement of human resources, planners traditionally seek to calculate manpower needs in the short, medium and long term. The devolution of aspects of manpower planning to the line manager, and indeed to the individual employee, associated with the practice of HRM, may lead to a situation where more diffuse lines of division undermine coherence and the strategic management of human resources.

- The traditional emphasis and faith in forecasting meant a considerable reliance on statistical methodologies. Only large organisations, such as the Civil Service and banks, seemed to pursue intricate statistical manpower planning. Perhaps this reflects the resources and expertise that they were able to invest in because of their insulation from the pressures and immediacy of market competition.

- The purported use of less mechanistic approaches to manpower planning, under the influence of human resource management, was seen to contain new lines of tension and division, that undermined a rational and coherent approach to the planning, organisation and distribution of resources.

- In the rhetoric of HRM we find a considerable emphasis on the 'needs' and aspirations of employees. However, there appears to be a serious potential conflict between the promise and expectations associated with HRM and the 'delivery' of responsibility, empowerment and career development.

170

• In the normative models of HRM (Legge, 1995) we find a considerable emphasis on strategic management and the importance of integrating human resource issues with business strategy. This chapter has argued for a holistic and contextual approach to human resource planning, one that recognises the interactions and contradictions associated with the play of economic, social and human relations.

**Activity**

Imagine that you are a regional personnel manager responsible for food retail stores in a growing regional economy. You have 36 stores in your area, ranging in size from small local grocery-style stores in which there are typically only about seven people employed, to large city centre superstores usually employing a store manager, two assistant managers, 12 line supervisors, 24 full-time employees working as check-out specialists, 45 full-time warehouse and stores staff, and 35 shopfloor assistants.

Over the last six months you have noticed a steadily increasing demand for your products within the region as a whole. Your chain is not renowned for paying particularly high wages relative to other employers in the area.

1  Carefully draw up an initial manpower plan for the organisation, indicating when and where staff are currently employed within the organisation, how long they are likely to stay in that position, and the future projections for staffing requirements. You can assume that within your region there are seven city centres in which you have two stores each. The remaining 22 stores are located in small to medium-sized peripheral towns.

2  Imagine now that you have been given the responsibility for designing an alternative method of planning and utilising labour. In your efforts to construct a new manpower plan and utilisation process you recognise that there are a number of aspiring career-minded individuals within the organisation. How are you going to reconcile the organisation's desire to maintain high productivity and low cost with individual employee requirements for progression and change?

3  How might the existence of a trade union affect the design and final outcome of a manpower plan?

## QUESTIONS

1  What is the point in preparing detailed manpower plans when there is so much economic and business uncertainty?

2  In what ways are manpower planners responsible for maintaining staffing levels?

3  What are the advantages and disadvantages of constructing a labour turnover index?

4  Is it fair to suggest that employees experience an induction crisis when first joining an organisation? Which type of people do you feel this is likely to affect more, and are there organisations where this phenomenon is potentially more damaging for the operational needs of the business?

5  In what ways does human resource planning differ operationally from manpower planning? Is there a significant philosophical and strategic difference between human resource planning and manpower planning?

6  How and why is manpower planning increasingly seeking to construct flexible organisations?

7  In what ways could it be suggested that manpower planning in the UK political and economic context is at a significant disadvantage from its European competitors?

171

## EXERCISES

1 Consider the reasons why the responsibility for manpower planning may have shifted away from head office personnel management. What is meant by organisational de-bureaucratisation, and in what ways may this interact with the supposed change from MP to HRP?

2 As a manpower planner in a large manufacturing firm producing components for television sets, prepare a report to senior management outlining the reasons for high turnover among recent inductees. Suggest methods and policies with which senior and line management may tackle this issue.

3 List those advantages and disadvantages that you associate with HRP in relation to MP.

## CASE STUDY

# Clarion call for a new social contract

**Robert Taylor** – What we expect from and are accountable for at work has drastically changed

The world of work is going through dramatic change but the institutions and policies that seek to support and govern it 'remain mired in the 1930s'. As a result the 'social contract' – what we expect from and are accountable for at work – has broken down'. Today's challenge in the US and elsewhere in the industrialised world is to update policies and institutions by the creation of a 'new social contract capable of meeting the needs and expectations of the workforce, economy and society of the new century'.

So argued Professor Thomas Kochan, outgoing president of the American Industrial Relations Association and a leading figure in MIT's institute for work and employment research, in a characteristically insightful address to last month's annual conference of the association in Boston.

He sees the term 'social contract' as a metaphor, which means 'the expectations and obligations that workers, employers and their communities and societies have for work and employment relationships'.

In his opinion, the 'good' employment relationship cannot be today's 'two-party instrumental exchange focused on only the narrow self-interest of the individual worker or their individual employer'. It must be enforceable, so that each party can be 'held accountable for keeping its part in the understanding'.

It also covers 'subjective principles and expectations that we bring to work as professionals, family members and community citizens'.

Kochan adds an ingredient that he describes as 'a uniquely American approach' reflecting its decentralising traditions which provide 'the parties closest to the workplace with the rights, power and capabilities needed to control their own destiny at work'.

Ever since Roosevelt's New Deal in the 1930s, US companies have had to balance competing responsibilities: to serve as agents for shareholders in maximising their wealth and to meet growing responsibilities focused on employment strategies.

In the US today, shareholder pressures have grown ever more intense but companies have discovered they need to recognise human capital, knowledge and learning as important critical assets for business success. We have also seen the transformation of the boundaries of the company, which have grown increasingly uncertain and blurred by corporate restructuring with an emphasis on core competencies.

Kochan argues that a 'new social contract' is needed that recognises companies now have 'multiple stakeholders to which they owe a fiduciary and social responsibility'.

Strategic partnerships between companies and their employees are one way forward, but few yet exist in the US. But in the dynamic and fluid US labour market he sees a possible advance by encouragement of a shift in employment policy away from a preoccupation with the individual enterprise to a focus on a wide network of intermediate labour market institutions and community bodies that facilitate employment mobility, and match people to jobs more efficiently.

Kochan pointed out in his Boston speech that there is evidence in the US that this is happening, with the creation of temporary help companies to meet recruitment needs in California's Silicon Valley and other tight labour markets; establishment of various family and work advisory services; and the formation of cross-company consortia.

172

But he would like to see much more experimentation in new forms of self-governance in workplaces.

Kochan's clarion call for action in workplace reform seems unlikely to interest any of this year's crop of US presidential candidates. But it deserves to be listened to and acted upon.

His demand for a national agenda on employment issues seems unlikely to meet with any favourable response. But it should. The breakdown between the world of work and the institutions and policies designed to provide employment with rules is not something that can be allowed to continue without adverse social and political consequences.

A recent elegantly written book by Professor David Marsden at the London School of Economics provides further evidence of the need for the closing of that perceived gap between work and how it is organised. He points out that, despite the hyperbole about the flexible labour market, as many as nine out of every 10 workers in the advanced industrialised world are still employed directly by companies under a relationship that gives them the right to determine the tasks their employees should undertake within specified but certain limitations.

However, those limits are vital for the durability of the open-ended and relatively stable employment relationship that remains the workplace norm despite the often-proclaimed arrival of the flexible labour market with its temporary, short-term and contract employees. The scope for what Marsden terms the 'opportunism' of employees in their relationship with their employers is considerable. The economic nature of the employment exchange and the costs of job changing for employees as well as replacement of workers with the required skills make 'the conditions for opportunism ripe'.

This might be expected to ensure chronic instability but in practice flexible limitations are provided to management's authority over work assignments and to employee obligations over performance that ensure the employment relationship can work for mutual benefit.

The existence of 'horizontal coordination' between companies over skill development and job design helps to underpin the relationship. Prof Marsden points to 'occupational communities' such as inter-firm chambers of commerce in Germany, UK professional associations and industrial districts in the US. It is also evident that the more one-sided the relationship, the greater reliance on legal regulation and stricter enforcement of task-centred rules, but this inhibits the flexibility required for workplace modernisation.

Prof Kochan's paper can be found at: http://mitsloan.mit.edu/iwer *A Theory of Employment Systems* by David Marsden, Oxford University Press.

*Source: Financial Times, 3 February 2000.*

---

1 Carefully consider what might be implied by the 'adverse social and political consequences' that Kochan warns us of in employment relations characterised by an absence of rules and regulations. What role can human resource planners play in the consolidation of a 'social contract' between capital and labour?

2 The boundaries of companies are growing increasingly uncertain and blurred, so Kochan seems to be telling us. What do you think Kochan means by this, and in what ways might we extend his analysis?

3 How might we interpret those 'community bodies that facilitate employment mobility' through the frame of reference provided by Foucault and his understanding of power?

---

## REFERENCES AND FURTHER READING

Those texts marked with an asterisk are particularly recommended for further reading.

Armstrong, M. (1979) *Case Studies in Personnel Management.* London: Kogan Page.

Armstrong, M. (1992) *Human Resource Management: Strategy and Action* London: Kogan Page.

Armstrong, P. (1995) 'Accountancy and HRM', in Storey, J. (ed.) *Human Resource Management: A Critical Text.* London: Routledge.

Armstrong, P. (1996) 'Productive and unproductive management', in Smith, C., Knights, D. and Willmott, H. (eds) *White Collar Work*, 2nd edn. Basingstoke: Macmillan.

*Atkinson, J. (1984) 'Manpower strategies for flexible organisations', *Personnel Management*, August, pp. 28–31.

Atkinson, J. (1985) 'Flexibility: planning for an uncertain future', *Manpower Policy and Practice*, Vol. 1, Summer.

Atkinson, J. (1989) 'Four stages of adjustment to the demographic downturn', *Personnel Management*, August, pp. 20–24.

Barker, J. (1993) 'Tightening the iron cage: concertive control in self managing teams', *Administrative Science Quarterly*, Vol. 38, pp. 408–437.

Barker, J. and Tompkins, P. (1994) 'Identification in the self-managing organisation: characteristics of target and

173

tenure', *Human Communications Research*, Vol. 21, No. 2, December.

Barthes, R. (1977) 'From work to text', in S. Heath (ed.) *Image–Music–Text*. London: Fontana.

Bartholomew, D. and Forbes, A. (1979) *Statistical Techniques for Manpower Planning*. Chichester: John Wiley.

Bataille, G. (1957/1987) *Eroticism*. London: Marion Boyars.

Bauman, Z. (1992) *Intimations of Postmodernity* London: Routledge.

*Bennison, M. and Casson, J. (1984) *Manpower Planning*. Maidenhead: McGraw-Hill.

Berman, M. (1982) *All That is Solid Melts into Air*. London: Verso.

*Beynon, H. (1973) *Working for Ford*. London: Allen Lane.

Bowey, A. (1974) *A Guide to Manpower Planning*. London: Macmillan.

*Bramham, J. (1989) *Human Resource Planning*. London: IPM.

*Bramham, J. (1990) *Practical Manpower Planning*. London: IPM.

Brown, W., Marginson, P. and Walsh, J. (1995) 'Management: pay determination and collective bargaining', in Edwards, P. (ed.) *Industrial Relations: Theory and Practice*. Oxford: Blackwell.

Burrell, G. (1997) *Pandemonium: Towards a Retro-Organization Theory*. London: Sage.

Casey, C. (1995) *Work, Self and Society: After Industrialism*. London: Routledge.

Castenada, C. (1971) *A Separate Reality: Further Conversations with Don Juan*. London: Penguin.

Clark, J. (ed.) (1993) *Human Resource Management and Technical Change*. London: Sage.

Clegg, H. (1975) 'Pluralism in industrial relations', *British Journal of Industrial Relations*, Vol. 13.

Clegg, H. (1979) *The Changing System of Industrial Relations in Great Britain*. Oxford: Blackwell.

Clegg, S. (1990) *Modern Organizations: Organization Studies in the Postmodern World*. London: Sage.

Cleverley, G. (1973) *Managers and Magic*. London: Pelican.

Cole, R. (1991) *Personnel Management: Theory and Practice*. London: DP Publications.

Cooper, G. (1998) 'Simulating difference: ethnography and the relations of intellectual production', *British Journal of Sociology*, Vol. 40, No. 1, pp. 20–35.

*Cooper, R. (1993) 'Technologies of representation', in Ahonen, P. (ed.) *Tracing the Semiotic Boundaries of Politics*, Berlin/New York: Mouton de Gruyter.

Cooper, R. and Law, J. (1995) 'Organization: distal and prox-imal views', in S.B. Bacharach (ed.) *Research in the Sociology of Organizations*. Greenwich, Conn. JAI.

Cowling, A. and Walters, M. (1990) 'Manpower planning – where are we today?', *Personnel Review*, Vol. 19, No. 3.

Cressey, P. and Scott, P. (1992) 'Employment, technology and industrial relations in the UK clearing banks: is the honeymoon over?', *New Technology, Work and Employment*, Vol. 7, No. 2, pp. 83–96.

Deal, T. and Kennedy, A. (1982) *Corporate Cultures: The Rites and Rituals of Corporate Life*. New York: Addison Wesley.

Delbridge, R. (1995) 'Surviving JIT: control and resistance in a Japanese transplant', *Journal of Management Studies*, Vol. 32, No. 6, pp. 803–817.

Donovan, Lord (1968) *Report of the Royal Commission on Trade Unions and Employers Associations*. London: HMSO.

*Edwards, P. (1986) *Conflict at Work. A Materialist Analysis of Workplace Relations*. Oxford: Blackwell.

Edwards, P., Hall, M., Hyman, R., Marginson, P., Sisson, K., Waddington, J. and Winchester, D. (1992) 'Great Britain: still muddling through', in Ferner, A. and Hyman, R. (eds) *Industrial Relations in the New Europe*. Oxford: Blackwell.

Eldridge, J., Cressey, P. and MacInnes, J. (1991) *Industrial Sociology and Economic Crisis*. Hemel Hempstead: Harvester Wheatsheaf.

Elger, T. (1990) 'Technical innovation and work reorganisa-tion in British manufacturing in the 1980s: continuity, intensification or transformation?', *Work, Employment and Society*, special issue, pp. 67–101.

Eurostat (1990) *Basic Statistics of the Community*. Luxembourg: Office for Official Publications of the EC.

Fayol, H. (1949) *General and Industrial Administration*. London: Pitman.

*Flanders, A. (1964) *The Fawley Productivity Agreement: A Case Study of Management and Collective Bargaining*. London: Faber & Faber.

Foucault, M. (1971) 'Nietzsche, genealogy, history', in Rainbow, P. (ed.) (1984) *The Foucault Reader*. Harmondsworth: Penguin.

Foucault, M. (1977) *Discipline and Punish*. Harmondsworth: Penguin.

Foucault, M. (1980) *Power/Knowledge* (ed. Colin Gordon). Hemel Hempstead: Harvester Wheatsheaf.

Foucault, M. (1984) *The History of Sexuality*, Vol. 1. Harmondsworth: Penguin.

Fox, A. (1985) *Man Mismanagement*. London: Hutchinson.

Freud, S. (1918/1991) 'The Wolf Man', in *Case Histories 2*, Vol. 9, The Penguin Freud Library. London: Penguin.

*Gabriel, Y. (1995) 'The unmanaged organization: stories, fantasies and subjectivity', *Organization Studies*, Vol. 16, No. 3, pp. 477–501.

Gabriel, Y. (1997) 'Meeting God: when organizational mem-bers come face to face with the supreme leader', *Human Relations*, Vol. 50, No. 4, pp. 315–342.

Game, A. and Metcalfe, A. (1996) *Passionate Sociology*. London: Sage.

Game, A. and Pringle, A. (1983) *Gender at Work*. Sydney: George Allen & Unwin.

Garrahan, P. and Stewart, P. (1992) *The Nissan Enigma: Flexibility and Work in a Local Economy*. London: Mansell.

Garsten, C. and Grey, C. (1997) 'How to become oneself: discourses of subjectivity in post bureaucratic organiza-tions'. *Organization*, Vol. 4, No. 2, pp. 211–228.

Giddens (1976) *New Rules for Sociological Method*. London: Hutchinson.

Golding, W. (1954) *Lord of the Flies*. London: Faber & Faber.

Grey, C. (1994) 'Career as a project of self and labour process discipline', *Sociology*, Vol. 28, No. 2, pp. 479–497.

174

Guest, D. (1989) 'Personnel and HRM: can you tell the difference?', *Personnel Managment*, January, pp. 48–51.

Guest, D. (1990) 'Human resource management and the American dream', *Journal of Management Studies*, Vol. 27, No. 4, pp. 377–397.

Guest, D. (1991) 'Personnel management: the end of orthodoxy?', *British Journal of Industrial Relations*, Vol. 29, No. 5, pp. 149–177.

Hakim, C. (1990) 'Core and periphery in employers' workforce strategies: evidence from the 1987 ELUS survey', *Work, Employment and Society*, Vol. 4, No. 2, pp. 157–88.

Hall, M. (1992) 'Behind the European Works Councils directive: the Commission's legislative strategy', *British Journal of Industrial Relations*, Vol. 30, No. 4, pp. 547–566.

Hall, M. (1994) 'Industrial relations and the social dimension', in Hyman, R. and Femer, A. (eds) *New Frontiers in European Industrial Relations*. Oxford: Blackwell.

Hall, S. and Jacques. M. (1983) *The Politics of Thatcherism* London: Lawrence and Wishart.

*Handy, C. (1989) *The Age of Unreason*. London: Business Books.

Handy, C. (1994) *The Empty Raincoat*. London: Hutchinson.

Harvey, D. (1989) *The Condition of Postmodernity*. Oxford: Blackwell.

Hassard, J. and Parker, M. (eds) (1994) *Postmodernism and Organisations*. London: Sage.

Hatch, M.J. (1997) *Organization Theory: Modem Symbolic and Postmodern Perspectives*. Oxford: Oxford University Press.

Hill, J.M.M. and Trist, E.L. (1953) 'A consideration of industrial accidents as a means of withdrawal from the work situation, *Human Relations*, 6, November.

Hill, J.M.M. and Trist, E.L. (1955) 'Changes in accidents and other absences with length of service', *Human Relations*, 8, May.

Hoskin, K. (1995) 'The viewing self and the world we view: beyond the perspectival illusion', *Organization*, Vol. 2, No. 1, pp. 141–162.

Hyman, R. (1975) *Industrial Relations: A Marxist Introduction*. London: Macmillan.

Hyman, R. (1978) 'Pluralism, procedural consensus and collective bargaining', *British Journal of Industrial Relations*, Vol. 16, No. 1, March.

Hyman, R. (1987) 'Strategy or structure? Capital, labour and control', *Work, Employment and Society*, Vol. 1, No. 1, pp. 25–55.

*Inayatullah, S. (1990) 'Deconstructing and reconstructing the future: predictive, cultural and critical epistemologies', *Futures*, Vol. 22, No. 2.

Industrial Relations Services (1995a) 'Customer service drive at BT', *Employment Trends*, 579, March.

Industrial Relations Services (1995b) 'New directions at Royal Mail', *Employee Development Bulletin* , 67, July.

Industrial Relations Services (1996) *Employment Trends* 604, March.

Institute for Employment Research (1995/6) *Review of the Economy and Employment: Occupational Studies*. University of Warwick.

Institute of Personnel Management (1975) *Manpower Planning in Practice*. London: IPM.

IRDAC (1990) [Industrial Research and Development Advisory Committee of the Commission of the European Communities] *Skill Shortages in Europe*. Luxembourg: Office for Official Publications of the European Communities.

Jackall, R. (1988) *Moral Mazes: The World of Corporate Managers*. New York: Oxford University Press.

Kallinikos, J. (1995) 'Mapping the intellectual terrain of management education', in French, R. and Grey, C. (eds) *Rethinking Management Education*. London: Sage.

Kanter, R.M. (1984) *The Change Masters*. London: Allen & Unwin.

Keep, E, (1989) 'Corporate training strategies: the vital component?', in Storey, J. (ed.) *New Perspectives on Human Resource Management*. London: Routledge.

Keep, E. (1994) 'The transition from school to work', in Sisson, K. (ed.) *Personnel Management in Britain*, 2nd edn. Oxford: Blackwell.

Keep, E. and Rainbird, H. (1995) 'Training', in Edwards, P. (ed.) *Industrial Relations: Theory and Practice*. Oxford: Blackwell.

Kondo, D. (1990) *Crafting Selves: Power, Gender and Discourses of Identity in a Japanese Workplace*. Chicago and London: University of Chicago Press.

Lasch, C. (1978) *The Culture of Narcissism*. New York: Warner Books.

*Lash, S. and Urry, J. (1994) *Economies of Signs and Space*. London: Sage.

Legge, K. (1995) *Human Resource Management: Rhetorics and Realities*. Basingstoke: Macmillan.

Linstead, S. and Banerjee, B. (1999) 'Organizational dreaming: modes of being: modes of knowing, and modes of organizing', paper presented to *Critical Management Studies Conference*, Manchester School of Management, 14–16 July 1999. 1st Annual International Conference in Critical Management Studies, Helm Hall, Machester, UK.

Lyotard, J. F. (1984) *The Postmodern Condition: A Report on Knowledge*. Manchester: Manchester University Press.

Mackay, L. and Torrington, D. (1986) *The Changing Nature of Personnel Management*. London: IPM.

Manpower Services Commission (1987) *People: The Key to Success*. London: NEDO.

Marcuse, H. (1964) *One Dimensional Man*. London: Routledge & Kegan Paul.

Marginson, P., Edwards, P.K., Martin, R., Purcell, J. and Sisson, K. (1988) *Beyond the Workplace: The Management of Industrial Relations in Large Enterprises*. Oxford: Blackwell.

McBeath, G. (1978) *Manpower Planning and Control*. London: Business Books.

Morgan, G. (1986) *Images of Organization*. London: Sage.

O'Doherty, D. (1992) 'Banking on part-time labour' *Occasional Paper*, Leicester Business School, De Montfort University.

O'Doherty, D. (1993) 'Strategic conceptions, consent and contradictions: banking on part-time labour?,'paper presented to the *Organisation and Control of the Labour Process, 11th Annual Conference*, Blackpool.

O'Doherty, D. (1994) 'Institutional withdrawal? Anxiety and conflict in the emerging banking labour process, or "How to

175

get out of it'", paper presented to *12th Annual International Labour Process Conference*, Aston University, Birmingham.

O'Doherty, D. (1996) 'Deflation and disappointment: the collapse of self and the failure of HRM in the banking industry', M*imeo, Department of HRM*, De Montfort University, Leicester.

O'Doherty, D. and Roberts, I. (2000) 'Career or slide: managing on the threshold of sense', in Collin, A. and Young, R. (eds) *The Future of Career*. Cambridge: Cambridge University Press.

*Organization* (1999) Thematic issue on organization as science fiction, Vol. 6, No. 4.

Peters, T. (1993) *Necessary Disorganisation in the Nano-second Nineties*. London: Macmillan.

Peters, T. (1994) *The Tom Peters Seminar: Crazy Times Call for Crazy Organizations*. London: Macmillan.

Peters, T. J. and Waterman, R. H. (1982) *In Search of Excellence: Lessons from America's Best Run Companies*. New York: Harper & Row.

Pollert, A. (1988) 'The flexible firm: fixation or fact?', *Work, Employment and Society*, Vol. 2, No. 3, pp. 281–316.

Pollert, A. (ed.) (1992) *Farewell to Flexibility?* Oxford: Blackwell.

Pringle, A. (1990) *Secretaries Talk: Sexuality, Power and Work*. London: Verso.

Quinn-Mills, D. (1985) 'Planning with people in mind', *Harvard Business Review*, July–August.

Rajan, A. (1993) *1990s: Where the New Jobs Will Be*. Centre for Research in Employment and Technology in Europe. CREATE, Tunbridge Wells.

Rose, N. (1990) *Governing the Soul: The Shaping of the Private Self*. London: Routledge.

Rowntree, I.A. and Stewart, P.A. (1976) 'Estimating manpower needs II: statistical methods', in Smith, A.R. (ed.) *Manpower Planning in the Civil Service*, London. HMSO.

Roy, D. (1958) 'Banana time: job satisfaction and informal interaction', *Human Organisation*, Vol. 18, No. 1, pp. 158–161.

Salaman, G. (1992) *Human Resource Strategies*. London: Sage.

Sewell, G. and Wilkinson, B. (1992) '"Someone to watch over me": surveillance, discipline and the just-in-time labour process', *Sociology*, Vol. 26, No. 2, pp. 271–289.

Sievers, B. (1994) *Work, Death and Life Itself. Essays on Management and Organization*. Berlin: De Gruyter.

Simon. H. (1957) *Models of Man*. New York: Wiley.

Sisson, K. and Marginson, P. (1995) 'Management: systems, structures and strategy', in Edwards, P. (ed.) *Industrial Relations: Theory and Practice in Britain*. Oxford: Blackwell, pp. 89–122.

Smith, A.R. (1971) 'The nature of corporate manpower planning', *Personnel Review*, Vol. 1, Autumn.

Smith, A.R. (ed.) (1976) *Manpower Planning in the Civil Service*. London: HMSO.

Starkey, K. and Barratt, C. (1994) 'The emergence of flexible networks in the UK television industry', *British Journal of Management*, Vol. 5, No. 4.

Storey, J. (1987) 'Developments in human resource management: an Interim report'. Warwick Papers in Industrial

Relations, No. 17. Coventry: Industrial Relations Research Unit.

Storey, J. (ed.) (1989) *New Perspectives on Human Resource Management*. London: Routledge.

Storey, J. (ed.) (1992) *Developments in the Management of HRM*. Oxford: Blackwell.

Storey, J. (ed.) (1995) *Human Resource Management: A Critical Text*. London: Routledge.

Storey, J. and Bacon, N. (1993) 'Individualism and collectivism: into the 1990s', paper presented to the *East Midlands Work, Employment and Society Seminar*, Leicester.

Taussig. M. (1993) *Mimesis and Alterity: A Particular History of the Senses*. London: Routledge.

Thrift, N. (1999) 'The place of complexity', *Theory, Culture and Society*, Vol. 16, No. 3, pp. 31–69.

*Timperley, S. and Sisson, K. (1989) 'From manpower planning to human resource planning', in Sisson, K. (ed.) *Personnel Management in Britain*. Oxford: Blackwell.

Tomkins, P.K. and Cheney, G. (1985) 'Communication and unobtrusive control in contemporary organization', in McPhee, R.D. and Tompkins, P.K. (eds) *Organizational Communication: Traditional Themes and New Directions*. Beverley Hills, Cal.: Sage.

Torrington, D. and Hall, L. (1989) *Personnel Management: A New Approach*. Hemel Hempstead: Prentice Hall.

Torrington, D. and Hall, L. (1995) *Personnel Management: HRM in Practice*. London: Prentice Hall.

Townley, B. (1994) *Reframing Human Resource Management: Power, Ethics and the Subject at Work*. London: Sage.

Turnbull, P. (1992) 'Dock strikes and the demise of the "occupational culture"', *Sociological Review*, Vol. 40, No. 2, May, pp. 294–318.

Turnbull, P. and Sapsford, D. (1991) 'Why did Devlin fail? Casualism and conflict on the docks', *British Journal of Industrial Relations*, Vol. 29, pp. 237–57.

Turnbull, P. and Sapsford, D. (1992) 'A sea of discontent: the tides of organised and "unorganised" conflict on the docks', *Sociology*, Vol. 26, No. 2, May, pp. 291–309.

Turnbull, P., Woolfson, C. and Kelly, J. (1992) *Dock Strike: Conflict and Restructuring in Britain's Ports*. Aldershot: Avebury/Gower.

Tyson, S. and Fell, A. (1986) *Evaluating the Personnel Function*. London: Hutchinson.

Tyson and York (1989) *Personnel Management*. London: Heinemann.

Urwick, L. (1947) *The Elements of Industrial Administration*. London: Pitman.

Valdez, S. (1997) *An Introduction to Global Financial Markets*, 2nd edn. Basingstoke: Macmillan Business.

Weber, M. (1948) *From Max Weber: Essays in Sociology*. London: Routledge & Kegan Paul.

Weber, M. (1964) *The Theory of Social and Economic Organization*. New York: Free Press.

*Willmott, H. (1993) 'Strength is ignorance; slavery is freedom: managing culture in modern organizations', *Journal of Management Studies*, Vol. 30, No. 4, pp. 515–552.

Wood, S. (ed.) (1989) *The Transformation of Work? Skill, Flexibility and the Labour Process*. London: Allen & Unwin.

176

# Job design: signs, symbols and re-signations

*Damian O'Doherty*

## OBJECTIVES

- To outline and detail the traditional, but still widely influential, 'Taylorist' form of job design and work organisation. An appreciation of Frederick Taylor and his management principles will prove indispensable for those human resource managers employed or seeking to understand the nature of work and the opportunities there may be for job redesign in the growing service sectors of the economy: the hotel, catering, retail, tourism and leisure industries.

- To consider the expectations and impact of Taylorism on the modern work organisation. By 'expectations' we mean the explicit and latent managerialist assumptions that inform the work of Taylor and his followers.

- To facilitate an understanding of the motivation and contribution of the human relations of work approach to the design of jobs and the organisation of work. This is often thought to come after Taylorism as an enlightened reaction to the degradation of jobs entailed in the adoption of scientific management.

- To explore the idea that we are undergoing an epochal shift in management and work organisation, a shift that many claim is slowly eliminating the prevalence of Taylorist forms of job design and the relevance of human relations style thinking. HRM is often considered to be a part of these wide-ranging changes, variously thought of in terms of the flexible work organisation, the post-bureaucratic firm, a post-Fordist regime of accumulation, and a postmodern social and cultural milieu.

- To critically evaluate the meaning and scope of the concept 'job design'. This will help us to develop a more sophisticated understanding of job design, one that understands it in terms of a politics of struggle and contest rather than the simple linear-rational outcome of managerial initiative.

- To explore the ideas and practices associated with teamworking, post-bureaucratic design, and business process re-engineering. We need to connect an understanding of these developments with the confusion and anxiety experienced by employees subject to these practices. If we are to appreciate the complex forces and dynamics in organisation that shape job design, we shall be obliged to examine the nature of 'agency' in the employment relation.

- To locate human resource management and the HR manager *within* the context of these wider socio-political forces. In this analytical move we begin to explore the conditions of possibility and constraint that encompass attempts to design and redesign jobs.

177

## INTRODUCTION

*Is it worth the aggravation*
*To find yourself a job when there's nothing worth working for*
*It's a crazy situation*
*But all I need are cigarettes and alcohol*

Noel Gallagher, 1994; Creation Records

Strange things are afoot in the field of job design. Making us slip. Kalashnikov rifles, murder, the Bacchic rites, Kevin Spacey, senility, and dandruff. Increasingly, practitioners are realising the limitations of the traditional prescriptive personnel management syllabus in allowing for a sophisticated understanding of the question of job design, an approach that in the main assumes that the design of jobs is the product of management initiative. Indeed, the very assumption that jobs can be 'de-signed' seems problematic today. This chapter explores these limitations. On one level it is exercised by the question of power and the complexity of social processes in organisation. On another, it begins to skirt deeper questions of rationality and meaning that permeate the subject of job design and the *writing on* the subject of job design. Job design is an inherently political subject. This is, then, the subject *of the subject* of job design. Many forget this. Or, perhaps it is more correct to say they wish to *repress* these difficult aspects of the subject. Let me explain.

Job design makes for hard reading. Now, I don't mean 'hard' in the sense that personnel managers will find contemporary developments in the understanding and practice of job design intellectually difficult or impenetrable. Far from it. Yet there are some of us who are worried that the technical training of traditional personnel managers has been or still is limited by the orthodox and provincial – limited by assumptions of modernity, science and rationality; assumptions that may no longer hold in contemporary work organisation. Consider recent developments in higher and management education as an exacerbation of these trends: financial poverty, student debts, working overnight in garages while attending university by day, modularity, semesterisation, accreditation, instrumental attitudes, broken classrooms, teachers moving from one class to the next without pause or breath. Remember, they no longer come out of their jobs feeling enriched – just knackered. Then think of the difference between education and training. A manager once said that he would rather employ a graduate of 'classics' than an MBA graduate, because at least the scholar of classics has been educated to *think* (Grey and Mitev, 1995). Is this not perhaps a little unfair?

So what is happening to the syllabus of personnel or human resource management? Is it more interesting than a rehearsal of how to recruit, how to select, how to train, how to develop, how to downsize, how to administer wages, the importance of fresh flowers in the restrooms? STRATEGY, STRATEGY, STRATEGY! declares the clarion call. We are probably now familiar with the mantras and litanies of the contemporary managerial sales pitch. Yet this is the syllabus that you probably will still be studying. However, HRM is spreading in weird and wonderful ways. Beware. Do you find it interesting? Is it relevant to you? Do you want a job? Are you in any position to tell? What would you rather be doing? Perhaps you have debts to pay off. You might want a mortgage and a more reliable car to shuttle you between your work and the mortgage. Casey (1995) reports that many managerial and white-collar employees employed at Hephaestus work 60–80 hour weeks, many priding themselves on being in seven days a week. Watson (1994) observes how managers would leave their offices for the night only to leave the lights on and their jackets slung over the back of their chairs so that colleagues leaving work would think

178

that they were still in the office working. This is the discipline of a panoptic society, hidden cameras, saturated news reportage, remote monitoring, live CAM broadcasts, smart technology, artificial intelligence, databases that automatically record information, interactive television, silent surveillance, the 'interview society' (Silverman, 1993), voyeurism and street 'security' cameras. The truth is out there . . . as many will have it.

Yet many come to tolerate and even to like this state of affairs. Even more accept it as an unnoticed background condition of everyday mundane life. We *want* to work longer hours – to develop, improve ourselves, move on, be a success, 'be more desirable' as a recent Open University advert proclaimed; 'fitter happier more productive comfortable not drinking too much regular exercise at the gym (three days a week) getting on better with your associate employee contemporaries', as Thom Yorke (1997), of Radiohead, sings. How does it happen that many of us end up working such long hours? Presumably, in reading this, you will be saying, 'This sounds a bit extreme'. Paranoia perhaps, existential angst, the indulgent ravings of deviants and outsiders. If so, reflect a little further on the possibility or likelihood of 'healthy' job design. Alongside repetitive strain injury, eye strain, skeletal deformity and tinnitus, employees today complain of dandruff and nervous eye twitches, the result, many argue, of badly designed offices and equipment and the dependence on computers and VDUs. Consider the number of head teachers interviewed on television during the 1980s and 1990s. Can you remember how many of them seemed to have slurred speech, nervous ailments, odd twitches, discoloured bags under their eyes, and bad haircuts? How many of you are saying, 'That'll never happen to me'?

During the 1980s and the ascendancy of Japanese organisations it used to be a common refrain heard in many a classroom that the Japanese live to work, whereas the English work to live. Unfortunately these distinctions between work and life, home and work, and even leisure and work, might be breaking down today. Certainly one doesn't so often hear the complaint these days that the Japanese live to work. Are we becoming then a more competitive and disciplined workforce – one that enjoys work, able to find interest and stimulation in jobs? Or are we becoming more like Coupland's (1991) generation X – bored; disillusioned; staring with an odd mixture of boredom and fascination at the flickering images on our television screens; playing minesweeper and solitaire on our computers at work (when we should be working); considering the possibility of medication (as a lifestyle choice); or filling in an application for *Who Wants to be a Millionaire* while dreaming of illicit sexual liaisons and the television show *Gladiators*? Yet, if you are asking questions of this sort, you have begun to exercise some of the qualities that make the human subject so difficult and intransigent, and the processes of management so troublesome and complex. Indeed, you are beginning to think about the design of your jobs.

Now come on – how many of you are told that work is good for you; that one is obliged to work? The sociologist Max Weber famously talked about the influence of Protestantism and the work ethic (Weber, 1965). Christian Schumacher (1999), similarly, writes today on the possibility of 'finding God' and the realisation of harmonious universal perfection through better job design. So it might seem that not only is work universal and necessary but it has become the means through which we realise individual and collective salvation. But is it true that we have to work? We need to know our history. In Greek times, of course, it was only the slaves who had to labour; the free citizen was at liberty to pursue the finer questions of Platonic philosophy, the contemplation of aesthetics and poetry. More recently, the novelist Douglas Coupland has begun to talk about a 'slacker' generation, a generation 'X' who shun slavery and hard

179

work, opting for low-responsibility jobs that do not interfere too much with their lifestyle pursuits – usually travel, drugs, music, video/television, shopping, and . . . well, more drugs. This has been explored more recently in the popular and Oscar-winning film *American Beauty*, in which the reformed slacker unfortunately gets murdered.

It would seem that questions of life and death surround the subject of job design. Is it possible that there is a relationship between the discharge of a Kalashnikov automatic rifle in a crowded McDonald's and the design of what Ritzer (1993) calls McDonaldized jobs and the Mcdonaldization of society? Open up any traditional introductory text-book on personnel management or human resource management and you won't find this being discussed. Nor will you find much in the way of cyborgs. Yet one of the most important developments in job design is the elimination of the 'human'. They're simply no longer needed. They cost too much. They're lazy. They are subject to inappropriate sexual impulses at work. They need to be fed, and need to sleep for 8 hours a day. Working conditions have changed too. This is not just a product of developments in e-commerce either. Think of the work of astronauts, off-world space engineering, deep sea divers, 'remote' medical operations, the NATO combat soldier, airline pilots, and the virtual worker – an example of which might be 'intelligent' software programs that filter information according to the user's needs and requirements as identified and established by the software program. All these designed jobs integrate the human and the non-human. In another sense it portents another kind of death for the individual human subject. They are beyond the simply human: hybrid jobs, part man, part machine – or, in other words, cyborgs (Featherstone and Burrows, 1995; Gray, 1995). Some now talk about the 'virtual organisation', the 'cyberorganisation', and the 'cyber-corporation', even the 'imaginary' organisation (Hedberg *et al.*, 1994). This goes way beyond a 'reconciliation' of those traditional categories used in the analysis of job design – the social and the technical – and the implications, far more profound.

To help us develop a critical appreciation of these issues, this chapter begins by discussing the influence of Frederick Taylor and the principles of scientific management. We begin by locating our study within the analytical frame of reference provided by labour process study. Moreover, we shall study the contribution of Braverman (1974) and the rise of labour process analysis as a way of understanding the impact and importance of deskilling on the nature of work organisation. One finds here that job design becomes a 'contested terrain', the contingent product of what some call a 'structured antagonism' (Edwards, 1986) between capital and labour. Rather than the determinist outcome of autonomous management initiative, the design of jobs is better thought of then as the precarious and unstable settlement of unequal power relations.

The negative implications associated with the impact of Taylorism prompted the study of human relations at work as a way of thinking about how jobs could be designed that secured some accommodation between the need for efficiency and individual 'needs', interest and motivation. In the main, the work of Mayo, Roethlisberger and Dickson, the UK-based studies emanating from the Tavistock Institute, and the various movements addressing the quality of working life, arose in response to the perceived failures of Taylorism; yet we shall find that these approaches inherit many of its problematic assumptions.

The chapter then moves on to consider the theoretical contributions made by the flexibility debate (Atkinson, 1984; Pollert, 1988), flexible specialisation (Kern and Schumann, 1987; Hirst and Zeitlin, 1991), post-Fordism (Aglietta, 1976); and postmodernism (Jameson, 1991; Smart, 1993) in order to explore the idea that we are undergoing an epochal shift in management and work organisation. For many this is a

180

systemic change that heralds the elimination of Taylorist forms of job design and the redundancy of human relations style thinking in the understanding and practice of job design. These theoretical proposals, however, operate at different analytical levels of abstraction and sophistication. Nevertheless, they all offer useful conceptual apparatus for assessing the development of human resource management and adjudicating the capacity of HRM to design jobs in innovative and novel ways. To extend our understanding of these issues we shall, following our discussion of the post-Fordist worker controversy, briefly read an etymology of 'design'. This allows us to unpack the conceptual assumptions that are built into the managerial understanding and use of job design. As an exercise in critical thinking this will further open up and extend our understanding of the tensions that exist between the nature of 'sign' and 'de-sign'. This adds further layers of complexity and struggle to the structured antagonism between capital and labour, an analytical move that works to further deflate and de-centre 'management' pretensions to rationality and control.

By locating our humble human resource manager *within* the context of these wider socio-political forces we can begin to explore the conditions of possibility and constraint that embrace attempts to design and redesign jobs. Seen as subject to forces over which they have little control or understanding, management and the process of job design begin to appear far less linear, rational and orderly. Even more, HRM may well prove to be part media and outcome of this growing irrationality or post-rational developments in management and organisation. Surrounded by the swarm of these cross-cutting tensions and struggles, the definition of a job – what it is, what it is composed of, where it 'starts' and 'finishes', and how it stitches in with other jobs in organisation – becomes vague and uncertain, stimulating further depths of confusion, struggle and anxiety.

We could extend this chapter by introducing an international dimension to the understanding of job design. For example, the German economy after the Second World War would offer an instructive example of nation state specificity in job design (Lane, 1989). This provides another way of thinking about the contextual location of management and the contingency of job design. We would find that global economic development is mediated by distinctive socio-political institutions and frameworks of governance, which place constraints on the 'freedom' and autonomy of management in the design of jobs. In many ways, Germany provides a useful contrast to the UK economy, illustrating how outcomes at the level of management and organisation can be shaped by wider political values and institutional structure. Given the limitations of this chapter we cannot develop a study of the other European economies other than to note that particular state institutions and legal frameworks in tension with an emergent pan-European series of coordinating regulations and institutions are likely to shape the development of very different patterns of job design. Nor can we, unfortunately, attempt to cover the burgeoning literature on gender, yet this too is of capital importance in any understanding of the thinking and practice of job design, a subject that has been dominated by masculine assumptions portrayed as universal.

## TAYLORISM AND THE DEGRADATION OF LABOUR

Frederick Winslow Taylor (1856–1917) was in many ways the founder of modern rationalised management methods of organising and disciplining work and employees. It was Taylor who systematised the practice of work study, piece-rate schemes, and the use of

181

time and motion studies in his drive towards redesigning jobs. What Taylor attempted to do was to break jobs down into their most basic and elementary components before reassembling them in more scientific and efficient ways. At least, this was the claim for rationality and science made by Taylor. Another way of looking at his work is to see the development of scientific management as part of a systematic attack by capital on the skilled craft traditions of organised labour. We first explore Taylor's life and early ideas before studying the ways in which he sought to secure management control over employment by means of the systematic deconstruction of work tasks. The role of financial reward occupied a central pillar in the system of scientific management, forming a major line of tension and disjunction in the employment relation, a medium through which its organisation was rendered fragile and insecure. Scientific management was to find its limitations attempting to repair and maintain organisation through this medium, generating tensions that prompted the development of 'human relations' study.

## Taylor's life and early ideas

Taylor dropped out of his study of law and, against the wishes of his affluent bourgeois Philadelphia family, took up a job as a manual craft apprentice in a firm whose owners were close friends of his parents. Later, Taylor became a gang boss in a lathe department at the Midvale steel works, one of the most technologically advanced companies in the steel industry. In his youth, Taylor apparently displayed odd behavioural quirks, counting his steps, calculating his time in performing various duties and tasks, and studying his bodily motions while doing basic domestic chores (Kakar, 1970). This obsessive and compulsive type of behaviour was explained, by some, as an early example of Taylor's desire to cut down and minimise waste and inefficiency. Even at this early stage in his life he seemed to be searching for the one best way to carry out tasks that would eliminate excessive bodily movements and reduce mental and physical effort.

While employed at the Midvale steel works he became preoccupied with what he called 'natural' and 'systematic' soldiering. The practice of soldiering was the result of what Taylor assumed to be the natural tendency and desire of workers to take it easy, to control the speed and effort with which they performed their jobs, and to work no harder than was absolutely necessary. 'Systematic' soldiering was for Taylor far more inefficient and pernicious because this type of soldiering was controlled, regulated and supported by informal social groups of employees. A body of 'rules' and norms, supported by the close social networks and relationships on the shopfloor, acted to regulate the speed and output with which employees were 'allowed' to perform their jobs. As a worker, Taylor claimed he never once broke the agreed norms on work restrictions, but once he became responsible for output and productivity in his capacity as 'gang boss', he was determined to reorganise and maximise production. In his own words, Taylor claims:

> As soon as I became gang boss the men who were working under me and who, of course, knew that I was onto the whole game of soldiering or deliberately restricting output, came to me at once and said, 'Now Fred, you are not going to be a damn piecework hog, are you?' I said, 'If you fellows mean you are afraid I am going to try to get a larger output from these lathes,' I said, 'Yes; I do propose to get a larger output from these lathes'. (Taylor, 1912; quoted in Clawson, 1980: 212)

For Taylor, the strength of the workers lay in the fact that it was they who had far more knowledge and understanding of jobs. How tasks were performed, the tools that were used, and the precise way and speed with which jobs were done, lay primarily in

182

the experience and the 'mysteries' of the 'craft' embodied in the work of the employees. We need to remember that the legacy of craft control was 'imported' into the early factories at the beginning of modern industry and the emergence of 'mass manufactures'. Under the craft system of production it was the workers themselves who organised the way work was to be done. Often this would extend to the management and control of recruitment and selection, training, development, and discipline – functions that were later colonised by management and appropriated within the terms of reference of the emerging specialist practice of personnel management. In many ways, what we have here is an example of semi-autonomous self-organisation. Jobs were designed and organised on the shopfloor by the employees themselves. Workers would deliberately keep management ignorant of the speeds that could potentially be achieved in the machine rooms and, as Taylor insisted, this was perfectly rational because of course as soon as management discovered the maximum potential speed of work tasks they would insist upon speed-ups and greater 'efficiency'. Systematic and natural soldiering are better thought of as rational attempts by workers to control the labour process, to control the speed and effort that they had to put into their jobs.

## The management prerogative and the deconstruction of work tasks

Taylor emphasised the importance of acquiring and monopolising the knowledge of work tasks so as to grant management better control and improve its capacity to discipline employees. Management were told they had to impose themselves on the shopfloor, to get down into the actual material work process in order to observe, measure and calculate how tasks were done and how jobs could actually and potentially be improved through better design and coordination. Taylor embarked on a series of 'scientific studies' of shopfloor practice with the intention of redesigning jobs in ways that recovered all knowledge and expertise – and hence control – in the hands of management. Jobs were broken down and fragmented into their most basic components. This resulted in the extreme division of labour. It was held, following Adam Smith and Charles Babbage, that by breaking down tasks into their most elemental structures, workers would become more efficient and productive in performing one routinised and repetitive task. If discretion and decisions could be entirely eliminated from workers – so that all they had to concentrate on was the maximisation of output through the repetitive exertion of physical effort – then productivity and efficiency in the factory would increase.

The writings of Adam Smith had previously argued that as a consequence of greater familiarity with work tasks workers would become progressively quicker and more efficient in the execution of those work tasks. If jobs could be made far more rudimentary, and broken down further through a detailed division of labour, then workers could more easily master the movements and motions necessary to perform work. As a result of carrying out one simple repetitive task over and over again, manual dexterity would increase and workers became far quicker in a far shorter period of time. According to Charles Babbage this had the additional advantage that it would reduce costs so that previously skilled labour could be replaced by unskilled labour. As jobs became fragmented there would be no need to employ and pay skilled workers as these newly designed jobs could be performed by unskilled labour.

This extreme fragmentation and division of tasks created a series of mundane and repetitive jobs. Instead of employing one person to do a 'whole job', a number of employees would now be required to work on highly specialised, routinised and simplified jobs.

183

**The Management of Human Resources**
**149**

Furthermore, the design and knowledge of tasks were secured by management so that they could far better control the labour process. As Clawson (1980) observes, as long as workers knew more than managers about how to do the work, 'management would have to find a way to get workers' voluntary cooperation' (p. 214). It was this 'voluntary' cooperation that provided the point of insecurity and uncertainty in organisation and the management of employment relations, a zone of indeterminacy that modern management science claims to be able to eliminate.

This led Taylor to entirely revise the design of machine and hand tools. In his book *On the Art of Cutting Metals* he devised an entirely new set of standardised tool sizes and shapes to which, he insisted, all tools should comply. Taylor bestowed upon these tools obscure titles, symbols, and names, so that only he and his management colleagues would understand what tools were going to be used and allocated to specific jobs. As a consequence, far more detailed instruction cards and job details needed to be written and transferred from management to the shopfloor. In designing new symbols and titles it would be far quicker for management to write down and record which tools were to be used on which jobs. Equally it meant that workers were unable to challenge the instructions on the job card until the very last moment, by which time it would be too late to resist or organise protest about the way that management wanted the job to be done. For example, what had previously been known as a horizontal miller No. 7 would have been retitled as a 7MH. Far more obscure symbols were used in an attempt by Taylor to appropriate and control the knowledge of how tasks were to be performed. This effectively meant replacing the knowledge that workers had previously held in the labour process with managerial knowledge. Hence management was trying to learn what the workers themselves already knew: how precisely work was done.

A major consequence of the system that Taylor was trying to introduce, a system he later proselytised through lecture programmes, was a concomitant increase in the number of managerial and administrative staff. Taylor insisted that the conception of work, and the way work was to be organised and performed, should be placed in the hands of a planning department. It was the responsibility of the planning department to devise the 'one best way' of carrying out jobs. This divorce between the conception and the execution of tasks left the 'science of work' in the hands and minds of management, leaving only the physical execution of work as the responsibility of manual labourers. This led Taylor to claim that workers were not supposed to challenge managerial instructions on how tasks were to be performed, nor indeed the speeds upon which management insisted. In Taylor's scientific management workers were not 'paid to think' but simply to perform their tasks as prescribed in their instruction cards, written, devised and planned by management. It was management's 'right' to correct or modify the way work was to be done, through the careful calculation and analysis of job record cards, instruction cards etc., and through shopfloor time and motion studies.

## The role of reward under the Taylor system: the 'rate busters'

In order to prove that jobs could be done far quicker, Taylor would often make use of what were known as 'rate busters' in his study of time and motion at work. The story goes that by offering a worker called Schmidt a higher rate to shift what would have been considered an impossible amount of pig iron, Taylor was able to show that effort and productivity could be improved through the combination of financial inducement and the detailed organisation of work by management. Essentially, Schmidt was offered more money to shift a greater amount of pig iron in a given period of time. In addition,

Taylor designed a new shovel with a scoop that was able to lift twice as much pig iron. Of course what was happening was that Taylor was extracting more effort and output than he was paying for – this is what made the system more 'efficient' – but, more importantly, by using Schmidt as an example, he was able to demonstrate that there was nothing natural, inevitable or sacrosanct in the work speeds that had been established by employee norms on the shopfloor. In this example, financial incentives were shown to complement and secure the control and monopoly of information and knowledge that management sought to gather and use in its control of the labour process. In Taylor's own words to Schmidt we read the commitment and importance that Taylor attached to the unilateral managerial design of jobs and the divorce in the conception and execution of work:

> Well, if you are a high-priced man, you will do exactly as this man tells you tomorrow, from morning till night. When he tells you to pick up a pig and walk, you pick it up and you walk, and when he tells you to sit down and rest, you sit down . . . And what's more, no back talk.
>
> (Taylor, quoted in Braverman, 1974: 105)

There are some who suggest that Schmidt later died tragically of a heart attack. One finds the history and contemporary practice of job design littered with similar tragedies and deaths. Taylor took the view that employees did not have the ability or intellect to be able to self-design and organise jobs effectively and efficiently. Therefore it needed to be left to a specialist elite of 'industrial engineers' in managerial planning departments. In the patronising and pretentious tone of Taylor's discussions with Schmidt, we catch a glimpse of this inherent elitism. This elitism seems to be further confirmed when we reflect upon his attempts to excuse his tone, claiming that this is the only kind of language that shopfloor employees are able to understand:

> This seems to be rather rough talk. And indeed it would be if applied to an educated mechanic, or even an intelligent laborer. With a man of the mentally sluggish type of Schmidt it is appropriate and not unkind, since it is effective in fixing his attention on the high wages.
>
> (Taylor, quoted in Braverman, 1974: 105–106)

For a man who was engaged in building his own house it is questionable whether this view of Schmidt, or indeed any manual employee, is justified.

In Taylor's ideal, therefore, workers should be left to perform those simple and routinised jobs for which they were inherently far better suited, leaving all 'possible brain work' in the hands of management. Taylor argued that efficiency and productivity could be guaranteed only if management took control over the design of and responsibility for the performance of jobs. This necessitated collecting all relevant information and knowledge over how jobs were traditionally done, and classifying, tabulating and restructuring work to prescribed rules, laws and formulae. Second, all possible brain work should be removed from the workers and the shopfloor and placed under the responsibility of the planning department. Finally, this knowledge and conception of work should be monopolised by management so that each stage of the production process is designed and controlled exclusively by management, who then simply give detailed instructions to workers. All pre-planning and pre-calculation is done by management at least one day in advance of its execution, so that all conception is removed from the imagination of the employee. In this way, according to Braverman (1974):

> Dehumanisation of the labour process, in which workers are reduced almost to the level of labour in its animal form, while purposeless and unthinkable in the case of the self-organised and self-motivated social labour of a community of producers, becomes critical for the management of purchased labour.
>
> (p. 113)

185

We have seen that scientific management seeks to redesign jobs in ways that reduce the exercise of initiative and discretion among shopfloor employees. It is perhaps a first attempt to design jobs that eliminate the human, and inaugurates a history that we find is strewn with corpses and bodily deformity – something Adam Smith (1982) was well aware of in *The Wealth of Nations*. We have also seen that financial reward provides the linchpin of the system. The work of Braverman allows us to extend and deepen our understanding of these developments in job design, exposing many of the tensions and antagonisms unleashed and exacerbated by this system, tensions that require considerable management attention and vigilance.

## Braverman and the labour process

For Braverman (1974), the scientific management principles of Frederick Taylor and his attempts to simplify and fragment jobs expressed the essence of capitalist management and rationality. Braverman argues that Taylorism remains the dominant form of management and job design to which all industries and indeed all forms of organisation – whether in extraction, production, service or distribution – would eventually conform. In locating job design and the work of Taylor within the conceptual frame of the labour process, Braverman illuminates the inherently political nature of 'scientific' management, showing that its science is not neutral but developed and specifically applied for the purposes of greater capitalist efficiency, profitability, and the subordination of labour. The labour process understands the employment relation in terms of its mediation of contradictory and antagonistic pressures, forces that pit capital against labour. Labour sells a capacity to work, but not a fixed quantity. In competition with other units of capital, the inherently malleable nature of this 'capacity' provides management with a means of pursuing competitive advantage. Job design, then, becomes a tool in this managerial pursuit. Deskilling work is a way of cheapening labour, of reducing labour costs while maintaining or increasing output. This means that labour and capital are at some loggerheads with 'interests' that are likely to diverge.

In a manner reminiscent of Weber's ideal type concept and his conception of the inevitability of bureaucratisation, Braverman posited a similar 'trend' towards deskilling and degradation in the design and control of jobs. The central concern for management was the necessity to maintain control and discipline in the labour process, and Taylor theoretically and practically showed how he thought this could be achieved. In this assumption Braverman has been criticised and amended, both for his mechanical-like determinism, and for what has been called his 'over-structuralist' reading of Marx, from where he draws his inspiration and main theoretical assumptions (Storey, 1983; Thompson, 1989; Knights and Willmott, 1990). In brief, an 'over-structuralist' approach tends to ascribe too much machine-like determinism to the system of capitalist production, where it seems that individual and collective subjects have no scope to change or shape the logic of industrial development.

It will not be necessary in this chapter to rehearse the entire theoretical and empirical amendments, corrections and modifications that have been made to Braverman, primarily through the auspices of the annual international labour process conference and its attendant series of papers, articles and books. However, the influence and take-up of Taylor's ideas have been important in the development of assumptions that understand management as a science, and its impact on job design has been profound.

According to the work of Craig Littler (1982) and Littler and Salaman (1984), however, Taylorism was never as popular as Braverman has suggested. In its purest form it is

186

difficult to find examples of the practice and successful application of concerted Taylorist deskilling and 'dehumanisation' of work tasks. In contrast to the USA, for example, Taylorism was far less popular in the UK and Japan. The existence of a stronger and more entrenched craft tradition in the UK and the paternalistic approach of many large-scale capital owners in the early twentieth century go some way to explaining the slow spread and unpopularity of Taylorism. In Japan the cultural traditions of teamwork and group fraternalism have acted both to resist Taylorist-style job design and to promote more participative and multi-skilled job design.

> Japanese factories depended on a tradition of work teams incorporating managerial functions and maintenance functions, with few staff specialists. There was a lack of job boundaries and continued job flexibility, unlike the prescriptions of Taylorism.　(Littler and Salaman, 1984)

This debate has been stimulated in part by the work of Andrew Friedman (1977, 1990), who has constructed an alternative approach to Braverman. Friedman questions the importance and centrality of deskilling and direct control. As Friedman argues, management itself is not primarily concerned with control, but with the profitability of business. If profit can be maintained or even enhanced through the continuation of skilled discretionary work then there will be little necessity or compulsion for management to seek to enhance control through deskilling and routinisation. Friedman goes on to develop a model that posits a continuum of job design and control structures. At one end of the pole we have direct control, deskilling, and low-trust employee relations; at the other we have high-skilled jobs based on flexibility and high-trust relations. Management is therefore assumed to have a choice, rather than the assumption made by Braverman, which sees management as inert pawns of an inevitable and predictable model of deskilling. The only historical role for management in the Braverman schema is to interpret correctly their role, which would anyway be difficult to interpret incorrectly because their job would ultimately depend on their ability to deskill and manage routinisation.

Friedman's work is important because it demonstrates both the *strategic choice* that management has and the constraints that partially 'guide' managerial practice. Direct control of the Taylorist type would be difficult to introduce in a situation where workers were currently highly skilled and discretionary. In these situations it would be better for management to seek a strategy of 'responsible autonomy', as the 'more complex and sophisticated the worker's knowledge and experience, the more difficult normally for management to prescribe tasks in detail and to monitor closely their performance' (Hyman, 1987: 39).

Management in these situations would be better advised to seek to manage and maintain a working relationship based on *trust,* where workers are not subject to intense direct control through detailed instructions, simplification and routinisation. Resistance is clearly going to be a problem if management looks to deskill workers who have previously been used to and socialised into high-discretion employment. Direct control is possible on work groups that are less central to the production process: those workers whom Friedman and others have called 'peripheral workers'. This form of labour can be more ruthlessly managed because they can be more easily replaced, and the insecurity associated with this form of employment does not bode well for collective organisation and resistance. Where this is the case management is likely to face less resistance in its attempts to impose deskilled low-trust work relationships. In the peripheral labour force, management may be able to pursue output maximisation and high volume intensity through repetitive and deskilled work tasks associated with the assembly line of car production (see also Fox, 1974).

187

| Stop and think | 1 How might the job of a BBC news presenter be 'Taylorised'? |
| | 2 To what extent is this a realistic form of job design? |
| | 3 How would Braverman have argued that the Taylorisation of the news media was inevitable? |
| | 4 Do you think this is 'inevitable'? If not, why not? |

## Summary

There is a considerable amount of evidence that suggests that Taylorism was not adopted in its pure form. Where it was adopted, it was renegotiated, contested and modified by craft and work group resistance. Moreover, we have seen that there has been some awareness of the deleterious effects on individuals and their jobs, which has continued to promote academic and managerial interest in alternative forms of job design. Some of these developments have gone beyond simply seeking alternatives to deskilling to advance broader critiques of the assumed rationality of Taylorism as a system of management control and utilisation of labour. For example, if all work is inevitably deskilled then everyone becomes a routinised and dehumanised worker, simply acting as an adjunct to a vast technological automaton. In this situation workers are homogenised, and so there arises the risk that a collective consciousness and a collective sense of power will emerge as workers realise their common interest in the resistance of forces that seek to reduce them to non-thinking degraded functionaries. In what sense could Taylorism be considered 'rational' if its consequences lead, paradoxically, to its own demise? In disregarding these outcomes of Taylorism, Braverman is perhaps a little guilty himself of accepting and inadvertently confirming the 'scientific' status of Taylor's management principles. Braverman assumes an immense amount of knowledge, foresight and cunning in those he assumes are able to design and implement such production systems. Yet he does not recognise the possibility, and indeed arguably the logical conclusion, of resistance and conflict to this attempted appropriation and monopolisation of knowledge and discretion. Nevertheless, a strength of Braverman's work is that his labour process perspective opens up the question of job design to issues of power and control – that is, the inherently *politicised* nature of the subject.

In what follows we trace the emergence of the 'human relations' study of work, which builds upon a critique of what is called *alienation* at work. One of the central criticisms made in response to Taylorism is that it is inhumane. Through the process of deskilling, Taylorism generates work that is not stimulating or challenging. Some argue that this is more a feature of a capitalist system than something that more rational 'management science' can address, and that deskilling remains the major tendency in mature capitalist economies (Thompson, 1989; Warhurst and Thompson, 1998). However, if we understand the negative consequences of Taylorism by means of the concept of *anomie* instead of alienation, there may be room within the constraints of competition and capitalist accumulation for management to develop methods of working that suspend and divert resistance and the paradox of systemic collapse.

# ALIENATION AND WORK

## Blauner's thesis

The concept of alienation is often drawn upon in any discussion of Taylor. To suffer from alienation is to experience an *estrangement* from what is assumed to be one's own natural physical, mental and/or intellectual essence. It is argued that human beings have an inherent need to express and control their surroundings so that they may experience fulfilment and development. Where this 'need' is suppressed or prevented from being expressed, it is suggested, individuals will suffer from alienation. More fundamentally, alienation is also associated with the idea that while individuals and their society produce economic goods collectively, the proceeds of production are appropriated privately. It is worth remembering that it is a relatively peculiar social situation that leaves individuals with nothing to sell but their own labour, the result of the usurpation of common land and the expropriation of land from the people undertaken in the UK from the late fifteenth century. Now, while the first definition of alienation provides some hope that more effective management can ameliorate some of the worst excesses of modern job design, in the latter, more enduring social-historical forces and power inequalities render alienation inevitable and systemic. Here, management in itself can do little to remove alienating work from the employment relation through better job design.

Robert Blauner (1964) is more concerned with the impact of Taylorist-style technology and work organisation on the attitudes and orientation of employees than with a historical analysis of power, property relations, and alienation. Blauner sought to analyse the worker's 'relationship' to the technological organisation of work in order to determine

> whether or not he [sic] characteristically experiences in that work, a sense of control rather than domination, a sense of meaningful purpose rather than futility, a sense of social connection rather than isolation, and a sense of spontaneous involvement and self expression rather than detachment and discontent.
>
> (Blauner, 1964: vii).

To suffer from a sense of powerlessness, according to Blauner, is where an individual experiences a lack of control over the pace and method of work. For example, assembly line work in which the machine sets the pace of work allows for little control and involvement of the employee. There is very little autonomy granted to the individual employee in this work situation, as generally the quality of work, the techniques of work and the time allowed to perform it are dictated by the machine. Hence there is a sense of powerlessness because there is no subjective input by the employee. Instead the employee becomes simply an object, controlled and manipulated by what seems to be an impersonal and alien system. In performing highly specialised and simplified tasks employees may also experience a sense of meaninglessness because they have no conception of the end product. In situations where there is an extreme division of labour, with employees performing repetitive work cycles, the scope and size of the individual's contribution to the end product is small. It may not be a car that the individual is producing, even though they may be considered a car worker. For the individual concerned it may simply be screwing and tightening three bolts to a gearbox in an engine. Such fractionalised jobs may result in the situation where individuals achieve no sense of purpose or satisfaction from their tasks:

189

Tendencies towards meaninglessness therefore stem from the nature of modern manufacturing, which is based on standardised production and a division of labour that reduces the size of the worker's contribution to the final product.

(Blauner, 1964: 22)

Blauner also suggested that self-estrangement arises because the worker becomes 'removed from themselves'. By this Blauner means that the extreme division of labour, in which tasks are broken down into their most simplified components, provides work that is somehow unnatural for human beings. Whereas independent craftworkers would actually manufacture and produce an entire product, a table or a chair for example, in modern industry a worker may continually and repeatedly put headlights on the front of a car, or cheese slices on a burger. This provides work that is repetitive and incessant in its regularity. It is work that allows for no variety in pace, method, location, or discretion. Hence, quoting Marx, Blauner (1964) writes that the employee: 'In his work . . . does not affirm himself, does not feel content but unhappy, does not develop freely his physical and mental energy but mortifies his body and ruins his mind' (p. 27).

Although this concept of alienation has its roots in a Marxist critique of capitalism, it can be seen to enter the work of the human relations school of job design. It does this through the slightly different but related concept of *anomie*, as first developed and applied by Emile Durkheim (1984) at the end of the nineteenth century. Anomie is that state of moral confusion and purposelessness consequent upon the extreme fragmentation of roles and tasks in contemporary society. An exclusive emphasis on individualism, encouraged by the routinisation and fragmentation of tasks in Taylor's system, would, in the absence of the strong guiding principles, norms and values associated with *social regulation*, inevitably lead to the breakdown of the social fabric. This arises because as more and more individuals begin performing highly individuated tasks, in isolation and distance from other individuals, problems of social solidarity emerge. Individuals no longer feel a part of societal community. For the individual, cut off from interaction and social relationships, the maintenance of community values will be at risk as work tasks become increasingly meaningless. The Kalashnikov in the restaurant becomes a possibility!

Blauner draws on both anomie and alienation in his critique of monotony and the assembly line production system. Despite some weaknesses in his approach – his technological determinism and over-optimistic projection of the possibilities of future technology – his work provides an interesting and stimulating account of the problems and 'injustices' associated with Taylorism and the one best way of production of scientific management. Via the concept of anomie, management is directed towards the recovery and reconstruction of strong binding, collective meaning and norms. We begin to see here the foundations of cultural management and the importance of 'strong' cultures (Deal and Kennedy, 1982).

## Elton Mayo's thesis

The human relations school of management, of which Elton Mayo is probably the best-known exponent and theorist, sought to attend to these anomic consequences of large-scale production and organisation. Mayo drew attention to the social needs of individuals. It is argued in this tradition that individual employees need a sense of social worth and satisfaction, which can only be developed if work is provided that allows for social interaction and communication. Furthermore, for Mayo, managers need to express a concern and interest in employees' personal problems, and to emphasise the importance of each individual for the organisation. Management needs to integrate the various elements of the organisation through the re-creation of those values and norms

190

lost as a consequence of modern industry and Taylorism. A sense of community and 'belongingness' needs to be created and fostered by managerial intervention designed to increase communication and participation (see Chapter 13), together with a greater understanding of those variables that motivate and demotivate individuals, instead of a reliance upon the cash nexus and the economic incentives detailed by Taylor. Hence Mayo emphasised the need for Durkheimian-style 'moral communities'. As Watson (1987) writes, Mayo teaches that it is only with 'the integration of the individual into the [management-led] plant community' that 'systemic integration be maintained and the potential pathologies of the industrial society avoided' (p. 40).

Within the field of the human relations approach to job design there have been repeated attempts to recreate 'social man' (Schein, 1965). If read through the frame of reference provided by Durkheim and his concept of anomie, human relations thinking ignores the underlying economic and historical forces of alienation to concentrate on those variables at work that management can influence through things such as job design. The idea that employees were 'social' beings as much as they were economic actors was uncovered through a series of studies of human relations in work organisations. One of the most important of these was the Hawthorne studies.

## Hawthorne studies: the informal work group

The Hawthorne studies in the mid-1920s appeared to show that informal work groups and associations were significant variables in explaining productivity and output performance. The Hawthorne studies were conducted in the Hawthorne plant of the United States Western Electrical Company, where 29 000 employees produced telephone equipment for the Bell system. Changing environmental variables such as the amount of lighting did not seem to have any consistent effects on the productivity of the work groups. Indeed, productivity would increase despite the contradictory changes in the degree of lighting and the number of rest pauses. This led the study to conclude that the work group was responding to the very act of being studied and analysed. Hence the result that paying attention and showing interest in work groups would itself lead to productivity increases: the Hawthorne effect.

In the later studies of the 'bank wiring room' the consultants and academics discovered, like Taylor, that work groups would systematically control and restrict output in order to maintain what they considered to be a fair day's work for a fair day's pay. Workers appeared to be responding to what in management's eyes were irrational sentiments such as 'fairness' and the 'right to work'. The recognition that informal groups, norms and attitudes could inhibit the efficient production and output of the enterprise led the leading authors of the study, Roethlisberger and Dickson (1939), to conclude that the best approach for management should not be to try and undermine and force the informal organisation to conform to the formal organisation. Rather, it was patently obvious that informal organisations would likely re-emerge and appear as a natural consequence of employees' needs for social solidarity, community and group association. The informal work groups in effect were substituting for the lack of social interaction and communication experienced in highly fragmented, individuated and specialised work tasks. Management were advised to attempt to engineer and channel sentiments and attitudes that prevailed in the informal work organisation. Through controlled participation, effective means and channels of communication, and socially skilled enlightened supervision, management could harness the strength and solidarity of the informal work groups to the productive needs of the 'formal organisation'.

191

**Stop and think**

1 How might an individual be alienated in their workplace yet not suffer from the condition of anomie?

2 How far did the Hawthorne studies demonstrate that management could only 'condition' the work *experience* of employees rather than materially re-design the employees' jobs?

## The work of the Tavistock Institute

These studies led to a number of further programmes and initiatives designed to release and tap into the assumption that individuals had an inherent need for creativity and social interaction. In Britain the Tavistock Institute for Human Relations contributed a number of important studies into the productivity of work organisations. They found that in the coal-mining industry, for example, productivity fell after the introduction of mechanised technology. The formal and elaborate division of labour that this entailed reduced the amount of social interaction, teamwork, discretion and 'responsible autonomy' to which miners had become accustomed (Trist and Bamforth, 1951). Tavistock researchers were firmly committed to an approach that emphasised the importance of providing individuals with the satisfaction of completing a whole task, of being able to control their own activities, and of organising work tasks so that individuals can develop satisfactory social relationships (Trist *et al.*, 1963). In their conclusion to the study of the coal-mining industry in the late 1940s and early 1950s, Eric Trist and his colleagues emphasised that the technical reorganisation of work needs to pay careful attention to the social aspects of work and the features of social organisation that exist within work groups. The tendency for managers and industrial engineers to introduce the most technically efficient system of production would result only in a low productive response from employees.

These studies have been influential in the development of ideas in job design such as job enlargement, job enrichment, teamworking, and semi-autonomous work groups. Job enlargement basically means that more tasks are added to the one that an individual employee is currently doing to add a variety in task, pace and location. Job enrichment, by contrast, attempts to add responsibility and discretion to an individual's job so that not only do they experience a variety of tasks but they are also provided with an opportunity for development and realisation of 'self-actualising needs' (Maslow, 1954). Teamworking and semi-autonomous work groups (SAWGs) attempt to restore the opportunity for social interaction and communication. These schemes usually include measures that allow teams to establish their own patterns and routines of working, electing their own leaders, organising their own rest periods, and scheduling their own workloads. The recent collapse of the SAWGs at the Volvo plant in Kalmar highlights a significant problem with these schemes, notably productivity. Indeed, criticism has been made of the tokenistic nature of many of these schemes, and in one famous quote an employee claims that this simply means that:

'You move from one boring, dirty, monotonous job to another boring, dirty, monotonous job, and somehow you're supposed to come out of it all "enriched". But I never feel "enriched" – I just feel knackered.'
(quoted in Nichols, 1980: 279)

Yet we need to ask how robust some of these assumptions are in the work of the human relations school of job redesign. We move on in the following section to examine issues concerned with the 'socialisation' of employees – in other words to examine

192

the conditions that might lead employees to accept and even welcome dirty, boring monotonous jobs. We find that, in many cases, employees adopt an 'instrumental' orientation to work, which means that they do not look to work for anything other than a wage, which then allows them to pursue gratification, meaning and fulfilment in areas outside the employment relation. We are beginning to enquire into what is called the *subjectivity* of employees – that is, the 'internal' existential and psychological processes common to the human subject – in our pursuit of an understanding of job design.

# SOCIALISATION AND ORIENTATIONS TO WORK

A common assumption made by theorists and consultants working in the field of job redesign, and especially the quality of working life movement, is the inherent or essential needs that individuals possess for creative employment. Buchanan (1989), for example, in his work on job design has stressed the debilitating effects of Taylorist-style work regimes and the stultifying impact on the physical, emotional and psychological well-being of individuals:

> people have higher levels of ability and higher expectations of working life . . . they have a physiological need for sensory stimulation, for changes in the patterns of information that feed to the senses to sustain arousal.
>
> (p. 80)

Similarly Michael Cross (1990) in his uncritical and prescriptive 'advice' to management suggests that, because of an inherent need for creativity and self-fulfilment, jobs need to be designed that test the initiative and ability of individuals so that they 'seek to provide meaningful jobs which build upon and stretch people's abilities so that they can realise their potential' (p. 29).

This essentialism has been the subject of a sustained critique by radical social psychologists (Knights and Willmott, 1989; Knights, 1990; Willmott, 1990), and indeed we can look back to studies of plant sociology for examples where frustration and dissatisfaction have not arisen from the experience interpreted by some as the hallmark of conditions fostering the alienation of human nature.

## Car workers

In their influential study of the Vauxhall car workers in Luton, Goldthorpe *et al.* (1968) discovered that, despite the machine-like Taylorist monotony of the work process, employees were neither militant nor sought to resist or renegotiate the content of jobs. The jobs themselves were the very ones that many in the school of human relations were arguing would lead to dissatisfaction and unrest because they denied the essential creativity and the self-actualising needs of human beings. Goldthorpe *et al.* found that certain groups of workers were not getting any intrinsic satisfaction from their work but equally were not prepared or inclined to do anything about it. This paradox was partly explained by what was identified as the employees' instrumental attitudes to work. This new class of affluent manual worker was prepared to labour on monotonous and intrinsically unrewarding work because they viewed employment as simply a means to pay for private housing, cars and other new consumer items proliferating during the 1960s. As the authors conclude, 'It is by no means those groups whose work-tasks and roles appeared least rewarding whose members had thought most often or most seriously about leaving' (p. 25). Furthermore, consumption and not production appeared as an equally important variable in employees' orientation to work:

193

> Workers within all groups in our sample tend to be particularly motivated to increase their power as consumers and their domestic standard of living, rather than their satisfaction as producers and the degree of their self-fulfilment in work.
>
> (Goldthorpe *et al.*, 1968: 38)

Studies such as these might suggest that deskilled jobs are not inherently frustrating or meaningless for employees. It prompts one to ask the question whether or not work necessarily has to be a source of fulfilment and meaning. Perhaps this is simply a modern bourgeois assumption. More than this, the Luton car workers study might suggest that organisation retains stability despite alienating conditions of work. In the work of Burawoy we are also offered ways of thinking how organisation is maintained and reproduced even where jobs are designed in traditional deskilled ways. The focus of Burawoy's work is, however, on the interaction of collective work groups with the existential forces that preoccupy individual subjects.

## The work of Burawoy

Theoretical and empirical studies have shown that a deskilling-resistance/frustration model is far too simple, and does not adequately explain adaptation and habituation to routine and monotony. Michael Burawoy (1979, 1985), drawing on the pioneering work of Donald Roy and Tom Lupton, has developed empirical work that demonstrates that workers adapt to what may be perceived as intolerable low-discretion roles through ritualised engagement in *game playing*. The resistance that many theorists had predicted would emerge from a Taylorist-style work regime needs to be countered, according to Burawoy, by an equal tendency by management–worker relations to generate or 'manufacture consent'.

In the study of the Allied Corporation, Burawoy (1979) describes how workers would both ease the routinised nature of Taylorist-style job design and actively create time and space for themselves within the working day. Through a game of *'making out'*, workers would gain a relative amount of satisfaction from low-discretion deskilled work by manipulating output levels through the banking or 'gold-bricking' of finished goods. In this way, quotas could be more easily achieved by workers while generating a sense of control in when and how fast they worked. In essence there were two types of job on the shopfloor: jobs where it was difficult to achieve quota levels, and 'gravy jobs' where it was relatively easy to reach quota. In order to 'make out', workers needed to manipulate work schedules, cajoling and bargaining with other workers whose cooperation was essential for success in the game of making out. Close working and social relations needed to be fostered with the scheduling man, the crib attendant, the truck driver bringing stock to the workstation, and also the set-up man.

Informally the work groups studied by Burawoy also maintained a restriction on output of 140%. It was believed that if you were able to produce in excess of this, then management would reduce the rate for the job, as it would become apparent to management that the job was a 'gravy job'. Workers would therefore hoard work in excess of 140% in a 'kitty' and keep the work for times when they were employed on difficult jobs, therefore creating margins of time and space for themselves in the future. Also, workers would 'chisel', which meant that time would be redistributed so that workers could maximise the time they spent on the 'gravy jobs', where they could turn out work in excess of 100%.

As Burawoy comments, on first entering the shop individual employees may have perceived the game as being banal and 'mindless', but after a while this aloofness tended to recede as all employees became caught up and preoccupied with the game of 'making

194

out'. Individuals would be evaluated by their peers and work group colleagues on their ability to make out, so that, as Burawoy writes, 'Each worker sooner or later is sucked into this distinctive set of activities' (Burawoy, 1979: 64).

This study of informal work groups and the restrictions and games in which they engage has long fascinated sociologists. At first sight it appears paradoxical. The game of 'making out' relieves the boredom of work, neutralises any discontent felt towards the job or towards management who were putatively 'responsible' for its design, and hence perpetuates the conditions for its ultimate survival. Employees appear to generate consent to the work process through this game of making out, ensuring profitability and the competitiveness of the organisation. For the employee:

> The rewards of making out are defined in terms of factors *immediately* related to the labour process – reduction of fatigue, passing time, relieving boredom, and so on – and factors that emerge from the labour process – the social and psychological rewards of making out on a tough job.
> (Burawoy, 1979: 64)

For the employer, production and output targets are maintained, and even, according to Burawoy, guaranteed, while deflecting concern over job content and work design. Conflict gets dispersed laterally to colleagues on whom individual employees are dependent in order to make out. Obstructive behaviour by other workers is likely to frustrate the ability to make out, and so potentially conflictual relations emerge among employees. The role of the foreman is seen as crucial in this respect, as it is he who 'referees' the game. Foremen can facilitate the game of making out by relaxing formal rules on health and safety – for example, running on the shopfloor may be overlooked – or they can obstruct the game by ensuring a strict adherence to formal rules and procedures. Hence conflict is dispersed down the organisation and laterally across the organisation, so that when 'the labour process is organised into some form of game involving the active participation of both management and worker, the interests of both are concretely coordinated' (Burawoy, 1979: 85).

## Subjectivity and identity

The work of Burawoy has been outlined in some detail because it has reworked many classic assumptions in labour process and industrial sociology theory. From Braverman's work on deskilling it is easy to assume that workers would have no interest in the perpetuation of deskilled Taylorist-style jobs. The conditions are restrictive, the discipline is harsh, and the jobs are of little interest and variety. However, from the work of Goldthorpe *et al.* we can see that workers may adapt and habituate to deskilled work for a variety of seemingly rational reasons. Second, this body of work challenges the school of human relations in their assumption that jobs need to be provided that offer a variety of pace, skill and initiative in order to counter the danger of alienation. We might be prompted to ask: What is the essential self of human beings? According to some readings of Marx it may be assumed that the self-actualising and developmental needs of individuals cannot be met in a production system continually forced to seek cheaper and more productive ways of carrying out labour. This implies that individuals will always feel estranged from themselves and hence likely to resist. However, the adaptive and acquiescent behaviour of employees that Burawoy and others have charted can be explained by reference to the dynamic existential nature of individuals (Fromm, 1991). Instead of employees confronting an intolerable situation, they tend to adapt themselves to external circumstances, creating something new in their

195

'nature'. Given time, what might have appeared an impossible and degrading situation becomes familiar and is soon made second nature. Employees' identity – that sense of 'who' they are, what it means to be 'me', for example – is open and dynamic. Yet this can be an anxious experience. We therefore find ourselves compelled to seek some secure identity, to define ourselves as 'this' or 'that'. Over time we can even become attached to very boring routines because they offer a semblance of security and familiarity. We know what we have to do and what is expected of us in these routines; in fact we know who we 'are'.

In terms of personal identity this might mean that individuals may feel 'threatened' by a change in routine or habit. As Willmott (1990) suggests, although Marx stated that employees come to the factory simply expecting a 'tanning', they may actually come to experience the tanning as quite tolerable or even desirable. It is quite possible that individuals come to accept and enjoy the habits and security afforded by deskilled work: hence 'the extent to which such opportunities are valued for the sense of security associated with a confirmation of the social identity of self' (Willmott, 1990: 363). In Camus's *The Outsider* the character of Salamano and his 'ugly brute' of a dog demonstrate this attachment to routinised work and relationships. Twice a day for eight years the two were seen dragging and fighting with each other during a monotonous regular walk. Salamano would beat and drag his dirty dog round the walk; 'Then they'd halt on the pavement, the pair of them, and glare at each other; the dog with terror and the man with hatred in his eyes' (Camus, 1961: 35). As soon as the dog runs away, though, Salamano is distraught and 'lost', declaring the dog to be a fine breed with a wonderful coat, and would not consider a replacement as, 'reasonably enough, he pointed out that he'd become used to this one, and it wouldn't be the same thing' (p. 51).

Work by Collinson and Knights (1986) shows how female employees in the life insurance industry come to internalise, resign themselves, and ultimately accept their jobs and the lack of promotion opportunities. What at first sight might appear intolerable, prompting overt expressions of resistance, is then made tolerable as the individual comes to 'adapt' to employment situations. Conflict and frustration gets channelled and redefined through the medium of identity, which might then find expression in anxiety, neurosis, or conservative inhibition. Organisation is made stable not so much by the design of jobs, as by existential processes that habituate employees to their work conditions. In Collinson and Knights (1986) a sense of security and the pursuit of a secure social identity prevents the female clerical support staff from challenging the restrictive and monotonous nature of their jobs. Sales and clerical workers internalise the assumptions that are used to justify gender segregation, and hence it can be seen that individuals accommodate to routine and restriction:

> In the context of highly subordinated, poorly paid positions which provide few opportunities to 'advance', indifference, as a defensive mode of managing to retain a measure of dignity in the face of its erosion, is all pervasive within contemporary work situations.
>
> (p. 161; see also Cohen and Taylor, 1992)

Confirmation of one's self and one's own identity provides a degree of certainty and security that can tend to provoke conservative tendencies in our behaviour and assumptions. Collinson and Knights (1986) observe these processes in the character 'Lyn', who, despite initial resistance to sex typing and segregation, ultimately acquiesced to others' (read men, managers) definition and view of her and her 'essential' female nature. In response to her lack of promotion she claims:

> 'Being female, you see, I'd have to be that bit older.'    (quoted in Collinson and Knights, 1986: 163)

196

We have been reviewing here a number of studies that challenge the idea that organisation is made vulnerable by Taylorist forms of job design. At first we have noted that Braverman's labour process framework adumbrates the political nature of job design. We then questioned the extent to which deskilling was as systematically determinist as Braverman argued. The work of the human relations school of job design both sought to address the negative consequences of scientific management and stood as some testimony to the argument that deskilling was an inevitable outcome of management and modern industry. In the latter part of this section we have begun to introduce ideas that open up the human subject in ways that help us to understand how organisation is maintained and reproduced even where overt deskilling and the degradation of work are evident. The politics of job design extends then to the question of subjectivity and identity. This prompts us to ask a series of questions: What is it that makes us what we are? What are the routines through which I might get ensnared? What is this work that I do? Is it what I want? What are the possibilities for change and personal growth offered in the job that I am currently doing? Do I want to be employed making weapons of mass destruction? Might I need to reach for my Kalashnikov?

## HUMAN RELATIONS REVISITED: CHANGE PROGRAMMES AND JOB DESIGN

In recent years there has been a marked revival in thinking that emphasises the possibility not only of reconciling individual and organisational goals but of creating the conditions for an existential and spiritual fulfilment that transcends the divisions between the employee and his or her work organisation. Job redesign programmes developed through human resource management, at least on the level of rhetoric (Legge, 1995), seek to empower and devolve responsibility to individuals. Yet there is considerable diversity and ambiguity in practice and rhetoric. For some companies, empowerment, paradoxically, is something that is given to employees, a product of top-down engineering; others, perhaps more radically, withdraw centralised bureaucratic rules and procedures far more extensively, leaving employees to 'pick up the pieces', redesigning their jobs in collaboration with colleagues.

Yet we find that many of the human relations and humanisation programmes adopted by contemporary management, employ simplistic assumptions with respect to change and development. Not only is it assumed that there is a *need* to provide 'stimulating' and rewarding jobs to counter frustration and resistance to 'dehumanised' Taylorist-style assembly line work, but that change is a rational process, one that can be introduced relatively easily through cause–effect-style thinking and planning. So, with sufficient managerial sensitivity and communication, it is assumed that consent and commitment to managerially designed change can be fostered and secured.

In order to come to terms more effectively with organisational change and management intervention in job design, we shall need to address the politics of organisation. Moreover we shall need to rethink habitual understandings of 'change'. Change is far better thought of as non-rational and non-linear; often unplanned and chaotic, change programmes discharge a whole series of untold and unintended consequences. At times this threatens the very fabric of organisation. The fabric of organisation is being stretched in all kinds of ways. Since the demise of 'Taylor', organisations are becoming 'unstitched'. In organisations today, bereft of institutional or bureaucratic anchor, it might be thought that de-sign is being replaced by a dehiscence of signs – contradictory, uncertain, floating, and ambiguous – manifest in the explosion of management

197

discourse and the whole plethora of buzzwords, fads and fashions. This is disorganisation, not organisation. More often than not what we are faced with today is not de-sign but re-signations. Like Kevin Spacey in the film *American Beauty*, there are many employees today quitting their jobs in search of something more meaningful. At one stage in the study of job design it was popular to ask the rhetorical question: 'If you won the lottery would you still do the same job?' Perhaps today a better question might be: 'If you didn't have a mortgage to pay would you still be in the job you are doing now?'

## The prescriptive advice on change and job redesign

Prescriptive advice on change programmes (Cross, 1990; James, 1992) increasingly emphasises the need to gain employee commitment to the goals of the organisation through the creation of *common values*, beliefs and assumptions. The development of a unitary organisational culture is seen by many today as the sine qua non of successful economic performance. According to Cross (1990), it is essential that the process of job redesign moves logically though a series of well-defined stages, 'moving through the various stages of gaining commitment to change' (p. 29). However, to introduce this change it is assumed that only management can recognise what employees need. Moreover, it is often assumed that the fear of change can be overcome by reassurance and involvement. Yet, as we have seen, routines, habit and innate conservatism may run a lot deeper than just the surface-conscious fear of change. More problematic still are the assumptions of the prescriptive approach. Equally problematic is the understanding that management somehow has a monopoly on what the organisation 'is', what its values and assumptions are, and where it 'needs to go'.

Cross (1990) suggests that a dynamic culture can be introduced through managerially led education and 'normative re-education' (p. 11). Despite the somewhat Orwellian nature of this statement, Cross makes the mistake to which many prescriptive management job design manuals seem to fall prey. This can be summarised as the uncritical acceptance of that kind of humanistic-psychological theory associated with the work of Abraham Maslow (1943), and the assumption that a 'culture of change' can be successfully manufactured, imposed, and administered by management. This takes a rather simplistic and naive approach to culture, one that neglects the theoretical discipline and complexity of the subjects from which it borrows – anthropology and sociology. Culture cannot simply be imposed. Rather, it develops over time in response to a number of variables, some of which cannot be controlled and 'scientifically measured'. To a large extent, culture is an emergent and unpredictable phenomenon partly 'constrained' by routinised social interaction that gets produced and reproduced over long periods of time (Giddens, 1991; Lynn-Meek, 1992).

This has a complicated theoretical and disciplinary heritage, to which we cannot do justice in this chapter. Yet this complexity is scarcely acknowledged in much of the post-Peters and Waterman management literature on organization and culture change programmes (Schein, 1985). Suffice it to say that culture is not something that can simply be turned on and off at the behest of management in some unitarist manner. Culture is as likely to emerge from a conflict of values and beliefs, 'particularly when we consider organisations where management tends to belong to one social class and workers to another. In such organisations, values, norms and social meanings are constructed by "class structures" and are a constant source for dispute' (Lynn-Meek, 1991: 197). Gender, age, ethnicity, religion and sexuality complicate the divisions and patterns in the cultural fabric of organisation and impart even greater degrees of vitality, conflict, and dispute to the processes of cultural emergence in organisation.

198

## Human resource management and job redesign

The enthusiasm with which HRM has been embraced by many working within the theory and practice of job (re)design is still founded on the prediction and promise that individuals need to be provided with stimulating and 'enriched' jobs, which tap those intellectual and cognitive domains left dormant by the traditions of organisation and management. Not only will individual employees perform far more varied and skilled jobs, but through the resulting quantitative and qualitative performance improvements organisations will become far more competitive. Hence one of the most important components of organisational effectiveness and economic prosperity is the attention and detail paid to the design of work tasks. It is proposed that 'multi-skilled' highly discretionary jobs will influence the critical psychological state of an employee, promoting a sense of meaningfulness, responsibility and value. Once an employee begins to experience a more positive psychological relationship with their job, their manager, the employer and organisation, it is expected that improved performance will follow (Hackman and Lawler, 1971; Hackman and Oldham, 1976).

In contrast to the rather jaded and in many ways discredited quality of working life movement in the 1960s and 1970s, it is argued that job design is back on the agenda as a critical component of organisational performance. This has emerged as a result of qualitative changes in product markets, communications and information technology, and trading conditions (Reich, 1983; Hirschorn, 1984). For many this promises, once again, to end the degradation and dehumanisation associated with the repetitive assembly line of mass production industries. A new utopia of management–worker consensus based on single-status empowered craft-style working practices is predicted within flatter, less hierarchical and autocratic organisational structures (Peters and Waterman, 1982; Deming, 1986). As Buchanan (1992) has claimed, acceptable worker control and autonomy have increased as a result of new environmental pressures, giving 'employees considerably more control over work activities, personal skills and development and career opportunities, and also offer[ing] significant opportunities for improved organisational performance' (p. 138). In contrast to the 'detailed' control of work tasks in the typical Western car factory, the contemporary worker is not only granted increased discretion and 'high trust' (Fox, 1974), but is also actually a functional prerequisite of successful economic performance (Piore and Sabel, 1984; Kern and Schumann, 1987).

Increased discretion and high-trust employment relations are often used as a justification for job redesign, a prerequisite it is claimed of competitiveness and market sustainability. However, the assumption remains that redesign initiatives remain the preserve of interventionist HR management. An assumption of linearity, even in those writers purporting to make a critical and interrogative examination (Buchanan, 1989, 1994) of job design, reduces change to something that HR order and channel into predictable and stable outcomes.

'Management' is seen in a relatively unproblematic manner – a delimited and well-defined 'category' of employee charged with the responsibility for the design, allocation, distribution and organisation of work. Given this assumption it then follows that change is formulated within the confines of this category and then filters down to have its effect downstream in the employment relation of shopfloor workers. The assumption remains that the high trust generated or granted to employees will be reciprocated by individuals. Work groups will now exercise vigilance and self-reflection in the conduct of their work, seeking continuous improvement through 'high performance work systems' (Buchanan, 1994). Subjectivity and the 'agency' status of employees is reduced to a level where it is assumed that they can only *respond* to higher managerial

199

initiatives. Management is the primary change agent: only management has the capacity to intervene, restructuring and redesigning work. If it does this correctly, new structures and order in the organisation of employment can be established, which can then be sustained and reproduced more efficiently by the autonomy vested in high-performance work teams.

What this overlooks is that individual employees are continually negotiating and redesigning their work in continuous interaction and struggle with management and other agents. Not only subordinates but management too is often 'in search of itself', as Watson (1994) writes, wondering what might happen next, how they might respond, what they are 'about', and how to 'carry on' in the performance and accomplishment of their job. In the subtle fabric of work organisation, the precise content and nature of work are being contested and redesigned – day in, day out. It is amorphous, fluid, and unpredictable. It is also partly irrational and uncontrollable. Work has to be interpreted and redefined every day – indeed every hour and minute. For example, what for years might have seemed a reasonable job, researching the subatomic processes of nuclear fission, suddenly becomes unethical in the eyes of the employee, complicit with the military–state–industrial complex and in part responsible for genocide and vast ecological devastation.

In the main, human resource management and job redesign overlook these issues. They tend to maintain faith in the progressive enlightenment of managerial thinking, and shy away from what Corbett (1994) and Burrell (1997) identify as the *underbelly* or *darker side* of organisation. History is examined from the standpoint of today, which confines managerial practice such as Taylorism essentially to an unenlightened past, which is overcome by the undisputed progress assumed in management development. Liberal-Whig-style interpretations such as this see history as a movement from ignorance to enlightenment, where managers learn from the mistakes of the past, enabling them to develop and introduce improved remedies and methods in the organisation and design of work. From the rather crude Taylorism of mass production, management thinking has progressed through the humanisation initiatives of Elton Mayo, the work of the Hawthorne studies and the Tavistock Institute, to contemporary 'radical' and enlightened job design. Contemporary job redesign, it is claimed, seeks a systemic or organisation-wide orientation through just-in-time, cellular organisation forms, and systematic and coherent business process re-engineering (Buchanan, 1994), correcting for the deficiencies of earlier approaches.

Conflict and tension in job-redesign initiatives are seen to stem simply from contingency and irrationality, features of organisation that can be eliminated and restructured by enlightened management. The usual recipe for eliminating such contingency is careful strategic planning, projection and negotiation among all relevant parties. This builds coherence initially through a process of political lobbying by attempting to mobilise sufficient political interest among organisational cliques (Storey, 1992: 118–161). Corbett (1997) offers an interesting essay on the job design implications of advanced manufacturing technology that illustrates how complex and multiple 'spheres of influence' shape the constitution of the 'problem', which is then addressed by solutions negotiated between a host of interested parties. While a narrow engineering-technological frame of reference predominates in the design and introduction of new technology, the 'web of dependency' that exists between the producer, shopfloor user, management development team and board of directors pulls and stretches the implementation process in different directions. In the light of the research carried out by Corbett, together with the important work of the actor-network theorists (Callon, 1986;

200

Latour, 1987), and the subsequent review by Whittington (1993), we can conclude that strategy does not proceed in a linear and rational way but is only ever partially emergent, subject to fragmentation and readjustment, contestation, struggle, spin-off 'sub-strategies', recovery programmes and deviation. If we contextualise HRM as a subject and practice bound up with this complex of political machinations, job redesign becomes more like an element in the will to power of managerial expertise, yet a contested terrain that mediates a whole host of political groups and factions, technical expertise, trade unions, informal shopfloor organisation, and user groups.

The practitioners of contemporary job redesign also tend to assume that technology remains essentially a means of improvement. It can only be successfully introduced and implemented, though, by management. Management will need to give due consideration to the concerns and needs of employees who might expect a degree of discretion, interest, and involvement, but management as a function is retained as the privileged agent of change. In this formulation of change management there is a signal lack of consideration or critical reflection brought to bear on the 'instrumentalism' and 'abstraction' involved in organisation, features of management that reduce and confine rationality to one of perpetuating mastery and objectification (Heidegger, 1977). As a recent commentary in the tradition of such critical theory argues, this epistemological straitjacket works to

> mark and reproduce an attitude whereby society and nature are looked on as if they were things to be made and remade, changed and transformed, corrected, amplified, destroyed, reconstructed, etc. (Kallinikos, 1996: 37–38)

A corollary of this is a certain subjectification and closure in the constitution of the human subject that dims down critical reflection on the alternative futures and possibilities of social relations, organisation, and the human being. A narrow instrumental orientation to control that seeks the subjugation of nature requires an ontology of human beings that represents humans as the centre and measure of all things. A technological order that subjugates, aligns, and coordinates individual and collective subjects restricts enquiry and action to an inexorable egotistical drive for 'instrumental rationality' (Weber, 1964). Human relationships are reduced to impersonal exchanges as technology and organisation concentrate on the means to ends rather than on the ends themselves. In the summary of Marcuse (1964), technology acts to *reify* organisation and social relations whereby 'The world tends to become the stuff of total administration, which absorbs even the administrators' (p. 169), and thus it is only

> in the medium of technology [that] man and nature become fungible objects of organization. The universal effectiveness and productivity of the apparatus under which they are subsumed veil the particular interests that organize the apparatus. (p. 168)

The 'one-dimensional' mindframe of human resource management seeks to suppress questions of power and inequality, and denies the legitimacy of plural contested values. As we have seen in previous chapters, this reflects the unitarist aspirations of HRM, where particular interests are represented as universal and necessary: 'We're here to serve the customer', for example, or 'Profit is the bottom line, the judge and jury'. Part of the legitimacy for these claims to 'universality' and 'necessity' is the connections that are made between job design and the rise of the flexible firm, flexible specialisation, and the post-Fordist economy. At times these arguments have been used to support the argument that the future of job design is one of semi-autonomous skilled craft-workers and the end of Taylorism.

201

# THE FLEXIBLE WORKER CONTROVERSY

## Post-Fordism

An influential current body of theory and writing has sought to demonstrate the breakdown of production systems based on Fordist assembly line methods (Aglietta, 1976; Piore and Sabel, 1984; Boyer, 1988). Each writer shades a nuanced approach to what is causing the breakdown, ranging from the inherent productivity limitations of Taylorism, to theories that emphasise the collapse and saturation of mass markets: that is, where consumers are now demanding individualised 'niche' products that require a more flexible approach to production. Here, workers are required who can exercise sufficient self-responsibility and initiative so as to go 'beyond contract' in the pursuit of skills and knowledge that ensure product innovation and competitiveness. It is argued that workers are required to embody a 'customer focus', developing and redeveloping, continually retraining in order to acquire new skills so that they can contribute to the design and production of goods that respond to the rapidly changing tastes and styles demanded by the product market.

The so-called Fordist system of manufacture was premised upon the systemic consistency between the existence of a mass of consumers demanding mass-produced invariant products. The standard cliché offered during Ford's early car factories was that consumers could have any colour of Model T car they wanted, so long as it was black. Aglietta (1976), in probably the most significant contribution to this debate, suggests three reasons internal to the labour process of Fordism that place constraints on its development as a system (pp. 119–121):

- There exist technical limits to the further fragmentation of assembly line tasks.
- Simply intensifying this process of production will lead to concomitant increases in absenteeism, and deterioration in the quality of the product: for example, in 1913 Henry Ford was to experience a turnover rate of 380%, which continued despite his famous $5 day.
- It becomes increasingly difficult and more 'expensive' to motivate employees: the five dollar day that Ford introduced in response to the above failed to significantly counter labour problems.

This kind of theoretical analysis has been taken up in many accounts within the critical theory of job redesign (Kelly, 1985; Littler, 1985). Kelly (1985), for example, suggests that a breakdown between product markets, labour markets, and the organisation of the labour process was expressed through a *disarticulation* of these various spheres of capital accumulation. The restructuring of organisations in response to global product market reorganisation and the domestic Thatcher-driven recession provided both a need for and the incentive to restructure production systems. This level of analysis is far more subtle and satisfactory than some overly deterministic accounts of job design (Piore and Sabel, 1984; Atkinson and Meager, 1986), integrating political economy, organisation, management and the labour process within its explanation. Management is repositioned and contextualised here, in ways that illuminate the mutual influence and interrelationship that exist between organisation and the wider political economy. The interaction of interfirm relations, product markets, labour markets, the spheres of consumption and production – are all included in these vast abstract theories of post-Fordism, providing a holistic-integrated account of change.

202

Management is therefore made subject to conditions that delimit a framework of constraints and opportunities in the redesign of jobs. This is clearly one of the strengths of these theories. One of the disadvantages is precisely its level of generality and abstraction, operating a degree of abstraction that occludes and precludes the presence of divergence, contingency and contradiction. Operating at a slightly less generalised level of analytical endeavour is the theory of flexible specialisation.

## Flexible specialisation

Piore and Sabel (1984) argue that a new system of flexible specialisation is emerging that demands a return to craft-style multi-skilled work. Flexible specialisation is seen as 'a new form of skilled craft production made easily adaptable by programmable technology to provide specialised goods which can supply an increasingly fragmented and volatile market' (Gilbert *et al.*, 1992). In order to make the best use of this programmable technology, workers are required who can be flexible, moving rapidly from one production set-up to the next, and capable of exercising greater levels of discretion in the monitoring and fine-tune adjustment of the technology. In a relatively early critical response to the promotion of flexible specialisation, Robin Murray (1985) argues that what is actually happening is that new technology is being used to further deskill work rather than reskill jobs. Instead of a return to the craft traditions of manufacturing and production, technology allows work to be outsourced to a host of small workshops, with a small central organising hub acting to coordinate production and exercise the strategic functions of management – in design, product development, marketing and investment.

This is what Murray calls the development of 'Benetton Britain'. So, in what might be thought of as an ideal-typical representation of flexible specialisation, Benetton organizations are assembled just in time, so to speak, combining and drawing upon a vast network of producer workshops. Flexible specialisation is accomplished by the temporary combination of different outsourced suppliers, who are able to provide particular products and styles. As fashion changes, the central coordinating hub drops individual outsourced workshops and draws upon others, reassembling organisation in response to market changes.

Like the Benetton product ranges, more and more products have a short lifespan today. Consider, for example, the pop music industry, where style and bands have a shelf-life approaching little more than three years. We now see a 'Greatest Hits' album hitting the shops after a group has been together in some cases for little more than two years. Moreover, like the Benetton 'organisation', the relationship between the product market and internal labour processes today is almost fully integrated and symbiotic, or de-differentiated, as Lash and Urry (1987) write. Sophisticated 'early warning' information technology connects up the central hub of these Benetton-style organisations with retail outlets, providing almost instantaneous feedback from current tastes and fashions located at the point of sale back to the internal labour process of Benetton. Within less than three days Benetton claim their production can respond to changing tastes and fashions. The design process is central to these production systems, where a high premium is placed on a quick 'turnover' in style and fashion. Companies increasingly compete on the basis of novelty and style, so that what was a fashionable item of clothing last week becomes an unfashionable garment this week. The role of marketing and advertising is obviously crucial in the promotion of this rapid style 'turnover'.

203

From this we can see how one might be led to suggest that the future for job design is based on flexibility and multi-skilling, a process of change driven by market imperative and fostered by intensive marketing and advertising. Alternatively, we might suggest that the future is one of insecurity and temporary employment, where increasing numbers of employees are condemned to work for subcontractors and outsourced suppliers subject to the beck and call of powerful multinational elites, who now have the technological capacity to shift sources of production from one part of the globe to the next (Burawoy, 1985). Either way, it seems the market decides. There is very little opportunity for choice in the development of job design. Management, then, becomes simply a cipher of broader market changes. It either interprets these changes 'correctly' or 'incorrectly': introduces the appropriate forms of job design, or makes mistakes that herald the onset of organisational collapse and insolvency. Perhaps what we are seeing is that management develops and preserves an elite workforce employed in the centre, who perform high-skilled and reskilled jobs, marketing, coordinating organisation, developing products, and exploring investment opportunities in new technology, while a mass of relatively unskilled labour is assembled as and when required. If we explore these subcontractors and suppliers we may find workshops that resemble, in many ways, the kind of deskilled Taylorist assembly lines to which we have become accustomed in our study of job design.

Walton (1985), in an influential account of forms of organisational restructuring that conform to the central tenets and philosophy of HRM, confirms that market necessity is prompting the restructuring, but that this was providing an opportunity to release and harness the frustrated but infinite potential of human labour rather than leading inevitably to deskilled and monotonous job design. Walton argues that workers respond best and most productively when they are not tightly controlled by hierarchical layers of management, and when they are provided with opportunities to move beyond narrowly defined and prescribed jobs. The influence of the early human relations philosophy and studies are clearly apparent here. We see this when Walton argues that workers *should be given* broader responsibilities, which will then harness commitment to the organisation, rather than nurturing conflictual relations at work that spiral into coercion and the adoption of regimes of direct control and harsh discipline. Walton seems to be able to find space in organisations where management is confronted with choice. Here, the market doesn't necessarily dictate outcomes at the level of job design. Moreover, management is using this space so that:

> Jobs are designed to be broader than before, to combine planning and implementation, and to include efforts to upgrade operations, not just to maintain them. Individual responsibilities are expected to change as conditions change, and teams, not individuals, often are the organisational units accountable for performance. With management hierarchies relatively flat and differences in status minimised, control and lateral coordination depend on shared goals.
>
> (Walton, 1985; quoted in Armstrong, 1992: 98)

## The flexible firm

In a series of articles on 'flexibility', however, John Atkinson and his colleagues at the Institute for Manpower Studies have argued that firms are responding to changing external market circumstances by restructuring their internal labour markets in ways similar to our critique of 'Benetton Britain'. Flexibility is achieved by combining functional, numerical, and financial flexibility. Functional flexibility represents attempts by management to develop broad-ranged polyvalent skills among their workforce. This provides organisations with the requisite flexibility to adapt to changing technology and product market fashions and tastes. In the 1980s, companies sought to remove internal rigidities between craft union lines of demarcation where workers combined production with maintenance work. Of course, while this might be considered flexible working, for some it might represent simply an intensification of labour. Yet within this group of employees it is argued that skills and training are extremely important in ensuring the adaptability of organisation. Atkinson describes these employees as the *core group* or the *primary labour market* in work organisations. Promotion, skill development and favourable terms and conditions of employment are the rewards offered to highly valued employees in this category. In contrast the *secondary labour market*, the peripheral group of employees and quasi-employees, is made up of part-time labour, short-term contracts, public subsidy trainees, job-sharing and 'delayed' recruitment. This provides the organisation with numerical flexibility. The peripheral group of employees can be quickly called in and disposed of in response to fluctuations in the product market. They can be seen as 'labour on call', providing a buffer stock of resources enabling the organisation to 'organically' expand and contract (see Chapter 4).

The concept and practice of flexibility has generated much academic and business interest, both favourable and critical. Some have questioned the empirical validity of the studies conducted by the IMS (Pollert, 1988; Marginson, 1989), drawing attention to figures that suggest there was only a small growth in the number of peripheral and core employees during the 1970s and 1980s. Pollert and Marginson also questioned whether UK management could introduce flexibility with the kind of strategic integrity and intent that its advocates suggested. In addition, studies have shown that it was in the management of the public sector, often driven by a political logic, where many of the changes associated with flexibility were introduced, rather than the cutting edge of market competition leading the way. This is an unusual finding in that Atkinson and Meager stressed that flexibility is primarily a radical private sector strategy designed to meet the requirements of changing manufacturing technology and shifting product market patterns. Clearly, the argument that flexible production systems are based on high-quality job design emphasising multi-skilling and functional flexibility is clearly inadequate in terms of both its empirical validity and its explanatory utility. The so-called leading-edge examples of these new production systems, Benetton and the Emilia-Romagna region in northern Italy, would appear to be founded on exploitative subcontract relationships that use the familiar Taylorist methods of low discretion and intensive labour input (Pollert, 1988, 1991; Elger, 1990).

Furthermore, our discussion above should lead us to question the analytical determinism built into some of these accounts in ways similar to those revisions and criticisms made of Braverman's work. Braverman, as was shown, posited only one future and direction for job design, one based on deskilling and intensification. In the accounts of flexible specialisation and multi-skilled craft working proposed by Piore and Sabel and Robin Murray, we are likewise presented with an account that posits unilinearity. Yet here the determinism works in the opposite direction – towards reskilling and empowerment. Common to those accounts premised on analytical determinism is the assumption that in the restructuring of organisations management retains a considerable amount of foresight and ability. Management also tends to be presented as a politically neutral agent, a change agent of organisations that are held together by a common set of integrating norms and values. As Kelly (1985) suggests, any consensus is undoubtedly temporary and fragile. Recession has provided management with both an

205

incentive and the rationale to drive through change in a situation in which individuals are glad just to have a job.

Many writers have attempted to account for the apparent contradiction in recent restructuring initiatives, which appear to be based simultaneously on reskilling and functional flexibility together with peripheralisation, intensification and deskilling (Shaiken *et al.*, 1986; Smith, 1989). This has been coined *neo-Fordism* in contrast to post-Fordism, and reflects a significant theoretical advance in moving away from overly deterministic 'uni-linear' accounts, which stress either deskilling or reskilling (Badham and Mathews, 1989; Lovering, 1990). As Batstone (1984) has argued, the development and form of labour relations outcomes must always be seen as provisional and contested, not simply between management and worker but within political struggles within management itself:

> Strategic change in organisations is accompanied by intra-management bargaining and micro-political struggles that make the outcome of the process of change uncertain and at the very least 'negotiable'. The ambiguities of the strategic process mean that the implications of strategy for labour relations are likewise uncertain, provisional and complex.　　(quoted in Hyman, 1987: 49)

Attempts by management to develop such production systems strategically are based on the simultaneous desire for commitment and consent from labour to work together with the retention of sufficient power within management to adjust the workforce numerically in response to market and technological developments. This contradiction has been usefully explored by Michael Burawoy (1979, 1985), who argues that *management simultaneously seeks to secure and obscure the power relations* in production. Ultimately management is responsible to the interests of capital, and if profitability is threatened management will need the power to preserve capital. The burden of adjustment to external market and technological shocks must fall asymmetrically on the quantitative and qualitative nature of labour. In our discussion of the flexible firm it can be seen that this contradiction has been partially 'managed' in organisations by obtaining numerical flexibility through peripheral labour and commitment and consent from a privileged core of employees.

## Postmodernism, replicants and the end of job design

Like post-Fordism, theories of postmodernism operate at an equally abstract and at times obtuse level of analysis. The diversity of writing collected under the title of post-modernism makes it very difficult to present a brief overview. In general the study of postmodernism has derived from the fields of media and cultural studies, drawing on a range of French theoreticians including Jean Baudrillard, Gilles Deleuze, Michel Foucault, Jacques Derrida, and Paul Virilio. Many argue that postmodernism first came into prominence in the late 1960s and early 1970s through art and architecture, but it wasn't until the 1980s that the study of postmodernism became associated with organisational analysis and management studies. A brief look at some so-called postmodern architecture proves instructive, however, in delineating what postmodernism might have to say about contemporary job design (Venturi *et al.*, 1972; Jencks, 1987; Betsky, 1990). We find that these buildings often seek to problematise the distinction between the real and the fictional, borrowing styles from the past, and mixing genres of historical architectural codes in a disjunctive bricolage-hybridity of style. Consider the building of contemporary shopping centres and the architecture of places like Las Vegas. Irony, quotation, and pastiche run riot in these buildings, where we might find

206

an exterior of 'fake' Greek temple-like pillars housing a three-year-old building, a surface that draws attention to itself as fake displaying its incongruity and artifice. If this marks the avant-garde in construction and design we might expect that contemporary work organisation will begin to follow its lead. It is increasingly being recognised in the field of job design that it is only in the presentation and packaging of ideas where there is anything new. Underneath the surface we find the persistence of Taylorised forms of job design. Yet one of the problems we might encounter in seeking to understand contemporary job design is where those distinctions between the authentic and fake, surface and depth, the real and the fictional, and/or objectivity and subjectivity no longer seem to hold. If we can no longer be sure what constitutes a 'job', or where its boundaries lie, and if the capacity of design is being overwhelmed by the explosion of 'signs' at work, we may be entering a period of postmodern employment where no one has a 'job', in that sense of a designed, delimited, bounded objective entity, and no one is sure any longer whether what they are doing constitutes something new or old, something 'skilled' or 'unskilled'.

There is a deconstructive impulse in the contemporary innovation and application of information and communication technology. Coupled with the growth in artificial intelligence and de-territorialising globalised trans-organisation, we seem to be threatened with a collapse in those spatial and temporal boundaries, borders and coordinates that we have traditionally used to orientate ourselves (Jameson, 1991). In work environments that are fluid and without geography, subject to perpetual construction and reconstruction, strange new evanescent forms seem to appear on the horizon. We are perhaps witness to the growth of 'virtual organisation': part workhouse, part shopping mall, part home, part slaughterhouse, Hybrid man–machine cyborgs (Haraway, 1985), and perhaps even the 'replicants' anticipated by science fiction writer Philip K. Dick, may be replacing the awkward, inefficient and recalcitrant bone–muscle–tissue– spirit that has evolved to take the form of the human body. Nexus 5 replicants, which for the moment remain only inhabitants of the fictitious world of science fiction and the films of Ridley Scott, may perhaps portent the future of contemporary movements in 'job design'.

These replicants are designed to work 'offworld' in basic engineering, maintenance and transportation employment in alien hostile conditions impossible for human subjects. Replicants are designed to perform with all the 'best' features of a human – intelligence, self-reflection, the capacity to learn from mistakes – but without the fallibilities and weaknesses of the human body. Whereas the human body 'naturally' gets tired and requires rest, occasionally questions the meaning and value of the work it is performing, gets hung up on the existential absurdity of it all, and remains subject to the inconvenience of emotional complexity and irrational interference, replicants are designed to work assiduously, efficiently, and without question. Does the future of job design entail the mass redundancy of traditional labouring subjects and their replacement by replicants and cyborgs, or does it perhaps spell the end of the human subject as we know it?

Strange questions to be asking in the context of a chapter on job design, but applications of new technology and organisational restructuring in manufacturing and engineering, and the emergence of the communications and education services, have led to job designs that not only disturb patterns of employment but also threaten the meaning of our categories 'job', 'technology', and 'human'. Contemporary education is not the exclusive preserve of lecturers and tutors who ply their trade in preparing weekly lecture and collective seminar material. Increasingly education takes the form of distant and isolated students surfing and interacting with other students on the

207

Internet, attending cyberspace courses and lectures from around the 'world'. The future student of job design theory and practice may attend a series of Internet workshops at the 'Virtual University' rather than sit in front of the ancient medium of a heavy 500-page textbook: a morning lecture at the University of California, lunch of Wiener schnitzel at a Viennese *Heurigen,* and an afternoon seminar organised by the Moscow Institute of Business Process Re-engineering. This would clearly have job design implications for the job of tutors and lecturers, but does it replace them? One can imagine self-selecting, structure and filtering software that designs courses of study for the student. Software programs may be designed to reflect and respond to academic text and articles, integrating and synthesising work in a field, summarising and even offering logical and 'intellectual' critique and beginning to produce text of its own (Woolgar, 1991). This may result in a situation where job design theory is split by the Warwick IBM 600 software dispute with the IBM 900 LSE program. One can imagine ideological hardware battles that may ultimately threaten Internet peace.

Applications of new computer and information technology are fundamentally redesigning jobs, in many cases blurring the distinction between organisational change and job design. In most academic texts on job design there is a signal lack of critical attention to and detail of the interaction between capital, technology and the complexity of social relations, complexity composed of centrifugal and centripetal forces. Job design, in the main, still tends to be seen in terms of a discrete and linear top-down intervention by representatives of some personnel department, which aims to restructure or transform the boundaries, allocation and distribution of job tasks. Yet deliberate and purposeful activity remains folded and shadowed by the accidental and contingent – what Cooper and Law (1995) call the proximal forces of organising. Management intention then, means what it says, that is 'in tension' – 'a pattern of actions that is distributed throughout such a field and which serves to maintain it or hold it together' (p. 246). Of course, this maintenance does not get reproduced unproblematically, but remains a contingent outcome of multiple and heterogeneous processes. In a remarkable and illuminating study, Yiannis Gabriel (1995) has illustrated one aspect of these processes, namely the marginal terrain he calls the 'unmanaged organization'. In this 'dreamworld', emotions, anxieties and desires find expression in stories, myths and fantasies, which refashion formal or official discourse and rhetoric for pleasure and perhaps simply for the 'kick'.

## CONTEMPORARY JOB DESIGN: AN ETYMOLOGY

Design is derived etymologically from the Latin *designare* and the French *designer.* Reflecting on these terms opens up a rather richer understanding of the complexity latent to the concept design than that typically employed by personnel and human resource managers. In exploring this complexity we actually capture a better sense of the subtle and contradictory nature of job design today, where order and disorder are beginning to emerge as *mutually overlapping forces* present in employment relations.

Design encapsulates a range of understandings. In one sense it implies a 'marking out', or a tracing and denoting. The *Oxford English Dictionary* suggests that design provides for the sense of giving 'something form, an outline and definition'. For example, ideas and material are fashioned and 'de-sign-ated' by a title, a profession or trade. It also implies a deliberate calculation, 'a purpose, an intention, plot, ambition . . . an end in view, a goal'. Yet a rather more circumscribed sense of design has typically been understood and appropriated in the field of personnel management, reducing it simply to one of *purposeful* change and reconstruction in the objective content of jobs. Moreover, it secures a definition and unity for the practice of job design that is unwarranted. As we have seen, job design is a contested medium, a political subject, one that exists in a state of perpetual processual struggle. These limiting assumptions in traditional personnel management are perhaps better seen as an element of this struggle, part of an instrumental agenda pursued in the interests of normalisation and control, but they have cost us considerable versatility and subtlety in our understanding of job design. Let us take another look at the word 'design'.

The word also captures the sense of contemplation – to contemplate or project a plan, to lay a plot. As the Renaissance architect Moxon claimed, 'Tis usual . . . for any person before he begins to erect a building, to have Designs or Draughts drawn upon paper' so that each floor of the building is 'de-lineated' in a flat, geometric, two-dimensional projection. In its *materialisation* we find that the *intention* (in-tension) is marked by a series of 'limits' that are expressed across a multidimensional realm, a realm made up of complex and contradictory pressures, intransigent forces of composition and decomposition that 'work on' the abstract geometric projection. These multidimensional forces can be thought of in terms of 'signs' that de-sign attempts to rationalise and limit, to prescribe and contain. Signs are less conclusive, open to interpretation; they merely suggest, perceive or indicate in some representative form or medium something often beyond rational cognition and the intellect. Signs have to wait to be coded, and are subject to recoding and reinterpretation; as the *Concise Oxford Dictionary* defines it, signs are 'actions or gestures to convey information'. As we shall see, job design never manages to circle and enclose 'signs' with definitional precision, and in fact in many contemporary organisations and workplaces, the boundaries and content of 'jobs' remain ambiguous and subject to various pressures of destabilisation.

It is worth noting that design evokes notions of 'crafty contrivance', where people are said to have cunning designs on others, a plot or intrigue in medieval court society in which political forces are realigned by the ambitions and designs of cliques, cabals and gangs. As the well-worn adage states, 'They who ask relief have one design; and he who gives it another'. Those organisations studied by Robert Jackall (1988) reflect this understanding of design as management coteries plot and design the downfall of other management groups, which generates repercussions in coups and counter-plots, all of which add contingency and ambiguity in the evolution of roles and responsibilities:

> Because of the interlocking ties between people, they know that a shake-up at or near the top of a hierarchy can trigger a widespread upheaval, bringing in its wake startling reversals of fortune, good and bad, throughout the structure.
>
> (p. 33)

Finally, design contains within it an important aesthetic dimension. One fashions or designs with artistic skill or decorative device. In contemporary job design this aesthetic dimension comes to play a fundamental role in which the 'dressage' of costume, language, posture, customer interaction rituals, and the furniture and stage props of employment take on significance in the efforts to structure and organise efficient work (Hochschild, 1983; Austrin, 1991). As Featherstone's research in contemporary culture (1988, 1991) has shown, there has been a generalised process of 'aestheticisation' where design proliferates in signs, symbols, myths and images that have saturated the fabric of everyday life. Lash and Urry (1994), similarly, argue that objects in contemporary political economies lose their spatial and temporal referents, becoming progressively emptied of objectivity and materiality:

209

objects in contemporary political economies are not just emptied out of symbolic content. They are progressively emptied out of material content. What is increasingly being produced are not material objects, but signs.

(pp. 14–15)

In contemporary work organisations the content of many people's jobs is arguably becoming more cognitive in nature and 'emptied out' as companies increasingly compete in the fields of information and ideas. Organisations often exist on the basis of networks of computer terminals that transcend the limitations of time, space and geography. The Californian advertising agency Chiat/Day, for example, offers its employees the option of working from home, and in any one day there are only 60% of staff on the premises. In addition, there are no private offices for employees of any status but rather collective 'living rooms', and for meetings, staff must book multi-purpose 'project rooms'. The accounting firm Ernst & Young has completely abandoned the traditional design and structure of jobs and offices, replacing its Chicago head office with a 'hotel'. A hotel coordinator books rooms, and arranges for special files or software to be available. Employees' jobs are designed to be mobile and flexible, 'out in the field', or in the relative peace of their home, where they can focus and study, complete reports, for example, in an environment they can better control. In giving employees more control and autonomy in the design of their own work routines, the quality of work, which in these sectors is increasingly of a cognitive nature, is likely to improve.

Oticon, the Danish hearing aid company, has abandoned offices and desks, taken out walls and barriers, erased job descriptions, and auctioned off all its office furniture to employees (Peters, 1994). Employees stow their effects in caddies or personal carts, and physically arrange themselves as they see fit and as the project or task demands. The plant is a completely open space, and employees have no fixed place but move around the interior of the plant as the job, which they themselves are responsible for organising and coordinating, changes and evolves. From a situation in which their market share had fallen by 50% in 1991, Oticon recovered and began to make record profits (Peters, 1994: 29). A similar idea of 'hot desking' has been introduced in many professional management service organisations. This removes all fixed furniture in a 'cordless office' designed with ponds and plants and infused by the Chinese philosophy of *feng shui* (Farmbrough, 1996). Workers become nomadic, equipped with their 'office in a briefcase', wired into the centreless organisation through mobile phones, car phones, paging systems, radio networks, portable fax machines, laptops and other portable technologies.

Organisational and job design initiatives in many sectors of the economy do not depend these days on centralised personnel management departments. In efforts to tap into the intangibles of ideas and imagination that now arguably fuel the competition in education, tourism, entertainment, management consultancies and services, job design becomes a less easily identifiable and delimited activity, but is diffused and decentralised so as to encourage networking, mobility and flexibility.

We can begin to see the relevance of this dematerialisation of work and the emptying out of objectivity when we look at the case of the Philip Morris company. When Philip Morris bought Kraft for $12.9 billion, the accountants were able to identify $1.3 billion of tangible assets. The remaining $11.6 billion dollars was defined as 'other', those intangibles including goodwill, brand equity, and ideas in the heads of the employees. Tom Peters (1994) calls this the 116/129 principle. Most management remains concerned with the 13/129 fraction, and the rest tends to get neglected. Peters also notes that only 6% of IBM staff actually work in the factory producing

210

'things'; the rest remain in design, servicing, product development, logistics and finance, in which the premium is on ideas and imagination. Even those in the factory mostly perform service tasks:

> Factory 'hands' (ah, words!) now spend much of their time working with outsiders in multifunctional teams that streamline processes, improve quality, or customize products.　(Peters, 1994: 14)

In the final sections of this chapter we attempt to trace the development of contemporary job design techniques against the background of these theoretical concerns. In particular we focus on the sustainability, consistency and order of design and its relation to breakdowns, accidents, contingencies and incoherence. This extends our concern with the development of a critical study of technology that gives due attention to the interaction of capitalist forces of production with organisation, and social relations in production that allow us to draw out the tension in design/sign. In current efforts to restructure and *reform* work organisations this tension may be reaching a new crisis in which ontological categories – man/technology–machine – and the horizontal and vertical boundaries and definition of 'jobs' are subject to decomposition. Here we reach the limits of our chapter, where we can only raise the question whether a new form of composition and organisational assembly is emergent or imminent in contemporary social relations.

## TEAMWORKING, BUSINESS PROCESS RE-ENGINEERING AND AESTHETICS: DISORIENTATION, SIMULATION AND RE-SIGN?

A relatively recent response to this putative crisis of modernity and Fordism has been the fervour surrounding the concept of business process re-engineering (BPR), sometimes peddled under the title 'business process transformation' or 'business process redesign'. The two key seminal articles propounding the miracle of BPR were published by Hammer in the July–August 1990 *Harvard Business Review,* and by Davenport and Short in the summer 1990 *Sloan Management Review.* Hammer and Champy's *Reengineering the Corporation: A Manifesto for Business Revolution* was published in the UK in 1993, and rapidly became a best-selling management text. The principles of BPR in themselves may not seem particularly revolutionary in the light of the above discussions, but the novelty seems to lie in the manner in which they are introduced, the holistic nature of the package, the synergy and coherence that the key principles are said to collectively deliver, and the inspirational and aggressive aesthetic of their texts. Tied in with these principles is the concomitant importance attached to human resource job design that drives through empowerment, devolution and autonomy. Managers are continually reminded of the market imperative that requires them to take a hammer, or an axe, to the structures and principles governing their organisation. Organisations require personality transplants; nothing less than a lobotomy will suffice, and employees who cannot and will not change need to be 'shot'.

Hammer and Champy claim that the origin of the problem is to be found in the propensity of capitalist organisations to develop large and unwieldy bureaucracies based on the separation of function, specialisation, hierarchy, long lines of authority relations, complicated structures of status, and layers of work task division and deskilling. Furthermore the products and services that organisations develop remain divorced from the customer, who gets easily forgotten, a remote element in this traditional supply-led

211

and production-dominant system. According to Hammer and Champy (1993), employees need to 'deeply believe' that they are working not for bosses or to keep pace with targets, but simply for the customers (p. 14). Authority needs to be vested in small, multifunctional teams who can develop the capacity to respond rapidly and competently to the vagaries and whim of customer requirements. Grint (1995) offers a useful example of the approach BPR takes by looking at an organisation selling books:

> if the business is concerned with selling books by post then a customer wanting to buy books from different departments, pay for them by credit card, and have them delivered by special delivery, should not have to be switched through departments that deal with different categories of books, then be switched to a new section that deals with accounts, and then find themselves trailing through the telephone network in an attempt to have the books sent out. (pp. 92–93)

Organisational barriers need to be smashed to create self-guiding, team-based process units. Although sceptical of much of BPR, Tom Peters recommends a similar reorganisation of job design, one that enables employees to get 'closer' to the customer. Union Pacific Railroad was in many ways a classic example of the ordered and structured bureaucratic, functional organisation. If a customer or a track inspector reported a problem it would be passed on to the manager of that yard. The manager would report this to his or her boss who would then subsequently pass the problem on to the divisional superintendent for transportation. Then it would go to the general divisional superintendent to be passed on to the region, and finally to the apex of the management structure. From there it would make a horizontal shift to sales and marketing and pass back down this convoluted hierarchy to the district sales representative, who would liaise with the customer (as Tom Peters adds, if the customer is still alive!):

> Today, if a track inspector discovers a problem at a customer-owned rail siding, he informs the customer directly. If the customer disagrees with the track inspector . . . then the customer can call the track inspector's boss, the Superintendent for Transportation Services. But the super will say in effect, 'Look, I don't know anything about track. I'm just a boss. Keep talking to the track inspector.' (Peters, 1994: 31–32)

BPR seeks to integrate a whole set of practices (Hammer and Champy, 1993), from flattening hierarchies to effecting a shift from a mentality based on 'training' to one that emphasises 'education'. BPR attempts to incorporate into organisations pay systems that calculate *added value* rather than reward attendance. Managers are made coaches rather than supervisors in BPR-designed organisations in an attempt to devolve responsibility and facilitate lateral working relations. Perhaps its singular most innovatory component, however, is the *evangelism* of the BPR message combined with an aesthetic of masculinity and aggression. Managers are exhorted to see the world in a new way, as dangerous, unstable and subject to rapid shifts. They are warned of the vagaries of fashion and style, where customers will no longer tolerate organisations that do not have the capacity for rapid and immediate, rather than incremental, change.

One of the interesting features of BPR discourse is its emphasis on those organisations that have failed. The figure of 80% is widely documented as the number of organisations that have not been sufficiently radical in adopting the BPR package (Willmott, 1995), creating a climate more amenable to the exhortations of continual pressure and badgering. It seems that managers need to be subjected to continual pressure to encourage attendance at the weekly ecclesiastical sermon – to strengthen their commitment and moral fibre in order that they remain faithful to the cause in the face of pressures to deviate and temptations to seek an easy answer. Moreover, once we turn to examine the processes involved in job redesign through a reading of case study research, we find that design and implementation remain subject to a host of forces and pressures, all working to pull and stretch design in a multitude of directions. Once again, we are reminded of the clash of organisation/disorganisation, where the complex movements of social relations condemn the pursuit of design and stability to the space of a 'contested terrain'. Only ever partially realised or materialised, job design is forever in the process of 'becoming', fluctuating and oscillating in a constant movement between order and disorder. This is the terrain where anything might happen next, the accidental, contingent, and spontaneous – those features of organisation over which management has only partial control.

## Teamworking at British Telecom

The recent customer service drive at British Telecom (IRS, 1995a: 579) seeks to develop team-based working that resonates with many of the job redesign implications of BPR. In the face of profound market changes – in the case of British Telecom, the product of political engineering, intervention, and state management – customers now have an increasing choice of suppliers for telephone equipment and maintenance. A BT marketing department survey found that 80% of customers wanted engineers to be available on Saturdays, and 25% of its customers wanted service availability on Sundays. Following a complicated and lengthy 18-month negotiation with the union, which ended in September 1994 with a union ballot returning an 85% rejection of the scheme, BT sought volunteers directly for their new attendance scheduling package. Engineers were offered the option of three different attendance patterns, ranging from intensive 12-hour, three-day working between Friday and Tuesday to a conventional five-day working week from Monday to Friday – but with evening work obligatory, and remunerated at standard rates. Management wanted to loosen up the rigid start and stop times that governed the traditional rostering system.

In addition to the change in attendance patterns, a vital component of the Customer Service Improvement Programme (CSIP) was the demand for flexibility that allowed management to call up engineers up to an hour before their scheduled shift start and insist upon their working, when required, an additional hour after the formal termination of their shift. This could be 'averaged out' and balanced over time by letting engineers go home early or start later as and when customer demand patterns dictated. As part of the CSIP, BT introduced a new Resource Administrative Management System (RAMS) that, able to store and load every individual engineer's roster in conjunction with derived data on customer orders, could automatically build work schedule rosters.

As part of this strategic programme BT sought to introduce small teams of field engineers who, instead of the traditional supervisory–management authority relations, would take on increased responsibility and initiative themselves. A major problem with the traditional structure was found to be the role of the first-line managers, who had increasingly become 'deskbound', tied up with administration and paperwork. BT wanted to get these managers back into the field, closer to the customer, and therefore they created a new role they designated as 'field manager'. This entailed a considerable effort in delayering organisational structure where the old supervisory grade had been made surplus to requirements. These new field managers were being trained to take on the role of 'coach' – managing, building, and developing teams through an attention to quality, workmanship and customer satisfaction. Field managers were not provided with dedicated office space, but were linked into a field support office by mobile phones and

213

home-based faxes. While they take on the appearance of 'coach', in many ways field managers are being made into conduits for the channelling of new modes of 'silent' discipline; less structured and hierarchical, or rule-bound and proceduralised, discipline is nonetheless an integral element in these new forms of job redesign. As Barker (1993) shows, teamworking operates to delayer discipline and embed its practice in forms of peer surveillance and sophisticated methods of performance monitoring. Rules and procedures then take on a kind of 'virtual immanence'; discipline is present but also absent in jobs that are empowered but also monotonous, de-signed and un-signed, stimulating many employees into re-sign-ation.

## Post-bureaucracy at W H Smith

WH Smith has embarked on a similar restructuring exercise following increased competition from supermarkets and petrol stations selling stationery, magazines and newspapers (IRS, 1995b: 596). A retail branch restructuring exercise sought a shift from a 'process' to a 'customer-driven' orientation, reducing unnecessary hierarchy, redefining job roles, rewriting job descriptions, and reducing the number of grades. The old paternal 'command-and-control' model that held the boundaries and structures of job design in place was deemed to be anachronistic given the present competitive climate. Departmental and assistant departmental managers were replaced with more flexibly defined customer service and support managers, with a team of customer support leaders responsible for coaching and developing their customer service teams. The guiding principles governing this change programme emphasised the importance of empowerment and flexibility:

> Managers and staff should feel a sense of personal ownership and accountability, making them quicker to respond to selling opportunities . . . We want to give people power to use their own initiative, make decisions and take responsibility.
>
> (IRS, 1995b: 6)

Similar to the changes taking place in the customer–employee interface in the high street retail banks (O'Doherty, 1994), employees are being refocused and reconstituted (Du Gay and Salaman, 1994) to service, satisfy and even 'excite' the customer, as Tom Peters has been proselytising throughout the 1980s and 1990s.

## Ethnographies of work and organisation

Most accounts of job redesign tend to present only the formal, or official, version of events. Typically, empirical research that has examined new innovations in teamworking and BPR has tended to rely on surveys of management, or on interview-based case-study material that again relies wholly or primarily on the accounts of those who have formally 'designed' the change programmes. Detailed longitudinal and ethnographic research is far more rare. That research which has adopted the more qualitatively rich methodology offered by ethnographic tradition (including Jackall, 1988; Kondo, 1991; Collinson, 1992; Casey, 1995; Watson, 1994) tends to emphasise the precarious and partial nature of these 'deliberate' interventions and design programmes. The work of Tony Watson illuminates the ever-present climate of uncertainty and anxiety that attends managerial work, especially where management is engaged in the exercise of organisation change. Existential preoccupations, in combination with the struggles to secure definition and objectivity in organisation, tend to destabilise and subvert management efforts to execute its functions in the prescribed manner of a dispassionate agent of rational–

214

technical calculation. Recent efforts to tap into the hearts and souls of employees attempt to constitute and appropriate some of these irrational and emotional aspects of employee behaviour (Hochschild, 1983; Burrell, 1992), with the intention of redirecting its energy in a more instrumentally useful and purposive manner. However, the same instability, if not heightened instability, often accompanies such efforts, as employees attempt to make sense of the ambiguity of devolved responsibility.

Managers are seen to be preoccupied with a search for themselves; in effect they are concerned with the management of themselves. Managers are seen to confront ambiguity and dilemmas in situations where they have to negotiate some compromise or trade-off between their own sense of identity and the demands of work. This often challenges and impinges on assumptions of self and identity. Steve Loscoe, a technical manager at ZTC Ryland, the pseudonym that Watson (1994) adopts for his case-study organisation, reflects on this ambiguity and complexity in defining both himself and his role in the corporation:

> I really do wonder what my bloody job is sometimes. I say to myself 'I'm in charge of this office and this office and the office in Birmingham' but then I ask whether I'm really in charge of even myself when it comes down to it. I get told to jump here, jump there, sort this, sort that, more than I ever did before I was a section leader.
> (p. 29)

Catherine Casey (1995) reports similar findings in her research at the 'Hephaestus' Corporation, where the interrelation between work, self and identity continually disrupts the smooth functioning and reproduction of the formal and technical relations in production. An employee she calls Hal reflects on the turbulence of change and the uncertainty that attends the development of his role where occupational boundaries are being destructured to make way for multifunctional organic 'product teams' (p. 106). Knowledge and skills that were previously valued under the former locus of occupational identity are now being made redundant, as fluidity and change disrupt former certainties, demanding of employees a continual investment and reinvestment of skill acquisition. Employees are left to search for the 'signs' of what is required as they are brought nearer to what Karen Legge has called the 'indiscriminate deconstructive impact of "free" market forces' (Legge, 1995: 244).

One manager in the Watson (1994) study had to reprimand Watson for using the redundant language of 'jobs': 'To use the term "job" was to be slapped down by, for example, the injunction to "wash your mouth out" (p. 115). On asking about job design the researcher was told 'For God's sake don't use that term; "job" is a dirty word here' (p. 115). Conventional job analysis assumes that there exists something stable called a 'job', which can be traced, marked and identified in terms of a stable set of tasks, responsibilities and knowledge. As one manager in the Jackall (1988) study comments, there are no rules, requirements or responsibilities that can be categorically defined as the boundaries of one's 'job'. Rather extreme, but perhaps reflecting the sentiments of those ambitious and desirous of success, is the following comment quoted in Jackall:

> The code is this: you milk the plants; rape the business; use other people and discard them; fuck any woman that is available, in sight and under your control; and exercise authoritative prerogatives at will with subordinates and other lesser mortals who are completely out of your league in money and status.
> (p. 97)

Where employees are 'positioned' in open and fluid skill grades, or in 'job clusters' in which the content and boundaries of jobs remain negotiable and subject to change, the security provided by status and identity, of knowing what is expected, is being slowly

215

eroded. Employees can now expect continual bouts of reskilling and deskilling as the life expectancy of skills is reduced to one in which last week's knowledge and skill today become redundant. Hal comments on the nature of his job, for example:

> My job? Well, it just changed. Yesterday, I think. Principal Information Systems Consultant is what it changed to. And I used to be Manager Assistant Projects, I think it was called.

Specialisation and demarcation are rapidly dissolving, leading to a synthetic post-occupational culture of flexibility and generalisation, precariously held together by the glue of corporate culture. In the absence of traditional forms of solidarity and community, organisations are busy providing a surrogate corporate collectivity. Corporate culture, for example, attempts to engineer and foster team-based harmony through the manipulation of myths, symbols and stories through which employees can identify and cohere around common purpose and identity. Class-based and occupational affiliations are giving way to simulated families, which tap into individuals' needs for direction and purpose (see also Willmott, 1993). However, this remains a precarious and unstable form of design as the existential concerns and questions of individuals and collectives can never be indefinitely secured in the artificial cocoon of corporate culture and charismatic leadership (Hopfl and Linstead, 1993). As Bauman (1995) argues, passion, emotion and what he calls 'new forms of togetherness' in a mode of 'Being-for' – that is concern, empathy and emotional commitment – always threaten this 'courthouse' of instrumental reason:

> In the garden of Reason, sentiments are weeds – plants that seed themselves in unexpected and inconvenient spots. The spots are inconvenient because they have not been allocated in advance – they are random from the point of view of the master plan, and hence undermine the design because the design is, first and foremost, about the impossibility of randomness. (p. 54)

However, a major problem with this critical *existential humanism* is its foundational reliance on the traditional ontological features of a human being. There has been a plethora of innovative scholarship recently, exploring the historical and cultural contingency of what it is to be human. The critical work of the University of Keele's Social Theory and Technology group (see Law, 1991, in the first instance) has done much to examine the historical relationship between power, self and technology in the constitution of notions about what is and what it means to be a 'human-self'. This work seeks to incorporate post-structuralist advances in social theory into the understanding of contemporary technological and organisational design. One of its main concerns is the boundary or difference between humans and technology. As our introduction suggests, hybrid forms of man/machine cyborgs may portend the future of job design. As Law (1991) suggests, 'the very dividing line between those objects that we choose to call people and those that we call machines is variable, negotiable' (p.17). To capture a sense of this complex literature, consider your own helplessness once your Internet port breaks down, or the next time your car won't start, or the sense of a limb missing when your word processor won't work. In fact, if you walk to work, instead of driving, you may experience a whole new sense of self as the route and surroundings take on new dimensions of sensuousness, of topographical and temporal meaning. Perhaps you may reflect on the extent to which the body has become composed, constituted and assembled by material computer and information technology.

Corbett (1995) examines contemporary fears and possibilities as the advance of computer and information technology creates simulated environments of artificial intelligence and virtual reality that break down comfortable definitions of the real and

216

the unreal. Machines that develop human characteristics and humans who increasingly resemble robots, as portrayed in the film *Bladerunner*, challenge the categorical divisions human/technology, reason/feeling and culture/nature. Is the future of job design one that undoes its own conceptual and practical foundations, where the notion of 'job' and 'design' as a top-down managerial delimitation and structure gives way to self-reflexive, quasi-organic cybernetic systems? Who (or what) remains in control here? Are we left with the rapid circulation of information bits, symbols and part-composed narratives, which float as 'signs' in an uncontrollable and unstable cyberspace (see Gibson, 1984)?

## CONCLUSIONS

Our chapter began with a brief essay reflecting upon the limitations of the traditional syllabus and the orthodox frames of reference in studying the complex dynamics inherent in job design. It was argued that in order to come to terms with contemporary job design we need to find new ways of thinking and writing about organisation, ways that enable us to analytically prise open that space of chance, spontaneity, and disruption in the employment relation. We have made an initial attempt to broaden the focus of job design study by attending to issues of power, control and technology. In our concern to address subjective aspects of work, those existential processes that preoccupy employees, we have extended an exploration of the complex forces of organisation and disorganisation that seem to render management–employee relations quite unstable, precarious, and contingent. A subtext in this chapter has been the recurring analytical problem of structure–agency: the extent to which job design can be thought of as the product of structural determinism against the 'free will' of management.

Braverman, for example, stressed that deskilling was inevitable, a structural necessity of capitalism driven by the continual need to increase productivity and output. Braverman understood the system of scientific management developed by F.W. Taylor as the apogee and perfection of management rationality. This sought a progressive deskilling of labour so that control and direction of the labour process could be effectively monopolised by management and colonised more effectively in order to determine and maximise levels of output and efficiency. However, from the discussion in this chapter, we have seen how this somewhat crude and mechanical view of management and job design was far too determinist in its assumptions.

Debates around the flexible firm, flexible specialisation, and especially post-Fordism, impart a degree of sophistication to the understanding of job design, drawing attention to a heterogeneous range of subjects focused upon the level of political economy and the interaction of product and labour markets. Nonetheless, these developments remain governed by a formal logic still inhibited by the problem of reconciling the degree of determinism with the scope for management autonomy and choice in job design initiative. Towards the end of the chapter we began to explore the non-rational aspects of organisation: that space that seems to lie forever beyond the instrumental-calculative efforts of management design and control. It is in the processual dynamics of organisation, in the social relations that day in/day out produce and reproduce organisation, that we find the elusive and inchoate flux that permeates the fabric of employment relations. Given the growth of postmodern phenomena and its extension into work organisations, more and more aspects of the employment relation seem to be subject to an ontological ambiguity whereby it might not even be that clear any more whether the categories that we have traditionally used to study job design – 'job',

217

'design', the 'social', 'human', the 'technological' – are going to prove useful in a future driven by the speed of de-differentiation, amorphous hybridity (Latour, 1993), and the abnormal collision of signs, symbols and re-signations.

We have also established that job design does not take place in some neat, well-defined managerial enclave or elite. Nor is it a coherent activity, the contents of which consist of fixed, objective-like elements that proceed along a linear rational line from cause to effect within discrete and coherent functional organisations. When we locate our human resource manager in the context of this swarming vitality and turmoil the prospects for the rational implementation and administration of job redesign seem a little bleak, to say the least. However, what we do recover from this analysis is a sense of the complexity of organisational life; its trials and tribulations; the frustration of sub-verted and aborted plans; a world of interrupted meetings and the hastily prepared management report left unread and filed for future reference; the arguments and con-fusions of daily organisational life. It restores that paradoxical sense we have of boredom and fascination that, in equal measure, seem to co-mingle and combine to generate the peculiar miracle of organisation. It's enough to set you off in a search for that Kalashnikov.

## SUMMARY

- The word and concept of 'job' is complex and ambiguous.

- The concept and practice of 'design' is multi-faceted and confusing.

- Issues of power, control and inequality are inextricably related to the practice of 'job design'. The practice of job design is therefore subject to interpretation, regulation and disagreement that renders 'organisation' precarious and at times unstable.

- Conflict and disorder are an ever-present feature of job design. These phenomena can be manifest, or latent and repressed – operating both within social relations and the individual psyche. The connections between these two sectors is usually considered the domain of social psychology.

- HRM is having a major impact on the sphere of resonsiblity and the content of jobs. We have tried to suggest that HRM is caught between contradictory demands or pres-sures. On the one hand, the practice of HRM is the 'object upon which' design is ultimately being directed. On the other, HRM is the subject that tries to indicate and exercise job design.

- The future of job design may well be one where both the terms 'job' and 'design' dis-appear. In some cases we might see the disappearance of the 'human' replaced by complex assemblages of man–machine hybrids. HRM is complicit with these historical tendencies, but may well turn out to be as much victim as perpetrator of those changes.

**Activity**    Imagine that your group represents the large personnel department of a car manufacturing company. The research department has recently passed on the research and results of the 'Affluent Workers' study by John Goldthorpe and his colleagues. Senior management within the company feel that this research largely debunks the notion and validity of job redesign, which, as a department, you have been actively sponsoring as part of your overall philosophy that good job design is fundamental to the success of the company. For many years you have been encouraging senior management to consider the possibilities of restructuring jobs as a means of reducing turnover, increasing commit-ment and morale, and generally improving the climate of employee relations.

218

Divide the group into three specialist working parties. Group A is required to prepare and present a short summary of the research and results of the Affluent Workers study, paying particular attention to its strengths and merits as a piece of academic research with important practical implications for companies such as yours. Group B is to critically evaluate the Goldthorpe study, drawing attention to its defects, oversights and methodological weaknesses. Group C is requested to adjudicate between Group A and B by presenting a short summary of the strengths and weaknesses of the Affluent Workers study, concluding by drawing together what appears to be the long-term impact of this study for the approach taken to job design by your department.

## QUESTIONS

1 Outline and define what is meant by a structuralist approach to job design and theory in contrast to an agency approach.

2 In what ways did Taylorism seek to 'degrade' workers?

3 In what ways may employees resist and/or consent to the deskilled nature of many of the jobs designed by Taylor and his methods of scientific management?

4 Do you think 'Taylorism' is justified in its claim to be a science? What is scientific about scientific management?

5 How might an 'essentialist' view of human nature lead one to the conclusion that job redesign is necessary?

6 What is meant by alienation and how does it differ from anomie?

7 Define what is meant by determinism in respect to job design. In what ways could it be suggested that theories of the post-Fordist worker are deterministic?

8 How may developments in the European Union actually promote UK companies to seek the redesign of their jobs?

9 How far are the claimed moves away from Fordism to do with technology and product markets in comparison to enlightened managerialism?

## EXERCISES

1 Consider any recent employment you may have had, and list all the positive sides of the job that you particularly enjoyed and found rewarding. Then list all the negative aspects of the job, and the reasons why you found them tedious, repetitive or monotonous.

2 What would you like in an ideal job in the situation you have outlined above? Consider how realistic your ambitions for this job may be. For example, it may well be that what seems rational and ideal to you may seem impossible operationally for production and line managers.

3 Then prepare a report for personnel outlining the assumed benefits of job redesign and the importance both for employees and the organisation of restructuring jobs and responsibilities more in tune with the philosophy of human resource management.

4 Consider the validity of the reasons that are suggested for the assertion that workers 'learn to enjoy' monotony in their jobs.

5 As a member of a head office personnel department in a large British bank you have been asked to consider the recent work of David Collinson and David Knights. Prepare a brief report with the

219

help of three of your colleagues outlining the theoretical approach adopted by Collinson and Knights, and the results they obtained. Present this report with the help of visual aids so that as a group your personnel department can quickly digest the information so that they can consider and reflect on the impact the work of Collinson and Knights is likely to have in your approach to job design. The rest of the personnel department is largely suspicious of the approach taken in the work of Collinson and Knights, and have come prepared to give the group a hard time in what it is hoped will be a lively and stimulating debate.

6 Imagine that your group represents a highly successful firm of management consultants. Divide the group into three working parties. Group A has recently been sent on a fact-finding mission to Germany, where they have discovered that the approach taken to job design in medium-sized engineering firms is far more progressive and advanced than typically found in similar-sized UK firms. On your return you are asked to present a summary of your findings. Critically reflect on the reasons why management appear to be more proactive in job design initiatives and more successful in the outcomes they achieve.

Group B has been sent on a similar tour of French banks, where, among other things, it has been discovered that individual employees do not appear to spend the vast majority of their time specialised in the dedication to one task. Present your findings to the group, outlining the distinctiveness of French job design programmes.

Group C has been requested to reflect on the lessons for British management that the work of groups A and B seems to suggest. In your terms of reference you have been asked to delineate between what British management can do within British organisations and the limitations they face within the context of a different political and economic structure.

Consider the role that governments play in facilitating job design initiatives.

---

## CASE STUDY

# Divine model for the seven work commandments

A guru of job design and organisation has revealed an unexpected source of inspiration for succesful theories, writes **Steven Overell**

Secular success has come to Christian Schumacher in prodigious quantities. After arriving daunted and unqualified in the job of manpower research officer at the British Steel Corporation in the early 1970s, he embarked on a feverish stint studying job design and work organisation. From this he forged seven principles of how work should be organised and set about putting them into practice at vast steel plants during the 1970s industrial boom.

For the next 25 years, word of mouth alone propelled him on a tour of ailing factories across blue-chip Britain. He took in Philips, Imperial Chemical Industries, Unilever, Courage and Pilkington Glass. More recently he has extended his work to central government, health authorities and zoos.

What he saw everywhere dismayed him. People did tiny, mindless tasks, alienated and de-humanised –

what he soon learned to call 'deformed' work. It was inefficient, destructive and unsustainable.

Instead, he said, work should be based around a fundamental transformation in the product, so that people could see the results of their labour, so that it formed a 'whole' task. Workers should be organised into small groups with several different roles, with a leader taking responsibility for the team. The teams should be able to 'plan, do and evaluate' their own work, and participation in the wider organisation should be encouraged.

As invitations to install his new regime flooded in, he checked to measure and verify with the true empiricist's devotion.

The hard measures were impressive: plant efficiency, on-time deliveries, faults per unit. So too were the softer ones: fewer industrial troubles, lower absenteeism, better motivation. Best of all were the anecdotes: people were less bored, a sense of thoroughness and responsibility pervaded, natural leaders gradually emerged. Work organisation, he reflected, had the power to make people more sensitive to one another. Unlike so many management consultants, Mr Schumacher's ideas created no losers. They have brought him great success, made him one of the best-known work structure specialists and forced him to take on seven more consultants to his company, Work Structure Limited.

And yet all this is really only the froth of his story. For Mr Schumacher had a secret, to which only his wife and a few trusted friends were party: the real source of his inspiration.

His ideas about the best way to organise work came from long and profound reflection on the Christian Trinity: God, as embodied in the Father, Son and Holy Spirit. His principles of job design were arrived at through 'a synthesis of theology and science'.

This revelation in his book *God in Work* has left him, he says, 'expecting mockery, but hoping for a serious debate about the role of theology – at least among the religious'. Had his clients known his source, one wonders, would Mr Schumacher have been such a success? Is he even guilty of a metaphysical hoax? He does not think so. 'The point is that my ideas work,' he says, 'not necessarily where they come from. Their source is obviously very important to me, but it is not to my clients.'

As he remarks in his book: 'There is no need to make explicit their (the ideas') theological antecedents any more than a doctor has to go through the theory of penicillin to a patient infected with a disease-causing bacterium.'

A book about theology and management is probably many people's idea of a literary felony, a cocktail of abstracts that do not belong together.

Mr Schumacher's book is nothing of the kind. Written in the style of a personal odyssey towards his conclusions, it is clearly the product of a well-organised mind, comprising a consistently argued attempt to answer the age-old question of how Christians are to interact with the world. It is almost certainly the first to splice the wisdom of Saints Augustine and Bonaventure with that of the twitchiest American organisational psychologists.

Mr Schumacher argues that the Trinity contains the functions of God towards His creation, which broadly corresponds to planning, doing and evaluat-

ing. The closer human beings can get to 'this divine exemplar', the better the result would be as 'good processes lead to good outcomes'.

God's relation to His 'work' would then be balanced by mankind's relation to work. Thus workers should 'plan, do and evaluate' as much of their work as is feasible. 'I honestly think,' he says, 'that many of the evils apparent in our society are rooted in job design – the loss of ownership, the task fragmentation, the de-skilling, the rendering of work psychologically meaningless to the worker.

'So when people see the results of my work reorganisation, they are always impressed by the compelling logic of the principles. If they asked, I could tell them the reason for that is that the relations they embody in the workplace are the same as the relations that exist in the Creator.'

Mr Schumacher – son of the late guru E.F. Schumacher of *Small is Beautiful* fame – describes himself as a 'very orthodox' member of the Church of England, and is anxious that no one think him 'fanatical or extreme'. He concedes that it is possible to stare at models of the Trinity and find all manner of distorted, sophistic reflections gawping back, but points out that the texts he has most relied on are those of the Medieval Church Fathers and that the theology is 'very mainstream'. It is the application that is radical.

The inspiration for Mr Schumacher's success in work organisation has not been heralded as a theological breakthrough. For six years he served on the snappily titled Industrial Committee of the Board of Social Responsibility of the Church of England, only to leave frustrated by colleagues' refusal to carry their belief beyond the level of individual consciousness and into the dimension of structures and systems. Mr Schumacher wanted to use theology directly as a model in that most worldly of worlds, business.

'The answers are actually there,' he says, 'but they have been overlooked because science and theology have drifted too far apart. Theology was once called the queen of the sciences.'

In contrast to the word of mouth that powered him through industry, interest in *God in Work* has been, he says, 'deep, but not wide. I may be wrong, of course, but my work is about synthesis and one part cannot be understood without the other.'

*Source: Financial Times*, 29 December 1999). Copyright © The Financial Times Limited. *God In Work*, Lion Books, 1999.

---

1  How important is the quest for 'meaning' in work organisations?

2  Discuss some of the theoretical sources that Schumacher draws upon to develop his ideas.

3  In the light of your reading in job design theory, what do you think of the likely success of this project? What are some of the obstacles that management may face if they try to introduce such a scheme?

---

221

## REFERENCES AND FURTHER READING

Those texts marked with an asterisk are particularly recommended for further reading.

Aglietta, M. (1976) *A Theory of Capitalist Regulation: The US Experience.* London: Verso (English trans. 1979).

Armstrong, M. (1992) *Human Resource Management: Strategy and Action.* London: Kogan Page.

Atkinson, J. (1984) 'Manpower strategies for flexible organizations', *Personnel Management,* Vol. 16, No. 8, pp. 18–31.

Atkinson, J. and Meager, N. (1986) 'Is flexibility just a flash in the pan?', *Personnel Management,* September.

Austrin, T. (1991) 'Flexibility, surveillance and hype in New Zealand financial retailing', *Work, Employment and Society,* Vol. 5, No. 2, pp. 201–221.

Badham, R. and Mathews, J. (1989) 'The new production systems debate', *Labour and Industry,* Vol. 2, No. 2, pp. 194–246.

Barker, J.R. (1993) 'Tightening the iron cage: concertive control in self managed teams', *Administrative Science Quarterly,* Vol. 38, No. 3, pp. 408–437.

Batstone, E. (1984) *Working Order.* Oxford: Blackwell.

Bauman, Z. (1995) *Life in Fragments.* Oxford: Blackwell.

Betsky, A. (1990) *Violated Perfection: Fragmentation in Modern Architecture.* New York: Rizzoli International Publications, Inc.

Blauner, R. (1964) *Alienation and Freedom.* Chicago: University of Chicago Press.

Boyer, R. (ed.) (1988) *The Search for Labour Market Flexibility: The European Economies in Transition.* Oxford: Clarendon Press.

*Braverman, H. (1974) *Labor and Monopoly Capital.* New York: Monthly Review Press.

*Buchanan, D. (1989) 'Principles and practice in work design', in Sisson, K. (ed.) *Personnel Management in Britain.* Oxford: Blackwell.

Buchanan, D. (1992) 'High performance: new boundaries of acceptability in worker control', in Salaman, G. (ed.) *Human Resource Strategies.* London: Sage.

Buchanan, D. (1994) 'Principles and practices in work design', in Sisson, K. (ed.) *Personnel Management: A Comprehensive Guide to Theory and Practice in Britain.* Oxford: Blackwell.

Burawoy, M. (1979) *Manufacturing Consent.* Chicago: University of Chicago Press.

Burawoy, M. (1985) *The Politics of Production.* London: Verso.

Burrell, G. (1992) 'The organisation of pleasure', in Alvesson, M. and Willmott, H. (eds) *Critical Management Studies.* London: Sage.

Burrell, G. (1997) *Pandemonium: Towards a Retro-Organization Theory.* London: Sage

Burrell, G. (1995) 'Normal Science Paradigms, Metaphors, Discources and Geneologies of Analysis', in Clegg, S. Hardy, C. and Walter, R. Nord (eds) *Handbook of Organization Studies.* London: Sage.

Callon, M. (1986) 'Some elements of a sociology of translation: domestification of the scallops and fishermen of St Brieuc Bay', in Law, J. (ed.) *Power, Action and Belief: A New Sociology of Knowledge?.* London: Routledge & Kegan Paul.

Camus, A. (1961) *The Outsider.* London: Penguin.

Casey, C. (1995) *Work, Self and Society: After Industrialism.* London: Routledge.

Clawson, D. (1980) *Bureaucracy and the Labour Process: The Transformation of US Industry, 1860–1920.* New York and London: Monthly Review Press.

Cohen, S. and Taylor, L. (1992) *Escape Attempts: The Theory and Practice of Resistance to Everyday Life.* London: Routledge.

Collinson, D. (1992) *Managing the Shopfloor: Subjectivity, Masculinity and Workplace Culture.* Berlin: Walter de Gruyter.

Collinson, D. and Knights, D. (1986) 'Men only: theories and practices of job segregation in insurance', in Knights, D. and Willmott, H. (eds) *Gender and the Labour Process.* Aldershot: Gower.

Cooper, R. and Law, J. (1995) 'Organization: distal and proximal views', *Research in the Sociology of Organizations,* Vol. 13, pp. 237–274.

Corbett, M. (1994) *Critical Cases in Organizational Behaviour.* London: Macmillan Business.

Corbett, M. (1995) 'Celluloid projections: images of technology and organizational futures in contemporary science fiction film', *Organization,* Vol. 2, No. 3/4.

Corbett, M. (1997) 'Designing jobs with advanced manufacturing technology: the negotiation of expertise', in Scarbrough, H. (ed.) *The Management of Expertise.* London: Macmillan Business.

Coupland, D. (1992) *Generation X; Tales for an Accelerated Culture.* New York: St Martin's Press.

Cross, M. (1990) *Changing Job Structures: Techniques for the Design of New Jobs and Organisations.* Oxford: Heinemann Newnes.

Davenport, T.H. and Short, J.E. (1990) 'The new industrial engineering: information technology and business process redesign', *Sloan Management Review,* Summer, pp. 11–27.

Deal, T. and Kennedy, A. (1982) *Corporate Cultures: The Rites and Rituals of Corporate Life.* New York: Addison Wesley.

Deming, W. (1986) *Out of Crisis.* Cambridge: Cambridge University Press.

Du Gay, P. and Salaman, G. (1994) 'The conduct of management and the management of conduct: contemporary managerial disclosure and the constitution of the "competent' manager", Making up Managers Working Papers Series, No. 1, The Open University.

Durkheim, E. (1984) *The Division of Labour in Society.* London: Macmillan.

Edwards, P. (1986) *Conflict at Work: A Materialist Analysis of Workplace Relations.* Oxford: Blackwell.

Elger, T. (1990) 'Technical innovation and work reorganisation in British manufacturing in the 1980s: continuity, intensification or transformation?', *Work, Employment and Society,* Special Issue, pp. 67–101.

Farmbrough, H. (1996) 'Man's journey desk into space', *Voyager,* March/April, pp. 30–36.

Featherstone, M. (1991) *Consumer Culture and Postmodernism.* London: Sage.

Featherstone, M. (ed.) (1988) *Postmodernism.* London: Sage.

Featherstone, M. and Burrows, R. (eds) (1995) *Cyberspace, Cyberbodies, Cyberpunk.* London: Sage.

222

Fineman, S. (ed.) (1993) *Emotion in Organizations*. London: Sage.

Fox, A. (1974) *Beyond Contract*. London: Faber.

Friedman, A. (1977) *Industry and Labour*. London: Macmillan.

Friedman, A. (1990) 'Managerial strategies, activities, techniques and technology: towards a complex theory of the labour process', in Knights, D. and Willmott, H. (eds) *Labour Process Theory*. London: Macmillan.

Fromm, E. (1991) *The Fear of Freedom*. London: Routledge & Kegan Paul.

Gabriel, Y. (1995) 'The unmanaged organization: stories, fantasies and subjectivity', *Organization Studies*, vol. 16, No. 3, pp. 477–501.

Gibson, W. (1984) *Neuromancer*. London: Victor Gollancz.

Giddens, A. (1991) *Modernity and Self Identity*. Cambridge: Polity Press.

Gilbert, N., Burrows, R. and Pollert, A. (1992) *Fordism and Flexibility: Divisions and Change*. London: Macmillan.

Goldthorpe, J.H., Lockwood, D., Bechhofer, F. and Platt, J. (1968) *The Affluent Worker: Industrial Attitudes and Behaviour*. Cambridge: Cambridge University Press.

Gray, C. H. (ed.) (1995) *The Cyborg Handbook*, London: Routledge.

Grey, C. and Mitev, N (1995) 'Management education: a polemic', *Management Learning*, Vol. 26, No. 1: pp.73–90.

Grint, K. (1995) *Management: A Sociological Introduction*. Cambridge: Polity Press.

Hackman, J.R. and Lawler, E.E. (1971) 'Employee reactions to job characteristics', *Journal of Applied Psychology*, Vol. 55, pp. 259–286.

Hackman, J.R. and Oldham, G.R. (1976) 'Motivation through the design of work: test of a theory', *Organisational Behaviour and Human Performance*, Vol. 16, pp. 250–279.

Hammer, M. (1990) 'Reengineering work: don't automate, obliterate', *Harvard Business Review*, July–August, pp. 104–112.

Hammer, M. and Champy, J. (1993) *Reengineering the Corporation: A Manifesto for Business Revolution*. London: Nicholas Brealey.

Haraway, D. (1985) 'A manifesto for cyborgs: science, technology and socialist feminism in the 1980s', *Socialist Review*, No. 80, pp. 65–107.

Hedberg, B., Dahlgren, G., Hansson, J. and Olve, N.-G. (1994) *Virtual Organization and Beyond: Discover Imaginary Systems*. Chichester: John Wiley.

Heidegger, M. (1977) *The Question Concerning Technology and Other Essays*. New York: Harper & Row.

Hendry, C. (1990) 'New technology, new careers: the impact of company employment policy', *New Technology, Work and Employment*, Vol. 5, No. 1, Spring, pp. 31–43.

Hirschorn, L. (1984) *Beyond Mechanisation*. Cambridge, Mass.: MIT Press.

Hirst, J. and Zeitlin, J. (1991) 'Flexible specialization versus post-Fordism: theory, evidence and policy implications', *Economy and Society*, Vol. 20, No. 1, pp. 1–55.

Hochschild, A. (1983) *The Managed Heart: Commercialization of Human Feeling*. Berkeley, Cal.: University of California Press.

Hopfl, H. and Linstead, S. (1993) 'Passion and performance: suffering and the carrying of organizational roles', in Fineman, S. (ed.) *Emotion in Organizations*. London: Sage.

Hyman, R. (1987) 'Strategy of structure: capital, labour and control', *Work, Employment and Society*, Vol. 1, No. 1, pp. 25–55.

Iles, P. and Salaman, G. (1995) 'Recruitment, selection and assessment', in Storey, J. (ed.) *Human Resource Management: A Critical Text*. London: Routledge.

Industrial Relations Services (1995a) 'Customer service drive at BT', *Employment Trends*, 579.

Industrial Relations Services (1995b) 'Putting the customer first: organisational change at WH Smith', *Employment Trends*, 596.

Information Technology Skills Shortage Committee (1985) *Second Report: Changing Technology, Changing Skills*. London: Department of Trade and Industry.

Institute of Manpower Studies (1984) *Competence and Competition: Training and Education in the FRG*, Report for NEDO and the MSC. London: IMS.

Jackall, R. (1988) *Moral Mazes: The World of Corporate Managers*. New York: Oxford University Press.

James, G. (1992) 'Quality of working life and total quality management', *International Journal of Manpower*, Vol. 13, No. 1, pp. 41–58.

Jameson, F. (1991) *Postmodernism or the Cultural Logic of Late Capitalism*. London: Verso

Jencks, C. (1987) *Postmodernism*. London: Academy Editions; New York: Rizzoli International Publications.

Kakar, S. (1970) *Frederick Taylor: A Study in Personality and Innovation*. Cambridge, Mass.: MIT Press.

Kallinikos, J. (1996) 'Mapping the intellectual terrain of management education', in French, R. and Grey, C. (eds) *Rethinking Management Education*. London: Sage.

Kelly, J. (1985) 'Management's redesign of work: labour process, labour markets and products markets', in Knights, D. *et al.* (eds) *Job Redesign: Critical Perspectives on the Labour Process*. Aldershot: Gower.

Kern, H. and Schumann, M. (1987) 'Limits of the division of labour: new production and employment concepts in West German industry', *Economic and Industrial Democracy*, No. 8, pp. 51–71.

Knights, D. (1990) 'Subjectivity, power and the labour process', in Knights, D. and Willmott, H. (eds) *Labour Process Theory*. London: Macmillan.

Knights, D. and Willmott, H. (1989) 'Power and subjectivity at work: from degradation to subjugation in social relations', *Sociology*, Vol. 23, No. 4, pp. 535–558.

Knights, D. and Willmott, H. (eds) (1990) *Labour Process Theory*. London: Macmillan.

*Knights, D., Willmott, H. and Collinson, D. (eds.) (1985) *Job Redesign: Critical Perspectives on the Labour Process*. Aldershot: Gower.

Kondo, D. (1991) *Crafting Selves: Power, Gender, and Discourses of Identity in a Japanese Workplace*. London: University of Chicago Press.

Lane, C. (1989) *Management and Labour in Europe*. Aldershot: Edward Elgar.

Lash, S. and Urry, J. (1987) *The End of Organized Capitalism*. London: Sage.

Lash, S. and Urry, J. (1994) *Economies of Signs and Space*. London: Sage.

Latour, B. (1987) *Science in Action*. Milton Keynes: Open University Press.

223

**The Management of Human Resources**
**189**

Latour, B. (1993) *We Have Never Been Modern.* London: Havester Wheatsheaf.

Law, J. (ed.) (1991) *A Sociology of Monsters? Essays on Power, Technology and Domination,* Sociological Review Monograph 38. London: Routledge.

Legge, K. (1995) *Human Resource Management: Rhetorics and Realities.* Basingstoke: Macmillan.

Lipietz, A. (1987) *Mirages and Miracles: The Crisis of Global Fordism.* London: Verso.

Littler, C. (1982) *The Development of the Labour Process in Capitalist Society.* London: Heinemann.

Littler, C. (1985) 'Taylorism, Fordism and job design', in Knights, D. *et al.* (eds) *Job Redesign: Critical Perspectives on the Labour Process.* Aldershot: Gower.

Littler, C. and Salaman, G. (1984) *Class at Work: The Design, Allocation and Control of Jobs.* London: Batsford.

Lovering, J. (1990) 'A perfunctory sort of post-Fordism: economic restructuring and the labour market segmentation in Britain in the 1980s', *Work, Employment and Society*, May, Special Issue, pp. 9–28.

Lynn-Meek, V. (1992) 'Organisational culture', in Salaman, G. *et al.* (eds) *Human Resource Strategies.* London: Sage.

Marcuse, H. (1964) *One-Dimensional Man.* London: Routledge & Kegan Paul.

Marginson, P. (1989) 'Employment flexibility in large companies: change and continuity', *Industrial Relations Journal*, Summer, No. 20.

Maslow, A.H. (1943) 'A theory of human motivation', *Psychological Review*, No. 50, pp. 370–396.

Maslow, A.H. (1954) *Motivation and Human Personality.* New York: Harper & Row.

Mayo, E. (1949) *The Social Problems of an Industrial Civilisation.* London: Routledge & Kegan Paul.

Mintzberg, H. (1978) 'Patterns in strategy formation', *Management Science*, Vol. 24, No. 9, pp. 934–948.

Murray, R. (1985) 'Benetton Britain', *Marxism Today*, September.

Nichols, T. (ed.) (1980) *Capital and Labour.* Glasgow: Fontana.

O'Doherty, D. (1994) 'Institutional withdrawal? Anxiety and conflict in the emerging banking labour process or "How to get out of it"', *Paper to the 12th Annual International Labour Process Conference*, Aston University.

Peters, T. (1994) *The Tom Peters Seminar: Crazy Times Call for Crazy Organizations.* London: Macmillan.

*Peters, T.J. and Waterman, R.H. (1982) *In Search of Excellence: Lessons from America's Best Run Companies.* New York: Harper & Row.

Piore, M. and Sabel, C. (1984) *The Second Industrial Divide: Possibilities for Prosperity.* New York: Basic Books.

Pollert, A. (1988) 'Dismantling flexibility', *Capital and Class*, (34), pp. 42–75.

Pollert, A. (ed.) (1991) *Farewell to Flexibility?* Oxford: Blackwell.

Reich, R.B. (1983) 'A structuralist account of political culture', *Administrative Science Quarterly*, Vol. 28, pp. 414–437.

Ritzer, G. (1993) *The McDonaldization of Society,* Newbury Park, Cal.: Pine Forge Press.

Roethlisberger, F.G. and Dickson, W.J. (1939) *Management and the Worker.* Cambridge, Mass.: Harvard University Press.

Schein, E.H. (1965) *Organizational Psychology.* Englewood Cliffs, NJ: Prentice Hall.

Schein, E.H. (1985) *Organizational Culture and Leadership.* San Francisco: Jossey-Bass.

Schumacher, C. (1999) *God in Work.* Lion Books: London.

Shaiken, H., Herzenberg, S. and Kahn, S. (1986) 'The work process under flexible production', *Industrial Relations*, Vol. 25.

Silverman, D. (1993) *Interpreting Qualitative Data: Methods for Analysing Talk, Text and Interaction:* London: Sage

Smart, B. (1993) *Postmodernity.* London: Routledge.

Smith, A. (1982) *The Wealth of Nations.* Harmondsworth: Penguin.

Smith, C. (1989) 'Flexible specialisation, automation and mass production', *Work, Employment and Society*, Vol. 3, No. 2, pp. 203–220.

Storey, J. (1983) *Managerial Prerogative and the Question of Control.* London: Routledge & Kegan Paul.

Storey, J. (1992) *Developments in the Management of Human Resources.* Oxford: Blackwell.

Thompson, P. (1989) *The Nature of Work.* London: Macmillan.

*Trist, E.L. and Bamforth, K.W. (1951) 'Some social and psychological consequences of the Longwall method of coal-getting', *Human Relations*, Vol. 4, No. 1, pp. 3–38.

Trist, E.L., Higgin, G.W., Murray, H. and Pollock, A.B. (1963) *Organisational Choice.* London: Tavistock.

Venturi, R., Scott-Brown, D. and Izenour, S. (1972) *Learning from Las Vegas.* Cambridge, Mass: Institute of Technology, MIT Press.

Walton, R.E. (1985) 'From control to commitment in the workplace', *Harvard Business Review*, No. 63, March/April, pp. 76–84.

Warhurst, C. and Thompson, P. (eds) (1998) *Workplaces of the Future.* London: Macmillan Business.

Watson, T. (1987) *Sociology, Work and Industry.* London: Routledge & Kegan Paul.

Watson, T. (1994) *In Search of Management: Culture, Chaos and Control in Managerial Work.* London: Routledge.

Weber, M. (1964) *The Theory of Social and Economic Organization.* New York: Free Press.

Weber, M. (1965) *The Protestant Ethic and the Spirit of Capitalism,* London: Allen & Unwin.

Whittington, R. (1993) *What is Strategy and Does it Matter?* London: Routledge.

Willmott, H. (1990) 'Subjectivity and the dialectics of praxis: opening up the core of labour process analysis', in Knights, D. and Willmott, H. (eds) *Labour Process Theory.* London: Macmillan.

Willmott, H. (1993) 'Strength is ignorance; slavery is freedom: managing culture in modern organisations', *Journal of Management Studies*, Vol. 30, No. 5, pp. 515–552.

Willmott, H. (1995) 'The odd couple? Reengineering business process, managing human resources'. *Mimeo, Manchester School of Management,* UMIST.

Wood, S. (ed.) (1982) *The Degradation of Work: Skill, Deskilling and the Labour Process.* London: Hutchinson.

Wood, S. and Kelly J. (1982) 'Taylorism, responsible autonomy and management strategy', in Wood, S. (ed.) *The Degradation of Work: Skill, Deskilling and the Labour Process.* London: Hutchinson.

Woolgar, S. (1991) 'Configuring the user: the case of usability trials', in Law, J. (ed.) *A Sociology of Monsters: Essays on Power, Technology and Domination.* London: Routledge.

224

# Chapter 13

# Flexibility

*Stephanie Tailby*

## Learning objectives

By the end of this chapter, readers should be able to:

- understand the reasons why labour flexibility became a central theme in public policy, academic and HRM practitioner debates in the 1980s and has remained so subsequently;

- understand the different dimensions of the flexibility debates of the 1980 and, in particular, those generated by theories of a transformation of work; government policies of labour market deregulation; and the policy-oriented model of the flexible firm;

- explain the meaning of the concepts of functional flexibility, numerical flexibility and working-time flexibility;

- evaluate employees' flexibility gains and losses under different forms of teamworking;

- explain the factors that have contributed to the growth of part-time work in the UK, and the forms of flexibility sought or attained by employers through the use of part-time contracts;

- explain the controversies that have surrounded the introduction of the EU Fixed-Term Work Directive and the proposed directive that aims to regulate employers' use of temporary agency staff.

## Introduction

Flexibility became a fashionable concept in government, business, media and academic circles from the end of the 1970s. It was applied in prescriptions for change in the organisation and management of work, the construction of working time patterns, and the regulation of pay and employment. Its currency drew sharp criticism. Pollert (1991: xix), for example, decried the 'flexibility fetish' and appealed for the application of 'sharper, more appropriate analytic instruments' in the examination of work and employment restructuring. Other commentators agreed that the concept's coherence attained at an ideological, rather than an analytical, level. Yet many were cautious in predicting any imminent collapse in its appeal (Hyman, 1991) – wisely, as it transpired.

Flexibility is an ambiguous concept. It denotes a quality that, like beauty, is largely in the eye of the beholder. It implies the absence of rigidity, even liberation, from oppressive constraints. Its application to the world of work and employment, however, raises the critical issue of whose interests are at stake? Structures and practices that employers characterise as rigid and inflexible may be a source of security and stability for employees. Exhibit 13.1 illustrates the point. It summarises a dispute that continued in 2001 between Post Office managers and employees at sorting centres around the UK. Immediately at issue were new shift start times and working patterns, although in the background were government initiatives to allow private sector organisations to operate in markets that hitherto had been the preserve of the public corporation. 'Flexible' work practices in this instance threatened for employees a disruption of work and domestic life and an erosion of employment security.

Flexibility remains a prominent and a contentious concept in the practice and analysis of employee relations, for reasons elaborated in this chapter. The discussion is organised in four sections. The first sketches the context in which flexibility became a central theme in government policy, and in management and academic discourse in the 1980s. It distinguishes three discrete but related dimensions of the flexibility debates of the period: theoretical accounts of a 'transformation of work'; government policies of labour market deregulation; and the policy-oriented 'flexible firm' model. The latter

---

**Exhibit 13.1**

## Postal worker strikes spread

Unofficial walkouts by thousands of postal workers spread across the country yesterday in the latest in a series of disputes about the imposition of 'flexible' working practices by Post Office managers, as the publicly owned business faces the threat of private competition.

The Communication Workers' Union, whose leaders met executives from Consignia – the newly named Post Office – to negotiate a return to work, estimated last night that up to 50,000 workers had joined the rolling unofficial stoppages, triggered by industrial action in Watford.

Mail centre and delivery office workers walked out in London, Liverpool, Cardiff, North Wales, Manchester, Preston, Teeside, Maidstone, Stockport and Chester, a spokeswoman for Consignia confirmed yesterday, in a dispute which could delay the delivery of election polling cards.

... The postal stoppages spread after managers tried to divert mail to Liverpool and other sorting centres from strike-bound Watford, where CWU members have been staging official walkouts in protest against new shift patterns, designed to deal with the rapid growth of junk mail.

The union agreed to flexible working in return for higher basic pay last year, but striking London postal workers said yesterday they were not prepared to accept the imposition of a move from 5.25 am to 4 am shift starts, and working patterns which entrenched part-time working.

Postal workers' discontent – which has already lost the Post Office 62,000 days through industrial action in the past year – has been further inflamed by threats from the government-appointed postal regulator, Martin Stanley, to introduce 'serious' private postal competition by the autumn.

*Source*: Seamus Milne, *The Guardian*, 24 May 2001. © 2002 Guardian Newspapers Limited

---

delineated an employer's core–periphery employment strategy to attain functional, numerical and financial flexibility – or the ability to adjust swiftly the skills deployed, numbers employed, and wage costs.

The debates on the transformation of work have focused attention on the forms of functional flexibility that employers have sought from 'core' employee groups and the extent to which employees have gained, in terms of skills, job satisfaction or autonomy at work. The issues are explored in the second section of the chapter, which looks at teamwork, and lean production systems.

The third and fourth sections of the chapter are concerned with 'non-standard' employment. The label denotes contractual forms of employment that deviate from the twentieth-century 'norm' (for men) of full-time and open-ended employment. The 'flexible firm' model identified the use of these contractual forms as the means through which employers could attain greater 'numerical flexibility': the ability to adjust the numbers of staff employed to meet fluctuations in the demand for the firm's goods or services. European Union policy and that of the government in the UK have developed, meanwhile, to identify non-standard forms of employment as responsive to employees' interests in attaining a better 'work–life balance' and as the means of widening the labour market participation of formerly 'disadvantaged' groups. In relation to these debates, section three of the chapter examines the growth of part-time employment and the forms of flexibility sought or achieved by employers through the use of part-time contracts. Section four focuses on temporary and agency employment. The chapter summary draws the different themes of the analysis together by addressing the flexibility gains and losses – for firms and for workers – of the past two decades.

## The flexibility debates

Employers' interest in labour flexibility is certainly not new or specific to the past two decades. Yet the upsurge of interest in flexibility from the late 1970s does require some contextualisation. Hyman (1991: 261–4) has identified seven relevant elements of change in the 'context, character and conceptualization of work'.

First, the 1970s and 1980s witnessed the 'first sustained and generalized crisis of the Western economies since 1945'. The long post-war boom, a 25-year period of sustained economic growth and relatively high levels of employment, had lost much of its momentum by the 1970s. Instability was exacerbated by 'shocks' such as the oil crises and the deregulation of financial markets. A brief period of economic growth intervened between the recessions of the early 1980s and early 1990s, and large-scale unemployment persisted in many European countries.

Secondly, the 'globalisation' of production and finance was thrust forward by interfirm competition and money market deregulation, and by the creation of regional economic blocs (such as the European single market) which stimulated ownership restructuring and the growth of multinational enterprise. Thirdly, corporations refined their internal control mechanisms. A trend was the devolution of operational policy-making although 'within tightly defined financial controls' (Hyman, 1991: 262). Local managers were empowered, or obliged, to experiment in the area of employee relations, in order to meet tight, centrally defined budget and financial targets.

Fourthly, the contraction of manufacturing employment and expansion of service sector employment, although long-term trends in many countries, accelerated in some. This was notably the case in the UK where the government's monetarist policies accentuated the scale of manufacturing redundancies in the early 1980s. Related to these sectoral shifts were changes in the occupational and gender composition of the workforce that, without innovation in trade unions' strategies, threatened a growth in the 'disorganised' workforce.

A fifth important factor was the political swing to the right in a number of countries. The new agenda 'encompassed a rejection of the "post-war settlement" – the consolidated balance of substantive rights of workers, unions and employers' (Hyman, 1991: 262). Keynesian 'full-employment' commitments were jettisoned, and the deregulation of product and labour markets became principal themes in government policy pronouncements. The Conservative administration in the UK between 1979 and 1997 appeared initially to be the most enthusiastic in its embrace of the neo-liberal agenda. There was a sustained attack on trade union legitimacy, activity and influence in addition to a programme of labour market deregulation that entailed the weakening of the force and coverage of employment protection law.

Sixthly, the development and application of new information and communication technologies provided 'novel opportunities for the reorganization of products, production systems and methods of deployment and control of labour' (Hyman, 1991: 263). As will be seen, some scenarios of the 'transformation of work' highlighted the potential for the application of the new technologies in manufacturing to develop new product market strategies that required for their success a more highly skilled, versatile and empowered workforce. More pessimistic accounts noted the potential for tighter management coordination of workflows and more perfect monitoring of employee performance.

Finally, Japan's rapid economic growth in the 1960s and 1970s and the location of Japanese manufacturing 'transplants' in the US, Europe and especially in the UK in the 1980s, fuelled western interest in 'lean production' and just-in-time inventory control systems. The academic debates on the 'Japanisation' of management techniques in the West paralleled, to a degree, those that were evolving on the application of new production technologies.

## Flexibility in work

One inspiration for the interest in flexibility has been the post-Fordist debate. This label can be applied to a set of academic studies that attempt to explain the economic and social dislocation experienced across the industrialised world from the late 1970s in terms of a transition from one distinct phase of capitalist development to a new one (Amin, 1994:1). Informed by a range of theoretical perspectives, these studies do not develop a single, uniform account. They agree that an earlier regime of Fordism was in decay by the 1970s, but differ in their interpretation of the causes of its demise and in their vision of the new regime in the making. The three most influential sets of interpretations are those of the 'regulation approach', pioneered by social scientists in France from the end of the 1970s and informed by a Marxist political economy framework; the 'new production concepts' approach, associated with the work of Kern and Schumann (1989) in Germany; and the 'flexible specialisation' thesis, which was the product of an Anglo-American collaboration (Sabel, 1982; Piore and Sabel, 1984; Sabel and Zeitlin, 1985; Hirst and Zeitlin, 1989). Of the three, the first contributes the most theoretically rigorous and challenging account of the 'crisis of Fordism' and the least optimistic vision of the future for labour in a regime of neo-Fordism. The third gained the widest audience in the UK in the 1980s and is summarised here.

## Flexible specialisation

The thesis suggests that alternative 'industrial paradigms' of mass production and flexible specialisation have been available since the nineteenth century. Neither has been destined to dominate, by virtue of technological superiority or economic efficiency. Rather, circumstances have combined at rare moments to present stark choices between the two. The turn of the twentieth century represented the first such 'turning point' or 'industrial divide'; the period since the 1970s has been the second.

The first was 'resolved' in favour of mass production. Epitomised by the moving assembly-line techniques pioneered by Henry Ford at his car plants in the US in the 1920s, mass production technology involved the use of dedicated (single-purpose) machinery and Taylorist forms of work organisation in the manufacture of standardised goods for distribution to large, undifferentiated markets. Economic competition was dominated by the logic of economies of scale under which large firms gained the competitive edge. These pursued volume growth, organised production into long runs of identical parts, and laid out factories to achieve a lineal flow of work between functionally specialised departments (machining, sub-assembly, final assembly, paint and inspection). The social organisation of production resonated with the rigidities of the technical system. The extreme horizontal division of labour deskilled production workers, who were paced by the speed of 'the line'.

Mass production technologies facilitated increases in labour productivity in the decades after the Second World War, and the Keynesian demand-management policies of western governments helped to support the paradigm. According to Piore and Sable (1984), however, its viability had been threatened from the end of the 1960s by the exhaustion of mass markets, 'external shocks' that disrupted the international economy, and an increase in competition from newly developing economies, able to draw on supplies of relatively cheap labour. While these authors admitted that the 'crisis of Fordism' could be resolved in favour of its renewal, they suggested that a shift to a new paradigm of flexible specialisation was the only viable solution.

Their argument, in brief, was that changing consumer tastes and the development of microelectronics production technology had coincided to support the re-emergence, in revitalised form, of nineteenth-century craft production. Flexible specialisation was characterised as the use of general-purpose machinery and skilled, adaptable workers in the manufacture of a wide and changing range of semi-customised goods for specialised niche markets.

Because the new production technologies were easily reprogrammed, they reduced the size of the economic batch. Firms were therefore able to reap economies of scope – the ability to shift cost-efficiently from the production of one good to another – and, with this, exploit the potential of the new market openings for quality, customised goods. As this potential was realised, economies of scale would become less significant as the basis of interfirm competition and small firms would be placed on a more equitable footing with large corporations.

The new product market strategy required far-reaching changes in workforce skills and methods of labour management, amounting to a reversal of the Taylorist and Fordist traditions of the past. Flexible specialisation demanded broadly skilled, adaptable workers who were able to use the new production technologies to engineer a variety of models and semi-customised goods and to switch flexibly between a variety of functions. Mental and manual work were in this way recomposed and tasks were reconstituted into more complete job roles. In short, flexible specialisation was presented as a progressive regime that conferred benefits on firms and workers alike. Jobs were enriched. Employment security was enhanced by virtue of the firm's dependence on employee skills that could not be replaced easily by recruiting from the external labour market. Labour had now to be treated as an asset, rather than as a variable cost, and in order to motivate employees and secure their commitment to enterprise goals, employers were obliged to modify hierarchical control in favour of a more participative approach in employee relations.

The flexible specialisation thesis aroused a good deal of academic interest in the 1980s. Most commentators agreed that it captured some of the features of current developments in manufacturing methods. However, its analysis of these developments and the broader theory of industrial change in which it was embedded were questioned (Williams *et al.*, 1987; Hyman, 1988, 1991). Critics argued that the analysis of economic change focused too narrowly on manufacturing technologies and market structures and that the mass production/flexible specialisation dichotomy was too rigid to capture past and current developments in production systems and labour utilisation. The thesis had little to say about the conditions of work in the expanding service occupations. More specific charges were that:

- it overstated the dominance of Fordist mass production in the twentieth century;
- it exaggerated the rigidities of mass production – Henry Ford was exceptional in insisting his customers could have any colour provided it was black;
- it relied on mainly impressionistic evidence of the break-up of mass markets;
- it overstated the flexibility of the new production technologies;
- it underestimated the continuing importance of scale economies.

The purported benefits of flexible specialisation for manufacturing employees were also questioned. Hyman (1988), for example, drew attention to the ways in which the new production and information technologies could be used by managements to direct and monitor more closely employee performance, that is, to reproduce and reinforce hierarchical management control.

## ■ Flexibility in the labour market

The theoretical debates considered so far have centred on flexibility at work. Flexibility in the labour market has also been a preoccupation since the 1970s, not least because of the political shift to the right in many countries. In the decades after the Second World War, governments in the West adhered broadly to the doctrine of Keynesianism. This legitimated state involvement in the (market) economy by proposing that, through demand-management policies, governments could attain the goals of full employment and price stability. Rising inflation in the 1970s, however, bolstered the challenge of neo-liberalism, the ideology of 'free markets'.

## Conservative government policies, 1979–97

The embrace of neo-liberalism was most obvious in the rhetoric and policies of governments in the US and UK, but was by no means confined to these (Hyman, 1991; Gamble, 2001). The Conservative government in the UK in its first term of office (1979–83), set out tight monetary targets and asserted that the control of inflation was to be the priority of macroeconomic policy. Unemployment, which was allowed to rise to over 3 million in the mid-1980s, was characterised as a problem originating in the supply side of the economy. It was argued that institutional 'rigidities' in labour markets had inhibited speedy wage and employment adjustments to changing economic conditions. More specifically, government ministers argued that:

- trade union demands and industry-wide collective agreements preserved wages in excess of market clearing rates, with the result that workers had been priced out of jobs;
- employees' statutory employment protection rights, by limiting employers' freedom to dismiss employees, impeded the reallocation of labour from declining to expanding industries and deterred employers from creating new jobs;
- welfare benefits dampened the incentive for the unemployed to seek work or to accept low-paid jobs.

The government's immediate objective was to erode the bases of trade union influence and to cede to company managers greater freedom in the conduct of industrial relations. This was pursued through a complex set of legislative reforms, enacted on a 'step-by-step' basis, and through reforms of public sector employment (see Chapters 4, 8 and 14). Labour market deregulation became a more prominent theme during the Conservatives' second term of office (1983–7). The reforms pursued included:

- the attenuation of individual employment rights; access to the right to make a claim of unfair dismissal, for example, was restricted, principally by raising the qualifying period of service from six months to two years;
- the elimination of minimum wage protection; the (traditionally weak) wages councils system that had set legally enforceable minimum terms and conditions for workers in some industries was abolished for all but agricultural workers from 1993;
- a reduction in the level and coverage of unemployment benefits.

At the same time, the Conservative government resisted strenuously the extension of EU social and employment legislation, which it viewed as antithetical to the aim of creating a 'competitive, efficient and flexible labour market' (Employment Department, 1994, cited in Beatson, 1995).

Evaluations of the impact of the Conservative government's industrial relations and labour market reforms differ greatly. These are most appropriately considered after empirical studies of employers' work reorganisation initiatives and use of 'flexible' contracts have been reviewed. It is worth noting here, however, that while a relatively early fall in unemployment after the 1990–2 recession was interpreted by some (e.g. Beatson, 1995) as a measure of increased labour market flexibility, authoritative studies continued to show a significant gap between UK labour productivity and that of other G7 (leading) industrial economies (McKinsey, 1998).

Critics of labour market deregulation have interpreted its emphasis on (downward) wage flexibility and the erosion of employment rights as inimical to long-term industry competitiveness, as well as socially iniquitous. In short, it is thought to be counterproductive to the reconstruction of industry and services on the basis of the high quality, high skill, high technology, high productivity 'production model' that is required to secure a competitive edge in the West *vis-à-vis* lower-waged economies. There are various permutations of this argument. For example, proponents of the flexible specialisation thesis argue that the development of such a regime requires state policies that encourage cooperation among networks of small firms and between firms and their skilled employees. Deregulatory measures that enhance employers' freedom to hire and fire, or to force down wages, as product market conditions dictate, are regarded as at best unhelpful (Hirst and Zeitlin, 1989). Analyses of the configuration of employee relations required to support 'high performance work systems' (discussed later) make similar arguments. Employee commitment is regarded as critical and not easily achieved where there is mistrust in the employer's commitment to a long-term employment relationship (for a summary, see Heery and Salmon, 2000). In other words, the development of flexibility in work is argued to require restrictions on employers' ability to adopt alternative routes to profitability, such as the use of a cheap and disposable workforce. However, employers' resistance to such restrictions may be strong. Thus, for many critics of neo-liberalism there is an essential congruity between its ideology and the aspiration of multinational capital not to be confined to any particular (local or national) workforce (e.g. Gamble, 2001).

## Labour market policies of Labour since 1997

To what extent have the policies of the Labour government since 1997 diverged from those of the preceding Conservative administration? Again, evaluations differ. Four successive electoral defeats prompted Labour leaders to transform the Party's relations with business and with the trade unions. By the time of the 1997 general election the former were being offered 'partnership' and the latter 'fairness not favours' (McIlroy, 1998). 'New' Labour espoused a 'third way' approach that to some (e.g. Giddens, 1998) promised a shift in UK state policy from neo-liberalism towards a European social market philosophy. Tony Blair defined the 'third way' as 'not laissez-faire nor state control and rigidity; but an active Government role linked to improving the employability of the workforce' (1998, cited in Undy, 1999: 316). This translated, in practice, into a continuing commitment to the control of inflation as the central objective of macro-economic policy, and to labour market flexibility as the route to employment growth. Hence, observers such as McIlroy (1998) concluded that Labour had accepted, in broad terms, the neo-liberal prescription that 'global trends' could be accommodated but not challenged by national governments.

The government's reforms of industrial relations and employment law, as previous chapters have noted, amount to change and continuity with the preceding Conservative administration. New *individual* employment rights have been enacted. These include:

- the statutory minimum floors to hourly earnings established under the National Minimum Wage Act 1998;
- entitlements to rest periods, paid holiday, and not to be required to work over 48 hours a week on average, established by the Working Time Regulations 1998;
- a reduction in the qualifying period of service required for general unfair dismissal protection, from two years to one (from 1999).

A number of the new individual rights have been concerned with the extension of 'family-friendly' policies, or have been labelled as such. Many of these have derived from EU directives that the UK has been obliged to adopt since the Labour government signed up to the Social Chapter in 1997. The provisions include:

- the right to take a reasonable period of time off work to deal with an emergency involving a dependant;
- a right to 13 weeks' (unpaid) parental leave;
- the right for part-time workers to be treated equally with similarly placed full-time workers in the same employment.

The Employment Bill introduced in November 2001 proposes also:

- a right to two week's paid paternity leave for working fathers;
- a right to 26 weeks' paid adoption leave, followed by 26 weeks' unpaid leave;
- an extended right to maternity leave (26 weeks with statutory maternity pay, followed by 26 weeks' unpaid additional maternity leave;
- giving powers to the secretary of state to make regulations implementing the 1999 EU directive on fixed-term work.

New collective employment rights were enacted, including the statutory union recognition procedure introduced as part of the Employment Relations Act 1999. At the same time, however, the Labour government retained much of the Conservative government's industrial relations legislation which had 'aimed to regulate, weaken and democratize the trade unions, in the interests of the Conservatives' wider economic, labour market and political objectives' (Undy, 1999: 326). Evidently the Labour government has a particular conception of the legitimate role of trade unions; the rights and restrictions are designed to encourage a form of unionism that is moderate in its object-ives and willing to work 'in partnership' with employers to achieve 'mutual gains'.

Labour's stated aim for its industrial relations and employment law reforms was to promote 'flexibility, efficiency and fairness at work' (DTI, 1998). When the detail of its proposed legislation became known in 1998, the *Financial Times* (21 May) argued that the proposals amounted to the 'biggest extension of rights and trade union opportunities in a quarter of a century'. Yet the content of Labour's legislative programme clearly reflects the tensions in its efforts to balance employment protection with labour market flexibility. The government has been anxious to keep business 'on board'. It has used consultation exercises and tripartite bodies (e.g. the Low Pay Commission) to achieve employers' consent for proposed measures. And it has advertised its commitment to 'light touch' legislation. Thus, while employers have complained about the volume of the legislation, its complexity, or the content of particular measures, trade unions and equal opportunities campaign groups criticised a number of provisions as insufficiently robust. The government has been accused of complying with European proposals in 'a minimalist fashion'. McKay (2001: 294–5) cites the example of its implementation of the EU Part-time Workers (Prevention of Less Favourable Treatment) Directive. The UK regulations were drafted initially to apply only to *employees*, that is those working under a contract of employment. Trade union representatives argued that they should apply to the broader category of *workers* in order to include temporary and agency staff and the self-employed, and meet the requirements of the EU directive. The threat of a legal challenge persuaded government ministers to amend the regulations accordingly.

## ■ The flexible firm

Different dimensions of the flexibility debates highlighted various forms of labour flexibility required to support enterprise competitiveness, and offered different interpretations of the industry structures and government policies necessary to achieve these. The flexible specialisation thesis urged firms to compete on quality and innovation, rather than on cost alone, and to invest in the development of workers with broad skills who would be interchangeable between work functions and tasks and motivated to contribute their creativity in support of the new product market strategy. The employment practices required to achieve such a degree of worker–management cooperation appeared to be at odds with the neo-liberal emphasis on labour market deregulation and erosion of employees' job protection rights. Yet the flexible firm model (Atkinson, 1984, 1985), which formed a third focus of the UK flexibility debates in the 1980s, suggested that these divergent labour management regimes could be combined within a single enterprise to yield a range of flexibility gains.

The model delineated an enterprise-level response to product market and technological uncertainty that centred on the reorganisation of the firm's internal labour market. The flexible firm segmented its workforce into core and peripheral groups in order to attain functional, numerical and financial flexibility. Core workers were those with key skills, or company-specific skills that were not readily available in the external labour market. Engaged on a full-time and permanent basis, they were trained and rewarded to supply *functional (or task) flexibility*. They were expected to have polyvalent skills that facilitated their allocation and reallocation among a wide range of tasks, and to acquire new competences as changes in technology or markets dictated. The peripheral workforce comprised those with skills that were more generally available in the external labour market and whose terms and conditions, as a result, could be constructed to emphasise the precariousness of their employment. Insecurely, irregularly or indirectly employed, they supplied the *numerical flexibility* that enabled company managers to adjust swiftly the level of labour inputs to meet fluctuations in demand for the organisation's goods or services, and to protect the employment security of the core. The peripheral workforce could include:

■ full-time workers who performed relatively routinised tasks which offered few career prospects and were vulnerable to market or technological change;
■ workers on 'non-standard' part-time or temporary employment contracts;
■ workers who were not employed directly by the company but rather supplied their labour (or were supplied as labour) under a contract for services: subcontractors, self-employed workers and agency temporary staff.

The advantages of a core–periphery strategy for an employing organisation were presumed to be higher productivity from the core workforce; lower wage and non-wage costs from the increased use of peripheral groups; and flexibility in wage costs as the size of the peripheral workforce could be adjusted to meet fluctuations in the demand for the firm's goods or services.

The flexible firm model attracted much interest from managers, academics and journalists in the UK in the 1980s, and from an international audience. Yet much of the academic attention was critical. The model was said to be ideologically charged, in the sense that it appeared to reiterate the neo-liberal preoccupation with labour market flexibility as the source of industry competitiveness (Pollert, 1987). Related criticisms were that it lacked conceptual clarity (Pollert, 1987; Wood, 1989); was ill-supported by empirical evidence (Hunter *et al.*, 1993); and neglected the tensions and new managerial problems to which a core–periphery employment strategy could give rise (Geary, 1992).

Certainly the model's status and purpose were ambiguous. Its proponents argued that it was 'only an analytical tool to help us understand what is going on'. However, they also suggested that firms were adopting the model and that 'this new division of labour' would be 'a permanent feature of the labour market for years to come' (Atkinson and Gregory, 1986: 4, 13). In other words, they presented the flexible firm model as a heuristic device and as a description and an explanation of what was actually taking place (Claydon, 1997), and this confused matters considerably.

The model's key concepts were imprecisely defined and therefore difficult to operationalise. This complicated its use as an analytical device and attempts to 'test' it against empirical evidence. The model suggested various ways in which 'core' and 'peripheral' groups might be identified: on the basis of employment security, contractual status (full-time, part-time, temporary, etc.), skills, tasks, and so on. Each of these and all combinations gave rise to difficulties:

> the identification of the core . . . can easily become circular; core workers have secure employment, and the fact of such employment is used as evidence for the presence of a core. If the core is more clearly defined by both its employment status (and especially its security and legal rights) and its tasks, there is a problem because some groups may have relatively secure employment but not be treated as part of the core of the business; whilst such 'peripheral' workers as part-time women in retailing may be central to the functioning and profitability of the business. (Wood, 1989: 5)

It is worth emphasising that any attempt to evaluate which skills are core is complicated by the fact that:

> 'skill' is socially constructed and also gendered. Thus, skills which are essential to an organisation, but are performed by women, may be socially constructed as semi- or unskilled, and may not be rewarded by the advantages of an internal labour market (by pay, promotion prospects and other non-wage benefits). (Pollert, 1987: 17)

There is therefore the danger of confusing new divisions with an existing, gender-based segmentation of the workforce.

As regards the model's fit with empirical evidence, survey and case study research in the late 1980s and early 1990s tended towards the conclusion that firms pursuing a core–periphery labour utilisation *strategy* were in a small minority (e.g. Hunter *et al.*, 1994). However, Procter *et al.* (1994) objected that researchers had employed a restrictive notion of management strategy, as top-down, conscious, planned and deliberate, rather than as emergent. The flexible firm model remains influential in the sense that its concepts of core and periphery, numerical and functional flexibility, have been absorbed into 'everyday' practitioner and academic vocabularies. As Kalleberg (2001: 480) suggests, however, research into organisational flexibility has tended to 'proceed along two relatively distinct streams'.

> The majority of studies emphasize the correlates of 'high performance work systems' that are believed to enhance functional or internal flexibility; the other group examines processes of externalization designed to reduce costs and provide organizations with numerical flexibility.

The discussion in this chapter is organised to review in turn each of these separate streams of research, before turning to consider the ways in which functional and numerical flexibility may be pursued simultaneously within an organisation or via its network of relations with other firms.

## Functional flexibility

Functional flexibility refers to a firm's ability to allocate and reallocate employees among a wide range of tasks. It is sometimes denoted as *internal* flexibility, to emphasise that the flexibility gains in question are derived from an existing workforce, as distinct from *external* flexibility which conveys the idea of bringing in additional workers and returning them to the external market when work levels fall (i.e. numerical flexibility). The pursuit of internal flexibility, however, can involve changes in the number and timing of working hours (working time, or temporary flexibility) in addition to the reconstruction of employees' job roles (functional flexibility).

Functional flexibility is a broad label and has been applied to a variety of types of change in working practices. These range from some relaxation and reorganisation of job boundaries – as, for example, where production employees are required to take on routine inspection or maintenance tasks – through to multiskilling and the introduction of teamworking. It is these latter forms that are given emphasis in more enthusiastic accounts of functional flexibility, or those that see its development as advantageous both for enterprise competitiveness and for employees who are thought to gain enriched jobs, greater security of employment, a more participative management regime and so on. The terms 'multiskilling' and 'teamworking', however, are often used loosely. Thus, while the former denotes the acquisition of additional skills – for example, where maintenance craftworkers become proficient in electrical as well as mechanical trades (or vice versa) – it is sometimes applied to the simple enlargement of jobs through the addition of further, routinised tasks. Moreover, empirical studies of multiskilling and teamworking 'proper' caution against the view that outcomes for employees are unambiguously positive.

Much of the research in this area has centred on manufacturing industry. This is not because work reorganisation initiatives have been confined to this sector – they have been in evidence in various branches of the private services and in public services. Rather, the manufacturing bias in academic studies of employers' pursuit of functional flexibility is to be explained, in part, by the trajectory of theoretical and practitioner debates. Claims of a 'transformation of work' in late-twentieth-century capitalism centred on work reorganisation initiatives in those industries most closely associated with the Fordist mass manufacturing model and have stimulated further studies and interpretations of the changes effected. Similarly, the 'pervasive ideology of Japanese manufacturing superiority' (Danford, 1998: 410) in the 1980s and 1990s generated much academic interest in the dimensions of a 'Japanese production model', of which functional flexibility and teamworking have been interpreted as among the most significant.

## Teamworking

Teamwork has been defined in general terms as 'a group of employees, normally between three and 15 members, who meet regularly in order to work independently on fulfilling a specific task' (Mueller *et al.*, 2000: 1399). At a conceptual level and in practice, however, it can take a great variety of forms. Many studies attempt to classify the forms that have, or are being developed within, a bipolar analytical framework of Swedish and Japanese 'models' of teamworking, or 'socio-technical' and 'Toyotist' teams. There are some difficulties with this approach, but the broad idea is that teamworking in conception and design can involve a significant departure from 'Taylorist' work principles or a reiteration of them.

The notion of socio-technical teams derives from ideas pioneered by researchers at the Tavistock Institute of Human Relations from the 1950s, and that were taken up in experiments with autonomous groupworking at the Kalmar and Uddevalla plants of the Swedish car manufacturer Volvo in the 1960s and 1970s. In the Swedish 'teamwork discourse', the 'emphasis was firmly placed on job-enrichment-orientated teamwork, in particular achieving over time a more ergonomical arrangement of work and a much greater degree of employee sovereignty which, it was hoped, would substantially reduce the strains which workers experienced' (Mueller *et al.*, 2000: 1394). Employees enjoyed 'sufficient freedom to influence such matters as goal formation, performance monitoring, production methods, labour allocation and choice of group leaders' (Danford, 1998: 410). It is against this Swedish model that social scientists have assessed forms of teamwork that, in their design and practice, draw on other traditions and, in particular, the 'Toyotist'.

Interest in teamwork has increased among management scientists in the past fifteen years. And the practice of teamwork has also grown in Europe and in North America: Benders *et al.* (1999, cited in Steijn, 2001) estimate that 36 per cent of workplaces in Europe now use some form of it. An important influence, certainly in the heightened curiosity in teamworking principles, although also in its 'diffusion' as a management practice, has been the 'challenge' of 'lean production', a system pioneered in Japan by Toyota and other large industrial corporations.

Proponents have interpreted lean production variously as a further stage of development beyond mass production (Womack *et al.*, 1990), and as a set of innovations that overcome the limitations of conventional mass production without departing from its basic principles (Wickens, 1993: 85). A central objective is the elimination of 'waste' – that is, human and material resources that are not considered by managers to be contributing continuously at maximum capacity. A key goal is low inventory/minimum 'buffer' stock production, which is pursued through a variety of interrelated practices:

- quick machine set-up times that offset the economies of long production runs and high levels of inventories of work in progress;
- a cellular as opposed to a sequential, production layout: the regrouping of machinery into manufacturing cells which reduces the physical distance between 'workstations' and inhibits the build-up of stocks of parts and work-in-progress inventories;
- the grouping of workers into teams that are assigned problem-solving and quality control responsibilities in addition to production tasks;
- just-in-time production scheduling: the principle that parts and sub-assemblies are produced and delivered for immediate use, at the next stage of production, rather than for stock.

In their influential study, Womack *et al.* (1990: 99) claimed that 'it is the dynamic work team that emerges at the heart of the lean factory'. Team-based work organisation, according to this view, is productive because it upgrades skills and empowers employees, and in this way strengthens their commitment to maintain the continuity of defect-free output, and to contribute their knowledge and skills to the continuous improvement of the production system. Alternative interpretations (e.g. Dohse *et al.*, 1985; Tomaney, 1994) emphasise the similarities with Taylorism. Continuous improvement involves the constant rationalisation of the production system, especially the elimination of 'wasteful' movements, and the standardisation of tasks. Productivity increases are achieved through the enlargement (as opposed to the enrichment) of production workers' jobs and the intensified pace of work achieved through just-in-time scheduling.

Studies of teamworking under the lean production regimes that have been developed in the UK by car manufacturers and firms supplying automotive components to these have tended to concur with the more critical evaluation (Danford, 1998; Delbridge, 1998; Garrahan and Stewart, 1992). Lean production admits adaptation at local level, and if introduced to a brownfield site will be shaped by the established configuration of labour relations. The results of empirical research, however, suggest that:

- multi-tasking – rather than multi-skilling – is the general theme;
- traditional, hierarchical forms of managerial supervision are in many instances retained;
- the elimination of buffers (excess stock, indirect quality inspection personnel), that is intended to accelerate the rate of throughput, results for employees in the experience of an intensified and more stressful pace of work.

Delbridge *et al.* (2000) draw on findings from an international study of management practices of plants in the automotive components industry to examine the distribution of responsibilities for different functions and tasks under lean teamworking. The study embraced 71 plants in nine countries. Delbridge *et al.*'s analysis focuses on the 30 plants that appeared to have the characteristics of 'lean teams'. It highlights three significant sets of findings that add up to the view that these teams are not independent and self-sustaining. First, the technical role of production workers appears to be rather limited. In the plants studied, operators have the principal responsibility for routine quality tasks, but they have not been upskilled to take on significant roles in activities such as maintenance, and do not have significant responsibility for production activities. As Delbridge *et al.* (2000: 1474) suggest, these findings 'question the claim that workers in teams have substantial autonomy and that lean teams are self-managing in any meaningful way'. Secondly, in contradiction to the notion of autonomous group working, the leaders of 'self-managing' teams have the main responsibility for the allocation and pace of work, and for settling grievances, 'implying that the team-leader is the front-line of management'. Thirdly, the roles of 'indirect', specialist occupational groups, have changed, although not always in the ways suggested by popular interpretations of lean production principles. For Delbridge *et al.*, the lack of evidence of upskilling among production workers suggests that the positions of skilled trades, in particular equipment maintenance workers, 'have been consolidated rather than eroded'. On the other hand, they note what 'appears to be a "hollowing out" of the roles of middle managers in the areas of engineering and quality' (2000: 1475), as these functions are transferred to shopfloor teams, or at least to the leaders of these.

Such evaluations have been taken up in the attempts to develop analytical taxonomies of teamworking. Bacon and Blyton (2000) suggest as an alternative to the Swedish–Japanese bipolar taxonomy that of 'high road' and 'low road' teamworking. The inspiration is the burgeoning literature on 'high performance work systems' (HPWS). As Ramsay *et al.* (2000: 502) explain, there has been much discussion among management scholars since the mid-1980s of a 'high road' approach to management, 'in which organizations choose to compete primarily on quality, and rely especially on human resource development and employee contributions to succeed in this'. In a sense, therefore, the debate recasts the themes of the flexible specialisation thesis. While the concept of the HPWS has become prominent in the discussion of high road approaches, it defies definition. Writers using it draw on a range of ideas, including those that have developed from Womack *et al.*'s (1990) study of lean production, and give emphasis to 'high commitment management', or 'high involvement' management, or 'total quality management' (see Wood, 1999, for an overview). The common theme (following Huselid, 1995), nevertheless, is that improvements in organisational performance are achieved through use of innovative HRM practices in particular combinations (or 'bundles') that are mutually reinforcing. Ramsay *et al.* (2000: 502) summarise the strategy prescribed as entailing 'managements ceding a degree of control to employees and introducing a range of progressive methods which increase employee welfare'. The workplace reforms recommended 'generally encompass any changes believed to introduce more flexible workplace practices and to enhance task discretion and responsibility, and usually revolve around the use of teamwork organization' (Godard, 2001: 25).

Bacon and Blyton develop their high road/low road taxonomy as a means of differentiating forms of teamworking and of exploring the links between these forms and outcomes. High road and low road teams are distinguished on the basis of the extent, or scale, of the reorganisation of work practices they represent; the former have more of the practices associated with socio-technical teams (the Swedish model in other taxonomies) and theories that stress participative management through teamworking. High road and low road teams are also distinguished, however, on the basis of the broader employment regimes they represent. This is useful in that it allows analysis of how low road teams 'may also deliver high performance but via a low skill–low wage strategy' (Bacon and Blyton, 2000: 1429). At the same time, however, it highlights the difficulties with bipolar taxonomies. Many analyses of lean production in Japan in the 1980s, for example, note employers' use of relatively high wages (and other internal labour market 'privileges') to secure from core workers cooperation with the continuing rationalisation and standardisation of the production process, in the interests of rising productivity and falling unit costs (Dohse *et al.*, 1985; Sayer, 1986).

## Teamworking in the UK

Survey data show that teamworking is increasing its hold on workplaces in the UK, in the service industries and public sector and not simply in manufacturing (Mueller *et al.*, 2000; IDS 2001a). In the national Workplace Employee Relations Survey (WERS), conducted in 1997/8, 83 per cent of managers reported that at least some employees in the largest occupational group worked formally in designated teams, and 65 per cent reported that most employees in this group worked in teams. Cully *et al.*'s analysis of the data, however, suggested that only 35 per cent of workplaces 'operated teams that corresponded approximately to a model of semi-autonomous teamworking' (1999: 42); that is, had teams that had responsibility for a specific product or service *and* allowed team members to jointly decide how work was to be done. Only 3 per cent of workplaces met these criteria and also allowed team members to appoint their own team leaders and, as such, approximated to a model of fully autonomous teamworking.

Other survey and case study evidence provides further insight into the forms of teamworking that have emerged. Ackroyd and Procter's (1998) analysis of work organisation and labour management at the plants of large British-owned manufacturing companies, based on a data archive compiled since 1996, suggests that, among these, teamworking is common, although it is predominantly teamworking of the 'low road' variety. The researchers argue that the arrangements do not depend on high levels of skill or high levels of investment. Rather,

> Output is achieved in part by some reorganization of machinery, but more significantly by a combination of a heavy dependency on the flexible use of relatively unskilled labour and a willingness to utilize external sources of production. The basic arrangement for manufacture is the use of standard technology by means of self-regulating and formally unskilled workers. Production is organized into a number of semi-autonomous segments, which also feature as cost centres. Each of these is periodically and individually assessed in terms of its costs and benefits, and this feature shapes most aspects of management organization and activity, including the control of labour. (Ackroyd and Procter, 1998: 171)

Functional flexibility has been developed, but it is of a particular kind. The erosion of traditional job demarcations, extension of cellular manufacturing and teamworking have allowed an increased use of semi-skilled or unskilled labour because the allocation of groups of employees to groups of machines 'limits the need for all employees to have a broad spectrum of skills' (Ackroyd and Procter, 1998: 174). The emphasis on teamworking, Ackroyd and Procter suggest, follows from its contribution to task coordination and wage cost reduction, 'rather than from any general attachment to the idea as such'. Profitability is maintained not through 'high surveillance management' but rather through regular assessment of the financial contribution of each manufacturing cell and the employment insecurity of production workers. Core employees – that is, those employed directly on full-time contracts – supply numerical as well as functional flexibility. The cellular manufacturing system allows capacity to be 'flexed' to meet demand fluctuations, and units deemed to be underperforming to be displaced by outsourced supplies.

Edwards and Wright's (1996) study of the 'high involvement work system' developed at Alcan's aluminium smelter at Lynemouth shows that 'high road' teamworking is also in evidence. Edwards and Wright report a positive employee response. Workers interviewed cited an increase in the stress and pressure of their work, although also increased job satisfaction, a greater ability to take decisions and better work relations with their colleagues. Three interrelated sets of factors are seen as supporting the success of the new work arrangements:

- the trauma of a recent and major redundancy programme;
- the continuous process technology and pre-existing division of labour which facilitated group work;
- support for the introduction of teamworking.

The plant was virtually 100 per cent unionised, and union involvement in the introduction of change satisfied employees that their interests had been represented. High involvement work systems are intended to deliver high performance, high commitment and high involvement. The success of the arrangements at Lynemouth was reflected in workers' increased job satisfaction (high involvement), improvements in productivity and decreases in overtime, absenteeism and accident rates (high performance). There were signs also of high commitment but expressed largely in terms of employees' greater diligence in the execution of job tasks. Evidence of greater employee identification with the company and its values, or of the emergence of 'high trust' worker–management relations, was thin. Edwards and Wright relate this in part to the continuing uncertainty over the future of the plant in the context of volatile product market conditions.

## Productivity, flexibility and partnership

The reassertion of managerial prerogative in the workplace was an objective of the Conservative government's restrictive trade union legislation. The impact of this legislation on economic performance remains a major area of controversy. Commentators such as Crafts (1991) and Metcalf (1989) have argued that by facilitating changes in work organisation and working practices, the government's industrial relations reforms made a major contribution to the upsurge in manufacturing productivity in the 1980s. Nolan (1996), in contrast, finds little evidence of a 'structural transformation' of the supply side of the economy. Highlighting the 'legacy of under-investment – in new technology, plant and people', he suggests that the productivity gains of the 1980s were rooted in three interlinked factors:

> labour shedding; incremental changes in production organisation; and what some analysts have referred to as the 'fear' factor, the central idea being that the threefold increase in unemployment in the early 1980s made employees more likely to acquiesce to new and more intensive (but not necessarily more efficient) work routines. (Nolan, 1996: 116–17)

This assessment suggests that the sources of change offer an insubstantial basis on which to build new 'high trust' production and work regimes (see also Heery and Salmon, 2000: 16–17).

From 1993 to 2001, unemployment in the UK economy was falling but manufacturing employment continued to contract, and accounted for only 14 per cent of all workforce jobs in June 2001. The Labour government since 1997 has championed the need for a 'partnership approach' in company and workplace employee relations on the grounds that this will increase workforce motivation and commitment leading to greater efficiency and productivity gains. The philosophy has been embraced by the TUC and the leaderships of many of the major British unions, and has been elaborated to include, as part of an 'integrative' bargaining agenda, a mutual – management, union and employee - commitment to 'bring together employment security and greater flexibility' (see Chapters 3 and 4).

Knell's (1999) influential study, conducted on behalf of the Department of Trade and Industry, examined 'the conceptual and practical foundations of partnership' among 15 organisations operating across a range of industries and selected because they were thought to have or to be developing a partnership approach. It found that these 'partnership firms' displayed:

> a high rate of innovation and have been successful in introducing new forms of work organisation and in managing the resultant changes. The erosion of hierarchy, the redefinition of roles, increased task discretion, flexible working practices, and the development of semi-autonomous teams were all widespread features of the case study firms. (Knell, 1999: iii)

Moreover, the employees who were interviewed were found to show 'high support for the principles and practices' being adopted by the case study firms. Some of these firms claimed a long-term commitment to a partnership approach (even if they did not label their approach explicitly as such). Others had been prompted by a commercial or financial crisis to engage in a change management programme that gave emphasis to employee or union involvement as the means of securing changes in working practices and performance. At one, Appor Ltd, the early changes, at the beginning of the 1990s, had resulted in a 50 per cent reduction in the size of the workforce (to 39 at the time of the research). Company managers suggested that 'many of those who left were those who didn't want to change – especially those who couldn't cope with the transition from "supervisor" to Coach' (Knell, 1999: 33).

A number of the firms were non-union (four of the nine in manufacturing). The research findings therefore lend some support to the critics of 'partnership' as a trade union renewal strategy. Union moderation may appeal to some employers (for example, those with a unionised workforce or a history of 'adversarial' employment relations), while others pursue partnership in tandem with union exclusion. There are, moreover, the risks for the trade unions of alienating members and potential members through compliance with change management programmes that achieve improvements in organisational performance through 'flexible' work practices that heighten the pace and stress of work for employees (Claydon, 1998).

## Part-time work

'Non-standard' employment denotes that which departs in some way from the twentieth century 'standard' of male full-time employment, on an open-ended contract at an employer's place of work. As such, it embraces a wide variety of types of work and contractual forms: part-time work, temporary work, working from or at home, and self-employment, each category of which is heterogeneous. Many of the workers in these forms of employment have fallen outside, or have been covered only partially, by the formal regulations surrounding labour markets – including statutory employment protection rights. Hence workers on non-standard contracts have been discussed as part of the 'insecure workforce' (Felstead and Jewson, 1999: 2), although the actual or felt degree of employment insecurity has been more acute for some than others. The growth in the proportion of the workforce engaged on non-standard contracts has stimulated academic interest in these types of labour contract, as has the trajectory of government labour market policies, and the attention that has been given to policy-oriented models, such as that of the flexible firm.

The flexible firm model identified the use of non-standard labour contracts as a principal source of the numerical flexibility that enabled an employing organisation to match staffing to fluctuations in the demand for its goods or services. Non-standard workers were the 'periphery' and were excluded from the firm's premium employment terms and conditions in order to protect the employment security of the 'core' workforce.

Much of the debate provoked by the flexible firm model centred on the extent to which firms were pursuing a conscious and planned 'core–periphery' employment strategy. New issues for research, however, have since emerged. One influence in the UK has been the Labour government's emphasis, in line with EU employment policy, on the need for employers to make provision for employees' interests in attaining a better balance between work and other interests and commitments. Flexible work arrangements and contractual forms of employment previously denoted as non-standard have been discussed in these terms. Similarly, these have been viewed by public policy-makers as supportive of opportunities for groups previously under-represented in the labour market to become economically active (Purcell, 2000: 130).

This section of the chapter and the next explore particular types of non-standard employment: part-time work and temporary work respectively. They outline the broad trends in the growth of these employment forms, discuss the reasons why people opt for or are relegated to these types of employment, and the reasons why employers use them. The discussion focuses largely on the UK but, where relevant, develops international comparisons.

## ■ Definitions of part-time work

In the UK, where the legal regulation of working time has been relatively restricted, there is no statutory definition of standard working hours or part-time work. The Working Time Regulations, introduced in October 1998 to give effect to the EU Working Time Directive, set a maximum limit on the average weekly hours that workers can be required to work by their employer. They do not prescribe 'standard' hours, however, or indeed minimum hours of work. The Part-time Workers (Prevention of Less Favourable Treatment) Regulations enacted in 2000 in compliance with the EU directive, define part-time work in relation to normal full-time hours. In essence, 'a worker whose hours are less than the normal full-time hours at his or her place of work is classified as a part-timer' (IDS, 2001b: 4).

Two main methods of defining part-time work are used in UK government databases: self-assessment and persons not working more than 30 hours a week. The former is used in the quarterly Labour Force Survey (LFS). The 30 hours 'cut-off' has been used in the UK by the Office for National Statistics (ONS) as a guide for participants in employer surveys.

Other definitions nevertheless have applied to employment rights and to social security benefits. UK employment law in the past 'was aimed primarily at work patterns associated with full-time employment' (IDS, 2001b: 4). Part-time employees were excluded from many statutory rights, including the right to claim unfair dismissal, unless they met the qualifying hours thresholds: 'For example, employees had to work at least 16 hours a week for that week to count towards their period of continuous employment (the threshold fell to eight hours after five years' service)' (IDS, 2001b: 4).

Many employers took 16 hours as the threshold at which employees became eligible for company benefits (holiday pay, sick pay, inclusion in company pension schemes and so on). The House of Lords ruled in 1993, however, that UK unfair dismissal and redundancy payments legislation breached EU equality law. The hours thresholds were judged to amount to indirect discrimination against women, who are the more likely to work part-time, and were subsequently removed by the Employment Protection (Part-time Employees) Regulations 1995. The need for a period of continuous employment (reduced from two years to one in 1999) and for employee status, nevertheless remain as obstacles, in particular for temporary and casual workers, many of whom work part-time (Purcell, 2000). Moreover, people who work relatively few hours or whose earnings fall below a specified level are often excluded from the National Insurance system.

On average, part-timers in the UK in 2000 worked 15.6 hours a week, according to LFS data, but there was a wide spread of hours: almost 2 million worked 12 hours or less a week, including more than 1 million who worked 8 hours or fewer (IDS, 2001b: 2). Part-timers' hours, on average, are rather shorter in the UK than in the EU as a whole. The average hours usually worked by male and by female part-timers in the UK in 1996 were 16.2 and 18.0, respectively, compared with EU averages of 19.3 and 19.8 (*Social Trends* 28 (1998): 83). A related factor that has set the UK apart, at least until fairly recently, has been the wide range of working time patterns. In most other European countries, part-time working is 'usually done in the morning, and tends to last at least 20 to 25 hours per week'. In the UK, such regularities have long since disappeared and it 'is hard to discern a typical pattern of part-time work' (Hegewisch, 1996). Thus while particular variants of part-time working have been identified – job-sharing, term-time-only working, Saturday-only working, twilight shifts, zero hours contracts – each forms a small proportion of all part-time employment and may in turn embrace a wide variety of practices.

## ■ The growth and composition of the part-time workforce

LFS data show that the number of people in part-time work in the UK rose by approximately 2 million since 1984, to 7.02 million in April/June 2001. The share of total employment (which includes employees, the self-employed, unpaid family workers and people on public subsidy training schemes) taken by those in part-time work has risen from one-fifth (21 per cent) to one-quarter (25 per cent). This expansion of part-time work continues a long-term trend, evident for much of the post-war period, however, and some analyses suggest that the rate of growth of part-time work was most vigorous in the 1960s (Bruegel and Perrons, 1998) or 1970s (Beatson, 1995). Full-time employment fell in the recession of the early 1980s and, among men, only began to recover towards the end of the decade. This context made salient the continuing growth of part-time work. Full-time employment among men and women contracted again in the downturn of the early 1990s and, among men, did not recover to the 1990 level before the end of the decade. Part-time employment grew more or less continuously over the 1990s. The increase in full-time employment after 1993, however, contributed slightly more strongly to the growth in total employment in the period to 2001, and therefore part-time employment's share of the total rose only modestly (see Table 13.1).

Table 13.1 Full-time and part-time employment in the UK, 1992–2001

| April–June | All in employment (000s) | Full-time (000s) | Part-time (000s) | Part-time as % all in employment |
|---|---|---|---|---|
| 1992 | 25,831 | 19,798 | 6,033 | 23.4 |
| 1993 | 25,575 | 19,489 | 6,086 | 23.8 |
| 1994 | 25,778 | 19,530 | 6,248 | 24.2 |
| 1995 | 26,136 | 19,791 | 6,345 | 24.3 |
| 1996 | 26,418 | 19,880 | 6,538 | 24.7 |
| 1997 | 26,982 | 20,266 | 6,716 | 24.9 |
| 1998 | 27,230 | 20,466 | 6,764 | 24.8 |
| 1999 | 27,592 | 20,747 | 6,845 | 24.8 |
| 2000 | 27,926 | 20,957 | 6,969 | 25.0 |
| 2001 | 28,176 | 21,158 | 7,018 | 24.9 |
| Change 1992–2001 (000s) | 2,345 | 1,360 | 985 | |
| % change 1992–2001 | +9.1 | +6.9 | +16.3 | +1.5 |

Source: LFS (ONS) Historical Supplement

Part-time work has grown in absolute and relative terms across the EU as a whole since 1980. In 2000, part-time jobs formed 18 per cent of total EU employment (European Commission, 2001: 11). However, the growth in part-time working has been distributed unevenly between different member states. Some countries that favoured full-time employment in the early 1980s have continued to do so; part-time work has risen, but not markedly as a share of all in employment. This is notably the case among the southern states of Greece, Italy and Spain (see Table 13.2). In contrast, Denmark, Norway and Sweden had the highest ratios of part-time to all in employment in the early 1980s and in each the share of part-time work has remained fairly constant. Indeed, in the five years to 2000, the share of those employed in part-time jobs increased in all EU countries except Sweden (European Commission, 2001: 19). The Netherlands had the highest proportion of part-time jobs to total employment in 1990 and the proportion continued to rise, from 32 per cent to 40 per cent in 2000. The UK had the fourth highest proportion of part-time employment among EU states in 1990, but has since moved to second place, behind the Netherlands. Across the EU, women form the majority of part-time workers. Those states with an above-average representation of part-time employment tend to be those with the highest rates of female labour market participation. Nevertheless, Finland and Portugal each have a high female activity rate and, in each, full-time employment remains more 'the norm' for women (Rubery and Fagan, 1995; and see Table 13.2).

Part-time work has increased among men in a number of countries, including the UK where it has more than doubled since the early 1980s. This growth was from a low base, however, and part-time work currently accounts for only 9 per cent of male employment in the UK. In contrast, 44 per cent of women in paid employment work part-time and women form 81 per cent of all those in part-time work (Table 13.3).

A majority of men in part-time work in the UK are aged either under 25 years or over 50 years. Around two-fifths of those in the younger age range report their reason for working part-time as being a student or at school (LFS, cited in Sly et al., 1998: 111). The abolition of student grants and the introduction of tuition fees have opened up an

## Table 13.2 Proportion of part-timers in the workforce in EU member states, 1999

| | All (%) | Men (%) | Women (%) |
|---|---|---|---|
| Netherlands | 39.4 | 17.9 | 68.6 |
| UK | 24.8 | 8.9 | 44.4 |
| Sweden | 23.8 | 9.4 | 40.0 |
| Denmark | 20.7 | 9.6 | 33.9 |
| Germany | 19.0 | 4.9 | 37.2 |
| Belgium | 17.5 | 4.2 | 35.8 |
| France | 17.2 | 5.6 | 31.7 |
| Austria | 16.8 | 4.4 | 32.6 |
| Ireland | 16.7 | 7.4 | 30.6 |
| Finland | 12.2 | 7.9 | 17.0 |
| Portugal | 11.0 | 6.3 | 16.7 |
| Luxembourg | 10.8 | 1.9 | 24.6 |
| Spain | 8.3 | 3.0 | 17.6 |
| Italy | 7.9 | 3.4 | 15.7 |
| Greece | 6.1 | 3.6 | 10.1 |

*Source*: European Commission (2000, cited in IDS, 2001b: 2)

## Table 13.3 Full-time and part-time employment in the UK by gender, 1992–2001

| April–June | Men in employment | | | Women in employment | | |
|---|---|---|---|---|---|---|
| | Full-time (000s) | Part-time (000s) | Part-time as % all men in employment | Full-time (000s) | Part-time (000s) | Part-time as % of all women in employment |
| 1992 | 13,351 | 1,006 | 7.0 | 6,473 | 5,022 | 43.7 |
| 1993 | 13,096 | 1,010 | 7.2 | 6,393 | 5,076 | 44.3 |
| 1994 | 13,121 | 1,089 | 7.7 | 6,408 | 5,159 | 44.6 |
| 1995 | 13,286 | 1,177 | 8.1 | 6,506 | 5,168 | 44.3 |
| 1996 | 13,324 | 1,239 | 8.5 | 6,556 | 5,229 | 44.7 |
| 1997 | 13,586 | 1,307 | 8.8 | 6,679 | 5,408 | 44.7 |
| 1998 | 13,741 | 1,327 | 9.7 | 6,725 | 5,436 | 44.7 |
| 1999 | 13,843 | 1,389 | 9.1 | 6,904 | 5,457 | 44.1 |
| 2000 | 13,995 | 1,393 | 9.1 | 6,962 | 5,575 | 44.5 |
| 2001 | 14,108 | 1,396 | 9.0 | 7,050 | 5,622 | 44.4 |
| % change 1992–2001 | +5.7 | +38.8 | +2.0 | +8.9 | +11.9 | +0.7 |

*Source*: LFS (ONS) Historical Supplement

increasing supply of young people (men and women) available for part-time work, although youth unemployment has also contributed and there are therefore similar trends in several other EU countries (European Commission, 2001). The age distribution of women working part-time in the UK is more even but has a distinct age-related profile.

Female economic activity rates increase with age, and in 1997 peaked at 78 per cent in the 40–49 year range (Sly *et al.*, 1998). LFS data for that year showed that part-time employment was higher among women over 25 years than under, and highest among women in their forties. This distribution, which conforms to the idea of women

Table 13.4 Labour market and family status of women, UK, summer 2001 (not seasonally adjusted)

| | All women | Women with dependent children (by age of youngest dependent child) | | | | | No dependent children | All men |
|---|---|---|---|---|---|---|---|---|
| | | All | | | | | | |
| | 16–59 | 0–18 | 0–4 | 5–10 | 11–15 | 16–18 | | |
| *Thousands* | | | | | | | | |
| All in employment | 12,101 | 4,791 | 1,592 | 1,610 | 1,187 | 402 | 7,310 | 15,335 |
| Full-time | 7,000 | 1,957 | 547 | 609 | 571 | 230 | 5,043 | 14,102 |
| Part-time | 5,099 | 2,833 | 1,045 | 1,000 | 616 | 172 | 2,266 | 1,230 |
| ILO unemployed | 607 | 231 | 89 | 76 | 75 | – | 376 | 956 |
| All economically active | 12,708 | 5,021 | 1,681 | 1,685 | 1,243 | 412 | 7,686 | 16,292 |
| Economically inactive | 4,719 | 2,385 | 1,306 | 633 | 355 | 91 | 2,334 | 2,896 |
| Total | 17,427 | 7,406 | 2,987 | 2,318 | 1,598 | 503 | 10,020 | 19,188 |
| *Percentages* | | | | | | | | |
| Employment rate (%) | 69.4 | 64.7 | 53.3 | 69.4 | 74.3 | 80.0 | 73.0 | 79.9 |
| Part-time as % all in employment | 42.1 | 59.1 | 65.6 | 62.1 | 51.9 | 42.8 | 31.0 | 8.0 |
| Economic activity rate (%) | 72.9 | 67.8 | 56.3 | 72.7 | 77.8 | 81.9 | 76.7 | 84.9 |
| ILO unemployment rate (%) | 4.8 | 4.6 | 5.3 | 4.5 | 4.5 | – | 4.9 | 5.9 |

*Source*: LFS, in *Labour Market Trends*, November 2001: 510

returning to (or switching to) work on a part-time basis after childbirth and child rearing, has remained fairly stable over the past 20 to 30 years. What has changed, however, is the age profile of women in full-time employment. Until the 1970s, women under 25 years were the most likely to work full-time. But full-time employment has declined among this group, partly because participation in higher education has risen. At the same time, the incidence of full-time employment among women in the 25–49 age range has increased (Harkness, 1998).

LFS data suggest that women's economic activity rates, their participation in employment and their participation on a full-time or part-time basis are influenced by whether or not they have dependent children and, among those with dependent children, the age of their youngest dependent child (see Table 13.4). Also of relevance among those women with dependent children is whether there is a second parent available to provide child care and/or an income from paid employment. Women with very young children (under five years) are the least likely to be economically active (that is, either in employment or unemployed and seeking work). That said, it is this group that contributed the most rapid increase in the rate of women's labour market participation in the ten years to 1998 (Sly *et al.*, 1998: 80). Financial need, together with improvements in statutory and employers' maternity pay and leave provision, have no doubt contributed to this increase in the number of women who do not quit employment at the time of childbirth, or who return swiftly to employment thereafter. The ability to return to work is nevertheless dependent on the availability of affordable child care. The UK, and also the Netherlands, have been distinguished among EU member states by their relatively poor provision of state-supported child care (Rubery and Fagan, 1995).

## ■ Industry and occupational distributions of part-time work

Table 13.5 shows the proportion of part-time employment in different sectors and industry groups in the UK. Most industries employ some workers on a part-time basis. It is evident, nevertheless, that part-time employment is concentrated in the service sector, and in particular industries within it. As a proportion of all in employment it is highest in industries with a high density of female employment. In the public sector, over one-third (34.6 per cent) of the workforce in the public administration, education and health industry group work part-time, and the proportion is significantly higher in education and in health (where women account for upwards of 70 per cent of the workforce). Among the private service industries, part-time workers represent over two-fifths of the workforce (41.5 per cent) in distribution, hotels and restaurants, and nearly one-fifth (18.9 per cent) of all workers in the financial services. In manufacturing, in contrast, less than one-tenth of the workforce is part-time. The sectoral recomposition of employment – the decline in manufacturing employment and expansion of service industries – offers part of the explanation for the growth in part-time work, a long-term trend dating from the 1950s. Some service industries have relied 'traditionally' on female and part-time labour. Their relative expansion has contributed to the growth of part-time employment and yet, the proportionate share of part-time employment has increased within a number of these service industries since 1980. Moreover, part-time employment has increased in proportionate terms in some industries that in the past were staffed primarily by full-time employees (e.g. the financial services).

The occupational segregation of women's employment, and of women's part-time employment in particular, is probably more pronounced than its industrial segregation. Hence, as Incomes Data Services reported in 2001: 'Although efforts have been made at European level to extend the breadth of part-time work, those employed on a part-time basis still tend to be in traditionally lower-paid, lower-skilled occupations' (IDS, 2001b: 3).

At the end of 2000, in the UK, part-timers accounted for 55 per cent of staff in selling, 45 per cent in personal and protective services, and 33 per cent in clerical and administrative positions. In contrast, only 5 per cent of workers in craft and related

Table 13.5 Part-time employment, by sector and industry group, 2000

| | Percentage of part-timers in sector/industry group |
|---|---|
| Public sector | 30.4 |
| Private sector | 23.3 |
| Distribution, hotels and restaurants | 41.5 |
| Other services | 36.7 |
| Public administration, education and health | 34.6 |
| Banking, finance and insurance, etc. | 18.9 |
| Agriculture and fishing | 16.5 |
| Transport and communications | 12.4 |
| Manufacturing | 8.2 |
| Construction | 6.4 |
| Energy and water | 5.4 |

Source: LFS (2000/1, cited in IDS, 2001b: 3)

positions, 10 per cent in managerial and administrative positions, and 17 per cent of people in professional occupations worked part-time.

The industry and occupational distributions of part-time work provide part of the explanation for part-timers' relatively low average hourly earnings. The gender pay gap has narrowed over the past 30 years, but the improvement has largely been confined to the ratio of female full-time to male full-time average hourly earnings (see Chapter 12). Moreover, an 'intra-gender pay gap' widened in the 1980s and 1990s. The average hourly earnings of female part-time employees were just 75 per cent of female full-time hourly earnings in April 2000, compared with 83 per cent in 1975 (New Earnings Survey data, cited in IDS, 2001b: 3). A partial explanation for this lies in the 'qualifications gap' between women in full-time and those in part-time work and, in relation to this, the skew of their distribution between different occupations.

Women with A-level or above educational qualifications have made some inroads into professional and managerial occupations – where full-time employment is generally the requirement, at least for career progression. The average of female full-time hourly earnings, in consequence, has been raised. Yet, 'qualified' women in full-time jobs often do not attain pay equality with their male colleagues. And women seeking part-time work – whether 'qualified' or not – have often been obliged to accept relatively low-paying jobs that do not provide access to other elements of the reward package offered to full-timers in the same organisation. Data relating to the early 1990s show that around one-third of female part-timers were in fact qualified to A-level or above. A similar proportion had no formal educational qualifications (Harkness, 1998). A significant proportion of the former may be in higher-paid part-time work (for example, in professional occupations in the education or health services). Gallie *et al.*'s (1998) analysis of survey data, however, found that a majority of part-timers reported that they had been recruited to jobs that required no qualifications. In other words, many part-timers are over-qualified for the job roles they fill.

## ■ A matter of choice?

The European Commission and the government in the UK have identified part-time work as a means of securing the labour market inclusion of formerly disadvantaged groups, including women with young children and, among these, lone parents. Part-time work has also been highlighted as a means through which employees – men and women – can attain a better work–life balance. Given that many part-time jobs are relatively low grade and low paid, however, it is relevant to ask why people opt for, or are relegated, to them.

The Labour Force Survey asks people in part-time work about their reasons for working part-time. Around four-fifths of women, although only between one-third and two-fifths of men, select the response that they 'did not want a full-time job'. Men are much more likely than women to report that they 'could not find a full-time job'. The exact proportions vary, principally with the state of the labour market. Nevertheless, while in the period 1992–2001 between one-fifth and one-third of men in part-time work gave this reason, it was cited by, at most, one-tenth of women in part-time work. Around one-third of men report being a student or at school as a reason for part-time work, and while the proportion of women giving this reason has risen steadily in recent years, in April/June 2001 it reached only just above one-tenth (*LFS Historical Supplement*). These data have been interpreted as evidence that, among women at least, part-time work is largely voluntary: a matter of choice, rather than of circumstance (e.g. European Commission, 2001). Hakim (1996) has elaborated on this interpretation to suggest there is an increasing polarisation among women. Those working part-time have made the conscious decision to maximise their preference for domestic as opposed to career, paid employment roles. They are 'willing slaves' to lower paid, part-time work, and this is exemplified by their failure to invest in the education and training that would equip them for better paid jobs, with promotion and pay prospects.

Critics argue that such interpretations underplay the influence of class and of gender relations (in the household, and in society more broadly) on women's preferences. Women have been defined and have seen themselves as having principal responsibility for social production, as well as reproduction, in the household and their integration into the 'public' world of the labour market, and paid employment has been structured in this way (Purcell, 2000). Coupled with the inadequacies of state-supported child care, this has meant that employers in the UK have been able to draw on a supply of female labour available and willing to work on part-time terms and conditions. The 'reserves' of labour supply have been supplemented by the rising numbers of students seeking part-time work, to gain work experience or simply to limit their debts. There are larger numbers also of older men who are relegated to part-time work because they cannot find alternative, full-time employment or who opt for it, for example, to 'wind down' from full-time employment prior to or after retirement.

## ■ Employers' use of part-time work

In surveys of employers in the UK, the most commonly cited reason for using or creating part-time contracts is to secure greater flexibility (e.g. IDS, 2001b). In the relatively 'tight' labour market context of the late 1990s and first years of the twenty-first century, the retention of skilled staff has also been cited by many employing organisations as a rationale for offering part-time work.

Labour flexibility can be developed in a variety of shapes and forms. Gallie *et al.*'s (1998) analysis of workforce survey data suggests that part-timers are unlikely to contribute greatly to the development of functional flexibility. Many part-time workers remained 'at a severe disadvantage in skill level and skill development' opportunities compared with full-timers in their workplace (Gallie *et al.*, 1998: 159). They were less likely than full-timers to report that they had discretion, in particular to introduce changes on the job.

Some types of part-time contract may be used by employing organisations to secure numerical flexibility, defined as the ease of engaging and dismissing staff in line with workload or product market fluctuations. These would include the 'zero hours' contracts that were used in the 1990s, in particular among large supermarket chains, and under which employees are 'on call' rather than having regular (or indeed, any guaranteed) working hours. Such types of contract illustrate the blurred line, or degree of overlap, between different forms of 'non-standard' work. Zero hours contracts are part-time and temporary and, until recently at least, have generally not been regarded by employers as contracts of employment. Part-time workers in general are more likely than full-timers to be in temporary employment. Yet the majority – Purcell (2000: 120) estimates 60 per cent – are in 'permanent' or, at least, open-ended employment. The hours thresholds that were required by employees to accrue continuous employment and in this way qualify for statutory unfair dismissal protection have been abolished. And since 1999, part-time employees, like full-timers, qualify for such protection after one year's employment. Thus they are, in principle, no more insecure than their full-time colleagues, provided their *employee status* is not in doubt.

A main attraction of part-time contracts for employers is their contribution to working time flexibility, that is the ability to adjust the pattern or timing of staff hours worked over a day, or week, to meet production or sales rhythms. In retailing, as in hotels and catering, it has for long been common for employers to organise shifts of part-timers to meet peak periods of customer trading: lunchtimes, early evening, weekends and so on. The extension of such practices has been encouraged by:

- the availability of information and communications technologies that allow the managers of supermarkets, banks and hospitals, to predict customer flows more accurately;
- investments in new technology, that require intensive use of the capital equipment to 'repay' the costs;
- the deregulation of business trading hours in the 1980s and 1990s.

Large employers in retailing, and in the financial services, now compete in their respective sectors by making their products and services available through a variety of channels (telephone banking, Internet shopping, the conventional high street bank branch) and over extended trading hours. A variety of types of part-time contract has been used to support these competitive strategies and to achieve cost savings. In large retail organisations, part-time employment has become more segmented. Pay and benefits have been improved for some part-timers, who are expected in return to cooperate in the pursuit of working time flexibility, for example, by working new shift patterns or, in some instances, longer hours. Alongside these, a 'periphery' of workers on very short or irregular (zero) hours has been developed (Neathey and Hurstfield, 1995: 206).

The retail banks formerly had well-defined internal labour markets. Pay and career progression to managerial level were the prospects for many (although not all) male entrants, who were recruited from school, trained to acquire 'general banking' skills, and who often remained with the bank for their working life. Many female employees worked full time but most were confined to back-office data processing or front-office customer service roles. Branch closures and redundancies in the 1980s and 1990s, however, have put paid to the idea that banking provides a job for life and have truncated career progression routes. Data processing has been removed from branches and concentrated in establishments that specialise in the work, which has been routinised. Shifts of full-timers and part-timers (employed directly or via an agency) are used to keep the 'machinery' operating virtually around the clock. The bank branches that remain open have been tiered, that is equipped to operate as sales or service-only outlets. The staffing of these, to match customer flows over longer opening hours, has been achieved by amending full-time contracts to include, for example, Saturdays as part of the regular working week, and through the use of a variety of part-time contracts. These include term-time-only contracts (for women) and Saturday-only contracts (for students). Call centres use full-time and part-time staff (agency-recruited or directly employed). The requirement, however, is for regular attendance: term-time-only contracts sometimes are not encouraged as managers believe staff lose their work-speed if they do not practise their 'skills' regularly (Tailby and Harrington, 2002).

The need to meet employees' working hours preferences, and in this way retain skilled and experienced staff, has been cited by a number of employers in recent surveys as a reason for their use of part-time contracts (e.g. IDS, 2001b). This is consistent with the Labour government's claim that work–life balance provision – working hours practices and contractual employment forms that are sensitive to employees' preferences and desires to balance work more effectively with other interests and commitments – yields business benefits as well as employee gains. The Department of Trade and Industry (DTI, 2000) lists work–life balance provision to include, in addition to part-time work:

- *flexitime*, where people can vary the timing of their working hours, although usually outside certain agreed core times;
- *staggered hours*, where employees in a workplace have different start, finish and break times;
- *job-sharing*, where two people carry out the duties of a post that would normally be done by one person;
- *compressed working hours*, which allow people to work their total agreed number of hours over a shorter number of working days;
- *self-rostering*, which gives team members greater control over their work times;
- *annual hours*, systems that organise working time on the basis of the number of hours to be worked over a year rather than a week (usually to fit in with peaks and troughs of work);
- *working at or from home*, for some or all of the time;
- *teleworking*, using a telephone and computer to keep in touch with work;
- *temporary and casual work*;
- *self-employment*, which, as the DTI hints, may involve very long hours of work rather than providing people with greater control over their working hours.

None of these practices is entirely novel and some (in particular, the last two listed) have been often been interpreted as the most 'precarious', or insecure, of all the forms of non-standard work. Many major employers in a range of industries and sectors have embraced the work–life balance agenda and some 'exemplars' have introduced, or have extended to a wider range of staff, access to some or most of the types of provision listed above. The relatively tight labour market of the late 1990s and early 2000s has been an influence, in particular for employers in public services such as education and health where there have been recurrent 'crises' of staff shortages. A strong commitment to become or remain an equal opportunities employer, nonetheless, has been a factor for some organisations. That said, survey data suggest that across all workplaces, provision of flexible working time arrangements is quite limited; part-time work (for women) and shift work for male full-timers remain by far the most common arrangements (Hogarth *et al.*, 2001: 14). In this context, it is relevant to note that studies have shown an upward trend in the proportion of women working full-time who would like to work shorter hours; an increase that is especially marked among women working in professional and managerial jobs. Yet they have also found evidence that 'qualified' women who have moved to a part-time or job-sharing contract after childbirth have experienced a significant downgrading of their conditions and career prospects (Wacjman, 1996, cited in Purcell, 2000).

UK employment legislation has changed since the mid-1990s. Part-time workers have acquired new statutory rights. These include the right to be paid at the statutory national minimum hourly rate, and the right to paid annual leave (introduced as part of the Working Time Regulations, 1998). The Low Pay Commission reported in 2000 that well over 1.5 million workers had benefited from the national minimum wage (NMW); that two-thirds of the beneficiaries were working women; and that two-thirds of these were part-time workers. Part-time workers in the past have been seen as offering employers a relatively cheap source of labour by virtue of their failure to qualify for shift or overtime premia and company benefits. Such discrimination is in principle ruled out by the Part-time Workers (Prevention of Less Favourable Treatment) Regulations that came into force in 2001. These introduce the principle of 'no less favourable treatment' between full-time and part-time workers. McKay (2001: 294) suggests, however, that the 'fact that it is limited to those working under the same type of contract and at the same location narrows the scope for comparison' and may limit the number of part-time workers who will benefit from the regulations.

## Temporary work

Temporary employment is 'unequivocally insecure' (Purcell, 2000: 121). This is regardless of whether people choose or are relegated to it. Temporary employment encompasses a range of employment relationships, and its diversity is suggested to an extent by its multiplicity of forms. It includes workers who are engaged directly by an employer either for a fixed term, or on a casual or seasonal basis, or as on-call workers with no regular or guaranteed hours, and staff who are supplied to an employing organisation by a third party recruitment or temporary work agency. Temporary workers are located in a wide range of occupations. Many are recruited to low-grade, low-paid jobs, but there has been growth in temporary employment in the past decade among professionals, managers and technically qualified personnel (TUC, 2001).

### ■ Extent and distribution of temporary employment

The LFS provides the principal source of data on the extent of temporary work and allows some assessment of trends. Its reliance on respondents' self-assessment of their employment status, however, may mean that it underestimates the extent of temporary work. Burchell et al.'s (1999) analysis, for example, shows that many workers on fixed-term appointments think they are in permanent employment and report this as their employment status in the LFS. Moreover, the LFS only questions respondents who have identified themselves as employees about the permanency, or otherwise, of their employment. It omits from this questioning the self-employed, a proportion of whom are akin to employees in respects other than the fact that they are engaged by an employing organisation on a 'contract for services' rather than a contract of employment. Burchell et al.'s (1999) analysis suggests that a significant proportion among these 'dependent self-employed' have jobs that are 'chronically insecure'.

Setting these difficulties to one side, it is clear that temporary employment in the UK has increased since the 1980s. In the second half of that decade, temporary employees accounted for a relatively stable 5 to 6 per cent of all employees in employment in the UK. Their numbers rose in the recession of the early 1990s and, according to LFS data, reached a peak of 1.8 million – or 7.8 per cent of all employees in employment – in 1997. The total and proportion have fallen slightly, to 1.7 million and 7 per cent, respectively, in 2001. The aggregate data, however, disguise some important growth trends. Fixed-term contract workers' share of the total of temporary employees rose slightly between 1992 and 1999, to 51 per cent. Seasonal and casual workers' share of the total fell slightly, to around 23 per cent. The proportion of agency temps more than doubled, from 6.6 to 15.5 per cent and has continued to rise.

LFS data show that women currently form a slim majority of all UK temporary employees, and that their share of the total has fallen from 57 per cent in 1992 to 54 per cent in 2001. Yet the gender composition of temporary employment varies with its type. Purcell (2000: 122) notes that men are more likely than women to work on fixed-term contracts, and women are more likely than men to be 'in other, generally more casual categories'.

Among all temporary workers, approximately equal proportions are in full-time and part-time work, but again there are variations by type of temporary employment. Drawing on the 1998 Temporary Employment Survey, IDS (2000: 2) reports that around 70 per cent of seasonal/casual workers are part-time, in contrast to 56 per cent of fixed-term contract workers and 36 per cent of agency workers. The TUC (2001) emphasises that young workers (under 30 years of age) and people from black and ethnic minority groups form significant proportions of the total of temporary employees: 44 per cent and 11 per cent, respectively. Approximately 50 per cent of all temporary agency workers are under 30 years old (TUC, 1999).

Among the different industry groups, the share of temporary to all employees is highest in public administration, education and health. LFS data show that in spring 1999 there were 0.5 million temps, representing 10 per cent of all employees in this public service group which had over half of the UK total of fixed-term contract workers (cited in IDS, 2000: 3). Government reforms of public sector employment have been an influence. Employers in the public sector have been obliged to operate within tight budgets, determined on an annual basis. Those in local government and health were statutorily required in the 1980s and 1990s to open to competitive tender with private sector organisations the provision of specified ancillary services, formerly performed in-house. Best Value has displaced compulsory competitive tendering since 1997 (see Chapter 14), but the pressures on public service organisations to reduce costs (or out-source activities) remain. Temporary workers represented 6.8 per cent of all employees in banking, finance and insurance in 1999 when this industry group accounted for one-third of all temporary agency workers recorded in the LFS. Distribution, hotels and restaurants had roughly one-third of all casual and seasonal workers (IDS, 2000: 2). Four per cent of manufacturing employees were temporary in 1999, but the pro-portion was higher in mechanical engineering and vehicle engineering (Gallie *et al.*, 1998: 173) which may reflect the extension of lean production regimes (*Financial Times*, 1 February 1996).

Temporary work is not the preserve of low-skilled and low-paid groups of workers and, as suggested, its growth has been recorded among professionals, managers and technically qualified employees in the past decade (TUC, 2001). Temporary workers in these occupations are likely to be engaged on fixed-term contracts, although among public service 'professionals', agency temping is increasingly common. Over half of those who are seasonal or casual workers are in craft, personal and protective services, plant and machine operative and other occupations. Over half of the temporary agency workers recorded in the 1998 Temporary Employment Survey were in clerical and secretarial positions (IDS, 2000: 2). A survey of recruitment agencies conducted for the DTI in 1999, however, found that 70 per cent of the temporary workers supplied by these labour market 'intermediaries' were men, and that one-fifth of the male total were classified occupationally as information technology, computing and telecommunications workers (Hotopp, 2000).

Temporary employment has grown across the EU as a whole since the mid-1980s. European Commission figures (cited in McKay, 2001: 291; see also European Commission, 2001) suggest that the proportion of jobs that were temporary contracts rose from 8.3 per cent in 1985 to 13.2 per cent in 2000. Some marked differences are apparent in temporary workers' share of total employment in different countries. Data relating to 1997 range from 6.3 per cent in Belgium to 13.1 per cent in France and 33.6 per cent in Spain (European Commission, 1998, cited in IDS, 2000: 15). Set in this context, the UK appears to have a relatively low incidence of temporary work (although, as will be seen, it has an above-average incidence of temporary agency workers).

Among the factors contributing to the cross-national variations are differences in national employment law. Legislation regulating dismissals and redundancies among 'permanent' employees (i.e. those on open-ended contracts) may provide, to differing degrees, an incentive for employers to create temporary jobs. Most EU countries, however, have legislation that regulates the types of tasks and work that can be constructed as temporary (and in some countries the maximum length of temporary contracts is also prescribed in law). The relatively high share of temporary employment in the Spanish economy has been attributed to the relatively strong 'job protection rights' enjoyed by 'permanent' workers and the introduction in the 1980s of legislation that extended the circumstances in which employers could use temporary contracts. Conversely, the UK's relatively low share of temporary to all employment has been attributed to the relatively weak employment protection that all workers have enjoyed under UK employment law (see, for example, Beatson, 1995).

In the past in the UK there has been no explicit legal distinction between permanent and temporary employees (IDS, 2000: 11). However, the length of continuous employment required to accrue the statutory right to claim unfair dismissal has meant that workers on short contracts have been especially insecure – that is, especially 'disposable', from an employer's point of view. Moreover, up until 1999, employers were able lawfully to require workers on fixed-term contracts to waive their statutory rights to claim unfair dismissal and financial compensation for redundancy. At the time of writing, the law has as yet to be amended to clarify the identity of the employer of temporary agency staff – the agency supplying these workers or the client organisation that uses their labour services. Some among the large agencies (e.g. Manpower) employ some temps directly, but many temporary work agencies do not – they simply act as a third party, placing workers temporarily with 'companies who have no legal employment relationship with them' (TUC, 1999: 9). As a consequence, many temporary agency staff have been unable to qualify for statutory unfair dismissal protection. The employment agency industry in the UK has been much less regulated by legislation than in most EU countries, and the Conservative government abolished the need for firms to obtain a licence to operate in it (see Exhibit 13.2 later in this chapter).

Surveys of employers' use of fixed-term and other directly employed temporary staff suggest that many have offered temporary workers the same basic pay as 'permanent' employees (and, in some instances, higher pay) and access to overtime and shift premium payments, although a significant proportion have not. Some employers have offered temps access to some of the company benefits extended to 'permanent' staff, but among these a number have insisted on a qualifying period of service. Outside the public sector, it has been rare for employers to provide temps with access to company or occupational pension schemes (TUC, 2001; see also IDS, 2000: 7). In short, it would appear that the attraction of temporary contracts for some employers has been the ability to save on pay and/or 'on-costs' as well as to secure gains in numerical flexibility. That said, it is evident that some employing organisations have been willing, or have been obliged, to offer premium rates of pay to secure the services of staff whose skills are in short supply, and who have opted to supply their labour on a temporary basis only.

## ■ Employees' preferences

Temporary work is by definition insecure and can involve working alongside 'permanent' colleagues whose terms and conditions are superior. As Gallie et al.'s (1998) analysis indicates, for many workers it is likely to mean limited job satisfaction and limited access to the on-the-job training that may be the prerequisite for progression to a 'permanent' appointment. Yet temporary work can offer attractions for some people. For professionals with qualifications and skills that are highly marketable, it may offer autonomy and flexibility and the opportunity to 'play the field' and bid up salaries (TUC, 2001). Students, who form a significant proportion of the temporary workforce, may fall between these two extremes. They may be forced into paid employment by virtue of spiraling debts and the pressure to accept whatever work is available. On the other hand, some may see temporary employment as a means of gaining the work experience that may enhance their subsequent marketability, or as a means of gaining a 'foothold in the door' of a company they would like to work for.

The LFS asks temporary employees about their reasons for having temporary employment. Its findings suggest that, alongside age, sex, ethnic origin, qualifications and occupation, the state of the labour market is an influence on whether workers opt for or are relegated to temporary work. In 1992, when the UK economy was barely recovering from recession, over two-fifths (43 per cent) of male temporary workers reported they were in temporary employment because they could not find a permanent job. By 2001, this proportion had fallen to less than one-third (31 per cent), whereas the proportion who reported that they did not want a permanent job had risen from one-fifth (20 per cent) to over one-quarter (26.3 per cent). Among female temporary employees, the proportion who reported they did not want a permanent job remained more stable, at around one-third, in the first half of the 1990s, although this rose in the second half of the 1990s to a peak of 37 per cent in 2000. The proportion who reported they could not find a secure job fell from a peak of above one-third (37 per cent) in 1994 to less than one-quarter (24 per cent) in 2001. The state of the labour market (the overall availability of employment opportunities) may therefore be taken as an influence on workers' preferences and opportunities. But the trends in the growth of types of temporary work have to be related also to the practices of employing organisations, the growth of the employment agency industry, and developments in UK employment law.

# ■ Employers' use of temporary labour

Incomes Data Services (IDS, 2000: 4) distinguish four employers' rationales for using fixed-term and other directly engaged temporary staff. These are:

- covering for the absence of permanent employees;
- coping with fluctuations in workload (often seasonal);
- completing specific projects or specialist projects;
- minimising redundancies where changes to working practices are anticipated.

To the list could be added the objectives of minimising pay or 'on cost' labour charges. It is important to note, however, that in surveys employers often report the disadvantages of using temporary staff (see TUC, 1999, 2001; IDS, 2000). A fairly common perception is that temporary employees are less committed and less reliable than staff whose employment security is not so immediately in doubt.

Employers' use of temporary agency staff has often been analysed from a 'transaction cost' theory perspective associated with the work of Williamson (1975, 1985). The idea is that employers secure administrative cost savings by outsourcing labour recruitment and labour management to an external organisation, in particular where their demand is for relatively small numbers of workers with general (as opposed to company-specific) skills. Yet, in practice, employers have used agency supply for a broader range of reasons; in construction, for example, an objective has been to avoid statutory obligations, such as the provision of sick pay, holiday pay and redundancy pay (TUC, 1999). In addition, the delegation of labour management functions to a third party may create its own difficulties, for example in terms of assuring the quality of labour supply (see Grimshaw *et al.*, 2001).

Employers traditionally have had available a range of means of covering short-term absences among permanent staff (on holiday or on sick leave). In addition to agency supply or use of a short contract, these means include asking permanent staff to work overtime. NHS hospitals have always had to resource a 24-hour, 365 day a year demand for medical and nursing services and many have used a 'bank' of nursing staff who are on call to fill in for staff absences or to meet workload peaks. 'Bank' nurses include not only those who work only on a casual basis, but also those who have a regular, full-time or part-time NHS job and undertake bank nursing as a second job. Until recently, many hospitals treated casual bank staff as akin to staff on zero hours contracts; they were not regarded as employees and were not given access to sick pay, holiday pay, the occupational pension scheme, etc. In short, their use offered the advantages of cheapness and flexibility.

Employers in some industry sectors have traditionally organised staffing to meet seasonal peaks and troughs in the workload; for example, via summer shutdowns in manufacturing plants, or the recruitment of casual and seasonal workers in hotels and catering. Employers in some sectors have become more attentive to the seasonality of trade and to the means of matching staff numbers and expertise to these rhythms. Retail banks, for example, now draw on their (student) supplies of Saturday-only staff to meet the Christmas peak in customer sales-flows in their branch networks.

Since seasonal peaks in workload are regular and recurrent, their staffing can be planned. Similarly, some retail banks use temporary agency workers to meet planned, temporary increases in the volume of customer enquiries generated by the launch of a new product (for example, a new mortgage repayment scheme). Most use agencies as a means of securing sufficient supplies of labour to meet staff turnover in their data processing centres, where the work is routinised, and some of the banks use agencies as a means of 'screening' recruitment to open-ended employment in their call centres. Staff are recruited by an agency and retained as agency staff for a period of weeks before being offered a 'permanent' appointment (or not). Practices vary among the banks, however, and agency recruitment to call centres and branch networks is eschewed by some on the grounds that it is expensive (agencies charge a commission for their services) and does not guarantee the calibre of staff to meet the quality or speed of customer service required. Thus in the 1990s, when banks were downsizing their branch networks, they tended to use fixed-term contract staff rather than temporary agency workers or, indeed, open-ended contracts, to fill vacant positions.

Much attention has been given to the increased use of temporary agency nursing staff in NHS hospitals since the late 1990s. Hospital managers have had to meet rising levels of patient demand for their services, and the more exacting performance targets instituted by government (e.g. to reduce the length of time patients have to wait for treatment). At the same time, they have experienced difficulties in recruiting and retaining staff on regular, open-ended contracts. This reflects an accumulation of staff grievances regarding workloads, pay and the inflexibility of working hours. Bank nursing supplies have proved insufficient to meet the staffing shortages on the wards, and hospital managers have been obliged to rely increasingly on agency supply. Indeed, some temporary work agencies have been adept in recruiting NHS nurses who want additional shifts, and now secure these through an agency rather than through the NHS hospital bank. Able to command high commissions for their services, these agencies have been able to offer nurses regular (additional) work at relatively attractive hourly pay rates, and with some choice as regards their preferred working hours.

## ◼ New rights for temporary staff

The framework of UK employment law has changed since the late 1990s. Temporary workers have made gains, although the law continues to allow discrimination against them in a range of respects. The Employment Relations Act 1999 circumscribed employers' right to oblige fixed-term contract staff to waive their statutory entitlement to unfair dismissal protection, although waiver clauses in respect of redundancy payments are still lawful. The length of service required for unfair dismissal protection has been reduced to a year, rather than abolished, and the requirement of 'employee' status remains. Therefore many workers on short contracts will continue to find it difficult to qualify for this statutory right, as will many of the 'dependent self-employed' and agency staff who are not employed by the agency through which they secure work. All workers are covered by the National Minimum Wage Act 1998 and by the provisions of the Working Time Regulations 1998. The latter initially restricted the right to paid annual leave to workers who had been employed continuously by the same employer for at least 13 weeks. The TUC challenged that this did not fulfil the UK's obligations under the EU Working Time Directive, and the length of service qualification – which discriminated against short-contract and freelance workers – has been abolished. IDS (2000) reports that the legal obligation to pay holiday leave has encouraged some employers to convert temporary jobs into 'permanent' appointments (i.e. because it has restricted the cost-cutting advantage of the former). 'Poor' employers, nevertheless, may find other ways of accommodating the legislation, and the TUC (1999:12) notes that some temporary work agencies have implemented holiday rights by 'leaving take home pay unchanged, but reducing basic pay and adding a notional holiday pay element to the wage packet'.

The European Commission has seen non-standard employment as a means of meeting employers' requirement for greater flexibility and of increasing labour market participation among 'disadvantaged' groups. At the same time, commissioners have acknowledged that labour market deregulation risks fuelling the growth of 'poor quality' jobs that do not contribute to productivity improvements (see, for example, European Commission, 2001). European trade unions have campaigned for higher 'labour standards' – better pay and conditions and stronger employment rights for workers – against European employers' appeals for further labour market deregulation. Some compromises have been reached. The Fixed-term Directive, adopted in June 1999, puts into effect the framework agreement on fixed-term work concluded earlier in that year by the European Trade Union Confederation and the European-level employers' organisations UNICE and CEEP. The directive aims to:

- prevent fixed-term employees from being less favourably treated than similar permanent employees;
- prevent abuses arising from the use of successive fixed-term contracts;
- improve access to training for fixed-term employees;
- ensure fixed-term employees are informed about available permanent jobs.

Member states were required to comply with its provisions by July 2001, but the UK government has made use of the additional year allowed for consultation 'to take account of special difficulties'.

At the beginning of 2002, details were 'leaked' of a draft EU directive that proposes to give temporary agency workers rights to the same remuneration as long-term employees doing comparable jobs. The proposals would cover pay, pensions, holiday and other benefits such as health insurance, interest-free loans, non-discretionary bonuses and share schemes (*Financial Times*, 17 February 2002). Among EU member states, the UK has one of the highest levels of use of temporary agency workers, and agency workers in this country have had fewer rights, *vis-à-vis* 'permanent' staff, than their counterparts elsewhere in Europe. In other words, they stand to gain most from the proposed directive. Whether it will be translated into EU legislation, however, remains to be seen. In the UK, employers' organisations and representatives of the major employment agencies have articulated their strong disapproval, claiming that, if passed, the proposed directive 'could damage the labour market irreparably' (see Exhibit 13.2).

## Chapter summary

Labour flexibility has been a central theme in public policy and in academic debates since the 1980s. The concept has been applied in prescriptions for change in the organisation and management of work, the construction of working time patterns, and the regulation of pay and employment. This chapter has explored different dimensions of the 1980s 'flexibility debates' and some of the issues in the restructuring of work and employment that continue to be discussed in the terms established by those debates.

Exhibit 13.2

## Fears over flexibility if temps get greater rights

The growing army of 'temps' in the workforce means that a draft Brussels directive giving agency workers greater rights would particularly affect employers in Britain.

As more temps are employed in the UK than in any other European country, the directive could be the most contentious European Union employment reform yet for the government to adopt.

And because Britain accounts for half the European total of agency workers, it could be hard for opponents of the proposals – and worried ministers – to win allies among other member states.

Employers are already arguing that the directive could damage the labour market irreparably.

James Reed, chief executive of Reed, one of the country's biggest recruitment agencies, said the directive was unworkable.

'It is bad news for the economy and for individuals, particularly the disadvantaged. Flexible labour has been a huge asset keeping unemployment at the lowest level in Europe', he said.

Behind Brussels' thinking is a recognition, welcomed by the trade unions, that the secretaries, clerical workers, computing staff, engineers, teachers and nurses employed by agencies do not enjoy the same rights as permanent colleagues.

With agency 'temping' growing fast, employers are able to tap a skilled and flexible labour resource, often at less cost than hiring staff themselves.

The problem is that agency workers can easily be exploited. Sarah Veale, of the Trades Union Congress, said: 'At call centres, it's not uncommon for people to have their contracts terminated and to be re-employed as agency workers on less pay and with fewer rights.'

To discourage substitution and abuse, Brussels wants agency workers to have the same remuneration as longer-term counterparts.

Employers have lobbied the European Commission to get the wording changed. Several commissioners are understood to have voiced concern about the draft and its publication is to be delayed, perhaps until after next month's EU summit in Barcelona.

Ministers are anxious about the directive's impact. Last year, the government reluctantly agreed to include pay and pensions when it implemented legislation giving fixed-term workers equal rights. In part, that decision was to emphasise that remuneration is an area of national discretion.

This time ministers could adopt a similar stance and try to resist including remuneration if the directive demands it.

Some member states, including Spain, France and Italy, already have stringent national legislation restricting the use of agency labour. In Germany and the Netherlands agencies have to reach agreements at a national level with trade unions. In Britain, most workers are not covered by collective agreements of this kind.

The Confederation of British Industry's case is that the directive is incompatible with UK practices and would damage competitiveness. The employers' organisation argues that a temp's relationship is with the agency, so comparisons with long-term staff are inappropriate. Agency work, it adds, is often a route into employment for young people and the long-term unemployed. Temping helps companies fill skills gaps and respond quickly to fluctuating demand.

But the TUC says legislation is needed because the rights of agency temps are weak. They cannot claim unfair dismissal and do not qualify for statutory redundancy. They are unlikely to be allowed to join the company pension scheme.

Requirements for employment agencies to be licensed disappeared under the previous Tory government.

'It is not a picture of non-stop abuse, but there are difficulties with agencies that spring up overnight', said Ms Veale. 'Unless you're caught not paying the minimum wage, you can get away with a lot.'

*Source:* Christopher Adams, *Financial Times*, 18 February 2002.
© 1995–2002 The Financial Times Limited

The 'flexible specialisation' thesis envisaged that firms and employees would secure mutual gains from the use of new information and communication technologies and 'flexible' forms of work organisation in the manufacture of quality goods for high value-added niche product markets. Government ministers in the UK in the 1980s mirrored their counterparts in the US by urging that industry competitiveness and the invigoration of employment growth required the deregulation of markets – the exposure of firms and, more especially, workers to the discipline of 'free market forces'. The flexible firm model attracted a good deal of academic and practitioner interest. It suggested that employers could use a numerically flexible peripheral workforce to underwrite the employment security of a core employee group whose commitment, flexibility and versatility could be tapped to secure productivity and quality gains.

The model's broad and bipolar categories of core and periphery, comprising skilled and secure full-time workers and those on insecure non-standard contracts respectively, proved overly rigid for the purposes of understanding the range of ways that employers could attain cost savings, productivity increases and other 'flexibility' gains. Ackroyd and Procter's (1998) study of the 'new flexible firm', for example, showed that large British-owned firms, operating in the manufacturing sector in the UK, had been able to cut costs by developing functional flexibility among relatively unskilled workers employed on a full-time basis. The employment security of these workers was threatened constantly by their employer's preparedness to outsource supplies if this contributed further labour cost savings.

It was evident by the early 1990s that certain forms of non-standard employment had become more common in the UK economy as a whole. Part-time work and self-employment increased in relative terms in the 1980s, and in the 1990s there was some growth in temporary employment and a marked increase in temporary agency work. There was clear evidence of the 'diffusion' of new forms of work organisation, although lean production regimes and a number of versions of teamworking were shown to reinforce rather than to depart from Taylorist principles. Yet core employment, if taken to mean relatively secure employment, was not greatly in evidence. Manufacturing and service sector employers met the recession of the early 1990s by downsizing. Journalists and academics drew on anecdotal and survey evidence to report a pervasive sense of job insecurity among most employee groups, including managers and professionals. The increased incidence of work-related stress was reported widely in the mid-1990s and, in relation to this, studies highlighted the UK's long-hours work culture.

Statistics showed that average full-time working hours were longer in the UK than in any other EU country. Yet Green's (2001) careful analysis suggests that the principal trend of the 1980s and 1990s was an increasingly uneven distribution of working hours, as between individuals and households. On the eve of the introduction of the Working Time Regulations in 1998, a higher proportion of the workforce was working long hours (in excess of 48 hours a week) in comparison with the position in the late 1970s, and a higher proportion was working short hours (fewer than 20 hours a week). There was an increased polarisation between work-rich and work-less households. In comparison with the late 1970s there were more dual-income households in which the male and female 'heads' each worked full-time. There were also more households in which no one of working age had paid employment.

Since 1997, government labour market policy in the UK has complemented rather than confronted directly that pursued at the level of the European Union, although this is partly because flexibility has become a stronger theme in the latter. The Labour government reiterated its Conservative predecessor's emphasis on the need for 'flexibility and efficiency' in the labour market but elevated 'fairness at work' as a policy goal. It retained much of the 1980s industrial relations legislation although it also enacted new collective employment rights, on the understanding that the trade unions will moderate their objectives and seek a 'partnership' relationship with company managers to secure flexibility and efficiency gains. The government delivered its commitment to enact certain minimum labour standards and has urged employers to attend to employees' aspirations for a better work–life balance. Yet various studies questioned the impact of the Working Time Regulations, which allow employers to secure individual and collective employee opt-outs from the 48-hour maximum working week provisions. And while relatively tight labour market conditions in the five years to 2002 encouraged many employers to extend employees' access to 'flexible' working hours, across all work-places it was part-time work (for women) and shift work (among males in full-time work) that remained the most common non-standard working time patterns.

EU directives that aim to reduce discrimination against workers on non-standard contracts have been proposed and some have been enacted. It remains to be seen how the new legal obligations will influence UK employers' use of the various types of non-standard work. It is evident, however, that the UK's implementation of EU legislation will continue to be shaped by the competing claims of employers and trade unions – for the freedom to use 'flexible' contracts and the obligation not to abuse the labour of workers engaged on them.

## Questions

1   Why has the concept of flexibility dominated discussion of work and employment restructuring in the advanced economies in the past two decades?

2   What is meant by the concepts of numerical flexibility, functional flexibility and working time flexibility?

3   Why do researchers analyse teamwork with reference to the 'Swedish model' and the 'Japanese model' of team-based work organisation ?

4   What factors have contributed to the growth of part-time employment in the UK since the 1980s?

5   What types of flexibility do employers seek or attain through the use of part-time contracts?

6   In what respects does temporary work form a heterogeneous employment category?

7   What is meant by 'work–life balance'? How might part-time work assist or undermine your efforts to attain such equilibrium?

## Activity

Study the section on temporary work, and Exhibit 13.2 in particular. Imagine you are (a) a senior civil servant in the Department of Trade and Industry in the UK, (b) a trade union official, (c) an employer, (d) a senior manager of a large temporary work agency, and (e) an agency temp. Sketch your response – in each role – to the proposed EU directive on temporary agency workers.

## Useful websites

*www.dfes.gov.uk* **Department for Education and Skills** Focuses on skills, training, productivity issues and government labour market policy.

*www.dti.gov.uk/er* **Department of Trade and Industry** Covers the work of the Employment Relations Directorate of the DTI, dealing with relations between workers and their employers, including individual and collective rights. Access for details of employment legislation (1998 Working Time Regulations, 1998 National Minimum Wage Act, etc.), research monitoring the impact of the legislation, consultation documents issued prior to the introduction of regulations, etc.

*www.eiro.eurofound.ie* **European Industrial Relations Observatory On-Line** Website of the European Foundation for the Improvement of Living and Working Conditions. For all 15 European Union member states there are three or four articles each month, as well as some comparative studies. Comprehensive coverage of new UK employment legislation and articles on the conflicting perspectives of the TUC and CBI on regulation and flexibility.

*www.eoc.org.uk* **Equal Opportunities Commission** The EOC is the leading agency working to eliminate sex discrimination in Britain. Apart from news, press releases, etc. there is extensive coverage of policy developments and campaigns, research and statistics, and aspects of the law.

*www.lowpay.gov.uk* **Low Pay Commission** Access to reports and publications of the UK Low Pay Commission established by the National Minimum Wage Act 1998 to advise the government about the National Minimum Wage.

*www.tuc.org.uk* **Trades Union Congress** The TUC's campaign sites focus on working hours, temporary workers, etc. Employment research section includes quarterly labour market briefings.

## References

Ackroyd, S. and Procter, S. (1998) 'British manufacturing organization and workplace industrial relations: some attributes of the new flexible firm', *British Journal of Industrial Relations*, 36(2): 163–84.

Amin, A. (1994) 'Post-Fordism: models, fantasies and phantoms of transition' in Amin, A. (ed.) *Post-Fordism: A Reader*. Oxford: Blackwell: 1–39.

Atkinson, J. (1984) 'Manpower strategies for flexible organisations', *Personnel Management*, August: 28–31.

Atkinson, J. (1985) 'Flexibility: planning for the uncertain future', *Manpower Policy and Practice*, 1: 26–9.

Atkinson, J. and Gregory, D. (1986) 'A flexible future: Britain's dual labour market', *Marxism Today*, 30(4): 12–17.

Bacon, N. and Blyton, P. (2000) 'High road and low road teamworking: perceptions of management rationales and organizational and human resource outcomes', *Human Relations*, 53(11): 1425–58.

Beatson, M. (1995) *Labour Market Flexibility*, Employment Department Research Series No. 48. London: Department of Employment.

Bruegel, I. and Perrons, D. (1998) 'Deregulation and women's employment: the diverse experiences of women in Britain', *Feminist Economics*, 4(1): 103–25.

Burchell, B., Deakin, S. and Honey, S. (1999) *The Employment Status of Individuals in Non-standard Employment*, Employment Relations Research Series No. 6. London: Department of Trade and Industry.

Claydon, T. (1997) 'Human resource management and the labour market', in Beardwell, I. and Holden, L. (eds) *Human Resource Management: A Contemporary Perspective*. London: Financial Times/Pitman Publishing: 73–117.

Claydon, T. (1998) 'Problematising partnership: the prospects for a co-operative bargaining agenda' in Sparrow, P. and Marchington, M. (eds) *Human Resource Management: The New Agenda*. London: Financial Times/Pitman Publishing.

Crafts, N. (1991) 'Reversing relative economic decline? The 1980s in historical perspective', *Oxford Review of Economic Policy*, 7(3): 81–98.

Cully, M., Woodland, S., O'Reilly, A. and Dix, G. (1999) *Britain At Work, As Depicted by the 1998 Workplace Employee Relations Survey*. London: Routledge.

Danford, A. (1998) 'Teamworking and labour regulation in the autocomponents industry', *Work, Employment and Society*, 12(3): 409–31.

Delbridge, R. (1998) *Life on the Line in Contemporary Manufacturing*. Oxford: Oxford University Press.

Delbridge, R., Lowe, J. and Oliver, N. (2000) 'Shopfloor responsibilities under lead teamworking', *Human Relations*, 53(11): 1459–80.

Dohse, K., Jurgens, U. and Malsch, T. (1985) 'From "Fordism" to "Toyotism"? The social organization of the labor process in the Japanese automobile industry', *Politics and Society*, 14(2): 115–46.

DTI (Department of Trade and Industry) (1998) *Fairness at Work*, Cm. 3968. London: The Stationery Office.

DTI (2000) *Essential Guide to Work–Life Balance*. www.dti.gov.uk/work-lifebalance

Edwards, P. and Wright, M. (1996) 'Does teamworking work and if so, why?', paper presented at ESRC seminar, the Manchester Series, 'Human Resource Management in Crisis?' Manchester Metropolitan University, 27 September.

European Commission (2000) *Employment in Europe 2000*. Brussels, European Commission, October.

European Commission (2001) *Employment in Europe 2001, Recent Trends and Prospects*. Luxembourg: Office for Official Publications of the European Commission.

Felstead, A. and Jewson, N. (1999) 'Flexible labour and non-standard employment: an agenda of issues' in Felstead, A. and Jewson, N. (eds) *Global Trends in Flexible Labour*. Basingstoke: Macmillan: 1–20.

Gallie, D., White, M., Cheng, Y. and Tomlinson, M. (1998) *Restructuring the Employment Relationship*. Oxford: Clarendon Press.

Gamble, A. (2001) 'Neo-liberalism', *Capital and Class*, 75 (special issue), Autumn: 127–34.

Garrahan, P. and Stewart, P. (1992) *The Nissan Enigma – Flexibility at Work in a Local Economy*. London: Mansell.

Geary, J. (1992) 'Employment flexibility and human resource management: the case of three American electronics plants', *Work, Employment and Society*, 6(2): 251–70.

Giddens, A. (1998) *The Third Way*. Cambridge: Polity Press.

Godard, J. (2001) 'Beyond the high-performance paradigm? An analysis of variation in Canadian managerial perceptions of reform programme effectiveness', *British Journal of Industrial Relations*, 39(1): 25–52.

Green, F. (2001) 'It's been a hard day's night: the concentration and intensification of work in late twentieth century Britain', *British Journal of Industrial Relations*, 39(1): 53–80.

Grimshaw, D., Ward, K.G., Rubery, J. and Beynon, H. (2001) 'Organisations and the transformation of the internal labour market', *Work, Employment and Society*, 15(1): 25–54.

Hakim, C. (1996) *Key Issues in Women's Work: Female Heterogeneity and the Polarisation of Women's Employment*. London: Athlone Press.

Harkness, S. (1998) 'The gender earnings gap: evidence from the UK', *Fiscal Studies*, 17(2): 1–36.

Heery, E. and Salmon, J. (2000) 'The insecurity thesis' in Heery, E. and Salmon, J. (eds) *The Insecure Workforce*. London: Routledge: 1–24.

Hegewisch, A. (1996) 'Part-time working in Europe', *Flexible Working*, May: 14–16.

Hirst, P. and Zeitlin, J. 1989. 'Flexible specialisation and the competitive failure of UK manufacturing', *Political Quarterly*, 60(2): 164–78.

Hogarth, T., Hasluck, C. and Pierre, G. with Winterbotham, M. and Vivian, D. (2001) *Work–Life Balance 2000: Baseline Study of Work–Life Balance Practices in Great Britain*, Summary Report. University of Warwick: Institute for Employment Research and Iff Research.

Hotopp, U. (2000) 'Recruitment agencies in the UK', *Labour Market Trends*, October: 457–63.

Hunter, L., McGregor, A., MacInnes, J. and Sproul, A. (1993) 'The 'flexible firm': strategy and segmentation', *British Journal of Industrial Relations*, 31(3): 383–409.

Huselid, M.A. (1995) 'The impact of human resource management practices on turnover, productivity, and corporate financial performance', *Academy of Management Journal*, 38: 635–72.

Hyman, R. (1988) 'Flexible specialisation: miracle or myth?' in Hyman, R. and Streeck, W. (eds) *New Technology and Industrial Relations*. Oxford: Basil Blackwell.

Hyman, R. (1991). '*Plus ça change*? The theory of production and the production of theory' in Pollert, A. (ed.) *Farewell to Flexibility?* Oxford: Blackwell Business: 261–83.

IDS (2000) *Temporary workers*. IDS Studies Personnel Policy and Practice, 689 (May).

IDS (2001a) *Teamworking*. IDS Studies Personnel policy and practice. December.

IDS (2001b) *Part-time Workers*. IDS Studies Personnel Policy and Practice, 715 (September).

Kalleberg, A. (2001). 'Organizing flexibility: the flexible firm in a new century', *British Journal of Industrial Relations*, 39(4): 479–504.

Kern, H. and Schumann, M. (1989) *Das Ende der Arbeitsteilung?* Munich: Beck.

Knell, J. (1999) *Partnership at Work*, Employment Relations Research Series No. 7. London: Department of Trade and Industry.

McKay, S. (2001). 'Annual review article. Between flexibility and regulation: rights, equality and protection at work', *British Journal of Industrial Relations*, 39(2): 285–304.

McKinsey Global Institute (1998). *Driving Productivity and Growth in the UK Economy*. London: McKinsey.

McIlroy, J. (1998) 'The enduring alliance? Trade unions and the making of new Labour, 1994–1997', *British Journal of Industrial Relations*, 36(4): 537–64.

Metcalf, D. (1989) 'Water notes dry up: the impact of the Donovan proposals and Thatcherism at work on labour productivity in British manufacturing industry', *British Journal of Industrial Relations*, 27(1): 1–31.

Mueller, F., Procter, S. and Buchanan, D. (2000) 'Teamworking in its context(s): antecedents, nature and dimensions', *Human Relations*, 53(11): 1387–424.

Neathey, F. and Hurstfield, J. (1995) *Flexibility in Practice: Women's Employment and Pay in Retail and Finance*, Equal Opportunities Research Discussion Series No. 16. London: Industrial Relations Services.

Nolan, P. (1996) 'Industrial relations and performance since 1945' in Beardwell, I. (ed.) *Contemporary Industrial Relations, A Critical Analysis*. Oxford: Oxford University Press: 99–120.

Piore, M. and Sabel, C. (1984) *The Second Industrial Divide: Possibilities for Prosperity*. New York: Basic Books.

Pollert, A. (1987) 'The "flexible firm": a model in search of reality (or a policy in search of a practice)?', *Warwick Papers in Industrial Relations No. 19*, Industrial Relations Research Unit, University of Warwick.

Pollert, A. (1991) 'Introduction' in Pollert, A. (ed.) *Farewell to Flexibility?* Oxford: Blackwell Business: xvii–xxxv.

Procter, S.J., Rowlinson, M., McArdle, L., Hassard, J. and Forrester, P. (1994) 'Flexibility, politics and strategy: in defence of the model of the flexible firm', *Work, Employment and Society*, 8(2): 221–42.

**The Management of Human Resources**

Purcell, K. (2000) 'Gendered employment insecurity?' in Heery, E. and Salmon, J. (eds) *The Insecure Workforce*. London: Routledge: 112–39.

Ramsay, H., Scholarios, D. and Harley, B. (2000) 'Employees and high-performance work systems: testing inside the black box', *British Journal of Industrial Relations*, 38(4): 501–32.

Rubery, J. and Fagan, C. (1995) 'Does feminization mean a flexible labour force?' in Hyman, R. and Ferner, A. (eds) *New Frontiers in European Industrial Relations*. Oxford: Basil Blackwell: 140–66.

Sabel, C. (1982) *Work and Politics*. Cambridge: Cambridge University Press.

Sabel, C. and Zeitlin, J. (1985) 'Historical alternatives to mass production: politics, markets and technology in nineteenth century industrialisation', *Past and Present*, 108: 133–76.

Sayer, A. (1986) 'New developments in manufacturing: the just-in-time system', *Capital and Class*, 30: 43–72.

Sly, F., Thair, T. and Risdon, A. (1998) Women in the labour market: results from the spring 1997 Labour Force Survey', *Labour Market Trends*, March.

Steijn, B. (2001) 'Work systems, quality of working life and attitudes of workers: an empirical study towards the effects of team and non-teamwork', *New Technology, Work and Employment*, 16(3): 191–203.

Storey, J., Wilkinson, A., Cressey, P. and Morris, T. (1999) 'Employment relations in UK banking' in Regini, M., Kitay, J. and Baethge, M. (eds) *From Tellers to Sellers*. London: MIT Press: 129–58.

Tailby, S. and Harrington, J. (2002) 'Contingent employment in retail banking', New Understanding of European Work Organisation case study research report (forthcoming).

Tomaney, J. (1994) 'A new paradigm of work organisation and technology?' in Amin, A. (ed.) *Post-Fordism, A Reader*. Oxford: Blackwell: 157–94.

TUC (1999) *Temporary Workers, Permanent Rights*. London: TUC.

TUC (2001) *Permanent Rights for Temporary Workers*. London: TUC.

Undy, R. (1999). 'Annual review article. New Labour's "industrial relations settlement": the third way?', *British Journal of Industrial Relations*, 37(2): 315–36.

Wickens, P. (1993) 'Lean production and beyond: the system, its critics and the future', *Human Resource Management Journal*, 3(4): 75–90.

Williams, K., Cutler, T., Williams, J. and Haslam, C. (1987) 'The end of mass production?', *Economy and Society*, 21(3): 321–54.

Williamson, O. (1975) *Markets and Hierarchies: Analysis and Anti-trust Implications*. New York: Free Press.

Williamson, O. (1985) *The Economic Institutions of Capitalism*. New York: Free Press.

Womack, J., Jones, D. and Roos, D. (1990) *The Machine that Changed the World*. New York: Rawson Associates.

Wood, S. (1989) 'The transformation of work?' in Wood, S. (ed.) *The Transformation of Work? Skill, Flexibility and the Labour Process*. London: Routledge: 1–43.

Wood, S. (1999) 'Getting the measure of the transformed high-performance organization', *British Journal of Industrial Relations*, 37(3): 391–418.

# CHAPTER 11

# DISCRIMINATION WITHIN
# THE EMPLOYMENT RELATIONSHIP

## INTRODUCTION

Discrimination at work is concerned with the unequal and inequitable treatment of some employees irrespective of their ability to perform their jobs (but see more detailed definition below). The main types of discrimination are:

- sex or gender discrimination;
- discrimination on the grounds of sexual orientation or sexuality;
- race discrimination;
- religious discrimination;
- discrimination on grounds of disability;
- discrimination on grounds of age;
- discrimination on grounds of trade union status;
- discrimination – against ex-offenders; and
- equal pay issues.

The traditional approach to the study of industrial relations as Liff (1995) points out, is overwhelmingly concerned with the white male worker, irrespective of fundamental changes in the labour market and the structure of work over the past few decades, thereby ignoring those groups which are prone to discrimination. The trade union movement, now amongst the foremost in fighting discrimination, used to be regarded as white and male dominated, as evidenced by membership composition and the very small proportion of full-time officers and executive staff who were black and female. Moreover, most managements have traditionally been male dominated (many still are) and white, and it is only in recent years that the proportion of women in management (and in trade unions for that matter) has risen.

Many of the changes in the labour market and patterns of working have been identified in Chapter 1. These changes have resulted in many more women entering the increasingly fragmented labour market. This, in turn, has raised the profile of 'equality' issues and influenced the emergence of **equal opportunities** initiatives and policies by both government and more 'progressive' managements during the past thirty years or so. The relevant legislation has been identified at the beginning of Chapter 9 and is considered in more detail in this chapter. Of particular and growing relevance to discrimination and equal opportunity issues is the direct and indirect influence and impact of European Community law, and this will be considered in some detail during the course of the chapter.

Discriminatory attitudes and practices impinge upon the employment relationship in a number of ways. For example, discrimination may be evident at the selection and recruitment stages of employment; opportunities for promotion may be restricted; there may be frequent instances of harassment and bullying within the workplace and equal opportunities policies, where they exist, may not be put into practice effectively enough. Occasionally, instances of discrimination may have more serious consequences both for employees and their organisation, and for the conduct of employment relations. The example of endemic racism at the Dagenham plant of the Ford Motor Company during October 1999, where workers staged a mass walkout after an Asian shop steward was pushed by a white foreman, is a case in point, and will be examined in greater detail later on in the chapter.

The main focus of the chapter will be upon the treatment of gender, race and disability discrimination. The equal pay issue will be dealt with mainly in connection with gender discrimination. Space will not permit a detailed examination of the other types of discrimination mentioned earlier, although these will be referred to where relevant. We start by examining some of the main theoretical perspectives and contextual developments in relation to gender and race discrimination, accepting the argument that discrimination in the workplace is a reflection of the wider patterns of discrimination, racial and gender inequality inherent within the wider society. We then look briefly at the legal changes which have taken place, both at national and European community level, which have sought to outlaw discrimination within the employment relationship. The chapter proceeds by looking at gender, race and disability discrimination in some detail, and the extent to which the relevant legislative and policy developments have influenced organisations in the adoption of equal opportunities and harassment policies and procedures.

## Learning objectives

When you have completed this chapter, you will be able to:

1. Describe the basics of theories explaining gender and racial inequalities within society as a whole.

2. Assess the extent to which these inequalities are reflected within the employment relationship.

3. Trace the development of national and European Community policies and legislation concerning gender, race, disability and equal pay.

4. Explain how organisations deal with discrimination through the operation of equal opportunities policies and procedures.

5. Identify the elements of other forms of discrimination based on age and trade union status.

6. Work through case examples of discrimination and harassment within the employment relationship.

## EXPLAINING GENDER AND RACIAL DISCRIMINATION

Evidence of discrimination within the employment relationship is not hard to find, and points to the fact that members of ethnic minorities do less well in the labour market than whites, despite having similar levels of qualifications (Jones, 1993). Reporting on the results of successive surveys conducted by the Policy Studies Institute (PSI), Jones found that despite certain ethnic groups (such as Indian, Chinese and African Asian males) being reasonably well represented in certain jobs up to and including professional level, all ethnic groups were significantly **under represented** in managerial grades. As Jones points out: 'men from certain minority groups have penetrated to a remarkable extent into certain professions, but to a much lesser extent into the management of large organisations' (p. 81). Later PSI surveys, such as that conducted by Modood, Berthoud *et al.* (1997) confirm the persistent labour market disadvantages faced by ethnic minorities. The extent of these disadvantages, or 'penalties' are revealed by Sly, Thair and Risdon (1998) who highlight certain factors based on their analysis of Labour Force Survey data:

- In 1997, 2.2 million people of working age belonged to ethnic minority groups (6.4 per cent of the total working-age population), half of them living in London.
- Black African men are most likely to have a higher qualification: Pakistani and Bangladeshi women tend to be the most poorly qualified.
- Economic activity rates for women vary widely between ethnic groups. In 1997, working-age Black Caribbean and White women had economic activity rates of around three-quarters compared with less than one-third for Pakistani/Bangladeshi women.
- Nearly half of Indian self-employed and employee men are in the top two social or occupational categories compared with only a quarter of Black Caribbean and Pakistani/Bangladeshi males. Black Caribbeans are the only group where women are more likely than men to be in the top two occupational categories.
- The unemployment rate for Black African men was more than three times (25 per cent) that for White men (7 per cent) in 1997. Pakistani/Bangladeshi men also have high rates. Black African and Pakistani women had unemployment rates (24 per cent and 23 per cent respectively) four times that of White women (5.4 per cent) in 1997.
- The ratio of the ethnic minority unemployment rate to the White unemployment rate has been higher in the 1990s than it was in the mid to late 1980s – for example, it was 1.7 in 1987–9 compared with 2.4 in Spring 1998.

The Commission For Racial Equality (CRE) in commenting upon the rising ratio of Black and Asian to White unemployment stated that:

*Some of this disparity can be explained by the different age profiles, qualifications and geographical distribution of the various ethnic groups, but these factors do not tell the whole story: there appears to be an undeniable, persistent overrepresentation of certain ethnic groups.* (CRE Annual Report, 1999, p. 5)

**Women workers** are still concentrated in poorly paid, routine occupations such as clerical and secretarial work. Far more women than men are in part-time occupations. To be sure, women have recently made some inroads into occupations defined as 'men's jobs' but only to a limited extent. Women are underrepresented in all the higher managerial and professional grades. Those women who are successful economically have to fit into a world of 'maleness' and masculine value systems where they feel they do not fully belong. One of the major factors affecting women's careers is the male perception that, for female employees, work comes second to having children. A survey by Homans (1987) investigating the views of managers interviewing female applicants for positions as technical staff in the health services revealed that the (male) interviewers routinely asked women applicants whether or not they had, or intended to have, children. Interviewers virtually never followed this practice with male applicants, and when asked why not, two themes ran through their responses:

- women with children may require extra time off for school holidays or if a child falls sick; and
- responsibility for childcare is seen as a mother's problem rather than a parental one.

Arguably, the bias in male attitudes may be less to do with the workplace itself than with the domestic responsibilities of parenting and as long as it is taken for granted that parenting cannot be shared on an equal basis, the problems facing female employees will persist, and 'it will remain a fact of life that women are severely disadvantaged, compared to men, in their career opportunities' (Cockburn, 1991, p. 123). The situation remains that, despite many advances in developing equality in the workplace, inequalities still exist: the EOC (1999) draws attention to the following facts:

- 67 per cent of women and 78 per cent of men of working age are employed.
- 43 per cent of women employees and 8 per cent of men employees work part-time.
- 52 per cent of employed women were in occupational groups in which more than 60 per cent of workers were women. These groups were: clerical and secretarial occupations; service occupations; and sales occupations.
- 54 per cent of employed men were in occupational groups in which more than 60 per cent of workers were men. These groups were: managers and administrators; craft and related occupations; and plant and machine operatives.
- Sexual harassment: in 1998, the EOC received more than 700 enquiries about sexual harassment.
- In 1998, women comprised 18 per cent of all executives (managers and directors); this compared with only 8.9 per cent in 1991. However, women comprised only 3.6 per cent of directors in 1998.

Moreover, persistent and institutional barriers to equality in the workplace remain. These include continuing job segregation in the labour market; the over-representation of women in part-time work and the inequality of treatment of part-time workers; women's over-representation in home working and the unequal treatment of home workers; women's under-representation in senior positions and the impact of double discrimination on many women in the labour market.

### Discrimination and prejudice

For our purposes, it is necessary to make a distinction between **discrimination** and **prejudice**. **Discrimination** refers to *actual behaviour* towards the other group. It can be seen in activities that disqualify members of one group from opportunities open to others, as when a black person is refused a job made available to a white person. **Prejudice** refers to *opinions or attitudes* held by members of one group towards another. A prejudiced person's preconceived views are often based on hearsay rather than on direct evidence, and are resistant to change even in the face of new information. Individuals may harbour favourable prejudices concerning groups with which they identify and negative prejudices against others.

Although prejudice is often the basis of discrimination, the two may exist separately. People may have prejudiced attitudes that they do not necessarily act upon. This is particularly the case within an organisation which acts upon discrimination legislation and equal opportunities policies and procedures. In such situations, an individual employee may have a predisposition to act in a prejudiced manner, but is constrained in doing so. However, the high incidence of racial and sexual harassment at work suggests that prejudiced attitudes are translated into action all too often, despite legislation and procedures.

Think of some examples of discrimination at work based on prejudiced attitudes.

# THEORIES EXPLAINING GENDER INEQUALITIES AND DISCRIMINATION

There are a number of interesting and important theories which attempt to explain and justify **differences** between men and women. These theories can be placed into two categories. The **first category** is based on **biology and the sexual division of labour,** and the **second category** is based on the premise that gender roles are **culturally** rather than **biologically** produced and which we may label **the social construction of gender roles.**

There are also theories which examine the basis of **inequalities** between men and women. Inspired by the development of the Women's Liberation Movement, attention is focused upon the **subordinate position** of women in society and the **feminist** approaches which attempt to explain this type of inequality. There are three main feminist approaches which can be identified:

- Radical feminism.
- Marxist and socialist feminism.
- Liberal feminism.

We will now look briefly at these theoretical categories.

## Biology and the sexual division of labour

Basically, the argument here is that biological differences between men and women lead them to occupy different social roles and exhibit different types of behaviours (the so-called **sociobiological** explanation). In terms of sexual behaviour, for example, men are more likely to be promiscuous, while women will be more circumspect in their pursuit of a 'suitable' male. Men will, in competing for the attention of women, be more assertive, physically stronger, more competitive and ultimately more dominant than women. Because of her biological function – that of childbearing – women are tied to the home base, and because of her physique, she is limited to less strenuous tasks. This sexual division of labour, it is claimed, is universal and accounts for the role of women in industrial society which is basically that of bearing and nursing children and providing them with warmth, security and emotional support in the home. In contrast to this, the male breadwinner spends his working day competing in an achievement-oriented society. The stress that this incurs in the male is relieved by the female through the provision of love, consideration and understanding. Sociobiological explanations of behaviour have been heavily criticised by feminists as a spurious attempt to provide 'scientific' justifications for male power. More specifically, Oakley, (1981), argues that:

- Gender roles are culturally rather than biologically determined.
- Evidence from a number of different societies shows that there are no tasks (apart from childbearing) which are performed exclusively by females.
- Biological characteristics do not bar women from particular occupations.

- The mother role is a cultural and not a biological construction. Evidence from several societies indicates that children do not require a close, intimate and continuous relationship with a female mother figure.

## The social construction of gender roles

This explanation of male/female differences rests on the assumption that gender roles are **culturally** rather than biologically produced. In other words, humans learn the behaviour that is expected of males and females within their society. Gender is **socially constructed** in the sense that differences in the behaviour of males and females are learned rather than being the inevitable result of biology. Initially, the parent-child relationship is important, and Oakley identifies four ways in which socialisation into gender roles take place:

1. The child's concept of himself/herself is affected by **manipulation**. For example, mothers tend to pay more attention to girl's hair and dress them in 'feminine' clothes.
2. Differences are achieved through the involvement and direction of boys and girls towards different objects and is particularly obvious in the provision of toys; girls are given dolls, soft toys and miniature domestic objects and appliances to play with, while boys are given toys which encourage more practical, logical and aggressive behaviour such as bricks and guns.
3. Parents and others such as primary school teachers will use verbal appellations such as 'You're a naughty boy', or 'That's a good girl'. This leads young children to identify with their gender and imitate adults of the same gender.
4. Male and female children are exposed to **different activities**. For example, girls are particularly encouraged to become involved with domestic tasks. In addition, much research has documented how stereotypes of masculinity and femininity are further reinforced throughout childhood and adult life. Portrayals by media advertising of men and women in traditional social roles have been criticised by feminists.

## Theories of gender inequality

The feminist preoccupation with the **position** of women in society, which they argue is a subordinate one, has generated a vast, but by no means unanimous, literature which can be broadly categorised into the three approaches described below:

### Radical feminism

Radical feminism supports the contention that men are responsible for the exploitation of women. Women are seen to be exploited because they undertake 'free' labour for men by carrying out childcare and housework, and because they are denied access to positions of power. Another argument that is commonly put forward is that society is regarded as **patriarchal** – dominated and ruled by men (see below).

### Marxist and socialist feminism

Women's exploitation is not attributed entirely to men, but to capitalism which is the main beneficiary. Housework and the 'job' of mother is 'oppressive' unpaid work from which capitalism benefits through the production of wealth. The exploitation of women in paid employment, and their generally subordinate position in the occupational hierarchy is held to be a consequence of the emergence of private property and the resultant lack of ownership of the means of production which deprives women of any power.

### Liberal feminism

This approach suggests that gradual change in the social and economic systems of society will lead to an improvement in the position of women. According to this perspective, no one benefits from existing gender inequalities; both men and women are harmed as the potential of females and males alike is suppressed. For example, many women with the potential to be successful and skilled members of the workforce, do not get the opportunity to develop their talents, while men are denied some of the pleasures of having a close relationship with their children. The explanation for this state of affairs lies not so much in the 'structures' and institutions of society, but in its culture and attitudes of individuals. Socialisation into gender roles produces particular expectations of men and women, while discrimination prevents women from having equal opportunities. The liberal feminist agenda includes:

- the creation of equal opportunities in all spheres and particularly in education and work contexts;
- the aim of creating equal opportunities is pursued through the introduction of legislation and the changing of attitudes. Measures such as the Sex Discrimination and Equal Pay Acts help to tackle discrimination; and
- the elimination of sexism and stereotypical views of women and men from children's books and the mass media.

Although the least radical of feminist perspectives, the liberal agenda could still lead to considerable social change, and at the very least, the changes it advocates could create the conditions whereby women have the same access as men to high status jobs.

---

**SE 11.2**  *The response is provided for only questions 2 and 3 at the end of the chapter*

---

1. Summarise the main theories which attempt to explain gender differences and gender inequality.

2. Identify what you think are the main characteristics of a 'patriarchal' (male-dominated) society.

3. To what extent do you think early 21st century Britain remains a patriarchal society?

---

### Explanations for gender inequality within the employment relationship

Gender inequality within the employment relationship, as we have noted previously includes important disadvantages experienced by women as compared with men in paid employment. These include:

- lower levels of remuneration;
- greater likelihood of being in part-time work;
- higher concentration of employment at lower occupational levels; and
- employment in low status jobs.

A number of explanations for these inequalities, which we now briefly consider, focus upon the labour market and the employment relationship.

## Human capital theory

Human capital theory argues that the apparent lack of commitment shown by women to paid employment is the cause of the disadvantages they suffer in the labour market. Because women are likely to abandon or interrupt their careers at an early age, they have less incentive to invest their time in lengthy programmes of training or education and are therefore of less value to employers than their more highly trained and more skilled male counterparts. For this reason, women will have less experience of their jobs than men which makes it difficult for women to be promoted to higher status and better-paid jobs. Women's lack of training, qualifications and experience resulting from the demands of childcare all contribute to their disadvantaged position in the labour market.

**SE 11.3**                                    *The response is provided at the end of the chapter*

Can you think of any criticisms of human capital theory?

## Dual labour market theory

Dual labour market theory distinguishes between **the primary labour market** which is characterised by high pay, job security, good working conditions and favourable promotion prospects, and the **secondary labour market** comprising lower paid jobs, poor job security, inferior working conditions and few opportunities for promotion. Both may exist within one organisation, but transfer from one to the other is difficult, if not impossible. Secondary sector workers are more dispensable and easily replaced and a high proportion of these workers are women. The relatively low status of women in society and their tendency not to belong to trade unions weakens their position further and makes it particularly difficult for them to get a foothold in primary sector employment. Once recruited to the secondary sector, women are likely to remain captives in it for the rest of their working lives. There are, however, some limitations and important exceptions which are not considered by the dual market approach:

● Some women in skilled manual jobs (for example, in the textile industry) are low paid even though their work may be very similar to primary sector men's jobs.
● Many women do have jobs in the primary sector, but not in manufacturing industry, as in the case of nurses, teachers and social workers.
● Dual labour market theory cannot adequately explain why women gain promotion less often than men, despite doing the same jobs.

## Gender and post-Fordism

This approach may be considered as an extension to the dual labour market theory, but takes into more detailed consideration the recent changes in the composition of the external and internal (to the organisation) labour market (See Chapter 1). McDowell (1992), for example, uses the assumptions of post-Fordism (See Chapter 5) in order to explain the increased use of part-time female labour and the reduction in the employment of males in full-time permanent jobs.

**SE 11.4**                                    *The response is provided at the end of the chapter*

Look back over Chapter 5 in order to identify the types of changes postulated by post-Fordism.

### Reserve army of labour

A Marxist explanation of the traditional role of women both within and outside the labour market argues that capitalism required a spare pool of potential recruits to the labour force. Because of their in-built contradictions, capitalist economies experience cycles of boom and recession accompanied by increases in labour demand during the former and shedding of labour during the latter phase of the cycle. Improvements in the efficiency of production technology together with market demands to produce new products also required a 'reserve army' to provide the necessary labour flexibility to deal with these changes.

One of the main functions of the reserve army is to reduce the wages of all members of the labour force as unemployed workers compete for jobs, thereby allowing employers to reduce wages and increase the rate and extent of exploitation. Beechey (1983) identifies a number of ways in which women have traditionally been particularly suited to the needs of this reserve army:

- Traditionally, women are less likely to be unionised and so are less able to resist redundancy than men.
- Women's jobs are least likely to be covered by redundancy legislation, making it more likely that women rather than men would be redundant at lower cost to the employer.
- Traditionally, unemployed women may not be eligible to state benefits if their husbands are working, and hence would not appear in the unemployment statistics: 'women who are made redundant are able to disappear virtually without trace back into the family' (Beechey, 1983, p. 203).
- Traditionally, women were prepared to work for less pay than men, even in equivalent jobs, because they could rely upon their husbands' wages as the main source of income for the family.

While the reserve army explanation appears to take into account at least some of the fluctuations in the employment of women during the course of the 20th century, for example, in appearing to account for the increased employment of women during the two World Wars, the theory may not adequately explain why a significant proportion of women are able to retain their jobs during periods of recession. Gardiner (1992), for example, argues that, according to **substitution theory**, there are advantages to the employer in allowing women to retain their jobs during times of recession and rising unemployment since they are a comparatively cheap substitute for male workers.

### Gender, labour markets and occupations: an integrated approach

Crompton and Sanderson (1990) argue that it is the structure of the labour market which shapes people's career choices, and that men who choose to follow traditional masculine careers, and women who choose to follow traditional feminine careers reinforce structural features of the labour market which produce gender differences, thereby making it difficult for other individuals to pursue careers which are not normally thought appropriate for their gender. Crompton and Sanderson identify a model of the labour market which takes into account these gender differences, making the following assumptions:

- The labour market and the position of individuals within it is partly determined by presence or absence of qualifications.

**The Management of Human Resources**

241

- The value of qualifications is not fixed; occupational groups can attempt to increase the value of qualifications they hold by restricting access to the profession and creating artificial shortages of qualified workers.
- A distinction can be made between **occupational labour markets (OLM)** which are external to the organisation, and **organisational labour markets** which are restricted to and controlled by firms or organisations.
- Amongst more skilled workers and professionals, there is movement between jobs and organisations; they are not tied to the internal labour market of a particular organisation and therefore are not restricted in their efforts to improve their pay or secure promotion.
- Those skilled professional workers whose status and rewards depend partly upon their skills and partly upon their position within their employing organisation (such as company lawyers and accountants) belong to what Crompton and Sanderson describe as the **occupational internal labour markets (OILM)**.
- Employees in **firm internal labour markets (FILM)** depend almost wholly on their position in a particular organisation or firm for their status and rewards, and any mobility there is is limited to similar types of organisation (for example, senior local authority workers are unlikely, on the whole, to find jobs in any other type of organisation). In firm internal labour markets an employee is normally a highly trained generalist rather than the mobile specialist of occupational or occupational internal labour markets.
- Use is made of dual labour market theory to indicate that workers with few skills in the occupational labour market tend to end up in the **secondary labour market (SLM)**.

For Crompton and Sanderson, **gender segregation** is:

*A product of the past sex-stereotyping of occupations and conventional assumptions relating to the domestic role of women, formal and informal exclusionary (discriminatory) practices, and fluctuations in both the demand for labour and the nature of female labour available.* (p. 46)

In some circumstances conventional expectations and exclusionary practices can be overcome, and women can break into those parts of the labour market to which they could not previously gain access. The researchers illustrate their theoretical assumptions by reference to four case studies within four areas of employment: pharmacy, accountancy, building societies and cooking and serving.

**Pharmacy**
Female membership of the Pharmaceutical Society increased dramatically during the course of the 20th century, and by 1983, a majority of undergraduates studying pharmacy were women. Crompton and Sanderson argue that pharmacy has not been 'sex-typed' even though it involves high levels of scientific training usually associated with mainly male professions. However, flexible patterns of employment within the profession are usually associated with predominantly female professions. Regulations mean that a pharmacist has to be present if drugs are to be dispensed. This has led to the creation of considerable amounts of part-time work which is attractive to women seeking to combine work with childcare.

However, although women have a high profile within pharmacy, they tend to be concentrated within the lower levels of the profession. Until the 1980s, part-time pharmacists in the NHS could not achieve promotion and in companies such as Boots, the requirement to be geographically mobile has discouraged women. Therefore, although women have been able to enter the occupational labour market in pharmacy, they have had limited success in gaining promotion within it.

## Accountancy

There are a number of different professional qualifications and associations, and while the careers of some accountants are closely bound up with the firm internal labour market of particular organisations, other accountants are self-employed or work in small independent practices and have occupational rather than organisational careers. The proportion of women in accountancy is relatively low compared with pharmacy, and even by the mid-1960s, less than 1 per cent of accountants were women, although by 1986 women comprised 36 per cent of those in accountancy training. Interviews with female qualified accountants revealed varying degrees of prejudice and discrimination amongst male colleagues and bosses as indicated by statements such as, 'I just think that that's where women are most fulfilled, at home having a family'. There were also few part-time opportunities in most firms which presented women accountants with a clear choice between their career or domestic childcare.

## Building societies

In contrast to accountancy, most building society workers are female and in their particular survey, Crompton and Sanderson established that 70 per cent of building society employees are women. (Since publishing their study, many building societies converted to banks, so while the building society sector has declined, the same employment patterns exist within the 'new' banks). The high concentration of women in building society employment has been attributed in part to the very rapid expansion of employment in these organisations during the 1970s, a time when many married women were deciding to seek employment or to continue in work despite having children.

As with accountancy, a large proportion of the female workforce tends to be concentrated at the bottom levels of the organisational hierarchy; clerical work is done by women, but senior managers are almost exclusively male. Crompton and Sanderson consider building societies as examples of *firm internal labour markets* with prospects largely tied to internal promotion opportunities. Men have been traditionally dominant in these labour markets and have used their dominance to exclude women. Women tend to lack the formal qualifications, the willingness to do irregular overtime and the ability to be geographically mobile, which are all necessary prerequisites for securing promotion.

There are also unofficial practices which tend to block women's promotion opportunities. For example, senior managers, who are invariably male occasionally act as 'sponsors' or 'mentors' for aspiring junior staff, assisting them with their careers. The process is discriminatory as the junior staff selected for mentoring are almost always male. Women also lack access to male-dominated informal networks and clubs which can provide the means to further career development. One building society (the Leeds) was found by the Equal Opportunities Commission (EOC) to adopt discriminatory practices by recruiting men to its management training programmes even when women candidates were younger, better qualified and had more relevant work experience. As a result of their interviews, Crompton and Sanderson revealed considerable evidence to suggest that exclusionary and discriminatory practices in building societies are widespread.

## Cooking and serving

Work in catering and hotels has normally been considered 'women's work' because of its similarity to unpaid domestic work. Such work is generally low paid and low status, although in some areas there are limited career prospects. Crompton and Sanderson looked at work in hotels and the school meals service. Not surprisingly, it was found that almost all school meals workers were women, and since the school meals service is widely regarded as 'women's work' and is seen as unskilled, there is little competition from men for the jobs. As with other work of this nature, women are attracted to the job owing to the availability of part-time employment during school hours, making it relatively easy to combine work with looking after school-age children.

The hotel context is slightly different in that there are areas where men predominate. For example, most porters and many of the most senior and well-paid chefs are men. Management is fairly evenly split between males and females, but women predominate in housekeeping and personnel, as managers within institutional catering and as proprietors of small establishments. At the lower levels of the hotel hierarchy, women are employed as counter and kitchen hands, waitresses, chambermaids, etc.

▶

Increasingly such workers are employed on a part-time and casual basis. The hotel trade is highly competitive and there is evidence from the case studies that employers are using greater numbers of casual workers who can be laid off during slack times in order to cut costs. Male employees therefore tend to have greater job security than female employees. Indeed, this is a classic example of women at the lower levels of hotel work being confined to a secondary labour market with little security and few prospects.

Adapted from Crompton and Sanderson (1990)

Crompton and Sanderson's research, therefore, indicates that women continue to suffer considerable disadvantages within the labour market and employment relationship. However, the precise reasons for these disadvantages, the degree of inequality and extent of discriminatory practices between men and women varies from industry to industry. Crompton and Sanderson nevertheless suggest that there is some evidence from their work of a reduction in gender divisions within employment, and point out that:

*The decline in manual occupations, and the intensification of competition between different types of disadvantaged labour at the lower levels of service employment, might be expected to result in a decline in sex-typed occupations in the (occupational) structure as a whole.* (p. 147)

At higher levels, more women have been using their educational success and the 'qualifications lever' to force their way into male strongholds, and that while gender difference might become less oppressive and inegalitarian, they will be a persisting feature within work and employment for the foreseeable future.

### Summary points concerning discrimination and theories of gender inequality

- There is plenty of evidence of sex and race discrimination within society, the employment relationship and the workplace. Many women are still concentrated in low paid, routine and part-time occupations and work. Black workers are often discriminated against in relation to selection, recruitment and advancement.
- It is important to make the distinction between prejudice (attitudes and opinions) and discrimination (actual behaviour) since the former underpins the latter. Legislating against discrimination may have no effect upon the nature of an individual's prejudices.
- Theories explaining gender inequalities within society include:
  - sociobiological explanations (biological differences lead to different social roles and behaviours);
  - social construction of gender roles through manipulation and social conditioning/engineering; and
  - feminism, incorporating radical, marxist and liberal feminism.
- Within the labour market, employment relationship and workplace, explanations for gender inequality include:
  - human capital theory (lack of commitment causes disadvantage at work);
  - dual labour market theory counterposing the primary and secondary labour markets;
  - post-Fordist assumptions concerning flexible specialisation; and
  - reserve army of labour thesis concerning the substitutability of labour.

**The Management of Human Resources**

● The integrated approach suggested by Crompton and Sanderson (1990) argues that the labour market structure influences career choice, thereby reinforcing through the pursuit of traditional 'masculine' and 'feminine' careers the occupational gender inequalities.

## ETHNICITY AND RACE

While Britain is becoming more ethnically diverse, divisions and inequalities between ethnic and racial groups continue to persist and are mirrored in the workplace. The term **race** is often used in an ambiguous and imprecise way, and there have been various attempts to establish racial categories based on biological differences; some researchers have distinguished four or five categories, while others have identified dozens. Obviously there are clear physical differences between human beings, and some of these differences are inherited. But the question of why some differences and not others become matters for social discrimination and prejudice has nothing to do with biology. Racial differences, therefore, should be understood as **physical variations singled out by the members of a community or society as socially significant** (Giddens, 1998). Differences in skin colour for example, are treated as significant, whereas differences in colour of hair are not. **Racism** is prejudice based on socially significant physical distinctions. A racist believes that some individuals and groups are superior or inferior to others as a result of these racial differences.

**Ethnicity** refers to cultural practices and outlooks of a given community of people that set them apart from others, that is, culturally distinct from other groups in society and are seen by others to be distinct. Different characteristics may serve to distinguish ethnic groups from one another, but the most usual are language, history/ancestry, religion, styles of dress or adornment. Ethnic differences are, therefore **entirely learned**. There are, therefore, many ethnic minority groups, and it is generally accepted that members of a minority group are **disadvantaged** as compared with the majority population and have some sense of **group solidarity**, of belonging together. The experience of being subject to prejudice and discrimination usually heightens feelings of common loyalty and interests. Members of minority groups often tend to see themselves as separate from the majority and are often physically and socially isolated from the larger community. Many minorities are both ethnically and physically distinct from the rest of the population, as with, for example, West Indians and Asians in Britain.

### Psychological interpretations of prejudice and ethnic inequality

There are two main explanations for ethnic differences and inequality of treatment. The **first** is based on **stereotypes and scapegoats** and the **second** is based on the **authoritarian personality**.

### Stereotypes and scapegoats

Prejudice operates mainly through the use of **stereotypical thinking**, that is, thinking in terms of fixed and inflexible categories. Stereotyping is often closely linked to the psychological mechanism of **displacement**, in which feelings of hostility or anger are directed against objects that are not the real origin of those feelings; people vent their anger against 'scapegoats' (people blamed for things/events which are not their fault).

**Scapegoating** is common when two deprived ethnic groups come into competition with one another for economic rewards. Those who direct racial abuse and attacks against blacks, for example, are often in a similar economic position; they blame blacks for grievances whose real causes lie elsewhere. Scapegoating is normally directed against groups that are distinctive and relatively powerless, because they make an easy target (Protestants, Catholics, Jews, Italians, Black Africans and others have played the unwilling role of scapegoat at various times throughout Western history. Finally, scapegoating frequently involves **projection** defined as the unconscious attribution to others of one's own desires and characteristics.

| **SE 11.5** | *This SE has no commentary* |
|---|---|

Think of examples of stereotypes and scapegoating and discuss these with your colleagues and tutor.

_____

### The authoritarian personality

Adorno *et al.* (1950) argued that some individuals may possess certain personality traits which predispose them to stereotypical thinking and projection, and as a result of their research diagnosed a personality type which they termed the **authoritarian personality**. The researchers developed a number of scales which, they argued, could determine levels of prejudice. On one scale, for instance, interviewees were asked to agree or disagree with a series of statements expressing strongly anti-Semitic views. Those who were diagnosed as prejudiced against Jews also tended to express negative attitudes towards other minorities. People with an authoritarian personality tend to be rigidly conformist, submissive to their superiors and dismissive towards inferiors, and tend to be highly intolerant in their religious and sexual attitudes and beliefs.

The research has been criticised, but at the very least, Adorno *et al.*'s ideas are valuable in assisting understanding of authoritarian patterns of thought in general and the psychological bases of prejudiced attitudes in particular.

## Sociological interpretations of prejudice and ethnic inequality

The psychological mechanisms of stereotypical thinking, displacement and projection are found amongst members of all societies, and help to explain why ethnic antagonism is such a common element in different cultures. However, they tell us little about the **social processes** involved in discrimination. Sociological concepts relevant to ethnic conflicts and disadvantage in society include:

- ethnocentrism;
- ethnic group closure; and
- resource allocation.

### Ethnocentrism

Ethnocentrism is defined as a suspicion of outsiders combined with a tendency to evaluate the culture of others in terms of one's own culture. Combined with stereotypical thought, ethnocentrism can give rise to particularly virulent forms of racial prejudice or **racism**. Outsiders are conceptualised as aliens, barbarians or as being morally and mentally inferior.

## Group closure

There is often a strong association between ethnocentrism and group closure. 'Closure' refers to the process whereby groups maintain boundaries separating themselves from others. These boundaries are formed by means of **exclusion devices** which accentuate the divisions between one ethnic group and another and include:

● limiting or prohibiting intermarriage between groups;
● restrictions on social contact or economic relationships such as trading; and
● physical separation of groups into 'voluntary' ghettos.

## Resource allocation

Groups of equal power may mutually enforce lines of closure; their members keep separate from one another, but neither group dominates the other. More usually, however, one ethnic group occupies a position of power over the other, and in these circumstances, group closure combines with resource allocation with the dominant group controlling the distribution of wealth and material goods. Some of the fiercest conflicts between ethnic groups centre on lines of closure between them, precisely because these lines signal inequalities in wealth, power and social standing. The concept of closure and unequal resource allocation assists our understanding of a whole range of differences, 'not just why the members of some groups get shot, lynched, or harassed, but also why they don't get good jobs, a good education or a desirable place to live' (Giddens, 1998, p. 215).

## Race, labour markets and the employment relationship

As with gender, the existence of a dual labour market where the secondary market comprises a relatively high proportion of ethnic minorities, is an important distinguishing factor. Workers of ethnic minority origin have also consistently suffered a disproportionately high level of unemployment. It would, however, be unhelpful to consider ethnic minorities as one homogeneous group, and the following factors suggest that there is a high degree of differentiation:

● With regard to **unemployment**, Pakistanis, West Indians and Guyanese do particularly badly, irrespective of their qualifications, while male Indians appear to be the most successful group in terms of using their qualifications to escape unemployment.
● Those with Indian origins are consistently better qualified than any other minority group, and as well qualified as, if not better qualified than, the white population.
● Those with Pakistani or Bangladeshi origins, and particularly the women from these two groups are the least qualified of all.
● The West Indian and Guyanese population traditionally have the highest employment rate for any group.

Ethnic minority groups in common with a significant proportion of the female labour force are disadvantaged with regard to qualifications and employment opportunities, levels of pay, differential recruitment policies and practices and trade union membership. Not only do ethnic minorities find access to organisations difficult, but once inside they generally find themselves discriminated against for reasons that are social rather than economic in origin, and for criteria that include not just skin colour but religious and political affiliation also (Doeringer and Piore, 1971). We now look briefly at two important sources of racial discrimination – selection and recruitment into employment, and trade unions and workers.

## Selection and recruitment

Since relatively few private firms in Britain undertake ethnic monitoring, it can be difficult to estimate the extent of discrimination at the selection and recruitment stage. Research by Jenkins (1988) indicates that managers involved in the recruiting process have a hierarchy of criteria for acceptability. The **primary criteria** involve appearance, manner and attitude, and maturity. **Secondary criteria** relate to 'gut feeling', employment history and experience, the ability to fit in, age, style of speech, literacy and marital status. **Tertiary criteria** concern references and English language competence.

In several areas minority workers are likely to face discrimination: they are less likely to fit the stereotypical 'married, two kids and a mortgage' pattern that recruiters seem to seek; their accent may well be regarded by white recruiters as inferior to white speech patterns; and they are less likely to 'fit in' to the existing organisation. Grint (1993) argues that:

> *Minority workers suffer the ignominies commonly associated with disparaging racial stereotypes. In many ways it seems that a large number of recruiters do not perceive themselves to be racist but prefer white workers on the grounds of expediency: the white workforce is racist, therefore, irrespective of their own liberal notions of 'fairness', white recruiters fear the consequences of recruiting minority workers. Inevitably, the failure to challenge assumed racism actually facilitates its reproduction; thus self-proclaimed liberalism acts merely as a conduit for the perpetuation of racism.* (p. 259)

Given the conventional recruitment procedures in many manufacturing firms – word of mouth and social networks – even conspicuously racist recruiters may never need to resort to racial discrimination in any open manner because the method of recruitment preselects ethnic minorities out of the pool through employee screening. This **informal recruitment** also implies that surveillance by state agencies is more difficult. Even where identically qualified individuals are interviewed, the emphasis placed upon the subjective assessment of the interviewer may ensure that the minority interviewee is not selected. A partial solution to this subjectivism is to formalise the procedure, and though this may not be the means to eliminate racial discrimination in the recruitment process, it may be regarded as a means by which its effects can be reduced.

---

**SE 11.6**                                   *The response is provided at the end of the chapter*

---

Can you think of one method whereby employers could recruit more employees from ethnic minorities?

---

## Examples of discrimination in recruitment

Within the **Civil Service**, there are no ethnic minorities amongst the top three grades and within the top seven grades there are only 207 out of 18 644 (1 per cent). This is not because ethnic minorities have avoided work in the Civil Service; on the contrary about 4 per cent of the total are minorities (Indians, Pakistanis and Bangladeshis and West Indians make up about 1 per cent each with a further 1 per cent for all minorities), marginally higher than the proportion for the total working population. These figures reveal a greater concentration of ethnic minorities within the lower reaches of the Civil Service (Grint, 1993). Within two areas of the Civil Service comprising 'general fast stream trainees' and 'examiners in insolvency' encouraging early trends were not maintained and 'in 1997 . . . there were no ethnic minority appointees in either area' (CRE, 1999, p. 28).

An investigation by the Commission for Racial Equality (CRE) into **chartered accountancy** (1987) revealed that members of ethnic minorities were three and a half times less likely to be offered a job than white applicants, and the discriminatory practices occurred at all levels of the screening process. It was not until 1998 that the Association of Chartered Accountants concluded an agreement with the CRE to keep ethnic records of all its UK members. The picture is the same in many other occupations; around 2 per cent of probation officers and 1 per cent of police officers are from minority groups, while only around 1 per cent of solicitors come from minorities, mostly working in the smaller law firms.

These examples indicate the need for managers to devise a more formal and less prejudiced approach to recruitment. After all, if discrimination hinders the recruitment of the most qualified and suitable individual for the particular job, then it must be against the interests of the company both morally and economically. However, formality does contain its own problems, as Grint (1993) points out:

> *Formality can actually provide the cover for more rather than less, manipulation of the recruitment procedure. Concomitantly, reducing informal procedures may actually undermine some of the shop floor patterns of trust between managers and workers. Since there can never be a sufficiently universal rule book to cover all contingencies there clearly is a problem regarding the manipulation or misinterpretation of rules. However, the ordinarily superior record of public employment regarding ethnic minorities suggests that formality should not be cast aside because of its inevitable problems.* (p. 264)

### Trade union and employee discrimination

British trade unions have a long history of exclusionary tactics and strategies against ethnic minorities, and racism within the indigenous British workforce is nothing new. Documented reports of racist attacks by British workers upon Irish workers in the 19th century, then Jewish workers at the turn of the century are early examples. The TUC has, until recently, often discriminated against minority workers. For example, as early as 1892 it made a declaration favouring the control of 'alien' labour. Grint (1993) identifies the following examples:

> *One of the earliest cases of official trade union hostility to their own minority members in Britain is that of the National Union of Seamen who were disinclined to support their minority members against the 1925 Special Restrictions (Coloured Alien Seamen) Order. Even Ben Tillet, an avowed socialist and radical union leader of the London dockers at the turn of the nineteenth century, was equivocal about the arrival of Jewish immigrants: 'Yes, you are our brothers and we will stand by you. But we wish you had not come' (quoted in Meth, 1973: 5). Similarly, the population as a whole seems to have been at best ambiguous about the status of the Jews. The Boer War was blamed by Keir Hardy (a trade unionist and founder of the Labour Party) and a substantial proportion of trade union leaders on the Army, composed as it allegedly was 'largely [of] Jews and foreigners'. Even during the Second World War indigenous anti-Semitism was ever present among the British working class, though they do not seem to have been as anti-Semitic as the government feared or the gutter press assumed (Kushner, 1989).* (pp. 266–7)

Interestingly enough, the influx of 'New Commonwealth' immigrants during the 1950s and 1960s during a period of full employment meant that labour shortages could be alleviated. For example, London Transport was active in recruiting bus conductors and drivers and underground railway staff through advertising and the provision of assisted passages for West Indians and their families. This ensured that there was little direct competition between white indigenous and minority workers. Similarly, in the North and Midlands where many Asian workers found manufacturing jobs, particularly in textiles, the general pattern was one where white employees left, leaving vacancies for Asian workers, rather than one where cheaper Asian workers pushed white workers out of the labour market. However, during the late 1960s onwards, with the increase in unemployment, there was a resurgence of racist attitudes by trade union members and white workers alike, based on the 'threat to jobs'. This type of 'occupational racism' was fuelled by the overt racism of some politicians, most notably Enoch Powell who gave his inflammatory 'rivers of blood' speech in 1968 which was supported by the London dockers. Even the Labour Party endorsed the establishment of immigration controls, while the TUC adopted policy statements explicitly linking the existence of immigrant workers to the issue of the 'coloured problem' and it was not until 1989 that the TUC at its annual conference supported the anti-racist resolution with a rule providing for expulsion of unions and members for 'deliberate acts of unlawful discrimination'.

Much empirical research suggests that, despite members of ethnic minorities being favourably inclined towards trade unions, white trade union members are generally less enthusiastic about anti-racist issues than their national officials (Lee, 1987; Commission for Racial Equality, 1981). There is, therefore, a distinction to be made between racist attitudes of a proportion of white trade union members and workers, and the official anti-racist pronouncements of full-time union officers. But even at the upper levels of trade union hierarchies, there appears to be a mismatch between rhetoric and reality, particularly in relation to the staffing of trade unions, as Grint points out:

*It is worth . . . acknowledging the extent to which trade union bureaucracies are themselves staffed by white employees. While there is little systematic evidence on this, because very few unions have ethnic monitoring, it is apparent that where studies do exist, they disclose a depressingly conservative picture of grossly under-represented ethnic minorities. The situation is worse than appears at first sight because the level of union density amongst ethnic minorities is substantially higher than the equivalent figure for white workers. In 1986 only thirteen of the main thirty-three British unions had any minority officials and many had only a token minority leader. Bill Morris . . . is the most senior minority union official. But although 56 per cent of minority employees were unionised in 1986, compared to 47 per cent of white employees, only 4 per cent of minority men held elected posts within their unions, compared to 11 per cent of white men. The figures were identical for white and minority women at 2 per cent (Policy Studies Institute, 1986).*

### Summary points concerning race discrimination

- The distinction between race (physical variations considered as socially significant) and ethnicity (cultural practices and outlooks of one group which distinguishes it from other groups), is important in understanding this type of discrimination.
- Prejudice is manifested by stereotypical thinking and scapegoating by, for example, targeting those groups that are 'distinctive' and/or powerless. Certain personality types such as the 'authoritarian personality' are, it is argued, more receptive to prejudice.

- Interpretations of prejudice and ethnic inequality include:
  - ethnocentrism (suspicion of 'outsiders');
  - group closure (groups segregating themselves from other groups); and
  - resource allocation (conflicts over scarce resources).
- Within labour markets and the employment relationship in Britain, ethnic and race inequality affects different groups in different ways, but in general they tend to be disadvantaged in terms of qualifications, employment opportunities, levels of pay, differential recruitment policies, trade union and employee discrimination.

## AN OVERVIEW OF DISCRIMINATION LEGISLATION

Here we look at the three main types of discrimination concerning sex, race and disability and identify the appropriate legislation and codes of practice. We firstly consider the national legislation and then any relevant Articles and Directives etc. emanating from the European Union.

### Sex discrimination

The national legislation recognises two important issues affecting men and women within the employment relationship:

- equal pay between men and women; and
- more general issues concerning sex discrimination.

#### Equal pay

##### The Equal Pay Act 1970

This was the first piece of legislation with the aim of promoting equality at work between men and women. The Act, which came into full force in 1975, has been amended by the Sex Discrimination Acts of 1975 and 1986, by the Equal Pay (Amendment) Regulations of 1983 and the Pensions Act 1995. The Industrial Tribunals Rules of Procedure (Amendment) Rules 1996 amend the procedure used to deal with equal value claims.

The Act provides that a woman's contract is to have an **equality clause** implied into it if the contract does not specifically contain one. The effect of the equality clause is to modify the woman's contractual conditions so that they are no less favourable than those of a man who is engaged on **like work** or on **work rated as equivalent**.

---

**SE 11.7**                                    *The response is provided at the end of the chapter*

---

Identify some instances or circumstances where you think a woman's pay should be equal to that of a man.

---

In order to demonstrate equivalence, the woman (or man) must know who to compare herself with, that is, the **comparator**. The comparator needs to be of a different sex, employed by the same employer and at an establishment covered by the same terms and conditions. She may then take her case to **employment tribunal** in order to seek redress. Should the job be considered equal by the tribunal (or subsequent courts of appeal), then she is entitled to receive equal pay backdated to a maximum of two years before the date at which she applied to tribunal. However, the employer, while accepting the principle of job equality could argue that the pay differential between the male and female employees concerned should be retained '**genuinely due to a material factor** which is not the difference of sex' (S.1 (3) Equal Pay Act). A genuinely material factor (**GMF**) for the same work and work rated as equivalent under a job evaluation scheme could be cited by the employer from a range of examples including a difference of personal factors such as length of service, superior skill or qualifications and higher productivity.

### The Equal Pay (Amendment) Regulations 1983

The regulations provide a new criterion and test under which pay parity between the sexes can be claimed – where the man is on **work of equal value** to that of the woman. **Equal value** is defined in terms of the demands made by the job, and includes skill, effort and decision making. An equal value claim is only relevant where the woman and her male comparator are not engaged in 'like work' or 'work rated as equivalent'. However, an important case, *Pickstone v Freemans plc (1987)* established that an employer cannot defeat an equal value claim by showing that there is another man engaged on like work or equivalently rated work (see below) as long as the male comparator selected by the applicant (the woman bringing the case) falls outside those categories.

The effect of the amendment is threefold:

- It has opened up a far wider field for claims than existed under the old law. Comparisons can now be made between totally dissimilar jobs, in different pay structures and across different collective bargaining groups.
- It allows for an independent expert to evaluate and compare jobs even where the employer has no job evaluation scheme. The 1996 amendments to employment tribunal rules mean that the tribunal can now decide whether or not an independent expert should be appointed in the particular case.
- It allows an existing job evaluation scheme to be scrutinised by the tribunal to ensure that there is no discriminatory bias within the scheme itself.

For **equal value** claims the **material factor** defence which the employer may use allows the employer to justify a difference on non-sex-based grounds relating to personal differences or market forces. The amendments apply equally to men who can, therefore, claim equality of terms with a woman on **like work**, **work rated as equivalent**, or on **work of equal value**.

## Sex discrimination

The Equal Pay Act and amendments cover the contractual aspects of discrimination concerning pay, while the Sex Discrimination Act of 1975 is designed to cover non-contractual discriminatory treatment.

### The Sex Discrimination Act 1975

The Sex Discrimination Act (SDA) promotes the equal treatment of women and men in employment, education and in the provision of goods and services and deals with discrimination against women or men and on the grounds of marital status at all stages of the employment relationship concerning selection, the availability of opportunities for training and promotion, the provision of benefits and facilities and dismissal.

The SDA was passed following increased concern over, and interest in, women's rights. Subsequent to Britain's membership of the EEC in 1973, Article 119 and associated Directives concerning equal pay and treatment have had an important influence on discrimination law in the UK. The SDA established the **Equal Opportunities Commission** with a remit to:

- eliminate discrimination on the grounds of sex or marital status;
- generally promote equal opportunities between men and women; and
- monitor the implementation of the SDA and Equal Pay Act.

The Act covers both **direct** and **indirect** discrimination.

### Direct discrimination

This is defined by section 1(1) as: *A person **discriminates against a woman** in any circumstances relevant to the purposes of any provision of this Act if on the ground of her sex he treats her less favourably than he treats or would treat a man.* It is also unlawful to **discriminate against married people** of either sex *on the ground of (an employee's) marital status (an employer) treats that person less favourably than he treats or would treat an unmarried person of the same sex.* It is worth noting that while the Act does not mention discrimination against employees on the basis of their unmarried status – and so is not unlawful, the European Community Equal Treatment Directive prohibits discrimination on the grounds of 'marital or family status' and so would include single people. Direct discrimination, therefore, involves two key elements:

- there must be **less favourable treatment**; and
- The treatment must be **because of sex or marital status**.

Clarke (1995) points out that direct discrimination is frequently **hidden or covert**:

*Many employers still discriminate against women by refusing to offer them jobs or promote them, but few employers admit that this is due to the woman's sex; some other reason will usually be given. It is the woman who has to prove that she has been discriminated against, and this is still a difficult task.* (p. 9)

---

**SE 11.8**                                           *The response is provided at the end of the chapter*

Provide an example of each of:

(a) 'Less favourable treatment'
(b) 'Treatment due to sex or marital status'.

---

In all cases of direct discrimination, it is necessary to compare a person's treatment with that of someone of the opposite sex. The comparison can be hypothetical – it is unnecessary for a woman, say, to show that a man was **in fact** treated more favourably than she was.

### Indirect discrimination

Indirect sex discrimination takes place when a requirement or condition is applied equally to men and women. However, the condition has the effect that in practice it disadvantages a much larger proportion of one sex than the other, because they find it harder to fulfil, and it cannot be justified on grounds other than sex. In the same way, an employer may discriminate indirectly against a married person of either sex on the ground of their **marital status**. Clarke suggests that:

> *Indirect discrimination is a concept which enables individuals to challenge seemingly innocent practices, such as requiring certain educational qualifications, or setting age limits, or insisting on physical characteristics, which appear to be neutral but which in fact operate so as to disproportionately exclude one sex. However, unlike direct discrimination which can never be justified, the employer may be able to show that the practice has some business-related purpose, even though it has an adverse impact on one sex.* (p. 9)

There are four criteria which must be satisfied in relation to indirect discrimination:

***Requirement or condition:*** The employer must have made a 'requirement or condition' such as a stipulation 'that only full-time employees were eligible for redundancy on a last in, first out basis' (Clarke, 1995, p. 10) which could be deemed to be indirectly discriminatory to women. Another example is the insistence that job applicants be under a certain age which could be indirectly discriminatory since women are more likely than men to have taken a number of years out of the labour market to care for children.

***Disproportionate effect:*** It should be established that the requirement, whatever it may be indirectly discriminates against a larger proportion of women than men.

***Detriment:*** A woman must demonstrate not only that she cannot comply with the requirement or condition, but also that this is to her detriment and that she is a real victim of the alleged discrimination.

***Justification:*** Even if a woman can show that there is a discriminatory requirement or condition which operates to her detriment, the employer may be able to justify the existence of such a requirement. If the employer is shown to be indirectly discriminatory, then the courts (following the precedent of a 'benchmark' case *Bilka-Kaufhaus GmbH v. Weber von Hartz*) must be satisfied that, in order to be justified, measures taken by the employer 'must correspond to a real need on the part of the undertaking and be appropriate and necessary to achieving the objectives pursued'.

### Unlawful discrimination

Within the employment relationship, the Act makes it unlawful to discriminate on the basis of sex or marital status in relation to **potential** and **present** employees. In relation to **potential employees**, it is unlawful to discriminate in recruitment arrangements such as advertising and interviewing and in the terms and conditions of a job offer. It is also unlawful to discriminate in the adoption of selection criteria and selection methods. In relation to **present employees** it is unlawful to discriminate in the provision of opportunities for promotion, transfer or training, and in the provision of opportunities for promotion, transfer or training, and in the provision of facilities or services such as study leave or company cars, and in unfavourable treatment such as dismissal.

There are some **exceptions** provided by the Act which permits **lawful discrimination** and are termed **genuine occupational qualifications (GOQs)**. These exceptions include occupations such as modelling, acting, or jobs such as toilet attendants. However, the Act does not permit **positive discrimination** where the employer may favour certain groups in the selection process. Nevertheless, the Act does allow **positive action** as in the example of the Metropolitan Police concerning race given earlier. Positive action, for example, would include situations whereby members of one sex have performed a job for the past twelve months and the employer feels that special training should be given exclusively for members of the opposite sex. Employers may also encourage applications from this group but not favour the applicants within the selection process.

The **enforcement** of the Act's provisions is through:

- The Equal Opportunities Commission (EOC) can, and does, take action concerning all aspects of discrimination considered above (the EOC Code of Practice. (1985) is dealt with later in the chapter).
- In instances which may lie outside the EOC's jurisdiction, individuals who feel they have been discriminated against can make a claim to the Employment Tribunal as detailed in the Equal Pay Act.

### Social Security Act 1989; Pensions Act 1995

The Social Security Act provides for entitlement to equal treatment in the provision of employment-related benefit schemes after a period of paid maternity leave or during a period of paid family leave. The Pensions Act acknowledges the EU Directive on equal treatment for men and women in relation to occupational social security schemes and in particular to occupational pension schemes.

### Employment Rights Act 1996

The Employment Rights Act (ERA) consolidated rights connected with pregnancy and maternity established by the Employment Act 1980, the Employment Protection (Consolidation) Act 1978 and the Trade Union and Employment Rights Act 1993. The rights concerning pregnancy and maternity are:

- **Time off for ante-natal care:** an employee who is pregnant and who has made an appointment to attend for ante-natal care on the advice of a medical practitioner, midwife or health visitor is entitled to take paid time off during working hours to keep the appointment.
- **Suspension on maternity grounds:** an employee is suspended on maternity grounds if she is suspended on the ground that she is pregnant, has recently given birth or is breast-feeding a child. As an alternative to suspension the employee has a right to be offered any suitable and appropriate alternative employment which the employer has available, and which is equivalent in terms and conditions. If an employee is dismissed in circumstances where she ought to be suspended under these provisions, she will be able to claim that her dismissal is automatically unfair.
- **Right to maternity leave for all employees:** there is a general right for employees to have 14 weeks' maternity leave regardless of the length of time for which they have been employed by their employer provided that they comply with all the notification requirements. Where an employee has a contractual right to maternity leave then she can 'pick and mix' her contractual and statutory rights to give herself the best composite right. If the employee is entitled, and wishes to exercise her right to return later than the end of the maternity leave period, within 29 weeks of the week of childbirth, then she must also inform her employer that she intends to exercise that right. If there is redundancy during the maternity leave period, then the employee is entitled to be offered any suitable alternative employment which is available on terms and conditions 'which are not substantially less beneficial' than those she enjoyed under her previous contract. Should the employer fail to provide suitable

available alternative employment or if the employee is selected for redundancy because of any reason connected with her pregnancy or maternity leave, the employee will automatically be treated as having been unfairly dismissed.

- **Right to return to work after extended maternity leave:** the 'right to return' is the right of an employee to return to work at any time from the end of her maternity leave period up to 29 weeks after the beginning of the week in which childbirth occurs. To be entitled to this 'right to return', the employee must fulfil the requirements to be entitled to maternity leave; have notified her employer that she intends to exercise her right to return to work; and at the beginning of the 11th week before the expected week of childbirth she must have been continuously employed for at least two years.

- **The right to return to what?** the employee's primary right to return is a right to return to work with the employer by whom she was employed at the end of her maternity leave period or his successor; in the job in which she was employed before she went on maternity leave on equivalent and no less favourable terms and conditions of employment and with seniority, pension and similar rights as if her employment up to the end of her maternity leave period was continuous with her employment after her return; otherwise on terms and conditions as if she had not been absent after her maternity leave period. If it is impracticable because of redundancy to permit the employee to return to work, she is entitled to be offered suitable, appropriate suitable alternative employment; if the employer fails in this, the employee will be deemed to have been automatically unfairly dismissed. Failure to permit a woman to return after maternity leave is considered to be unfair dismissal. There are two exceptions to this general position:
  - where the employer employs five or fewer employees immediately before the end of her maternity leave period and it is not reasonably practicable for the employer to offer suitable alternative employment or to allow the woman to return to her original job, then the woman will not be treated as having been dismissed; and
  - if it is not reasonably practicable for reasons other than redundancy, for the woman to be allowed to return to her original job and the employer offers the woman suitable alternative employment and she accepts or unreasonably refuses that offer, then again, the woman will not be treated as having been dismissed by being refused the right to return to work.

- **Dismissal of a temporary replacement:** where a temporary replacement is engaged to do the work of an employee who is suspended on maternity grounds or absent because of pregnancy or confinement, then provided:
  - the replacement is informed of this fact when they take the job on; and
  - the replacement is dismissed to allow the woman to return to work; the employer will still have to show that he acted fairly.

- **Right not to be dismissed because of pregnancy or childbirth:** an employee is considered to be automatically unfairly dismissed if she is dismissed for any reason related to her pregnancy; where her maternity leave period is ended by dismissal for any reason connected with:
  - the fact that she has given birth to a child; or
  - the fact that she took maternity leave or the benefits attached to it;
  - when she ought to have been suspended on maternity grounds;
  - where her maternity leave period, extended or otherwise, is ended by dismissal because of redundancy and she was not offered suitable alternative employment which was available; or

- where she is ill at the end of her maternity leave, has given the employer a medical certificate covering the period of her illness (up to four weeks) and she is dismissed during the currency of the medical certificate.
- **Right to pay in lieu of notice whilst absent due to pregnancy or maternity:** employees who are given notice when they are away from work due to pregnancy or confinement are entitled to be paid in lieu of notice provided that their notice entitlement is not over a week more than the statutory minimum notice entitlement. Where it was the employee who gave notice, the requirement for the employer to pay for the notice period in such cases only applies if the employee actually leaves the employer's employment.
- **Automatic right to written reasons for dismissal in pregnancy and maternity cases:** A woman who is dismissed while pregnant or in trying to exercise her right to return to work is entitled to be given written reasons for dismissal without asking for them.

### Employment Relations Act 1999
Based substantially upon the proposals contained in the *Fairness at Work* White Paper, the 'family-friendly' provisions include:

- the extension of maternity leave to 18 weeks in line with maternity pay;
- giving employees rights to extended maternity absence and to (unpaid) parental leave after one year's service;
- provision for the contract of employment to continue during the whole period of maternity or parental leave, unless it is expressly terminated by either party, by dismissal or resignation;
- provision of similar rights for employees to return to their jobs after parental leave as currently apply after maternity absence;
- provision of the right to three months' parental leave for adoptive parents;
- provision of a right to reasonable (unpaid) time off work for family emergencies, which will apply to all employees regardless of length of service; and
- ensuring that employees are protected against dismissal or other detriment if they exercise their rights to parental leave and time off for urgent family reasons.

## Summary points concerning sex discrimination legislation
- National legislation is concerned primarily with equal pay between men and women and more general issues concerning sex discrimination.
- Equal pay legislation provides for an 'equality clause' to be included in the woman's contract of employment in respect of like work and equivalently-rated work.
- The employer could justify pay differentials on grounds of a 'genuinely material factor' (GMF) such as length of service, superior skill or qualifications. Legislation since 1983 also provides for equality of pay for work of equal value.
- The SDA which established the EOC covers both direct and indirect discrimination. Direct discrimination involves intentionally less favourable treatment because of sex or marital status. Indirect discrimination occurs where a requirement or condition affecting both sexes equally nevertheless has a disproportionate effect upon one sex.
- The SDA permits lawful discrimination in certain instances which the Act calls 'genuine occupational qualifications' (GOQs). The Act does not permit 'positive discrimination' but does not sanction 'positive action'.
- Other relevant legislation includes:
  - Social Security Act 1989
  - Pensions Act 1995

- Employment Rights Act 1996 (pregnancy and maternity provisions)
- Employment Relations Act 1999 ('family friendly' provisions)

## Race discrimination

Legislation concerning discrimination on grounds of race and ethnicity is largely based on the Race Relations Act 1976 which makes discrimination unlawful on the grounds of colour, race, nationality or ethnic or national origin in employment and other fields. It is unlawful to discriminate against a person either directly or indirectly on these grounds. The Act does not, however, apply to the police or the public services.

### Race Relations Act 1996

The Act has been amended slightly by the Employment Act 1989, the Further and Higher Education Act 1992, the Education Act 1993, the Race Relations (Remedies) Act 1994, and the Police Act 1997. The Act also established the Commission for Racial Equality (CRE) whose duties are:

- to work towards the elimination of racial discrimination;
- to promote equality of opportunity and good relations between persons of different racial groups generally; and
- to monitor the working of the Act and to make recommendations to the Secretary of State to amend the Act if and when necessary.

The CRE is given wide powers of investigation and power to draw up codes of practice to eliminate discrimination in employment (see p. 603). An employee or applicant for a job who has been discriminated against may be awarded compensation by an employment tribunal.

It is important to note that the Race Relations Act (RRA) has not been directly subject to the European Community legislation which has so influenced the case law and statutory development of domestic sex discrimination law in the employment field. It is likely, however, that the EC will assume a more prominent role as a result of the inclusion of a general non-discrimination clause into the Treaty of Rome as a result of the ratification of the recent Treaty of Amsterdam. This will enable the Council of Ministers, acting unanimously on a proposal from the European Commission after consultation with the European Parliament to take 'appropriate action to combat discrimination based on sex, racial or ethnic origin, religion or belief, disability, age or sexual orientation'. In a recent communication: *An Action Plan Against Racism*, the Commission indicated its intention to table proposals for legislation to combat race discrimination before the end of 1999. In addition, the CRE in 1998 put forward a comprehensive set of proposals and recommendations to the Home Secretary which would, if adopted, substantially reform the RRA. The proposals focused on the following areas:

- increasing the duties on public bodies to promote racial equality and eliminate discrimination;
- tackling institutional discrimination;
- strengthening the law enforcement powers of the Act;
- compulsory ethnic monitoring for all private employers with more than 250 employees and for public bodies;
- clearer definitions of key concepts, such as positive action; and
- removal of some of the existing exceptions to the Act.

The basic structure of the RRA is to define discrimination in Part 1. This covers:

- direct and overtly less favourable treatment on racial grounds;
- indirect or institutional discrimination which results from the imposition of apparently racially-neutral requirements or conditions which have a 'disproportionately deleterious' impact on a particular racial group and which cannot be objectively justified; and
- discrimination by way of victimisation (because, for example, an individual has previously brought proceedings under or makes allegations in relation to the RRA).

Having so defined what amounts to discrimination, the RRA goes on to say that discrimination of that kind, as manifested in certain separate fields, amounts to unlawful conduct. In relation to employment and recruitment for employment, the relevant provisions are contained in Part II of the Act. Later parts of the Act deal with the constitution and powers of the CRE, enforcement of the Act and remedies.

### Direct discrimination

Direct discrimination occurs when, on the grounds of race, a person is treated **less favourably**, or would be treated less favourably, than other persons. Note that the difference in treatment has to be on grounds of race, although this does not have to be the sole reason, as long as it is a substantial or important factor.

**SE 11.9**                                  *The response is provided at the end of the chapter*

Identify one or two examples of direct discrimination.

### Indirect discrimination

Indirect discrimination occurs when a person applies to another a condition or requirement which he applies or would apply equally to persons not of the same racial group as that other but:

- which is such that the proportion of persons of the same racial group as that other who can comply with it is considerably smaller than the proportion of persons not of the racial group who can comply with it;
- which he cannot show to be justifiable irrespective of the colour, race, nationality or ethnic or national origins of the person to whom it is applied; and
- which is to the detriment of that other because he cannot comply with it.

Relevant examples include:

In *Perera v Civil Service Commission* (1982), the Employment Appeals Tribunal (EAT) decided that, 'taking account of the fact that a larger proportion of "coloureds" are adult immigrants, placing an upper age limit of 32 on trainees for certain posts in the Civil Service made it harder for "coloured" immigrants to apply'.

In *Bohon-Mitchell v. Common Professional Examination Board* (1978) an industrial tribunal decided that the Board's requirement for non-law graduates from overseas universities to complete a two-year course of legal study before becoming barristers while only one year was required for non-law graduates from British and Irish universities was indirect discrimination. Fewer graduates from overseas countries could comply with this requirement.

## Victimisation

Victimisation occurs when an employer treats any person less favourably than others because that person threatens to bring proceedings, to give evidence or information, to take any action or make any allegation concerning the employer with reference to the RRA, or has already taken such actions.

## Genuine occupational qualifications (GOQs)

Employers may lawfully discriminate in certain jobs where being a member of a particular racial group is a genuine occupational qualification (GOQ). The main GOQ's are:

### Authenticity

Relevant to: the **entertainment** field such as participating in a dramatic performance where it is necessary to have a person of a particular racial group to achieve an authentic act; **modelling or photographic work** where it is necessary to use persons from particular racial/ethnic groups to provide authenticity for a work of art; **the restaurant business** where it is necessary to have a person from a particular ethnic group, for example, an Indian waiter in an Indian restaurant to contribute to an authentic atmosphere.

### Personal welfare or educational services

Where an employee's duties include providing individuals with personal services promoting their welfare or education, or similar personal services, and those services can most effectively be provided by a member of a particular racial group.

## Racial harassment

Racial harassment constitutes unlawful race discrimination and often also constitutes a criminal offence such as assault or incitement to racial hatred. Examples of harassment include: personal attacks; verbal or written threats or insults; damage to property; victimisation; intimidation.

## Disability discrimination

### The Disability Discrimination Act 1995

The Disability Discrimination Act (DDA) makes it unlawful for employers with **more than twenty** employees to discriminate against existing or prospective staff for a reason relating to their disability. A person has a disability 'if he has a physical or mental impairment which has a substantial and long-term adverse effect on his ability to carry out normal day-to-day activities'. The definition therefore covers impairments affecting the senses, such as hearing and sight, together with learning difficulties or a mental illness which is clinically well recognised. However, addictions, tattoos and body piercing are all excluded from the protection of the Act. For these purposes an impairment has a long-term effect only if it has lasted for at least twelve months, is likely to do so, or is likely to last for the rest of the life of a person. Day-to-day activities are normal activities carried out on a regular basis and must involve one of the following:

- mobility;
- manual dexterity (which covers the ability to use hands and fingers with precision);
- physical co-ordination;
- continence;
- the ability to lift, carry or move everyday objects;

- speech, hearing or eyesight;
- memory or ability to concentrate, learn or understand; and
- perception of the risk of physical danger.

Severe disfigurements are treated as disabilities although they have no effect on a person's ability to carry out normal day-to-day activities. Medication or equipment is not taken into account when assessing whether an impairment has a 'substantial effect' (one exception to this is when people wear glasses or contact lenses). Where a progressive condition has resulted in an impairment which has affected a person's day-to-day activities, but that effect is not yet substantial, it is to be treated as having a substantial effect if that is the likely prognosis. The examples given of progressive conditions are: cancer, multiple sclerosis, muscular dystrophy and HIV infection. It should be noted that the DDA does not cover those with a latent genetic predisposition to disability such as Huntington's chorea, unless the disability develops.

### Direct discrimination by the employer

An employer discriminates against a disabled person if, for a reason relating to that person's disability:

- he treats him less favourably than he treats, or would treat others to whom that reason does or would not apply; and
- he cannot show that the treatment in question is justified.

For example, where an advertisement might reasonably be understood to have indicated that a person might not get the job because of their disability or that an employer is unwilling to make adjustments for disabled people, and a disabled person who was not offered the post complains, the employment tribunal must take the advertisement into account. Unless it can be proved otherwise, the tribunal will assume that the reason the complainant did not get the job related to his or her disability.

### Victimisation

It is unlawful for a person to victimise another for:

- bringing proceedings under the DDA;
- giving evidence or information in connection with such proceedings;
- doing anything under the DDA; or
- alleging that another person contravened the DDA (unless the allegation was false and not made in good faith).

As with race and sex discrimination, anything done by a person in the course of employment is treated as also done by the employer, whether or not it was done with the employer's approval. However, employers will not be liable if they can show that they took such steps as were reasonably practicable to prevent the employee's action.

The DDA established a **National Disability Council** with lesser powers than the EOC and CRE to advise government on ways to reduce or eliminate discrimination. However, the Council was abolished by the Disability Rights Commission Act 1999 (see below).

#### The Disability Rights Commission Act 1999
The main purpose of the Act is to establish a Disability Rights Commission (DRC) for Great Britain. The Act makes provision as to the DRC's functions which are similar to those of the EOC and CRE. These functions are:

- to work towards the elimination of discrimination against disabled people;
- to promote the equalisation of opportunities for disabled people; and
- to keep under review the workings of the DDA and the DRC Act.

The DRC is expected to **encourage good practice** in the treatment of disabled people; to advise ministers on existing and proposed legislation emanating from Britain and the European Union where issues arise which are connected with the elimination of discrimination against, or equalisation of opportunities for, disabled people; and to provide information and advice to employers (among others) in particular sectors on, for example, making reasonable adjustments.

The DRC will provide a **central point of information and advice** for employers, service providers and disabled people. They will be able to go to the DRC for information about the law, their rights and responsibilities under it and advice about how best to comply with it. They may also seek help on good practice; the DRC will also have an important promotional role in spreading the message that discrimination is unacceptable and helping people to understand how it can be avoided.

With regard to unlawful discrimination, the DRC has the same power as the EOC and the CRE:

- to conduct formal investigation in order to determine whether unlawful discrimination has taken or is taking place;
- to issue non-discrimination notices to those who have been subject to a formal investigation, where they are found to be discriminating unlawfully.

Like the CRE and EOC, the DRC will issue its own Code of Practice which will provide employers with practical guidance on how to avoid discrimination, promote the equalisation of opportunities and encourage good practice. Courts and tribunals will be able to take account of any provision of the Code which may be relevant to the particular case being scrutinised.

### Age discrimination

Age discrimination has been outside the scope of legislation, but the current Labour government's intention to initiate a consultation process and then to draft a non-statutory Code of Practice is a first stage towards fulfilling its manifesto commitment that age discrimination would be made illegal (DfEE, 1998). Evidence of age discrimination is revealed in surveys undertaken by the Equal Opportunities Review (1993, 1998). The 1993 survey looked at discrimination in recruitment and found that around 25 per cent of advertisements contained a requirement that applicants should be under 45, and 50 per cent of these advertisements specified an age limit of 35 or under. The survey also discovered that discrimination in job advertisements is much more prevalent in the private than in the public sector. Discrimination is also rife in training and promotion/advancement within the organisation. The 1998 survey of over 7000 job advertisements found that the use of formal age barriers discriminating against older workers has dropped sharply since 1993, with 8 per cent of job advertisements in the *Sunday Times* stating a numerical age preference. While this is an improvement on 1993, the improvement may well conceal more subtle discriminatory changes in job advertisements:

*However, some advertisements, while not specifying a numerical age range for candidates, used language that clearly signalled they were looking for someone from a particular age group. This was done in two main ways: by using language which either related to the preferred person, e.g. 'young' or 'articulate youngsters', or to the working environment, e.g. 'young, dynamic environment'.* (IRS 666, 1998)

The government's consultation process (1998) concluded that 'it is clear that age discrimination does exist against older workers (and occurs) across the whole spectrum of employment and can affect both old and young people'. The report emphasises that in common with sex, race and disability discrimination, both direct and indirect age discrimination exist within the employment context and occurs more obviously where people 'hold strong, stereotypical views about a person's ability to do a job or to be developed because of their age'. The report identifies certain initiatives consistent with 'defeating unjustified age discrimination' including:

- 'the introduction of revised policy appraisal guidelines which highlight the need for all government departments to take account of equal opportunities issues – including age – when developing policy, and the introduction of monitoring arrangements to ensure departmental compliance;
- recognition of the need to take into account the views and concerns of older people before developing policies;
- setting a good example in the way the government takes account of age discrimination issues in terms of the employment and recruitment of its own staff, including issuing guidance on avoiding unfair age discrimination in employment within the Civil Service' (IRS 1998).

While it is not, therefore, unlawful to discriminate on grounds of age, Clarke (1995) points out that age discrimination is a form of indirect sex or race discrimination:

*So in* **Price v. Civil Service Commission** *(1977), job applicants had to be between 17 and 28. It was held that this was a requirement or condition and that a smaller proportion of otherwise suitably qualified women could comply with the requirement in practice than the proportion of men who could comply, because of women's child-rearing responsibilities. Nor could the employer justify the requirement.*

*However, it is not easy to successfully claim indirect discrimination based on age:*

- *First, the employee must show that the age limit was an absolute bar, rather than simply a preference on behalf of the employer for employees under a particular age.*
- *Secondly, the employee has to show that the proportion of people of a particular sex or racial group who can comply with the requirement or condition is considerably smaller than the proportion of people of the opposite sex or not of that racial group who can comply.* (p. 112)

### Trade union status

Legislation prohibits discrimination owing to trade union status. The relevant legislative provisions are found in the Trade Union and Labour Relations (Consolidation) Act 1992 (TULR(C)A) and the Employment Rights Act 1996. In the area of **recruitment** it is unlawful to deny a person employment on grounds of union membership or non-membership, and as with sex and race discrimination, the job applicant must prove that they were refused employment on these grounds. It is also **automatically unfair** to dismiss an employee either for being or proposing to become a trade union member; for taking or proposing to take part in union activities; for not being a member, and for refusing to become a member or remain a member of a trade union

(See Chapter 12). Finally, it is unlawful for an employer to victimise an employee on grounds of union membership.

### Summary points concerning discrimination on grounds of race, disability and trade union membership

- The RRA established the CRE, and like the SDA, distinguishes between direct and indirect discrimination.
- Again, as with the SDA, the RRA identifies instances where employers may lawfully discriminate on GOQ grounds.
- The Disability Discrimination Act (DDA) makes it unlawful for employers with more than twenty employees to discriminate on grounds of disability.
- The Disability Rights Commission Act, 1999, abolished the largely ineffective National Disability Council (set up by the DDA) and replaced it with a Disability Rights Commission (DRC) with similar powers to those of the CRE and EOC.
- There is no legislation at the moment concerning age discrimination, although the government through a consultation process will draft a non-statutory code of practice.
- It is unlawful for employers to discriminate against employees and potential employees on grounds of trade union membership.

## THE EUROPEAN UNION AND DISCRIMINATION

Since joining the European Community in 1973, the British government, employers and employees have been increasingly affected by the various Treaty provisions and Directives relating to equal rights for men and women. Much of European law is concerned with sex discrimination, but there has been increased concern about race discrimination.

**Treaty provisions** create rights enforceable by individuals which enable individuals to bring legal action in the national courts of member states. Hence, a person can initiate action concerning an equal pay claim against her employer by relying on Article 119 of the Treaty of Rome without having to resort to the Equal Pay Act, 1970.

**Directives,** as we have seen in Chapter 4, operate as instructions to member states to introduce legislation giving effect to these Directives. If a member state does not introduce such legislation, then individuals can still enforce their rights under a particular Directive against their employer, provided that the employer is an **organ of the state**. An organ of the state is broadly defined as a result of the case *Foster v. British Gas* (1990) as *'a body, whatever its legal form, which has been made responsible by the State for providing a public service under the control of the State and has for that purpose special powers beyond those which result in the normal rules applicable in relations between individuals'*. So, for example, a person can rely on the Equal Treatment Directive (see below) in order to establish that it is unlawful for a local authority or health authority to set different retirement ages for men and women employees. While Directives directly benefit public sector employees using the 'organ of the state' criterion, it is possible for private sector employees to claim damages from the British government where they have suffered some loss because of the government's failure to implement a Directive. There are two ways in which to do this:

1. Judge made decisions in many cases will interpret British legislation so that it is congruent with the meaning of the relevant Directive.
2. Where a member state has failed to implement a Directive, an individual may be entitled to damages from the government provided:
   - the result required by the Directive includes conferring rights for the benefit of the individual;
   - the content of those rights can be determined by reference to the provisions of the Directive; and
   - there is a causal link between the breach of the obligation by the State and the damage suffered by the individuals so affected.

In addition, Clarke (1995) points out that it is possible to seek **judicial review** where European law is incompatible with domestic law.

*In R v. Secretary of State for Employment ex parte EOC (1994), the EOC argued that the hours threshold contained in the Employment Protection (Consolidation) Act 1978 was contrary to Community law as it indirectly discriminated against women. The House of Lords held that the EOC was entitled to bring the action, and further held that the hours provisions were incompatible with Community law. As a result, the Government was forced to introduce the Employment Protection (Part-time Employees) Regulations 1995: the Regulations removed all hours qualifications for unfair dismissal, redundancy, maternity rights and other statutory rights.* (p. 3)

## Equal pay and equal treatment

**Article 119 of the Treaty of Rome** as amended by the Maastricht Treaty, and currently being replaced by a new Article 119 as a result of the Amsterdam Treaty, 1997 enshrines the principle that:

*All member states should ensure and maintain the principle that men and women should receive equal pay for equal work.*

**Directive 75/117 (1975)** deals directly with issues concerning equal pay for equal value, and this eventually resulted in the UK Equal Value Regulations 1984.

**Code of Practice concerning Implementation of Equal Pay for Work of Equal Value for Women and Men (COM(96) 336).** The Code was introduced in 1996 to address the continuing problems concerning the still considerable differences in pay between men and women with the aim of eliminating sex discrimination in pay structures determined by job classification and job evaluation schemes.

**Directive 76/207 (1976) – Equal Treatment Directive** deals with discrimination on the grounds of sex in all aspects of employment (access to employment, vocational training, promotion and working conditions). The corresponding UK legislation was the SDA (1976) and the Employment Act (1989).

**Directive 79/7 (1979)** – progressive implementation of the principle of equal treatment for men and women in matters of social security.

**Directive 86/378 (1986)** – implementation of the principle of equal treatment for men and women in occupational social security schemes.

**Directive 86/613 (1986)** – application of the principle of equal treatment between men and women engaged in an activity, including agriculture, in a self-employed capacity, and on the protection of self-employed women during pregnancy and motherhood.

**Directive 92/85 (1992)** – introduction of measures to encourage improvements in the safety and health at work of pregnant workers who have recently given birth or are breast-feeding.

**Directive 96/34 (1996)** – the result of the **First European Framework Agreement** introduced measures concerning **parental leave** whose provisions included:

- three months unpaid leave for both parents before the birth or adoption of a child;
- protection from dismissal for requesting parental leave;
- the right to return to work after leave protected; and
- additional time off if for reasons that cannot be avoided as a significant means to reconcile family and personal life.

The Parental Leave Directive will be implemented in Britain as part of the Fairness at Work Act 1999.

**Directive 97 (1997)** – the result of the **Second European Framework Agreement** 'to provide for the removal of discrimination against part-time workers and to improve the quality of part-time work'. The main provisions are:

- that the conditions of employment for part-time workers should not be less favourable than for comparable full-time workers; and
- that the conditions of employment must be pro-rata with those of full-time employees wherever appropriate.

**Directive 98 (1998)** – concerns **burden of proof** in sex discrimination cases and provides that the person bringing the complaint to employment tribunal establishes 'facts from which it may be presumed that there has been direct or indirect discrimination' then the employer has to prove 'that there has been no breach of the principle of equal treatment' (IRS, 671, 1999). The new regulations will necessitate changes to the SDA regarding direct discrimination only; no amendments are required in relation to indirect discrimination and equal pay. The Directive has to be implemented in the UK by 13 July 2001.

A change of government has seen a more pro-European approach with 'New' Labour endorsing a new Social Chapter arising from the Amsterdam Treaty which emphasises, amongst other things, the commitment to achieve equality between men and women while Article 119 is amended by the Treaty to incorporate specific reference to work of equal value. **Future EU proposals** include legislation to combat racism which will be brought forward under a new Article to be inserted into the Treaty of Rome which provides that the European Council 'may take appropriate action' against discrimination on grounds of sex, race, ethnic origin or belief, disability, age or sexual orientation. With regard to sexual harassment, it is likely that the European Commission may issue either non-binding Recommendations to member states or a binding instrument as an amendment to the 1976 Equal Treatment Directive.

## DISCRIMINATION AND MANAGEMENT POLICIES

Having considered the extent of discrimination in Britain with particular emphasis upon the employment relationship and the UK and European Union legislation which seeks to eliminate discriminatory practices, we now consider what employers can and should do to achieve the aims of the legislation within the workplace. In relation to **sex discrimination**, we look in particular at some equal pay issues and at sexual harassment in the workplace, together with EOC prescriptions for 'best practice'. We then go on to consider other forms of related discrimination involving sexual orientation. The section continues with an overview of management policy and practice in relation to workplace **sex and race discrimination**. Finally, we place the entire issue of work-related discrimination within the context of **equal opportunities policies and practices**.

## Sex discrimination: the EOC Code of Practice 1985

The EOC and CRE Codes of Practice adopt a procedural approach to managing equal opportunities which is based on efforts to control managerial behaviour by tightly specifying what management should do in order to avoid sex discrimination and encourage equal opportunities. While a failure to observe the Code cannot itself give rise to proceedings, in any proceedings before an industrial tribunal such a failure will be taken into account if it is relevant to the case. The first part of the Code deals with the role of good employment practices in eliminating sex and marriage discrimination while the second part deals with promoting equality of opportunity. The main elements of the Code are provided below:

(a) *Responsibilities of employers:* The primary responsibility at law rests with each employer to ensure that there is no unlawful discrimination. It is important, however, that measures to eliminate discrimination or promote equality of opportunity should be understood and supported by all employees. Employers are therefore recommended to involve their employees in equal opportunities policies.

(b) *Responsibilities of trade unions:* Trade unions should:
- encourage and press for equal opportunities policies so that measures to prevent discrimination at the workplace can be introduced with the clear commitment of employers and trade unions;
- pay careful attention to claims from members alleging discrimination;
- ensure that deliberate acts of discrimination are treated as disciplinary offences;
- train and inform all officials and representatives on their role and responsibilities for equal opportunity;
- examine their own procedures to ensure they do not contain any discriminatory requirements or conditions.

(c) *Implementing an equal opportunities policy:* The Code states that the formulation and implementation of an equal opportunities policy 'will ensure the effective use of human resources in the best interest of both the organisation and its employees' and a statement clearly detailing the central relevance of equal opportunities to effective people and business performance will reinforce the organisation's commitment.

(d) *Code points for successful implementation are:*
- the policy must be seen to have the active support of top management;
- the policy should be clearly stated and, where appropriate, included in a collective agreement;
- overall responsibility for implementing the policy should rest with senior management;
- the policy should be made known to all employees and, where reasonably practicable, to all job applicants; and
- trade unions have an important part to play in implementing genuine equality of opportunity and will obviously be involved in the review of established procedures to ensure they are consistent with the law.

(e) *Monitoring policy:* The policy should be monitored regularly to ensure that it is working in practice. In a small organisation or enterprise it may be quite adequate to assess the position of

▶

employees from personal knowledge. In a large, complex organisation a more formal analysis will be necessary, for example, by sex, grade and payment in each unit. This may need to be introduced by stages as resources permit. Sensible monitoring will show, for example, whether members of one sex:

- do not apply for employment or promotion, or that fewer apply than might be expected;
- are not recruited, promoted or selected for training and development or are appointed or selected in a significantly lower proportion;
- concentrate their applications in certain jobs, sections or departments.

A system of structured exit interviews and occasional skills audits will help assess the effectiveness of the equal opportunities programme.

(f) *Positive action:* The Code stresses that selection for recruitment and promotion must be on merit, irrespective of sex. However, it also refers to s. 48 of the SDA which allows certain steps to be taken by employers to redress the effects of previous unequal opportunities. The act, where there have been few or no members of one sex in particular work in their employment for the previous 12 months, allows employers to give special encouragement to and provide specific training for the minority sex. Positive action measures suggested by the Code include:

- training employees for work traditionally the preserve of the other sex;
- positive encouragement to apply for management posts for which special courses may be required;
- advertisements which encourage applications from the minority sex, but make it clear that selection will be on merit, irrespective of sex; and
- notifying job agencies that as part of a positive action programme the employer wishes to encourage members of one sex to apply for vacancies, where few or no members of that sex are doing the work in question. In these circumstances job agencies should tell both men and women about the posts and, in addition let the under-represented sex know that applications from them are particularly welcome.

The Code's warning is to be noted; that withholding information from one sex in an attempt to encourage applications from the opposite sex would be unlawful.

---

**SE 11.10**                                             *The response is provided at the end of the chapter*

---

In your opinion, do you think that discrimination legislation and Codes of Practice are effective in eliminating workplace discrimination?

---

## Equal pay issues which employers should consider

Pay inequalities are deeply rooted. Special rates of pay for women doing the same job as men became illegal in 1975 when the Equal Pay Act of 1970 came into force in 1975. Many jobs, however, have traditionally been assigned to one sex or the other and in many areas this demarcation continues. Other factors contributing to the income gap include stereotyping and occupational segregation in other ways; for example, maternity leave can mean losing out on performance-related pay. The net effect has been to depress 'women's' rates. This is one factor which continues to produce a situation where overall women's earnings are still only around 70–80 per cent of male earnings (See Table 11.1) while women part-timers were paid a mere 58 per cent of men's full-time hourly pay (LRD, 1999). The fact that women tend to work in a sex-segregated labour market and the devaluation of skills traditionally associated with 'women's work' contributes to the problematic nature of pay inequity. The success of equal pay legislation needs to be measured against its effectiveness in tackling these

**Table 11.1 The pay gap: average gross weekly earnings of employees in selected occupations**

| Occupation | Women's earnings (£) | Men's earnings (£) | % of Men's earnings |
|---|---|---|---|
| General administrators and national govt. | 501.00 | 563.40 | 88.9 |
| Treasurers and company financial managers | 680.10 | 1070.30 | 66.5 |
| Medical practitioners | 767.60 | 945.70 | 81.2 |
| Solicitors | 597.30 | 756.80 | 78.9 |
| Nurses | 366.40 | 391.20 | 93.7 |
| Chefs/cooks | 202.70 | 255.00 | 79.5 |
| Bar staff | 156.50 | 193.20 | 81.0 |
| Care assistants and attendants | 197.30 | 229.30 | 86.0 |
| Sales assistants | 184.00 | 229.40 | 80.2 |
| Cleaners/domestics | 181.40 | 221.20 | 82.0 |

Source: EOC Annual Report, 1999

problems, but as we have already noted, legislation can inevitably have a marginal effect in changing what are primarily structural problems in pay systems. These problems and others concerning the processing of cases relate to:

- overtime payments, bonuses and allowances for which many women may not be eligible, or may receive them at a lower rate;
- the discriminatory nature of payment systems themselves;
- part-time workers (of which over 4.5 million or around 85 per cent are women) often have limited pay and career prospects;
- discriminatory pay practices have traditionally been sustained by collective agreements;
- employee's lack of knowledge of their rights under UK and EU equal pay and equal value legislation; the legislation is relatively complicated and relies on the individual to take action; and
- delays in tribunal procedure may discourage genuine applicants; it is not unusual for a case to take three or four years through the tribunal and appeals system.

### The extent of the problem

An EOC briefing paper (January 1997) argues that if the trend towards greater pay equality continues at its present rate, it will be another forty-five years before women achieve equal pay with men:

> It is over 20 years since the Equal Pay Act came into force yet there is still an average pay gap of 20 per cent. At this rate women will wait until the year 2040 to achieve equality in pay. There can be no equality of opportunity without equality in pay. Throughout their working lives women earn less than men, whether they are lawyers or sales assistants. Unless significant changes are made in the way the pay gap is tackled, women face a future of continuing inequality. The EOC wants to see simplified and more effective equal pay legislation and greater recognition by employers that pay must be at the heart of their equal opportunity policies and practices.

The EOC's proposal for a new sex equality law contains recommendations aimed at closing the income gap, and the Commission is hopeful that pay equality can be achieved in the near future. However, a less optimistic view of the situation is provided by the argument that, despite some notable successes, attempts by individuals and trade unions to gain equal pay are a waste of time for, behind all the convoluted explanations of unequal pay lies the real question: who is doing what and how do we rank their efforts? In addition, the essence of differential pay may lie in our acceptance of the traditions of a workforce so segregated along gender lines that we barely notice it and that no matter what sphere of work women are hired for or select, like sediment in a wine bottle they settle to the bottom.

## What can be done about the problem?

The approach of the EOC is to work in partnership with government on the National Minimum Wage, the Lower Earnings Limit and other proposed measures affecting pay. The EOC also seeks to work in partnership with employers, trade unions and voluntary organisations on equality issues in relation to income; and to raise awareness among individuals of their rights and the issues in relation to equal pay and other income.

Despite pessimistic views about the nature of pay inequality, a number of the larger trade unions have had some successes in pursuing equal pay claims, and this is borne out by survey data which reveal that for 1998, equal pay claims showed a record rise of 11 per cent and settlements are at an all-time high of £8 million (LRD, 1999). Successful claims concerning, for example, 250 UNISON members who won a £1.2 million settlement against St. Helens Metropolitan Borough Council may encourage others to come forward. In the wake of this success, UNISON has launched its strategy to gain equal pay for one million women employed mainly within the local authority sector through negotiations, and if negotiation does not succeed, then through the courts. Similarly, Manufacturing Science and Finance (MSF) has initiated a claim on behalf of several thousand women employed in the NHS which is based on the successful claim of Pam Enderby, an equal pay for equal value 'benchmark' case. Recent decisions of the European Court of Justice mean that women workers in different NHS professions can claim equal pay across the entire service, not just within trusts or authorities. The MSF claim and other pay problems within the NHS has led to a government commitment to review and fundamentally restructure the NHS pay system, but whether this will satisfy equal pay campaigners such as MSF remains to be seen.

### The Enderby case

**Enderby v. Frenchay Health Authority (1983–1994)**
Pam Enderby was a senior speech therapist whose rate of pay was set by a collective agreement. Her union also negotiated with her employer, under a different collective agreement, on behalf of a group of people including pharmacists and physiotherapists. The latter's pay rates, at the same level of seniority, were significantly greater than Enderby's. She therefore brought an equal pay claim, based on the work of pharmacists and physiotherapists being of equal value to her own work as a speech therapist. The industrial tribunal dismissed Enderby's claim on a preliminary point – namely that the difference in collective bargaining machinery had given rise to the difference in pay, and that there had been no discrimination in the evolution of the separate collective bargaining machinery for two classes of employee.

The tribunal rejected the employer's alternative defence based on genuine material differences/ material factors of 'market forces'. The health authority had argued that market forces justified the difference in pay: that pharmacists could work in the private sector and needed to be paid more to attract them. However, it was established that only some 10 per cent of the pay differential could be explained by the shortages of pharmacists and therefore the difference in pay was much greater than was required by market forces.

Enderby appealed to the Employment Appeals Tribunal (EAT) which upheld the tribunal's decision. Since the difference in pay arose from the different collective bargaining machinery used to negotiate pay, and since there was no discrimination in the setting up of the two collective bargaining structures, the pay differential was justified. On the question of the employer's **alternative** defence, the EAT overruled the tribunal and found for the health authority.

Enderby went to the Court of Appeal, which in turn sent a number of questions on the construction of the European equal pay legislation to the European Court of Justice.

**The judgment** of the European Court of Justice was based on the fact that once it is shown that there is a significant difference in pay between two jobs which are of equal value, one of which is carried out predominantly by men and one predominantly by women, Article 119 of the Treaty of Rome (to be amended by the Treaty of Amsterdam) shifts the burden of proving that the difference is objectively justified by factors which are unrelated to sex discrimination to the employer. If it were otherwise it would be impossible for employees to enforce their rights to equal pay. The fact that different rates of pay arose from separate negotiations between the same union and employers was not sufficient justification for the difference in pay between the two jobs, even though there was no discrimination within either sets of negotiation themselves. On the question of whether or not and to what extent the difference in pay could be justified by market forces, the European Court of Justice's answer was that it was up to the national court to quantify how much of the difference is attributable to market forces.

The **relevant legislation** considered here is:

1. Article 119 of the Treaty of Rome.
2. Article 1 of Directive 75/117/EEC which says: 'The principle of equal pay for men and women outlined in Article 119 of the Treaty of Rome . . . means, for the same work or for work to which equal value is attributed, the elimination of all discrimination on grounds of sex with respect to all aspects and conditions of remuneration'.
3. Equal Pay Act s. 1 (2c and 3) as added to by the Equal Pay (Amendment) Regulations 1983.

---

**SE 11.11**                                             *The response is provided below*

What steps should employers take in order to ensure that equal pay policies are effective? (The Enderby case above will be useful).

---

**Employers** bear much of the responsibility for ensuring equality of pay. The **EC and EOC's new Code of Practice** which came into force in 1997 recommend that employers should adopt an equal pay policy and provides detailed guidance on how employers should conduct internal pay reviews in order to eliminate pay inequality. The EOC Code is admissible as evidence in tribunal proceedings, but there is no legal obligation on employers to carry out a pay review or introduce an equal pay policy. The main points of the **EC Code of Practice on Equal Pay** are:

1. Employers should study their pay structures 'to reveal any possible undervaluation of work typically carried out by women in comparison with that typically carried out by men and vice versa' (p. 11). The study should comprise three main stages. **Firstly, the relevant information** should be collected across the whole of the organisation's workforce. **Secondly,** the relevant information gained should be **assessed** and **thirdly,** particular aspects of the pay system should be examined, especially those which might prove to be discriminatory.
2. The **relevant information** would include:
   - **Information about employees** such as gender, grade, job title, hours of work excluding breaks, required entry qualification, other relevant qualifications, length of service, basic pay, additional payments.

- **Pay arrangements and practices** such as job descriptions, grading, classification and evaluation systems, job evaluation manual, performance pay handbook, rules concerning bonus and incentive schemes, piece-work or contract work pay arrangements.
3. **Assessing the relevant information.** Key indicators of potential sex bias include:
   - women have lower average earnings than men with the same job title
   - women have lower average earnings than men in the same grade
   - women in female-dominated unskilled jobs are paid less than men in the lowest male-dominated unskilled job
   - women are paid less than men with equivalent entry qualifications and length of service
   - the majority of men and women are segregated by different grading, classification and evaluation systems
4. **Particular aspects of the pay system.** Practices which prove to be discriminatory include basic pay issues, bonus/performance pay and piece rates, pay benefits, part-time workers, job classification, grading, evaluation and skills/competency-based systems. The example of **basic pay** discriminatory practices together with the advice given in the Code is given below.

   *Women are consistently appointed at lower points in a pay scale than men are.*
   - Examine recruitment and promotion records to see if different treatment is objectively justifiable irrespective of sex.
   - Are qualifications rewarded by allowances necessary for the posts? Is the way qualifications are defined adversely affecting women?

   *Women are paid less than male predecessors in the job.*
   - Check if job duties and responsibilities are the same or have changed. Do the changes justify any pay reduction?

   *Women progress more slowly through incremental scales and/or seldom reach higher points.*
   - check whether service pay is linked to ability to do the job rather than length of service. Where women have broken or shorter periods of service because of family responsibilities, they may be less able to meet length of service criteria.
   - investigate criteria by which employees are progressed through a scale.

   *Men are paid more, by supplement or by a higher grading, because of 'recruitment and retention' policies.*
   - Adopt measures to deal with recruitment and retention problems, e.g.: existing staff could be trained and then avail of development initiatives. The pool from which staff are normally drawn could be expanded. For example, clerical and non-manual staff might be considered for management training and apprenticeships through the use of positive action.

5. Once the pay structure study is completed, **follow-up action** is needed to tackle every instance of sexual discrimination detected in the pay structure. The follow-up action should then be **evaluated** to avoid perpetuating sexual discrimination.

---

## Sexual harassment

*Sexual harassment is one of the most offensive and demeaning experiences an employee can suffer. (It) can reduce the productivity or efficiency of an organisation and can have considerable cost implications where management fails to take appropriate action. Evidence also suggests that harassment can seriously affect employees' confidence and self-esteem as well as leading to absenteeism, poor morale and resignation. In addition, since sexual harassment is unlawful under the Sex Discrimination Act 1975, employers may find that, in certain circumstances, they are liable for the actions of employees who sexually harass other employees in the course of their work. (IRS September 1996)*

**SE 11.12**                                    *The response is provided at the end of the chapter*

Identify examples of what might constitute sexual harassment. How widespread do you think the phenomenon is?

## Legislation dealing with sexual harassment

As we mentioned earlier, sexual harassment is unlawful under the SDA, which means that if an employee has been harassed, he/she can take the case to employment tribunal. The tribunal will consider the SDA's criterion concerning 'less favourable treatment' and that the applicant was dismissed or subjected to some other detriment. The principle underlying this criterion was established by *Strathclyde Regional Council v. Porcelli*. Sexual harassment claims can be brought against the harasser and the employer. Under the SDA the employer is liable for the discriminatory acts of employees at the workplace, whether or not they were committed with the employer's knowledge and approval. Irrespective of liability, tribunals also expect employers to have harassment policies in operation. If an employee is forced to quit her job as a result of harassment she/he may claim unfair (constructive) dismissal under the 1996 ERA provided they have been employed continuously for a period of two years. The tribunal can award compensation for losses resulting from the discrimination including wages and medical treatment costs. As a result of a ruling by the European Court of Justice (1993), there is no upper limit for compensation which, prior to 1993 was fixed at £11 000.

---

### Strathclyde Regional Council v. Porcelli

This case was the first sexual harassment case to reach the appeal courts establishing that sexual harassment constituted direct discrimination under the SDA. The complainant, Mrs Porcelli, was a laboratory technician employed by the regional council in one of its schools. She claimed she had been unlawfully discriminated against when she had been compelled to seek a transfer to another school because of a deliberate campaign of vindictiveness against her by two male colleagues, some of it of a sexual nature. She claimed that the regional council was vicariously responsible for the behaviour of the two men.

The industrial (now employment) tribunal rejected Porcelli's application even though it accepted that the men's behaviour had been extremely unpleasant. However, the Employment Appeals Tribunal (EAT) rejected the decision of the industrial tribunal and allowed Mrs Porcelli's appeal. According to the court of appeal, even if only some of the treatment complained of was sexually oriented, there was less favourable treatment on grounds of sex. What mattered was the treatment, not the motive for it, and therefore if any material part of the treatment included elements of a sexual nature to which the woman was vulnerable, but a man was not, then she had been treated less favourably on grounds of her sex. It was also held that conduct falling short of physical contact could still constitute sexual harassment.

Clarke (1995) comments:

> *Porcelli* was important in establishing that unlawful sexual harassment encompasses more than simply a woman's being dismissed for refusing to have a sexual relationship with her boss. It is now clear that the existence of an unpleasant and intimidating work environment is sufficient detriment to establish a case. If the less favourable treatment is on the ground of sex, then this is unlawful, regardless of the motive for the behaviour. It is also clear from the case law that whether a particular course of conduct amounts to sexual harassment depends upon how that conduct is viewed by the woman at whom it is aimed; comments and behaviour that some women find inoffensive can be highly intimidating to others. (p. 33)

## EU law

The EC Council of Labour and Social Ministers adopted a resolution relating to sexual harassment at work and in 1991, as part of its third action programme on equal opportunities the EC adopted a Recommendation and Code of Practice on the protection of the dignity of women and men at work. The Recommendation asks member states to:

> take action to promote awareness that conduct of a sexual nature, or other conduct based on sex affecting the dignity of women and men at work, including conduct of superiors and colleagues, is unacceptable if:
>
> 1. such conduct is unwanted, unreasonable and offensive to the recipient
> 2. a person's rejection of, or submission to, such conduct on the part of employer or workers (including superiors or colleagues) is used explicitly or implicitly as a basis for a decision which affects that person's access to vocational training, access to employment, continued employment, promotion, salary or any other employment decisions; and/or
> 3. such conduct creates an intimidating, hostile or humiliating work environment for the recipient;
>
> and that such conduct may, in certain circumstances, be contrary to the principle of equal treatment within the meaning of (the Equal Treatment) Directive 76/207/EEC.

The **Code of Practice** recommends that senior management should develop and communicate a policy statement which should:

- expressly state that sexual harassment will not be permitted or condoned;
- set out a positive duty on managers and supervisors to implement the policy and to take corrective action to ensure compliance with it;
- explain the procedure which should be followed by employees subjected to sexual harassment at work in order to obtain assistance;
- contain an undertaking that the allegation will be dealt with seriously, expeditiously and confidentially, and that the complainants will be protected against victimisation; and
- specify that disciplinary measures will be taken against employees guilty of sexual harassment.

Certain cases have established that employment tribunals will expect to see evidence of implementation of the Code of Practice on sexual harassment, and that any oversight on the part of the employer will not be considered favourably. The ET will also use the Code to help establish whether the conduct to which the complainant was subjected, amounted to sexual harassment.

### Taking action on harassment: employers' responsibilities

#### The grievance procedure route

IRS (1996) found that in organisations without harassment policies 'a victim of sexual harassment is expected to lodge a complaint through the organisation's formal grievance procedure' and in many such organisations, resort to the grievance procedure is the **only** option open to complainants. The grievance procedure route has its **limitations**.

**Firstly,** where the victim is expected to complain in the first place through her/his immediate line manager, women will normally be faced with approaching their immediate superior who may be a man: 'the embarrassment involved in raising a complaint with their line manager and the fear some women have of being taken seriously may dissuade them from pursuing a complaint through the organisation's formal grievance procedure' (IRS 1996). **Secondly,** grievance procedures often fail to take account of the fact or possibility that the accused harasser is often the immediate superior, so it is most unlikely that the victim will pursue her complaint via that channel. Nevertheless, Hawkins (1994) points out that 'requiring line managers to take on the role (of investigator) reinforces their day-to-day managerial responsibility for eliminating harassment ... (although) allowing line managers to investigate complaints of harassment unassisted, particularly in the early stages of a policy, is likely to be very risky' (p. 28).

### Counselling

In organisations with a harassment policy and procedure there will normally be provision for counselling support for complainants throughout the procedure. Where counsellors are included as a feature of the harassment policy, the role needs to be clear to the counsellors themselves, to supervisors and managers and to employees. Hawkins identifies two alternative counselling roles, depending upon the nature of the policy and procedure. These are:

- *Where the policy requires the complainant to take full responsibility for the complaint, the role may be restricted to one of pure counselling comprising an empathic ear, an explanation of procedural options, and, perhaps, behind-the-scenes support through assisting in the preparation of any written complaint or statement.*
- *Where the policy provides a higher level of support, the role must extend to accompanying the complainant at meetings with the alleged harasser or, less commonly, taking up the complaint on their behalf informally.* (p. 28)

### Developing policies and procedures

The following is an extract from the EOC booklet 'Consider the cost – sexual harassment at work' (1997).

---

**Sexual harassment at work: what employers should do**

1. Issue a policy statement concerning sexual harassment
   The statement should:
   – define unacceptable behaviour
   – make clear that sexual harassment can be treated as a disciplinary offence
   – point out that both sexes can be subject to harassment
   – explain that it is for the person on the receiving end of any behaviour to decide whether she or he finds it unacceptable.
2. Lay down a procedure for dealing with complaints of sexual harassment
   This can be included in the existing disciplinary and/or grievance procedures, but experience suggests that for most organisations a separate procedure for investigating complaints is needed. The procedure should:
   – specify to whom a complaint should be made, and provide an alternative
   – ensure that complaints are treated seriously and sympathetically
   – wherever possible provide for a manager of the same sex as the complainant to hear the complaint

▶

---

- ensure that any complaint is dealt with promptly and with due care. The investigation of the complaint should be carried out objectively and independently, and by someone with sufficient authority to be able to handle the matter effectively. If a complaint is upheld the harasser should be dealt with under the normal disciplinary procedure. If dismissal is a possible outcome, it is important that the usual procedures should be followed, i.e. an investigation and proper hearing at which the alleged harasser can comment on the case against them

- ensure that any panel set up to investigate the complaint has at least as many women as men on it. Very often such panels include only one woman who is often of lower status than the men. A woman in this position will find it difficult to be effective

- ensure that procedures set out a time frame for the investigation. The complainant and the alleged harasser should be told at the outset how long the investigation is likely to take, and who will be communicating with them. Complainants should be kept well informed at every stage.

3. Ensure that, if it becomes necessary, either during the investigation or afterwards, to separate the complainant and the alleged harasser, no pressure is put on the complainant to transfer.

   While it is acceptable to ask the complainant if they wish to move, they should not be presumed to do so. If there is a problem over them continuing to work together, it is the harasser who should be moved.

4. Introduce the policy statement and associated procedures in consultation with any workplace trade unions.

5. Ensure that the individual is not victimised either by line management or by their colleagues for having made a complaint.

(Adapted from IRS)

---

**SE 11.13**                                              *The response is provided at the end of the chapter*

---

Can you think of any reasons why employers should introduce sexual harassment policies?

---

Policy statements concerning sexual harassment should take the form of **either** a separate part of a general equal opportunities policy **or** a written policy statement dealing specifically with sexual harassment. Most firms in the IRS survey had both an equal opportunities policy and a separate policy for sexual harassment, although sexual harassment policies increasingly are part of a more general policy dealing with all types of harassment. The policy statement should incorporate all the points referred to in the EOC booklet, and in addition should make it clear that all employees have a right to be treated with dignity and respect; state that sexual harassment is unlawful and will not be permitted; define what is unacceptable behaviour; state that appropriate disciplinary action will be taken against those found guilty and point out that both sexes suffer harassment.

A specific **complaints procedure** for dealing with harassment cases should give employees confidence that their allegations will be taken seriously and that complaints will be dealt with quickly and confidentially. They should also aim to provide a fair outcome to complaints, enforce penalties against harassers and protect against victimisation of the complainant. The formal procedure should be supplemented wherever possible with informal methods for dealing with the victim's situation. Provided below is the City of Liverpool local authority procedures for dealing with harassment, discrimination and bullying.

## Liverpool City Council

### Complaints procedures

#### Informal procedures

1. Employees are strongly advised to keep a written record of the incidents including the following information: time, date and place the incident occurred, a full description of what happened, and name(s) if known of the alleged perpetrators and any witnesses.
2. All employees have the right to confidential support, advice and representation, and there are trained Advisory Officers in each directorate who can provide this. A current list of Advisory Officers will be displayed on notice boards and is available from the Equal Opportunities Team on . . .
3. There are a number of ways of dealing with incidents of harassment, discrimination and bullying which include:
   - telling the person(s) involved that the behaviour in question is offensive, unwanted and that it must stop immediately.
   - enlisting the help of an Advisory officer, personnel officer, trade union representative, specialist equalities officer or a colleague, for advice, assistance and support.
   - reporting the matter to your line manager and asking him/her to respond informally by speaking to the alleged perpetrator. Consideration may also be given by line managers to dealing with the issue indirectly without mentioning that a complaint has been made and/or by rearranging desks or work allocations to reduce the risk of contact.
   - managers may wish to provide training either for individuals or work groups
   - copies of this Policy, Code of Practice and publicity materials should be visible and available in the workplace
   - managers may wish to raise the complaint in an informal way and clearly inform the employee that harassment, discrimination and bullying are disciplinary offences.

#### Formal procedures

1. At all times, whether or not informal steps have been taken, any employee who feels that they or others have been harassed, discriminated against or bullied may make a formal complaint by using the Grievance Procedure.
2. Because of the sensitivity of such complaints and the need to resolve them speedily, the complaint should be made in writing and sent to your head of service or to an officer designated to deal with such complaints.
3. Should the complaint be made against a head of service, the complaint should be made to the relevant director. A complaint against a director should be made to the Chief Executive.
4. The first stage of the procedure (discussion with supervisor) may be omitted.
5. The investigating officer, together with a senior personnel officer or specialist Equality Officer, will conduct the investigation.
6. The complainant and the person against whom the allegations are made will be interviewed separately, and the proceedings will be confidential.
7. Both the complainant and the person against whom the allegations are made may be accompanied/represented at all stages of the procedure by either an employee of their choice, a trade union representative, or a friend.
8. The investigation, which will include the interviewing of witnesses, should take a maximum of six weeks through investigation to conclusion.
9. An accurate record will be made of the investigation and its conclusion. The investigating officer will write to the complainant and the person against whom the allegations are being made, detailing the findings of the investigation and the action to be taken. The letter will contain an undertaking that the complainant will not be victimised or suffer any detriment. In the case of complaints concerning race and sex discrimination, complainants will be advised of their rights to apply to the Industrial Tribunal for a decision on the matter.
10. If the complainant is dissatisfied with the outcome s/he must submit a written request to the directorate's personnel officer within seven working days. The matter will then be referred to the Chair and the decision here will be made in writing to both parties.

▶

**The Management of Human Resources**

11. If the investigating officer or the Chair find that disciplinary action is justified then this decision will be notified to the complainant and the person against whom the allegations are being made. A disciplinary hearing normally will be convened within five working days and the person against whom the allegations are made will have the opportunity to challenge any of the evidence and/ or make any submissions in mitigation.
12. During these proceedings it should not normally be necessary to repeat detailed interviews unless necessary in the interests of natural justice.
13. In some cases where it is considered appropriate to issue a disciplinary warning, it may be necessary to consider an alternative post or reallocation of work for the offender in order that s/he and the complainant do not continue to work in close proximity.

**Conclusion**

Employees will be protected from intimidation, victimisation, discrimination or bullying resulting from making a complaint or assisting in an investigation. Retaliating against an employee for making a complaint is a disciplinary offence. During an investigation, or where a complaint is upheld, counselling support must be offered to the complainant. Making false or unsubstantiated allegations with malicious intent will result in the disciplinary procedure being invoked.

Finally, the **successful implementation** of a sexual harassment policy requires, **firstly,** the communication of the policy to the entire workforce in order to make employees aware of the company's procedures for tackling the problem. **Secondly,** all managers concerned with the operation of the policy will require training in all aspects of their role; and **thirdly,** it is essential to review and monitor the policy regularly in order to develop and improve it.

## Discrimination against homosexuals and transsexuals

There is no law in the UK which prohibits discrimination on grounds of sexual orientation. It was thought that the SDA did not provide any assistance for those discriminated against on grounds of sexual orientation, as the Act was confined to protection against gender-based discrimination – but this may be about to change, particularly if the EU takes a lead in this area. Early attempts to use the SDA against discrimination on grounds of sexual orientation had failed until the decision in the groundbreaking *P v. S and Cornwall County Council* (1996) case. In this case the applicant was employed as the general manager of a unit of an educational establishment operated by the county council. The applicant was taken on as a male employee but in April 1992 she informed her head that she proposed to have a gender reassignment. She wrote to her line manager explaining that she was to embark on a life test, which is a one-year period during which a patient planning to undergo an operation for gender reassignment lives in the mode of the proposed gender. The governors of the establishment were informed and during the summer P took sick leave for initial surgical treatment. However, at the beginning of September 1992 she was given three months notice of dismissal. She was not permitted to return from sick leave in her female gender role. The final surgical operation took place before the notice of dismissal expired. The European Court of Justice held that:

*The Directive cannot be confined simply to discrimination based on the fact that a person is one or other sex. In view of its purpose and the nature of the rights which it seeks to safeguard, the scope of the Directive is also such as to apply to discrimination arising from the gender reassignment of the person concerned. Such discrimination is based essentially if not exclusively, on the sex of the person concerned.*

Further cases confirmed the European Court of Justice ruling and would appear to protect transsexuals and presumably homosexuals employed in the private sector against discrimination. However, there still appears to be some inconsistency of judgment in cases of this type. For example in *Grant v. South West Trains Ltd* (1998), the Advocate General found in favour of the lesbian railway clerk who complained that she had been discriminated against because her lover was refused the travel concessions from her employer, South West Trains, she would be entitled to if her lover was of the opposite sex. The Advocate General said it would have been all right to limit concessions to an employee's married partner, but as South West Trains had made this concession available to common law partners, they had to include employee's homosexual partners. However, the European Court of Justice unexpectedly ruled that a lesbian employee was not entitled to the same employee benefits as a heterosexual employee and concluded that the scope of the Treaty of Rome could not be extended beyond the 'competencies of the Community'. New rules are therefore needed to provide for this type of discrimination which the implementation of the Treaty of Amsterdam will provide by extending discrimination provisions to sexual orientation. The government, having published a consultation paper entitled '*Legislation regarding discrimination on grounds of transsexualism*' aims to provide express provision in the SDA to protect transsexuals from discrimination. Employers will, therefore, need to take this into account when devising or revising equal opportunities policies and practices.

## Employers' responsibilities concerning race and ethnicity

Like the SDA, an employer is vicariously liable under the RRA for the actions of his or her employees undertaken in the course of employment, whether or not the employer was aware of the racial discrimination. The employer can only avoid liability for acts or omissions of his/her employees undertaken in the course of employment if the employer can show that he/she has taken all reasonable steps to prevent unlawful race discrimination generally or of the type complained of. The existence of an equal opportunities policy covering all aspects of discrimination together with evidence that the policy is put into practice in appropriate ways will assist the employment tribunal in its proceedings and judgment. Similar remedies for those who are sexually discriminated against are also available to those who are subject to unlawful racial discrimination should they take their case to employment tribunal.

Specific responsibilities of employers have been identified by the CRE and EOC Codes of Practice. Codes of practice, as we have seen, exist to encourage and promote effective management practices, and these practices need to be implemented and enforced in the following areas (CRE 1984):

- ethnic monitoring;
- recruitment;
- selection;
- promotion, transfer, training and appraisal;
- employment conditions and pay;
- harassment and grievance handling; and
- discipline, dismissal and redundancy.

### Ethnic monitoring
The CRE Code recommends that employers regularly monitor the effect of selection decisions, personnel practices and procedures in order to ensure that the criteria within

an equal opportunities policy are being met. While the method of monitoring is left to each employer to determine, the CRE recommends comprehensive monitoring to include:

- the ethnic composition of the workforce of each workplace, section, shift and job category, and changes in distribution over periods of time;
- selection decisions for recruitment, promotion, transfer and training according to the ethnic group of candidates and reasons for these decisions;
- an estimation of the geographical areas from which employers expect to recruit different types of employees and the proportions of the various minority ethnic groups within these areas;
- devising a suitable method for obtaining relevant information (self-assessment questionnaires for this purpose have been used successfully by many organisations);
- communicating the purpose for which the information is being collected.

Monitoring data should be collected from all applicants, since, without this information employers may be unaware that they are discriminating against particular groups. The CRE recommends the use of nine categories comprising White, Black-African, Black-Caribbean, Black-Other, Indian, Pakistani, Bangladeshi, Chinese, Other. The information should be separate from other types of information required (for example, the application form) and should not be used as part of the recruitment or selection process.

### Recruitment

Organisations committed to equality of opportunity should ensure that the recruitment (and selection) process itself is not discriminatory. It is unlawful to discriminate, outside of there being a *genuine occupational qualification (GOQ)* by mentioning or indicating the race of the preferred applicant in advertising; offering less favourable terms of employment; refusing the employment on grounds of race; affording less favourable terms in respect of promotion, training opportunities, facilities, benefits or services.

Assuming that there are no GOQs, employers should review **job descriptions** to ensure that they are based on current requirements and then draft a **person specification** containing objective criteria based on the actual qualifications, skills, experience and aptitude required from any person to be considered to fill the post, thereby ensuring that all candidates are compared against objective criteria rather than with one another. It is important to ensure that **job advertisements** are designed in such a way that they do not discriminate against specific groups. Specifically, employers:

- should not confine advertisements unjustifiably to those areas or publications which would exclude or disproportionately reduce the number of applicants of a particular ethnic group or groups;
- should review current employment advertising in order to attract applicants from the ethnic minority communities more effectively;
- should avoid recruiting by 'word of mouth', through existing employees where the workforce is predominantly white or black and the labour market is multi-racial;
- should avoid arrangements where applicants are mainly or wholly supplied through trade unions where this means that only members of a particular racial or ethnic group, or a disproportionately high number of them, come forward;
- should avoid prescribing requirements such as length of residence or experience in the UK, and where a particular qualification is required it should be made clear that

a fully comparable qualification obtained overseas is acceptable as a UK qualification; and

- should demonstrate their commitment to equality of opportunity by including a statement that they are equal opportunity employers in literature sent to applicants.

In cases where a particular race or ethnic group has been under-represented in the previous 12 months, the company should have a **positive action** programme whereby the advertisement can explicitly encourage applications from the ethnic minority population. If employment agencies are used, they should be told that such applicants are particularly welcome (provided that no applicant is excluded, denied information or the opportunity to apply). The employment agency itself should be fully aware of equal opportunities policies and ensure that it does not discriminate unlawfully in its recruitment process.

### Selection

Selection criteria should be specifically related to the requirements of the job to be performed, and this should be made clear to the candidate. In addition, employers should not disqualify applicants because they are unable to complete an application form unassisted, unless personal completion of the form is a valid test of the standard of English required for the safe and effective performance of the job. Employers should ensure that adequate records, including reasons for selection and rejection, are kept for each stage of the selection process, as this will be relevant if any unsuccessful applicant does bring a discrimination claim. Other selection methods such as tests should be carefully chosen in order that they do not discriminate unfairly. Concern has been expressed by both the EOC and CRE over the potential race and sex bias in certain forms of psychometric testing; for example it is claimed that in some tests questions are asked that lean towards knowledge and experience that would be more readily available to a white male. During the interview questions which could be interpreted as discriminatory should be avoided. If it is necessary to ask about qualifications or experience gained overseas 'this should not be done in a way that may make it appear that the qualifications or experience are being undervalued' (Clarke, 1995, p. 100). Finally, those responsible for selection should be made aware of the possible misunderstandings that can occur in interviews between persons of different cultural backgrounds.

### Promotion, transfer, training and appraisal

It is unlawful to discriminate on racial grounds in affording access to promotion, transfer or training. Age limits for promotion, transfer or training should be questioned as they could lead to indirect discrimination. Many of the issues considered within the areas of selection and recruitment are also relevant here. Clarke (1995) refers to the following example:

> In 1990, the CRE carried out an investigation into promotion procedures at London Underground and found that they operated in a way which discriminated against ethnic minority staff. None of the 63 senior managers recently appointed had been from an ethnic minority; vacancies were not advertised internally or externally; and candidates for promotion were selected on the recommendation of their superiors. The employer could have used the provisions of section 38 of the RRA to actively encourage employees to apply for promotion. (p. 103)

With regard to **promotion**, employees should be made aware of promotion arrangements, job requirements and method of application; promotion systems should be closely examined to ensure that the criteria employed do not adversely affect employees on the grounds of race. Employers can usefully adopt monitoring arrangements analysing the results of promotion and appraisal systems. These arrangements should include analysis of the promotion success rates and length of time taken for people of differing ethnic groups to progress within the organisation. It is likely that most organisations will have concentrations of jobs in which employees of one racial group are concentrated and from which **transfers** are traditionally restricted. Efforts should be made to open up opportunities for more flexible career routes as, for example, with transfer skills training and work shadowing. **Training** records of employees should be kept to facilitate monitoring of the numbers of different racial groups who undergo training, day release and personal development; and where an imbalance is identified the causes should be analysed to ensure they are not discriminatory. Care should be taken to ensure that, as far as is practical, all eligible employees have the opportunity to attend training and development courses and it is important to ensure that the facilities available at the venue are suitable for people from differing ethnic backgrounds.

### Terms of employment

It is unlawful to offer employment on discriminatory terms by, for example, offering ethnic minorities employment on lower pay than whites or only to offer jobs on the night shift to ethnic minorities. The CRE Code of Practice recommends that 'where employees have particular religious and cultural needs which conflict with existing work requirements, it is recommended that employers should consider whether it is reasonably practicable to vary or adapt these requirements to enable such needs to be met'. For example, orthodox Jewish employees are unable to work on Friday evenings and Saturdays and Sikhs as part of their religious culture are required to adopt certain dress codes.

### Racial harassment

Racial harassment can take the form of violence or ostracism and will amount to direct discrimination which is unlawful. Many of the measures that employers could take to prevent sexual harassment as previously discussed apply to instances of racial harassment. However, the important issue of whether an employer can be held liable for the harassment of its employees by third parties who are not in its employment was raised in the case of *Burton v. De Vere Hotels* (1996) as described below:

Miss Burton and Miss Rhule, who were of Afro-Caribbean origin, were employed by De Vere Hotels as casual waitresses. On the night in question they were waiting on 400 guests, all men, and the guest speaker was Bernard Manning. While clearing the tables the women heard Mr Manning make sexually explicit and racially abusive jokes and comments, some aimed directly at them. After Mr Manning's act was over, the guests started to make sexually and racially offensive remarks to both women. The next day the hotel manager apologised to the women for what had happened. The women alleged that their employer had discriminated against them on racial grounds by subjecting them to the detriment of racial abuse and harassment contrary to the RRA. Initially the industrial tribunal found that there was racial harassment but it was Mr Manning and the guests, not the employer who had subjected the women to this and therefore their claims were dismissed. However, the EAT considered that the employer can be viewed as subjecting an employee to harassment if he/she causes or permits the harassment to occur in circumstances in which he/she can control whether it happens or not. The key question was whether the event was something which was sufficiently under the control of the employer that he/she could, by the application of good employment practice, have prevented the harassment or reduced the extent of it. If he/she could, then the employer had subjected the employee to harassment. Applying this to Miss Burton's case, it was held that the employer could have prevented or reduced the extent of the harassment but had failed to do so. (*Adapted from Painter and Puttick (1998) p. 128*)

### Discipline, dismissal and redundancy

*It is unlawful to discriminate in the operation of grievance, disputes and disciplinary procedures, for example by victimising an individual through disciplinary measures because he or she has complained about racial discrimination or given evidence about such a complaint.* (CRE Code)

The employer must ensure that appropriate consideration concerning racial abuse or other racial provocation, communication and comprehension difficulties and differences in cultural background or behaviour be given in the operation of disciplinary procedures. Therefore discriminatory offences should be regarded as a disciplinary matter and extreme forms of discrimination (such as severe harassment and racially motivated attacks) can often be regarded as gross misconduct carrying the penalty of summary dismissal.

It is also unlawful to discriminate on racial grounds in dismissal, and should there be any redundancies, selection criteria for redundancies (See Chapter 12) should not be indirectly discriminatory.

**SE 11.14** *This SE has no commentary*

Described below is a case which requires urgent action to be taken to rectify the situation. Indicate what action should be taken by reference to both sections 11.6.6 and 11.6.7

You are a newly appointed HR manager in a company employing 850 people on one site, and have a special interest in the development of equal opportunities policies, which is one reason why you were appointed. The company, in its various policy statements says it is committed to equal opportunities, but as far as you can ascertain, very little, if anything has been put into practice. The company is located on the fringes of an inner city area which is ethnically diverse; in fact over 70 per cent of the inner city population is non-white. As one of your first tasks, you have decided to undertake an audit of the workforce, concentrating in the first instance on its ethnic composition. The initial results of the audit give you great cause for concern as they reveal, amongst other findings, that only 1.5 per cent of the entire workforce is non-white, and is almost wholly concentrated on the manual worker's night shift. There are no non-white employees on the manual day shift or amongst the non-manual or managerial staff.

After you report your initial findings to the managing director together with suggestions for remedial action, you have been told to 'get on with it'. Outline the action you would now take.

---

#### Racism at Ford's Dagenham plant

During September and October 1999, a number of race and race-related incidents occurred at Ford's Dagenham plant. A dispute concerning shift work and rostering concerning Asian employees led to rioting, vandalism of vehicles and a walk-out of night-shift workers. This incident was followed two days later by another walkout involving 800 workers after a complaint by an Asian shop steward that he was pushed by a white foreman. These incidents occurred only weeks after another Asian worker who claimed he was a victim of bullying, won a case he brought to an employment tribunal. As a result of short-time working and demands for increased productivity, workers on the assembly line were feeling particularly pressurised by supervisors, the situation being compounded by the fact that ▶

whereas more than 40 per cent of assembly line workers are from ethnic minorities, only 10 per cent of their supervisors are. The Asian shop steward allegedly pushed by a white foreman was discussing racial harassment with a colleague when the incident took place. The situation at the Dagenham plant could be regarded as a failure of management to take its equal opportunities policies sufficiently seriously (see below). The alleged culture of institutional racism at the Dagenham plant has been reinforced in recent years by a number of revelations in the media detailing Ford's insensitivity towards its ethnic minority workforce. The main revelations are detailed below.

**February 1996:** Ford pays £1500 to four black workers after digitally altering a picture to give them white faces for an advertisement to be used in Poland. The company's claim that it was advised by its advertising agency to do this evoked little sympathy.

**June 1996:** £70 000 is paid to seven black and Asian workers after a 'kith and kin' policy is found to have existed. The men were proved to have been unfairly denied jobs on the company's truck fleet.

**March 1998:** A TV advertisement spoofing *The Full Monty* is withdrawn by Ford following a complaint that, unlike in the film, no black actor is present in line-up.

**September 1999:** An Asian assembly-line worker tells a tribunal how he has been banished to a 'punishment cell', being refused protective clothing and found the word 'Paki' written on his payslip.

**September 1999:** Workers stage a mass walkout after an Asian shop steward was pushed by a white foreman.

## Equal opportunities and managing diversity

As we have seen, legislation is extremely important as a means for combating discrimination and enforcing appropriate behaviour through the 'stick' of legal sanctions. The various commissions set up by the discrimination Acts, such as the CRE and EOC play a significant 'overseeing' role in seeking to ensure that employers and others adhere to the legislation. Against the background of the discrimination legislation, the voluntary Codes of Practice developed by these commissions and by the European Union which concern equal pay, harassment and the development of equal opportunities policies, provide further encouragement for employers to adopt 'good practice'.

**SE 11.15**                                    *The response is provide at the end of the chapter*

Apart from the legal and quasi-legal reasons referred to above can you think of any other reasons as to why organisations should develop equal opportunities policies?

### Managing diversity

The 'managing diversity' approach to managing discrimination claims that the traditional focus of equal opportunities policies is misplaced, and that rather than concentrating upon *groups* of employees who fall within particular categories (based on gender, ethnicity, and disability, for example), the focus of employers should be upon *all the individuals* within the organisation. Clarke (1995) argues that:

> *The advantage of this approach is that it includes everybody within its scope and concentrates on the **diversity** of all individuals within the organisation, rather than just looking at a woman worker as a woman. Family-friendly policies, for example, should examine men's problems in reconciling work and family life, as well as women's. This approach*

*can feed into a good equal opportunities policy by concentrating on the advantages to everyone rather than by simply avoiding disadvantages to particular groups.* (p. 136)

Although we argue that managing diversity (MD) should be incorporated within an effective equal opportunities (EO) policy, there are important differences between the two approaches which we shall now briefly consider:

- Equal opportunities approaches have sought to adopt a **legislative solution** to prevent discriminatory practices, while MD approaches emphasise the benefits of such approaches to the **business and economic well being** of the organisation.
- Equal opportunities approaches emphasise **moral, social and ethical** issues concerning individuals within society generally, while MD approaches argue that **employers benefit economically** 'if they invest in ensuring that everyone in the organisation is valued and given the opportunity to develop their potential and make a maximum contribution'. (Torrington and Hall, 1998, p. 351)
- Equal opportunities approaches aim to ensure an adequate and fair representation of disadvantaged groups in the workplace in order to reflect the distribution of those groups within the community and wider society through, for example **positive action** campaigns. MD approaches do not use positive action but focus upon improvement of opportunities of **all** employees, involving and benefiting everyone.
- Equal opportunities policies are mainly the responsibility of personnel and HRM departments which are expected to put these policies into practice, while implementation of MD approaches is deemed to be the responsibility of every department and all managers.
- Equal opportunities approaches are oriented towards equality of treatment of particular disadvantaged groups and ignore the needs of individuals, whereas MD approaches acknowledge that each and every individual is unique and should be treated accordingly.

While EO approaches have been criticised (Heilman, 1994) for the inadequacy of positive or 'affirmative' action policies in that they may alienate large sections of the 'non-disadvantaged' workforce who perceive no advantages of the policy to themselves, MD approaches have also been criticised for diverting attention from disadvantaged groups in the interests of business advantage and benefits for all. However, Ford (1996) suggests that the two approaches are not mutually exclusive and can co-exist within an **integrated policy** whose objective is the elimination of discrimination. The example of Marks & Spencer's *Equal Opportunities Statement* reflects this integrated approach:

---

### M & S Equal Opportunities Statement

Marks & Spencer is committed to an active Equal Opportunities Policy from recruitment and selection, through training and development, appraisal and promotion to retirement.

It is our policy to promote an environment free from discrimination, harassment and victimisation where everyone will receive equal treatment regardless of age, colour, disability, ethnic or national origin, gender, marital status, religion or sexual orientation. All decisions relating to employment practices will be objective, free from bias and based solely upon work criteria and individual merit.

The company is responsive to the needs of its employees, customers and the community at large and we are an organisation which uses everyone's talents and abilities **where diversity is valued.**

---

**The Management of Human Resources**

### Elements of a good equal opportunities policy

Although organisations have different requirements depending upon the nature of the workforce, the product market, the size and complexity of structures and operations, there are, as Clarke (1995) points out, a number of key points applicable to all organisations.

As a **first step** in devising an EO policy, it is important to secure the commitment of all organisational participants to the aims of the policy, and not just the personnel or HRM department. 'Drafting an equal opportunities policy should not be left to the personnel or human resource division alone. Here the approach of focusing on managing diversity, rather than simple non-discrimination, can be important, as is awareness of the possible business advantages to the whole organisation' (Clarke, p. 137).

**Secondly,** Clarke suggests that the organisation should undertake an equal opportunities audit 'in order to see where any problems lie' and will include a consideration of all aspects of the employment relationship such as recruitment, training, promotion, dismissal, redundancy, staff turnover and pay structures.

**Thirdly,** on completion of the audit (which should then be undertaken regularly on an annual basis), potential problems may be revealed which should then be addressed:

> *In addition to developing an overall strategy, specific solutions should be sought for specific problems. For example, the company may have a very poor record of women returning to work after maternity leave. Why? What can be done to improve the position? Is turnover higher amongst women or ethnic minorities? In either case, is this because of a lack of opportunity for career development? Does the selection process produce fewer non-white applicants than would statistically be predicted for the locality? If so, is it because the company relies on word-of-mouth recruitment, or advertises in ways that do not reach ethnic minorities, or has a poor reputation for employing non-whites? . . . There may be many other issues revealed by an equal opportunities audit. It is important to realise, furthermore, that monitoring should be continuous: the problems, and the solutions required, will change over time. (ibid., p. 137)*

**Fourthly,** to be effective there should be a clear structure of responsibility for equal opportunities which should involve everyone, particularly those in managerial positions, in equal opportunities training.

**Fifthly,** the equal opportunities policy, having been introduced, should be continually reviewed and monitored in order to ensure that new problems are effectively dealt with. The policy itself should be modified where appropriate according to changes in legislation and in the internal labour market.

### From policy to practice: rhetoric or reality?

#### Equal opportunities at Ford Dagenham

The incidents concerning ethnic minorities at Ford's Dagenham plant in recent years have aroused suspicions concerning the operation of equal opportunities policies within Ford UK. A senior TGWU official stated that 'In Britain, "people problems" – racism, bullying and grievance problems are not being treated as seriously as commercial and productivity problems' (Lamb, 1999). Although there is much talk of 'diversity in the workplace' at the top of the organisation, the policies do not appear to have filtered down to the shopfloor. The workforce claim that management pays only lip service to equal opportunities; bullying is one result and limited opportunity for promotion is another. The gap between policies as written and as implemented could be the result of poor promotion of these policies or the refusal of managers to embrace them, which in turn perpetuates and reinforces the workplace culture.

In October 1999, Ford's global president Jac Nasser took personal control of the growing crisis over racism at Dagenham after flying in from Detroit to sign a comprehensive agreement with the unions to stamp out discrimination and harassment. The agreement, hailed by Bill Morris, leader of the TGWU as the 'fresh start that Dagenham needs', will set up joint equal opportunities committees at every Ford plant in Britain, backed by anti-racist policies for recruitment, promotion and corporate image-making. The new structure will be overseen by a new diversity manager, already dubbed Ford's 'anti-racism tsar'.

The evidence suggests that while many organisations purport to have equal opportunities policies (Torrington and Hall (1998) cite research which they conducted in 1994 and found that 89 per cent of their sample organisations had equal opportunities policies), a much smaller proportion put these policies into effect. The CRE (1995) found that while around 90 per cent of the large companies it surveyed had EO policies which specifically incorporated provisions for racial equality, only 45 per cent of them had taken any measures to implement the policy. Liff (1995) argues that there are three important factors which make implementation problematic: 'the relationship between line managers and personnel; the conflicts between EO and other priorities facing managers; and resistance from employees' (p. 480). We now look briefly at each of these factors:

1. *Line managers and personnel*: As we noted earlier, traditional EO approaches assume that the main responsibility for implementing EO policies rests with the personnel department, while the responsibility for MD lies with management in general. Liff cites a study by Collinson *et al.* (1990) which attempts to demonstrate that personnel managers' influence in implementing equality measures particularly with regard to recruitment and selection matters is limited owing to lack of intervention in decisions involving line managers; undue deference shown to line management under the assumption that line managers had a better understanding of the situation; and reluctance to take responsibility for making 'wrong' decisions. The general problems besetting personnel management discussed in Chapter 2 may well contribute to personnel's relative ineffectiveness in implementing EO policies.

2. *EO and other priorities*: Managers may regard the formal approaches recommended for adoption in the various Codes of Practice concerning recruitment and selection, for example, as unnecessarily time-consuming and costly, particularly when faced with production and staff shortage problems. It may therefore be tempting for managers to resort to informal methods of recruitment (which may include 'word of mouth') which are cheaper and quicker than formal methods, but also potentially discriminatory. Action based on economic expediency does not necessarily indicate that managers are opposed to EO practices; managers may, as Liff suggests, 'not be simply for or against equal opportunities. In some situations they may find it acceptable or may even be favourably disposed towards it. In other cases they may find it objectionable' (p. 481).

3. *Employee resistance*: Liff points out that 'groups who currently have a dominant position within the workforce are likely to feel threatened by EO initiatives' (p. 481). These groups normally comprise white male employees who may resent EO policies which favour minority groups who may be perceived to have been given 'special treatment' with regard to promotion and other opportunities for advancement.

**The Management of Human Resources**

A recent comprehensive survey of NHS hospital trusts (Hurstfield 1999) reveals that there is a considerable gap between formal policies and their implementation. Summary details of the survey are given below:

### NHS Trusts: a suitable case for treatment?

The survey was carried out by Industrial Relations Services Research (IRSR) in order to provide data on the extent to which NHS trusts have adopted EO policies and practices. During 1998, 420 or 99 per cent of all trusts in England were surveyed and case studies of 25 trusts were undertaken to examine issues in greater depth.

**The findings**

- Almost every trust has a general policy statement on EO, but there were wide variations in the extent to which trusts have introduced policies on specific subjects (see table below).
- Where subjects are covered, trusts prefer separate policies for different subjects rather than incorporating them in different policies (see table). For example, paternity leave is covered by a separate policy in 83 per cent of the trusts compared with 4 per cent that incorporate it in their general EO statement. The only exception to this is childcare.
- The majority of trusts collect monitoring data on their workforce by gender, ethnic origin, disability and full or part-time working, and nearly two-thirds also produce a report on the monitoring data for the trust board.
- Only a minority of trusts use their monitoring data to help produce forecasts or goals for the representation of women, ethnic minorities or disabled people in their workforces, with the highest proportion – one in three -setting targets for women, while 25 per cent had set targets for employing ethnic minorities and even fewer (13 per cent) for disabled people.
- The main initiatives the trusts identified for the previous two years were in the areas of disability (16 per cent of trusts), gender (14 per cent of trusts), while only 10 per cent of trusts cited initiatives aimed at assisting ethnic minorities by increasing the proportion of ethnic groups in their workforces and senior management posts and strengthening links with local ethnic minority communities.
- While a high proportion of trusts operate EO policies, the case studies reveal the extent of the gap between the espousal of formal policies and their effective implementation, with poor communication and dissemination of policy details to staff, and inconsistent implementation of policies by line managers.

The survey indicates that there is considerable room for improvement when it comes to implementing EO policies in most hospital trusts.

**Coverage and content of EO policies in NHS trusts**

| | Included in general EO policy | Covered by separate policy |
| --- | --- | --- |
| Maternity pay/leave | 5% | 96% |
| Recruitment/selection | 32% | 85% |
| Adoption leave | 3% | 84% |
| Paternity leave | 4% | 83% |
| Carer leave | 4% | 83% |
| Harassment by staff | 23% | 81% |
| Jobsharing | 9% | 73% |
| Harassment by patients | 12% | 59% |
| Other special leave | 3% | 55% |
| Retainer schemes | 3% | 38% |
| Childcare | 38% | 5% |

*Source:* IRS Employment Trends 671 (1999)

## Summary points concerning the management of equality

- The European Union, through Treaty Articles and Directives has become increasingly influential in encouraging member states to introduce discrimination and equal pay legislation. Much of European law in this area is concerned with sex discrimination and equal rights for men and women.

- With regard to sex and race discrimination, employers should follow the procedural approaches suggested by the EOC and CRE Codes of Practice. The EOC Code deals with the importance of developing good employment practices in order to eliminate sex discrimination and promote equal opportunities.

- Pay inequality is an important ongoing issue as there is still a considerable pay gap between women and men which, at the current rate of progress will not be eliminated until 2040.

- The EOC Code of Practice concerning equal pay aims to provide concrete advice for employers and collective bargaining partners to ensure that the principle of equality between men and women performing work of equal value is applied to all aspects of pay and to eliminate sexual discrimination whenever pay structures are based on job classification and evaluation systems.

- Sexual harassment is common and widespread, but under-reported. Sexual harassment is unlawful under the SDA and under EU law. The EU Code of Practice concerning sexual harassment identifies measures which employers should take to deal with the problem.

- There are no statutory provisions expressly prohibiting discrimination on grounds of sexual orientation.

- The CRE has produced a Code of Practice which aims to encourage effective management practices in order to rectify and prevent race discrimination. Areas covered include ethnic monitoring, recruitment, selection, promotion, transfer and appraisal, terms of employment, racial harassment, discipline, dismissal and redundancy.

- While we may distinguish between 'equal opportunities' and 'managing diversity', the two should be seen as complementary and as part of an overall approach which organisations should adopt to encourage and promote equality amongst employees.

## REFERENCES

Adorno, T.W. *et al.* (1950): *The Authoritarian Personality*. New York, Harper and Row

Beechey, V. (1983): 'The sexual division of labour and the labour process: a critical assessment of Braverman' in Wood, S. (ed.): *The Degradation of Work; Skill, Deskilling and the Labour Process*. London, Hutchinson

Clarke, L. (1995): *Discrimination*. London, IPD

Cockburn, C. (1991): *In the Way of Women*. London, Macmillan

Collinson, D.L. *et al.* (1990): *Managing to Discriminate*. London, Routledge

CRE (1981): *BL Cars Ltd . . . Report of a Formal Investigation*. London, CRE

CRE (1987): *Chartered Accountancy Training Contracts*. London, CRE

CRE (1984): *Code of Practice for the Elimination of Racial Discrimination and the Promotion of Equality of Opportunity in Employment*. London, CRE

CRE (1996): *Positive Action and Equal Opportunity in Employment*. London, CRE

CRE (1999): *Annual Report 1998*. London, CRE

Crompton, R. and Sanderson, K. (1990): *Gendered Jobs and Social Change*. London, Unwin-Hyman

Dale, A. (1995): 'Occupational inequality, gender and life-cycle'. *Work, Employment and Society*, vol. 9, no. 3 pp. 326–51

Department for Education and Employment (1998): *Action on Age: Report of the Consultation on Age Discrimination in Employment*. DfEE Publications

Doeringer, P. and Piore, M. (1971): *Internal Labour Markets and Manpower Analysis*. Lexington, Mass. D.C. Heath

EOC (1985): *A Code of Practice for the Elimination of Discrimination on Grounds of Sex and Marital Status in Employment*. Manchester, EOC

EOC (1997): 'Consider the cost: sexual harassment at work'. Manchester, EOC

EOC (1997): *Briefings on Women and Men in Britain*. Manchester, EOC

EOC (1999): *Annual Report 1998*. Manchester, EOC

European Commission (1996): *A Code of Practice on the Implementation of Equal Pay for Work of Equal Value for Men and Women*. ECSE-EC-EAEC, Brussels

Ford, V. (1996): 'Partnership is the secret of progress'. *People Management*, February

Gardiner, C. (1992): *Gender and Substitution Theory*. Cambridge, Polity Press

Giddens, A. (1998): *Sociology*. Cambridge, Polity Press

Grint, K. (1993): *The Sociology of Work*. Cambridge, Polity Press

Hawkins, K. (1994): 'Taking action on harassment'. *Personnel Management*, March

Heilman, M.E. (1994): 'Affirmative action: some unintended consequences for working women'. *Research in Organisational Behaviour*, vol. 16

Homans, H. (1987): 'Man-made myth: the reality of being a woman scientist in the NHS' in Spencer, A. and Podmore, D. (eds), *In a Man's World: Essays on Women in Male-Dominated Professions*. London, Tavistock

Howe, S. (1999): 'Discrimination' in Hollinshead G. *et al.* (eds.) *Employee Relations*. London, Financial Times, Pitman Publishing

Hurstfield, J. (1999): 'Equal opportunities and monitoring in NHS trusts', *IRS Research*, Department of Health

IRS (1998): 'Tackling age bias: code or law?' *Equal Opportunities Review*, no. 80

IRS Employment Trends (1996): 'Sexual harassment at work' *IRS*, no. 615

IRS Employment Trends (1998): 'Government sets out its stall on tackling age discrimination'. *IRS*, no. 666

Jenkins, R. (1988): 'Discrimination and equal opportunity in employment: ethnicity and "race" in the United Kingdom' in Gaillie, D. (ed.): *Employment in Britain*. Oxford, Blackwell

Jones, T. (1993): *Britain's Ethnic Minorities*. London, Policy Studies Institute

Labour Research, (1999): *Pay Inequalities*. London, LRD

Lamb, J. (1999): 'Race for a solution at Dagenham': *People Management*, October, pp. 20–1

Lee, G. (1987): 'Black members and their unions' in Lee, G. and Loveridge, R. (eds.) *The Manufacture of Disadvantage*: *Stigma and Social Closure*. Milton Keynes, Open University Press

Liff, S. (1995): 'Equal opportunities: continuing discrimination in a context of formal equality' in Edwards, P.K. (ed.), *Industrial Relations Theory and Practice in Britain*. Oxford, Blackwell

McDowell, L. (1992): 'Gender divisions in a post-Fordist era: new contradictions or the same old story?' in McDowell, M. and Pringle, R. (eds). *Defining Women: Social Institutions and Gender Divisions*. Cambridge, Polity Press

Modood, T. and Berthoud, R. (1997): *Ethnic Minorities in Britain*. London, Policy Studies Institute

Oakley, A. (1981): *Subject Women*. Oxford, Martin Robertson

Painter, R.W. and Puttick, K. (1998): Employment Rights. London, Pluto Press

Policy Studies Institute (1986): *Black and White Britain*. London, Macmillan

Rees, T. (1992): *Women and the Labour Market*. London, Routledge, *Resource Manual*. London, IRS Eclipse Group Ltd

Rubenstein, M. (1996): *Preventing and Remedying Sexual Harassment at Work: A Sex or Marital Status in Employment*. EOC, Manchester

Sly, F., Thair, T. and Risdon, A. (1998): 'Labour market participation of ethnic groups', *Labour Market Trends*, December 1998, pp. 601–15

Stanford, J. and Gardiner, J. (1993): 'Sexual harassment: how it happens and how to beat it'. *The Industrial Society*. London

The *Guardian*: February 8, 1999

Torrington, D. and Hall, L. (1998): *Human Resource Management*. Hemel Hempstead, Prentice Hall Europe

Walby, S. (1986): *Patriarchy at Work*. Cambridge, Polity Press

Walby, S. (1990): *Theorising Patriarchy*. Oxford, Blackwell

Witz, A. (1993): 'Women at work' in Richardson, D. and Robinson, V. (eds). *Introducing Women's Studies*. London, Macmillan

## RESPONSES TO SELF EVALUATIONS

### SE 11.1
With regard to **sex discrimination**, the following examples are relevant:

#### *Promotion*
If promotion vacancies are filled solely on the basis of informal selection using a subjective procedure which excludes women from senior jobs. In one case, a clothing manufacturer employed two trainee supervisors, one male and one female. The male trainee was offered the post of assistant manager, with the intention that he takes over the manager's job at a later date. The post was never advertised and the female trainee was not informed of the vacancy (*Schofield v. Double Two: 1992*).

#### *Sexual harassment*
Harassment can take many forms and is a very difficult issue for women to cope with. In the case *Van Den Burghen v. Nabarro Nathanson: 1992*, Miss Van Den Burghen, a trainee solicitor had her breasts squeezed by a male trainee solicitor at a Christmas lunch during which their secretaries presented solicitors with chocolate penises. She complained to a senior partner, who later told her that following investigation he considered the matter closed due to lack of witnesses. Miss Van Den Burghen was then 'sent to Coventry' by her colleagues and three months later was made redundant.

There are many examples of **race discrimination** at work of which two will suffice:

#### *Terms of employment*
There are many instances where employers discriminate in the terms of employment they provide. In 1993, John Haggas plc, a mill in West Yorkshire, was found to have discriminated against Asian night shift workers. The night shift was all-Asian and had been threatened with dismissal if they refused to take on extra duties, whereas this had not happened to the all-white day shift. The Asian workers were not paid overtime, received four days' less holiday a year than white workers, and had no chance of promotion.

#### *Racial harassment*
Again, there are many examples, although racial harassment has received less attention than sexual harassment. Use of terms such as 'black bastards', uttered in the presence of employees constitutes unlawful harassment. In one case (*Mann v. Moody: 1993*) a Department of Social Security line manager made a reference to 'Paki shops' in the presence of an Asian employee and was held to constitute racial discrimination. In another case, an employee was subjected to serious racial abuse by his fellow employees and was called names, had metal bolts thrown at his head, and was branded with a hot screwdriver.

### SE 11.2
2 and 3. Walby (1986) identifies the following areas as still being 'male dominated':

#### *Paid employment*
This remains a key structure in creating disadvantages for women. Nineteenth century regulations excluded women from whole areas of work altogether, while at the same time permitting women to work in mines and factories. Male dominated trade unions and the state ensured that opportunities were severely restricted. In the 20th century, women, and particularly married women were able to take employment, but not on equal terms with men, and in recent years the degree of inequality between men and women, and access to well-rewarded occupations has declined only very slightly. The gender pay gap has declined somewhat, but women continue to be over represented in low-paid and part-time employment. In theory, governments since 1946 have supported greater equality in the labour market, but in practice such policies are not pursued as vigorously as they should be.

### Household production

According to Walby (1990), patriarchal dominance was common in the household; men would exploit women by benefiting from women's unpaid labour. This was most marked during the 19th century when most women were excluded from the labour market. In the 21st century, however, exploitation of this nature has declined as women spend more time in paid work, although it has not disappeared. Women who are housewives spend as much time on domestic labour as they did decades ago, and women with children who leave their husbands are disadvantaged in a patriarchally structured labour market and are unlikely to find a job with reasonable pay so that 'liberation from marriage is then usually a movement into poverty' (Walby, 1990, p. 56). It is likely that this situation will persist well into this century.

### Culture

The culture of Western society has consistently distinguished between men and women and has expected different types of behaviour from them. During the 19th century, womens' confinement to domesticity was thought to refine their femininity and increase their sexual attractiveness to men. The escape from the confines of domesticity for some women at least during the 20th and 21st centuries has replaced one form of cultural patriarchy by another. For example, the spread of pornography, Walby argues, increases the freedom of men while reducing that of women by encouraging the degradation of women by men and promoting harassment and sexual violence.

### The state

State policies relating to gender have changed considerably since the 19th century. There has, according to Walby (1990), been:

> the cessation of legal backing to exclusionary (discriminatory) practices in employment; the increased ease of divorce and financial provision for non-wage earners; the ending of state backing to exclusionary practices in education and the removal of most forms of censorship of pornography; the decriminalisation of contraception and abortion under most circumstances; and minor changes in the law making it marginally easier for a woman to leave a violent man.
> (p. 87)

State policies are no longer directed at confining women to the private sphere of the home, but there has been little progress made in improving women's position in the public sphere. Womens' pay is still lower than men's over a whole range of occupations and equal opportunities legislation is not often enforced. Women in one-parent families get little state benefit and women have been harmed by the greater availability of pornography. While the state is not so manifestly patriarchal as it used to be, it still, according to Walby, does little to protect women from patriarchal power in society.

### SE 11.3

Witz (1993), in criticising human capital approaches, argues that even when women do work continuously without taking career breaks, they still tend to end up in lower-paid and lower-status jobs. Rees (1992), who reviewed research within the American context discovered that about half the pay differentials between men and women could be explained in terms of human capital theory, and also ignores the causes of inequality between male and female employees located within the structure of the labour market.

### SE 11.4

The changes relevant to McDowell's argument include:

- the move away from mass production towards flexible production of small batches of specialised products;
- the subsequent employment of a highly skilled 'core' group of workers within an organisation who are capable of using their skills to produce a wide variety of products; and

● the use of part-time, short-term contract and/or contracted-out labour to perform relatively unskilled work.

McDowell argues that these changes are reflected in the increased use of part-time female labour and the reduction in the employment of males in full-time permanent jobs. Certainly during the past twenty-five years or so, the decline in male employment has been more than matched by the increase in female employment – a process described as the 'feminisation' of the labour market. As we have explained above, women have been employed in increasing numbers within secondary labour markets, and particularly within the service sector of the economy as women are traditionally cheaper to employers and more easily dispensable than male employees. Owing to the 'need' for employers to cut costs and to have a more flexible labour force in order to cope with repeated recessions and increased competition, McDowell suggests that part-time flexible work has not been created in response to 'demand' on the part of employees, whether men or women. Rather, many have had part-time or temporary jobs imposed on them or have taken them for want of alternatives while continuing to seek full-time and stable work.

## SE 11.6

The Metropolitan Police Force, (and police forces generally) have been criticised for their reluctance to recruit from ethnic minorities. For example, the CRE (1999) expressed disappointment that the latest version of the initial police recruitment test 'had a statistically significant adverse impact on ethnic minority applicants' (p. 9). Within many police forces accusations have been made of 'institutional racism', both within the forces and in their treatment of members of ethnic minorities within the community. The Metropolitan Police is keen to dispel (however justified or unjustified) its image of racism. One method of doing this is to publicise 'positive action' initiatives in recruitment and elsewhere. In February 1999, the Metropolitan Police decided to make its most controversial attempt to recruit ethnic minorities into the service:

*A group of Brixton rappers are producing a sound track and video for the Met that both criticises the police and calls on black people to join it. The idea is that of music producer and filmmaker Charles Bailey. The soundtrack has already been made, and filming with a cast of around 100 extras will start shortly. Bailey says he is putting the package together because he does not believe that the black community will receive the policing they deserve until they are properly represented within the service . . . Currently there are around 900 ethnic minority officers, or 3 per cent of the service, when a representative figure would be six times that number.*

> *Rap attack*
> *Now if we the ethnic minorities*
> *Want security, safety and unity*
> *Let's get in . . .*
> *Let's get unified*
> *Uniformed*
> *Strictly dressed to address*
> *No contest*
> *'Cos we invest in justice*
> *No stress*
> *Dressed in blue to fill the gap*
> *Yes!*

(The *Guardian*, February 8, 1999)

## SE 11.7

● One of the most obvious and clear-cut instances is where a woman works alongside a man and performs exactly the same work as the man. For example, a woman operating a garment-making machine alongside a man operating the same type of machine; or a woman working on the assembly-line with men doing the same job of dealing with the same items; or in an office performing the same type of clerical tasks as a male office worker. In all these instances women, according to the Act, should receive the same amount of pay as their male counterparts.

- A less obvious circumstance is where a woman is performing tasks which are rated as equivalent to (but are different from) the tasks being undertaken by male colleagues. In this instance, the woman would have to demonstrate that she is performing tasks rated as equivalent to those performed by men. Equivalence-rating is facilitated if the company has a job evaluation scheme in operation and the woman's job is given the same rating as a different job done by a man.

### SE 11.8

(a) Dale (1995) provides the following case examples:

> 'Less favourable treatment' involves some detriment to the person concerned. In Peake v. Automotive Products Ltd (1978) women were allowed to leave the factory five minutes before male employees. The Court of Appeal refused to hold that this was sex discrimination, as the employer's motive was to prevent the women from being jostled, and it would be very wrong, according to Lord Denning, if the law was 'to do away with the chivalry and courtesy which we expect mankind to give to womankind'. Fortunately, subsequent cases took a more robust approach: in Ministry of Defence v. Jeremiah (1980) the Court of Appeal held that it was sex discrimination to stipulate that only men could work in the 'colour-bursting shell shop' because the women's hair would be messed up. This counted as less favourable treatment. In Gill and Coote v El Vinos Co. Ltd (1983) it was held to be less favourable treatment to refuse to serve women at a bar; and in R. v. Birmingham City Council ex parte EOC (1989) the loss of a chance of a grammar school place was held to be less favourable treatment.

(b) Treatment on the grounds of sex does not mean that the employer necessarily **intends** to discriminate as motive is irrelevant. Clarke cites the case of *James v. Eastleigh Borough Council (1990)* in which a swimming pool allowed women over the age of 60 free admission, whereas men had to pay until they reached 65 (based on the state pension age). The Lords held that this was unlawful sex discrimination, and the nature of the Council's motive was irrelevant: the test for sex discrimination was whether the men would have been treated differently but for their sex. In *Hurley v. Mustoe (1981)* a woman with three young children was refused a job because the employer believed that mothers were unreliable workers. This rule only applied to women with young children, and therefore constituted direct discrimination. Men with young children were not, in practice, excluded. In this case the employer acted on the basis of stereotyped assumptions, instead of looking at the particular individuals and their circumstances.

### SE 11.9

In *R v. Commission for Racial Equality ex parte Westminster City Council* (1985), the Council appointed a black refuse collector, but then withdrew his appointment because there was concern that the other (white) refuse collectors would take industrial action. This was racial discrimination, because the decision was taken on racial grounds, even though the motive was to avoid industrial action.

Discrimination on grounds of national origin is discrimination on racial grounds within s. 3(1) of the Act. In *Northern Joint Police Board v. Power* (1997), an Englishman claimed that he had not been short listed for the post of Chief Constable of the Northern Constabulary because he was English rather than Scots. The claim was upheld.

In the case of *Weatherfield Ltd t/a Van and Truck Rentals v. Sargent* (1998), Mrs Sargent, a white European, was instructed to inform 'coloureds and Asians' that no vehicles were available. She felt she had been put in an intolerable position and consequently resigned.

**SE 11.10**

As we have seen Britain, in common with other EU nations, has adopted the so-called 'legislative approach' which incorporates EU Articles and Directives. The legislative approach has certainly been effective in raising the profile of workplace sex (and race) discrimination and in encouraging organisations to adopt equal opportunities policies and practices. However, as Howe (1999) points out:

> In areas of both sex discrimination and race discrimination, criticisms have been voiced about the overall effectiveness of the legislative approach. The difficulties and costs involved in bringing cases to an industrial tribunal and the delays in hearing cases prevent many victims of discrimination from pursuing their struggles. Industrial tribunals, which were originally designed to be less formal and more accessible to individuals, have become increasingly burdened with bureaucracy and case law complications (and) the supremacy of EU law also makes the validity of industrial tribunal judgments open to question, further delaying the outcomes. Investigations needed to pursue an equal pay claim are costly and difficult to enact, despite some notable successes. (pp. 428–9)

The persistence of inequality and discrimination within the workplace where women continue to lag behind men is of concern to the EOC (1999) which believes that 'measures to tackle structural discrimination against women in the workplace are needed to achieve equality at work and help to create a competitive workforce'.

**SE 11.12**

The EC Code of Practice dealing with sexual harassment defines it as **'unwanted conduct of a sexual nature or other conduct based on sex affecting the dignity of women and men at work'** and includes unwelcome physical, verbal or non-verbal conduct which creates an intimidating, hostile or humiliating working environment. In its most recent survey of 65 employers, the IRS (1996) found that the following actions constituted sexual harassment:

- Demands for sexual favours in return for promotion, etc.
- Sexual assault.
- Unwanted physical contact such as unnecessary touching, patting or pinching of another employee's body.
- Unwelcome sexual advances or propositions.
- Offensive flirtations.
- Continued suggestions for social activity outside the workplace after it has been made clear that such suggestions are unwelcome.
- Derogatory remarks which are gender-related.
- Offensive comments about appearance and dress which are gender-related.
- Suggestive remarks, innuendoes or lewd comments.
- Leering/'eyeing-up' a person's body.
- Sexist or patronising behaviour.
- Display of sexually aggressive pin-ups or calendars.

Sexual harassment is a common and widespread phenomenon. The Industrial Society (1993) revealed that 54 per cent of working women experience sexual harassment in the workplace while the IRS (1996) survey found that harassment was equally widespread with 54 per cent of organisations reporting such cases during 1995. There is, however, good reason for arguing that harassment cases are under-reported to a very large extent, and therefore that the incidence of harassment is much more widespread than reported cases suggest. One reason for the reported increase in cases is the existence of sexual harassment policies; organisations without such policies may encourage a climate of intimidation which may make it difficult for victims to come forward (Rubenstein, 1996).

### SE 11.13

In the second part of their survey, IRS (1996) identified four main reasons for introducing policies. These were:

- the need to ensure equal opportunities at work (cited by 95 per cent of respondents);
- to avoid legal action and potential costs such as increased absenteeism, higher sickness levels and lower productivity (cited by 66 per cent of respondents);
- in response to developments within the European Union cited by 18 per cent of respondents; and
- to aid recruitment and retention, cited by 14 per cent of employers.

No employer mentioned trade union pressure as a reason for introducing harassment policies.

### SE 11.15

Perhaps the main reason for developing equal opportunities policies is that such policies make sound business sense. Discrimination in employment can be potentially costly to the employer, particularly as a result of the lifting of ceilings on compensation levels for sex and race discrimination. In addition, discriminatory recruitment policies could mean that the best person for the job is not being appointed. Training policies which are discriminatory means that abilities and potential of employees are being wasted.

# Chapter 2

# Selection and assessment as an interactive decision–action process

Sue Newell and Viv Shackleton

## Introduction: selection from a decision-making perspective

A given topic can always be viewed from a number of different perspectives. Traditionally, selection and assessment has been viewed from a psychometric perspective. It is treated as representing a measurement problem. There are clearly individual differences (both physical and psychological), which mean that certain people will be more suited to some jobs than others. From a psychometric perspective then, selection and assessment is concerned with finding methods to measure these individual differences more accurately so that individuals and jobs can be appropriately matched.

In this chapter, while not ignoring this psychometric tradition, we will adopt a rather different perspective, which can help us to explore some issues in selection and assessment that may be underemphasised by the traditional perspective. We will view selection and assessment from a decision-making perspective (Brunsson, 1982), where a decision is a conscious choice between at least two alternative actions. In this chapter we will consider decisions that are made in respect of both selection and development, both of which involve making decisions based on the assessment of individuals. Thus, in terms of selection, a representative (or group of representatives) of the recruiting organisation chooses between a number of candidates in order to select the individual who best fits the requirements of a particular job for which there is a vacancy. These decisions are made on the basis of some kind of assessment of the suitability of a group of potential individuals who might fill the vacancy.

While selection involves decisions about who will best fit a particular job vacancy, the same or similar processes of assessment are also increasingly used within organisations to make developmental decisions related to the promotion potential of internal employees. Thus, it is recognised that it is necessary to pre-pare current employees for taking on more senior roles within the organisation, so that leadership crises are averted. However, it is also recognised that not all exist-ing employees will be suitable for these more senior roles. Assessment methods are therefore used to identify the developmental potential of existing employees. The result is that choices are made about who will be groomed and developed and for which senior jobs.

The emphasis in the selection literature has typically been on the decision made by the recruiting organisation. However, it is also the case that candidates are making decisions – to apply (or not) for a particular job vacancy, to turn up (or not) to an interview, or to take (or decline) an offered job. In terms of assessment for developmental purposes there has always been more recognition that the can-didate is making decisions as well as the assessors. Indeed, with the increasing emphasis on self-direction, assessment exercises are used as much to provide the individual with evidence to make career path choices as they are for the organisa-tion to make promotion decisions. In this chapter we will consider the selection and assessment decision-making process from the perspective of both the organisa-tion and the candidates.

The decision-making perspective has been dominated by normative research, which prescribes how decisions should be made (Brunsson, 1982). This assumes that the desire is to make decisions as 'rational' as possible. The prescription for making decisions rational is to follow a sequence of specified steps: understand the situation and identify the problem(s); generate potential solutions to the problem(s); systematically evaluate each solution; select the best solution; monitor and evaluate the results; identify the problem(s) etc. This rational decision-making model has also implicitly underpinned selection and assessment research. Thus, in selection or development decisions, the objective has been to make this decision as objective and rational as possible in order to select the 'right' or 'best' person for the job. It is possible therefore to look at the steps prescribed in the rational deci-sion-making process and apply them to the literature on selection and assessment.

## Selection and assessment as a rational decision-making process?

Each of the steps in the rational decision-making model can be applied to the steps in selection and assessment:

### 1. Understand the situation and identify the problem(s): organisational review and job analysis

The first step typically identified in the selection process is to undertake a review of the situation to determine that a recruitment need actually exists. Even if an individual has left a job, this should not automatically mean that a job vacancy is presumed. It is necessary to establish that there are not alternative and more effective ways of filling the gap left by the departing employee. For example, it may provide the opportunity for reassigning these tasks to other employees. Alternatively, the tasks may be automated so that human resources are no longer required. Prior to developmental assessment, the rational model would see the need for succession planning to identify the predicted gaps at senior levels for which people need to be groomed.

Once the situation has been reviewed to ensure that a job vacancy or succession gap does actually exist, the next step is to conduct a thorough analysis of the particular job. Job analysis is used to gather information about a job in order to determine the key tasks and role requirements and so specify the kind of person most likely to be successful in that job. A problem with traditional job analysis is that it collects information about the job as it currently exists on the assumption that it will be similar in the future (Schneider and Konz, 1989). Unfortunately, given the dynamic environment in which organisations operate, this is increasingly an unwarranted assumption. As a result, there is a need to develop new methods of job analysis which can identify the key tasks and the associated knowledge, skills and abilities (KSAs) that are required for jobs that are changing (Landy *et al.*, 1995). In this light, Landis *et al.* (1998) describe the process of conducting a future-oriented job analysis. This begins with a traditional job analysis, collecting relevant information about the target jobs as they currently exist and then using panel discussion groups to develop a comprehensive list of tasks and KSAs. Then subject-matter expert groups are involved to identify how these tasks and KSAs are likely to change in the future.

The traditional person specification has given way to a focus on competencies (Boam and Sparrow, 1992). Competencies are behavioural indicators that have been identified as relevant to a particular context. There are a number of different approaches to identifying competencies, but they have a common focus on specifying 'outputs'. These are 'couched in terms of what an individual achieves and produces from a situation by managing it effectively' (Sparrow and Bognanno, 1993: 51). The advantage of using a competency framework is that the focus is on actual behaviour – what a person can do or needs to be able to do – and there is no need to make inferences about personal qualities that might underpin this. Theoretically, this should allow for the fact that different individuals can achieve the same output, but using a rather different approach because of different knowledge, skills and abilities. Unfortunately, while this is true in theory, in practice competency approaches are often used in ways which specify process criteria as well as output or task criteria. In other words, the person is assessed not simply in terms of whether they successfully completed the task but also in terms of dimensions that are 'normally' expected to underpin successful task completion. This means there is a presumption of 'the right way' to complete a task, and the individual will be assessed against this 'right way', as well as against the task output itself.

Nevertheless, whether a job analysis (traditional or future-oriented) or competency analysis is undertaken, the goal is to describe the particular job, identify the task requirements and specify the kind of person most likely to fulfill these requirements.

## 2. Gather information and materials to help solve the problem: identify appropriate assessment methods

Once the job analysis has been completed, the next step is to identify methods that will allow individuals to be assessed and compared on the various KSAs or competencies identified as crucial for job success. Much effort has been devoted to this step from the psychometric perspective. The reason for this is that traditional assessment methods – unstructured interviews and references – have, until recently, been shown to be very poor at measuring these important individual differences. The development of newer methods of assessment is considered in more detail below.

## 3. Generate potential solutions to the problem: recruitment

Once this initial phase has been completed and there is a clear idea about the kind of person wanted and the methods to be used to assess individuals, the next step is to attract a pool of applicants from which the 'right' person can be chosen. Where assessment is used for developmental purposes, recruitment will be internal and typically based on information gathered during appraisals as to which individuals are 'ready' and have the potential to be developed. Where an organisation is selecting for a particular job vacancy recruitment can be internal or external. External recruitment is expensive. In the UK, over £1 billion was spent in 1997 on recruitment advertising (Merrick, 1997). Matthews and Redman (1998) found that, despite such a large amount being spent on recruitment advertising, recruiters were not making the most effective use of it, because generally the ads were not well tailored to managerial requirements. In particular, they argue that recruitment advertisements need to be more specifically targeted to the group they are trying to attract. They advocate that this targeting should be done on the basis of market research to identify what the potential applicant is looking for in a recruitment advertisement. With regard to the content of advertisements they suggest that many do not contain enough information to attract the initial interest, especially of the casual job seeker. For example, they found that one in five advertisements gave no details of salary level and job location, which have been shown to be key to gaining attention. Once attracted, potential applicants then seek further information from the advertisement to decide whether to apply. However, 59 per cent of the advertisements gave no information on minimum qualifications, which is useful to help applicants self-screen. At the same time, 71 per cent did give information on personal attributes required, despite this being condemned by prescriptive models of 'good' adverts (Redmond, 1989).

Increasingly, companies have started to use information and communication technologies (ICTs) for recruitment purposes. For example, the internet is now a common medium for advertising job vacancy information, having the advantage of reaching a global audience, at least of potential recruits with access to this technology. Similarly, applicants are using the internet to submit their CVs, thus potentially speeding up the process of applying. A key advantage of such electronic applications is that CVs can be coded (e.g. in terms of the applicants' competencies) and stored electronically so that they can be easily searched, both for current job vacancies and for jobs in the future. This search can be done on a global basis provided that a company has a shared electronic database for storing and retrieving applicant information. The use of ICTs for both advertising and applying is likely to increase as accessibility and familiarity with this medium grow (Batram, 2000).

### 4. Systematically evaluate each solution: assessment methods applied to candidates

Once a pool of recruits has been attracted, the assessment methods are applied in order to evaluate each individual against the KSAs or competencies identified as important for job success. For selection, presuming that there are more applicants than vacancies, a first step will be to pre-select those applicants who look potentially suitable. This is done typically on the basis of the application form and/or CV that has been sent in. Despite the widespread use of such pre-screening methods, research evidence suggests that they are not designed or used systematically (Keenan, 1995). A growing trend is to use telephone interviews as a more interactive and potentially valid method of pre-selecting. Evidence about the effectiveness of this method is not yet very clear. From this initial screening, a smaller number of applicants will be assessed more fully, using whatever is considered to be the appropriate assessment method(s). The different methods of assessment are considered more fully later in the chapter.

### 5. Select 'best' solution: selection or development decision

This step in the decision-making cycle is seen to be the logical outcome of the previous steps. Once each candidate has been measured using the particular assessment methods the data can be evaluated in a logical manner in order to select the 'best' candidate. Each candidate can be rated against the person specification or competency profile. The candidate who has all the specified essential characteristics and the most desirable characteristics should be selected for the job. Where assessment is used for developmental purposes the decision is more about which candidates are suitable for which senior positions within the organisation. Nevertheless, there is the same assumption that this can be done rationally and logically on the basis of the data accumulated from the assessment exercises.

### 6. Monitor and evaluate results: validation

Ratings of employee potential estimated during the selection or developmental assessment process can be compared with subsequent performance on the job. This provides the measure of validity. High correlations between the selection or development ratings (referred to as the predictor) and performance ratings (referred to as the criterion) would indicate that the decisions made during the assessment process were valid (and hence rational). Low correlations would indicate that decisions were not valid. Evidence of the criterion-related validity of traditional methods used to make selection decisions, i.e. the unstructured interview and references, suggests that neither of these methods results in valid predictions.

One particular problem with such validity studies is that the criteria against which the selection or development decisions are compared (i.e. measures of job performance) may themselves be inaccurate (Campbell, 1990). The most typical criterion used is supervisory ratings, but research has demonstrated that these may vary widely in terms of accuracy. For example, Sundvik and Lindeman (1998) found that accuracy was dependent on the opportunity the supervisor had to observe the subordinate, especially in terms of the length of the supervisor–subordinate relationship. They also found that female supervisors are more accurate at rating than are males.

From the rational decision-making perspective, however, the key issue is to identify where selection or development decisions have been made that have not been good (i.e. where validity is poor) and to take this as the starting point for repeating the decision-making cycle in order to improve validity.

### 7. Identify problem

And so the circle repeats itself!

## The selection and assessment decision-making process in practice

While the rational decision-making model can be applied to the selection and assessment process, and indeed underpins much of the literature on improving the validity of such decisions, research evidence suggests that, in practice, the decision process is often far removed from this ideal. This is true for decisions of all kinds, not just selection and development decisions. Thus, research has demonstrated that such rational decision-making does not equate with reality. Rather, empirical research gives mostly examples of irrational decisions when compared to the normative standard (Cyert and March, 1963; March and Olsen, 1976; Nisbett and Ross, 1980). This is the case even where the decision is taken by a group rather than an individual. Indeed, Janis (1972) demonstrated how groups making extremely important strategic decisions failed to adopt the rational, normative approach. Janis used the term 'groupthink' to refer to the fact that, within the decision-making groups he observed, disturbing information was suppressed, immense and unjustified risks taken, and individuals censored their own concerns. The result was an illusion of unanimity for the decision taken, despite individual group members not really agreeing.

Given that research evidence does not support a rational decision-making process in practice, other models have been developed which attempt to mirror reality rather than idealism. Simon (1960) introduced the concept of bounded rationality, which acknowledged the fact that decision-makers, in practice, were under pressure to make decisions so that they did not have time to search exhaustively for all possible solutions. He coined the term 'satisficing' to describe how the search for solutions was not exhaustive, but continued only until a satisfactory solution had been found. Another model of decision-making that has attracted attention recently has been the intuitive decision-making model (e.g. Agor, 1989; Behling and Eckel, 1991). This assumes that managers make decisions by relying on past experiences and their general sense of the situation. Intuition is essentially an unconscious process created out of distilled experience. When managers face complex decisions and cannot get accurate information, they tend to rely on hunches, intuitions and general experiences. As Bazerman (1994) concludes: 'Most significant decisions are made by judgement, rather than by a defined prescriptive model'. Such intuition, however, is not really acceptable in cultures where rational analysis is the approved way of making decisions, such as North America and the UK. So intuition is often disguised or hidden. For example, one of the executives in the study by Agor (1986) commented: 'Sometimes one must dress up a gut decision in "data clothes" to make it acceptable or palatable, but this fine-tuning is usually after the fact of the decision.'

A final, non-rational model of the decision-making process is the garbage can model developed by Cohen *et al.* (1971). They described decision-making processes in terms of a 'garbage can', rather than a rational process. This model suggests that decisions have a random and haphazard element to them – that is, decisions are sometimes made from the random interaction of problems, solutions, choice situations and participants, rather than from intentions, plans, and consistent decisions. Various kinds of problems, solutions and energy ('garbage') are dumped into a garbage can by participants. The decision process may then just as well start with the solution as the problem.

These models of decision-making acknowledge the limits or 'bounds' to rational decision-making, including:

1. Perceptual limitations and biases
2. Limited availability of information
3. Prediction is an art not a science so it is not possible to evaluate options as rationally as proposed
4. Organisational goals constrain decisions
5. Conflicting goals of different stakeholders mean that interpersonal conflicts, personal biases and power struggles are an inherent part of the decision process.

## The irrationality of the selection and assessment decision-making process

The irrationality of decision-making processes has been confirmed in studies focusing on selection and assessment decisions. A brief look at the steps in the decision-making cycle and evidence of what happens at each stage highlights the continued 'irrationality' of the selection process in practice.

## 1. Understand the situation and identify the problem

The idea that someone leaving an organisation should be used as an opportunity to rationally consider whether or not a replacement is 'really needed', ignores the political realities of organisations (Pfeffer, 1981). Power within organisations is at least partly a function of resources that are controlled, including human resources. While individuals are recruited to work for a particular company, in reality they are recruited to particular departments or divisions. A department is unlikely to admit voluntarily that they do not need to replace a particular person since that will diminish their 'empire'. The department may actually be more likely to argue that they 'need' two people to replace the one leaver! Someone leaving may be an opportunity for a renegotiation of resources within the organisation, but this needs to be understood as an inherently political process. 'Need' is not something that can be established as fact, but is socially constructed through a process of negotiation and sense-making until a 'workable version of reality' is produced (Weick, 1990).

## 2. Gather information and material to help solve the problem

Despite the extensive effort put into developing new, more valid methods to measure and assess individuals during the selection process, evidence suggests that unstructured interviews and references remain the most dominant methods (Shackleton and Newell, 1991; Keenan, 1995). This can be related to the human fallacy of us each believing that we are a 'good judge of people', despite evidence to the contrary (see section below on person perceptions errors). Later in this chapter we will also consider another reason for the continued use of the interview – that is, that selection is not simply about 'valid' selection, but also about commitment and motivation to follow up the decision with behaviours that encourage the individual selected to integrate into the organisation. A recruiter who feels that s/he has personally selected the candidate is much more likely to feel committed and motivated to helping achieve that integration. Similarly, the selected candidate may well be more committed to the organisation because unstructured interviews are more likely to provide the opportunity to negotiate a 'mutually agreeable psychological contract' (Dipboye, 1997).

## 3. Generate potential solutions

While the rational model of selection suggests that the recruitment stage is about generating the widest search possible in order to ensure the 'best' pool of applicants, evidence suggests that, in reality, the alternatives considered are often less than exhaustive. For example, some organisations only go to Oxford and Cambridge universities to recruit graduates. While these universities may well have some of the brightest graduates, there will certainly be bright graduates at other universities. Other evidence suggests that the so-called 'old boy network' is still actively used across organisations (Coe, 1992). In other words, it is very often personal contacts that provide job openings rather than systematic recruitment and selection procedures.

## 4. Systematically evaluate each solution

The evidence suggests that assessors, whatever method they are using, do not systematically use the evidence that is collected. For example, the evidence about assessment centres, reviewed below, suggests that assessors are unable to distinguish between different aspects of behaviour within a given exercise, but instead give ratings based on their overall assessment of the candidate's performance on that particular exercise. Research on interviews suggests that decisions are often made very quickly and are subjective, unreliable and vulnerable to bias (Arvey and Faley, 1992; Dipboye, 1992; Janz, 1989).

## 5. Select best solution

A truly rational decision process would have assessors numerically rate each candidate on each dimension or competency; give the different dimensions or competencies specific weightings depending on their relative importance for the job in question; and then total the score for each candidate, taking into account the relative weightings. The candidate with the highest total would be selected. This can be described as the actuarial method as it is based purely on a numerical calculation of the collected data (although the ratings themselves are subjective). In practice, however, the decision is much more likely to be based on a process of clinical judgement. The ratings may be numerical but these will be evaluated subjectively by the assessors and weightings will be assigned to justify decisions rather than to make the decisions. So leadership skills become more important than numerical skills, if this allows the favoured candidate to come out top! As Beach (1990: xiii) states: 'most decisions are made quickly and simply on the basis of "fittingness", and only in particular circumstances are they made on the basis of anything like the weighing and balancing of gains and losses that is prescribed by classical decision theory'.

## 6. Monitor and evaluate results

In practice it seems that very few organisations carry out a systematic evaluation of their selection process (or indeed any other human resource practice). Moreover, where validity studies have been conducted, they demonstrate low levels of validity even when using methods that can potentially provide reasonable or good levels of validity (see below). These results confirm that selection methods are not used in the prescribed way and that efforts to improve validity have had rather limited impact on actual practice.

The conclusion drawn from such research is that the prescriptive, rational decision-making process does not typically equate with what happens in practice and that methods of selection actually used by practitioners are often not high on criterion-related validity. Exactly the same points could be made with reference to decisions made during developmental assessment processes. The response from those researching and writing about selection and assessment has been to attempt to improve the validity of the methods used to measure individual differences. In other words, the focus has been on trying to find ways of improving the extent to which the rational, normative decision-making model is actually followed.

## Improving the validity of selection and assessment decisions

In particular, attention has focused on introducing methods which provide a better basis on which to make rational decisions. Considerable progress has been made here, which demonstrates how the validity of the selection and assessment decision-making process can be improved.

### Structured interviews

The interview is the most common selection tool used within organisations across many countries (DiMilia et al., 1994; Shackleton and Newell, 1994). Early research demonstrated that the traditional unstructured interview had very low validity (e.g. Mayfield, 1964; Ulrich and Trumbo, 1965). Given the ubiquity of the interview, effort has been devoted to improving its validity, primarily by increasing the structure of the interview, so that at least all candidates are asked the same sorts of questions (if not the identical questions) and all interviewers use the same dimensions to assess candidates. Research looking at the validity of structured interviews suggests that they can indeed improve validity. For example, McDaniel et al. (1994), in a large meta-analytic study, reported that structured interviews were more valid than unstructured interviews. Structuring interviews can therefore potentially improve the quality of decisions made, although there appears to be a ceiling on this, beyond which increasing structure does not improve validity (Heffcutt and Arthur, 1994).

### Biographical measures

Biographical measures, or biodata, attempt to capture directly the past behaviour of a person and use this as the basis for predicting future behaviour. Since they are based on actual behaviour, the idea is that they are less prone to misinterpretation, resistance and distortion (Stricker and Rock, 1998). Research has indeed demonstrated that biographical measures can produce good levels of predictive validity (e.g. Mumford and Stokes, 1992; Stokes et al., 1993; Hesketh, 1999). Nevertheless, there remain a number of concerns about the appropriate item content and about test construction methods (Mael, 1991). For example, in terms of content many biographical measures contain questions which are indistinguishable from items on an attitude scale (e.g. What is your attitude towards working mothers?); or items that call for subjective judgements (e.g. How punctual are you?); or items that are not under the control of the assessee and so are dubious on ethical grounds (e.g. How many sisters and brothers have you got?). In terms of test construction, a key problem is that because most measures are empirically keyed to predict particular criteria, they cannot be used in different settings. There is also the problem that this method can produce a very homogeneous workforce, since those selected will have very similar backgrounds and experiences. This may be problematic in a dynamic environment where the ability to adapt to change is important.

## Psychometric tests

Essentially, there are two kinds of tests used for selection or developmental assessment – cognitive and personality tests. Cognitive tests, especially tests of general intelligence, have typically been found to have high predictive validity across a wide range of jobs (Hunter and Hunter, 1984), but it is debatable how much additional information they provide since there are other ways of estimating ability, especially from academic qualifications.

Personality tests have typically been found to have a low validity for predicting job performance (Ghiselli, 1973; Schmitt *et al.*, 1984). However, more recently, evidence has been established to suggest that personality measures can be valid predictors of job performance (e.g. Day and Silverman, 1989; Robertson and Kinder, 1993; Salgado, 1996). One reason for the early pessimism was that there was no generally accepted model of personality. More recently, the so called 'Big 5' have emerged around which there is substantial agreement. Research using the Big 5 model has shown that measurement of these five traits can help to predict job performance. For example, Barrick and Mount (1991) found that conscientiousness is a valid predictor for all occupational groups and all criterion types. And Hough *et al.* (1990) found that neuroticism is negatively related to general performance measures. Moreover, researchers have begun to consider more thoughtfully the relationship between particular aspects of personality and particular aspects of performance that might logically be related; not assuming that a measure of personality will be related to just any criterion measure.

## Assessment or development centres

Assessment or development centres make use of a variety of exercises over a period of time (typically 2 days) to assess a small group of candidates on a number of dimensions (often defined in terms of competencies) that are deemed relevant to the particular job and organisation. Ratings are made by a small group of trained assessors who observe the candidates on the different exercises. Exercises might include: a group decision-making exercise, a presentation, a role play, an in-basket test, psychometric tests, and interviews. In the UK, the use of assessment centres is increasing more rapidly than any other selection procedure, with 65 per cent of large firms (over 1,000 employees) using them (Industrial Relations Service, 1997). Research evidence using meta-analysis demonstrates that they can have a relatively high level of predictive validity (Gaugler *et al.*, 1987) and are seen as fair and thorough by candidates (Macan *et al.*, 1994).

Despite this good predictive validity, research has demonstrated that assessment and development centres do not have good construct validity (Kauffman *et al.*, 1993). In particular, research has demonstrated that within each exercise, ratings across the different dimensions are not clearly differentiated, while correlation of a given dimension across exercises is low (Joyce *et al.*, 1994; Kaufman *et al.*, 1993; McCredie and Shackleton, 1994). One suggested reason for this is that the information-processing load on assessors is too high, so that they selectively attend to only certain behaviours, misinterpret key behaviours, and/or confuse categorisation of behaviours by dimensions (Fleenor, 1996; Thornton, 1992). Schema-driven theory suggests that this occurs because people use established schemata to interpret and evaluate the observed behaviour of others (Fiske and Taylor, 1991; Zedeck, 1986). Schemata refer to the mental representations that an individual has built up over time to structure and cluster their understanding of perceived phenomena. Any new input will be interpreted on the basis of the assumptions which underpin these schemata. Traditionally, the recommended way to overcome this problem has been to separate the steps of observation and classification – recording behaviours longhand while observing, classifying behaviours according to the defined dimensions for the exercise, and only then rating the individual on each dimension (Bray and Grant, 1966; Boyle *et al.*, 1995). While this does help to overcome some of the perceptual problems of assessors, the requirement to write detailed notes of the observation can be a distraction and means that the assessor might miss some behavioural information.

Hennessy *et al.* (1998), in an attempt to overcome this problem, experimented with the use of a Behavioural Coding method of assessment. This provides a list of key behaviours for each of the dimensions rated and requires observers to code the frequency of behaviours as they occur. They are not required actually to note the behaviours per se, but only tally the frequency of the specified behaviours. This has the advantage that information-processing demands are reduced and also limits the extent to which personal schemata will direct the observation. The results of their research demonstrated that this Behavioural Coding method was as accurate as the traditional method of assessment and reduced differences between raters in their judgements. They suggest that its simplicity in comparison with the traditional method, and its theoretical basis in schema-driven theory, may make this a preferred method for overcoming the construct validity problem of assessment or development centres.

On the basis of reviewing a number of studies which have attempted to improve the construct validity of assessment and development centres, Lievens (1998) makes a number of practical recommendations. For example, in terms of:

1. Dimensions: use only a small number of conceptually distinct dimensions and define these in a concrete and job-related way.
2. Assessors: ensure assessors are trained, especially in relation to understanding the dimensions and categorisation schemes used.

3. Situational exercises: develop exercises which generate a large amount of dimension-related behaviour and avoid exercises which elicit behaviours potentially relevant to many dimensions.
4. Systematic observation, evaluation and integration procedures: Provide assessors with an observation aid (a checklist), which operationalises each dimension with 6–12 key behaviours.

## The rhetoric versus the reality of the selection and assessment decision-making process

These newer assessment methods appear to offer significant benefits since they can improve objectivity and criterion-related validity. However, as seen, research into actual practice suggests that, in reality, selection and development decisions continue to be dominated by more subjective approaches. Moreover, even where so-called 'objective' approaches are used, their interpretation remains highly subjective. That is, the fact that a structured interview or an assessment centre has the potential to reach high levels of validity does not mean that it will be used in ways to guarantee this. For example, DiMilia and Gorodecki (1997) evaluated the reliability and use of a commercially available structured interviewing system. They found that, in practice, the reliability achieved was much lower than considered in the literature to be an acceptable level. This was because there was a lack of role clarity for interviewers, interviewers had different expectations of the job specification and there was inconsistency in the application of the rating system. They conclude that: '. . . whilst an interviewing system can have a number of features described in the literature as necessary conditions for better validity, the actual result of the system is in the hands of the user' (DiMilia and Gorodecki, 1997: 198).

Similarly, while psychometric tests can potentially add valid information to the selection or development decision, it is also clear that this will only occur if tests are used appropriately (Newell and Shackleton, 1993). Rees (1996) identifies a number of common misunderstandings among test users which suggest that tests are not always used in a valid and ethical way. For example, a frequent misconception is that it is acceptable to use a poor test to structure a subsequent interview. Rees concludes that such misunderstandings may, over time, undermine the case of those attempting to use psychometric tests 'effectively and appropriately in the occupational setting'. He argues that there are too many test users who are unable to recognise technically poor test material and so use such tests inappropriately to help them make decisions that affect both individuals and organisations.

These observations are not confined to selection decision methods. Other attempts to improve the rationality of decision-making, for example by introducing cost-benefit analysis, computer-based information systems or other decision support systems, demonstrate that, in practice, these solutions are not used in the prescribed way (e.g. Ackerman *et al.*, 1974; Argyris, 1977). Essentially, the normative model of the selection and assessment decision-making process does not equate to reality because selection and assessment is a process that inherently depends on an interaction between two or more parties. Such interpersonal *interactions* involve two (or more) parties who are simultaneously providing input (which the other is evaluating) and evaluating the other. Such interactions are inherently subjective, involving processes of impression management and interpretation.

### Impression management

Decisions made about candidates during selection and assessment depend on the concrete experiences that are provided. These experiences of the 'target person' (i.e. the candidate) may be indirect (e.g. information from an application form or a personality test) or direct (e.g. behaviour exhibited during an interview). The newer methods of assessment attempt to ensure that the event provides assessors with an accurate reflection of the person being assessed. This assumes that the candidate is passively responding to the various assessment experiences. In reality, of course, candidates are actively attempting to create a certain image of themselves. This is especially the case in the 'high stakes' selection situation. Candidates will attempt to create and maintain a particular impression of themselves which coincides with what they believe the assessor is looking for. Thus, to some extent at least, the assessor only sees what the target person wants him/her to see. This is referred to as Impression Management (Rosenfeld *et al.*, 1995). Arnold *et al.* (1997) identify a variety of techniques that can be used to convey a particular impression. For example, ingratiation ('I have always wanted to work for this firm'), selective description of events (candidate ignoring details of failed examinations they have taken), positive descriptions of self ('I am a very hard-working person'). While it might be obvious to appreciate that candidates are engaging in impression management tactics, it is also the case that assessors are simultaneously attempting to 'create an impression' because they want to attract or retain the 'best' candidates.

### Interpretation

The assessor has to make sense of the data that is accumulated about the candidate and this sense-making process is inherently subjective. At the same time, the candidate is also trying to 'make sense' of the situation – what would it be like to work for this company, or what would my colleagues be like, or what are my implied career opportunities? For both parties, there is a stimulus ('evidence' from the candidate to the assessor and vice versa) and a response (a job offer or an acceptance of a job offer). However, the key to understanding this is that between these two observable phenomena are the unobservable processes of perception.

Perception, by definition, is a subjective process by which individuals attend to, organise and so interpret their sensory input in order to give meaning to their environment. Subjective processes, including selective attention, personal judgement and interpretation, will therefore affect the decision. Behaviour is based on the world as it is perceived and a number of factors operate to shape and sometimes distort perception, including personal characteristics, motives, interests, past experiences, and expectations. This will result in biases, such as:

1. *Selective attention* – as we cannot attend to everything, we only attend to some things, but this is not random. Rather, what we attend to is chosen according to our interests, background, experience and attitudes. This allows us to draw conclusions from an ambiguous situation.
2. *Halo/horn effect* – we tend to draw a general impression about an individual on the basis of a single characteristic, such as intelligence.
3. *Contrast effects* – evaluations of a person's characteristics can be affected by comparisons with other people recently encountered. So, in an interview situation, if someone has just been interviewed who was judged very poor, the next candidate may be more positively evaluated in contrast. Conversely, following a very good candidate, an average candidate may be rated poorly.
4. *Projection* – there is a tendency to attribute one's own characteristics to other people. So if I want challenge and responsibility in a job, I assume that others want the same.
5. *Stereotyping* – this involves judging someone on the basis of one's perceptions of the group to which that person belongs.
6. *Heuristics* – these are judgemental short cuts in decision-making. Two common heuristics are availability and representativeness. The availability heuristic is the tendency for people to base their judgements on information that is readily available to them. For example, if there is an internal and an external candidate, the internal candidate may be preferred simply because more information is readily available about him/her ('better the devil you know!'). The representative heuristic is the tendency to assess the likelihood of an occurrence by drawing analogies and seeing identical situations where they do not exist. So, for example, if four graduates from the same college had all been recruited but none had been very satisfactory, then another applicant from this college might be rejected on the assumption that they also would not be good.

It is just these sorts of impression management problems and perceptual biases that 'new' assessment methods have attempted to overcome. They structure and standardise the information gained during the assessment process, so that decisions are less likely to be biased by these perceptual short cuts that we use in our everyday judgements of other people, to a greater or lesser extent. To the extent that these new assessment methods can reduce these biases, they can improve validity. The research evidence presented earlier suggests that this is indeed the case. However, as we have also seen, while newer, more valid assessment methods have been developed, and can improve the validity of selection and development decisions, in practice they are often not used in quite the 'rational' way anticipated. Human subjectivity and the political reality of organisations mean that the normative decision model can never be an entirely realistic account of decision-making in practice.

## Unfounded assumptions: selection as an interactive process

While human perception and organisational politics limit the extent to which a selection or development decision can ever be entirely rational, there is an even more fundamental problem with the normative decision model. The normative approach makes the assumption of a 'right' or 'best' person for the job and assumes that there is one key decision, i.e. to select or reject the candidate, which is the crucial point. The important issue is to select the 'right' person and then this will solve the organisational problem because this person will be able successfully to carry out the particular tasks where there is currently a vacancy (although this may be only after training has been given). However, this ignores the fact that successful performance on a job is rarely, if ever, dependent solely on a particular individual. The individual job exists within a complex network of structures, processes and relationships, which will affect and interact with the actions of the particular individual employee. So a potentially very competent recruit can be thwarted in their ability to perform to a high standard by a whole multitude of events – a lack of adequate resources, poor training, an unhelpful supervisor, colleagues who are not supportive, etc. On the other hand, a barely competent recruit can perform to a high standard if she/he is exposed to a supportive or benign situation.

In other words, it is not helpful to look at the selection decision itself in isolation from the stream of events that occur both before and after this. Vaughan (1996, 1997) made a similar point in analysing the Challenger space shuttle disaster. She points out that the explosion should not be viewed as the unfortunate result of one bad decision to launch on that day in January 1986. Rather, it was the outcome of an accumulation of many launch decisions over the course of the shuttle programme. So instead of focusing on single decisions, she advocates the analysis of cycles of decisions or networks of decisions. This is equally the case in terms of analysing selection or development decisions. Thus, whether a decision to select (or reject) can be described as 'good' or 'bad' is the result of a network of interacting decisions. These decisions are made by both the individual and the organisational representatives, over a period of time, starting well before the actual advertisement of a job. For example, individuals will form an impression of a particular company based on what they know about its products and services or what they know about the organisation itself. These impressions may be formed either on the basis of direct experience (e.g. good or bad experience of service as a customer) or indirect experience (e.g. reading something good or bad about the company in the press). These impressions will influence how an individual responds to a recruitment advertisement. So a potentially ideal candidate may not even apply if s/he has formed a negative impression. Moreover, decisions made subsequent to the selection decision, will have a considerable impact on the extent to which the recruit performs the job effectively. Particularly important in this respect is the socialisation experience of the new recruit (Anderson and Ostroff, 1997). This suggests the need to see selection as an interactive process in which the expectations of both parties are intertwined in a process of continuous exchange, which does not begin and end at the point of the selection decision. Again, exactly the same points can be made with reference to development decisions. Whether the 'right' career path is chosen for and by a particular individual on the basis of evidence from a development centre will depend on a host of decisions made prior and subsequent to this choice.

What this analysis implies is that the normative, rational model of decision-making isolates the decision from subsequent action, including subsequent decisions (Brunsson, 1982). Brunsson argues that the normative decision-making perspective fails to recognise that a decision is not an end product but simply a step towards action of some kind. In the case of selection, this equals the effective deployment of human resources. More importantly, Brunsson points out that rational decisions are not always good bases for appropriate and successful actions: 'Since decision processes aim at action, they should not be designed solely according to such decision-internal criteria as the norms of rationality; they should be adapted to external criteria of action' (1982: 32). The selection or development decision per se is only one episode in the successful integration of the individual in the organisation. Successful integration is more likely to occur where there are positive expectations, motivation and commitment from both parties. Thus, the stronger the expectation, motivation and commitment expressed in a decision, the more power that decision exerts as a basis for action. However, Brunnson argues that to achieve such expectation, motivation and commitment breaks all the rules for rational decision-making:

1. Few alternatives should be considered: while the rational model assumes that many (all) alternatives should be considered, from a decision-action perspective parsimony is more appropriate. Considering multiple alternatives generates uncertainty and this reduces commitment and motivation.
2. Only positive consequences of the chosen decision should be analysed: the rational model advocates considering all consequences of a decision, both positive and negative. From a decision-action perspective it may be more sensible to search for consequences in only one direction since this reduces inconsistency which can stimulate doubt.
3. Objectives should not be predefined: the rational model assumes that objectives should be predefined so that all alternatives can be considered against these objectives. For producing action, a better strategy may be to start from the consequences and invent the objectives afterwards (Lindblom, 1959).

This action-oriented perspective can help to explain some of the research findings on the selection and assessment decision process, which suggest that it remains less rational than prescribed best practice would advocate. Examples of this are given below.

1. Continued use of unstructured interviews – the belief that 'I am a good judge of character' allows the interviewer to be confident in his/her decision and so increases commitment and motivation to make the chosen individual 'fit'.

2. Continued use of subjective (clinical) rather than objective (actuarial) choice criteria – again this empowers the assessor to believe that they were influential in the decision and so makes him/her more committed to ensuring the decision translates into effective action – i.e. successful integration of the chosen candidate within the organisation.

3. Less than exhaustive search of alternatives – making decisions quickly makes life more comfortable for managers. It allows them to use heuristics or 'short-cuts' to solving problems. Predefined recipes for successful selection decisions can increase confidence in the decision and so raise expectations of subsequent success by the candidate.

4. Little systematic evaluation of selection decision – while academic research has focused on establishing the predictive validity of selection decisions, in practice few organisations systematically monitor the success of their decisions. Again, from an action perspective this is sensible since it allows those involved to be confident in their decision-making qualities and so more confident about and committed to the decisions they make. It also reduces the possibility of cognitive dissonance (Festinger, 1957). Cognitive dissonance is the uncomfortable feeling that occurs when people hold inconsistent or conflicting beliefs – I made the decision to hire this person, I am good at making these kinds of decisions, this person is not a good employee. Cognitive dissonance can be avoided if systematic evaluation of selection decisions is avoided.

5. Overemphasis of negative data – research has demonstrated that negative information about a candidate is given more weight than positive information. Many of the newer assessment methods are aimed at reducing this effect. However, from a decision-action perspective this is entirely rational. Negative information raises doubts about the suitability of a candidate and so will undermine confidence that the person can be successful. So if there are two candidates, and from an objective evaluation of the evidence, candidate A is 'best', having more of the essential and desirable characteristics than candidate B, then rationally that candidate should be selected. However, if there is also one piece of negative information about candidate A (for example a question mark over their willingness to collaborate), while there is nothing negative about candidate B, then from an action-decision perspective, candidate B would be preferable. If candidate A were selected there would remain doubts, which might undermine motivation and commitment to the decision.

In each case, the decision-action criteria improve the positive expectations of those involved over the purely rational decision criteria. This is important since expectations can become self-fulfilling prophecies. For example, Eden and Shani (1982) informed the instructors of a command course for the Israeli Defence Forces that one-third of the 105 soldiers on the course had high potential, one-third had normal potential and the rest were of unknown potential. In reality, the soldiers had been randomly assigned to one of these three groups. However, at the end of the 15-week course, those trainees who were given the high potential label scored significantly higher on objective achievement tests and exhibited more positive attitudes to the course and the instructors, than did the rest.

## Interactive action-oriented perspective, fairness and justice

One particular problem in selection and development decisions has been the issue of 'fair' discrimination. Thus, while selection is based on making discriminations between people, the objective has been to make these discriminations on the basis of relevant criteria, i.e. ability to do the job effectively, rather than irrelevant criteria like sex, ethnicity, and disability. One of the key benefits of the psychometric perspective is that it presents a very rational and objective view of the whole process. It assumes that the 'best' person for the job can be clearly specified in advance, with selection and assessment processes essentially presented as a set of 'rational' choices based on objective evidence gained about the candidates from the various selection methods deployed. This allowed companies to defend against claims of unfair discrimination. Essentially, the traditional approach may be considered to have a high level of procedural justice (Lind and Tyler, 1988) since it theoretically treats everyone the same. In this chapter, we have argued that this semblance of rationality is actually a myth. Moreover, it could be argued that the psychometric perspective actually increases the opportunity for distributive injustice (Singer, 1993), because its starting premise is that there is one 'best' way to do the job. This 'best' way is likely to be a reflection of the way previous job incumbents have done the job. So if the previous job incumbents have all been white males who have adopted fairly autocratic management styles, worked long hours, relied on a lot of electronic communication, etc., then the assumption will be that these are the characteristics to look for in a replacement. This may perpetuate the status quo and thus the segregation that exists within organisations, although the process may look procedurally 'fair'.

Adopting the interactive, action-oriented perspective provides the opportunity to break through this barrier by recognising that people can do jobs in very different ways but equally effectively. The problem with this perspective, however, is that it acknowledges the subjectivity of the selection process and so could be used as a vehicle to increase unfair discrimination even more. This is entirely true but it will depend on the motives of those involved. If there is a belief in equal opportunities, or, perhaps even better, in the advantages of diversity in the workforce, then this perspective can help to increase these opportunities. The psychometric perspective simply hides behind a façade of objectivity so that it remains easy to perpetuate discrimination even while presenting the whole process as fair. The interactive action-oriented perspective does not have this façade to hide behind so that any continuation of segregated workforces must, by implication, be the result of prejudice and unfair discrimination.

## Conclusion

Understanding the selection and assessment process from a decision-making perspective highlights issues that are otherwise not brought into focus. In this chapter, this perspective has been used to contrast the traditional psychometric perspective with its implicit acceptance of the normative rational decision-making model, with an interactive decision-action perspective. The decision-action perspective leads us to recognise both that the process of selection and assessment can never be entirely rational and objective and that the decision per se (to accept or reject) is not necessarily the crucial point in the process. Rather, it is a stage in the ultimate goal of achieving the effective integration and socialisation of an individual within the organisation. Effective integration is clearly unlikely if an entirely unsuitable person is chosen for a job. However, the assumption that there is a fixed type of person for a particular job and that the only goal of selection and assessment is to ensure accurate measurement in order to be able to identify this right type, is inappropriate. It is inappropriate both because of its assumptions about individual differences and our ability to assess these accurately in a selection or development situation and because it ignores the criteria for translating the decision into action.

Successful performance on the job is dependent on motivation as well as ability. Ability is dependent not only on fixed characteristics, but also on opportunities for training and development that are provided. An 'ideal' person selected for a job but then given no training or development opportunities is more likely to fail than a moderately suitable person who is given such opportunities.

More importantly, in terms of motivation, success or failure will depend on both the individual's own self-beliefs and on the beliefs of those around him/her. If these significant others have been involved in the selection and assessment process and believe that the person selected is 'the best', then they will be committed to ensuring he/she is successful, regardless of whether or not he/she is best according to some objective rational decision criteria. An entirely rational, actuarial evaluation of data collected during an assessment centre that results in the selection of a person that those involved do not 'like' or do not think is 'best' (for whatever reason), is unlikely to translate into active commitment aimed at helping that individual succeed. As seen, such commitment is more likely to follow a selection decision-process that is less than entirely rational, but that gives those involved the belief that they have chosen someone who will be successful. Similarly, motivation is likely to be high if the selection or development experience results in positive but realistic expectations on the part of those assessed. Self-efficacy beliefs, an individual's belief that s/he is capable of performing the task selected for (Bandura, 1977), will be high and these beliefs have been shown to be important in influencing the persistence and effort that someone will put into ensuring success (Gist, 1987).

An action-decision perspective can help to identify those selection and assessment processes that can generate such high levels of self- and other belief and expectation that lead, in turn, to high levels of commitment and motivation. Of course, measurement of individual differences will remain important in selection and development decisions. However, the recognition that accurate measurement per se is not enough (even if it were possible), can help us focus on the ultimate goal of successful person-organisation fit, rather than just valid and rational decisions that might not readily translate into action. The decision-action perspective, therefore, compliments the more traditional psychometric perspective and can help to ensure not only that decisions are made on the basis of reasonably good individual assessment but also that those decisions get translated into successful organisational performance.

# Assessment at Newsco, Pharmco and Retailco

Sue Newell and Viv Shackleton

Taking a decision-action perspective suggests that processes involved in selection and assessment should differ depending on the particular context and, in particular, on the intended action outcome. In order to demonstrate this diversity, we consider three separate cases in the following section. Each had a different objective and so a different design.

## Newsco

### Introduction

The first example of the application of the assessment techniques we have talked about in this chapter concerns Newsco, a large and successful company in the business of selling news and information. It is a truly international company, operating as it does in most countries of the world. It divides the world up into three zones. We are concerned here with the European part of the operation.

### The brief

The company decided to assess the top 50 or so of its managers in this region. The stated purpose was assessment for development. That is to say, the managers would go through a development centre (an assessment-type centre designed with development in mind) in order for them to assess what sort of development they needed. 'Development' is a word that is frequently misunderstood. Here, it does not necessarily mean promotion or acquiring new responsibilities. It means training in techniques or skills, or acquiring new information, that would help them in their present or future roles. The traditional 'sheep dip' approach to management development, training and learning, where everyone receives the same training, regardless of need, is often not appropriate at any level in an organisation. It can be particularly inappropriate for senior people where the opportunity cost of having them away from their desks on a course is very high. This organisation wanted to target training only on those who needed it, in the areas they most needed.

The role of those participating in the development centre was mostly that of 'country manager', the people who headed up the business in each country, although there were also specialists of various kinds.

### The design

The start of the process of designing the development centre began with an assessment of competencies, just as we described in the section on the traditional approach to assessment in this chapter. This involved interviewing people in the organisation to establish what the competencies were, both for the present job and for the ways in which the jobs might develop. The interviews were based on in-depth reviews of the role in question and how the organisation might develop. Two other kinds of interview were also used, the repertory grid technique and the critical incident technique. The repertory grid technique asks the interviewee to think of a number of people known to him or her who do, or have done, the job and to compare the way that they perform that role. From this information, the interviewer can work out the key skills, knowledge, abilities or competencies that effective job holders need and which differentiate the effective from the less effective. The critical incident technique asks interviewees to think of times in the job when they or their team were particularly successful or unsuccessful. The interviewee is encouraged to say what it was that made this particular incident successful or unsuccessful. From this evidence, the experienced interviewer can work out some of the competencies needed in the job.

Some of the competencies in this case were:

- *Managing change*
  - Continually challenging the status quo
  - Generating innovative ideas and solutions
  - Driving change through and overcoming resistance

- *Thinking for the future*
  - Anticipating future trends and identifying new opportunities
  - Thinking strategically
  - Retaining a global perspective

- *Working with customers*
  - Building partnerships with customers by knowing their business
  - Consulting with customers to understand needs and provide the best service
  - Promoting a positive image of the company

Exercises were then designed to give the opportunity to assess these and the other competencies. Exercises included:

- a role play with a customer, where the customer had a serious complaint about the level of service and support he or she was receiving
- a competitor analysis, where participants were given information about three competitors and asked to do a SWOT (strengths, weaknesses, opportunities and threats) analysis of their own organisation and the competition
- giving a presentation on issues of their own choosing from their own country business to the top management from the head office

- a group discussion on a strategic issue facing the whole organisation
- some psychometric tests

### The workshop

Each development centre lasted two days. Managers from all corners of Europe and North Africa arrived, eight at a time, for the programme. There were external consultants and managers from head office running the programme and assessing the participants on the competencies. A crucial element of the two days was a one-to-one feedback, lasting around an hour, conducted by the external consultant with each of the participants. The purpose of this meeting was to review the performance of the participant on each of the exercises and competencies, and to get his or her agreement to the accuracy of the assessment. Most importantly, it was also an opportunity to discuss what the participant proposed to do about developing the strengths and remedying the weaknesses exposed by the programme.

### The outputs

Following the workshop, the consultant wrote a report on the participant, summarising his or her performance and outlining a development plan. In effect, the report summarised and formalised the one-to-one discussion at the end of the centre. The report was sent to the participant and to his or her human resources manager. Participants themselves only showed it to their line manager or others in the organisation if they so wished. It was a confidential report and the recommendations were to be implemented by the participant in the manner most likely to achieve the development proposed. Development methods included secondments, job shadowing, training courses, self-directed learning, distance learning, job changes, and even withdrawal from the organisation if this was what the participant wanted.

After the development centre, there was no follow-up to check that the participants at the workshop had done any development after the event, and no attempt to evaluate the benefits of the programme. It was sufficient for the participants to say that the workshop had been useful and enjoyable. The feedback was essentially positive. This is not to say that the development centre was anodyne. There was some indication of how they could do even better. It pointed out that, where the participant had demonstrated excellent skills, he or she might coach others in these skills or seek opportunities to use them even more. Where there were skills that needed improving, suggestions were made on how this might be accomplished. But the whole development centre, and the feedback in particular, was geared to reinforcing, motivating and encouraging, rather than assessing and measuring. The participants were generally very positive about the event, after some initial reservations. They pointed out the many considerable advantages of the programme, including the opportunity to meet others in similar roles, to reflect on their own progress in the organisation, to think about themselves for a change, rather than the job in hand, and to consider how they might change or reinforce certain aspects of their own behaviour. In summary, the opportunity to reflect and learn was very motivating and satisfying for them.

## Pharmco

### Introduction

The second case concerns a long-established German corporation, Pharmco. Its early beginnings were in the traditional 'smokestack' industries of iron and steel, but since the Second World War it has moved into pharmaceutical manufacture and retail, along with the manufacture of medical and other technical equipment and a number of other businesses. In the more recent past, it has also started to expand beyond its national border and acquire and develop businesses in other European countries, including Britain, France and Spain. It is still predominantly a German company, though, with 90 per cent of its manufacturing and retail business conducted within the country.

### The brief

We meet up with the company at the point when it was thinking of investing in the development of its young managers to groom them for more senior appointments. In typical German style, it placed great emphasis on the importance of formal, high-quality education. It planned to offer the chance for some of the young managers to broaden their education and experience out of their technical and functional expertise and into a general management education. They would offer the opportunity to enrol in a part-time MBA at a prestigious international business school for those who were assessed as having the potential to profit from it. But who would benefit?

### The design

The method they chose to select those who would be offered the opportunity was an assessment centre. Germany, like Britain and America, has a long tradition of using assessment centres, right back from the days of officer selection in the Second World War. But here, there was the additional complication of having to design an assessment centre for candidates from a number of different European countries. Although the language of the centre would be English, the exercises would be taken by people from four or five different countries. Of course, Newsco was a very international group, and consideration was given to designing exercises that would not favour one culture rather than another. But here, the cultural fairness issue was considered even more carefully by the designers. This is because this centre was seen as more akin to a traditional assessment centre, where fairness of treatment and equal opportunity to display skills are paramount. As we will discuss shortly, though, this objectivity and equal treatment were more apparent than real.

Once again, the first issue was what knowledge, skills and abilities should be assessed. And again, the favoured means of acquiring that knowledge was a competency analysis. Methods adopted to decide on the required competencies were very similar to those already described for Newsco. Competencies included:

■ *Cross-cultural sensitivity*
- Demonstrating curiosity and open-mindedness about other national cultures
- Acting to promote mutual understanding of other cultures
- Demonstrating sensitivity when working with people from other cultures

■ *Leadership*
- Focusing a group on generating a range of new ideas and possibilities
- Demonstrating confidence and a sense of responsibility
- Developing subordinates by making demands on them

■ *Orientation to the task*
- Agreeing clear and realistic actions
- Prioritising
- Taking decisions
- Reviewing progress towards achieving the task

Participants were nominated by their line managers and by human resource professionals in their separate companies, in whichever country they worked. Participants were assessed at the centre by both company managers and by outside consultants, using competency-based rating scales.

Exercises were designed with the multicultural audience in mind. They included one on cultural sensitivity, where participants discussed their perception of their own culture and the German culture, as they had experienced it. They had to meet to discuss what recommendations they would make to improve cross-cultural working and how they would know if their recommendations were effective.

When designing assessment centre exercises, it is important to keep these and other cultural dimensions in mind. So, for example, it is important to make sure that exercises have many routes to success for a participant. An example of this need to provide many routes to success (and failure) in a multicultural environment is provided by an exercise used in this case. The exercise involved a customer service manager who was new to the post, and a subordinate, a customer service team leader, who had been in post for a long time. This was a role play exercise. An 'actor', a manager who had been in that post in the past, played the team leader. The participant played the superior, the customer service manager. There was some written material on the team leader, such as previous performance appraisal reports and statistical data on the subordinate's performance, available to the new boss. The issues were that the team leader was very good with customers, being liked and respected by them, but not good at developing his or her team, in part because s/he spent so much time with customers. In addition, they were not good at organising the work of the team since they were too busy doing the work themselves. The exercise could be done in a number of ways. It could be done from a relationships-building point of view, where, for example, the new boss could coach or mentor the old hand into new ways of working. Or it could be done from a very task-focused point of view, such as saying that this style and level of performance is not acceptable and you should be working in a different way and here are some targets and a timetable to achieve a different level of achievement. Or it could be successfully tackled in ways between those two extremes, such as helping the individual to explore alternative ways of doing the job over the next month and coming back to discuss progress after that time interval. What was important was that the individual was guided to seeing that the job involved two sets of customers, internal and external, and that it was important for the team leader to give attention to both. How participants achieved that aim was up to them.

## Retailco

### Introduction

The third case is a British-based retailer, Retailco. Like many large retailers in Britain, it was finding organic growth within Britain hard to achieve. It was already market leader, with the market dominated by about five players. Growth in its main market was less than 5 per cent a year, with it achieving this or a little more, year by year. This was likely to be the case for the foreseeable future. It was innovative in expanding in other businesses, but its main core business was unlikely to grow substantially.

An obvious route for a company in this position is growth by acquisition. While this was an option, a few big players dominated the market, so, realistically, a major acquisition in its home market was unlikely. Another route was expansion into other markets, and this it was pursuing. A third route was expanding overseas, and it is this route which concerns us here.

Recently, the markets of Eastern Europe have opened up considerably. Our case organisation saw this as an opportunity. In four or five countries in that part of the world, it acquired small businesses in its market sector, or, in some cases, developed those businesses from scratch.

### The brief

But this presented the organisation with a difficulty from a human resources point of view. It was completely new to the issue of recruiting and employing a non-British workforce. To start with, it sent experienced, specialist managers from Britain and recruited skilled and semi-skilled workers locally. But this was only a stopgap measure. For the longer term it needed to develop indigenous managers. In Britain, it had a well-designed and long-standing assessment centre for the selection of graduates who would become the senior managers of the future. This selection centre was regularly revised and checked for criterion validity. But could this centre be used for the assessment and selection of foreign graduates?

### The design

The answer was a firm 'no'. The exercises and tests were not appropriate for candidates from outside of Britain. It was not just the obvious differences, such as use of the English language or measurements in miles and gallons rather than kilo-metres and litres. It was the nature of the exercises themselves. Topics for group discussion, such as use of drugs by young people, have different meanings and importance for people from other cultures. Exercises dealing with the design of supermarkets are unlikely to work as well in countries less familiar with them. Tests not only have to have local norms and validation studies, but may not be as appropriate in countries where the whole concept of testing is unfamiliar and even disapproved of.

There was also the issue of whether the competencies were the same for gradu-ates being selected for a post within their own country and for a well-established, brand name company in its local market, compared to a start-up enterprise for a company which was small and unknown in its local market. Obviously, the compe-tencies were different. A competency analysis, similar to that described in the first two cases, was conducted. This revealed that being able to be independent of much day-to-day support was important. These managers would be big fish in small ponds, the opposite of new recruits in Britain. So they needed considerable confi-dence to back their own judgements and to act independently, when they were hundreds or thousands of miles from their head office in England. Similarly, the capacity for innovation and entrepreneurialism was much more important in Eastern Europe than it was in the home country. In effect, these managers would be in charge of their own business in a more fundamental way than they would be if running a store in Britain. Finally, a capacity for cultural awareness was important. The candidates would be groomed for the role of international manager. They would spend time in Britain, getting to know the business. They would spend time in their home country, learning about and, hopefully, expanding the business there. But this organisation had big expansion plans. It was considered likely that the European managers would often be transferred to foreign postings outside of their home market. So it was important for them to have not just the capacity to work in English, the international business language, but to be able to have some cultural sensitivity and awareness to be able to relate to, and work with, people from a wide range of different cultures. This was not a fundamental requirement for most of the British graduates being recruited in the organisation's home country.

So the whole assessment process was redesigned. Out went those stalwarts of the assessment centre, psychometric tests, since appropriate norms of sufficient sample size were not available. In addition, there were doubts about their accept-ability in cultures unfamiliar with such things.

Exercises which could assess the required competencies, such as cultural sensi-tivity, entrepreneurialism and independence, were designed. An exercise designed for the cultural issue was a group discussion, which involved candidates describing how they saw their own culture and the cultures represented in the group. Observers were trained to look for behaviours which indicated that a candidate was open-minded towards different views of his or her own culture, and aware of the ways in which his or her own culture could be viewed. Defensiveness about others' negative perceptions of one's own culture was a contraindication.

This approach is very much in the psychometric tradition: job analysis, followed by description of the job in competency terms, then design of exercises to assess that competency. What is different from the usual approach to the design of selection centres, though, is the cross-cultural dimension. This brings enormous challenges, as described in the case of Pharmco. Once again, the exercises were designed so that there was more than one route to success. How candidates tackled the exercise was much less important than the outcome.

Even here, though, the rational decision-making model was not adopted to the full. Candidates were expected to gain an 'acceptable' score on all competencies, but this was not always adhered to. Rules were 'broken' when a candidate was seen to perform exceptionally well in one or two exercises. There was no attempt to base decisions on a statistical or mathematical calculation of marks (sometimes called the actuarial method) whereby scores given for each competency are summed or weighted in some way. The decision was much more an intuitive feel (sometimes called the clinical approach) for what final grade a candidate should be given based on an impression of the suite of marks. In the early centres the assessors were a mix of expatriates and indigenous managers. The power and influence in contentious decisions about a certain candidate tended to lie with the expatriate. As the company became more established in the foreign market, and more and more expatriates became replaced with indigenous managers, the power shifted. So, even in this more traditional example, the rational decision-making model is found not to explain all purposes and outcomes.

## Questions

1. Compare the three cases according to how far they conform to the rational decision-making perspective (i.e. the psychometric tradition) or to the interactive action-oriented perspective described in this chapter.

2. On the surface, the case of Newsco illustrates the design of a fairly standard assessment for development workshop in the psychometric tradition. What evidence is there to suggest that assessment is not the sole purpose? What other purposes might the centre serve?

3. In what ways is Pharmco an example of an assessment centre, a development centre, or a mix of the two?

4. Why is it important to consider the national/cultural dimension in the design of centres?

# References to Chapter 2

Ackerman, B., Ross-Ackerman, S., Sawyer, J. and Henderson, D. (1974) *The Uncertain Research for Environmental Quality*, New York: Free Press.

Agor, W. (1986) 'The logic of intuition: How top executives make important decisions', *Organizational Dynamics*, Winter: 5–15.

Agor, W. (1989) *Intuition in organizations*, Newbury Park, CA: Sage.

Anderson, N. and Ostroff, C. (1997) 'Selection as socialization', in Anderson, N. and Herriot, P. (eds) *International Handbook of Selection and Assessment*, Chichester: Wiley.

Argyris, C. (1977) 'Organizational learning and management information systems', *Accounting, Organizations and Society*, 2: 113–123.

Arnold, J., Cooper, C. and Robertson, I. (1997) *Work Psychology: Understanding Human Behaviour in the Workplace*, London: Financial Times/Pitman Publishing.

Arvey, R.D. and Faley, R.H. (1992) *Fairness in Selecting Employees* (2nd edn), Reading, Mass: Addison-Wesley.

Bandura, A. (1977) 'Self-efficacy: Toward a unifying theory of behavioural change', *Psychological Review*, May: 191–215.

Barrick, M. and Mount, M. (1991) 'The big five personality dimensions and job performance: A meta-analysis', *Personnel Psychology*, 44: 1–26.

Batram, D. (2000) 'Internet recruitment and selection: kissing frogs to find princes', *International Journal of Selection and Assessment*, 8(4): 261–74.

Bazerman, M. (1994) *Judgement in managerial decision-making* (3rd edn), New York: Wiley.

Beach, L. (1990) *Image Theory: Decision Making in Personal and Organizational Contexts*, Chichester: John Wiley.

Behling, O. and Eckel, N. (1991) 'Making sense out of intuition', *Academy of Management Executives*, February: 46–54.

Boam, R. and Sparrow, P. (1992) *Designing and Achieving Competency: A Competency-Based Approach to Managing People and Organizations*, London: McGraw-Hill.

Boyle, S., Fullerton, J. and Wood, R. (1995) 'Do assessment/development centres use optimal evaluation procedures?', *International Journal of Selection and Assessment*, 3: 132–140.

Bray, D. and Grant, D. (1966) 'The assessment centre in the measurement of potential for business management', *Psychological Monographs*, 80(17) (Whole No. 625).

Brunsson, N. (1982) 'The irrationality of action and action rationality: decisions, ideologies and organizational actions', *Journal of Management Studies*, 19(1): 29–44.

Campbell, J.P. (1990) 'Modeling the performance prediction problem in industrial and organizational psychology', in Dunnette, M.D. and Hough, L.M. (eds) *Handbook of Industrial and Organizational Psychology* (2nd edn), Vol. 1, Palo Alto, CA: Consulting Psychologists Press.

Coe, T. (1992) *The Key to the Men's Club: Opening the Doors to Women in Management*, Corby: IM Foundation.

Cohen, M., March, J. and Olsen, J. (1971) 'A garbage can model of organizational choice', *Administrative Science Quarterly*, March: 1–25.

Cyert, R. and March, J. (1963) *A Behavioural Theory of the Firm*, Englewood Cliffs, NJ: Prentice Hall.

Day, D. and Silverman, S. (1989) 'Personality and job performance: Evidence of incremental validity', *Personnel Psychology*, 42: 25–36.

DiMilia, L., Smith, P. and Brown, D. (1994) 'Management selection in Australia: A comparison with British and French findings', *International Journal of Selection and Assessment*, 2: 80–90.

DiMilia, L. and Gorodecki, M. (1997) 'Some factors explaining the reliability of a structured interview at a work site', *International Journal of Selection and Assessment*, 5(4): 193–199.

Dipboye, R. (1992) 'Selection interviews: Process perspectives', Cincinnati, Oh.: South-Western.

Dipboye, R. (1997) 'Structured selection interviews: Why do they work? Why are they under-utilized?' in Anderson, N. and Herriot, P. (eds) *International Handbook of Selection and Assessment*, Chichester: John Wiley.

Eden, D. and Shani, A. (1982) 'Pygmalion goes to boot camp: Expectancy, leadership and trainee performance', *Journal of Applied Psychology*, April: 194–199.

Festinger, L. (1957) *A Theory of Cognitive Dissonance*, New York: Harper Row.

Fiske, S. and Taylor, S. (1991) *Social Cognition*, New York: McGraw Hill.

Fleenor, J. (1996) 'Constructs and developmental assessment centres: Further troubling empirical findings', *Journal of Business and Psychology*, 10: 319–333.

Gaugler, B., Rosenthal, D., Thornton, G. and Bentson, C. (1987) 'Meta-analysis of assessment centre validity', *Journal of Applied Psychology*, 72: 493–511.

Ghiselli, E. (1973) 'The validity of aptitude tests in personnel selection', *Personnel Psychology*, 26: 461–77.

Gist, M. (1987) 'Self-efficacy: implications for organizational behaviour and human resource management', *Academy of Management Review*, July: 472–485.

Heffcut, A.I. and Arthur, W. (1994) 'Hunter and Hunter (1984) revisited: interview validity and entry level jobs', *Journal of Applied Psychology*, 79: 184–190.

Hennessy, J., Mabey, B. and Warr, P. (1998) 'Assessment centre observation procedures: an experimental comparison of traditional, checklist and coding methods', *International Journal of Selection and Assessment*, 6(4): 222–31.

Hesketh, B. (1999) 'Introduction' to the *International Journal of Selection and Assessment* special issue on biodata: *International Journal of Selection and Assessment*, 7(2): 55–56.

Hofstede, G., (1984) *Culture's Consequences: International Differences in Work-Related Values*, Sage Publications: London.

Hough, L., Eaton, N., Dunnette, M., Kamp, J. and McCloy, R. (1990) 'Criterion-related validities of personality constructs and the effect of response distortion on those validities', *Journal of Applied Psychology*, 75: 581–585.

Hunter, J. and Hunter, R. (1984) 'Validity and utility of alternative predictors of job performance, *Psychological Bulletin*, 96: 72–98.

Industrial Relations Service (1997) 'The state of selection: an IRS survey', *Employee Development Bulletin*, 85: 8–18.

Janis, I. (1972) *Victims of Groupthink*, Boston, Mass: Houghton Mifflin.

Janz, T. (1989) 'The patterned behaviour description interview: the best prophet of the future is the past', in Eder, R.D. and Ferris, G.R. (eds) *The Employment Interview: Theory and Practice*, London: Sage.

Joyce, L., Thayer, P. and Pond, S. (1994) 'Managerial functions: An alternative to traditional assessment centre dimensions?', *Personnel Psychology*, 47: 109–121.

Kauffman, J., Jex, S., Love, K. and Libkuman, T. (1993) 'The construct validity of assessment centre performance dimensions', *International Journal of Selection and Assessment*, 1: 213–23.

Keenan, T. (1995) 'Graduate recruitment in Britain: A survey of selection methods used by organizations', *Journal of Organizational Behaviour*, 16: 303–17.

Landis, R., Fogli, L. and Goldberg, E. (1998) 'Future-oriented job analysis: A description of the process and its organizational implications', *International Journal of Selection and Assessment*, 6(3): 192–97.

Landy, F., Shankster-Cawley, L. and Moran, S. (1995) 'Advancing personnel selection and placement methods', in Howard, A. (ed.) *The Changing Nature of Work*, San Francisco, CA: Jossey-Bass.

Lievens, F. (1998) 'Factors which improve the construct validity of Assessment Centres: A review', *International Journal of Selection and Assessment*, 6(3): 141–152.

Lind, E. and Tyler, T. (1988) *The Social Psychology of Procedural Justice*, New York: Plenum Press.

Lindblom, C.E. (1959) 'The science of "muddling through"', *Public Administration Review*, 19: 79–88.

Macan, T.H., Avedon, M.J., Paese, M. and Smith, D.E. (1994) 'The effects of applicants' reactions to cognitive ability tests and an assessment centre', *Personnel Psychology*, 47(4): 715–38.

Mael, F. (1991) 'A conceptual rationale for the domain and attributes of biodata items', *Personnel Psychology*, 44: 763–92.

March, J. and Olsen, J. (1976) *Ambiguity and Choice in Organizations*, Bergen: Universitetsforlaget.

Matthews, B. and Redman, T. (1998) 'Managerial recruitment advertisements – Just how market-orientated are they?', *International Journal of Selection and Assessment*, 6(4): 240–48.

Mayfield, E.C. (1964) 'The selection interview: A re-evaluation of published research', *Personnel Psychology*, 17: 239–60.

McCredie, H. and Shackleton, V.J. (1994) 'The development and interim validation of a dimensions-based senior management assessment centre', *Human Resources Management Journal*, 5(1): 91–101.

McDaniel, M.A., Whetzel, D.L., Schmidt, F.L. and Maurer, S.D. (1994) 'The validity of the employment interviews: a comprehensive review and meta-analysis', *Journal of Applied Psychology*, 79: 599–616.

Merrick, N. (1997) 'Big thaw shows up on recruitment market', *People Management*, 3(2): 10–11.

Mumford, M. and Stokes, G. (1992) 'Developmental determinants of individual action: Theory and practice in applying background measures', in Dunnette, M. & Hough, L. (eds) *Handbook of Industrial and Organizational Psychology*, 2nd edn, Vol. 3, 61–138), Palo Alto, Ca: Consulting Psychologists Press.

Newell, S. and Shackleton, V. (1993) 'The use (and abuse) of psychometric tests in British industry and commerce', *Human Resource Management Journal*, 4(1): 14–23.

Nisbett, R. and Ross, L. (1980) *Human Inference*, Englewood Cliffs, NJ: Prentice-Hall.

Pfeffer, J. (1981) *Power in organisations*, Marshfield, Mass: Pitman Publishing.

Redmond, S. (1989) *How to Recruit Good Managers*, London: Kogan Page.

Rees, C. (1996) 'Psychometrics: Topical misunderstandings amongst test users', *International Journal of Selection and Assessment*, 4(1): 44–48.

Robertson, I. and Kinder, A. (1993) 'Personality and job competences: The criterion-related validity of some personality variables', *Journal of Occupational and Organizational Psychology*, 66: 225–44.

Rosenfeld, P., Giacalone, R.A. and Riordan, C.A. (1995) *Impression Management in Organizations*, London: Routledge.

Salgado, J. (1996) 'Personality and job competences: a comment on Robertson and Kinder's (1993) study', *Journal of Occupational and Organizational Psychology*, 69: 373–75.

Schmitt, N., Gooding, R., Noe, R. and Kirsch, M. (1984) 'Meta-analyses of validity studies published between 1964 and 1982, and the investigation of study characteristics', *Personnel Psychology*, 37: 407–22.

Schneider, B. and Konz, A. (1989) 'Strategic job analysis', *Human Resource Management*, 28: 51–63.

Shackleton, V. and Newell, S. (1991) 'Management selection: a comparative survey of methods used in top British and French companies', *Journal of Occupational Psychology*, 64: 23–26.

Shackleton, V. and Newell, S. (1994) 'European selection methods: a comparison of five countries', *International Journal of Selection and Assessment*, 2: 91–102.

Simon, H. (1960) *The New Science of Management Decision*, New York: Harper and Row.

Singer, M. (1993) *Fairness in Personnel Selection*, Aldershot: Avebury.

Sparrow, P. and Bognanno, M. (1993) 'Competency requirement forecasting: issues for international selection and assessment', *International Journal of Selection and Assessment*, 1(1): 50–58.

Stokes, G., Hogan, J. and Snell, A. (1993) 'Comparability of incumbent and applicant samples for the development of biodata keys: the influence of social desirability', *Personnel Psychology*, 46: 739–62.

**The Management of Human Resources**

Stricker, L. and Rock, D. (1998) 'Assessing leadership potential with a biographical measure of personality traits', *International Journal of Selection and Assessment*, 6(3): 164–184.

Sundvik, L. and Lindeman, M. (1998) 'Performance rating accuracy: convergence between supervisor assessment and sales productivity', *International Journal of Selection and Assessment*, 6(1): 9–15.

Thornton, G. (1992) *Assessment Centres in Human Resource Management*, Reading, Mass: Addison Wesley.

Trompenaars, F. (1993) *Riding the Waves of Culture: Understanding Cultural Diversity in Business*, Nicholas Brealey Publishing: London.

Ulrich, L. and Trumbo, D. (1965) 'The selection interview since 1949', *Psychological Bulletin*, 53: 100–116.

Vaughan, D. (1996) *The Challenger Launch Decision: Risky Technology, Culture, and Deviance at NASA*, Chicago, Il: University of Chicago Press.

Vaughan, D. (1997) 'The trickle-down effect: policy decisions, risky work and the Challenger tragedy', *California Management Review*, 39(2): 80–102.

Weick, K.E. (1990)'Technology as equivoque: sensemaking in new technologies', in Goodman, P.S., Sproull, L.S. and Associates, *Technology and Organisations*, Oxford: Jossey-Bass.

Zedeck, S. (1986) 'A process analysis of the assessment centre method', in Shaw, B. and Cummings, L. (eds) *Research in Organizational Behaviour*, 8: 259–96, Greenwich, CT: JAI Press.

# Human resource development: the organisation and the national framework

*Len Holden*

**OBJECTIVES**

● To examine the strategic nature of HRD and its relationship to the individual and to organisational development.

● To outline and explain a human resource development plan including the assessment of training needs, an outline of training methods, and the processes of monitoring and evaluating the plan.

● To examine the concepts of the learning organisation and knowledge management.

● To examine vocational education and training in the leading industrial nations, with an in-depth investigation of the training systems of Germany, Japan and France.

● To examine the implications of these international comparisons for the UK.

● To examine the national framework for vocational education and training in the UK.

● To outline possible future policy developments in vocational education and training.

● To identify some controversial issues in the field of vocational education and training.

## INTRODUCTION

As we have seen from the previous chapter on employee development, it is difficult to arrive at a consensus definition of terms such as 'development', 'education' and 'training' because of the varied ways in which they are translated into work and life situations.

The Manpower Services Commission, set up by the 1973 Employment and Training Act but replaced in 1988, defined training as

> a planned process to modify attitude, knowledge or skill behaviour through learning experience to achieve effective performance in an activity or range of activities. Its purpose, in the work situation, is to develop the abilities of the individual and to satisfy the current and future needs of the organisation. (Manpower Services Commission, 1981)

This definition is no longer adequate or wide enough in a world where organisations are in a constant state of transformation in a turbulent and rapidly changing economic environment. Training was seen as a series of mechanistic interventions through which trainers poured knowledge into an employee's head, with the expectation of automatic improvement in individual and organisational performance.

Such a concept is too narrow for the modern organisation. First, the skills and knowledge that employees need are rapidly changing, and what is relevant now may not be relevant in the future. Second, there is an increasing need for employees to 'own' their learning. This means being aware of their own needs for both the organisation's requirements and their own long-term development. In other words, individuals also need to be aware of their own learning strategies. Third, increasing competition is forcing organisations to improve the quality of the products and services they provide, and this requires a closer relationship with the customer, empowerment of employees, and improved communication for exchanging knowledge and skills. Some commentators have suggested that this need to constantly improve knowledge and skill must lead to an environment where learning and sharing knowledge are at the centre of the organisation's operation – what has come to be called the *learning organisation* or the *knowledge-based organisation* (Senge, 1990; Nonaka, 1991; Pedler *et al.*, 1997; Dixon, 2000).

However, even in a learning environment there may be a conflict between developing the skills of employees and the future needs of the organisation. For example, many organisations prefer to train employees in firm-specific skills rather than transferable skills, and thus these two objectives may prove mutually exclusive or, at best, only partly achievable. A survey in the early 1990s concluded:

> Much of the training reported was for organisational rather than individual development, suggesting that many employees would not regard the training they receive as training at all, since it neither imparts transferable skills nor contributes to personal and educational development.
>
> (Rainbird and Maguire, 1993)

There is little to suggest that this situation has changed radically at the start of the new millennium. The loss of employees in whom considerable sums have been invested in training and development influences some employers to concentrate on training in areas that are specific to their organisation, while the 'poacher' organisations use money as an attractor and invest little or nothing in training their employees.

Other commentators believe that the idea of transferable skills is used far too widely, and that many processes are particular to organisations and their products and services. Even in a country such as Japan, whose training systems are much admired, the programmes involve a considerable proportion of training for firm-specific skills (Dore and Sako, 1989).

## THE NEED FOR TRAINING

Until the 1980s, training and development in British organisations were inadequate compared with some other industrialised countries. This was confirmed by a number of surveys (Coopers & Lybrand, 1985; Industrial Society, 1985; Mangham and Silver, 1986; Constable and McCormick, 1987; Handy, 1987), which collectively had a considerable impact on the nation's consciousness. This added to an increasing awareness of the importance of change and the key role that training had played in helping that process.

325

Encouragingly, surveys in the early 1990s revealed that British companies seemed to be taking training more seriously (Saggers, 1994). The Price Waterhouse Cranfield Project Surveys indicate that training and staff development is the leading issue for most personnel departments across Europe, including the UK (Brewster and Hegewisch, 1993).

This growing awareness of the importance of training over the past decade was also supported by reports that employers were spending more in aggregate terms on training activities (Training Agency, 1989). However, the measurement of training expenditure is still controversial, and those figures that do exist are open to question, interpretation and political manipulation (Finegold, 1991; Ryan, 1991).

Thus there seems to be a gap between the perceived importance of training and the willingness to do something about it. The view strongly persists in the commercial and industrial culture of the UK that training is a 'cost' and not an 'investment.'

## HRD and human resource management

Recognition of the importance of human resource development (HRD) in recent years has been heavily influenced by the intensification of overseas competition and the relative success of economies such as Japan, Germany and Sweden, where investment in employee development is emphasised. Technological developments and organisational change have gradually led some employers to realise that success relies on the skills and abilities of their employees, and this means considerable and continuous investment in training and development.

This has also been underscored by the rise in human resource management, with its emphasis on the importance of people and the skills they possess in enhancing organisational efficiency. Such HRM concepts as 'commitment' to the company and the growth in the 'quality' movement have led senior management teams to realise the increased importance of training, employee development and long-term education. There has also been more recognition of the need to complement the qualities of employees with the needs of the organisation. Such concepts require not only careful planning but also a greater emphasis on employee development. Indeed, some commentators have seen this aspect of HRM as so important that they see HRD as an equally important discipline in its own right (Hall, 1984; Nadler, 1984).

In HRM companies such as Hewlett-Packard, Xerox, IBM, Caterpillar and The Body Shop, HRD is seen as a major key to the success of the organisation, and is emphasised at all levels. HRD has also served as an agent for change or even survival in organisations such as Harley Davidson and Euro-Disney.

HRD programmes are continuous, and shaped to fit the culture changes in the organisation in relation to the needs of the individual. In this way training and HRD become tools for effecting change, and the policy ramifications can be wide ranging and strategic. As a result, HRD takes on a variety of forms and covers a multitude of subjects.

HRD is just one of the instruments at the disposal of the HR department and the organisation in creating HR strategy, and as Keep (1989) reminds us:

> The interrelationship between training and recruitment strategies is usually a very close one, not the least because if an organisation wishes to improve the skills of its workforce, it has the choice of either training its existing employees or recruiting pre-skilled labour that has been trained elsewhere.

326

## Employee development needs

As noted in the previous chapter, HRD has significance for employees in fulfilling their own needs. One problem is that individuals are often unaware of those needs. It is important to help them towards some awareness, especially in terms of the emphasis on self-development, another important issue raised in the previous chapter.

Sadly, the further down the organisational ladder one descends the less money is spent on training. Thus managers and professionals generally receive more financial support for training than clerical and manual workers do (Price Waterhouse Cranfield Project, 1990; Brewster, 1999: 16). Given the need to encourage individuals to recognise their training needs and, more importantly, to seek ways to improve their knowledge and skills to advance their career prospects, the advantage seems to lie with individuals further up the organisational hierarchy.

The divide between professional and non-professional workers is increasing with the growing use of flexible work patterns, which emphasise core and periphery workers engaged on part-time or restricted contracts (see Chapter 3 and elsewhere). As a result of these changes, management is less likely to be committed to training periphery workers, and this is reflected in the time and money devoted to training and developing these groups (Syrett and Lammiman, 1994).

Another issue that further emphasises the status divide is that non-professional and non-managerial employees are less aware of the need for training and, more importantly, less able to do something about it, which places considerable barriers in the way of improving their working life prospects. Professionals are imbued with the value of education and self-development, which is often acquired in the routes to, and in, higher education. This need for continual self-development is becoming increasingly important throughout the working life of most professionals, who continue to embark on courses of varying kinds into their 40s and 50s.

Importantly, this process also helps them to cope with change. Awareness of the power of education and training leads to self-activation in meeting career changes and organisational change. By contrast, non-professional workers often rely heavily on the services of external agencies to help them cope with redundancy resulting from skills obsolescence. In the UK in the past agencies such as Employment Training have been less than adequate in dealing with the needs of the long-term unemployed and those wishing to retrain for employment that needs new skills, such as a redundant coalminer seeking to learn computer skills. Most importantly, once new skills are acquired there must be opportunities to practise them. This is difficult in areas undergoing structural change or industrial decay, such as mining and shipbuilding areas. This subject will be explored more fully later in the chapter.

## CREATING A HUMAN RESOURCE DEVELOPMENT PLAN

There are no set procedures that organisations should follow in creating a human resource development plan, but the eight points listed in Table 8.1 should act as guidance. This can also be summed up diagrammatically as in Figure 8.1.

This has strong elements of the systems approach to training (SAT), but the mechanistic overtones of SAT should be moderated by recognising the human needs of employees and the changes (sometimes rapid) that can affect organisations. Therefore a more flexible or 'organic' approach is recommended: training schemes that are patently

327

### Table 8.1  A human resource development plan

- Discern the training and development requirements from the organisational strategy and business objectives
- Analyse the training requirements for effective work performance in organisational fuctions and jobs
- Analyse the existing qualities and training needs of current employees
- Devise an HRD plan that fills the gap between organisational requirements and the current skills and knowledge of employees
- Decide on the apropriate training and development methods to be used for individuals and groups
- Decide who is to have responsibility for the plan and its various parts
- Implement the plan, and monitor and evaluate its progress
- Amend the HRD plan in the light of monitoring/evaluation and changes in business strategy

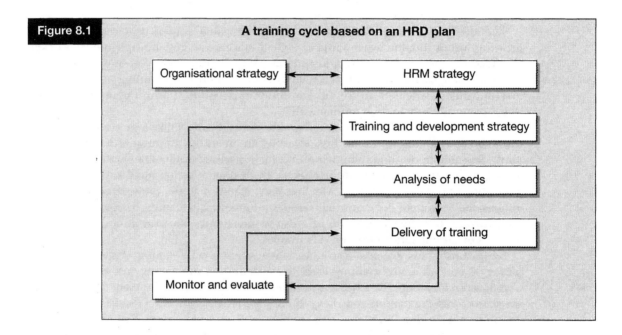

**Figure 8.1**  A training cycle based on an HRD plan

not working, perhaps because of changes in personnel, occupations, job specifications, personal relationships, business plans or economic performance, should be abandoned, or adapted to accommodate the change.

## Analysing training needs

The first vital step in HRD is 'the identification of needed skills and active management of employees learning for their long-range future in relation to explicit corporate and business strategies' (Hall, 1984).

For training to be effective it is necessary to discern not only the training needs of the individual and the group, but also how their needs fit the overall organisational objectives. As we have already suggested, this may be more difficult to achieve than it appears.

Researchers and commentators doubt whether managerial hierarchies recognise the importance of these relationships in training initiatives or, if they do, doubt whether they have the will or the ability to carry them out. As Hall (1984) comments:

328

Many organisations invest considerable resources in training and development but never really examine how training and development can most effectively promote organisational objectives, or how developmental activities should be altered in the light of business plans.

Bernhard and Ingolis (1988), in studying training and its strategic implementation in US companies, believe that a considerable amount of money is 'thrown away' mainly because fundamental issues such as analysis of training needs in relation to the short- and long-term business plans have not been addressed.

A prominent French bank witnessed less than beneficial results after a huge investment in an extensive training scheme. This was seen to be primarily a consequence of the failure to analyse training needs within the organisation (Holden and Livian, 1992). Investors in People (IIP) schemes have been set up by numerous organisations in the UK in an attempt to align training needs to organisational strategy. However, as we shall see on examining IIP in greater depth later in this chapter, the results have been variable.

An integral part of analysing training needs is recognising what will 'fit' the company culture, as well as the company strategy and objectives. The training scheme that fits one company may not fit another, and these company differences can only be ignored at great cost. This is part and parcel of the organic approach to HRD, and a view shared by those organisations that claim to be (or on their way to being) learning organisations.

The training and development needs of the individual must be reconciled with those of the organisation. Conflicts here need to be resolved, for the benefit of both. Unfortunately, this may be easier to achieve for professional and managerial employees than for the workforce lower down the organisation. For example, many companies recognise the advantages of having managers with an MBA degree or a Diploma in Management Studies, a situation mutually beneficial to the individual and the organisation. Professionals such as accountants and lawyers have the advantage of transferable knowledge and expertise. But a shopfloor worker in a production company is much more likely to be trained in firm-specific skills that cannot be easily transferred to other organisational contexts.

### For the job

#### Job description

Given the recent popularity of flexible work practices in many organisations, criticism has been levelled at job descriptions that are too highly structured. Critics claim that this narrows too strictly the perceived responsibilities of the employee, and can be counterproductive, by creating protectionist attitudes in employees towards their jobs, which could lead to demarcation disputes and other problems related to work roles.

Nevertheless, employees are usually hired to take a specific responsibility within the organisation (whether that be accountant, receptionist or cleaner), but they may have to take on other responsibilities in times of emergency, to enhance organisational efficiency. Therefore job descriptions are necessary in order to give employees a sense of purpose, and to enable their immediate superiors to appraise their performance, but a culture must prevail that enables employees to deal with problems that may be outside their immediate work domain.

#### Job analysis

Job analysis is a more sophisticated method of evaluating job functions, and is often used to discern the levels of skill necessary to do a job, primarily for the purpose of creating pay structures. Many modern organisations have rejected such techniques, as one executive of IKEA states: 'We reward individuals and not the job' (Pickard, 1992).

329

However, the information gleaned from such procedures can be useful in analysing the skill needs and requirement of jobs.

### Interview with jobholders

This is one of the most commonly used methods: a manager, supervisor or member of the personnel department interviews the current jobholder about the duties and functions of the job. The interview can be structured, in the sense of having a series of questions framed to cover all aspects of the job.

### Interview with managers and supervisors

Alternatively, a personnel manager or senior manager can interview the immediate supervisors of the job. Often descriptions arising are compared with the interview responses of the jobholder to act as a double check for discrepancies or elements missed by either party.

### Performance objectives

The aim of increased quality, for example, will require performance objectives to be laid down. In doing so, assessment must take place as to whether current employees need training to reach these objectives. This has become increasingly popular in organisations that have adopted performance management programmes or *high-performance work systems* as they are known in the USA.

### Analysis of competences

An analysis of competence requirements could be useful to match 'NVQ (National Vocational Qualification) or MCI (Management Charter Initiative) standards which are considered relevant to the various jobs involved. These can be compared with assessments of the current general levels of employee skills and abilities' (Fowler, 1991).

## For the individual

Concomitant with an analysis of organisational needs is the analysis of the training needs of current employees. Much information about employees can be gleaned from organisational records, including original application forms and other databases.

### Characteristics of people required (person specification)

In the effort to identify skills and competence requirements, the characteristics of the people required for the job are often forgotten. This will to some extent emerge in the competences analysis. For example, sales personnel would need an ability to deal with people, and this would undoubtedly be identified as an essential part of the job; but in other occupations and jobs, personal characteristics are often forgotten in the desire to isolate purely functional job requirements.

### Personal profiles

Personal profile records are increasingly used in organisations, and useful for training needs analysis. They also include information on employees' career aspirations, which may well be of significance in creating training initiatives.

### Appraisal

Appraisal has come in for much criticism recently, but a good appraisal can reveal much about the strengths and weaknesses of individuals in terms of their performance. Indications of areas where training and development programmes could improve perfor-

330

mance are vital to both the individual and the organisation. Indeed the appraisal and variations of it are now used in many organisations as a central part of the learning organisation concept, whereby individuals can negotiate their training needs with their line manager. Some organisations have allocated training budgets for individuals to use for their own development in negotiation with their line managers. In this way an employee gains a sense of ownership of their development, with positive results for the organisation.

### Assessment centre techniques

Though rather elaborate and expensive, assessment centres are the most thorough way of analysing individual strengths and weaknesses. Using a variety of methods including in-depth interviews and re-interviews, psychometric tests, team performance simulation exercises and other techniques, a detailed profile of employees can be constructed, which is useful for analysing training needs. Caution must be counselled, however, in terms of cost-effectiveness and an unrealistic expectation that infallible results are produced (Dulewicz, 1991).

### Global review and training audits

The most wide-ranging method of training needs analysis is a global review, or more modestly a training audit. These are usually undertaken when far-reaching changes are planned within an organisation. Survey questionnaires and in-depth interviews are often used, together with all, or combinations of, the approaches previously mentioned.

### Relating resources to the training objective

An across-the-board use of all these methods could be too expensive in terms of both time and money. Reid *et al.* (1992) point out that the global review could end up producing large amounts of paperwork, unjustified by the returns gained. It is therefore essential to assess the cost-effectiveness of training needs analysis in relation to the outcomes and returns expected.

Hirsch and Reilly (1998) warn that 'organisational structures and employee attitudes have an impact. Simply having appropriately skilled individuals does not automatically yield high performance' (p. 40). They give the example of the UK Post Office, where managers have learned that thinking through the skill implications of organisational change early enough gives them time to change the composition of the workforce. Hirsch and Reilly also stress that it may 'be important to design jobs and technology around the skills of the workforce, rather than to assume that the workforce will adjust to the new situation'.

## Training methods

A careful use of training methods can be a very cost-effective investment in the sense of using the appropriate method for the needs of a person or group. However, many commentators have mentioned that organisations often use inappropriate methods, which can be both costly and time wasting and bring very little improvement in the performance of the employee. Storey (1991), in a comparative analysis of training in British and Japanese organisations, found that some British training is wasted as it is not embedded in the organisation as is the Japanese. British organisations also suffered from the 'bandwagon effect' and what he calls 'programmitis' – a constant series of newly launched programmes and initiatives which led to chopping and changing rather than consistently coherent long-term training initiatives.

331

In general, training can be divided into *on-the-job* and *off-the-job* methods. There is a place for both types, and each can be effective at meeting certain training requirements.

## On-the-job training

On-the-job training (OJT) is probably the most common approach to training. It can range from relatively unsophisticated 'observe and copy' methods to highly structured courses built into workshop or office practice. Cannell (1997) defines OJT as

> training that is planned and structured that takes place mainly at the normal workstation of the trainee – although some instruction may be provided in a special training area on site – and where a manager, supervisor, trainer or peer colleague spends significant time with a trainee to teach a set of skills that have been specified in advance. It also includes a period of instruction where there may be little or no useful output in terms of productivity. (p.28)

### *'Sitting by Nellie' and learning by doing*

These traditional methods are still very popular ways of teaching new skills and methods to employees, and they can be very effective. However, there are many acknowledged weaknesses that still persist in many organisational practices. Some people are better at it than others, and 'Nellie' may not be trained herself in the methods of transmitting knowledge and skills. There is often a lack of structure and design in the training given, which leads to the passing-on of bad or even dangerous working practices (Cannell, 1997).

Far more successful is to use a senior or experienced worker who has been trained in instruction or training methods and whose teaching skills are coordinated with a developed programme linked to off-the-job courses. Self-proclaimed learning organisations such as Analog Devices make very effective use of OJT, and claim that people learn and retain more of the training by performing the actual process at the place of work.

### *Mentoring*

This is another version of the system, in which a senior or experienced employee takes charge of the training and development of a new employee. This suggests a much closer association than master–apprentice, and elements of a father–son or mother–daughter relationship can exist, whereby the mentor acts as an adviser and protector to the trainee. A study by Brockbank and Beech (1999) of mentors in the health sector reveals that overemphasis on the technical side of the mentoring process and an underestimation of the emotional side can have negative results. They recommend that appropriate support should be provided for mentors themselves. This dual role of providing professional and emotional support may clash, and it might be advisable for the two roles to be performed by different people.

### *Shadowing and job rotation*

*Shadowing* is another oft-practised on-the-job training method. It usually aims to give trainee managers a 'feel' for the organisation by providing experience of working in different departments. It is an old technique, and has been criticised not so much for the concept itself as for the way it is often implemented. Trainees may feel it is time wasting, and people in the various departments in which they are temporarily working must also feel committed to and involved in the training if it is to work. Trainees are often not warmly welcomed, and are seen by supervisors and workers in the department as obstacles to the daily routines. However, if well structured, and planned with the cooperation of all departmental supervisors, this method can be a worthwhile learning experience.

332

Another version of training by switching roles is *job rotation*, which became popular in the 1970s to help relieve boredom and thereby raise the productivity of shopfloor workers. If appropriately implemented, it can be an excellent learning experience for workers, and it fits suitably with HRM concepts of teamworking and empowerment, whereby people are encouraged to take greater responsibility for their work and that of the team. On the negative side there have been criticisms that not enough structured training is given to enable workers to do these jobs well, and that it is also bound up with functional flexibility initiatives, often criticised for their deskilling and exploitative propensities.

## Off-the-job training

Courses and other types of 'off-the-job' training have come in for much criticism, and are often viewed by both recipients and fellow employees as a waste of time and money. Yet off-the-job training is sometimes necessary to get people away from the hustle and bustle of the work environment. This enables the trainee to study theoretical information or be exposed to new and innovative ideas. The problem arises when those ideas or learning experiences do not appear to relate to the work situation. As we have seen from the research of Storey (1991), the predilection for sending employees on courses that do not appear to have much relevance to the employee or the job ('programmitis') only enhances the negative view of this type of training.

### Perceptions of courses

Being sent on a course can be interpreted by the trainee as a sign of official approval or disapproval. For example, an approval sign would be that you are considered suitable for promotion, and the course is part of the training required for that position. A negative perception could be that the employee feels that they are being sent on a course because they are not very efficient in their job. Sending the correct messages to the trainees is also an important aspect of training initiatives.

## A variety of methods

It is impossible to cover in depth in this book all the rich variety of approaches to training. Many of these the reader will have experienced before – sometimes with negative consequences. It is best to bear in mind that there may be nothing wrong with the methods, but that they may be utilised ineffectively by the trainer or the learner. In other words, the key is to make the appropriate match between the training requirements of the employee and the training methods available.

## Active and passive learning

Much traditional training is a one-way learning process, in which the student is a passive learner receiving information from a lecturer, tutor or instructor. This can be an efficient way of imparting information, but all education theorists agree that the best form of learning is one in which the student is actively involved in the learning process.

### Interactive learning methods

There are a wide variety of interactive learning techniques, some of them adaptations of one-way approaches:

- workshops;
- case studies;

333

- role play;
- simulations;
- interactive computer learning packages;
- video and audio tapes (interactively used);
- the Internet (web sites), intranet (organisational systems);
- problem solving.

For a fuller explanation of these techniques and others see Harrison (1997) and Barrington and Reid (1999).

## Responsibility for and delivery of training

It is important to consider who is to be responsible for training, and who will deliver training.

### Training departments

From the 1950s and (particularly) the 1960s, the responsibility for and delivery of training in many large organisations rested very much with specialist departments. By the 1980s and 1990s, however, training departments had come in for considerable criticism. They were accused of:

- being too rigid to respond to the changing needs of the organisation;
- being too much of an administrative expense;
- having lost contact with the changing skills needed on the shopfloor or at the place of work;
- being self-serving and bureaucratic;
- providing off-the-job training at their various centres that did not match up to 'on-the-job' needs;
- providing training that was too theoretical and not sufficiently practically based;
- not providing training and development that met individual needs – courses were too class/group based.

Despite these criticisms, training departments remain important in many organisations because they have personnel who have specialised knowledge and skills in the provision of training. As HRD becomes more important in the organisation the role of providers is becoming increasingly pivotal as facilitators of learning and the exchange of information and knowledge. The concepts of the learning organisation and the knowledge-based organisation place learning and HRD at the very heart of the organisation. HRD departments also act as internal consultants giving support to line managers alongside the HR department.

### Training consultancies

Over the last decade the number of consultancies, many of them specialising in training, has burgeoned into an industry. While there are many excellent consultancies, there are also the inevitable 'cowboy' operations, which sometimes have unqualified, inexperienced and untrained staff, and at present there is no regulation to stop such operations from being set up. Some client companies and organisations have spent considerable sums on ineffective programmes, or to be told things they already knew. Of course, it is in the interest of the consultancy to push sometimes costly and unwarranted programmes on to unsuspecting clients, in order to drum up business.

334

It would be naive to believe that consultants are brought into organisations only to provide training programmes. They are also used to resolve political conflicts, to add kudos and status, to justify having larger budgets, to support political manoeuvring, and for other questionable reasons.

However, used carefully, reputable consultancies can provide invaluable specialist services and expertise that are often not available within client organisations, particularly small and medium-sized ones.

### Training and the line manager

In order to counteract the perceived inflexibilities of training and personnel departments, there has been a notable trend to devolve many functions to line managers, including training policy. The justification is usually couched in terms of meeting the needs of people where it matters – at workplace level. Part of the line manager's brief is to discern the training needs of individuals in their department, and to suggest suitable training for them, usually in consultation with the personnel or training department. Training budgets have increasingly been devolved to line managers, in the belief that funding can be spent most effectively at the point where needs have been identified.

This can be very effective, because the assessment and delivery of training is more closely attuned to people in their working environment, but its efficacy depends very much on how it is carried out.

Research by the Price Waterhouse Cranfield Project team shows that there are many problems in splitting responsibilities between line managers and the personnel department:

> First there is often a dichotomy between the decentralised role and increasing responsibility of line managers, and the centralised role of the personnel/human resource function which must act as an interpreter of organisation-wide information and as a creator of human resource strategies. Secondly, the desire to empower the line manager may lead to sacrifices by the central personnel function in ensuring the relevant information is being relayed back.　　(Holden and Livian, 1992)

For example, 41% of personnel departments in the UK survey did not know how much money was spent on training, and 38% did not know the average number of training days allocated per person in the organisation (Holden, 1991; Holden and Livian, 1992).

## Evaluation and monitoring of training

The penultimate stage in the training strategy is the evaluation and monitoring of training. It is one of the most important but often the most neglected parts of the training process.

This stage can be viewed as both simple and complicated. It is simple in that monitoring consists in gleaning information from the trainees and then amending the courses and programmes in the light of these comments. But it is also complex because there are other stakeholders in the process as well as the trainees: the designers of the courses, the trainers, and the sponsors. Each have their own purposes, aims and objectives, and these must be clearly identified before evaluation can proceed (Easterby-Smith and Mackness, 1992).

Another problem is that, while it is relatively easy to evaluate a formal off-the-job course, much on-the-job training often takes place in an informal way, which is usually subjective and open to interpretation (Holden, 1991).

Methods of evaluation include the following:

- *Questionnaires* (feedback forms) or 'happiness sheets' are a common way of eliciting trainees' responses to courses and programmes.

335

- *Tests or examinations* are common on formal courses that provide a certificate, such as a diploma in word-processing skills, and end-of-course tests can be provided after short courses to check the progress of trainees.
- *Projects* are initially seen as learning methods, but they can also provide valuable information for instructors.
- *Structured exercises and case studies* are opportunities to apply learned skills and techniques under the observation of tutors and evaluators.
- It is important to have the opinions of those who deliver the training. *Tutor reports* give a valuable assessment from a different perspective.
- *Interviews of trainees* after the course or instruction period can be informal or formal, individual or group, or by telephone.
- *Observation* of courses and training by those devising training strategies in the training department is very useful, and information from these observations can be compared with trainee responses.
- *Participation and discussion* during training must be facilitated by people who are adept at interpreting responses, as this can be highly subjective.
- Over the past decade *appraisal* has become an increasingly important method of evaluation. It has the advantage that the line manager and trainee can mutually assess the training undergone in terms of performance and employee development.

A combination of these approaches is advisable. It is also wise to receive feedback from the trainees and the tutors or trainers, and others involved in the assessment process.

## Amending the HRD plan

While many organisations carry out excellent training programmes, the final and perhaps most vital stage is often ignored. As Easterby-Smith and Mackness (1992) wryly state:

> Training evaluation is commonly seen as a feedback loop, starting with course objectives and ending by collecting end-of-course reactions which are then generally filed away and not acted on.

Adjustments can be carried out after a small course to tighten up its effective operation, or when a training strategy cycle has been completed after six months or a year. At the end of such a phase it is essential to see whether training has effectively met the business objectives. Usually adaptations and changes are necessary, and the evaluation and monitoring process is invaluable in ensuring that these are appropriate.

### Comment

In reading this section on training strategy two points need to be borne in mind:

- These training prescriptions can appear too simplistic, particularly in a textbook that has limited space to give to this complicated subject. The reality of creating training strategies is much more complex, and frustration and failure to achieve objectives are common, even in organisations that take such approaches seriously.
- There is limited evidence of a positive link between training and organisational efficiency and profitability, although there is a widespread belief that this is the case.

336

# THE LEARNING ORGANISATION

The approach described above in the HRD strategy has been rejected by a number of organisations as far too mechanistic, controlling and inefficient. Writers such as Senge (1990) and Pedler *et al.* (1997) have put forward the concept of the *learning organisation,* in which learning and HRD are central functions of the organisation. In such an organisation the learning process is so embedded that learning and development become subconscious acts through which the business of the organisation operates. In this way its adherents claim that HRD becomes automatically strategic.

## What is a learning organisation?

A clear definition of the learning organisation is elusive. Pedler *et al.* (1997) suggest that it is a vision of what might be possible when organisations go beyond merely training individuals towards developing learning at the whole organisation level. Their definition states:

> A Learning Company is an organisation that facilitates the learning of all its members and consciously transforms itself and its context. (p. 3)

Dixon (1994) added to the concept, suggesting that organisational learning, a key characteristic of a learning company, can be defined as

> the intentional use of learning processes at the individual, group and system level to continuously transform the organisation in a direction that is increasingly satisfying to its stakeholders.

Senge (1990) states that the basic meaning of the learning organisation is:

> an organisation that is continually expanding its capacity to create its future. For such an organisation it is not enough to merely survive . . . for a learning organisation 'adaptive learning' must be joined by 'generative learning', learning that enhances our capacity to create. (p.14)

## Why the need for the learning organisation?

The concept has gained popularity in recent years because of the turbulent and increasingly competitive business environment. The impact of new technology and changing organisational forms that cater for customer needs mean dealing with continual change. This has led to what learning organisation (LO) adherents feel is *not* an add-on HRD system that is a lowly function driven by corporate strategy, but one that is central to the strategy of the organisation. The ability to respond swiftly to product and market developments is crucial. There has also been an increasing recognition of the importance of utilising not just the physical abilities of employees but also their mental powers. Senior managers are becoming aware that if their people are their greatest resource, they are also the source of any longer-term competitive advantage. This realisation has led to increased competition for skilled, flexible, adaptable staff, and to the development of organisational programmes that attempt to fully utilise the talents and knowledge of the workforce. It is also being recognised that international competitiveness means raising the standards of training to world-class levels. Failure to meet these pressures leads to organisational stagnation and ultimately organisational death.

337

# Pedler *et al.*'s view of the learning organisation

A learning company is one that looks beyond mere survival. By developing an ability to constantly adapt its operations it is able to sustain market leadership. Such companies not only change with differing contexts but learn from their people and their environments while 'contributing to the learning of the wider community or context of which they are part' (Pedler *et al.*, 1997: 4). As leading-edge organisations they move beyond the visions of their founders or the conservatism of many companies formed in the same era or culture, evolving through an allegiance between internal and external environments.

Thus for Pedler *et al.* (1988: 4) a learning organisation is one that:

● has a climate in which individual members are encouraged to learn and develop their full potential;
● extends the learning culture to include customers, suppliers and other significant stakeholders;
● makes human resource development strategy central to business policy;
● is in a continuous process of organisational transformation.

While it is not possible to construct a model of a learning company, principally because there is no predetermined structure, Pedler *et al.* (1997: 15–17) identify 11 key characteristics that a learning company must possess:

● a learning approach to strategy;
● participative policy making;
● 'informating' (information technology is used to inform and empower people to ask questions and take decisions);
● formative accounting and control (control systems are structured to assist learning from decisions);
● internal exchange of ideas and knowledge;
● reward flexibility to promote performance and reward learning;
● enabling structures that remove barriers to communication and learning;
● boundary workers as environmental scanners benchmarking and using knowledge gained by sales staff and those who deal with the organisation's suppliers and customers. Seeing what rival oganisations are doing;
● inter-company learning;
● a learning climate;
● self-development opportunities for all.

# Knowledge-managing organisation

Another concept that emerged in the 1990s was the *knowledge-managing organisation*. It is also known as the *knowledge-based organisation* or the *knowledge-creating company* (Nonaka, 1991). The process by which it is carried out is often known as *knowledge management* (Mayo, 1998).

A definition of knowledge management offered by Mayo (1998: 36) states that the following processes are essential:

● managing the generation of new knowledge through learning;
● capturing knowledge and experience;
● sharing, collaborating and communicating;
● organising information for easy access;
● using and building on what is known.

338

This list contains elements not greatly different from the learning organisation concept, and some observers claim that in effect they are the same phenomenon. Both concepts rely heavily on the exchange of knowledge and the desire of employees to be receptive to knowledge and learning – employees are the repositories of the organisation's knowledge and wisdom. As Tom Watson, former president of IBM, states: 'If you burnt down all our plants and we just kept our people and our files, we would soon be as strong as ever.' This underscores and adds to the strength of HRM and HRD departments, many of which have been preaching for years that 'our people are our greatest assets', often with the reality not living up to the slogan.

While the visionary concepts of knowledge management and the LO are inspiring, the reality is that, like most large-scale initiatives, implementation of such systems requires a massive change of attitude in most organisations that is not always easy to achieve. Success rests in creating a high-trust organisation where knowledge is readily exchanged. In practice there are many barriers. Knowledge is seen as power, and jealously guarded. Its possession and use can further ambitions. A culture of openness may be difficult to achieve, particularly in organisations where suspicion has been the norm. Knowledge management thus has serious implications for communication structures, employee involvement systems, reward systems and industrial relations.

There are many examples of companies that claim to be, or are on their way to being, learning organisations, including Anglia Water, Transco, IBM, Analog Devices, Nokia, GM, ICL, Xerox, and Hanover Insurance.

## e-learning

A more recent concept of the informational and learning exchange environment is *e-learning*. This emphasises the use of new technology such as email, Internet, intranet and computer software packages to facilitate learning for employees whenever they need it. As one of its advocates (Masie, 1999) states:

> I expect to see an increasing alignment between e-learning and e-commerce. Information collected on the World Wide Web about product knowledge, for example, can be accessed in the same way for someone else to learn from. Organisations are even focusing on delivering knowledge and competencies to their whole supply chain by this method.    (p. 32)

The adoption of on-line learning is attractive to organisations because the required data is available when learners want to learn. This will speed up the learning process and knowledge exchange. It also allows for 'granularisation' of learning. Until recently a unit of learning was expressed in terms of a three-day course, a morning course or a two-hour course. Granularisation can deliver a course in bite-sized chunks when the learner needs it. The e-learning forms can be formal (an actual course delivered via software or the Internet) or informal (exchange of information and knowledge via email or an intranet). The recently established University for Industry (UfI) in the UK will base a great deal of its approach to learning and delivery of courses on the use new technology, a trend that is increasing rapidly in universities and other educational institutions.

## Criticisms of the learning organisation concept

Despite its relatively new entrance on the corporate scene there have already been a number of critical studies that have highlighted the weaknesses of LO. Garvin (1993) partly blames academics such as Senge, whose writings are often 'reverential and

339

utopian (and) filled with near mystical terminology. Paradise, they would have you believe, is just round the corner.' He continues:

> Nonaka suggested that companies use metaphors and organisational redundancy to focus thinking, encourage dialogue, and make tacit, instinctively understood ideas explicit. Sound idyllic? Absolutely. Desirable? Without question. But does it provide a framework for action? Hardly. These recommendations are far too abstract, and too many questions remain unanswered. How, for example, will managers know when their companies have become learning organisations? What concrete changes in behaviour are required? What policies and programmes must be in place? How do you get from here to there? (p. 49)

Sloman (1999) believes that 'the concept of the learning organisation should be redefined or declared redundant' (p. 31). The language and vocabulary of the learning organisation need to make sense to the hard-pressed line manager, and for these reasons alone the concept 'is in urgent need of review.'

An international study carried out by Chase (1997) for the *Journal of Knowledge Management* examined approaches to creating knowledge-based organisations. He found that while organisations acknowledge 'the importance of creating, managing and transferring knowledge, they have so far been unable to translate this into need into organisational strategies. Mayo (1998: 38), cited in Chase's work, believes that 'most organisations are also struggling to use information technology to support implementation' and a learning organisation. Chase's survey also pointed out that the biggest obstacles to creating a knowledge-based organisation were the existing company culture, lack of ownership of a problem, lack of time, inappropriate organisational structure, lack of senior management commitment, inappropriate rewards and recognition, and an emphasis on individuals rather than team work.

Lähteenmäki *et al.* (1999) have pointed to a number of criticisms that can be levelled at the concept:

● lack of clarity and multiplicity of definitions;
● lack of explanation of the detailed implementation of LO systems;
● lack of explanation as to how these systems are integrated;

(all these factors point to the need for a holistic model of the learning organisation, which should convincingly link theory and practice, bringing together 'pieces of theory')

● too much stress on learning by individuals and not by the organisation;
● a dearth of research on measurement of the learning process in organisations;
● a need to recognise the historical antecedents of the learning organisation;
● a need to recognise the relationship of the LO with organisational change literature;
● the need for further investigation of the link between HR strategy and change;
● the need for more research on LO in the international context, particularly the transfer of learning between units within multinational organisations, and the cultural barriers that may exist in that process.

## The failure of LOs

Lähteenmäki *et al.* (1999), in summing up a number of research projects, emphasised these reasons for failure:

● failure to deal with feelings of uncertainty and insecurity in employees during periods of intense competition and culture change;
● a work situation that lacks trust – this can only make failure more certain, because it inhibits the learning process, as employees recede into defensive coping styles;

340

- poor feedback, limited encouragement, insufficient discussion of mistakes and the lack of empowerment, which serve to further undermine the effectiveness of LO initiatives;
- failure to give all employees the responsibility for learning;
- failure to understand the linkages between the LO and HRM strategy.

They suggest some recommendations in moving towards a learning organisation:

- An environment of openness and trust, must be created.
- An atmosphere of certainty and security must be generated.
- This can be achieved by developing strategy from the bottom up, through building a shared vision, team learning, and developing core competences that are recognised and valued by all.
- It is essential to have objectives that are clearly and positively linked to HRM strategy.
- It must be recognised that measurement of learning can feed more positively into an evaluation of the effectiveness of the learning process.
- Finally, it is of paramount importance to create a learning atmosphere that all members of the organisation share.

There are no easy prescriptions for creating a learning organisation; it takes a considerable time to engender the right attitudes and conditions in the change process. Those organisations that can learn these lessons not only are well on the way to becoming learning organisations, but also are more likely to have the skills, competences and, above all, the right attitudes for survival in our increasingly competitive globalised environment.

# HRD AND THE NATIONAL FRAMEWORK FOR VOCATIONAL EDUCATION AND TRAINING

### Introduction

Learning and development are not solely matters of concern for individuals and their employers. An educated and skilled workforce is essential for the effective functioning of the economy, for the competitiveness and wealth of the nation, and for the overall well-being of society. Indeed, Tyson and Fell (1995) suggest that 'the future will see a world of work based more on skills than organisations' (p. 45). To ensure that a nation achieves the level of skills it needs, its government therefore puts in place the vocational education and training (VET) policies and systems that will facilitate their development. Such national strategies therefore form an important part of the context (see Chapter 2) of individual learning and organisational human resource development.

As new technology progresses, replacing jobs and changing skill requirements, there is an increasing need for a skilled and highly trained workforce able to meet these changing situations. Traditional skills, for example in the engineering and construction industries, are rapidly changing, and the type of economy in which a young person can receive an apprenticeship that would stand them in good stead for a lifetime career is dwindling.

This trend is international, and poses problems for the USA, Japan, Germany, France, Sweden and other industrialised nations. However, comparisons with competitor nations indicate that Britain is suffering from a severe skills shortage. Its 'first ever

341

national audit of job skills', which the government published in 1996 to accompany its third 'competitiveness' White Paper, compares Britain with France, Germany, Singapore and the USA:

> Its findings confirm fears that Britain's skills are lagging behind those of Germany, which has had a policy of investment in vocational training for years. More worrying is the rapidly shrinking gap between the UK and Singapore in the league tables.
> (Welch, 1996c: 11)

Britain's greatest deficiency is in basic and level 2 skills, (low-level NVQ skills including numeracy and literacy) though 'Britain is ahead of its competitors both on quality and the quantity of its population' possessing degrees and vocational qualifications of a comparable level.

Many see the solution to be the investment of more capital in education and training, and the creation of an ever more skilled and knowledgeable workforce, partly because the industrialised countries can never compete with developing world economies in terms of cheap labour. The developments in VET in Britain, as elsewhere, have to be seen within this context. However, the efficacy of VET to achieve such national needs is not fully demonstrated. For example, the relative economic decline in Britain has led to much debate as to the adequacy of training in helping to arrest this trend. (This is a controversial issue that will be discussed in a later section.)

There has been considerable criticism of training policy in the UK at both national and organisational level (though other views are also now being expressed: see Harrison, 1995 and Merrick, 1995). As a later section will show, Britain has not compared favourably with Germany, Japan, Sweden or France in VET terms. Many surveys throughout the 1980s and 1990s have shown that employers regard training as being important, but the problem seems to be that, despite this recognition, not enough training has been done to meet the changing needs of the economy. What we have therefore seen is the British government tackling the training needs for the economy in an energetic way, and introducing many new policies and systems. These are having a major impact upon how learning individually and in organisations takes place by providing a framework of philosophies (such as competences), structures (such as the National Council for Vocational Qualifications), resources (such as the Training and Enterprise Councils), and incentives (such as the Investors in People award).

The purpose of this section is to outline some of the VET policies and systems currently in place in Britain, and to indicate possible future developments. However, it first recognises the key stakeholders in VET, and then sets British provision in the context of that of some of its major competitors.

## Stakeholders in vocational education and training

Chapter 7 identified several stakeholders in the individual's learning and development, and it examined the needs and responses of the individual and the employer in particular. There are several stakeholders in VET too, and their values and actions constitute the framework within which individual learning and development and organisational HRD have to take place. The part the government plays in this field will be examined in some detail later in this chapter. Note that in Britain the departments concerned with education and employment have both been involved, and they were eventually merged to form the Department for Education and Employment.

Employers are also significant stakeholders in VET. This is apparent in the international comparisons in the following section. During the 1990s, the British employers'

342

body, the Confederation of British Industry (CBI), played an influential role. For example, recognising the need for a 'skills revolution' (Confederation of British Industry, 1989), it proposed training targets (later adopted by the government) for the minimum standards needed to increase Britain's competitiveness.

The trade unions are further stakeholders in VET. At present the role of British unions in this regard is somewhat limited compared with that of their counterparts in France and Germany:

> where unions are involved widely at national, regional, sectoral and company levels in promoting and regulating the training process. This role is supported in France by law. In Germany it constitutes one part of the corporatist system of compromise and consensus between the 'social partners'. (Claydon and Green, 1992).

However, British trade unions have recently been examining their role in the economic system, particularly in the light of their decline over the past decade. One strategy they have begun to adopt is to advocate training as a collective bargaining issue other than in the narrow context of setting wages and conditions for apprentices (Kenney and Reid, 1988). Some unions, for example the EETPU, have advocated a policy of training their members to update their skills and improve their employability, in order to demonstrate to employers that the presence of unions can be beneficial (Lloyd, 1990). The TUC discussed training initiatives in *Skills 2000* (TUC, 1989) and *TUC: Joint Action over Training* (TUC, 1990), and has advocated greater 'involvement in the planning and provision of training and educational opportunities through participation at European, national and firm levels' (TUC, 1991; quoted in Claydon and Green, 1992).

Since the election of the Labour government in 1997, unions have been welcomed into a partnership with employers and the government, and have collectively been a large contributor to the National Skills Task Force (NSTF), which has investigated national skills shortages and has produced several reports and recommendations. Regional TUC organisations are also involved in implementing and operating Learning and Skills Councils, which replaced Training and Enterprise Councils (TECs) in April 2001.

## VET IN THE LEADING INDUSTRIALISED NATIONS

This section compares and contrasts VET in six leading industrialised nations: Britain and five competitor countries. There are a number of similarities. All six countries have compulsory education of similar ages (Table 8.2) and therefore recognise the importance of at least a basic education in a modern industrialised society. All six countries experienced decline in the number of children of school-leaving age in the 1990s (Table 8.3); Germany experienced the most severe decline.

**Table 8.2  Compulsory school education ages**

| | |
|---|---|
| Britain | 5–16 yrs |
| Germany | 6–15 yrs |
| France | 6–16 yrs |
| Sweden | 7–16 yrs |
| Japan | 6–15 yrs |
| USA | 6–16 yrs[a] |

[a] Varies from state to state

343

**Table 8.3  Indices of the 16 to 18-year-old population and participation in education rates**

| | 16 to 18-year-old population indices (year) | | | 16 to 18-year-old participation in education and training (%) | | |
|---|---|---|---|---|---|---|
| | *1980* | *1990* | *2000* | *Full* | *Part* | *All* |
| Britain | 121 | 106 | 94 | 33 | 31 | 64 |
| Germany | 125 | 83 | 72 | 47 | 43 | 90 |
| France | 100 | 103 | 90 | 66 | 8 | 74 |
| Sweden | 99 | 102 | 86 | 76 | 2 | 78 |
| Japan | 91 | 114 | 92[a] | 77 | 3 | 79 |
| USA | 102 | 83 | 85[a] | 79 | 1 | 80 |

100 = 1970
[a] 1996
*Source*: DES (1990). Reproduced by permission of the Controller of Her Majesty's Stationery Office.

**Table 8.4  Proportion of salaries and wages spent on training 1990–91**

| | *UK* | *France* | *Spain* | *Sweden* | *Germany* |
|---|---|---|---|---|---|
| 0.01–1.0% | 21 | 4 | 33 | 9 | 20 |
| 4% and above | 11 | 27 | 13 | 16 | 11 |
| Don't know | 41 | 2 | 25 | 48 | 47 |

*Source*: Price Waterhouse Cranfield Survey (Holden, 1991: 120).

**Table 8.5  Proportion of salaries and wages spent on training 1991–92**

| | *Switzerland* | *Germany* | *Denmark* | *Spain* | *France* | *Italy* | *Norway* | *Netherlands* | *Sweden* | *UK* |
|---|---|---|---|---|---|---|---|---|---|---|
| 0.01–2.0% | 64 | 61 | 66 | 76 | 25 | 76 | 63 | 65 | 57 | 62 |
| 4% and above | 11 | 16 | 13 | 10 | 32 | 9 | 19 | 16 | 25 | 18 |
| Don't know | 25 | 42 | 33 | 18 | 2 | 24 | 30 | 23 | 44 | 38 |

*Source*: Price Waterhouse Cranfield Survey (Holden and Livian, 1992: 15). Reproduced with permission of MCB University Press.

An examination of the statistics for 16- to 18-year-olds shows that the majority continue with some form of education or training, either full or part time (Table 8.3). Britain, however, has the fewest involved, being 10% below the comparable French figure, for example.

There are also significant differences between these countries in the amount of financial investment that their organisations make in training. This is demonstrated in Tables 8.4 and 8.5.

Germany has a thoroughgoing VET infrastructure, and Sweden has a well-established vocational system, which begins when children are 14 years old. These countries therefore, while having a large proportion of organisations ignorant of their training expenditure, have tried and tested systems of VET. The large UK 'don't know' figures are therefore all the more ominous given the unclear and contradictory approaches to VET.

## VET policies and practices

An examination of the VET systems beyond compulsory school age for the same six countries reveals a varying, and sometimes widely varying, set of practices (see Table 8.6). They can be roughly divided into *voluntarist* and *directed*. By voluntarist is meant a

344

## Table 8.6 VET policies and practices

**Britain**
- New Deal – Training for 18-24-year-olds out of work longer than 6 months, and training for over-24-year-olds out of work for longer than 2 years
- National Training Organisations (NTOs) – sectoral bodies whose function is to analyse skills gaps using international benchmarking, scenario planning and local focus groups
- National Skills Task Force (NSTF) – body composed of government, employees and union representatives investigating skill shortages nationally and recommending proposals
- Learning and Skills Councils – regional bodies set to replace TECs in April 2001
- National Vocational Qualifications (NVQ) levels 1 to 5
- Competence movement, e.g. Management Charter Initiative (MCI)
- Investors in People (IIP) – to encourage companies to attain a recognised level of strategic training
- New apprenticeships – set up in the early 1990s to encourage quality skilled training
- Colleges of higher and further education
- Universities (including the 'old polytechnics')
- Business schools, usually part of universities

Training culture – voluntarist: finance rather than industry orientated; class based; public/private education

**Germany**
- Dual system – in-company training (practical); vocational school (theoretical)
- Apprenticeships – 319 000 places, though demand is decreasing
- Technical colleges
- Universities

Training culture – directed: functionalist; industry orientated, particularly engineering

**France**
- Much VET in school system
- Apprenticeship places 300 000
- University institutes of technology
- Universities
- Grandes écoles
- Law requiring employers to spend 1.2% of total gross salaries on training employées

Training culture – directed: mathematical/engineering orientation; centralised; elitist, e.g. grandes écoles; the educational establishment attended often decides career prospects

**Sweden**
- Upper secondary school – large vocational content
- Technical and specialist universities
- Universities
- VET in most organisations is strong; heavy emphasis on HRD
- Retraining for unemployed
- Labour Market Training Board (AMU) is very influential
- Considerable free adult education
- Emphasis on 'self-development' and open learning systems

Training culture – directed: state will use training to affect labour market policy. Companies are strongly encouraged to train

**Japan**
- High schools take up to 90% of pupils up to 18 years
- Two-year college – vocationally specific training
- Four-year university courses
- Five-year college of technology courses
- Considerable continuous in-company training

Training culture – directed/voluntarist: central and local government set and enforce training standards; meritocratic – top companies will take from top universities etc.; lifetime employment and training in large companies; self-development emphasised

**USA**
- Junior or community college two-year associate degree course
- Technical institutes
- Vocational, trade and business schools
- 'GI Bill' federal loans/grants for four years' higher education after completion of four years' military service
- Private schools and colleges
- University courses
- Apprenticeships are increasingly less common and of low status
- Excellent training by leading companies but this is not universal

Training culture – voluntarist: anti-federalist in nature with wide variation; uncoordinated, with emphasis on individual effort and individual payment

*Source*: Dore and Sako (1989); Carnevale *et al.* (1990); Brewster *et al.* (1992), DfEE web page.

345

system that has little or no government interference, and effectively leaves training to the choice of the individual or the organisation. By directed is meant the existence of state legislation or regulation that has an element of compulsion for employers to train their staff.

Britain and the United States clearly have voluntarist systems and Germany, France and Sweden have directed systems, whereas Japan, while not having legislation that makes VET compulsory, has strong directives set by local and central government that enforce high-quality training standards (Dore and Sako, 1989). The Japanese also have a culture that values training and education highly, and such policies have a collectivist rather than an individualist imperative (Hofstede, 1984).

What can also be discerned is that in each country there are a considerable number of routes through vocational education and training, which vary from relatively low-grade schemes such as Training for Work in Britain to university graduate and postgraduate degrees. However, it is apparent that the British system lacks homogeneity and consistency in courses and standards of occupational qualifications compared with those of Japan, Sweden and Germany.

In Europe there are two main types of vocational training: the sequential and the dual systems. The *sequential system* is practised in France, Italy, Belgium, the Netherlands and Sweden, and is conducted in specialist vocational training colleges, which school leavers attend full time. The German *Berufsbildungssystem* is the main exemplar of the *dual system,* and is described below.

## The German system of VET

The German 'directed' and dual system of vocational training has frequently been referred to as an example of excellent practice. A common misunderstanding is that the VET is funded and run by the state. In reality employers fund two-thirds of VET, and employers and trade unions have a considerable influence on the control of the system, together with central and local government. Laws and guidelines of VET regulate the system so that employers are duty bound to provide funding and resources for training. The institutions and procedures that operate the system are, however, administered jointly by employers, unions and the state.

There are three stages in the dual system (see Figure 8.2). The first begins in the latter years of school, where emphasis is placed on a high level of education for all. A good general education, it is recognised, provides the solid basis for later learning. Nearly all young school leavers enter apprenticeships, as do a quarter of youths with qualifications similar to A levels; the rest enter the college and university system (Rose and Wignanek, 1990).

The dual system stresses the strong relationship between theoretical and practical training; part of the apprentice's time is taken up in attending vocational college, and part in receiving structured training from a *meisterwerker* (skilled craftsman) in the workplace. The *meisterwerker,* it must be stressed, is also trained in instruction techniques (Thorn, 1988). On-the-job and off-the-job instruction is carefully coordinated to produce a vocational course that gives a thorough grounding in the skills of the apprentice's trade, and this, once acquired, is acceptable in all parts of the German labour market.

The costs of the dual system are shared by firms, government and youths. Firms pay for on-the-job training, youths accept relatively low wages, and the vocational colleges are paid for by public funds (Rose and Wignanek, 1990). There are approximately 319 000 apprenticeship places available in Germany compared with approximately

346

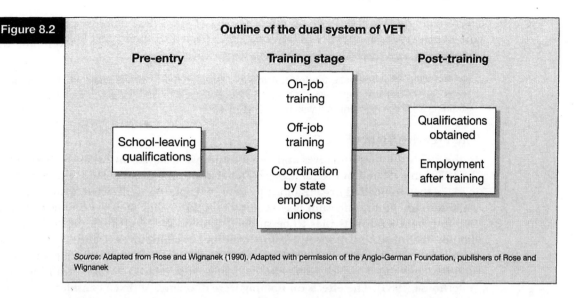

**Figure 8.2** Outline of the dual system of VET

Pre-entry | Training stage | Post-training

School-leaving qualifications → On-job training, Off-job training, Coordination by state employers unions → Qualifications obtained, Employment after training

Source: Adapted from Rose and Wignanek (1990). Adapted with permission of the Anglo-German Foundation, publishers of Rose and Wignanek

13 000 in Britain. However, since 1986 young people in Germany have taken up only about 172 000 apprentice places, but that number may have declined with the advent of more difficult times in the 1990s(Gaugler and Wiltz, 1992).

Germany has three times more skilled workers than Britain, even though the labour force of each country is of similar size (Rose and Wignanek, 1990). Nevertheless, as will be noted in the section on controversial issues, Germany's much admired VET policies and practices are apparently no longer effective in reducing the number of the unemployed.

### The Japanese system of VET

While the German system illustrates the comparative efficiency of its youth training programmes, an examination of the Japanese system of VET reveals the advantages of continuous development of employees throughout their careers. 'Lifetime employment' is a much referred to Japanese employment practice, although in reality '40% of new recruits leave within three years of entering their first job' (Dore and Sako, 1989). However, there is still a considerable proportion of lifetime employment in large-scale companies among the managerial and professional workforce in particular, who tend to form the core (those with relatively permanent positions and career structures) of company employees.

Lifetime employment allows for the long-term development of employees, and enables the creation of a structured succession programme that is mutually beneficial to the organisation and the individual employee. Decision-making is shared at all levels, there is a strong sense of collective responsibility for the success of the organisation, and cooperative rather than individual effort is emphasised, although achievement is encouraged. Training and development are an integral part of company policy in helping to reinforce these working practices, and in improving skills in technology and other related working practices. Training and development are thus 'embedded' in Japanese companies, rather than extraneous as in British organisations. A study of eight comparable British and Japanese companies recently revealed the inherent weaknesses of the British system (Storey, 1991). While the study concentrated on management development, the fact that the Japanese have no term for this was significant. They believe all workers should be

347

developed, and this should be an ongoing part of systematic employee development. Line managers in Japanese organisations are expected to spend time developing their subordinates, and this is deeply imbued in their expectations:

> In the main, the Japanese treated training and development more seriously. In Britain, despite many good intentions and recent advances, there was a level of ambiguity about the real value of training and development that was not found in Japan.
>
> (Storey, 1991)

### The French system of VET

In the 1970s training initiatives and expenditure were similar in Britain and France. In the 1970s and 1980s, however, successive French governments initiated a number of training laws that compelled organisations to train, making this a 'directed' system. The *taxe d'apprentissage* (apprenticeship tax) required employers engaged in commercial, industrial and handicraft activities to be subject to a tax of 0.6%, which was to be used to finance technical and apprenticeship training. An employee training tax was also introduced, which compelled employers of nine people or more to allocate a minimum amount equal to 1.2% of total annual wages and salaries to staff training (Price Waterhouse, 1989). The effects on training were dramatic. At first a considerable number of training consultancies came into existence to cater for the expected demand (Barsoux and Lawrence, 1990). Another longer-term factor was that, as companies were forced to train, many found that it brought benefits, and they began to spend above the 1.2% requirement, as Tables 8.4 and 8.5 indicate.

French organisations, in conforming to French law, have a much greater knowledge of their training expenditure compared with other European countries, as the Price Waterhouse data consistently show in both years of the survey, even when extended from five to ten countries (see Tables 8.4 and 8.5). Only 2% of French organisations did not know how much they spent on training, but well over 40% did not know this in the UK, Sweden and Germany. Similar figures can be found in the 1991–92 survey.

Overall, French organisations

> have been forced to pay more attention to training since under law they also have to draw up a training plan to be submitted and discussed with the *comité d'entreprise* [works council] [and] . . . gradually firms have begun to look on it [training tax] as an investment that can be integrated into the firm's strategy.
>
> (Barsoux and Lawrence, 1990)

## The implications of these international comparisons for Britain

Statistics reveal that Britain has one of the lowest percentages of young people between the ages of 16 and 18 years of age staying on at school or undertaking vocational education schemes (see Table 8.3), compared with other industrialised countries of the European Union and the world (DES, 1990). A more recent report published by the OECD stated that of 14 countries studied in depth only Hungary and Portugal had a record as poor as the UK for smoothing the transition from school to work. Of those students staying on in full-time education 20% dropped out within one year, and an astonishing 10% could not be traced as in work or in education. It also stated that 40% of British young people aged 19–24 had not reached what the OECD considered to be a minimum-level qualification (Atkinson and Elliott, 2000: 6).

Concerns have also been raised regarding the relative decline of literacy and numeracy among school leavers and the relevance of the school curriculum to the world of

348

work, for example the narrow and restrictive role of A levels. Moreover, there is also considerable concern about long-term unemployed people condemned to a life of inactivity because they have not been able to receive adequate training to create a suitable career. There has been disquiet regarding the role of training and education policy in helping to halt or reverse that trend. Yet despite high unemployment in some areas there are organisations experiencing difficulties in recruiting certain highly skilled positions. The comparisons made above between the British system of VET and those of some of its major competitors do little to allay such concerns. Recent nationwide skills audit reports show that Britain's workforce has slipped further behind its main economic rivals in training and education. In comparing Britain with France, Germany, Singapore and the United States, the report indicated that, while the number of young people staying on in full-time education in Britain had improved, it was still behind the other four nations. It was in VET, particularly in craft and technical skills, that the report stated that Britain still had much to do to equal its rivals (Targett, 1996: 3; Macleod and Beavis, 1996: 6).

Some critics claim that Britain is becoming a 'low-tech' (untrained and unskilled), cheap-labour economy, with an increasing proportion of the potential labour force condemned to a lifetime of economic inactivity. In the early 1990s Layard stated that 'two-thirds of British workers had no vocational or professional qualification, compared with only a quarter in Germany' (Anon, 1992a).

These issues raise many questions as to the scope and type of training that is needed. The following subsections outline some of the recent VET initiatives designed to improve Britain's competitiveness. It is too soon to judge their effects, but the conclusion that Britain lags behind its competitors is now being questioned: 'the UK system may eventually be seen as an example of how to create a more flexible workforce' (Merrick, 1995: 8).

## VET IN BRITAIN

### The involvement of government in VET in the UK

With its voluntarist system of VET, Britain has traditionally left the provision of training and employee development to employers, and has largely had an educational system that was geared to preparing young people as members of society rather than as workers. However, the experience of relative economic decline in Britain has raised a number of questions regarding the role of education and training policy in helping to halt or reverse that trend. It has become clear that employers by themselves cannot achieve the major investment needed by the nation in training and development. This is not only because they serve their own self-interest rather than that of the economy at large, but also because they have had to operate within a patchwork of complex and poorly integrated VET courses, standards and qualifications. The only way to deal strategically with the nation's shortfall in skills has been for the government to modify its voluntarist approach and develop an overall framework for VET. However, whether voluntarism should be abandoned entirely is being currently debated, although in February 2000 the Labour government stated that it will not be adopting a training levy proposal at present, an indication that the voluntarist approach will remain predominant (see the subsection on Labour government policies later in this chapter).

349

## The recent history of government involvement

The history of government initiatives in training is a relatively short one. Not until 1964, when Industrial Training Boards (ITBs) were set up, was there an attempt by government to influence employer training behaviour. Subsidies were given to companies that were able to show that they were carrying out training programmes of a type approved by the Training Boards, and Boards were set up to oversee most sectors of the economy.

The ITBs did have some impact on popularising training by pointing to its benefits, which also helped to influence companies to set up training departments and improve their training methods (Manpower Services Commission, 1981).

The neo-liberalist Conservative governments from 1979 were directly opposed to any form of compulsion, and thus the voluntarist tradition was re-emphasised and bolstered. It is surprising, therefore, that more government policies directed at improving training were initiated than before. The Employment and Training Act 1981 abolished most of the ITBs, and the government stressed that 'it is for employers to make the necessary investment in training for the work that they require' (IMS, 1984).

During this same period the government introduced initiatives in education that were intended to generate an enterprise culture. Moreover, the new national curriculum for schools was designed expressly to meet the needs of employers. The merging of the Department for Education and Department of Employment into one ministry expressed how close the relationship between education and employment was deemed to be.

## Government training initiatives

A further impetus for the government's increasing involvement in VET during the 1980s and 1990s was the dramatic rise in unemployment among young people and adults, with a high incidence of long-term unemployment. Consequently, a plethora of initiatives in the fields of education and training were introduced. These included schemes for training the unemployed, the establishment of bodies to initiate, foster and undertake training of direct relevance to employers (the Training and Enterprise Councils), the development of a comprehensive national framework of vocational qualifications, and national targets for training. The following subsections will outline the major elements of this context.

## Youth Training Scheme and Employment Training

Increasing unemployment in the recession of the early 1980s forced the government to take action. In particular, youth unemployment, combined with the impact of the inner-city riots in 1981, led to the creation of youth schemes, and the Youth Opportunities Programme (YOP), introduced by the previous Labour government in 1978, was revived. This later became the Youth Training Scheme (YTS). However, there was considerable criticism levelled against YOPs and YTSs: that they were ineffective, and merely a way of relieving unemployment statistics by involving unemployed school leavers in poor-quality and, in some cases, exploitative work experience programmes.

The equally pressing need to help the adult unemployed back into the job market, particularly those who had been without work for a considerable time and those made redundant as a result of changing technology, led the government to set up Employment Training (ET) in 1988. ET was considered by critics as an even worse failure than YOP and YTS and by the end of 1992 ET 'had petered out through lack of

350

cash and commitment' (Lowe, 1992). It was later merged with the Employment Action programme and retitled Training for Work. One review body stated:

> The concern is that both YT and ET (now Training for Work) are headed for low skill, low quality, low expectation, low takeup, and low prestige 'aid of last resort' position.
>
> (G10 Group of Training and Enterprise Council Chairmen, House of Commons, 1993: 4, quoted in Felstead, 1994: 1)

### Training and Enterprise Councils

Another major Conservative government initiative was the setting-up of Training and Enterprise Councils (TECs) in England and Wales, and Local Enterprise Companies (LECs) in Scotland. Between 1991 and 1992, 82 TECs and 22 LECs were set up. Local business people were to be encouraged to sit on the TEC and LEC boards, as it was felt they would be in tune with local business needs and thus able to direct training schemes that would have relevance to local employers. The emphasis was put on closing the 'skills gap': that is, training people, such as the unemployed, to be able to fill jobs where there were shortages, which were often in skilled areas such as computer skills and electrical engineering skills. Training providers were not allowed to join the main board.

TECs and LECs have come in for a barrage of criticism, not only from political opponents but from the world of industry and commerce and those administering the schemes themselves (Milne, 1991; Anon, 1992b; Felstead, 1994). Many argue that leaving training to the voluntary decisions and exigencies of the business community cannot succeed, because it has repeatedly been shown that many business organisations will not train enough to suit the needs of the economy, but only their own needs. Critics further claim that voluntary systems have not worked, and that either a form of compulsion to force employers to train or an increase in direct government involvement is needed.

In addition, TEC board members have reproached the government for not providing enough funding to make the scheme viable and for leaving resources far too stretched to fulfil their aims (Graham, 1992; Wood, 1992).

There were also devastating criticisms of irregular practices by private training companies in collusion with TECs, leading to accusations of funding for jobs and training being given to people already about to be employed or even in employment. Felstead (1994) summed up the position by the mid 1990s:

> the prospect of TECs/LECs curing Britain's well known deficiencies in intermediate skills therefore looks bleak, the more likely outcome is the production of more and more workers with low level skills in business administration, community care and retailing. The 'skills revolution' that TECs/LECs were meant to prompt looks a long way off. (p. 21)

The Labour government has decided to replace TECs in April 2001, and their role will be taken over by the Learning and Skills Councils and National Training Organisations (see below).

## Competences

Chapter 7 has identified competence as one of the outcomes of learning and development. Defined as the ability to apply knowledge and skills with understanding to a work activity and, importantly, assessed via performance, the notion has resonated with the values that have come to pervade the recent thinking of government policy makers on VET, with their increasing emphasis upon outcomes rather than inputs into education and training. During the later 1980s, therefore, competence and competency was

351

adopted as a major building block in the new thinking about VET, and has now achieved wide currency in this field.

However, these notions are not universally accepted, and there has been considerable debate about the way they have been conceptualised and used in practice (Kandola, 1996). A key issue for those critical of this approach is the status given to the knowledge underpinning the performance of skills. The issue rumbles on in the various debates (e.g. Armstrong, 1996).

Nevertheless, the competency approach has been a major innovation in the field of HRD, and has permeated it widely during the 1990s. Although it may be applied in different ways (Kandola, 1996), there is no sense yet that it is fragmenting or fading. Buttressed by its adoption in various government-led VET initiatives (see below), it is likely that it will withstand its critics for some time yet, and will therefore continue to influence the format of and philosophy underpinning much individual and organisational training and development activity.

## A national framework of vocational qualifications

The establishment in 1986 of the National Council for Vocational Qualifications (NCVQ) and the Scottish Vocational Educational Council (SCOTVEC) institutionalised the competency approach. These bodies provide a framework of National Vocational Qualifications (S/NVQs, or VQs), which accredit competencies across organisations so that an individual's performance at work can now be taken into account in an educational qualification. In addition, GNVQs are an alternative to academic A levels for those preparing for the world of work.

S/NVQs are statements 'confirming that the individual can perform to a specified standard' and that he or she 'possesses the skills, knowledge and understanding which makes possible such performance in the workplace' (Harrison, 1992: 28). There are five levels of S/NVQ: from the most basic level through craft, technician and lower-level professional skills to the higher professional levels. The standards of competence for particular occupations and professions are, after a lengthy analytical and consultative process, set by industry lead bodies, which include representatives of employers and trade unions, as Townsend (1992) illustrates in the work of the Personnel Standards Lead Body, to ensure that the standards are relevant to work and are valued by employers.

There is a wide range of lead bodies, such as the Small Firms Lead Body and the Guidance and Counselling Lead Body. The comparable body in the field of management is the Management Charter Initiative (MCI), the work of which is described in Chapter 9. Many occupational areas are therefore embraced in the new qualifications' framework: bouncers, caterers, translators, teachers etc. Awarding bodies such as City and Guilds, RSA and BTEC have changed their awards to meet S/NVQ criteria. The nature of the lead bodies has evolved, and some have formed themselves into occupational standards councils (OSCs) for particular sectors of employment. For example, the Personnel Standards Lead Body, the Training and Development Lead Body and the Trade Union Sector Development Body merged in 1994 to become the Employment OSC. This has not always been a smooth process, as Welch (1996a) indicates when reporting the eventual accreditation by NCVQ of the IPD's new qualifications in personnel, training and development.

The developments so far, however, have not been an unqualified success. There have been criticisms of definitions, purposes and methodology. There has been considerable frustration with their excessive bureaucracy and the 'jargon-ridden language' of

352

the standards, and recognition of the need for the lead bodies or OSCs to provide external quality checks on the standard of assessment. The controversy and debate surrounding this issue will undoubtedly exercise the minds of the interested parties for some time to come.

Nevertheless, like the competency approach, the language and framework of VQs are influencing how individuals construct their own development, and how organisations approach and deliver HRD, and hence the nature of the learning environment they offer their employees.

## Investors in People

Investors in People (IIP) was launched in 1991 and created out of the collaborative work of the National Skills Task Force (NSTF), CBI, Department of Employment, TUC and IPD. Since 1993 it has been a private company limited by guarantee – Investors in People UK (IIP UK, 1995; Taylor and Thackwray, 1995). Based on 'the practical experience of businesses that have improved their performance through investing in people' (Employment Department Group, 1990), IIP gives a national framework that specifies 'the principles which tie training and development activity directly to business objectives', ensures that the 'resources committed to training and development are put to the most effective use', and provides 'a clear benchmark of good practice . . . against which any organisation, large or small, can measure progress towards improved business performance' (IIP UK, 1995: 1).

The Employment Department Group's (1990) brochure *What is an Investor in People?* states:

An Investor in People makes a public commitment from the top to develop all employees to achieve its business objectives.

- Every employer should have a written but flexible plan which sets out business goals and targets, considers how employees will contribute to achieving the plan and specifies how development needs in particular will be assessed and met.
- Management should develop and communicate to all employees a vision of where the organisation is going and the contribution employees will make to its success, involving employee representatives as appropriate.

An Investor in People regularly reviews the training and development needs of all employees.

- The resources for training and developing employees should be clearly identified in the business plan.
- Managers should be responsible for regularly agreeing training and development needs with each employee in the context of business objectives, setting targets and standards linked, where appropriate, to the achievement of National Vocational Qualifications (or relevant units) and, in Scotland, Scottish Vocational Qualifications.

An Investor in People takes action to train and develop individuals on recruitment and throughout their employment.

- Action should focus on the training needs of all new recruits and continually developing and improving the skills of existing employees.
- All employees should be encouraged to contribute to identifying and meeting their own job-related development needs.

An Investor in People evaluates the investment in training and development to assess achievement and improve future effectiveness.

353

- The investment, the competence and commitment of employees, and the use made of skills learned should be reviewed at all levels against business goals and targets.
- The effectiveness of training and development should be reviewed at the top level and lead to renewed commitment and target setting.

By December 1999, 16 454 organisations (or units within them) had achieved the national standard as Investors in People, and almost 22 000 had made a commitment to gaining the award (IIP, 2000). Taylor and Thackwray (1995) report that organisations find considerable benefit in working for and achieving the standard. They quote a survey and case studies that suggest that the benefits derive from ensuring that training is strategic and relates to the organisation's business needs. In particular, organisations cite that working towards IIP helps to clarify and communicate business objectives, stimulates continuous improvement initiatives (see Chapter 7), increases the involvement of managers in individuals' development, brings together some seemingly unrelated activities, and gives attention to administrative staff who are often otherwise overlooked. Taylor and Thackwray (1995: 30) also note that some organisations believe that through IIP they have increased profitability, efficiency, sales and income, and reduced costs.

Alberga (1997) in a survey in 1996 warns that there could be difficulties over re-recognition as organisations seek to retain the reward after three years: 'The problem is that it enables people to let things slide and then drag them up just in time for the re-recognition process' (p. 32). The achievement of this standard calls for considerable effort, but it is becoming clear that its benefits lie in the diagnostic and reflective process that it sets in train rather than, perhaps, in the award itself.

## New developments in education to increase flexibility

During the 1980s there were a number of developments that have made educational provision more flexible and the qualifications system more responsive to the needs of individuals. These are:

- the *Credit Accumulation and Transfer Scheme* (CATS) to help non-traditional entrants and eliminate unnecessary repetition of learning, by giving credit for learning achievements, the transfer of credits from one educational institution or programme to another, and so the possibility of exemption from relevant parts of a course;
- *Accreditation of Prior Learning* (APL) to give credit for previous learning, whether certificated or uncertificated;
- *Accreditation of Experiential Learning* (AEL) to give credit for learning from life and work experiences;
- *modularisation*.

## National training targets

These various VET initiatives are pulled together by the setting of national training targets, first proposed by the CBI in 1989 to benchmark the UK's skills base against that of other nations, and launched in 1991. The National Advisory Council for Education and Training Targets (NACETT) came into being in 1993 to monitor and report on progress towards achievement of the targets. While targets were well received, Armstrong (1996) warned that the 'qualification cuckoo should not be allowed to push competence-based learning out of the nest' (p. 23). This is an issue for many commentators on the British VET policy. Welch (1996c) reports that 'a quarter of large British firms' do not see higher academic qualifications 'as reliable indicators of skills', and 40% do not consider that they indicate 'basic skills'.

354

The targets are ambitious, and despite wide consultation and updating in 1995 the revised targets for the year 2000 were not met. New targets have been set for 2002 to improve the UK's international competitiveness by raising standards and attainment levels in education and training to world-class levels through ensuring that:

1 All employers invest in employee development to achieve business success.
2 All individuals have access to education and training opportunities, leading to recognised qualifications, which meet their needs and aspirations.
3 All education and training develops self-reliance, flexibility and breadth, in particular through fostering competence in core skills (NACETT, 1996).

The National Learning Targets for the year 2002 are as follows:

1 Targets for 11 year olds – 80% of 11 year olds reaching the expected standard for their age in literacy and 75% reaching the standard for numeracy.
2 Targets for 16 year olds – 50% of 16 year olds getting five higher-grade GCSEs and 95% at least one GCSE.
3 Targets for young people – 85% of 19 year olds with a 'level 2' qualification and 60% of 21 year olds with 'level 3 'qualification.
4 Targets for adults – 50% of adults with level 3 qualification, 28% with level 4 qualification and 7% reduction in non-learners – the learning participation target.
5 Targets for organisations – 45% of medium-sized or large organisations recognised as Investors in People and 10000 small organisations recognised as IIP. (DfEE, 2000)

(*Note*: At the time of writing Scotland, Wales and Northern Ireland were making their own separate arrangements, which had not been published.)

NACETT charts the progress so far. Again, there is speculation whether the targets will be achieved. However, these targets also serve the important purpose of directing, motivating and reinforcing the various other VET initiatives already referred to in this chapter, so that what is emerging in the UK is a systematic, self-reinforcing framework for VET rather than, as hitherto, a patchwork of piecemeal initiatives. A common characteristic of the elements of this framework is the emphasis upon observable, tightly defined and often measurable outcomes. This, in some respects, contrasts with other contemporary developments. For example, as noted in Chapter 2, in the fields of philosophy and the social sciences those (positivist) approaches that favour measurement are being increasingly challenged by those favouring interpretation; in organisations, multi-skilling and flexible working are to some extent eroding the traditional boundaries and definitions of jobs; while notions of total quality management and of the learning organisation are breaking down traditional internal and external organisational boundaries. This contrast prompts the question whether the underpinning philosophy of today's VET will remain unchallenged for long, and what would become of the VET framework if its philosophy were undermined.

## RECENT VET DEVELOPMENTS

Industry is no longer drawn to the comparative advantage of abundant natural resources, but instead to pools of human skills. American – and British – governments neither provide the education nor the training in depth, nor the infrastructural foundations necessary for the post-electro-mechanical society. (Ford, 1993; in Thurow, 1992)

355

Advanced economies of the future will not be based on a cheap and unskilled work-force. As we have noted, Britain and similar economies can never compete with Third World countries on these terms. If economies are to remain relatively prosperous, one of the policy imperatives for the future must be a considerable investment in education and training by both organisations (public and private sector) and governments.

There will have to be greater accessibility to universities for more of the population, a coherent system of VET in which harmonised qualifications are accredited and appreciated by all employees, and a commitment to lifelong learning. This implies an increase in funding for education. As noted in Chapter 7, the future organisation is a learning organisation, and future employees are those who are continually seeking to develop themselves.

Further developments in VET are therefore inevitable in the UK. The Labour government elected in 1997 strongly recognised this, and put in their election manifesto that one of their primary aims would be 'education, education education'. It is clear that further attention will be paid to education and VET in the UK for some time to come, although critics within the system at school, college and university levels claim that there is insufficient funding to meet all their needs.

## Compulsory or voluntary VET?

One major issue will be whether training should be voluntary or compulsory. Observers and interested bodies are divided on the issue. The Liberal Democrats, the TUC, the Commission for Social Justice and, previously, the Labour Party have argued 'that the problem must be tackled with legislation. Employers should be compelled to provide training' (Harrison, 1995: 38). On the other hand, a strong case can be made for 'voluntarism' (Harrison, 1995). The Labour Party has now moved its position from one where organisations should be compelled to provide training (the levy system) to the most recent proposal, *learning accounts*, which backs away from elements of compulsion and retains the elements of persuasion (Littlefield and Welch, 1996). This approach has been reinforced recently with the rejection of a levy system, with its elements of compulsion, after the publication of the third report by the National Skills Task Force in January 2000. While welcoming the partnership approach, John Monks of the TUC expressed concerns about the emphasis on voluntarism (Rana, 2000:13).

The CBI, the Institute of Directors and the IPD have argued for 'carrot' rather than 'stick' measures, as levies or compulsory learning accounts could act as a tax on jobs. In the face of the failure of the Australian levy system and the fact that proposals for levy systems in New Zealand, Ireland and Sweden have not been taken up, it would appear that the Labour Party has seen these as precautionary tales (Beresford and Gaite, 1994; Harrison, 1995).

## Labour government initiatives: building a VET framework

As we have already noted, the Labour government claims that one of its primary concerns has been education and training, and it visualises these as being fundamental tools to create a viable economic future for all in Britain in the twenty-first century. These are lofty but necessary ambitions, and – building on Conservative reforms – the Labour government has attempted to create a VET framework for all. We have already noted

356

that training and education targets have been set for school pupils, students, young employed 16–21-year-olds, adults and organisations. Building on the Dearing Report's recommendations, attempts have been to harmonise diverse qualifications in the academic and technical worlds, with mixed results and some more development needed.

Since Labour has come to office VET initiatives have been abundant. The following section briefly describes the major initiatives that have been instituted to date.

## The New Deal

This initiative is an attempt to provide training for 18–24-year-olds who have been out of work for more than six months, and 25-year-olds and over who have been unemployed for longer than two years. The idea behind the scheme is to make the unemployed more employable by providing them with skills. It offers four options (Pickard, 1997):

- a job subsidised for six months with an employer;
- six months' work with a governmental environment task force;
- six months' work with a voluntary sector employer;
- a year's full-time education and training for people who do not hold an NVQ level 2 or equivalent.

Scepticism has been expressed, partly because of the negative experiences of previous schemes such as YTS and ET, but also because of the failure of the Australian New Deal scheme, where employers were not enthusiastic about taking on the long-term unemployed because of 'low skills, poor attitudes to work and low levels of motivation' (Pickard, 1997: 34). These are concerns that remain in the minds of members of the CBI and other employer bodies, but nevertheless they are willing to cooperate with the TUC and other bodies. The government has made provisions to overcome these predicted difficulties by proposing the following:

- There will be a prolonged 'gateway' of up to four months' intensive counselling for the unemployed before being presented to an employer.
- Each individual will get an Employment Service case worker, who will stay with them throughout the programme.
- Each client will have a 'mentor' – someone from the community or local company but independent of the scheme's organisers – who can represent their interests.

The nationwide launch of the scheme took place in April 1998. Concerns have already been expressed about too much red tape, the low quality of the recruits, the lack of support from the Employment Service, and the fact that case workers have been overloaded with clients and do not have enough time to deal with individuals (Rana, 1999a: 14). Further criticisms are that the scheme has not met the needs of single parents, and has failed ethnic groups – claims rebutted by Andrew Smith, Minister of State for Employment (Smith, 1999: 33). A study of employers found that one in three have failed to train their New Deal recruits, and that 21% had no training planned for them. 'This is exactly what happened to YTS recruits and it discredited the scheme' claims Nick Isles, an IPD representative (Rana, 1999b: 18)

At present the jury is still out, with supporters such as Smith and David Blunkett, Secretary of State for Education and Employment, claiming that the New Deal has achieved far more than any previous scheme. If cooperation between the partners does break down, then the government may have to resort to more compulsory measures.

357

## National Training Organisations

National Training Organisations (NTOs) were launched in May 1998 to replace Industry Training Organisations (ITOs). They are government-supported sectoral bodies, rather like the old ITBs, charged with the task of anticipating and analysing skill gaps using international benchmarking (comparing UK skills with other nations), scenario planning (plans to improve skills in given sectors of the economy) and local focus groups. The main idea is an 'investment framework' of voluntary measures that could be backed up by legislation if they failed to work. Among the more radical voluntary measures is the development of sector-based 'learning institutes' – physical or virtual – that would join forces with firms to allow workforce development (Pickard, 1998: 15).

With the demise of the TECs in April 2001, NTOs will take on some of their role. David Blunkett has made NTOs key players in the proposed reforms of post-16 education and training laid out in the *Learning to Succeed* White Paper (Rana, 1999c). It is suggested that the legal framework will encourage employers and employees to take up their training responsibilities rather than return to the old levy system. In 1999 85% of sectors reported recruitment problems, with acute shortages in manufacturing, but fewer than a third offered their workforce any training (Whitehead, 1999).

## Learning and Skills Councils and the Small Business Service

From April 2001 TECs will be replaced by Learning and Skills Councils (LSCs), and the Small Business Service will replace Business Links (bodies that promised training and development of local companies). The role of LSCs will be to

> build a new culture of learning which will underpin national competitiveness and personal prosperity, encourage creativity and innovation and help build a cohesive society.　　(DfEE, 1999)

The role of the Small Business Service will be

> to provide a single gateway for all government programmes directed primarily at mainly small business . . . and it will have the right to monitor all and existing proposals for business support.
> 　　(DfEE, 1999)

There will be 47 local LSCs and 45 Small Business franchises, their boundaries being co-terminous. These will be overseen by a national LSC that will, among other things:

● work to a three-year plan;
● assess national skills and learning needs;
● allocate budgets to local LSCs;
● set strategy on attainment of the National Learning Targets;
● secure information, advice and guidance for adults;
● develop national partnerships with local authorities and local education authorities, the Employment Service, the University for Industry, NTOs, trade unions, new support services for young people, major and multisite employers, and education and training providers.

These bodies, along with NTOs and the NSTF, will obviously play an important part in defining the role and structure of VET.

## Other VET measures

A number of other initiatives are worth mentioning, although space does not permit extensive information. They include the following:

358

*Modern apprenticeships*

These are mainly for 16- and 17- year-old school leavers and training includes at least an NVQ at level 3, showing that the apprentice can do the job to the standard that industry and commerce require. Over 82 frameworks have been approved so far, from accountancy to warehousing.

*National traineeships*

These are aimed at a lower level than modern apprenticeships, and are for school leavers from 16 upwards. They offer quality training to industry standards at NVQ level 2. They are designed by employers for employers. Trainees, like apprentices, can earn while they learn.

*Learning Card*

The Learning Card is issued to young people in their final year of compulsory education. It acts as a reminder to young leavers of their right to further learning and careers information and guidance. The card entitles holders to discounts from a number of organisations, such as BT, YHA, National Express, Letts and BSM. It also gives access to a Career Bank to help in the choice of careers.

*Lifelong learning*

Lifelong learning is an ill-defined concept, although its name suggests the encouragement of continuous learning for all throughout their lives. Various initiatives have been set up by the government in collaboration with universities, local authorities and employers to examine the possibilities of regional lifelong learning projects and support mechanisms. Local authorities have been cast in the leading role, but they have been sluggish in taking the initiative (Pollock, 1999). By implication they will have to turn themselves into learning organisations, and one – Norwich, a pioneer in the initiative – calls itself a 'Learning City.' One of the problems is that the lifelong learning brief maybe too wide and thus too amorphous to manage effectively. If the idea is to create a learning climate for citizens in general, then there needs to be a considerable degree of coordination of existing support mechanisms in cooperation with the various partners and local bodies.

*Learning accounts*

The Labour government espouses the use of learning accounts rather than training levies. These will be 'targeted at people in most need of basic training. One million people will each be given £150 if they contribute £25 from their own pocket. This would allow individuals to take the first step up the learning ladder by enrolling on, say, an IT course for beginners or taking basic literacy skills' (Littlefield and Welch, 1996: 5). This 'Learn as You Earn' proposal 'is designed to give people the freedom to choose the training courses and skills which fit with their aspirations' (Butters, 1996: 2). It will also form the cornerstone for lifelong learning initiatives.

*University for Industry*

The University for Industry was proposed in 1996 by the Labour Party and came into being in November 1999. Its aim is to prepare individuals for the rapid economic and social changes in the modern, more flexible world of work, where there are 'weaker relationships between employers and employees' (Hillman, 1996: v). Among its aims are to:

359

- be the hub of a national learning network extending to workplaces, homes and local learning centres;
- provide access to user-friendly services on the Internet and create links with tutors, experts and other learners;
- commission new learning programmes in strategic areas;
- sustain an accessible system of support and guidance services;
- stimulate mass-marketing of learning opportunities.

It would also become a main support for lifelong learning. One of its principal aims to this effect is to widen accessibility of learning opportunities, in terms of time, place and pace. This obviously suggests the use of individualised programmes on the Internet, CD-ROMs and distance learning initiatives, combined with local learning support mechanisms. At the time of writing, 68 Learndirect centres had been set up across England that will work with UfI to develop a new approach to the delivery of flexible learning. Centres will also be set up in Wales, Northern Ireland and Scotland, and will be parallel but distinct organisations.

### Conclusion

The Labour government hopes that these VET initiatives will provide a framework for the encouragement and development of a learning atmosphere in the nation as a whole. Whether this is the case or not depends on the enthusiasm, funding and continuing importance that the government places on the overall strategy and its individual programmes and institutions. It also remains to be seen whether these become a number of disparate schemes desperately operating to keep afloat despite lack of funding and support at national level. They will also be a test as to the success of the voluntarist system that the Labour government has continued from its Conservative forebears.

## CONTROVERSIAL ISSUES

### The contribution of training to national competitiveness

In the past, economic growth has been seen to have been bound up as much with the wealth of a nation's 'human capital' as with its material resources. Japan and Germany are two oft-cited cases. Both countries have relatively few natural resources, and both have relied heavily on the development of the skills, aptitudes and efforts of their people.

Both had suffered considerable wartime destruction by 1945, but had largely rebuilt their economies by the 1960s as a launch pad from which to challenge world markets.

The problem with training and education is that, although most observers acknowledge their importance, it is very difficult, if not impossible, to correlate directly their contribution to economic growth. Attempts have been made by some researchers to do this, albeit with questionable results (Prais and Steedman, 1986; Steedman, 1988; Prais and Wagner, 1988; Prais et al., 1989). Comparative economic research by Freeman (BBC, 1996) finds that although the Philippines has increased and improved education, it is not doing as well economically as China, which has not significantly increased its education and training but is experiencing high economic growth. He warns that education and training alone are not a prescription for pulling a country out of low economic growth, and other writers from developing nations have also attested that the hopes invested in education in the 1960s and 1970s have not been realised in economic terms for many Asian and African countries (Halls, 1990).

However, Ashton and Sung (1994) cite the impressive economic growth of the Singaporean economy in recent years, and claim that much of this growth can be related to a comprehensive state-directed VET programme integrated into the Singaporean government's long-term economic aims. They claim that 'the relative autonomy of the state apparatus is the ability of the political elite to define long-term goals for political and economic action' (p. 5). From these examples we can at best conclude that the experience of developing economies is varied, and that the way VET policy is conceived and implemented is of utmost importance: this is an area of research that is receiving increasing attention.

Note also that in recent years the much vaunted German VET system has come under criticism, mainly because training for the unemployed is not affecting the labour market in the way it had done previously, and levels of unemployment are now equivalent to, if not greater than, those in Britain. It would seem that in certain areas of the economy training and retraining in practical skills are proving less effective, largely because of the changing nature of the economy, which is requiring fewer and fewer engineering, construction and other manual skills. As world competition increases, and new technology replaces many occupations that would once have absorbed the unemployed, retraining schemes appear increasingly out of date and ill equipped to help the 'new' unemployed (BBC, 1996). Unification has also had a negative economic impact on the new German state. The changing labour requirements of the economy in terms of numbers of employees and skills needed will be an increasingly pressing problem for the major economies, having ramifications for social as well economic policy making.

Similarly, while in-firm training has increased considerably in France, there remains the problem of what to do with the unemployed, particularly unemployed youth, in whom there has been a considerable increase. Long-term unemployment in France has also risen over the past decade, and labour-market policies have not been particularly effective in providing the skills-based training needed to help these people find jobs. France, like Britain, has not succeeded in bridging the skills gap, and this may be partly due to the low esteem in which vocational training initiatives are held (Bournois, 1992).

Training is also regarded as an instrument for solving specific economic problems such as unemployment, and for bridging the skills gap. Many advanced economies have pursued such training policies with, at best, mixed results and usually little long-term effect on the unemployment register. Social arguments seem to fare better, and according to Lord Young it is preferable to have unemployed youngsters on training schemes than out 'ram-raiding' (BBC, 1996). In addition, as we shall see in Chapter 15 on international HRM, factors such as the influence of national institutions, social attitudes and culture are also bound up with explanations of the economic success of these nations and their education and training systems. Nevertheless, comparative study can highlight weaknesses and strengths in national systems of training and education, from which we may learn some vital lessons.

361

## SUMMARY

- This chapter examined the practicalities of human resource development, offering a definition and highlighting the problem of transferable and non-transferable skills. Although there has been a growing recognition of the need for training in organisations, controversy still exists as to the extent and quality of training required.

- Training is seen as a key instrument in the implementation of HRM policies and practices, particularly those involving cultural change and the necessity of introducing new working practices. Of equal importance in the training process is the recognition of individual needs. These may, however, clash with organisational needs, and it is crucial to harmonise these demands, to the mutual benefit of both parties.

- The first part of the chapter dealt with the practicalities of creating a human resource development plan. The first and most vital step in an HRD plan is to analyse the training needs of the organisation in relation to its strategy, and equate these with the needs of the individuals within it. Proposals were then made as to how this might be effected, including the use of various forms of analysis of job requirements and personnel performance. A choice of methods was then outlined, which fell into the basic categories of on-the-job and off-the-job training, followed by the equally important consideration of who was to deliver the training. The last and perhaps least well-performed part of the HRD plan is evaluating and monitoring the training. This section reviewed various methods by which this can be carried out, the results of which should be fed back into the HRD process to improve the effectiveness and increase the relevance of future programmes.

- The notion of the learning organisation and the knowledge-based organisation, and the difficulties in defining, modelling and implementing these concepts, were examined.

- The second half of the chapter examined the stakeholders in the individual's learning and development, concentrating on the role of the employer, the state and the trade union movement.

- An examination was undertaken of training in a comparative international context, which made an in-depth exploration of vocational training policies and practices in Germany, Japan and France, and outlined some of the lessons they might afford for the British experience.

- This was followed by an in-depth critical examination of the recent history of training in the UK context. Recent and past public policy training initiatives were examined such as the YTS, ET, TECs, the competency approach, vocational qualifications, Investors in People, national training targets, the New Deal, NTOs, and more recently the Learning and Skills Councils and the University for Industry.

- The chapter also examined the debate concerning whether or not training policies should be compulsory or voluntary, and the contribution of training to national competitiveness.

362

**Activity**  **A debate on national vocational education and training**

Divide the lecture group/class into groups.

One group is to assume the position of Secretary of State for Education and Employment and his/her supporters.

Another group is to assume the critical position of members of the parliamentary opposition.

A third group is made up of critics of the voluntarist approach to vocational education and training (VET): the TUC, for example.

By referring to this chapter, its references and further reading and other sources, each group must state its position. This should include a critique of the other two groups' case, and the reasons why you support your present views.

Elect a chairperson to order the debate.

## QUESTIONS

1 The learning organisation is purely an aspiration, and can never be achieved in reality. How far would you agree with this statement?

2 What are the advantages of organisations adopting a learning organisation or knowledge-based approach to HRD? What difficulties could possibly develop in the implementation and operation of these systems?

3 Examine the experience of those countries mentioned in the international section, and comment on whether Britain can learn from their policies and approaches.

4 What are the potential effects of government initiatives such as National Training Targets, Vocational Qualifications (S/NVQs) or the Investors in People award upon the human resource development of an organisation?

## EXERCISES

1 Divide into three groups. One group should identify the particular strengths of the French VET as compared with the British; the second should do the same for the German; and the third for the Japanese. Report back to the whole class.

2 Outline the strengths and weaknesses of the Investors in People programme. How does it fit in with government overall VET strategy? You may wish to contact your local IIP office or the national office: Investors in People UK, 7–10 Chandos Street, London W1M 9DE. Email: information@iipuk.co.uk

3 What steps would you follow if you were charged with devising an IIP programme for your company or organisation?

Below are two IIP case studies that may guide you. They are both actual case studies. The first shows how one organisation achieved IIP status and how it helped their organisation. The second sets the problem, and the *Lecturer's guide* that accompanies this textbook gives you the full report.

363

## CASE STUDY 1

## The Cumberland Hotel

### The organisation

The Cumberland Hotel, Harrow, Middlesex, grew from a small guest house established in 1956 to its present size of 84 bedrooms with a capacity for over 140 guests, an award-winning restaurant and the recent extension of its conference and leisure facilities. This privately owned hotel employs 100 people, and has progressed to 4 Crown Commended status from the English Tourist Board for its facilities and quality of service, together with three-star AA and RAC rating.

The hotel serves the international business market for Wembley and the north-west London area, providing a service for visitors to the capital and, increasingly, for overseas guests from France, Germany, Japan and the United States. Investors in People has been crucial to the success of the Cumberland Hotel in what is, after all, a people-led business.

The hotel is unique in having recently won the prestigious London Regional Training Award for the exceptionally high standard of staff training: in 1996 it also won the Rubicon Award for Employer of the Year.

### The challenge and the strategy

The principal elements of the strategy needed to meet defined business priorities required the following:

- hotel management and staff to perform to their maximum potential;
- the business to develop the ability to change and become more efficient and profitable;
- systematic sales and marketing activity, particularly regarding competition and the identification of new markets;

- a culture change for the recognition of the importance of new skills;
- the increasing amounts of new legislation covering health and safety and food hygiene to be understood and applied;
- improvement of personnel practices encompassing employee induction, ongoing training provision and performance appraisal;
- elimination of wastage, reducing operating overheads and preserving margins;
- improvement in continuity of action between departments and functions through better communication and interpersonal skills;
- consistent standards that met or exceeded the expectations of customers.

### The results

Implementation of this strategy has resulted in significant business performance, including:

- increase in revenue of 50% in the past three years;
- growth in gross operating profit of 200%;
- reduction in labour costs and staff recruitment;
- savings used to invest in a £500 000 conference and banqueting suite.

### Investors in People

The Cumberland Hotel was formally recognised as an Investor in People in 1993 and successfully reassessed in 1996. The hotel's recognition sets it apart from all competition in the area, and will continue to ensure high standards of customer service.

(Printed with the kind permission of Investors in People.)

## CASE STUDY 2

## Wealden District Council

### The organisation

Wealden District Council was established as a local authority in 1974. Embracing 320 miles of East Sussex, it stretches from the Kent borders to the sea, and is the largest district council in the South East. Its 135 000 population is scattered among rural villages and four substantial market towns.

It provides a range of services, including planning and development, refuse collection, environmental health, housing and leisure services. A staff of 560 is divided between two offices, four leisure centres, two depots and 19 sheltered dwellings. The Council, with no overall control, has 58 elected councillors, serving on ten committees and subcommittees.

364

## The challenge

The Council aims to offer the highest possible standard of service within the constraints of its budget, customer care being of paramount importance.

Particular challenges have continued to include:

- the introduction of compulsory competitive tendering, with the cost of services being tested in the open market against commercial operators;
- new legislation affecting large areas of the Council's work;
- the consolidation of Audit Commission performance indicators against which service performance is stringently measured;
- the requirement to work to constrained budgets, while delivering consistently high levels of service;

- introducing and developing new indicators for the benefit of the customer.

The objective continues to be to deliver a consistently high standard of service across an organisation widespread in location and function, with all the elements working harmoniously together, against a background of change.

(Printed with the kind permission of Investors in People.)

What strategy would you recommend Wealden District Council to follow in order to achieve its aims?

(A full answer to this question is given in the *Lecturer's Guide* that accompanies this textbook)

## REFERENCES AND FURTHER READING

Those texts marked with an asterisk are particularly recommended for further reading.

Alberga, T. (1997) 'Investors in People: time for a check up', *People Management*, 6 February, pp. 30–32.

Anon (1992a) 'Call for training system reform', *Financial Times*, 11 December, p. 2.

Anon (1992b) 'TECs must get the resources to do the job, CBI director warns', *Personnel Management*, May, p. 6.

Armstrong, G. (1996) 'A qualifications cuckoo in the competency nest?' *People Management*, 16 May, p. 23.

Ashton, D. and Sung, J. (1994) *The State, Economic Development and Skill Formation: A New Asian Model?* Working Paper No. 3, Centre for Labour Market Studies. Leicester: University of Leicester.

Atkinson, M. and Elliott, L. (2000) 'UK fails to provide path from school to work', the *Guardian*, 11 February, p. 6.

*Barrington, H. and Reid, M.A. (1999) *Training Interventions: Promoting Learning Opportunities*, 6th edn. London: Institute of Personnel and Development.

Barsoux, J.-L. and Lawrence, P. (1990) *Management in France*. London: Cassell.

BBC (1996) 'Train and prosper', *Analysis*, BBC Radio 4, broadcast 11 April.

Beresford, K. and Gaite, J. (1994) *Personnel Management*, April, pp. 38–41.

Bernhard, H.B. and Ingolis, C.A. (1988) 'Six lessons for the corporate classroom', *Harvard Business Review*, Vol. 66, No. 5, pp. 40–48.

Bournois, F. (1992) 'France', in Brewster, C., Hegewisch, A., Holden, L. and Lockhart, T. (eds) *The European Human Resource Management Guide*. London: Academic Press, pp. 113–162.

Brewster, C. (1999) 'Who is listening to HR?' *People Management*, 25 November, pp. 16–17.

Brewster, C. and Hegewisch, A. (1993) 'A continent of diversity', *Personnel Management*, January, pp. 36–40.

Brewster, C., Hegewisch, A., Holden, L. and Lockhart, T. (eds) (1992) *The European Human Resource Management Guide*. London: Academic Press.

Brockbank, A. and Beech, N. (1999) 'Guiding blight', *People Management*, 6 May, pp. 52–54.

Butters, T. (1996) 'Labour's plans for a skills revolution', the *Guardian*, Careers Supplement, 27 April, pp. 2, 3.

Cannell, M. (1997) 'Practice makes perfect', *People Management*, 6 March, pp. 26–33.

Carnevale, A., Gainer, L. and Schulz, E. (1990) *Training the Technical Workforce*. San Francisco, Calif.: Jossey-Bass.

Chase, R. (1997) 'The knowledge based organisation: an international study,' *Journal of Knowledge Management*, Vol.1, No. 1, pp. 38–49.

Claydon, T. and Green, F. (1992) *The Effect of Unions on Training Provision*. Discussion Papers in Economics, No. 92/3, January. Leicester: University of Leicester.

Confederation of British Industry (1989) *Towards a Skills Revolution*. London: CBI.

Constable, J. and McCormick, R. (1987) *The Making of British Managers*. London: British Institute of Management.

Coopers & Lybrand Associates (1985) *A Challenge to Complacency: Changing Attitudes to Training*. London: MSC/National Economic Development Office.

Department for Education and Employment (1999) *Learning to Succeed: A New Framework for Post 16 Learning*. Nottingham: DfEE publications.

Department for Education and Employment (2000) *National Learning Targets for England for 2002*, DfEE web page, 1 March, dfee.gov.uk/nlt/targets.htm

Department of Education and Science (1990) 'International statistical comparisons of the education and training of 16 to 18 year olds', *Statistical Bulletin*, 1/90, January. London: DES.

Dixon, N. (1994) *The Organisational Learning Cycle*. London: McGraw-Hill.

365

## The Management of Human Resources

*Dixon, N. (2000) *Common Knowledge*, Cambridge, Mass: Harvard Business School Press.

*Dore, R. and Sako, M. (1989) *How the Japanese Learn to Work*. London: Routledge.

Dulewicz, V. (1991) 'Improving assessment centres', *Personnel Management*, June, pp. 50–55.

Easterby-Smith, M. and Mackness, J. (1992) 'Completing the cycle of evaluation', *Personnel Management*, May, pp. 42–45.

Employment Department Group (1990) *What is an Investor in People?*, IIP 17, September. London: Employment Department Group.

Felstead, A. (1994) *Funding Government Training Schemes: Mechanisms and Consequences*. Working Paper No. 3, Centre for Labour Market Studies. Leicester: University of Leicester.

Finegold, D. (1991) 'The implications of "Training in Britain" for the analysis of Britain's skills problem: a comment on Paul Ryan's "How much do employers spend on training?"', *Human Resource Management Journal*, Vol. 2, No. 1, pp. 110–115.

Ford, G. (1993) 'Losing ground', *New Statesman*, 19 March, p. 41.

Fowler, A. (1991) 'How to identify training needs', *Personnel Management Plus*, Vol. 2, No. 11, pp. 36–37.

Garvin, D. (1993) 'Building a learning organisation', in *Harvard Business Review on Knowledge Management*. Cambridge, Mass: Harvard Business School Press, pp. 47–80.

Gaugler, E. and Wiltz, S. (1992) 'Federal Republic of Germany', in Brewster, C., Hegewisch, A., Holden, L. and Lockhart, J. (eds) *The European Human Resource Management Guide*. London: Academic Press, pp. 163–228.

Graham, A. (1992) 'YT funding and the TECs: a tragedy in the making', *Personnel Management*, February, p. 4.

Hall, D.T. (1984) 'Human resource development and organisational effectiveness', in Fombrun, C., Tichy, N. and Devanna, M. (eds) *Strategic Human Resource Management*. New York: John Wiley.

Halls, W. D. (1990) *Comparative Education: Contemporary Issues and Trends*. London: Jessica Kingsley Publishers for UNESCO.

Handy, C. (1987) *The Making of Managers: A Report on Management Education, Training and Development in the United States, West Germany, France, Japan and the UK*. London: NEDO.

Harrison, R. (1992) *Training and Development*. London: Institute of Personnel Management.

Harrison, R. (1995) 'Carrots are better levers than sticks', *People Management*, 19 October, pp. 38–40.

Harrison, R. (1997) *Employee Development*. London: Institute of Personnel and Devlopment.

Hillman, J. (1996) *University for Industry: Creating a National Learning Network*. London: Institute for Public Policy Research.

Hirsch, W. and Reilly, P. (1998) 'Cycling proficiency: how do large organisations identify their future skill needs among their thousands of employees?' *People Management*, 9 July, pp. 36–41.

Hofstede, G. (1984) *Culture's Consequences*. Newbury Park, Calif.: Sage.

Holden, L. (1991) 'European trends in training and development', *International Journal of Human Resource Management*, Vol. 2, No. 2, pp. 113–131.

Holden, L. and Livian, Y. (1992) 'Does strategic training policy exist? Some evidence from ten European countries', *Personnel Review*, Vol. 21, No. 1, pp. 12–23.

House of Commons (1993) *The Work of the Training and Enterprise Councils, Minutes of Evidence*, House of Commons Session 1992–93 (cited in Felstead, 1994).

Industrial Society (1985) *Survey of Training Costs: New Series No. 1*. London: Industrial Society.

Institute of Manpower Studies (IMS) (1984) *Competence and Competition: Training and Education in the Federal Republic of Germany, the United States and Japan*, MSC/NEDO.

Investors in People (IIP) UK (1995) *The Investors in People Standard*. London: Investors in People UK.

Investors in People (IIP) UK (2000) *Management Report 1999, No. 10*. London: Investors in People UK.

Kandola, B. (1996) 'Are competencies too much of a good thing?', *People Management*, 2 May, p. 21.

Keep, E. (1989) 'Corporate training strategies: the vital component?', in Storey, J. (ed.) *New Perspectives on Human Resource Management*. London: Routledge.

Kenney, J. and Reid, M. (1988) *Training Interventions*, 2nd edn. London: IPM.

Lähteenmäki, S., Holden, L. and Roberts, I. (eds) (1999) *HRM and the Learning Organisation*. Turku, Finland: Turku School of Economics and Business Administration, Series A-2.

Littlefield, D. and Welch, J. (1996) 'Training policy steals the political limelight', *People Management*, 4 April, pp. 5, 6.

Lloyd, J. (1990) *Light and Liberty: The History of the EEPTU*. London: Weidenfeld & Nicolson.

Lowe, K. (1992) 'End of the line for ET', *Personnel Today*, 8 December, p. 14.

Macleod, D. and Beavis, S. (1996) 'Britain trails rivals for want of skills', the *Guardian*, 14 June, p. 6.

Mangham, I.L. and Silver, M.S. (1986) *Management Training: Context and Practice*, ESRC/DTI Report. Bath: University of Bath, School of Management.

Manpower Services Commission (1981) *A Framework for the Future: A Sector by Sector Review of Industrial and Commercial Training*. London: MSC.

Manpower Services Commission (1981) *Glossary of Training Terms*. London: HMSO.

Mase, E. (1999) 'E-learning: joined-up thinking', *People Management*, 25 November, pp. 32–36.

Mayo, A. (1998) 'Knowledge management: memory bankers', *People Management*, 22 January, pp. 34–38.

Merrick, N. (1995) 'Moving up the class?', *People Management*, 30 November, pp. 8–9.

Milne, S. (1991) 'TECs failing to back training guarantees', the *Guardian*, 4 November, p. 6.

Nadler, L. (1984) *The Handbook of Human Resource Development*. New York: John Wiley.

National Advisory Council for Education and Training Targets (1996) *Skills for 2000: Report on Progress Towards the National Training Targets for Education and Training*. London: NACETT.

366

Nonaka, I. (1991) 'The knowledge creating company', in *Harvard Business Review on Knowledge Management*, Cambridge, Mass.: Harvard Business School Press, pp. 21–45.

Pedler, M., Burgoyne, J. and Boydell, T. (1988) *Learning Company Project Report*, Sheffield: Training Agency.

*Pedler, M., Burgoyne, J. and Boydell, T. (1997) *The Learning Company: A Strategy for Sustainable Development*, London: McGraw-Hill.

Pickard, J. (1992) 'Job evaluation and total management come under fire', *Personnel Management*, May, p. 17.

Pickard, J. (1996) 'Barriers ahead to a single currency', *People Management*, 21 March, pp. 22–27.

Pickard, J. (1997) 'The New Deal: just the job', *People Management*, 28 August, pp. 32–35.

Pickard, J. (1998) 'New training bodies focus on skills gap', *People Management*, 14 May, p.15.

Pollock, L. (1999) 'Upskill task,' *People Management*, 14 October, pp. 58–60.

Prais, S. and Steedman, H. (1986) 'Vocational training in France and Britain', *National Institute Economic Review*, No. 116, May, pp. 45–56.

Prais, S. and Wagner, K. (1988) 'Productivity and management: the training of foremen in Britain and Germany', *National Institute Economic Review*, No. 123, pp. 34–37.

Prais, S., Jarvis, V. and Wagner, K. (1989) 'Productivity and vocational skills in services in Britain and Germany', *National Institute Economic Review*, No. 130, November, pp. 52–74.

Price Waterhouse (1989) *Doing Business in France*. Paris and London: Price Waterhouse.

Price Waterhouse Cranfield Project (1990) *Report on International Strategic Human Resource Management*. London: Price Waterhouse.

Price Waterhouse Cranfield Project (1991) *Report on International Strategic Human Resource Management*. Cranfield: Cranfield School of Management.

Rainbird, H. and Maguire, M. (1993) 'When corporate need supersedes employee development', *Personnel Management*, February, pp. 34–37.

Rana, E. (1999a) 'Dim view of New Deal,' *People Management*, 3 June, p. 14.

Rana, E. (1999b) 'New Deal firms come under fire for training deficiencies', *People Management*, 19 August, p. 18.

Rana, E. (1999c) 'NTOs debate radical plans for voluntary investment', *People Management*, 16 September, p. 17.

Rana, E. (2000) 'National Skills Task Force rules out levy,' *People Management*, 20 January, p. 13.

Reid, M.A. and Barrington, H. (1997) *Training Interventions: Managing Employee Development*, 5th edn. London: Institute of Personnel and Development.

Reid, M.A., Barrington, H. and Kenney, J. (1992) *Training Interventions: Managing Employee Development*, 3rd edn. London: Institute of Personnel Management.

Rose, R. and Wignanek, G. (1990) *Training Without Trainers? How Germany Avoids Britain's Supply-side Bottleneck*. London: Anglo-German Foundation.

Ryan, P. (1991) 'How much do employers spend on training? An assessment of "Training in Britain" estimates', *Human Resource Management Journal*, Vol. 1, No. 4, pp. 55–57.

Saggers, R. (1994) 'Training climbs the corporate agenda', *Personnel Management*, July, pp. 40–45.

Sako, M. and Dore, R. (1986) 'How the Youth Training Scheme helps employers', *Employment Gazette*, June, pp. 195–204.

*Senge, P. (1990) *The Fifth Discipline: The Art and Practice of the Learning Organisation*. London: Century.

Sloman, M. (1999) 'Learning Centre: seize the day', *People Management*, 20 May, p. 31.

Smith, A (1999) 'Get with the programme', *People Management*, 3 June, p. 33.

Steedman, H. (1988) 'Vocational training in France and Britain: mechanical and electrical craftsmen', *National Institute Economic Review*, No. 126, November, pp. 57–71.

*Stewart, J. and McGoldrick, J. (1996) *Human Resource Development: Perspectives, Strategies and Practice*. London: Pitman.

Storey, J. (1991) 'Do the Japanese make better managers?' *Personnel Management*, August, pp. 24–28.

Syrett, M. and Lammiman, S. (1994) 'Developing the peripheral worker', *Personnel Management*, July, pp. 28–31.

Targett, S. (1996) 'Shepherd admits skills shortage', *Times Higher Education Supplement*, 14 June, p. 3.

Taylor, P. and Thackwray, B. (1995) *Investors in People Explained*. London: Kogan Page.

Thorn, J. (1988) 'Making of a Meister', *Industrial Society Magazine*, June, pp. 19–21.

Thurow, L. (1992) *Head to Head: The Coming Economic Battle Among Japan, Europe and America*. London: Nicholas Brealey.

Townsend, T. (1992) 'How the lead body sees it', *Personnel Management*, November, p. 39.

Trades Union Congress (1989) *Skills 2000*. London: TUC (quoted in Claydon and Green, 1992).

Trades Union Congress (1990) *TUC: Joint Action over Training*. London: TUC (quoted in Claydon and Green, 1992).

Trades Union Congress (1991) *Collective Bargaining Strategy for the 1990s*. London: TUC (quoted in Claydon and Green, 1992).

Training Agency (1989) *Training in Britain*. Norwich: HMSO.

Tyson, S. and Fell, A. (1995) 'A focus on skills, not organisations', *People Management*, pp. 42–45.

Welch, J. (1996a) 'HR qualifications get the go-ahead at last', *People Management*, 30 May, p. 11.

Welch, J. (1996b) 'YT alternative comes out of the shadows', *People Management*, 30 May, p. 12.

Welch, J. (1996c) 'Britain slipping behind in the race for skills', *People Management*, 27 June, p. 11.

Whitehead, M. (1999) 'Firms ignore staff needs in key areas of the economy', *People Management*, 11 February, p. 16.

*Wilson, D.A. (1996) *Managing Knowledge*. Oxford: Institute of Management/Butterworth Heinemann.

Wood, L. (1994) '"Urgent need" found for government to examine TECs funding', *Financial Times*, 25 March.

367

# Chapter 3

# Performance appraisal

Tom Redman

## Introduction

The practice of performance appraisal has undergone many major changes over the last decade or so. In the main developments have been driven by large-scale organisational change (see Chapter 1) rather than theoretical advances in the study of performance appraisal. Particularly prominent here are the advent of downsizing, decentralisation and delayering, flexibilisation of the workforce, the move to teamworking, and wave after wave of culture change programmes and new managerial initiatives such as TQM, BPR, competency and in particular Investors in People. The most recent WERS data finds that organisations which are recognised as an Investor in People were significantly more likely to have a performance appraisal scheme in use (Cully *et al.*, 1999). Changes in payment systems have also fuelled the growth and development of performance appraisal. Developments in integrated reward systems, harmonisation and the increased use of merit- and performance-based pay have been strongly associated with the growth of performance appraisal.

Two main implications for performance appraisal practice arise from the new organisational context. Firstly, it would be clearly inappropriate to expect that those appraisal schemes operating ten years or so ago could be effective in many organisations today (see Case Study 3.1). Secondly, rather than new developments heralding the end of performance appraisal or diminishing its importance, they appear to have enhanced its contribution to helping achieve organisational objectives and stimulated considerable experimentation and innovation in its practice. Performance appraisal, as we discuss below, has in fact become more widespread. It has grown to include previously untouched organisations and occupational groups. In particular, performance appraisal has moved down the organisational hierarchy to encompass blue-collar, secretarial and administrative staff, and from the private to the public sector. New forms of appraisal have also emerged. We thus now have competency-based appraisal systems, staff appraisal of managers, team-based appraisal, customer appraisals and the so-called '360°' systems.

This chapter's main aim is to review some of the key developments in the practice of performance appraisal. Firstly, a brief history of performance appraisal is presented and its current practice examined by considering how widespread it is, what it is used for, and its role as a managerial control tool within broader performance management systems. Secondly, we review some of the major innovations in the practice of performance appraisal. Thirdly, some of the problems of performance appraisal in practice are considered – in particular, we examine here the compatibility of performance appraisal with TQM and customer service initiatives. Finally, in light of the growing criticisms, we conclude by considering whether performance appraisal has a future in HRM practice.

## Development of performance appraisal

Informal systems of performance appraisal have been around as long as people have worked together; it is a universal human tendency to make evaluations of our colleagues at work. Formal performance appraisals have a shorter but still considerable history. Grint (1993) traces it back to a third-century Chinese practice. In the UK Randell (1989) identifies its first use via the 'silent monitor' in Robert Owen's textile mills. Here a multi-coloured block of wood was hung over the employee's workspace with the front colour indicating the foreman's assessment of the previous day's conduct, from white for good through to black for bad. Owen also recorded a yearly assessment of employees in a 'book of character'.

Since these early developments performance appraisal has now become a staple element of HRM practice, although personnel managers have tended to be much keener on it than their line manager colleagues (see below). Accompanying practitioner interest in performance appraisal has been a mushrooming of academic research, notably by occupational psychologists. A key thrust of much of this research has been on improving performance appraisal's effectiveness, and in particular, its accuracy in assessing employee performance. We know rather less about a more strategic use of performance appraisal as an organisational change lever and managerial control tool. There is now a wealth of academic studies on performance appraisal. A computer literature search of one year alone in the USA reports a 'conservative' figure of 11 articles per month appearing with 'performance appraisal' in their titles (Halachmi, 1993). Despite the large and growing volume of research work on the subject, however, it is debatable how much influence such studies have had on the actual practice of performance appraisal (Maroney and Buckley, 1992). It seems that managers are peculiarly reluctant to heed the advice of researchers in this area of business practice and there is an increasing gap between research and practice (Banks and Murphy, 1985).

This lack of impact of research on practice is not simply a question of general managerial indifference to the academic researcher, especially when compared to the wide influence of consultants and popular management gurus. Rather, one explanation is that little of the research has considered the implications for practitioners who are faced with a plethora of organisational constraints not encountered in the research laboratory. More damning perhaps is the view that much of the research has had little to offer HR managers, except for the recommendation to train appraisers, as it has generally been unable to provide much improvement – in terms of accuracy at least – over the simplest of supervisory ratings systems (Giffin, 1989).

## The practice of performance appraisal

### How widespread is performance appraisal?

Performance appraisal has become more widespread in Western countries. For example, surveys report performance appraisal in the USA increasing from 89 per cent of organisations surveyed in the mid-1970s to 94 per cent by the mid-1980s (Locher and Teel, 1988). Similar surveys in the UK by the Institute of Personnel and Development report increasing coverage of formal appraisal arrangements (Long, 1986; Armstrong and Baron, 1998). Performance appraisal is also now more common in many other non-Western countries, such as China (Chow, 1994), Hong Kong (Snape et al., 1998), Japan in the form of Satei (see Endo, 1994); Africa (Arthur et al., 1995) and India (Lawler et al., 1995).

Appraisal is particularly prominent in some industrial sectors in the UK, such as financial services (IRS, 1994, 1999), and it has grown rapidly in the public sector of late. The last decade has seen its introduction in schools, hospitals, universities, local authorities, the civil service, etc. For example, some 80 per cent of local authorities surveyed either operated or were currently introducing performance appraisal (IRS, 1995a). It has also grown from its main deployment in the middle of organisation hierarchies, particularly in middle management and professional occupations, to include a much broader group of manual and clerical employees (Cully et al., 1999). Increasingly it seems, in line with harmonisation policies, that all employees in an organisation are included in the performance system appraisal. An IRS survey found that 39 per cent of organisations applied appraisal to every employee (IRS, 1994) and a replication of the survey five years later found 75 per cent to do so (IRS, 1999). The coverage of employees in the public sector, given the relative infancy of many schemes, is still rather more limited than the private sector. The IRS found only 17 per cent of public sector organisations surveyed included all employees in the scheme. However, these claims can be misleading. Employers who include the growing numbers of 'contingent' or 'peripheral' workers, such as part-time and contract staff, in performance appraisal schemes appear to be the exception rather than the rule (Syrett and Lammiman, 1994).

## How is appraisal conducted?

A wide range of methods are used to conduct performance appraisals, from the simplest of ranking schemes through objective-, standard- and competency-based systems (see below) to complex behaviourally anchored rating schemes (see Snape *et al.*, 1994). The nature of an organisation's appraisal scheme is largely a reflection of its managerial beliefs (Randell, 1994), the amount of resources it has available to commit, and the expertise it possesses. Thus, smaller organisations with limited HR expertise tend to adopt simpler ranking and rating schemes whilst the more complex and resource consuming systems, such as competency-based and 360° appraisal, are found mainly in larger organisations.

Most employers use only one type of appraisal scheme, often a 'hybrid form' of a number of methods and a few companies even provide employees with a choice of methods in how they are appraised. The IRS surveys (IRS, 1994, 1999) found many organisations with more than one system of performance appraisal operating. The main reason behind multiple systems was the wish to separate out reward and non-reward aspects of appraisal, and to provide different systems for different occupational groups (e.g. managerial and non-managerial employees), and separate systems for different parts of the organisation.

## What is it used for?

Organisations use performance appraisal for a wide range of different purposes. Surveys commonly report the use of performance appraisal for clarifying and defining performance expectations; identifying training and development needs; providing career counselling; succession planning; improving individual, team and corporate performance; facilitating communications and involvement; allocating financial rewards; determining promotion, motivating and controlling employees, and achieving cultural change (Bowles and Coates, 1993; IRS, 1994, 1999).

Recent trends suggest that the more judgmental and 'harder' forms of performance appraisal are on the increase and that 'softer', largely developmental approaches are declining (Gill, 1977; Long, 1986; Armstrong and Baron, 1998). Thus there has been a shift in performance appraisal away from using it for career planning and identifying future potential and increased use of it for improving current performance and allocating rewards. Here the arrival of flatter organisations has given rise to the need to uncouple to some extent performance appraisal and promotion whilst competitive pressures have emphasised the need to incentivise improvements in short-term performance.

There are both advantages and disadvantages to such broad demands upon performance appraisal systems. A wide use helps to integrate various, often disparate, HRM areas into a coherent package of practices. For example, by providing a link between performance and rewards, and development needs and succession planning, more effective HRM outcomes are possible. However, it also gives rise to the common criticism that performance appraisal systems are simply too ambitious in that managers expect them to be able to accommodate a very wide range of purposes. The breadth of use thus results in appraisal becoming a 'blunt instrument that tries to do too much' (Boudreaux, 1994).

Further, many of the above purposes of appraisal are seen as being in conflict. Thus, recording the past and influencing future performance is difficult to achieve in a single process. The danger is that appraisal, particularly given the trends identified above, concentrates on the past at the expense of the future performance, with a common analogy being that this is rather like using the rear view mirror to drive future performance. Similarly, allocating rewards and identifying training needs are often seen as being incompatible objectives in a single appraisal scheme. The openness required for meaningfully assessing development needs is closed down by the need for the employee to 'explain away' performance problems in order to gain a merit rise. However, the danger of disconnecting reward allocation from appraisal is that appraisers and appraised would not treat the process as seriously because without it appraisal lacks bite and 'fires blank bullets' (Lawler, 1994). Increasingly, as we now examine, performance appraisal is used as one element of a much broader performance management system.

## Performance management

Performance management, like many HRM innovations, is an American import that has been a major driver in the increased use of performance appraisal by British organisations. Performance management has been defined as 'systems and attitudes which help organisations to plan, delegate and assess the operation of their services' (LGMB, 1994). Bevan and Thompson (1991) describe a 'textbook' performance management system thus:

- a shared vision of the organisation's objectives communicated via a mission statement to all employees
- individual performance targets which are related to operating unit and wider organisational objectives
- regular formal review of progress towards targets
- a review process which identifies training and development needs and rewards outcomes
- an evaluation of the effectiveness of the whole process and its contribution to overall organisational performance to allow changes and improvements to be made.

A principal feature of performance management is thus that it connects the objectives of the organisation to a system of work targets for individual employees. In such models of performance management objective setting and formal appraisal are placed at the heart of the approach. The development of performance management systems has had major implications for performance appraisal. A key trend has been away from stand-alone performance appraisal systems and towards individual appraisal becoming part of an integrated performance management system. Bevan and Thompson's survey for the IPM found some 20 per cent of British organisations had introduced performance management systems.

There is a growing critique of performance management systems. Firstly, they are seen as adding more pressure to a short-term view amongst British managers, which may well hamper organisational performance over the long term. Secondly, they are often proffered in a very prescriptive fashion, with many writers advocating a single best way for performance management, to the neglect of important variables such as degree of centralisation, unionisation, etc. This is in contrast to the actual practice of performance management in the UK, which is 'extremely diverse' (Fletcher and Williams, 1992). The real danger is that performance management systems cannot be simply borrowed from one organisation and applied in another, as many advocates appear to suggest. Thirdly, although performance management is supposed to be line management 'driven' (Fowler, 1990), case studies of its practices report the motivating forces in organisations as being chief executives and HR departments with often questionable ownership and commitment from line managers (Fletcher and Williams, 1992). Fourthly, there is a growing concern that performance management systems, because of their dedicated focus on improving the bottom line, have added unduly to the pressures and stresses of work-life for many employees. Many systems have been introduced with scant regard for employee welfare (see Box 3.1). Lastly, and perhaps more damning, is the view that it is ineffective. The main driver of performance management is the improvement of overall organisational effectiveness. However, there is little support from various studies that performance management actually improves performance. For example, Bevan and Thompson's survey of performance management in the UK found that there was no relationship between high-performing UK companies (defined as those demonstrating pre-tax profit growth over a five-year period) and the operation of a performance management system.

## Performance appraisal as managerial control

With the decline of careers in the flat, delayered organisation, HRM techniques such as performance appraisal have become more significant managerial tools in motivating and controlling the workforce. Appraisal is now seen by some commentators as being much more significant in maintaining employee loyalty and commitment than in directly managing performance (Bowles and Coates, 1993). Its use provides managers with a major opportunity to reinforce corporate values and attitudes and so it appeals as an important strategic instrument in the control process. Thus, we find a growing use of appraisal systems for non-managerial employees that are based on social, attitudinal and trait attributes (Townley, 1989). Employees are increasingly being appraised not only on 'objective' measures such as attendance, timekeeping, productivity and quality but also on more subjective aspects such as 'dependability', 'flexibility', 'initiative', 'loyalty', etc.

Recent analyses of performance appraisal, based upon the work of Foucault, have given particular emphasis to the power relations implicit in performance appraisal. For Townley performance appraisal has the potential to act as the 'paper equivalent' of the panopticon with its 'anonymous and continuous surveillance'

**BOX 3.1**

## Stretching the American workforce

A new approach to performance management in the USA is the so-called 'stretch management'. Instead of a traditional approach of generating more output by committing more input 'corporate America seems to be trying to get more output just by demanding more output' (Sherman, 1995: 231). It is being applied in US companies such as Boeing (to drive down costs) and 3M (to improve product innovation). Stretch management involves setting demanding objectives – 'stetch targets' – for the organisation.

Accounts chronicle its success in achieving major performance improvements in areas such as return of investment, product innovation, productivity, capital utilisation (Tully, 1994). Alcoa, the world's largest aluminium company, provides a good example. Following the appointment of a new chief executive, a large scale TQM programme was initiated in 1987 and, by many standards, proved highly successful (Kolesar, 1993). However, by 1991 a new strategy emerged due to the CEO's frustration with the slow pace of TQM. The new strategy demanded intense and focused commitment to 'quantum leap' rather than continuous improvement management.

Given its recent introduction it is perhaps too early to write off 'stretch management'. Nevertheless, its sustainability must be open to question and critics view it simply as one of the latest and most intense forms of 'management by stress'. Indeed, early reports show an especially high casualty rate amongst middle managers, with estimates of between a third and a half of managers being unable to cope (Tully, 1994). Some companies have now 'softened' their stretch programmes. At General Electric its role is seen as an 'artificial stimulant' for new and more effective ways of working and employees are not punished for failing to achieve demanding targets (Sherman, 1995). This leads to a particular problem with stretch management: its demotivation potential. The danger is that such a system of performance management which sets truly stretching goals, which employees thus often fail to achieve, results in high-performing staff feeling like losers. In an attempt to get employees to buy into stretch programmes some companies are now linking the achievement of targets to gainsharing programmes.

(1993: 232). Recent developments in appraisal, which have both broadened the range of, and increased the number of appraisers, via 360° appraisal, upward appraisal and the use of external customers (see below), have increased the potential for managerial control and the utilisation of the panoptical powers of performance appraisal. In such systems the employee is now continually exposed to the appraiser's 'constant yet elusive presence' (Fuller and Smith, 1991: 11). Every customer, peer, subordinate and colleague is now also a potential appraiser. Thus it is hardly surprising that employees have nicknamed peer reviews of performance 'screw your buddy' systems of appraisal.

Managers themselves are not immune from the disciplinary 'gaze' of performance appraisal (see next section). Managerial attitudes, especially at middle management levels, have often been identified as a barrier to the introduction of new ways of managing, such as employee involvement and empowerment. The use of upward appraisal of managers by staff is increasingly being used to link managerial behaviour more closely with corporate values and mission statements by incorporating questions on these into appraisal instruments which are completed by the employee (Redman and Snape, 1992). Thus at one and the same time organisations promote their required values to their employees and evaluate the commitment of their managers to these. Managers scoring badly in such appraisals are often 'culled' (see Redman and Mathews, 1995). Thus, for example, at Semco, the much-discussed Brazilian company, managers are upwardly appraised every six months using a scale up to 100. The results are then posted on a notice board and those who consistently underperform are squeezed out or simply 'fade away'.

## Recent developments in performance appraisal

As we noted in the introduction, there have been many innovations in performance appraisal practice. In this section we discuss some of the more influential of these.

### Upward appraisal

Upward appraisal is a relatively recent addition to performance appraisal practice in the UK. Although it is still far from common, the 1990s have witnessed the introduction of upward appraisal in a range of UK companies. Upward appraisal is more common in the USA and appears to have spread from US parent companies to their UK operations (e.g. at companies such as Federal Express, Standard Chartered Bank, and AMEX) and from these to UK companies such as WH Smith, The Body Shop and parts of the UK public sector (see Redman and Mathews, 1995). Upward appraisal involves the employee rating their manager's performance via, in most cases, an anonymous questionnaire. The process is anonymous to overcome employees' worries about providing honest but unfavourable feedback on managerial performance. Anonymity limits the potential for managerial retribution or what is termed the 'get even' factor of upward appraisal.

Advocates claim significant benefits for upward appraisal (see Redman and Snape, 1992) including improved managerial effectiveness and leadership through 'make-you-better' feedback and increased employee voice and empowerment. Equally, upward appraisal is seen as being more in tune with the delayered organisation where managerial spans of control are greater and working arrangements much more diverse. In such situations employees are in much greater contact with their manager than is the manager's manager and thus traditional top-down boss appraisal is seen as being less effective. Upward appraisal, because of the use of multiple raters, is also seen as being more robust to legal challenge of performance judgements. Given the increasingly litigatious culture in the UK, Townley (1990) has noted that it is surprising that performance appraisal methods and the systems in which they are embedded are not attacked in the courts more often.

Managers have been reported as not being especially fond of upward appraisal systems. In part this may stem from the career-threatening use of upward appraisal schemes in some organisations. For example, one of BP Exploration's objectives in introducing upward appraisal was to return to individual contribution roles those managers 'clearly not cut out to manage people' (Thomas *et al.*, 1992). Often it appears to the manager on the receiving end of upward appraisal that, according to Grint (1993), '. . ."the honest opinions" of subordinates look more like the barbs on a whale harpoon than gentle and constructive nudges'. Such a lack of managerial acceptance of upward appraisal, especially at middle and junior levels of management, may go some way to explaining its relatively low uptake in the UK after a flurry of activity in the early 1990s.

### 360° performance appraisal

The so-called 360° appraisals appear to be taking root and becoming an established form of appraisal in the UK (see Box 3.2). A survey by consultants Pilat reported up to 40 per cent of FTSE companies are now using it. Although considerable, such a usage rate is somewhat behind the three-quarters of Fortune 500 companies reported as employing 360° appraisal in a similar US survey (*Personnel Management*, July, 1995 p. 15). Dudgill (1994) traces the origins of 360° appraisal to the US army in the 1970s. Here military researchers found that peers' opinions were more accurate indicators of a soldier's ability than those of superiors were. The term '360°' is used to describe the comprehensive nature of feedback derived from a composite rating from peers, subordinates, supervisors and occasionally customers. Again, it is normally conducted via an anonymous survey, although some recent innovations include the use of audio and videotape to record feedback answers. Some organisations also use on-line computerised data-gathering systems as well as more informal systems where managers simply pass a disk around a number of appraisers. One management consultancy, in order to encourage responses, is experimenting with 'fun' methods of collecting data such as using short statements comparing individual managers with well-known characters (CPCR, 1995).

There is a wide variation in what is appraised in 360° feedback. Many companies use fully structured questionnaires based upon models of managerial competency. Others, such as Dupont, which uses 360° appraisal in its Individual Career Management programme, employ a much less structured approach. Here appraisers respond to open questions, which ask for descriptions of the appraiser's 'major value-adding areas for the year'; summaries of the manager's strengths; descriptions of key improvement needs, and a request for other general comments. Unstructured systems of appraisal have advantages in tapping into key aspects of managerial performance. Nevertheless, the danger of using an unstructured approach is that the popular but incompetent manager may well fare better than one who is highly effective but not particularly pleasant. Mostly the appraisers remain anonymous but some systems, such as Dupont's, leave the option open to

## BOX 3.2

### 360° appraisal at Northumbrian Water

Following the hot dry summer of 1995 and accompanying water shortages, adverse public relations and intense media interest, life has been particularly difficult for managers in the newly privatised water companies. One company, Northumbrian Water, has been helping its managers to cope with a range of management development practices, including 360° appraisal.

Northumbrian Water introduced a 360° feedback programme for its managers in 1990 via a pilot group of 35 managers. A key reason behind the introduction was to provide data for the company's development centre for senior managers. The development centre was designed to enable managers to move to a position of managing their own career development. It was considered important that individual managers should have a view from their colleagues about their performance, potential and development needs in order to facilitate sound career decisions. The 360° appraisal instrument consists of a bank of questions asking respondents to comment on the effectiveness and performance of the appraised manager against three main categories: competence, style and role. Appraisers, for example, are asked to say how often they see the candidate behave in a particular fashion which is consistent with the behaviours listed for a senior manager. Space is also provided for open comments on the manager's performance and the company feels it is often these which prove the most enlightening.

The system is based upon a refined competency model originally developed in 1981. The competencies model was further developed following privatisation of the industry as the roles and styles of management appropriate to the company's new values were developed. For example, commercial awareness and customer care were not present in the original formulation. A study of HRM practices in the post-privatization water industry considers Northumbrian Water to have introduced the 'most dramatic changes' of all the companies (IRS, 1992).

The feedback forms are distributed to 10–12 of the manager's colleagues in some form of distribution such as two above, five sideways and four below the individual manager. Internal customers are often part of the process but the company has yet to incorporate external customers. The forms are returned directly to the company's consultants who produce a summary data booklet, discuss the results with the manager, and help prepare them for the development centre.

The main benefit the company perceives it has obtained from 360° feedback is in providing individual managers with vital insights into some of their shortcomings, which would otherwise remain unaddressed. Although it has been somewhat of a shock for some, managers are considered to be much more self-aware about their leadership qualities and are felt to be working better with their staff. 360° appraisal is also seen as making a valuable contribution in encouraging managers to engage in continuous professional development and encouraging an approach where performance problems can be positively tackled through training and development. One of the main problems the company has found with its implementation is that in the early programmes there was some difficulty in convincing managers that such feedback was of value because their development and career planning was within their own remit rather than that of their boss. A few individuals also had great difficulty in accepting the feedback and searched for reasons to rationalise it.

*Source*: interviews with managers

the appraiser whether or not to add their name to the appraisal form. However, unless a composite rating only is presented to the manager – and this tends to counter the value of having multiple perspectives in 360° – it is very difficult to provide the immediate supervisor with anonymity.

It seems that 360° appraisal is edging away from a management development tool and towards a broader organisational role. Increasingly, and controversially, it seems that organisations are also experimenting with linking 360° appraisal and managerial remuneration. The press has recently reported companies such as 3M and British Aerospace as introducing 360° appraisal and feeding the results into the formula for performance-related pay for managers. Rather a lot is claimed for 360° appraisal and, as in the case of many new initiatives, we have seen a rash of articles announcing how it can 'change your life' (O'Reilly, 1994), and deliver competitive advantage for the organisation (London and Beatty, 1993). Because of its use of multiple raters with different perspectives – a sort of safety in numbers approach – it is often suggested that it provides more accurate and meaningful feedback. However, as Grint (1993) notes, this often simply replaces the subjectivity of a single appraiser with the subjectivity of multiple appraisers.

Undoubtedly, many organisations have gained some advantages from using 360° appraisal, particularly in management developmental terms. It has proved especially useful for providing feedback for senior managers who are often neglected at the top in appraisal terms. A strength of 360° appraisal is that management consultants proffering systems will tailor a basic questionnaire to meet the organisation's characteristics such as culture, mission, business values, and structure and management practices. It remains to be seen whether the benefits gained are outweighed by the considerable time, effort and costs involved. Indeed it seems some management consultants are 'gravy training' on the back of the current enthusiasm for 360° appraisal with week-long feedback courses, facilitated by themselves, recommended to debrief managers.

One key advantage of the broad group of appraisers used in this method is that it can provide a more meaningful appraisal for employees with little contact with their workplace. In such situations traditional top-down appraisals are of little value. A good example is provided by Burger King, which in a recent re-organisation, now has over half of all managerial staff working in the field (*Financial Times*, 13 September, 1995, p. 15). Such managers are based at home and communicate with head office via computerised telecommunications equipment. The aim of the reorganisation was to force managerial staff into closer contact with the restaurant staff. Clearly, top-down appraisal is of little value in such a low-contact working relationship. Thus Burger King introduced 360° assessment whereby up to 10 colleagues provide an assessment of the manager against some 83 behavioural characteristics. Although the system is not perfect – one manager described the process as having your personality dissected by ten people you have hardly met – the company feels that it provides a more meaningful assessment process for its field managers.

A number of questions remain unanswered about 360° appraisal – not least whether the data generated is accurate, valid and, more importantly, meaningful for the appraisee and whether the organisation stands to benefit from it. Ratings are only as good as the questions asked and often the interpretation of question wording is far from clear in many instruments. Such questions as 'Does the manager deal with problems in a flexible manner?' are not uncommon in appraisal instruments. Items need to be clear, easy to understand and easy to rate given the rater's contact with the appraisee. One particular criticism of many 360° systems is that all raters are given the same instrument, despite the different nature of the contact with the appraisee. Some issues are clearly more visible to the rater from different vantage points and questionnaires should ideally be constructed accordingly. Items based on actual behaviours, key organisational competencies, or critical incidents observed in the workplace indicative of superior-performing managers tend to be more effective. However, respondents will usually provide ratings on whatever questions are asked, whether they are in a position to do so or not.

There is also a tendency to produce overly bureaucratic systems. The danger here is that one common cause of failure in performance appraisal – that of requiring participants to fill in large quantities of paperwork – is being ignored. Making the feedback meaningful is also a challenge to which many users of 360° appraisal fail to rise. To ensure meaningful feedback a process of self-appraisal, comparison against other managers' ratings and follow-up with facilitators and those who provided the ratings are the minimum required. Also there is an implicit expectation on the part of those providing the ratings that such feedback will lead to improvements and that managers will change their behaviour for the better. However, there is as yet little evidence that this actually occurs (e.g. Redman and McElwee, 1993).

Lastly, many so called 360° appraisal systems are far from an all-round view of managers; the external customer as a reviewer is often left out but, as we discuss in the next section, customers are an increasingly heard voice in the assessment of employee performance. 360° appraisal, it seems, is also only a starting point and as management consultants 'discover' new sources of raters we can look forward to such innovations as 450° and even 540° appraisal.

### Customer appraisal

TQM and customer care programmes are now very widespread in both private and public sectors in the UK. One impact of these initiatives is that organisations are now increasingly setting employee performance standards based upon customer care indicators and appraising staff against these. A mix of 'hard' quantifiable standards such as 'delivery of a customer's first drink within two minutes' and soft qualitative standards such as 'a warm and friendly greeting', as used at Forte Roadside Restaurants, are now used in performance appraisal systems (IRS, 1995b). Employee performance standards, when linked into customer care policies, need to be realistic, achievable, and measurable. The use of service guarantees, which involve the payment of compensatory moneys to customers if the organisations do not reach the standards has also led to a greater use of customer data in performance appraisal ratings.

Customer service data for use in appraising employees is gathered by a variety of methods. Firstly, there is the use of a range of customer surveys, via the completion of customer care cards, telephone surveys, interviews with customers, postal surveys, etc. Organisations are now using such surveys more frequently and are increasingly sophisticated in how they gather customer views (Silvestro, 1990). Secondly, there is a range of surveillance techniques used by managers to sample the service encounter. Here the electronic work monitoring of factory workers is being extended into the services sector (Laabs, 1992). For example, customer service managers at Mercury Communications spend some 30 hours of their time each month reviewing staff performance by taping staff–customer conversations and giving immediate feedback as well as using the data for the regular formal review process.

Third, and even more controversial, is the increasing use of the so-called 'mystery shopping'. For some commentators customer service can only be really effectively evaluated at the boundary between customer and organisation and this view has fuelled the growth of shopping as a data capturing process (Miles, 1993). Here staff employed by a specialist agency purport to be real shoppers and observe and record their experience of the service encounter. It is now commonly used in banks, insurance companies, supermarkets and parts of the public sector (see Moores, 1990; Ring, 1992). For example, an element of the Citizen's Charter requires the setting of performance indicators on answering telephone calls and letters. Some local authorities evaluate the quality of telephone responses by employing consultants to randomly call the authority and assess the quality of the response (IRS, 1995b).

Mystery shopping is argued to give a company a rich source of data that cannot be uncovered by other means, such as customer surveys. Such surveys, although useful for some purposes, are often conducted many months after the service encounter and thus exact service problems are difficult to recollect. Mystery shopping is also seen as being particularly useful in revealing staff performance that causes customers to leave without purchasing. In many service sector organisations a natural consequence of the use of mystery shoppers has been to utilise the data in the performance evaluations of staff (Fuller and Smith, 1991).

These data gathering methods are, as one could well expect, not very popular with staff. Employees often question the ethics of introducing shoppers and feel that it represents a distinct lack of managerial trust in them. Thus employees describe shoppers in terms of 'spies' and 'snoopers' and react with hostility and 'shopper spotting' to their introduction. The introduction of mystery shopping for the largely negative reason of catching staff performing poorly only fuels such reactions. Cook (1993) advises that using shoppers as a means to reward staff for good performance, rather than to punish staff for poor performance, can help their acceptance. Staff who obtain good mystery shopping ratings should be rewarded and recognised whilst those who obtain poor ones should use them as a way of identifying training needs.

In an increasing number of organisations internal service level agreements are also being established. The introduction of compulsory competitive tendering has given considerable impetus to such agreements in the public sector. Often in such agreements there is an internal customer-service 'guarantee' stating what level and the nature of services the supplier will provide. It has been a natural progression of such a development for organisations such as Federal Express and Digital to incorporate performance data from service level agreements into the appraisal process (e.g. Milliman *et al.*, 1995). A key advantage claimed for using internal customers in this way is that joint goal-setting helped to give both internal customer and provider a greater understanding of the roles that individuals and departments fulfil. It thus helps in breaking down internal barriers between departments.

## Team-based appraisal

Work is increasingly being restructured into highly interdependent work teams, yet, despite this, performance appraisal often remains stubbornly based on the individual. In some cases teams are being given more responsibility for allocating work tasks, setting bonuses, selecting new staff, and even disciplining errant members. For such organisations it has thus been seen as entirely appropriate that performance appraisals should also be based upon and even conducted by the team themselves.

Two main variants of team appraisal can be identified. In some approaches the manager appraises the team as a whole. Targets are set, performance measured and assessments made, and rewards are allocated as with traditional individual appraisals. The manager makes no attempt to differentiate one member from another in performance terms, in fact, the creation of internal inequity with respect to rewarding performance is a deliberate aspect (Lawler, 1994). Equal ratings and rewards ensue for all the team, regardless of performance. The team are then encouraged to resolve internally any performance problems or competence deficiencies in order to facilitate overall team performance and development. Team members themselves may then provide informal awards or recognition of superior performance. The other main variant is where individual appraisals of each team member are still made but not by management. Rather, in a form of peer appraisal, team members appraise each other, usually via the use of anonymous rating questionnaires.

## Competency-based appraisal

Interest in the concept of competency has been one of the major HR themes of the last decade. Connock (1992) describes it as one of HRM's 'big ideas'. One consequence of this has been the attempt by some organisations to use the competency approach to develop an integrated human resource strategy. This has been particularly pronounced in HR practices targeted at managers but is also growing for non-managerial groups. A consequence of the development of organisational competency models has been that employers have increasingly extended their use from training and development, selection and reward uses into the area of appraisal (e.g. Mitrani *et al.*, 1992). For example, the most widely reported innovation in performance appraisal systems during the 1990s has been the linking of appraisals to competency frameworks (IRS, 1999).

The assessment of competencies in the appraisal process has a number of bene-fits. The evaluation of competencies identified as central to a good job performance provides a useful focus for analysing the progress an individual is making in the job rather than the static approach of many ability- or trait-rating schemes. Thus competency-based assessment is especially useful in directing employee attention to areas where there is scope for improvement. The use of competencies broadens appraisal by including 'How well is it done' measures in addition to the more traditional 'What is achieved measures'. It also helps to con-centrate the appraisal process on the key area of performance and effectiveness and provides a language for feedback on performance problems (Sparrow, 1994: 9). This latter benefit overcomes one of the problems of traditional objective-based appraisal systems in which the appraiser is often at a loss as to how to counsel an employee on what they should do differently if the appraisal objectives have not been achieved. However, these benefits must be set against the development and running costs involved and the wider critical debate surrounding the 'competency movement' in general.

## Problems of performance appraisal

Performance appraisals appear to be one human resource activity that everyone loves to hate. Carroll and Schneier's (1982) research found that performance appraisal ranks as the most disliked managerial activity. It is frequently suggested in the popular management literature that most managers would prefer to have a dental appointment rather than conduct a performance appraisal. Many appraisees, it seems, would also prefer this! According to Grint (1993: 64) 'rarely in the history of business can such a system have promised so much and delivered so little'.

The critics of performance appraisal claim that it is expensive; causes conflict between appraised and appraiser; has limited value and may even be dysfunctional in the improvement of employee performance; and, despite the rhetoric its use con-tributes little to the strategic management of an organisation. It is also held to be riddled with so many distorting 'effects' that its accuracy in providing an indicator of actual employee performance must also be called into question (see Box 3.3). Some appraisal systems, especially the more judgmental, those tied in to merit pay systems and those with forced distributions are argued to be especially problematic in these respects. Thus, for many writers performance appraisal is 'doomed' (Halachmi, 1993); a managerial practice 'whose time has gone' (Fletcher, 1993; Bhote, 1994) and whose end is imminently predicted (Roth and Ferguson, 1994).

Why does performance appraisal not work? One reason is that, despite their widely held belief to the contrary, most managers are not naturally good at conducting performance appraisals. According to Lawler (1994: 17), it is an

---

**BOX 3.3**

## Cronies and doppelgangers in performance appraisal

The search for accurate performance appraisals is a seemingly illusory one, with many pitfalls and distorting effects strewn in the appraiser's path. Some of the main ones are:

- *Halo effects* – This is where one positive criterion distorts the assessment of others. Similarly the *horns effect* is where a single negative aspect dominates the appraisal rating.

- *Doppelganger effect* – This is where the rating reflects the similarity between appraiser and appraised.

- *Crony effect* – This is the result of appraisal being distorted by the closeness of the relationship between appraiser and appraised.

- *Veblen effect* – This is named after Veblen's practice of giving all his students the grade C irrespective of the quality of their efforts. Thus all those appraised received middle-order ratings.

- *Impression effect* – This is the problem of distinguishing actual performance from calculated 'impression-management'. The impression management tactics of employees can result in supervisors liking them more and thus rating their job performance more highly. Employees often attempt to manage their reputations by substituting measures of process (effort, behaviour, etc.) for measures of outcome (results), particularly when the results are less than favourable.

---

'unnatural act' for managers, with the result that, if they are not trained properly, it is done rather poorly. Appraisal meetings are thus reported as being short-lived, ill-structured and often bruising encounters. Studies find that appraisers are ill-prepared, talk too much, and base much of the discussion on third-party complaints with many of the judgements made on 'gut feelings' (e.g. Finn and Fontaine, 1993). It is then of little surprise when we find reports of how it takes the average employee six months to recover from it (Peters, 1987).

Appraisals are also discredited by being subject to 'political' manipulation (Tziner, 1999). Managers, it seems, frequently play organisational games with performance ratings (Snape *et al.*, 1994). Longenecker's (1989) research found that managers' appraisal ratings are often manipulated to suit various ends. Sometimes ratings were artificially deflated to show who was the boss; to prepare the ground for termination; to punish a difficult and rebellious employee and even to 'scare' better performance out of the appraisee. One manager we interviewed described how he deflated the performance ratings of all new graduate trainees for their first few years of employment in order to 'knock some of the cleverness out of them' and show them that they 'did not know everything'. Equally, a poor performer may be given an excellent rating so that they will be promoted up and out of the department and managers may inflate ratings in the hope that an exemplary set of appraisals reflects favourably on the manager responsible for such a high-performing team.

The move to more objective forms of performance appraisal, particularly encouraged by performance management models, and increasingly reported for managerial grades is often argued to overcome some of the above 'subjective' problems. Legal challenges to personality- and trait-based performance appraisal schemes, particularly in North America and increasingly in the UK (Townley, 1990) have also encouraged the move away from personality- and trait-based systems. However, the so-called objective-based schemes are not without difficulties. Firstly, measurement is often difficult and according to Wright (1991) 'there are a number of jobs where the meaningful is not measurable and the measurable is not meaningful'. The tendency is also to simplify measurement by focusing on the short rather than the long term. Secondly, since objectives are set for individual employees or teams under such systems, it can be especially challenging to achieve equitable ratings. Equally problematical is that the actions of the employee may account for little of the variability in the outcomes measured (a key criticism of the quality gurus – see below) and thus the extent to which they are achievable is not within the employee's control. This has posed real problems with appraisals in industries such as financial services where the economic climate and general business cycle arguably affect outcomes far more than individual effort. The potential here is thus for employee demotivation and disillusionment, especially when many such systems are now linked to reward structures.

Kessler and Purcell (1992) identify a range of further specific problems with objective-based systems. These include the difficulty in achieving a balance between maintenance and innovator objectives; in setting objectives that cover the whole job so that performance does not get skewed to part of it; and the lack of flexibility to redefine objectives as circumstances change during the appraisal cycle. The introduction of performance appraisal into the public sector has also given rise to many concerns. In particular there are worries about its potential to undermine professional autonomy, with this concern being strongly expressed by clinicians in the NHS. A more general concern is that such a 'managerialist' intervention would undermine the public service values and public accountability of employees (Redman et al., 2000).

A range of more practical difficulties also results in problems with performance appraisal. Often the paperwork used to support the system can become excessive and give rise to a considerable bureaucratic burden for managers, particularly as spans of control grow. Some organisations have attempted to reduce this problem by designing paperless systems (Anderson et al., 1987), requiring the employee to complete the bulk of the paperwork (Wilson and Cole, 1990) or moving to computer-based systems (Angel, 1989). A real danger in many systems is that the paperwork dominates and the process is reduced to an annual 'cosy chat' and a ritual bureaucratic exercise devoid of meaning or importance for all concerned. Thus, according to Barlow (1989: 503), the performance appraisal of managers is little more than the 'routinized recording of trivialities'. Appraisers and appraised go through the motions, sign the forms and send them to a central personnel department who simply file them away rather than utilising the data in a meaningful way (Snape *et al.*, 1994). Given the lack of follow-up in many appraisal systems, it is hardly surprising when they fall into disrepute and eventual decay.

Lastly, the growth of TQM and customer care programmes has triggered a considerable debate and a reassessment of the organisational value of appraisal. On the one hand, there has been a high-profile barrage of criticism rejecting appraisal as being incompatible with TQM. In its strongest formulation it is suggested that managers face a stark choice between choosing either TQM or performance appraisal (Scholtes, 1993; Bowman, 1994). On the other hand, some have suggested that appraisal may play a key role in developing, communicating and monitoring the achievement of quality standards (Deblieux, 1991; Fletcher, 1993) and many organisations have been spurred by the introduction of TQM to revise their appraisal schemes in more customer-focused ways.

TQM has thus highlighted both old and new problems with performance appraisal. In relation to old problems some of the quality gurus, most notably Deming (1986), maintain that performance appraisal is inconsistent with quality improvement. He argues that variation in performance is attributable mainly to work systems rather than to variations in the performance of individual workers. Quality improvements are thus found mainly by changing processes rather than people, and the key is to develop co-operative teamwork. This, he claims, is difficult to do where the focus is on 'blaming' the individual, as in traditional appraisal, and where, as a result, there is a climate of fear and risk-avoidance, and a concern for short-term, individual targets, all of which undermines the co-operative, creative, and committed behaviour necessary for continuous improvement.

Deming is careful to argue, in rejecting performance appraisal, not that all staff perform equally well but that appraisers are incapable of disaggregating system effects from individual staff effects. Thus, what is needed for TQM is a shift away from the traditional focus on results and individual recognition, towards processes and group recognition. The TQM critics also raise some new problems with performance appraisal, in particular that it 'disempowers' employees by reducing variety and increasing homogenisation of the workforce whereas for meaningful customer care we need the 'empowered' employee.

## Conclusions

Performance appraisal is now more widespread than at any time in its history and the organisational resources consumed by its practice are enormous. At the same time its critics grow both in number and in the ferocity of their attacks. It is thus tempting to adopt a somewhat sceptical view of the value of performance appraisal. Following the rise of TQM and the prominence of its, mainly American, management gurus, it has become rather fashionable of late to reject performance appraisal outright. Pathological descriptions of performance appraisal as a 'deadly disease' and an 'organisational virus' are increasingly common.

However, it would appear that the danger here is that such views are often based on little more than anecdote rather than solid empirical research. For example, one survey of employer reasons for introducing appraisal systems in the UK found that in over a third of cases they were developed to provide support for quality management initiatives (IRS, 1994). Our studies of managers' actual experience of being appraised finds many reporting its overall value to them and the organisation, with few suggesting that it should be discarded altogether (e.g. Redman and Mathews, 1995; Redman et al., 2000). Many of the criticisms are based upon a hard and uncompromising model of performance appraisal that is now less commonly found in practice, and on the ineffective way in which many organisations implement appraisal. The critics all too often have rather conveniently ignored many of the new developments we discuss above, which act to alleviate some of these problems. Many of the problems of performance appraisal can be ironed out over time as experience with its practice accumulates. Indeed, there is some evidence to suggest that employers who have used performance appraisal for longer report fewer problems (Bowles and Coates, 1993).

Further, performance appraisal's detractors are usually silent on what should replace it. A common response is to suggest that this is an unfair question in that it is the organisational equivalent of asking, 'What you would replace pneumonia with?' (e.g. see People Management, 13 July 1995, p. 15). The question of how to assess individual performance, determine rewards and promotion, provide feedback, decide training and career needs and link business and individual goals without a performance appraisal system, however, cannot be so easily shrugged off.

Performance appraisal emerged in the first place to meet such needs and employees still need guidance in focusing their skills and efforts on important organisational goals and values. Hence we would suggest that performance appraisal will continue to have an important role in HRM practice. A good example here is that organisations often struggle to get managers committed to taking health and safety management as seriously as other aspects of their jobs. Tombs (1992) reports that 'safety leaders' in the chemical industry ensure that managers give safety management the attention it deserves by developing a 'safety culture', a key part of which is achieved by incorporating safety objectives into their performance appraisals. Thus the first objective of all ICI plant managers is always a safety one.

This is not to argue that the current practice of performance appraisal is unproblematic. Certainly some of the evidence presented above would suggest that there are many concerns with its application. However, although these problems are persistent they are certainly not insurmountable and it is argued strongly that organisations should think very carefully before abandoning performance appraisal altogether. Rather, the evidence would seem to support the view that the key task facing most organisations in the new millennium is the upgrading, renewal and reinvention of performance appraisal such that it is more compatible with new business environments. The evidence above and elsewhere (e.g. IRS, 1999) suggests that many employers are rising to such a challenge.

**Case study 3.1**

# Performance appraisal at North Trust

Tom Redman, Ed Snape, David Thompson and Fanny Ka-ching Yan

## Organisation background

This case study examines the practice of performance appraisal in an NHS trust hospital. North Trust (NT) is a whole district trust in the North-east of England serving a community of quarter of a million people. It provides 32 major health care services, including the full range of inpatient, day case and outpatient services alongside a comprehensive primary care service including health visiting and district nursing services. It employs some 2,200 'whole time equivalent' (wte) staff. The trust has recently been relatively successful, meeting all its financial targets thus far. However, at the time of the study (1995–97), it was, like many other trusts, experiencing increasing difficulties in meeting the demand for healthcare services within the constraints of its current resources.

## The development of appraisal at NT

Appraisal at North Trust, a variant of the national Individual Performance Review scheme, was first implemented for senior managers in 1988. Between 1988 and 1994 it was largely restricted to managerial and senior professional groups. In 1994 a review of IPR was conducted. An initial analysis found patchy coverage of IPR and a half-hearted commitment to it. Following the review, a decision was taken to revise and relaunch the IPR scheme and roll it out to a wider group of staff. There were two key influences underpinning this decision. Firstly, a new chief executive with a much greater belief in the value of performance management was appointed. Secondly, a decision to pursue the Investors in People award resulted in a decision to commit more time and effort to making IPR work. The next 18 months thus saw the revising of policy, the redesigning of supporting paperwork, and the committing of major training resources to IPR.

Final written agreement was secured in March 1995 and the new policy and procedure were approved by the chief executive in June 1995. The key aims of IPR at NT were articulated in the new policy document as ensuring that all staff understand the trust's goals and strategic direction; are clear about their objectives, how these fit with the work of others and the organisation as whole and are aware of the tasks they need to carry out; are given regular feedback and explicit assessment of performance; and are developed to improve their performance. The revised policy document made an explicit commitment to implement IPR for all employees.

The revised IPR policy at NT placed greater emphasis on measurability as a key aspect of the setting of individual objectives. The policy document outlines the principles underpinning individual objective setting as following the acronym 'SMART'. Here objectives should be specific, measurable, agreed/achievable, realistic and time-bound with the form of measurement for each objective to be agreed at the time when they are set. According to the CEO, when he first arrived, this aspect was perceived as being very weak in practice:

> Most people didn't know what an objective was if it sat up and bit them on the backside. Objectives here tended to be half-a-dozen or so generalised statements with no measurable outcome, no timescale, no agreement about how something is to be judged and whether it has been done or not with the result that there is little accountability.

For the CEO the result of this was major problems in 'getting things done' at the trust:

> We don't have a performance culture here. This place was just great for talking about things. Only talking about things, not actually doing them.

Thus, a key aim for the CEO was to 'toughen up' IPR. This was to be attained in part by an increased emphasis on the evaluation of the achievement of work objectives and to encourage detailed measures to be established for all new objectives. However, the CEO's view of the direction in which IPR should go did not seem to be shared by its 'owners' – the personnel department. Here a softer, more developmental focus for IPR was envisioned:

> What is important is the manager taking the time out to talk to the individual about how they are progressing. How they feel things are going. And talk about training and development. These things really help morale. Forget the form filling and objectives, and all the other bits. It is these things that really make the difference.

In the remainder of this case study we describe the practice of performance appraisal in North Trust.

### The IPR process

#### Mechanics

IPR at NT is designed to cascade downwards through the organisation. The business plan is formulated by December/January each year and reviews conducted during February and March for senior managers. The majority of appraisals for other staff take place during April and May. A minority of managers, because of the large number of appraisals they conducted, in one case over 50, scheduled the appraisals over the full year, which, in effect, largely undermined the direct link with business planning for the majority of their staff. However, linkages with the business plan, especially for lower levels of staff, were also difficult to discern in the accounts of the IPR reviews conducted by those managers who did these in phase with the business planning process. Here managers' descriptions of how they appraised healthcare assistants, porters, domestics, catering staff, laundry workers, nurses rarely mentioned anything other than the loosest of connections with the business plan.

The IPR policy specifies very much a 'top-down' process, noting that only occasionally it might be beneficial to involve another manager closely concerned with the objectives being measured (such as a project manager). In practice, no examples of this were found. A particular problem reported by the interviewees was that of continuity of appraisers between appraisal cycles. Due to high levels of managerial turnover, caused by resignations, promotions, transfers, and secondments, etc. of both appraisees and appraisers, nearly a third of interviewees reported having different appraisers from one cycle to the next. This level of managerial change, because of the need for a close working relationship between manager and employee for appraisal to be effective (see below), was felt to generally limit IPR's potential. Interviewees described how continuity between appraiser and appraisee was important because reviews were generally perceived as improving as both parties got to know each other better and the discussion became more useful and open.

### Coverage

There was an uneven application and use of IPR. Despite the avowed intention of the new policy to roll out IPR uniformly over the trust, its use appeared to be distinctly patchy. The personnel department estimated that only around 25–30 per cent of staff received a performance review and that below management levels 'huge swathes' of staff were not involved. One of the tools to encourage its greater uptake was that senior managers were now being given personal objectives in their own appraisals to introduce IPR for all their staff. However, this strategy alone did not seem sufficient to gain their commitment to making IPR process effective. As one manager explains:

> Appraisal for lower-level staff is a five-minute wonder, get it out of the way. The supervisors say . . . 'I have got to go through this with you. You haven't been too bad a lad this year, have you? See you next year.' We get the odd constructive thing coming out of it but the main thing is that the director will be happy that he can report we have now appraised all the staff in our department when he has his next IPR.

Such cynical attitudes were a source of irritation to the majority of managers who spent considerable time and effort in conducting IPRs in their departments. Here it was particularly resented that their managerial colleagues either did not conduct appraisals ('It's not fair that I have to do it if others don't'; 'Other staff feel they are missing out because they are not getting it') or gave mere lip service to them ('It brings the whole IPR process into disrepute and makes it much more difficult for me to get my staff to take it seriously').

### Documentation

The standard trust documentation was used for fewer than half of our interviewees' appraisals. The standard forms were felt to be too cumbersome and somewhat of an administrative chore, especially for use with employees at lower levels in the organisation. Thus, those responsible for IPR often tailored the forms, usually reducing their length. A problem with some of the customised forms was that questionable performance categories, such as an appraisee's 'personality', featured prominently in these versions. In contrast, some professional groups found the forms rather too simplistic to capture the nature of their roles and again customised the standard forms to suit their needs. In a number of departments reviews were conducted without the aid of either customised or standard forms, and in one case an appraiser admitted that this was because he had never got round to actually reading them.

### The IPR encounter

The heart of the IPR process, and the main source of participants' evaluation of it as either a success or failure, is the face-to-face meeting between appraiser and appraisee. Here for IPR is its 'moment of truth'. Table 3.1 shows that the majority of our appraisees reported interviews of at least 30 minutes, with 47 per cent having interviews of more than an hour. Judging from Table 3.2, appraisers were not usually dominating the interviews. The impression gained is that the majority of appraisees were having a sufficiently long and participative appraisal interview, an encouraging finding when we note that those who reported longer and more participative interviews also tended to report greater satisfaction with the appraisal process.

**Table 3.1  How long did the appraisal interview last?**

| Time | Percentage of total appraisals |
| --- | --- |
| Less than 30 minutes | 11 |
| Between 30 minutes and an hour | 43 |
| Between one and two hours | 35 |
| More than two hours | 12 |

**Table 3.2  During the appraisal interview approximately what proportion of the time did you and the appraiser talk?**

| Proportion of time spent talking | Percentages of total appraisals |
| --- | --- |
| Mainly me (more than 75%) | 13 |
| Approximately 60% me | 26 |
| Approximately equal | 48 |
| Approximately 60% appraiser | 12 |
| Mainly the appraiser (more than 75%) | 1 |

Table 3.2 sets out the extent to which various issues were discussed during the appraisal, as reported by our appraisees. The main emphasis appears to be on the achievement and planning of work objectives and on the planning of training and

**Table 3.3  To what extent were the following issues covered in your appraisal?**

| Issue | Percentage of total appraisals | | |
|---|---|---|---|
| | 3 Thoroughly discussed | 2 Briefly discussed | 1 Not discussed at all |
| Your achievement of work objectives | 63 | 32 | 5 |
| Your future work objectives | 65 | 31 | 4 |
| Your personality or behaviour | 17 | 42 | 42 |
| Your skills or competencies | 35 | 52 | 13 |
| Your training and development needs | 45 | 43 | 12 |
| Your career aspirations and plans | 30 | 43 | 27 |
| Your pay or benefits | 3 | 12 | 85 |
| Your job difficulties | 24 | 57 | 19 |
| How you might improve your performance | 16 | 40 | 44 |
| How your supervisor might help you to improve your performance | 15 | 45 | 40 |
| Your personal or domestic circumstances | 4 | 20 | 76 |

development. Not surprisingly, given the absence of performance-related pay for most staff, pay and benefits were only discussed in any detail during the appraisal interview. Overall, the approach seems to be one of performance management and development rather than of judgement and reward allocation.

A strong theme in the accounts of those who were positive about the overall IPR process was the notion that the interview represented 'quality time' between manager and managed. For some it was an 'employee's right' to have meaningful 'one-on-one time' with their manager and:

> People value quality time to talk through with their immediate manager what they are doing, why they are doing it, and what they need to do in the future.

As we have seen, in these 'quality-time' appraisals, which were often two to three hours in duration for managers, appraisees reported that a broad range of issues were discussed.

In contrast, the focus for lower-level grades was much more restricted and our in-depth interviews suggested that for such staff the time spent on the IPR's interview varied between 10 and 45 minutes. Typical descriptions of the nature of appraisals for lower-grade staff were:

> I discuss with them how they have worked this year. I say 'You've been a bit slack in these things. You are bloody good at that. You are one of my key workers for this. But your time-keeping wants pulling up a bit and your general attitude is not what it should be.

> To be honest there is very little to say to someone who feeds sheets into a machine five days a week. I have found it hard to think of positive things.

One manager reported the difficulty of getting lower-grade staff to relax during their review because prior to IPR's introduction the only time such staff were called to her office was for a 'rugging'. Perhaps unsurprisingly given such an approach, lower-grade staff were often reported as being 'indifferent' to and 'disinterested' in the IPR process.

> It's the lower grades that feel 'Do I have to go through this again? I don't know why. I only want to do the job I'm doing and get my money at the end of the week.' These tend to be short interviews, most are less than 10 minutes.

Managers appeared to be coping with this lack of interest via a number of strategies. Firstly, by renewing efforts to encourage active staff participation and using developmental 'carrots'. Secondly, individual sceptics were labelled 'lost causes' and managers simply went through motions in IPR and waited for such staff to leave. A more difficult problem was with clusters of IPR-resistant employees. Here a coping strategy, often sold under the guise of self-development, appeared to be one of 'sharing the misery' more evenly with more junior managers and supervisors. The responsibility for conducting IPRs for 'difficult', 'obstructive', and 'awkward' staff was spread between the managerial team.

Generally, appraisees felt that their managers were good at giving performance feedback but fewer felt that they received regular feedback on their progress towards objectives (Table 3.4). The need for appraisal to be an ongoing, year-round exercise was emphasised in the IPR system (see below). It seems that at NT, significant minorities of appraisers were neglecting to do the expected follow-up. Judging from our interviews, constructive feedback was especially welcomed by the appraisees in providing direction ('You realize you are getting there'; 'Gives me some comfort I am getting there') and helping to boost confidence ('You know what you are doing is being done correctly'). Critical feedback was also valued but not often received by the interviewees, who in part blamed appraisal training here, which overly emphasised the positive nature of IPR. Around a third of interviewees said they often watered down their feedback in the reviews to ensure a positive IPR event and harmony within their work-teams. Appraisees, especially female managers, emphasised the value of constructive criticism and 'meaningful' appraisals, with cosy chats being seen as a waste of their time.

Sound personal relationships between appraiser and appraised were emphasised by our interviewees as being a necessary but not sufficient condition for the review to be effective. The large majority of appraisees considered that their managers were professional enough not to reward favourites, thought that appraisers were objective, felt they could talk freely, were confident enough to challenge their appraisal, and believed that keeping on good terms with their manager was not a requirement in order to obtain a good appraisal (see Table 3.4). However, this still leaves a minority of appraisers whose appraisal behaviour was less positively rated by appraisees. Thus, some interviewees reported a poor relationship with their manager, describing IPR reviews in terms of conflict, verbal confrontation, point-scoring,

**Table 3.4  Perceived supervisor behaviour**

| | Percentage of total appraisals | | | | |
|---|---|---|---|---|---|
| | 5<br>*Strongly agree* | 4<br>*Agree* | 3<br>*Neither agree nor disagree* | 2<br>*Disagree* | 1<br>*Strongly disagree* |
| **Positive aspects** | | | | | |
| My supervisor is good at giving me feedback on my performance. | 7 | 51 | 19 | 19 | 4 |
| I receive regular informal feedback from my supervisor regarding my progress towards agreed targets and objectives. | 4 | 37 | 19 | 30 | 9 |
| My supervisor takes my appraisals very seriously. | 21 | 50 | 15 | 12 | 2 |
| My supervisor takes my career aspirations very seriously. | 5 | 50 | 24 | 17 | 3 |
| I am confident that my supervisor is as objective as possible when conducting appraisals. | 10 | 60 | 20 | 8 | 1 |
| **Negative aspects** | | | | | |
| I have to keep on good terms with my supervisor in order to get a good appraisal rating. | 2 | 10 | 21 | 52 | 14 |
| Supervisors use appraisals to reward their favourites. | 2 | 6 | 16 | 54 | 23 |
| I am not entirely happy about challenging my supervisor's appraisal of my performance. | 3 | 18 | 17 | 52 | 11 |
| I found it difficult during my performance appraisal to talk freely with my supervisor about what I wanted to discuss. | 4 | 14 | 9 | 52 | 21 |

and 'edging about the real issues'. At its worst, this reduced appraisers using IPR to list what the appraisee had done wrong or badly over the year. A few appraisers, particularly those in clinical posts, described the problems of achieving an appropriate environment for conducting appraisal in a busy, emergency-led hospital.

> When I had my IPR the phones were going, people were coming in and out of the office, the manager got called away. It spoke volumes to me about the value that was attached to IPR here.

> Conducting IPRs on nights, at 2 am, when people are not at their best, is hardly conducive to a quality process.

### Mini-reviews

The formal annual reviews are supported by mini reviews. The policy document sees these as a 'crucial element' of IPR, providing constant review and monitoring such that the annual review itself becomes 'mainly a confirmation of agreements made during the year', or, as the title of the IPR training video suggests, appraisees should experience *No Surprises*. However, these appear to be rather sporadic in practice and, as we saw in Table 3.4, only 41 per cent of survey appraisees said that they received regular feedback from their supervisor on their progress towards their objectives.

A few departmental heads formally scheduled three-monthly reviews for all employees. The norm for the mini-reviews was a six-monthly, informal discussion, with a minority of interviewees receiving only the annual appraisal. Below management and professional levels, the impression gained was that mini-reviews were extremely rare or very ad hoc and rushed at best – 'corridor and canteen chats' – with managers struggling to find the time to conduct even the annual appraisal for some groups. However, the interviewees themselves often stressed the value of mini reviews, not only in providing a measure of progress and attainment but in a general updating of performance objectives. Several interviewees reported requesting, and receiving, additional mini reviews. Here mini reviews were especially useful to fine-tune, and often to replace personal objectives that had been rendered obsolete by a rapidly changing organisational environment. Given the current level of change and 'churn' in the NHS, we suggest that it may now be appropriate to consider it a 'high-velocity' environment requiring fast strategic decision-making. In such circumstances static yearly objectives are clearly inappropriate. Interviewees reported how objectives set in April of one year were often irrelevant and obsolete by the following year. Mini reviews allowed for individual objectives to be kept in line with changes in business strategy.

### Objective setting

As we have seen, the increased emphasis on work objectives and measurability desired by the CEO is reflected in the issues covered in the appraisal process, with appraisees reporting that the achievement and planning of work objectives were the most thoroughly discussed issues in the appraisal meeting. Generally, appraisees found the emphasis on objectives a useful part of the IPR process. A picture that emerges from the survey findings is that objectives are generally clear, cover the most important parts of the job, and that appraisees are actively involved in the objective-setting process (see Table 3.5). Interviewees reported being reassured they were on the 'right track', 'working along the right lines', 'on-line', and 'knowing where they stood' ('You might think you are doing a good job but you need some one to tell you that and vice versa') in their jobs. For example:

> Without IPR it would be so easy for you to drift and not do anything. It keeps you on your toes. It keeps you focused. You know exactly what you are aiming for. It makes you look at what you do and what the organisation's trying to achieve. If you didn't have appraisal it would be so easy just to not do anything. You'd just drift. It makes you think about where you are going and where you would like to be.

**Table 3.5  Objectives and feedback**

| | Percentage of total appraisals | | | | |
|---|---|---|---|---|---|
| | 5 Strongly agree | 4 Agree | 3 Neither agree nor disagree | 2 Disagree | 1 Strongly disagree |
| The goals that I am to achieve are clear. | 8 | 61 | 13 | 15 | 2 |
| The most important parts of my job are emphasised in my performance appraisal. | 3 | 58 | 24 | 13 | 2 |
| The performance appraisal system helps me understand my personal weaknesses. | 5 | 48 | 19 | 26 | 3 |
| My supervisor allows me to help choose the goals that I am to achieve. | 13 | 65 | 10 | 10 | 1 |
| The performance appraisal system helps me to understand my job better. | 3 | 37 | 27 | 31 | 1 |
| The performance appraisal system gives me a good idea of how I am doing in my job. | 6 | 55 | 23 | 14 | 2 |

The setting of objectives provided direction in an increasingly complex and fast-moving organisational environment. The view of one manager was that, by appraising her staff, she:

> Gives them something to hang onto. The job description is so vast and we are facing so many changes. The objectives give direction. It's a stepping stone for them. They give staff guidance and something to aim for, something constructive to aim for.

Interviewees reported how they often tended to 'push' and 'challenge' themselves to make 'progress', attain 'personal development' and 'growth' via the objective-setting process. The general view was that in this respect the objectives they set for themselves were more challenging (and interesting) than those produced by their managers. For example:

> Generally, I can take them in my stride. There are one or two demanding ones but they are actually objectives I have brought forward myself. I probably tend to push myself harder than the organisation does.

> I always put a new really challenging one in each time, like reducing sickness absence. I tend to challenge myself.

However, for some interviewees their accumulated experience of objective-setting had taught them not to challenge themselves 'too much' and restrict both the scope and the number of the objectives they set for themselves. Here we find managerial appraisees becoming sensitised to the objective-setting 'game'. For example:

What I've learnt, as time goes by, is you've got to be careful, right at the outset, how you set your objectives because you can be overoptimistic, unrealistic. There's a danger of sitting down and thinking of all the things you'd love to do, or ideally should do, forgetting that you've got lots of constraints and you couldn't in a month of Sundays achieve it. So I think quite a few of us have learnt there is a skill in setting objectives which are reasonable and stand a chance of being achieved. I think that that bit is probably more important than anything else. There is nothing more demoralizing than being measured against something which you yourself have declared as being in need of being done and finding that you couldn't possibly do it.

Some appraisees felt that objectives were 'imposed' on them but most accepted that this was 'just part of the job'. Occasionally, though, this caused considerable irritation and anger, particularly in the clash with IPR's espoused developmental focus. One manager described 'ending up with nothing you really wanted to do' from his IPR and another described how, when she pushed her appraiser to include a particular objective that she perceived as being a key issue for the department and which fitted well with her personal development needs, she was told '...either forget it or fit it into your own time'. The danger with imposing objectives on staff reluctant to accept them was that all that was achieved was lip service and half-hearted commitment, accompanied by subsequent 'fudge' in the appraisal review on the measures of achievement. For example:

I've got to do them (objectives). I don't not do them but I don't give them the commitment they need if I don't feel it's right. And it never gets picked up at the next appraisal.

### Measuring achievement

The use of data in measuring and evaluating individual performance was reported by interviewees as being very reactive on the part of appraisers. Here if the appraisee did not produce data there tended to be very little use of anything other than informed opinion in assessing whether objectives had actually been achieved. An effect of this lack of data use appears to be that although a majority of appraisees felt that IPRs represented an accurate measure of their performance, a substantial number were unclear on the standards used to evaluate performance (see Table 3.6).

Some appraisees were prolific in their use of data in the IPR process. Interviewees who had also undertaken NVQ management programmes described a considerable use of reports and the production of memorandums to measure their achievement of objectives. It seems that the NVQ requirement to produce a portfolio causes managers to start to document their work – at least until they attain the award. Our findings suggest this new-found enthusiasm for the memorandum and report generated by NVQs found a further outlet in the IPR process. Further, such documentation and the generally greater level of preparation on the part of the appraisee enabled them to control, to a considerable extent, the content and outcomes of the IPR process. For example:

I took lots of things along (to the IPR meeting). One of my objectives was to set up team objectives on the ward. I copied examples of these objectives and took them along. I

**Table 3.6  Measuring performance**

| | Percentage of total appraisals | | | | |
| --- | --- | --- | --- | --- | --- |
| | 5<br>Strongly<br>agree | 4<br>Agree | 3<br>Neither<br>agree nor<br>disagree | 2<br>Disagree | 1<br>Strongly<br>disagree |
| My performance appraisal for this year represents a fair and accurate picture of my job performance. | 7 | 68 | 11 | 13 | 1 |
| My supervisor and I agree on what equals good performance in my job | 6 | 67 | 14 | 12 | 1 |
| I know the standards used to evaluate my performance | 2 | 40 | 26 | 29 | 4 |

showed reports I had done on the empowerment of patients and gave her copies of patients' meetings. I used information to show that I had done things. I used these things to prove to her that I had achieved them.

In contrast, other managers usually reported a much less documented measuring process under IPR. The effective use of documentation by this group of managers and professionals thus raises the issue of 'impression management' in the performance measurement process. Impression management is a process by which people attempt to create and sustain desired perceptions of themselves in the eyes of others. In the employment context such others are colleagues, peers, internal customers, clients, and especially bosses. The theory of impression management suggests that employees attempt to control, sometimes consciously and sometimes unconsciously, information on themselves which positively shapes others' perceptions of them. The performance appraisal process is a particularly important arena for the creation of favourable impressions at work. The effective use of performance documentation on the part of appraisees thus appears to be a very powerful tool in the production of an overall favourable impression of their managerial capability. A number of appraisers appeared to be very aware of staff's attempts at impression management via the IPR process. Such appraisers reported how they supplemented data from the IPR interview with views from an appraisee's peers and the 'grapevine'. Some declared that they were very wary of the accuracy of views offered by 'mouthy' and 'gobby' staff. For example:

A nurse who's an extrovert, who does a lot of mouthing off, may give the impression that they are doing a really wonderful job and the lass who is quiet could be doing an even better job. But because she's not there selling herself, telling you how wonderful she is, she often loses out here.

I am always wary of the gobby ones. Those who are always telling you how wonderful [they are] and how hard worked [they are].

It appears that the key for managers in measuring individual performance under IPR was distinguishing between 'real' and 'created' performance achievements, the danger being that managers may actually measure an employee's ability to perform in a 'theatrical' rather 'task-orientated' sense.

### Objectives and teamwork

The CEO was also keen to encourage wider sharing of objectives, particularly between managers. Here the IPR policy's emphasis on the confidentiality of the appraisal process and its individual nature was seen as discouraging the formal communication of personal objectives with others. The individualistic nature of IPR thus fitted rather uneasily with the considerable growth in teamwork across the trust. For example, according to one manager:

> My boss knows how my objectives fit in with my colleagues', but I don't because I never see them.

The CEO was attempting to introduce change here by leading by example and then encouraging other managers to do the same. After setting objectives for his executive directors, all objectives for each manager, including his own, were circulated to the entire senior management team and also sent out to the clinical divisions. However, generally there did not seem to be much formal sharing of objectives amongst other managers and professionals. Many of our interviewees felt that greater sharing of objectives would be valuable, not least in creating a better understanding of performance priorities within and between departments. On an informal level some staff were actively sharing objectives. One manager describes how she encourages this at team meetings with her managers and supervisors:

> I'll say at meetings 'Have you looked at your IPR lately? Who's got that in their IPR? Somebody's got that in their IPR.'

Interviewees expressed how they found it easier to prepare their own objectives when their appraising manager provided copies of his or her own objectives in advance of the review process. Appraisees also reported that much of their work was now conducted in teams, and many felt that more team-based appraisals and the setting of team objectives would helpfully supplement the individualistic nature of IPR. For example:

> I think IPR needs to achieve a better balance between individual performance and team performance. We need a much greater emphasis on team performance. Nowadays at NT we are all about teamwork. The IPR approach is too preoccupied with individual performance. It can become too narrow and it is often divisive.

A number also suggested that wider collaboration on the setting of objectives with other managers, project leaders, working parties, etc. would be beneficial in encompassing the full range of their activities.

## IPR outputs

In this last section we report our findings on what the IPR process actually achieves. Here we structure our discussion under four main headings: management control; employee motivation; training and development; and rewards.

### Management control

Clearly, as we discuss above, the setting and measuring of work objectives facilitates a direct form of managerial control over the labour process. Despite the rhetoric and policy of development, appraisers seemed to use IPR to exert their managerial authority. Occasionally, this was done in a very crude way. For example, a number of interviewees reported problems with managers waiting for the IPR to settle scores for past conflicts. IPR was thus perceived by some appraisees as a vehicle for the line manager to 'tell me what I should be doing', and to 'tell me what I am not doing right in my job'. There is also evidence that IPR acts as a less obvious and more indirect form of managerial control. Here IPR appears to act as a means to encourage self-discipline and responsibility amongst staff and thus to promote the reshaping of staff attitudes to fit new managerial values and beliefs in line with the changing form of work organisation. Even some of the sternest critics of IPR noted its subtle effects on them:

> I achieve nothing from it. I suppose the main benefit is I actually discipline myself more with my time management. I think 'Oh I have got to do so and so' and I chart out my work better so that I'll take all that in. I give myself deadlines for my work, saying 'I'll achieve that by March.'

The direction of control in the IPR process, however, is far from one-way. Some managers described how their staff turned the IPR tables on them:

> The cooks use IPR to say 'This is why I cannot do my job. This is why I cannot achieve this objective.' And then they trot out a great list of problems with the job.

One manager described why he hated doing appraisals with lower-level staff because they were reduced to 'a managerial witch-hunt and a general gripe and groan session about what I had or hadn't done over the year'. The manager became so fed-up with being on the receiving end of this that he had written to all staff reminding them of the nature of the IPR process and asking for a more positive attitude and less moaning about perceived managerial inadequacies. However, the memorandum had only served to highlight his discomfort with the process and to increase the level of complaining behaviour from appraisees, such that he now admitted to merely '. . .going through the motions with IPR to get it over with as quickly as possible'.

### 'It's good to talk': motivation and morale

IPR, as we discuss above, was often perceived by appraisers and appraised as a good opportunity for managers and managed to talk meaningfully, and engage in 'quality time' together. Not only did IPR visibly and symbolically demonstrate to staff their value and importance to the organisation but that the manager also personally cared about their wellbeing. In some of the accounts of appraisers there were classic human-relations descriptions of the IPR encounter going well beyond the boundaries of work relations. Here interviewees reported appraisals discussing broader personal and social issues and referred to this as 'getting to know your staff'.

IPR helps people in knowing where their professional career and their lives are going.

It's your time that you devote to them. And some of them have aspirations that you wouldn't know about until you sit down and talk to them. You show that you are genuinely interested in them as people as well as nurses.

The language used to describe these encounters was often heavily redolent of the unitary ideology of human relations. Appraisees' and appraisers' stories were littered with references to 'progress', 'going forward together', 'participation', 'empowering the appraisee', 'boosting morale', 'becoming a proactive team', 'harnessing our collective energies' via IPR. Interviewees emphasised the importance of good communication, listening and being listened to particularly, as being a manager was often described as being a 'lonely job'. Thus some two-thirds of interviewees felt that they performed the duties of the post better and that IPR contributed positively to their personal motivation and job satisfaction:

If they scrapped it tomorrow, I don't think I would go home in tears but I would miss it. It helps me keep going, helps me keep motivated. It gives me some comfort, considering all the problems we have at the moment – I've got a service with a lot of problems – that I am achieving what I am supposed to do in my job.

In contrast, other managers, again especially in relation to lower-level staff, were not convinced that IPR reviews delivered much other than a lot of 'hot air' and wasted time that could have been much more profitably employed doing other things. For example:

I have 49 staff. Appraisal takes at least 30-40 minutes each. That's a lot of man-hours to get nothing out of it other than hot air.

Senior management would like to think that if you appraise everybody it would instil in them some kind of belonging, some kind of corporate feeling. But for the rank and file they are just not interested.

### Training and development

Despite the emphasis of IPR on training and development by the personnel department, as we can see from Table 3.3, the discussion of an appraisee's training needs takes second place to that on work objectives. Some 12 per cent of appraisees reported that training and development issues were not discussed at all. The majority of those interviewed emphasised training and development as an outcome of the IPR process. All interviewees claimed to have discussed their own 'personal development plan' (PDP) during the interview. However, this was often reported to be a relatively unfocused and vague discussion. Indeed, few interviewees, under persistent probing, could actually give details of what was in their PDP. The impression gained was that the PDP title signified a much more formalised, more detailed and rather grander training and development document in theory at least if not in practice. Many of the interviewees described a rather mechanical process whereby training and development was discussed as a distinct, almost stand-alone issue. The appraiser was often perceived as running through a check list of items to be covered in the interview, of which training and development was one, rather than the identification of training needs emerging from a grounded discussion of appraisee performance. The large majority of interviewees felt that much of the training and development that was taking place would still have occurred without the use of IPR but possibly less systematically and at a slower pace.

Managers reported problems with the IPR process – especially coupled with the decision to pursue the IiP award – giving rise to appraisees producing training and development 'wish lists' . Here the key difficulty was finding the training resources to fund costly external courses in the face of increasingly tight training budgets. The demand for degree and diploma courses – particularly amongst nursing staff – fuelled in part by IPR, was causing managers problems in maintaining staff commitment to the appraisal process, given that few employees could be supported in this way. Managers described a coping strategy here of encouraging employees to consider alternative, and less costly, development activities such as short secondments, work shadowing and job exchanges. Interviewees were also critical of the personnel department pushing the current training 'flavour of the month' via the IPR process. At the time of our study this was reported as being the managerial NVQ programme running in-house in conjunction with a local university.

### Rewards

The PRP element of IPR was not particularly popular with either appraisers or appraisees. Whereas the general view of IPR was that a majority of both appraisees and interviewees considered it to be an overall positive experience, at least for managers and professionals, the views expressed in relation to performance-related pay were all negative. A strong view from those receiving PRP was that it was: a lot of 'hassle' for little reward; more influenced by quotas than real performance; did little to motivate yet was often demotivating; unfair; arbitrary; inequitable; highly subjective; bias-laden; ineffective and detrimental to professionalism; created dysfunctional interpersonal competition; and undermined the developmental focus of IPR. For some IPR was 'sullied' by its linkage with PRP. At best, appraisees felt that PRP might possibly work with better and more stringent guidelines, where performance targets were clear and easily measurable rather than subject to an assessment based on ratings, and when they got on well with their line-manager. PRP also ensured that appraisals were treated seriously. Many of these issues are very familiar 'moans and groans' from the growing PRP literature. A particular problem identified at NT was that performance was highly dependent on team effort and work was increasingly being reorganised along teamwork lines yet PRP was individually based. The team–individual conflict in

PRP may be at least partially resolved by including teamwork objectives in the appraisal process but as we discuss above this was rarely done at NT. Thus:

> To achieve my objectives I have to rely on all my heads of departments. I have to rely on people outside of our division to co-operate or to take things on board. It's a team effort, yet I receive an individual reward that's largely determined on things beyond my control

Equally, those who did not receive PRP were not keen to be subject to it. This seems to contradict the view that PRP is like an extra-marital affair where those with no experience of such things think they are missing out on something terribly exciting and rewarding whilst those who were involved simply felt miserable. For example:

> I don't need someone wielding a financial stick to tell me how to do my job or push myself.

> PRP wouldn't affect me in the slightest. A few hundred pounds is neither here nor there for me.

Only one of the non-PRP managers was concerned that he was not receiving PRP. In essence, this stemmed from his belief that it was unfair for some managers to receive PRP whilst others (such as himself) did not, rather than any great desire to be subject to it himself:

> IPR was first introduced here for senior managers and was linked to their pay. Then they brought it down to other managers. This is not sour grapes, but when it got down to my level of management the pay was wiped out and just the appraisal was left.

> *Note* This case study draws on four main sources of data: interviews with managers and professionals; a fully structured postal questionnaire administered to a sample of 270 managers and professionals; the analysis of internal documents and procedures manuals and fourthly, the observation of training workshops on appraisal and several senior management meetings reviewing appraisal practice in the organisation (see Redman *et al.*, 2000).

## Questions

1. Is IPR a failure at North Trust?
2. Should IPR be retained by the organisation? If you recommend retention, what changes would you advise? If you recommend that it should be scrapped, what would you advise should replace it?
3. According to Wright (1991) a paradox of performance management systems is that the meaningful is rarely measurable and the measurable is rarely meaningful. What evidence is there to support such a criticism in North-Trust?
4. A key for managers in measuring individual performance under systems of performance appraisal is distinguishing between 'real' and 'created' performance achievements, the danger being that managers may actually measure an employee's 'ability to perform in the theatrical rather than task-oriented sense' (Randle and Rainne, 1997). What evidence is there that this is a problem at North Trust? How can the problems of impression management be minimised?

5. It has been suggested that the key challenge now facing performance appraisal systems is their upgrading, renewal and reinvention such that they are more compatible with business environments. To what extent does IPR fit the business environment of the 'new, modern and dependable NHS' (Department of Health, 1997)?

6. Some analysts have suggested that the NHS is moving from a bureaucratic mode of organisation to a network mode of organising. What are the implications of such a development for IPR practice?

## References

Department of Health (1997) *The New NHS: Modern, Dependable*, London: The Stationery Office.

Randle, K. and Rainnie, A. (1997) 'Managing creativity, maintaining control: a study in pharmaceutical research', *Human Research Management Journal*, 7(2): 32–46.

Redman, T., Snape, E., Thompson, D. and Ka-ching Yan (2000) 'Performance appraisal in an NHS hospital', *Human Resource Management Journal*, 10(1): 1–16.

Wright, V. 1991. 'Performance related pay' in Neale, F. (ed) *The Handbook of Performance Management*, London: Institute of Personnel Management.

# Appraisal at Bankco

Tom Redman and Adrian Wilkinson

Jim is a branch manager at Bankco, a large retail bank. The branch comprises 20 staff with a mix of front desk, sales and back office roles. There has been a lot of pressure on the bank in the last two years or so with threats of takeover and merger, and branch managers have had rigorous financial targets to meet. Jim has managed to achieve these but at the cost of bearing down on staff. He is known as a strict disciplinarian and is known to berate staff in front of customers if they have failed to meet targets. The result is low morale and increasing staff turnover. A branch inspection has raised HR issues. Jim has not done much induction or many appraisals this year and few staff have been on training programmes. Staff see his manner to them as offhand and very directive. At the same time the bank has promoted 'a profits through people' philosophy and has a mission statement which places great emphasis on staff value to the organisation and how the organisation will treat them with respect.

Corporate principles refer not only to business objectives and shareholders but also to the organisation's commitment to its employees, the community, customers and the environment. The section on employees in the booklet which is issued to all staff places great stress and emphasis on teamworking, involvement and communication, training and development and welfare. In particular, the booklet states that:

- We will seek to achieve an atmosphere conducive at all levels to effective teamwork.
- We will encourage involvement in decision-making within the scope of an employee's responsibilities.
- We will ensure that each employee receives all relevant information necessary for the performance of duties and an understanding of how these relate to the Bank as a whole.
- We will provide for the possibility of developing the potential of employees by means of training and development, education, job rotation, and performance appraisal.
- We treat employees fairly and with dignity.

You (the Divisional Head, Fred) are now appraising Jim. You are anxious to be sympathetic as he is an experienced and capable manager, but at the same time you need to put the message across that he has to change his attitude to staff. Jim has a reputation for being confrontational and aggressive. You are not looking forward to this meeting.

## Instructions for exercise

Carry out an appraisal role play with Fred and Jim. The observing group should review the following issues:

1. Did Fred put the message he wanted across?
2. Did Jim accept this? If not, what was the resolution? If so, what were the required standards for the future?
3. How well did Fred question and listen?

# References to Chapter 3

Anderson. G.C., Young, E. and Hulme, D. (1987) 'Appraisal without form-filling', *Personnel Management*, 19(2), 44–7.

Angel, N.F. (1989) 'Evaluating employees by computer', *Personnel Administrator*, November: 67–72.

Armstrong, M. and Baron, A. (1998) *Performance Management*, London: IPD.

Arthur, W., Woehr, D.J., Akande, A. and Strong, M.H. (1995) 'Human resource management in West Africa: practices and perceptions', *International Journal of Human Resource Management*, 6(2): 347–67.

Banks, C.G. and Murphy, K.R. (1985) 'Toward narrowing the research–practice gap in performance appraisal', *Personnel Psychology*, 38: 335–45.

Barlow, G. (1989) 'Deficiencies and the perpetuation of power: latent functions in management appraisal', *Journal of Management Studies*, 26(5): 499–517.

Bevan, S. and Thompson, M. (1991) 'Performance management at the crossroads', *Personnel Management*, November: 36–39.

Bhote, K.R. (1994) 'Boss performance appraisal: a metric whose time has gone', *Employment Relations Today*, 21(1): 1–8.

Bowman, J.S. (1994) 'At last, an alternative to performance appraisal: total quality management', *Public Administration Review*, 54(2): 129–36.

Bowles, M.L. and Coates, G. (1993) 'Image and substance: the management of performance as rhetoric or reality', *Personnel Review*, 22(2): 3–21.

Boudreaux, G. (1994) 'What TQM says about performance appraisal', *Compensation and Benefits Review*, 26, 3: 20–24.

Carroll, S.J. and Schneier, C.E. (1982) *Performance Appraisal and Review Systems: The Identification, Measurement and Development of Performance in Organisations*, Glenview, Il: Scott Foresman.

Chow, I. (1994) 'An opinion survey of performance appraisal practices in Hong Kong and the Peoples' Republic of China', *Asia Pacific Journal of Human Resources*, 32: 62–79.

Coates, G. (1994) 'Performance appraisal as icon: Oscar-winning performance or dressing to impress?', *International Journal of Human Resource Management*, 5(1): 165–191.

Connock, S. (1992) 'The importance of "big ideas" to HR managers', *Personnel Management*, 21(11): 52–56.

Cook, S. (1993) *Customer Care*, London: Kogan Page.

CPCR (1995) *The Right Angle on 360-degree Feedback*, Newcastle: CPCR.

Cully, M., Woodland, S., O'Reilly, A. and Dix, G. (1999) *Britain at Work*, London: Routledge.

Deblieux, M. (1991) 'Performance reviews support the quest for quality', *HR Focus*, November: 3–4.

Deming, W.E. (1986) *Out of the Crisis: Quality, Productivity and Competitive Position*, Cambridge: Cambridge University Press.

Dent, M. (1995) 'The new National Health Service: a case of postmodernism?', *Organisation Studies*, 16(5): 875–99.

Dugdill, G. (1994) 'Wide angle view', *Personnel Today*, 27 September: 31–32.

Endo, K. (1994) 'Satei (personal assessment) and interworker competition in Japanese firms', *Industrial Relations*, 33(1): 70–82

Finn, R.H. and Fontaine, P.A. (1983) 'Performance appraisal: some dynamics and dilemmas', *Public Personnel Management Journal*, 13(4): 335–43.

Fletcher, C. and Williams, R. (1992) 'The route to performance management', *Personnel Management*, October 24(10), 42–47

Fletcher, C. (1993) 'Appraisal: an idea whose time has gone?', *Personnel Management*, September: 25(9), 34–38.

Fowler, A. (1990) 'Performance management: the MBO of the 1990s?', *Personnel Management*, July: 47–51.

Fuller, L. and Smith, V. (1991) 'Consumers' reports: management by customers in a changing economy', *Work Employment and Society*, 4(1): 1–16.

Giffin, M.E. (1989) 'Personnel research on testing, selection and performance appraisal', *Public Personnel Management*, 18(2): 127–37.

Gill, D. (1977) *Appraising Performance: Present Trends and the Next Decade*, London: IPD.

Grint, K. (1993) 'What's wrong with performance appraisals? A critique and a suggestion', *Human Resource Management*, 3(3): 61–77.

Halachmi, A. (1993) 'From performance appraisal to performance targeting', *Public Personnel Management*, 22(2): 323–44.

Illes, P. and Salaman, M. (1995) 'Recruitment, selection and assessment', in Storey, J. (ed) *Human Resource Management. A Critical Text*, London: Routledge.

IRS (1992) 'Industrial relations developments in the water industry', *Employment Trends*, 516: 6–15.

IRS (1994) 'Improving performance? A survey of appraisal arrangements', *Employment Trends*, 556: 5–14.

IRS (1995a) 'Survey of employee relations in local government', *Employment Trends*, 594: 6–13.

IRS (1995b) 'The customer is boss: matching employee performance to customer service needs', *Employment Trends*, 585: 7–13.

IRS (1999) 'New ways to perform appraisal', *Employment Trends*, 676: 7–16.

Kessler, I. and Purcell, J. (1992) 'Performance related pay: objectives and application', *Human Resource Management Journal*, 2(3): 16–33.

Kolesar, P. (1993) 'Vision, values and milestones. Paul O'Neil starts total quality at Alcoa', *California Management Review*, 35(3): 133–65.

Laabs, J. (1992) 'Measuring work in the electronic age', *Personnel Journal*, 71(6): 35.

Lawler, E.E. III (1994) 'Performance management: the next generation', *Compensation and Benefits Review*, May–June: 16–28.

Lawler, J.J., Jain, H.C., Ratnam, C.S.V. and Atmiyanandana, V. (1995) 'Human resource management in developing economies: a comparison of India and Thailand', *International Journal of Human Resource Management*, 6(2): 320–46.

LGMB (1994) *Performance Management and Performance Related Pay. Local Government Practice*, London: LGMB.

Locher, A.H. and Teel, K.S. (1988) 'Appraisal trends', *Personnel Journal*, 67(9): 139–43.

London, M. and Beatty, R. W. (1993), '360-degree feedback as a competitive advantage', *Human Resource Management*, Summer/Autumn: 353–72.

Long, P. (1986) *Performance Appraisal Revisited*, London: IPD.

Longenecker, C. (1989) 'Truth or consequences: politics and performance appraisals', *Business Horizons*, November–December: 76–82.

Maroney, B.P. and Buckley, P.P.M. (1992) 'Does research in performance appraisal influence the practice of performance appraisal? Regretfully not.' *Public Personnel Management*, 21(2): 185–196.

Miles, L. (1993) 'Rise of the mystery shopper', *Marketing*, 29 July: 19–20.

Milliman, J.F., Zawacki, R.A., Schulz, B., Wiggins, S. and Norman, C. (1995) 'Customer service drives 360-degree goal setting', *Personnel Journal*, June: 136–41.

Mitrani, A., Dalziel, M.M., and Fitt, D. (1992) *Competency Based Human Resource Management*, London: Kogan Page.

Moores, B. (1990) 'The service excellence experience', *Marketing Intelligence and Planning*, 8(6): 19–24.

O'Reilly, B. (1995) '360-degree feedback can change your life', *Fortune*, October 17: 55–58.

Peters, T. (1987) *Thriving on Chaos*, London: Macmillan.

Randell, G. (1994) 'Employee appraisal', in Sisson, K. (ed) *Personnel Management in Britain*, Oxford: Blackwell.

Redman, T. and Snape, E. (1992) 'Upward and onward: can staff appraise their managers?,' *Personnel Review*, 21(7): 32–46.

Redman, T., and McElwee, G. (1993) 'Upward appraisal of lecturers: lessons from industry?', *Education + Training*, 35(2): 20–26.

Redman, T. and Mathews, B.P. (1995) 'Do corporate turkeys vote for Christmas? Managers' attitudes towards upward appraisal', *Personnel Review*, 24(7): 13–24.

Redman, T., Snape, E., Thompson, D. and Ka-ching Yan, F. (2000) 'Performance appraisal in the National Health Service: a trust hospital study', *Human Resource Management Journal*, 10(1): 1–16.

Ring, T. (1992) 'Managing quality: efficiency on the line', *Personnel Today*, 14 July: 25–26.

Roth, W. and Ferguson, D. (1994) 'The end of performance appraisals?', *Quality Digest*, 14(9): 52–57.

Scholtes, P.R. (1993) 'Total quality or performance appraisal: choose one', *National Productivity Review*, Summer: 349–63.

Sherman, S. (1995) 'Stretch goals: the dark side of asking for miracles', *Fortune*, November: 231–32.

Silvestro, R. (1990) 'Quality management in service industries', *International Journal of Service Industry Management*, 1(2): 54–56.

Snape, E., Redman, T. and Bamber, G. (1994) *Managing Managers*, Oxford: Blackwells.

Snape, E., Thompson, D., Ka-ching Yan, F. and Redman, T. (1998) 'Performance appraisal and culture: practice and attitudes in Hong Kong and Great Britain', *International Journal of Human Resource Management*, 9(5): 841–61.

Sparrow, P. (1994) 'Organizational competencies: creating a strategic behavioural framework for selection and assessment', in Anderson, N. and Herriot, P. (eds) *Assessment and Selection in Organizations*, Chichester: John Wiley.

Syrett, M. and Lammiman, J. (1994) 'Developing the "peripheral" worker', *Personnel Management*, July: 28–31.

Thomas, A., Wells, M. and Willard, J. (1992) 'A novel approach to developing managers and their teams: BPX uses upward feedback', *Management Education and Development*, 23(1): 30–32.

Tombs, S. (1992) 'Managing safety: could do better...', *Occupational Safety and Health*, 9–12.

Townley, B. (1989) 'Selection and appraisal: reconstituting "social relations"', in J. Storey (ed) *New Perspectives on Human Resource Management*, London: Routledge.

Townley, B. (1990) 'A discrimination approach to appraisal', *Personnel Management*, December: 34–37.

Townley, B. (1993) 'Performance appraisal and the emergence of management', *Journal of Management Studies*, 30(2): 221–38.

Townley, B. (1994) *Reframing Human Resource Management*, London: Sage.

Tully, S. (1994) 'Stretch targets', *Fortune*, 14 November: 83–90.

Tziner, A. (1999) 'The relationship between distal and proximal factors and the use of political considerations in performance appraisal', *Journal of Business and Psychology*, 14(1): 217–31.

Wilson, J. and Cole, G. (1990) 'A healthy approach to performance appraisal', *Personnel Management*, June: 46–49.

Winstanley, D., Dawson, S., Mole, V. and Sherval, J. (1995) 'Under the microscope: performance management and review for senior managers in the NHS', paper presented at BUIRA annual conference, Durham.

Wright, V. (1991) 'Performance related pay', in Neale F. (ed) *The Handbook of Performance Management*, London: IPM.

# Chapter 34    Strategic aspects of payment

Pay is all sorts of different things. It is basically a transaction, as an employer pays £X in exchange for generally specified time, skills, commitment and loyalty. But pay is also a label (the £2,000-a-day libel lawyer), a status symbol (professors are paid more than senior lecturers) and a determinant of standard of living. Pay is also likely to be a discriminator according to gender (average earnings are lower for women than for men) and social class (average earnings are lower for manual workers than for non-manual workers), and is one of the main influences on the degree to which people value their employment. It is not just the amount they are paid, but the nature of the contract. Salaried posts in the main are for what a person *is* as well as for what he or she does. The government minister in charge of the treasury is paid to *be* Chancellor of the Exchequer, not just to prepare and deliver an annual budget.

The reason why pay is a crucial issue for managers is that managers decide what employees should be paid, so they influence all of these factors in the lives of John Brown and Mary Smith. Managers mediate between the customer and the worker as a supplier of goods and services, and we are all highly sensitive to issues like our social status. This is why trade unions were created and pay review bodies formed. This is why we have laws to control at least some aspects of the pay bargain. If you are an employee at any level someone decides what you are worth, and few things matter more to us than how we are valued.

This type of management mediation between customer and worker applies only to employees; it is different for the self-employed and sole traders. In writing this book we have one thing in common with J.K. Rowling and Delia Smith: we have all recently published books. Every copy of this book that is sold puts a modest amount of money in our pockets, that is predetermined by a royalty agreement. There is no employer intervention to vary the amount. If the publisher sells a huge number, then our royalty payments rise in strict proportion. If they sell few, then our royalty payments are disappointing, but there is no argument about worth or value, because there is no mediation.

## Management approaches to payment

A strange thing about payment is that managers seem to shy away from actually using the word. We hear about 'compensation', 'reward' or 'remuneration', yet the idea of compensation is that it involves making amends for something that has caused loss or injury. Do we want to suggest that work necessarily causes loss or injury? Reward suggests a special payment for a special act. Much current management thinking on pay issues concerns the need to induce more special effort by employees, but the bulk of the pay bargain for an individual is not affected by performance. Remuneration is a more straightforward word which means exactly the same as payment but has five more letters and is misspelled (as renumeration) more often than most words in the human resource manager's lexicon.

We use the general term 'payment' as this part of the book includes material about pensions, sick pay and other benefits, but the current general term is certainly 'reward'. This term is used to identify the system of payment as a central, integrated feature of the approach to HRM. The traditional collective bargain was separated from the management of the people receiving the money: the concept of reward is to have some sort of multiple helix, where motivation, skill, career and performance are all intertwined to produce added value to the individual career and corporate aspects, with the pay reflecting, describing and moving with the other elements continuously.

The approach to payment adopted by employers typically takes one of three forms, the focus being on *service*, on *skills* or on *performance*. The focus on service is characterised by open-ended agreements about continuity of employment, incremental pay scales and annual reviews. Focusing on skills produces higher rates of pay with greater or rarer skills, while a focus on performance emphasises target setting, adapting to change and a close relationship between what the employee achieves and what the employee is paid. The first is sometimes referred to as 'traditional' (Mahoney 1989) in that it focuses on the rate for the job. By contrast, the second and third can be seen as different kinds of 'non-traditional' approach with their emphasis on rewarding individual contribution. In practice the various approaches are not incompatible and all are widely used. Most people are therefore paid a rate for the job they are employed to do, but have pay rises or incentive payments determined by some aspect of their personal contribution.

In the following chapter we look in detail at the measurement and grading of jobs. In Chapters 36 and 37 the focus is on incentives and employee benefits. Here we introduce some of the fundamental choices that managers have to make in deciding how much and in what form to pay their employees. We also acknowledge the constraints faced when making these decisions and describe recent academic debates about 'strategy' in reward management. We start by focusing on the different objectives that employers and employees have in respect of payment.

## Employee objectives for the contract of payment

Those who are paid and those who administer payment schemes have objectives for the payment contract which differ according to whether one is the recipient or the administrator of the payments. The contract for payment will be satisfactory in so far as it meets the objectives of the parties. Therefore we consider the range of objectives, starting with employees.

### First objective: purchasing power

The absolute level of weekly or monthly earnings determines the standard of living of the recipient, and will therefore be the most important consideration for most employees. How much can I buy? Employees are rarely satisfied about their purchasing power, and the annual pay adjustment will do little more than reduce dissatisfaction. The two main reasons for this are inflation and rising expectations.

## Second objective: felt fair

Elliott Jacques (1962) averred that every employee had a strong feeling about the level of payment that was fair for the job. In most cases this is a rough, personalised evaluation of what is appropriate. The employee who feels underpaid is likely to demonstrate the conventional symptoms of withdrawal from the job: looking for another, carelessness, disgruntlement, lateness, absence, and the like. Perhaps the worst manifestation of this is among those who feel the unfairness but who cannot take a clean step of moving elsewhere. They then not only feel dissatisfied with their pay level, but also feel another unfairness too: being trapped in a situation they resent. Those who feel they are overpaid (as some do) may simply feel guilty, or may seek to justify their existence in some way by trying to look busy. That is not necessarily productive.

## Third objective: rights

A different aspect of relative income is that concerned with the rights of the employee to a particular share of the company's profits or the nation's wealth. The employee is here thinking about whether the division of earnings is providing fair shares of the Gross National Product. The focus is often on the notion of need – the idea that someone has a right to a greater share because they or their families are suffering unjustly. These are features of many trade union arguments and part of the general preoccupation with the rights of the individual.

## Fourth objective: relativities

'How much do I (or we) get relative to ... group X?' This is a version of the 'felt fair' argument. It is not a question of whether the employee believes the remuneration to be reasonable in relation to the job done, but of whether they believe it reasonable in relation to the jobs other people do. There are many potential comparators, and the basis of comparison can alter. We may compare our own pay with that of the person sitting in the next desk, with an opposite number in a competitor company or we may be concerned more generally about comparisons with other professional or occupational groups.

Whichever comparator is chosen, it is often difficult to make a fair comparison. For example, basic pay may be very different from overall earnings, while jobs themselves can share a title or job description in common while carrying rather different levels of real responsibility.

## Fifth objective: recognition

Most people have an objective for their payment arrangements, of their personal contribution being recognised. This is partly seeking reassurance, but is also a way in which people can mould their behaviour and their career thinking to produce progress and satisfaction. It is doubtful if financial recognition has a significant and sustained impact on performance, but providing a range of other forms of recognition while the pay packet is transmitting a different message is certainly counter-productive.

## Sixth objective: composition

How is the pay package made up? The growing complexity and sophistication of payment arrangements raises all sorts of questions about pay composition. Is £400 pay for 60 hours' work better than £280 for 40 hours' work? The arithmetical answer that the rate per hour for the 40-hour arrangement is marginally better than that for 60 hours is only part of the answer. The other aspects will relate to the individuals, their circumstances and the conventions of their working group and reference groups. Another question about composition might be: is £250 per week plus a pension better than £270 per week without? Such questions do not produce universally applicable answers because they can be quantified to such a limited extent, but some kernels of conventional wisdom can be suggested as generalisations:

1 Younger employees are more interested in high direct earnings at the expense of indirect benefits, like pensions, which will be of more interest to older employees.
2 Incentive or performance-related payment arrangements are likely to interest employees who either see a reliable prospect of enhancing earnings through the ability to control their own activities, or see the incentive scheme as an opportunity to wrest control of their personal activities (which provide little intrinsic satisfaction) away from management by regulating their earnings.
3 Women with children are less interested in payment arrangements that depend on overtime than men often are.
4 Overtime is used by many employees to produce an acceptable level of purchasing power particularly among the lower-paid.
5 Pensions and sickness payment arrangements beyond statutory minima are a *sine qua non* of white-collar employment, and are of growing importance in manual employment.

**Activity 34.1** Which of the above objectives do you consider to be most important to you? How far do you think priorities in this area change with age?

## Employer objectives for the contract for payment

In looking at the other side of the picture, we consider the range of objectives in the thinking of employers, or those representing an employer interest *vis-à-vis* the employee.

## First objective: prestige

There is a comfortable and understandable conviction among managers that it is 'a good thing' to be a good payer. This seems partly to be simple pride at doing better than others, but also there is sometimes a feeling that such a policy eliminates a variable from the contractual relationship. In conversation with one of the authors a chief executive expressed it this way:

> I want to find out the highest rates of pay, job-for-job, within a fifty-mile radius of my office. Then I will make sure that all my people are paid 20 per cent over that. Then I know where I am with them as I have taken money out of the equation. If

they want to quit they can't hide the real reason by saying they're going elsewhere for more cash: they can't get it. Furthermore, if I do have to fill a job I know that we won't lose a good guy because of the money not being right.

Whether high pay rates succeed in getting someone the reputation of being a good employer is difficult to see. What seems much more likely is that the low-paying employer will have the reputation of being a poor employer.

## Second objective: competition

More rational is the objective of paying rates that are sufficiently competitive to sustain the employment of the right numbers of appropriately qualified and experienced employees to staff the organisation. A distinction is drawn here between competition thinking and prestige thinking, as the former is more designed to get a good fit on one of the employment contract dimensions rather than simply to overwhelm it. It permits consideration of questions such as: how selective do we need to be for this range of jobs? and: how can we avoid over-paying people and inhibiting them from moving on? Every employer has this sort of objective, even if only in relation to a few key posts in the organisation.

## Third objective: control

There may be ways of organising the pay packet that will facilitate control of oper-ations and potentially save money. The conventional approach to this for many years was the use of piecework or similar incentives, but this became difficult due to the unwillingness of most employees to see their payment fluctuate wildly at the employer's behest. Theoretically, overtime is a method of employer control of output through making available or withholding additional payment prospects. In practice, however, employees use overtime for control more extensively than employers. Other ways in which employers could control their payroll costs have been eliminated or made more difficult by legislation. Redundancy, short-term lay-off and unfair dismissal are all now more expensive, and it is unlawful to regard women as a reservoir of inexpensive, temporary labour as once was common.

## Fourth objective: motivation and performance

Employers also seek to use the payment contract to motivate employees and thus to improve their work performance. The subject of incentive payment systems is discussed in detail in Chapter 36, but some features of payment and its influence on performance are worth mentioning here.

Prior to the 1980s incentive payment systems were primarily used as part of the payment package for manual workers and sales staff. The design of such schemes is simple, with a built-in bias towards rewarding the volume of products manu-factured or sold. Wherever the quality of output is a matter of significance such approaches are, therefore, inappropriate. Two extreme examples indicate the weakness of this approach. Someone engaged in the manufacture of diamond-tipped drilling bits would serve the employer poorly if payment were linked to output. If it were possible to devise a payment system that contained an incen-tive element based on high quality of workmanship or on low scrap value that might be more effective. If schoolteachers were paid a 'quantity bonus' it would presumably be based either on the number of children in the class or on some

> ### WINDOW ON PRACTICE
>
> ### The case of the AIDS counsellor
>
> The difficulty of determining a fair and satisfactory rate of pay for particular individuals is illustrated in the following example of a nurse employed by a large NHS hospital as a counsellor for haemophilia patients who have contracted AIDS through blood transfusion.
>
> The nurse concerned was employed on a senior sister's grade but was required to work in the community, undertaking counselling duties with patients and their families. The nature of the job, however, meant that she was required to work very irregular and unpredictable hours and could not delegate duties to anyone else or share the burden of cases with others. She requested a regrading with the full support of her managers who perceived her to be a uniquely good performer. No performance-related scheme had, however, been developed and regrading the nurse was not straightforward. The first stumbling block came when her duties were assessed according to grading criteria negotiated by the relevant NHS Whitley Council. Although several attempts were made to try to make the job fit the criteria for the higher grade, the task proved impossible. Authorising a regrading on these grounds would have set a precedent leading to large numbers of regrading claims.
>
> The next approach taken was to analyse the nurse's job using the hospital's computerised job evaluation system. This route also failed because the results of the analysis suggested that the job was already graded too highly. To regrade in spite of this would render the decision indefensible were an equal value claim to be brought by a male nurse employed at the same grade.
>
> Finally an attempt was made to justify the proposed regrading by discovering at what level other hospitals paid nurses undertaking similar roles. It was found, however, that other AIDS counsellors were paid on the same or lower grades.
>
> It thus proved impossible to pay the nurse concerned a rate which she and her managers regarded as 'fair' because no decision to regrade could be objectively justified.

indicator like the number of examination passes. The first would encourage teachers to take classes as large as possible, with probably adverse results in the quality of teaching. The second might increase the proportion of children succeeding in examinations, but would isolate those who could not produce impressive examination performance.

In recent years a great deal of attention has been paid to the development of incentive payment systems which go beyond rewarding the quantity of output to take account of job performance as a whole. In particular there has been a marked increase in the use of performance-related pay (PRP) for management and professional staff, especially for senior managers; organisations have sought either to re-establish or to introduce for the first time schemes which reinforce the messages required to produce improved performance and increased productivity. Private sector employers in particular now increasingly believe that they are not providing an appropriate or competitive package for their directors and senior executives unless there is some element of risk money to add on to the basic salary and reward the achievement of company growth, profitability and success. At the same time, companies have been re-examining the use of bonus schemes for more junior employees in order to increase motivation and to reward them for their contribution. The use of PRP is also growing in the public sector following active promotion of its benefits by government ministers.

## Fifth objective: cost

Just as employees are interested in purchasing power, the absolute value of their earnings, so employers are interested in the absolute cost of payment, and its bearing on the profitability or cost-effectiveness of their organisation. The importance of this varies with the type of organisation and the cost of employees relative to other costs, so that in the refining of petroleum employment costs are modest, in teaching or nursing they are substantial. The employer interest in this objective is long term as well as short term. Not only do employees expect their incomes to be maintained and to carry on rising, rather than fluctuating with company profitability, but the indirect costs of employing people can also be substantial.

## Sixth objective: change management

Pay can be used specifically as one of a range of tools underpinning change management processes. The approach used is to tie higher base pay, bonuses or promotion to the development of new behaviours, attitudes or skills gained by employees. Pay works far more effectively than simple exhortation because it provides a material incentive to those whose natural inclination is to resist change. It also sends out a powerful message to employees indicating the seriousness of the employer's intentions as regards proposed or ongoing changes.

## Approaches to setting base pay rates

One of the most important decisions in the design of payment systems concerns the mechanism or mechanisms that will be used to determine the basic rate of pay for different jobs in the organisation. There are, of course, restrictions on management action in this area provided by the law. Since 1999 the UK has had a National Minimum Wage (£3.70 an hour in 2001) to which workers over the age of 22 are entitled; a lower minimum rate is set for those aged 18–22. Equal pay law is a further way in which the state intervenes, providing a mechanism for employees to complain when they consider their pay to be unjustifiably lower than that paid to a colleague of the opposite sex. Moreover, in many countries incomes policies are operated as tools of inflation control. These restrict the amount of additional pay that people can receive in any one year while remaining in the same job. While formal incomes policies were abandoned in the UK after the 1970s, similar thinking continues to underpin government decision making in the area of public sector pay (Thorpe 2000, pp. 34–5).

A further restriction on management action is the nature of the product markets in which their organisations operate. The extent of this influence varies according to how important labour costs are in deciding product cost, and how important product cost is to the customer. In a labour-intensive and low-technology industry like catering, there will usually be such pressure on labour costs that the pay administrator has little freedom to manipulate pay relationships. In an area like magazine printing, the need of the publisher to get the product on time is so great that labour costs, however high, may be of relatively little concern. In this situation the pay negotiators have much more freedom of manoeuvre.

It is possible, notwithstanding the above restrictions, to identify four principal mechanisms for the determination of base pay. They are not entirely incompatible, although one tends to be used as the main approach in most organisations.

## External market comparisons

In making external market comparisons the focus is on the need to recruit and retain staff, a rate being set which is broadly equivalent to 'the going rate' for the job in question. The focus is thus on **external relativities.** Some employers consciously pay over the market rate in order to secure the services of the most talented employees. Others 'follow the market', by paying below the going rate while using other mechanisms such as flexibility, security or longer-term incentives to ensure effective recruitment and retention. In either case the decision is based on an assessment of what rate needs to be paid to compete for staff in different types of labour market. Going rates are more significant for some than for others. Accountants and craftworkers, for instance, tend to identify with an external employee grouping. Their assessment of pay levels is thus greatly influenced by the going rate in the trade or the district. A similar situation exists with jobs that are clearly understood and where skills are readily transferable, particularly if the employee is to work with a standard piece of equipment. Driving heavy goods vehicles is an obvious example, as the vehicles are common from one employer to another, the roads are the same, and only the loads vary. Other examples are secretaries, switchboard operators and computer operators. Jobs that are less sensitive to the labour market are those that are organisationally specific, like most semi-skilled work in manufacturing, general clerical work and nearly all middle-management positions.

There are several possible sources of intelligence about market rates for different job types at any one time. A great deal of information can be found in published journals such as the pay bulletins issued by Incomes Data Services (IDS) and Industrial Relations Services (IRS), focusing on the hard-to-recruit groups such as computer staff. More detailed information can be gained by joining one of the major salary survey projects operated by firms of consultants or by paying for access to their datasets. Information on specific types of job, including international packages for expatriate workers, is collected by specialised consultants and can be obtained on payment of the appropriate fee. White (2000, pp. 44–5) identifies a range of other sources of UK pay data including the Confederation of British Industry's Pay Databank and the Office of Manpower Economics. In addition there are more informal approaches such as looking at pay rates included in recruitment advertisements in papers and at job centres. New staff, notably HR people, often bring with them a knowledge of pay rates for types of job in competitor organisations and can be a useful source of information. Finally, it is possible to join or set up salary clubs. These consist of groups of employers, often based in the same locality, who agree to share salary information for mutual benefit.

## Internal labour market mechanisms

Just as there is a labour market of which the company is a part, so there is a labour market within the organisation which also needs to be managed so as to ensure effective performance. According to Doeringer and Piore (1970) there are two kinds of internal labour market: the enterprise and the craft. The enterprise market is so called because the individual enterprise defines the boundaries of the market itself. Such will be the market encompassing manual workers engaged in production processes, for whom the predominant pattern of employment is one in which jobs are formally or informally ranked, with the jobs accorded the highest pay or prestige usually being filled by promotion from within and those at the bottom of the hierarchy usually being filled only from outside the enterprise. It is, therefore, those at the bottom that are most sensitive to the external labour market. Doeringer and Piore point out that there is a close parallel with managerial jobs, the main ports of entry being from management trainees or supervisors, and the number of appointments from outside gradually reducing as jobs become more senior. This modus operandi is one of the main causes of the problems that redundant executives face.

Recent American research has stressed the importance of this kind of internal labour market in determining pay rates. Here the focus is on **internal differentials** rather than external relativities. An interesting metaphor used is that of the sports tournament in which an organisation's pay structure is likened to the prize distribution in a knock-out competition such as is found, for example, at the Wimbledon Tennis Championships. Here the prize money is highest for the winner, somewhat lower for the runner-up, lower again for the semi-final losers and so on down the rounds. The aim, from the point of view of the tournament organisers, is to attract the best players to compete in the first round, then subsequently to give players in later rounds an incentive to play at their peak. According to Lazear (1995, pp. 26–33), the level of base pay for each level in an organisation's hierarchy should be set according to similar principles. The level of pay for any particular job is thus set at a level which maximises performance lower down the hierarchy among employees competing for promotion. The actual performance of the individual receiving the pay is less important.

The second type of internal labour market identified by Doeringer and Piore is the craft market, where barriers to entry are relatively high – typically involving the attainment of a formal qualification. However, once workers are established in the market, seniority and hierarchy become unimportant as jobs and duties are shared among the individuals concerned. Such arrangements are usually determined by custom and practice, but are difficult to break down because of the vested interests of those who have successfully completed their period of apprenticeship. Certain pay rates are expected by those who have achieved the required qualification and it is accepted by everyone that this is a fair basis for rewarding people.

## Job evaluation

We assess job evaluation in some detail in the next chapter. Here it is necessary only to define the term and identify it as one of the four principal mechanisms of pay determination. Job evaluation involves the establishment of a system which is used to measure the size and significance of all jobs in an organisation. It is defined by Bloom (1998, p. 185) as follows:

> Job evaluation is a systematic process designed to aid an establishment in establishing differentials across jobs within a single employer ... The culmination of this appraisal process is a hierarchy of jobs denoting their relative complexity and value to the organisation.

The focus is thus on the relative worth of jobs within an organisation and on comparisons between these rather than on external relativities and comparisons with rates being paid by other employers. Fairness and objectivity are the core principles, an organisation's wage budget being divided among employees on the basis of an assessment of the nature and size of the job each is employed to carry out.

## Collective bargaining

The fourth approach involves determining pay rates through collective nego-tiations with trade unions or other employee representatives. Thirty years ago this was the dominant method used for determining pay in the UK, negotiations commonly occurring at industry level. The going rates for each job group were thus set nationally and were adhered to by all companies operating in the sector concerned. Recent decades have seen a steady erosion of these arrangements, col-lective bargaining being decentralised to company or plant level in the manu-facturing sector. Meanwhile the rise of service sector organisations with lower union membership levels has ensured that collective bargaining arrangements now cover only a minority of UK workers. According to Cully *et al.* (1999, pp. 241–2) only 41 per cent now have any of their terms and conditions determined in this way. The experience of many other countries is similar, but there remain regions such as eastern Europe and Scandinavia where collective bargaining remains the major determinant of pay rates. Where separate clusters of employees within the same organisation are placed in different bargaining groups and represented by different unions, **internal relativities** become an issue for resolution during bargaining.

In carrying out negotiations the staff and management sides make reference to external labour market rates, established internal pay determination mechanisms and the size of jobs. However, a host of other factors come into the equation too as each side deploys its best arguments. Union representatives, for example, make reference to employee need when house prices are rising and affordable accom-modation is hard to find. Both sides refer to the balance sheet, employers argu-ing that profit margins are too tight to afford substantial rises, while union counterparts seek to gain a share of any increased profits for employees. However good the case made, at the end of the day what makes collective bargaining dif-ferent from the other approaches is the presence of industrial muscle. Strong unions which have the support of the majority of employees, as is the case in many public sector organisations, are able to ensure that their case is heard and taken into account. They can thus 'secure' a better pay deal for their members than market rates would allow.

---

**Activity 34.2**   Which of the four mechanisms outlined above do you think is usually most efficient for setting the following?

1 Base pay

2 Annual cost of living increases

3 Executive remuneration packages

4 Bonus schemes

## The elements of payment

Once the mechanisms for determining rates of pay for jobs in an organisation have been settled, the second key strategic decision relates to the make-up of the pay package. Here there is a great deal of potential choice available. What is included and to what extent are matters which should be decided with a view to supporting the organisation's objectives and encouraging the necessary attitudes and actions on the part of employees. The payment of an individual will be made up of one or more elements from those shown in Figure 34.1. Fixed elements are those that make up the regular weekly or monthly payment to the individual, and which do not vary other than in exceptional circumstances. Variable elements can be varied by either the employee or the employer.

### Basic rate

The irreducible minimum rate of pay is the basic. In most cases this is the standard rate also, not having any additions made to it. In other cases it is a basis on which earnings are built by the addition of one or more of the other elements in payment. Some groups of employees, such as operatives in the footwear industry,

**Figure 34.1 The potential elements of payment**

| | | | |
|---|---|---|---|
| **Bonus** | Profit allocation | | |
| | Discretionary sum | | **Variable elements**<br>• Irregular<br>• Variable amount<br>• Usually discretionary |
| **Incentive** | Group calculation basis | | |
| | Individual calculation basis | | |
| **Overtime payment** | | | |
| **Premia** | Occasional | | |
| | Contractual | | |
| **Benefits** | Fringe benefits | | |
| | Payments in kind | Other | **Fixed elements**<br>• Regular<br>• Rarely variable<br>• Usually contractual |
| | | Accommodation | |
| | | Car | |
| | Benefit schemes | Other | |
| | | Pension | |
| | | Sick pay | |
| **Plussage** | 'Fudge' payments | | |
| | Special additions | | |
| **Basic rate of payment** | | | **Basic** |

have little more than half of their earnings in basic, while primary and secondary schoolteachers have virtually all their pay in this form.

## Plussage

Sometimes the basic has an addition to recognise an aspect of working conditions or employee capability. Payments for educational qualifications and for supervisory responsibilities are quite common. There is also an infinite range of what are sometimes called 'fudge' payments, whereby there is an addition to the basic as a start-up allowance, mask money, dirt money, and so forth.

**Activity 34.3**   If your employer offered you a 'remuneration package', which could be made up from any of the items in Figure 34.1 provided that the total cost was no more than £X, what proportion of each item would you choose and why? Does your answer suggest ideas for further development of salary policies?

## Benefits

Extras to the working conditions that have a cash value are categorised as benefits and can be of great variety. Some have already been mentioned; others include luncheon vouchers, subsidised meals, discount purchase schemes and the range of welfare provisions like free chiropody and cheap hairdressing.

## Premia

Where employees work at inconvenient times – or shifts or permanently at night – they receive a premium payment as compensation for the inconvenience. This is for inconvenience rather than additional hours of work. Sometimes this is built into the basic rate or is a regular feature of the contract of employment so that the payment is unvarying. In other situations shift working is occasional and short-lived, making the premium a variable element of payment.

## Overtime

It is customary for employees working more hours than are normal for the working week to be paid for those hours at an enhanced rate, usually between 10 and 50 per cent more that the normal rate according to how many hours are involved. Seldom can this element be regarded as fixed. No matter how regularly overtime is worked, there is always the opportunity for the employer to withhold the provision of overtime or for the employee to decline the extra hours.

## Incentive

Incentive is here described as an element of payment linked to the working performance of an individual or working group, as a result of prior arrangement. This includes most of the payment-by-results schemes that have been produced by work study, as well as commission payments to salespeople, skills-based pay schemes and performance-related pay schemes based on the achievement of agreed objectives. The distinguishing feature is that the employee knows what has to be done to earn the payment, though he or she may feel very dependent on other people, or on external circumstances, to receive it.

### Bonus

A different type of variable payment is the gratuitous payment by the employer that is not directly earned by the employee: a bonus. The essential difference between this and an incentive is that the employee has no entitlement to the payment as a result of a contract of employment and cannot be assured of receiving it in return for a specific performance. The most common example of this is the Christmas bonus.

We include profit sharing under this general heading although the ownership of shares confers a clear entitlement. The point is that the level of the benefit cannot be directly linked to the performance of the individual. Rather, it is linked to the performance of the business. In some cases the two may be synonymous, with one dominant individual determining the success of the business, but there are very few instances like this, even in the most feverish imaginings of tycoons. Share ownership or profit sharing on an agreed basis can greatly increase the interest of the employees in how the business is run and can increase their commitment to its success, but the performance of the individual is not directly rewarded in the same way as in incentive schemes.

## The importance of equity

Whatever methods are used to determine pay levels and to decide what elements make up the individual pay package, employers must ensure that they are perceived by employees to operate equitably. It has long been established that perceived inequity in payment matters can be highly damaging to an organisation. Classic studies undertaken by J.S. Adams (1963) found that a key determinant of satisfaction at work is the extent to which employees judge pay levels and pay increases to be distributed fairly. These led to the development by Adams and others of **equity theory** which holds that we are very concerned that rewards or 'outputs' equate to our 'inputs' (defined as skill, effort, experience, qualifications, etc.) and that these are fair when compared with the rewards being given to others. Where we believe that we are not being fairly rewarded we show signs of 'dissonance' or dissatisfaction which leads to absence, voluntary turnover, on-job shirking and low-trust employee relations. It is therefore important that an employer not only treats employees equitably in payment matters but is *seen* to do so too.

While it is difficult to gain general agreement about who should be paid what level of salary in an organisation, it is possible to employ certain clear principles when making decisions in the pay field. Those that are most important are the following:

- a standard approach for the determination of pay (basic rates and incentives) across the organisation;
- as little subjective or arbitrary decision making as is feasible;
- maximum communication and employee involvement in establishing pay determination mechanisms;
- clarity in pay determination matters so that everyone knows what the rules are and how they will be applied.

These are the foundations of procedural fairness or 'fair dealing'. In establishing pay rates it is not always possible to distribute rewards fairly to everyone's satisfaction, but it should always be possible to do so using procedures which operate equitably.

## A strategic approach to payment administration

Since the late 1980s a number of authorities have expressed the view that the way payment is managed is undergoing a fundamental change. This view has been most eloquently expressed by Armstrong and Murlis in successive editions of their book, *Reward Management*, where they describe the way they perceive the role of the salary administrator to have changed since the early 1980s:

> Salary administration was very much seen as a back-room function in which numerate specialists worked out details of policies that came from elsewhere – from government, from head office or from general management. There was little obvious link between what happened on the remuneration front and over all business strategy, let alone an organization's human resource strategy – if it had one. There was certainly little line management involvement in, or ownership of, the pay practice that emerged. (Armstrong and Murlis 1994, p. 16)

In this and a more recent edition of their book (Armstrong and Murlis 1998) they go on to describe how they perceive practice to have changed. In particular they stress the significance of reward strategies which have led to the replacement of traditional grading structures with less bureaucratic means of determining an individual's pay. As a result it is possible to reward individual contribution to organisational success through payments related to profit, performance or skills acquisition to a far greater extent than was previously the case.

While there has, unquestionably, been a greater interest in incentive payments during the past 10–15 years, it is unclear whether this represents a shift in employer practice of the degree described above. Criticism of this view has been expressed by Smith (1993) who questions the extent to which the various developments in incentive pay have in fact derived from a new-found strategic approach to pay. Rather, he believes, they amount to 'no more than a collection of expedient manoeuvres to deal with the boom conditions of the late 1980s'. According to this view, the continued growth in profit-related pay owes more to government encouragement than to a serious attempt on the part of employers to use pay strategically as a means of improving productivity. The argument that developments in incentive pay are born of short-term considerations on the part of employers is further backed up by evidence of declining labour productivity during the late 1980s and early 1990s. Poole and Jenkins (1998) give a measure of support to Smith in their finding of considerable gaps in many organisations between the rhetoric and reality of strategic activity in pay management. They did, however, find evidence of the adoption of genuinely original approaches which were fundamentally new in some larger private sector organisations.

## Summary propositions

**34.1** In payment matters employees are principally concerned with purchasing power, fairness and recognition of effort and skills. Employers are concerned with recruitment, retention, motivation and minimising the wage budget.

**34.2** Employers are restricted in pay matters by the law and the realities of their product markets.

**34.3** There are four main alternative methods of setting base pay rates: external labour market comparisons, internal labour market mechanisms, job evaluation and collective bargaining.

**34.4** The main elements of payment are basic rate, plussage, benefits, premia, overtime, incentives and bonus.

**34.5** Procedural equity is essential to the design of successful payment systems.

**34.6** Analysts disagree about how far UK managers have embraced more strategic approaches to reward management in recent years.

## References

Adams, J.S. (1963) 'Towards an understanding of inequity', *Journal of Abnormal and Social Psychology*, Vol. 67, pp. 422–36.

Armstrong, M. and Murlis, H. (1994) *Reward Management: A handbook of salary administration*. London: Kogan Page.

Armstrong, M. and Murlis, H. (1998) *Reward Management: A handbook of remuneration strategy and practice*. London: Kogan Page.

Bloom, M.C. (1998) 'Job evaluation methods', in L.H. Peters, C.R. Greer and S.A. Youngblood (eds), *Blackwell Encyclopedic Dictionary of Human Resource Management*. Oxford: Blackwell.

Cully, M., Woodland, S., O'Reilly, A. and Dix, G. (1999) *Britain at Work: As Depicted by the 1998 Workplace Employee Relations Survey*. London: Routledge.

Doeringer, P.B. and Piore, M.J. (1970) *Internal Labour Markets and Manpower Analysis*. Washington, DC: Office of Manpower Research: US Department of Labor.

Jaques, E. (1962) 'Objective measures for pay differentials', *Harvard Business Review*, January–February, pp. 133–7.

Lazear, E.P. (1995) *Personnel Economics*. Boston: Massacheusetts Institute of Technology.

Mahoney, T. (1989) 'Multiple pay contingencies: strategic design of compensation', *Human Resource Management*, Vol. 28, No. 3, pp. 337–47. Also in G. Salamon (ed.) (1992) *Human Resource Strategies*. London: Sage.

Poole, M. and Jenkins, G. (1998) 'Human Resource Management and the Theory of Rewards: Evidence from a national survey', *British Journal of Industrial Relations*, Vol. 36, No. 2, pp. 227–47.

Thorpe, R. (2000) 'Reward Strategy', in R. Thorpe and G. Homan (eds), *Strategic Reward Systems*. London: Financial Times/Prentice Hall.

Smith, I. (1993) 'Reward management: A retrospective assessment', *Employee Relations*, Vol. 15.

Torrington, D.P. and Tan Chwee Huat (1994) *Human Resource Management for South East Asia*. Singapore: Simon & Schuster.

White, G. (2000) 'Determining pay', in G. White and J. Druker (eds), *Reward Management: A Critical Text*. London: Routledge.

## General discussion topics

1 Can payment ever be truly fair?

2 The chapter lists employer and employee objectives in relation to payment. What changes would you make to these lists?

3 Do you think it is possible to identify 'best practice' in payment policy? What elements would you consider should make up any such package?

# Chapter 4

# Reward management

Philip Lewis

## Introduction

Reward has traditionally been thought of as the poor relation of personnel management. It has been seen as part of 'the turgid, unimaginative and inflexible world of wage and salary administration' (Smith, 1993: 45). But this world has changed in recent years for many organisations. This chapter reflects this new thinking about reward. Indeed, many writers have argued that thinking about wage and salary administration is in itself new. Livy (1988) typifies this scepticism in describing most reward systems as 'chaotic' with 'employers having little idea about what their pay systems are supposed to achieve'. Smith (1983: 12) is equally sceptical:

> Repeated questions to managers and employees about why they pay and accept certain levels of remuneration usually result in replies which boil down to the same answer: that is the pay level is as it has always been or, in harsher terms, we don't really know. There are very few organisations where the answer is clear and positive.

Pay does not have to be so 'chaotic'. The orthodoxy which has arisen in recent years under the heading of 'new pay' (Lawler, 1990; Schuster and Zingheim, 1992) argues that the business strategy of the organisation determines the behaviours employees need to demonstrate in order that the strategy may be implemented effectively. These behaviours may, in part, be delivered by the reward strategy. Lawler (1995) notes that the reward strategy consists of three key elements: the values which underpin the reward strategy; the reward structures and reward processes.

This chapter uses the 'new pay' approach, and in particular Lawler's theory. This serves as a point of departure and a device for structuring the chapter. Using this perspective ensures that the emphasis is upon the major concern of many organisations: the role that reward strategy redesign may play in contributing to organisational change.

## Strategic reward management

Consideration of the relationship between reward management and changing employee behaviours in order to complement business strategy must begin with a clarification of what it is the organisation wishes to change and why. It was pointed out at the beginning of this chapter that a logical starting point for this process is to clarify what it is that the organisation wishes employees to do which may be different from what they are currently doing. Equally logical is the rationale for such changed employee behaviours: that is, they should be consistent with what the organisation is seeking to achieve through its business strategy. This sits easily with the strategic HRM literature (see, for example, Mabey, Salaman and Storey, 1998).

The strategic reward model in Figure 4.1 below suggests that reward strategy starts with a consideration of the business strategy. This is based upon the organisation's external and internal operating environments. (Armstrong (1993) notes that the internal environment consists of the organisation's culture, structure, technology, working arrangements, processes and systems.) The business strategy implies the need for the development of particular employee behaviours appropriate to the strategy. This may be, for example, the acquisition of more 'commercially aware' attitudes and behaviours and greater preparedness and ability to undertake a wider range of tasks.

Lawler's model proposes that the compensation strategy can make a valuable contribution to the development of these employee behaviours. As such, compensation is, of course, only part of the wider HR strategy. Lawler (1984) argues that there should be congruence between these various aspects of the HRM strategy in that the reward system needs to fit the other features of the HR strategy, such as job design and managers' leadership styles, to ensure that total human resource management congruence exists.

According to Lawler (1995) the reward strategy consists of three components:

- the organisation's core reward values
- structural issues
- process features

The organisation's core reward values are what the organisation stands for, which informs the principles on which the reward strategy is founded. Structural issues include the strategy features (e.g. performance-related or profit-related pay) and the administrative policies surrounding these features. Process features include principally how the strategy is communicated and implemented and the extent to which employees are involved in the design and implementation of the strategy.

Each of these is considered in the remainder of this chapter. Lawler makes the point that the stronger the alignment between the core reward values, structural features and processes, the more effective the reward strategy will be. He argues that the key consideration is the level of consistency between what organisations say and what they do. In the event of inconsistency, Lawler notes that there is likely to be employee misunderstanding about how the reward strategy works, with a consequence being a failure to generate the required behaviours.

### Challenging the assumptions underlying strategic reward management

On first examination this model of strategic reward management seems highly rational, but it makes significant assumptions. First, consider the main driving force of the reward strategy – the business strategy. Two of the complications are well rehearsed in the literature. First, the assumption that business strategy is a rational, top-down process rather than emerging as a result of a pattern of management actions over time (Mintzberg and Waters, 1989; Whittington, 1993). Even if the business strategy is clearly formulated, it is by no means certain that the HRM strategy will follow this lead. Indeed, if this is contemplated, it is often not possible to promote wholesale changes to, for example, recruitment and selection, training, appraisal and career development. What is more likely is that such changes happen incrementally over time.

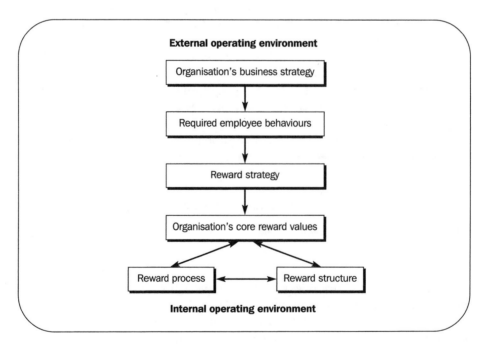

**Figure 4.1 Key elements of reward system design**
*Source*: developed from Lawler, 1995

In addition, the model is essentially unitarist in that it assumes employees will endorse the business strategy and wish to demonstrate the behaviours it implies. Moreover, it assumes that they will accept the organisation's reward strategy if the values, structure and process are consistent. This may be the case if the employees' interests are not threatened. But such reward changes under the heading of 'new pay' may not be received favourably by employees. Indeed, if, as is often the case, one of the strategic driving forces is cost saving, such a threat is almost inevitable.

As well as being unitarist, the strategic reward management model is highly deterministic. It reflects a very 'bottom line' orientation (Beaumont, 1993: 205) which assumes that an effective reward strategy will have a beneficial effect upon the performance of the organisation. This is a significant assumption because of the difficulty in subjecting it to empirical test. The model masks the complexities of organisational life. To think that simply designing the reward strategy in accordance with the prescription will yield 'success' ignores the host of variables which may conspire to render such an outcome unlikely. Managers often take 'short cuts' due to the pressure to produce quick results exerted by senior managers obsessed with short-term goals (Storey and Sisson, 1993; Monks, 1998). There is often opposition to changing reward strategies from trade unions as well as managers who feel their interests threatened. In short, the deterministic perspective is based on assumptions of rationality and unitarism which disregard the political realities of organisational life (Keenoy, 1990).

There is also a major assumption which dominates reward management thinking in general and the model in Figure. 4.1 in particular. This is that pay has the ability to motivate employees to behave in a way in which they might not otherwise behave. The theory that tends to dominate is that of the rational economic person. This has its roots in the work of F.W.Taylor (1911) who assumed that workers were lazy and needed money to motivate them to expend greater effort. The prevalence of payments-by-results schemes this century, in particular for blue-collar workers, testifies to the influence of this way of thinking about the relationship between pay and employee effort. Later, this approach was questioned by the human relations school, which queried the overreliance on money as a motivator and argued that social relationships were an important determinant of employee productivity.

The theories of Maslow (1943) and Herzberg (1968) are equally well known. Maslow's 'hierarchy of needs' suggests that people's needs change as they ascend a hierarchy which has basic needs for food, security, etc. at the lowest level, ranging to self-actualisation at the highest. Herzberg argued that employees were more likely to be motivated by factors such as achievement and the work itself rather than simply money. While money has only limited power to motivate, it does have the ability to demotivate employees if they are dissatisfied with the amount they receive or the way in which this amount is determined.

It is beyond the scope of this chapter to go into detail on these and the many other motivation theories. What is clear is that the relationship between pay and motivation is highly complex. Perhaps the best that can be said is that money may motivate some people to behave in particular ways some of the time, in some circumstances. What cannot be assumed is a clear relationship between pay and motivation. Indeed, as Pfeffer (1998) suggests, overreliance on pay to secure the motivation of employees may be at the cost of more powerful motivators such as meaningful work in a high-trust, friendly environment.

Clearly, caution needs to be exercised in assuming that the implementation of strategic reward management will lead to a reward strategy that will automatically change employee behaviours in line with the organisation's business strategy. There are far too many variables which may conspire against such a straightforward cause–effect relationship. However, it would be foolish to abandon the possibility that reward strategy may play a role in contributing to organisational change.

## Ethical concerns of strategic reward management

In addition to the assumptions of rationality, unitarism and determinism, the strategic reward management model promotes ethical concerns. Heery (1996) argues that there are three concerns with new pay. First, strategic reward management poses a threat to the wellbeing of employees. New pay advocates suggest reducing the proportion of pay that is fixed, thus putting a proportion of the pay packet 'at risk' through techniques such as performance-related pay or profit-related pay. Wellbeing is threatened by an increased amount of insecurity and unpredictability that is potentially harmful both economically and psychologically. Additionally, putting a proportion of employees' income at risk may lead to such behaviours as overwork which may damage both mental and physical health.

Second, Heery argues that new pay may be unjust. This may be at two levels. It may be procedurally unjust in terms of the way in which the element of pay at risk is determined, usually by line managers. This is considered later in this chapter under the heading of individual performance-related pay. It also may be unjust in a distributive sense. New pay theory has it that employees take their share of the hardship when the organisation is doing less well, for example, through lower or non-existent profit-related pay. In this way employers are transferring an element of risk from their shareholders to their employees. But as Heery points out, shareholders are often better equipped to spread their risks than employees, who often are dependent on their salary as the sole source of income.

Thirdly, Heery (1996: 62) suggests that new pay 'affords little scope for the exercise of democratic rights by citizens at the workplace'. It is suggested earlier in this chapter that new pay has a highly unitarist ring. If it is assumed that there is no essential conflict of interest between employer and employees then the right of employees to have their views represented is of little importance. Indeed, trade unions and collective bargaining have little coverage in the new pay literature. On the other hand, there is emphasis on employee involvement, but this tends to focus on securing commitment of employees to the goals of the organisation and new pay rather than representing the interests of employees. In this sense, new pay may be seen as part of a sophisticated edifice to marginalise the democratic rights of employees at the workplace and the mechanisms for securing those rights. There is little evidence, however, of such a sophisticated level of strategic thinking in the UK. Wood's (1996) survey of UK manufacturing plants found little systematic association between pay systems such as performance-related pay and profit-related pay and so-called high commitment work practices such as teamworking, quality circles, employee communication, multiskilling and single status terms and conditions. These are the sort of HR practices, when aligned with new pay techniques, which one would expect to see if management were making concerted efforts to ensure that employees adopted the goals of the organisation.

The remainder of this chapter examines the components of Figure 4.1. The purpose of the analysis is to explain how integration between the HRM strategy and the reward strategy, and integration between the three components of the reward strategy itself, may contribute to changed employee behaviours.

The analysis starts with a consideration of the employee behaviours employers may wish to encourage. The relationship between HRM strategy and reward strategy is then examined briefly. The main part of the analysis is devoted to a consideration of the reward strategy's values, structure and processes.

## What employee behaviours may organisations wish to encourage?

The strategic HRM literature (e.g. Beer *et al.*, 1984; Guest, 1987) reflects the desire for certain key goals: employee commitment to the organisation's aims; employee competence; flexibility and the production of quality goods and services. The way in which many organisations have sought to ensure the acquisition of appropriate employee behaviours is through the definition of key competencies for particular jobs. Typical of this approach is the competencies required by Standard Chartered Bank (IDS, 1992). Box 4.1 (overleaf) lists the generic competencies employees are expected to develop if they are to perform their jobs satisfactorily and generate individual performance-related pay awards.

At the end of this chapter is a case study of Lincoln Insurance. It is clear in this case that Lincoln wished to develop the range of skills of its employees to make them more flexible. This was a response to the need to restructure the work processes to provide a better service to customers

## What part do reward management values, structures and processes play in changing employee behaviour?

The importance Lawler (1995) placed on consistency between the three components of reward strategy, values, structure and processes, is noted above. In particular, Lawler claimed that an inconsistency between what the organisation says and does in its reward strategy may lead to employee discontent. It follows from this that the reward values which employers espouse are of great significance.

---

**BOX 4.1**

### Generic competencies used by Standard Chartered Bank for performance-related pay awards

- *Job and professional knowledge* which includes keeping abreast of the latest technology developments in the employee's professional field and knowledge of other areas of the bank.

- *Commercial customer awareness*, including understanding the financial and competitive forces affecting the bank and keeping informed of customer needs.

- *Communication*, which includes speaking and writing clearly.

- *Interpersonal skills*, which include interacting effectively with colleagues and responding productively to constructive criticism.

- *Teamwork*, including fully contributing to the team effort by relating well to others.

- *Initiative/adaptability/creativity*, which includes seeking out opportunities for innovation, setting priorities and goals.

- *Analytical skills/decision-making*, including understanding data and information in order to solve problems.

- *Productivity*, which assesses the quantity of performance such as volume of work.

- *Quality*, for example, freedom from errors.

- *Management/supervision*, which includes reviewing performance, counselling and staff development and delegation.

- *Leadership*, including the ability to inspire, motivate and give confidence.

(IDS, 1992)

---

This section analyses four values which organisations may consider in reward management design. These are the degree to which the organisation believes in:

- paying for performance
- equity
- employees sharing in the organisation's success
- combining financial and non-financial rewards

The analysis that follows considers each of these values and the ways in which the values are reflected in the pay structure. There is also some consideration of key implementation processes.

### The value of paying for performance

Paying for individual job performance is, for many organisations, at the heart of a reward strategy. This raises what for many employees is a highly contentious issue: the putting at risk of a proportion of their salary. Most employees think about pay in terms of base pay (Schuster and Zingheim, 1992): the fixed amount which traditionally has increased yearly to reflect inflation and, often, length of service. Base pay will also change, of course, upon promotion to a more responsible job. This embodies the values of predictability, security and permanency – none of which are characteristics consistent with the desire to change employee behaviours. From a managerial perspective, it is not necessarily the best form of reward strategy. The very permanency which employees value is expensive. Increasingly employers are asking themselves why they should build into their fixed salary costs a permanent salary bill which takes little account of changing external, organisational and individual circumstances. Pay strategies which rely exclusively on base pay enshrined in salary scales through which employees move annually until the top of the scale is reached, or promotion achieved, are typical in the public sector. Such strategies assume that length of service equates with experience and loyalty. Neither tends to be as prized by organisations now as in the past. Such is the pace of change that yesterday's experience may be an impediment to change. It is accepted that loyalty to one employer, typified by a career spent with that employer, is an increasingly outdated concept in an age where employees may have a number of different careers as well as employers. In addition, pay strategies which rely on promotions for employees to grow their salaries do not take into account the fact that organisations now have flatter structures, with the consequence that promotion is less available. The desire of employees only to move to jobs within their own organisation which result in a minor promotion, and therefore, regrading, is a major obstacle to developing employees into different roles where they learn new skills. This was precisely the problem which Lincoln experienced. It proved a major incentive for the company to reduce the amount of levels in its pay structure.

For some organisations base pay is of declining importance. This raises the question: 'How can the traditional reward objectives of attracting, retaining and motivating people be achieved while making the pay budget more cost-effective?' The answer for many organisations has been to make base pay reflect the market rate for the job and to supplement this with a variable pay element related to individual performance, team performance, organisational performance and individual competence acquisition – or a combination of these. One of the key decisions that needs to be taken into account is whether to pay the variable element as a lump sum bonus or to consolidate this into salary. The trend in the USA has been for variable pay to be one-off cash bonuses (Kanter, 1987). This is hardly surprising given the cost saving that the organisation enjoys. By not raising base pay, one-off cash bonuses do not affect future base pay increases or other associated payments such as overtime and, of course, pensions.

A shift from all base pay to a combination of base and variable pay does, of course, signal the organisation's desire to move from paying for the job to paying the person. Therefore, the reliance on traditional bureaucratic forms of job evaluation is less pronounced. However, job evaluation is still relevant. Base pay still needs to be set at a level consistent with the external labour market. Therefore, some method of determining the relative importance of jobs is needed. It is that definition of importance that is likely to be different in the organisation which places more significance in a combination of base and variable pay. Such a definition is likely to reflect the changed employee behaviours the organisation wishes to encourage in order to meet its changed organisational circumstances. What is clear, according to Schuster and Zingheim (1992), is that internal equity will no longer be the dominant consideration. The market value of jobs, and employees' skills and their impact on the organisation's strategy will take precedence over internal equity. Such a strategy, however, runs the risk of contravening the legislation on equal pay if, for example, women are systematically disadvantaged in that they have fewer opportunities to demonstrate good performance or achieve competence. This may be, for example, as a consequence of the greater likelihood of women working part-time.

Below is a brief consideration of some of the main structural and process issues in relation to two pay for performance initiatives: individual performance-related pay and competence-based pay (pay linked to organisational performance is considered in the section on employees sharing in the organisation's success). Both of these are exemplified in the Lincoln case study at the end of this chapter.

### Individual performance-related pay

Individual performance-related pay (PRP) is defined by ACAS as: 'a method of payment where an individual employee receives increases in pay based wholly or partly on the regular and systematic assessment of job performance' (ACAS, 1990: 2). It has been adopted with great enthusiasm in many areas of white-collar employment, for example local government and financial services.

PRP has been introduced in many organisations to change the culture to reflect the 'new' values which senior managers think are necessary. Lawler (1984: 128) argues that reward systems can 'cause the culture of an organisation to vary quite widely. For example they can influence the degree to which it is seen as a human-resource oriented culture, an entrepreneurial culture, an innovative culture, a competence-based culture, and a participative culture'. There is also a strong thread of felt-fairness about PRP. Most employees (Kessler, 1994) agree with the principle of PRP: that the able and industrious employee should be rewarded more generously for that ability and industry than the idle and incompetent.

However, it is the implementation of PRP that seems to cause problems of perceived unfairness. Lewis (1998), in a study of PRP for first-level managers in three financial services organisations found evidence of their managers imposing objectives upon them, with the result that the objective-setting process was 'something that was done to them rather than something in which they played an active part'

(Lewis, 1998: 70).The employees interviewed by Procter *et al.* (1993) in an electronics plant expressed concerns about favouritism, in particular, the arbitrary way in which managers applied measurement criteria and the ways in which grades were distributed. In two of the three organisations Lewis (1998) researched he noted little attention paid to the giving of performance feedback to employees. There were similar implementation problems in the pharmaceutical company studied by Randle (1997: 198) such that performance-related pay emerged as 'one of Pharmex's most consistently disliked management practices'.

An important part of the implementation of PRP is that managers are put in a position where they must differentiate between the level of reward of their team members. This decision process effectively creates increased dependency of the team member on the line manager, and less dependency on, for example, the trade union (Kessler, 1994). Consequently, some organisations have seized this opportunity to expect greater management accountability. ACAS (1990: 8) point out that the role of managers and supervisors is critical to the implementation of PRP. It is they who must define the required standards of performance and behaviour; explain these to their team members; take tough decisions about assessments; communicate these decisions to team members and defend their judgements if asked (Storey and Sisson, 1993). But often managers find this differentiation difficult, with the result that they produce statistical distributions that concentrate on the middle rank of performance, thus defeating the object of paying for differentiated performance. Kessler and Purcell (1992: 22) found evidence of the desire to 'make managers manage' in their research. They note, 'PRP is often seen as a means of forcing a manager into a direct one-to-one, usually face to face relationship with their employees'.

The outcome of these implementation weaknesses is that the value of paying for performance is not practised. What seems a good idea in principle becomes overtaken by perceived problems, with the result that employees lose faith in the concept. It seems that teachers have learned the lessons from other employment sectors in developing their opposition to PRP (*The Guardian*, 1999).

### Competence-related pay

Competence-related pay can be defined as 'a method of rewarding people wholly or partly by reference to the level of competence they demonstrate in carrying out their roles' (Armstrong and Murlis, 1998). It is predictable that interest in competence-related pay should grow in view of the enormous amount of attention given to the definition of competencies for purposes of selection, training and appraisal in recent years.

One of the frequent complaints of the first-line managers in a bank (Lewis, 1998) was that it was really only the 'hard' outputs (e.g. the number of mortgages sold) rather than the 'soft' processes (e.g. the way in which they led their branch team) that counted when performance measurement was carried out. Their managers were not too concerned with how the job was done, provided that results were achieved. Competence-related pay overcomes this alleged weakness of PRP by ensuring that, usually, both processes and outputs are taken into account when pay-related measurement is made.

Armstrong and Murlis's (1998) definition of competence-related pay captures the most important difference between competence-related pay and PRP. This is that PRP is essentially retrospective in that it measures performance over the past pay period (often one year). However, competence-related pay is more forward-looking. It identifies those competencies that are likely to be associated with effective job performance.

Flannery *et al.* (1996: 92) define competencies as 'sets of skills, knowledge, abilities, behavioural characteristics, and other attributes that, in the right combination and for the right set of circumstances, predict superior performance'. So the technical skill to do the job is clearly not enough. The successful job-holder must ally this skill (e.g. introducing clients to new products) with other attributes (e.g. the desire to enhance the performance of the branch or team). In other words, competence-related pay is highly contextual. It also has, potentially, strong links to organisational strategy. The question which may be asked at business strategy level is 'What competencies do we want our people to demonstrate in order that we may achieve our business goals?'

Managers concerned with 'hard' outputs would be comforted by the fact that many organisations introducing competence-related pay accompany competence-related ratings with performance output measurements, the market rate for the job, and the position of the individual on the pay scale in determining salary level. As can be seen in the following case study, this is the case at Lincoln.

With PRP, it was noted that managers can apply measurement criteria in an arbitrary way, which creates in employees problems of a lack of felt-fairness. This is no less true of competence-related pay. In fact, the more the approach moves from one where identifying discernible skills and outputs is possible, the more subjective the measurement process becomes. As yet, little empirical research has been done on the operation of competence-related pay, but it would be surprising were it to uncover anything other than the same sort of employee dissatisfactions as PRP. However, the measurement criteria themselves may be more acceptable to employees than in the case of PRP. This is often because there is some form of employee involvement in the development of the competence statements (Armstrong and Murlis, 1998), albeit that line managers are making the assessment of the extent to which they have been demonstrated. This is unlike PRP, where it is usually the manager who defines the performance objectives and assesses performance.

### The value of equity

It would be an exaggeration to say that the value of equity may be a major contributor to the promotion of changed employee behaviours. But if employees feel their pay to be inequitable then the changed employee behaviours managers hope for in their new reward strategy are unlikely to materialise. Employee acceptance is a key determinant of reward strategy success (Lawler, 1990) and perceived inequity by employees will lead to a lack of employee acceptance of the reward strategy.

There are two ways in which employees may feel their pay is inequitable. First, there is the issue of external equity and internal equity. External equity refers to the extent to which the employee feels his/her pay is fair in relation to those doing similar jobs in other organisations. Internal equity relates to the same feeling in comparison with those doing similar jobs in his/her own organisation. Armstrong (1993) points out that in many organisations there is a tension between the two. The desire to be competitive in the labour market for some jobs, thus ensuring external equity, may lead to feelings of lack of internal inequity among those employees whose external labour market appeal does not afford them similar power. What is implied here is the necessity for the employer to take a clear policy decision on the value it places in equity and the way in which this value is expressed.

The second way in which employees may feel their pay is inequitable is less about the amount of pay than the way in which it is determined. This raises issues concerning structure and process, which are considered below.

One of the most potent symbols of perceived inequity which has gained considerable publicity in recent years is that of directors' pay. The image of directors gaining huge pay increases at a time when their organisations have been declaring redundancies and trimming general pay costs is one that has created significant employee and trade union discontent. The facts appear to justify this discontent. Armstrong (1996) notes that in the period between 1985 and 1990, according to a survey by the UK National Institute of Economic and Social Research, directors' pay rose in real terms by 77 per cent while the equivalent figure for all employees was 17 per cent. Reports from the Cadbury and Greenbury committees of the mid-1990s, which were designed to secure greater openness and accountability, seem to have done little to improve the public perception of unfairness. Clearly, employee acceptance of reward strategy change is unlikely if the general impression is that 'fat cats' are getting an unfair share of organisational rewards.

But it is not just directors' pay that fed the impression of inequity. Inequality between the pay of men and women is such that, despite the three decades of equal pay legislation, the gross hourly earnings of women in 1998 were significantly lower than men's. Manual women earned 71.6 per cent of the equivalent gross hourly figure for men. For non-manual women the figure was 69 per cent (*Labour Market Trends*, 1998).

Less often discussed is the possibility of perceived inequality in the comparison between white- and blue-collar workers. This is a wider issue than simply pay. It relates to a range of terms and conditions of employment. Many organisations which have been at the forefront of change, in particular Japanese manufacturing companies, have featured initiatives designed to harmonise terms and conditions of employment between white- and blue-collar workers in an attempt to foster a greater feeling of 'community' in their workforce (Price and Price, 1994).

There may be a similar feeling of inequity among these employees who may be called 'solid citizens'. These are the employees who add a good deal to every organisation but who do not pursue promotion. The move to broad banding has the capacity to reduce some of these feelings of inequity. Broad banding is defined by Armstrong (1996: 224) as 'the compression of pay grades and salary ranges into a small number (typically four or five) of wide bands. Each of the bands will therefore span the pay opportunities previously covered by several separate pay ranges'. The advantages of broad banding noted by Armstrong (1996) suggest that this pay reform has, potentially, a powerful role to play in complementing, if not generating, organisational change. Among these are:

- facilitation of movement of employees across the organisation without the necessity for promotion to a higher grade to be obtained
- development of employees' skills and competencies by removing perceived barriers to movement
- the support of multiskilling and teamwork by removing barriers to lateral movement
- enabling line managers to accept greater responsibility to reward with salary increases those employees who demonstrate a greater 'contribution' (however defined) to the organisation.

Wider pay ranges give the 'solid citizens' the opportunity to 'grow' their salaries without hitting the barriers imposed by narrower bands which can only be surmounted by promotion. The role broad banding plays in changing employee behaviours is potentially very important. It complements the efforts which many organisations are currently making to achieve greater flexibility in the organisation of work. The Lincoln case study at the end of this chapter is an excellent example of an organisation introducing broad banding for this purpose.

### The value of employees sharing in the organisation's success

Organisations that wish to promote a high level of employee identification with the pursuit of success are likely to have an element of sharing in that success built into their reward strategy. The most popular form this has taken is profit-related pay, although other forms of profit-share schemes are explained below. These schemes may not play the major role in changing employee behaviours due to the remote connection between effort and reward. However, they are likely to form an increasingly significant portion of the employee's pay and have the potential to foster a greater bond between employers and employees.

#### *Profit-related pay*

Profit-related pay has grown considerably in recent years to the point where in 1994 1.8 million private sector employees were covered by such a scheme (IDS, 1994). Such schemes are most popular in the utilities sector (water, gas and electricity) and financial services where 81 per cent and 80 per cent of workplaces reported their existence in the 1998 Workplace Employee Relations survey (Cully *et al.*, 1999). Overall, the survey noted that 47 per cent of private sector workplaces had profit-related pay schemes.

The reasons for this are easy to guess since it has been possible for employees to have as much as £4,000 of salary per year free of income tax. This tax advantage was introduced by government to promote a stronger awareness of the commercial performance of the employer among employees and to encourage employees to greater effort. It is doubtful if it has achieved that effect since many organisations have seen it as little more than a tax-efficient way of structuring salary. However, the last Conservative budget in 1997 announced the gradual withdrawal of the tax advantage by the year 2000. This may see the growth of other forms of profit-sharing and share option schemes which have the capacity to enhance employee awareness of profit performance.

### Profit-sharing schemes

The concept of the profit-sharing scheme is quite simple: the company pays a bonus to eligible employees, based on company profits, which the employee must use to buy shares in the company. Unlike profit-related pay, this is not a part of the employee's salary – it is a discretionary bonus. However, like profit-related pay, it gives tax advantages to the employee because the share bonus is tax-free provided that the scheme is approved by the Inland Revenue. In order for the scheme to meet this approval the employer must meet a number of criteria including:

- the necessity to set up a company-wide scheme
- the payment of bonuses must be in free shares of the company, not in cash
- the necessity to set up a special trust with appointed trustees. (The trust purchases the shares for employees and sets these aside)
- the stipulation that no more than £3,000 p.a. per employee or, if it is a greater amount, 10 per cent of salary, up to a maximum of £8,000 in any tax year (at 1999) must be set aside as bonus.

The employee has no tax liability if the bonus shares are not sold for at least three years. To gain Inland Revenue approval, all employees who have been employed by the company for five years must be eligible, although in many cases companies allow employees to participate with much shorter service periods (e.g. six months at Severn Trent Water (IDS, 1998)). Payments are made from a profit-related pool. This pool may be determined by a published formula or be at the discretion of the directors at the time of the payout. For example, at Barclays Bank in 1997, 5 per cent of company profits made up the profit-share pool (IDS, 1998).

In his November 1999 pre-Budget report, the Chancellor announced that companies will be able to give their employees £3,000-worth of shares tax free with no capital gains to pay after 5 years. This can be restricted to a single department, division or subsidiary of the company. In addition, employees will be able to buy another £1,500-worth of shares out of their pre-tax pay. If they do so the company can give them another £3,000-worth of shares (*Daily Telegraph*, 1999).

Profit-sharing schemes are likely to become more widespread in future years. In 1995/6 around 740,000 UK employees were enjoying the benefits of profit-sharing schemes (IDS, 1998). The 1998 Workplace Employee Relations survey (Cully *et al.*, 1999) reported that 25 per cent of private sector workplaces had some sort of employee share ownership scheme. According to IDS (1998) the average value in shares allocated as bonus to each participant was £640.

### Savings-related share option schemes

Unlike the typical profit-sharing scheme, the savings-related share option scheme requires a contribution from the employee. In a savings-related share option scheme the employee saves for a specified period (three, five or seven years). The scheme specifies that employees can buy shares at the end of the savings period with the savings fund accumulated. The price of the shares will be the market price at the start of the savings contract or at an agreed discount, that discount rate being agreed at the start of the contract. The shares bought at the end of the savings contract attract tax relief.

With the three-year savings contract the employee saves a fixed amount monthly (it cannot exceed £250) and at the end of the term a cash bonus of 2.75 months' payments is added. At the end of a five-year contract a cash bonus of nine months' payments is added. At the end of the three or five year term the employee uses the amount saved and the bonus to buy shares in the company. For employees who have saved for five years there is the option of saving for seven years, in which case 18 months' payments are added as a cash bonus. However, this means that the employee can still only buy shares with the amount saved after five years.

The price at which employees have the opportunity to purchase shares must not be below 80 per cent of the market value at the start of the contract. This seemed to be the typical price determined by employers in an IDS study (IDS, 1998).

As with profit-sharing schemes, all employees who have been employed by the company for five years must be eligible to participate in savings-related share option schemes if the scheme is to gain Inland Revenue approval. However, one year appears to be a more usual minimum service period (IDS, 1998). In 1995/6, 610,000 employees were in 1,305 schemes.

### Company share option plans

Inland Revenue approval may also be gained for schemes that grant share options to employees. These have usually been aimed at directors and senior managers and have therefore become known as 'executive share options'. However, some companies, like Kingfisher, run all-employee share option schemes. The scheme allows employees to buy shares at a future date but at prices operating at the time the share option is granted. There is a £30,000 limit on the amount of shares that may be granted under this and other approved share option schemes. In addition, the Inland Revenue rules forbid the granting of shares at a discount.

At Kingfisher (IDS, 1998), all full-time and part-time employees employed on the date at which the company results are announced are included in the scheme and therefore have the option to buy. All eligible Kingfisher employees were granted 200 shares (companies may also base the grant allocation on a percentage of salary) at a price of £6.57 per share in April 1997. In order to gain tax relief on the shares Kingfisher employees must take up the option to purchase shares from their allocation of 200 between April 2000 and April 2007 (i.e. between three and ten years after the date of the grant). Kingfisher employees are able to buy and sell the shares and take any gain at no cost to themselves.

### Gainsharing

Gainsharing is more popular in the USA than in Britain. In a gainsharing scheme the relationship between employees' efforts and their eventual reward is more direct than with profit-related pay. Gainsharing plans are designed so that employees share the financial results of improvements in productivity, cost saving or quality. The resultant payment is paid from costs savings generated as a result of such improvements. Employees participating in the gainsharing plan are normally part of a discernible group who have had a direct effect upon the cost savings. The gainshare plan payment to them may be made in three ways: as a percentage of base pay; as a one-off cash bonus or as a payment per hour worked. Schuster and Zingheim (1992) make the point that the same payment would normally go to all members of the group. They are also careful to point out that the organisation must design safeguards to ensure that it derives financial value from the results generated from the project linked to gainsharing. This type of gainsharing differs from more traditional forms of gainsharing which have operated in manufacturing under the heading of Scanlon and Rucker plans. The principal difference is that the foundation of this new type of gainsharing is the future goals of the organisation whereas that of more traditional gainsharing plans is the historical performance standards of the participating employees. The key point here, of course, is that historical performance standards may be achieved or exceeded while the organisation's overall goals are not met.

### The value of combining financial and non-financial rewards

The extent to which an organisation combines financial and non-financial rewards in its reward strategy reflects a clear value position. Overreliance on pay as a motivator is likely to be accompanied by other human resource policies which assume a scientific management perspective (e.g. no involvement in management decisions, minimum employee control over the way in which jobs are performed). Recognition by the employer that non-financial rewards may play an important part in attracting, and more particularly retaining, employees suggests a view of humanity which recognises that individuals require more for their efforts than monetary reward.

Armstrong (1996) notes that there are five areas where employees' needs may be met by non-financial rewards: achievement, recognition, responsibility, influence and personal growth. Of these, it is likely that the first two, achievement and recognition, will apply to virtually all employees. Responsibility, influence and personal growth will apply to many more than may be realised. Everyone likes to feel that they have achieved something in their work – pride being derived from a job well done. In addition, most managers realise that a simple 'thank you' and a pat on the back for a job well done have enormous motivational power. It has to be recognised that not all employees seek greater responsibility in their jobs, or greater influence over decisions which directly or indirectly influence those jobs. This may be related to the individual's personal characteristics. But it may also be a consequence of a history of organisations not giving people the opportunity to exercise responsibility or influence. Semler's (1993) account of the management style in his Brazilian company is an excellent example of how employees accept responsibility when they are treated in such a way that they are obviously valued. The desire of many individuals to seek opportunities for personal growth through their work is very powerful. It may seem odd that this could be termed an employee reward rather than a vital prerequisite of organisational success. Yet many individuals rate the opportunity for personal growth more highly than financial reward.

Non-financial rewards may be particularly important as motivational tools for some employees. Noted below are some of the structures which may need to be in place in order for employee needs for achievement, recognition, responsibility, influence and personal growth to be realised. Meeting these needs increases the possibility of more positive employee attitudes and behaviours.

The first of these structures is probably the easiest to put in place. This is a communication strategy which broadcasts the successes of individuals and teams. Many organisations do this through their in-house magazines. This combined with special 'thank you' prizes (e.g. a weekend in Paris) often will have more motivational influence than direct financial rewards. Most of us like our colleagues to know when we are successful!

Performance appraisal systems also have a significant role to play in meeting employees' needs for recognition and a feeling of achievement. Goal-setting and giving feedback to employees about their performance in pursuit of those goals are key performance appraisal activities. A developmental perspective to performance appraisal rather than seeing it as a management control mechanism is likely to result in employees defining their own training and career development needs. However, this approach to performance appraisal does depend on line managers having the appropriate attitudes and skills to manage in such a way that the individual is given sufficient autonomy for personal growth to be developed. This implies a clear training need for managers to shed the 'technician' label they often possess and embrace new ways of managing which have leadership and facilitation as their guiding principles. These 'new ways of managing' are central to the concept of change, given the key role line managers play in managing the change process.

Employees' needs for responsibility, influence and personal growth may also be met through imaginative job design. Among the elements of job design which Armstrong (1993) advocates to enhance the interest and challenge of work are:

greater responsibility for employees in deciding how their work is done; reducing task specialisation; allowing employees greater freedom in defining their performance goals and standards of performance and introducing new and more challenging tasks. In addition, more opportunities for employee involvement may also foster responsibility, influence and personal growth among employees. They may be achieved through such activities as quality circles and problem-solving groups.

## Conclusions

'New pay' is the philosophy which underpins this chapter. It is a useful way of thinking about reward management because it has the potential to complement, if not generate, organisational change.

Organisational change begins with a clarification of what it is the organisation wishes to change and why. A starting point is to clarify what it is that the organisation wishes employees to do which may be different from what they are currently doing. Such changed employee behaviours should be consistent with what the organisation is seeking to achieve through its business strategy. The aim of the reward strategy is to contribute to the generation of these changed employee behaviours.

If the reward strategy is to contribute to changing employee behaviours it must contain three key components: the values which underpin the strategy; the structures which are in place to promote these values and the processes involved in the design and implementation of the strategy.

The four values which underpin the reward management strategy are: the degree to which the organisation believes in: paying for performance; equity; employees sharing in the organisation's success and combining financial and non-financial rewards.

Important structures to promote the reward values are: making a clear division between base pay and variable pay; individual performance-related pay; team-based pay; broad banding; profit-related pay; gainsharing; performance appraisal and job design. It is important that the way in which these structures are communicated and implemented is consistent with the values which the organisation is seeking to pursue.

Many of the concepts in this chapter are being introduced in a piecemeal fashion by UK organisations. But Lincoln Insurance is introducing them in an integrated way. An examination of that organisation's reward strategy is conducted below.

---

**Case study 4.1**

# Introducing a new pay structure at Lincoln

Philip Lewis

---

## Background to Lincoln

In the UK, Lincoln is a leading provider of life assurance, pensions and investment plans. The company has grown quickly, both through acquisition and putting customers first. At the time of writing Lincoln has assets of over £4.9 billion and there are more than one million client policies in existence. The UK group is owned by Lincoln National Corporation, whose business was founded in the USA in 1905. The company was named after the former American President, Abraham Lincoln. It manages total assets of nearly $134 billion and at March 1999 had $6 billion in annual revenues. In the UK Lincoln sells its range of financial services through self-employed financial advisers. It has approximately 1,500 UK employees, based primarily on two operational sites in Uxbridge and Gloucester and 60 branch offices.

The company operates a divisional structure, the main divisions being finance, actuarial, legal, operations (e.g. customer services, IT), sales, investment and HR. Some of these divisions, e.g. HR and operations, operate on both sites.

In common with most financial services organisations, Lincoln is going through a period of significant change. This is due to its growth and the necessity to seek competitive advantage in an increasingly aggressive product market. Lincoln's principal goal is to grow sales faster than the industry average. To achieve this it aims to be more customer-focused, to develop products in line with customer requirements and to embrace new technology.

The way in which HR in general, and pay in particular, can contribute to achieving Lincoln's aims is through generating greater employee flexibility. As the introductory details for managers on the new pay structure note:

> . . . we need to create an environment which encourages the development and utilisation of each employee's skills so they can achieve results for us by becoming multi-skilled and flexible.

Nowhere illustrates this need for flexibility and multiskilling better than the image and workflow system which has been introduced in Customer Services. In essence, this means that paper is only evident at two stages in the work process: at the beginning and the end. Initially, the client's paper post is scanned on to the computer system, indexed with the policy number and a process number and delivered into an electronic 'pot' of work. Work is then taken electronically from the 'pot', sent to employees' screens and processed. At the end of the process relevant completed documents are printed in paper form and mailed to the client. This system means that employees need to possess both a wide range of skills and knowledge of technical processes because managers require them to perform a variety of functions on the client's policy work. For example, staff who have only worked on applications enquiries are required in the new system to deal with renewals or payments. In addition, staff also need to be accomplished in their operation and knowledge of the software necessary to perform the various processes.

The major benefits of the image and workflow system are that instant data retrieval will be possible on any post received and replies sent in the past six months, meaning that client enquiries can be handled more quickly and efficiently. The system also means that work can be balanced between the two operational sites more effectively. Employees on both sites have been trained to operate the system, thus enabling work to be allocated to the site where resources are best able to deal with the work.

### The 'old' pay structure

The pre-1998 pay structure was a hierarchical, incremental ladder which had 16 grades. Pay progression for individuals was through moving up to the next rung on the ladder, provided that there was a job available. The consequence was that staff became, as the compensation and benefits manager put it, 'grade-fixated'. This was because jumping to the next grade not only generated a salary increase but sent a powerful message to the Lincoln world that 'here was someone on the way up'. Managers too saw upgrading as the only way of achieving salary increases for their staff outside the annual review. This was particularly important in times of low inflation and low general pay awards.

Often the means by which managers secured such upgradings was by claiming that the job had grown and this warranted an increase. Agreeing to such requests created the problem of 'leap frogging' where an upgrading in one area created pressure elsewhere for another to maintain a perceived differential status. Over time this had the effect of undermining the integrity of the grade structure. This led to senior managers asking 'Why should we feel we have to promote someone every time we want to reward them?'

The old system also paid employees more on the basis of their length of service and, therefore, experience in the company. It was clear that this was no longer a sustainable basis for the pay structure, given the amount of change that was taking place. In fact, 'unlearning' traditional ways of doing jobs was becoming even more important than adhering to old methods.

### The new pay structure

The old pay structure was characterised by paying for jobs rather than paying the person and it was felt that it encouraged a value of 'job ownership'. Lincoln wished to change the pay structure so that employees defined themselves in terms of the contribution they could individually make to achieving the company's business aims. As the guidance notes for managers put it:

> We want to reward people for the knowledge and skills they have and how they apply them, not simply for the job they do. Of course, the make up of duties, tasks and responsibilities remains important but we want to move towards rewarding people for the results they achieve. Carrying out a series of rigidly defined jobs is not, we believe, the best way for people to develop and grow.

Lincoln's principal aim is to create a pay structure that complements business needs more effectively. In people terms these business needs are for a more flexible organisation, flexible work patterns with expanded job roles requiring broader skills and competencies and greater responsiveness to client demands. In addition, managers are to be given greater scope to reward good performance by their employees and respond more swiftly to changes in individual employee contribution and responsibility.

The specific objectives of the new pay structure are to:

- create a clearer, flatter structure with fewer grades which would be simpler to manage
- put greater emphasis on the individual, not the job
- increase the focus on individual growth and lateral career development
- motivate individuals to acquire new skills and responsibilities to enhance their career progression
- empower managers to make decisions about pay to reward good performance and increased responsibilities
- streamline the job evaluation process, making it more responsive to business needs.

### Decreasing the amount of grades

The new grade structure reflects the process of broad banding. It consists of eight broad-banded levels rather than sixteen. Each of the eight levels contains roles with common responsibilities and a comparable impact upon organisational success. Thus, the grade levels reflect what the company calls 'value added tiers'. Roles add value to the organisation's success to an increasing degree as the levels ascend.

For each level there is a general statement of the responsibilities entailed and skills required. The responsibilities are illustrated in Table 4.1. opposite. Role titles are harmonised within each division to ensure consistency with the role holder's role and responsibilities and with general industry practice.

Each level has defined key skills and behaviours (KSBs). These are deemed necessary requirements for effective completion of the role. These KSBs effectively change the emphasis from the content of the role to the way in which the role is performed. More detail on the role of these KSBs is given opposite.

### Determining the pay level of the individual employee

One of the key principles of the new pay structure is the flexibility it affords managers to make their own decisions about the pay of individual employees for

**Table 4.1. Definition of responsibilities for each of the grades in the new pay structure at Lincoln**

| Level A | Former grades 1–4 | Responsibility for processing a variety of high-volume, well-defined activities in a variety of contexts under direct supervision. |
|---|---|---|
| **Level B** | Former grades 5–6 | Responsibility for processing a variety of high-volume, well-defined and some less well-defined activities in a variety of contexts. Requires close supervision for some of the time. |
| **Level C** | Former grades 7–8 | Responsibility for processing a variety of high-volume, non-routine activities in a variety of contexts. Requires some supervision as well as being capable of some independence. May have responsibility for leading a small team. |
| **Level D** | Former grades 9–10 | Responsibility for a variety of complex non-routine activities. Capable of a large degree of independence. Performs some specialist or professional activities and/or has responsibility for the direction and guidance of a team. |
| **Level E** | Former grade 11 | Involves some accountability and autonomy. Performs specialist or professional activities and/or has responsibility for the direction and guidance of a team. |
| **Level M1** | Former grades 12–13 | Involves significant accountability and autonomy. Competence in a broad range of complex specialist or professional activities and/or has responsibility for the direction and guidance of others. |
| **Level M2** | Former grades 14–15 | Involves comprehensive accountability and autonomy. Competence in an extensive range of complex specialist or professional activities, including accountability for analysis and diagnosis, design, planning, execution and evaluation. Has responsibility for the direction and guidance of others and for substantial resources. |
| **Level M3** | Former grade 16 | Involves the allocation of a significant range of fundamental principles and complex techniques across a wide and often unpredictable variety of contexts. Complete personal autonomy and responsibility for the work of others and for the allocation of substantial resources. |

*Source*: Lincoln internal document.

whom they have responsibility. Consequently, there are no rigid guidelines which managers must follow. An example of this is the lack of mid-points in the new salary ranges, which means that managers and employees do not have an immediate reference point that indicates the 'typical' salary of a 'typical' employee. However, within each level there is a benchmark role. There is a target salary rate set for each benchmark role. The benchmark role is intended to be useful in providing guidance to managers on locating the position of job roles in the new structure and determining individual salaries.

Target rates are based on an assessment of four considerations:

- the local labour and, where appropriate, national market rate for comparable roles
- the average basic salary for staff undertaking the same or a similar role within the same department or division

- the average basic salary for staff undertaking the same or a similar role within Lincoln
- budgetary considerations.

Target rates are set by HR. They are deliberately not called market rates because this does not capture the full range of criteria used. It also prevents employees asserting that the company is paying less than market rate by producing job advertisements for similar roles in other companies which are, in all probability, selectively chosen. Target rates are based, in part, upon data from specialist pay consultancies such as Hay, Watson Wyatt and Remuneration Economics. In addition, the compensation and benefits manager attends a number of HR forums on a regional and national basis where pay is the main agenda item.

Further assistance is given to managers in that a pay zone is defined for each benchmark role. This pay zone is based on the target rate for a fully competent performer. The pay zone establishes a *minimum* recommended salary for a given role which is below the target rate. The pay zone figure is regularly reviewed by HR in order that it may remain competitive. Lincoln's policy is to pay a fully competent employee within the pay zone for any role. The fact that there is a minimum recommended salary for a given role which is below the target rate means that there is scope for the employee to grow his or her salary dependent on individual circumstances. The level of this pay zone will be influenced by the amount of time the employee needs to achieve target rate related to a fully competent employee. The more technical the role content, the longer the period necessary to become fully competent. The aim is to enable employees to achieve target rate as soon as full competence is demonstrated. This contrasts sharply with the old pay structure where salary was grown through length of service. It is important to note in this respect that there are no maxima to the pay zones. Therefore individuals can progress their salaries in a way that was not possible under the old structure. In that case employees had to secure promotion to progress their salaries beyond the grade maximum. The pay zone is useful for two additional reasons. First, it provides managers with a useful reference point to help guide pay decisions. Second, it serves as a valuable means of assuring internal equity.

Salaries at Lincoln are reviewed on February 1 each year. It is more likely that employees progress their salaries through horizontal moves across their existing grade level than by being promoted to a new level. Examples of the ways in which an individual employee's salary may be enhanced are:

- permanent additional responsibilities
- sustained high-quality performance
- development of competencies and/or the acquisition of experience leading to more effective role performance or the ability to assume greater responsibilities
- acquisition of full or part professional qualification.

The extent to which each of these is applicable is dependent upon the individual employee and the role that employee is performing.

In the event of the first of these, permanent additional responsibilities, it is necessary for the line manager to make a case for the employee. This case is made to the job evaluation committee, which consists of two representatives from HR (the compensation and benefits manager and the HR director) and four managers from different parts of the business. It is important to note here that the claim must be made on the basis of permanent role responsibility growth rather than because the line manager wishes to secure an increase for the employee. The intention of the new pay structure is to give line managers sufficient flexibility to increase the salary of individuals without the necessity to 'bid up' the importance of the role. The key question for the job evaluation committee to ask is: 'Has the role changed significantly such that it warrants an upgrading?' The old argument of needing to pay more to retain an employee is no longer applicable given the breadth of the pay bands.

Sustained high-quality performance relates to the performance of the role holder against predetermined objectives. Each individual employee has role objectives set between that employee and the line manager. The employee is measured against these objectives. There are three reviews per year. But objectives need not necessarily change three times in the year. This depends on the level of the role. Level A and level B role objectives may change more frequently than the more all-embracing objectives of higher-level roles.

The third way in which an individual employee may enhance salary is the development of competencies and/or the acquisition of experience leading to more effective role performance or the ability to assume greater responsibility. Lincoln put a great deal of work into the development of these competence statements. This involved pilot groups involving over 100 managers and employees, and structured questionnaires and interviews with members of the workforce. As noted above, the development of these competencies is seen as the key to creating the multiskilled, flexible workforce Lincoln need.

As noted above, the competence statements are based on the principle of key skills and behaviours (KSBs). There are four areas in the company where all employees need to excel. These are grouped under four general headings:

■ developing the business (the KSBs necessary to ensure the successful planning and co-ordination of work)
■ developing the role (the KSBs necessary to ensure that tasks are completed in the most efficient and effective way)
■ developing relationships (the KSBs necessary to work effectively with colleagues, customers and other stakeholders)
■ developing self (the KSBs necessary to develop continually both professionally and personally).

Each employee has an information pack which describes all the competence statements related to his or her level. Table 4.2 is an example from level B (roles with responsibility for processing a variety of high-volume, well-defined and some less well-defined activities in a variety of contexts and which requires close supervision for some of the time). It relates to the second KSB area of 'developing the job'.

**Table 4.2 Competence statements relating to the KSB area 'developing the job'**

| Key behaviours | Examples of how my customers will know I am achieving this are when I . . . | Key skills |
|---|---|---|
| Ensuring communication is clear and simple | Speak and write clearly<br>Avoid or explain jargon<br>Adhere to company written and telephone standards | Telephone techniques<br>Written communications |
| Resolving problems and passing on information | Reach solutions that take account of others' needs<br>Refer queries or complaints above my authority level | Customer care |
| Supporting colleagues to achieve objectives | Help colleagues to meet deadlines<br>Achieve my personal and departmental goals<br>Highlight tasks not allocated | Problem solving |
| Paying attention to detail | Adhere to company standards<br>Plan time to check my work<br>Keep mistakes to a minimum | Adaptability |
| Approaching all tasks conscientiously and with a sense of urgency | Undertake all tasks with enthusiasm<br>Accept responsibility for non-routine tasks<br>Accept responsibility for completing tasks<br>Undertake all work professionally and with equal effort<br>Don't avoid doing the tasks I dislike | Accuracy<br>Planning |
| Sharing and requesting information | Seek and distribute information as appropriate<br>Update correspondence and files | Handling information |

*Source*: Lincoln internal document

Underpinning the move to competence development is the principle that employees should take charge of their own development. This is important if they are to progress their salaries and their careers. Lincoln has set up a learning centre with a full set of learning resources (e.g. self-learning packs in technical and management development skills) in order to assist employees.

These competence statements form the basis of the performance reviews. They cover all Lincoln's employees from levels A–M3. Employees are defined as 'fully competent' when they use their knowledge and skills effectively and possess the personal attributes required to achieve the results managers expect from them. It is possible for individuals to progress beyond the salary which relates to 'fully competent'. This would be the consequence of the acquisition and application of additional competencies as the individual's career develops.

In the view of the compensation and benefits manager, success of the change in the pay structure depends on two principal factors. First is the willingness and ability of managers to recognise the extent to which employees are displaying the competencies in their work. In addition, managers need to become skilled at working with the employee to ensure that competencies which have not been achieved are developed. The second factor is the readiness with which employees grasp the importance of competencies, both to Lincoln's success and to the development of their own careers both with Lincoln and, in the longer term, other employers.

The fourth way in which an individual employee can progress salary is through the acquisition of full or part professional qualifications. This may be, for example, in accountancy, actuarial, IT or taxation. The company pays the relevant fees and gives necessary time-off for study.

### Maintaining the pay structure

Job evaluation still has a role to play at Lincoln, despite the assertion by the compensation and benefits manager that the technique is insufficiently sensitive to market pressures and places undue emphasis upon measuring the job rather than the person. Job evaluation remains useful in ensuring internal equity by measuring the relative worth of jobs through defining the boundaries of the eight levels. In addition, it is useful in deciding whether roles should be allocated to new levels, although the role of job evaluation in deciding on grading appeals has diminished, as is explained later. The compensation and benefits manager is also mindful of the role job evaluation plays in the avoidance of claims under the 1970 Equal Pay Act. At Lincoln the scheme is sufficiently analytical to merit the basis of a defence against claims brought under the legislation. This may be where a woman (for example) claims that her work is equivalent to a man's if her job and his have been given equal value in a job evaluation study undertaken to evaluate the jobs done by the organisation's employees.

The job evaluation committee meets monthly. Its role is to decide on the appropriate level for new jobs and jobs that may need upgrading. For upgradings, managers make a claim to the committee based upon significant permanent change to the responsibilities of the job. In the event of a job not reflecting significant permanent change to merit an upgrading, the flexibility given to managers under the new structure means that managers may award an increase in pay.

### Communication of the new pay structure

The initial stage in the communication process took place during April 1998. This involved a series of two-day workshops for managers, which focused on the new pay structure in general and the KSBs in particular. It was then for managers, with the aid of a briefing pack, to brief their staff. All staff attended KSB briefings run by the HR team. This included an explanation of KSBs, the rationale for their introduction, a video and role plays of a performance review and an introduction to broad banding.

All employees received a letter informing them of their level and salary range together with their new role title as from July 1, 1998.

## Progress so far

As with any major change, some employees greeted the new pay structure with caution. They had become familiar with the old structure and understood the principle of being rewarded for length of service and promotions. Reducing the number of grades from sixteen to eight meant that promotions were no longer the frequent occurrence that they had been. Employees voiced the fear that they had lost their familiar 'signposts' – the steps on the promotional ladder. With that had gone the opportunity to gain public esteem through highly visible promotions. Some employees were more positive about the new structure. Those in more prescribed and constrained roles – in particular, those at level A – had traditionally seen little prospect of promotion in the old structure. However, the new structure meant that they could grow their salary through acquiring new competencies. As the new pay structure complemented the introduction of the new image and workflow system, it meant that the development of new individual competencies was not only a realisable ambition, but also an organisational necessity.

Similarly, some managers have adopted a very positive attitude to the new pay structure while some have been more circumspect. This is best illustrated in the way in which managers have used their allocated pay 'pot'. Some have, as the compensation and benefits manager said, 'bitten the bullet' and given a wide range of awards, including zero increase. Other managers have given virtually all their employees the average increase, which in February 1999 was 3.6 per cent. Employees given a zero increase were typically those being paid in excess of the maximum salary for their level or those who were not effective performers. This suggests that they may receive zero increases in the foreseeable future unless performance or competence acquisition merits otherwise. High performers have received increases paid for by the zero increases applicable to less effective performers.

HR managers have welcomed the fact that the job evaluation committee has seen a marked drop in the number of submissions from line managers for job upgradings. Prior to the introduction of the new structure, managers would go to the committee with outdated job descriptions and incomplete data on the revised content of the job. The real reason for the upgrading appeal was often that the manager would fear losing the employee if a salary increase was not forthcoming, and an upgrading was the way to secure an increase. The compensation and benefits manager gave a typical example:

> A manager came to me and said that he wanted to promote one of his old level 8 (new level C) employees to a level D role because he was afraid of losing him. It was clear that the person warranted an increase but the role did not. I encouraged him to use the flexibility of the new structure to award a salary increase based on contribution, which the manager willingly accepted.

It is too early to judge the overall effectiveness of the new pay structure at Lincoln. However, early evidence suggests that managers are using the greater flexibility offered them because they are awarding increases outside the annual review cycle. This is the result of giving managers an annual pay budget which they have the power to spend as they think fit, although the compensation and benefits manager sees all managers' increase decisions and has the authority to recommend rejection of some of these. This has appeased some employee grumbles because they see that it is now possible to earn increases other than as a consequence of the annual review or promotion.

*Savings-related share option scheme*

The aim of the Lincoln savings-related share option scheme is to encourage a sense of employee ownership. According to the published set of shared values this means that:

> employees should feel a strong sense of ownership of their work and be proud of, and committed to, the company. One tangible way to make that commitment is to have a financial stake in it. Lincoln UK encourages its staff to own shares in the parent company, LNC, so that they can gain from the growth and prosperity of the group.

In addition, the scheme provides enhanced benefits for employees, thus making the benefits package more competitive.

Employees may save £10–£250 monthly: the average contribution is £90 per month. The scheme is administered by Abbey National, who invest the employee's savings in a fund which, at the end of three years, can be used to buy shares at the price operative at the start of the savings contract. Abbey National add to this fund a bonus of 2.75 times the monthly savings amount (e.g. £275 for the employee saving £100 per month.)

Approximately 40 per cent of Lincoln UK employees have joined the scheme, distributed evenly across the levels.

*Note*: Phil Lewis would like to thank Steve Glover, Compensation and Benefits Manager at Lincoln, for his valuable help in preparing this case study.

## Questions

1. What do you think are the potential strengths and weaknesses of Lincoln's new pay structure?

2. The case explains that target rates are based on an assessment of four considerations: the local labour and national market rate for comparable roles; the average basic salary for staff undertaking the same or a similar role within the same department or division; the average basic salary for staff undertaking the same or a similar role within Lincoln and budgetary considerations. What tensions do you think these may produce and how may these tensions be resolved?

3. One consequence of Lincoln's new pay structure is that employees are less likely to be promoted. What problems may that create and how may the impact of these problems be lessened?

4. The measurement of competencies may cause particular problems for line managers. What techniques may be used by managers in establishing the extent to which employees are displaying competencies in their work?

5. If you had to develop a training programme for Lincoln line managers in order to ensure they implemented the new pay structure effectively what would be the programme's objectives and content?

## References to Chapter 4

ACAS (1990) *Appraisal-related Pay*, London: ACAS.

Armstrong, M. (1993) *Managing Reward Systems*, Buckingham: Open University Press.

Armstrong, M. (1996) *Employee Reward*, London: Institute of Personnel and Development.

Armstrong, M. and Murlis, H. (1998) *Reward Management: A Handbook of Remuneration Strategy and Practice,* 4th edition, London: Kogan Page.

Beaumont, P.B. (1993) *Human Resource Management : Key Concepts and Skills*, London: Sage.

Beer, M., Spector, B., Lawrence, P.R., Mills, Q.N., and Walton, R.E. (1984) *Managing Human Assets*, New York: Free Press.

Cully, M., Woodland, S., O'Reilly, A. and Dix, G. (1999) *Britain at Work*, London: Routledge.

*Daily Telegraph* (1999) 'Green budget maps out the way ahead', 15 November.

Flannery, T., Hofrichter, D. and Platten, P. (1996) *People, Performance and Pay*, New York: Free Press.

Guest, D. (1987) 'Human resource management and industrial relations', *Journal of Management Studies*, 24(5): 503–21.

Heery, E. (1996) 'Risk, representation and the new pay', *Personnel Review*, 25(6): 54–65.

Herzberg, F. (1968) *Work and the Nature of Man*, London: Staples Press.

Income Data Services (1992) *Skill-based Pay*, Study No. 500, February.

Income Data Services (1994) *Profit-related Pay*, Study No. 564, October.

Income Data Services (1998) *Profit-sharing and Share Options*, Study No. 641, January.

Kanter, R.M. (1987) 'The attack on pay', *Harvard Business Review*, March–April: 60–67.

Keenoy, T. (1990) 'Human Resource Management: rhetoric, reality and contradiction', *International Journal of Human Resource Management*, 1(3): 363–84.

Kessler, I. (1994) 'Performance pay', in Sisson, K. (ed) *Personnel Management*, Oxford: Blackwell.

Kessler, I. and Purcell, J. (1992) 'Performance-related pay: objectives and application', *Human Resource Management Journal*, 2(3): 16–33.

*Labour Market Trends* (1998), 'Patterns of pay: results of the New Earnings Survey 1998', December: 623–34.

Lawler, E.E. (1984) 'The strategic design of reward systems', in Fombrun, C., Tichy, N.M. and Devanna, M.A., *Strategic Human Resource Management*, New York: John Wiley.

Lawler, E.E. (1990) *Strategic Pay: Aligning Organisational Strategies and Pay Systems*, San Francisco: Jossey Bass.

Lawler, E. (1995) 'The new pay: a strategic approach', *Compensation and Benefits Review*, July–August: 14–22.

Lewis, P. (1998) Managing performance-related pay based on evidence from the financial services sector', *Human Resource Management Journal*, 8(2): 66–77.

Livy, B. (1988) *Corporate Personnel Management*, London: Pitman.

Mabey, C. , Salaman, M. and Storey, J. (1998) *Human Resource Management: A Strategic Introduction*, 2nd edition, Oxford, Blackwell.

Maslow, A. (1943) 'A theory of human motivation', *Psychological Review*, 50: 370–96.

Mintzberg, H. and Waters, J. (1989) 'Of strategies deliberate and emergent', in Asch, D. and Bowman, C., *Readings in Strategic Management*, Basingstoke: Macmillan.

Monks, J. (1998) 'Trade unions, enterprise and the future', in Sparrow, P. and Marchington, M., *Human Resource Management: the New Agenda*, London: Financial Times Pitman Publishing.

Pfeffer, J. (1998) 'Six dangerous myths about pay', *Harvard Business Review*, May–June: 109–119.

Price, L. and Price, R. (1994) 'Change and continuity in the status divide', in Sisson, K. (ed) *Personnel Management*, Oxford: Blackwell.

Procter, S., McArdle, L., Rowlinson, M., Forrester, P. and Hassard, J. (1993) 'Performance-related pay in operation: a case study from the electronics industry', *Human Resource Management Journal*, 3(4): 60–74.

Randle, K. (1997) 'Rewarding failure: operating a performance-related pay system in pharmaceutical research', *Personnel Review*, 26(3): 187–200.

Schuster, J. and Zingheim, P. (1992) *The New Pay: Linking Employee and Organisational Performance*, New York: Lexington.

Semler, R. (1993) *Maverick! The Success Story Behind the World's Most Unusual Workplace*, London: Arrow Business Books.

Smith, I. (1983) *The Management of Remuneration: Paying for Effectiveness*, London: Institute of Personnel Management.

Smith, I. (1993) 'Reward management: a retrospective assessment', *Employee Relations*, 15(3): 45–59.

Storey, J. and Sisson, K. (1993) *Managing Human Resources and Industrial Relations*, Buckingham: The Open University Press.

Taylor, F.W. (1911) *Principles of Scientific Management*, New York: Harper and Row.

*The Guardian* (1999) 'A stick in carrot's clothing', 9 April.

Whittington, R. (1993) *What is Strategy and Does it Matter?*, London: Routledge.

Wood, S. (1996), 'High commitment management and payment systems', *Journal of Management Studies*, 33(1): 53–77.

# Chapter 8

# Regulating the employment relationship through employee participation and involvement

At the end of this chapter you should be able to:

■ define and differentiate terms used in relation to employee participation and employee involvement;

■ recognise philosophical differences between employee participation and employee involvement, and analyse their differing aims;

■ examine forms of employee participation and employee involvement, and evaluate differing strategies underpinning the use of methods such as employee communication and joint consultation;

■ evaluate attitudes towards the use of employee participation and employee involvement;

■ analyse the role of European legislation for the future of employee participation and employee involvement.

## 8.1 Introduction

Concepts related to employee participation and employee involvement have a long history. Sometimes these concepts have been used in an undifferentiated way, which generates a degree of complexity and even confusion. Our aim in this chapter is to analyse the relationship between employee participation and employee involvement, in order to be able to differentiate between their aims and intended outcomes. Section 8.2 commences this discussion.

Section 8.3 focuses on the nature of employee participation and its occurrence in practice. Section 8.4 focuses on the nature of employee involvement and its use in organisations.

Differentiating between employee participation and employee involvement is made more difficult by the fact that some of the methods used to achieve either approach overlap in relation to their terminology. It is therefore necessary to differentiate between forms of information provision, communication and consultation to be able to understand how these techniques may be used to support either approach (Section 8.5). Section 8.6 analyses developments emanating from the European Union for the future of employee participation and employee involvement. After studying this chapter, we hope that you will be able to relate the aims and practices associated with employee participation and with employee involvement to other aspects of the management of the employment relationship. A case study exploring these approaches within an organisation is included at the end of the chapter.

| 8.2 | Understanding the terminology of and philosophical differences between employee participation and employee involvement and their differing aims |
|---|---|

Over several decades a number of terms or concepts have emerged that categorise approaches to the participation of employees in relation to the making and implementation of organisational decisions that affect them. These terms include *employee* or *worker participation* and *employee involvement*. An agreed set of definitions does not exist through which we may understand and differentiate these terms. In some cases, these terms are used as synonyms. For example, Marchington *et al.* (1992: 7) reported that 'the [British] Employment Department ... consider[ed] the terms "employee participation" and "employee involvement" to be synonymous.' This is partly understandable in terms of the way in which participation and involvement may be used in relation to one another. For example, to participate voluntarily is likely to lead to a feeling of involvement, and a sense of involvement is likely to lead to some level of participation.

However, a significant conceptual simplification is created if we think of employee participation and employee involvement as synonymous concepts, or if we simply see one as an input and the other as an outcome. The range of definitions that have been advanced through the course of time suggests that participation and involvement should not be treated as a single concept (Wall and Lischeron, 1977). Instead, employee participation and employee involvement strategies will be designed to pursue different aims and outcomes. This was recognised by Brannen (1983: 13), who understood that if these concepts are merged, this would imply that: 'individuals or groups may influence, control, be involved in, exercise power within, or be able to intervene in decision-making within organisations.' Processes or outcomes such as *influence, control, involvement,* the *exercise of power* and *interventions in decision-making* imply many different types of practice and intention. Even where an umbrella term has been used to consider different forms of participation, such as by Eldridge *et al.* (1991) who asked, 'Whatever happened to industrial democracy?', significant distinctions are evident in the resulting analysis related to the exercise of power and control and the nature of employee influence.

Consideration of some definitions for employee participation and employee involvement respectively allow us to start to recognise important differences that exist between these concepts in relation to the exercise of power, the locus of control, the nature of employee influence, and the driving force behind each approach in practice. These are set out in Box 8.1.

These definitions indicate a contrast between employee participation and employee involvement. This contrast is evident in relation to a number of dimen-

> **Box 8.1** Definitions of employee participation and employee involvement
>
> The Royal Commission on Trade Unions and Employers' Associations (Donovan, 1968: 257) included a brief chapter on 'Workers' participation in management', and referred to this as 'participation by workers and their representatives, over and above issues dealt with in collective bargaining, in decisions concerning the running of the undertaking'.
>
> Brannen (1983: 16) said that 'workers' participation is about the distribution and exercise of power, in all its manifestations, between the owners and managers of organisations and those employed by them. It refers to the direct involvement of individuals in decisions relating to their immediate work organisation and to indirect involvement in decision-making, through representatives, in the wider socio-technical and political structures of the firm.'
>
> Hyman and Mason (1995: 21) used participation to 'refer to State initiatives which promote the collective rights of employees to be represented in organisational decision-making, or to the consequence of the efforts of employees themselves to establish collective representation in corporate decisions, possibly in the face of employer resistance.'
>
> In contrast, the CBI defined employee involvement in 1988 (cited in Kessler and Bayliss, 1998: 125) as 'a range of processes designed to engage the support, understanding and optimum contribution of all employees in an organisation and their commitment to its objectives'.
>
> In 1991, the CBI and the then Department of Employment launched an initiative called 'Managing for Success – Improving business performance through employee involvement'. This described the purpose of employee involvement as being to 'promote business success through a combination of practices and systems designed to secure the maximum awareness and commitment of all employees in an enterprise to its objectives' (CBI/EDG, 1991).
>
> The Chartered Institute of Personnel and Development and the Industrial Participation Association developed an Employee Involvement Code, dating back to 1982, one of whose aims was to 'generate commitment of all employees to the success of the organisation' (IPM/IPA, 1982).

sions. These relate to the promotion of participation or involvement, its intended purpose, the exercise of power, locus of control, and the nature of employee influence. Further dimensions related to the practice of employee participation and employee involvement have been identified that help to differentiate between these approaches. These relate to the scope, level and form of employee participation or involvement (e.g. Marchington *et al.*, 1992). We shall now explore each of these sets of dimensions to differentiate between these approaches, first in relation to employee participation and then in relation to employee involvement.

## 8.3 Employee participation

### Promotion of participation

Employee participation has been promoted in three principal ways. Participation has been promoted by the State; at a supra-governmental level by the European Union (EU); and more generally through the activity of trade unions and workforce agitation. We shall consider the promotion of employee participation by the EU in a later section in this chapter, when we look at the establishment of European Works

Councils and the requirement for structures to be set up within organisations for the purpose of informing and consulting employees within Member States. The discussion that follows considers the attitude of the British State to employee participation over recent decades and its status in UK employing organisations as a result, as well as its attempted promotion more generally through activities by trade unions and groups of employees.

This discussion initially focuses on events in the 1970s, as this was a 'high-water mark' for employee participation in the context of the UK. Following the return of a Labour government in 1974, a Committee of Inquiry chaired by Lord Bullock was established in 1975 to consider how 'a radical extension of industrial democracy in the control of companies by means of representation on boards of directors' could be achieved (Bullock, 1977: v). This was to be designed to incorporate trade union representation as an essential element of this form of employee participation.

Before this period in the UK, the idea of this type of employee participation had not received such State support. The reference in Box 8.1 to the Royal Commission on Trade Unions and Employers' Associations between 1965 and 1968, chaired by Lord Donovan, is revealing in the sense that the ensuing report included only one chapter (of just 10 paragraphs) out of 16 that explicitly considered employee participation. The report acknowledged the importance of this aspect of industrial relations, but gave two reasons for considering this matter only briefly:

> First, we are agreed that any changes which might be made in order to facilitate and encourage such participation should be subsidiary to our main proposals for the reform of collective bargaining; and, secondly, we have been unable to agree upon changes which might be expected to have the desired effect. (Donovan, 1968: 257)

A significant reason underpinning the lack of agreement about how to promote employee participation in company decision-making at this time (Brannen *et al.*, 1976) was the prevalence of the view that had been advanced by the eminent industrial relations academic, Hugh Clegg (1951, reproduced in McCarthy, 1972: 74), that 'trade unions [are] an Opposition which can never become a Government.' Participation in corporate decision-making, according to this view, would have significantly compromised what was seen as the essentially oppositional role that the trade unions needed to play.

Having stated that employee participation essentially required board-level representation for employees and trades unions, the Bullock Committee suggested how this should be implemented, as we outline briefly below. However, this proposal for board-level employee participation was highly contested. The Committee actually produced two reports: a main report signed by its trade union and academic members, who constituted a numerical majority, and a minority report signed by its employers' representatives. The main report recommended the introduction of employee representatives onto redefined company boards, in private sector organisations over a certain employment size, in equal numbers to shareholder board members, with a third group of directors to be co-opted through agreement between these employee and shareholder representatives.

Those signing the minority report disagreed not only with the recommendations in the main report but also about the remit given to the Committee. They believed that

'"Industrial democracy" is a term which can all too easily be applied to a wide range of developments, some good, some in our view, bad. ... Certainly it is unwise to impose "democracy" on those who are unwilling or unready to receive it' (Bullock, 1977: 171). However, the views expressed in the minority report were but a 'pale reflection' of the depth of feeling of many British employers against the proposals being made for corporate-level employee participation at this time (Cressey *et al.*, 1985: 2). This was in spite of the fact that the authors of the main report promoted their recommendations in terms of a model of participation that they believed would incorporate employee interests with those of employers in order to produce greater efficiency:

> Sooner or later, we believe, this is a decision which will have to be taken... We believe the change in attitude of the TUC and their willingness to accept a share of responsibility for the increased efficiency and prosperity of British companies offer an opportunity to create a new basis for relations in industry which should not be allowed to pass. ... For if we look beyond our immediate problems it appears to us certain that the criterion of efficiency in the world of tomorrow ... will be the capacity of industry to adapt to an increasing rate of economic and social change. (Bullock, 1977: 161)

This aim of incorporation of employee interests with those of employing organisations is one view of the intended purpose of employee participation. We shall consider this and other views in more detail below.

A White Paper on Industrial Democracy was subsequently published in 1978. This proposed establishing a two-tier board structure with a statutory right for employee representatives, following an employee ballot, to sit on an envisaged policy (as opposed to a management) board in companies with over 2000 employees (Cressey *et al.*, 1985). However, with the return to power of a Conservative government in 1979 these proposals for a statutory approach to participation were eschewed. The stated preference of this government was to leave any arrangements for participation as a voluntary matter for companies to make decisions about how they might wish to involve employees (e.g. Kessler and Bayliss, 1998). This remained the view of the Conservative governments throughout the 1980s and 1990s.

The result of this failed attempt in the 1970s and the continued espoused policy of voluntarism throughout the 1980s and 1990s meant that the UK did not develop a statutory framework for employee participation. Only two countries in the EU at the beginning of this century did not have a statutory framework for consultation or participation – Ireland and the UK. We return to consider the recent establishment of such a statutory framework – albeit limited to information and consultation rights – in the section below that examines recent developments in the EU.

Of course, other forms of employee participation had long existed below company board level. The Bullock Committee's main report (1977) believed that such forms were necessary, and that these would be complementary to their proposals for statutory employee participation on company boards. Participation at below board level was seen in this report as any form that permitted employees, or more particularly trade unions, jointly to regulate issues affecting employment in an organisation. Three main categories relating to participation at this lower level have usually been identified. *Collective bargaining* has traditionally been seen as the primary means of joint regulation and participation. *Consultation* that effectively allows for some sort of veto over particular management proposals has also been seen as an important means to permit participation. Finally, the *provision of information* has been seen as necessary for participation but not as a form in its own right, according to Bullock.

The strength of the trade unions, at least in general terms, was seen as great enough in the 1970s to promote the development of employee participation at below board level. However, over the next two decades the reduced power of the trade unions and the diminishing scope and effectiveness of collective bargaining (discussed in Chapter 7) reversed their ability to promote employee participation at this level.

## ▧ The intended purpose of participation, nature of employee influence, exercise of power and locus of control

In the definitions cited above and discussion so far, employee participation has been used to emphasise some degree of power sharing and regulatory ability in relation to organisational decision-making, by (or on behalf of) a group of employees. However, even within analyses that consider only employee participation (as opposed to involvement) there are different views about the extent of power sharing and therefore the nature of employee influence and the locus of control. In broad terms, participation can be used to describe a range of situations where employees exercise either less than equal power over decision-making in comparison with management, or equal power, or even greater power than management where workers determine the outcome (Brannen, 1983).

The latter scenario is often referred to as *workers' control* (e.g. Coates and Topham, 1970; Eldridge *et al.*, 1991). These alternative situations indicate a very different approach to and outcome from employee participation in each case. A question has also been raised about the types of decision that may be open to employee influence. It is therefore useful to discuss a number of dimensions of employee participation that have been identified, to be able to analyse different types of participation in practice. These dimensions relate to the degree or depth, scope, level and form of employee participation (e.g. Schuchman, 1957; Poole, 1975; Marchington, 1980; Marchington *et al.*, 1992; Blyton and Turnbull, 1998). We shall now consider these four dimensions and use them to analyse types of employee participation.

*Degree* of participation relates to the extent of employees' influence, or the level of their control, over the way in which a decision is reached. As indicated in the previous paragraph, this may vary along a continuum that ranges from no influence through to control over a particular decision. In between these two extremes lie a number of possibilities. One of the earliest attempts to categorise these possibilities (Schuchman, 1957) recognised a number of key points along such a continuum. In ascending order of influence, these are rights to receive information, raise objections, make suggestions, be consulted, reject a proposal either temporarily or permanently, make a decision jointly with management, and exercise sole control over a decision (Poole, 1975; Marchington, 1980). The first four points of this continuum indicate a low level of participation, as we now consider.

As we referred to above, the Bullock Report (1977) recognised that the provision of information, although necessary for participation, should not be seen as a form in its own right. Any right to raise objections or make suggestions, although permitting some level of employee influence, does little to alter management's power to determine any decision. The Bullock Report also recognised that the nature of consultation varied, and believed that only those forms that permit some sort of veto over particular management proposals should be seen as a means to permit participation. For such reasons, these activities (providing information through to non-veto forms of consultation) have been seen as being promoted by management to encourage 'cooperation' (Schuchman, 1957; Poole, 1975; Marchington, 1980) (see Figure 8.1). In terms of our differentiation here between employee involvement and employee participation, these activities would be manifestations of the former rather than the latter. Participation in this sense must therefore be seen as commencing from the point where employees have a right either to veto a proposal advanced by management or to be involved in the conception of proposals from their earliest formulation (see Figure 8.1). Consequently, *joint regulation* and/or *co-determination*, indicating the exercise of equal power, are usually used as terms to indicate employee participation in decision-making.

Pateman's (1970) categorisation differentiates between three degrees of participation indicated by *full*, *partial* and *pseudo* approaches. Only the first is seen as proper participation. Joint regulation or co-determination would be an example of full participation in decision-making. Non-veto forms of consultation and similar activities exemplify partial participation, indicating the exercise of less than equal influence over decision making in comparison to management. Managerial activities, such as the dissemination of information (discussed later), that seek to persuade employees about decisions that have already been made are seen as pseudo participation. Pseudo participation in this categorisation would again be analogous to employee involvement.

However, even if we have reached an understanding about what is meant by participation in relation to the degree of influence conferred by such activity, there is still a weakness inherent in this approach related to the types of decision that may be open to such employee influence. In this way, participation in some decisions may apparently

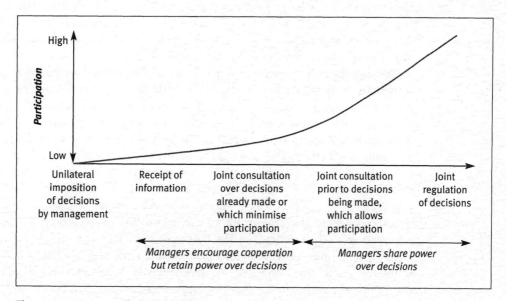

Figure 8.1  **Degree of participation**

confer a high level of influence; however, the limited nature of these decisions in relation to the functioning of an organisation may result in the maintenance of a high level of managerial control and a low level of employees' control. Examples of this would include full participation in relation to choosing the employee of the year or the charging policy about parking at work but only partial or pseudo participation in relation to matters of a more strategic or direct operational nature. The *scope* of the decisions that are subject to employee participation is therefore a critical aspect in assessing the nature of employees' influence and the locus of control in an organisation.

The scope of decisions that might be subject to employee participation may be placed into one or more different categories that in turn help us to understand the nature of employees' influence and control in a given organisation. For example, Marchington (1980) and Marchington *et al.* (1992) differentiate between the scope to participate in decision-making about strategic, operational and individual task issues. Scope to engage in decision-making about task matters, perhaps through collective bargaining, while providing a significant means for participation will, however, prove to be considerably different from the scope to participate in strategic decision-making in the way envisaged in the Bullock Report (1977; see also Kessler and Bayliss, 1998). Of course, in practice participation may range across more than one of these domains, as well as none. It is therefore important to identify not only whether participation exists but also the range of activities included in a given organisation in order to be able to assess the nature of employees' influence.

This provides a link to the *levels* at which employee participation may take place within a particular organisation. We recognised above that participation has been associated with employee influence at the strategic decision-making level of an organisation, through some form of representation at board level. Such representation may occur at main board level, or at the subsidiary board of an operating unit within a multidivisional type of organisation. For the Bullock Committee, representation at such strategic decision-making boards was the key to employee participation. Other types of employee participation at a lower level within an organisation were seen as being complementary. Such other forms, referred to above and discussed in detail below and elsewhere in this book, include collective bargaining and participation through works council style representation.

The significance of employee participation occurring at board level has been recognised in the literature. Poole (1975) and Brannen (1983), for example, elaborated on the significance of participation occurring at a strategic level. It has been recognised that, where participation only occurs at an operational level, whether in a division, business unit or department, its scope is likely to be limited significantly by decisions taken at a higher strategic level. It has also been recognised that participation may occur at such strategic and operational levels but be restricted to particular issues, such as health and safety, the transfer of undertakings, redundancies or the management of pension funds, because specific statutory rights underpin its use in these areas. It is also important to recognise that, even where participation has occurred at a strategic level in the UK context in a limited number of cases in the past, its scope has been limited *in practice* by a range of logistical and attitudinal problems (see Brannen *et al.*, 1976; Brannen, 1983; Cressey *et al.*, 1985; Eldridge *et al.*, 1991). For example, greater management familiarity with, and in-depth knowledge of, strategic matters, as well as their control over information, gives them a significant advantage over employee representatives. This is an issue that we return to when we discuss the practice of European Works Councils below.

As we have recognised, employee participation is likely to manifest itself in the *form* of formal and elected representation on established organisational decision-making bodies, such as board-level participation, or on other specially convened bodies such as works councils, or through the machinery established for collective bargaining. It is therefore likely to be indirect to the majority of employees whose interests are being represented at these decision-making bodies. Those who hold such representative positions may be personally known to those whom they represent, or they may be fairly distant from them in the sense of being elected as professional trade union officials who have little day-to-day contact with an organisation's workforce.

Through these dimensions, it is possible to differentiate employee participation from employee involvement (discussed in detail below). We shall use these dimensions in our discussion of employee involvement to compare its aims in relation to those for employee participation. These dimensions also provide a means to analyse practices across a range of countries, of which we shall include a discussion about developments in the European Union later in this chapter. However, it is important that we examine the extent to which employee participation, according to this differentiation, is seen in action in the current UK context.

## Participation in practice

There is little evidence of employee participation at the level of corporate decision-making in the UK context in the early twenty-first century, in the way envisaged in the Bullock Committee's main report in 1977. References to such forms of participation are historical and refer to experiments in the steel industry and in the Post Office, as well as to a small number of other cases (e.g. Brannen *et al.*, 1976; Eldridge *et al.*, 1991). There are nevertheless employee representatives on the corporate boards of some organisations in the public sector/services. For example, if you are reading this chapter as a student at a university or a college, there are likely to be student and employee representatives on its governing body. However, the proportion of student and employee representatives in relation to the total number of people sitting on this body is likely to be small, suggesting a limited degree of participation.

The prevalent forms of employee participation in the UK context centre on the existence of collective bargaining, joint consultation arrangements and works councils. The extent of these forms, as well as their depth and scope, has been reported through the Workplace Employee Relations Survey (WERS) series (e.g. Millward *et al.*, 1992; Cully *et al.*, 1999; Millward *et al.*, 2000) and the Employment in Britain research programme (Gallie *et al.*, 1998). Collective bargaining is explored in Chapter 7. However, it is worth briefly considering some of the available data about collective bargaining, to understand the extent of employee participation that this process permits through scope for joint regulation of aspects of the employment relationship.

Millward *et al.* (2000) report that the coverage of collective bargaining has reduced significantly over the past two decades. In 1984, 86 per cent of employees in unionised workplaces employing 25 or more people had their pay and conditions determined through collective bargaining. In terms of all workplaces employing 25 or more people, 70 per cent of employees were covered by collective bargaining in

1984. By 1998, only 67 per cent of employees in unionised workplaces of this size were covered by collective bargaining. In terms of all workplaces with 25 or more employees, by 1998 only 40 per cent were covered by collective bargaining. Complementary data taken from employee perceptions about levels of union influence over decision-making at the workplace have been produced by Gallie *et al.* (1998). They report (1998: 101) that 'while 63 per cent believed that the unions had either a great deal or a fair amount of influence over pay, only 25 per cent thought this was true for the way in which work is organised.' Given the reduced presence of unions and generally lower membership densities in workplaces by 1998 compared with earlier years, particularly in the private sector (Millward *et al.*, 2000), this indicates a somewhat limited scope for collectively based forms of employee participation. The possibility for participation in decision-making will be constrained both by the restricted presence and strength of unions in the workplace and by limitations placed on their scope to negotiate about broader issues affecting their members even where they are present.

Given the limited extent and scope of employee participation through collective bargaining, we now consider whether forms of consultation offer some means to participate in the regulation of the employment relationship. Cully *et al.* (1999) report that 53 per cent of all workplaces with 25 or more employees in the 1998 WERS had some form of joint consultative arrangement. These take different forms in relation to the organisational level at which consultation occurs. Seventeen per cent of all workplaces of this size were reported as only having a workplace-based consultation committee. Twenty five per cent only have access to a committee at a higher organisational level to facilitate consultation across the organisation. Eleven per cent had arrangements both at individual workplace level and at a higher level to permit consultation to occur across the organisation. Smaller organisations, measured by number of employees, were found to be less likely to engage in formal consultation (80 per cent of organisations employing less than 100 were reported as not having a committee, whereas the opposite was the case for organisations employing over 10 000 employees). Formal consultation arrangements are also much more prevalent in the public, as opposed to the private, sector. Over half of private sector organisations did not have such an arrangement (57 per cent), whereas less than one-fifth of public sector organisations were without a consultative committee (18 per cent). Cully *et al.* (1999) also found that the attitude of management towards employee consultation and the existence of unions was positively related to the likelihood of formal consultation arrangements existing within organisations.

A key question for our consideration is the extent to which these consultation committees permit participation, or at least some level of influence, in the regulation of the employment relationship. Earlier WERS data covering the 1980s (Millward *et al.*, 1992) indicate that about 3 out of 10 consultative committees engaged in both consultation and bargaining. The incidence of bargaining, as opposed to just consultation, was reported as being twice as frequent in the public sector and in private sector manufacturing, compared with private sector services in this period. These sectors (the public sector and private sector manufacturing) were also the ones where union organisation was likely to be more prevalent (Millward *et al.*, 1992).

The 1998 Workplace Employee Relations Survey also offers some information about the extent to which consultative and employee representative arrangements provide a forum for participation through negotiation of issues raised. In organisations where consultative arrangements exist, Cully *et al.* (1999) found that employee participation was restricted in both degree and scope. Negotiation, as opposed to just consultation, occurred only as a minority activity in relation to each of nine issues discussed with survey participants (including pay and conditions, handling grievances, health and safety, and pay systems). In about half of the organisations where consultation occurred, it was reported that there was an absence of any negotiation. The number of issues subject to negotiation in relation to the nine discussed averaged only 1.1 in organisations where there were union representatives and 0.9 where there were non-union representatives (Cully *et al.*, 1999).

From these findings, we may conclude that formal participation in the regulation of the employment relationship is constrained in the current climate. Cully *et al.* (1999) offer two factors to explain this conclusion, which relate to our earlier discussion. First, scope to participate in decisions that affect many workplaces is constrained by the fact that many of these are taken at a higher organisational level, reducing the potential for local managerial as well as employee influence. It was at this higher organisational decision-making level that the political attempt to introduce employee participation in the UK in the 1970s failed. Second, managerial attitudes to employee participation may not be favourably disposed towards joint regulation of the issues that the workforce would like to influence in respect of the decisions to be made. The main report from the Bullock Committee sought to promote participation at the strategic level through a rationale based on achieving the incorporation of employee interests with those of their employing organisations, and through envisaged gains related to greater efficiency and adaptation to change (see page 251 above). However, its means to achieve this, through power sharing, did not find favour with employers, as we recognised above. The power-sharing nature of participation clashed with the unitary conception of governance that appears to be the preferred approach of most employing organisations. For reasons related to this preference, Ramsay (1977) believed that, whenever employing organisations had acquiesced with forms of employee participation in the past, this had been motivated by a desire to offer some degree of influence in order to contain a potentially more fundamental challenge to management's control. His *cycles of control* thesis suggests that management have been willing to adopt a pragmatic approach to forms of employee participation during periods of labour shortages and unrest. Once the period of labour market problems had subsided, management allowed these participative activities to disappear or become trivial.

Ramsay's thesis to explain periods of employee participation principally as the result of a subtle managerial strategy to accommodate tensions arising from labour shortages and unrest has been criticised (e.g. Ackers *et al.*, 1992). The forms of employee involvement that we now consider are motivated by a different and wider managerial strategy than the temporary accommodation of labour market tensions. Hyman and Mason (1995) and Blyton and Turnbull (1998) recognise that employee involvement strategies are not so much about coping with labour market issues, but are a means to address tensions created by competitive product markets, where a key HR strategy is to optimise employee commitment and contribution. We therefore now move to examine employee involvement.

self-check question **8.1** Think of an organisational situation with which you have some familiarity.

What forms of employee participation, if any, exist in this organisation?
What authority promotes the existence of these forms of employee participation?
Evaluate the practice of these forms of employee participation using the dimensions of degree or depth, scope, level and form.
What practical problems exist in relation to the exercise of employee participation?

## 8.4 Employee involvement

### Promotion of employee involvement

In contrast to the promotion of employee participation as a means of sharing some degree of power in relation to organisational decision-making, employee involvement is promoted by management on a voluntary basis to influence employees' attitudes and workplace behaviours. This approach was supported, in the UK context, by the Conservative governments of the 1980s and 1990s (e.g. CBI/EDG, 1991). These Conservative governments supported the philosophy of voluntarism, aimed at allowing management to introduce forms of involvement as they saw fit rather than having a standard model imposed from some external source. In this way, this support was also a reaction against attempts by the European Commission to promote forms of employee participation. Michael Howard, the Conservative Secretary of State for Employment in the early 1990s, summed up this view in a speech to promote involvement:

> Those who have practical experience in the day-to-day business of industrial relations in this country know that our voluntary approach is the most effective one because it means that firms are free to establish the arrangements which are best suited to their own individual circumstances. A specific model of consultation imposed by community-wide legislation would destroy the flexibility which we believe is essential for effective employee involvement. (Howard, 1991: 14).

### The intended purpose of involvement, nature of employee influence, exercise of power and locus of control

The nature and purpose of employee involvement has been characterised along a number of dimensions. These allow it to be clearly differentiated from the concept of participation discussed above. One of these dimensions relates to its underpinning philosophy. As we saw in the quotation from Michael Howard's speech in 1991, the philosophy of involvement is related to a free market, non-interventionist stance. Management is promoted as knowing best, and according to this view should be allowed to introduce those initiatives that it wishes to, without outside intervention. Voluntarism is a form of self-determination and is related to non-intervention. This position of managerial ascendancy is also strongly unitarist. The definitions of employee involvement in Box 8.1, with their emphasis on employee awareness of, support for, and commitment and contribution towards organisational objectives, emphasise the underpinning unitary and managerialist nature of involvement initiatives as a further key dimension.

Another dimension flows from this recognition. For the unitary nature of employee involvement to be realised, it is designed primarily as a set of initiatives to appeal to and address employees as individuals. The concept of involvement is an essential component of a range of other individually focused human resource strategies, such as performance and reward management (see Chapter 10).

A further dimension is related to the level at which involvement initiatives are designed to operate within an organisation. These are focused either at the task and workgroup level, or at the corporate level but limited to the provision of information directly to employees rather than being related to any form of power sharing, or more generally through forms of financial involvement. These dimensions are summarised in Table 8.1. We explore these dimensions further through a discussion of the analytical framework that we used above to analyse participation, this time related to employee involvement.

**Table 8.1 Dimensions of employee participation and involvement**

| Participation | Involvement |
|---|---|
| Fostered by trade unions and through interventionist-style governmental and European Union regulation | Fostered by employers/managerial interests on a voluntary basis, supported by free-market style governments |
| Pluralist and rights-centred | Unitarist and business-centred |
| Collectivist in nature | Individualist in nature |
| Intended to gain representation via employee representatives, who may be members of trade unions | Intended to generate employee commitment and contribution to their employing organisation |
| Indirect means of participating for most employees | Directly focused on employees, bypassing indirect employee forums in many cases |
| Power centred, with the aim of achieving operational and strategic influence | Task-centred and focused also on generating communicative and/or financial involvement |

Employee involvement initiatives are designed to generate no more than a low or localised *degree* of employee influence. As we recognised in the discussion above about participation, possible involvement through the dissemination of information, communication, the making of suggestions or consultation (see Table 8.2 below for a list of methods for each of these categories) offers employees only very limited influence over decision-making. These are all limited in relation to the degree of power conferred on employees. Although there may be some degree of employee influence exercised through one or more of these means, management's right to make decisions is not subject to any formal means of joint decision-making, and employees do not exercise any right of veto. This is consistent with the essentially unitarist nature of such strategies, where the underlying belief is in the existence of common interests between employees and their employer. With management left to identify what that common interest may be, the intention behind such involvement initiatives is to develop employee cooperation, commitment and contribution, not to share power (e.g. Schuchman, 1957; Poole, 1975; Kessler and Bayliss, 1998).

The involvement initiatives referred to in the above paragraph, ranging from information dissemination to consultation, are labelled as *communicative involvement* by Gallie *et al.* (1998: 96). This allows them to differentiate these initiatives from those that they term *direct participation*. For Gallie *et al.* (1998: 90), 'direct participation is most likely to occur with respect to relatively local decisions about work organisation, since these are the types of decisions where management is particularly likely to benefit from employees' technical knowledge.' This type of involvement is therefore concerned with the granting of some localised employee influence over the way in which work is scheduled and undertaken. The rationale for such task-level involvement, recognised in the Gallie *et al.* quotation, is related to managerial attempts to generate greater efficiency (such as through the reduction of supervisory time) and effectiveness (by tapping into the know-how of employees). Geary (1994) identifies ways in which task involvement may be achieved, including through the use of semi-autonomous work groups, team working and quality management techniques to involve employees. It is important to recognise that granting employee discretion over aspects of work is capable of leading to a higher level of employee influence in comparison with communicative involvement, albeit that any such influence will be very localised and may be more illusory than real. This type of direct involvement is often referred to as *empowerment*, and has been recognised as being a difficult concept to realise in practice, given the nature of the employment relationship in many real-life instances (e.g. Geary, 1994; Marchington, 1995; Cunningham *et al.*, 1996). We return to this issue below when we discuss employee involvement in practice.

The *scope* of decisions that might be subject to employee involvement is therefore limited to task-level issues, indicating a sharp contrast to the nature of decisions that are intended to be subject to employee participation. The scope to become involved in strategic and operational, as opposed to individual task, issues (e.g. Marchington *et al.*, 1992) is restricted to the receipt of information, engagement in communication, opportunities to make suggestions and perhaps also to engage in consultation. This is again consistent with the underpinning unitary approach that drives this strategy, whether this is explicitly recognised and expressed or not. Management strategy in relation to decisions taken at strategic and operational *levels* is to offer scope to receive information about these and perhaps to be able to discuss them, but not to engage in the decision-making process when such decisions are being made. In this sense, involvement is about creating awareness and understanding of strategic and operational issues, with a view to engendering cooperation, commitment and contribution, through the explanation and justification of decisions made by management.

In broad terms, this indicates two principal *forms* of involvement so far: *task-level involvement* and *communicative involvement*. In addition, there is a need to recognise a third form of intended employee engagement with corporate objectives through *financial involvement*. Financial involvement seeks to link some proportion of an employee's reward to organisational performance through schemes such as profit-related pay and employee share ownership. The Conservative governments of the 1980s and 1990s sought to encourage the widespread development of schemes for financial involvement through an extension of related tax relief. This had a considerable impact during this period in terms of the number of schemes that were introduced, with over 2 million employees being covered by such arrangements.

The effectiveness of each of these approaches to employee involvement, in terms of altered attitudes and behaviours, is likely to be dependent on a number of factors, and is a far from simple matter to assess. An important part of any assessment of employee involvement in practice is likely to include employee perceptions about managerial actions and style of leadership. This is likely to be a significant way of assessing whether managerial strategies to engender employee involvement are perceived as marginal, 'bolt-on' approaches, or as a more fundamental and genuine approach to influence and perhaps change the culture of an organisation positively. For this reason, *managerial style* has been judged to be an integral component of involvement, and is recognised to have an important relationship to perceptions about employee involvement in practice (e.g. Marchington, 1992; Storey, 1992; Guest *et al.*, 1993). We may therefore treat managerial style as a means to affect employee involvement, even though it may be seen as a somewhat diffuse and less tangible form of involvement. Conversely, by ignoring managerial actions and style of leadership, an organisation may invest in forms of communicative and task-level involvement but fail to develop any sense of credibility in relation to these where its prevailing style of management is seen as being incongruent with the aims of such initiatives.

In summary, we have identified a number of important principal forms of employee involvement. Related to these, the earlier definitions of employee involvement in Table 8.1 referred to *a range of processes* and *a combination of practices and systems*. These processes, practices and systems may be listed under the principal categories or forms that we have discussed above. Table 8.2 presents these categories of employee involvement, and lists related forms that are associated with each category, together with a brief management rationale.

## Employee involvement in practice

Millward *et al.* (2000: 136) conclude that by 1998 'there had been a major shift from collective, representative, indirect and union-based voice, to direct, non-union channels.' We review the forms that this major shift took using the typology outlined in Table 8.2, by analysing reported developments in the use of communicative involvement through the provision of downward information and two-way communication, task involvement and financial involvement.

Forms of communicative involvement measured in the Workplace Employee Relations Survey series demonstrate that these continued to develop in terms of their use across the 1980s and 1990s (Cully *et al.*, 1999; Millward *et al.*, 2000). In relation to the provision of information to employees, two-thirds of workplaces provided information about their financial position in 1998. Similarly, over 6 out of 10 organisations composed of multi-site operations provided information to their employees about their financial position. Managers provided information about investment plans to employees in just over half of organisations in 1998. Managers in 6 out of 10 workplaces also provided information to employees about staffing plans in 1998. Only about one in six organisations across all sectors did not provide any of these types of information to their employees according to this survey data. Of particular interest, the 1998 survey data reveal that the increase in the provision of information directly to employees was most pronounced in unionised organisations. Forty-nine per cent of unionised workplaces provided information to employees about their

## Table 8.2  Categories and forms of employee involvement

| Main categories of employee involvement | Examples of related forms | Management's likely rationale |
|---|---|---|
| Communicative involvement: information provision/downward communication | Team briefing; other briefing groups; corporate newspapers, journals and reports aimed at employees; videos; audiotapes; email; recorded telephone briefings | To provide information; uniform messages; to be educative or re-educative |
| Communicative involvement: problem-solving involvement and upward, two-way communication | Briefing groups with feedback and managerial response loops; quality circles; quality action teams; quality improvement teams; suggestion schemes; employee surveys | Explicit access to employees' experience and skills; gain cooperation and opinions |
| Communicative involvement: consultation | Joint consultation committees, working parties or groups; staff forums | Providing information and testing reactions |
| Task involvement at job and work organisation levels | Job redesign: job enlargement and job enrichment. Work reorganisation: team working; (semi) autonomous working groups; 'empowerment'. See also problem-solving involvement | To be re-educative; providing greater levels of motivation and satisfaction; empowering |
| Financial involvement | Employee share ownership plans; profit-related pay; performance-related pay; bonus schemes | To be re-educative; providing incentives and promoting effort |
| Managerial actions and style of leadership | Participative managerial style; being visible; accessible and informal; creating credibility; ensuring actions in line with key messages | To provide support; encourage positive working relationships and trust; reduce barriers |

*Sources*: Developed from: CBI/EDG (1991); Ackers *et al.* (1992); Marchington (1992); Storey (1992); Guest *et al.* (1993); Marchington (1995); Kessler and Bayliss (1998); Thornhill *et al.* (2000)

financial position, investment and staffing plans, compared with just 27 per cent of non-union workplaces that provided all three of these types of information (Cully *et al.*, 1999; Millward *et al.*, 2000). One of the principal means of disseminating information is through the issue of organisational newsletters. By 1998, half of organisations were found to be distributing these to employees, with Cully *et al.* (1999) noting that smaller organisations (with fewer than 1000 employees) were also increasingly using this method (just under one-third). This means of disseminating information to employees remained most common in large organisations and in the public sector.

Direct communication of a more two-way nature has been measured in the WERS series through the incidence of regular meetings between senior managers and employees, meetings or briefing groups involving more junior managers and employees, and other forms of problem-solving communication (Cully *et al.*, 1999; Millward *et al.*, 2000). It has been estimated that, by 1998, regular meetings between senior managers and employees occurred in just under half of workplaces, having risen from one-third in 1984. By the late 1990s, it has also been estimated that about two-thirds of workplaces were using team briefing or briefing groups on a regular basis. The increase in the use of briefings over the 1990s has been particularly concentrated in private sector workplaces without recognised unions and joint consultation arrangements (Millward *et al.*, 2000).

The use of problem-solving groups in the workplace also increased significantly over the 1990s, rising from 35 per cent of workplaces in 1990 to just under half by 1998 (Millward *et al.*, 2000). Suggestion schemes were operating in one-third of workplaces in 1998 (Cully *et al.*, 1999). The increasing use of problem-solving groups and suggestion schemes over the 1990s, as well as the greater incidence of workgroup-level systems for briefing employees, may also be seen as an indication of managerial attempts to broaden the extent of task-level involvement during this period.

Gallie *et al.* (1998) found that the use of communicative involvement was positively associated with the presence of particular organisational characteristics. These include the incidence of higher skill levels in the organisation, the use of new technology, which may itself facilitate greater direct communication, and organisational size as we noted above. They also found that forms of communicative involvement are more likely to be more developed in organisations with systems of performance and reward management. This approach to management involves performance appraisal, the establishment of targets and setting performance-related pay, with effective communication being seen as a necessary prerequisite for this approach to work (see Chapter 10).

Forms of financial involvement also continued to be used at the end of the 1990s. Of the two principal forms briefly described above, schemes for profit-related pay were the most widely used during the 1990s, with arrangements for profit-sharing being used to some extent in 44 per cent of private sector workplaces with over 25 employees in 1990 and in 46 per cent of such workplaces in 1998. Employee share ownership schemes were also evident in about one-quarter of the private sector by 1998 (Cully *et al.*, 1999).

 **8.2** Think of an organisational situation with which you have some familiarity.

What forms of employee involvement, if any, exist in this organisation?
. Who is responsible for promoting these forms of employee involvement?
Evaluate the practice of these forms of employee involvement.
What practical problems exist in relation to the exercise of employee involvement?

##  Common terms but different intentions: differing roles for communication, information and consultation

Our discussion of employee participation and employee involvement has recognised that there are common terms used in relation to each approach, but with the intention of achieving a different purpose. For example, the provision of information in relation to employee participation is seen as being a prerequisite to the sharing of power. In relation to employee involvement, information provision is aimed instead at generating employee attitudes that are congruent with those espoused by managers and the organisational goals that they wish to achieve, as well as providing knowledge-based workers in particular with necessary data (e.g. Townley, 1994; Marchington and Wilkinson, 2000).

Any requirement placed on management to provide information to employees, their representatives or trade unions is known as *disclosure of information*. Management may be obliged to disclose information through having entered into a recognition and/or collective agreement with one or more trade unions. Effective collective bargaining is likely to rely on the disclosure of some management information, and disclosing a high level of information may help to promote a more integrative approach to bargaining (see Chapter 7) (Salamon, 1992, 2000). Such disclosure may be in relation to negotiations that generally cover the regulation of the employment relationship, or it may be more narrowly focused, for example in relation to specific organisational changes that have been made the subject of some form of employee participation, such as restructuring and redundancies.

Perhaps the most widespread obligation on employers in this respect stems from their statutory requirement to disclose information. Townley (1994) provides a brief résumé of this statutory requirement, commencing with the initial and unfulfilled proposal for the disclosure of information in 1969, through a series of legislation dating from the early 1970s. This includes the Health and Safety at Work etc. Act 1974 and the Employment Protection Act 1975, as well as the 1977 ACAS Code of Practice, which promoted the disclosure of information to trade unions for the purpose of collective bargaining. More recently, the statutory requirement to disclose information has grown, boosted by legislation emanating from the European Union requiring the disclosure of information to, as well as consultation with, employee representatives. This includes the European Works Councils, Acquired Rights, Collective Redundancies and Health and Safety Framework Directives. EU directives such as these have led to legislation in the UK including the Collective Redundancies and Transfer of Undertakings (Protection of Employment) (Amendment) Regulations 1995 and the Health and Safety (Consultation with Employees) Regulations 1996. These regulations have spread the right to information disclosure and consultation into non-union situations (e.g. Hall, 1996; Terry, 1999). We return to the role of EU legislation in promoting disclosure of information in the following section.

In contrast to enforced disclosure, *dissemination of information* refers to a situation where an organisation voluntarily informs its employees about any matter affecting itself. This is the type of information provision and communication linked with employee involvement, aimed at developing employees' identification with, as well as commitment and contribution to, their employing organisation. This approach is also intended to optimise work effectiveness. However, its achievement in practice is likely to be problematic. Linked to this, strategies based on the dissemination of information and communication may be poorly conceived and inadequately implemented, as we now discuss.

Part of the rationale behind any strategy to disseminate information may be to 'educate' employees about the economic circumstances of their employing organisation, thereby shaping their attitudes to generate expectations that are seen by management as being more realistic. This type of strategy is therefore also intended to assert the authority of managers and to improve organisational effectiveness (Townley, 1994). However, lowering employee expectations and seeking to improve effectiveness in the same period, for example, is likely to be a very difficult mix to achieve and sustain. The outcome of this strategy from an employee perspective may be the adoption of an instrumental approach to work and/or a position of passive compliance (Marchington and Wilkinson, 2000). Employment relationships based on employee compliance are generally judged to be inappropriate, particularly in relation to competitive environments where commitment to an organisation is seen as likely to aid competitive advantage (e.g. Walton, 1985). Forms of information dissemination and communication that seek to generate commitment to an organisation therefore need to recognise employees' interests, their reactions to any changes occurring around them, and the organisation's responsibility to and for its employees.

Different writers have variously labelled the distinction between these two approaches to information dissemination and communication. Townley (1994) refers to the former approach as being designed to have an educative function and to the latter approach as being part of a strategy to engender commitment. Salamon (1992, 2000) refers to the former approach as having corporate-centred aims and the latter approach as having employee-centred aims. These two sets of labels are clearly complementary and conceptually useful in conjunction with one another. Townley (1994) argues that the 'educative' (and corporate-centred) approach to communication is likely to be based on the exercise of managerial power but is unlikely to be integrated with other human resource policies. Conversely, the commitment-based communication strategy will not only be more employee-centred, emphasising a cooperative and joint problem-solving approach, but is also more likely to be part of an integrated human resource strategy. The distinction being drawn here is akin to the difference in managerial style between an authoritarian approach and a more sophisticated human relations strategy (see Chapter 4) (e.g. Purcell and Sisson, 1983; Purcell and Gray, 1986).

Another set of distinctions can be drawn around the use of joint consultation. We have already recognised that consultation that allows some degree of joint decision-making is distinct from forms that do not permit this type of outcome. Marchington (e.g. 1988, 1994) has developed a typology of four models of consultation, each of which demonstrates a distinct purpose. These are labelled as:

- the non-union model;
- the marginal model;
- the competitive model;
- the adjunct model (Marchington, 1988).

Marchington analyses each of these models in relation to the presence of trade unions and collective bargaining, so that the *non-union model* of consultation is fostered in organisations to resist any attempt at unionisation and the collectivisation of the employment relationship. An employer's strategy in this approach may combine an educative function, through the provision of information about the enterprise to influence the attitudes of employee representatives on the committee, with a more sophisticated approach, by responding to employee concerns in the hope of preventing any momentum to unionise.

In the *marginal model* consultation is seen as being unimportant, because unions are established and other fora exist for collective bargaining and employee participation. However, there may be some motivation for retaining this type of consultative arrangement because of its symbolic value (to show corporate concern), or because it provides a means to absorb the time of employee representatives and unions without the organisation having to concede much by the way of tangible outcomes.

The third type of model of consultation potentially accords greater value for an organisation in the sense that it is used to *compete with collective bargaining*. Issues of substance will be discussed with union representatives through this type of consultative arrangement, with the intention of creating an educative forum to persuade these representatives about the economic circumstances of the organisation and to move their perceptions towards those of management. In conjunction with this approach to enjoin union representatives in management thinking, the organisation is also likely to deploy employee involvement initiatives directly at its employees to justify managerial actions and to gain commitment. Success in this strategy will perhaps reduce the necessity for negotiation, moderate demands made when collective bargaining occurs, and possibly reduce its scope.

In the fourth type of model, consultation is not used to supplant collective bargaining but to operate alongside it in a meaningful way. As an *adjunct to collective bargaining*, this model of consultation provides a means to cover those issues that are not dealt with through negotiation. This model is likely to exist in workplaces where union organisation is not only strong but also where there are particularly competent union representatives who are less prone to accept attempts by management to affect their perceptions and alter their attitudes. A key point to emerge from Marchington's typology is that management may actively use forms of consultation to pursue their own aims, rather than simply agree to take part in this at the behest of a recognised trade union.

These alternative approaches to information and communication, and models of consultation, demonstrate not only a fit with our earlier discussion about employee participation and employee involvement, but also the existence of different strategies that the parties to the management of the employment relationship may adopt in particular circumstances. Marchington (1994) recognises, for example, that changing circumstances may alter the nature of the model of consultation that is used at different points in time. A consultation committee may commence its existence as a means to prevent unionisation but later be used to compete with the functions of a union if one subsequently gains recognition. In contrast to this situation, a consultative committee that functioned effectively as an adjunct to collective bargaining may become marginal where unionisation itself withers in a workplace. These potentially changing scenarios demonstrate the dynamic nature of the employment relationship in many workplaces over time and the scope for change to occur in a number of ways. The principal type of change that we have witnessed so far, of course, in the recent past relates to the growing use of forms of employee involvement. However, a question may be posed about the future in respect of the nature of both employee involvement and employee participation.

**self-check question**

**8.3** In relation to the organisational situation that you used for the self-check questions above:

What types of information are disclosed to employees and what types are disseminated? What do you think is management's rationale for disseminating particular types of information?
Where employee consultation is evident in this organisation, how does this relate to the typology described above, and is there any evidence that the purpose of consultation has changed, or is changing?

## 8.6 The role of the European Union for the future of employee participation and involvement

The reported decline of forms of employee participation and growth of employee involvement, as discussed above, indicate one trend towards employer-led initiatives. However, there is also some evidence for the development of partnership agreements in the regulation of the employment relationship (see Chapter 5). Unions also continue to have at least some presence in about half of workplaces with 25 or more employees and to be recognised in about 4 out of 10 organisations of this size, within which about two-thirds of employees are covered by collective bargaining (Millward *et al.*, 2000). These data indicate that some forms of employee participation will continue into the future and will be a significant feature of the employment relationship for many people.

A major stimulus to promote certain forms of employee participation comes from recent European Union social legislation. Several EU Member States have a tradition of employee participation of the type that has caused a high level of resistance from British employing organisations. Earlier we charted the attempt in the 1970s to introduce some form of statutory board-level representation into the UK context. This attempt failed. In contrast, about two-thirds of European Union Member States have introduced statutory board-level representation to some extent. Some countries, such as Denmark, Germany and the Netherlands, have two-tier board structures, with employees being represented on a higher-level supervisory board. Statutory requirements vary between countries depending on the nature of their enabling legislation, with the requirement for this type of employee participation being dependent on factors including a minimum organisational size, the nature of its ownership and legal form, and industrial sector. For example, some countries, such as Greece and Ireland, confine this type of statutory employee participation to state enterprises. The extent of employee participation also varies from minority level representation to *full parity* co-determination, where employees make up half of the supervisory board (e.g. IRS, 1990; Brewster *et al.*, 2000).

Recent legislation from the EU is being used to promote forms of employee participation at below board level. The Member States except the UK adopted the Community Charter of Fundamental Social Rights, known as the Social Charter, in December 1989. This included recognition of the need for rights to information, consultation and participation relating to matters such as technological and organisational change and redundancies (e.g. Kessler and Bayliss, 1998). We referred earlier to a number of EU directives that have led to legislation in Member States to enact particular requirements for information disclosure and consultation. These include directives relating to European Works Councils, Acquired Rights and Collective Redundancies. Of particular significance in the UK context, the regulations that finally led to the intended implementation of the latter two Directives, in 1995, introduced the right to information disclosure and consultation in non-union situations in respect of collective redundancies and the transfer of undertakings (Hall, 1996; Terry, 1999).

The European Works Councils (EWCs) Directive was adopted in 1994 and came into force in September 1996. Initially, this was introduced into 17 of the 18 Member States of the European Economic Area (EEA), with the exception of the UK. Its provisions were designed to affect *Community-scale* companies, defined as those having at least 1000 employees within these Member States, with 150 or more employees in each of at least two such countries. Affected companies are obliged to set up a European Works Council (EWC) within a given period following a properly constituted request and subsequent negotiation in order to provide information to and consult with their workforce, through representatives, on a transnational basis. The process of establishing an EWC may be triggered by a company's central management or by a request from 100 or more employees or their representatives in at least two Member States.

Initially, during the two years between September 1994 and 1996, Article 13 of the Directive permitted companies to reach a voluntary agreement for the establishment of an EWC. As this route to establishing an EWC exempted companies from the specific provisions of the Directive, allowing the parties greater scope when negotiating an agreement, there was an initial flurry of activity, with some 450 EWCs being set up by 22 September 1996 (IRS, 2000a). An analysis of 386 Article 13 EWC agreements (Marginson *et al.*, 1998; IRS, 1998a) found that these varied from the statutory provisions of the Directive in respect of four principal aspects. Voluntarily agreed EWCs were often found to cover a broader geographical area than just EEA countries, and to include the UK; however, some agreements imposed an employment size threshold below which direct representation on the EWC from that country's operations would not be allowed. Some voluntarily agreed EWCs also established structures at divisional level in the company, where these divisions operated across EEA countries, rather than set up a corporate level or group-wide structure in line with the statutory requirement of the Directive. Most voluntarily agreed EWCs were also established as joint management–employee councils rather than following the Directive's statutory provision for the establishment of employee-side-only EWCs. Although the Directive does not specifically grant trade unions a role, unions nevertheless became signatories to the establishment of just under half of voluntarily agreed EWCs. Of particular interest, the involvement of trade unions was associated with the establishment of joint management–employee EWCs rather than the German model of employee-only councils. Although all voluntarily agreed EWCs were concerned with receiving information and consultation, some 4 per cent were also given the right to make recommendations and proposals, and a further 2 per cent were granted negotiating rights (Marginson *et al.*, 1998; IRS 1998a, 1998b).

Of the EEA Member States, the UK was not directly covered by the 1994 EWCs Directive because of its opt-out from the Social Chapter of the 1991 Maastricht Treaty of the European Union, negotiated by John Major's Conservative government. However, many of the voluntarily agreed EWCs negotiated through Article 13 included British workforces. Indeed, it has been reported that, of the 250 companies with operations in the UK that agreed to set up Article 13 EWCs, only seven excluded their British workforce (Marginson *et al.*, 1998; IRS, 1998a). Many of these companies were British owned and headquartered but were still affected by the Directive because of the size and nature of their operations in other EEA Member States. Cressey (1998) reports the TUC finding that over 50 British-based companies agreed to set up Article 13 EWCs. These companies include many well-known names such as Barclays Bank, British Airways, BT, Coats Viyella, Courtaulds, GKN, ICI, Marks and Spencer, NatWest Bank, Pilkington, Scottish and Newcastle, and Unilever (a fuller list is shown in Wills, 1999). We return to the ending of the UK opt-out from the Social Chapter below.

After 22 September 1996 the Directive came into effect and the procedure for introducing EWCs changed. The creation of EWCs in the 17 EEA Member States was then governed by the Directive (or more specifically its transposition into national law). Article 5 required that a request to establish an EWC should become the subject of negotiation by setting up a *special negotiating body* (SNB) of employee representatives to reach agreement with management. An agreement has to fulfil the requirements laid down in Article 6 about the coverage of the EWC, its composition, functions, meetings and facilities (IRS, 1999a). Negotiations may continue for a period of up to 3 years, after which if agreement is not forthcoming the Directive provides for the establishment of a statutory EWC model in the company. This provision clearly acts as an incentive to reach agreement. Similarly, when a company's employees make a valid request for a council to be set up but its central management refuses to enter negotiations within 6 months, this statutory EWC model will also be applied.

Since 1996 the rate at which new EWCs have been created has slowed. The number of transnational organisations potentially affected by the 1994 EWCs Directive is thought to be about 1200. IRS (2000a) estimates that the total number set up by early 2000 is about 600, including those established under Article 13. Negotiations to set up new EWCs will also be in progress. Table 8.3 shows some of the range of companies that are reported to have established an EWC under Article 6.

The UK's opt-out from the Social Chapter and from this Directive was ended in 1997, with the return of a Labour government. An EWC 'extension' directive was formally adopted in December 1997, which gave affected organisations 2 years to reach a voluntary agreement in line with Article 13 of the original Directive. This was subsequently transposed into UK law through the Transnational Information and Consultation of Employees Regulations 1999, closely following the requirements of the Directive outlined above (IRS, 1999b).

The statutory functions of an EWC relate to the disclosure of information and consultation. This will be of a transnational nature and may be intended to supplement and enhance arrangements to undertake consultation within the national or local settings of a company's operations. The need for these linkages to occur in practice has been recognised in order to promote EWCs as a meaningful way of consulting with employees, although their ability to facilitate this in the way that they

**Table 8.3 Some organisations reported as establishing EWCs under Article 6**

| | | |
|---|---|---|
| Air France | France | Air transport |
| Akzo Nobel | Netherlands | Chemicals |
| American Express | USA | Financial services |
| BTR | UK | Engineering |
| Bosch | Germany | Engineering |
| Cadbury Schweppes | UK | Confectionery |
| Campbell Bewley | Ireland | Food |
| Carlsberg | Denmark | Beverages |
| Cummins | USA | Diesel engines |
| Dalgety | UK | Food and agricultural |
| General Electric | USA | Plastics and power systems |
| Glaxo Wellcome | UK | Pharmaceuticals |
| Heineken | Netherlands | Brewing |
| IBM | USA | IT |
| Michelin | France | Rubber and tyres |
| Nissan | Japan | Motor manufacturing |
| Nortel | Canada | Telecommunications |
| Sara Lee Douwe Egberts | USA | Food and personal |
| Swedish Match | Sweden | Matches and tobacco |

*Source*: IRS / ETUC

are currently being run has been questioned, as we discuss below. Certainly, by intention, the nature of envisaged information disclosure is designed to allow employee representatives to get closer to corporate-level issues. The Directive envisages that EWCs will be provided with information about substantial matters affecting employees' interests, including company performance and prospects, production and sales, investments, the employment situation, organisational changes, introduction of new working methods or production processes, production transfers, mergers, closures or cutbacks and collective redundancies. Consultation may cover any of these aspects.

However, the extent to which the operation of EWCs is advancing employee participation is open to question. Cressey (1998) points to trade union awareness that EWCs are restricted in their capacity to promote employee participation because they are limited to a consideration of corporate-level issues. Wills (1999) believes that management interest in establishing EWCs, particularly in relation to Article 13, has been driven by their attempts to use these councils as a vehicle to promote their own agenda and vision, and to help to build a European corporate culture. She also points to a strategy in some companies where an EWC has been used to create a competitive situation between unions and non-unionists to represent employee interests. This may suggest scope to develop a typology similar to that of Marchington (1988, 1994) described above. The effectiveness of EWCs may also be limited by the way in which they are constituted. The European Trade Union Confederation (ETUC) would like to see the employment size thresholds for the establishment of EWCs reduced. The Directive requires only that EWCs meet on an annual basis, although exceptional circumstances, such as relocations, closures or collective redundancies, may require that additional meetings occur. The ETUC also believe that the procedures for information disclosure and consultation need to be made more effective. In addition, consulting with representatives on a transnational basis, while allowing links to corporate management and to other national unions and company operations (Cressey, 1998), may make this process appear remote to the majority of a company's workforce.

In their proposals the European Trade Union Confederation include the following suggestions for the reform of EWCs to improve their effectiveness from the trade union perspective:

■ Information needs to be more continuous and to be provided in good time.

■ Consultation should take place well before management takes decisions, to enable employees' views to be considered.

■ Meetings other than the existing annual information and consultation meeting need to be planned 'with a view to reaching agreement' on matters discussed.

■ Representatives on EWCs need to be given greater rights, including access to training, time off work, and the resources to disseminate information from EWC meetings to lower-level employee representatives, to establish linkages to these structures.

■ Representatives need to be able to meet together outside the formal EWC meeting and to be allowed greater access to expert assistance, including enjoining union officials (see IRS, 2000b).

These proposed extensions to the operation of EWCs would alter the nature of the process towards one that was more power centred and away from a narrowly defined information-sharing and consultation remit. They are not supported by the European employers' organisation, UNICE. Employee participation clearly remains a topical issue that exercises the minds of various stakeholders to this process.

**8.4** How would you analyse the position of EWCs in relation to the dimensions used to analyse employee participation and employee involvement, relating to degree or depth, scope, level and form?

The extension of statutory information and consultation rights to the national level has been at issue in the EU since late 1998, when the European Commission adopted a draft Directive on this matter. This statutory extension was finally resolved when a Directive for the provision of information to and consultation with employees' representatives within Member States was agreed in February 2002 (2002/14/EC). This agreement was partly reached when it was accepted that a long timetable would be allowed to transpose this Directive into national legislation. This was because Ireland and the UK do not already have national-level systems for employee information and consultation. Consequently, Member States do not have to transpose this Directive into national legislation before March 2005, and it does not have to be implemented for all affected organisations, depending on their size, until 2007 or 2008. However, once it is implemented in practice, affected organisations will have to provide information about their activities and economic situation and also undertake consultation in respect of their employment situation (including threats to employment) and on decisions likely to introduce substantial changes to the organisation of work or contractual relations. Such consultation will have to take place with a view to reaching agreement about the introduction of substantial changes to the organisation of work or contractual relations.

## 8.7 Summary

- This chapter has differentiated between the concepts of employee participation and employee involvement. Employee participation is used essentially as a power-centred concept, fostered by trade unions and through governmental and European Union regulation. Employee involvement is recognised as a unitarist and business-centred concept, fostered by employer and managerial interests, designed to generate employee commitment and contribution.
- Participation takes three principal forms: board-level representation; joint regulation of employment issues; and joint consultation, where this allows an employee veto over particular managerial proposals. The nature and extent of employee participation may be analysed through four dimensions that relate to its degree, scope, level and form.
- In the UK, collective bargaining remains the most widespread means of permitting some degree of employee participation, although this has reduced significantly over the past two decades. The scope of such bargaining has also been reduced. The scope for participation through forms of employee consultation is also limited.
- In contrast, there has been a significant shift to forms of employee involvement in the UK over the past two decades. These include a range of channels that are focused directly towards employees, including forms of communicative involvement, task-level involvement and financial involvement. Employee involvement will also be affected and moderated by managerial actions and styles of leadership.
- There are differing strategies underpinning the use of methods such as employee communication and joint consultation in relation to the pursuit of employee participation or employee involvement. This emphasises the need to differentiate between these approaches and to understand the purpose of communication, information-sharing and consultation strategies in practice.
- Recent legislation emanating from the European Union has helped to promote some forms of limited employee participation, notably in relation to the introduction of European Works Councils in affected organisations and through the impending development of a national system for informing and consulting employees. Although these measures establish systems for consultation, the degree of participation permitted through these approaches falls short of power sharing and joint regulation.

## References

Ackers, P., Marchington, M., Wilkinson, A. and Goodman, J. (1992) 'The use of cycles? Explaining employee involvement in the 1990s', *Industrial Relations Journal*, 23:4, 268–83.

Blyton, P. and Turnbull, P. (1998) *The Dynamics of Employee Relations*, Basingstoke, Macmillan.

Brannen, P. (1983) *Authority and Participation in Industry*, London, Batsford Academic.

Brannen, P., Batstone, E., Fatchett, D. and White, P. (1976) *The Worker Directors: A sociology of participation*, London, Hutchinson.

Brewster, C., Mayrhofer, W. and Morley, M. (2000) *New Challenges for European Human Resource Management*, Basingstoke, Macmillan.

Bullock, A. (1977) *Report of the Committee of Inquiry on Industrial Democracy* (Cmnd 6706), London, HMSO.

CBI/EDG (1991) *Managing for Success*, launch issue, April, London, CBI/EDG.

Clegg, H.A. (1951) *Industrial Democracy and Nationalization*, Oxford, Blackwell.

Coates, K. and Topham, A. (1970) *Workers' Control*, London, Panther Books.

Cressey, P. (1998) 'European works councils in practice', *Human Resource Management Journal*, 8:1, 67–79.

Cressey, P., Eldridge, J. and MacInnes, J. (1985) *Just Managing: Authority and democracy in industry*, Milton Keynes, Open University Press.

Cully, M., Woodland, S., O'Reilly, A. and Dix, G. (1999) *Britain at Work as Depicted by the 1998 Workplace Employee Relations Survey*, London, Routledge.

Cunningham, I., Hyman, J. and Baldry, C. (1996) 'Empowerment: the power to do what?', *Industrial Relations Journal*, 27:2, 143–54.

Donovan, T.N. (1968) *Royal Commission on Trade Unions and Employers' Associations 1965–1968* (Cmnd 3623), London, HMSO.

Eldridge, J., Cressey, P. and MacInnes, J. (1991) *Industrial Sociology and Economic Crisis*, London, Harvester Wheatsheaf.

Gallie, G., White, M., Cheng, Y. and Tomlinson, M. (1998) *Restructuring the Employment Relationship*, Oxford, Clarendon Press.

Geary, J.F. (1994) 'Task participation: employees' participation enabled or constrained?', *in* Sisson, K. (ed.), *Personnel Management: A comprehensive guide to theory and practice in Britain* (2nd edn), Oxford, Blackwell, pp. 634–61.

Guest, D., Peccei, R. and Thomas, A. (1993) 'The impact of employee involvement on organisational commitment and "them and us" attitudes', *Industrial Relations Journal*, 24:3, 191–200.

Hall, M. (1996) 'Beyond recognition? Employee representation and EU law', *Industrial Law Journal*, 25:1, 15–27.

Howard, M. (1991) Speech to the Department of Employment and CBI Conference on Employee Involvement, Monday 22 April, London.

Hyman, J. and Mason, B. (1995) *Managing Employee Involvement and Participation*, London, Sage.

IPM/IPA (1982) *Employee Involvement and Participation Code*, London, IPM.

IRS (1990) *Employee Participation in Europe*, EIRR Report No. 4, London, Industrial Relations Services.

IRS (1998a) 'An analysis of Article 13 EWC agreements', *European Industrial Relations Review 296*, London, Industrial Relations Services, September, 16–18.

IRS (1998b) 'EWCs are achieving new and effective forms of employee-interest representation', *IRS Employment Trends 669*, London, Industrial Relations Services, December, 2.

IRS (1999a) 'Article 6 agreements in focus', *European Industrial Relations Review 305*, London, Industrial Relations Services, June, 25–8.

IRS (1999b) 'UK draft EWCs legislation', *European Industrial Relations Review 307*, London, Industrial Relations Services, August, 28–9.

IRS (2000a) 'European Works Council update', *European Industrial Relations Review 316*, London, Industrial Relations Services, May, 20–2.

IRS (2000b) 'Commission issues EWCs report', *European Industrial Relations Review 317*, London, Industrial Relations Services, June, 19–22.

Kessler, S. and Bayliss, F. (1998) *Contemporary British Industrial Relations* (3rd edn), Basingstoke, Macmillan.

Marchington, M. (1980) *Responses to Participation at Work*, Farnborough, Gower.

Marchington, M. (1988) 'The four faces of employee consultation', *Personnel Management*, May, 44–7.

Marchington, M. (1992) *Managing the Team: A guide to successful employee involvement*, Oxford, Blackwell.

Marchington, M. (1994) 'The dynamics of joint consultation', *in* Sisson, K. (ed.), *Personnel Management: A comprehensive guide to theory and practice in Britain* (2nd edn), Oxford, Blackwell, pp. 662–93.

Marchington, M. (1995) 'Involvement and participation', *in* Storey, J. (ed.), *Human Resource Management: A critical text*, London, Routledge, pp. 280–305.

Marchington, M. and Wilkinson, A. (2000) 'Direct participation', *in* Bach, S. and Sisson, K. (eds), *Personnel Management: A comprehensive guide to theory and practice in Britain* (3rd edn), Oxford, Blackwell, pp. 340–64.

Marchington, M., Goodman, J., Wilkinson, A. and Ackers, P. (1992) *New Developments in Employee Involvement*, Employment Department Research Series No. 2, London, HMSO.

Marginson, P., Gilman, M., Jacobi, O. and Krieger, H. (1998) *Negotiating European Works Councils: An analysis of agreements under Article 13*, Report prepared for the European Foundation for the Improvement of Living and Working Conditions and the European Commission.

McCarthy, W.E.J. (ed.) (1972) *Trade Unions*, Harmondsworth, Penguin Books.

Millward, N., Bryson, A. and Forth, J. (2000) *All Change at Work?*, London, Routledge.

Millward, N., Stevens, M., Smart, D. and Hawes, W.R. (1992) *Workplace Industrial Relations in Transition: The ED/ESRC/PSI/ACAS surveys*, Aldershot, Dartmouth.

Pateman, C. (1970) *Participation and Democratic Theory*, Cambridge, Cambridge University Press.

Poole, M. (1975) *Workers' Participation in Industry*, London, Routledge & Kegan Paul.

Purcell, J. and Gray, A. (1986) 'Corporate personnel departments and the management of industrial relations: two case studies in ambiguity', *Journal of Management Studies*, 23:2, 205–23.

Purcell, J. and Sisson, K. (1983) 'Strategies and practice in the management of industrial relations', *in* Bain, G.S. (ed.), *Industrial Relations in Britain*, Oxford, Blackwell, pp. 95–120.

Ramsay, H. (1977) 'Cycles of control: worker participation in sociological and historical perspective', *Sociology*, 11:3, 481–506.

Salamon, M. (1992) *Industrial Relations: Theory and practice* (2nd edn), Hemel Hempstead, Prentice Hall.

Salamon, M. (2000) *Industrial Relations: Theory and practice* (4th edn), Harlow, Financial Times Prentice Hall.

Schuchman, A. (1957) *Co-determination, Labor's Middle Way in Germany*, Washington DC, Public Affairs Press.

Storey, J. (1992) *Developments in the Management of Human Resources*, Oxford, Blackwell.

Terry, M. (1999) 'Systems of collective employee representation in non-union forms in the UK', *Industrial Relations Journal*, 30:1, 16–30.

Thornhill, A., Lewis, P., Millmore, M. and Saunders, M. (2000) *Managing Change: A human resource strategy approach*, Harlow, Financial Times Prentice Hall.

Townley, B. (1994) 'Communicating with employees', *in* Sisson, K. (ed.), *Personnel Management: A comprehensive guide to theory and practice in Britain* (2nd edn), Oxford, Blackwell, pp. 595–633.

Wall, T.D. and Lischeron, J.A. (1977) *Worker Participation*, London, McGraw-Hill.

Walton, R.E. (1985) 'From control to commitment in the workplace', *Harvard Business Review*, 85:2, 77–84.

Wills, J. (1999) 'European Works Councils in British firms', *Human Resource Management Journal*, 9:4, 19–38.

# self-check Answers

**8.1** *Think of an organisational situation with which you have some familiarity.*
*What forms of employee participation, if any, exist in this organisation?*
*What authority promotes the existence of these forms of employee participation?*
*Evaluate the practice of these forms of employee participation using the dimensions of degree or depth, scope, level and form.*
*What practical problems exist in relation to the exercise of employee participation?*

Inevitably, the organisation you are thinking of is unlikely to be one with which we are familiar. However, in relation to the series of questions posed, you will be able, perhaps following some enquiry, to find out whether some form of participation exists at board level, or at a lower level related to joint regulation or collective bargaining of particular terms and conditions of employment. You will also be able to find out whether any form or forms of joint consultation exist within the organisation.

In relation to the authority that promotes any employee participation, you will be able to find out whether this is underpinned by legislation, or through prior trade union recognition and agreement within the organisation. The degree of participation will inform you about the extent of employees' influence in relation to organisational decision-making, and the scope of participation will provide you with information about which types of decision are subject to this influence. Consideration of the levels at which participation occurs within the organisation will allow you to understand how this works in practice, as will consideration of the forms that participation takes.

Using these dimensions to analyse and evaluate participation within an organisation should help you to consider what practical problems exist in its usage. These may, for example, relate to a sense that participation forms are somewhat remote and that they do not affect most employees' working lives. There may also be a management attitude that this is something that they are forced to engage in and which they seek to use for their own purpose. Alternatively, where participation exists in your organisation, you may have reached the conclusion that in overall terms it is accepted as part of the operation of the organisation and is valued by those engaged in or affected by its practice.

**8.2** *Think of an organisational situation with which you have some familiarity.*
*What forms of employee involvement, if any, exist in this organisation?*
*Who is responsible for promoting these forms of employee involvement?*
*Evaluate the practice of these forms of employee involvement.*
*What practical problems exist in relation to the exercise of employee involvement?*

Reference to Table 8.2 will have provided you with a checklist to use to identify the forms of employee involvement that exist within your organisational context. It may be interesting to identify the relative usage of involvement forms within this organisation, using the categorisation offered in Table 8.2. Involvement also includes, or is affected by, the nature of managerial actions and styles of leadership, and it may therefore be interesting to evaluate the extent to which the use of forms of involvement is congruent within the organisation.

It is likely that you will have identified that management is responsible for promoting employee involvement within the organisation. Hopefully, you will have been able to identify the levels of management at which specific forms of involvement are promoted. Again, recognising that involvement also includes, or is affected by, the nature of managerial actions and styles of leadership, it will be significant to recognise that, if involvement is to be engendered within an organisation, it will need to be promoted by all levels of management.

This recognition will hopefully help you to evaluate the practice of employee involvement within the organisation. You may have found it useful to use Tables 8.1 and 8.2 to evaluate employee involvement in your organisational context.

The comments above allude to possible practical problems arising from any attempt to promote employee involvement. Practical problems may arise in particular ways: for example, they may occur where the use of forms of communicative involvement is not reinforced by managerial actions within the organisation (see Table 8.2). There may also be a number of espoused aims for employee involvement within an organisation (see for example Table 8.1), although these may not be transferred into organisational practice, perhaps being 'crowded out' by other organisational imperatives related to cost pressures, resource allocation pressures and competition. Alternatively, employee involvement may be evaluated as a valuable component of organisational culture and the management of the employment relationship.

**8.3** *In relation to the organisational situation that you used for the self-check questions above:*
*What types of information are disclosed to employees and what types are disseminated?*
*What do you think is management's rationale for disseminating particular types of information?*
*Where employee consultation is evident in this organisation, how does this relate to the typology described above, and is there any evidence that the purpose of consultation has changed, or is changing?*

You are very likely to have found that the types of information that are disclosed to employees are related to those required by legislation. For example, this will include those related to business transfers, collective redundancies and health and safety matters. Those types of information that are disseminated to employees relate to a broader range of subjects about which management voluntarily wishes to inform the workforce. The rationale for disseminating such information is likely to be related to an educative, or re-educative, purpose designed to shape attitudes and expectations, and consequently to affect employee behaviour.

Your response to the third question in this series will also depend on the organisational context that you have used to explore and answer it. Hopefully, however, you will be able to relate the use of consultation in this context to Marchington's typology related to the non-union model, the marginal model, the competitive model and the adjunct model. You may also be able to recognise how the purpose of consultation is changing, or has changed, within this organisational context.

**8.4** *How would you analyse the position of EWCs in relation to the dimensions used to analyse employee participation and employee involvement, relating to degree or depth, scope, level and form?*

Degree of participation will be determined by the extent to which employee representatives are able to influence organisational decision-making. The purpose of EWCs is to receive information and to be consulted rather than to engage in negotiation. The extent to which EWCs may be able to influence decision-making will depend on the nature of the consultation process in practice, its timeliness, and the capabilities of those representing employee interests. Reform of the type requested by the ETUC may increase the degree of participation that EWCs permit in organisational decision-making. The potential scope for participation granted to EWCs appears to be extensive, although of course this will be limited by the nature of their engagement in decision-making. The Directive envisages that EWCs will be provided with information about substantial matters affecting employees' interests, including company performance and prospects, production and sales, investments, the employment situation, organisational changes, introduction of new working methods or production processes, production transfers, mergers, closures or cutbacks, and collective redundancies. Consultation may cover any of these aspects. However, consultation at the EWC level will be related to transnational corporate matters and will need to be underpinned by effective national level consultation, as well as by coordination between these levels. As EWCs work on the basis of an indirect, representational form of employee participation at a transnational level, there is also a danger that they will appear to be somewhat remote to most employees. This impression is likely to be reinforced by the relative low frequency of their meetings.

## CASE 8  Participation and involvement at The Grange Community School[1]

The Grange Community School is located on the eastern edge of Bristol, in Warmley. Its 885 pupils are drawn from the urban fringes of north-east Bristol, including Kingswood. The Grange is controlled by the South Gloucestershire Local Education Authority, and was threatened with closure in recent years. The Grange has a teaching staff of 58, who together with about 30 support staff are led by the headteacher, Steve Colledge.

Steve Colledge became headteacher at The Grange in early 2002, and the other members of its senior management team were also appointed to their posts during this year. These comprise a deputy headteacher, who is responsible for staffing, staff development and operational management issues, and two assistant heads, who are responsible for curriculum and teaching matters, and pupils and learning respectively. These other members of the senior management team were appointed to their posts from within the staff of the school. The fifth member of The Grange's senior management team, its director of resources, has responsibility for the support staff who work at the school.

Teaching at The Grange is organised into nine academic faculties. The assistant head for curriculum and teaching has line management responsibility for the nine heads of faculty. Within each faculty there are about six academic members of staff, together with faculty-based support staff such as technicians. Like many other secondary schools, The Grange also operates a house-based system for pupils, which is concerned principally with pastoral care. There are four such houses at The Grange, each run by a head of house, who is responsible to the assistant head for pupils and learning. The Grange also runs a sixth form, managed by a head, which offers a range of AS/A2 level subjects that cater for the 45 per cent of pupils who stay on at the school.

---

[1] The assistance of Steve Colledge in the preparation of this case is gratefully acknowledged.

Like all schools, The Grange is subject to a range of environmental influences and pressures that impact on the way it is managed and its scope for development. Central government continues to lay stress on improving standards in education. To this effect, the Department for Education and Skills generates a range of information, consultation documents and proposals for legislation. More locally, local education authorities have a range of concerns that are outlined in statutory obligations and an education development plan. Each school also has a governing body, which helps to shape its direction and provides a source of guidance and accountability for its management.

In addition, the main terms and conditions of employment of those who teach in the maintained schools sector in England and Wales are determined by the School Teachers' Review Body (STRB). This was established in 1991 to consider and report on the conditions of employment of school teachers in England and Wales. The establishment of this review body saw the ending of collective bargaining between the employers' body and trade unions in this sector of education. The STRB produced its eleventh report in 2002, which made a number of recommendations about the pay and career structure of classroom teachers, performance thresholds for progression onto the upper pay scale for teachers, the pay of heads, deputies and assistants, and other issues (Vineall, 2002). This report was presented to the Prime Minister and the Secretary of State for Education and Skills, who then decide whether to accept and implement each of the recommendations made. In arriving at its recommendations, the STRB consults with a range of organisations including the trade unions representing school teachers and head teachers.

Although the trade unions no longer engage in collective bargaining to determine the pay and conditions of those they represent, they are able to participate in more local-level discussions about conditions of employment through joint standing consultative committees at local education authority level.

The existence of these forms of intervention to determine conditions of employment affects the scope for and nature of employee participation and involvement in schools. Steve Colledge refers to this as 'working within someone else's set of rules'. The scope to reach a school-based agreement on particular issues is tempered by the existence of nationally determined conditions, such as those that affect the nature of teacher contracts. Nevertheless there is a need for the management of a school to offer leadership in respect of its development and an expectation by those involved that this will be offered. The senior management of a school will need to identify the expectations of government and the opportunities that these provide, and to identify how it should respond to specific government initiatives. This will include identifying what the school needs to do, what its targets will be, when these need to be met, and how to achieve them. This might include responding to the offer of government grants, applying to become a specialist school, or attaining progressive educational standards. There is also a need to recruit and retain high-quality staff, which requires a recruitment and retention strategy at a time of teacher shortages.

Within this framework of intervention and regulation there is scope for determined and effective leadership, and for employee involvement and participation, in the running of schools. At The Grange some degree of participation occurs through meetings that involve some negotiation about conditions within the school between

Steve Colledge and representatives of three teacher unions – the Association of Teachers and Lecturers (ATL), the National Union of Teachers (NUT), and the National Association of Schoolmasters Union of Women Teachers (NASUWT). Steve Colledge meets with union representatives on a regular basis to inform and consult them about developments in the school. He is willing to meet with them to present options about change and to talk these through before making a decision. Such discussions with the representatives of these teacher unions tend to occur around 'a single table', where they meet together with Steve Colledge, although there is also scope for individual discussion. There is also scope for the district representative of one or more of these teacher unions to visit the school to discuss aspects of the performance of the teaching contract, such as the level of cover required. Steve Colledge also meets with support staff, some of whom are members of Unison (see Chapter 5), to keep them informed and to consult with them as a group. In addition to these union-based forms of employee participation, there is also provision for some degree of employee participation through the election of two teachers and one member of the support staff employed at The Grange to its governing body. However, these staff governors do not sit as representatives of any trade union and are not expected to consult formally with the rest of the staff about the views of and decisions taken by the governing body.

An attempt is made to weave employee involvement into the management and operation of the school. The organisation of work in the school is based on the principle of a number of overlapping teams. These include the senior management team, faculty-based teams and house-based teams. At the faculty level within the school, the heads of faculty are seen as a key group to influence its effectiveness and development. Most heads of faculty are recent appointments and are sent on a range of training courses to become familiar with new educational initiatives. They hold faculty meetings of their staff every three weeks to discuss the work of their areas and to consider how to respond to new initiatives. Heads of house also hold team meetings at the school. Minutes from these meetings are circulated with the school. Meetings of the heads of faculty and the heads of house are also held, sometimes jointly, to consider initiatives and to evaluate progress. A member of the senior management team of the school attends these meetings. Meetings between the senior management team and these groups of heads are also held. More generally, meetings involving all academic staff in the school are held eight times a year. Support staff attend some of these meetings, with additional meetings being held specifically for this group.

The use of these types of meeting to seek to involve staff at a range of levels within the school requires a delicate balance to be reached in relation to the nature of its leadership. The senior management team of The Grange has attempted to develop a style of leadership where the resulting agenda is not seen to be dominated by it. There is nevertheless a need to offer leadership, particularly in relation to the options open to the school that arise from the external initiatives and challenges that affect its future. Members of the school's senior management team are allowed time within their schedule of work to meet with heads of faculty and of house to listen to and understand different points of view and to discuss matters. This also provides an opportunity to identify misconceptions and to discuss these.

The role of the senior management often involves understanding the direction of change, interpreting what this will mean for the way the school operates, and promoting involvement from staff to help to meet this need for change. Involvement is encouraged in this context by asking heads what they would like to do to meet a target rather than imposing a means to achieve this. There are also a growing number of 'toolkits' for faculties to use regarding the Key Stage 3 strategy, teaching and learning in the foundation subjects and the OFSTED model for self-evaluation. Discussion about such ideas leads to reflection and the possible modification of a proposal, and avoids the imposition of a strategy from above to bring about change. Steve Colledge also promotes the idea of sitting down with anyone who objects to a change, or who requires convincing, to discuss this with them. This consumes both time and energy but provides the opportunity to ask them whether they have seen the documentation that originated the need to consider change and how they would seek to approach this need.

### Questions

1 How does the context of the education system in the maintained schools sector affect the scope for and nature of employee participation?

2 How would you evaluate the nature of employee involvement at The Grange?

### Reference

Vineall, T. (2002) *School Teachers' Review Body: Eleventh Report 2002* (Cm 5353), Norwich, The Stationery Office Limited. Available through the website of the Office of Manpower Economics: <http://www.ome.uk.com/stp_review.cfm> (Crown copyright).

# Chapter 3

# The role of power, justice and culture in the regulation of the employment relationship

At the end of this chapter you should be able to:

- define the concept of power and analyse its use in organisations;

- explore the role of power in the regulation of the employment relationship;

- define the concept of organisational justice and analyse its significance in organisations;

- explore the role of justice in the regulation of the employment relationship;

- define the concept of culture and explain its importance to understanding the employment relationship;

- explore the role of culture in the regulation of the employment relationship.

## 3.1 Introduction

This chapter considers a range of concepts that are integral to the conduct of the employment relationship. These are *power*, *organisational justice* and *culture*. More traditional employee relations textbooks either have taken these three concepts for granted, or have virtually ignored them altogether. Related concepts to those in this chapter that have featured in some earlier texts are *equity* and *fairness*. Although these concepts undoubtedly reside at the centre of the employment relationship, they may be seen as lacking analytical precision and are sometimes used as little more than synonyms. Fairness lies at the heart of justice, and organisational justice theory may be seen as a development from earlier equity theory. Consideration of theories of organisational justice and power offer much greater analytical development and depth through which to explore the employment relationship. In relation to context, it has been usual to include at least one chapter in an employee relations textbook that examines a number of external contextual variables, related to economic, political, social and legal factors and perhaps others as well. This book includes such a chapter. However, it has been less usual to include an extended discussion related to the importance of organisational culture in particular.

This chapter is designed, or least intended, to cover these aspects. It seeks to examine the role of power, justice and culture in the regulation of the employment relationship. Power pervades this relationship, and, rather than implicitly refer to aspects of power, Section 3.2 reviews a range of approaches to and definitions of organisational power. This leads to a consideration of power relations in the employment relationship. The concept of organisational justice has led to the development of three overlapping theories that have been subject to a considerable level of research that relates to the employment relationship. The development of these theories provides a rich analytical framework to explore and to relate to the subject of this book in Section 3.3. Section 3.4 seeks to demonstrate how the culture of an organisation affects both the formulation and the use of power in organisations, and helps to shape perceptions about organisational treatment and justice. A case study is included, based on reported experiences in a real organisation, which explores the relationship between power, organisational justice and culture in the employment relationship.

## 3.2 The role of power in the regulation of the employment relationship

Power is an integral part of the employment relationship. R. Martin (1992: 2) wrote: 'Orthodox industrial relations scholars have recognized the central importance of power.' More recently, Rose (2001: 4) commented that 'the employment relationship is ... characterised by power relationships between employer and worker.' Yet in spite of such clear statements about the role and importance of power in the employment relationship, it has often been overlooked as a subject of discussion in many previously published employee relations textbooks (Kelly, 1998). Kirkbride (1992) refers to the concept of power often being used in a 'taken-for-granted' way in the employment relations literature. Nevertheless, as Townley (1994: 1) states: 'Whether explicitly acknowledged, or not, the experience of work is located in, and constituted by, power relations.'

### Attempting to define power and recognising its use in organisations

Our purpose here will therefore be to describe and discuss the principal ways in which power has been defined, and to consider, albeit succinctly, its use in organisations. This will allow us to develop a discussion about the nature of power relations in the employment relationship.

A frequent starting point in terms of defining power is the work of Weber (1978) and of Dahl (1957). Weber's definition of power stressed the ability of a person to get others to do what he or she wants, including acting against their will. Dahl's definition says that one person has power over another to the extent that this second person does something that he or she wouldn't do otherwise. These definitions of power may be seen as emphasising behavioural control, and they stress the notion of one person having 'power over' others (Lukes, 1986; Hardy and Clegg, 1996). Earlier work in the field of employee relations by Fox (1974) appears to recognise and follow this approach to power. Fox (1974: 14) wrote that: 'Power ... enables the few to minimise the discretion of the many in the making of decisions deemed by the few to be important for their purposes.' Fox goes on to state that the likely outcome of the use of such power will be to create employment relations that are characterised by distrust. The original use of this power will, according to Fox, be based on distrust and will in turn lead to the reciprocation of distrust by those who are subject to it.

However, the limitation of a person's discretion to act according to his or her own will (even where this is feasible) does not have to rely on the overt use or behavioural exercise of power. More subtle or covert forms of power may be used to limit discretion and action. Dahl's work, and that of other researchers on power in the 1950s and 1960s, focused on community-centred decision-making processes in the USA. It led to the finding that participation was open to all of those affected by such decisions. This is the ideal position of a fully participative democracy. Others recognised, however, that participation in decision-making processes might be restricted to particular groups in society. Similarly, the range of issues to be subject to participative decision-making processes might also be restricted. These issues were therefore likely to be restricted to matters that didn't threaten the position of those elite groups who already enjoyed a position of power. Schattschneider (1960) referred to this outcome as the *mobilisation of bias*. In this way, the issues and grievances of some groups will not be considered and will remain outside any formal decision-making processes. Schattschneider saw organisations as being based on the mobilisation of bias, with the outcome that participation either would not be allowed, or would be controlled, in respect of the issues of particular groups within an organisation.

Bachrach and Baratz (1962) identified what they labelled as a *second face of power*, based on Schattshneider's idea of the mobilisation of bias. For them the investigation of power needed to commence by seeking to understand the mobilisation of bias in an organisation. This could be done by analysing the dominant values and political procedures of the organisation, with a view to understanding which groups in the organisation benefited from the bias that would be revealed and which groups were disadvantaged by it. This second face of power is essentially a restrictive one, preventing or reducing the effective and meaningful participation of some groups in an organisation. In this sense the notion of what was called *non-decision-making* is at least as important as decision-making in terms of understanding the nature and dynamics of power in organisations. Those who control 'non-decision-making' can effectively maintain the status quo and the existing structures of power within an organisation.

In this way, those who control the ability of others to raise issues or grievances that would conflict with the status quo exercise power. This amounts to control over the organisational agenda and over those issues that may be debated openly or bargained over. Bachrach and Baratz (1970) refer to a number of strategies that those in power may use to achieve this control. A dissenting voice either may be prevented from being raised at all, or may be restricted to nothing more than a covert utterance, or if raised openly it may be checked from advancing to any organisational decision-making forum, or it may be rejected at such a stage.

Lukes (1974) argued that there is another dimension of power that is important to its understanding. The work of Dahl and that of Bachrach and Baratz, which Lukes respectively termed the *one-dimensional view* and *two-dimensional view* of power, both focus on 'actual behaviour' and 'actual, observable conflict' (Lukes, 1974:

21–2). Lukes recognised, however, that conflict is not necessary to exercise power and that power may be used to avoid the incidence of overt conflict. Indeed, the incidence of overt conflict and attempts to use power openly may actually indicate a position of weakness rather than one of strength:

> ... very often, it is not those groups which have most frequent recourse to overt use of coercion who have most power; frequent use of coercive sanctions indicates an insecure basis of power. (Giddens, 1968: 261, cited in Barker and Roberts, 1993: 197)

The more effective use of power will involve preventing this type of outcome. Power can thus be seen as a potential and latent capacity rather than something that needs to manifest itself openly, in order to exist. Lukes develops this idea in his suggestion that:

> ... is it not the supreme and most insidious exercise of power to prevent people, to whatever degree, from having grievances by shaping their perceptions, cognitions and preferences in such a way that they accept their role in the existing order of things, either because they see or imagine no alternative to it, or because they see it as natural and unchangeable, or because they value it as divinely ordained and beneficial. (1974: 24)

In this way, Lukes' *three-dimensional view of power* suggests that power may be used to alter or shape the views of those affected so that their 'real interests' are excluded or suppressed by those who exercise it (Lukes, 1974, 1986). Such an outcome would create a *hegemonic* effect (Clegg, 1989), where the interests of those who exercise power would be universally accepted by all, leading to a situation where this informed and shaped an organisation's culture.

The implications of this view of power have been criticised on the grounds not only that the identification of 'real interests' is highly problematic, but that these will be shaped by the conditions in which a person finds herself or himself. Thus, although some may consciously or unconsciously accept the values projected through the prevalence of power, this may also be seen as reflecting their best interests in such circumstances. However, even in this case there is scope to question whether such an acceptance is real or self-serving and how this affects behaviour as a consequence. In addition, there is scope to question whether those affected universally share perceptions about prevailing conditions. Such perceptions may vary, for example, between participants in different areas of an organisation, between women and men, between those in different occupational groups and so forth (e.g. see the discussion in Barker and Roberts, 1993). Where this type of fragmentation occurs, this is likely to prevent the development, or reduce the prevalence, of an ideological and cultural hegemony based on the existence of latent power.

This discussion points to the sociological relationship or dualism between structure and agency (e.g. Townley, 1994). *Structure* refers to the existence of factors such as the ownership and control of resources that help to determine people's attitudes, behaviour and the nature of power relations. *Agency* refers to the voluntary nature of human action based on will and the exercise of choice. Barker and Roberts (1993: 210) state that the 'debate over the theory of power (became) stuck in the gravitational pulls between individual action and social structure.' However, they use

Benton's (1981) work that considers how interests are identified and the nature of conflicts that arise in this process to develop this debate. Benton points out that people's interests in practice are unlikely to be straightforward and simple. These are likely to be characterised by conflicting identifications, loyalties and beliefs. The tension between structure and agency is therefore open to intervention. Those who exercise power have the scope to intervene actively to shape, for example, employees' perceptions about their interests. Power may therefore be exercised deliberately to shape perceptions of interests, attitudes and behaviour. Such a position appears to support the structural determination of 'interests' through the exercise of power, but also implicitly recognises the existence of human agency and the conflicts to which this can lead. Bachrach and Baratz (1970) identified a number of types of power that may be exercised, and these are shown in Box 3.1.

---

**Box 3.1  Types of power**

- *Force*. Power is exercised through ensuring an absence of choice, where those affected are aware of this action and its originator.

- *Manipulation*. Power is exercised through ensuring an absence of choice, where those affected are unaware of this action and its originator.

- *Coercion*. Power is exercised through the threat of sanctions in the case of non-compliance.

- *Influence*. Power is exercised without implying the use of threats.

- *Authority*. Power is exercised when one person recognises another's instruction as being based on some form of legitimacy and procedural reasonableness.

*Source*: Adapted from Bachrach and Baratz (1970)

---

So far, we have tended to define and use power in a negative way. The 'power terms' in Box 3.1 refer to a number of negative uses of power, related to the use of force, manipulation and coercion. These reinforce the notion of someone or something having 'power over' a person or a group, etc. Use of power in this way may be unrecognised, related say to Lukes' three-dimensional view, or may be more overtly exercised, related to the use of force or coercion and backed up by the threat or use of sanctions. These forms suggest the idea of a *zero-sum* approach to power, with winners and losers, where the interests of some (however determined) are supported over those of others (e.g. Mumby, 2001). This leads to notions of domination and potential resistance. In relation to the overt exercise of power in an organisational context, management would rely on a 'command–obedience relationship' (Lukes, 1986: 3). We recognised earlier that the use of more subtle forms of power, related to its conscious or unconscious acceptance, is likely to be more effective. One way in which power may be exercised and accepted is related to the final concept listed in Box 3.1. We therefore now consider the concept of authority and the notion of legitimate power in organisations.

Organisational strategy determines the purpose and goals of an organisation. To achieve this, an organisation will need to establish a formal organisational structure composed of a necessary range of roles and relationships including hierarchical ones. Those who hold positions of responsibility within such a structure are granted formal authority, which may be seen as a legitimised form of power. The intention is that their authority will be recognised and accepted by those with whom they interact, including those in subordinate positions (e.g. Morgan, 1997). This approach is linked to Talcott Parsons' concept of power as being a *system resource* (Lukes, 1986). The fulfilment of social or organisational goals requires and legitimises a situation whereby some people enter positions of authority over others in order to achieve these goals. In theory, this type of rational–legal authority will be limited to the formalised functions of a postholder in an organisational structure. It would not extend to power exercised in a more discretionary way. This approach essentially characterises the operation of organisations as bureaucracies, where work is conducted according to systems of rules. However, as we consider in the following subsection, managers may seek to exceed their authority by engaging in forms of discretionary power, while those subject to rules may also use these to gain control in relation to their job performance.

The exercise of authority and other organisational characteristics such as an organisation's structure and culture are therefore 'invariably saturated and imbued with power' (Hardy and Clegg, 1996: 629). This has not prevented strands of the literature viewing the exercise of power by management as being legitimate while seeing its use by others outside the formal organisation as illegitimate, reflecting a unitarist perspective as discussed in Chapter 1. Where a unitarist perspective prevails, the pursuit of goals other than those sanctioned by the organisation, as well as any conflict associated with these demands, will be seen as dysfunctional. In more critical strands of the literature this narrow approach to defining what is 'legitimate' power in organisations is seen as promoting only the interests of organisational elites and reinforcing the structural nature of power (see the discussion in Hardy and Clegg, 1996).

The work of Foucault provides an alternative and yet relevant approach for understanding the nature of power in organisations. Foucault saw power as pervading every social relationship rather than emanating from particular sources in a downward direction. Each individual is seen as a vehicle of power and as a result power should be viewed not just as a centralised entity but as something that circulates through all social networks (Foucault, 1980). Foucault's analytical emphasis is therefore placed on understanding *relationships of power* rather than seeing power as something that is possessed by a relative few and exercised over the remainder. In this way, 'power is relational: it is not a possession' (Townley, 1994: 7). This places emphasis on a micro-level of analysis, and on analysing the practices and techniques used in everyday life to understand the ways in which power relations affect our lives.

Foucault treated power and knowledge as interrelated concepts; hence what he terms *power/knowledge*. Put simply, power requires knowledge, and knowledge provides a basis for power. This leads to power potentially being seen as 'positive and creative, not just negative and repressive' (Townley, 1994: 8). This power/knowledge linkage led to his conceptualisation of *disciplinary power*: 'power is conceived of as a technique which achieves its strategic effect through its disciplinary character' (Clegg, 1989: 153). Foucault's analysis identified practices, or *disciplines*, that 'create both knowledge and power. Disciplines are techniques designed to observe, monitor, shape and control behaviour' (Townley, 1994: 5). A central theme related to this understanding is that of *surveillance*: 'Foucault sees the methods of surveillance and assessment of individuals, which were first developed in state institutions such as prisons, as effective tools developed for the orderly regimentation of others...' (Clegg, 1989: 153). According to this approach, disciplinary power provides a regulatory means of effective control that operates through various forms of surveillance at, and assessment of, work. This suggests the means to ensure behavioural compliance. Disciplinary power may even lead to the internalisation of surveillance behaviours where the subject obediently disciplines himself or herself (Clegg, 1989). This ultimately suggests some form of psychological compliance. This approach therefore appears to provide an alternative way to conceive of power, related to its diffuse, pervasive, potentially internalised and continually recreated nature, rather than something that is just centralised, external and essentially stable.

This brief discussion of several, often conflicting, theories of power has been intended to provide an overview of its nature and use in organisations. Although power remains a highly problematic and contested concept, this discussion has nevertheless illustrated that it is an important theme to seek to understand in terms of studying the employment relationship. We therefore turn to discuss the nature of power relations in the employment relationship, which will allow us to apply and consider further some of the ideas introduced above.

**3.1** Think of an organisational situation with which you have some familiarity. How does power manifest itself in this situation, and what types of power are exercised?

## Power relations in the employment relationship

Townley (1994: 13) states that the central issue in the employment relationship is 'the indeterminacy of contract, the naturally occurring space between expectation and deliverance of work'. Each employee or worker may be seen as representing a particular capability and a capacity to work. The realisation of these attributes is the objective of effective management. However, the nature of this capability and the extent of this capacity may be contestable areas for discussion and negotiation, and they indicate a forum for the exercise of power. Whereas managers will seek to formulate expectations and targets about work, individual employees will develop views about their willingness to conform to these expectations and to accede to forms of managerial control. They will also form perceptions about the nature and fairness of their organisational treatment. Edwards (1995: 13) states that: 'expectations about standards of performance have to be built up during the process of production.' These factors suggest the scope to exercise some level of discretion in the employment relationship. Employees will thus be able to exercise some control over the conduct of their work and the level of their effort in terms of what they do and how they do this. Whereas management will attempt to find ways in which to control the conduct of work, employees will also seek to exercise, or to find new ways of maintaining, some level of discretion.

In the previous section we referred to the distinction between *legitimate* and *illegitimate* forms of power. Authority conferred by holding a position in a formal organisation is seen as a legitimised form of power. Attempts by employees to exercise some discretion over the conduct of their work, or job controls, have been equated with the use of unauthorised or illegitimate power. This distinction also points to the incidence of *actual* power, as opposed to the exercise of formal authority. Past organisational research identified the basis (or bases) for the exercise of this type of power. Early research in this area found that groups of workers who possess particular technical knowledge or sets of competence that are not easily substitutable, and which are exercised in the context of high interdependence, where their role is central to the achievement of production, will be in a position to exercise such power (e.g. Thompson, 1956; Mechanic, 1962).

Power is also generated through the ability to exercise control in situations of uncertainty. For example, Crozier's famous study (1964) identified the maintenance workers in a French state-owned factory as holding power because of their ability to exercise control in relation to the production process. Given the bureaucratic systems in place in the organisation, machine breakdowns were the major remaining source of uncertainty relating to production. Based on the system of rules operating in this organisation, this gave these maintenance workers a position of considerable discretionary power over both production workers and production supervisors. These maintenance workers were able to defend their privileged position in relation to this particular task. Production supervisors were not able to check on maintenance or exercise control over these workers, given the nature of the organisation. Their central position in relation to resolving uncertainty in this system therefore gave them considerable power.

The development of the 'strategic contingencies theory of intra-organisational power' (Hickson *et al.*, 1971) recognised that uncertainty, substitutability and centrality were key variables affecting the nature of power in organisations (Mumby, 2001). Power will vary between organisational sub-units according to their relationship to these variables. The most powerful parts of an organisation will be those that are central to its working, whose work is not easily substitutable and least dependent on other parts, and which are best able to deal with factors that create uncertainty (e.g. Hardy and Clegg, 1996). Although these parts of an organisation may themselves be characterised by internal differences, strengths and weaknesses, these factors may nevertheless confer power on some who work within them in relation to those who work in other parts of an organisation. The nature of such power is likely to devolve on managers as much as, or perhaps more than, other types of workers.

A related theory of power is known as the *resource dependency theory*. This views the relative power of organisational sub-units and individuals as depending upon their possession and use of scarce resources. Many potential bases of power resources have been listed, and Hardy and Clegg (1996) comment that these are potentially infinite in the absence of the identification of possible contexts. Perhaps the best known is that of French and Raven (1959), who identify five that are common and important and which relate to influence on individuals. These are reward, coercive, legitimate, referent and expert power. We summarise these in Box 3.2.

As indicated in the discussion above, there are potentially numerous bases of power, including those that exert influence on organisational groups as well as on individuals. For example, Hardy and Clegg (1996) also refer to the power that derives from control over information and contacts with senior managers. Morgan (1997) includes in his list of power resources the formation and use of networks and interpersonal alliances. We have already referred to other bases, such as the ability to manage or exploit uncertainty.

| Box 3.2 | Bases of power |
| --- | --- |

- *Reward power*. Power based on the ability to reward, for example in relation to pay rises, whose strength increases with magnitude and expectation
- *Coercive power*. Power based on the ability to punish, for example in relation to dismissal, whose strength depends on the magnitude of the punishment and its likelihood
- *Legitimate power*. Power based on the internalisation of values that indicate the legitimate right of another person to influence a subject's behaviour and the obligation to accept this. This is the same as authority, discussed above
- *Referent power*. Power based on the identification of a person with another, or with a group leading to a desire to join or maintain membership
- *Expert power*. Power based on the knowledge of a person, or another's perception of this, in relation to a given area

*Source*: Adapted from French and Raven (1959)

However, although factors such as being best able to deal with uncertainty, low substitutability and centrality may confer a degree of labour power on some employees, other variables will affect its realisation. Most obviously, the incidence of product market competition and rising levels of unemployment will be likely to weaken the realisation of labour power. Even without such external environmental influences, employees may not be aware that they possess such power, or they may not have the motivation to attempt to use it. The recognition and realisation of power is likely to be related to the development of group cohesion and consciousness among employees, as we saw in relation to the case of the maintenance workers reported above (Kelly, 1998).

More fundamental than this perhaps is the fact that employees will have a number of interests in relation to their role as workers, and that although some of these may be seen to oppose those of their employers, others will not, requiring at least some form and level of cooperation. A number of different shared, or common, interests between employees and employers may be identified. These will include a shared interest in relation to the economic need to generate income from work. Given that performance standards need to be devised and revised during the process of production, some level of cooperation as opposed to simple compliance will also be necessary. In more general terms, Blyton and Turnbull (1998: 31) recognise that many people 'identify with and define themselves in relation to their work.' Work may therefore provide a form of intrinsic motivation, a means of identification and a sense of purpose.

Some interests will therefore be shared, or at least overlap, but the nature of the employment relationship will nevertheless be contradictory and antagonistic (Edwards, 1986, 1995). According to Edwards, it will be contradictory because management need to provide employees with some level of autonomy to be able to benefit from their creative capabilities, while at the same time exercising various forms of control over them. Antagonism will follow from the use of managerial strategies designed to optimise the generation of surplus value from employees' labour and minimise their discretion (Edwards, 1995). In overall terms, and on a day-to-day basis, cooperation between employers, or managers, and employees will be necessary to realise the interests of both, particularly in the face of uncertainty, although the actual conduct of the employment relationship is likely to be characterised by what Edwards (1986) terms *structured antagonism*.

In spite of the structured antagonism that underpins the employment relationship, shared or common interests and the need for cooperation will have implications for the identification and use of employees' discretionary power. The presence of interests that are common with those of employers, as well as the existence of employees' interests that conflict with one another, suggests that these will have a moderating effect on the use of discretionary power. It also suggests a situation of greater complexity in reality, compared with the rather notional scenario of conflict arising from the identifiable and distinct interests of employers on the one hand and employees on the other. This situation will also have implications for the use of power by employers and management. Given the messy scenario where the employment relationship is in practice characterised by the occurrence of forms of antagonism and conflict but where there is also a need to ensure some level of employee consent and cooperation, there will be an active need to seek the latter. Edwards (1995: 11) cites Alan Fox's (1966: 14) phrase that 'cooperation needs to be engineered.' We discuss the role of managerial strategies to exercise control and to seek cooperation further in Chapter 4. However, we conclude this part of our discussion by specifically discussing the nature of employers' power.

Employers will have some interests in common with those who work for them, as well as a measure of shared dependence where the parties in the relationship each provide something that the other cannot, but they will also have other interests that are clearly identifiable and discrete. Employers will possess power and exercise control as the owners of the assets of an organisation, or as their agents. Although the owners or agents of such assets may be equivocal about the nature and extent of power conferred in this way, ownership will be likely to focus and shape their beliefs and values, particularly in relation to any challenge to their sense of legitimacy and authority. Using the concept of power in an aggregated sense, there are frequent references in the literature to the balance of power between the parties involved in the employment relationship. Reference is sometimes made to the balance of power shifting between the parties involved depending on factors such as the level of employment or a willingness on the part of unionised employees to engage in industrial action. However, this type of analysis has been questioned because of the underlying asymmetry of power based on the ownership of organisational resources. Such asymmetry of power related to ownership leads to the dominance of organisational elites, whose power is either drawn directly from the ownership of these resources, or arises because of their relationship to those who own them.

In this way, Hardy and Clegg (1996) suggest that any focus on the *balance of power* within an organisation is likely to be related only to the superficial aspects of organisational politics rather than to its deeper foundations. One way in which employees have sought to counter this underlying asymmetry of power has been to form and join trade unions, and we consider the power resources of trade unions later in this book, particularly in relation to their relative decline over recent decades. This discussion is located in Chapter 5 and also in Chapter 6.

The studies and theories to which we have referred in this section indicate that power relations pervade employment relationships. It is not possible to reduce the role of power in these relationships to a simple prescription. Our discussion has instead been intended to convey something of the complexity of this issue, while attempting to provide a systematic review of the theories of power that have been developed. We shall explore aspects related to this discussion in subsequent chapters, although we now turn to discuss the role of justice in the regulation of the employment relationship.

<table>
<tr><td>

*self-check question*

</td><td>

**3.2** Think of an organisation with which you are familiar.

Which functional groups in this organisation appear to be able to use their knowledge or situation as a power resource over and above the authority formally granted to them? What are the particular bases of their power?

</td></tr>
</table>

## 3.3 The role of justice in the regulation of the employment relationship

Organisational justice theory (Greenberg, 1987) focuses on perceptions of fairness in organisations. It seeks to categorise and explain the views and feelings of employees about their own treatment and that of others within an organisation. Cropanzano and Greenberg (1997) point out that organisational justice theory is descriptive in nature. It does not seek to prescribe how justice may be achieved. Instead, it is concerned with understanding the subjectively held perceptions of employees that result from the outcomes of decisions taken in an organisation, the procedures and processes used to arrive at these decisions, and their implementation.

Organisational justice has developed to offer theories in relation to each of these issues. Employees' perceptions about the outcomes of decisions taken in an organisation and their responses to these form the basis of *distributive justice* (Homans, 1961; Leventhal, 1976). Perceptions about the fairness of the processes used to arrive at, and to implement, organisational decisions form the basis of two types of justice theory – *procedural justice* and *interactional justice* (e.g. Cropanzano and Greenberg, 1997). We consider each of these types of organisational justice in turn to understand their role in the regulation of the employment relationship.

### ■ Distributive justice

Organisational decisions affect the allocation of resources and the nature of outcomes in organisations. Distributive justice is concerned with perceptions of fairness about organisational allocations and outcomes. In this sense, the concept of distributive justice provides the basis of an analytical framework that can be used to understand the perceptions of those affected in relation to many different types of organisational allocation and outcome.

Perceptions about the fairness of organisational allocations and outcomes will be largely reactive in nature (Greenberg, 1987). Homans (1961) conceived of distributive justice as arising from the outcomes of a social exchange in relation to inputs previously made. Perceptions about fairness will be based on a subjective assessment of outcomes in relation to the costs incurred or investments made in an exchange. For example, others would see a promotion as fairer where they perceived this as recognition of the appointed person's experience, previous effort, achievement, and suitability for the intended role. Such an allocation would be likely to be seen as unfair where it arose simply as the result of favouritism.

Adams (1965) proposed that feelings of inequity would arise where the ratio of a person's outcomes in relation to their inputs from an exchange was perceived as disproportionate, as the result of a comparison with others. The significance of this comparison with others and the ways in which this may be formulated are discussed below. This theory allows for the recognition of positive and negative forms of inequity. Perceptions of unfairness may lead to positive inequity, where the person experiencing this state feels that others had a greater claim to a particular reward or outcome compared with himself or herself. It has been suggested that this may lead to the person feeling guilty. A person experiencing this state may undertake a revaluation of their contribution, to alleviate this feeling. This might lead them to think their contribution is worth more than they did so originally! On the other hand, perceptions of unfairness may lead to negative inequity, where those experiencing this reaction feel that they had a greater claim to a particular reward or outcome in relation to others who receive this benefit, leading to feelings of anger and possibly alienation. A number of potentially adverse behavioural reactions may follow from this perception, such as reduced job performance, embarking on the use of withdrawal behaviours such as absenteeism, and reduced cooperation (Folger and Cropanzano, 1998).

More generally, different allocations of resources or rewards between occupational groups may adversely affect perceptions of fairness in relation to their differential treatment. For example, there are likely to be negative perceptions about distributive justice where outcomes such as redundancies and increases in workload are seen to affect some groups of workers disproportionately in relation to others (Brockner, 1992). This type of scenario is likely to lead to perceptions of inequity and distributive injustice. It emphasises that distributive justice may be applied to situations where organisational outcomes, such as involuntary job losses or increased workload, are negative and where there is an issue about the distribution of such outcomes. Punishments or other negative outcomes for those adversely affected (such as disciplinary action or failure to achieve a performance-related pay rise) may also generate perceptions of unfairness and negative inequity, where these are perceived by the subject of the decision as unjust.

A key question relates to the causes of perceptions about distributive justice: what factors influence employees' perceptions about whether an outcome is seen as fair or unfair, and whether such perceptions are strongly or weakly felt? As we referred to earlier in relation to the development of distributive justice, perceptions will be largely based on comparisons with others (Adams, 1965; Greenberg, 1987; Cropanzano and Greenberg, 1997). In this way, perceptions about outcome fairness will not be simply related to an absolute measure, such as the more money or better treatment that a person receives, but will also be based on one or more social comparisons. These are termed *referent standards*. This raises a supplementary question about how referent standards are chosen. A number of bases of such standards have been advanced in the literature. An important basis is likely to be comparisons made with specific others working nearby. For example, an employee may seek to compare her or his treatment with co-workers by observing the way in which they are treated. This type of comparison is likely to be important in relation to the allocation of tasks and the setting of performance targets. This comparison may be more generalised so that the referential standard becomes an external group (Greenberg, 1987), allowing generalised comparisons to be made with those who work elsewhere, in relation to a person's occupational group or a similar type of organisation. This type of comparison may be important in terms of relative pay levels, leading to perceptions about external equity related to comparative levels of reward. More generally still, an employee may make a comparison with a broader social or societal norm or expectation.

The basis on which organisational decisions are made may also help to explain why employees see some organisational outcomes as unfair. A number of bases have been identified in the literature (Leventhal, 1976; Lerner, 1977; Greenberg, 1987; Cropanzano and Greenberg, 1997). These include allocations based on the principle of equity, where contribution is recognised and used to decide the nature of an allocation; equality, where an allocation is shared irrespective of contribution; and needs, where an allocation may be divided unequally based on greatest need. Many organisational decisions are ostensibly based on the principle of equity, although employees observing such allocations may perceive that published business-related criteria do not match their judgements about effective prior performance. This is likely to lead to perceptions of unfairness in relation to resulting outcomes. Where the principle of equity is used in situations requiring a high degree of group cohesion, the result is likely to be detrimental where any resulting unequal allocation of resources is felt to be unjustified by those affected (Deutsch, 1975; Greenberg, 1987). The use of the equity principle is also likely to lead to perceptions of unfairness where employees' economic needs to maintain organisational membership are threatened by an outcome such as selecting redundant staff only according to an organisation's pursuit of cost minimisation. This is particularly likely to be the case where some staff have a reduced need to work and are willing to leave voluntarily, provided that they receive a reasonable level of redundancy compensation (Brockner and Greenberg, 1990).

Organisational communication may play at least some role in helping to alleviate some negatively held perceptions about outcomes, by providing an explanation for the decision underpinning an outcome. This leads us to a consideration of procedural justice.

## ■ Procedural justice

Assessments of organisational justice depend not only on perceptions about the fairness of allocations and outcomes but also on perceptions about the procedures used to arrive at such decisions. Procedural justice is concerned with perceptions of fairness about the procedures and processes used to arrive at decisions. Since the conceptual development of procedural justice in the mid-1970s (e.g. Thibaut and

Walker, 1975; Leventhal, 1976), the importance of this concept for many aspects of human resource management has been recognised (Folger and Cropanzano, 1998). A key finding emerges from numerous studies conducted in different areas of decision-making that affect people in organisations: decisions based on procedures that are perceived as fair are more likely to be accepted by those they affect, than decisions arising from procedures that are not perceived as fair (Cropanzano and Greenberg, 1997). Genuinely fair procedures and processes are also likely to moderate the impact of negative reactions that arise from decisions leading to undesirable employee outcomes. For example, whereas the use of redundancies is likely to generate negative reactions, Brockner (1990) concluded that genuine procedures to help those being made redundant should help to generate a perception of fairness amongst those who remain in employment. This type of impact has been termed a *fair-process effect*, where perceptions about the fairness of the process help to promote an acceptance of the outcomes even where these have adverse implications (Folger *et al.*, 1979; Folger and Cropanzano, 1998).

Organisational studies designed to understand the dynamics of procedural justice have focused on the related concepts of *voice* (Folger, 1977) and *process control* (Thibaut and Walker, 1975). These concepts are linked to the scope for the subjects of organisational decision-making to participate in the process of arriving at, including being able to influence, the decisions that are made. Participation or voice allows those affected to exercise some degree of process control, or personal influence, in relation to the process of reaching a decision (Thibaut and Walker, 1975; Greenberg and Folger, 1983). The ability to exercise process control has been linked to a number of positive attitudinal and behavioural reactions. Davy *et al.* (1991) found that process control positively affects perceptions about fairness and job satisfaction, which in turn influence levels of commitment to the organisation and intention to stay. Other positive attitudinal and behavioural reactions have been reported in the literature arising from perceptions about procedural justice and the exercise of process control, including improved trust in management and some evidence for increased job performance (for a review of sources see Cropanzano and Greenberg, 1997).

Leventhal's (1976, 1980) work details other facets that have been found to promote procedural justice. These relate to the following list:

- the consistent application of organisational procedures between individuals and across an organisation;
- the avoidance of self-interest in the application of procedures;
- accuracy in their use based on reliable information;
- scope to evaluate the application of procedures and alter outcomes where necessary;
- allowing for the representation of differing interests during their use; and
- the adoption of ethical standards through their use.

Representation of differing interests during the application of organisational procedures is related to the concept of voice, although many of these other facets suggest a stage beyond the process of applying such procedures. These facets therefore point towards and suggest a link with the theory of interactional justice, which we discuss next (Folger and Cropanzano, 1998).

## ▒ Interactional justice

Perceptions about procedural justice, related to the way in which decisions are made, may be differentiated from justice considerations arising from their implementation. There are two principal aspects to this differentiation. The first of these relates to different stages of the process. Initially, perceptions about procedural justice will arise in relation to the scope for those who are likely to be affected by a decision to be able to exercise voice and to engage in some level of process control. Those affected may develop perceptions about whether the decision-making procedure is just or unjust, depending on whether they are able to exercise voice and whether this is seen to be effective. This perception may inform the way in which they continue to perceive the remainder of the process. However, perceptions of fairness developed at this stage may be altered by the subsequent implementation of the decisions that are made.

The second aspect of this differentiation therefore relates to the way in which decisions are applied in practice. Decision-makers may intend their decisions to be interpreted and applied in a particular way. However, those charged with applying decisions might interpret and implement them in a way that contravenes the original intention of the decision-makers. This may be related to a lack of clarity about what was intended, or because of other reasons such as contravention of Leventhal's (1976) principles relating to the avoidance of self-interest and the adoption of ethical standards on the part of the implementers. In reality, these principles are idealistic and even where broadly followed in practice are likely to lead to a range of interpretations. However, where principles such as consistency of treatment and post-implementation evaluation are not adequately applied, it may be that biased implementation leads to perceptions of unfairness and injustice.

Interactional justice (Bies and Moag, 1986) is thus concerned with perceptions about the fairness of the interpersonal treatment received by those affected during the implementation of decisions. This has been identified as being composed of two principal elements relating to the explanations and justification offered for decisions made, and the level of sensitivity of treatment of those affected during the implementation of decisions. Justification of organisational decisions through effective explanations has been found to produce an effect similar to that of process control: justification has been related positively to procedural fairness and, in turn, to intention to stay (Daly and Geyer, 1994). This may be explained through the finding that employees are more likely to accept a decision, even an unfavourable one, when given an adequate and genuine reason for it (Brockner *et al.*, 1990; Brockner and Wiesenfeld, 1993; Daly and Geyer, 1994). Similarly, the way in which people are treated during a period of implementation has also been found to affect their perceptions about the fairness of the process (Folger and Cropanzano, 1998). This suggests a clear role for line managers in relation to the development of their subordinates' perceptions about fairness. Part of this will involve communicating decisions, providing reasons for these, and consulting about their impact on the future nature of work with those affected in the area that they manage. The nature of the way in which affected employees are treated is therefore likely to have a significant impact on the perceptions that they form about the fairness not only of the process of implementation but also of the decisions that underpin this process.

*self-check question* **3.3** Think of a decision that has been taken in an organisational situation with which you have some familiarity, or indeed in another social situation of which you are aware. What were your reactions to this decision and to the way in which it was arrived at and carried out? Analyse these by using the three strands of organisational justice theory.

## 3.4 The role of culture within the employment relationship

Culture is one of the most widely written about concepts in management literature, typified by writers such as Handy (1993), Peters and Waterman (1995), Tayeb (1996) and Hofstede (2001). Messages relating to organisational culture from these and a vast range of other publications have been summarised as twofold by Hendry (1995): first, organisational culture matters, and the right culture can lead to improved performance; second, organisational culture is a tangible phenomenon, which can be managed and will impact upon all aspects of the organisation, including the management of the employment relationship. In addition, publications focusing on national cultures highlight the importance of understanding the implications of these for human resource practices in both multinational firms and uninational firms employing a multicultural workforce. Within this they argue that the national cultures within which an organisation is situated and from which its workforce are drawn will have a major influence on the organisation's culture. This implies that although it might be possible for an organisation to manage some aspects of its own culture and thus its impact upon the employment relationship, external influences such as national cultures will also have an impact.

In this section we have chosen to use Brown's (1998: 9) definition as the basis of our discussion:

> Organisational culture refers to the patterns of beliefs, values and learned ways of coping with experiences that have developed during the course of an organisation's history, and which tend to be manifested in its material arrangements and in the behaviours of its members.

This definition uses the term *culture* collectively to refer to more than a single set of beliefs and values within any one organisation. Through doing this the possibility of more than one culture coexisting within an organisation is acknowledged, as is the possibility of a multinational organisation having differing cultures in different countries owing to the influences of national cultures. By implication, this means that we have adopted a combination of J. Martin's (1992) differentiation and integration perspectives on the study of culture. These will be discussed as part of our consideration of frameworks for understanding cultures. Following this we shall consider typologies of culture and the implications of these for managing the employment relationship.

### ■ Frameworks for understanding cultures

Work by Schein (1992) and Hofstede (2001) emphasises that cultures manifest themselves in many ways. Some of these are visible and therefore relatively easy to discern when studying an organisation but, because of their shallow or superficial nature, the true meaning is difficult to decipher. These manifestations are Hofstede's *symbols*, *heroes* and *rituals* and Schein's *artefacts* (Figure 3.1). The deepest levels of culture (Hofstede's *values* and Schein's *basic underlying assumptions*) are invisible and, as a consequence, extremely difficult to discover. They provide what Argyris (1995: 21) terms the *theories in use* upon which the more visible practices or artefacts of culture are built. Hofstede (2001: 10) refers to these values as the *core* of culture. Such values are likely to have become so taken for granted that there would be little variation in them within a culture or subculture (Schein, 1992). They will be communicated to new members, thereby transferring the culture. If these basic underlying assumptions are strongly held then group members will find behaviour on any other premise inconceivable. For this reason employee relations practices that run counter to these underlying assumptions are unlikely to find support within the organisation. Similar considerations also need to be made in relation to national cultures. For example, different cultures attach different values to different types of reward and the extent to which reward should be individual or collective. Reflecting upon this, Schneider and Barsoux (1997) contrast the relative importance of financial and non-financial incentives between cultures. They compare the Swedish preference for time off with monetary rewards with Japan, where many employees take only half their 16-day holiday entitlement.

Between the deepest and shallowest levels Schein (1992) introduces *espoused values*. These are values connected with moral and ethical codes, and determine what people think ought to be done, rather than what they necessarily will do. Often organisations present a particular view of their culture through formal documents, such as annual reports, mission statements and speeches by senior managers. These predict much of the behaviour that is observed at the practice or artefact level, especially with regard to what people *say*, but they may conflict with what people *do* (Schein, 1992). In research we undertook in an English county council there appeared at first to be almost universal acceptance of management's desire to create a 'can do' culture, and the intention to improve its levels of public service. However, subsequent in-depth interviews revealed that those who felt they had been treated

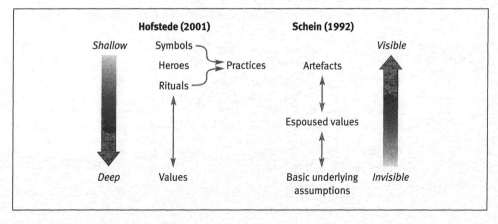

**Figure 3.1  A comparison of Hofstede's and Schein's representations of cultures**

©2000 Thornhill *et al.* Reproduced with permission

**The Management of Human Resources**

unjustly were only espousing the new culture, their behaviours reflecting their basic underlying cynicism about the new culture (Saunders *et al.*, 2002).

J. Martin (1992) identifies three perspectives for looking at organisations' cultures. These she termed *integration*, *differentiation* and *fragmentation*. The integration perspective implies that all members of an organisation share a common culture, and there is consensus regarding the beliefs held and the behaviours expected. This concept of one culture is easy to comprehend, but our discussion of the nature of power relationships between employees and managers earlier in this chapter suggests that it is unlikely to exist in its purest form. Although there may be some aspects of the way in which people in organisations behave and beliefs that are accepted by everyone, it is unlikely that all the beliefs and behaviours of those who exercise power will be universally accepted. Rather, employees and their representatives are likely to have different beliefs about some aspects of the employment relationship. Martin terms this perspective *cultural differentiation*, arguing that, for this, within-organisation manifestations of culture will be inconsistent. Only subcultures, perhaps formed round different work groups such as shopfloor workers and management, will exist with consensus being found within as opposed to between these groups. Martin's fragmentation perspective offers a further, if somewhat extreme, alternative to the other two. Within this researchers argue that they can detect very little cultural consensus in what they are studying other than around time-specific sensitive issues such as an imminent downsizing. Inevitably, these issues will change over time and, as a consequence, cultures are ambiguous and uncertain.

In reality, therefore, the idea of an integrated whole-organisational culture in which all members hold precisely the same beliefs is unlikely to occur in practice. Rather, organisations will exhibit only some organisation-wide cultural consensus and consistency. In addition there will be differentiation between groups of employees. Our research at the global nylon manufacturer Dupont's Gloucester site (Thornhill *et al.*, 2000) emphasises this, highlighting how some employees had embraced the 'trust culture' introduced by management as part of a change process. Although these employees were now taking responsibility for their own actions, others, in particular production workers, still believed that this was not part of their job. This example also emphasises that culture is not a static entity, but rather an organic process that is created, sustained and changed by people (Bate, 1995).

**self-check question**

**3.4** Think of an organisation with which you are familiar.

a What do you think are the main artefacts of its culture?

b Can you distinguish any subcultures within the organisation using different artefacts?

## Typologies of cultures and their implications for managing the employment relationship

Over the last 30 years a large number of typologies of both national and organisational cultures have been developed. These provide differing overviews of the variations that exist between cultures and some indication of the associated dimensions. Although these typologies are not applicable to all organisations or nations, they provide a series of idealised types through which to begin to understand aspects of cultures and subcultures and explore the implications of these for the employment relationship. To this end we begin by considering national cultures.

## The influence of national cultures

As we suggested earlier, one of the influences upon an organisation's culture is the national culture within which it is located. Within the literature, there is a long-standing discussion as to whether national cultural differences and their impact are declining or increasing. This is known as the *convergence–divergence debate*. Those favouring the convergence view argue that the rapidly increasing use of technology and the growing numbers of multinational organisations will result in a convergence of organisational configurations in terms of strategy, structure and management (Senior, 2002). As a consequence the impact of national cultures on organisational cultures will decline as organisations have no national allegiance, only an international common purpose (Ohmae, 1994). In contrast writers like Tayeb (1996) and Hofstede (2001) argue that, despite the growth in multinational organisations, between-country differences in language, religious beliefs, laws, political systems, education and the like will mean that their cultures will diverge. Consequently, organisations will need increasingly to be aware of differences in national cultures, their influence upon the organisation's culture or subcultures and the implications for the organisation's policies and procedures. Our discussion in Chapter 2 highlighted how advances in telecommunications technology were increasingly enabling organisations to locate work anywhere, thereby taking advantage of economic differences between countries. The management of such changes in the location of work also needs to take account of cultural differences between countries. These will influence both the culture of organisations operating within these countries and the employment relationship within these organisations. In addition an increasingly culturally diverse workforce within countries such as the UK further emphasises the need to understand the implications of national cultures for organisational employee relations practices.

The best-known work on national cultures has been undertaken by the Dutch academic Geert Hofstede, the most recent version being published in 2001. In this Hofstede focuses on the differences and similarities between national cultures using five dimensions based upon survey data drawn from employees of IBM worldwide, first in the 1960s and continuing through the next three decades. These are power distance, individualism/collectivism, masculinity/femininity, uncertainty avoidance and Confucian dynamism.

*Power distance* relates to the extent to which less powerful employees accept that power is distributed unequally. Thus within low power distance countries such as the UK, Sweden and Denmark, inequalities between people are likely to be minimised and consultative decision-making is likely to be used. In contrast, in high power distance countries such as Malaysia and the Philippines, inequalities are considered desirable and there are greater differentials between employers and senior managers in terms of pay and privileges.

*Individualism/collectivism* refers to the extent to which individuals are orientated to themselves and their immediate family rather than wider, strong, cohesive in-groups that offer protection in exchange for unquestioning loyalty. In high-individualism countries, such as the USA and the UK, contracts of employment are based on mutual advantage in which employer-provided training and good physical conditions are taken for granted and are hence relatively unimportant. For low-individualism countries, such as Pakistan and Indonesia, contracts with employers tend to be viewed in moral terms like a family relationship. Consequently, hiring and promotion decisions are more likely to take into account the employee's in-group. The provision of training, and the like, is less likely to occur, and where it does it is unlikely to be taken for granted.

The *masculinity/femininity* dimension refers to the extent to which assertiveness and decisiveness are prioritised over more caring values such as nurturing and concern for quality of life, Hofstede's label attributing these to specific genders. In 'masculine' countries, such as the UK and Italy, managers place greater emphasis on competition and high performance. Employment disputes tend to be resolved by conflict, and there is often a stronger ethos of living to work. In more 'feminine' countries, such as Sweden and the Netherlands, conflicts tend to be resolved by compromise and negotiation, and there is often an ethos of working to live.

*Uncertainty avoidance* relates to the extent to which people feel threatened by ambiguous or unknown situations. In low uncertainty avoidance countries, such as the UK and Hong Kong, there is greater tolerance of risk and ambiguous situations, and people are likely to be motivated by achievement and by esteem. For high uncertainty avoidance countries, such as Portugal and France, there is a fear of ambiguous situations, and people are more likely to be motivated by security and esteem.

Hofstede's final dimension, *Confucian dynamism*, captures the long- or short-term orientation of culture. Countries with a high long-term orientation, such as China and Japan, emphasise the adaptation of traditions to a modern context, are sparing with resources, and stress perseverance. In contrast, countries with a low long-term orientation, such as the USA and the UK, tend to have less respect for traditions, place lower emphasis on the importance of social and status obligations, approve conspicuous consumption, and demand quick results.

Table 3.1 notes the relative scores on Hofstede's dimensions of national culture for selected countries. Hofstede has emphasised that although his work, and that of others such as Laurent (1983), on upper and middle managers has focused on the nature of national cultures, these nations are largely a creation of the twentieth cen-

**Table 3.1 Relative scores on Hofstede's dimensions of national culture for selected countries**

| Country | Power distance | Individualism/ collectivism (high=individualism) | Masculinity/ femininity (high=masculinity) | Uncertainty avoidance | Confucian dynamism (high=long term) |
|---|---|---|---|---|---|
| Germany (West) | Low | High | High | Moderate | Moderate |
| Hong Kong | High | Low | Moderate | Low | High |
| Japan | Moderate | Moderate | High | High | High |
| Netherlands | Low | High | Low | Moderate | Moderate |
| Pakistan | Moderate | Low | Moderate | Moderate | Low |
| Sweden | Low | High | Low | Low | Moderate |
| Taiwan | Moderate | Low | Moderate | Moderate | High |
| UK | Low | High | High | Low | Low |
| USA | Low | High | High | Low | Low |

*Source*: Developed from Hofstede (2001)

tury. Indeed, within the past two decades, we have seen the dissolution of the Soviet Union and Yugoslavia into constituent countries and the reunification of Germany. Despite this, differences between countries in language, education and laws mean that national cultures are still powerful forces in shaping the patterns of beliefs, values and learned ways of coping with experiences for employees within organisations.

**self-check question** | **3.5** Examine Table 3.1. Use Hofstede's dimensions to suggest how the view of employee relations of a Japanese company setting up a manufacturing operation in the UK might differ from that of a potential UK workforce.

## The influence of organisational cultures

Our exploration of Hofstede's work on national cultures has further emphasised the importance of power and the way it is exercised for the management of the employment relationship. However, it has also highlighted the importance of other factors such as the importance of the way in which conflicts are resolved and justice is seen to be done. Alongside this it has also emphasised that the tolerance of employees of uncertainty, the focus on the individual or the collective, and whether the time orientation is over the shorter or longer term, are also likely to influence the way in which the employment relationship operates.

Structural views of organisational culture inevitably use structural artefacts or symbols as outward expressions of an organisation's culture. Of these, the most widely known and influential is probably Handy's (1993) typology. This was developed in the 1970s from work by Harrison (1972) and is concerned with how authority is exercised within an organisation and is the basis for power. These artefacts through which power is expressed can be used to help explore the likely cultural implications for managing the employment relationship. Handy proposes four main types of organisational culture: power, role, task and person. He argues that although these types do not have a high level of rigour, the differing power structures they encapsulate impact upon the way the organisation does things – in other words the organisation's ways of coping with experiences that have developed during the course of its history.

In a *power culture*, Handy argues, there is a single source of power from which rays of influence spread out. The internal organisation of power is highly dependent upon trust, empathy and personal communication for its effectiveness. Authority comes from the resources controlled and the leader's charisma. This means that the strength of the culture comes from the willingness of employees to defer to the leader and, presumably, accept her or his power. Within such a culture, Handy argues that employees are unlikely to be concerned about taking risks or issues of job security. In contrast, power in a *role culture* comes from the bureaucracy (rules and procedures) and the logic and rationality of the way functions/specialisms are organised. Position power and to a lesser extent expert power are therefore the main bases for authority, and such organisations attract employees who value security and predictability.

Power in a *task culture* is based upon employees' expertise rather than their charisma. This is likely to necessitate a different approach to managing the employment relationship, as flexibility and adaptability are valued, and authority is based

**The Management of Human Resources**

upon the employee's ability rather than their position or seniority until a crisis occurs. When this happens, such cultures can, Handy argues, quickly change into a power or role culture with rules or procedures or internal political influences becoming the dominant way of managing employees. Within Handy's fourth type, the *person culture*, power and authority lie within each of the individual members, and rules and procedures are of minimal importance. This, Handy argues, occurs in very few organisations and represents a group of people who decide that it is in their own interests to come together as a group rather than individually. Later work by Pheysey (1993) has linked task and person cultures in particular with processes of support and achievement used within organisations, thereby emphasising the importance of culture in motivating and controlling employees.

Work by Quinn and McGrath (1985) uses the nature of information exchange within organisations to distinguish between different organisational cultures. Within their typology the focus is on how things are done rather than the status that these processes give to both individuals and groups within the organisation. As part of their work, they argue that the manner in which these transactions are conducted (the artefact) is governed by a set of norms, which reflect the basic underlying assumptions within the organisation. From this they identified four generic cultures determined by these dominant beliefs: rational or *market* culture, ideological culture or *adhocracy*, consensual or *clan* culture, and the hierarchical culture – *hierarchy*. Although there is a concern about the nature and use of power within these, they also appear to have some parallel with Hofstede's individualism/collectivism and masculinity/femininity dimensions.

A *market culture* is directive and goal orientated, with individuals being judged according to their output and achievement. The 'boss' is firmly in charge of the organisation, and their competence is the basis of authority. Decisions are made decisively and compliance is guaranteed by employees' contracts. In contrast, within an *adhocracy* individuals are judged according to their intensity of effort rather than achievement. Authority in an adhocracy is maintained by charisma, and power comes from referring to organisational values. Decisions are taken intuitively.

Authority in the *clan culture* is based upon the informal status of organisation members. Decisions are made participatively, and employees comply because they have shared in the process by which these were reached. Individuals are evaluated in terms of the quality of relationships they enjoy with others and are expected to show loyalty to the organisation. In a *hierarchy culture* authority is vested in the rules, and those with technical knowledge exercise power. Decisions are made on the basis of factual analysis, and leaders are conservative. Compliance of employees is maintained by surveillance and control, and they are evaluated against formally agreed criteria. They are expected to value security. Thus the artefact of the nature of transactions within an organisation provides a means of helping to distinguish the underlying culture.

The typology of organisational culture of Deal and Kennedy (1982) is explained through artefacts related to the importance of the marketplace. They identify four generic cultures based upon the interaction of two marketplace factors: the degree of risk associated with companies' activities, and the speed at which company and employees receive feedback on their decisions and strategies (Figure 3.2). The latter factor, speed of feedback, can be argued to incorporate aspects of the short- or

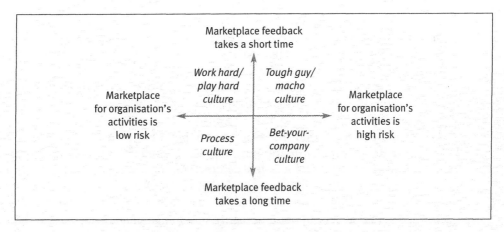

**Figure 3.2 Deal and Kennedy's typology of organisational culture**
*Source*: Developed from Deal and Kennedy (1982)

long-term orientation of the culture – Hofstede's Confucian dynamism dimension. Whilst Deal and Kennedy recognise that organisations will not fit into any one of their four cultures perfectly, they argue that this framework is useful in helping managers to identify their own organisation's culture(s).

Within *tough guy/macho cultures* the focus is on speed and the short term, which places enormous pressures on employees to take risks and get results quickly. As a result internal competition, tension and conflict are common, suggesting both masculine and individualist dimensions in which employees are unlikely to make a long-term commitment to the organisation. *Work hard/play hard cultures* also focus on short-term feedback for performance, but at the same time each individual action is unlikely to have high risks for the organisation as a whole.

*Bet-your-company cultures* are associated with risk, but feedback takes a long time. As a consequence decision-making tends to be top down, and there is a strong respect for authority, technical competence and cooperative working linking to power distance and uncertainty avoidance dimensions. The *process culture* is a low-risk and slow feedback culture, which operates well in a known predictable environment with employees receiving relatively little feedback on their work and memos and reports seemingly disappearing into a void. Those employees who remain in such organisations tend to be orderly, punctual and attentive to detail.

## Managing the employment relationship as cultural artefact

Organisational culture is therefore likely to influence and be reflected in the way that an organisation manages its employment relationship. This in turn will have been influenced by external factors including the national cultures within which it operates. Earlier in this section we defined an organisation's culture in terms of artefacts, espoused values and basic underlying assumptions. Artefacts as the most visible of these often have symbolic value for employees over and above their normal associations. Most of this book focuses upon the relationship between management and employees, but it is worth considering that the manifestations of this relationship can also be thought of as cultural artefacts.

Within an organisation, aspects of the way in which the employment relationship is managed are likely to have strong symbolic associations for employees. These may manifest themselves in particular procedures or policies, such as a partnership agreement between an organisation and a trade union (Chapter 6) or an avoidance of redundancy procedure (Chapter 12), but are likely to be based upon the underlying basic assumptions of that organisation. From these sources, individuals are likely to obtain the information that they need to understand how the employment relationship operates within the organisation and what forms of behaviour are acceptable and unacceptable. In addition, the way in which employee relations are managed may also provide a focus for identification or loyalty such as a bargaining group or perhaps a trade union with which they can identify.

Considering an organisation's culture in the way that we have in this chapter suggests that it is as an objective entity, and in particular 'something an organisation has' (Legge, 1994: 405), which manifests itself visibly in the organisation's features and behaviours, including its systems, procedures, policies and processes. In doing this we are considering culture as one of a number of variables that an organisation has, such as the set of psychological predispositions that employees possess that lead them to act in certain ways (Schein, 1992). This implies that culture is a distinct influencing variable that needs to be understood in managing the employment relationship.

## 3.5 Summary

- This chapter has examined the role of power, justice and culture in the regulation of the employment relationship.
- Power is a problematic concept to define, and yet the theories of power that have been advanced lead to a number of insights when applied to organisations and to the employment relationship. The employment contract, in its broadest sense, is one that is constructed through the course of the employment relationship and thus provides scope to act as a forum for the exercise of power. Power may be seen to pervade this relationship. There are potentially many bases of power, some of which are seen as legitimate, but there are also others that indicate 'actual power', which are generally labelled as illegitimate. However, the realisation and exercise of forms of labour power are likely to be moderated by a number of variables. These include the need to develop forms of cooperation in the employment relationship. The basis of employers' power may be seen to include interests that are clearly identifiable and discrete. References to the 'balance of power' between employers and employees, and shifts in this, are seen to be superficial, given the underlying asymmetry of power that exists because of structural factors that favour employing organisations.
- Organisational justice theory focuses on perceptions of fairness. It is concerned with understanding the subjectively held perceptions of employees that result from the outcomes of decisions taken in an organisation, the procedures and processes used to arrive at these decisions, and their implementation. Distributive justice is concerned with perceptions of fairness about organisational allocations and outcomes. Perceptions about fairness will be based on comparisons made with others. Perceptions of unfairness are likely to lead to adverse psychological and behavioural

reactions. Assessments of organisational justice also depend on perceptions about the procedures used to arrive at such decisions, or procedural justice. Decisions based on procedures that are perceived as fair are more likely to be accepted by those they affect, than decisions arising from procedures that are not perceived as fair. Genuinely fair procedures and processes are also likely to moderate the impact of negative reactions that arise from decisions leading to undesirable employee outcomes, leading to the notion of a 'fair process effect'. Finally justice considerations also arise from the implementation of organisational decisions. Interactional justice is composed of two principal elements relating to the explanations and justification offered for decisions made, and the level of sensitivity of treatment of those affected during the implementation of decisions.

- Organisational and national cultures will impact on the nature of the employment relationship. Strongly held beliefs and values will affect the nature of the employee relations policies and practices that are established in an organisation. However, there may be a distinction between espoused policies and the way in which these operate in practice. Organisational cultures are likely to be differentiated, with a range of subcultures existing in an organisation. These will impact on the nature and conduct of the employment relationship. The attributes of national cultures will also affect facets of the contract of employment and the employment relationship, although this is likely to occur in a way that is taken for granted by those within a particular culture. A number of organisation culture typologies have been outlined in order to consider the implications of each type for the nature and management of the employment relationship. Organisational culture will thus influence and be reflected in the way that an organisation manages the employment relationship.

## References

Adams, J.S. (1965) 'Inequity in social exchange', in Berkowitz, L. (ed.), Advances in Experimental Social Psychology Vol. 2, New York, Academic Press, pp. 267–99.

Argyris, C. (1995) 'Action science and organizational learning', Journal of Managerial Psychology, 10:6, 20–6.

Bachrach, P. and Baratz, M.S. (1962) 'Two faces of power', American Political Science Review, 56, 947–52.

Bachrach, P. and Baratz, M.S. (1970) Power and Poverty: Theory and practice, New York, Oxford University Press.

Barker, R. and Roberts, H. (1993) 'The uses of the concept of power', in Morgan, D. and Stanley, L. (eds), Debates in Sociology, Manchester, Manchester University Press, pp. 195–224.

Bate, P. (1995) Strategies for Cultural Change, Oxford, Butterworth-Heinemann.

Benton, T. (1981) 'Objective interests and the sociology of power', Sociology, 15, 161–84.

Bies, R.J. and Moag, J. (1986) 'Interactional justice: communication criteria of fairness', in Lewicki, R., Sheppard, B. and Bazerman, M. (eds), Research on Negotiation in Organizations Vol. 1, Greenwich, CT, JAI Press, pp. 43–55.

Blyton, P. and Turnbull, P. (1998) The Dynamics of Employee Relations (2nd edn), Basingstoke, Macmillan.

Brockner, J. (1990) 'Scope of justice in the workplace: how survivors react to co-worker lay-offs', Journal of Social Issues, 46:1, 95–106.

Brockner, J. (1992) 'Managing the effects of layoffs on survivors', California Management Review, Winter, 9–28.

Brockner, J. and Greenberg, J. (1990) 'The impact of layoffs on survivors: an organizational justice perspective', *in* Carroll, J.S. (ed.), *Applied Social Psychology and Organisational Settings*, Hillsdale, NJ, Lawrence Erlbaum Associates, pp. 45–75.

Brockner, J. and Wiesenfeld, B. (1993) 'Living on the edge (of social and organizational psychology): the effects of job layoffs on those who remain', *in* Murnighan, J.K. (ed.), *Social Psychology in Organizations*, Englewood Cliffs, NJ, Prentice Hall, pp. 119–40.

Brockner, J., DeWitt, R.L., Grover, S. and Reed, T. (1990) 'When it is especially important to explain why: factors affecting the relationship between managers' explanations of a layoff and survivors' reactions to the layoff', *Journal of Experimental Social Psychology*, 26, 389–407.

Brown, A. (1998) *Organisational Culture* (2nd edn), London, Financial Times Pitman Publishing.

Clegg, S.R. (1989) *Frameworks of Power*, London, Sage.

Cropanzano, R. and Greenberg, J. (1997) 'Progress in organizational justice: tunnelling through the maze', *in* Cooper, C.L. and Robertson, I.T. (eds), *International Review of Industrial and Organizational Psychology*, Vol. 12, Chichester, Wiley. *Reprinted in* Cooper, C.L. and Robertson, I.T. (eds) (2001), *Organisational Psychology and Development*, Chichester, Wiley, pp. 243–98.

Crozier, M. (1964) *The Bureaucratic Phenomenon*, Chicago, University of Chicago Press.

Dahl, R. (1957) 'The concept of power', *Behavioral Science*, 2, 201–15.

Daly, J.P. and Geyer, P.D. (1994) 'The role of fairness in implementing large-scale change: employee evaluations of process and outcome in seven facility relocations', *Journal of Organizational Behaviour*, 15, 623–38.

Davy, J.A., Kinicki, A.J. and Scheck, C.L. (1991) 'Developing and testing a model of survivor responses to layoffs', *Journal of Vocational Behaviour*, 38, 302–17.

Deal, T.E. and Kennedy, A.A. (1982) *Corporate Culture: The rites and rituals of corporate life*, Reading, MA, Addison-Wesley.

Deutsch, M. (1975) 'Equity, equality and need: what determines which value will be used as the basis for distributive justice?', *Journal of Social Issues*, 31:3, 137–49.

Edwards, P. (1986) *Conflict at Work*, Oxford, Blackwell.

Edwards, P. (1995) (ed.), *Industrial Relations Theory and Practice in Britain*, Oxford, Blackwell.

Folger, R. (1977) 'Distributive and procedural justice: combined impact of "voice" and improvement on experienced inequity', *Journal of Personality and Social Psychology*, 35, 108–19.

Folger, R. and Cropanzano, R. (1998) *Organizational Justice and Human Resource Management*, Thousand Oaks, CA, Sage.

Folger, R., Rosenfield, D., Grove, J. and Cockran, L. (1979) 'Effects of "voice" and peer opinions on responses to inequity', *Journal of Personality and Social Psychology*, 37, 2243–61.

Foucault, M. (1980) *Power/Knowledge: Selected Interviews and Other Writings 1972–1977*, New York, Pantheon.

Fox, A. (1966) *Industrial Sociology and Industrial Relations*, London, HMSO.

Fox, A. (1974) *Beyond Contract: Work, Power and Trust Relations*, London, Faber & Faber.

French, J.R.P. and Raven, B. (1959) 'The bases of social power', *in* Cartwright, D. (ed.), *Studies in Social Power*, Ann Arbor, MI, University of Michigan, pp. 150–67.

Giddens, A. (1968) 'Power in the recent writings of Talcott Parsons', *Sociology*, 2, 257–72.

Greenberg, J. (1987) 'A taxonomy of organizational justice theories', *Academy of Management Review*, 12:1, 9–22.

Greenberg, J. and Folger, R. (1983) 'Procedural justice, participation, and the fair process effect in groups and organizations', *in* Paulus, P.B. (ed.), *Basic Group Processes*, New York, Spinger-Verlag, pp. 235–56.

Handy, C. (1993) *Understanding Organisations*, London, Penguin.

Hardy, C. and Clegg, S.R. (1996) 'Some dare call it power', *in* Clegg, S.R., Hardy, C. and Nord, W.R. (eds), *Handbook of Organization Studies*, London, Sage, pp. 622–41.

Harrison, R. (1972) 'Understanding your organization's character', *Harvard Business Review*, 50: May–June, 119–28.

Hendry, C. (1995) *Human Resource Management: A strategic approach to employment*, Oxford, Butterworth-Heinemann.

Hickson, D.J., Hinings, C.A., Lee, C.A., Schneck, R.E. and Pennings, J.M. (1971) 'A strategic contingencies theory of intraorganizational power', *Administrative Science Quarterly*, 16:2, 216–29.

Hofstede, G. (2001) *Culture's Consequences: Comparing values, behaviours, institutions and organisations across nations*, Thousand Oaks, CA, Sage.

Homans, G.C. (1961) *Social Behavior: Its elementary forms*, New York, Harcourt Brace Jovanovich.

Kelly, J. (1998) *Rethinking Industrial Relations Mobilization, Collectivism and Long Waves*, London, Routledge LSE.

Kirkbride, P. (1992) 'Power', *in* Hartley, J. and Stephenson, G.M. (eds), *Employment Relations: The psychology of influence and control at work*, Oxford, Blackwell, pp. 67–88.

Laurent, A. (1983) 'The cultural diversity of Western conceptions of management', *International Studies of Management and Organization*, 13:1–2, 75–96.

Lerner, M.J. (1977) 'The justice motive: some hypotheses as to its origins and forms', *Journal of Personality*, 45, 1–52.

Leventhal, G.S. (1976) 'Fairness in social relationships', *in* Thibaut, J.W., Spence, J.T. and Carson, R.C. (eds), *Contemporary Topics in Social Psychology*, Morristown, NJ, General Learning Press, pp. 211–39.

Leventhal, G.S. (1980) 'What should be done with equity theory?', *in* Gergen, K.J., Greenberg, M.S. and Willis, R.H. (eds), *Social Exchanges: Advances in theory and research*, New York, Plenum, pp. 27–55.

Lukes, S. (1974) *Power: A radical view*, London, Macmillan.

Lukes, S. (1986) *Power*, New York, New York University Press.

Martin, J. (1992) *Cultures in Organizations: Three perspectives*, New York, Oxford University Press.

Martin, R. (1992) *Bargaining Power*, Aldershot, Gower.

Mechanic, D. (1962) 'Sources of power of lower participants in complex organizations', *Administrative Science Quarterly*, 7:3, 349–64.

Morgan, G. (1997) *Images of Organization*, Thousand Oaks, CA, Sage.

Mumby, D.K. (2001) 'Power and politics', *in* Jablin, F.M. and Putnam, L.L. (eds), *The New Handbook of Organizational Communication*, Thousand Oaks, CA, Sage, pp. 585–623.

Ohmae, K. (1994) *The Borderless World: Power and strategy in the interlinked economy*, London, HarperCollins.

Peters, T.J. and Waterman, R.H. (1995) *In Search of Excellence*, London, HarperCollins.

Pheysey, D.C. (1993) *Organizational Cultures: Types and transformations*, London, Routledge.

Quinn, R.E. and McGrath, M.R. (1985) 'The transformation of organizational cultures: a competing values perspective', *in* Frost, P.J., Moore, L.F., Louis, M.R., Lundberg C.C. and Martin, J. (eds), *Organizational Culture*, Beverly Hills, CA, Sage, pp. 315–34.

Rose, E. (2001) *Employment Relations*, Harlow, Financial Times Prentice Hall.

Saunders, M.N.K., Thornhill, A. and Lewis, P. (2002) 'Understanding employees' reactions to the management of change: an exploration through an organisational justice framework', *Irish Journal of Management*, 23:1, 85–108.

Schattschneider, E.E. (1960) *The Semi-Sovereign People*, New York, Holt, Rinehart and Winston.

Schein, E.H. (1992) *Organizational Culture and Leadership* (2nd edn), San Francisco, Jossey-Bass.

Schneider, S.C. and Barsoux, J.L. (1997) *Managing Across Cultures*, London, Prentice Hall.

Senior, B. (2002) *Organisational Change* (2nd edn), Harlow, Financial Times Prentice Hall.

Tayeb, M.H. (1996) *The Management of a Multicultural Workforce*, Chichester, Wiley.

Thibaut, J. and Walker, L. (1975) *Procedural Justice*, Hillsdale, NJ, Erlbaum.

**The Management of Human Resources**

Thompson, J.D. (1956) 'Authority and power in identical organizations', *American Journal of Sociology*, 62, 290–301.

Thornhill, A., Lewis, P., Millmore, M. and Saunders, M.N.K. (2000) *Managing Change: A human resource strategy approach*, Harlow, Financial Times Prentice Hall.

Townley, B. (1994) *Reframing Human Resource Management: Power, ethics and subjects at work*, London, Sage.

Weber, M. (1978) *Economy and Society: An outline of interpretive sociology* (ed. Roth, G. and Wittich, C.), Berkeley, CA, University of California Press.

## *self-check* Answers

**3.1** *Think of an organisational situation with which you have some familiarity. How does power manifest itself in this situation, and what types of power are exercised?*

Inevitably the organisation you are thinking of is unlikely to be one with which we are familiar. However, you will be likely to have considered the manifestation of power within this organisational context along one or more dimensions. Following the discussion in the chapter you will probably have evaluated the way in which power is exercised over others and the extent to which the organisation is participative (democratic) or non-participative (authoritarian). Where the organisation appears to be more participative you may have considered the scope of that participation. Which issues are open to decision-making and which are in the realm of 'non-decision-making'? You may have also considered the extent to which conflict is present or absent, the nature of any conflict, and the reasons for this. To what extent is power used overtly or covertly? The use of power may of course vary within the organisation and between different participants in similar roles.

Your conclusions about the way in which power manifests itself within this organisational setting will be linked to the types of power that are used. You may have found it useful to draw on the types listed in Box 3.1. However, you may have also developed the depth of your analysis by thinking about the practices and techniques used in this setting that demonstrate the exercise of power. This may have also led you to think about the difference between power that is accepted as legitimate and that which is seen as discretionary or personal.

There are a number of ways to respond to this question, and the main point perhaps is to start to relate the analysis in the chapter to an organisational setting with which you have some familiarity, to test these ideas.

**3.2** *Think of an organisation with which you are familiar.*

*Which functional groups in this organisation appear to be able to use their knowledge or situation as a power resource over and above the authority formally granted to them? What are the particular bases of their power?*

This question will again require you to conduct an analysis that is specific to an organisation known to yourself. Your answer will therefore be specific to this context. However, you will be likely to have drawn on a number of the concepts briefly outlined and discussed in the chapter. These are likely to include the following:

- the nature of the technical knowledge of the group or groups that you have identified;
- their central role in the organisational system;

- the difficulty of finding an alternative way of conducting the work that they undertake (which may be due to technical or political reasons); and
- their ability to deal with uncertainty, or perhaps their ability to create it.

You may have also drawn on other bases of power to recognise the power resources of the functional group or groups that you have analysed.

**3.3** *Think of a decision that has been taken in an organisational situation with which you have some familiarity, or indeed in another social situation of which you are aware. What were your reactions to this decision and to the way in which it was arrived at and carried out? Analyse these by using the three strands of organisational justice theory.*

Your reactions to this decision and the processes of making and implementing it may be broadly positive or negative, or may reflect a shift between these two types of reaction. Organisational justice theory allows you to analyse your reactions by examining these in relation to the outcomes of the decision that was taken in the organisation, the procedures and processes used to arrive at this decision, and its implementation. Your feelings may therefore be positive or negative in relation to all three aspects, or they may reflect different reactions in relation to each aspect. For example, the decision may have initially led you to react negatively, but knowledge about the procedure used to arrive at this may have helped to moderate your view. Alternatively, the decision-making procedure may have appeared fair, but the way in which the decision was implemented may have led you to feel negative. These are just examples of how you may have reacted. The value of organisational justice theory is that it provides a fairly simple but effective means of understanding reactions. As such it is a useful tool to explore and understand employees' reactions in the employment relationship.

**3.4** *Think of an organisation with which you are familiar.*

**a** *What do you think are the main artefacts of its culture?*
**b** *Can you distinguish any subcultures within the organisation using different artefacts?*

Inevitably the organisation you are thinking of is unlikely to be one with which we are familiar. However, the following discussion of a small sample of a university's cultural artefacts may give some clues to the nature of your answer.

**a** Within the university, the main artefacts of the culture include the learning centre (library), and the lack of any reserved car parking spaces. The naming of the library as a 'learning centre' is a strong symbol of the importance of learning within the university; the lack of reserved car parking spaces is a symbol of the egalitarian nature of the culture. Other artefacts, which are perhaps less visible, include written documents such as the student charter (explaining amongst other things students' rights to high-quality teaching), the ethical code, and the plagiarism policy. The former of these again emphasises the learning culture within the organisation, and the latter two point to the university's ethical beliefs of not causing harm to others and fairness.

**b** Different subcultures also exist within the university between, for example, academic and support staff as well as between different departments. Academic and support staff are, for example, represented by different trade unions (NATFHE and Unison respectively) and have different conditions of service. Some departments focus predominantly on undergraduate teaching whereas others, such as the Business School, deliver courses to both undergraduate and postgraduate students.

**The Management of Human Resources**
527

**3.5** *Examine Table 3.1. Use Hofstede's dimensions to suggest how the view of employee relations of a Japanese company setting up a manufacturing operation in the UK might differ from that of a potential UK workforce.*

The UK scores lower on the power distance dimension than Japan. According to Hofstede, this suggests that potential UK employees will be less likely than Japanese employees to accept uneven distributions of power within the workplace and will expect more consultative decision-making. Potential UK employees are also less likely to be happy with large pay and reward differentials than Japanese employees.

Hofstede's research suggests that UK employees are likely to be more individualistic than Japanese employees. This suggests that the potential UK employees are more likely to view their contract of employment from an individual perspective of their own exchange relationship with the organisation.

Both UK and Japanese employees are likely to place emphasis on performance at work, both having scored towards the masculine on Hofstede's masculinity/femininity dimension. This means there are less likely to be differences in the view of employee relations in this area.

However, Hofstede's work highlights the fact that UK and Japanese employees differ markedly on uncertainty avoidance. This suggests that potential UK employees are likely to have a lower level of uncertainty avoidance, and implies that they are less likely to be motivated by long-term job security. This means that the reward package developed is likely to differ from that which would be developed for Japanese employees.

Finally, Hofstede's work highlights the fact that Japanese employees are likely to have a longer-term view than their UK employees. This may be reflected in the focus on longer-term targets rather than quick results more normally expected in UK organisations.

---

**CASE 3** | **Power, justice and culture in Publicservice.org[1]**

Publicservice.org exists to provide a specific range of services in a given geographical area, and obtains most of its funding from the state. The nature of these services is not particularly important in relation to the purpose of the case study. One aspect of organisational context that is important is the role of government in terms of establishing initiatives that need to be implemented and targets to be achieved, and as a source of funding.

Employees point to an increasing number of government initiatives and related priorities that affect them. They are also aware of the implications of this governmental intervention in relation to the services that they provide and the expectations that are associated with this. Some employees commented that it was increasingly difficult to sustain the effort that was required to cope with the initiatives that were being introduced. One employee stated, 'I feel that there is a loss of professional control; we are expected to do more and more but it is increasingly difficult to cope even where you give up your own time.' Another thought that the organisation had become increasingly reactive in its planning as it sought to introduce new initiatives. One

[1] The organisation and the people working within it are fictional.

**The Management of Human Resources**

employee felt that there was a danger of creating additional bureaucracy to cope with these initiatives. Another believed that the organisation's decision-making and policies were increasingly being skewed by the need to respond to these central government initiatives, not least because the attainment of additional resources was tied to the achievement of centrally determined standards. This person also commented that important information for the implementation of the initiatives with which they were involved was centrally devised and often took a considerable period of time to arrive. As a result of these changes, several employees felt that the level of resources available and the demands made upon them were becoming an acute issue. Those in areas where new initiatives were being implemented indicated in particular that the workload associated with this often resulted in staff feeling anxiety and stress.

Employees often recognised that the 'difficulties' the organisation faced and the stress evident within it were caused by a lack of resources and the advent of government initiatives that were outside management's control, but many nevertheless felt that management was rather remote. One person commented that 'Management sometimes appear to have little idea about what is really going on.' This belief broadly typified that of several others. Higher tiers of management were referred to as being 'remote', 'distant', 'unaware' and 'rarely seen'. An employee commented that, 'They don't really understand the work, the pressures, and the diversity needed.' Many felt that management didn't reciprocate the level of commitment to staff that employees were offering to the organisation to help to fulfil its goals related to service.

Although management was felt to be 'remote' and 'distant', they were nevertheless praised by many for their attempts at top-down communication. However, some commented that, although top-down communication had improved over the recent past, there was insufficient attempt to promote 'pathways of communication from the bottom up'. One commented that management was engaging in 'rhetoric'; others said that they wished to feel more involved and to receive more support. Another stated that 'management are good at "talking the talk", but I'd like to see them "walking the talk" much more; coming to find out how they can help us and how we can help the organisation.' In spite of these comments about the role of management in general, which generally referred to more senior managers, many stated that their line managers were very supportive in terms of helping them to cope with the changes that were introduced as well as with their high workloads.

Management was seen as being driven by external forces, and many employees perceived that organisational planning was restricted to the organisation's most senior managers. One commented that 'the corporate plan is the product of the senior management team'. This led to a feeling that while 'some policies appear to be well worked through, others seem pretty unrealistic and baffling in terms of the decisions made and their practical effects.' An employee summed up the views of several with the comment that 'little notice is taken of front line staff when decisions are taken.' This often led to other comments associated with frustration and even anger. One person said, 'Decisions are taken without much thought for the effect that these will have on people at the sharp end of delivery. These are often associated with a message such as, you are the expert, you need to deal with this....' Another commented that 'decisions are taken that affect my work but no

▶

**The Management of Human Resources**

one bothers to talk to me about this before the decision is taken. This has happened a couple of times and I feel quite demoralised about it.'

This situation was associated with reports that rumours frequently circulated about future plans and decisions. In this sense, the attempts that were being made to cascade communication from the top and throughout the organisation were strongly welcomed by most employees. However, these attempts were associated with problems. Those who worked in facilities that were physically distant from the central location of the organisation, as well as many who worked in departments where services were delivered, complained that they often did not receive the same level of communication about organisational developments as those who worked 'in the centre'. Many commented that they were so busy that they had little time to search available internal media to obtain news about the organisation. In particular the organisation had recently established an intranet, which was used to convey a wide range of information to employees who had access to a personal computer.

There was a general feeling that employees would value the opportunity for face-to-face consultation to a far greater extent than was apparent in the organisation. Many also felt that there was scope for more local decision-making. One person commented that 'I rarely feel that my experience and feelings as a practitioner are taken into account in relation to the decisions that affect our work, but with so many government targets and political issues, I wonder if that will ever be possible?'

## Questions

1 How would you analyse the nature of power relations in Publicservice.org?

2 How may the three facets of organisational justice theory be applied to the case study organisation to help to analyse the perceptions of employees?

3 How would you characterise the organisational culture of Publicservice.org?

## Chapter 5

# The role of trade unions and employers' associations in regulating the employment relationship

At the end of this chapter you should be able to:

- define the purpose of trade unions and employers' associations and analyse their roles and functions;

- analyse the changing structure and nature of trade unionism;

- analyse recent trends in trade union membership and recognition, and consider the implications of these for the future unionisation of the workforce;

- evaluate the promotion of partnership in the workplace;

- analyse the role and activities of union officials and workplace representatives, including those engaged on health and safety duties.

## 5.1 Introduction

This chapter commences by exploring the purpose and functions of trade unions, in Sections 5.2 and 5.3. It then seeks to explain the structure of trade unionism and the way in which this is changing in Section 5.4, exploring some of the implications that have arisen from the nature of trade unionism in Britain. These implications relate to mergers between unions, multi-unionism in the workplace, the emergence of a small number of proportionately large unions, the development of single union agreements, and single table bargaining. Section 5.5 discusses the role and functions of the Trades Union Congress in Britain and of the European Trade Union Confederation. Section 5.6 defines the nature of employers' associations in Britain, discusses their changing functions, and describes the role of the Union of Industrial and Employers' Confederations of Europe.

Recent trends relating to trade union membership and recognition are examined in Section 5.7. This section explores employers' attitudes to unionisation, the advent of union derecognition in the 1980s and 1990s, and the ways in which unions responded to declining levels of union membership and recognition through this period. This establishes the context for discussion of the introduction of the statutory recognition of trade unions in 2000, and this section discusses the initial impact of this change. Section 5.8 explores the nature of partnership approaches in the work-

**The Management of Human Resources**

**531**

place and the impact that this may have on union membership and recognition. The case study at the end of this chapter, based on the TUC Partnership Institute, permits this approach to be explored in greater detail. Sections 5.9 and 5.10 describe the role of trade union officials and workplace representatives, and the involvement of union representation in health and safety committees. This final section also briefly outlines the nature and functions of the Health and Safety Commission and Health and Safety Executive.

## 5.2 Defining the purpose of trade unions

You may have asked yourself the following questions. How relevant are trade unions in the early twenty-first century? More particularly, what are they for? If you have had similar thoughts to these, you will not have been alone. The role of trade unions has always been subject to question, and they have often operated in an environment characterised by at least some degree of hostility. The work of Allan Flanders, an important theorist of industrial relations, helps us to understand the nature of reactions to trade unions over a long time span. In 1961, Flanders wrote that,

> Increasingly the unions are accused of being out of date, of clinging to restrictive practices that have outlived their usefulness, of failing to adapt their organisation to present needs, of being ... unresponsive to the challenges that contemporary society presents. (1975: 13)

These comments were related to the context of that time, but they may resonate in the current period in relation to calls for employment modernisation and greater flexibility. In 1968, Flanders asked the question, 'What are trade unions for?' (Flanders, 1975: 38–47). His response is still highly relevant today in helping us to answer this question and, in so doing, to define, and understand the purpose of, trade unions.

Flanders believed that the primary responsibility of a trade union was to protect the welfare of its members. Its membership will have come together in the union because they will have recognised some level of common interest. The union offers a means to identify and give voice to such common interests, and to require some level of collective discipline and action to protect or pursue them. In conventional terms this means defending and where possible improving the terms and conditions of employment of the union's membership. In even more concrete terms, Flanders wrote that unions 'are out to raise wages, to shorten hours, and to make working conditions safer, healthier and better in many other respects' (1975: 41). In seeking to achieve these outcomes, their purpose is sectional, which means that they promote 'the interests of the section of the population they happen to organise' (Flanders, 1975: 41). In doing so, the purpose of trade unions is to engage in the regulation of the employment relationship. For Flanders,

> The constant underlying social purpose of trade unionism is participation in job regulation. But participation is not an end in itself, it is the means of enabling workers to gain more control over their working lives. (1975: 42)

Much of this analysis reflects the earlier definition of trade unions by the labour movement historians Sidney and Beatrice Webb. The Webbs defined a trade union as 'a continuous association of wage earners for the purpose of maintaining or improving the conditions of their working lives' (1920, cited in Clegg, 1979: 182). The idea of being a continuous association indicates a state of permanence. Flanders recognised that, for this to be the case, trade unions also needed to be dynamic organisations. In order to be dynamic, trade unions require an active core of membership, for many who are members of a union do not take an active part in their affairs. Trade unions are also affected by the environment within which they operate. Many trade unions have developed to become numerically large before losing the bulk of their membership through commercial, industrial or technological events. A current example of this in the UK is the National Union of Mineworkers. Many unions in the past, faced with a diminishing level of membership, have sought a defensive merger with another, more numerically strong union. We shall return to some of the implications of this later in the chapter.

Acts of Parliament since the nineteenth century have sought to define the purpose of trade unions. The current definition is contained in the Trade Union and Labour Relations (Consolidation) Act 1992. Section 1 of this Act defines a trade union as an organisation, whether temporary or permanent, that consists wholly or mainly of workers whose main purpose is the regulation of relations between these workers and employers or employers' associations. The law goes further in terms of identifying those organisations that may legally call themselves trade unions. In order to be recognised legally in the UK, the Certification Officer must officially list a trade union. Many statutory rights for trade unions, their officials and members are available only to unions certified as being independent. A trade union will be able to obtain a Certificate of Independence from the Certification Officer only if it is able to demonstrate that it is not under the control, or financial influence, of any employer. The Certification Officer is appointed by the Secretary of State for Trade and Industry. Box 5.1 briefly describes the functions of this official.

However, even a legal definition does not fully represent the complex nature of what trade unions are for and how they function in practice. Blackburn and Prandy (1965: 119) recognised that 'trade unionism is not an "all or nothing" quality, but one which can exist in varying degree.' They developed the concept of *unionateness*

---

**Box 5.1    Functions of the Certification Officer**

The home page of the website of the Certification Officer says that this statutory official is responsible for:

- keeping lists of trade unions and employers' associations;
- receiving and examining the annual returns from these organisations;
- investigating complaints about trade union elections and alleged breaches of union rules;
- making sure that the statutory requirements established for mergers between trade unions and between employers' associations are properly observed;
- overseeing the finances and political funds of these organisations;
- certifying those trade unions that meet the criteria of independence.

*Source*: Adapted from Certification Officer's website at <http://www.certoffice.org>

---

to characterise differences between trade union policies and activities as a means of measuring the extent to which such an organisation is 'a whole-hearted trade union, identifying with the labour movement and willing to use all the powers of the movement' (Blackburn, 1967: 18). Blackburn and Prandy (1965) and Blackburn (1967) identified a number of elements of unionateness. These relate to the following questions, first about a trade union's identification and affiliation:

- Does the organisation call itself a trade union?
- Has it been listed as a trade union?
- Is it affiliated to the Trades Union Congress?
- Is it affiliated to the Labour Party?

Second, about the way in which it functions:

- Does it operate independently of any employer?
- Is its principal purpose to engage in collective bargaining and other forms of job regulation to protect the interests of its members?
- What forms of industrial action are its members prepared to use to pursue their interests? Are they prepared to engage in strike action?

These elements are useful to identify the degree of unionateness of a trade union. Where the answer to all, or nearly all, of these questions is 'yes' in respect of a particular trade union, this would indicate a high degree of unionateness. For example, the four largest trade unions in the UK (see Table 5.3) – UNISON, Amicus, the Transport and General Workers' Union and GMB – would each be categorised as highly unionate. Some organisations combine the role of being a professional association with that of a trade union. For example, in the Health Service a number of professional health bodies are also listed and certified as independent trade unions as they fulfil the function of regulating the employment relationship of their members with the employers of these people. These include the British Medical Association, the Royal College of Midwives, and the Royal College of Nursing of the UK. These organisations fulfil some of the criteria in the list above and therefore demonstrate an intermediate degree of unionateness. Where the answer is 'no' to many of the questions listed above, this would indicate a low degree of unionateness.

However, the reality may be more complex than it first appears in some cases. The Certification Officer's list of trade unions for March 2002 includes several that are referred to as being staff associations within specific employing organisations, although they have also met the criteria established to receive a certificate of independence as a trade union. These particular staff associations are therefore likely to demonstrate a higher degree of unionateness than may at first be evident from looking at their name. As Farnham and Pimlott (1995) recognised, several trade unions commenced their existence as staff associations and then developed a higher degree of unionateness through broadening their membership base, or by merging with external unions. The Certification Officer's Annual Report in 2000 provides two examples of this type of development. The banking and finance union, UNIFI (see Table 5.3), was created in May 1999 as the result of the amalgamation of three employee organisations: the Banking Insurance and Finance Union (BIFU); Unifi, the staff union of Barclays Bank; and the NatWest Staff Association. The second example was the merger of several company-based staff associations, many of which already had certificates of independence, into the Manufacturing, Science and Finance Union (now itself part of Amicus: see Table 5.3). These examples indicate how degree of unionateness develops for many trade unions during the course of their existence.

Any attempt to define what a trade union is for therefore needs to consider all of the dimensions to which we have referred. The definitions cited above are useful in general terms, but it is nevertheless important to recognise that the specific purpose and values of one trade union may vary, albeit perhaps only slightly, from that of another. To return to the work of Flanders briefly, he argued that the best way of seeking to define the purpose of trade unions is to examine their behaviour: 'to infer what they are for from what they do' (Flanders, 1975: 41).

## 5.3 The functions of trade unions

The primary function of trade unions is related to the regulation of the employment relationship. Other related functions include recruiting new members and retaining existing ones, pursuing issues for particular groups of members, providing member services, pursuing institutional goals related to the development of the union (or perhaps even its survival), and realising some measure of personal fulfilment for those who work for it. We shall discuss each of these. We start briefly with the recruitment and retention of members, and broaden this particular discussion to explore the relationship between levels of membership and the nature of union power.

### ■ Recruiting new members and retaining existing ones: building union density and union power?

A key function of trade unions relates to their efforts to build and retain membership. Although the power of a trade union cannot be measured simply in relation to the size of its membership, its ability to attract members from particular groups of workers will be important to influence employers to recognise the union to act for these members. This is an obvious although important point. Millward *et al.* (2000) recognise that levels of membership and employer recognition of unions mutually reinforce each other, so that a high level of membership will encourage recognition, and in turn this will encourage employees to join a recognised union. Employees joining a trade union expect to benefit from the greater protection and scope for improvement that its collective resources offer, in comparison with remaining outside its membership. However, these benefits need to be evident and to outweigh any costs of joining.

Unions that build up high levels of membership density, whereby the considerable majority of those eligible to join actually do so, should be able to exercise much greater power and influence, where other circumstances are also favourable, than poorly organised groups. In theory, the power of union and individual should be enhanced together in these circumstances. Batstone (1988), in discussing the power resources of trade unions, suggested that these are composed of two basic factors. These relate to the power resources of individual workers and the ability of a union to combine these resources and to mobilise, or use, them.

The level of power that workers may exercise depends on their scarcity value in the production process or the provision of services, the extent to which they are required given the state of the labour market, their ability to disrupt production or service provision, and their political influence (Batstone, 1988). Some workers will be able to exercise a higher level of power than others, when 'measured' in relation to these elements. For example, highly skilled workers will possess much greater scarcity value in relation to lower-skilled ones in the same industry, although the state of the labour market may adversely affect this value where demand is depressed. Batstone's (1988) second factor, relating to a union's ability to combine workers effectively and to use their power resources, indicates that level of membership by itself will not ensure the realisation of this power. Mobilisation of potential power resources will depend not only on level of membership but also on the extent to which members identify with, are committed to and involved in realising the goals of the union. Underpinning this will be the extent to which a union is effectively structured and defined by a clear strategy around which members may identify. The action taken by the members of the Fire Brigades Union (FBU) in 2002 indicates an example of a clear aim and strategy around which its membership coalesced. Batstone (1988) also recognised that the role and attitude of the state will affect union power, and we return to this aspect in a later section of this chapter when we look at the role of the Trades Union Congress.

## ■ Regulating the employment relationship

Clegg (1979) summarised the four principal ways in which the employment relationship is regulated. *Collective bargaining* involves trade unions and managers jointly regulating aspects of the employment relationship, although the exact level at which this activity takes place and its scope will vary (see Chapter 7). *Employer regulation* or *managerial regulation* relates to aspects of the employment relationship being decided unilaterally by either employers or managers respectively. *Trade union regulation* involves an attempt by a union to determine particular conditions unilaterally and to impose these on an employer. *Statutory regulation* relates to those aspects of the employment relationship governed by legislation. Within organisations more than one of these forms of regulation may operate, perhaps emphasising the different organisational levels at which the employment relationship is regulated. In addition, particular forms of legal regulation will affect aspects of the employment relationship, for example in relation to equality of opportunity and health and safety at work. Statutory regulation will also affect classes of workers such as those covered by the national minimum wage.

It has been widely recognised that collective bargaining is the key method used by trade unions to protect or improve the interests of their members (e.g. Thornley *et al.*, 2000). Collective bargaining is discussed in detail in Chapter 7, so we will only refer to it briefly at this point in order to recognise it as a major union function. The term developed from the fact that union organisation of employees led to the collective representation of their interests to employers and involved the process of bargaining at which each side sought to apply pressure, including contemplating forms of industrial action, to seek to resolve differences between them. In the past, collective bargaining was the predominant method used to determine many aspects of the employment relationship; however, its use has reduced significantly in the UK.

Millward *et al.* (2000) report on the reduced coverage of collective bargaining during the last two decades of the twentieth century. In 1984, 86 per cent of employees in unionised workplaces employing 25 or more people had their pay and conditions determined through collective bargaining. In terms of all workplaces employing 25 or more people, 70 per cent of employees were covered by collective bargaining in 1984. By 1998, 67 per cent of employees in unionised workplaces of this size were covered by collective bargaining. In terms of all workplaces with 25 or more employees, by 1998 only 40 per cent of employees were covered by collective bargaining. This reduced coverage was also accompanied by a narrowing of the range of subjects that were subject to collective bargaining (see Chapter 7 for further discussion of the reduced scope of bargaining). However, the recent increase in trade union recognition deals (discussed later in this chapter) may indicate the end of this downward trend.

Trade union recognition and collective bargaining also lead to other forms of employee representation that help to regulate the employment relationship. Collective bargaining is likely to lead to two types of collective agreement. The first type leads to agreements about *substantive issues* such as levels of pay, hours and patterns of work and contractual entitlements such as annual leave. The second type leads to agreements about a range of *procedural issues* to deal with problems that arise during the course of employment. These will be likely to include agreed procedures for handling collective disputes, individual grievances and disciplinary actions, as well as in relation to other areas where trade union representation is permitted. Procedural agreements will also cover arrangements for bargaining and facilities for union representatives at the workplace. Trade unions will also gain rights in relation to the disclosure of information for collective bargaining purposes and in relation to consultation (see Chapter 10).

Trade unions can therefore seek to regulate or influence aspects of the employment relationship through a number of means including collective bargaining, joint consultation and individual representation. As we recognised earlier, individual unions are also likely to focus on particular objectives, and this will affect the way in which they function. These objectives may be promoted by the nature of environmental factors that affect the industrial or occupational sectors within which the union operates. For example, UNISON, which is the largest union in Britain (see Table 5.3), is currently focusing on the ownership of public services in the UK through its 'Positively Public' campaign, aimed at 'keeping the public services public'. It is against the creation of Private Finance Initiatives (or PFIs) and public–private partnerships (or PPPs), which it believes are against the public interest as well as the interests of its members (IRS, 2002a). Public campaigning such as this indicates that trade unions may also engage in a broader range of activities with the aim of seeking to regulate the employment relationship through such indirect means.

## Pursuit of issues for particular groups of members and the provision of services for all members

Recently, trade unions have focused more on issues affecting particular groups of members. IRS (2002a) report that the TUC has promoted a range of diversity and equal opportunities work-related issues. These include issues related to the treatment of women, gay and lesbian workers, part-time employees, and disability and racism in the workplace. The Union of Shop, Distributive and Allied Workers, or USDAW, whose membership is approximately two-thirds female, has been promoting a range of issues that relate particularly to its female members. These issues include equal and low rates of pay, part-time working, harassment and maternity rights (IRS, 2002a). Through the pursuit of these types of issue, unions attempt to influence and regulate the employment relationship, albeit in relation to particular groups of members and in specific areas that relate closely to their personal experiences of work.

Unions have also sought to widen their appeal by offering a range of non-traditional services to existing members that may also encourage non-members to join. These have included a range of financial services such as insurance, loans, mortgages and purchase discounts, offered in association with financial services organisations, and access to legal advice. The success of these additional services in attracting members is open to evaluation.

## ▓ Institutional and personal goals

It is common to refer to a trade union and its members, as opposed to a union being composed of its members where the two would be thought of as indivisible. References to organisations in general make the same assumption. All organisations are composed of people, and when we refer to a distinction between the two it is likely that we are tacitly referring to 'the organisation' as being the group within it who exercise greatest power over its strategy and structure. In this way, all organisations including trade unions can be seen as being composed of different sets of interests, rather than all within an organisation or union somehow sharing the same set. We have already considered the idea of a trade union as being a continuous association, indicating some sense of permanence. Trade unions, as we shall consider further in the next section of this chapter, have had to adapt through the course of time in order to survive. Some unions had to abandon exclusive policies so that they could broaden their membership base in order to survive, or so that they could merge with another union whose membership was more inclusive in relation to different occupations and levels of skill. However, such a change may indicate the dilution of some members' interests in order to secure the wider goal of maintaining the union into a future period.

The continuation of a union in a particular form, the pursuit of broader principles of trade unionism, or the nature of a union's direction may therefore conflict with the interests of members at particular points in time. These issues will indicate conflict between sections of a union's membership and its leadership. One of the authors recalls a regional official of a large union in the early 1980s recounting that 'when the union was on the defensive it had to encourage its members, whereas when it experienced periods of militancy it had to try to constrain them!'

Participation in the operation of a union's functions offers opportunities to individual members to take part in types of activity that most would not experience otherwise. Unions require organisational structures that encompass workplace, local and national levels. This creates opportunities for union members to become involved as workplace-based representatives (usually on a part-time basis); or district, divisional, regional or national officials depending on the particular structure of a union; or even to aspire to nationally elected office as general secretary, or deputy general secretary, of their trade union for one or more terms of office. These activities offer the opportunity to participate in, for example, employee representation at a range of levels and for different purposes, the recruitment of members, health and safety matters, negotiation and bargaining, policy-making and implementation, and the management of the union's affairs. Participation in such activities may therefore offer scope for development and personal fulfilment (although not all experience of union affairs leads to positive outcomes!). The capabilities of those involved and the way in which these activities are conducted will also have a direct relationship to the internal efficiency of the union and to its external effectiveness in terms of its overall scope to exercise influence in the regulation of the employment relationship.

**self-check question**

**5.1** How may the other trade union functions discussed above be related to a union's primary function to become involved in the regulation of the employment relationship?

## 5.4 The changing structure of trade unionism in Britain

### Number of trade unions

Table 5.1 shows the number of trade unions and level of membership in Great Britain over recent years.

**Table 5.1 Number of trade unions and level of membership: Great Britain, 5 year intervals, 1975–2000**

| Year | Number of unions | Membership (millions) |
| --- | --- | --- |
| 1975 | 446 | 11.7 |
| 1980 | 467 | 12.6 |
| 1985 | 391 | 10.8 |
| 1990 | 306 | 9.8 |
| 1995 | 260 | 8.0 |
| 2000 | 221 | 7.8 |

*Source*: Adapted from Certification Officer's Annual Reports

The number of trade unions decreased steadily over the course of the twentieth century. At the beginning of the twentieth century there were 1323 unions (Donovan, 1968), whereas at the start of the twenty-first century there were 221 unions listed in Great Britain. This reduction was accompanied by the increasing concentration of membership in a few, proportionately very large, unions. By 2000, the 16 largest trade unions in Great Britain accounted for just under 6.5 million members out of a total membership of 7.9 million, or 82 per cent of all union members (Whybrew, 2001) (see also Table 5.3). This demonstrates a situation in the UK of a small number of large unions and a much larger number of smaller ones. However, trying to categorise these different unions according to which groups of workers they organise is problematic.

## Classifying trade unions

The way in which trade unions developed and evolved in the UK became a source of frustration for those who have tried to classify them into meaningful analytical categories. A number of bases for organising different types of workers in unions have been identified. These organising bases, or boundaries, form the traditional way of classifying unions into types. These are shown in Table 5.2, together with the generic name given to each type of union organisation.

**Table 5.2 Traditional classification of trade unions**

| Organising basis or boundary | Generic union name |
| --- | --- |
| Within an employing organisation | Company unionism<br>Employment unionism |
| Within a craft or group of skills | Craft unionism |
| Within an occupational group | Occupational unionism |
| Within an industry | Industrial unionism |
| According to a religious or political affiliation | Ideological unionism |
| Based on inclusion, not bound by any of the above | General unionism<br>(Class unionism) |

We shall briefly consider each of the categories listed in Table 5.2.

### Company unionism and employment unionism

*Company unionism* generally refers to a union that is not only restricted to organising within a particular employing organisation but also sponsored or even controlled by it. This strategy has been used to restrict recognition to the company union, and the only encouragement to join a union will be limited to membership of this organisation. Employing organisations resorting to this approach in the past have actively discouraged membership of any independent trade union. The term company unionism has therefore been used in a pejorative way to indicate an inferior form that is not independent of the employer and which is controlled or influenced by this organisation to prevent conflict from occurring, at least overtly.

A potentially less negative form of union organisation restricted to those in the employment of a particular concern has been termed *employment unionism* (Turner, 1962). We noted earlier that several unions or staff associations that only organise within one company and that bear its name have obtained certificates of independence in the UK. The key to this single-employer form of employee organisation is therefore the degree to which the union is independent of the employer rather than the fact that membership is restricted to within the company.

### Craft unionism

The power of *craft unions* rested on the organisation of highly skilled workers who were central to the production process in which they were employed (Chapter 3). These skilled workers were able to limit the supply of new labour through their exclusive position in being able to train and pass on their skills to entrants to the particular craft. However, the exclusiveness of many different craft unions was eroded through time by industrial and technological changes. Technological changes allowed employers to develop new production processes that permitted them to use other workers with lower levels of skill, thereby displacing craft workers. The rise of the car industry through the twentieth century provides an example of this type of development, although examples of skill displacement continue to occur as new technology allows for the replacement of particular groups of workers. Many craft unions, such as the Amalgamated Engineering Union (now part of Amicus), either had to open up their membership to groups of lesser-skilled workers to survive, or had to merge with another union, or face extinction. These developments meant that craft unions lost the basis of their power in the labour markets within which they organised.

## Occupational unionism

*Occupational unions*, like craft ones, organise workers who undertake the same type of job. This involves organising an occupational group across employment boundaries. In some cases this will involve a union organising an occupational group who work within the same industry or sector. In this way, the National Union of Teachers or the National Association of Schoolmasters and Union of Women Teachers recruit teachers irrespective of their employer. Some occupations spread across industrial sectors, and an occupational union will expand its recruitment across these industrial boundaries. For example, Unison organises those in similar types of 'support' jobs who work in local government, education or the health service. The scope of organisation for this type of union therefore spreads *horizontally* across employers and industrial boundaries.

## Industrial unionism

*Industrial unionism* adopts a different basis for the way in which it seeks to organise workers and build a union movement. Its strategy is based on organising all workers within a particular industry irrespective of their occupation or level of skill. These unions have been characterised as being '*vertically*' oriented in terms of their approach to building membership. This model of, or approach to, unionism has never been firmly established in Britain. Some industries have witnessed the existence of a dominant union, in terms of membership levels, but these unions have never established exclusive rights to organise all workers in a particular industry. For example, the National Union of Mineworkers was the dominant union in the British coal industry, but other unions existed to organise and represent supervisory and managerial grades of employees. Similarly, the former National Union of Railwaymen, now part of the National Union of Rail, Maritime and Transport Workers, faced competition to organise train drivers from the Associated Society of Locomotive Engineers and Firemen.

The early model of trade unionism in Britain was based on the creation of craft unions, around which the early general unions sought to organise lower-skilled groups of workers irrespective of the industry in which they were employed. This historical basis has subsequently affected the shape of trade unions in Britain. This may be contrasted with the situation in Germany, where the structure of trade unionism was reshaped after the Second World War. This led to the creation of 16 industrially based unions affiliated to the German Trade Union Confederation, Deutscher Gewerkschaftsbund (DGB). This union federation incorporated members from across the range of occupational levels in each industry, although smaller union federations also formed for white-collar workers (the DAG) and civil servants (DBB), as well as the Christian Federation of Trade Unions (CGB). In spite of these other federations, the DGB operated as the predominant union grouping for all occupations. However, in response to membership losses, several of the industrial unions affiliated to the DGB embarked on a series of mergers from 1996, with the result that German trade unions have taken on a multi-sectoral approach, with a smaller number of unions operating across various industries. Even with this development, however, at the level of the company or the workplace the principle of a single union remains (Jacobi *et al.*, 1998).

### Ideological unionism

Political affiliations and religious beliefs have also shaped the basis of trade union organisation in some European countries. These considerations have been superimposed on top of the other dimensions of union structure discussed in this section. For example, trade unions in France and in Italy have traditionally been influenced by ideological and, to some extent, religious beliefs and aligned according to political affiliations. This has led to the fragmentation of the union movements in these countries (e.g. Goetschy, 1998; Regalia and Regini, 1998). These dimensions affecting the shape of trade unions have not been so evident in Britain, although see the discussion later relating to the determinants of union mergers.

### General unionism

*General unionism*, in theory, is designed to be open to any grade of worker, or occupation, across any industrial sector. The earliest attempts at general unionism, in the nineteenth century, were designed to organise all grades of worker as a political class. However, any attempt to develop *class unionism* was abandoned by the later, more successful generation of general unions that developed, as these general unions made agreements with other unions, including craft ones, to regulate the scope of their organising activities (see example, Turner, 1962).

### ■ The nature of trade unionism in Britain

As a result of these different approaches to the development of trade unionism in Britain, compounded by several decades of union mergers, growth and decline, and industrial and technological changes, the nature of trade unions in Britain presents a somewhat unclear picture. In the 1960s, Turner (1962: 240–1) noted that many unions 'including certain of the biggest are now virtually unclassifiable.' He went on to comment that, 'The difficulty in confining such unions to a category is partly that the categories themselves often fail to yield a sharp jurisdictional definition in practice.' For example, it is often difficult to offer a precise definition of particular industries and occupations. In the period since Turner wrote these comments, unions in Britain have continued to merge and, as we discussed earlier, to form proportionately larger bodies that have often been referred to as *super-unions*. In this way, many of the largest unions in Britain may best be thought of as multi-sectoral employee organisations, recruiting a range of occupations at different grades in a way that has been shaped by a number of historical reasons. Table 5.3 shows the membership of the 15 largest trade unions in the UK in 2001, which account for 82 per cent of all union members. Box 5.2 briefly describes the sectors within which each of the four largest unions organise, together with some indication of the types of workers they recruit.

**Table 5.3 Membership of the 15 largest trade unions in the UK, 2001**

| | Union | TUC affiliated | Membership |
|---|---|---|---|
| 1 | Unison: The Public Service Union | Yes | 1272470 |
| 2 | Amicus[a] | Yes | 1079185 |
| 3 | Transport and General Workers' Union | Yes | 858804 |
| 4 | GMB | Yes | 683860 |
| 5 | Royal College of Nursing of the United Kingdom | No | 334414 |
| 6 | Union of Shop, Distributive and Allied Workers | Yes | 310222 |
| 7 | National Union of Teachers | Yes | 286245 |
| 8 | Communication Workers' Union | Yes | 284422 |
| 9 | Public and Commercial Services Union | Yes | 267644 |
| 10 | National Association of Schoolmasters and Union of Women Teachers | Yes | 255768 |
| 11 | Graphical Paper and Media Union | Yes | 200008 |
| 12 | Association of Teachers and Lecturers | Yes | 178697 |
| 13 | UNIFI | Yes | 160267 |
| 14 | Union of Construction Allied Trades and Technicians | Yes | 114854 |
| 15 | British Medical Association | No | 111055 |

[a] Amicus was created on 1 January 2002 from a merger of the Amalgamated Engineering and Electrical Union and the Manufacturing Science and Finance Union. The table shows the combined membership for the year 2001–02.

*Source*: Adapted from Certification Officer's Annual Report of 2001–02: see Cockburn (2002); and ⟨http://www.tuc.org.uk/tuc/unions_list.cfm⟩

Box 5.2 illustrates a complex pattern of organising activities for the four largest trade unions in the UK. Each of these unions is the result of several or many mergers through time. Some of the other 15 largest unions have a narrower organising focus, within particular occupational groups, industrial or employment sectors. However, attempting to apply a categorical label to several of these unions is still problematic (see Table 5.2). This is due partly to the problem of being able to define a particular industry or occupation adequately. Irrespective of this definitional problem, however, most of these unions attempt to recruit across a range of occupations and employment sectors, and none can be said to have an exclusive right to organise all workers within a particular industry.

So why is the nature of trade unionism in the UK 'messy' in terms of the attempts that have been made to categorise it? One obvious reason is that it has a relatively long history that reflects its struggle to develop as well as the subsequent way in which it has done so in practice, as we noted above. It is also the product of real events and real people, rather than existing for convenient academic categorisation. The resultant pattern of trade unionism in the UK has often led to the issue of *multi-*

| Box 5.2 | Main trades and sectors within which each of the four largest UK unions organises |
| --- | --- |

**UNISON: The Public Service Union**

Local government, health care, the water, gas and electricity industries, further and higher education, schools, transport, voluntary sector, housing associations, police support staff.

**Amicus**

Manufacturing, engineering, energy, construction, IT, defence aerospace, motor industry, civil aviation, chemicals and pharmaceuticals, steel and metals, shipbuilding, scientists, technologists, professional and managerial staff, electronics and telecommunications, tobacco, food and drink, textiles, ceramics, paper, professional staff in universities, commercial sales, the voluntary sector, financial services, NHS.

**Transport and General Workers' Union**

Administrative, clerical, technical and supervisory; agriculture; building, construction and civil engineering; chemical, oil and rubber manufacture; civil air transport; docks and waterways; food, drink and tobacco; general workers; passenger services; power and engineering; public services; road transport commercial; textiles; vehicle building and automotive.

**GMB**

Civil air transport, security, AA, aerospace, defence, clothing, textiles, food production and distribution, retail, hotel, catering, chemicals and process, construction, building supplies, furniture and timber, local government, NHS, care, education, engineering, offshore, shipbuilding, energy, utilities.

*Source*: Trades Union Congress at <http://www.tuc.org.uk/tuc/unions_list.cfm>

*unionism,* and the mergers that occurred between unions have taken place for a number of reasons, some of which may not appear to the external observer to be entirely objective. We now discuss briefly the nature of and reasons for union mergers in the context of the UK, to help to understand the nature of trade unionism in Britain, and the nature and issue of multi-unionism, before briefly looking at the advent of single-union agreements over recent years.

## Union mergers

Union mergers are regulated by the Trade Union and Labour Relations Act 1992 and by other statutory regulations. These statutory instruments define two types of union merger. The first of these involves a *transfer of engagements*, where a union agrees to transfer its membership into another union, following a postal ballot of all of its members that is subject to independent scrutiny and which produces a favourable vote. The second of these involves an *amalgamation*, where the members of two or more unions vote by the required majority in each case to merge their memberships into a new union. The statutory regulations that govern union mergers are principally designed to facilitate these changes and to protect the interests and rights of the members involved (Cockburn, 2002).

Union mergers have been a continuing feature of trade unionism in Britain. Undy *et al.* (1981) produced a threefold categorisation to explain the reasons for mergers between trade unions. One of these categories covers a *defensive merger*, where a union suffering from membership decline and reduced income merges with another union that is more powerful. A second category covers a *consolidating merger*, where a union seeks to consolidate its organising position through a merger with another union. The third category covers an *expansionist merger*, where a union merges with another in order to expand its membership and to organise in an industry or amongst an occupation that is new to it. A general motive underlying each of these reasons for merging is the desire to retain or enhance a critical level of power that stems from collective organisation. Without this, a union's purpose to engage in the regulation of its members' employment relationships will be diminished.

IRS (1992a) identified a number of reasons for the union mergers that were taking place in the 1990s. These included financial, industrial, organisational, political and technological reasons as well as a competitive effect. Declining membership at this time reduced union income from subscriptions, pushing some unions towards merger. Conversely, mergers offered greater economies of scale and cost-effectiveness to the larger unions that resulted. The decentralisation of collective bargaining (see Chapter 7) that was increasingly occurring in this period added to unions' costs because they needed to train and resource local union officials and workplace representatives (discussed later in this chapter) to undertake this work. Industrial and technological changes were also affecting traditional boundaries between particular occupations and between grades of skill. Such changes threatened previously understood recruitment boundaries between unions for members, as well as creating new opportunities leading to increased competition between these unions. These factors helped to push some unions towards merger.

However, not all of the union mergers that resulted did so for such rational reasons. Some mergers have taken place over time for reasons that are more political. Consequently, many merged unions have been seen as being politically to the 'right', 'centre' or 'left' of the trade union movement. In some cases, political alignment may be seen to have taken precedence over the industrial logic of the situation, where there was a more obvious alternative partner for merger. IRS (1992a) also recognised that some mergers have caused some smaller unions to seek a merger for themselves for fear that they will be left vulnerable to a hostile merger at a later date.

Table 5.4 lists the major recent mergers that have taken place in the UK.

## Multi-unionism

The Royal Commission on Trade Unions and Employers' Associations (Donovan, 1968) recognised two types of *multi-unionism*. The first type involved the situation where each occupational group in a workplace is organised by a different union. This situation was recognised as being common at that time in Britain, given the absence of industrial unionism. The second type involved a situation where two or more unions compete 'for membership within a given group of workers' (Donovan, 1968: 179). This second type of multi-unionism was seen as less desirable. The Report of this Royal Commission discussed a number of possible solutions to the issue of multi-unionism. These included promoting industrial unionism, although this was not seen as practicable given the entrenched position of the existing unions in Britain

Table 5.4 **Recent major union mergers in the UK**

| Merged union | Former unions | Year of merger | Membership strength, 2001 |
|---|---|---|---|
| Unison – The Public Service Union | National and Local Government Officers' Association (NALGO), National Union of Public Employees (NUPE) and Confederation of Health Service Employees (COHSE) | 1999 | 1272470 |
| Amicus | Amalgamated Engineering and Electrical Union (AEEU) and Manufacturing Science and Finance Union (MSF) | 2002 | 1079185 |
| Communication Workers Union | Union of Communication Workers (UCW) and National Communications Union (NCU) | 1995 | 284,422 |
| Public and Commercial Services Union | Civil and Public Services Association (CPSA) and Public Services Tax and Commerce Union (PTC) | 1998 | 267644 |
| Graphical Paper and Media Union | National Graphical Association (NGA) and Society of Graphical and Allied Trades (SOGAT) | 1991 | 200008 |
| UNIFI | Banking, Insurance and Finance Union (BIFU), Unifi and NatWest Staff Association | 1999 | 160267 |

by this time. Two other possible solutions were discussed. These were seen as complementary and involved 'agreements between unions on recruiting rights and negotiating rights' and 'many more mergers between unions' (Donovan, 1968: 182).

In spite of union merger activity over recent decades, multi-unionism is still evident in the workplace. The Workplace Employee Relations Survey of 1998 found that while 43 per cent of unionised workplaces with 25 or more employees had one union present, 57 per cent had two or more unions present. One quarter of unionised workplaces with 25 or more employees had four or more unions present. As nearly half (47 per cent) of workplaces with 25 or more employees were reported as not having any unions present in 1998, it is useful to look at union presence and multi-unionism in relation to this proportion. In this way, the WERS data show that while 47 per cent of workplaces of this size did not have any union present, 23 per cent had one union present and the remaining 30 per cent had two or more unions present (Cully *et al.*, 1999). Not all of the unions present were recognised, however. Of the 53 per cent of all workplaces of this size where a union was present, 45 per cent had a recognition agreement and the other 8 per cent did not recognise a union. The average number of unions at workplaces of this size where unions were present in 1998 was 2.4 (Millward *et al.*, 2000).

There are a number of ways in which the potentially adverse effects of multi-unionism can be reduced. One of its potentially adverse effects relates to conflict between unions in respect of the second type of multi-unionism, where unions compete for members from within the same group of workers. Union mergers may eliminate this type of conflict, where the unions involved merge. However, the nature of union mergers, as we noted above, has not always been based on industrial grounds. IRS (1992a: 13) commented that 'mergers may coexist with enhanced inter-union competition for members.' Although this may only occur in particular cases, it demonstrates that union mergers do not necessarily eliminate inter-union competition and conflict, given the underlying nature of unionism and the types of merger that result in particular cases. Another potentially adverse effect of multi-unionism can be the development of fragmented structures for collective bargaining (Cully *et al.*, 1999), whether at the workplace or at a higher level of bargaining. To overcome this effect, significant proportions of employing organisations have promoted the use of single-union agreements or single-table bargaining. We now discuss the use of these strategies in this context.

## Single-union agreements and single-table bargaining

Single-union agreements, as defined below, developed in the 1980s. They were most often associated with the establishment of new production plants on 'greenfield' sites, often involving inward investments by foreign-owned companies, and where union recognition was new. In a *single-union agreement*, one union represents all relevant employees for collective bargaining and representation purposes. However, the price of being recognised as the single trade union sometimes involved competing unions going through a 'beauty contest', perhaps with the effect of undercutting one another to gain the sole right of recognition in the workplace concerned. Single-union agreements also became associated with the following terms:

■ union support for the organisation's goals;
■ single-status employment;
■ flexible working arrangements, multiskilling and the eradication of demarcation boundaries between jobs;
■ training to promote multiskilling, flexibility and team working;
■ initiatives to promote employee involvement, with a company or staff council to deal with both consultation and negotiation issues composed of employee representatives who may not be union members;
■ a no-strike clause and binding arbitration for the resolution of disputes incorporating the principle of pendulum arbitration, where the arbitrator has to decide between the management's offer and the union's claim rather than seek to reach a compromise deal (e.g. IRS, 1992b).

These single-union agreements were seen to avoid multi-unionism and the problems that may arise in relation to inter-union competition and conflict, and to promote a culture that emphasised the company, flexibility, cooperation and consensus. However, the recently elected joint General Secretary of Amicus, Derek Simpson, has written about the operation of some single-union agreements in less than complimentary terms. He is quoted in IRS (2002c: 2) as follows:

Many deals did not recognise the role of shop stewards, nor the right of the trade union to negotiate over pay on behalf of the members. We had the farcical situations of shop stewards denied time off for trade union duties under a single union agreement, no access to staff in order to recruit and, most ridiculous of all, pay negotiations conducted with a company-appointed staff council with no role for the union.

The nature of single-union agreements may vary in practice, but the comments above indicate the way in which managerial power over the employment relationship was exercised in some of these arrangements.

An alternative means to avoid fragmented bargaining structures where a number of unions are already recognised in a workplace involves the introduction of *single-table bargaining*. This strategy copes with the presence of several recognised unions by bringing these around a single table to negotiate jointly. This avoids not only the fragmentation of bargaining but also the associated past tendency to make claims characterised by 'leapfrogging', where one union sought to improve on the previous deal made by another union on the basis of maintaining traditional wage differentials (e.g. Gall, 1994). The WERS data indicate that, where collective bargaining was used to determine pay settlements in 1998, 77 per cent of such workplaces were using single-table bargaining. This compares with 40 per cent in 1990. Millward *et al.* (2000: 203) comment that, 'This shift, most marked in the public sector, but still very pronounced in the private sector, possibly represents one of the most striking changes in the nature of British industrial relations in the 1990s'.

## 5.5 Trades Union Congress and European Trade Union Confederation

### The Trades Union Congress

The Trades Union Congress, or TUC, describes itself as 'the voice of Britain at work'. Founded in 1868, it is the representative body of the trade union movement in the UK, with approximately 70 affiliated unions that collectively represented about 6.7 million workers, or roughly 85 per cent of those who were members of a union, in 2002. In this way, the TUC is a secondary organisation, representing unions that have decided to affiliate to it. Kessler and Bayliss (1998: 184) refer to the TUC as being 'the servant of its affiliated unions and not their master'. The majority of its income is derived from the fees paid by these unions. Table 5.3 shows that all but two of the 15 largest unions in the UK are affiliated to the TUC. These two unions are the Royal College of Nursing and the British Medical Association.

Box 5.3 summarises the key functions of the TUC.

The way in which the TUC seeks to operationalise these functions is expressed in the organisational objectives that it publishes. The TUC's objectives for 2003 are summarised in Box 5.4.

The TUC has experienced a number of significant changes since 1980. These have affected its internal organisation and its relationship with the government in particular. The TUC conducted a number of reviews from 1980 into its internal organisation that led to significant changes in its operating structures and staffing. The traditional policy-making body of the TUC has been its annual Congress, which meets each September for a period of four days. Affiliated unions send delegates to Congress on a proportionate basis. This annual meeting considers a range of motions, or resolutions, that, if agreed, form the basis of the work of the TUC for the following year. In between the annual Congress, policy-making is entrusted to the TUC's General Council, which meets every two months. This is

---

**Box 5.3    Functions of the TUC**

- The TUC is the means through which British trade unions formulate common policy positions about issues that affect them as a whole.
- It provides an important means to lobby government about trade union, employment, economic and social issues.
- More broadly, the TUC campaigns about issues that affect people at work.
- It also conducts research related to these issues.
- The TUC provides the means through which unions are represented on different public bodies in the UK, in the European Union and at the International Labour Organisation of the United Nations. It also develops links to other trade union bodies internationally, and is a member of the International Confederation of Free Trade Unions (ICFTU).
- It operates education and training programmes for union representatives through its network of staff in England, Scotland and Wales. Accredited programmes are organised for workplace representatives, safety representatives and pension scheme trustees.
- The TUC helps to promote cooperation between unions and to resolve disputes where these arise.
- The TUC has also been active in developing financial and some other services for union members.

*Source*: Adapted from the TUC website at ‹http://www.tuc.org.uk/›

---

**Box 5.4    Objectives of the TUC for 2003**

- Securing improved workplace rights and raising public awareness of the need for these.
- Campaigning for high-quality public services that are provided from within the public sector and resolving issues about the pay and conditions of those who provide these services.
- Promoting the European Social Model and engaging in issues related to the enlargement of the EU and the euro referendum.
- Promoting trade unionism and working with unions to organise those in work through various initiatives.
- Raising awareness about pensions reform and promoting new pensions policies.
- Promoting equality though initiatives including publicity about the continuation of pay discrimination, involvement in legislation about equality issues, continued anti-racism work, and highlighting age discrimination.
- Working with national and international trade union organisations to consider and coordinate approaches to a range of international economic and labour issues.
- Working at regional and sectoral levels to improve the effectiveness and influence of the trade union movement.
- Promoting and spreading the partnership model of industrial relations, easing tensions between trade unions relating to membership and recognition, and ensuring greater coordination between them.
- Developing the services of the TUC for affiliated unions and strengthening relations between them.

*Source*: Summarised and adapted from the TUC website at ‹http://www.tuc.org.uk/the_tuc/tuc-5927-f0.cfm›

**The Management of Human Resources**

also broadly representative of the unions that are affiliated to the TUC. The composition of the Council is structured according to a number of sections that permit representation from:

- different-sized unions (calculated on a sliding scale, with 6 seats for a union of 1.2 million members or more);
- women members (for whom 4 seats are specifically reserved from amongst unions with fewer than 200 000 members); and
- black members (for whom 1 seat is for a member from a union with over 200 000 members; 1 seat is for a member from a union with under 200 000 members; and 1 seat is reserved for a woman).

In 1994, an Executive Committee of the TUC was established. This meets monthly to oversee the implementation of policy and its development, and to manage the financial affairs of the organisation as well as to deal with any urgent matters that arise. The General Council decides the membership of the Executive. The TUC employs over 200 people, who are organised into seven departments, about 100 of whom are located at its headquarters in the centre of London. There are also offices in Glasgow for the TUC of Scotland and Cardiff for the Wales TUC, in Birmingham, Bristol, Leeds, Liverpool, London and Newcastle for the six Regional Councils in England, and in Brussels.

The 1980s and 1990s also saw changes to the TUC's relationship with the government. There was a significant reversal of the corporatist approach that had developed since 1945, which manifested itself in the creation of a number of tripartite bodies that brought government, employers and the trade unions together to consider a range of important economic, industrial and social issues. The Conservative governments of 1979–1997 espoused a non-interventionist approach that was anti-corporatist (see Chapter 6). However, they did intervene to introduce a range of legislation that codified many trade union activities and that was not seen as sympathetic to the aims and methods of trade unionism. They also operated a policy of seeking to reduce public expenditure, and introduced cash limits in the public sector that effectively operated as an indirect form of policy on incomes (see Chapter 6; Kessler and Bayliss, 1998). Relative salaries in many public sector occupations declined as a result.

Many of the tripartite bodies, where the TUC enjoyed representation, were gradually abolished through the period of these Conservative governments. The National Economic Development Council (NEDC), which had been chaired by the UK's prime minister, had its activities reduced in 1987 before being abolished in 1992. In the area of training policy a succession of tripartite bodies were abolished through the 1980s: the Industrial Training Boards (ITBs), the Manpower Services Commission (MSC), and its successor the Training Commission. These were replaced by the employer-led Training and Enterprise Councils (TECs) (see Chapter 6). Kessler and Bayliss (1998: 196) indicate that tripartite representation continued only for those bodies whose 'function ... is hardly conceivable except on a tripartite basis'. These bodies include the Health and Safety Executive (HSE) and the Advisory, Conciliation and Arbitration Service (ACAS) (see Chapters 2, 6 and 7). More generally, the TUC found that the frequency and quality of its meetings with government departments had diminished.

The return of a Labour government in 1997 resulted in a change of attitude to the role of trade unions in the UK. Chapter 6 outlines several of the ways in which this change has been demonstrated. In particular this includes the restoration of trade union rights at GCHQ, ending the UK's opt-out from the Social Chapter of the Treaty of Maastricht, and statutory recognition of trade union rights, where the majority of employees are in favour (see Chapter 7). However, these changes have not led to a return to the old corporatist approach, or to the more widespread use of tripartism. As the quotation of Tony Blair's words in Chapter 6 indicates, the view of the government has been that governing the country and running the unions are and should be seen as discrete matters. This suggests the continuation of a more limited role for the TUC, although it would also be unwise to exaggerate the level of its pre-1979 influence when it enjoyed a wider range of representation in some of the consultative structures that had been established to advise and inform government.

## The European Trade Union Confederation

John Monks, General Secretary of the TUC from 1993 to 2003, was the sole nominated candidate to become the General Secretary of the European Trade Union Confederation from 2003. The ETUC was established in 1973, 'to provide a trade union counterbalance to the economic forces of European integration', according to its website (ETUC, 2002). Following political changes in central and eastern Europe, a number of trade union bodies have recently joined the ETUC, so that in 2002 its membership stood at 76 national trade union confederations from 35 countries, together with a further 11 European industry federations, giving it representation of some 60 million members. The ETUC is recognised by the European Union, the Council of Europe and the European Free Trade Association as the representative body of the trade union movement at the European level. The principal objectives of the ETUC are to:

- influence the direction of European-level legislation and policy-making through representations to the institutions of the EU and by participating in consultation processes including at the EU's Economic and Social Committee;
- engage in the regulation of employment with employers at the European level through the European social dialogue process. The ETUC and UNICE (discussed below) are recognised by the EU as Social Partners and are permitted to negotiate framework agreements at the European level. This has resulted in three such agreements relating to parental leave, part-time work and fixed-term contracts, which are now part of EU legislation following ratification by the EU's Council of Ministers;
- campaign for employment rights through trade union action, including the organisation of demonstrations within European cities to promote trade union causes (ETUC, 2002).

## 5.6 Employers' associations and the Union of Industrial and Employers' Confederations of Europe

### Defining employers' associations

Like trade unions, employers' associations are defined in law. The current definition is contained in the Trade Union and Labour Relations (Consolidation) Act of 1992. Section 122 of this Act defines an employers' association as an organisation, whether temporary or permanent, that consists wholly or mainly of employers whose main purpose includes the regulation of relations between these employers and workers or trade unions. Associations in particular industries operate as both trade and employers' organisations, so that their functions cover commercial representation as well as the regulation of the employment relationship.

The Certification Officer's report for 2002 lists 94 employers' associations covering England, Scotland and Wales. However, as listing is a voluntary matter, this report notes that a further 90 employers' associations had submitted an annual return to the Certification Officer in line with their statutory requirement to do so although these organisations had not applied to be listed. The largest employers' associations include the Engineering Employers' Federation (EEF), which is made up of 16 member associations that have several thousand organisations in their collective membership; the National Farmers' Union, with 137 492 members in 2002; the National Federation of Retail Newsagents, with 21 855 members; the Federation of Master Builders, with 13 450 members; the Freight Transport Association, with 10 996 members; and the Retail Motor Industry Federation, with 9710 members. Many employers' associations cover, or predominantly cover, very small employing organisations, with fewer than 20 employees, and fairly small ones, with 20–500 employees. Notable among these associations is the Federation of Small Businesses, with over 174 000 members.

As these data indicate, an employers' association may operate as a national federation of other associations, such as the EEF. Conversely, it may operate as a local association of employers, which may or may not be associated to a national federation. An example of the former case, where an employers' association is part of a national federation, is the EEF West Midlands Association, with 991 members in 2002. Alternatively, an association may represent the employers in a particular industry without adopting a dual structure: for example, in addition to the cases listed above, the Chemical Industries Association had 166 members in 2002. Specialist associations also exist in particular industries, such as the Vehicle Builders and Repairers Association in the motor industry and the Newspaper Society in publishing. Employers' associations also exist in the public sector, such as the Representative National Organisation of Employers of Local Authority Staff, the Association of Colleges, and the Universities and Colleges Employers' Association (see Cockburn, 2002).

### The changing role and functions of employers' associations

Traditionally, the principal role of an employers' association has been to represent its members at multi-employer collective bargaining with recognised trade unions, which generally led to industry-wide collective agreements for terms and conditions of work. As Chapter 7 outlines, the incidence of multi-employer bargaining has declined considerably in recent years (Cully *et al.*, 1999). This has raised a question about the continuing role of employers' associations. However, they have managed to adapt to place greater emphasis on other functions and to serve the needs of smaller employing organisations in particular, who often do not have the resources to invest in specialist functions within their own businesses, as we outline in the following paragraphs.

Although multi-employer bargaining continues in some industries, employers' associations now place much greater emphasis on providing advisory services to their members, representing these in a number of ways and operating disputes procedures when required. Employers' associations are able to invest in the specialist provision of these services, which smaller employing organisations in particular would not have the resources to be able to provide for themselves. IRS (2002b) report that employers' associations provide advice to their members on a wide range of topics. These include advice on health and safety, employment law, disciplinary, equal opportunities, pay, welfare, recruitment, change and partnership matters. They are also able to organise and offer training courses and consultancy, for which additional fees are likely to be payable.

Employers' associations are also able to invest resources to represent the interests of their members to a range of other organisations. A key role for employers' associations is to lobby government at both national and local levels. IRS (2002b) found that 90 per cent of its sample of employers' associations represented the interests of their members to government departments. Representing the interests of members to the departments and institutions of the EU was also found to be highly important (IRS, 2002b). Employers' associations also provide a means to represent the common interests of their members to the trade unions recognised within an industry, even where multi-employer bargaining no longer takes place.

Employers' associations provide other services for their members including advice and representation in relation to employment tribunal cases, the operation of disputes procedures, provision of model policies for members to adopt or adapt, dissemination of current employment issues, and the opportunity for networking within the membership (e.g. IRS, 2002b). Employers' associations have had to adapt to structural changes, related to industrial change and the levels at which collective bargaining occurs in many industries and occupational sectors, but they have been able to secure an important role, particularly in relation to serving the specialist needs of smaller employing organisations. These associations may also be affiliated to employers' organisations that have a wider remit and that help to represent employers' interests at the European level. In this way, many employers' associations are members of the Confederation of British Industry (CBI), which in turn is a member of UNICE.

## Union of Industrial and Employers' Confederations of Europe (UNICE)

The Union of Industrial and Employers' Confederations of Europe, or UNICE, describes its role as the 'the voice of business in Europe'. Founded in 1958, its membership is made up of 34 business federations from 27 countries in Europe. Its mission is to promote the common interests of the businesses that are represented by its member organisations, to influence the decision-making processes at the European level so that these take account of business needs, and to represent its member organisations at the European social dialogue process.

It wishes to see 'improving labour market flexibility' and 'a well functioning internal market, including less and better legislation' (UNICE, 2002). Based in Brussels, it is recognised by the EU as one of the Social Partners that are permitted to negotiate framework agreements at the European level. There are two other employers' organisations that are also recognised as partners in the European social dialogue process. These organisations are the European Centre for Public Enterprises and Services of General Economic Interest (CEEP) and the European Association of Craft, Small and Medium-Sized Enterprises (UEAPME).

UNICE announced in late 2002 that the Social Partners in the European social dialogue process (ETUC, CEEP, UEAPME and UNICE) had agreed their programme of work for the period of 2003–2005 to cover 19 industrial relations and employment regulation issues (UNICE, 2002).

> **self-check question** **5.2** What can an employers' association do to help an individual employer?

## 5.7 Trade union membership and recognition

### Trade union membership

Table 5.1 shows levels of union membership in Great Britain at five-year intervals between 1975 and 2000. Union membership peaked at just over 13.2 million members in 1979. This equated to approximately 57 per cent of those in employment at this time (although union density amongst the actual workforce would have been lower as not all union members were in employment). By 2000, union membership had fallen to 7.8 million people, a decline of approximately 40 per cent, so that only 29 per cent of those in employment were union members. In fact, trade union membership in Great Britain has remained around 7.8 million since 1997, according to the Certification Officer's annual reports.

The Labour Force Survey (LFS) reveals data about union densities in Great Britain, although this only considers the union status of those in employment (Brook, 2002). *Union density* is the unionised workforce expressed as a percentage of potential membership. Union densities may be calculated in relation to the total in employment, or for particular industries, sectors, occupations and workplaces, or in relation to individual and job-related characteristics, as we now describe. In 2001, according to the LFS, 29 per cent of employees were members of a union in Great Britain. There was a slight variation according to gender: 30 per cent of males in employment were members and 28 per cent of females. Young employees were significantly less likely to join a union: only 5 per cent of those under 20 years of age were members in 2001. In contrast, 38 per cent of those in employment aged 40–49 years old were members. According to the LFS classification, 30 per cent of black or black British employees were union members in 2001, 29 per cent of white employees,

25 per cent of Asian or Asian British employees and 22 per cent of Chinese and other ethnic groups. Employees with a degree or other higher education qualification were more likely to join a union in comparison with employees generally. In contrast, those with GCSEs as their highest qualification or employees without any qualifications were less likely to join a union.

Length of service is also positively related to union membership. In 2001, only 12 per cent of employees with less than one year's service were union members. In contrast, 45 per cent of employees with 10–20 years' service were members, rising to 60 per cent of those with 20 years' service or more. The very high proportion of managers and supervisors who are union members in the public sector means that, in aggregate terms, these groups are more unionised than non-managers or non-supervisors (managers, 30 per cent; supervisors, 37 per cent; other employees, 27 per cent). Those in permanent employment are more likely to be union members (30 per cent density) than those in temporary employment (19 per cent density). This is also the case for those in full-time employment (32 per cent density) in comparison with those in part-time employment (20 per cent density).

Significant differences in union densities exist in relation to industrial sector and size of workplace. Fifty-nine per cent of those employed in the public sector were union members in 2001; in the private sector, union membership was just 18 per cent. Within the private sector there are also some noticeable differences: union densities remain relatively high amongst those employed in energy and water (53 per cent) and transport and communication (37 per cent), but are much lower for those employed in hotels and catering (4 per cent), wholesale and retail jobs (12 per cent) and construction (14 per cent). People employed in the same industrial classification, for example in education and in health, are far more likely to be union members if they work in the public sector than in the private sector. In workplaces employing fewer than 25 people, only 15 per cent of employees were union members in 2001, whereas 36 per cent were members in workplaces employing 25 or more (Brook, 2002).

A number of reasons have been advanced to account for the decline in trade union membership between 1979 and 1997. Metcalf (1991: 22) stated that changes in union membership are

> determined by the complex interaction of five factors: the macroeconomic climate, the composition of jobs and the workforce, the policy of the state, the attitude and conduct of employers, and the stance taken by unions themselves.

Chapters 2 and 6 discuss how some of these factors changed during this period. Studies of the decline of trade union membership have emphasised different factors. Carruth and Disney (1988) and Disney (1990) place emphasis on the role of macroeconomic factors in this decline, with high unemployment and real wage growth acting to depress union density. In contrast, Freeman and Pelletier (1990) place emphasis on the role of changes in labour law in the UK during the Conservative governments of the 1980s to explain the reduction in union density during that period. Yet other studies have placed emphasis on changes in the composition of jobs and the workforce during this period to explain this decline (e.g. Millward and Stevens, 1986, 1988). Metcalf (1991) rejects the idea that only one of these factors could largely explain the decline in union membership and density that occurred in the UK in the period to 1997. His view is that,

It seems much more plausible that macroeconomic factors, industry composition, and industrial relations law *each* played a part: the authors [of the various explanations advanced] are all *partly* right.' (Metcalf, 1991: 23) (original emphasis)

He also places emphasis on the roles and attitudes of employers and the unions in this decline.

### ■ Employers' attitudes to unionisation, union recognition and derecognition, and how unions responded: from 1979 to the late 1990s

The policy of an employer towards unionisation is an important factor in determining level of union membership (e.g. Metcalf, 1991; Millward *et al.*, 2000). According to the WERS series, unions were present in 54 per cent of British workplaces in 1998, having declined from 73 per cent in 1984 (Millward *et al.*, 2000). *Union presence* is defined as one or more union members in a workplace. The presence of unions also varies by sector. In 1998, union presence was 97 per cent in the public sector, 42 per cent in private sector manufacturing and 35 per cent in private sector services (Millward *et al.*, 2000). However, as Metcalf (1991: 25) stated, 'recognition is the fulcrum on which membership moves.' According to the WERS series, trade union recognition declined significantly through the 1980s and 1990s. In 1984, unions were recognised in 66 per cent of workplaces. By 1998, this had fallen to 42 per cent of workplaces. In the public sector there was some reduction in recognition for the purpose of collective bargaining, so that unions were recognised in 87 per cent of this sector in 1998. This reduction in the public sector is largely explained by a small number of structural changes, such as the ending of the national pay bargaining system for teachers by the government in 1987 and the establishment of a pay review body to recommend pay increases (Millward *et al.*, 2000).

Recognition fell much more significantly in the private sector between 1980 and 1998. Half of workplaces in the private sector recognised unions in 1980; by 1998 this had fallen to a quarter of private sector workplaces (Millward *et al.*, 2000). Millward *et al.* (2000: 97) comment that,

> The decline in the incidence of union recognition from 1980 onwards was thus almost a wholly private sector phenomenon. From 1990 onwards it was entirely so.... Manufacturing and service industries were equally affected. Almost all of the broad industrial sectors experienced a substantial fall in union recognition between 1990 and 1998.

As with the decline in union membership discussed above, there is more than one reason for this decline in union recognition. Linkages are also evident to the reasons presented above for the decline in union membership. For example, industrial restructuring led to the closure of many organisations in 'mature' and 'declining' industries. These older and generally larger employing organisations in the private sector had traditionally granted union recognition. They were composed mainly of full-time, male workers who undertook manual work, of which a high proportion were union members. By the late 1990s, the relative decline of this type of workplace meant that Millward *et al.* (2000) were able to report that these no longer stood out as the bedrock of union representation and recognition in relation to other categories of workplace. By the late 1990s, smaller establishments and organisations were also significantly less likely to recognise unions than larger ones, as were younger workplaces than older ones. While union recognition was diminishing in the declining parts of the economy in particular, it was not being replenished in the new and developing sectors. The reduction in union presence, reported above, to only 42 per cent in private sector manufacturing and 35 per cent in private sector services workplaces in Britain by 1998 appears to provide evidence for this: without union members being present, recognition will not occur.

The decline in recognition also occurred because of union derecognition in some employing organisations that altered their policy towards trade unions. Claydon (1989: 215) defines derecognition 'as a decision to withdraw from collective bargaining in favour of other arrangements for regulating employment relations.' His study of derecognition in Britain in the 1980s found that this should not be equated with deunionisation, where unions are not given any rights to organise or operate within an employing organisation (Claydon, 1989). Derecognition took a number of forms along two dimensions, breadth and depth. *Breadth of derecognition* contains three categories:

■ general, where the union's bargaining rights on behalf of all employees are withdrawn;
■ grade specific, where these rights are withdrawn in respect of a particular grade of employee in an organisation;
■ plant specific, where bargaining rights are withdrawn at a particular plant, establishment or workplace (Claydon, 1989).

*Depth of derecognition* refers to the nature of the bargaining and representation rights that are withdrawn. Depth in this context contains four possibilities or categories, where derecognition:

■ is partial, so that a union loses bargaining rights in respect of pay determination but retains these rights for other issues;
■ involves the union losing its status as a bargaining agent, so that it loses all bargaining rights but still retains the right to be consulted and to represent individual members in respect of grievances etc.;
■ involves the union losing its status for all collective issues, so that it retains representation rights only in respect of matters affecting individual members.
■ involves the union losing all rights over collective issues and individual representation. This amounts to deunionisation (Claydon, 1989).

Studies of derecognition in the 1980s and 1990s nevertheless found that this was a limited phenomenon. For example, Claydon (1996) identified 170 cases for the period between 1984 and 1993, with the greatest concentration occurring between 1988 and 1993. In the period to 1988, cases of derecognition occurred most often in the publishing, paper and print industries (12), followed by cases involving companies operating in ports, shipping and transport (11), and 6 cases each in broadcasting and communications, petroleum and chemicals, and food manufacture (Claydon, 1996). In the period between 1988 and 1993, Claydon (1996) identified 112 cases, with the greatest number still in publishing, paper and print (25), followed by cases in the metal, engineering and vehicle industries (16), and 15 cases each in the petro-leum and chemicals, and the wholesale, retail and distribution industries. Gall and McKay's study (1994) identified just under 400 cases between 1988 and 1994. Their study confirms the relatively high level of cases in the industries identified above, with the National Union of Journalists, Graphical, Paper and Media Union, Transport and General Workers' Union and Amalgamated Engineering and Electrical Union most frequently confronted by cases of derecognition.

Claydon (1996) identified two broad approaches to union derecognition. The first of these involves management acting in a *reactive* way to the decline in union mem-bership by seeking to derecognise the union or unions involved. Millward *et al.* (2000) report from the WERS series data that managers interviewed who had been involved in cases of derecognition justified these in just over half of cases by saying that union membership had declined or union activity was absent. The second approach to union derecognition involves management acting in a *purposive* way to get rid of unions from the regulation of the employment relationship. Claydon (1996) describes how this approach often involved an incremental strategy to elimi-nate union presence by allowing areas of weak unionisation to wither in an organisation and targeting hard or strong areas of union membership, particularly where these existed in a strategically important area of the production process. Such targeting appears to have been associated with organisational restructuring, downsiz-ing and the announcement of redundancies, contracting-out of some functions, and the introduction of incentives to encourage employees to sign up to individual con-tracts that eradicated the need for collective bargaining (e.g. Claydon, 1996).

Although cases of derecognition are important in terms of understanding the way in which the regulation of the employment relationship for some groups of employees has changed, its incidence in the 1980s and 1990s was limited. By the late 1990s, it appears to have declined significantly, so that the ACAS Annual Report of 1999–2000 reports only one case of full union derecognition (ACAS, 2000), and the Report of 2000–2001 refers only to two cases of partial derecognition (ACAS, 2001).

Union strength and managerial policy are seen as important determinants of dere-cognition. Claydon (1989, 1996) concluded that a crucial factor in many cases of derecognition was union strength, as measured by membership density in an organisa-tion, support for the union from members and the resources available externally to support the union at the workplace. Whereas these indicators of union power, where evident, may be countered by a highly determined and well-resourced employing organisation and its management, the existence of reasonably effective unionisation in many workplaces may have reduced attempts at union derecognition. Conversely, the policy of management in many organisations is likely to have been sufficiently accept-ing of union recognition not to invest in the effort to derecognise, especially in a period when unions were weakened. This presents a complex scenario where both union strength and its relative weakness may potentially avert union derecognition. The crucial factor may therefore be the attitude and policy of an employing organisa-tion's management. Management may support the regulation of the employment relationship through collective relations, it may accept this on pragmatic grounds, or it may oppose this, sometimes, given particular circumstances, being prepared to attempt to operationalise this opposition. Of course, within particular employing organisations this situation is likely to be more complex, perhaps with support for the collectivisation of some employment relationships but not others, or with some managers supporting union presence and others opposing. A weakened union presence may be accepted in particular cases, although where the legitimacy of union presence is threatened, derecognition may follow. This has happened in cases where national collective bargaining arrangements have ceased and the legitimacy for union recognition has consequently reduced in workplaces where its strength was low, leading to cases of derecognition (e.g. Metcalf, 1991; Claydon, 1996; Millward *et al.*, 2000).

Trade unions responded to their membership losses in a number of ways. These included continuing to recruit members in traditional areas, attempting to recruit in new areas, attempting to broaden the appeal of the union by offering new services, resisting attempts at derecognition, entering single-union agreements, and engaging in union mergers. We have already considered some of these strategies. Many single-union agreements were seen to offer too many concessions to employers. A union entering this type of arrangement gained recognition and the sole right to recruit amongst an organisation's workforce, but its attractiveness to potential members may have been decreased by the terms of the agreement that gave it single-union status. Unions also broadened the range of services offered to members, although these remain marginal to their core functions of engaging in the regulation of the employment relationship, including the negotiation of pay increases and the promotion and protection of employees' rights (e.g. Waddington and Whitston, 1997).

Unions were active in the recruitment of new members as a means to counter membership losses. While total union membership declined by about 40 per cent between 1979 and 1997, unions were nevertheless investing considerable resources to recruit new members. Some unions continued to recruit large numbers of new members, although their membership levels still show an overall decline. The largest union in Britain in 1979 with two million members, the Transport and General Workers' Union (TGWU), continued to increase its recruitment though the 1980s, with 245 000 recruits in 1988 alone (Metcalf, 1991). In overall terms, however, the TGWU continued to lose members through the 1980s and 1990s, standing at just 858 804 members in 2001 (see Table 5.3). This equated to a loss of about 59 per cent of its level of membership in 1979. Metcalf (1991) also referred to the Union of Shop, Distributive and Allied Workers (USDAW) losing about one-quarter of its membership each year in the 1980s. In 1979, the membership of USDAW stood at just over 460 000; by 1996 this had declined to about 282 000, although by 2001 it stood at about 310 000, a loss of about one-third in terms of its overall level of membership between 1979 and 2001. Although both of these unions lost members in overall terms, the fact that they were able to recruit large numbers of new members demonstrates scope to expand membership in sectors where union density is low or volatile. Both of these unions also have fairly open approaches to recruitment (see the discussion earlier).

Other unions with scope to improve the density of membership in the industry, employment sector or occupation within which they organised were also able to recruit large numbers of new members. Some unions were able to increase their levels of membership against the trend of overall decline between 1979 and 1997. The teacher unions and the Royal College of Nursing of the United Kingdom (RCN) were able to stand out against the trend of overall decline. Notably, the membership of the RCN increased from about 160 000 in 1979 to 334 000 by 2001. Conversely, unions with a relatively closed approach to recruitment, or which organised in a declining industry or employment sector, suffered losses that were closer to the overall trend or greater than the trend. The most notable case in this respect is the National Union of Mineworkers, which had a quarter of a million members in 1979, but which was reduced to a few thousand members by the mid 1990s.

One further strategy that helped some unions to respond to membership losses was to merge with another union. Table 5.4 outlines a number of mergers that helped each of the unions formed to become one of the largest in Britain. These include Unison, Amicus, the Communication Workers' Union, the Public and Commercial Services Union, the Graphical, Paper and Media Union, and UNIFI. These mergers helped these unions to consolidate their organising positions and to provide a resource base for expansion in particular cases. Throughout the 1980s and 1990s unions ran various campaigns aimed not only at increasing membership levels in general but also at targeting particular groups who were less well represented. Although recruitment gains were made, these campaigns were not always successful. For example, the campaigns organised under the auspices of the TUC in Manchester and at the Docklands in London were described as 'relative failures' (IRS, 1993). Despite the efforts made to recruit new members and the relative success achieved in some cases, union membership declined significantly between 1979 and 1997, as we recognised above.

## The impact of statutory recognition: union recognition from 2000

As we noted above, the return of a Labour government in 1997 resulted in a change of attitude to the role of trade unions in the UK. The Employment Relations Act of 1999 introduced provisions for the statutory recognition of trade unions, which were implemented on 6 June 2000. These provisions are outlined in Chapter 7, together with a brief description of the role of the Central Arbitration Committee (CAC), which is the independent body provided with statutory powers to adjudicate on applications related to statutory recognition and derecognition (Table 7.2). This statutory recognition procedure complements the traditional route to recognition, where unions approach an employer, to be either rebuffed or voluntarily accepted. The opportunity to use a statutory route to gain recognition is clearly seen as being advantageous for trade unions, provided that the qualifying conditions are not too onerous (see Chapter 7).

In fact, according to Gall and McKay (1999), the trend away from derecognition had already begun to change in the mid-1990s, with cases of union recognition exceeding cases of derecognition in Britain. Following the implementation of legislation for the statutory recognition of unions in June 2000, the incidence of union recognition in employing organisations increased significantly, as Table 5.5 shows.

In addition to the 450 recognition agreements reached voluntarily during the first full year after the introduction of provisions for the statutory recognition of trade unions, a further 20 cases were approved statutorily through the CAC (TUC, 2002a). According to these data, the average number of union recognition agreements, through both voluntary and statutory means, was 39.2 per month during the period from November 2000 to October 2001, indicating a significant increase on the

**Table 5.5 Cases of union recognition, 1996–2001**

| Period | Number of months | Number of voluntary agreements | Average number per month during period |
|---|---|---|---|
| January–December 1996 | 12 | 110 | 9.2 |
| January 1997–February 1998 | 14 | 81 | 5.8 |
| March 1998–October 1999 | 20 | 109 | 5.5 |
| November 1999–October 2000 | 12 | 159 | 13.3 |
| November 2000–October 2001 | 12 | 450 | 37.5 |

Source: Adapted from TUC (2002a)

1990s. Agreements reached voluntarily provided for full recognition in 94 per cent of these cases, according to the TUC. This included recognition for collective bargaining in relation to pay, hours of work and holidays, member representation and time off for union duties. These agreements were reached with a range of private sector organisations and involved 23 unions, with Amicus involved in 136 cases, the GMB in 109 cases, the Graphical, Paper and Media Union in 72 cases, TGWU in 58 cases, Unison in 20 cases, and the National Union of Journalists in 19 cases (TUC, 2002a). Some of these recognition agreements involved more than one union.

The statutory provisions that were introduced have undoubtedly bolstered the increased trend in cases of voluntarily agreed recognition. David Yeandle, deputy director of employment policy at the Engineering Employers' Federation, comments in *IRS Employment Review* that,

> ... there seems little doubt that the existence of the statutory procedure – and sometimes the threat of its use – has led to a number of organisations adopting a different approach to union recognition ... (resulting) ... in an increasing number of voluntary recognition agreements being reached.... (IRS, 2002d: 2)

This early period since statutory recognition raises questions about whether unions will only regain recognition in some areas where they lost it previously, whether their attempts to gain recognition will slow after an initial period of activity, and whether union membership will increase in response to wider recognition. Unions will also need to build membership and gain recognition in areas where they have tradition-ally been weak, or where they have lost their presence as we described earlier, especially as unions were present in only 54 per cent of British workplaces in 1998. The provisions for statutory recognition also exclude employers with fewer than 21 employees, relieving these employers of attempts by unions to gain recognition backed by this means. Conversely, the TUC (2002a) reports that, where voluntary agreements have been reached, these have been prompted not only by the existence of these statutory provisions but also through successful union campaigns to pro-mote membership and recognition in these workplaces. In this way, these statutory provisions may provide a focus around which some recovery may take place, leading to greater numbers of union recognition agreements and some improvement in the overall level of union membership.

## 5.8  Partnership approaches in the workplace: the way forward?

Another means to promote trade unions in the workplace and union membership is through partnership agreements. Union recognition agreements may be reached as the result of management realising that it has no choice where a union is able to apply successfully for statutory recognition. This may mean that recognition is granted somewhat reluctantly, even though this attitude may change. Partnership agreements are likely to commence from a different basis. They are more likely to develop in organisations where unions are already recognised and where management and union wish to develop or restructure the nature of their relationship. Traditional union–employer relationships may be based on an adversarial model of interaction. Partnership in this context is based on a joint commitment, by the union as well as management, to work for the successful development of a business or employing organisation. This implies a model of mutual gain, where employees benefit from collective representation, and the interests of the business are enhanced by the release of added value from this relationship. The TUC believes that union membership and recognition will be promoted through the process of working in partnership with employing organisations in this way. It has established a TUC Partnership Institute to help to promote the dissemination of workplace-based partnership. The TUC has also defined six key principles for partnership, which help to make clear its rationale for this approach. These are outlined in Box 5.5.

This approach emphasises a model for mutual gain that may allow it to be differentiated from more traditional approaches to trade union recognition and collective representation. It also allows partnership to be differentiated from the approach taken to single-union agreements in the 1980s. Earlier we quoted the views of Derek Simpson, the joint General Secretary of Amicus, about the nature of many of these single-union agreements in the 1980s. In these comments, he goes on to say that,

> When I say I will renegotiate agreements that do not meet the needs and aspirations of our members, I mean I want to close the book on the dark days of the 1980s and replace them with a redefined template for partnership. ... We only seek a fair deal for our members and meaningful partnerships with their employers. (IRS, 2002c: 2)

The extent to which partnership agreements deliver mutually beneficial gains, help to develop union membership and recognition, and meet the needs and aspirations of union members will need to be evaluated as this approach develops. Some employers and employers' organisations may attempt to promote the idea of partnership with the workforce without seeking to recognise or work with trade unions. In 1998, the Institute of Personnel and Development issued a 'position paper' that stated:

> IPD believes it is entirely sensible that, where a majority of employees in a relevant business unit want to have a trade union recognised, the employer should reach such an agreement. However, it seems to IPD that 'partnership' has more to do with an approach to the relationship between employers and employees, individually and in groups, than it has to do with trade unions as such. (IPD, 1998: 8–9)

Partnership may be associated more with a unitarist approach to the management of the employment relationship in the strategy of some organisations than with the development of a pluralist approach that actively involves trade unions. Kelly (1996,

---

**Box 5.5   The TUC's principles for partnership**

**Principle 1: Joint commitment to the success of the enterprise**

Effective partnerships will be developed where both unions and employers understand an organisation's strategy and are committed to its success. This requires the replacement of any adversarial approach to regulating the employment relationship.

**Principle 2: Recognition of respective legitimate interests**

Genuine partnerships will recognise the legitimate existence of different interests and views between unions and employers. Arrangements are required to resolve these differences in an atmosphere of trust.

**Principle 3: Commitment to security of employment**

Partnership needs to embrace employment security to complement the existence of forms of flexibility in the workplace. Flexibility should not be used at the expense of employment security. This will mean restricting the use of compulsory redundancy and developing employability where appropriate.

**Principle 4: Focus on the quality of working life**

Partnership should provide opportunities for employees to participate in the making of decisions that affect their working lives and for improved terms and conditions of work. It should also broaden the scope of organisational issues that are considered jointly by unions and employers.

**Principle 5: Transparency and sharing of information**

Partnership is based on transparency and the sharing of information at an early stage, with opportunities for meaningful consultations to be conducted with unions and employees.

**Principle 6: Mutual gains and adding value**

Effective partnerships will lead to improved organisational performance, terms and conditions, and develop employee involvement, commitment, and mutual gains.

*Source*: Adapted from ‹http://www.tuc.org.uk/pi/partnership.htm› and related material (TUC, 2002b)

---

1998) has observed that hostility to union presence has developed in the recent past, and that 'It is, after all, difficult for a union to construct a partnership with an employer who would prefer that the union simply did not exist' (Kelly, 1998: 63).

*self-check question*

**5.3** What opportunities exist for trade unions to recover some of their losses of the last two decades, and what factors may threaten any such recovery?

## 5.9   Union officials and workplace representatives

Different types of union official manage trade unions. In the British context in particular, those who manage union affairs may be divided into two main types. The first type that unions employ are generally referred to as *full-time officials*. These officials work at national or regional level. This organisational arrangement is similar to that

**The Management of Human Resources**

of the TUC described above. The chief officer of most unions is referred to as its General Secretary. For example, the Graphical, Paper and Media Union (GPMU), the eleventh largest union in the UK in 2001 with 200 000 members (Table 5.3), has an organisational structure that includes a general secretary, deputy general secretary, general president, national officer(s) with particular sectoral responsibilities, and financial secretary to manage its affairs (GPMU, 2000). These officers are elected by the union's membership. The GPMU also employs industrial officers who may work at the union's head office or in its regions. This union is organised into 10 regions, covering Great Britain and the Republic of Ireland. Within these regions, the union is organised into branches, which are run by a number of branch officials including a chairperson or president, secretary, committee members, auditors and health and safety advisor, elected by the branch membership. At company level, where there are two or more GPMU members a union chapel is formed, and the member who oversees this is known as the father/mother or clerk of the chapel (GPMU, 2000).

*Lay officials* or *workplace representatives* make up the second type of union official. The existence of these representatives provides an important indication of trade union strength at the workplace. They provide an important means of representing the interests of union members to management not only because of their locational proximity but also because they share a close understanding of the issues of the particular employment relationship. Workplace representatives are formally accredited to represent the interests of the members of a recognised trade union in an employing organisation and thus are recognised by its management for this purpose. They are employed by this employing organisation, within which they are very likely to receive time off from their normal duties to operate as workplace representatives. They can be differentiated from other union officials at national and regional levels where these are employed by the union itself. Workplace representatives of different unions may be known by different terms including shop stewards, corresponding members or staff representatives. The senior workplace representative of a union may be referred to as its convenor, or as we saw in relation to the example of the GPMU the father/mother or clerk of the chapel.

Workplace representatives may be involved in a range of union activities, which may be classified into two main categories. The first of these relates to the functions that they carry out on behalf of the trade union as an *external organisation*. This principally involves:

- recruiting other eligible employees to join the union;
- promoting the benefits of membership to potential and actual members;
- receiving information from the union externally and communicating this to members within the workplace;
- making contact with other workplace representatives, and with branch, regional or perhaps national officials for advice and assistance in relation to casework, negotiating and dispute situations;
- reporting any breaches of agreement to branch, regional or perhaps national officials.

The second category relates to involvement in union processes at the *workplace*, which principally involves:

- representing the interests of members to the management of an employing organisation to endeavour to promote or protect these, and to respond to the treatment of members by management;

- protecting and promoting members' interests in relation to health and safety at work (discussed below);
- advising and representing members in relation to discipline and grievance cases (see Chapter 9);
- negotiating about pay and conditions of work where this is devolved to workplace level (see Chapter 7);
- engaging in the process of joint consultation at the workplace (see Chapter 8);
- involvement in collective disputes where these arise at the workplace;
- reporting outcomes to members, consulting with them and encouraging them to become more active in the union.

However, the proportion of workplaces with union representatives fell significantly between 1980 and 1998. In 1980, union representatives were present in at least 53 per cent of workplaces with 25 or more employees; by 1998 this had fallen to 33 per cent. Non-union representatives were reported in a further 41 per cent of such workplaces in 1998. The remaining quarter of such workplaces did not have any workplace representatives (Millward *et al.*, 2000).

In 1998 union representatives were present in 74 per cent of workplaces with 25 or more employees that recognised trade unions. Private sector services organisations of this size that recognised unions were least likely to have union representatives (58 per cent), whereas they were present in 93 per cent of private sector manufacturing firms that recognised unions. The WERS data also show that whereas there was a decline in the proportion of workplaces with union representatives in the 1980s, their presence stabilised in the 1990s in organisations with recognised unions (Cully *et al.*, 1999; Millward *et al.*, 2000).

In 1998 each union representative in the workplace represented an average of 29 members compared with 32 members in 1990, although this varied significantly depending on workplace size and industrial sector (Cully *et al.*, 1999; Millward *et al.*, 2000). In organisations with 25–49 employees, the average number of members represented by each union representative was 17. This compares with 53 members per union representative in organisations with 500 or more employees (Cully *et al.*, 1999). These data in the last three paragraphs indicate that although the presence of union representatives is restricted to a smaller proportion of organisations than in 1980, there nevertheless remains a reasonably well-organised infrastructure of workplace representatives in organisations where unions are recognised (see Godfrey and Marchington, 1996; Millward *et al.*, 2000).

 **self-check question** **5.4** This chapter has referred to a number of different ways of identifying trade union power. What determinants of trade union power have been identified in the chapter?

## 5.10 Health and safety committees and union representation

The Health and Safety Regulations of 1996 mean that all employing organisations in the UK should now consult with employees or their representatives about health and safety matters. This consultation may take place in different ways. These include the use of health and safety committees and consulting directly with safety representatives. Slightly fewer than 4 out of 10 workplaces had health and safety committees and in marginally less than 3 out of 10 workplaces consultation took place directly with safety representatives in 1998 (Cully *et al.*, 1999; Millward *et al.*, 2000).

However, although legislation has promoted the development of workplace representation for the purpose of health and safety consultation, the most recent WERS data suggests that unions appointed representatives to health and safety committees in only about one-third of cases by 1998 (Millward *et al.*, 2000). The Health and Safety Commission's guide to the health and safety system in Great Britain (HSC, 2002: 32) states that, 'in workplaces where trade unions are recognised, the unions have the right to appoint safety representatives to act on the employees' behalf in consultations with their employer....' As Millward *et al.* (2000) suggest, in those organisations where they are recognised but do not have representatives, unions are not able to establish these in practice. The right to appoint representatives exists, but in practice the lack of workplace-based strength does not allow this to occur. It also appears to indicate an area in which the presence of non-union representatives has become more evident.

## The Health and Safety Commission and Health and Safety Executive

At national level in the UK the Health and Safety Commission (HSC) and the Health and Safety Executive (HSE) are the two principal governmental organisations responsible for the regulation of health and safety at work. The Health and Safety at Work etc. Act 1974 led to the establishment of these two institutions. The HSC is a tripartite body consisting of 10 commissioners whose role is to introduce arrangements for the health, safety and welfare of people at work and for the public from the way in which businesses and organisations operate. The functions of the HSC include proposing new laws, regulations and standards, promoting research and training, providing information and advice, and maintaining the Employment Medical Advisory Service. The HSE is appointed by the HSC, with government approval and advice, and assists the Commission. The HSE is responsible for the enforcement of health and safety law. It operates through a board that is composed of several directorates. Its staff of approximately 4000 is organised within these directorates and includes inspectors, scientists, technologists, medical experts, policy advisors and lawyers (HSC, 2002; HSE, 2002).

## 5.11 Summary

- Trade unions may be defined in relation to their functions to protect their members' welfare and to participate in job regulation with employers. Unions may be differentiated according to their degree of unionateness.
- Other union functions include recruiting new members and retaining existing ones, pursuing issues for particular groups of members, providing member services, and pursuing institutional goals related to the union's development, or even its survival.
- The number of trade unions in Britain has steadily declined. By 2000 the 16 largest trade unions in Great Britain accounted for almost 6.5 million members out of a total membership of 7.9 million, or 82 per cent of all union members. The development of trade unionism in Britain makes classification problematic, although many unions may be described as multi-sectoral in terms of the scope of their organising activities.

■ Union mergers and multi-unionism are continuing features of trade unionism in Britain. Recent employer strategies to overcome problems of multi-unionism include the introduction of single-union agreements and single-table bargaining.

■ The Trades Union Congress, or TUC, is the representative body of the trade union movement in the UK, with approximately 70 affiliated unions that collectively represented about 6.7 million workers, or roughly 85 per cent of union members in 2002. The TUC has experienced a number of significant changes over the last two decades.

■ With the decline in the incidence of industry level or multi-employer collective bargaining, many employers are no longer members of employers' associations. Many employers' associations continue to function by placing much greater emphasis on advisory services for their members and servicing the needs of small employers in particular.

■ Trade union membership fell significantly between 1979 and 1997, although this has since stabilised. However, the incidence of union presence and union recognition in employing organisations, particularly in the private sector, also declined significantly in this period.

■ The introduction of statutory recognition of trade unions and the promotion of partnership agreements by the TUC and its affiliates offer these unions some hope to expand their membership and the incidence of union recognition.

■ This chapter also describes the role and activities of union officials and workplace representatives including those engaged on health and safety duties.

## References

ACAS (2000) *Annual Report, 1999–2000.*

ACAS (2001) *Annual Report, 2000–2001.*

Batstone, E. (1988) 'The frontier of control', *in* Gallie, D. (ed.), *Employment in Britain*, Oxford, Blackwell, pp. 218–47.

Blackburn, R.M. (1967) *Union Character and Social Class*, London, Batsford.

Blackburn, R.M. and Prandy, K. (1965) 'White-collar unionization: a conceptual framework', *British Journal of Sociology*, 16:2, 111–22.

Brook, K. (2002) 'Trade union membership: an analysis of data from the autumn 2001 LFS', *Labour Market Trends*, 110:7, 343–54.

Carruth, A. and Disney, R. (1988) 'Where have two million members gone?', *Economica*, 55:1, 1–19.

Claydon, T. (1989) 'Union derecognition in Britain in the 1980s', *British Journal of Industrial Relations*, 27:2, 214–24.

Claydon, T. (1996) 'Union derecognition: a re-examination', *in* Beardwell, I.J. (ed.), *Contemporary Industrial Relations: A critical analysis*, Oxford, Oxford University Press, pp. 157–74.

Clegg, H. (1979) *The Changing System of Industrial Relations in Great Britain*, Oxford, Basil Blackwell.

Cockburn, D. (2002) *Annual Report of the Certification Officer, 2001–2002* [online] [cited 19 November] Available from <http://www.certoffice.org/annualReport/pdf/2001-2002A.pdf>

Cully, M., Woodland, S., O'Reilly, A. and Dix, G. (1999) *Britain at Work as Depicted by the 1998 Workplace Employee Relations Survey*, London, Routledge.

Disney, R. (1990) 'Explanations of the decline in trade union density in Britain: an appraisal', *British Journal of Industrial Relations*, 28:2, 165–78.

Donovan, T. N. (1968) *Royal Commission on Trade Unions and Employers' Associations* (Cmnd. 3623), London, HMSO.

ETUC (2002) 'About the ETUC' [online] [cited 26 November] Available from <http://www.etuc.org/en/about_etuc>

Farnham, D. and Pimlott, J. (1995) *Understanding Industrial Relations* (5th edn), London, Cassell.

Flanders, A. (1975) *Management and Unions: The theory and reform of industrial relations*, London, Faber & Faber.

Freeman, R. and Pelletier, J. (1990) 'The impact of industrial relations legislation on British union density', *British Journal of Industrial Relations*, 28:2, 141–64.

Gall, G. (1994) 'The rise of single table bargaining in Britain', *Employee Relations*, 16:4, 62–71.

Gall, G. and McKay, S. (1994) 'Trade union derecognition in Britain, 1988–1994', *British Journal of Industrial Relations*, 32:3, 433–48.

Gall, G. and McKay, S. (1999) 'Developments in union recognition and derecognition in Britain, 1994–1998', *British Journal of Industrial Relations*, 37:4, 601–14.

Godfrey, G. and Marchington, M. (1996) 'Shop stewards in the 1990s: a research note', *Industrial Relations Journal*, 27:4, 339–44.

Goetschy, J. (1998) 'France: the limits of reform', *in* Ferner, A. and Hyman, R. (eds), *Changing Industrial Relations in Europe* (2nd edn), Oxford, Blackwell, pp. 357–94.

GPMU (2000) *Rules of the Graphical, Paper & Media Union*, Bedford, GPMU.

Health and Safety Commission (2002) *The Health and Safety System in Great Britain*, HSE Books and available at <http://www.hse.gov.uk/aboutus/hsc/index.htm>

Health and Safety Executive (2002) 'About us' [online] [cited 12 December] Available from <http://www.hse.gov/aboutus/index.htm>,

<http://www.tuc.org.uk>,

<http://www.tuc.org.uk/tuc/unions_list.cfm>

IPD (1998) *Employment Relations into the 21st Century*. IPD position paper, London, Institute of Personnel and Development.

IRS (1992a) 'Unions respond to membership losses', *Employment Review 519*, London, Industrial Relations Services, September, pp. 13–15.

IRS (1992b) 'Single-union deals in perspective', *Employment Review 523*, London, Industrial Relations Services, November, pp. 6–15.

IRS (1993) 'New union recognitions embrace over 60,000 workers', *Employment Review 545*, London, Industrial Relations Services, October, p. 2.

IRS (2002a) 'What do unions want – apart from a pay rise?', *Employment Review 746*, London, Industrial Relations Services, February, pp. 14–16.

IRS (2002b) 'Stormy waters ahead for employers' associations?', *Employment Review 748*, London, Industrial Relations Services, March, pp. 7–13.

IRS (2002c) 'Trade unions: Expert view: Goodnight sweetheart', *Employment Review 761*, London, Industrial Relations Services, October, p. 2.

IRS (2002d) 'Trade unions: Expert view: The limits on union organisation remain', *Employment Review 745*, London, Industrial Relations Services, February, p. 2.

Jacobi, O., Keller, B. and Muller-Jentsch, W. (1998) 'Germany: facing new challenges', *in* Ferner, A. and Hyman, R. (eds), *Changing Industrial Relations in Europe* (2nd edn), Oxford, Blackwell, pp. 190–238.

Kelly, J. (1996) 'Union militancy and social partnership', *in* Ackers, P., Smith, C. and Smith, P. (eds), *The New Workplace and Trade Unionism*, London, Routledge.

Kelly, J. (1998) *Rethinking Industrial Relations*, London, Routledge.

Kessler, S. and Bayliss, F. (1998) *Contemporary British Industrial Relations* (3rd edn), Basingstoke, Macmillan.

Metcalf, D. (1991) 'British unions: dissolution or resurgence?', *Oxford Review of Economic Policy*, 7:1, 18–32.

Millward, N. and Stevens, M. (1986) *British Workplace Industrial Relations 1980–1984*, Aldershot, Gower.

Millward, N. and Stevens, M. (1988) 'Union density in the regions', *Employment Gazette*, 96:5, 286–95.

Millward, N., Bryson, A. and Forth, J. (2000) *All Change at Work?*, London, Routledge.

Regalia, I. and Regini, M. (1998) 'Italy: the dual character of industrial relations', *in* Ferner, A. and Hyman, R. (eds), *Changing Industrial Relations in Europe* (2nd edn), Oxford, Blackwell, pp. 459–503.

Thornley, C., Ironside, M. and Seifert, R. (2000) 'UNISON and changes in collective bargaining in health and local government', *in* Terry, M. (ed.), *Redefining Public Sector Unionism*, London, Routledge, pp. 137–54.

TUC (2002a) *Focus on Recognition, 2002*, London, TUC.

TUC (2002b) *TUC Partnership Institute* [online] [cited 12 December] Available from <http://www.tuc.organisation.uk/pi/partnership.htm>

Turner, H.A. (1962) *Trade Union Growth, Structure and Policy*, London, Allen & Unwin.

Undy, R., Ellis, W., McCarthy, W. and Halmos, A. (1981) *Change in Trade Unions*, London, Hutchinson.

UNICE (2002) UNICE website [online] [cited 12 December] Available from <http://unice.org/unice/Website.nsf/>

Waddington, J. and Whitston, C. (1997) 'Why do people join unions in a period of membership decline?', *British Journal of Industrial Relations*, 35:4, 515–46.

Webb, S. and Webb, B. (1920) *The History of Trade Unionism 1666–1920*, London, Longman.

Whybrew, E.G. (2001) *Annual Report of the Certification Officer, 2000–2001* [online] [cited 12 December] Available from <http://www.certoffice.org/annualReport/pdf/2000-2001.pdf>

## *self-check* Answers

**5.1** *How may the other trade union functions discussed above be related to a union's primary function to become involved in the regulation of the employment relationship?*

The effectiveness of a union depends, to varying degrees, on each of the functions outlined and the way in which these are seen to support one another. One dimension of union power is related to its membership. The level of, as well as the 'qualities' exhibited by, its membership will affect the willingness of employers to recognise and to bargain with a union. This has recently been reinforced by the conditions that underpin the statutory recognition of trade unions, discussed in Section 5.7 and Chapter 7. Level of membership also affects the union's resource base, which will in turn affect its ability to pursue a range of agendas for members and to arrange services that appeal to these members. Conversely, the pursuit of interests that relate closely to the experiences and concerns of employees at work should help to attract them into membership. The effectiveness of a union also depends on the existence of an active core of members, especially those who put themselves forward to become workplace representatives and full-time officials. Through these examples, we can recognise that the effectiveness of a union is bound to the way in which its functions mutually support one another.

**5.2** *What can an employers' association do to help an individual employer?*

Employers' associations may negotiate with trade unions in multi-employer collective bargaining structures where these continue to be used to determine levels of pay and conditions of employment. They may also devise and operate formal procedures for resolving disputes and advise in relation to difficulties with pay settlements.

**The Management of Human Resources**

Employers' associations also provide advice on a wide range of issues including those related to employment legislation, health and safety and other employee relations and personnel matters. This is likely to include the dissemination of information and model procedures to members. Advice in relation to employment tribunal cases and representation at these may be provided. They may also provide consultancy services and offer training courses. Employers' associations also offer the specialist capability to represent members' interests to government, at local and national levels and at the European level, sometimes via other employers' organisations. This final function indicates the importance of pressure group activity.

**5.3** *What opportunities exist for trade unions to recover some of their losses of the last two decades, and what factors may threaten any such recovery?*

The principal opportunities outlined in this chapter for unions to recover some of their losses relate to the introduction of the statutory recognition of trade unions and the development of partnership agreements. The incidence of union recognition had already started to rise at the beginning of this decade, and partnership agreements have been introduced in a number of organisations. The TUC reports that union recognition has been gained not only because of the existence of these statutory provisions but also because of successful campaigns to develop membership at particular workplaces. However, a number of questions may be raised in relation to these strategies. These include whether unions will only regain recognition in some areas where they lost it previously, whether their attempts to gain recognition will slow after an initial period of activity, and whether union membership will increase in response to wider recognition or where partnership agreements are reached.

A number of factors threaten the prospect of a union recovery. A number of key measurements indicate the way in which unions were adversely affected during the 1980s and 1990s. Union density in relation to total employment stood at only 29 per cent in 2000, with total union membership at about 7.9 million. According to the WERS data series, unions were present in only 54 per cent of British workplaces in 1998, and recognised in only 42 per cent, with recognition in the private sector standing at just 25 per cent. Significant variations within the private sector indicate areas where unions struggle to promote recognition and membership. Even within workplaces where unions are recognised, union activity may be low, and in 1998 union representatives were present in only 74 per cent of such workplaces with 25 or more employees. These factors indicate that any recovery is likely to be limited or slow, and it may be focused in particular parts of the economy and amongst specific sectors of employment.

**5.4** *This chapter has referred to a number of different ways of identifying trade union power. What determinants of trade union power have been identified in the chapter?*

The power of a union will depend on the level and nature of its membership as well as on other factors. A union's ability to attract members from particular groups of workers will be important to influence employers to recognise the union, although the attitude of an employer is likely to have a moderating effect in terms of the decision taken by many employees about whether to join. Unions that build up high levels of membership density should be able to exercise much greater power and influence, although other circumstances need to be favourable. This recognises that union power is based on factors other than the level of union membership, although this is an important, underlying factor. Other factors relate to the power resources of individual workers and the ability of a union to combine these resources to mobilise, or use, them. The power resources of workers are related to their scarcity value in the production process or the provision of services, the extent of demand for their type of labour, and their ability to disrupt production or service provision. A union's power will also depend on its ability to combine workers effectively to use these power resources. Mobilisation of potential power resources will also depend on the extent to which members identify with, are committed to and involved in realising the goals of the union. Underpinning this will be the extent to which a union is effectively structured and defined by a clear strategy around which members may identify. Traditionally, the power of craft unions was also defined by the ability of skilled workers to limit the supply of new labour through their exclusive position in being able to train and pass on their skills to entrants to the particular craft. The existence of representatives and activity in the workplace also provides an important indication of trade union power.

## CASE 5 The TUC Partnership Institute

The TUC launched its Partnership Institute in January 2001, with the aim of developing partnerships between unions and employing organisations that will improve employee relations. Partnerships are designed to develop a joint focus that improves people's working lives and the performance of the businesses for which they work. The TUC believes that partnership in the workplace is capable of producing a range of benefits both for employees and for the organisations that employ them, as well as in terms of promoting union membership and organisation.

The TUC believes that a successful approach to partnership is based on six principles (TUC, 2002b). These are:

- *Joint commitment to the success of the enterprise*. Effective partnerships will be developed where both unions and employers understand an organisation's strategy and are committed to its success. This requires the replacement of any adversarial approach to regulating the employment relationship.
- *Recognition of respective legitimate interests*. Genuine partnerships will recognise the legitimate existence of different interests and views between unions and employers. Arrangements are required to resolve these differences in an atmosphere of trust.
- *Commitment to security of employment*. Partnership needs to embrace employment security to complement the existence of forms of flexibility in the workplace. Flexibility should not be used at the expense of employment security. This will mean restricting the use of compulsory redundancy and developing employability where appropriate.
- *Focus on the quality of working life*. Partnership should provide opportunities for employees to participate in the making of decisions that affect their working lives and for improved terms and conditions of work. It should also broaden the scope of organisational issues that are considered jointly by unions and employers.

■ *Transparency and sharing of information.* Partnership is based on transparency and the sharing of information at an early stage, with opportunities for meaningful consultations to be conducted with unions and employees.

■ *Mutual gains and adding value.* Effective partnerships will lead to improved organisational performance, terms and conditions of work, and develop employee involvement, commitment, and mutual gains.

The TUC Partnership Institute is based at its National Education Centre in north London and is composed of a small team of staff supported by a larger group of associates. The Director of the TUC Partnership Institute, Linda Kelly, is responsible for its strategic direction. The TUC's Economic and Social Affairs Department is also responsible for promoting partnership to employers, government and the unions as well as conducting research into this concept. An Advisory Board to the Partnership Institute has been established. Chaired by Professor William Brown of Cambridge University, this is composed of union, employer, academic and other representatives.

The TUC Partnership Institute provides a range of support to promote the development of partnership at work. This includes the provision of advice, diagnostic assessment, training and consultancy about partnership working to both unions and managers. The Partnership Institute recognises that the introduction of partnership working is likely to be problematic, often changing the behaviours and attitudes of those involved for this to be successful. Success in this context requires the development of trust between those involved and their commitment to the approach of partnership, as well as the sustained operationalisation of these attributes in practice. Underpinning the approach to partnership is a commitment to joint decision-making and problem-solving. The TUC Partnership Institute states:

> In our view, partnership is about real joint decision making and problem solving, it is about unions having more influence in the workplace, and employees exercising greater control over their immediate working environment. (TUC, 2002b)

The agenda for partnership encompasses consideration of business strategy, the organisation of work, collective bargaining and issues that affect the quality of working life.

The consultancy work undertaken for the Partnership Institute includes running workshops for union representatives and managers and developing partnership agreements. The provision of training covers the development of skills required for partnership working, including those related to information sharing, developing consensus and jointly solving problems. Training is offered to organisational managers and union representatives, and where this is undertaken jointly it may help to develop a partnership culture within the organisation. The Partnership Institute also uses a diagnostic approach to assess the nature of working relationships between organisational managers and union representatives and the way in which these impact on performance and quality of working life, which may also be benchmarked to other organisations. This allows positive attributes of union–employer relationships to be identified, as well as areas where these could be developed. Independent consultants who demonstrate impartiality in their work with unions and organisational managers are used to provide these services (TUC, 2002b).

The TUC Partnership Institute recognises that there will be a number of aspects that will be common in all cases for partnership to work effectively. These include:

- building a common understanding of the situation and the need for change;
- the establishment of trust between those involved;
- developing an open approach to information and channels for effective communication;
- allowing unions to become more involved in decision-making and developing the participation of employees in respect of operational decisions that affect their work;
- establishing partnership working as part of the culture of an organisation (TUC, 2002b).

## Questions

1 Based on your reading of the chapter as well as the case study, how does the TUC's approach to partnership relate to previous approaches to promote unionisation in the workplace?

2 How would you evaluate the prospects for the success of this approach?

# Chapter 14

# New management techniques in small and medium-sized enterprises

Tony Dundon, Irena Grugulis and Adrian Wilkinson

## Introduction

This chapter is concerned with New Management Techniques (NMTs) in small and medium-sized enterprises (SMEs). Structurally, this chapter differs from others in the book. This is partly because of the need to understand the employment relationship in the context of a small social setting and partly because of the differences in managerial strategies between small and large firms. Most HRM textbooks have relatively little to say about smaller companies, despite the importance of this sector in many industrialised economies (Lane, 1995). This importance is evident both by their centrality to the economy and by the statements of policy makers and mainstream politicians, who argue that it is the growth and prosperity of smaller firms that will stimulate growth in the economy as a whole (Department of Employment, 1992). In Britain, SMEs account for 99 per cent of all companies and 57 per cent of non-government employment (DTI, 1998). However, there are dangers in using these figures in a homogeneous and deterministic way. One SME may not resemble another and lessons obtained in one sector may not necessarily be generalisable elsewhere. It is for these reasons that this chapter presents four brief case studies since these can help to explore the significance of both organisational context and management practice in smaller firms.

The key theme of the chapter is the uses (and abuses) of 'soft HRM and NMTs' in SMEs. Techniques such as cultural change programmes, employee involvement schemes, teamworking and devolved control systems are evident among SMEs (Duberley and Walley, 1995; Bacon et al., 1996; Wilkinson et al., 1998; Downing-Burn and Cox, 1999; Cully et al., 1998) but, as in larger firms, this development is not necessarily positive. Many HRM practices implicitly and explicitly rely on the existence of such managerial techniques to justify 'harder' employment outcomes

(Keenoy, 1997). Moreover, as noted above, SMEs are heterogeneous. In such diverse organisational contexts the use of NMTs needs to be assessed against a variety of influences: product and labour market factors, their dependency on larger firms, as well as the internal dynamics of a small social setting.

Despite the general consensus that employment relations in this sector are worthy of study (Westhead and Storey, 1997), there is a tendency in the existing literature to oversimplify the practices found among SMEs into one of two divergent perspectives (see Table 14.1). The first is the view of the Bolton Commission (Bolton, 1971) that 'small is beautiful'. Here, a low incidence of strikes among SMEs is used to argue that the close proximity of owner-managers to employees ensures informal and harmonious relations, good communications and greater flexibility. This is problematic since, as Edwards (1995) argues, strikes are only one (particularly dramatic) form of industrial discontent and, while the absence of strikes may demonstrate high or increasing levels of trust, communication and commitment between employer and employee, it may also show a fear of management and an abuse of the managerial prerogative. In practice, there is rather more evidence to suggest that discontent is taking forms other than the withdrawal of labour, than there is to suggest that high levels of trust have replaced industrial unrest (Kelly, 1998).

In contrast is Sisson's (1993) 'Bleak House' perspective which indicates that the small firm may manage its labour in ways that are authoritarian, dictatorial and exploitative (see also Goss, 1988; Rainnie, 1989, 1991; Ram, 1991; Ram and Holliday, 1993). Indeed, as Philpott (1996) notes, the majority of employees who earn less than £3.50 per hour can be found within the SME sector. Conflict is not lacking but rather expressed through high levels of absenteeism and labour turnover, as well as a greater propensity for problematic 'interpersonal' relations to develop and ferment over time. In practice, owner-managers tend to take a unitarist view of the enterprise that aspires to a 'happy ship', assuming 'what is good for their business is good for employees' (Goodman *et al.*, 1998).

**Table 14.1  From small is beautiful to Bleak House**

| Positive HR | Negative HR |
| --- | --- |
| Harmonious | Hidden conflict |
| Good HR | Bleak House |
| Little bureaucracy | More instability |
| Family style | Authoritarian |

Source: Wilkinson, 1999: 207

Interesting as these two divergent perspectives are, theorising about human resource management techniques for such a large proportion of Britain's working population in such extreme 'either-or' terms tends to oversimplify and polarise practices that are, in fact, remarkably diverse and complex. Nor in this sector have the empirical studies or core textbooks on HRM helped to counter such simplifications, since the bulk of evidence and theoretical models presented in these is drawn from large organisations (see, for example, Storey, 1992, 1995; Guest and Hoque, 1993; Beardwell and Holden, 1997; Gratton *et al.*, 1999; Bach and Sisson, 2000). These issues and debates are explained later in the chapter, after the significance of the SME sector in Britain is briefly outlined.

## The SME sector

There is no single or acceptable definition of a small firm (Storey, 1994: 8). In Britain, firms that employ fewer than 200 workers are defined as small, while in France, Germany and America the figure is 500 (Odaka and Sawai, 1999). One difficulty is that size can be defined by a combination of indicators, including profitability, rate of tax returns (pre-and post-tax), sales, annual turnover, or the number of employees and there is no clear agreement about which are the most acceptable. Of equal significance here is the issue of organisational context. For example, a hairdressing salon with 20 staff would be small in relation to a chemical plant with 100 workers. However, in the *context of their respective industries*, the hairdressing establishment would be large (possibly with a working owner on site) and the chemical plant small (but subject to greater technological control and possibly collective bargaining). These contextual issues suggest that a range of other factors need to be examined when exploring management strategy in smaller firms, such as the relationships that exist between small and big business, the role of product and labour markets along with the ideologies of owner-managers.

The Bolton Report (1971) defined a small firm as one with fewer than 200 employees and a medium-sized company as one which employed up to 500 workers. For particular sectors a combination of other measures have been used: in road transport the size of a firm was related to both the number of employees and vehicles owned by the organisation; in the retail sector, financial turnover was the main criterion. More recently, the Department of Trade and Industry (DTI, 1998) have adopted a (non-binding) European recommendation that defines smaller firms either as a *micro, small* or *medium*-sized enterprise (see Table 14.2). This appears to fit with recent evidence confirming that organisations are now generally smaller. According to the latest research (Cully *et al.*, 1999: 18; Millward *et al.*, 2000: 29) the typical workplace size is just over 100 employees, with SMEs accounting for 99 per cent of all businesses in Britain (DTI, 1998).

However, such strict statistical definitions can be misleading when used to inform assumptions about employment practices, as SMEs are characterised by high heterogeneity (Curran and Stanworth, 1979; Goss, 1988; Rainnie, 1991). Research suggests that labour–management relations in a small social setting can be complex, diverse, and above all, informal (Scott *et al.*, 1989; Roberts *et al.*, 1992; Ram, 1994). Take the hairdressing salon and chemical plant mentioned earlier. Each would be subject to quite specific internal and external factors that could influence managerial strategies. Managing people at a small chemical plant may be influenced by the dependency of a few (even single) large customers,

**Table 14.2 European Commission SME definitions**

| Criterion | EC SME Definitions | | |
| --- | --- | --- | --- |
| | Micro | Small | Medium |
| Max. number of employees | 10 | 50 | 250 |
| Max. annual turnover | – | 7 m–ecu | 40 m–ecu |
| Max. annual balance sheet total | – | 5 m–ecu | 27 m–ecu |
| Max. % owned by one, or jointly by several, enterprise(s) not satisfying the same criterion. | – | 25% | 25% |

Note: To qualify as an SME, both the employees and the independence criteria must be satisfied and either the turnover or the balance sheet total criteria.

Source: DTI, 1998

capital-intensive process technologies and possibly collective negotiation with trade unions. By contrast, the hairdresser's may be dependent on a large number of individual customers and rely on part-time and casual non-union employees who are subject to managerial autocracy (paternalism), with the owner-manager actually working alongside other employees. It is these contextual variations which suggest that deterministic definitions of the small firm sector ought to be treated with caution. One major problem is the assumption that HRM in larger organisations can be easily transposed to SMEs without an appreciation of the contextual diversity of smaller firms.

## Diversity of NMT in SMEs

There is a growing debate about the use of managerial techniques in smaller firms (Duberley and Whalley, 1995; Bacon *et al.*, 1996; Kinnie *et al.*, 1999) that mirrors 'best practice HRM' (Pfeffer, 1998; Wood, 1995). Examples include devolved managerial responsibilities, cultural change programmes, teamworking and a range of employee involvement (EI) initiatives (Wilkinson *et al.*, 1999). The WERS survey found that in firms employing fewer than 100 people, 28 per cent had introduced 'five or more' NMTs (see Table 14.3). Further evidence suggests that, when it comes to the introduction of these initiatives, SMEs may not be too far behind their larger counterparts. In a study among small engineering firms it was shown that managerial techniques such as teamworking and quality audits are on the increase (Downing-Burn and Cox, 1999). According to Bacon *et al.* (1996), the use of such management techniques among many SMEs may not even be 'new'. In a survey of over 200 SMEs they discovered that management change programmes were introduced in less formal ways than those found among many larger firms. They conclude that smaller businesses offer a better setting for the implementation of HRM initiatives, given their existing flat hierarchy and the organic nature of communication flows between employee and employer.

It is also possible that in smaller firms the 'type' of manager is changing, many of whom can more easily adopt the role of 'champion' for certain HRM practices

**Table 14.3 Examples of new management initiatives in smaller firms***

|  | % of workplaces |
| --- | --- |
| No 'new' management practices or employee involvement schemes | 8 |
| Five or more of these practices and schemes | 28 |
| Joint consultative committee at workplace | 17 |
| One or more equal treatment practices | 24 |
| Union presence | 22 |
| Union recognition | 12 |
| Worker representative at workplace | 10 |
| Employees with one or more flexible/family-friendly working arrangements | 48 |
| Employees with high or very high job satisfaction | 61 |
| Low-paying workplaces (quarter or more earn below £3.50 per hour) | 21 |
| High productivity growth | 33 |
| Industrial tribunal complaints (rate per employee) | 2.4 |

Note:* Stand-alone private sector workplaces with 10–99 employees.
Figures are weighted and based on responses from 250 managers and 2,957 employees.

Source: Cully et al., 1998:26

(Marchington, 1992). For instance Bacon *et al.* (1996: 90) report that several SMEs were run by owner-managers who had been made redundant from larger firms and used that experience to introduce sophisticated HR practices into their smaller business. They show that a new managerial agenda was not intended to replace informal practices with formal systems, it was to maintain the informality associated with a small social setting while at the same time promoting professional managerial techniques.

Reports from workers employed in SMEs have also been surprisingly positive. Guest and Conway (1999: 397) comment that there are discernible 'shades of grey and occasional shafts of light' emerging from the 'black hole' of SMEs. In their survey 29 per cent of employees said they were 'very satisfied' with their job and 31 per cent displayed 'a lot of loyalty' to their firm. Similarly, the WERS data show that workers in both big and small firms display broadly similar (positive) patterns of workplace 'wellbeing' (Cully *et al.*, 1999: 179, 271). In explaining these results Guest and Conway (1999) suggest that employees in smaller firms appear to experience several features related to the psychological contract, such as perceptions of fairness and trust, that may be characteristic of social harmony.

Yet the interpretation of these survey results can be problematic. In the WERS survey, for example, while 65 per cent of all managers reported that most employees work in designated teams, only 3 per cent confirmed that such teams were fully autonomous in deciding how the work will be performed with self-appointed team leaders (Cully *et al.*, 1999:43). Other evidence suggests that broader 'soft' HRM practices can actually translate to 'hard' employment outcomes (Keenoy, 1997; Bacon, 1999). Research suggests that the majority of smaller firms tend to recruit workers through word-of-mouth, and few SMEs provide any formal training for employees (Holliday, 1995; Carroll *et al.*, 1999; Westhead and Storey, 1997). Moreover, industrial relations tends to be based on systems of 'unbridled individualism', with informality the central *modus operandi* in the day-to-day management of people (Scott *et al.*, 1989; Lucas, 1996). Many of those employed in smaller firms experience work-related illness, face dismissal and have less access to union representation than their counterparts in larger organisations (Millward *et al.*, 1992; IRS, 1998; Cully *et al.*, 1999: 272).

## Explaining management diversity among SMEs

The risk of oversimplification notwithstanding, two broad approaches can be identified within the existing literature to account for the diversity of managerial techniques in SMEs.

### The political economy of small business

The first approach focuses on the political economy of small business. This seeks to assess the pattern of management action against four types of relationship: *dependent*, *dominated*, *isolated* or *innovative* links between big and small firms (Rainnie, 1989, 1991). *Dependent* SMEs rely on large firms for their survival. Blyton and Turnbull (1998) show the implications of such a *dependency* relationship for a small clothing firm that manufactures garments for Marks & Spencer (M&S). In this case authoritarian management, strict supervision and piece rate wages reflect the relationship between the small firm and M&S rather than the unique features of the clothing industry. In other organisations a similar relationship led workers to view 'the customer as being in charge', rather than the company management (Delbridge, 1998). However, these dependency relationships can also influence HR practices among the smaller partners in less direct ways. MacMahon (1996) found that outsourcing was little more than a shift in 'risk' from larger firms to the workers of many smaller enterprises. In this way small subcontracting firms became vulnerable as they were dependent on supplying the products and services deemed non-essential by large corporations. These included catering, cleaning, security, construction, food and drink and transport, where a significant number of employees work part-time on low-paid casual and temporary contracts (Dale and Kerr, 1995; Guest and Conway, 1999).

*Dominated* SMEs exist in (very) competitive markets. Many offer lower rates of pay and fewer employee benefits in order to compete with larger firms. Examples include corner shops that have to compete with new (and large) out-of-town supermarkets. Employees tend to be those with weak bargaining power – women, family members, the young and ethnic minorities – and are often employed on a short-term and casual basis. Barrett and Rainnie (1999) challenge current government thinking by arguing that these working conditions are closer to those of a flea market than a sector which is viewed as the engine of economic recovery.

Once workers had been recruited, management techniques sought to develop them in line with the company's 'culture statement' (see Box 14.1). Top of the list was 'having fun at work', which was actively encouraged by the owner-manager through an open and friendly style. There was a strong emphasis on mutual trust and respect both inside and outside the workplace, with employees at all levels on first name terms.

These interventions were underpinned by social activities funded from the 'culture budget'. They included weekend trips to Dublin, white-water canoeing in Wales and a river cruise-cum-office party. There were regular inter-company football tournaments among staff when the men played and the women dressed as American-style cheerleaders as well as fancy dress and dress down days in the office. More serious matters were also mixed with humour to engender an informal atmosphere. Individual appraisal interviews and group induction events for new staff were regularly held as a social event at the company's expense.

These social events were time-consuming and attendance was only notionally voluntary yet workplace controls, by contrast, were much more relaxed. Consultants were free to determine their own work schedules: they could base themselves at home, in the office or spend weeks at client sites across the globe.

Considerable emphasis was also placed on personal and professional development. All 12 directors were studying for the Institute of Directors professional examination, another 30 staff had attained the Institute of Electronic Engineers membership, four had doctorates and several were working toward MBAs. In addition, two separate company-wide training days were held each year when the whole workforce would be taken to a hotel to discuss new projects and receive company information.

Many employees were enthusiastic advocates of these NMTs. Most valued their in-house friendships and many enjoyed the social events. But tensions and problems still existed. Pay was set by the owner and no formal criteria were published on how individual performance was evaluated. This research was conducted when the company was performing well and the majority of employees were extremely well satisfied with the pay awards. However, one clerical worker complained about the lack of overtime pay, and other employees lower down the hierarchy were critical of both the long hours and difficulties in achieving a performance pay award as few worked exclusively on client (fee-earning) projects. Consultants were engaged in interesting and responsible work, but taking ownership for decisions, actively negotiating contracts with clients and participating in social activities often demanded long hours at work. During the research at Consultancy Co, a group of consultants worked through the night to complete a client project on time.

### Motor Co: Management style and exploitation in the Bleak House

Motor Co is a family-run enterprise that displayed many of the hallmarks of a *dominated* SME. Established in 1987, Motor Co is the largest of three separate dealerships owned by the same family in the North-west of England. The company employs 65 workers, including motor mechanics in a garage workshop, clerical support staff, warehouse stores and forecourt sales. The company's main business is the sale and leasing of trucks and coaches to local bus companies and HGV hauliers. These on-going commercial arrangements account for approximately 80 per cent of all business, which includes the regular servicing and replacement of vehicles. Individual customers account for the remaining 20 per cent of business, usually in the form of one-off sales or vehicle repairs. In the past, the reputation of high-quality vehicles has ensured a relatively stable market position for Motor Co.

However, by the late 1990s the company faced a sharp rise in local market competition. A number of other garages had opened up in the region as direct competitors, and the vehicle manufacturer was in the process of reviewing all existing franchise dealers. In response to this commercial uncertainty, the family-owners introduced several NMTs to formalise and restructure employment arrangements (see also Dundon *et al.*, 1999). A new general manager was appointed in the hope of reassuring the vehicle manufacturer as to the company's management structure during the franchise review. Younger and increasingly assertive line managers were hired to take on greater departmental responsibilities and the daughter of the founding-owner was appointed as the personnel manager. Formal procedures were introduced and policies such as recruitment changed, with a combination of formal applications and interview selection replacing more *ad hoc* means of seeking potential employees from friends and acquaintances in the motor trade. Individual appraisals, regular communications and employee involvement techniques were also introduced in an attempt to formalise employee relations.

Yet while the managers emphasised the use and utility of these NMTs, no workers did. Among the eight employees interviewed, none could recall staff appraisals being conducted and in a survey of the whole workforce (n=45) only 11 per cent spoke favourably of management communications. Most respondents referred to what was perhaps a well-intentioned but nonetheless insensitive pay review policy. One garage mechanic commented that:

> I know when we get a rise. It's each Christmas. It's not automatic though, you only get a rise if they think you should have a pay rise [and] . . . that's based on not dropping a bollock in the year . . . It's a letter in the Christmas card saying we're getting a rise . . . it really pisses the lads off. I mean a little card, 'all the best and all that', but naught about your money and so and so next to you gets something.

Against the rhetoric of so-called enlightened NMT, the family-owners maintained a 'no work – no pay' policy at all levels of the organisation. This even applied to employees who had sustained injuries at work. When a garage mechanic lost two fingers in an industrial accident not only did he have his wages stopped, but Motor Co also began dismissal procedures because of his prolonged absence from work. The personnel manager had little sympathy for him:

> Two people have been off for a long time this year. The first person had a bad workplace accident here – both people were blue-collar. The first guy was suing for loss of earnings – but that case might have been dropped, he's gone to work for another company so he's not too badly damaged. Though he has lost his (two) fingers.

A more common effect of this policy was that employees were required to use holiday leave to cover periods in which they were ill. As one clerical employee said:

> A sick pay scheme should be introduced. Either lose a day's pay or take holidays – which they don't let you take now at short notice. It reminds me of a Victorian mill-owner, and make sure [the personnel manager] doesn't hear that.

The new management techniques and new managerial structure at Motor Co were intended to mark a departure from earlier informal relations in which 'walking the shopfloor' was the main way owner-managers engaged with employees. But their introduction was not accompanied by a shift in power relations nor (despite the customary association of employee commitment with 'soft' HR practices) did it involve any increase in trust. As one employee concluded: 'The firm is run by "family-men". What they say goes. It's as simple as that.'

## Conclusion and discussion

This chapter has been concerned with the impact of NMTs in four case studies broadly based on Rainnie's (1991) SME typologies. However, none of the explanations reviewed in this chapter can fully account for the diversity in employment relations at these organisations. The NMTs introduced at Motor Co had little substantive impact on employment relations in the firm, employees at Care Co gained satisfaction from their relationship with residents but this did little to lessen the tensions between workers and the owner-manager, consultants at Consultancy Co were trusted and well rewarded but only as long as they conformed, and NMTs in Compu Co meant additional administrative burdens and work intensification for staff. Given this, it is difficult to argue that NMTs are all necessarily 'good' or 'bad' in themselves or that their presence in an organisation signifies a certain managerial strategy.

Throughout this chapter relationships between small and large firms have been emphasised. This has the advantage of locating analysis in relation to wider macro factors that may shape managerial action in a micro context. In each of the four case studies the categories suggested by Rainnie (1991) help understand the patterns of NMT found in these firms. For example, the *dependency* experiences reported at Compu Co and the *dominated* market of Motor Co were a function of their relations with large firms.

The framework does, however, have a significant disadvantage: its comparative neglect of factors internal to each SME. Yet, as seen here, management style had a significant influence on the pattern of employment relations. While Consultancy Co would appear to be an *innovative* SME, its distinctive features of freedom at work and constraint over social life are equally (if not more) important than the organisation's place in Rainnie's typology in understanding both managerial and worker behaviour. In these four case studies the uses (and abuses) of new managerial techniques translate into both the exploitative use of labour

**The Management of Human Resources**

through low wages and casualisation, and also the intensification of highly paid professional work.

By reporting direct research evidence this chapter has been able both to illuminate the dynamic nature of NMTs in smaller organisations and to subject existing frameworks to critical analysis. It is the complex interplay of external and internal factors, relationships with large firms, management style and the nature of the employees' work, which supports the view that theorising about human resource management in polarised perspectives (small is beautiful or Bleak House) simplifies complicated processes. Further, reliance on self-reported surveys is problematic because this form of evidence does not necessarily demonstrate that employees are being treated as an asset. Yet until the processes of change management in small firms are explored more fully and the complexity used to inform and shape current debates about HRM, then theoretical models can only ever be partial. Above all, there is a need for more study into the management of people employed in SMEs, both to construct a more grounded and complex picture of activity and to influence the way HRM is currently defined and taught.

### Case study 14.1

# Cultural management in Consultancy Co

Tony Dundon, Irena Grugulis & Adrian Wilkinson

### Introduction

Managing culture is often portrayed as a key lever to win employees' 'hearts and minds', that will secure competitive advantage (Deal and Kennedy, 1982; Schein, 1985). By targeting employees' attitudes and norms, companies can eliminate the need for irksome systems of control and effectively substitute 'active employee commitment' for 'resigned compliance' (Ogbonna, 1992/93).

In this particular case study the management of 'corporate culture' was not intended to change the organisation's values or atmosphere, but actively preserve them during a period of growth. The key objective at Consultancy Co was cultural *continuity* rather than culture change (Grugulis *et al.*, 2000).

### The company

Consultancy Co specialises in computer software and security technologies. The company was founded in 1992 by one owner, 'Ian Reese', and is based in the North of England with subsidiary offices in Edinburgh, Dublin and Dallas (USA). Ian started the company with 11 colleagues, all of whom previously worked together for the same large organisation. In commercial terms Consultancy Co's results are impressive. It has maintained an annual 30 per cent increase in turnover for the past 5 years, has grown from 12 to 150 people and has won several small business and quality excellence awards.

It is important to note that the founding members were all friends as well as co-workers. Not only did they work together on a daily basis, but they also socialised together. This helped create a bond of interpersonal loyalty as well as a strong sense of identification with 'their' organisation. Quite often they raised money for charity, participated in local sports activities and enjoyed weekends away together. It was this friendly relationship between Ian Reese and his colleagues that helped shape Consultancy Co's approach to managing culture.

### The culture: work hard and play hard

As the company grew, the links between work and socialising became a central feature of management activity. In 1997 Ian appointed 'Anna Culbertson' as culture and training manager. Anna had been one of the company's first employees.

She was allocated 2 per cent of company turnover (£250,000) to manage and preserve a culture defined as 'work hard and play hard'.

One area to which Anna paid particular attention was the recruitment of people. Here technical and job competency was viewed as secondary to the behavioural attributes and attitudes of prospective employees. Most recruits were carefully selected through a combination of formal and informal techniques. Each year Anna organised a graduate recruitment event to coincide with 'Red-Nose Day', when most of the employees arrived in fancy dress. Applicants' reactions were assessed and used as criteria for short-listing. If they displayed any sign of criticism, their application went no further. Once these 'suitable souls' had been recruited, Anna's role focused on supporting employees in line with the company's culture statement.

Consultancy Co. culture is one where individuals are encouraged to:
■ Have fun and enjoy work
■ Always put the client first
■ Make quality a part of everything we do
■ Share knowledge with others
■ Work as a team
■ Develop your full potential
■ Make decisions
■ Take ownership and resolve problems
■ Learn from mistakes without fear or recrimination

'Having fun and enjoying work' was actively promoted by Ian Reese through an open and friendly style of *paternalistic* management. Informal social relations were encouraged among staff both inside and outside the workplace. The emphasis was on mutual trust and respect with employees and managers on first name terms. Sean, an office junior, remarked:

It's a happy office, everyone's approachable, you're never left on your own and being a good team member is regarded as an important thing. I mean, there's no problem having a laugh with anyone. [Ian] is as approachable as anyone.

A range of social activities were financed by the company. These included weekend trips to Dublin, regular office parties and an internal company football tournament. Other formal work processes were mixed with fun and humour to engender an informal and relaxed atmosphere. Individual appraisals were held as coffee afternoons and staff induction events were regularly undertaken during a 'night out' financed by the company. Anna explained:

It's important to involve new starters in our extra curricular activities. . . I'm thinking of a few things at the moment, which has been prompted by new people coming in. I don't know whether to have a night out bowling or just pick up the bar bill in a pub. I quite fancy a Chinese meal night – I just don't know yet. We like new people to feel part of the culture right from the start and get involved with everyone socially – this is work hard, and then we all play hard.

In practice, there was a great deal of freedom for employees at Consultancy Co. Consultants were free to determine their own work schedules as long they satisfied client demands. They could work at home, in the office or spend weeks at client sites. It was common practice for staff to work and mix with colleagues in other sections of the firm and learn different aspects of the business, which helped develop cross-functional team working.

In supporting this distinctive culture company training was high on the agenda, as Ian Reese commented: 'Our people are a key asset and we regard their training and development as vital to the business.' The most extensive of these training initiatives were two company-wide training days held each year. During these events two telephonists were left to staff the office while all other employees would spend the day at a local hotel developing team skills, playing games and receiving presentations from Ian Reese about the future plans of the company.

Between these training events Consultancy Co supported other activities to help develop staff. The company subscribed to a number of professional journals that were scattered around the office, was willing to invest in the latest software and allowed consultants to 'play around' with the technology in designing new client products. There was also 'Consultancy Co University'. Here consultants presented seminar papers to other staff members about client projects, outlined new technological developments or talked about the fun in their work. Senior consultants were also expected to give formal papers at international business and technology management conferences. This supported both their own personal development and helped to market Consultancy Co to prospective clients. Finally, consultants were encouraged to obtain professional qualifications at the company's expense. All 12 directors were studying to become members of the Institute of Directors, another 30 staff attained graduate membership of the Institute of Electronic Engineers and several consultants were studying for MBAs.

### Attitude survey at Consultancy Co

Table 14.5 is a summary of results from an attitude survey conducted by the authors at Consultancy Co. Overall, this shows that high numbers of employees trusted management, felt they were part of a family and were generally supportive of the values espoused by firm.

### Culture and (mis)behaviour

Yet, despite such high levels of satisfaction, it is difficult to argue that all employees' 'hearts and minds' were entirely given over to the company.

Many employees were dissatisfied with communications. In the above survey the negative results all relate to a lack of information between employee and employer. Indeed, over half the sample (59 per cent) disagreed with the statement that management involved them in decisions. At one staff briefing the communication was all one way. Ian Reese and other directors made very quick statements to

**Table 14.5  Percentage of respondents agreeing / disagreeing with question items**

| Question item | Agree | Not sure | Disagree |
| --- | --- | --- | --- |
| On the whole, I feel I can trust the information provided by management at Consultancy Co. | 85 | 11 | 4 |
| People are treated fairly by the management of Consultancy Co. | 83 | 12 | 5 |
| Working here is like being part of a team and family. | 79 | 10 | 11 |
| The values and beliefs of Consultancy Co. are very similar to my own personal beliefs. | 74 | 18 | 8 |
| Communications here are very informal and relaxed. | 28 | 34 | 38 |
| Employees are kept fully informed of changes within Consultancy Co. | 26 | 32 | 42 |
| Management involve employees in decisions at Consultancy Co. | 18 | 23 | 59 |
| I regularly have the chance to discuss my pay with management | 14 | 20 | 66 |

Note: $N = 82$

the workforce and questions or comments from staff were actively discouraged. The meeting started at 8 am (with breakfast provided) and employees returned to their desks ready for work by 8.30 am.

In addition, pay and hours were at times problematic at Consultancy Co. While consultants were relatively well paid (earnings varied between £28,000 and £45,000, plus benefits such as a car and health insurance), they were also expected to work extremely long hours in return. Most seemed to accept this, something that was not necessarily true of their less well-rewarded colleagues. One clerical employee was critical of the lack of overtime pay and the long hours.

The voluntary nature of participation in social events was only notional. While this research was being conducted the HR manager, 'Helen', was sacked, not because of poor work or lack of competence but because, as Anna argued, 'she did not fit in with the "people" way of doing things' at Consultancy Co. Helen's participation in company socials was seen as reluctant and both Anna and Ian wanted enthusiasm. The dismissal was acrimonious and a settlement was only agreed after Ian Reese was advised that an employment tribunal was unlikely to rule in the company's favour. The repercussions of this on other employees and company culture were predictable. The same week that Helen was dismissed, other employees received their individual appraisal reports in envelopes marked 'Confidential'. Several workers feared that they were also being dismissed. Anna's attempt to reassure them was not successful:

> When I said (rhetorically), 'Do you really think we'd ever do anything like that?', they said 'Yes, isn't that how it happened to Helen?'

ten employees who all work on different production lines, which make food and drink flavourings, including vanilla, coke, soup, and meat additives. A similar team structure exists at the head office. Here, the majority of employees are clerical workers involved in administration, sales and marketing. There is no union recognition for these employees and, despite several requests from the GMB union, management has decided to keep this side of the business non-unionised.

In the late 1990s Beverage Co experienced a period of commercial uncertainty. It faced increasing UK competition for food and drink flavourings, lost a few important export contracts and, in 1997, made ten workers redundant. This was the first time that Beverage Co had ever experienced any form of job losses. The company had been owned by members of the same family for more than a century and their management style was characterised by benevolent paternalism. However, with increased market competition, declining profits and redundancy, the company's owners decided to distance Beverage Co from its informal industrial relations history. In its place they introduced a more strategic form of human resource management, much of which included several employee involvement schemes.

### EI techniques and management style at Beverage Co

This new HR strategy had a profound impact on organisational culture and management style. In the past family-owners were highly paternalist and the industrial relations procedures were informal. Indeed, the previous chairman and managing director, descendants of the founding owner, were known for stopping production quite regularly and asking manual employees to help repair the family Bentley, Jaguar and collection of classic sports cars. This all changed when non-family members were appointed to senior management and board-level positions. A personnel department was established with the aim of formalising HR policies and practices across the two sites. Key performance targets for profits, quality and customer satisfaction were linked to staff appraisals and merit pay was introduced, based on individual targets. In addition, production supervisors and team leaders were given responsibility for staff appraisals and team meetings. In describing this approach the new MD regarded the strategy as 'a route to building a world-class organisation'. The range of EI techniques that helped support this objective are summarised in Table 14.6.

'Downward communication' was the most extensive of all forms of EI at Beverage Co. These included a quarterly staff newsletter, monthly team briefings, formal presentations by the MD to the whole workforce (held twice a year in the staff canteen), a staff suggestion scheme, e-mail communications and electronic message boards. The latter included e-mails for clerical staff in the head office and electronic display screens for manual workers, which were located at various points across the manufacturing plant. The underlying objective was to inform employees about new products, encourage quality and share financial information. For example, the company-wide presentations by the MD explained company objectives, profit details and more general HR developments to staff,

**Table 14.6  EI techniques introduced at Beverage Co**

| EI category | EI technique introduced |
|---|---|
| Downward communications | Staff newsletter |
| | Notice boards |
| | Electronic message boards (manual staff only) |
| | E-mail communications (clerical staff only) |
| | Site-wide meetings led by MD |
| | Team/cell briefings by team leaders |
| | Personnel management surgeries |
| | Individual performance reviews/appraisals |
| Upward problem solving | Staff suggestion scheme |
| | Staff attitude surveys |
| Task participation | None |
| Financial involvement | Merit pay |
| Representative participation | Company joint consultative committee |

including the merit pay scheme or Beverage Co's attempt to achieve Investors in People (IiP) accreditation.

However, the introduction of these communication techniques was met with some suspicion among employees. Team leaders who held monthly briefings were regarded as 'supervisors on the cheap' by many staff. In effect, team leaders were the same grade as other workers but were also required to carry out briefing sessions without extra pay. The personnel manager compiled the information and team leaders then cascaded this down to shopfloor level. The site-wide meetings introduced by the new MD were also questioned. Several workers suggested that the information presented was often partial, with management controlling the agenda for discussion or questioning. A middle manager explained:

> There's a reluctance to show the whole picture. We have canteen meetings but they're controlled, the information is very selective. That's a general feeling that not all the info is given out.

Across the manufacturing plant, electronic notice boards would regularly 'flash' with messages from the personnel department. Typical examples included the latest figures for customer complaints, current absenteeism rates or the volume of products made hour by hour and compared against (management's) expected target. As one process operator commented during his lunch in the canteen: 'There's no getting away from them [i.e. management messages] here.'

Other EI mechanisms included a 'weekly surgery' held by the personnel manager. The aim was to allow employees to discuss issues of concern in private without appointment. In addition, a staff suggestion scheme was introduced to encourage workers to make improvements to product quality. A financial payment ranging from £10 to £1,000 was given for adopted suggestions. Individual staff appraisals were also introduced where supervisor and worker could discuss objectives for the coming months.

In practice, these EI techniques fell short of their intended objective. Few employees would attend the surgery. Indeed, according to the personnel manager, this time was often used to meet with the shop steward or to inform team leaders about the next briefing. Several clerical employees were also critical of the staff suggestion scheme, especially the lack of any formal criteria for determining the amount of financial award. In response, the MD explained that any individual award depended on the 'quality of the idea' as well as the 'cost savings' for the company. Further, employees at both sites commented that any 'discussion' about appraisal plans was a myth, as supervisors tended to 'inform' workers about new targets without any agreement or discussion.

The range of EI at Beverage Co can be seen to fit broadly those categories where management maintains greatest control, namely downward communications. Moreover, the use of communications tended to bureaucratise and formalise management style, as one production supervisor commented:

> Too much communications in one sense – we've forgotten to use general conversation. They try and make things too formal, thinking it's a better way, which isn't always the case.

Indirect forms of EI were reduced at Beverage Co in favour of the more direct techniques described above. Representative participation remained with the GMB union for manufacturing employees, although a former bi-monthly joint consultative committee (JCC) met on a quarterly basis, and its remit was restricted to heath and safety matters, whereas it had formerly dealt with all employment terms and conditions. Similarly, collective bargaining became the responsibility of two local shop stewards, the MD and personnel manager. Previously, a full-time regional official had negotiated pay with family-owners. The pay rise for non-union clerical employees was reviewed by the personnel manager, and usually set in accordance with the negotiated settlement for manual workers. In addition, merit pay accounted for up to 10 per cent of the gross salary for most staff. This was determined on the basis of set targets from the performance appraisal, which was assessed by line managers.

Table 14.7 provides a summary of employee responses to a survey conducted at Beverage Co by the authors. While workers confirmed that management pass on information (52 per cent) and encouraged staff to make suggestions (82 per cent), only 15 per cent of respondents said that management acted on such suggestions. Overall, there were few positive responses to the range of EI techniques introduced. One-quarter of employees suggested that management sought their views while over 80 per cent disagreed with the statement that management involved them in decisions.

### Workplace sabotage at Beverage Co

Shortly after these EI techniques were introduced a series of sabotage attacks was carried out at the manufacturing plant. The production unit in question manufactured food flavourings for a Far East contract, which Beverage Co eventually lost.

**Table 14.7  Employee responses (%) to EI at Beverage Co**

| EI Indicator | Agree | Not sure | Disagree |
|---|---|---|---|
| At Beverage Co management regularly seek the views of employees | 25 | 21 | 54 |
| Employees are kept informed about changes at Beverage Co | 36 | 7 | 57 |
| Management pass on information regularly | 52 | 12 | 36 |
| Management involve employees in decisions at Beverage Co | 9 | 10 | 81 |
| Management encourage staff to make suggestions | 82 | 13 | 5 |
| Management at Beverage Co act on staff suggestions | 15 | 25 | 60 |

Note: N = 67

The sabotage took a variety of forms. Flavouring products were labelled incorrectly, such that beef stocks were marked as vegetable soup ingredients and garlic batches packaged as cola additives. Other acts included racial and sexual graffiti written inside cartons. The commercial impact of these events was highly significant. Beverage Co flavourings form essential ingredients for food and drinks made by other organisations. Not only did this sabotage damage Beverage Co's reputation it also, owing to the intermediary character of the products, resulted in lost production of thousands of tonnes of food and drinks products. When incorrectly labelled food flavourings were used to produce final goods manufactured by Beverage Co's customers, these subsequently had to be destroyed.

Management were anxious to attribute these problems to the youth and immaturity of workers involved. One production supervisor attributed the sabotage to the use of agency staff brought in to help meet sudden demand. For the shop steward, however, the sabotage was a form of resistance to increased supervisory powers and poor working conditions. The nature of work was explained as dirty, dusty and intense. Interestingly, the system of cell working meant that management failed to identify the culprits. It was common for employees to work on several flavouring production lines simultaneously and switch to packaging duties during the same shift. As a result, management could not identify the employees who had been working on specific duties at the time of the sabotage.

### Questions

1. What are the likely benefits for workers of employee involvement as practised at Beverage Co? Are these likely to differ in each of the union and non-union parts of the company? Why?/Why not?

2. The family owners of Beverage Co have asked you to produce a report (or a short presentation) on the efficacy of EI in the company. Using the information in the case study, identify the main barriers to EI and make recommendations to help the new management team gain the commitment of staff to these (or other) techniques.

3. What influence has the small firm context had on EI at Beverage Co?

4. Should trade unions be worried about the introduction of EI techniques? Why?/Why not?

5. To what extent has the change in management style and HR strategy exacerbated the tensions and contradictions in the employment relationship at Beverage Co?

## References

Marchington, M., Goodman, J., Wilkinson, A. and Ackers, P. (1992) *New Developments in Employee Involvement*, Employment Department Research Paper, Series No. 2.

Marchington, M. and Wilkinson, A. (2000) 'Direct participation', in Sisson, K. and Bach, S. *Personnel Management in Britain*, 3rd edition, Oxford: Blackwell.

Pfeffer, J. (1998) *The Human Equation: Building Profits by Putting People First*, Boston, Mass: Harvard Business School Press.

Roberts, I., Sawbridge, D. and Bamber, G. (1992) 'Employee relations in smaller enterprises', in Towers, B. (ed) *Handbook of Industrial Relations Practice*, London: Kogan Press.

Scott, M., Roberts, I., Holroyd, G. and Sawbridge, D. (1989) *Management and Industrial Relations in Small Firms*, London: Department of Employment Research Paper, No. 70.

Schuler, R. and Jackson, S. (1987), 'Linking competitive strategies with human resource management', *Academy of Management Executives*, 1(3): 206–19.

Wilkinson, A., Dundon, T. and Grugulis, I. (1999) 'Exploring employee involvement in SMEs', Paper delivered at the British Universities Industrial Relations Association, HRM Conference, Cardiff University, January.

Wood, S. (1995) 'The four pillars of HRM: are they connected?', *Human Resource Management Journal*, 5(5): 49–59.

# References to Chapter 14

Atkinson, J. B. and Storey, D. (1994), 'Small firms and employment', in Atkinson, J.B. and Storey, D. (eds) *Employment, the Small Firm and the Labour Market*, London: Routledge.

Bach, S. and Sisson K. (2000) (eds) *Personnel Management*, 3rd edition, Oxford: Blackwell.

Bacon, N. (1999) 'Union de-recognition and the new human relations: a steel industry case study', *Work, Employment & Society*, 13(1): 1–17.

Bacon, N., Ackers, P., Storey, J. and Coates, D. (1996) 'It's a small world: managing human resources in small businesses', *International Journal of Human Resource Management*, 7(1): 82–100.

Barrett, R. and Rainnie, A. (1999) 'We've gotta get out of this place! Assessing the state of industrial relations theory and research in small firms', *Employment Studies Working Paper 31* (UHBS 1999: 24), University of Hertfordshire Business School.

Beardwell, I. and Holden, L. (1997) (eds) *Human Resource Management: A Contemporary Perspective*, 2nd edition, London: Pitman Publishing.

Blyton, P. and Turnbull, P. (1998) *The Dynamics of Employee Relations*, 2nd edition, London: Macmillan.

Bolton, J.E. (Chair) (1971) *Report of the Commission of Inquiry on Small Firms*, Cmnd 4811, London: HMSO.

Carrol, M., Marchington, M., Earnshaw, J. and Taylor, S. (1999) 'Recruitment in small firms: processes, methods, and problems', *Employee Relations*, 21(3): 236–50.

Cully, M., O'Reilly, A., Millward, N., Forth, J., Woodland, S., Dix, G. and Bryson, A. (1998) *Workplace Employee Relations Survey: First Findings*, London: Routledge.

Cully, M., Woodland, S., O'Reilly, A. and Dix, G. (1999), *Britain at Work: As depicted by the 1998 Workplace Employee Relations Survey*, London: Routledge.

Curran, J. and Stanworth, J. (1979) 'Worker involvement and social relations in the small firm', *Sociological Review*, 13(3): 317–42.

Dale, I. and Kerr, J. (1995) 'Small and medium-sized enterprises: their numbers and importance to employment', *Labour Market Trends*, December: 461–66.

Delbridge, R. (1998) *Life on the Line in Contemporary Manufacturing*, Oxford: Oxford University Press.

Department of Employment (1992) *People, Jobs and Opportunities*, London: Department of Employment/HMSO.

Department of Trade and Industry (1998) *Small and Medium Sized Enterprise Statistics for the UK*, Ref: P/98/597, London: Department of Trade and Industry/HMSO.

Downing-Burn, V. and Cox, A. (1999) 'Does size make a difference?', *People Management*, 5(2): 50–3.

Duberley, J. and Walley, P. (1995) 'Assessing the adoption of HRM by small and medium-sized manufacturing organizations', *International Journal of Human Resource Management*, 6(4): 891–909.

Dundon, T., Grugulis, I. and Wilkinson, A. (1999), 'Looking out of the black hole: non-union relations in an SME', *Employee Relations*, 21(3): 251–66.

Edwards, P. (1995) 'Strikes and industrial conflict', in Edwards, P. (ed) *Industrial Relations: Theory and Practice in Britain*, Oxford: Blackwell.

Goodman, J., Earnshaw, J., Marchington, M. and Harrison, R. (1998) 'Unfair dismissal cases, disciplinary procedures, recruitment methods and management style', *Employee Relations*, 20 (6): 536–50.

Goss, D. (1988) 'Social harmony and the small firm: a reappraisal', *Sociological Review*, 36(1): 114–32.

Goss, D. (1991) *Small Business and Society*, London: Routledge.

Gratton, L., Hope Hailey, V., Stiles, P. and Truss, C. (1999) *Strategic Human Resource Management*, Oxford: Oxford University Press.

Grugulis, I., Dundon, T., and Wilkinson, A. (2000) 'Cultural control and the "culture manager": employment practices in a consultancy', *Work, Employment & Society*, 14(1): 97–116.

Guest, D. and Conway, N. (1999) 'Peering into the black hole: the downside of the new employment relations in the UK', *British Journal of Industrial Relations*, 37(3): 367–89.

Guest, D. and Hoque, K. (1993) 'The good, the bad and the ugly: employment relations in new non-union workplaces', *Human Resource Management Journal*, 5(1): 1–14.

Hilbert, J., Sperling, H.J. and Rainnie, A. (1994) *SMEs at the Crossroads?: Scenarios on the Future of SMEs in Europe*, FAST – Future of Industry in Europe, Vol. 9, Brussels: European Commission.

Holliday, R. (1995) *Investigating Small Firms: Nice Work?*, London: Routledge.

IRS (1998) 'Predicting union membership', *Employment Trends*, No 669, Industrial Relations Service, December.

Keenoy, T. (1997) 'Review article: HRMism and the language of re-presentation', *Journal of Management Studies*, 34(5): 825–41

Kelly, J. (1998), *Rethinking Industrial Relations: Mobilization, Collectivism and Long Waves*, London: Routledge.

Kinnie, N., Purcell, J., Hutchinson, S., Terry, M., Collinson, M. and Scarbrough, H. (1999) 'Employment relations in SMEs: market-driven or customer shaped?', *Employee Relations*, 21(3): 218–35.

Lane, C. (1995) 'The small-business sector: source of economic regeneration or victim of economic transformation?', in Lane, C. *Industry and Society in Europe*, Aldershot: Edward Elger.

Lucas, R. (1996) 'Industrial relations in hotels and catering: neglect and paradox?', *British Journal of Industrial Relations*, 34(2): 267–86.

MacMahon, J. (1996) 'Employee relations in small firms in Ireland: an exploratory study of small manufacturing firms', *Employee Relations*, 18(5): 66–80.

Marchington, M. (1992) *Managing the Team: A Guide to Successful Employee Involvement*, Oxford: Blackwell.

Marchington, M., Goodman, J., Wilkinson, A. and Ackers, P. (1992) *New Developments in Employee Involvement*, London: Department of Employment Research Series No. 2 (May).

Millward, N., Stevens, M., Smart, D. and Hawes, W.R. (1992) *Workplace Industrial Relations in Transition. The ED/ESRC/PSI/ACAS Surveys*, Aldershot: Dartmouth.

Millward, N., Bryson, A. and Forth, J. (2000) *All Change at Work? British Employment Relations 1980–1998, as portrayed by the Workplace Industrial Relations Survey series*, London: Routledge.

Philpott, J. (1996) *A National Minimum Wage: Economic Effects and Practical Considerations.* Issues in People Management No. 13, London: Institute of Personnel and Development.

Odaka, K. and Sawai, M. (1999) *Small Firms, Large Concerns: The Development of Small Business in Comparative Perspective*, Oxford: Oxford University Press.

Pfeffer, J. (1998) *The Human Equation*, Boston, Mass: Harvard Business School Press.

Rainnie, A. (1985), 'Small firms, big problems: the political economy of small businesses', *Capital & Class*, 25, Spring: 140–68.

Rainnie, A. (1989) *Industrial Relations in Small Firms: Small Isn't Beautiful*, London: Routledge.

Rainnie, A. (1991) 'Small firms: between the enterprise culture and new times', in Burrows, E. (ed) *Deciphering the Enterprise Culture*, London: Routledge.

Ram, M. (1991) 'Control and autonomy in small firms: the case of the West Midlands clothing industry', *Work, Employment & Society*, 5(4): 601–19.

Ram, M. (1994) *Managing to Survive: Working Lives in Small Firms*, Oxford: Blackwell.

Ram, M. (1999) 'Management by association: interpreting small firm–associate links in the business service sector', *Employee Relations*, 21(3): 267–84.

Ram, M. and Holliday, R. (1993) 'Relative merits: family culture and kinship in small firms', *Sociology*, 27(4): 629–48.

Roberts, I., Sawbridge, D. and Bamber, G. (1992) 'Employee relations in smaller enterprises', in Towers, B. (ed) *Handbook of Industrial Relations Practice*, London: Kogan Press.

Scase, R. (1995) 'Employment relations in small firms', in Edwards, P.K. (ed) *Industrial Relations in Britain: Theory and Practice,* Oxford: Blackwell.

Scase, R. and Goffee, R. (1987) *The Real World of the Small Business Owner,* 2nd edition, London: Croom Helm.

Scott, M., Roberts, I., Holroyd, G. and Sawbridge, D. (1989) *Management and Industrial Relations in Small Firms,* London: Department of Employment Research Paper, No. 70.

Sisson, K. (1993) 'In search of HRM', *British Journal of Industrial Relations,* 31(2): 201–10.

Storey, D. (1994) *Understanding the Small Business Sector,* London: Routledge.

Storey, J. (1992) *Developments in the Management of Human Resources,* Oxford: Blackwell.

Storey, J. (1995) (ed) *Human Resource Management: A Critical Text,* London: Routledge.

Westhead, P. and Storey, D. (1997), *Training Provision and the Development of Small and Medium Sized Enterprises,* London: Department for Education and Employment, Research Report No. 65.

Wilkinson, A. (1999) 'Employment relations in SMEs', *Employee Relations* (Special Issue), 22(3): 206–17.

Wilkinson, A., Redman, T., Snape, E. and Marchington, M. (1998) *Managing with Total Quality Management: Theory and Practice,* London: Macmillan.

Wilkinson, A., Dundon, T. and Grugulis, I. (1999) 'Exploring Employee Involvement in SMEs', Paper delivered at the British Universities Industrial Relations Association, HRM Conference, Cardiff University, January.

Wood, S. (1995) 'The four pillars of HRM: are they connected?', *Human Resource Management Journal,* 5(5): 49–59.

The Management of Human Resources
596

# International human resource management

*Len Holden*

## OBJECTIVES

- To define and distinguish between international HRM and comparative HRM.

- To examine the debate over whether HRM systems are converging or will remain divergent.

- To examine comparative HRM models, and to review some international and comparative surveys.

- To explore country of origin and host country effects on international HRM.

- To examine mechanisms used by multinational corporations to control and coordinate HRM activities in and between their subsidiaries.

- To investigate expatriation management issues.

- To examine some models of international HRM.

## INTRODUCTION

There is increasing recognition of the importance of human resources in international competition. Porter (1990) states that the most important factors that influence national competitiveness are skilled human resources and the scientific base. He asks: Why does a nation achieve international success in a particular industry? Switzerland, for example, is a landlocked nation with high-cost labour, strict environmental law, and few natural resources – least of all cocoa. Yet it is a world leader in chocolate, not to mention pharmaceuticals, banking and specialised machinery. Similarly, Japan has few natural resources and yet from a shattered post-war position has built itself up into one of the most formidable economies in the world, rivalling, and in some industries, surpassing the United States. What both Switzerland and Japan lacked in natural resources they compensated for strongly in human resources, nurturing the education, skills and abilities of their populations. Porter (1990) claims that for nations wishing to achieve competitive advantage understanding these lessons is vital.

Similarly, multinational companies (MNCs) are beginning to understand the strategic importance of the resourcing and deployment of their human resources. Initially much of this concern has been with the development of expatriate managers, but increasingly there is concern about the export of managerial

633

systems, and how local subsidiary managers and staff can be induced to cooperate and absorb these ways of working. It is being increasingly recognised that the malfunctioning of managerial and HRM systems can have far-reaching consequences for the effective operation of MNCs in an overseas context.

# INTERNATIONAL HRM: SOME ATTEMPTS AT DEFINITION

The recognition of the significance of human resources to organisational and national productivity has led to a surge of interest in international human resource management (IHRM), but there is still some confusion as to what it means. IHRM can be studied in an organisational and a comparative context. Definitions would therefore need to recognise the locations of, and the approaches to, IHRM. Boxall (1995) arrives at similar conclusions, and defines international human resource management as being 'concerned with the human resource problems of multinational firms in foreign subsidiaries (such as expatriate management) or, more broadly, with the unfolding HR issues that are associated with the various stages of the internationalisation process' (p. 5). This accords with Dowling *et al.* (1994: 2) and Briscoe (1995: 9), and also Torrington (1994) who sees IHRM as 'simply HRM on a larger scale' (p. 6).

Comparative HRM, on the other hand, has much wider significance both in terms of the HRM role, which Boxall (1995) states 'should be interpreted as the comparative study of labour in its broadest sense' (p. 6) and in the national contexts in which it exists. He points out that HRM as such was initially perceived in mainly Anglo-American terms, but the comparative label would suggest a move beyond this 'into an intellectual and cultural terrain where there may well be diverse notions of management itself and of labour management institutions and practices' (p. 6).

Here he suggests an examination of the richer vein of comparative industrial relations and comparative labour market theory, incorporating the historical development of management labour systems, as for example in the work of Gospel (1992), which attempts to offer explanations of poor British productivity throughout the preceding century by an examination of internal and external labour markets.

Boxall also notes the lack of rigour in the theoretical development of the subject, and comparative studies that have been conducted to date tend to lack depth of analysis as a result. Other commentators have suggested that a move towards the comparative case study approach may prove more fruitful. Clark *et al.* (1999), in examining a wide variety of IHRM and comparative HRM and contingent literature, lament the lack of progress in theoretical, conceptual and research methodological terms. We shall return to some of these themes later in this and subsequent chapters.

# APPROACHES TO INTERNATIONAL AND COMPARATIVE HRM: CONVERGENCE AND DIVERGENCE, THE STUDY OF COMPARATIVE HRM

In studying comparative and international HRM from a number of perspectives, writers have borrowed freely from theories of various philosophies and academic disciplines, and these approaches can be categorised into four main areas:

- the convergence or contingency perspective;
- Marxist theory;

634

- the cultural approach;
- the institutionalist perspective.

These categories follow closely those of Lane (1989, 1995). Each approach attempts to examine the relationship between social settings and organisational forms, and the similarities and differences that would point to convergence or divergence. One main problem with each approach is that it tends to exclude or play down factors that other perspectives emphasise. This results in a less rounded and thus less satisfactory analysis of the forces influencing IHRM. Cultural theorists are thus inclined to play down or ignore institutional or economic factors. Those advocating a contingency approach and those coming from a Marxist perspective are often suspicious of the dangers of national and racial stereotyping that could emanate from the cultural approach. Institutional theorists, while acknowledging the influence of cultural values, are wary about becoming too involved in examining the 'black box' of culture, given the difficulties in defining and researching it.

## A synthesis of approaches

Each of the four approaches listed above has its weaknesses and limitations, which many adherents as well as critics acknowledge. A synthesis of the major ideas and approaches that have influenced the scope, direction, and ideological interpretation of international and comparative HRM may prove a useful way forward.

The four approaches to the employment relationship in a comparative context can be placed in convergent and divergent categories as illustrated in Table 15.1. Most observers have to come to the view that in an evolving and globalising world economy both convergent and divergent forces have considerable impact. Child (1981) claims that there is evidence for both convergence and divergence; Child and Tayeb (1983) emphasise the evolutionary nature of managerial and HRM development and the fact that, while culture may be regarded as a contextual contingency, over time cultural differences are of diminishing importance. Prentice (1990) goes so far as to say that there will be a best management style for the future. The problem with this view is: How far in the future will that be? Evidence seems to suggest that while some aspects of employee relations are converging, the influence of culture and national institutional factors remains strong. Kidger (1991), Sparrow and Hiltrop (1994), Sparrow and Wu (1999) and others have come to the view that separating these influences out is the present concern of research. This will be examined in more detail in the sections dealing with international HRM, but at this point it is worth examining each of the convergent and divergent perspectives in more detail, and exploring some of their weaknesses.

**Table 15.1  A synthesis of theoretical approaches to comparative HRM**

**Convergent**

Convergence or contingency perspective: Kerr et al., Purcell and Mueller, McLuhan
Marxist theory: Braverman, Friedman, Edwards, Burawoy, regulationist school (Aglietta, Boyer and Lipietz)

**Divergent**

Cultural theorists: Hofstede, Laurent, Trompenaars, Hall, Tayeb
Institutional perspective: Aix school (Maurice et al.), Lane, Sorge and Warner, Dore, Whitley, Crouch, Sisson, Fulcher

635

## Convergence approaches

### Convergence or contingency perspective

This perspective on industrialisation and its influence on management and labour relation systems originated from the writings of Kerr *et al.* (1960). They posited the view that technological change ultimately creates similar industrial systems. These systems are rooted in the industrial organisation, where technology imposes the need for similar structures and work forms. This growth in similarity of organisational structures over time Kerr *et al.* called *convergence theory*.

An argument of the convergence school claims that, when organisations reach a certain scale, defined by the numbers of employees, it becomes necessary to introduce functional specialisation. To coordinate and control these functions results in a more formalised system of organisation, with rules, regulations and hierarchies. More staff are thus needed to perform these roles, with parallel development of more centrally controlled systems. Probably the most overt example of convergence has been Fordist systems, where the logic of the assembly line controls and constrains the ability of workers to take initiatives in the work process.

In this manner ways of working in countries throughout the world become similar when influenced by the same technologies and organisation of production. For example car plants, whether in Brazil, South Africa, Britain or the United States, will have similar production lines, which in turn influence the kind of human resource and work policies each nation will tend to follow, for example speed of the line, control over the work process and payment systems. Mueller and Purcell (1992) for example, claim that in the automobile industry 'convergent forces in the shape of globalisation of markets, European legislation and common product standards, as well as the easing of cross border shipments of components or half finished products, have led to the emergence of remarkably similar operational requirements in management policies in various countries' (p. 15).

A more recent interpretation of convergence theory has been proposed by Ritzer (1998) in what he calls the *McDonaldization thesis*. Here we can see the application of Fordism to the growing service sector, in which attempts are made by global organisations such as McDonalds, to achieve homogeneity not only of product but also of service. Close controls are created through training employees to perform a given script when customers enter the restaurant. In this way the consumers are also controlled and conditioned by the dialogue with the server, and by the way the restaurant is designed for fast turnover of customers. Thus

> Europe and the rest of the world are moving towards business and cultural worlds dominated by the principles of efficiency, predictability, calculability, and control through the substitution of non-human for human technology. In other words, we are moving towards a world in which business and culture in one region will be indistinguishable from the business and culture of every other.
>
> (Ritzer, 1998:75)

Cultural and institutional theorists would take issue with such a unidimensional view of how management and HRM operate in different national contexts. Even Kerr *et al.* (1971) revised their views on convergence theory, and claimed that they had been far too simplistic in explaining how technology influences organisational structure and behaviour. Other critics claimed that the convergence approach considers only the formal structures, and remains insensitive to informal structures within organisations. Another problem with the convergence approach as posited by Kerr *et al.* is that there is an assumption that only technology, work organisation and organisational forms drive convergence. The work of Mueller and Purcell (1992: 15) shows clearly that the globalisation of markets, regional legislation such as in the European Union, and common product standards also affect convergence. To this can be added the cross-border integration of products and services within MNCs and the influence of 'Japanese' methods across the globe, such as lean production and just in time. Convergence thus can take a number of forms and emanate from a number of sources. Nevertheless, it has enjoyed some revival in a revised form in recent years, and globalisation provides some compelling reasons for this.

## Marxist theory

Another form of convergence theory emanates from the ideas of Karl Marx and his view of the development of capitalism. Like the convergence perspective this view ignores cultural and other informal influences on organisational development.

Essentially, this view sees capitalism as a mode of production in which the primary features are private ownership of capital, and competition between capitalist enterprises. The need for profit drives the system, and this is achieved by appropriation of surplus value from labour – that is, paying a wage that is lower than the value of the goods. Therefore in order to be competitive there is a need to exploit labour for ever-higher productivity for comparatively less reward.

A relatively recent development of the Marxist view of capitalism was advanced by Braverman (1974). The Marxists, unlike the convergence theorists, shift the emphasis from the structure of the organisation to the relationship between management and labour. In other words, there is a focus on the actors in relation to the processes of production. Braverman and his followers stress the importance of managerial control over the workforce, deskilling, and the cheapening of labour. They emphasise the importance to management and owners of the necessity of breaking down skill processes by the use of new technologies and the implementation of flexible work practices. The variety of management–labour relations throughout the world merely reflects the various stages of capitalism through which economies are passing. As developing economies grow they will pass through similar stages to advanced ones, with, presumably, the development of similar management–labour systems.

This deterministic view has been reinforced by writers positing what has become known as the *Fordist* view of capitalist development in terms of the organisation of production. This 'regulationist' school of Marxist theorists (Aglietta, Boyer and Lipietz) believes that developments of economic growth through periods of boom and slump lie in 'the rise and decline of a particular form or regime of economic organisation and regulation' (Meegan, 1988:138). The era of Fordism up to the 1960s and 1970s was the main form of industrial organisation upon which Western capitalism was built. The slumps in the 1970s and 1980s witnessed a crisis of capitalism and consequently a breakdown in the Fordist system. Fordism is predicated on mass production, often on an assembly line system, which enables the fragmentation of the labour process (job tasks etc., which each worker can perform, usually with little training). It is mostly heavily associated with car and vehicle production – hence the term 'Fordism' – and latterly with white goods and electrical appliance manufacture. Like the convergence theorists, the regulationists assume that the mode of production will create similar systems of control through machine pacing, and there will be less need for supervisors or foremen and a greater need for managers. Using 'scientific' methods such as those advocated by

637

Frederick Taylor, managers would seek ways of increasing employee productivity. The assumption was that these scientific methods would be applicable in all work contexts.

Marxists believe that the competitive world of capitalism will eventually lead to a crisis in production whereby too many goods will be produced for the market to absorb. However, while there have been crises in capitalism they have not led to its breakdown. They claim that the adoption of neo-Fordist or post-Fordist techniques of manufacture that emphasise customer differentiation in an attempt to meet individual customer needs through flexible specialisation has created new forms of work organisation that have given capitalism a new lease of life. This means giving greater autonomy to the workforce by introducing measures such as teamworking, job enrichment, cellular manufacture and forms of functional flexibility. In the 1980s and 1990s HRM strategy and policy has been used to support these forms of flexible specialisation. In this way another regime or regulationist paradigm has been created in the intensive search for markets, by lowering costs and increasing quality of product or service. These work forms have been increasingly extended beyond those industries associated with mass production, particularly as there has been considerable restructuring of advanced economies, shifting the emphasis of labour force employment to the service sector. In this way the new work forms and management systems that emanate from them become widespread globally.

## Divergence approaches

### The cultural approach

Writers who emphasise divergence in managerial and HRM forms tend to view convergence theories as being overly simplistic in their applicability to all work contexts. The cultural approach is one of the most important schools that criticises convergent theories, and one of the most notable writers in the field is Geert Hofstede, who believes 'that there is no evidence that the cultures of present-day generations from different countries are converging' (Hofstede, 1991:17). He believes that cultural influences play an enormous part in the way employees behave in organisations, and that the introduction of technology produces only superficial similarities.

Culture is in itself notoriously difficult to define. It can mean many things, ranging from expression through the arts and other creative media to societal perceptions of history and spirituality. The most commonly accepted definition is the one put forward by Kluckhohn (1951) after studying over a hundred definitions:

> Culture consists of patterns, explicit and implicit of and for behaviour acquired and transmitted by symbols, constituting the distinctive achievement of human groups, including their embodiment in artefacts; the essential core of culture consists of traditional (i.e. historically derived and selected) ideas and especially their attached values; culture systems may, on the one hand, be considered as products of action, on the other as conditioning elements of future action.        (p. 86)

Even with this definition the multiplicity of meaning makes social investigation using empirical tools very difficult.

### The work of Hofstede

Hofstede's research into IBM is one of the most groundbreaking and important pieces of research into the cultural influences on the management process. Using the responses of managers from 66 different countries produced some interesting if contro-

638

versial evidence on cultural differences. He found that managers and employees vary on four primary dimensions, which he called: *power distance, uncertainty avoidance, individuality* and *masculinity* (Hofstede, 1980).

### Power distance

By power distance (PDI) Hofstede means 'the extent to which the less powerful members of institutions and organisations within a country expect and accept that power is distributed unequally' (1991: 28). For example, in democratic societies the distance between the government and the governed is narrower than in dictatorships. In other words a worker in the Philippines will have far less chance of influencing the decisions of the government than would a worker in Sweden; and the same applies in the workplace. There is thus a high PDI in the Philippines and a low PDI in Sweden. Such work attitudes, Hofstede believes, are culturally determined and are liable to be accepted as much by the workforce as by the managers.

### Uncertainty avoidance

The definition of uncertainty avoidance involves, *inter alia*, the creation of rules and structures to eliminate ambiguity in organisations and support beliefs promising certainty and protecting conformity. In simple terms, this means that human beings try in various ways to avoid uncertainty in their lives by controlling their environment through predictable ways of working. For example, France and Germany are much higher in uncertainty avoidance than Britain and Sweden. In other words, the Germans and French feel a much greater need to adhere to rules and regulations than do the Swedes and British.

### Individualism

Individualism describes the relationship between the individual and the group to which he or she belongs, or the preference for living and working in collectivist or individual ways. Not surprisingly, the USA and Britain score high on the individual index, and South American and Asian countries score low. In the latter there is much more reliance on the extended family and the subsuming of the individual identity within the group, whereas in countries with high individual indexes, such as the USA and the Northern European countries, there is a tendency to revere individual achievement.

### Masculinity

Hofstede's last and perhaps most controversial index of culture is masculinity. This pertains to societies in which social gender roles are clearly distinct: that is, men are supposed to be assertive, tough and focused on material success. Femininity pertains to societies in which women are supposed to be more modest, tender and concerned with the quality of life (Hofstede, 1991: 82). In his index, masculine and feminine values can apply to both men and women. Thus we find that in Sweden, the least masculine country in the index, feminine values apply also to men. However, in the most masculine country, Japan, women seem to retain their feminine values.

Some commentators have pinpointed feminine values as being those most required in management practices in the organisation of the future. If that is the case, then some cultures will have considerable problems in adapting to those values immediately, if we are to believe Hofstede's masculinity index. The Netherlands comes very low on the masculinity index (MAS score 14) and the USA quite high (MAS score 62). Naturally, managerial practices could pose cultural misunderstandings between managers and workforces from the two countries.

639

### The research of Trompenaars

Trompenaars has also examined cultural differences in a world context. He uses seven dimensions of culture, each of which has within it a tension as exemplified by two opposite or polarised values. These measures are:

- **Universalism–Particularism**, in which individuals from a 'universalist' culture would focus on rules, and from a 'particularist' culture on relationships (Trompenaars, 1993: 29). For example, he asked respondents to state whether they would tell the truth to the authorities if they were accompanying a friend who, driving at 35 mph in a 20 mph speed-restricted zone, knocked down a pedestrian. In universalist cultures the respondents would feel a greater obligation to state that the friend had been travelling at 35 mph, but in a particularist culture respondents felt a greater obligation to the relationship by protecting the friend from a possible serious conviction.
- The **Analysing–Integrating** dimension examines the tension between the tendency to 'analyse phenomena into parts i.e. facts, items, tasks, numbers, units, points, specifics, or . . . to integrate and configure such details into whole patterns, relationships, and wider context' (Hampden-Turner and Trompenaars, 1994: 11).
- **Individualism–Collectivism** is the 'conflict between what each of us wants as an individual, and the interests of the group we belong to' (Trompenaars, 1993: 47).
- The **Inner Directed–Outer Directed** scale ranges from individuals who are influenced to action by 'inner directed judgements, decisions and commitments, or signals, demands and trends in the outside world to which we must adjust' (Hampden-Turner and Trompenaars, 1994: 11).
- **Time as Sequence–Time as Synchronisation** is the preference for doing 'things fast, in the shortest possible sequence of passing time, or to synchronise efforts so that completion is coordinated' (Hampden-Turner and Trompenaars, 1994: 11).
- **Achieved Status–Ascribed Status** examines the view that 'the status of employees depends on what they have achieved and how they have performed, or on some characteristic important to the corporation, i.e. age, seniority, gender, education, potential, strategic role' (Hampden-Turner and Trompenaars, 1994: 11).
- **Equality–Hierarchy** asks the question: 'Is it more important that we treat employees as equals so as to elicit from them the best they have to give, or to emphasise the judgement and authority of the hierarchy that is coaching and evaluating them?' (Hampden-Turner and Trompenaars, 1994: 11). This dimension has similarities to Hofstede's power distance index. Table 15.2 indicates where some major industrial powers would be located on Trompenaars' scale of cultural measures.

### The work of André Laurent

André Laurent of INSEAD in France has also achieved considerable recognition through his research on work-related values. He studied the attitudes of managers in Western European countries, the United States and two Asian countries, Indonesia and Japan (Laurent, 1983). He asked managers from these countries to describe their approaches to over 60 normal work situations. He discovered that managers of each of these countries fitted four clear groupings concerning perceptions of the organisation as a political system, authority system, role formulation system and hierarchical relationship system.

For example, when he posed the statement, 'The main reason for hierarchical structure is so that everybody knows who has authority over whom,' there were a variety of responses. Americans tended to disagree with the statement, believing the purpose of

640

**Table 15.2 The position of some major industrial countries on Trompenaars' cultural dimensions**

| | |
|---|---|
| Universalism | Britain, Sweden, USA, Germany, the Netherlands |
| Analysis | Britain, Sweden, USA, the Netherlands |
| Individualism | Britain, Sweden, USA, the Netherlands |
| Inner direction | Britain, USA, Germany |
| Time as sequence | Britain, Sweden, USA, Germany, the Netherlands |
| Status by achievement | Britain, Sweden, USA, Germany, the Netherlands, Japan |
| Equality | Britain, Sweden, USA, Germany, the Netherlands |
| Particularism | France, Japan |
| Integration | France, Germany, Japan |
| Collectivism | Germany, France, Japan |
| Outer direction | Sweden, the Netherlands, France, Japan |
| Synchronised view of time | France, Japan |
| Status by ascription | France |
| Hierarchy | France, Japan |

*Source*: Hampden-Turner and Trompenaars (1994: 301). Reprinted from *The Seven Cultures of Capitalism* by permission of Piatkus Books.

hierarchy is to organise tasks to assist in problem solving. The Americans tended to appreciate an organisation with as few levels of bureaucracy or hierarchy as possible. By contrast many Southern European and most Asians managers strongly agreed with Laurent's statement. These managers regard hierarchy as important in making sense of work structures and thus work itself. The structure being distinct enables them to know more clearly where they fit in and what their role is in the work process.

In response to the statement 'In order to have efficient work relationships, it is often necessary to bypass the hierarchical line' cultural differences were also revealed.

On this index the Swedes scored the lowest, which is consistent with the Swedish style of working, in which employee involvement is emphasised and many responsibilities are given to the workforce compared with other countries. However, cultural theorists would regard it as being simplistic and unjustified to place a value judgement on these attitudes, as they are rooted very much in the values of a society. In Italy, for example, it would be considered disrespectful and even challenging to bypass the boss, even to solve a problem advantageous to the organisation. This would be regarded as a challenge to the boss's authority.

In other words, while employees in different countries outwardly appear to be carrying out the same type of work processes, the cultural values that each individual carries shape both their perception and understanding of the workplace and their preferences for certain styles of working.

## High and low context cultures

Hall (1976; Hall and Hall, 1990) has made a comparative study of national attributes in the setting of *high context* and *low context* cultures.

Low context people appreciate explicit, clear written forms of communication, as provided by computers, books and letters. In contrast high context peoples, such as the Japanese, Arabs and Southern Europeans, divulge less information officially in written forms, but tend to be better informed than low context people, since they tend to develop extensive informal networks for exchanging information verbally face to face or by telephone. High context people are also more adept in interpreting non-verbal aspects of communication, and seeing the significance of what is implicit or not said, pauses, silence, tone, and other subtle signals.                    (Leeds *et al.*, 1994: 12)

641

One could say that the British 'old boy network' falls very much into this high context category, as does the felt need for exclusive clubs and societies, providing an entrée into various influential networks, which pervades British society. See Table 15.3.

**Table 15.3 Locating low and high context cultures**

| Country | High context | Low context |
|---|---|---|
| West Germany | | XXXX |
| German Swiss | | XXXX |
| Scandinavian | | XXX |
| North American | | XXX |
| Belgium, the Netherlands, Denmark | | X |
| France | | X |
| Britain | XX | |
| Southern Europe | XXX | |
| Middle East | XXX | |
| Asia, Africa, Latin America | XXX | |
| Japan | XXXX | |

Source: Leeds *et al.* (1994: 13).

## Criticism of the cultural approach

Attempts at measuring attitudes in human beings are difficult enough (as the wealth of research work in the social sciences testifies), but the application of numerous cultural values to the equation makes the work of disentangling one value from another extremely difficult, if not impossible. The cultural values of the researcher must be considered, and how much they are embodied in the research, from its conception to the analysis of the findings.

The cultural approach to HRM has received considerable criticism from academics working in HRM and related fields. Research such as that of Hofstede, Trompenaars and Laurent, which uses a positive approach, has been attacked for being too narrow in focus, and that using ethnographic approaches as often being too nebulous (Hollinshead and Leat, 1995: 3). Altman (1992) sums up the dilemma of the positive approach:

> Hofstede's strength lies in a finely tuned and rigorously applied research design. This is also his limitation. His approach can be likened to a powerful torch – sending a concentrated and bright, extremely sharp, ray of light, but, necessarily, leaving much in the dark. (p. 36)

In addition, the focusing of cultural values on bipolar dimensions has its difficulties. Individualism, for example, can have widely differing interpretations from one society to another, and may not necessarily mean the opposite of collectivism. Both Sweden and the USA are seen as high in individualism, but they do not have the same type of individualism. Swedish individualism resides very much within a welfare society, and American individualism within a neo-liberalist one. This begs the question of what these indices are actually representing.

Hofstede and Trompenaars also tend to assume clear relationships between attitudes and behaviours. There is an assumption that certain cultural attitudes will automatically lead to specific types of behaviour. They also ignore the wider context of culture, and their work suffers from being a static analysis in that it does not locate values in real historical development patterns and relationships between social groups and institutions –

642

an approach that the institutional perspectives attempts to address. Other critics claim that not all important value dimensions are represented, and that 'the structure of those four dimensions . . . can be challenged. The Masculinity/Femininity dimension is perhaps misnomered; it invites interpretation in terms limited to sexism' (Mead, 1994: 74).

There is also the problem of ascribing one culture to a whole national context. Very few societies are culturally homogeneous (Clark *et al.*, 1999: 521). For example, it would be difficult to sum up culturally what Englishness is, given the variety of regions and classes within England. Summing up Britishness will have greater problems given the diversity of Welsh, Scottish, English and Irish cultures.

In addition Sparrow (1995) astutely points out that

> The 'culture bound' perspective runs the gauntlet between generalizability and stereotyping and fails to consider the equally pervasive impact of both individual differences and organisational choice over its resource development. We need to know how all the operationalised dimensions relate to each other, and to the different levels and concepts of culture? Which dimensions have the greatest utility in shaping or influencing HRM when translated to the work of organisations?
>
> (p. 949)

Thus while many observers point to the importance of culture and the understanding of cultural differences in the HRM context, there are still considerable problems concerning definitions and approaches to meaningful and applicable research.

## The institutional perspective

A more wide-ranging divergence perspective on international HRM emanates from institutional theory. This view essentially sees the business environment as socially constituted. In other words, the influence of national and regional institutions and the historical traditions from which they have emerged is important in understanding why institutions differ throughout the world.

This perspective on the employment relationship suggests not only that business systems vary, but also that there are different models of capitalism. Until the 1980s much emphasis was placed upon four business systems or modes of industrial organisation: the American, European, Japanese and Soviet systems. Work by Sisson (1987), Lane (1989, 1995), Fulcher, (1991), Whitley (1992), Crouch (1993) and others has shown the complexity of industrial systems rooted in national institutional frameworks. For example, to speak of a 'European model' is patently absurd given the wide-ranging differences within the European Union alone, let alone the whole of what may qualify as Europe and indeed the world. In addition, since the collapse of the Soviet system another hybrid form of capitalism has emerged rooted in Soviet and Russian pre-existing systems and thus possessing unique characteristics of its own.

Such influential factors as the role of the state, financial systems, systems of education and training, national labour markets, culture, employment relations and systems of industrial bargaining, for example, have evolved in diverse ways in different national contexts that in turn affect the way organisations develop.These factors create a variety of configurations of institutional systems that have a considerable impact on the way human resource management is conducted. Given such diversity of national institutional frameworks Whitley (1992) has argued that creating a European system of HRM will prove virtually impossible, certainly for the foreseeable future.

The corporatist systems of Sweden, Germany and France, for example, are not only radically different from the neo-liberalist systems of the United States and the UK but also have considerable differences between themselves. These differences originate in

643

the way in which each nation's institutions have historically evolved, affected not only by the changing economic structure but also by historical events that impact on the national psyche at crucial points in institutional development. For example the Ådalen Strike in Sweden in 1931, in which a number of workers were killed by government troops, came to symbolise the old conflictual industrial relations. This had a considerable impact on the Saltsjöbaden Agreement 1938 between employers and unions, which implemented controls over the use of the strike weapon and the lockout in the resolution of disputes (Martin, 1984). This in turn had an impact on the creation of the Swedish Model in the 1950s, one of the main purposes of which was to resolve disputes and subsequently avoid such drastic incidents (Hadenius, 1988).

Lane (1989, 1994, 1995) has compared the industrial orders of Britain, Germany and France, and points to five institutional effects on business systems: the state, the financial system, the system of education and training, trade associations and chambers, and the system of industrial relations. For example, Lane (1992) shows that the state has a much higher profile in Germany than in Britain by endeavouring to provide 'a stable economic environment as well as uniform regulatory frameworks resulting in considerable national homogeneity of structural arrangements' (p. 67). State regulation of the British industrial order is much less than in Germany, particularly where the state acts as a coordinator for the integration of local and national policy with local government and other relevant regional bodies. The German and British financial systems are also structured differently. There is a heavy reliance on the stock market for large capital investment in the UK compared with Germany, with the result that short-termism predominates as investors desire to see immediate gains, and the capital markets are more prone to fluctuations. By contrast the German stock market is less developed. The role of capital provider is filled by large universal banks that maintain close links with industry. This interconnected system of mutual support makes events such as a hostile takeover rare, and viewed with suspicion if not hostility, as illustrated by the attempt by Vodafone to take over Mannesmann in early 2000.

In Germany there is strong structural support for training by government, although the costs are borne mainly by employers. By contrast, in the UK, structural supports, while existing, have emerged from different sociopolitical traditions, and the emphasis at present is on a voluntarist approach, which relies on organisations being willing to participate in government-inspired schemes. Vocational education and training (VET) has greater prestige in Germany, and the institutions (government, local government, private and public sector organisations, unions and educational institutions) that will benefit from such arrangements readily cooperate in providing support. The result is a high level of technical competence within the German workforce which is able to cope with forms of functional flexibility, and the productivity of German workers is thus much higher than that of their British counterparts.

In Germany, trade associations and chambers of industry and commerce also perform a crucial role in maintaining the craft tradition of high skill that keeps abreast of modern technical developments. Their importance is underscored by legislative support, and as statutory bodies they can impose levies on firms. In Britain, chambers of commerce do not have statutory status, and therefore have a more marginal role in the institutional framework of the industrial order.

The systems of industrial relations in the two countries also have different structures and influence. The German system is nationally homogeneous, with considerable legal underpinning. There is employee representation through works councils, the right to join unions and engage in collective bargaining is legally supported, and the system is

644

geared towards conflict resolution at all times rather than shaped by the determinants of market forces as in the UK. The British system has emerged through custom and practice over a long period of time, and has experienced intense conflict at certain periods. This has been partially explained by the lack of strong employer associations and the practice in the past of backing up demands by industrial action. However, over the past 20 years there has been a considerable shift in collective bargaining from national to organisational levels, with a subsequent decline in union influence at national level. Legislation has also had the effect of curbing union power, and while union density remains relatively high militant activity has receded considerably. The lack of national bargaining arrangements compared with the German system has served to undermine British trade union power further. We can thus see that while both countries are European and ultimately subscribe to capitalist values each system is substantially different from the other in the way in which it deals with employment relation issues.

Supporters of the institutional perspective claim that it avoids the controversial issues associated with cultural theory, which can be heavily laden with culturally based value judgements. However, significant work using an institutional perspective does rely to some extent on the interpretation of culture. Dore's work comparing a British and a Japanese corporation shows how the Japanese employment system is 'partly an adaption of earlier pre-industrial patterns, partly a conscious attempt to create new arrangements consonant with dominant cultural values, and partly the result of borrowing elements from industrialised nations' (Dore, 1973, quoted in Lane, 1989: 32). He finds, for example:

- adaption of earlier pre-industrial patterns – that is, European and US;
- adaption of Japanese values – 'Bushido spirit', loyalty, group work, respect, duty;
- elements borrowed from other industrialised nations, such as Deming's ideas on total quality management.

Another perspective on the institutional approach has been provided by Whitley (1992), in what he calls *business systems*. He views economic systems as being socially constructed in that 'major differences in dominant institutions result in different kinds of leading firms becoming established and following different growth patterns in different European economies' (p. 1). To understand its management structures, industrial and employment relations and HRM, an understanding is also needed of how the market is organised and of the nature of firms, and how this influences their authority, coordination and control systems. The way these three elements interact results in the unique business system of each national economic entity.

## Convergence or divergence?

Despite the simplicity of the convergence perspective and the limitations of the Marxist view there is some evidence to support increased convergence. Sparrow *et al.* (1994) conclude that there is a convergence in the use of HRM for competitive advantage, although they counsel caution in the interpretation of their findings, and still believe that cultural and institutional differences have some influence on divergent practices. Similarly, the Price Waterhouse Cranfield Surveys (Cran E net) reveal similar trends within corporations operating in different national settings: for example, greater use of flexible employment policy, the devolvement of HRM to line managers, an increase in spending on training and management development, and a greater strategic use of HRM initiatives (Brewster and Hegewisch, 1994). McGaughey and De Cieri (1999) have

645

also taken up the theme of convergence recently, and have refined convergence to macro-level variables in HRM and divergence to micro-level ones, focusing on individual attitudes, performance and behaviours. These are generally variables that are psychological and behavioural.

Another support for the convergence view is the widespread dissemination of managerial practices that has had the effect of creating a degree of managerial homogeneity (Celestino, 1999). The export of American managerial practices and ideas has been under way since the Second World War, and since the 1970s Japanese managerial styles have had a considerable influence on managerial theory and practice. The ubiquity of the Masters in Business Administration (MBA) has also witnessed the spread of ideas, together with popularity of managerial fashions such as TQM, quality circles, empowerment schemes, performance management and numerous other initiatives propagated by the 'business and management industry' and the media. These have been extensively disseminated through business sections in newspapers, the proliferation of managerial journals, consulting practices and the growth in popularity of business and management courses worldwide.

This archetypal form of modernism, some claim, has been superseded by postmodernist work forms in which decentralisation and flexibilities pervade the new working environment (Harvey, 1989). Others have refuted this postmodernist view and believe that this flexibilised world hides types of Fordism, which remains strongly influenced by the capitalist organisation's compulsion to produce profit.

This limited evidence does not really disturb the view that divergence remains strong in cultural and institutional terms throughout the world. The recognition of this has been acknowledged with the growth of expatriate management training and development programmes, the increasing popularity of which in MNCs and other overseas organisations is clearly evident in the cultural, societal and institutional barriers that can create huge problems for companies operating in a foreign context. (See below in the expatriation section for a fuller discussion). There is also considerable evidence that the transposition of a management system that has worked well in one national setting will not work in others. The work of Dore (1973) and more recently Broad (1994) has clearly shown the difficulty of implanting Japanese management systems even within the same company from one national sociocultural context to another – from Japan to Britain, for example. Research on quality circles and TQM in the 1980s and 1990s also illustrated that a wholesale adoption of an imported approach from Japan can have even less success when adopted by companies that have little or no connection with the country where they originated (see Chapter 13 for an in-depth discussion of such initiatives). Subsequently such systems survive only when considerable adaptations are made to accommodate the customs and practices of the indigenous country.

Blyton and Turnbull (1996), in reply to Warhurst's (1995) article (on HRM convergence in European airlines in seeking competitive advantage), point to the limitations of the convergence versus divergence approach. They argue that comparative analysis should focus on modes of labour regulation rather than institutions of industrial relations. In doing so, a more profitable approach to understanding the dynamics of comparative HRM would be the exploration of how 'different choices are open to management (and) how they might interact with, rather than simply be determined by the external environment, and how this might affect industrial relations' (p. 14). In a sense this is an application and extension of the business systems approach advocated by Whitley (1992).

646

Whatever comparative method or combination of methods we choose to use, uncertainty and inexactitude will remain important weaknesses in all approaches. With so many influential factors playing on the employment relationship and the relationship of organisations to governments, there will always be considerable room for debate and controversy.

## COMPARATIVE HRM

The separation of international HRM and comparative HRM is a useful way to untangle the various debates that surround the area of international HRM as a whole. International HRM we have defined as the creation and implementation of HRM strategy and policies and issues of international organisations, and comparative HRM as dealing with HRM concerns in national and regional contexts. Comparative HRM encompasses a wider area, and can range from comparing national employment systems rooted in ideologies, to aspects of HRM and related subjects such as training systems, pay systems, and the extent of the spread of flexible work systems. Comparative HRM can also vary in its approaches and meanings. One approach is to compare one nation state's HRM advantage with another. This approach often rests on a comparison of predominant national economies such as USA and Japan.

Economists and labour market theorists have undertaken considerable research into the essential properties that these regional and national contexts possess as drivers for successful economic growth. Unsurprisingly, the more successful these economies are (the USA and Japan, for example,) the more likely they are to be imitated or held up as exemplars of managerial efficiency. The US origin of HRM has been alluded to by a number of writers, who have attributed American values and even ideology to its theory and practice. This has led to a consideration of the transferability of HRM, both ideologically and as a set of employment issues, to other national and regional contexts, and whether other nations and global regions have HRM characteristics separate from American ones (Guest, 1990; Brewster, 1994; Clark and Mallory, 1996).

Another approach to comparative HRM is to draw a number of variables together into an analytical framework or model to help understanding of a nation's uniqueness in terms of its employment structure, industrial relations system and deployment of human resources. This poses many difficulties. Nevertheless, there have been some attempts to construct models to help understand these processes in a comparative context, and in this limited work we shall examine three: Poole's adaptation of the Harvard model, Brewster and Larsen's European model of HRM, and Sparrow and Hiltrop's comparative model of European HRM.

### Comparative HRM models and frameworks

The growth of interest in international HRM issues has led observers to attempt to systematise its processes and influences. The first attempts to create a coherent framework were extensions of already existing models rooted in Anglo-American experience. Thus Poole (1990) in the first issue of the *International Journal of Human Resource Management* begins the process by examining the Harvard model for its suitability for international application. The Harvard model of Beer *et al.* (1984) is very much reflective of its North American origins. Nevertheless, Poole argues that the Harvard model lends itself readily to international HRM because of its pluralist nature, in that it accepts differing

647

approaches and attitudes to the employment relationship. While Poole's model may be seen to be comparative, the fact that it is rooted in the Harvard model, which tries to explain HRM in an organisational context, also suggests that there is some confusion as to whether it is a comparative or an international model. In this sense it reflects the early stages of research in the subject, and in some senses it is a hybrid. Nevertheless it is a useful model, as it sets out the key elements in the study of comparative (and international) HRM.

## Poole's adaption of the Harvard model

Because some of the key features of the Harvard model reflect its North American origin, Poole (1990: 3) believes three key modifications are necessary for it to be accommodated into a new framework of international HRM:

- the global development of business;
- the power of different stakeholders;
- the more specific links between corporate and human resource strategies.

Taking his cue from writers on other aspects of the international employment relationship, including his own work on comparative industrial relations (Poole, 1986), Poole emphasises the notion of strategic choice in international HRM. The main areas of strategic human choice he sees as:

- employee influence;
- human resource flow;
- reward systems;
- work systems.

### Employee influence

The concept of empowerment of the workforce has long been recognised as an important in employee relations, and it has taken many forms in national and organisational cultures, including quality circles, job enrichment, union representation, works councils, co-determination, producer cooperatives, and self-management. Not all of these forms of participation will fit into HRM frameworks, but 'most are (a) relevant and (b) are the subject of vibrant comparative research' (Poole, 1990: 5).

### Human resource flo w

This is divided into *inflow* (recruitment, assessment and selection, orientation and socialisation), *internal flow* (evaluation of performance and potential, internal placement, promotion and demotion, education and training), and *outflow* (termination, outplacement and retirement). Each of these policy levers is governed by the government legislation, educational institutions, unions, societal values and public policy of each national and regional context.

### Reward systems

These would include in the framework not only the traditional methods of rewards such as pay, but also intrinsic rewards such as employee satisfaction and motivation to work.

### Work systems

The aim of all organisations is to gain high commitment from employees, and the various ways of achieving this reflect work-related value systems that need to be recognised and integrated.

648

Apart from these additions and adaptions to the Harvard model, Poole emphasises the need to recognise the role of globalisation, power and strategy in the evolution of international HRM.

The transcendence of national boundaries by multinational enterprises* (MNEs) and their relation to supranational bodies such as the European Union are becoming crucially important in the HRM process. Intertwined are the power structures of such bodies, which may conflict strategically and politically at company, country or regional level. The creation of strategies to take account of these possibilities becomes crucial in shaping the strategy of human resources. New technologies, the economies of large markets and market competition are other important factors to add to this strategic melting pot.

Poole sums up this process by quoting Adler and Ghadar (1989): 'the central issue of MNEs is not to identify the best international HRM policy per se, but rather to find the best fit between the firm's external environment, its overall strategy, and its HRM policy and implementation.'

As an early model it was useful in conceptualising some of the major issues that confront organisations in framing IHRM strategy, and acted more as a pointer towards research and theory building rather than being an end in itself.

## Brewster and Larsen's model of European HRM

The uniqueness of Brewster and Larsen's model of comparative HRM is that it is rooted in, and has emerged from, an extensive comparative research data bank. The Price Waterhouse Cranfield Surveys (Cranet -E) compared HRM practices initially in five countries (France, Germany, Spain, Sweden and the UK) in 1989–90, and then ten countries (the original five plus Denmark, Italy, the Netherlands, Norway and Switzerland) in 1990–91. The survey was extended to 16 countries in 1995 with the addition of Finland, Ireland, Turkey, East Germany, Greece and Belgium, more recently has been expanded to Eastern European states, and there are plans to extend it beyond Europe.

Brewster claims that his European model attempts to break away from American-influenced conceptualisations of HRM (Brewster and Bournois, 1991; Brewster, 1993). One major problem, however, is the lack of homogeneity of European employment systems (despite the attempts of the European Union social action programme), which creates considerable difficulties for model building. Yet European HRM systems are different from American ones, and this difference and diversity requires a distinctly different model.

The Brewster/Larsen model, like later ones developed by Brewster, emphasises the strategic positioning of HRM in the organisational context. HRM is considered part of the strategic apparatus, and it should also inform the business strategy and not be merely a tool to enact HRM aspects of the business strategy. The model rests on two dimensions that they argue are crucial to HRM being strategic: the integration and devolution of HRM. By integration is meant 'the degree to which HRM issues are considered part of the formulation of business strategy' (Brewster and Larsen, 1992: 411). HRM is thus integrated with technological, financial and human considerations of strategy implementation. Devolution concerns the transference of HRM functions to line managers and others at the operational levels within the organisation. HRM policy and functions are thus shared between the HRM department and line managers. The two dimensions are placed on a matrix, allowing an analysis both of the roles of the HRM department and of HRM as a general management activity (Figure 15.1).

* The terms MNE (multinational enterprise) and MNC (multinational company) are interchangeable.

649

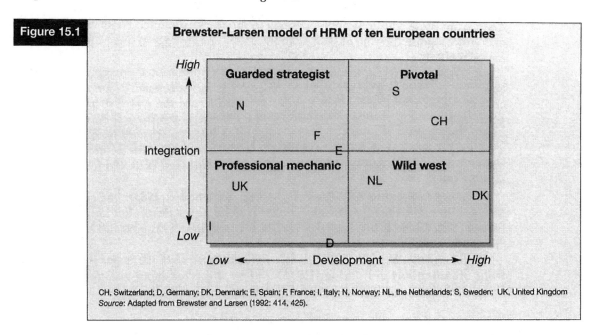

**Figure 15.1**        **Brewster-Larsen model of HRM of ten European countries**

CH, Switzerland; D, Germany; DK, Denmark; E, Spain; F, France; I, Italy; N, Norway; NL, the Netherlands; S, Sweden; UK, United Kingdom
*Source*: Adapted from Brewster and Larsen (1992: 414, 425).

Within the matrix are four types of HRM. The bottom left box indicates that business strategy is low, and there is little devolvement of HRM to the line. They have called this the *Professional mechanic* 'to emphasise the specialist, but limited skills and interests of practitioners' (Brewster and Larsen, 1992: 414). The professional role of the HRM department is emphasised, cherishing its HRM expertise and viewing it as not transferable to the line to any great extent. It thus has an increasing distance from strategic interests. The bottom right-hand box is called the *wild west*, because while a considerable amount of HRM is devolved to the line, the integration of HRM with business strategy remains low. In the top left-hand box is the *guarded strategist*, where integration of HRM with the business strategy is high, but devolvement to the line is low. This type of HRM is usually found in large and influential departments. The top right-hand box, the *pivotal*, represents the situation where HRM is fully integrated with business strategy and there is a high degree of devolvement to the line.

The UK, Germany and Italy emerge as professional mechanics, the Netherlands and Denmark as wild westers, Norway, France and Spain as guarded strategists, and the most integrated with the business strategy and the most devolved are Sweden and Switzerland in the pivotal box.

While presenting an interesting analysis of European HRM this does also pose a number of problems. First, these findings need to be put in the context of the national institutional environments in which HRM operates. These factors have a considerable impact, and it is hard to accept that the UK, Germany and Italy are similar in their HR practices because they appear in the same box based on only two dimensions. Institutional theorists would argue strongly how different HR is in these countries in terms of labour law, VET systems and collective bargaining, which could have a strong bearing on integrational and devolutional approaches to HRM. Second, these countries are very different culturally, and although the authors make some attempt to place the findings against the cultural dimensions of Hofstede and Laurent this has limitations. Third, there is always a methodological question mark over postal surveys and the drawing of wide generalisations based on them. Only personnel/HR managers were asked to complete the questionnaire, and large staff sections of the organisation were excluded. There are also ontological and epistemological limitations to the final analysis. Without other data, for example qualitative research, these results must be viewed with some scepticism. The authors do acknowledge some of these limitations, and we must also bear in mind that this is the only Europe-wide survey that has been conducted consistently over a period of a decade. It would be interesting in future works emanating from the Cran E survey material to attempt to contextualise the findings more deeply.

In later works Brewster (1994, 1995) has tried to address some of these concerns, and has developed models that attempt to give explanations of the influence on HRM of factors external to the organisation, such as culture, legislation, patterns of ownership, sector, size, trade union representation, employee involvement and communication, bargaining arrangements, labour markets, education and training. European organisations operate with restricted autonomy owing to the constraints of the European Union (for those member countries) and, at national level, the constraints of legislation and culture. These features, he claims, need to be integrated into the concept of HRM.

Clark and Mallory (1996) have criticised these models on the grounds that there cannot possibly be a European model of HRM given the diversity of European cultures. They also accuse Brewster of being Anglo-American in that he takes the parameters of the HRM debate purely from the literature of the UK and USA without due regard to writings in related areas in European organisations. While these criticisms have some validity, Brewster would claim that they are by no mean perfect models but merely steps in our thinking towards devising better ones.

## The Sparrow and Hiltrop model

Sparrow and Hiltrop's model also aims to differentiate European HRM from its American origins. They state 'that if European management exists it is in terms of greater cautiousness, sophistication of methods, and pursuance of elitist reward and career systems' (Sparrow and Hiltrop, 1997: 201). They suggest that a European perspective needs to take these factors into account:

- more restricted levels of organisation autonomy in HRM decisions such as recruitment, dismissal and training;
- a history that has produced a lower exposure of organisations to market processes;
- a greater emphasis on the role of the group over the individual;
- the increased role of social partners (trade unions and employee representatives) in the employment relationship;
- higher levels of government intervention in the management of business and the people within it.

In examining comparative HRM their aim is to make a dynamic model that is orientated towards the process of change, as they claim that the field hitherto has been 'long on description but short on analysis' (p. 202). The subject of their model centres on the factors that result in distinctive national differences; unlike Brewster's model it does not try to place emphasis on HRM practices in the organisation. The *force field* framework that they develop (Figure 15.2) is constructed around four sets of factors:

- cultural factors, such as national understandings of distributive justice and the manager–subordinate relationship;

651

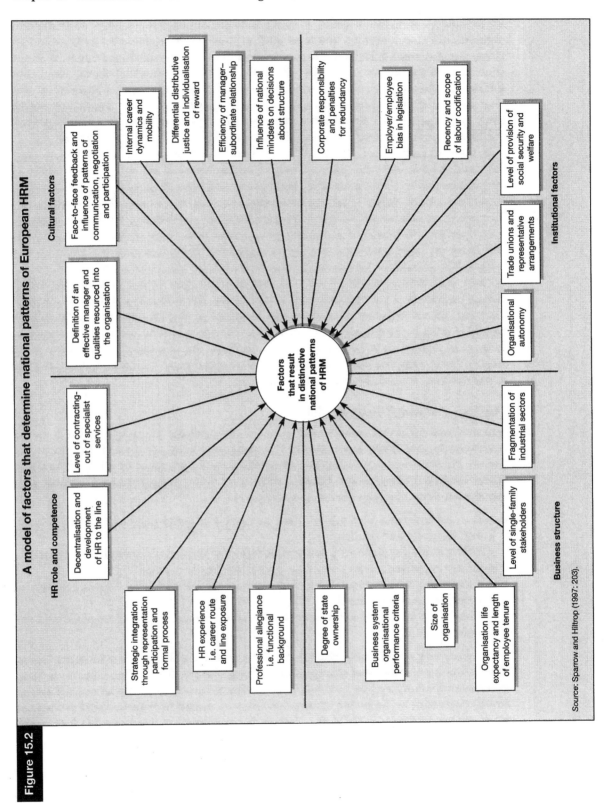

**Figure 15.2**

A model of factors that determine national patterns of European HRM

**Cultural factors**

- Face-to-face feedback and influence of patterns of communication, negotiation and participation
- Internal career dynamics and mobility
- Differential distributive justice and individualisation of reward
- Efficiency of manager–subordinate relationship
- Influence of national mindsets on decisions about structure
- Corporate responsibility and penalties for redundancy

**HR role and competence**

- Definition of an effective manager and qualities resourced into the organisation
- Level of contracting-out of specialist services
- Decentralisation and development of HR to the line

**Institutional factors**

- Employer/employee bias in legislation
- Recency and scope of labour codification
- Level of provision of social security and welfare
- Trade unions and representative arrangements
- Organisational autonomy
- Fragmentation of industrial sectors

Factors that result in distinctive national patterns of HRM

- Strategic integration through representation participation and formal process
- HR experience i.e. career route and line exposure
- Professional allegiance i.e. functional background
- Degree of state ownership
- Business system organisational performance criteria
- Size of organisation
- Organisation life expectancy and length of employee tenure
- Level of single-family stakeholders

**Business structure**

*Source: Sparrow and Hiltrop (1997: 203).*

- institutional factors, including the scope of labour legislation and social security provisions, and the role of trade unions;
- differences in business structures and systems, such as the degree of state ownership and fragmentation of industrial sectors;
- factors relating to the roles and competence of HRM professionals.

Organisations respond to their immediate business environments, and thus economic activities are controlled and coordinated differently in each national business system setting. For example, the impact of social and economic legislation of the European Union will be mediated by differing organisational strategies in the context of the national business system. Factors such as the degree of state ownership, the way public sector organisations connect to the business environment, and the number of small family-owned businesses are crucial to understanding different national business systems. For example, the preponderance and influence of small family-owned businesses in Italy has a powerful impact on the way HR issues are dealt with. In large organisations a greater number of employees tend to create more formalised HR structures compared with the informal practices of small businesses.

Institutional factors provide a second force field framework in their model. The role of the state, financial sectors, national systems of education and training and labour relations systems create unique 'logics of action' in each country, which guide different management practices (Whitley, 1992). The impact of national cultures (the third force field framework) shapes behaviour and perceptions, and there is a wide diversity of culture within Europe. The variations in culture will thus give widely differing approaches to management and HRM in terms of attitudes and definitions as to what makes an effective manager. HRM practices such as recruitment, selection, training, employee involvement, feedback, negotiation, communications, reward and performance will be perceived differently in divergent cultural settings.

The final force field framework relates to HR roles and competence and how these are interpreted at organisational levels in different national contexts. The levels of competence, career paths and the professional background of European HRM managers vary considerably. Thus the 'German HR professional with their strong legalistic background will have a very different mindset when compared to their less formal Anglo-Saxon colleagues, while the financial backgrounds of many Dutch and Italian HRM professionals produce yet a different focus' (Sparrow and Hiltrop, 1997: 208).

These force field frameworks are themselves open to different pressures from an ever-changing business environment that is experiencing rapid and discontinuous change as a result of the globalisation of markets and production and service systems. This in turn leads to choices within nations as to levels of taxation, investment in training and education, degrees of regulation or deregulation of labour markets and a number of other decisions. Sparrow and Hiltrop believe that the working out of responses to these changes will be most immediately felt at organisational level, perhaps by the adoption of 'best practices' in management and HRM. MNCs often act as a conduit for Anglo and Japanese approaches to HRM for example. In this sense a degree of convergence begins to overlay national HRM and managerial settings.

The Sparrow and Hiltrop model is a useful theoretical advance in aiding our understanding of comparative HRM, but in this short exposition of their work we cannot do justice to its complexity. They also clearly point to the sterility of strategic models of HRM, which do not consider the importance and influence of wider contextual factors. Strategic models that have emerged particularly from the American context embody

653

American values either explicitly or implicitly, and in many ways are inapplicable to other national and regional contexts. The strength of this model, given the fact that it has not been rigorously tested in the field, is that there is a recognition of the influence of cultural and institutional factors peculiar to business environments within which organisations have to operate.

## Some comparative HRM studies

Comparative studies into international aspects of the employment relationship have been carried out for a number of years and in their widest sense cover an enormous area of research, from an industrial relations and labour market perspective (Wilczynski, 1983; Bean, 1985; Poole, 1986; Bamber and Lansbury, 1987, 1998; Lane, 1989; Baglioni and Crouch, 1990; Hyman and Ferner, 1994; Ferner and Hyman, 1992, 1998; Ruysseveldt, *et al.*, 1995; Ruysseveldt and Visser, 1996; Cooke and Noble, 1998) to a broad raft of managerial issues including management development (Handy *et al.*, 1988; Randlesome, 1990; Kakabadse, 1991; Storey *et al.*, 1991; Storey, 1992; Lawrence, 1992; Brewster *et al.*, 1993). While such studies inform aspects of the employment relationship, human resource management is not their central concern.

Other studies have taken aspects of the employment relationship and have compared policy and practice in a number of national or regional contexts: for example, comparisons of employee involvement systems (Poole, 1986; Lincoln and Kalleberg, 1990; Gill, 1993; IDE, 1993; Holden, 1996). However, there is still a dearth of research that examines overarching HRM strategy and various HRM-related issues in a comparative context. There are many single-country studies, and while these may be informative, collectively they lack the unifying research methodology that allows rigorous comparability. Purcell (1993: 508–509) made a plea that comparative HRM research should examine different industry settings, and the extent to which capital markets and accounting practices affect HRM, as well as the impact of organisational size and ownership. This research agenda still remains relevant.

There have been studies of comparative and contrasting aspects of personnel management, management, management styles, international business and organisational behaviour, but in many ways they illustrate the hybrid nature of the relatively new discipline of HRM. There have been a number of single-nation surveys of aspects of HRM (Brewster and Tyson, 1991; Tyson *et al.*, 1993), and various dual or multiple-country qualitative studies and case studies, but there have been few internationally comparative quantitative surveys. One such survey is the Price Waterhouse Cranfield Survey on international strategic human resource management, referred to earlier.

### Price Waterhouse Cranfield Survey of International HRM

The research team were confronted with many methodological problems, and so the results have to be handled with care. For example, the creation of a questionnaire that would be completely compatible in all national employment settings posed enormous difficulties. Meanings of words change in context and in translation. For example, in France three general staff categories are used:

> Cadres, referring to managers and some professional employees, ETAM who are administrative, technical and advisory staff and ouvriers or operatives. These are not only the customary definitions but are also defined in law. There is little point therefore in trying to force French personnel managers into the customary British fourfold division of: 'management'; professional/ technical; 'clerical', and 'manual'. (Brewster et al., 1991)

654

Meanings of work typologies alluded to earlier in this chapter also presented problems of interpretation. Another restricting factor was that the survey dealt only with organisations in European countries, although a number were owned by American, Japanese and other non-European based companies.

The survey questionnaire was also directed at personnel managers, and therefore responses could well be flavoured with their interests and biases. Despite these and other methodological problems, observable trends were in evidence. Strategic HRM, as we have noted in Chapter 1, is concerned with the view that the creation of HRM policy is aligned to, and is an important part of, business strategy. In companies employing over 200 people the survey revealed that the HRM function seems to be becoming a more important part of organisations, as indicated by the high percentages of HRM managers or their equivalents with places on the board of directors.

The survey also revealed that the Scandinavian countries (Denmark, Norway, Sweden) had the highest percentage of organisations (over 60%) that had written personnel or HR strategies, and the Netherlands and Switzerland had over 50%, while the rest, including the UK, had less than 50%. Of those that had a personnel/HR strategy, only half to three-quarters translated these into work programmes, and 'this raises a substantial question mark over the extent of strategic human resource management in Europe' (Price Waterhouse Cranfield Project, 1991: 8).

The survey, however, confirmed a number of trends, including the continuing devolution of some aspects of HRM to line managers, particularly in recruitment and selection. Training is also tending to be devolved much more, albeit with consultation from the HR function. Industrial relations, however, remains typically within the personnel department's purview, which clearly indicates some of the differences between American organisational autonomy and the more centralised and coordinated European systems of collective bargaining. This, of course, is reflected in pay bargaining, which, while indicating a drop at national level in Britain and France, still remains relatively strong in these countries, and very strong in the rest of the survey countries, particularly Scandinavia (Price Waterhouse Cranfield Project, 1991; Brewster and Bournois, 1991). Trade union strength, while showing a relative decline in some countries, still retains a strong influence, and even low-density figures in France and Spain belie the considerable political power that the trade union movement can exert in these countries (Segrestin, 1990; Estevill and de la Hoz, 1990).

As we have noted in Chapter 13, employee communication is one of the central tenets of HRM, and the survey indicates a significant increase in its use; but in many European countries it is supported by legal requirements (and EC Directives) to consult and inform the workforce, another element that does sit well with American views of HRM (Brewster and Bournois, 1991: 9).

Atypical working or forms of flexibility (e.g. part-time workers) have increased in recent years, and have significance both for organisations that practise 'soft' HRM, associated with unitarist concepts aligned to internal labour markets, and for 'hard' HRM, associated with the core–peripheral external labour market model. Evidence from the survey shows a distinct increase in part-time working, and to a lesser degree fixed-term contracts. 'There is some evidence from the survey that Germany approximates more to the internal labour market model and Britain to the external' (Brewster and Bournois, 1991:10). 'Currently, however, there are indications here that support the view that European organisations are looking to create a more controlled external labour market for themselves' (Brewster and Bournois, 1991:11).

655

The survey gives credence to the views of Guest, Poole and others that HRM trends in Europe must be put in context against many different working practices (both internal and external to organisations) resting on different legal requirements and national assumptions, which contrast strongly with American HRM. Only further research will make it possible to develop and refine an international model and a European model.

### The Towers Perrin survey

Another survey conducted by Towers Perrin and analysed by Sparrow *et al.* (1994) looked at 12 countries worldwide. They asked the question: Do firms in different parts of the world practise HRM for competitive advantage differently? Data gathered from a questionnaire postal survey of chief executive officers and human resource managers revealed after analysis that there was convergence in the use of HRM for competitive advantage. These included:

- changes in organisational culture to create greater empowerment and equality of employees and greater diversity in their roles;
- organisational restructuring to reduce the number of vertical layers (delayering) and increase employee flexibility;
- an increase in the number and variety of performance management policies;
- improvements in resourcing – acquiring personnel and training and developing them;
- improvements in communication and corporate responsibility.

There were divergences in the way that specific aspects such as culture, work structuring, performance management and resourcing were utilised, but these, they claimed, differed more in degree than in kind (Sparrow *et al.*, 1994: 295).

It would seem that the influence of HRM and management trends is beginning to have a global impact on organisations, and that there is a degree of convergence of practices and approaches.

Easterby-Smith *et al.* (1995), using a case study approach in conducting a comparative piece of research between Chinese and UK companies, also found a convergence of approaches. However, they associated this convergence with 'hard' HRM policies such as manpower planning, and they noted divergence in 'soft', culture-sensitive areas, bound up with motivational issues such as remuneration and reward.

The research findings in the above surveys seem to suggest that the impact of managerial education, through international management programmes such as the MBA, and the increase in the worldwide popularity of management issues with an ever-increasing profile in the media, is influencing a convergence of policy and practice in HRM. Equally, however, we must recognise that these practices are not implemented in the same way in each country and organisational context.

## Problems of international research

The astute and experienced observer will note that there are considerable problems confronting the researcher of comparative aspects of HRM. Apart from the expense and communicational problems involved in conducting such undertakings there are considerable methodological mountains to climb. We have alluded to some problems already in examining the Price Waterhouse data. Although research is increasing there is still a considerable lack of reliable information, and that which does exist poses problems of interpretation. These include the following:

- There is a *lack of data*. It is only relatively recently that many countries have begun to keep detailed records of their economic performance, such as GNP, growth rate, unemployment, trade balances, and workforce statistics.
- Even though advanced industrial nations have been keeping such statistics for many years, there is still a *lack of comparative data*: for example, trade union statistics, GNP and unemployment can all be measured quite differently in different countries.
- *Statistics and similar data are highly political and open to manipulation and bias*, both in the way they are collected and in the way they are presented for public consumption.
- Another difficulty is to find a *series of figures that do not have a break in consistency*. For example, is it possible to meaningfully compare unemployment statistics of the 1930s with those of the 1980s?
- International statistics are also noted for having *time lags where one economy is behind in furnishing statistics*. Thus one country may be giving data pertaining to a period as much as one year behind another country's data on the same subject.
- *Language and meaning can be diverse*: even though the same words are often used they can cause confusion. Job titles vary widely from country to country. For example, the equivalent term for 'management' in France is 'cadre', although the meanings are not the same. In consequence the English term 'manager' is increasingly being used in French organisations. Japanese corporations have no concept of management development; they prefer what can only be described as 'capability development', and this includes all employees.
- Some national economies emphasise *some aspects of economic performance* rather than others, because these are the areas in which they are strong – agriculture, new technology or engineering for example – and this can skew comparisons.
- *Cultural differences can give quite differing approaches to the same data*. This can affect interpretation and meaning.
- *Generalisation is necessary but leads to dilution to the point where the interpretation of the data can become meaningless*. For example, regional differences could be ignored because they do not fit the national pattern closely.

Thus the area of comparative study is fraught with many pitfalls and difficulties.

## INTERNATIONAL HRM

At the beginning of this chapter we made a distinction between comparative HRM and international HRM in that the latter exists primarily in multinational companies (MNCs) and the former has a wider contextual setting. This section will explore developments in international HRM. There is a considerable overlap between international and comparative HRM in that both examine aspects of HRM policy and practice in a world or regional context. Comparative HRM is concerned more with examining trends in HRM practice and comparing HRM and business systems between nations. International HRM is concerned with how HRM is carried out purely within the international organisational context: for example, how international HRM strategy is conceived and implemented in an MNC, and how the parent company relates to the overseas subsidiaries in terms of the amount of control it exercises over them and the amount of autonomy it gives them. It is concerned with what kind of HR policies should

657

be adopted and how they should be implemented. It is also concerned with the strategy makers and the implementers themselves – that is, the attitudes and approaches of the parent company's HR managers and overseas subsidiary staff, including expatriate managers and host country staff. It is also concerned with how HR policy and practice will vary within different organisational parameters such as size, sector and ownership (public, private and non-governmental organisations).

Despite the burgeoning literature concerning international HRM, comparatively little is known about how such firms manage their human resources, particularly across national borders. The literature to date has concentrated largely on MNCs and mainly on issues of expatriation (Scullion, 1995), though the subject is now receiving increasing attention from researchers. However, MNCs have been increasingly aware of the growing need to have not only international business strategies but also international human resource strategies (Pucik, 1984). Attention has been focused on HRM by such issues as global management succession planning, recruitment, selection and training for the expatriation process, recruitment from the indigenous population, and awareness of labour and human resource practices in different countries and regions.

## Expatriation

Expatriation has been a dominant theme in the literature of IHRM, and an understanding of the reasons for this is an appropriate point to start an examination of IHRM. MNCs are now recognising that internationally minded management teams of expatriate managers with international skills and experience are becoming a major competitive advantage. Increasingly, multinational corporations are expecting their senior executives to have had international experience. The implications for management training and development are enormous (see Chapter 9), a fact that nations and companies ignore at their peril (Pucik, 1984: 404).

Brewster and Scullion (1997) have identified a number of key reasons why expatriates are used extensively by MNCs. The first is the transmission of technical and management skills from the parent to the subsidiary. Often this takes place in the early stages of international development particularly in countries that lack these skills. Expatriates thus perform not only a management and technical operational role but often also a training and development role in which they pass on these skills to the indigenous workforce. Second, expatriates are used as a control mechanism to ensure that the company strategy, policies and procedures are being correctly followed by the subsidiary. Edström and Galbraith (1977) identified three types of control mechanism, two of which have expatriate managers in a pivotal role.

- *Bureaucratic.* Bureaucratic control is indirect and impersonal. This allows some discretion at the local level, where procedures and processes (such as financial) are put in place to monitor activities, and therefore decisions can be delegated to lower levels locally.
- *Geocentric.* Control is through expatriate managers. The advantage is increased communication between HQ and the subsidiary. The approach is personal, allowing face-to-face communication. It can make company policy more acceptable at local levels, and it allows local discretion and responsiveness while maintaining a level of control from the centre.
- *Socialisation.* This is achieved through expatriate managers building social networks for informational and communicational interaction between HQ and subsidiaries

658

and between subsidiaries. Functional behaviours and rules determining them are learned by individuals. This obviates the need for procedures, hierarchical communication and surveillance. This approach emphasises loyalty to a person as well as to the organisation (Edström and Galbraith, 1977).

Organisations will not necessarily use only one of these control mechanisms, but are more likely to use a combination of some or all of them. Ethnocentric organisations (high parent company control – see below for a fuller explanation) seeking greater degrees of control may well use combinations of all. Polycentric organisations (high subsidiary company control – see below for fuller explanation) may be seeking to keep a lower ownership profile for political reasons, and may be more inclined therefore to use bureaucratic control mechanisms perhaps setting financial or production targets. If the subsidiary meets them then it is allowed to sustain a large degree of autonomy. But as Adler and Ghadar (1990) suggest, organisational HQs are more than likely to emphasise different aspects of control at different periods in the organisation's development.

## Expatriation failure and its prevention

Considerable attention in the literature on expatriation has been concerned with the failure of expatriate assignments and with methods to prevent this (Brewster, 1991). Support for expatriate managers is expensive for companies. They are often required to pay high salaries, and additional costs are incurred such as relocation costs for the expatriates and their families involving travelling expenses, accommodation, schooling and other factors not directly paid for in the parent company environment. If an assignment fails then the company stands to lose considerable money and has to replace the repatriated manager. There has recently been a debate as to the extent of failure rates, and Harzing (1995) has claimed that the figures have been considerably inflated and based on dated and limited research that has been repeated in the literature without being examined or questioned. While Forster (1997) agrees with Harzing's critique he nevertheless believes that the definition of failure has been too narrow, and must include 'the stresses and strains experienced by a minority of staff who are under performing; the poaching of successful managers by other companies while they are abroad . . . ; the often negative outcomes of the repatriation experience . . . ; the negative (and largely unreported) effects on some families and their career prospects of partners and negative views about the prospect of overseas postings in the future' (p. 414). Indeed, a growing subsidiary but, nevertheless, equally important concern is the high failure rate of assignments associated with the unhappiness of the spouse and the family (Black and Stephens, 1989).

Failure of assignments has also focused significantly on the difficulties of acculturation in terms of a 'culture clash' between expatriate managers and the host country environment and employees (Torbiörn, 1982). Failure to understand a foreign culture can lead to feelings of alienation and depression in the expatriate manager and his or her family.

As a result of these concerns there is a considerable literature concerned with expatriate selection, training, development and career succession (Brewster, 1991). Torbiörn (1982) has made a close examination of the adjustment process that expatriate managers experience in postings abroad, and as we have already noted, Hofstede (1980) and Laurent (1983) have examined cultural differences of managers.

Considerable attention has therefore been given to recruitment, selection and training of potential expatriate managers and acculturation and acclimatisation issues (Dowling et al., 1994, 1999). There is also a growing body of research on repatriation

659

issues, particularly the re-acculturation of expatriates who have spent considerable time abroad (as many as 10 or 20 years) and the problems of 're-entry' into not only their home country culture, but also their HQ organisational culture (Black and Gregersen, 1991; Forster, 1994). Another area of growing interest is the experience of the international woman manager (Adler and Izraeli, 1994).

In recent years there has been speculation that expatriate managers are being used less in MNCs because of their high cost, the increasing levels of education and technical expertise in foreign countries, and the increase in communications making contact between parent and subsidiaries much easier. However, research by Scullion (1992) shows that the majority of the British and Irish MNCs in his study used expatriate managers, and the shortage of such managers was of considerable concern to them. These findings are similar to research into American MNCs (Dowling *et al.*, 1994, 1999).

Kobrin's (1994) research also emphasises the importance of expatriates and claims that their training, development and experience are essential for creating a geocentric mindset (a global perspective of the organisation and its goals). Kobrin proposes a tentative hypothesis that the need to transmit knowledge and information through the global network may lead, through increased interpersonal interaction, to organisational geocentrism in terms of attitudes and IHRM policies. The latter point is interesting in that his research reveals a growing interest in IHRM among major MNCs as it is perceived to have a crucial link to effective policy implementation.

## Globalisation and the effects of country of origin and host country on HRM

As globalisation proceeds apace, MNCs and other cross-national organisations are becoming increasingly important, and one of the chief concerns of observers of the globalisation phenomenon is the key role played by MNCs in influencing change. Where MNCs locate production plants can have considerable impact on employment at home and abroad. Critics have pointed to the power that MNCs have in persuading national governments to be amenable in their labour practices in return for large investments in their economies (Hirst and Thompson, 1996). With the increase of globalisation there has been a growth in the number of transnational companies. These are companies that have no national adherence that are globally free floating, with the ability to switch resources to different global arenas to gain competitive advantage. A number of observers have noted that this argument has been considerably exaggerated, and that the transnational is still a rare phenomenon. Having examined the evidence, some writers believe that national economies are still important in shaping MNCs' strategies (Porter, 1990; Ruigrok and Van Tulder, 1995; Hirst and Thompson, 1996) and most MNCs are strongly rooted in their country of national origin, but nevertheless pay particular attention to host country influences such as laws, customs and practices (Whitley, 1992).

The country of origin of most MNCs is still a powerful influence on the strategy, structure and managerial and HRM policy implementation worldwide. The major assets as well as the key strategic decision-making groups reside, in the overwhelming majority of cases, with the parent company. While there has been some interest in the way in which companies control and manage their subsidiaries from headquarters there has been little in the way of research conducted into the effects of country of origin on organisational and HRM issues (Ferner, 1997). This perspective emphasises the way in which developments in HRM are informed by trends within the parent company and its national context. The United States has had the most significant impact in

660

promoting innovative HRM, but this raises questions as to the exportability of HRM policy and practice from one national socio-economic context to another – a theme touched on in the section on comparative HRM above. Early literature tended to ignore these questions, and there was an assumption that convergence would readily take place between the parent company policy and practice and that of the subsidiary – the view that international HRM was HRM 'writ large.' Researchers working from cultural and institutional perspectives have clearly indicated the complexity of transposing HRM policy and practices from one national context to another, even within the same organisational culture. The variety of influences on the creation and implementation of strategic IHRM is thus one of the major themes demanding the attention of researchers in the field.

There has also been recognition that subsidiaries can play important and varied roles in HRM strategy formulation and implementation. Strategic HRM becomes increasingly complex as companies expand overseas, and it would be naive to assume that once HQ decisions are made they are automatically implemented as intended. Thus the influence of subsidiaries in interpreting and implementing becomes an important element in the internationalisation of the HR process; and the way subsidiaries execute HR policy is also conditioned by host country environmental factors. Seminal writers in the field of international management have recognised that the pressures for global integration and the forces for national differentiation are the two major environmental factors in the practice of international management and HRM processes (Bartlett, 1986; Hedlund, 1986; Bartlett and Ghoshal, 1989; Doz and Prahalad, 1991). The balancing of these forces is thus a pivotal element in the management of international HRM. An understanding of the headquarters–subsidiary relationship has therefore become the focus of considerable research (Hedlund, 1980; Ghoshal and Nohria, 1989; Forsgren 1990; Nohria and Ghoshal, 1997).

This raises questions of power and control in the implementation of strategy – how much power and control reside in different parts of the organisation. Simplistic conceptualisations assume that control is automatically imposed by HQ on the subsidiary, but Perlmutter (1969) has created a typology that proposes that the subsidiary role can vary widely in organisations.

## Perlmutter's headquarters–subsidiary orientations in MNCs

Four approaches have been identified to describe the way MNCs conduct their international HRM policies: ethnocentricism, polycentricism, geocentricism and regiocentrism.

### The ethnocentric approach
This approach has all key positions in the host country subsidiary filled by parent company nationals. It therefore offers the most direct control by the parent company over the host country subsidiary, when there is a felt need to maintain good communication between the subsidiary and the MNC HQ. This is common in the early stages of internationalisation, when the MNC is establishing a new business process or product in another country. It may also be used because there is a lack of qualified host country nationals.

### The polycentric approach
This is directly opposite in approach to ethnocentricity: host country nationals are recruited to manage the subsidiary in their own country. This allows the MNC to take a lower profile in sensitive economic and political situations, and to avoid intercultural management difficulties.

661

### The geocentric approach

This approach utilises the best people for the key jobs throughout the organisation, drawing on all parts of the world MNC operation. This makes it possible to develop an international executive team.

### The regiocentric approach

In this approach an MNC divides its operations into geographic regions and moves staff within these regions, such as Europe, America, or the Asia Pacific rim. Some see such regionalisation as an effective way of developing management succession programmes.

An MNC may pass through several of these stages depending on its familiarity with the host country setting, the calibre and quality of its host country national staff, and the degree of direct control that is felt necessary to impose on the subsidiary. These decisions are all bound up with wider economic, political and social concerns.

While this approach provides a useful framework for conceptualising managerial approaches in MNCs, it lacks explanations of change and fails to take into account the dynamics of turbulent changes in the global environment. Perlmutter acknowledges that companies could change from an ethnocentric to a polycentric orientation (and vice versa) but he offers no explanation as to why or how this is accomplished.

## Adler and Ghadar's phases of internationalisation

Adler and Ghadar (1990) have attempted to develop a framework to explain the changing nature of international HRM by relating HRM strategy and policy changes to product life cycles. As companies expand their activities from domestic to overseas markets and operations they concentrate on different aspects of organisational development. They perceive this organisational development moving through four phases (summarised in Table 15.4).

### Phase I: Domestic

Phase I concentrates mainly on the home market, with some overseas sales through agents, and as a result international HRM is non-existent.

### Phase II: International

The international phase witnesses a definite commitment to overseas markets, marked by the creation of subsidiaries or joint ventures. Expatriate managers are assigned positions overseas, and bring with them managerial and technical expertise and financial control. This phase is characterised by the passing on of skills and knowledge to locally recruited employees, some of whom may assume managerial positions in running the operation at a later time. Human resource issues become important in terms of recruiting, selecting, training, developing and rewarding expatriate and host country staff. The expatriate managers will need language and cultural awareness training, among other things, and the host country staff will need to learn the skills and knowledge of the business.

### Phase III: Multinational

In the multinational phase the organisation seeks to gain competitive advantage by high sales and low cost. The emphasis in this phase is on creating cohesion through the spread of the organisation's aims and values and inculcating them into a developing

662

## Table 15.4 Globalisation and human resource management

| | Phase I<br>Domestic | Phase II<br>International | Phase III<br>Multinational | Phase IV Global |
|---|---|---|---|---|
| **Primary orientation** | Product or service | Market | Price | Strategy |
| **Strategy** | Domestic | Multidomestic | Multinational | Global |
| **Worldwide strategy** | Allow foreign clients to buy product/service | Increase market internationally, transfer technology abroad | Source, produce and market internationally | Gain global strategic competitive advantage |
| **Staffing expatriates** | None (few) | Many | Some | Many |
| **Why sent** | Junket | To sell control or transfer technology | Control | Coordination and integration |
| **Whom sent** | | 'OK' performers, salespeople | Very good performers | High-potential managers and top executives |
| **Purpose** | Reward | Project 'To get job done' | Project and career development | Career and organisational development |
| **Career impact** | Negative | Bad for domestic career | Important for global career | Essential for executive suite |
| **Professional re-entry** | Somewhat difficult | Extremely difficult | Less difficult | Professionally easy |
| **Training and development** | None | Limited | Longer | Continuous throughout career |
| **For whom** | No one | Expatriates | Expatriates | Managers |
| **Performance appraisal** | Corporate bottom line | Subsidiary bottom line | Corporate bottom line | Strategic positioning |
| **Motivation assumption** | Money motivates | Money and adventure | Challenge and opportunity | Challenge, opportunity, advancement |
| **Rewarding** | Extra money to compensate for foreign hardship | | Less generous, global packages | |
| **Career 'fast track'** | Domestic | Domestic | Token international | Global |
| **Executive passport** | Home country | Home country | Home country, token foreigners | Multinational |
| **Necessary skills** | Technical and managerial | Plus cultural adaption | Plus recognising cultural differences | Plus cross-cultural interaction, influence and synergy |

Source: Alder and Ghadar (1990).

**The Management of Human Resources**

management cadre. Managers may be drawn not only from the country of origin and from host country staff, but also from third country staff (staff from neither the home or host country moved from one subsidiary to another in a different country). In HRM terms emphasis will be placed on career development, management development and management succession.

### Phase IV: Global

In the global phase the company will become a truly international player, operating worldwide in a wide variety of countries and regions. Management cadres will reflect this approach by creating strategies to gain advantage from global integration with local responsiveness. Differentiation will be welcomed as staff become increasingly skilled and knowledgeable. They will be able to utilise their local knowledge in coordination with their company skills to create competitive advantage. Human resource management issues will be continued from phases II and III, and ideally forums will be created to facilitate the exchange and development of knowledge, transforming the company into a learning and knowledge organisation on a global scale.

One of the problems with this conceptualisation is that it makes huge assumptions about what constitutes an MNC or an international organisation in general. Such organisations could take many forms in terms of size, ownership, distribution or sectoral characteristics, all of which could defy the developments predicted in the framework outlined.

Adler and Ghadar's phases of internationalisation also do not address issues of HRM beyond expatriation, and there is no attempt to explain the linkages between parent and subsidiaries in terms of HRM strategy and its implementation. Some observers have attempted to do this by building models, and the next section explores this.

## Models of strategic international human resource management

The difficulties of attempting to create a model of HRM have already been noted even within the cultural context of one country, the United States, and the further complexities of attempting to apply such models to other national settings. This is also compounded by the variety of organisational and managerial styles that abound within different organisations in different sectors depending on the products they make and the services they perform within the diversity of national and regional cultures. A further drawback is the relative lack of research that has taken place in the field of IHRM. Research emphasis has been very much in the realm of expatriation, while questions of IHRM strategy and its operationalisation have been relatively neglected. Thus model building has tended to lean towards theoretical considerations, resting on prescriptions rather than rooted in research. Other writers, most notably Pieper (1990), hold the view that no universal model of HRM is possible. Pieper bases this argument on the fact that the variations are too wide in terms of institutions and working practices between nations.

Since Pieper wrote this a decade ago there have been some significant developments in international HRM. It has also become clear from comparative surveys available that there have been, if not degrees of convergence in HRM practice, at least trends that indicate the adoption on a worldwide basis of many managerial initiatives associated with HRM.

664

### Schuler *et al.*'s integrative framework of international HRM

The most comprehensive model in the field to date is that proposed by Schuler *et al.* (1993) (Figure 15.3). They have linked human resource management with organisational strategy into a framework of strategic international human resource management (SIHRM), that they hope will be useful to both academics and practitioners alike. They claim that a considerable amount of the research literature has concentrated on the problems of expatriation, and that the 'next task for researchers is to examine the influence of exogenous and endogenous factors on strategic international HRM and to consider the consequences of these influences and interrelationships' (p. 753). By exogenous factors they mean those external to the MNE, such as industry characteristics and country/regional characteristics. By endogenous factors they mean those internal to the MNE, such as the structure of international operations, headquarters international orientation, competitive strategy and the experience in managing international operations.

These endogenous and exogenous factors influence the organisation's strategic IHRM, which in turn affects the MNE's competitiveness, efficiency, local responsiveness, flexibility and transfer of learning. Of vital importance in the creation and enactment of strategic IHRM is the way units within MNEs link and how they can be integrated, controlled and coordinated. This concerns how much autonomy can be granted to

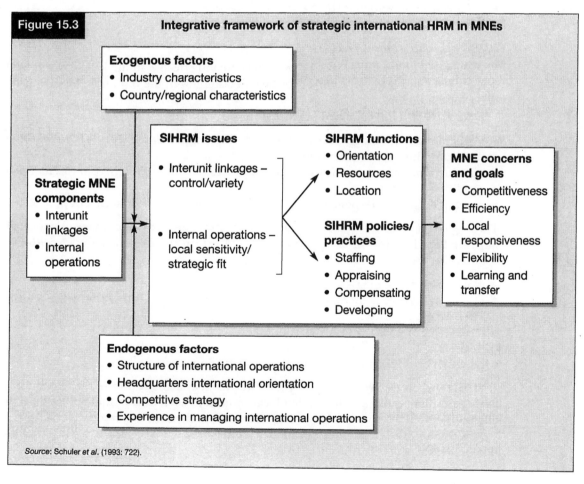

**Figure 15.3**  **Integrative framework of strategic international HRM in MNEs**

**Exogenous factors**
- Industry characteristics
- Country/regional characteristics

**Strategic MNE components**
- Interunit linkages
- Internal operations

**SIHRM issues**
- Interunit linkages – control/variety
- Internal operations – local sensitivity/strategic fit

**SIHRM functions**
- Orientation
- Resources
- Location

**SIHRM policies/practices**
- Staffing
- Appraising
- Compensating
- Developing

**MNE concerns and goals**
- Competitiveness
- Efficiency
- Local responsiveness
- Flexibility
- Learning and transfer

**Endogenous factors**
- Structure of international operations
- Headquarters international orientation
- Competitive strategy
- Experience in managing international operations

*Source:* Schuler *et al.* (1993: 722).

665

**The Management of Human Resources**

local units, how they are coordinated and controlled, and how much control the MNE will exercise over internal operations. It also involves decisions on whether to export people or the HR function.

### SIHRM concerns at headquarters

Schuler *et al.* state that SIHRM functions at HQ level will have three areas of concern:

- the MNE's HR orientation;
- the time, energy and financial resources devoted to operating the human resource organisation in the MNC;
- the location of those resources and the human resource organisation – centralised or localised, or a combination of both.

Policies and practices will be designed in accordance with the way individuals will be managed and the way specific practices are developed – for example, how performance is rewarded, and how staffing, appraising and developing are carried out. This will also mean that the HQ will be concerned with three issues:

- maintaining a mix and flow of parent country nationals (PCNs or expatriates), host country nationals (HCNs) and third country nationals (TCNs – managers and employees from neither host or parent country);
- systematically developing HR policies and practices;
- using management development as the glue.

### SIHRM concerns at local level

The main task of local units is to be responsive to and effective in the local environment yet be willing and ready to act in a coordinated fashion with the rest of the MNE units in order to achieve this.

Relevant SIHRM policies and practices are:

- matching and adopting HR practices with the competitive strategy of the unit and the local culture and legal system;
- creating a modus operandi whereby HR practices can be modified to fit changing conditions;
- developing global HR policies flexible enough to be adapted for local HR practice.

Throughout the balancing and coordination of these processes a number of concerns must be kept in mind in the practice of HRM within the organisation's worldwide context:

- global competitiveness – a main concern;
- efficiency – HRM is increasingly seen as a source of competitive advantage and its effective use as crucial;
- local responsiveness (sensitivity);
- flexibility;
- organisational learning (the transfer of information across units).

SIHRM may travel well, and policy and practice may actually transfer across cultures more easily than is often assumed, but local conditions such as laws and culture make it imperative for MNEs to be aware of the need to adapt their human resource practices.

As a result of the creation of this model Schuler *et al.* (1993) came to a 'final' definition of SIHRM:

666

developing a fit between exogenous and endogenous factors and balancing the competing demands of global versus local requirements as well as the needs of coordination, control and autonomy.                                                                                     (p. 753)

The model is highly complex, and space dictates that we cannot do justice to it here, but it points a way forward to further refinements to future models and theorisation. However, critics have pointed to its still highly prescriptive nature, and the fact that it does not explain the political micro processes that take place between HQ and the subsidiaries (Quintanilla, 1998). Ferner (1994) has also pointed out that that it is primarily concerned with senior management, and not the workforce as a whole.

### Taylor *et al.*'s integrative model of strategic IHRM

Taylor *et al.*(1996) build on previous work on IHRM by drawing on concepts from the resource-based view of the firm to develop a theoretical model of the determinants of SIHRM systems in MNCs (Figure 15.4). Resource-based theory adds to prior models of SIHRM the fundamental notion that, in order to provide value to the business, the SIHRM system of global firms should be constructed around specific organisational competences that are critical for securing competitive advantage in a global environment (Pucik, 1992). The resource-based framework helps to identify those situations in which MNCs will exercise control over the SIHRM system of their affiliates. The authors define SIHRM as

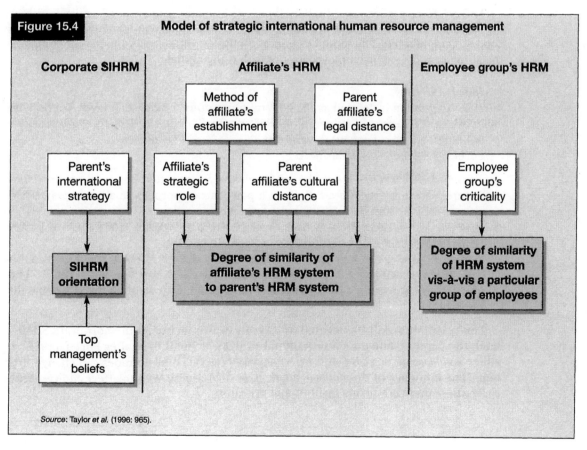

**Figure 15.4**        **Model of strategic international human resource management**

Source: Taylor et al. (1996: 965).

667

> human resource management issues, functions and policies and practices that result from the strategic activities of multinational enterprises and that impact the international concerns and goals of those enterprises.
>
> (Taylor *et al*,. 1996: 961)

They quote Lado and Wilson's (1994) definition of the resource-based view of HRM:

> The resource-based view suggests that human resource systems can contribute to sustained competitive advantage through facilitating the development of competencies that are firm specific, produce complex social relationships, are embedded in a firm's history and culture, and generate tacit organisational knowledge.
>
> (p. 699)

HRM competence is viewed as both the *tangible* resources (e.g. HR planning systems, selection tests) and *intangible* resources (e.g. shared mindset, ability to attract qualified employees) that allow a firm to outperform its competitors. Using the resource-based theory approach, they distinguish between resources at three levels in the MNC:

- parent company *resources* developed from a particular configuration of economic, cultural, human and other resources in a country – not differentiated domestically, but can give an MNC an advantage when competing outside its home country (e.g. German apprenticeship system);
- parent company *unique bundle of assets and capabilities* developed over its lifetime;
- affiliate *resources,* which may provide a competitive advantage at the local, regional or global levels (e.g. developing HRM selection policies to deal with high labour market mobility).

The origin of the resource (national, firm or affiliate) is likely to affect its usefulness in other locations. Resources, including HRM competence, can be context specific or context generalisable. The model examines SIHRM at three levels: the parent company, the affiliate, and specific employee groups within the affiliate.

### Corporate SIHRM

SIHRM orientation is defined as the general philosophy or approach taken by top management in the design of its overall IHRM system. This will reflect the organisation's overall approach to managing the *differentiation vs integration dilemma.*

Three orientations are identified:

- *Adaptive.* HRM systems are designed for affiliates that reflect the local environment. Differentiation is emphasised. Reflects a polycentric approach in all aspects of HRM, with virtually no transfer of policies and practices.
- *Exportive.* An ethnocentric approach in which there is complete transfer of the parent firm's HRM systems. The emphasis is on high integration.
- *Integrative.* Attempt to take the 'best' approaches and use them across the organisation in the creation of a worldwide system (Bartlett and Ghoshal, 1989). This approach incorporates substantial global integration, with an allowance for some differentiation.

The orientation will be decided as a result of two factors at the corporate SIHRM level: the parent company's international strategy, defined here after Porter (1986) as either *multidomestic* or *global*; and *top management beliefs.* These attitudes can change over time. The influence of the *national origin of the MNC* is also seen to affect choices, especially where there are strong institutional pressures.

668

## Affiliate's HRM system

The degree of similarity of an affiliate's HRM system is assessed via its strategic role using the resource-based approach – that is, how reliant the subsidiary units are on the parent company's unique resources. Under this approach, the strategic role of an affiliate can be defined by the amount and direction of the resource flows between the parent company and the overseas affiliate. Four types of role are distinguished:

- *global innovator*, with high outflow of resources to the parent company and low inflow of resources to the affiliate;
- *integrated player*, with a high outflow and high inflow;
- *implementer*, with low outflow and high inflow;
- *local innovator*, with low outflow and low inflow.

As the resource flows between the affiliate and the parent company increase, the resource dependence and hence the need for control will also increase. The resource dependence of the parent company on its affiliates is greatest for global innovators and integrated players.

Three other factors constrain the exercise of control of the parent company over the affiliate. The first is the method of affiliate establishment, with affiliates established as greenfield operations being seen to have a greater degree of similarity in their HRM patterns than those that were acquired or established as shared partnerships. The second and third constitute the cultural and legal distances of the affiliate from the parent company. The authors propose that the greater the cultural distance between the host country of the affiliate and the home country of the MNC, the less similarity between the parent and affiliate's HRM system. Likewise the greater the legal distance between the host country of the affiliate and the home country of the MNC, the lower the degree of similarity between the parent and affiliate's HRM systems. Once again, it is acknowledged that such relationships evolve over time.

The final part of the model, focusing on *employee group's criticality*, again adopts the resource dependence perspective, and argues that the HRM system will be different depending on the nature of the employee groups within the affiliates. It is proposed that the highest degree of similarity between a parent company's HRM system and an affiliate's HRM system will be in relation to the groups of employees who are most critical to the MNC's performance.

## Implications of the model

The authors see the following main implications from their model. First, it acknowledges the critical role that the HRM competence of the parent firm plays in the transfer of HRM policies to affiliates and how this can contribute to competitive advantage. Second, it recognises the pivotal role of top management in SIHRM. The authors see a key research area in an analysis of the factors that influence top management's ability to perceive an MNC's HRM competence and those factors that lead management to decide whether the firm's HRM competence is context specific (that is, cannot be transferred) or context generalisable and hence, transferable. Third, there is a need to reconsider the assumption that the critical groups of employees at affiliate level are either expatriates or white-collar workers. On a more general level, Taylor *et al.* argue that further research is needed into the determinants of the context generalisability of a resource and the ways in which managers can judge whether a particular resource is useful beyond the context in which it was created. However, the authors dismiss country

669

of origin as a determinant without saying why, and omit to state what is actually transferred in strategic international HRM.

While these frameworks and models are ways forward in helping us towards an understanding of the complexities of IHRM, there is also a need for research on operational issues.

## Issues in international HRM

As we have already noted, an increasingly important concern in the IHRM literature is how it is operationalised. Much of this research has centred on which aspects of HRM are exportable from the parent country and which are not exportable, a question tentatively explored in examining the host country influence on IHRM, and examined more fully in the work of Rosenzweig and Nohria.

### Rosenzweig and Nohria and the influence of local isomorphism

Rosenzweig and Nohria (1994) explore a key concern in IHRM – the tension between the pressures for internal consistency and local isomorphism (the influence of local culture, institutions and working practices on MNCs' HRM policies). From a research base of 249 US affiliates of foreign-based MNCs they argue that, of all organisational functions, HRM tends to most closely adhere to local practices as they are often mandated by local regulation and shaped by strong local conventions. Within HRM, they see the order in which six key practices will most closely resemble local practices as:

- time off;
- benefits;
- gender composition;
- training;
- executive bonus;
- participation.

This order is predicated on the assumption that HRM practices for which there are well-defined local norms and which affect the rank and file of the affiliate organisation are likely to conform most to practices of local competitors.

Three other factors are identified as being important in determining the extent of internal consistency or local isomorphism. The first is the degree to which an affiliate is *embedded* in the local environment. This refers to its method of founding and its age, as well as its size, its dependence on local inputs, and the degree of influence exerted on it from local institutions. The second is the strength of the flow of resources, such as capital, information and people, between the parent and the affiliate. The third relates to characteristics of the parent, such as the culture of the home country, with a high degree of distance between cultures being predicted to lead to more internal consistency (that is, an ethnocentric approach). Two final characteristics relate to the parent organisation's orientation to control and the nature of the industry, with greater local isomorphism in a multi-domestic industry as opposed to a global industry (Porter, 1986; Prahalad and Doz, 1987).

Other areas of international HRM are related to issues concerning the management and motivation of host country staff by expatriate managers, and issues of compensation and staff promotion. For example, a performance-related pay scheme that works in the USA (a highly individualistic culture) may well prove disastrous in Indonesia (a highly collectivist culture). Thus the way in which HRM policies are transferred and translated into subsidiary host country contexts can prove crucial to their success.

Training and development has been emphasised by many writers as an important aspect in the implementation of HRM strategy and as helping to create an 'organisational glue' in terms of binding subsidiary units into the aims, objectives and values of the company as a whole. Training is not only essential in imparting technical know-how, it is also crucial in enabling employees to imbibe the organisational culture as well as providing forums for the imparting and exchange of information. Some writers conceptualise forms of an international learning organisation or a knowledge-based organisation (Kamoche, 1997; Bonache and Fernández, 1999) in which the creation of a learning climate for the sharing and transfer of knowledge is crucial in the international context. This is a move away from the goal-measuring orientations that have become popular in recent years under the guise of performance management, but which have encountered considerable problems in the domestic context let alone within the complexities of the international context.

In addition HRM impacts more widely on the international organisation than the individually prescribed subjects of recruitment, selection, training and development, management development, reward, outplacement, employee involvement might suggest. As we have seen in other chapters in this book HRM is also concerned with organisational change and the implementation of new work practices that have important strategic implications. The work of Broad (1994), Tayeb (1998), Muller (1998), Martin and Beaumont (1998, 1999) and others has illustrated how difficult this process can be. Their work also reveals how simplistic, and even primitive, the models and frameworks that have emerged so far are as a tool in aiding analysis of the transference of HRM from one national context to another.

## CONCLUSION

The forces of globalisation have clearly created convergences of more flexibilised systems of work and employment, although these will be operationalised in differing ways in different institutional and cultural settings. Research and theory building still have some way to go, but developments of the global economy in the 1990s saw much more attention from researchers to the importance of international and comparative HRM as part of the equation that gives companies and economies their competitive edge.

Limited space forbids an in-depth examination of individual aspects of HRM such as recruitment, selection, reward, training and development, employee involvement and industrial relations. For more detailed aspects of international and comparative HRM the following chapters will be of value:

- human resource planning: developments in the UK and Europe: Chapter 4;
- multi-skilling and European developments: Chapter 5;
- international perspectives on recruitment and selection: Chapter 6;
- vocational education and training in the leading industrial nations: Chapter 8;
- international management development: Chapter 9;
- variable pay – results from across nations and international remuneration policies – remuneration and reward: Chapter 12;
- international aspects of employee involvement: Chapter 13;
- HRM and Europe: Chapter 16;
- HRM and the Asia Pacific Rim: Chapter 17.

671

# SUMMARY

- This chapter examined the increasing importance of human resource management in an ever-changing competitive international environment and the growth of multinational corporations. The distinctions between comparative HRM and international HRM were examined: this saw international HRM located in multinational organisations, and comparative HRM being concerned with the comparison of HRM systems within the context of countries and regions.

- Various major theories relating to comparative HRM were explained: convergence theory, which poses the view that technological developments create homogeneous global work practices; Marxist theory, with its class-based view of the processes of work in capitalist organisations; cultural theory, which emphasises the differences in work practices influenced by cultural values; and the view of how work practices in different national settings are influenced by institutional aspects such as legal and political structures, which are in turn affected by social factors. An attempt was made to synthesise these convergent and divergent approaches to comparative HRM.

- Comparative HRM models by Poole, Brewster and Larsen, and Sparrow and Hiltrop were outlined and critiqued. A review of the quantitative survey conducted under the banner of the Price Waterhouse Cranfield Project revealed the similarity of a number of trends across Europe, such as moves towards atypical working, decentralisation and devolvement of HRM practices, particularly to line managers, increases in direct communication channels to the workforce, the decline in influence of trade unions, and the increasing decentralisation of pay bargaining. The survey researchers warn, however, that practices still vary widely and are still heavily influenced by national employee relations laws and practices. The Towers Perrin survey analysed by Sparrow *et al.* concluded that there was a convergence in the use of HRM for competitive advantage.

- Problems of international research were outlined that often hinge on differing practices in collecting data and varying interpretations based on cultural and linguistic influences.

- Within the international HRM part of the chapter the effects of globalisation on MNCs were examined, as were the effects of country of origin and host country on HRM strategy and policy formulation. Perlmutter's typology of headquarters–subsidiary orientations was also outlined, with comment on its shortcomings. Adler and Ghadar's phases of internationalisation were explained in the context of HRM. The use of a variety of mechanisms to control subsidiaries within MNCs was then discussed.

- Expatriation issues such as assignment failure were also examined, and suggestions made as to how organisations could make provisions to prevent this happening.

- Two international HRM models were explored in detail: Schuler *et al*'.s integrative framework of SIHRM, and Taylor *et al.*'s integrative model of SIHRM. Each was critiqued from both theoretical and practical positions.

- The last section dealt briefly with the difficulties of the practical applications of IHRM policy. Rosenzweig and Nohria's local isomorphism model was taken as a starting point in considering which HRM practices were exportable and which were not.

- Given the relative infancy of IHRM the chapter indicates the need for more research and theorising if our knowledge of this increasingly important subject is to be extended.

672

## QUESTIONS

1  In what ways does international HRM differ from HRM?

2  What problems are expatriate managers liable to find in a foreign assignment, and how could these problems be prevented in future?

3  Is there increasing convergence in human resource management practices worldwide?

4  How much do parent company culture and strategy influence the practice of HRM in overseas subsidiaries?

5  What control mechanisms can MNCs use to ensure that their aims and objectives are being fulfilled across the organisation?

6  Of the models of international HRM examined in this chapter which seem the most feasible as a guide to the formulation and implementation of IHRM?

## EXERCISES

1  A British expatriate manager undertakes an assignment at a UK-owned subsidiary in Malaysia. Given the following Hofstede cultural indices, with what problems is he likely to be confronted and why? In the light of this information what management approaches would you advise him to adopt in the subsidiary?

|  | UK | Malaysia | Difference |
|---|---|---|---|
| Power distance | 35 | 104 | 69 |
| Uncertainty avoidance | 35 | 36 | 1 |
| Individualism | 89 | 26 | 63 |
| Masculinity | 66 | 50 | 16 |

2  Devise a training and development programme for expatriate managers and their families for pre-departure, overseas assignment experience and re-entry. How could the experience of expatriate managers be utilised by the company for future training and development?

673

**The Management of Human Resources**
**637**

## CASE STUDY

### Pharmco International

Hugo Bradshaw is a senior executive of Pharmco International, a large multinational pharmaceutical company. He has just returned from a fact-finding tour of its operations in the Asia Pacific Rim (Hong Kong, Taiwan, Japan and Malaysia). He presents his report to the board, and it makes sobering reading. Sales are down in some areas and not progressing in others. Hugo believes that the company is not using its local personnel effectively.

The products have proved to be of a high standard but have failed to penetrate the market deeply. Hugo believes there is too much control from HQ and not enough initiative allowed to the local workforce.

The Head of HRM, Carol Johnson, has proposed areas that would help the company to fulfil its new strategy: a new HRM strategy including recruitment initiatives, training and development, reward, management development policies and team building and communicational and networking structures.

---

How would you suggest Carol Johnson implements these policies? Could you make any other suggestions that might help Pharmco International to create an effective HRM strategy to help solve their problems?

## REFERENCES AND FURTHER READING

Those texts marked with an asterisk are particularly recommended for further reading.

*Adler, N. (1997) *International Dimensions of Organizational Behavior* 3rd edn. Cincinnati, Ohio: South Western College Publishing.

Adler, N. J. and Ghadar, F. (1989) 'International business research for the twenty first century: Canada's new research agenda', in Rugman, A. (ed.) *Research in Global Stratgic Management: A Canadian Perspective*, Vol. 1. Greenwich, Conn.: JAI Press.

Adler, N.J. and Ghadar, F. (1990) 'Strategic human resource management: a global perspective', in Pieper, R. (ed.) *Human Resource Management: An International Comparison*. Berlin: De Gruyter, pp. 235–260.

Adler, N. and Izraeli, D. (1994) *Competitive Frontiers: Women Managers in a Global Economy*. Cambridge, Mass.: Blackwell.

Altman, Y. (1992) 'Towards a cultural typology of European work values and work organisation', *Innovation in Social Science Research*, Vol. 5, No. 1. pp. 35–44.

Baglioni, G. and Crouch, C. (1990) *European Industrial Relations*. London: Sage.

Bamber, G. and Lansbury, R. (eds) (1987) *International and Comparative Industrial Relations: A Study of Developed Markets*. Sydney: Allen & Unwin.

Bamber, G. and Lansbury, R. (eds) (1998) *International and Comparative Industrial Relations: A Study of Industrialised Market Economies*. London: Sage.

Bartlett, C. (1986) 'Building and managing the transnational: the organisational challenge', in M. Porter (ed.) *Competition in Global Industries*. Boston Mass.: Harvard Business School Press, pp. 367–404.

Bartlett, C. and Ghoshal, S. (1989) *Managing Across Borders: The Transnational Solution*. London, Hutchinson.

Bean, R. (1985) *Comparative Industrial Relations*. London: Croom Helm (reprinted by Routledge, 1994).

Beer, M., Spector, B., Lawrence, P.R., Quinn Mills, D. and Walton, R.E. (1984) *Managing Human Assets*. New York: Free Press.

Black J.S. and Gregersen, H. (1991) 'When Yankee goes home: factors related to expatriate and spouse repatriation adjustment', *Journal of International Business Studies*, Vol. 22, No. 4, pp. 671–694.

Black, J.S. and Stephens, G. (1989) 'The influence of the spouse on American expatriate adjustment and intent to stay in Pacific rim overseas assignments', *Journal of Management*, Vol. 15, No. 4, pp. 529–544.

Blyton, P. and Turnbull, P. (1996) 'Confusing convergence: industrial relations in the European airline industry – a comment on Warhurst', *European Journal of Industrial Relations*, Vol. 2, No. 1, pp. 7–20.

Bonache, J. and Fernández, Z. (1999) 'Strategic staffing in multinational companies: a resource based approach', in Harris, H. and Brewster, C. (eds) *International HRM: Contemporary Issues in Europe*. London: Routledge, pp. 163–182.

Boxall, P. (1995) 'Building the theory of comparative HRM', *Human Resource Management Journal*, Vol. 5, No. 5, pp. 5–17.

Braverman, H. (1974) *Labour and Monopoly Capitalism*. New York: Monthly Review Press.

Brewster, C. (1991) *The Management of Expatriates*. London: Kogan Page.

Brewster, C. (1993) 'Developing a European model of human resource management', *International Journal of Human Resource Management*, Vol. 4, No. 4, pp. 765–784.

Brewster, C. (1994) 'European HRM: reflection of, or challenge to, the American concept?', in Kirkbride, P. (ed) *Human Resource Management in Europe: Perspectives for the 1990s*. London: Routledge, pp. 56–92.

Brewster, C. (1995) 'Towards a "European" model of human resource management', *Journal of International Business Studies*, 1st quarter, pp. 1–21.

674

Brewster, C. and Bournois, F. (1991) 'Human resource management: a European perspective', *Personnel Review*, Vol. 20, No. 6, pp. 4–13.

Brewster, C. and Hegewisch, A. (eds) (1994) *Policy and Practice in European Human Resource Management: The Price Waterhouse Cranfield Survey*. London: Routledge.

Brewster, C. and Larsen, H. (1992) 'Human resource management in Europe: evidence from ten countries', *International Journal of Human Resource Management*, Vol. 3, No. 3, pp. 409–434.

Brewster, C. and Scullion, H. (1997) 'A review and agenda for expatriate HRM', *Human Resource Management Journal*, Vol. 7, No. 3, pp. 32–41.

Brewster, C. and Tyson, S. (eds) (1991) *International Comparisons in Human Resource Management*. London: Pitman.

Brewster, C., Hegewisch, A. and Lockhart, T. (1991) 'Researching human resource management: methodology of the Price Waterhouse Cranfield Project on European trends', *Personnel Review*, Vol. 20, No. 6. pp. 36–40.

Brewster, C., Lundmark, A. and Holden, L. (1993) *A Different Tack: An Analysis of British and Swedish Management Styles*. Lund: Studentlitteratur.

Briscoe, D. (1995) *International Human Resource Management*. Englewood Cliffs, NJ: Prentice Hall.

Broad, G. (1994) 'The managerial limits to Japanization: a manufacturing case study', *Human Resource Management Journal*, Vol. 4, No. 3, pp. 39–51.

Celestino, M. (1999) 'Graduate education programs with international vision: how graduate business schools are transcending borders', *World Trade*, Vol. 12, No. 7, pp. 86–92.

Child, J. (1981) 'Culture, contingency and capitalism in the cross-national study of organizations', in Staw, B. and Cummings, L. (eds) *Research in Organizational Behaviour*. Vol. 3, London: JAI Press.

Child, J. and Tayeb, M. (1983) 'Theoretical perspectives in cross-national organizational research', *International Studies of Management and Organization*, Vol. 7, Nos. 3–4, pp. 23–70.

Clark, T. and Mallory, G. (1996) 'The cultural relativity of human resource management: is there a universal model?', in Clark, T. (ed.) *European Human Resource Management*. Oxford: Blackwell, pp. 1–33.

Clark, T., Gospel, H. and Montgomery, J. (1999) 'Running on the spot? A review of twenty years of research on the management of human resources in comparative and international perspective', *International Journal of Human Resource Management*, Vol. 10, No. 3, pp. 520–544.

Cook, W. and Noble, D. (1998) 'Industrial relations systems and US foreign direct investment abroad', *British Journal of Industrial Relations*, Vol. 36, No. 4, pp. 581–610.

Crouch, C. (1993) *Industrial Relations and European State Traditions*. Oxford: Clarendon Press.

Dore, R. (1973) *British Factory–Japanese Factory: The Origins of National Diversity in Industrial Relations*. London: Allen & Unwin (quoted in Lane, 1989: 32).

Dowling, P., Schuler, R. and Welch, D. (1994) *International Dimensions of Human Resource Management*. Belmont: Wadsworth.

*Dowling, P., Welch, D. and Schuler, R. (1999) *International Human Resource Management: Managing People in a Multinational Context*. Cincinnati, Oh.: South Western College Publishing.

Doz, Y. and Prahalad, C. (1991) 'Managing DMNCs: a search for a new paradigm', *Strategic Management Journal*, No. 12, pp. 145–164.

Easterby-Smith, M., Malina, D. and Yuan, L. (1995) 'How culture sensitive is HRM? A comparative analysis of practice in Chinese and UK companies', *International Journal of Human Resource Management*, Vol. 6, No. 1, pp. 31–59.

Edström, A. and Galbraith, J.R. (1977) 'Transfer of managers as a coordination and control strategy in multinational organisations', *Administrative Science Quarterly*, Vol. 22, June, pp. 248–263.

Estevill, J. and de la Hoz, J. (1990) 'Transition and crisis: the complexity of Spanish industrial relations', in Baglioni, G. and Crouch, C. (eds) *European Industrial Relations*. London: Sage, pp. 265–299.

Ferner, A. (1994) 'Multinational companies and human resource management: an overview of research issues', *Human Resource Management Journal*, Vol. 4, No. 2, pp. 79–102.

Ferner, A. (1997) 'Country of origin effects and HRM in multinational companies', *Human Resource Management Journal*, Vol. 7, No. 1, pp. 19–37.

Ferner, A. and Hyman, R. (eds) (1992) *Industrial Relations in the New Europe*. Oxford: Blackwell.

*Ferner, A. and Hyman, R. (eds) (1998) *Changing Industrial Relations in Europe*. Oxford: Blackwell.

Forsgren, M. (1990) 'Managing the international multi-centred firm', *European Management Journal*, No. 8, pp. 261–267.

Forster, N. (1994) 'The forgotton employees? The experience of expatriate staff returning to the UK', *International Journal of Human Resource Management*, Vol. 5, No. 2, pp. 405–426.

Forster, N. (1997) 'The persistent myth of high expatriate failure rates: a re-appraisal', *International Journal of Human Resource Management*, Vol. 8, No. 4, pp. 414–433.

Fulcher, J. (1991) *Labour Movements Employers and the State: Conflict and Cooperation in Britain and Sweden*. Oxford: Clarendon.

Ghoshal, S. and Nohria, N. (1989) 'Internal differentiation within multinational corporations', *Strategic Management Journal*, No. 10, pp. 323–337.

Gill, C. (1993) 'Technological change and participation in work organization: recent results from a European Community survey', *International Journal of Human Resource Management*, Vol. 4, No. 2, pp. 325–348.

Gospel, H. (1992) *Markets, Firms and the Management of Labour in Modern Britain*. Cambridge: Cambridge University Press.

Guest, D. (1990) 'Human resource management and the American dream', *Journal of Management Studies*, Vol. 27, No. 4, pp. 377–397.

Hadenius, S. (1988) *Swedish Politics During the 20th Century*. Stockholm: The Swedish Institute.

Hall, E. (1976) *Beyond Culture*. New York: Anchor Press Doubleday.

675

**The Management of Human Resources**

Hall, E. and Hall, M. (1990) *Understanding Cultural Differences*. Yarmouth: Intercultural Press.

Hampden-Turner, C. and Trompenaars, F. (1994) *The Seven Cultures of Capitalism*. London: Piatkus.

Handy, C., Gordon, C., Gow, I. and Randlesome, C. (1988) *Making Managers*. London: Pitman.

Harvey, D. (1989) *The Condition of Postmodernity*. Oxford: Blackwell.

Harzing, A.-W. K. (1995) 'The persistent myth of high expatriate failure rates, *International Journal of Human Resource Management*, Vol. 6, No. 2, pp. 457–474.

*Harzing, A.W. and Van Ruysseveldt, J. (eds) (1995) *International Human Resource Management*. London: Sage.

Hedlund, G. (1980) 'The role of foreign subsidiaries in strategic decision making in Swedish multinational corporations', *Strategic Management Journal*, No. 1, pp. 23–36.

Hedlund, G. (1986) 'The hypermodern MNC: a heterarchy, *Human Resource Management*, pp. 9–35.

Hirst, P. and Thompson, G. (1996) *Globalisation in Question*. Cambridge: Polity Press.

Hofstede, G. (1980) *Culture's Consequences: International Differences in Work Related Values*. Beverly Hills, Calif.: Sage.

Hofstede, G. (1991) *Cultures and Organisations: Software of the Mind*. London, McGraw-Hill.

Holden, L. (1996) 'HRM and employee involvement in Britain and Sweden: a comparative study', *International Journal of Human Resource Management*. Vol. 7, No. 1, pp. 59–81.

*Hollinshead, G. and Leat, M. (1995) *Human Resource Management: An International and Comparative Perspective*. London: Pitman.

Hyman, R. and Ferner, A. (eds) (1994) *New Frontiers in European Industrial Relations*. Oxford: Blackwell.

IDE (1993) *Industrial Democracy in Europe Revisited*. Oxford: Oxford University Press.

Kakabadse, A. (1991) *The Wealth Creators*. London: Kogan Page.

Kamoche, K. (1997) 'Knowledge creation and learning in international HRM', *International Journal of Human Resource Management*, Vol. 8, No. 3, pp. 213–225.

Kerr, C., Dunlop, J.T., Harbison, F. and Myers, C.A. (1960) *Industrialism and Industrial Man*. Cambridge, Mass.: Harvard University Press.

Kerr, C., Dunlop, J.T., Harbison, F. and Myers, C.A. (1971) 'Postscript to industrialism and industrial man', *International Labour Review*, 103.

Kidger, P. (1991) 'The emergence of international human resource management', *International Journal of Human Resource Management*, Vol. 2, No. 2, pp. 149–164.

Kluckhohn, C. (1951) 'The study of culture' in Lernex, D. and Lasswell, H. (eds) *The Policy Sciences*. Stanford, CA: Stanford University Press, pp. 61–90.

Kobrin, S.J. (1994) 'Is there a relationship between a geocentric mind-set and multinational strategy?', *Journal of International Business Studies*, 3rd quarter, pp. 493–511.

Lado, A. and Wilson, M. (1994) 'Human resource systems and sustained competitive advantage: a competency-based perspective', *Academy of Management Review*, Vol. 19, pp. 699–727.

Lane, C. (1989) *Management and Labour in Europe*. Aldershot: Edward Elgar.

Lane, C. (1992) 'European business systems: Britain and Germany compared', in Whitley, R. (ed.) *European Business Systems: Firms and Markets in their National Context*. London: Sage, pp. 64-97.

Lane, C. (1994) 'Industrial order and the transformation of industrial relations: Britain, Germany and France compared', in Hyman, R. and Ferner, A. (eds) *New Frontiers in European Industrial Relations*. Oxford: Blackwell, pp. 167–195.

Lane, C (1995) *Industry and Society in Europe: Stability and Change in Britain, Germany and France*. Aldershot: Edward Elgar.

Laurent, A. (1983) 'The cultural diversity of Western conceptions of management', *International Studies of Management and Organisation*, Vol. 13, Nos. 1–2, pp. 75–96.

Lawrence, P. (1992) 'Management development in Europe: a study in cultural contrast', *Human Resource Management Journal*, Vol. 3, No. 1, pp. 12–24.

Leeds, C., Kirkbride, P. and Durcan, J. (1994) 'The cultural context of Europe: a tentative mapping,' in Kirkbride, P. (ed.) *Human Resource Management in Europe: Perspectives for the 1990s*. London: Routledge, pp. 11–27.

Lincoln, J. and Kalleberg, A. (1990) *Culture, Control and Commitment: A Study of Work Organization and Attitudes in the United States and Japan*. Cambridge: Cambridge University Press.

Martin, A. (1984) 'Trade unions in Sweden: strategic responses to change and crisis', in Gourevitch, P., Martin, A., Ross, G., Bornstein, S., Markovits, A. and Allen, C. (eds) *Unions and Economic Crisis: Britain, West Germany and Sweden*. London: George Allen & Unwin, pp. 190–342.

Martin, G. and Beamont, P. (1998) 'Diffusing "best practice" in multinational firms: prospects, practice and contestation', *International Journal of Human Resource Management*, Vol. 9, No. 4, pp. 671–695.

Martin, G. and Beamont, P. (1999) 'Co-ordination and control of human resource management in multinational firms: the case of CASHCO', *International Journal of Human Resource Management*, Vol. 10, No. 1, pp. 21–42.

McGaughey, S. and De Cieri, H. (1999) 'Reassessment of convergence and divergence dynamics: implications for international HRM', *International Journal of Human Resource Management*, Vol. 10, No. 2, pp. 235–250.

Mead, R. (1994) *International Management: Cross Cultural Dimensions*. Oxford: Blackwell.

Meegan, R. (1988) 'A crisis of mass production', in Allen, J. and Massey, D. (eds.) *The Economy in Question*. London: Sage.

Mueller, F. and Purcell, J. (1992) 'The Europeanisation of manufacturing and the decentralisation of bargaining: multinational management strategies in the European automobile industry', *International Journal of Human Resource Management*, Vol. 3, No. 1.,

Muller, M. (1998) Human resource and industrial relations practices of UK and US multinationals in Germany', *International Journal of Human Resource Management*, Vol. 9, No. 4, pp. 732–749.

676

Nohria, N. and Ghoshal, S. (1997) *The Differentiated Network: Organizing Multinational Corporations for Value Creation.* San Francisco, Calif.: Jossey-Bass.

Perlmutter, H.V. (1969) 'The tortuous evolution of the multinational corporation', *Columbia Journal of World Business*, Vol. 4, pp. 9–18.

Pieper, R. (ed.) (1990) *Human Resource Management: An International Comparison.* New York: Walter de Gruyter.

Poole, M. (1986) *Industrial Relations: Origins and Patterns of National Diversity.* London: Routledge & Kegan Paul.

Poole, M. (1990) 'Editorial: Human resource management in an international perspective', *International Journal of Human Resource Management*, Vol. 1, No. 1, pp. 1–16.

Porter, M. (1990) *The Competitive Advantage of Nations.* London: Macmillan.

Porter, M. (ed.) (1986) *Competition in Global Industries.* Boston, Mass.: Harvard Business School Press.

Prahalad, C.K. and Doz, Y.L. (1987) *The Multinational Mission: Balancing Local Demands and Global Vision.* New York: The Free Press.

Prentice, G. (1990) 'Adapting management style for the organisation of the future', *Personnel Management*, Vol. 22, No. 6, pp. 58–62.

Price Waterhouse Cranfield Project (1991) *Report on International Strategic Human Resource Management.* Cranfield: Cranfield School of Management.

Pucik, V. (1984) 'The international management of human resources', in Fombrun, C.J., Tichy, N.M. and Devanna, M.A. (eds) *Strategic Human Resource Management.* New York: John Wiley, pp, 403–419.

Pucik, V. (1992) 'Globalisation and human resource management', in Pucik, V., Tichy, N. and Barnett, C. (eds) *Globalising Management: Creating and Leading the Competitive Organisation.* New York: John Wiley, pp. 61–84.

Purcell, J. (1993) 'Developing research in comparative human resource management', *International Journal of Human Resource Management*, Vol. 4, No. 3, pp. 507–510.

Quintanilla, J. (1998) 'The configuration of human resource management policies and practices in multinational subsidiaries: the case of European retail banks in Spain', Unpublished PhD Thesis, University of Warwick.

Randlesome, C. (ed.) (1990) *Business Cultures in Europe.* London: Heinemann.

Ritzer, G. (1998) *The McDonaldization Thesis.* London: Sage.

Rosenzweig, P. and Nohria, N. (1994) 'Influences on human resource management practices in multinational corporations', *Journal of International Business Studies*, No. 25, pp. 229–251.

Ruigrok, W. and Van Tulder, R. (1995) *The Logic of International Restructuring.* London: Routledge.

Ruysseveldt, J. and Visser, J. (eds) (1996) *Industrial Relations in Europe.* London: Sage.

Ruysseveldt, J., Huiskamp, R. and van Hoof, J. (eds) (1995) *Comparative Industrial and Employment Relations.* London: Sage.

Schuler, R., Dowling, P. and De Cieri, H. (1993) 'An integretive framework of strategic international human resource management', *International Journal of Human Resource Management*, Vol. 4, No. 4, pp. 717–764.

Scullion, H. (1992) 'Strategic recruitment and development of the "international manager": some European considerations,' *Human Resource Management Journal*, Vol. 3, No. 1, pp. 57–69.

Scullion, H. (1995) 'International human resource management', in Storey, J. (ed.) *Human Resource Management: A Critical Text.* London: Routledge, pp. 352–382.

*Scullion, H. and Holden, L. (2001) *International HRM: A Critical Perspective.* London: Macmillan.

Segrestin, D. (1990) 'Recent changes in France', in Baglioni, G. and Crouch, C. (eds) *European Industrial Relations.* London: Sage, pp. 97–126.

Sisson, K. (1987) *The Management of Collective Bargaining: An International Comparison.* Oxford: Blackwell.

Sparrow, P. (1995) 'Towards a dynamic and comparative model of European human resource management: an extended review', *International Journal of Human Resource Management*, Vol. 6, No. 4, pp. 935–953.

Sparrow, P. and Hiltrop, J.-M. (1994) *European Human Resource Management in Transition.* Hemel Hempstead, Prentice Hall.

Sparrow, P. and Hiltrop, J.-M. (1997) 'Redefining the field of European human resource management: a battle between national mindsets and forces of business transition?', *Human Resource Management*, Vol. 36, No. 2, pp. 201–219.

Sparrow, P. and Wu, P.-C. (1999) 'How much do national value orientations really matter? Predicting HRM preferences of Taiwanese employees', in Lähteenmäki, S., Holden, L. and Roberts, I. (eds) *HRM and the Learning Organisation.* Turku School of Economics and Business Administration Publication, Series A-2, pp. 239–284.

Sparrow, P., Schuler, R. and Jackson, S. (1994) 'Convergence or divergence: human resource practices and policies for competitive advantage worldwide', *International Journal of Human Resource Management*, Vol. 5, No. 2, pp. 267–299.

Storey, J. (1992) 'Making European managers: an overview', *Human Resource Management Journal*, Vol. 3, No. 1, pp. 1–11.

Storey, J., Okazaki-Ward, L., Gow, I., Edwards, P.K. and Sisson, K. (1991) 'Managerial careers and management development: a comparative analysis of Britain and Japan', *Human Resource Management Journal*, Vol. 1, No. 3, pp. 33–57.

*Tayeb, M. (1996) *The Management of a Multicultural Workforce.* Chichester: John Wiley.

Tayeb, M. (1998) Transfer of HRM practices across cultures: an American company in Scotland', *International Journal of Human Resource Management*, Vol. 9, No. 2, pp. 332–358.

Taylor, S., Beechler, S. and Napier, N. (1996) 'Toward an integrative model of strategic human resource management', *Academy of Management Review*, Vol. 21, No. 4, pp. 959–985.

Torbiörn, I. (1982) *Living Abroad: Personal Adjustment and Personal Policy in the Overseas Setting.* Chichester: John Wiley.

Torrington, D. (1994) *International Human Resource Management: Think Globally, Act Locally.* Hemel Hempstead: Prentice Hall.

Trompenaars, F. (1993) *Riding the Waves of Culture.* London: Nicholas Brealey.

677

**The Management of Human Resources**

641

Tyson, S., Lawrence, P., Poirson, P., Manzolini, L. and Soler, C. (1993) *Human Resource Management in Europe: Strategic Issues and Cases*. London: Kogan Page.

Warhurst, R. (1995) 'Converging on HRM? Change and continuity in airlines' industrial relations', *European Journal of*

*Industrial Relations*, Vol. 1, No. 2, pp. 259–274.

Whitley, R. (ed.) (1992) *European Business Systems: Firms and Markets in National Contexts*. London: Sage.

Wilczynski, J. (1983) *Comparative Industrial Relations*. London: Macmillan.

# Chapter 14

# Public sector employment

*Martin Upchurch*

## Learning objectives

By the end of this chapter, readers should be able to:

■ discuss the origins and current composition of public sector employment;

■ consider the special features of public sector employee relations and, in relation to this, discuss the concept of model employer;

■ examine recent developments and contemporary issues in public sector employee relations, in particular the attempted transition from an industrial relations to an HRM context.

## Introduction

Employee relations in the public sector have experienced a major transformation since the 1970s. The reasons for this change are located in a reversal of the state's approach to the public sector, in terms of both the scope and scale of its activity and the relationship it has with the public as a 'provider' of public services. Ideological commitment to market forces combined with a concentration on supply-side economic forces has meant that public spending is no longer been seen by governments as a panacea for economic ills during downward swings of the business cycle. The role of the public sector as a vehicle for boosting demand has been replaced by notions that 'excessive' public spending is harmful to the national economy. Indeed, the Conservative government in the 1980s and into the 1990s was not alone among advanced industrial countries in being openly distrustful of the public sector, and often sought to 'scapegoat' public spending as the cause of economic demise (Ferner, 1994). The consequences for employee relations have been severe, involving restrictions on the growth of the wage bill, a cutback in levels of staffing in the drive for efficiency, and the introduction of new management initiatives designed to reflect financial accountability within a market environment. Two results of this 'wind of change' have been a thorough overhaul of much of the organisational culture and structure of the public services and an increase in industrial disputes, both in absolute terms and in relation to the traditionally more strike-prone private manufacturing sector. The return of Labour to government in 1997 made little difference to this approach, with inherited spending limits being adhered to in the first years of the government's first term. Policies to inject private finance into the public sector are now part of government objectives through various Private Finance Initiatives (PFIs)[1] and public private partnerships (PPPs).

While the size of the public sector as an employer has been reduced with privatisation and contracting out, it nevertheless still employs one-fifth of the UK workforce in total, and so an understanding of developments remains important in its own right. The total employed in public administration and defence, education, and health and social work totalled just under 6 million in 2001. Those directly employed by the state, as Crown civil servants, equalled some 501,000 in 2000. The NHS has more than 1 million employees and is the largest employer in Europe; local government is the largest sector with approximately 2.5 million employees, mainly concentrated in education, social services and the police and fire services. The remaining nationalised industries or public corporations such as the Post Office and Bank of England have less direct control from central government but nevertheless are subject to Parliamentary accountability and restrictions on trading. Total employment in this sector is just over half a million. Finally, 113,000 people work in over 1,000 public bodies or 'quangos' (quasi-autonomous government organisations) which carry out functions at an 'arm's length' to government, but which have some government financial support. Examples of these include the Arts Council and the Health and Safety Commission and Executive.

This chapter begins with an overview of the development of the public sector prior to the onset of change in the mid to late 1970s. The structure of employment within the sector is then described before analysing why change occurred in the 1980s and 1990s. New management initiatives are then outlined as well as the mechanisms for establishing the difficult question of public service pay. A profile of public sector trade unionism is then given together with some analysis of disputes and strikes. Finally, the chapter seeks to address the approach of the Labour government and the agendas for further change in this century.

## From 'model employer' to 'winter of discontent'

From the end of the First World War in 1918 through the development of the post-1945 welfare state, successive governments adopted a 'model employer' approach to the public service (Fredman and Morris, 1989). In practice this meant that the government, as employer, should set some example to the private sector in terms of fair treatment of employees and recognition of representation rights in collective bargaining. Fair treatment meant not only the benefits of pay and conditions but also high levels of job security, good (non-contributory and index-linked) pensions and generous sick pay schemes. 'Fair' pay was achieved by the establishment of an elaborate set of 'comparability' mechanisms that sought to assess the skills of public servants with the nearest equivalents in the private sector and to set the resultant pay level in the 'average-to-good' range of the private comparators.[2] The role of trade unions as bargaining partners was also thoroughly institutionalised by the establishment of pay review bodies[3] and councils such as the National Whitley Council for the civil service or the Burnham Committee for teachers, which allowed for formal consultation and negotiation on pay and conditions. Such a recognition of the role of trade unions came as a result of the perceived need to contain and control the growing trade union movement in the immediate aftermath of war. J.H. Whitley, deputy speaker of the House of Commons, had produced his committee report in March 1917, which recommended the establishment of joint councils between employers and employees 'to give opportunities for satisfying the growing demands made by trade unions for a share in industrial control' (quoted in Wigham, 1980). Most public sector unions were naturally quick to campaign for the introduction of the 'Whitley Councils' into the public service. Rules and procedures were also subject to joint consultation and implemented through code books, which allowed for national standards to be maintained (for example, the Pay and Conditions of Service code for the civil service included over 11,500 paragraphs of regulations, from major pay scales down to the comparative obscurity of 'daily pedal cycle allowances'). In cases of dispute, an elaborate procedure of appeals and arbitration was constructed that allowed full trade union representation and staged involvement during the appeal process.

Other reasons for the establishment of this model employer approach were as follows.

First, there was recognition in the inter-war period that a modern industrialised society was becoming more complex and complicated to administer and hence a professional civil and public service was needed as a result. To recruit and retain good staff it was therefore necessary to ensure that pay levels and other conditions of service were 'fair' and comparable with the private sector.

Secondly, the achievement of this comparability and the associated development of an effective internal labour market for professionals within the public service were in themselves difficult to accomplish. Sophisticated machinery (the pay review bodies) were therefore needed to overcome this problem.

Thirdly, it was important to 'legitimise' the process of the establishment of fairness and comparability by the involvement of trade unions within the institutional structures as representatives of staff. Thus, the formalised involvement of trade unions, including the positive official encouragement to all staff to join the appropriate and recognised union, helped the senior management of the public service in the task of maintaining a sense of fairness as well as easing the considerable administrative burden of assessing hundreds of separate pay scales over a huge range of crafts and occupations. To help ease the burden further, the process of comparability was best served by the establishment of strict incremental progress through the pay scales, which recognised seniority of service and could be applied easily if the employee moved jobs within the service or moved to another part of the country.

The concept and practice of model employer thus created a bureaucratic and centralised machinery in which employee relations were conducted, and which gave some concession and advantage to public sector unions and their members. The associated rules and regulations governing the employment relationship consolidated the growing hierarchical organisation structure of large ministries and government agencies bound by statute in their tasks and functions.

## ■ Keynesianism and the birth of the welfare state

The concept of the model employer continued through and after the Second World War. The public sector became more important in the atmosphere of post-war reconciliation and reconstruction for two reasons.

First, the fear of a return to the depression years of the 1920s and 1930s had created political space for the adoption of John Maynard Keynes's theories of demand management of the economy. In 1944, the government had published a White Paper arguing the necessity for policies likely to produce 'high and stable levels of employment' in the post-war period, and by the end of the war Keynesian economics had been accepted as orthodoxy by the Treasury. From the 1950s through to the mid-1970s, both Conservative and Labour governments then sought to maintain full employment by a variety of fiscal and monetary measures that ensured a major role for the public sector in boosting domestic demand to avoid recession.

Secondly, the value of public spending as a counter to recession was boosted by the perceived political need to both reconstruct British industry and society and head off social discontent with the creation of a post-war welfare state. The wartime coalition government had produced the Beveridge Plan in 1942, which emerged as a 'new declaration of human rights brought up to date for an industrial society and dealing in plain and vigorous language with some of the most controversial issues in British politics'. After this post-war 'political settlement' the 1945–50 Labour government proceeded to bring in the enabling legislation creating the pillars of the welfare state, together with legislation to nationalise certain industries in an effort to rationalise and modernise. The central aspects of legislation and their practical outcomes can be summarised as follows.

The National Insurance Act 1946 and the National Health Service Act 1946 laid down the principles of universality, which gave equal right of access to a developing range of social benefits and free medical treatment. Such 'rights' as sickness and unemployment benefit were made available to those who had paid their share of National Insurance contributions and were available for a limited period only. The NHS legislation would, of course, mean the building of new hospitals as well as the expansion of general practitioners' workload. The Housing Acts 1946 and 1949 released local authorities from the obligation that they should build accommodation only for the 'working class', but in reality allowed councils to raise money and begin a process of building housing for the masses, first as post-war prefabricated bungalows to house the homeless and later as mass council estates on compulsorily purchased land. The Education Act 1944 formed a fourth pillar of the welfare state and granted free secondary education for all up to the age of 15. The combined effect of the legislation was to massively boost the role and scope of the public sector within the economy, leading to the creation of hundreds of thousands of jobs which included, in particular, new and expanding opportunities for female employment in the so-called caring occupations, such as nursing and teaching. Another important consequence of this post-war expansion was the creation of large numbers of new jobs in lower-paid areas that serviced the public functions of the welfare state (cleaners, porters, junior clerks, etc.). An expanding economy meant that labour shortages were a problem, and so it was necessary to draw not only more women into employment, either as full- or part-time workers, but also, in the 1950s and 1960s, to recruit immigrant labour from the Caribbean and Indian sub-continent. Special recruitment drives took place in the West Indies, for example, to fill new and vacant posts in areas such as public transport and nursing. By 1980, 2.3 million people were employed by central government and just over 3 million by local authorities.

The profile of those employed within the public sector also changed dramatically as a result of the post-war programme of nationalisation. The first organisation to be nationalised was the Bank of England, on 1 March 1946, but this was followed by the nationalisation of civil aviation (1946), coal, cable and wireless (1947), transport and electricity (1948), gas (1949) and iron and steel (1951). By 1961 the nationalised industries and public corporations employed 2.2 million people, and throughout the next two decades, until the era of privatisation, the total employed stabilised around 2 million. All in all, by the end of the 1970s, almost 30 per cent of all employment in the UK was in the public sector.

## Employee relations during the period of model employer

Employees in the public sector, especially in the post-war period, enjoyed some distinctly superior terms and conditions compared with their private sector counterparts as a result of the model employer approach. First, their pay was generally set, under the terms of fair comparison, within the average-to-good range of those equivalent jobs in the private sector. While inflation was relatively low (as it was through the 1950s and 1960s), any period of 'catching up', in terms of waiting for the results of comparability exercises, was not an insurmountable problem. In addition to pay, most white-collar civil and public servants also enjoyed the benefits of a good non-contributory pension scheme (the contributions being offset against pay levels) and job security for the more senior grades in return for contractual obligation to accept transfer anywhere within the relevant branch of the public service (enhanced with generous relocation packages). Benefits for junior white-collar grades and industrial grades were less good. Pay was generally low but other conditions of service schemes (pensions, sick pay, etc.) were superior to those found in most of the private sector.

However, public sector employee relations in this period were not without their problems. One particular concern, the role and status of women in the public service, had dogged industrial relations since the 1920s over the two issues of equal pay and the 'marriage bar' (which denied employment to those, such as women teachers, who married). Campaigns were launched by the unions in favour of equal pay in the 1930s but were unsuccessful. Some of the public sector unions restored the campaign after the war but were not supported by the TUC until 1950. It was not until 1955 that the government agreed to gradually introduce equal pay into the public services in stages until full operation in 1961. This, of course, predates the Equal Pay Act 1970, for which women in the private sector had to wait before justice was done.

The campaign to end the marriage bar on married women's employment actually split the trade unions in the immediate post-war period. The Union of Post Office Workers, together with some of the senior grade civil service unions, wanted to keep the bar based on arguments that men were family breadwinners. Others, such as the Civil Service Clerical Association, wanted to abolish it. Similarly, in teaching, the National Association of Schoolmasters (NAS) was in favour of retention while the National Union of Teachers (NUT) and Union of Women Teachers (UWT) favoured abolition. However, the experience of women working in the war and their increased absorption into the labour force clearly made the bar anomalous, leading to eventual abolition by the government in phases during the lifetime of the 1945–50 Labour administration.

Public sector employees have also been restricted in some of the 'rights' to participate in political affairs such as standing for local councillor or parliamentary positions as members of a political party. The rules disallowing open political sympathy, or campaigning or standing in elections, have generally been applied to the more senior grades or those in 'politically sensitive' posts. Political vetting of candidates for some posts (with questions geared at political sympathy or parents' nationality) have also been designed to preserve the alleged neutrality of civil appointments in the public service. The trade unions were also affected by the provisions of the Trades Disputes Act 1927 which, in the aftermath of the defeated General Strike (1926), removed the 'right' of civil service and some other public sector unions to affiliate to either the TUC or the Labour Party. These particular restrictions were repealed after the war.

As the immediate post-war period receded, many of the unions became increasingly aggressive towards government restrictions on pay, particularly as it affected the public sector. Government incomes policy aimed at restricting wage increases was always enforced more rigorously in the public sector (with the government as employer) than it was in the private sector. This, combined with increasing fears of inflation, problems of low pay, and some dissatisfaction with the machinery of pay comparison and its ability to provide compensatory increases, led to the first pay strikes throughout the public sector in the 1970s. Local authority unions conducted their first coordinated national strike over pay in the autumn of 1970 and they were followed by the Union of Post Office Workers, which led its first national strike in 1971 (ending in defeat). In 1973, the civil service also experienced its first national pay strike. Meanwhile, in 1972 and again in 1974 the National Union of Miners went on all-out strike to re-establish their pay position in the 'earnings league' – a reference to their perceived worsening pay in comparison with other manual groups in the private sector. The miners were victorious in both their strikes and caused an election in 1974 after the Conservative prime minister, Edward Heath, threw down the election gauntlet in the aftermath of his attempt to control coal stocks by ordering a 'three-day working week' for all industrial and domestic coal consumers. The resultant victory for the Labour Party did not prevent public sector industrial strife. In 1977, firefighters in the Fire Brigades Union secured a new pay comparison formula after a short all-out strike. Finally, after two years of wage restraint in the public sector under the 1974–9 Labour government, the pay dam finally burst in the 1978/9 'winter of discontent' as NHS and local authority workers conducted a series of all-out and selective strikes designed to restore public sector pay levels to private sector equivalents. A new pay comparability body (the Clegg Commission) was created as part of the settlement of the strikes.

The arrival of militancy in the public sector in the 1970s was also accompanied by internal factional strife in some of the white-collar unions as left-wing 'opposition' groups began to challenge the trade union leaderships' more moderate influence. In unions such as the NUT, the Civil and Public Services Association (civil service clerks), and the local authority white-collar union NALGO, these groups were backed by organisations such as Militant and the Socialist Workers' Party. They were often separate from the more established Communist-Party-led 'broad lefts' within the unions and grew to have some influence as militancy increased generally in the 1970s (see Seifert, 1987; Kelly, 1988).

In summary, with the government as direct or indirect employer and the continuation of the model employer policy, many policy issues covering social affairs, such as equal pay, took place in the public sector in advance of the private sector. The experience of public sector employee relations in the 1970s and the increased tensions over pay meant that the period was very much a 'coming of age' of the unions and their relationship with the government after the more genteel approach of the 1950s and 1960s. It is now necessary to examine the 'wind of change' that swept through the public sector in the aftermath of Margaret Thatcher's Conservative Party election victory in 1979.

## Monetarism, Thatcherism and public spending cuts

The crisis of public sector funding can be traced to the onset of economic recession following the oil 'shock' of 1973/4 and the consequent hike in inflation. The new phenomenon of 'stagflation' – rising prices combined with rising unemployment – threw the Labour government (1974–9) into crisis and sounded the death knell of Keynesian economic management. Inflation in 1975 reached 24 per cent and, as the economy slowed and unemployment rose, public spending as a proportion of GDP soared to average 43.7 per cent in the period from 1974 to 1985 (compared to 37.7 per cent in 1970–3). Part of this increase was related to expanded social security payments to cover increased unemployment but part was also the result of the increased wage bill for public sector employees as comparability awards raced to keep up with inflation. In 1976, faced with a balance of payments crisis and increasing national debt, the Labour government was forced to seek a loan from the International Monetary Fund (IMF), which was granted on condition that the Chancellor (Denis Healey) introduced a monetarist economic programme aimed at capping public spending and reducing the public sector borrowing requirement (PSBR). The consequent programme of 'cash limits' for the public sector was designed to control public spending plans of individual departments and ushered in recruitment freezes and a variety of other cost-cutting measures throughout the sector.

### ■ The period of retrenchment: the 1980s and 1990s

While the 1974–9 Labour government had set in train the reversal of policy towards public sector spending, the incoming Thatcher administration stepped up the attack with extra ideological vigour. The new government's attitude to the public sector was one of hostility as a result not only of monetarist orthodoxy but also of a perceived need to liberate market forces in an effort to boost Britain's competitive position in the world economy. It was argued that the public sector was a burden to the economy in that it did not create wealth and it 'crowded out' investment opportunity that could otherwise be allocated to the profit-making private sector (Bacon and Eltis, 1978). In addition, the public sector unions, and their increasingly powerful influence and militancy, were seen as obstacles to the restructuring of the British state and the introduction of *laissez-faire* market forces. As a consequence, the Thatcher administration embarked on a programme of policy measures designed both to reduce the size of the public sector and to confront the public sector unions and the ever increasing wage bill. The various policy initiatives are listed below.

### Privatisation and contracting out

The privatisation programme was launched by the government in the 1980s in line with the 1979 Conservative manifesto commitment. This was to be achieved primarily with the public offer of shares and involved a total of 43 companies by the end of 1996. The share sales had the added advantage of raising revenue for the government and temporarily reducing public sector debt. In 1983–4, for example, over £1 billion was raised, and in 1984–5 over £2 billion. The peak years were 1988–9 (£7.1 billion: BP, gas and steel) and 1992–3 (£8.2 billion: BT and electricity). Programmes of the contracting-out of services to the private sector (involving a tendering process) were confined to a range of services in local authorities, the NHS and the civil service, such as cleaning, rubbish collection and catering. In terms of employee relations, most of the privatisations and contracting out were bitterly opposed by the unions concerned, involving one-day strikes by BT unions against job losses and fears of reduced services (such as the potential loss of rural telephone kiosks), and selective strikes against the loss of jobs and introduction of inferior conditions of service for those areas of work threatened by contracting out (Fairbrother 1996; Foster and Scott 1998). Both privatisation and contracting out also fragmented the collective bargaining framework and reduced the power and influence of public sector unions, particularly in local authorities where workers in key areas of 'industrial muscle', such as refuse collectors, now found themselves working (if they were taken on) in un-unionised and anti-union companies. In many respects this entailed a significant shift in employee relations whereby the pattern began to resemble that of the private sector (Carter and Fairbrother, 1999).

## Confrontations with the unions

The system of 'cash limits' on departmental spending engendered a series of confrontations with the unions forced to make a 'choice' between increased pay and job loss (given the restrictive limit on budgets). The increased tensions resulted in an upsurge of industrial disputes in the public sector throughout the 1980s including the civil service (1981 and 1987), hospital and railway workers (1982), social workers (1983), teachers (1985, 1986 and 1987), local authority white-collar staff (1989) and ambulance workers (1989). Apart from the two disputes in 1989, in every case the unions were defeated in their key objectives of either winning pay demands or opposing programmes of public spending cuts. Industrial action against specific programmes of spending cuts was particularly difficult to sustain. The NHS, for example, saw some flashpoints when staff occupied wards that were threatened with closure programmes (Seifert, 1992: chapter 7). The general pattern of defeats for the unions meant that a period of demoralisation set into the ranks of the public sector unions. The government offensive against the unions also included attacks on the 'fair comparison' principle of pay determination. In the civil service the pay comparability machinery for all but senior civil servants was withdrawn and teachers lost their rights to negotiate on pay. These defeats for the unions opened the door for a further erosion of relative pay and enabled the government to achieve more easily some of its objectives in cutting the public sector pay bill. The institutional status of trade unions was also downgraded by employer action to redefine facilities agreements in the civil service, and many local authorities reduced the 'time off' allocated to trade union local representatives to conduct their trade union business. The 'check-off' arrangement, whereby trade union subscriptions were deducted from wage packets automatically by employers, was also withdrawn in many areas of the public service. Finally, the provision that new staff were 'recommended' in the civil service to join the appropriate trade union was dropped by the new Conservative government.

In the nationalised industries, confrontation was just as sharp. British Steel management defeated the unions in an all-out national strike in 1980, and decentralised collective bargaining to business divisions and rationalised jobs throughout the industry in the process (see Blyton and Turnbull, 1998: chapter 7). Most important of all was the defeat of the year-long strike conducted by the National Union of Mineworkers in 1984–5 over the withdrawal of coal price subsidies and the introduction of a pit closure programme. The defeat of the miners, and the consequent authority it placed in the hands of the government, had clear ramifications for trade union 'solidarity' in Britain, and led to some soul searching within the trade union movement. One other point of interest concerning government attacks on the public sector trade unions was the banning in 1984 of trade union membership for 8,000 employees at the Government Central Headquarters (GCHQ) in Cheltenham. For 40 years previously, GCHQ collated signals intelligence worldwide. The ban was imposed by ministerial decree (i.e. without the necessity of a parliamentary vote) by the Foreign Secretary, Sir Geoffrey Howe, on the presumption that intelligence-gathering and trade union membership were incompatible. The banning followed the case of 'spying' for the Soviet Union by an employee at Cheltenham. Civil service unions opposed the ban and alleged that it was instigated by President Reagan in the US as a condition for continuing US financial support for the centre (the US government also proposed the introduction of the polygraph – lie detector – as a test for all new recruits). Fears that the ban might spread to other civil servants in politically sensitive areas were allayed after the general secretary of the TUC, Len Murray, went on television to call a one-day general strike in protest at the ban. With only a few days' notice, more than 1 million people went on strike in response to the TUC's call. One of the first tasks of the incoming Labour government in May 1997 was to reinstate trade union recognition at GCHQ.

It can be seen from the above that the concept of model employer no longer applied under the Conservative governments in the 1980s. The attacks on trade union power and influence, combined with their 'deinstitutionalisation' and redefining of the value of pay comparison, changed the framework of public sector industrial relations. Spending cuts, privatisation and contracting out also reduced the size of the public sector. The net effect of the cuts in the size of the sector are apparent in the fall in the number of those employed. More than 1.9 million jobs were cut between 1981 and 1994 as a result of either privatisation and contracting out (a transfer to the private sector) or spending cuts in remaining public services. Totals employed in the civil service, for example, fell by 20 per cent between 1981 and 1994. The public sector share of employment in the economy has fallen from a high of 30 per cent to just over 20 per cent as a result.

While the institutional role of trade unions had changed and cuts in spending had taken place, the government and public sector employers also attempted to alter management style and techniques. It is to this issue that we now turn (see Exhibit 14.1).

## 'Marketisation' and new public management

The Conservative government was also concerned to introduce the ethos of 'marketisation' into the public sector as a way of injecting some 'discipline' into decision-making and offering market choice to potential consumers of services. This process of marketisation, typified by the breakdown of units and divisions into cost and/or budget centres, has been accompanied by new levels of financial and administrative accountability for managers and new forms of management practice designed to motivate the workforce in the absence of profit-related market discipline.

Local managers, whether heads of schools, chief nursing officers, governors of penal establishments or commanders of units within the armed forces, are now responsible for offsetting pay increases against productivity and efficiency savings. Headteachers, for example, can now choose between separate items of budget expenditure, such as

Exhibit 14.1

# UK public sector strikes and the search for private finance

For those of a nervous disposition, last week's strikes by the UK Post Office and the London Underground might suggest a return to the bad days of the late 1970s. Taken with the likely return of a Labour government, the spectre is all too familiar: chaos in the capital, unburied corpses and rubbish in the streets. Calmer reflection suggests nothing of the kind. Transport and postal strikes catch the nation's attention, but across the economy as a whole, the reality is that strike figures are still the lowest on record. Critics might pose a different question. Recent strike threats in the private sector, such as that by British Airways pilots, have been quietly averted. Why do public sector managers seem so much less adroit in handling disputes?

The answer comes in two parts. First, today's public sector managers often come from the private sector. The Post Office chairman is an ex-director of personnel at Unilever. The head of London Underground was formerly with British Airways. His boss, the chairman of London Transport, comes from Harvard Business School, McKinsey and P&O. The second part of the answer goes to the heart of what the two disputes are about. In both cases, management is trying to change the organisation's culture: to make it less rigid and more capable of change. The ultimate goal, in both cases, is to make the workers think and act more like their private sector counterparts.

Thus, the Post Office is trying to move away from its old hierarchical culture towards a system of teamwork. London Underground is trying to reform structure in which, for instance, holiday rotas are still organised by the workforce rather than the management.

The ultimate driving force in both cases is the same: the need to attract private sector finance. At the extreme, this means privatisation: explicitly advocated by Post Office management and unlikely to be opposed by London Transport. It might seem an odd time for managers to be thinking in those terms. Even in the unlikely event of a Tory election victory, privatising the Post Office, while still a Tory objective, would prove difficult and contentious.

As for London Underground, privatisation has apparently been dropped from the Tory manifesto as being too politically sensitive. For a Labour government, of course, privatisation – under that title, at any rate – would be anathema. But the main issue would remain. The Post Office and London Underground need to invest heavily if they are to carry on doing their jobs. The more they can present themselves in private sector guise, the easier it will be to attract private finance.

In the Post Office's case, this might seem perverse. Investment is certainly needed to keep pace with the rapid development of electronic media and digital information. But in a private sector context, the Post Office would have no trouble at all in raising the money. Its management, after all, would have a good story to tell: a consistent record of profit, strong cash flow and a remarkable level of customer satisfaction. At present, the Post Office is not allowed to borrow, since that would count as government debt. But as a private company, its balance sheet would allow it to borrow well over £1bn without strain.

The case of London Underground is less clear cut. If its accounts were drawn up in private sector fashion, its operating loss might be relatively small. But by comparison with the Post Office, it is hugely capital intensive. This year, it will swallow close to £1bn of taxpayers' money, of which more than half will be spent on the new extension to the Jubilee Line.

Attempts to help out with private finance have so far proved tough going. The £2bn-plus London CrossRail project, providing an underground link between the capital's railway termini, is supposed to contain an element of private funding. But the main burden will fall upon the taxpayer. Unsurprisingly, therefore, the project has been postponed to the next century.

The government's Private Finance Initiative is supposed to help here, but the results so far are not encouraging. The Northern Line of the Underground is being supplied with some £800m worth of new trains through a leasing arrangement with the suppliers, GEC Alsthom. But even that was opposed by the Treasury as being in breach of its rules, as was a plan to lease out some of the automatic barriers at Underground stations. It would be perhaps unfair to single out the Treasury as the culprit. The history of

**Exhibit 14.1** *continued*

nationalised industries in the UK has left its scars. In their heyday, investments by nationalised companies too often proved disastrous. An important reason was that since spending was ultimately backed by government, managers lacked the guidance of the market on the balance between risk and opportunity.

Given the context, today's public sector managers might well feel occasionally helpless. Their ownership structure is unsuited to the job they have to do. Their workers, meanwhile, have no incentive to speed the transition to a private sector model, since they have every evidence that it means upheaval and insecurity.

There is a central irony to all this. The City and the financial markets are criticised for being short-termist. In the closing years of the century, the reality

is just the other way round. Governments – not only in the UK – are increasingly weighed down by the fiscal burden of pensions and unemployment. Long-term capital projects are no longer to be thought of, especially by governments which know that proposing taxes to pay for them would spell doom at the polls. The world is therefore reverting to a 19th century model, whereby long-term private savings are channelled by the financial institutions into long-term investments. The problem is not one of a shortage of funds. The question is rather how public sector managers, squeezed between hostile owners and resentful employees, can gain access to the money.

*Source:* Tony Jackson, *Financial Times*, 12 August 1996. © 1996 The Financial Times Limited

staff requirements, books and equipment, or administrative items (Menter *et al.*, 1997). The principle of 'consumer choice' must again be seen as an attempt to introduce market discipline. Prime Minister John Major's (1991–7) initiative on the Citizen's Charter[4] sought to empower consumers of public services if targets for service provision failed. Parental choice in schooling or penalty clauses for service operators of contracted-out services, such as refuse collection or road sweeping, are examples.

The principal changes can be summarised as follows:

- Reorganisation of the civil service into executive agency status and further decentralisation into non-departmental public bodies (NDPB). Staff remained civil servants in status but the overall head of the agency, the chief executive, could be appointed from either the public or the private sector. Links were maintained with the appropriate government department through a contractual 'framework document'. Pay, conditions of employment and gradings from April 1996 were decentralised to each agency and NDPB. These changes follow the Next Steps policy introduced into the civil service in 1988 designed to break up the civil service into more discrete accounting units.[5]
- Simulation of competition through the purchaser–provider division (commonly called the internal market[6]). Introduced in 1981, this is now apparent in the NHS, NHS trusts and local authorities. NHS trusts, for example, have powers to appoint staff, establish their own conditions of service, and shape their own industrial relations procedures. Within the NHS, the market measures have led to competition between hospitals and their departments for internal 'contracts'. Labour savings have clearly been identified as an aid to competitiveness, and fears over job security have arisen as a result. Employers have often responded to their new powers by challenging working practices, and tightening up on discipline and sickness procedures. The conflict between 'cost-cutting' and quality service provision has also been apparent, and this in particular has led the Labour government in 2002 to rethink the logic of these market reforms within the NHS environment.

■ Within local authorities the ability to raise revenue through local taxation has been curtailed by the 'rate capping' procedure enacted by central government, meaning some spending cuts and service withdrawal as a result. Decentralised and devolved managerial accountability also means that many sections of local government now operate within their own budgets and staffing arrangements. Similar arrangements also exist in the school sector through the local management of schools (LMS) initiative. This substitutes local authority planning in the schools sector in favour of more direct headteacher responsibility combined with parental choice for state school places. The ability of local secondary schools to opt out of local authority financial control and to raise additional monies reinforces this process of consumer 'choice', especially when combined with the publication of school 'league tables' giving results of examination performance.[7] Both the programme of school opt-outs and league tables were initially opposed by the NUT, leading to dispute. The failure of the campaign to prevent the measures led to the NUT withdrawing its opposition.

Management style and technique in the public sector have been much influenced by the emphasis on performance, objectives and targets. This focus reflects the primary change of devolving financial accountability but also mirrors parallel changes in management techniques much associated with HRM or 'Japanisation' in the private sector, as well as competitive costing programmes involving a potential private sector service provider as is the case with Best Value[8] (local authorities) or the Private Finance Initiative (Kerr, 1997). The forms of 'New Public Management' that have evolved have sought to break down the traditional bureaucratic and hierarchical organisation structures that were previously dominant. In addition, this renewed emphasis on rational managerial accountability has acted to allay some of the blame for service cuts from government policy and transfer them to the individual decisions of managers (Winchester and Bach, 1995). In many instances the change has resulted in a downgrading of the traditional importance of negotiated procedures as unions have become de-institutionalised, work has intensified, and collective bargaining has fragmented. Many of the old conditions of service handbooks, which formerly laid down rules and regulations of conduct, working procedures and conditions of service, have been downgraded in importance or abandoned. In some cases, new local agreements have been negotiated with local trade unions, but in other cases, such as in further education colleges, attempts have been made to completely redefine contract terms and impose new ones. Large-scale, long-running disputes with the unions concerned have resulted.

As an alternative management approach, personnel practices have concentrated much more on appraisal systems, the use of direct communication with employees (rather than through trade unions) and on quality initiatives such as total quality programmes or quality circles. Teamworking (particularly in the NHS) has also been emphasised. Such changes have posed considerable problems, either because of trade union opposition or because of the difficulties of assessing 'performance' in the public service when no 'value added' contribution can be identified. What measures of performance, for example, can be applied to nurses when the fate of the sick is dependent on so many other factors than simply the care given by an individual nurse? Similarly, how can the performance of a social worker or teacher be assessed when caseloads or class size are possibly more important variables in performance outcome? Such problems manifested themselves in difficulties for the government's policies. In the NHS, for example, local trust managers have attempted to raise productivity by reducing staff, changing the mix of required skills, extending working time flexibility and casualisation of contracts, and reducing wage costs by reducing overtime premia, sick and holiday pay (Fisher, 1999). The result has been a deterioration in staff–management relations and, in some cases, an increase in trade union activity. Recent research by Marsden and French (2000) also reports the general experience of staff in the public sector when confronted with new forms of performance-related pay (PRP). Among their main findings were that:

- most staff believed that PRP was divisive, undermined morale, caused jealousies and inhibited workplace cooperation;
- most staff believed that PRP had not raised their motivation;
- many believed that line managers used PRP to reward their favourites;
- many line managers believed PRP had reduced staff cooperation with management.

Despite these general misgivings from staff on new pay determination it is in the field of pay that the most important changes have taken place, and it is this area which is now examined.

## Pay determination: comparability, indexation and performance

We have already seen how the government, in abandoning the model employer approach, has sought to shift the emphasis away from pay being determined by 'fair comparison' to that of 'affordability'. This shift of emphasis has also corresponded to devolved managerial authority and the perceived need to encourage individual performance and flexibility by using pay as the incentive. Despite these trends, nearly three-quarters of public sector employees still had their pay determined by collective bargaining (Millward *et al.*, 1992), with the remainder attached to some form of indexation or review by a third party. To a large extent this reflects the difficulties of assessing performance of the public servant (as already discussed) as well as the entrenched opposition of trade unions to the break-up of more collectively beneficial systems. A summary of the major sectoral differences is given below.

### ■ The civil service

The pay comparability machinery associated with 'Whitleyism' and the model employer was abandoned by the government in 1981 (despite trade union opposition involving a 20-week dispute of selective strikes). In the aftermath of the dispute, the government established an enquiry into civil service pay (the Megaw Report) which concluded with recommendations that maintained 'informed' collective bargaining and which geared pay awards to the priorities of 'recruitment, retention and motivation'. Performance-related pay was introduced shortly afterwards for senior grade staff and the system of 'automatic' yearly incremental progression up long scales was altered to allow for performance-only related 'merit' increases to be reserved at the higher end of the scales for most white-collar grades. The extra flexibility in the system satisfied some management criteria but the unions were successful in retaining automatic incremental progression for at least some part of the pay scale. The agreement was achieved on the basis that the outside pay comparisons would be at the lower end of the 'league table' rather than in the average (median) to good range.

However, the introduction of agency status into the civil service in the 1980s and 1990s led to a fragmentation of paymasters and a devolution of collective bargaining to more discrete areas of work within the service. As a consequence, the determination of the pay scales and the mix of automatic and merit increments have become much more diverse. Pay bands are now commonplace, linked to job-evaluated regrading of skills, tasks and responsibilities. The Treasury, as overall paymaster, retains some control over pay within agencies and has the power to reverse decisions. On the other hand, some civil service departments are likely still to be fully privatised (Amersham International – a scientific establishment formerly part of the civil service – was in fact the first government privatisation) and would consequently be completely outside the scope of public sector pay determination.

## The National Health Service

The NHS contains a multitude of occupational grades covered by numerous bargaining units and trade unions. Ten separate Whitley Councils have traditionally acted as forums for negotiations based within the fair comparison remit. In addition, doctors and dentists have been catered for by a review body that, after consultation with all interested parties, has made recommendations on pay and conditions to the government. This highly centralised system has been altered rather than fundamentally challenged in the 1980s and 1990s. Following a lengthy dispute over pay in 1982, the government created two new pay review bodies for nurses and midwives, and employers and government have since sought to influence the outcomes of these reviews by incorporating greater elements of affordability at the expense of comparability. This has resulted in continuing skirmishes between the various unions representing nurses and midwives and the government as ultimate paymaster. In particular, there has been a determined effort to relate nurses' pay to local, rather than national, labour market conditions with proposals for basic increases that could be 'topped up' (or not) by the need to recruit and retain within the local labour market. Despite this, it has been possible to enhance nurses' pay relative to others within the NHS, either by better than average pay awards or by reassessing the grading criteria on which individual nurse's pay is assessed.

The difficulties of localising nurses' pay have been caused not just by opposition from unions but also by the problems of defining a local labour market for nurses, many of whom relate to a *national* occupational labour market and have highly individual personal profiles relating to skills, grade and contractual status. It is for these reasons that 90 per cent of NHS trusts have reverted to national, as opposed to local, pay rates for nurses (*People Management*, 25 September 1997).

One other issue which has clearly upset union negotiators has been the tendency of governments to 'stage' awards of the pay review body and save money by delaying full implementation of any award. This pattern has been repeated by the Labour government in its decision to stage the 1998 award for nurses.

Elsewhere within the NHS, the system of collective bargaining through Whitley Councils continues. The government has been more than willing, however, to utilise its policy of 'cash limits' to suppress pay rises, and in 1989 this policy caused confrontation with ambulance workers, who staged a 'work to rule' in order to secure a pay review index similar to that enjoyed by the emergency services of the police and fire services. While securing a higher pay settlement than previously offered, the ambulance workers failed in their attempt to establish indexation. National agreements for Whitley-related grades have nevertheless shown signs of fragmentation as more discrete elements of local pay linked to 'recruitment and retention' have emerged and managers have begun to exercise power in seeking more flexibility in pay with links to new working arrangements.

## Local government

Similar patterns of change are recorded in local authorities, with moves by the individual employers to establish local rates outside of the national collective agreement. The employers (i.e. the management of individual local authorities) are members of separate institutions (representing Scotland or the metropolitan or county councils), which for bargaining purposes has led to some discrepancy of position in key disputes. This was highlighted in 1989 during a dispute with the union representing white-collar staff (NALGO) when the employers failed in their efforts to dismantle and break the national collective agreement and impose more locally based agreements in its place. However, within local authorities there remains much scope for variation in pay that can be engineered through grading agreements struck at local level. Thus, it is perfectly possible for differences in remuneration for skills and occupations to arise between authorities as different interpretations of grading formulas are imposed or negotiated. The evaluation of jobs and skills by formal (and sometimes informal) means has thus been a central issue in local authority employee relations, sometimes with important equal opportunities implications when it can be demonstrated that particular jobs are gender specific (e.g. canteen assistants compared with 'binmen').

More significant changes have taken place within education (see Exhibit 14.2). Further education colleges and the former polytechnics were removed from local authority financial control in the early 1990s, resulting in attempts by the college management and employers' forums to break with the traditional national collective agreements. This led to two national one-day strikes in the former polytechnics in order to preserve national conditions of service. The end settlement led to a revision of contractual obligations for lecturers and the establishment of local agreements within a national 'framework agreement'. National bargaining on pay was preserved, but since the transformation of the former polytechnics into 'new' universities with similar funding arrangements (but dissimilar conditions of work) to the 'old' universities there has been division of opinion between the union representing 'new' staff (NATFHE) and 'old' (Association of University Teachers) as to whether or not lecturers would be better served with national bargaining or a pay review body. The introduction of new contractual arrangements into the further education sector proved much more contentious, leading to a series of national and college-based disputes as lecturers' teaching hours were lengthened and holidays reduced. The bitterness of many of these disputes was compounded by the ability of college principals to award themselves (with governing body approval) large salary increases. To date there remains no agreed outcome to this dispute and in fact, in 1995 and 1996 at least, the sector has recorded in official statistics a significant proportion of 'working days lost' through strikes (see later section).

Exhibit 14.2

# Plan to boost pay for top teachers

The government yesterday called for a new salary structure to reward a class of advanced skills teacher it wants to introduce. In advice to the schoolteachers' review body, Mr David Blunkett, education and employment secretary, said he wanted a 'distinct new role' for particular teachers in raising standards by 'supporting and mentoring' trainee and newly qualified teachers.

Mr Blunkett has expressed concern that the only avenue for career advancement for good teachers is to go into administration. He acknowledges that under the present system there is no financial incentive for them to remain in the classroom. In his letter to Mr Tony Vineall, the review body chairman, Mr Blunkett made clear he wanted a tight pay settlement to ensure most of the extra £1bn announced for education in the Budget went to improving standards.

Mr Blunkett is having to reconcile a financial squeeze on education with the government's crusade to raise standards – to be the centrepiece of a 200-clause education Bill in the next parliamentary session. However, he indicated he was amenable to funnelling more money to the new grade of teacher and asked the review body to consider how best to achieve that. 'Skilled and experienced teachers are

the key asset of our schools and we need to retain them in the profession', Mr Blunkett said.

Teachers' unions condemned the proposal. Mr Doug McAvoy, general secretary of the National Union of Teachers, called for 'a significant increase' for all teachers. Mr Phil Willis, Liberal Democrat education spokesman, said: 'Increased salaries for advanced skills teachers can help improve schools, but they will only affect a very small proportion of teachers. The government must not allow this to become a case of robbing Peter to pay Paul.'

The review body will make its recommendations on pay for all 400,000 teachers in England and Wales in time for the government to announce the 1998–99 pay round in February. 'We need to ensure those who are in the service for 20–30 years have a career structure', Mr Blunkett said. Plans for the new 'super-teachers', as Mr Blunkett dubs them, were outlined in a government White Paper last month. Mr Blunkett also asked the review body to consider reinforcing headteachers' management role by requiring them to report to governors each year to ensure individual performance did not fall below recognised standards.

*Source*: John Kampfner, *Financial Times*, 7 August 1997. © 1997 The Financial Times Limited

In secondary and primary education there has been a long history of disagreement between the unions and employers as to the outputs of the Burnham Committee negotiating forum. A series of disputes led eventually to the government deciding to abolish the system of national collective bargaining in 1987 and through the Teachers' Pay and Conditions Act 1987 to enable the Secretary of State to impose pay rates on the teaching service. In 1991 a pay review body was established for teachers with a part remit to establish performance-related pay within schools. However, the introduction of performance systems within schools has been very limited. Schools rely on trust and teamwork between teachers, and few heads are likely to be willing to threaten this by the introduction of potentially divisive merit-based pay. Opposition from the teaching unions would also mean a difficult path would lie ahead in its introduction.

## ■ Indexation

Both the police and fire service (representing 200,000 employees) have their pay determined by indexed attachment to outside movements in earnings. The police are the one sector of civilian public employment denied by law a 'right' to strike, having lost this right in the aftermath of their strike defeat in 1919. Their indexation formula was established after a campaign organised by the Police Federation (the police union) in 1979, and initially linked annual increases to the increase in the whole economy average earnings. Since 1994 their pay increases have been linked to the median increase in private sector non-manual settlements. Other issues affecting police pay have been the baseline level (again subject to dispute in 1979) and the possibility of the introduction of performance-related pay. The latter issue again raises questions of the efficacy of linking pay to performance in a public service occupation. Firefighters won an indexation system in the aftermath of their dispute with the Labour government in 1977. Their pay is linked to the top quartile of male manual earnings. As mentioned in the previous section, ambulance workers failed in 1989 to secure an indexation system; their case at the time rested on the proposition that they should be considered an equivalent 'emergency' service to the police and fire service. During the life of the 1979–97 Conservative governments it was mooted within government circles that a strike ban should be introduced in the emergency services. However, legislation, although often expected, failed to materialise before the election defeat of May 1997.

## The public sector under 'new' Labour

The first two years of the Labour government after 1997 saw little change within the sector. The spending limits of the previous Conservative government were adhered to by the Chancellor. However, new agendas for the public service have since begun to emerge in terms of the government's commitment to modernising government, as expressed in its 1999 White Paper. This White Paper had as its declared objectives to:

- break down barriers between departments and local authorities;
- get the best people for the job – whether public, private or voluntary;
- create a greater say for people in forming policies;
- recognise and reward the best staff;
- tackle the fear of taking risks within the sector.

Examples of new initiatives under these declared objectives are plans to extend the hours by which public services can be accessed. In the NHS, for example, walk-in centres and direct line Internet access have been established. Civil servants are also encouraged to develop cost-cutting initiatives by pooling resources across departments and avoiding duplication, and to adopt a system of peer review to assess progress in achieving the necessary cultural changes within the service. The government also established a series of focus groups and 'peoples' panels' to enact some level of feedback on satisfaction or otherwise with the level and state of public services.

Beyond these cultural and organisational initiatives the government has shown a renewed determination to inject private finance into public service provision either through the PFI (Private Finance Initiative) or PPP (public private partnership) programmes. It is in these areas that controversy has arisen and some confrontation with public service trade unions has occurred. PFI has been aimed especially at hospital provision and is a continuation of the Conservative policies introduced in 1993. No public money is released for major hospital works unless the relevant NHS trust has first drawn up a plan for a private finance initiative within the building programme. Private companies might then build hospitals and let them over a contracted period to the NHS. The Labour government has adopted this programme and announced in 2000 that it was on course for the private funding of public projects worth £20 billion by 2003 (*Financial Times*, 16 March 2000). New arrangements whereby private finance is introduced are to be extended into primary care facilities and social services and in 850 schools (*Guardian*, 17 July 2001). The main public service union, Unison, however, has taken issue with the government over the programme, claiming that private finance initiatives 'are an inefficient means of financing improvements to public services . . . for every £1bn of PFI contracts, the cost to the public purse is £50m per year more than if the public sector could borrow directly' (Unison, 2001). The union also claims that the costs of PFI may then be directly met by cuts in services and in the employment conditions of public service workers. During 2000, a long-running dispute took place at Dudley hospital over such issues. Some parallel union concern has taken place in local authorities whereby the government Best Value initiative (see Boyne, 2000), designed to improve service accountability, has been perceived by some union members as an extension of compulsory competitive tendering.[9] A flashpoint with the PPP initiative was the long-running argument between the government and the newly elected mayor of London, Ken Livingstone, centred on the proposed new funding arrangements for London Underground. The continuation of the privatisation drive also touched one of the last remaining nationalised industries – the Post Office. The overall corporate management body for Royal Mail was renamed Consignia and during 1999 the Postal Services Bill was announced, freeing the Post Office to engage in more commercial undertakings, eventually becoming a government-owned plc. The Post Office has now been transformed into 12 business units with separate profit accountability. Lastly, the government took a decision in October 2001 to revise the arrangements for the privatised Railtrack by introducing parliamentary legislation to turn the company into a not-for-profit organisation without shareholders. In summary, the issue of privatisation proved a contentious one during the second term of the Labour government. Potential confrontation with unions meant that the 2001 Trades Union Congress was likely to be a focal point of union discontent and potential opposition to many of the government's plans. The GMB union, for example, had threatened to withdraw £250,000 annual funding to the Labour Party if its plans were not revised. Other union leaders, such as Sir Ken Jackson, general secretary of the Amalgamated Engineering and Electrical Union (AEEU), have on the other hand been supportive of the government's privatisation agenda. In the event, the key debates at the TUC were curtailed as the 2001 Congress itself was ended before the debate could take place in response to the terrorist attacks on New York and Washington on September 11.

## Assessment: employee relations or industrial relations?

No assessment of the public sector is complete without recognition of the fact that the sector stands apart from the private sector in that there has been a continuing relative resilience of trade union membership and density and a higher propensity in recent years for industrial dispute. In 2000, average union density in public administration was 61 per cent, in education was 58 per cent and in health was 64 per cent. This compares with a density rate of 29.4 per cent for all employees in Britain (*Labour Market Trends*, September 2001). Overall union density in the public sector is around three times greater than in the private sector. In terms of industrial disputes during the 1990s, the public sector has consistently provided the most significant proportion of 'working days lost'. Some of the key areas of disputes were as follows:

- 1991 – a strike by council workers over redundancy matters accounted for 102,000 working days lost (13 per cent of the annual total).
- 1992 – a similar strike by council workers accounted for 81,000 working days lost (15 per cent of the 0.5 million total).
- 1993 – a strike by civil servants over market testing, privatisation and cuts in service accounted for 162,000 working days lost (25 per cent) out of 0.6 million days total. The workers involved in this one-day strike accounted for 42 per cent of all workers on strike in 1993.
- 1994 and 1995 – a strike by college lecturers over the introduction of new contracts of employment accounted for 63,000 (22 per cent) of the 0.28 million days lost in 1994 and 39,000 (9 per cent) of the 0.41 million days lost in 1995.
- 1996 – a strike by university staff (all grades) over pay accounted for 111,700 (9 per cent) of the 1.3 million days lost. Sixty-eight per cent of all days lost in this year came as a result of productivity disputes in the London Underground and Royal Mail.
- 1997 – the largest single number of disputes in any sector was in education, which recorded 35 stoppages and 27,900 working days lost. The Royal Mail also recorded another significant number of disputes.
- 2000 – one-quarter of all working days lost were due to ten stoppages in health and social work.

Part of the increasing prominence of the public sector in strike statistics is the result of the decline of *individual* propensity to strike in the private sector (Dickerson and Stewart, 1993). However, the continued propensity of public sector workers both to remain relatively well unionised and to strike, does need some explanation. In addition, the relative resilience of collective bargaining as a form of pay determination and the continued legitimacy of the trade union role in the face of new management techniques need some analysis. In many respects, traditional forms of adversarial bargaining have kept pace in the public sector with employer- and government-driven attempts to inject employee relations techniques designed to 'individualise' and 'de-collectivise' the employment relationship. Some reasons for this lingering 'industrial' rather than 'employee' relations framework are now suggested.

## Trade union attachment

Membership of the public-sector-based trade unions grew dramatically in the post-war period alongside the growth of the public sector. However, the growth in density outstripped the growth in membership potential in most areas. For example, union membership in national and local government, education and health increased from 1.46 million in 1948 to 2.25 million in 1968 and 5.76 million in 1979, while density rates increased from nearly 60 per cent to nearly 80 per cent over the same period (Waddington, 1992). Job cuts and privatisation from 1979 on took their toll on membership in these sectors and totals fell to 3.8 million in 1987. Density, however, remained stable at just under 79 per cent before some slippage occurred in the 1990s. The pattern of membership in some of the larger unions can be seen from Table 14.1.

Table 14.1 **Membership of selected public sector trade unions**

| Union | 1979 | 1997 | 2000 |
|---|---|---|---|
| GMB (local authority manual grade workers) | 967,000 | 709,708 | 712,010 |
| CWU (communications) | 333,453 | 273,814 | 287,732 |
| National and Local Government Officers Association (NALGO) | 753,000 | na | na |
| National Union of Public Employees (NUPE) | 692,000 | na | na |
| Confederation of Health Service Employees (COHSE) | 213,000 | na | na |
| Unison (1993 merger of above three unions) | (1,657,926)[a] | 1,300,451 | 1,272,350 |
| Public and Commercial Services Union (PCS) | (445,329)[b] | 265,902 | 258,278 |
| National Union of Teachers (NUT) | 290,740 | 191,828 | 201,297 |
| National Association of Schoolmasters/Union of Women Teachers (NAS/UWT) | 152,222 | 172,852 | 180,682 |

[a] NALGO, COHSE and NUPE   [b] PCT plus CPSA
*Source*: Certification Office and TUC annual reports

There exists a mixture of occupational, craft and industrial unions within the sector. For example, in the NHS, manual grades are represented by Unison (the result of a merger in 1993 of NALGO, NUPE and COHSE) or GMB, whereas nurses might join the professionally oriented and non-TUC-affiliated Royal College of Nursing (RCN) or Unison. Staff technicians are generally represented by MSF (Manufacturing, Science and Finance) and maintenance grades by AEEU (Amalgamated Engineering and Electrical Union). In the civil service, unions have historically been split by occupation and grade for white-collar staff in separate unions. However, a series of mergers have created one 'conglomerate' union (PCS) for many other grades, including administrative and executive officers, security officers and Inland Revenue staff. Technical staff can join the IPMS (Institute of Professional Managers and Specialists) while the Association of First Division Civil Servants (FDA) recruits the senior 'mandarin' grades. In primary and secondary education, the major unions are the NUT and the NAS/UWT (and the EIS in Scotland). The NUT has the majority membership in primary schools whereas the NAS/UWT shares membership in the secondary sector. Headteachers can join the National Association of Head Teachers (NAHT). Further education college lecturers and those in the 'new' universities are generally represented by NATFHE (National Association of Teachers in Further and Higher Education) while those in the pre-1992 universities are represented by the Association of University Teachers. Talks on a confederation or merger between these unions is ongoing. Administrative staffs in local authorities, education and the NHS are usually represented by Unison and sometimes MSF (now renamed Amicus, after merging with the AEEU in 2002).

The growth in membership of the public sector unions has given them more weight and influence within the TUC and the trade union movement in general. In the 1970s, the public sector unions gained more seats on the TUC General Council at the expense of some declining private sector and manually based unions. Since its creation by amalgamation in 1993, Unison is now Britain's largest union with over 1.3 million members against the Transport and General Workers' Union's 800,000. The merger of the CPSA and PTC in the civil service into the Public Commercial Service Union (PCS) had been held up in the past because of fears in the junior grade union (CPSA) that their members would be in the same union as their executive grade 'bosses' in the PTC. It is also worth noting that many of these 'public' sector unions also have substantial membership bases in the private sector following privatisation or 'hiving-off' of government departments and nationalised industries.

The relatively high density of membership for many of these unions is partly a legacy of the model employer years when trade unions established strong membership bases aided and abetted by the legitimacy given to them by their institutionalisation in the process of collective bargaining and working procedures.

The fact that managerial grades have also been traditional union members throughout much of the public sector may also have helped to make union membership socially acceptable within the workplace without a 'fear' of victimisation for joining.

The sustained growth of membership throughout the 1960s and 1970s is more complex to explain. White-collar staff in general were drawn into unions during this period at a greater rate than average in all sectors, leading to some debate as to the cause of this new 'white-collar' unionism. Instrumental reasons, linked to the perceived ability of unions to deliver wage increases within a framework of collective bargaining, were undoubtedly important. Further debate surrounds the contention that white-collar staff were becoming more collectivised and identifying themselves as working class within an increasingly large, bureaucratic and 'Taylorised' public sector work environment increasingly typified by automated routine work procedures and the emergence of 'clerical factories' (see Prandy *et al.* (1982) for a contemporary review of the debates). Public sector unions have exhibited more 'unionateness' in recent years, with the decision of some of the unions to newly affiliate to the TUC or to establish political funds for campaign purposes (although falling short of affiliation to the Labour Party).

In the 1980s and 1990s, individual workloads increased as a result of recruitment freezes, cutbacks and cash limits. The need to monitor service outputs and record information for budgeting purposes has also created extra administrative burdens. More government interference and suppression of wage and salary increases have also occurred. The potential role of trade unions as defenders of terms and conditions has become much more important as a result, and where an attempt has been made to fulfil this role the resultant increase in levels of activism within the unions at local level is likely to have enhanced participation and encouraged membership recruitment and retention (Fairbrother, 1996). Pressures on individual managers to meet financial targets and to provide a public service within strict cash limits have also led to a tightening of discipline over such issues as sickness and unauthorised absence as well as the adoption of a more aggressive management style (Edwards and Whitston, 1991). Workers, in other words, are working harder within the public sector, and if so then a sense of injustice is likely to arise if there is no corresponding revision of the effort-bargain. This again, within the workplace, is likely to increase feelings of 'them and us' and create opportunities for active unions to polarise feelings and cement loyalties towards the trade union case.

Many of the trade unions in the sector have also played a dual role as trade union defenders of terms and conditions and representatives of the 'professional' interests of their members. This has enabled them in many instances to offer a service to their members on training provision and career advice that enhances their appeal. In fact many of these 'professional associations', which are not affiliated to the TUC, have seen significant growth of membership over the 1990s against the general trend (Farnham and Giles, 1995). The Royal College of Nursing, for example, has grown from 134,689 in 1979 to over 360,000 in 2000. Other growing associations include the Secondary Heads Association, the British Association of Occupational Therapists, and the Association of Teachers and Lecturers. In some cases the professionally oriented approach of such associations has meant that they have adopted a 'no strike' policy (e.g. the RCN and Professional Association of Teachers), but in some cases (e.g. the RCN and Royal College of Midwives) this policy has seen some relaxation in the 1990s, reflecting a heightening of industrial relations tension within the public sector.

The final explanatory factor for trade union attachment in the sector has been the common cause established by the unions between the defence of jobs and the defence of service provision. The deleterious effects on service provision caused by spending cuts (hospital ward or library closures, for example) have meant that unions have gained extra legitimacy for their cause in defending both jobs *and* services. The likelihood of some success, however minimal, in resisting closure plans or cutbacks has improved as a result, particularly where it is clearly possible to reverse spending cuts within the local process of political accountability. This added political and social dimension to the role of public sector unions, if effectively deployed, gives the unions an enhanced identity which may well have acted as a spur to membership recruitment and retention.

The choice dilemmas within the sector, between service provision, cost and efficiency, have also set limits to the degree of flexibility that could be expected in terms of employers' strategies to change working practices. It is to these dilemmas that we now turn.

## Service provision versus cost cutting: a management dilemma

The pressures on managers to continue to provide a public service against the background of public spending cuts have meant that efforts to introduce many aspects of performance incentives and HRM techniques have been dampened. The difficulties of setting targets and performance objectives for individual staff in public services have already been discussed. In particular, the problems of isolating 'value added' in monetary terms are apparent where no test of increased profits or market share can be made. In some cases it will be possible to determine 'outputs' if these relate, for example, to identifiable performance indicators such as increased student numbers in education or decreased empty bed space in hospitals. However, such targets, if pursued uncautiously, may well have deleterious effects on 'quality' of service or level of provision that may have contradictory effects on other performance 'indicators' that are quality related or which relate to customer/client/public satisfaction. Such policy dilemmas are also likely to create some cynicism among employees unless the performance criteria are transparent and seen to have accommodated some of the more difficult policy contradictions.

These problems, combined as they are with an increasingly low-trust working environment inspired by pay restrictions and job cuts, have meant that some newer personnel practices such as appraisal, merit pay or 'quality' programmes have often met with resistance from staff and their unions. Thus, proposals for a teachers' performance appraisal system have created disputes in schools, and in further and higher education continual union resistance meant that new systems in many instances were effectively imposed by college employers (and their developmental value reduced as a result). Within schools, the government finally succeeded in establishing its 'threshold' system of individual performance-related pay. However, morale and productivity have not necessarily been improved. A government commissioned Mori survey in 2001, established as part of the Department of Education and Skills review, found that two-thirds of teachers who had succeeded in obtaining the £2,000 per year performance bonus said it had done little to boost their confidence. For the one in seven teachers who refused to apply, the scheme was reported to be a major factor in any decision to leave the profession (*Times Educational Supplement*, 21 September 2001 – see Exhibit 14.3). Similarly, proposals for quality circles in departments of the civil service in the 1980s were withdrawn after union boycotts amid fears that any emerging proposals would inspire non-negotiable service or job cuts.

---

**Exhibit 14.3**

# Performance-related pay for teachers

The following case study examines the introduction of performance-related pay for teachers, the union response, and the workings of the scheme in practice.

### 1   The government's threshold plan

Qualified teachers with a good honours degree and seven years' teaching experience, together with other teachers with nine years' experience, will be able to apply for the scheme. The cash for the threshold payments comes from a separate government fund over and above that reserved for teachers' salaries. Schools will have available in their budgets an extra £2,000 annually for each full-time teacher who crosses the threshold which will be in place until at least March 2002. Teachers applying for the money had to fill in an application form and headteachers then made an assessment drawing on the opinions of senior staff and line managers as appropriate. External assessors would then verify the headteachers' recommendations through a sample. Pay increases would be backdated to September 2000. A successful High Court challenge was made by the unions to certain aspects of the scheme's operation, but eventually the scheme was introduced after some changes were made by the government.

### 2   The union view

**Cash first, details of performance pay later, unions say**
Teachers' leaders are to accept the link between pay and pupil progress in an attempt to get threshold cash to members as quickly as possible. Only the National Union of Teachers will press for the controversial link to be dropped, as the government attempts to get the policy on to the

statute book after its High Court defeat. However, a new survey of teachers who applied for the pay rise shows they have little confidence in the standards they must meet to get their extra £2,000-a-year. Only four in 10 believed the eight standards – which include the pay and results link – described good teaching, the Association of Teachers and Lecturers' survey found. Eight out of 10 said filling in the forms had been a 'bad experience', with half believing performance pay would divide staff.

Education Secretary David Blunkett will refer the eight standards to the School Teachers' Review Body, asking it to report back by the end of September. That could mean some teachers get their rise as early as November. All payments will be backdated to September 1.

The NUT this week warned the review body it risked getting into a 'constitutional dispute' over devolution if it accepted responsibility for the standards. The union believes ministers should let standards in Wales be decided by the Welsh Assembly.

Tony Vineall, the review body chairman, is understood to have told the union it was a matter for the government. The NUT denied applying pressure. Most unions fear infuriating members who would have to repeat the time-consuming application process if the standards changed. The ATL found that the 197,000 applicants took an average of 16 hours to fill in the forms. These unions will instead press for changes next year. Once the criteria become part of the review body's remit, they could be debated annually.

Even the NUT, whose action led to the standards being ruled unlawful, is pressing for a quick solution: drop the results link and debate the standards next year. The union's general secretary Doug McAvoy said: 'We oppose payment by results and will continue to do so. What we have done is ensure there is a statutory vehicle open for us to use.' The National Association of Head Teachers and the Secondary Heads Association said any change this year

▶

**The Management of Human Resources**

**Exhibit 14.3** *continued*

would be unacceptable to members assessing applications. NAHT general secretary David Hart said: 'There is no way headteachers would go through the process again.'

The National Association of Schoolmasters Union of Women Teachers said there had been plenty of informal consultation over the standards. Deputy general secretary Eamonn O'Kane said repeating the exercise would be 'utterly unacceptable'. (Nicolas Barnard, *Times Educational Supplement*, 8 September 2000)

### 3  The scheme in practice

■ When the scheme was finally in place, 201,000 teachers, around 80 per cent of those eligible, applied to be assessed for performance-related pay by presenting the appropriate portfolio of evidence and achieving the necessary threshold of performance.

■ If successful, a teacher would receive a salary enhancement of £2,000 for that year.

■ Thirty-seven per cent of the 201,000 applications were from primary teachers, 52 per cent from secondary teachers, 5 per cent from centrally employed local education authority staff, and 4 per cent from special schools.

■ A total of 1,300 schools did not apply i.e. the head-teachers did not enter into the scheme.

■ Men and women applied in equal proportions, but 4.6 per cent of men failed, compared with 2.2 per cent of women.

■ Common failings were teaching and classroom management.

■ Assessors overturned decisions in 315 cases (0.2 per cent).

■ Teachers were assessed in five areas: knowledge and understanding, teaching and assessment, pupil progress, wider professional effectiveness, and professional characteristics.

### 4  Comment: performance pay, teacher morale and productivity

A team from Exeter University examined in detail the workings of the performance pay scheme for teachers. The study showed that only 3 per cent of teachers who applied to cross the threshold to a higher scale of pay for an immediate £2,000 rise were turned down. A team of external assessors, appointed by the government and paid £300 per day, had interviewed staff, but spent virtually no time observing them teaching. In only a very small number of cases (1 in 270) did the assessors disagree with the headteacher's judgement on whether the teacher concerned should pass the threshold. Heads spent an average two hours examining each application and, according to the Exeter study, teachers who failed to cross the threshold felt shocked, upset and bitter, while heads who had to give the bad news found the experience stressful and demoralising. Most importantly, the study suggests that three-quarters of heads felt that the threshold had made little or no difference to the way teachers behaved and taught in the classroom. Only one in five believed it had any impact. In summary, the main impact of the performance pay scheme has been to make staff keep more detailed records of childrens' work as evidence to present to assessors.

The risks attached to the development of lower-trust relationships between management and staff as a result of cutbacks will also reflect on attempts to reorganise work. Efforts to introduce elements of employee participation and involvement, such as the Best Value initiative for local authorities, might often be perceived by staff as attempts to intensify work. Data collected by the University of Warwick's 'Trade Unions into the 1990s' project, for example, indicate that there is a lesser incidence of the introduction of quality circles and teamworking into the public sector but a higher incidence of team briefing, suggesting difficulties in establishing more radical change (Waddington and Whitston, 1996). Similarly, the survey reports a higher incidence of grievances over workload and staffing levels in the public sector. A study of work intensification in UK workplaces by Green (2001) also found that there was considerable intensification of work in the public sector throughout the 1990s. In schools, for example, new demands were placed on teachers as a result of the introduction of the National Curriculum and a rise in pupil–teacher ratios, while in universities new external pressure to produce more research output were placed on lecturers. The long-running series of disputes in the Royal Mail since 1988, often initiated by rank-and-file union members against the wishes of the leadership, over the introduction of total quality management (TQM) and team-working is a case in point. Management proposals to introduce these more HRM-based techniques have followed a programme of 'delayering' of management strata and a staff redundancy programme. Industrial relations tensions were therefore heightened in the process such that 'the re-organisation of Royal Mail left the personnel function in a somewhat ambiguous situation within an increasingly complex and politically charged industrial relations environment' (Martinez Lucio and Noon, 1994). While the number of strikes in Royal Mail was especially high in the 1990s, there was a fall in strike rates recorded in 2001. This came after a deal was struck between the employer and the Communication Workers' Union (CWU) whereby Royal Mail agreed not to implement any unagreed changes in working practices at local level in return for a union commitment to suspend industrial action (*People Management*, 25 October 2001).

All of these factors have imposed some limitation on the degree to which new management techniques have been able to be introduced within the public sector. The continued relative resilience of public sector unions, despite their being placed on the defensive, has meant that employers have been forced to negotiate change where they might otherwise have sought to bypass or marginalise unions. Often such change has had to involve re-examining grading structures and realigning pay through job evaluation studies (Waddington and Whitston, 1996). Derecognition of unions in the public sector, or partial derecognition involving managerial grades, has been much rarer than in the private sector, and has been generally confined to those instances where services have been contracted out or privatised (e.g. managerial staff in British Telecom following privatisation). As a result, the climate of adverserial 'industrial' relations, established in particular in the 1970s, has lingered on and processes designed to individualise the employment relationship have proved more difficult to establish.

## Chapter summary

This chapter explores the structure and growth of the public sector in the UK. The history from 'model employer' to 'new' Labour is assessed, and the tensions between providing a public service and managing within budgetary constraints are explored. A description of the key industrial relations concerns is given together with a commentary of major disputes.

## Questions

1   How can you explain the high density of union membership in the public sector when compared to the private sector?

2   Discuss the problems of introducing 'new public management'. How might the problems be overcome?

## Activities

1 Reread Exhibit 14.1 about public sector financing and answer the following questions.

   (a) Why might modern governments be keen to finance public services by private money?

   (b) What problems, if any, might follow from such a strategy?

2 The following questions related to the case study presented in Exhibit 14.2 on performance-related pay for teachers.

   (a) Why did the government face so much opposition from teachers' unions to the introduction of performance-related pay?

   (b) Given the obvious difficulties of the scheme, how might a satisfactory system of performance measurement be established for teachers?

   (c) In introducing the scheme the government has argued that the wider interests of parents and children are at stake. Should public sector trade unions such as the teachers' unions have limitations imposed on them in any action they may take which opposes government policy?

## Notes

1 The Private Finance Initiative (PFI) was introduced during the Conservative administration by the Chancellor of the Exchequer in his Autumn Statement in September 1992. The catchphrase of the initiative was 'private opportunity, public benefit', and the aim was to allow the private sector to assume the management of public services where an improvement in efficiency and a reduction in costs may arise. While the PFI approach may be more expensive than using public finance, ongoing savings may be made by later cost savings in the operation of the service. Despite some opposition to the scheme from Labour prior to its 1997 election victory, the incoming government retained the scheme.

2 The principle that the pay of particular groups of public sector employees is to be determined through comparison with comparable private sector occupations has been superseded since 1979 by the concept of affordability, the idea that pay should be related to the financial circumstances of the employing organisation.

3 Pay review bodies are standing bodies appointed by government and able to take an independent view on medium-term developments in pay for the public service occupations covered. There are pay review bodies for nurses and midwives, doctors and dentists, other health service professionals, school teachers, the armed forces and 'top salaried' senior military officials, civil servants and judges. A total of 1.5 million employees are covered. While this is rather less than one-quarter of the public sector workforce, pay review body awards have influenced pay settlements for other groups within the public sector. Pay review bodies take evidence each year from relevant sources and make recommendations to government. The presumption is that, unless there are compelling reasons to do otherwise, the government will accept the recommendations.

4 The Citizen's Charter initiative was proposed by the government in 1991 through the Citizen's Charter White Paper which emphasised four themes: quality, choice, standards and value in the provision of public services. The objectives were to improve service provision and to instil in providers a more customer-oriented culture. Service providers were required to establish and monitor performance targets along prescribed dimensions, and performance

**The Management of Human Resources**
**668**

is subject to independent validation. Charters for particular services were introduced and a central unit established to oversee their development.

5 *Improving Management in Government: The Next Steps* was a report by Sir Robin Ibbs, head of the government's Efficiency Unit, published in 1988 and critical of the impact of the government's management reforms on the civil service. It suggested that the civil service was 'too big and too diverse to be managed as a single unit', and advocated the reorganisation of the executive activities of government (as distinct from policy advice) into separate agencies with specific responsibilities and targets. Headed by chief executives, often recruited from outside the civil service, these agencies were granted greater flexibility in financial and personnel matters. Variations between agencies (in terms of size, activities, financial regimes) in part explain the uneven pace of decentralisation of pay and conditions. Nevertheless, this has been given further impetus by subsequent central government initiatives, and devolution is increasing quite rapidly.

6 The aim of the internal market has been to stimulate greater competition between providers of public services and in this way to improve performance. In the NHS from 1991, for example, the main purchasers of health care (health authorities) were separated from providers of the services (hospitals and community units). The internal market has been supported by devolved budgets and financial management. General practitioners can acquire fundholder status and purchase hospital provision. Similar arrangements now exist across most public sector employers although the major tenets of the internal market in the NHS were substantially downgraded after the election of the Labour government in 1997.

7 In education, the term 'opting out' applies to around 20 per cent of secondary schools that, after a ballot, became grant-maintained schools, no longer subject to local education authority control. All schools are covered by the Local Management of Schools structure of devolved financial management. The policy of opting out of schools has been put on hold by the Labour government.

8 Best Value (BV) was introduced as a new regime for local authorities in England and Wales under the Local Government Act 1999. It was intended as a replacement for the compulsory competitive tendering programme of the outgoing Conservative government. The government's expectations of Best Value is 'continuous improvement' in local authority performance, assessed through changes in service costs and standards, as well as 'better services . . . with significant efficiency improvements'. This involves performance plans, five-yearly reviews of progress with evidence of comparison and competition, and action plans which may involve private finance initiatives. In terms of employee relations, BV authorities are required to adopt a 'partnership' approach to employees and trade unions embodied in a framework agreement signed by the major employers and trade unions.

9 Public sector service organisations were legally obligated under Conservative legislation to allow private contractors to bid for the right to carry out specified services. In the NHS, compulsory competitive tendering (CCT) was introduced initially in 1983 for cleaning, catering and laundry services. In local government, the initiative started in direct labour organisations (e.g. in building work) and was extended into cleaning, refuse collection and maintenance functions by the Local Government Act 1988. The tendering exercise required local authorities to separate the 'client' and 'contractor' roles and hence resulted in a radical restructuring of internal management and organisation in local government. 'Market testing' is closely associated with CCT and was later extended to white-collar central government and local authority services.

## Useful websites

*www.newdeal.gov.uk* **Welfare to Work** Government website on the Welfare to Work initiatives.
*www.pcs.org.uk* **Public Commercial and Services** Website of the trade union for the civil service.
*www.ukonline.gov.uk* **Statistical information** Government website which provides statistical and other information.
*www.unison.org.uk* **Unison** Website of the trade union Unison (local government employees), with many useful links.

## References

Bacon, R. and Eltis, W. (1978) *Britain's Economic Problem: Too Few Producers*, 2nd edn. London: Macmillan.

Blyton, P. and Turnbull, P. (1998) *The Dynamics of Employee Relations*, 2nd edn. London: Macmillan.

Boyne, G. (2000) 'External regulation and Best Value in local government', *Public Money and Management*, July–September.

Carter, B. and Fairbrother, P. (1999) 'The transformation of British public-sector industrial relations: from "model employer" to marketized relations', *Historical Studies in Industrial Relations*, 7: 119–46.

Dickerson, A. and Stewart, M. (1993) 'Is the public sector more strike prone?', *Oxford Bulletin of Economics and Statistics*, 55(3): 253–84.

Edwards, P.K. and Whitston, C. (1991) 'Workers are working harder: effort and shop floor relations in the 1980s', *British Journal of Industrial Relations*, 29(4): 593–600.

Fairbrother, P. (1996) 'Workplace trade unionism in the state sector' in Ackers, P., Smith, C. and Smith, P. (eds) *The New Workplace and Trade Unionism*. London: Routledge.

Farnham, D. and Giles, L. (1995) 'Trade unions in the UK: trends and counter-trends since 1979', *Employee Relations*, 17(2).

Ferner, A. (1994) 'The State as employer' in Hyman, R. and Ferner, A. (eds) *New Frontiers in European Industrial Relations*. London: Blackwell.

Fisher, L. (1999) 'Strong workplace union fights health "Reforms"' in Cohen, S. (ed.), *What's Happening? The Truth about Work and the Myth of Partnership*. London: Trade Union Forum Pamphlet.

Foster, D. and Scott, P. (1998) 'Conceptualising union responses to contracting out municipal services, 1979–97', *Industrial Relations Journal*, 29(2): 137–50.

Fredman, S. and Morris, G. (1989) *The State as Employer: Labour Law in the Public Services*. London: Mansell.

Green, F. (2001) 'It's been a hard day's night: the concentration and intensification of work in late twentieth-century Britain', *British Journal of Industrial Relations*, 39(1): 53–80.

Kelly, J. (1988) *Trade Unions and Socialist Politics*. London: Verso.

Kerr, D. (1997) 'The PFI miracle', *Capital and Class*: 64.

Marsden, D. and French, S. (2000) *What a Performance*. London: London School of Economics.

Martinez Lucio, M. and Noon, M. (1994) 'Organisational change and the tensions of decentralisation: the case of Royal Mail', *Human Resource Management Journal*, 5(2).

Menter, I., Muschamp, Y., Nicholls, P., Ozgal, J. and Pollard, A. (1997) *Work and Identity in the Primary School*. Milton Keynes: Open University Press.

Millward, N., Stevens, M., Smart, D. and Hawes, W.R. (1992) *Workplace Industrial Relations in Transition*. Aldershot: Dartmouth.

Prandy, K., Stewart, A. and Blackburn, R.M. (1982) *White Collar Work*. London: Macmillan.

Seifert, R. (1987) *Teacher Militancy: A History of Teacher Strikes, 1896–1987*. Brighton: Falmer Press.

Seifert, R. (1992) *Industrial Relations in the NHS*. London: Chapman & Hall.

Unison (2001) *Public Services Manifesto*. London: Unison.

Waddington, J. (1992) 'Trade union membership in Britain 1980–87: unemployment and restructuring', *British Journal of Industrial Relations*, 30(2): 287–324.

Waddington, J. and Whitston, C. (1996) 'Empowerment versus intensification – union perspectives of change at the workplace' in Ackers, P., Smith, C. and Smith, P. (eds) *The New Workplace and Trade Unionism*. London: Routledge.

Wigham, E. (1980) *From Humble Petition to Militant Action: A History of the Civil and Public Services Association 1903–1978*. London: CPSA.

Winchester, D. and Bach, S. (1995) 'The public sector' in Edwards, P. (ed.) *Industrial Relations Theory and Practice*, 3rd edn. London: Prentice Hall.

## Further reading

Beaumont, P.B. (1992) *Public Sector Industrial Relations*. London: Routledge.

Corby, S. and White, G. (1999) *Employee Relations in the Public Services*. London: Routledge.

Farnham, P. and Horton, S. (1993) *The Political Economy of Public Sector Change*. London: Macmillan.

Millward, N. (1993) *The New Industrial Relations*, London: PSI.

Monbiot, G. (2000) *Captive State: the corporate take-over of Britain*, London: Macmillan.

Rajan, A. and Pearson, R. (1986) *UK Occupation and Employment Trends to 1990*. London: Butterworths.

Salamon, M. (2000) *Industrial Relations*, 4th edn. London: Prentice Hall.